SORAYAMA

COMPLETE MASTERWORKS

SPECIAL EDITION · REVISED AND ENLARGED

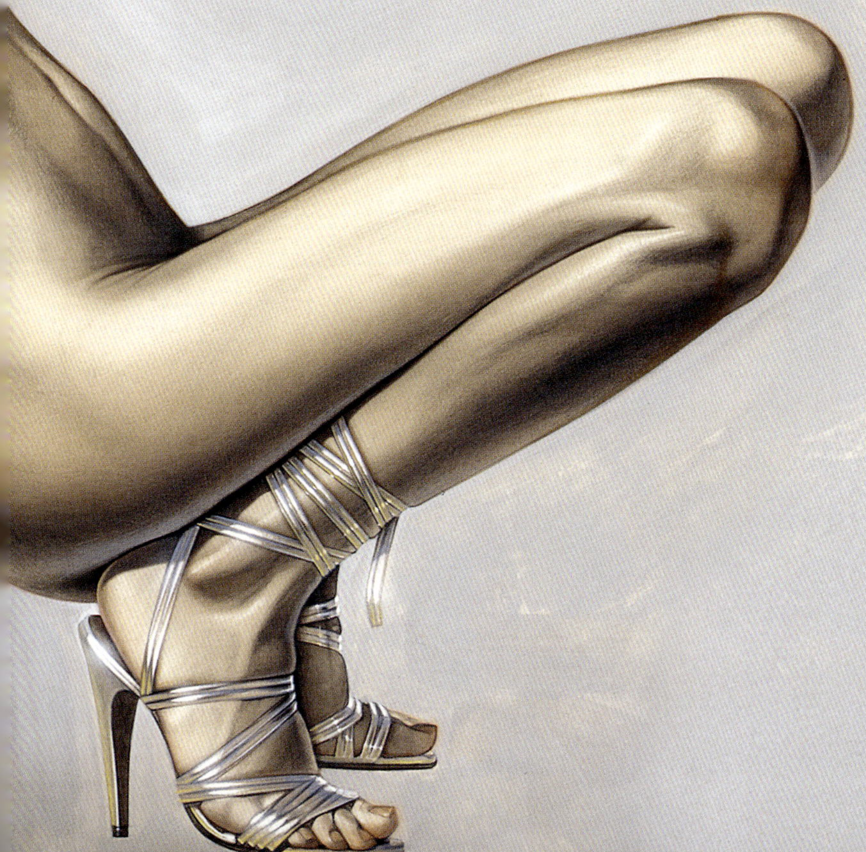

EDITION *Skylight*

Third Edition, revised and enlarged 2021
Second Edition 2017
First Edition 2010

EDITION SKYLIGHT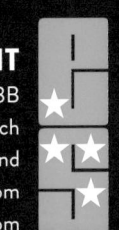
Rosengartenstrasse 13B
CH-8608 Bubikon / Zürich
Switzerland
info@edition-skylight.com
www.edition-skylight.com

ISBN 978-3-03766-678-4

Bibliographic information published by Die Deutsche Bibliothek
Die Deutsche Bibliothek lists this publication in the
Deutsche Nationalbibliografie; detailed bibliographic data
are available in the Internet at http://dnb.ddb.de.

Design:
Weiß-Freiburg GmbH – Grafik und Buchgestaltung

Hajime Sorayama is represented by NANZUKA
https://nanzuka.com/en

Printed in Czech Republic

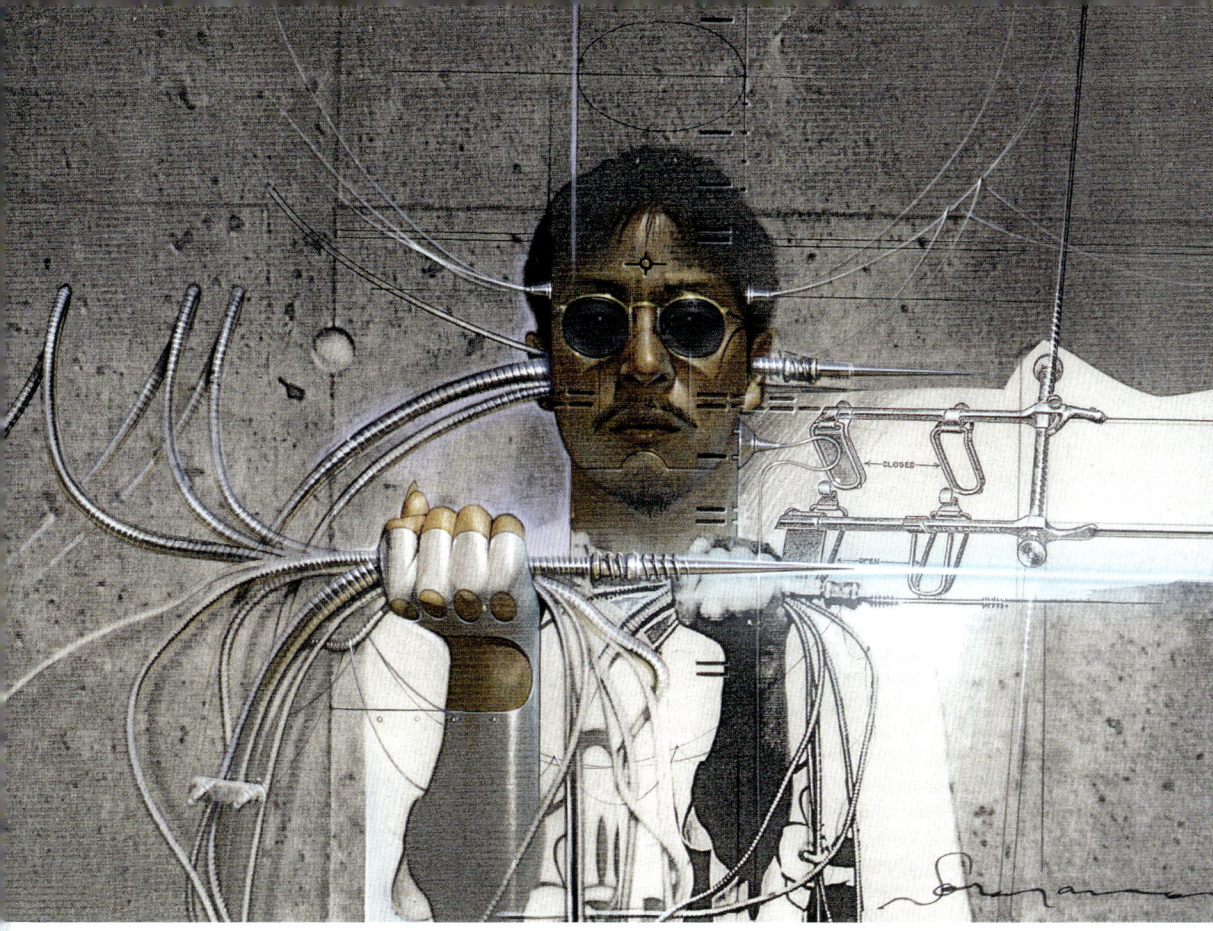

HAJIME SORAYAMA

was born in 1947 in the Ehime prefecture in Japan, and studied at Shikoku Gakuin University in 1965. His subjects were Greek and then English, but he remained uninspired. It was Sorayama's childhood talent for drawing that helped him into Japan's Chuo Art School in 1967. Graduating in 1969, he was employed by the advertising firm Asahi Tsushin sha in Tokyo as an all-round illustrator. He became freelance in 1972.

In 1978 he drew his first organic lifelike robot, and soon began to make a name for himself. In the 1980s, artist HAJIME SORAYAMA's Sexy Robots series were completed and published in Japan. They depicted the organic human form, but with life-like, muscular metallic skins; later "the Gynoids" book followed, influencing both the fashion and movies industries. Almost 20 years later, the first AI robotic pet (AIBO) came available as a people companion. AIBO grew out of Sony's Computer Science Laboratory (CSL). Together

with the famous Sony engineers, Hajime Sorayama was recruited to create the initial organic metallic skin designs. These are now part of the permanent collections of Museum of Modern Art and the Smithsonian Institution, with later versions of AIBO being used in studies in Carnegie Mellon University. Sorayama has also produced works for Disney's "Future Mickey" .
At the same time, a favorite subject remains the erotically charged female nude, although his masterful technique lends itself to many different subjects. A special Sorayama article appeared in the Silver Anniversary issue of Penthouse Magazine, for which he secured a long-term contract the following year. He designed the organic form of "Sony Aibo" the first intelligent pet robot, earning himself the highest level design awards from the Japanese government. He also worked on several movie projects, producing conceptual designs for the movie characters, such as a mechanical warrior for the science

fiction film "Space Trucker", an assassin woman in "Spawn" and other works by major filmmakers like George Lucas and Dino and Martha De Laurentiis.

About his art he says, "It is a kind of tenacity, an insistence upon asserting your own originality. By contrast, super realism deals with the technical issue of how close one can get to one's subject. Unlike art, illustration is not a matter of emotion or hatred, but an experience coming naturally through logical thinking."

In retrospect, Sorayama's work has been remarkably prescient. Beginning in the 1970's and still evolving, his amazing range of futuristic robots and mythical fantastic figures always look ahead of their time.

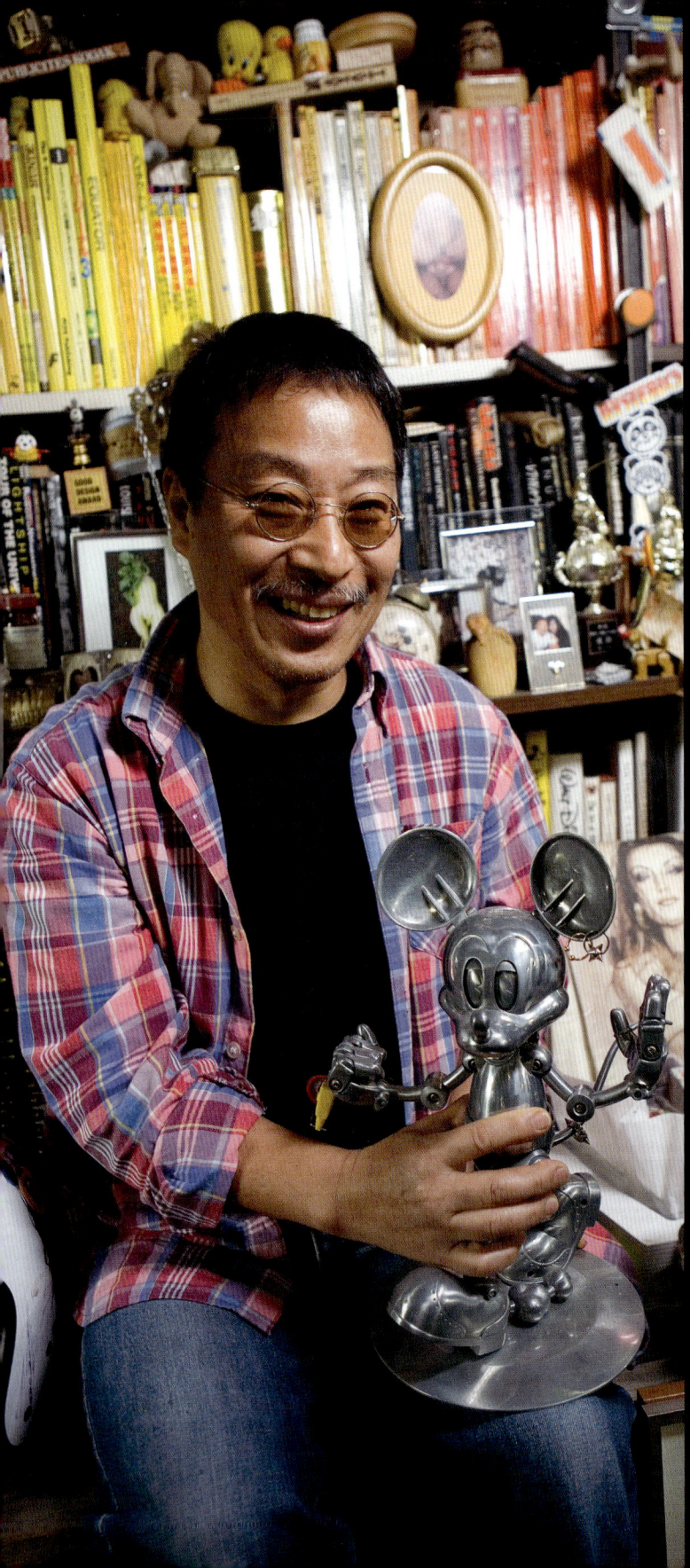

HAJIME SORAYAMA

PROFILE

1947   Born in Ehime, Japan
1969   BFA, Chuo Bijutsu Gakuen,
           Tokyo, Japan
           Lives and works in Tokyo

SOLO EXHIBITIONS

2021   "SORAYAMA SHARK",
           chi K11 art space, Guangzhou, China
           "Metropolis", HOW Art
           Museum, Shanghai, China
           "Dinosauria", NANZUKA
           2G, Tokyo, Japan
2020   "SEX MATTER", NANZUKA,
           Tokyo, Japan
           "TREX", NANZUKA
           2G, Tokyo, Japan
2019   "SORAYAMA Space Park", Central
           Embassy, Bangkok, Thailand
2018   "Sorayama Explosion 💥",
           NANZUKA, Tokyo, Japan
           "editions", AISHONANZUKA,
           HongKong, China
2017   "Sawasdee Sexy Robot by
           Hajime Sorayama", EchoOne
           ArtSpace, Bangkok, Thailand
           "Club Sorayama", LANDMARK,
           Hong Kong, China
           "空山基的械慾論", Wrong
           Gallery Taipei, Taipei, Taiwan
2016   "Sorayama", Jacob Lewis Gallery, New
           York, NY, USA
           "An actress is not a machine, but
           they treat you like a machine",
           NANZUKA, Tokyo, Japan
2015   AISHONANZUKA,
           Hong Kong, China
           Little High, Tokyo, Japan
           FIFTY24SF GALLERY, San
           Francisco, CA, USA
2014   Stussy Guest Artist Series — HAJIME
           SORAYAMA Exhibition Curated by
           NANZUKA, STUSSY HARAJUKU
           CHAPTER, Tokyo, Japan
2013   AISHONANZUKA,
           Hong Kong, China
           Hajime Sorayama x graniph
           Exhibition, graniph Harajuku
           Gallery, Tokyo, Japan
2011   "Hajime Sorayama: 1970–2010",
           Gering & Lopeg Gallery,
           New York, NY, USA
           "NEO DISCIPLINE", Span Art
           Gallery, Tokyo, Japan
           "Neo Japonism & Obsession",
           TOKYO CULTUART by BEAMS/B
           GALLERY, Tokyo, Japan
2010   NANZUKA UNDERGROUND,
           Tokyo, Japan
           Span Art Gallery, Tokyo, Japan
2008   Opera Gallery, New York,
           NY, USA
           WEAM, Miami, FL, USA
2007   "EROTOVISION", Mondo
           Bizzarro Gallery, Rome, Italy
2005   Hysteric Mini 20th Anniversary Art
           Exhibition, Tokyo/Osaka/HK

6

Show Room, New York, NY, USA

2003 Ginza Graphic Gallery,
Tokyo/Osaka, Japan

2002 Bape Gallery, Tokyo, Japan

1999 Tamara Bane Gallery,
Los Angels, CA, USA

1998 Tamara Bane Gallery,
Los Angels, CA, USA
ECR, Cologne, Germany

1994 UP'S Gallery
Tamara Bane Gallery,
Los Angels, CA, USA
the Castlegate Hotel and Conference
Center, Atlanta, GA, USA

1988 The Seibu Department Store
Gallery, Hakodate, Japan

GROUP EXHIBITIONS

2021 "POP-ING NANZUKA at
AKI Gallery", AKI Gallery,
Taipei, TAIWAN

2020 "H.R.GIGER x SORAYAMA",
PARCO MUSEUM TOKYO,
Tokyo, Japan
"Underground of Diversity", Art Basel
Miami Beach Online 2020
"GROBAL POP UNDERGROUND"
PARCO MUSEUM TOKYO, Tokyo,
Japan
"JP POP UNDERGROUND",
Shinsaibashi PARCO
14F, Osaka, Japan

2019 "Arsham x Sorayama", NANZUKA
2G, Tokyo, Japan
"TOKYO POP UNDERGROUND",
Jeffrey Deitch, LA, US
"TOKYO POP UNDERGROUND",
Jeffrey Deitch, NY, US
"Art Basel Hong Kong 2019", Hong
Kong Convention and Exhibition
Center, Hong Kong
"Span Art Gallery Collection
2019", Span Art Gallery,
Tokyo, Japan
"MUZAN -cruel and beauty-",
VANILLA GALLERY, Tokyo, Japan
"I draw", D MUSEUM, Seoul,
South Korea
"PEOPLE", Jeffrey Deitch,
Los Angeles, USA
"Taipei Dangdai", Taipei Nangang
Exhibition Center, Taipei, Taiwan

2018 "AAF - AUTOMOBILE ART
FEDERATION vol.7", gallery
YAMAWAKI, Tokyo, Japan

2017 "Exhibition of Mythical beast IV",
TOKYO KOTSU KAIKAN,
Tokyo, Japan
"Alice 2017", ROPPONGI
STRIPE'S SPACE, Tokyo, Japan
"Blood and Roses", SPAN ART
GALLERY, Tokyo, Japan
"AUTOMOBILE ART
FEDERATION(AAF)" YAMAWAKI
GALLERY,
Tokyo, Japan
"ARRIVAL XX PLANET THE
COLLECTION - EXHIBITION OF
KAWS × MURAKAMI
TAKASHI'S WORKS" Je Fine

Art Gallery Shanghai, Shanghai
The Encyclopedia of Masamichi
Katayama "Life is hard... Let's go
shopping.", Tokyo Opera City
Art Gallery, Tokyo, Japan
"THE UNIVERSE AND ART",
ARTSCIENCE MUSEUM,
Singapore
"Hello, Robot: Design Between
Human and Machine",
Vitra Design Museum,
Weil am Rhein, Germany
"The Encyclopedia of Masamichi
Katayama", Tokyo Opera City
Art Galleryz, Tokyo, Japan
"TENGAI 3.0"(Traveling exhibition),
hpgrp GALLERY TOKYO,Tokyo,
Japan
"頽恋期", Mangasick, Taiwan

2016 "Desire", Moore Building,
Miami, FL, USA
"TENGAI 3.0", hpgrp GALLERY
NEW YORK, New York, NY, USA
"The Universe and Art",
Mori Art Museum, Tokyo, Japan
"Cosmic Fusion 4",
O Museum, Tokyo, Japan
"TRIBUTE TO KOW YOKOYAMA",
TOKYO CULTUART by BEAMS,
Tokyo, Japan
"ALLOY & PEACE",
Spiral, Tokyo, Japan

2015 "Unorthodox", The Jewish Museum,
New York, NY, USA
"Exhibition of Mythical beast II",
Bunkamura, Tokyo, Japan
"MEDICOM TOY EXHIBITION'15",
PARCO MUSEUM, Tokyo, Japan
"The Aesthetics of Fantasy – Japanese
Erotica in Contemporary Art",
Bunkamura, Tokyo, Japan
"Here is ZINE tokyo 10", Tokyo
Cultuart BEAMS, Tokyo, Japan
"FELIX THE CAT – Cats Out
Of The Bag", SLOW CULTURE,
Los Angeles, CA, USA

2014 LEATHER JAPAN 2014,
New York, NY, USA
Amalia Ulman + Hajime Sorayama
Exhibition, London, UK
"JAPAN EROTICA",
Musee de l'erotisme, Paris, France
"with Hello Kitty", MDP GALLERY/
SPACE M,
Tokyo, Japan
"PUSSYCAT! KILL! KILL! KILL!",
Vanilla Gallery/Kinokuniya Gallery,
Tokyo, Japan
"O's story", billiken Gallery,
Tokyo, Japan
"atrocity beauty", Vanilla Gallery,
Tokyo, Japan
HORIYOSHI THE THIRD x Hajime
Sorayama, Galleria Harajuku, Tokyo,
Japan
KITAHARA COLLECTION,
Takamatsu city museum of Art,
Takamatsu, Japan
Span Art Gallery, Tokyo, Japan

2013 "The Pop Surrealism Show", Opera

Gallery, New York, NY, USA
"UKIYOE Roman Exhibition", Span
Art Gallery, Tokyo, Japan
"ALICE Fantasy tale exhibition",
Bunkamura, Tokyo, Japan

2012 "Cosmic Fusion III", O museum,
Tokyo, Japan
The ObsessionArt 5th Anniversary
Exhibition, The Gallery in
Cork Street, London, UK
"Artist's book by Treville 1985–2012",
Kinokuniya Gallery,
Tokyo, Japan
"Monster", billiken Gallery,
Tokyo, Japan
"Japanese Erotic Artsts",
Jinbocho Gallery, Tokyo, Japan

2011 "MEDICOM TOY 15th
ANNIVERSARY",
PARCO MUSEUM, Tokyo, Japan
"Here is ZINE tokyo 2", Tokyo
Cultuart BEAMS, Tokyo, Japan
Hamamatsu Municipal Museum of Art
40th Anniversary Special Exhibition,
Hamamatsu Municipal Museum of
Art, Shizuoka, Japan
"Märchenism",
The Tobu Department Store
Gallery, Tokyo, Japan

2010 "CODE : EROTICA", Bunkamura,
Tokyo, Japan
KITAHARA COLLECTION, Mori
Arts Center Gallery, Tokyo, Japan

2009 "Almost There" Time Tunnel
Series Vol.29, G8, Tokyo, Japan

2008 "CARNIVORA", FUSE Gallery,
New York, NY / L'Imagerie
Gallery, Los Angeles, CA / CPOP
Gallery, Detroit, MI, USA

2007 20th Anniversary Exhibitions
„Graphics & Messages",
GGG, Tokyo, Japan

2006 Ginza Recruit Gallery, Tokyo, Japan

2005 "Winter Invitational",
Art At Large, New York, NY, USA

1997 "Forum--Gelande",
Castrop-Rauxel, Germany

1989 "Ferrari Hall", Munich, Germany

AWARD

2001 Inventor's Award – Asahi newspaper

1999 Good Design Grand Prize Award
Media Art Festival Grand Prize Award

1996 Vargas Award

PUBLIC COLLECTIONS

Museum of Modern Art,
New York, USA

Smithsonian
Institute of Technology Museum. Washington
DC, USA

World Erotic Art Museum,
Miami, USA

US Library of Congress.
Washington DC, USA

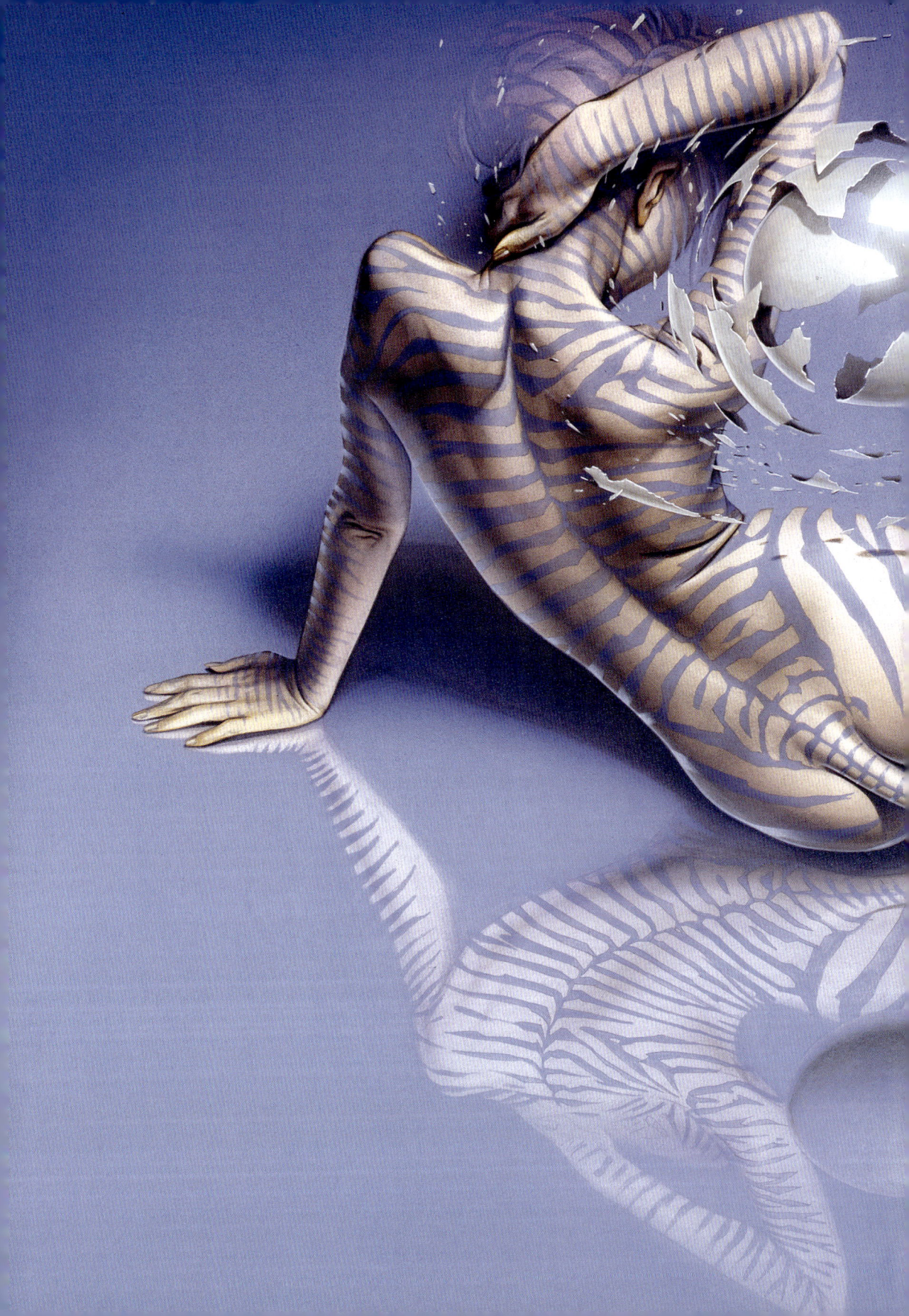

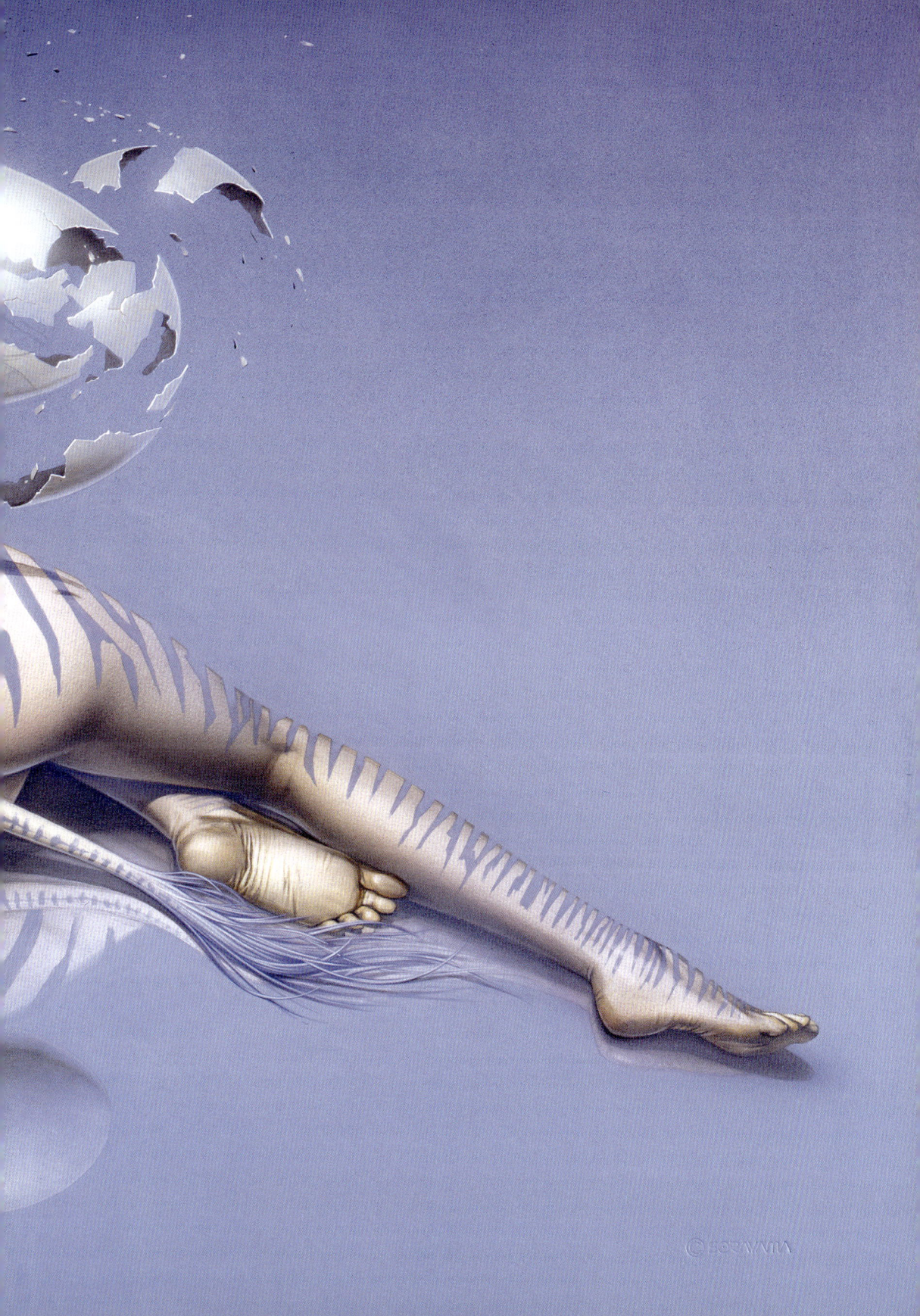

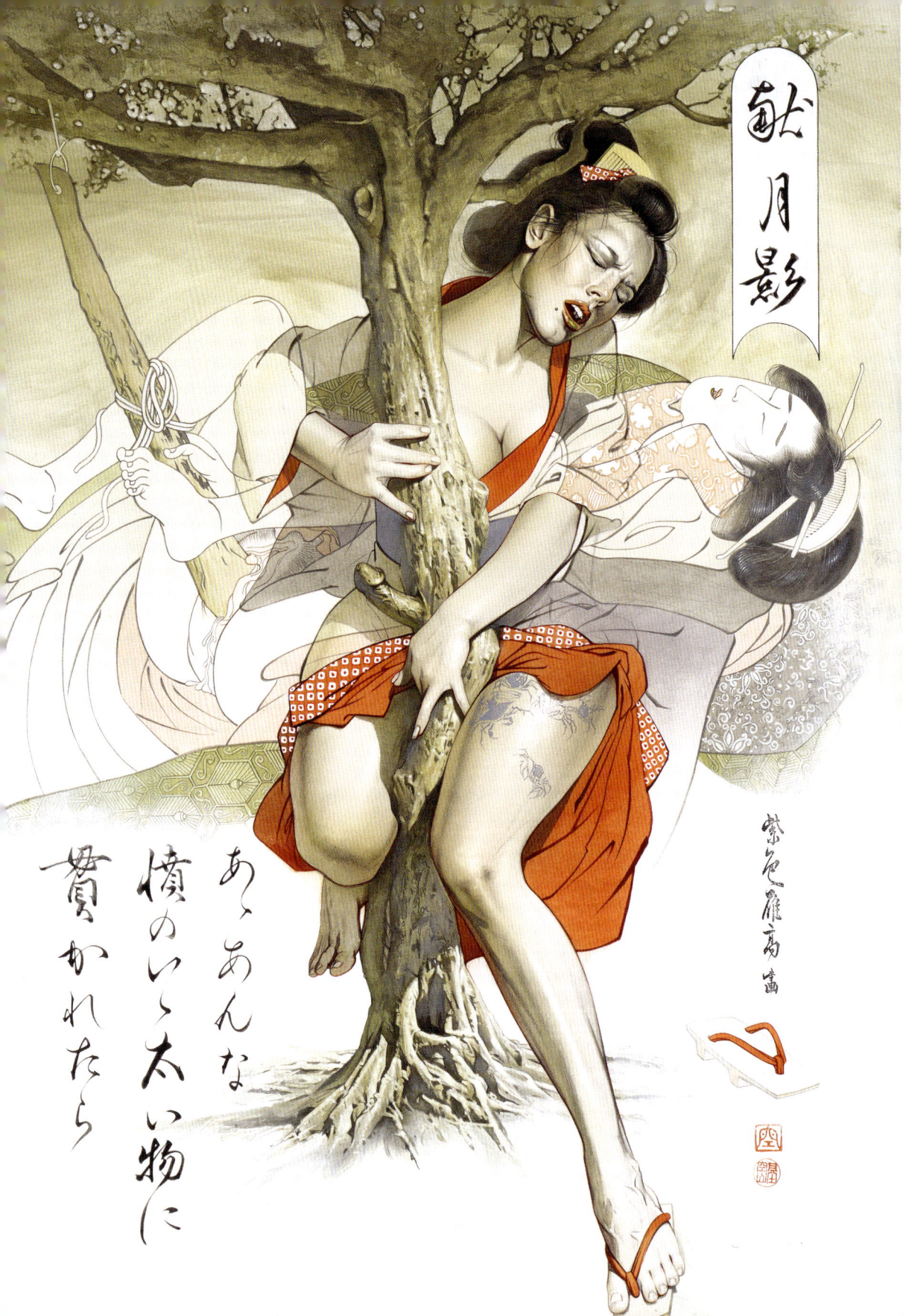

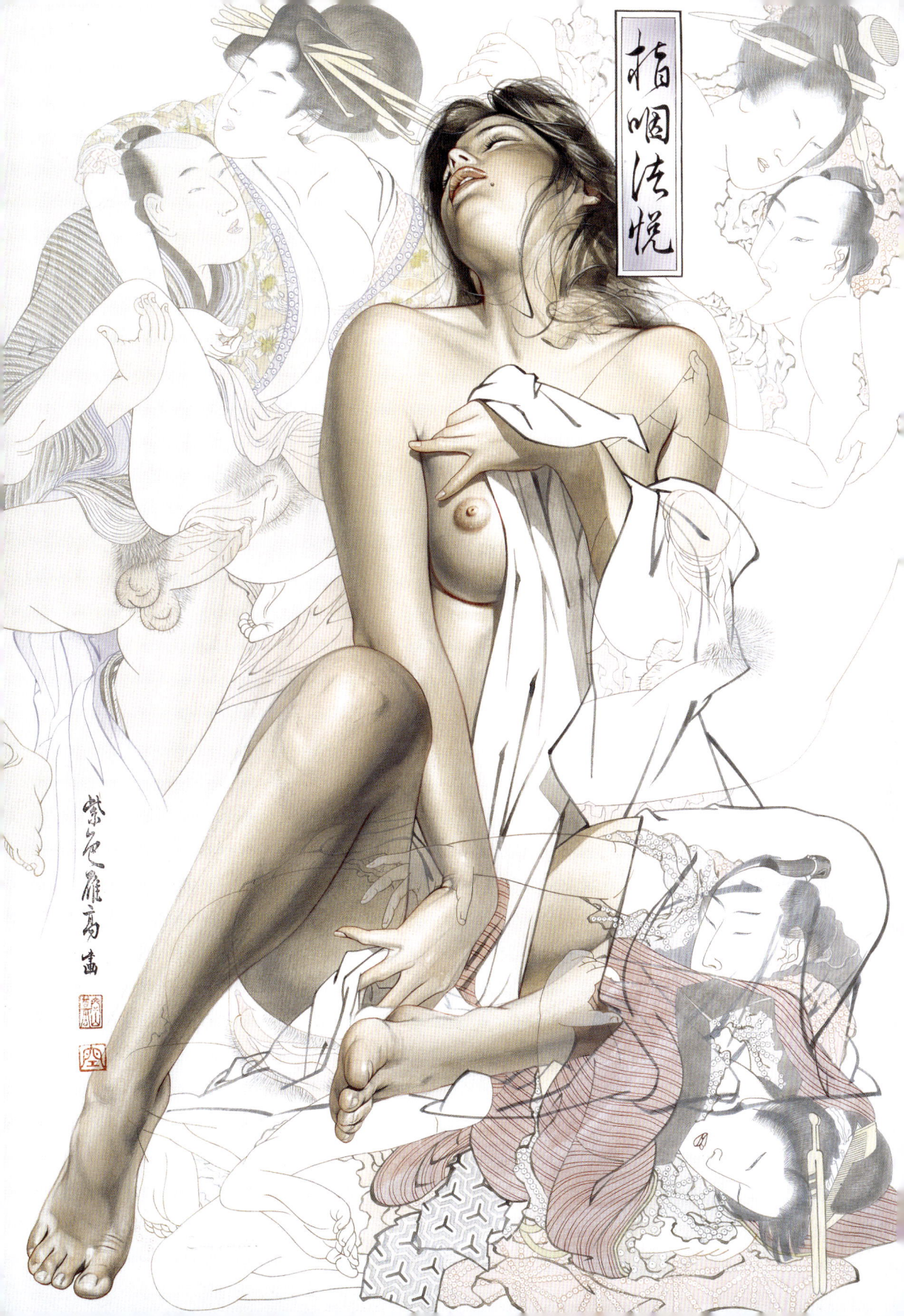

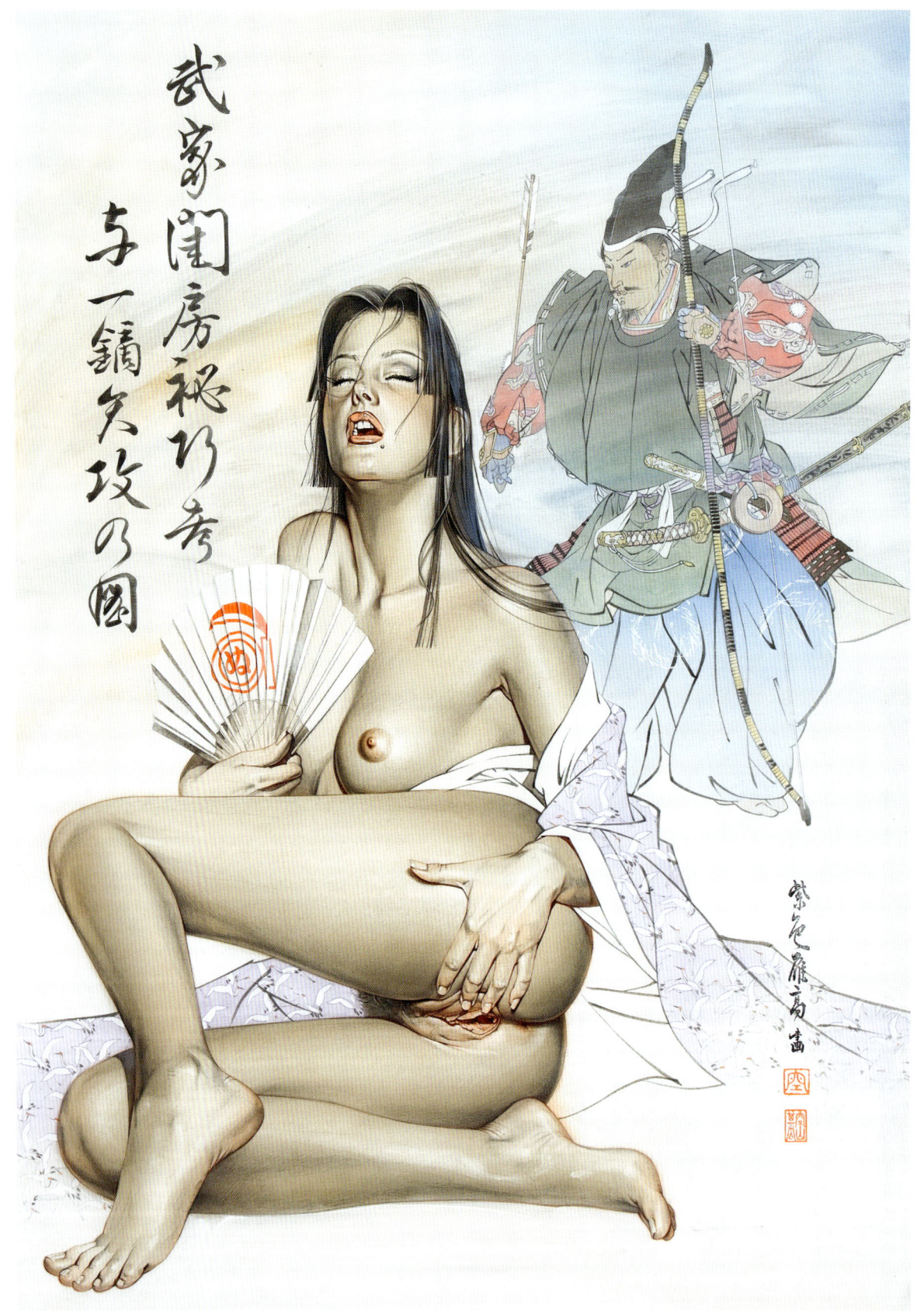

武家閨房裲杖考
与一鏑矢攻の図

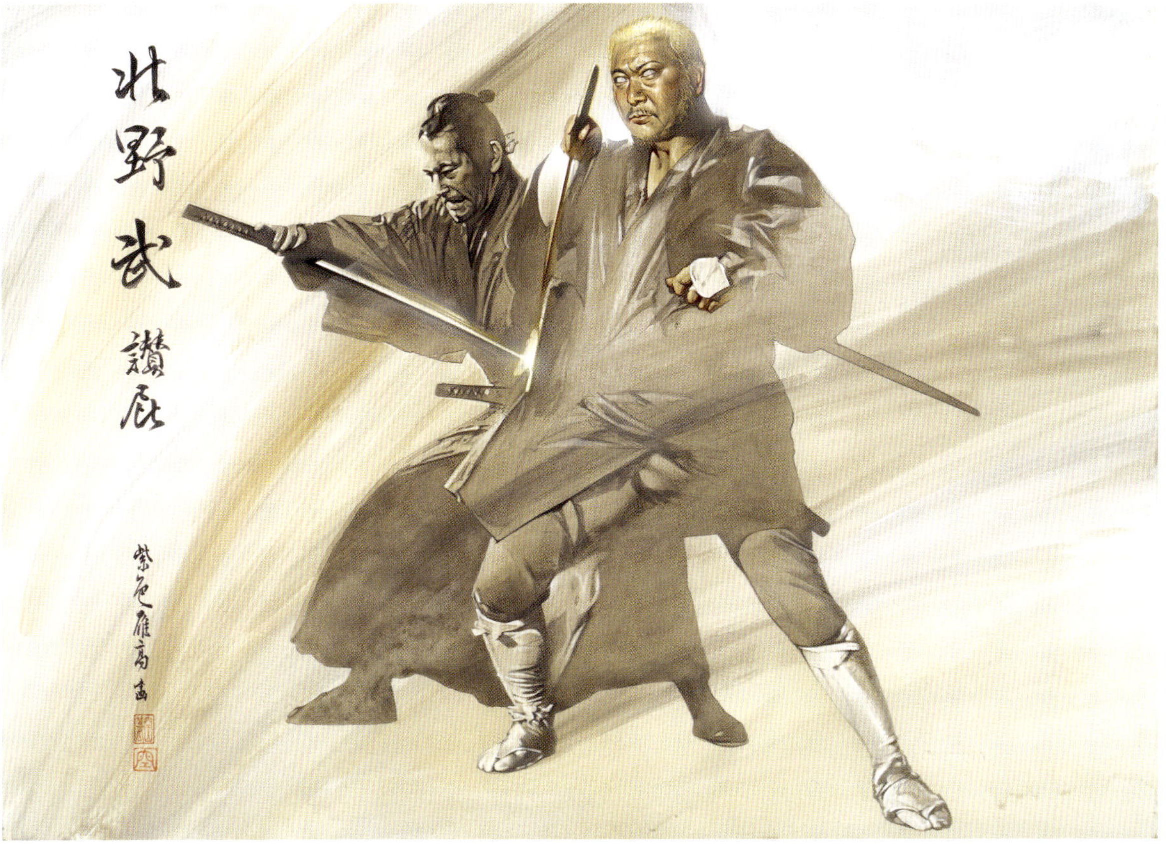

北野武 讃屁

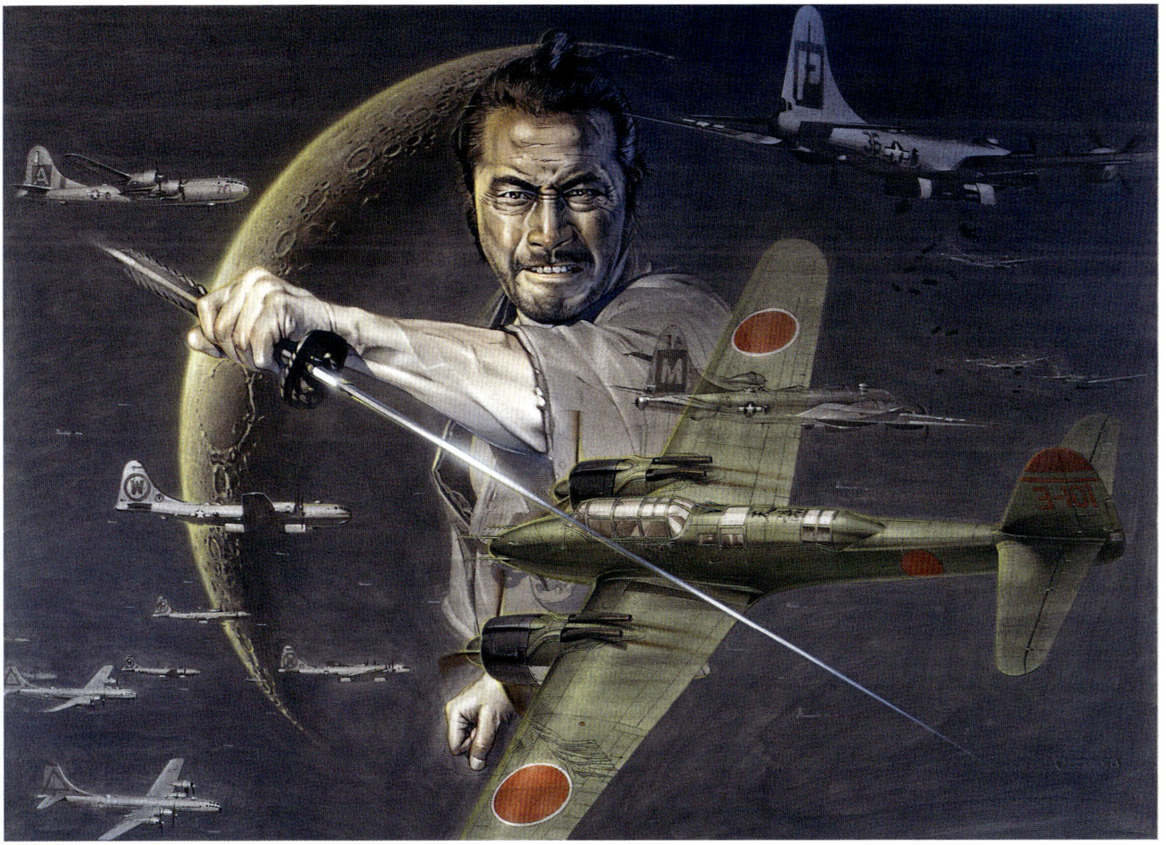

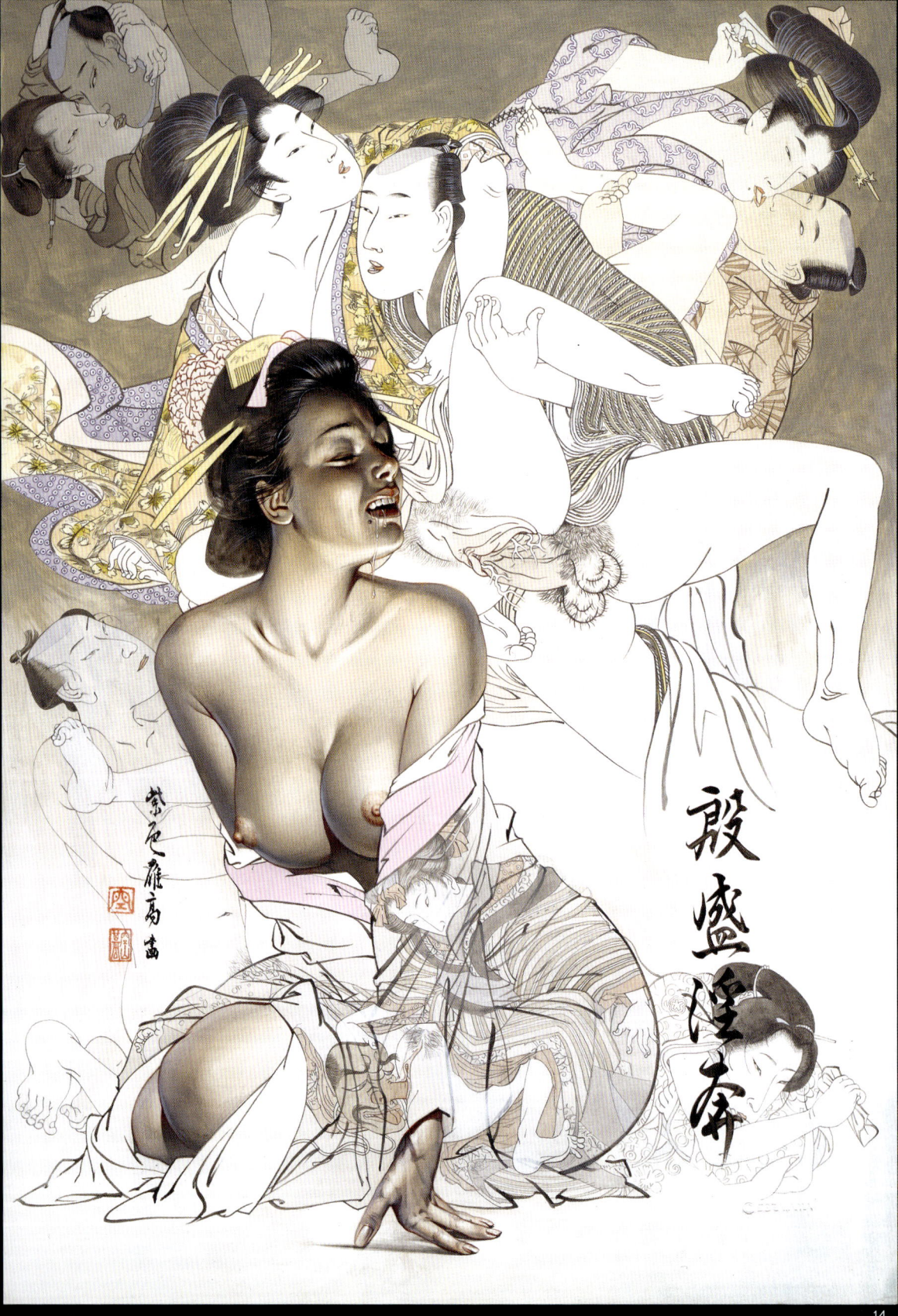

殷盛淫奔

14

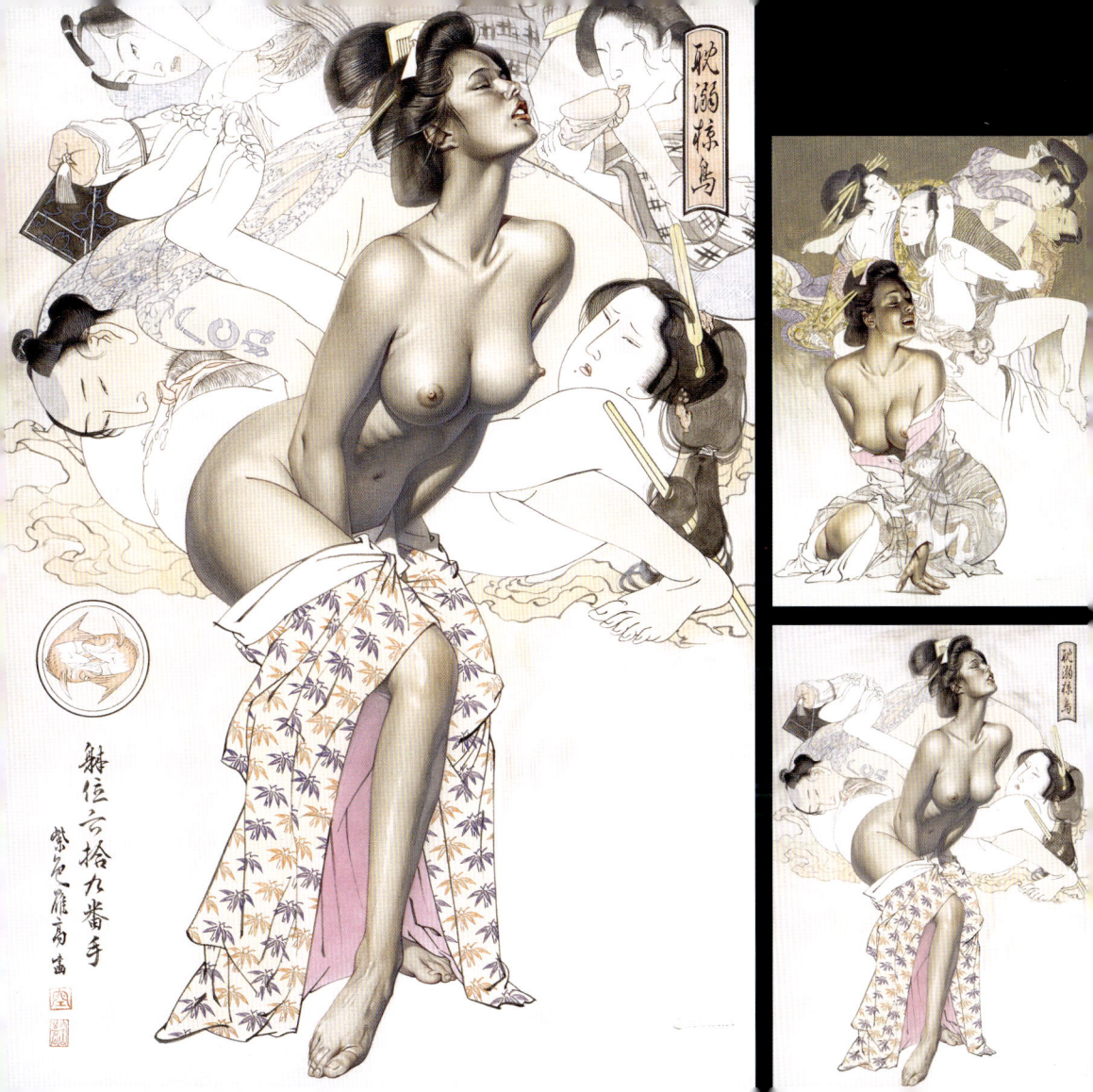

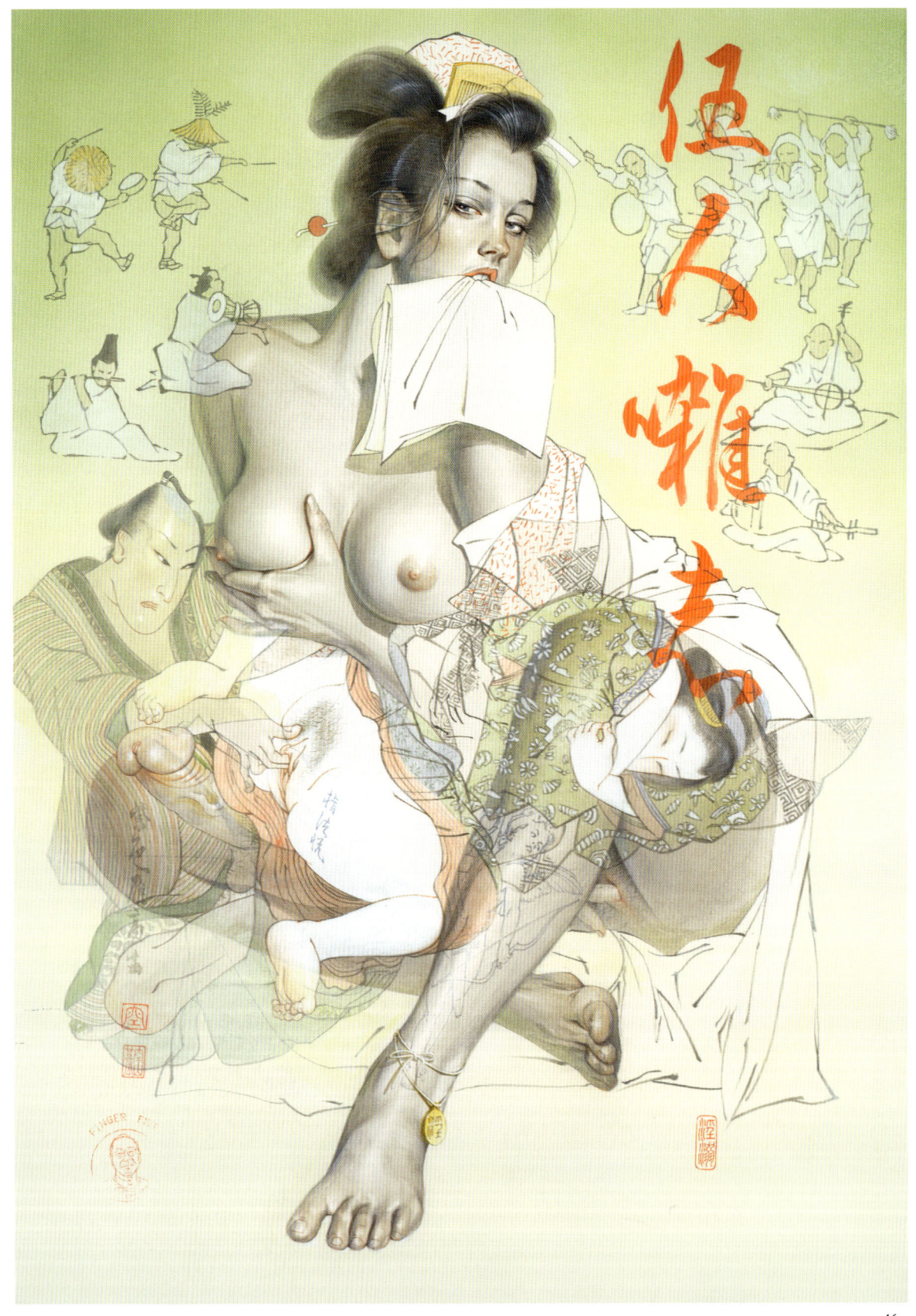

16

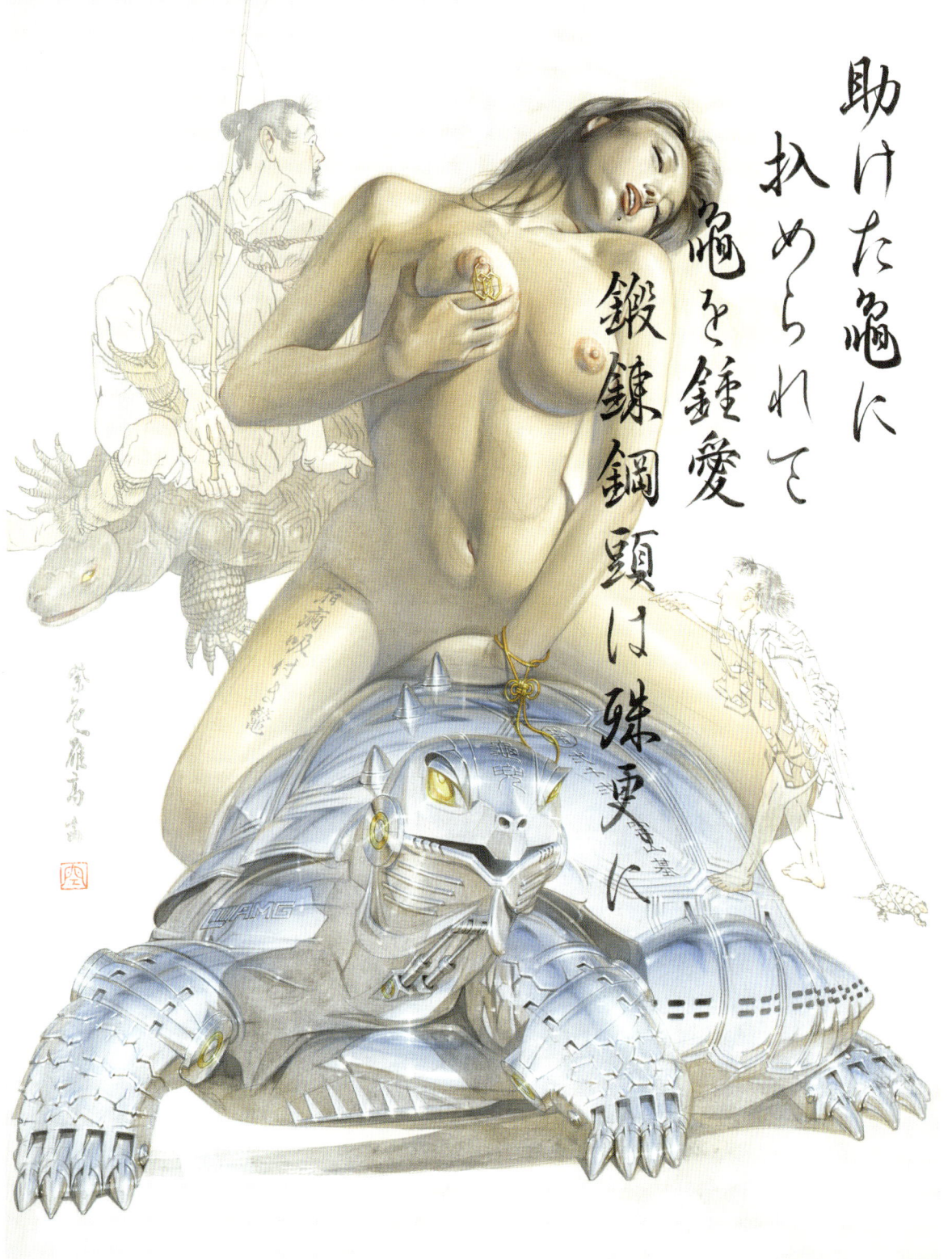

助けた亀に拉められて亀を鍾愛

鍛錬鋼頭は殊更に

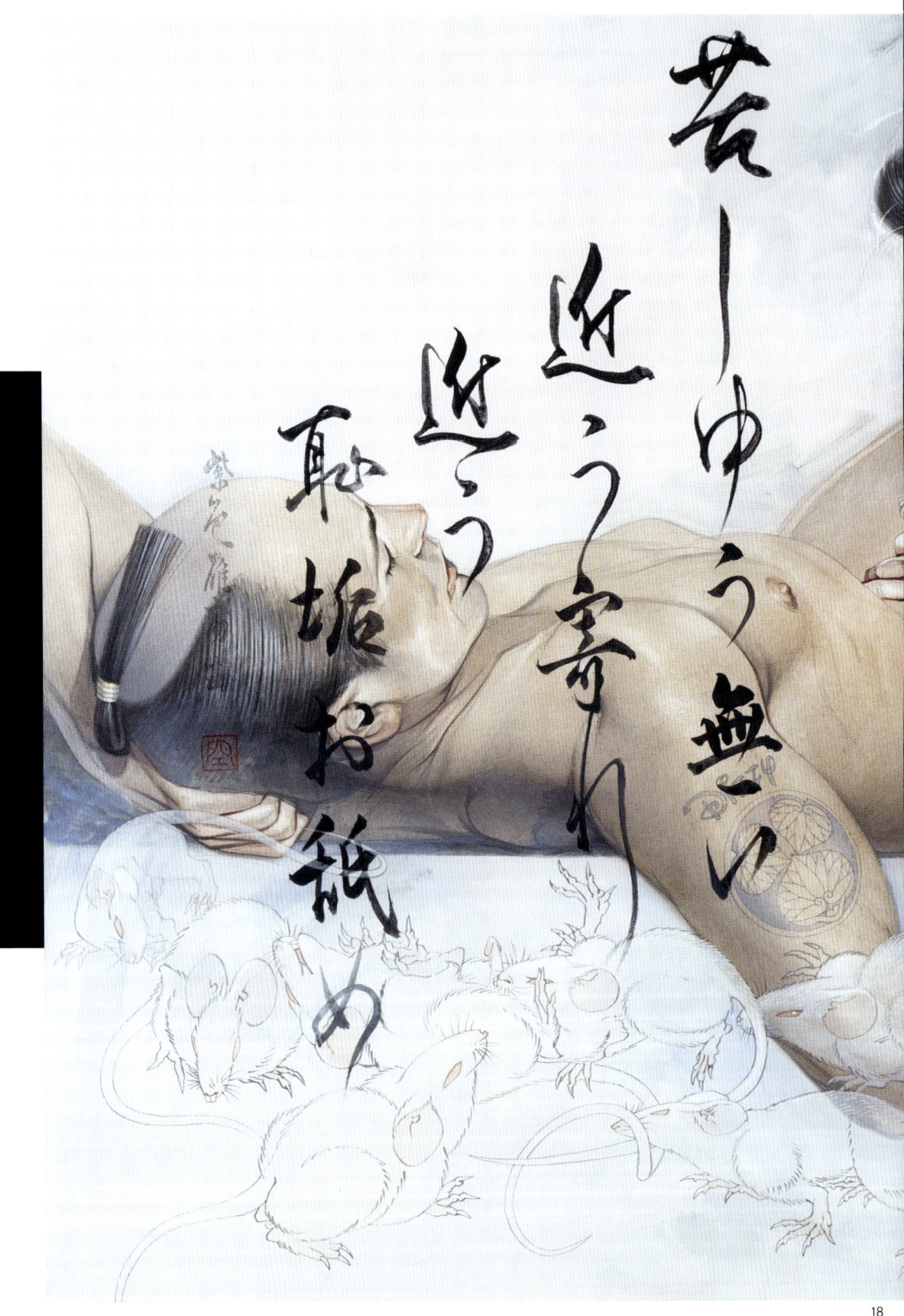

18

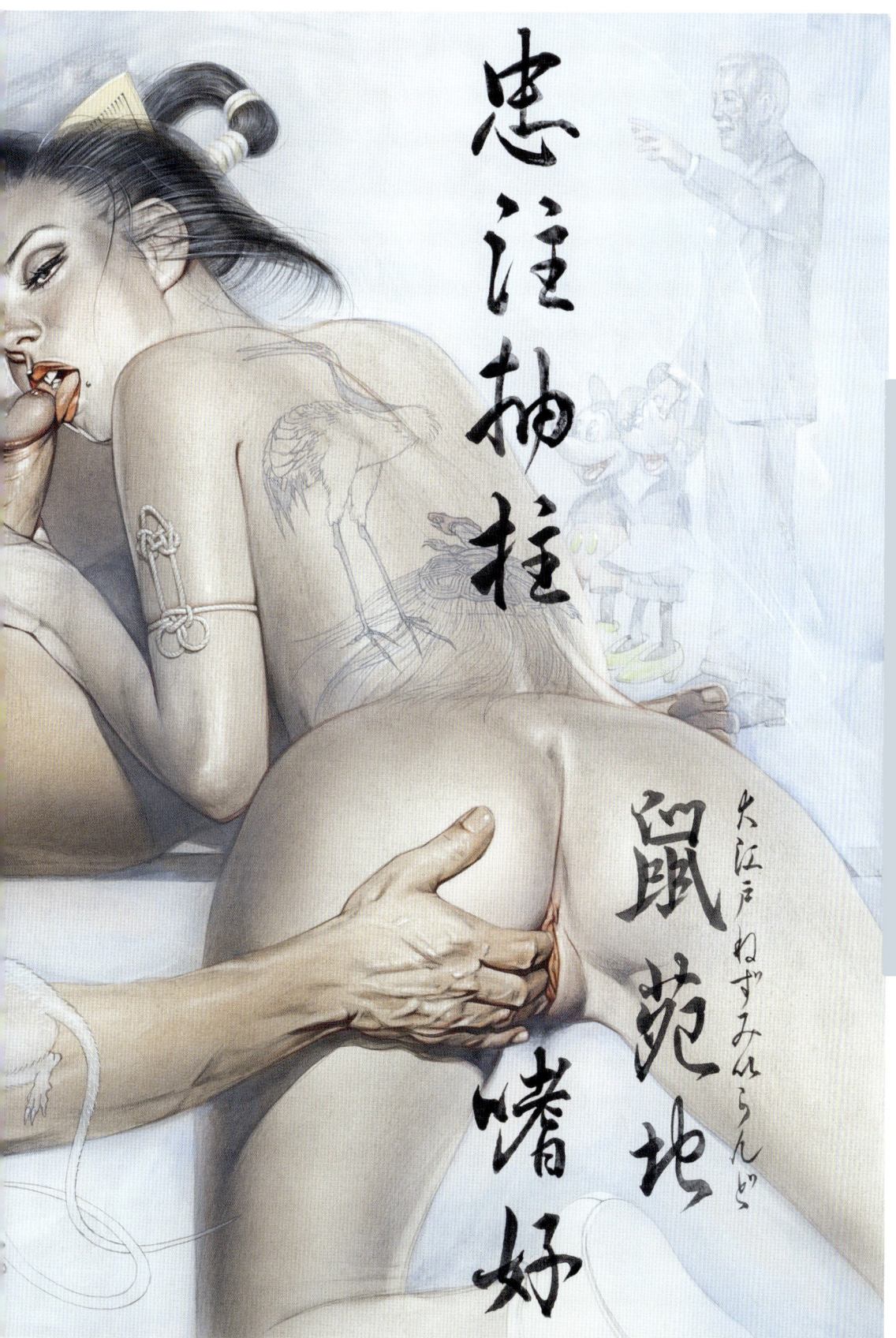

忠涯柚桂

大江戸ねずみらんど

鼠苑地

嗜好

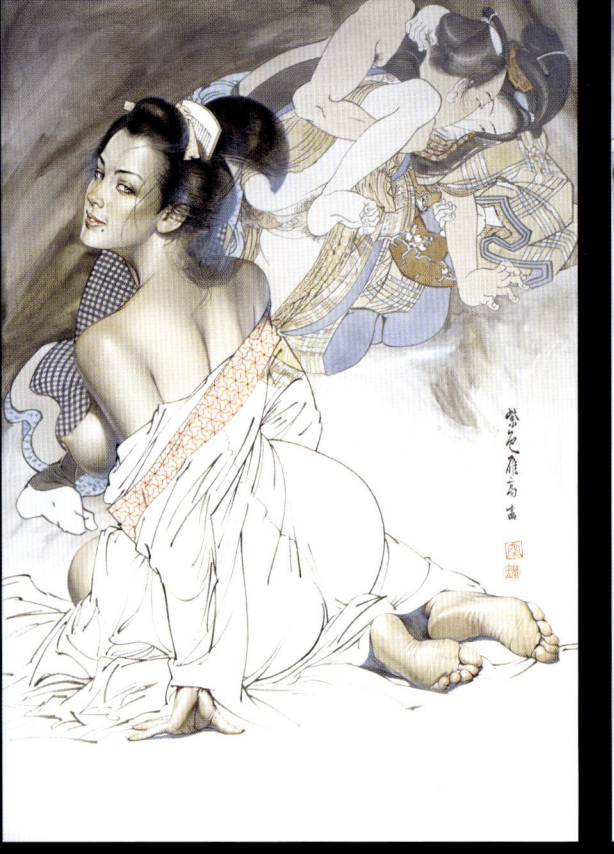

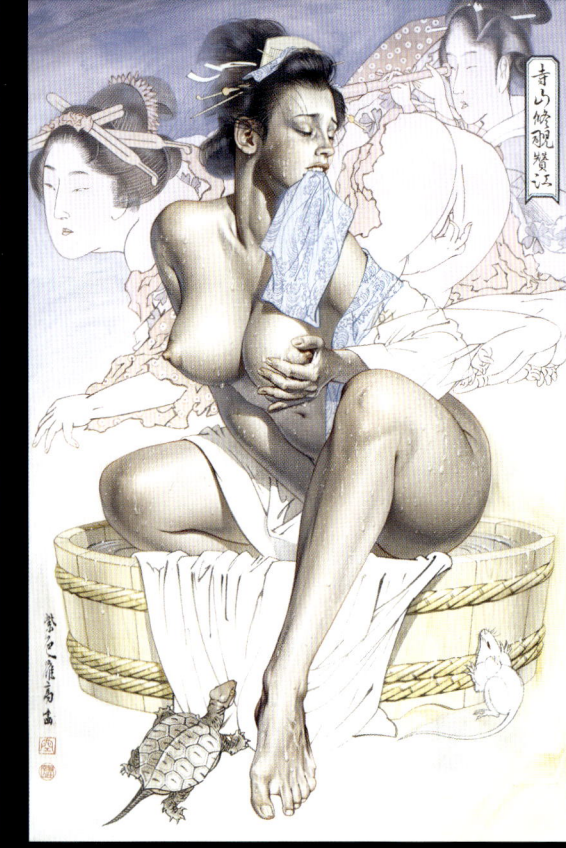

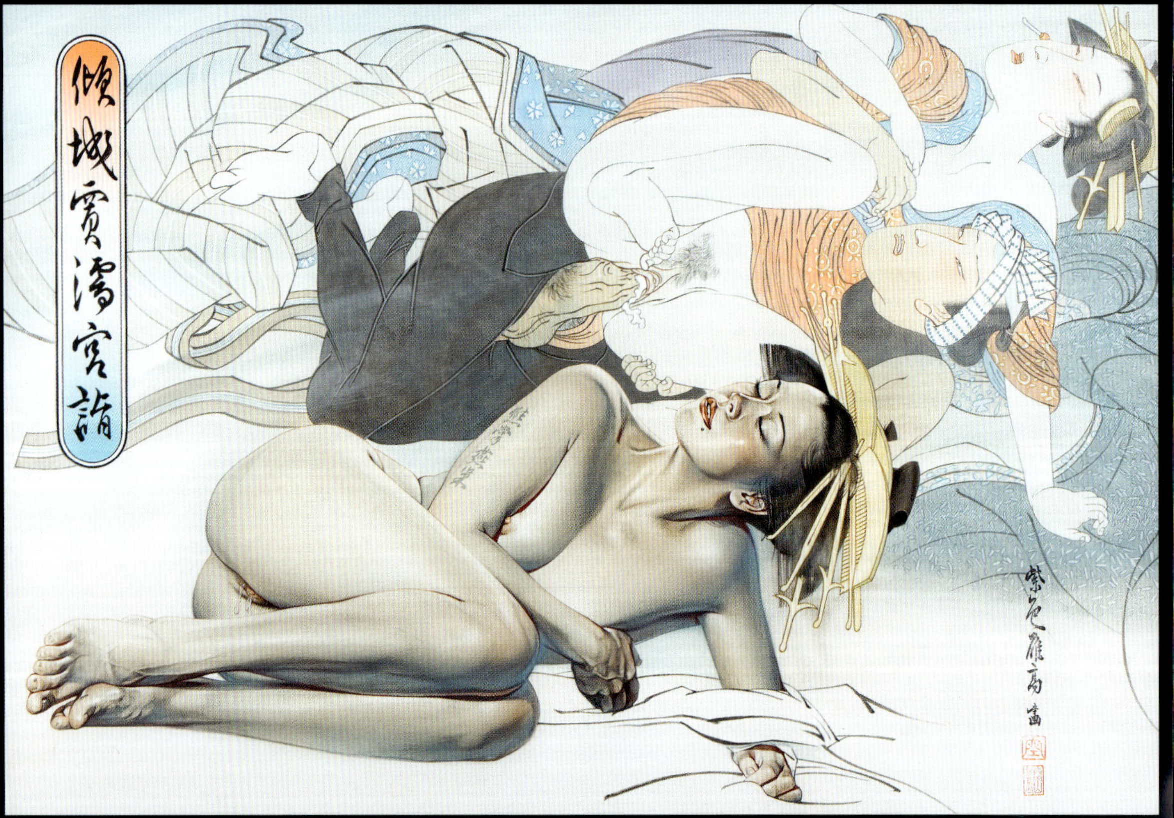

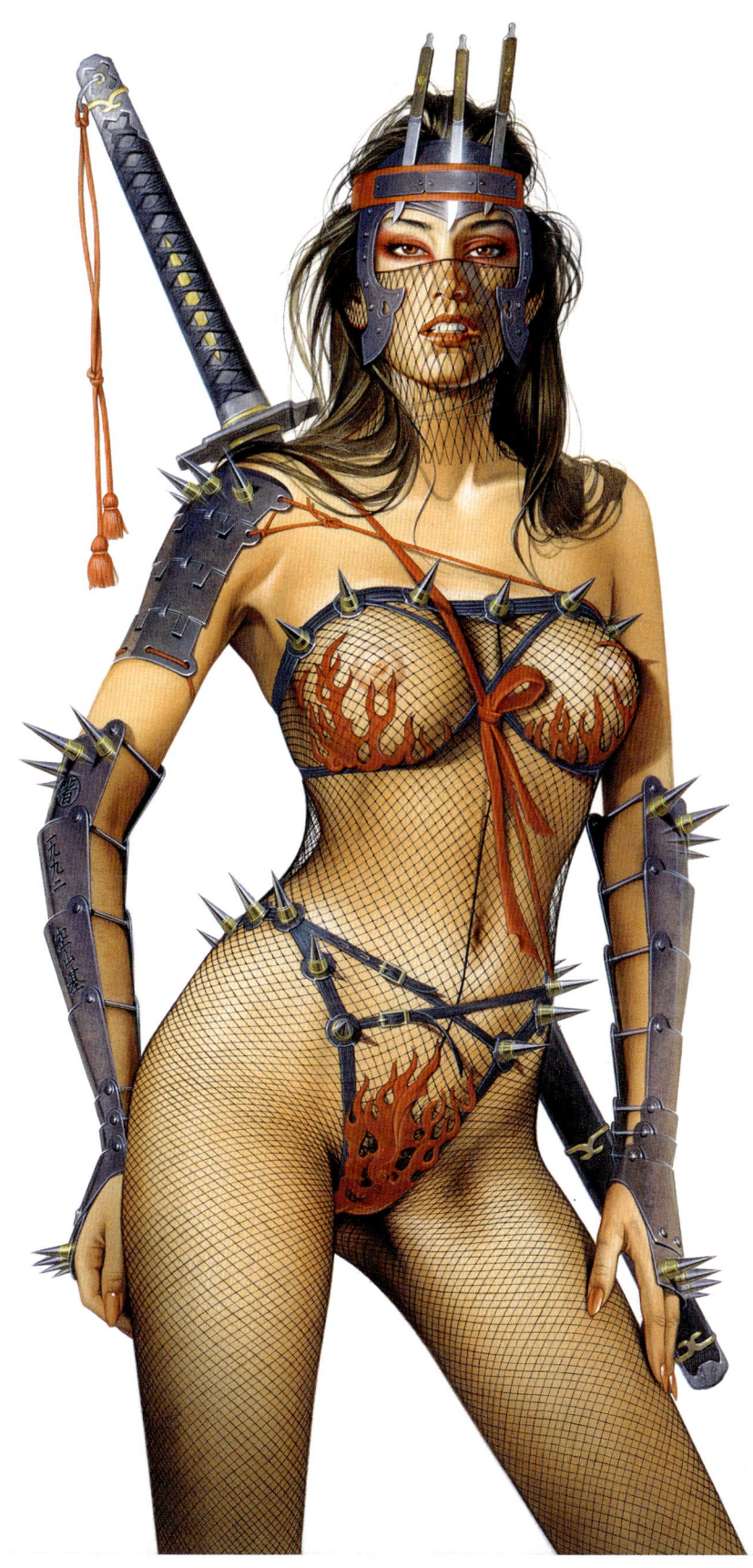

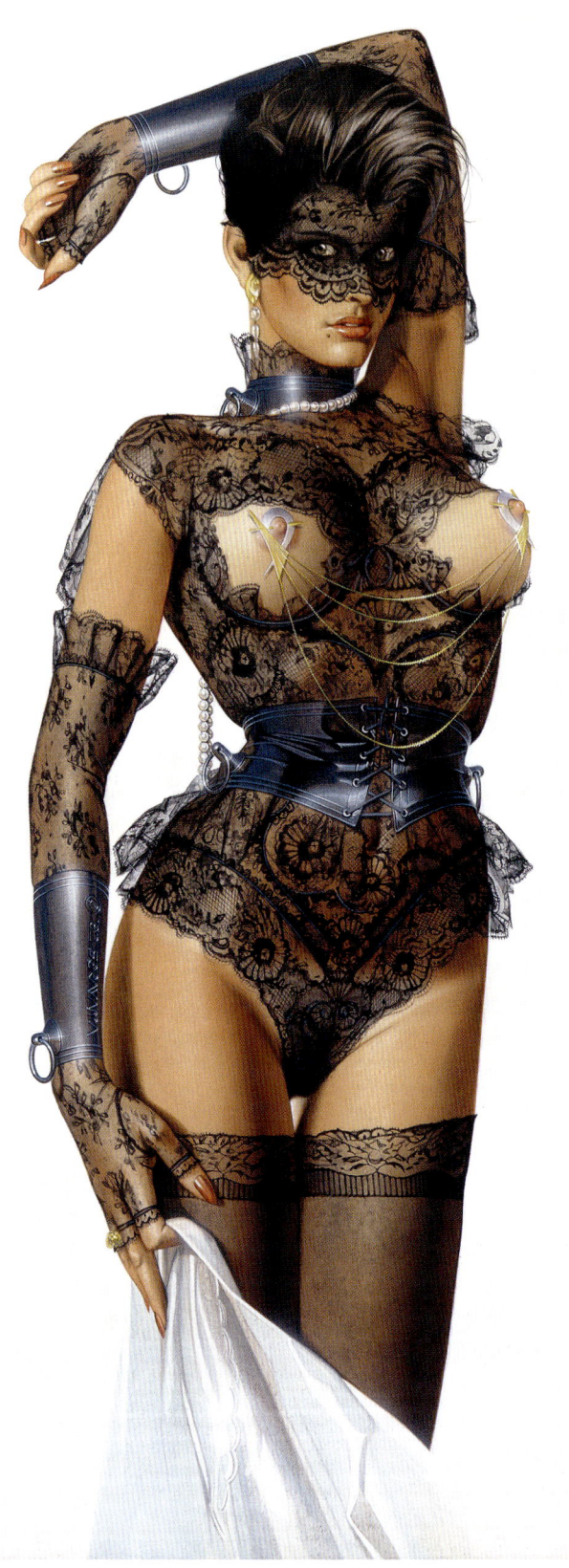

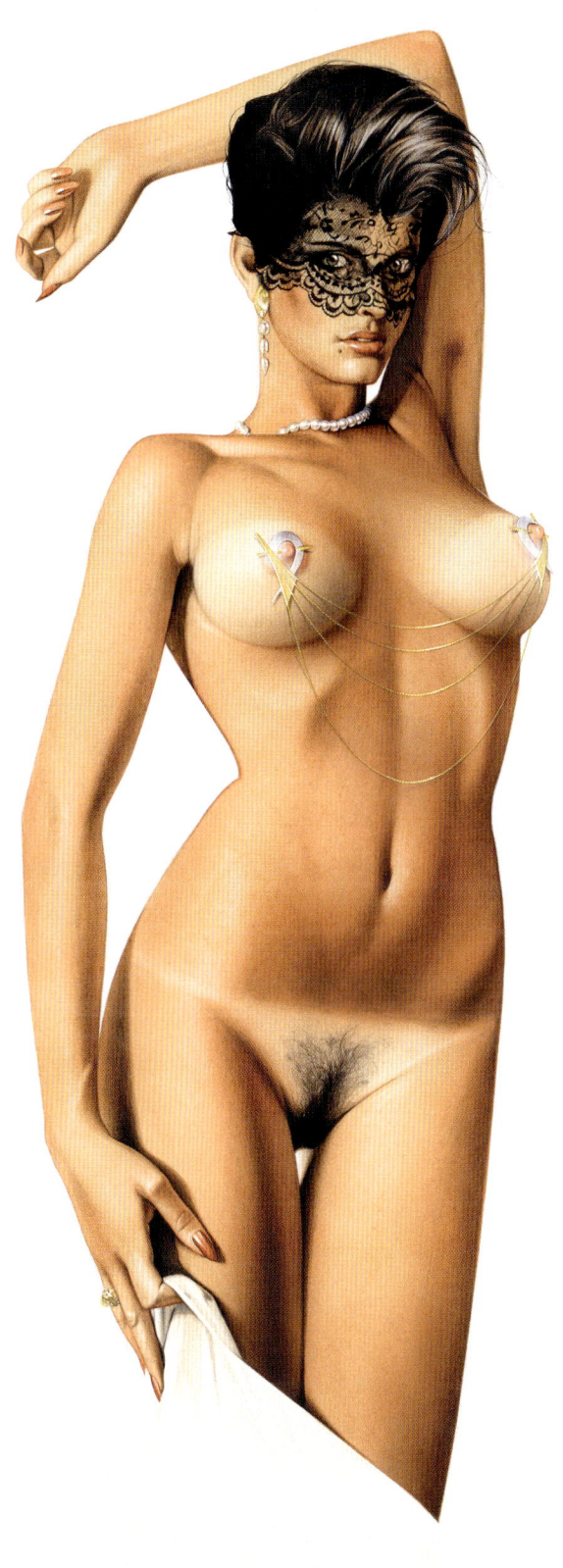

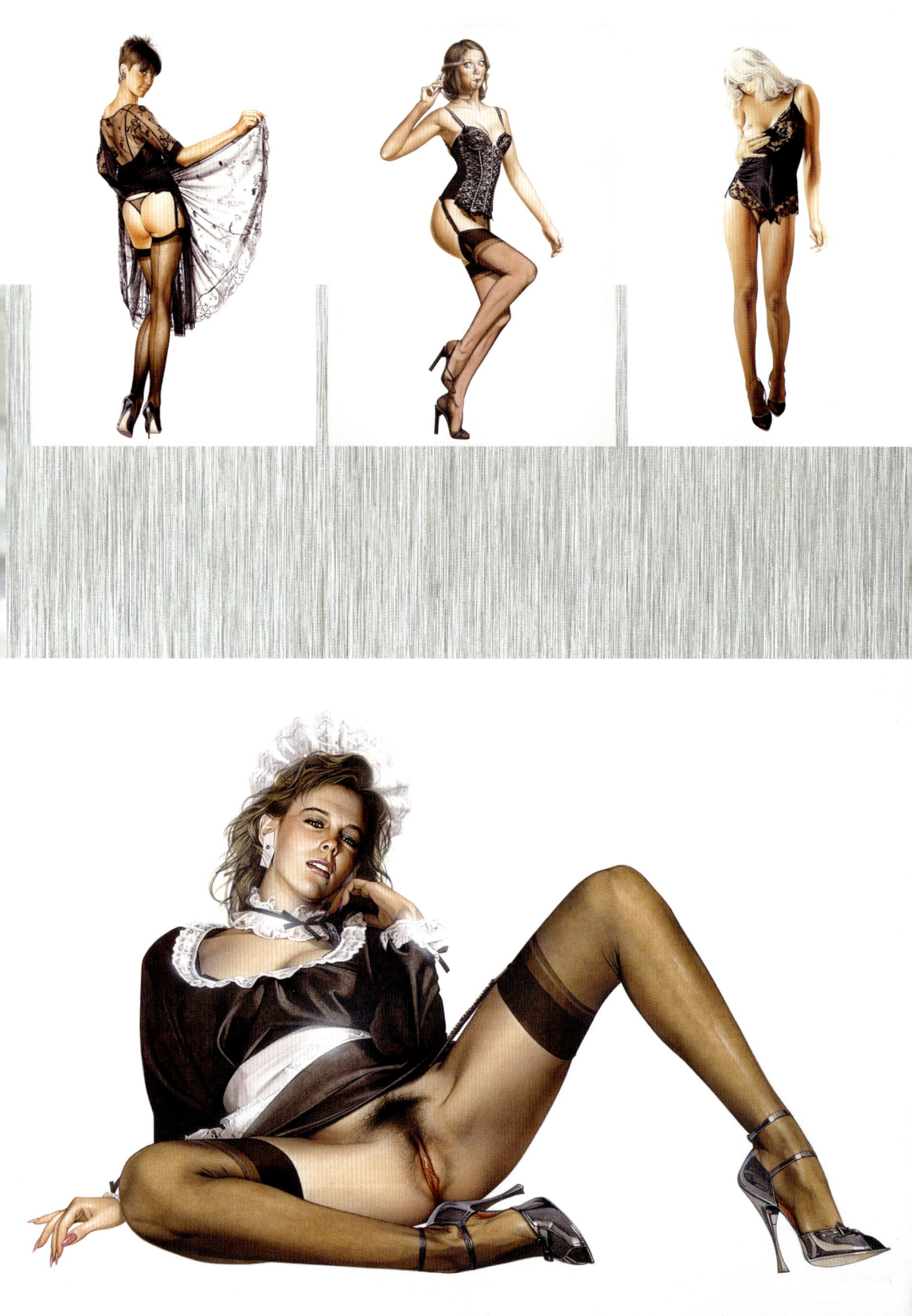

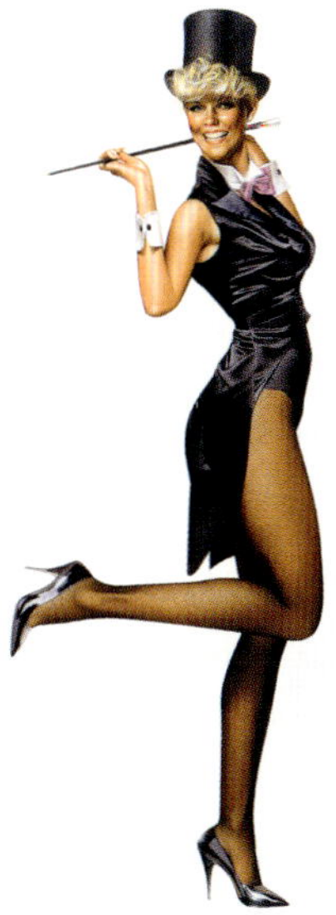

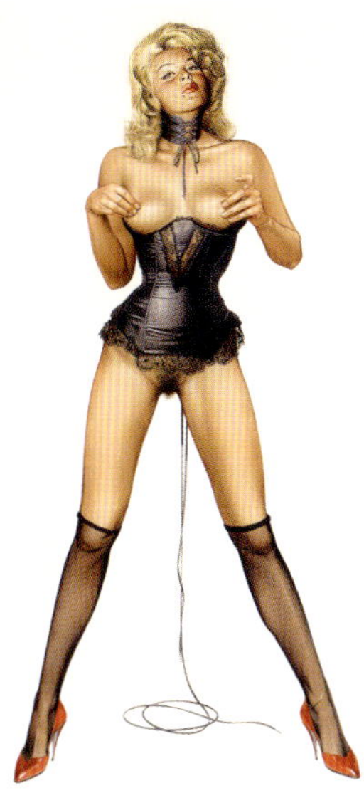

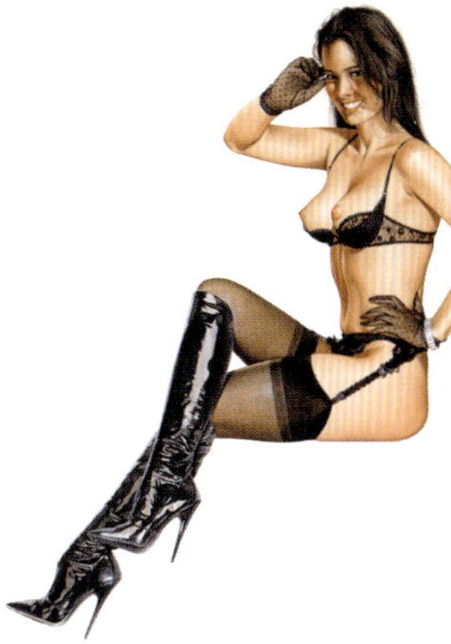

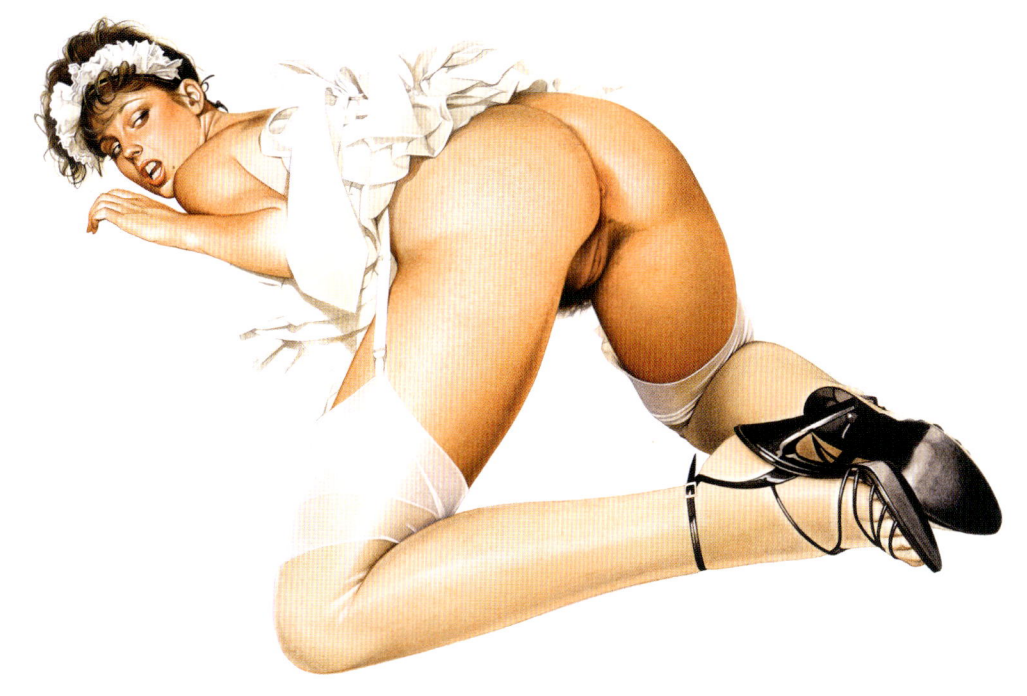

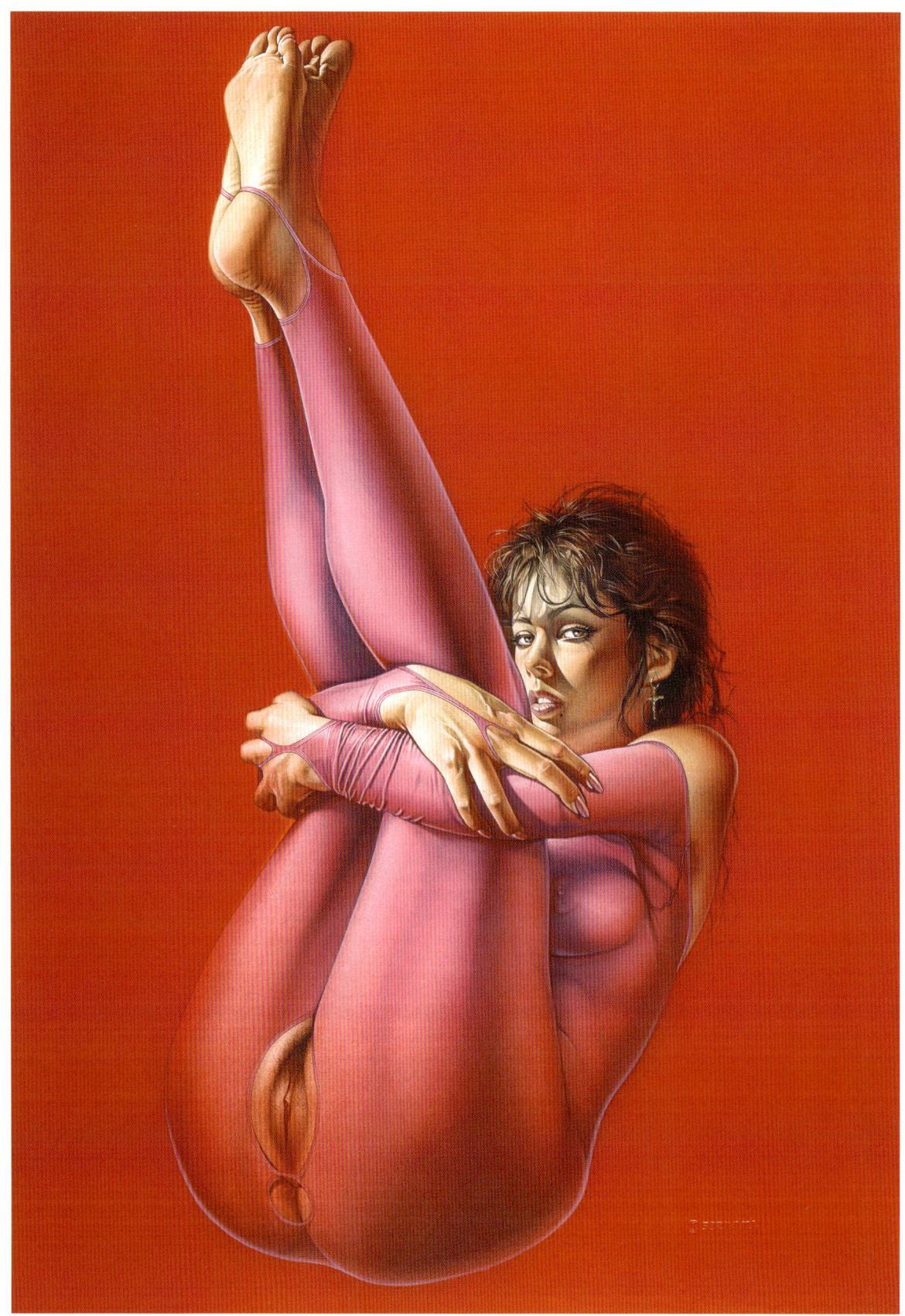

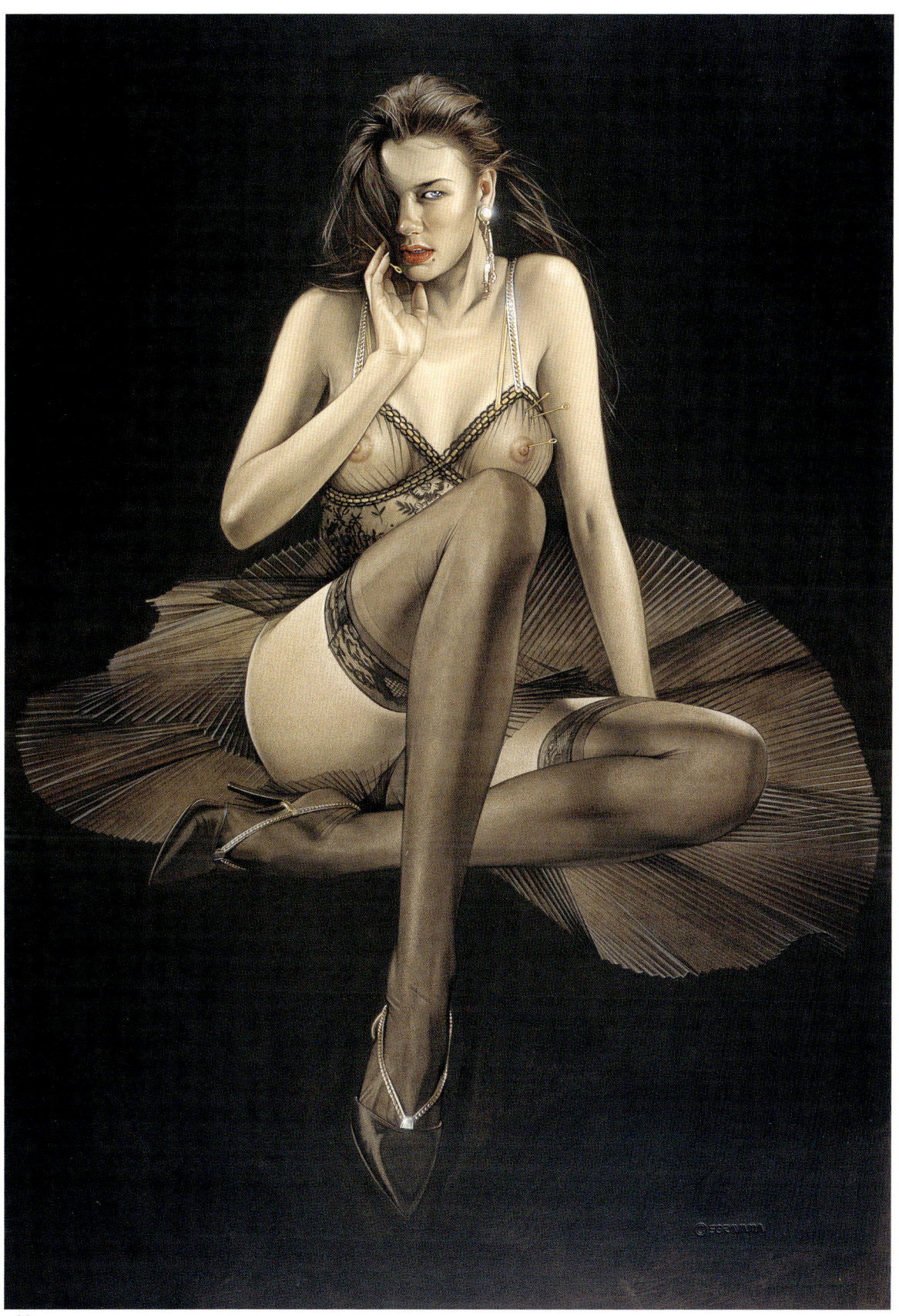

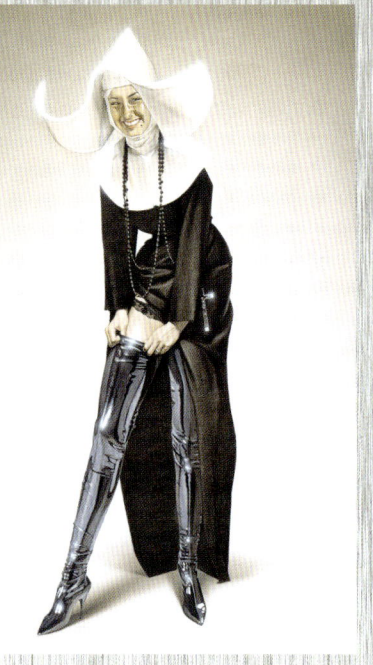

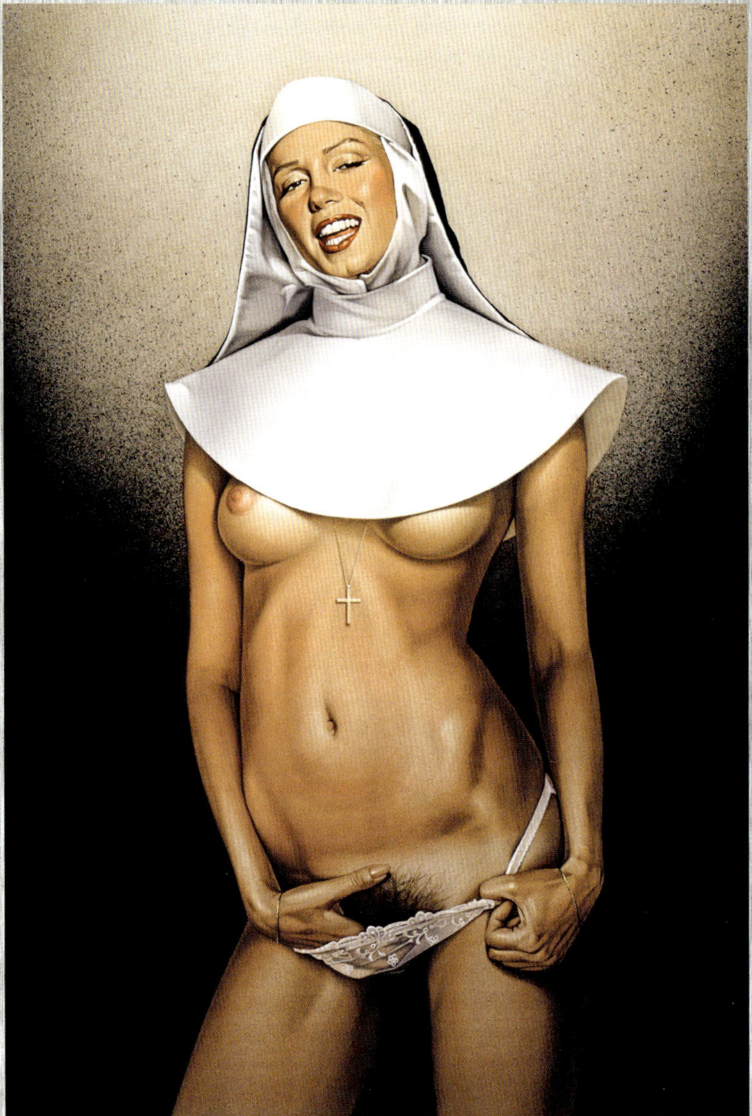

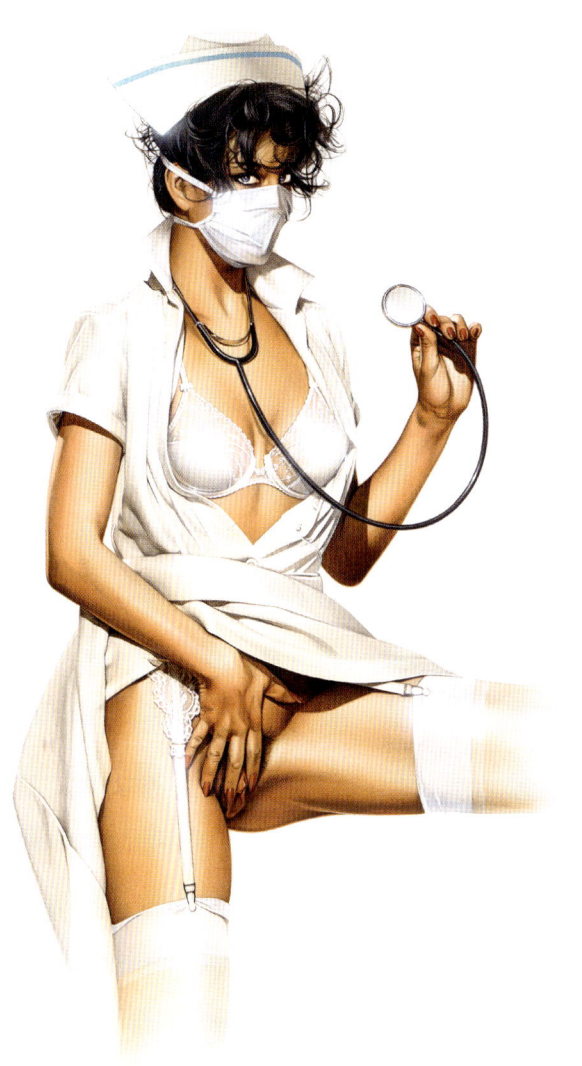
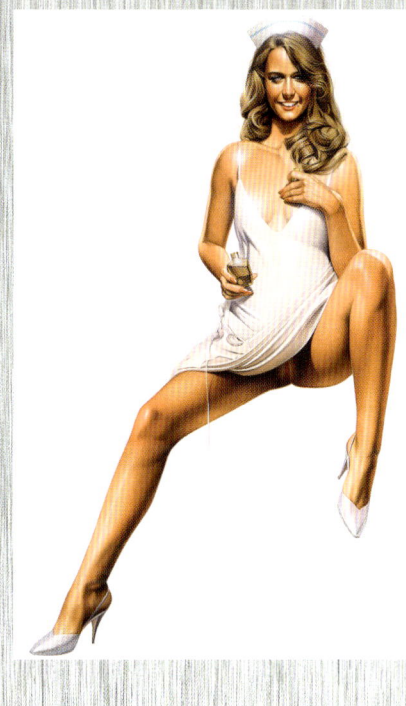

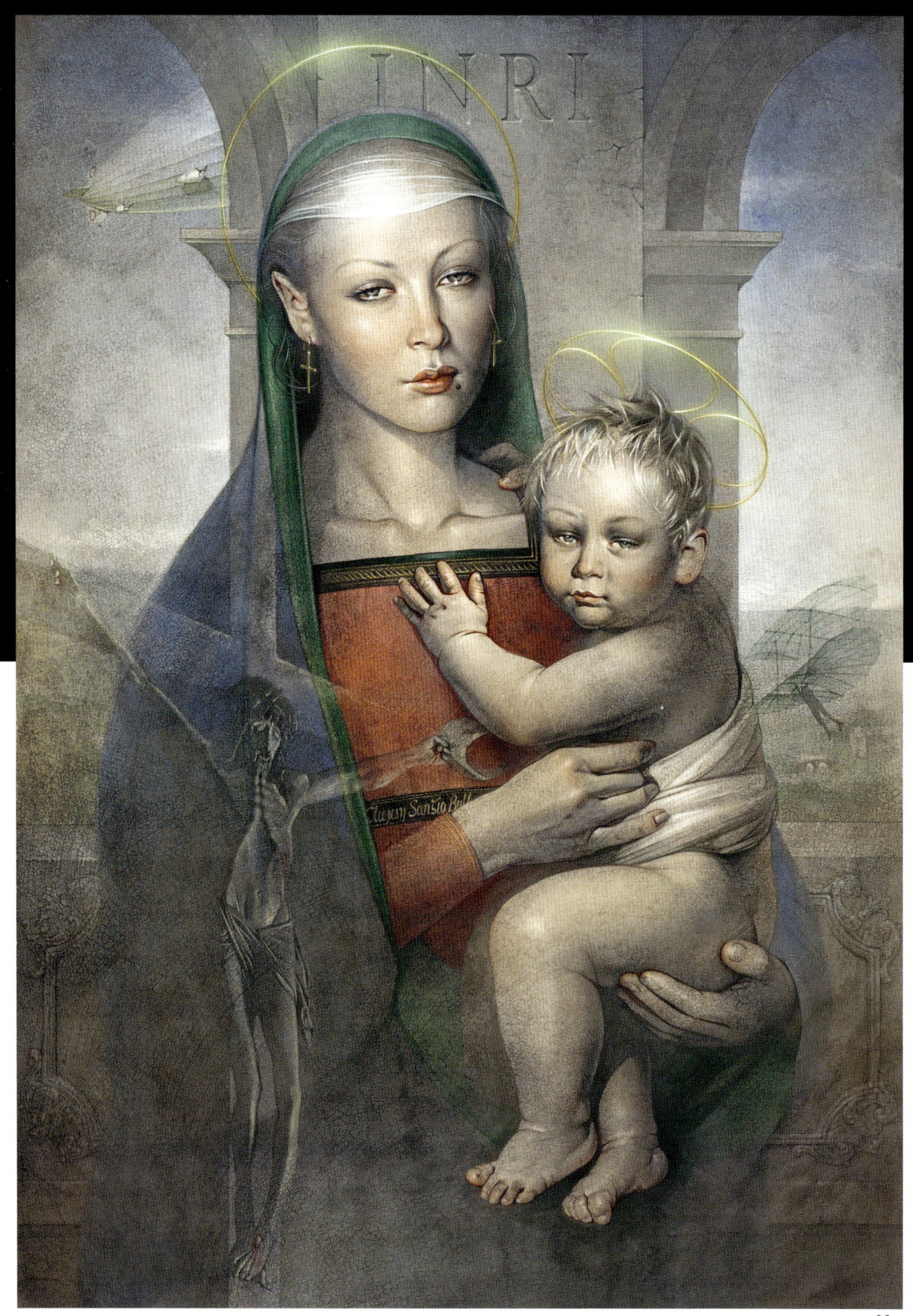

INRI

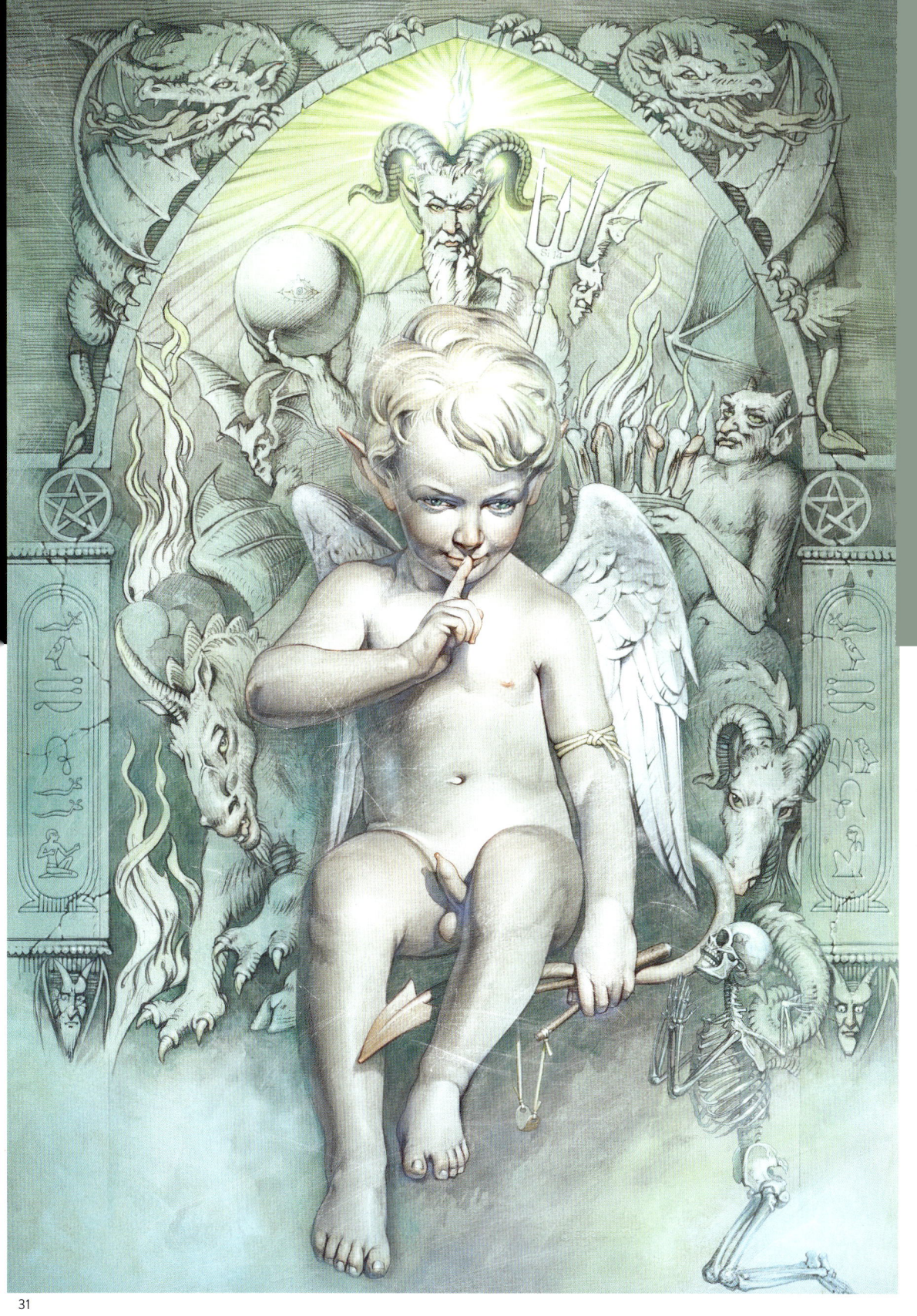

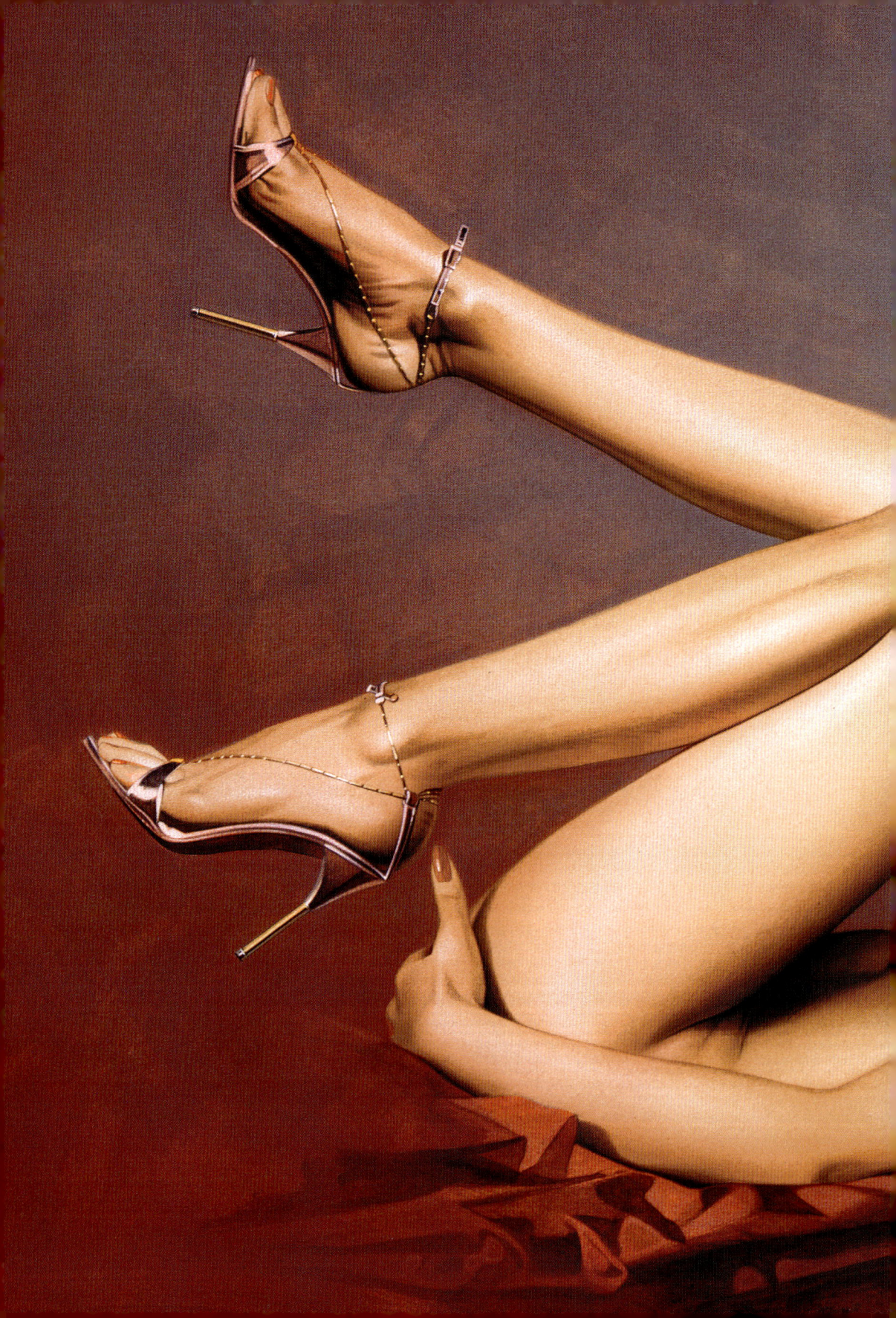

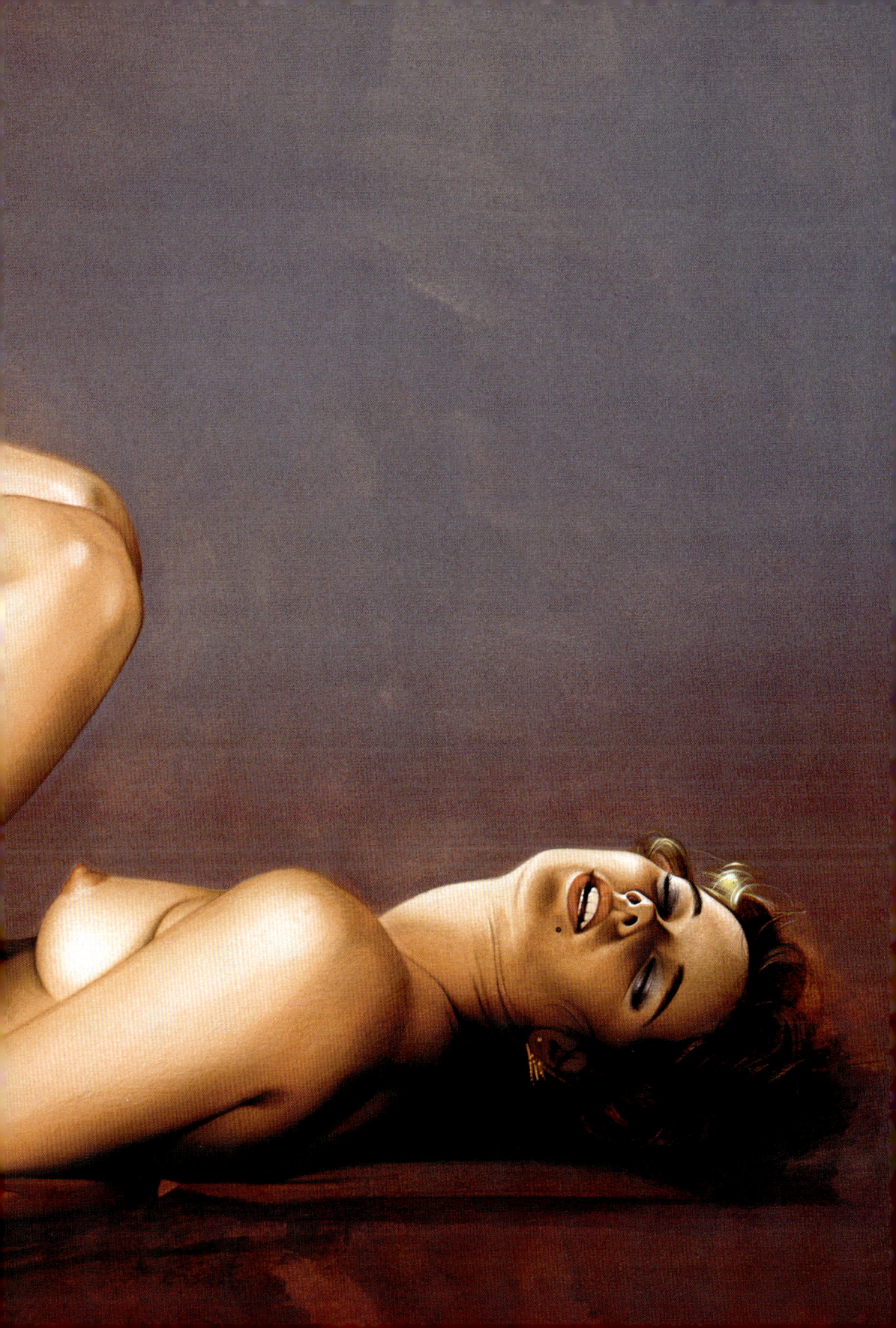

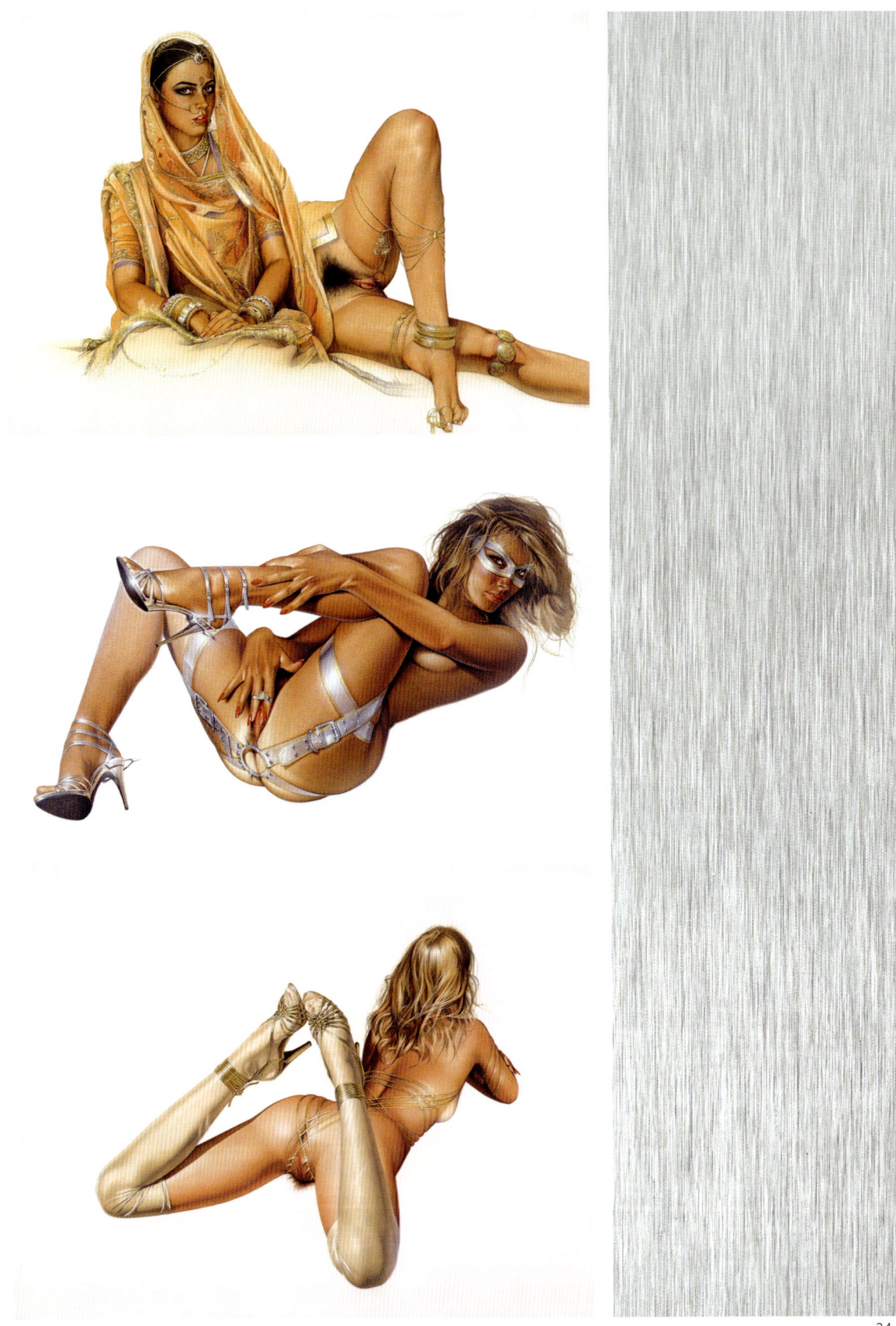

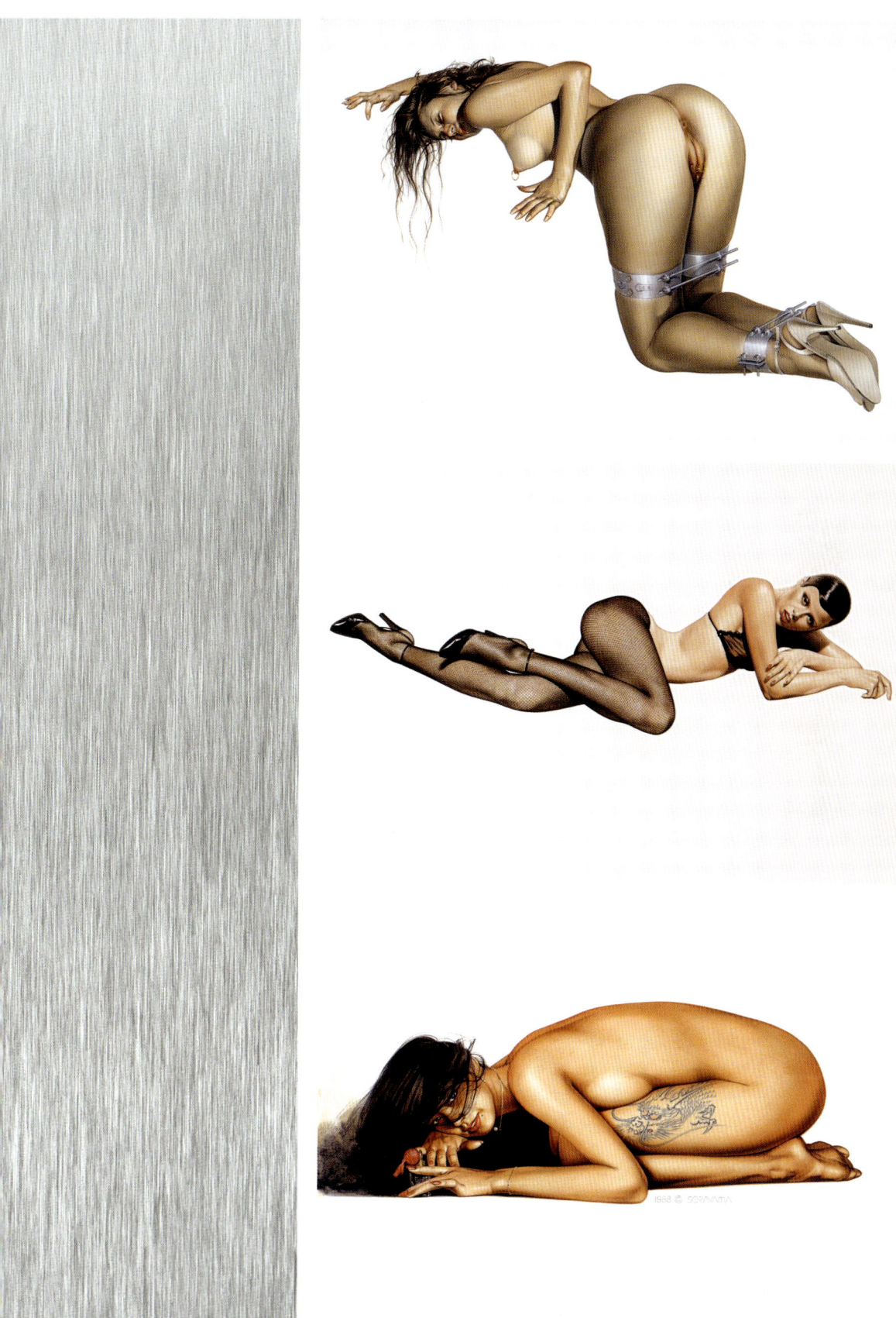

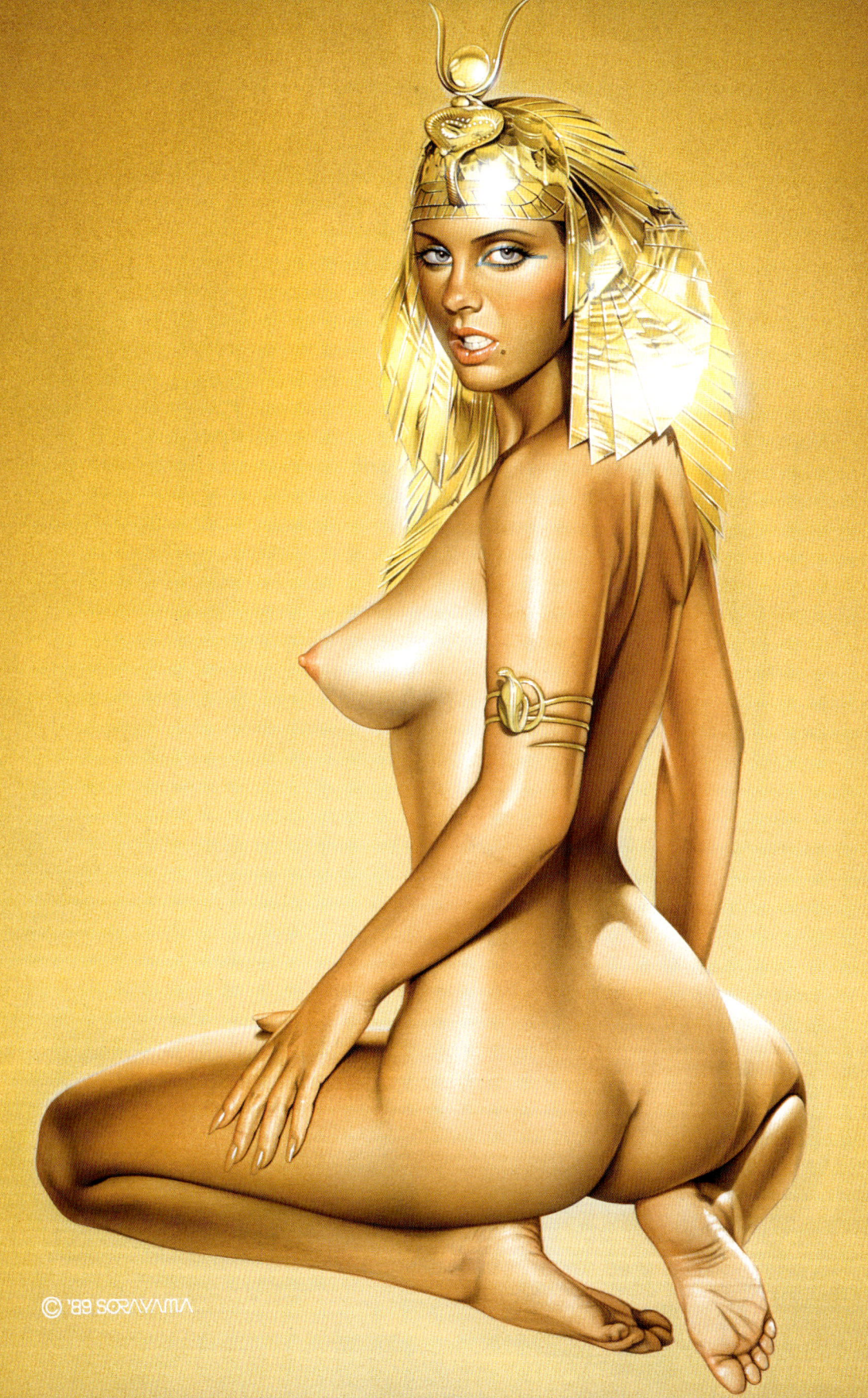

© '89 SORAYAMA

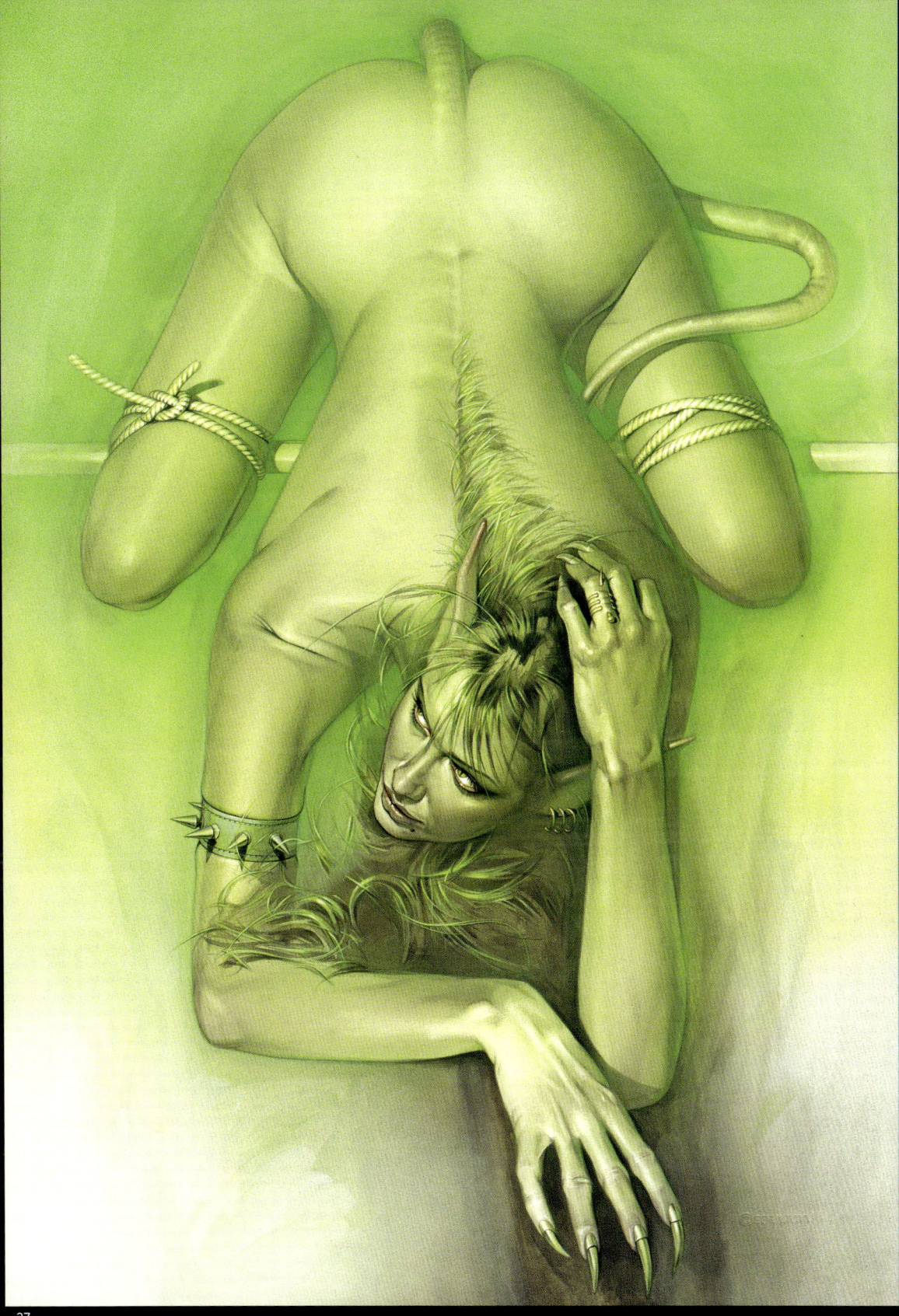

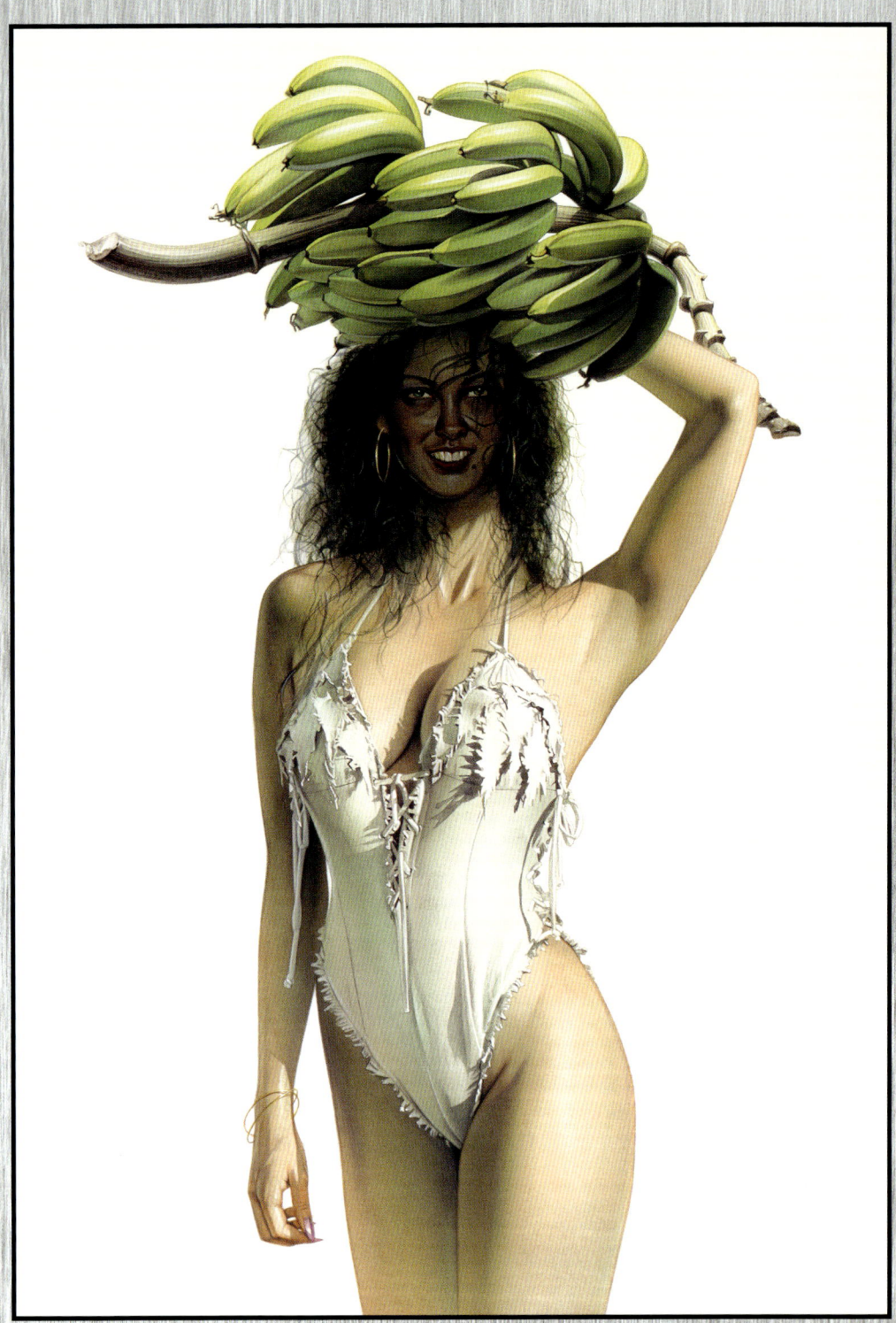

推　薦　文

北 野　武
（映画監督・小説家・俳優・タレント・たけし軍団殿ほか多数）

北野 武

「彼にいろんな才能があるのは、各方面の仕事を見せてもらって理解していたが、
こんな凄い絵が描けるとは思わなかった。また一人あぶな絵師の登場だ。」

棟方死行（ビートたけし幼なじみ）

「人間は生まれながらに平等だと言うのは嘘だ。
一人の男に、これほどまでの画才をあたえていいのだろうか？
私は創造の神を恨む。」

通称；足立区ダヴィンチ山本（廃品回収業）

「もっと細部まで、しっかり見せろ。」

浅草ロック座客：渡辺和夫（野ばとバス運転手）

장말 굉정하네요　ソラヤマ　マンセイ!!

~~金正日~~
金正雲

هذا شيء لا يتصوّره العقل.

川口スナック　アルジャジーラ

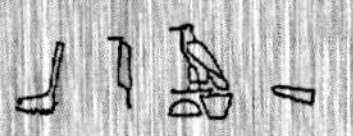

𓃀𓏏𓆑𓈖

高価買入　吉村作治（古物商）

Ах, как велико!

沖縄料理　プーチン

39

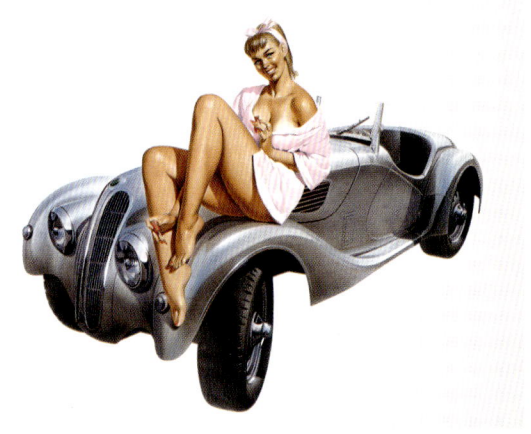

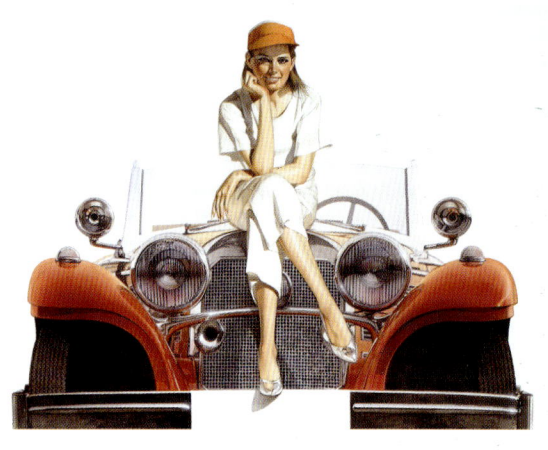

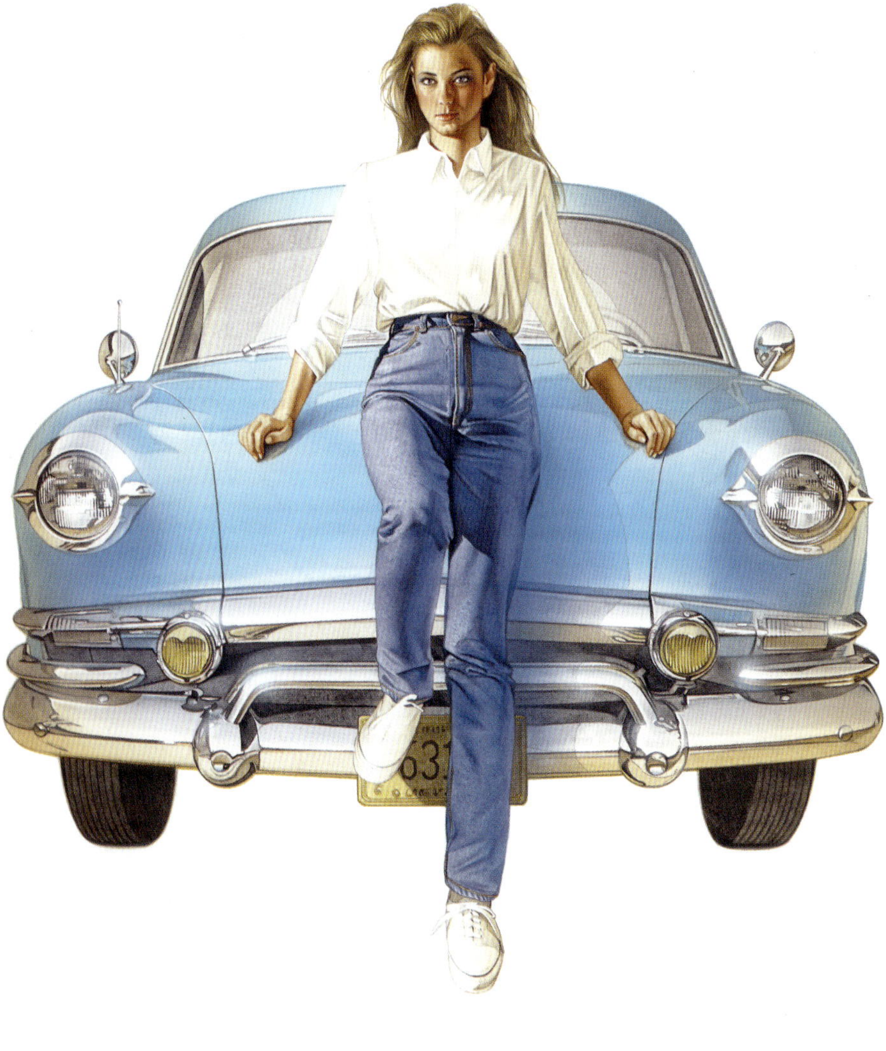

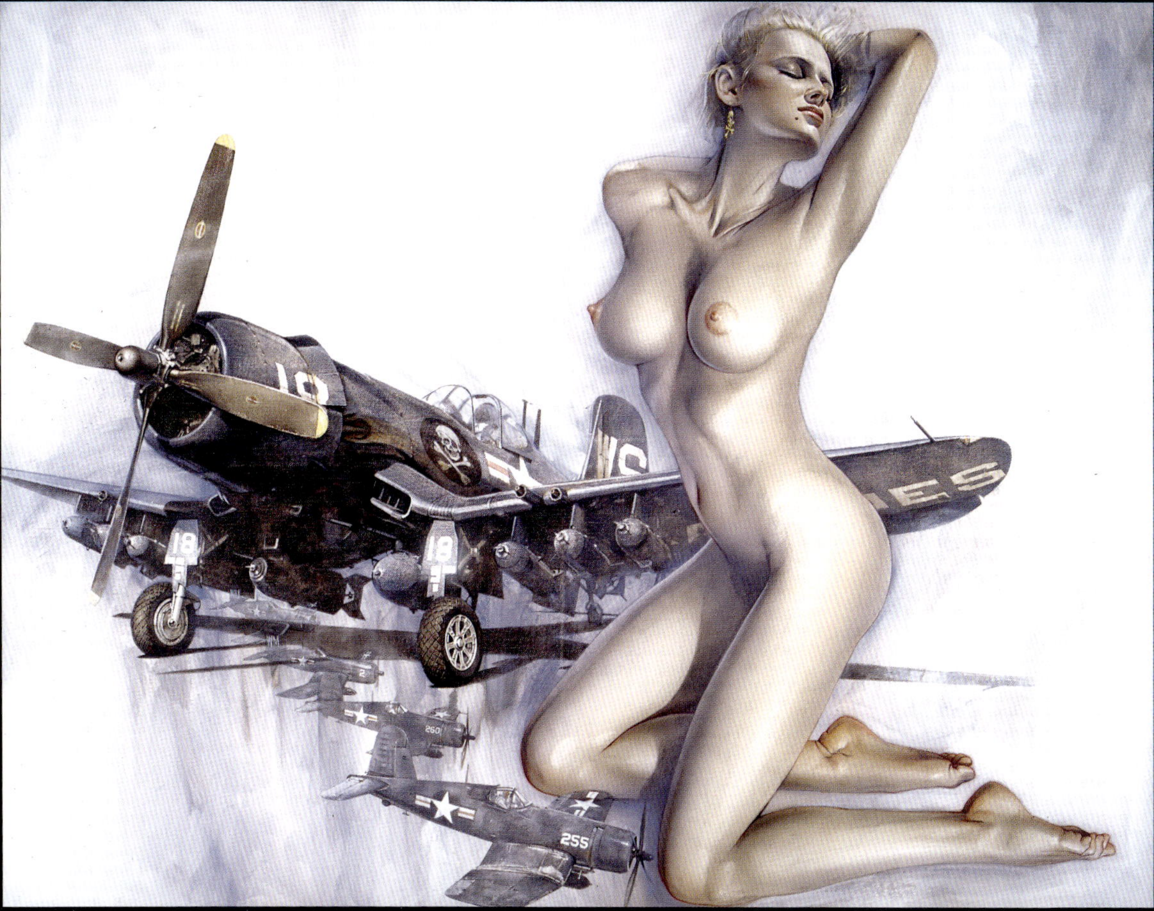

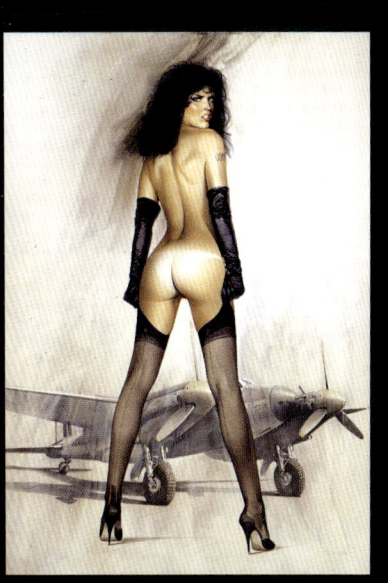
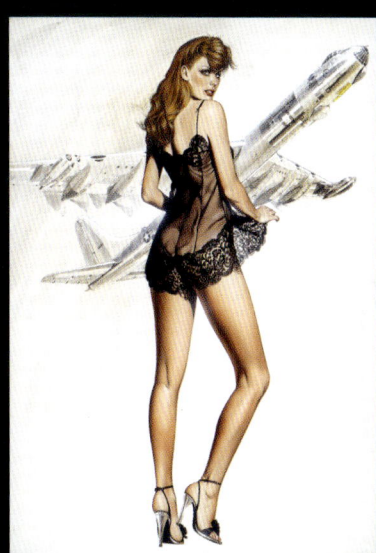
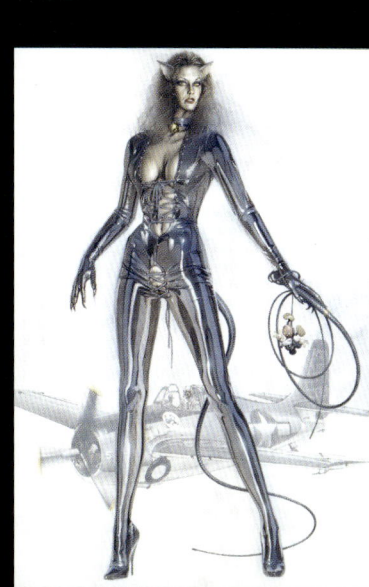

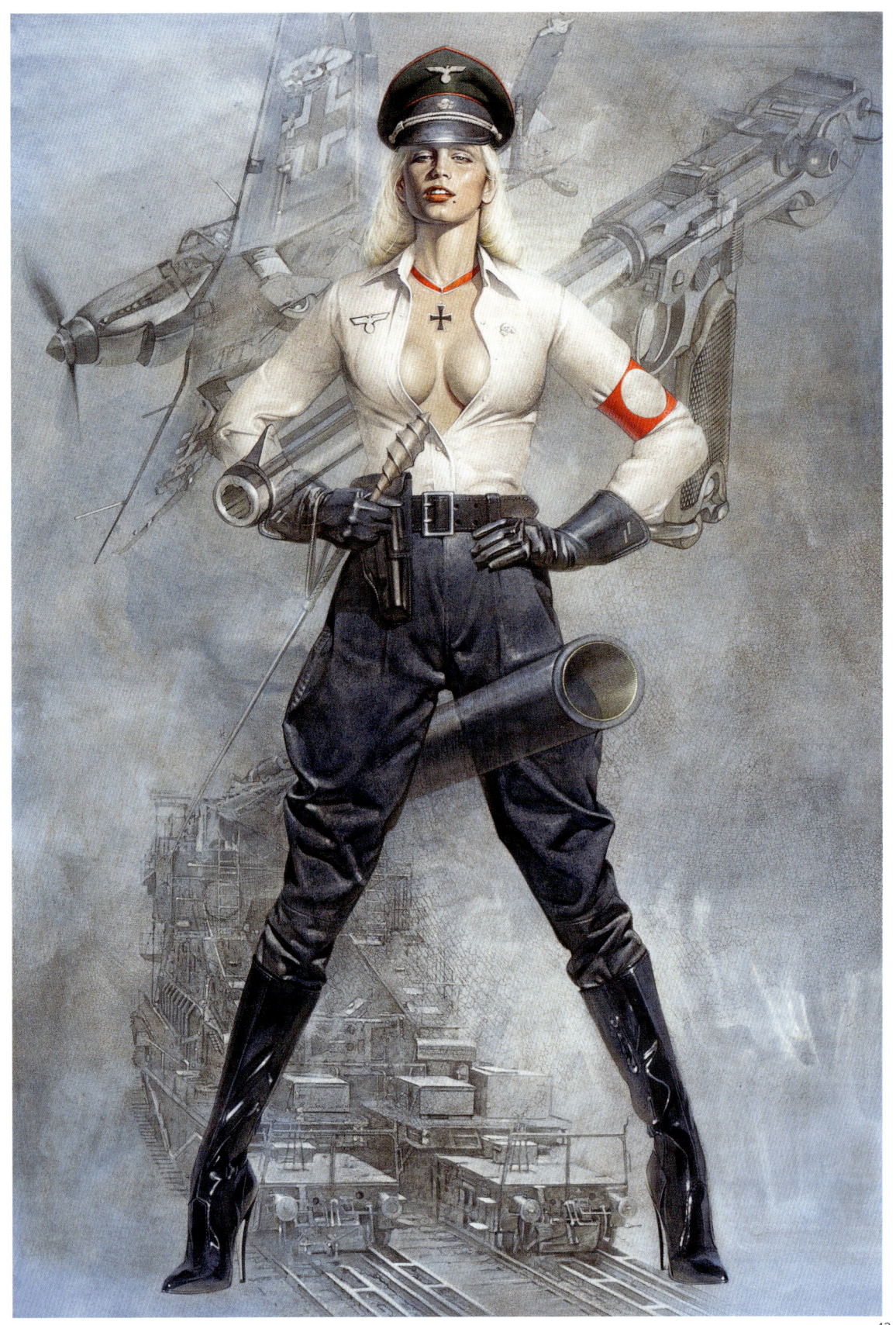

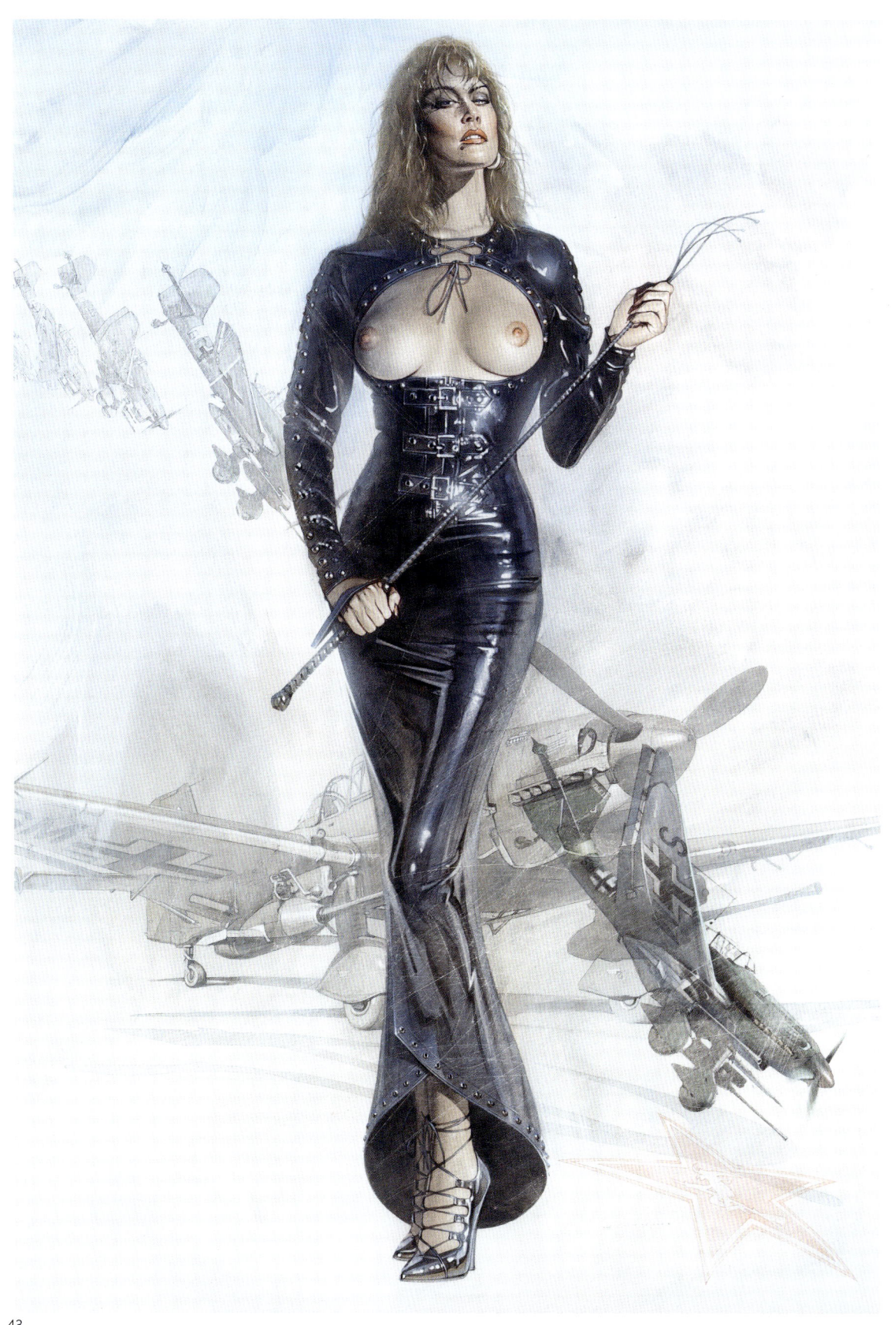

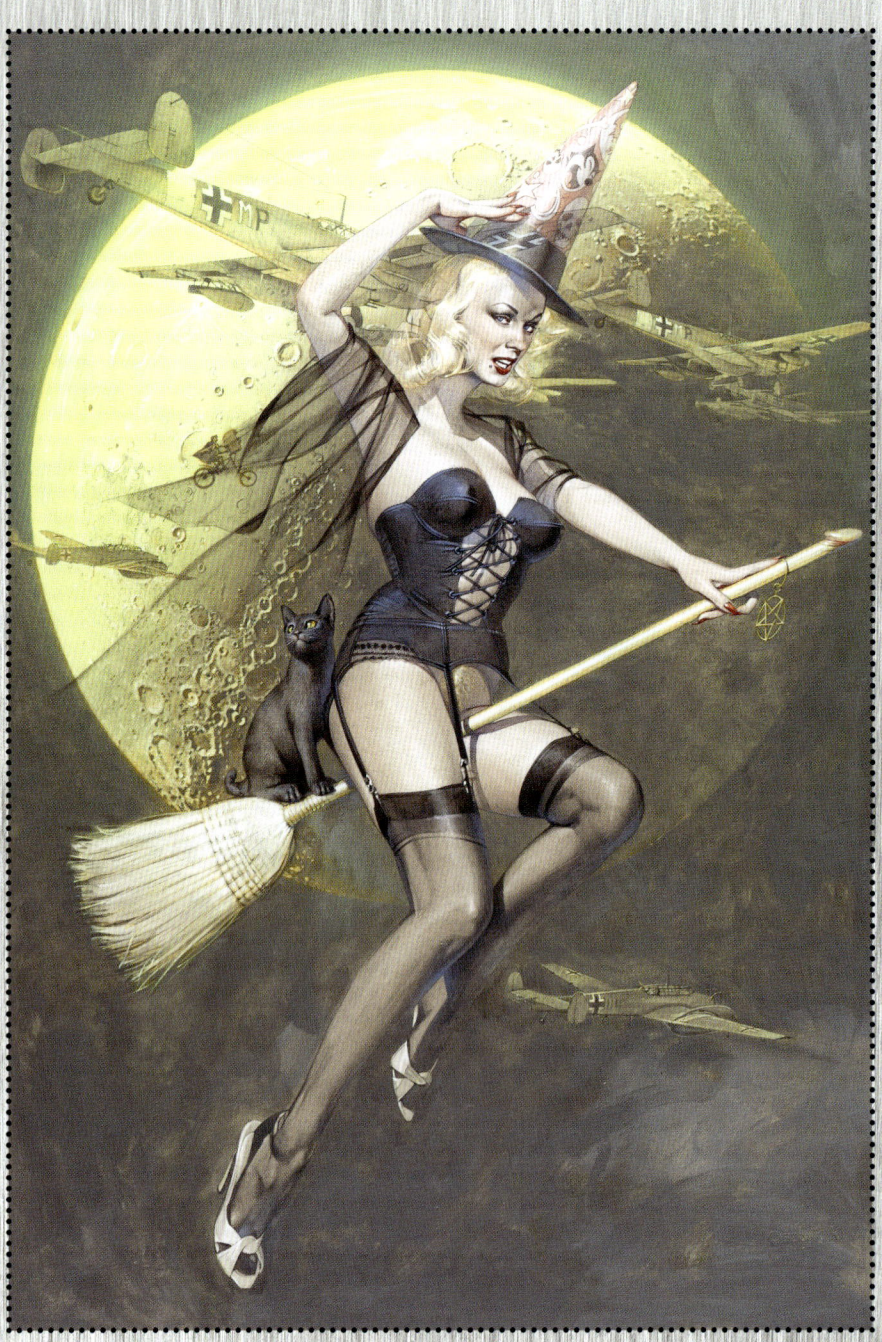

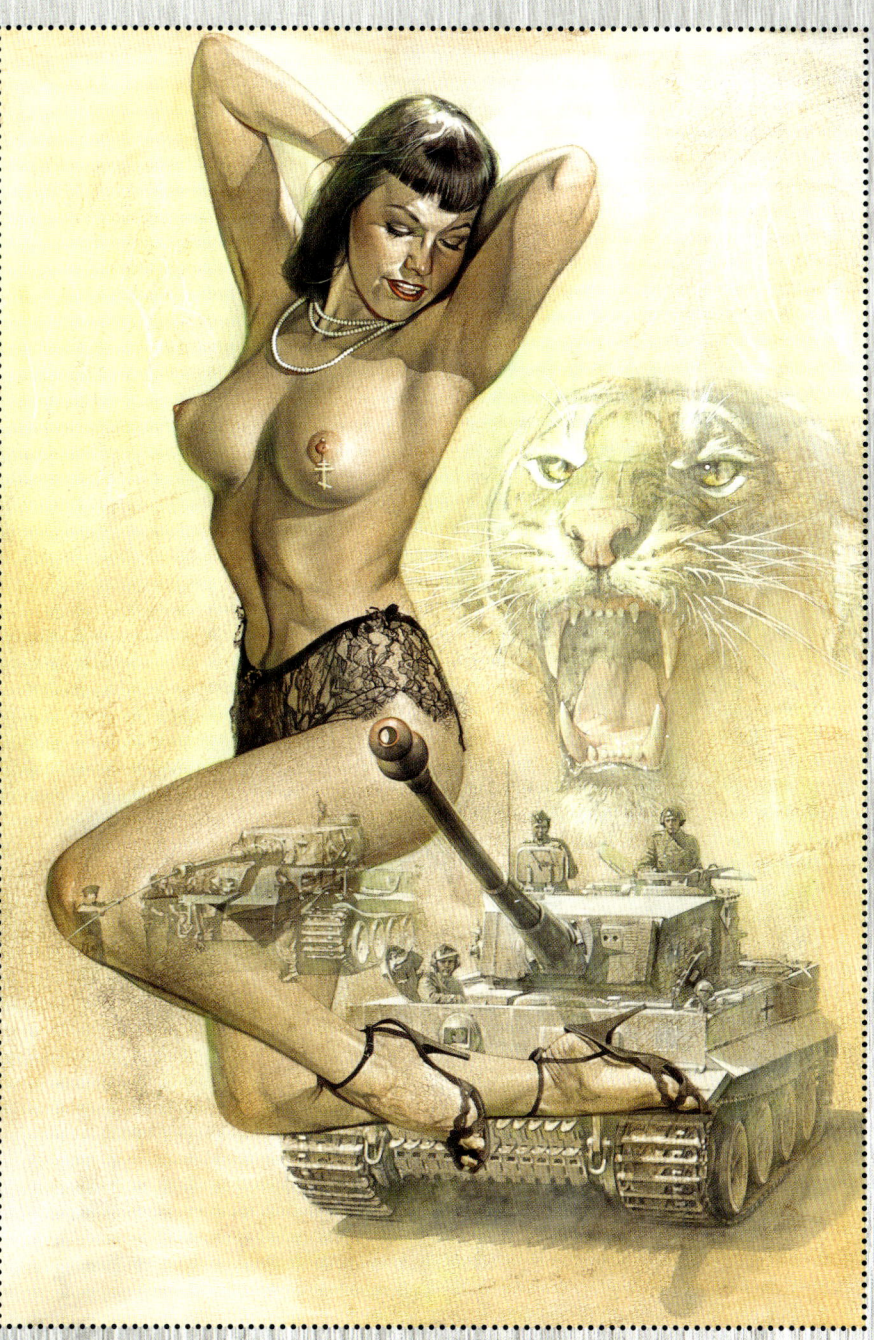

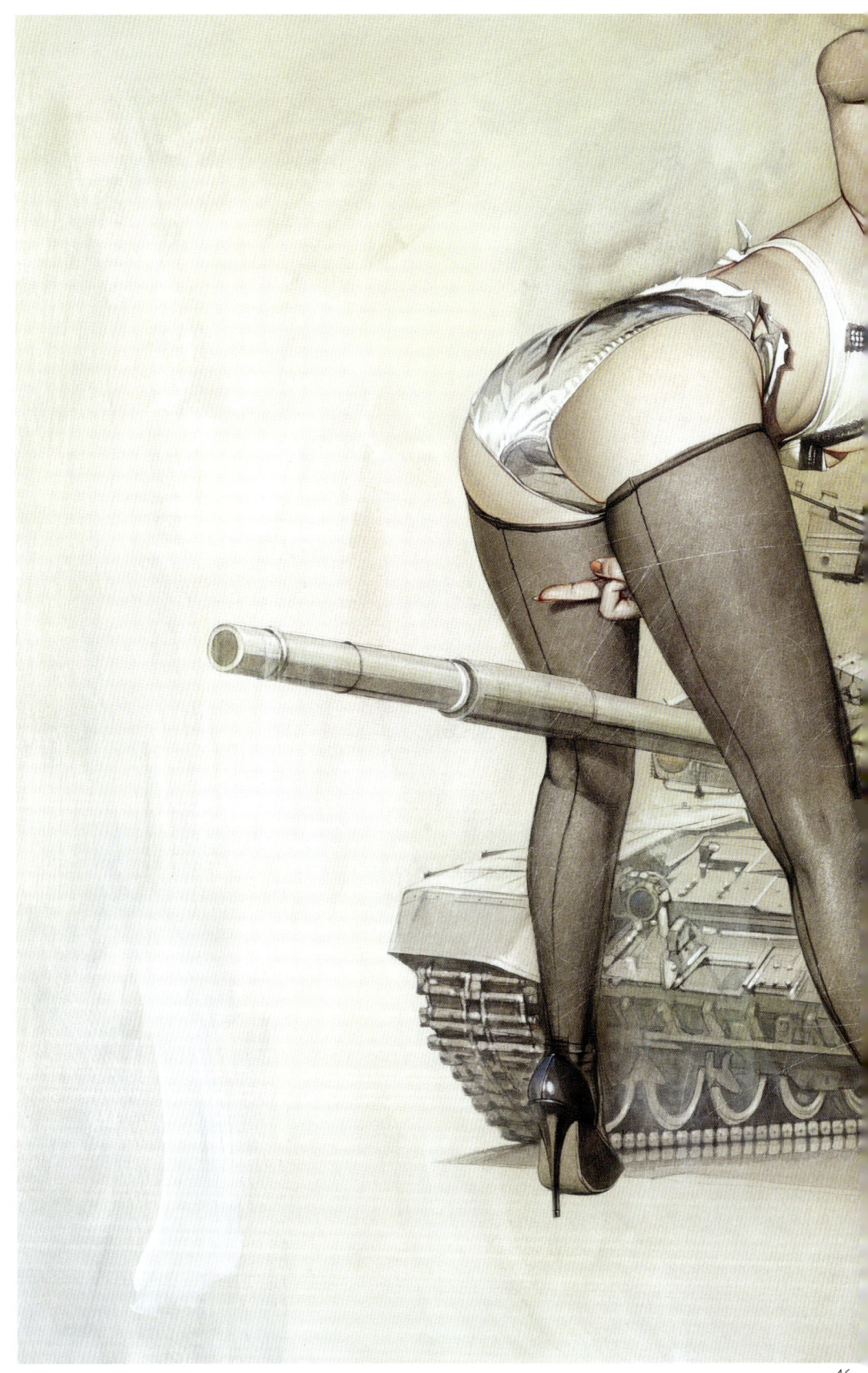

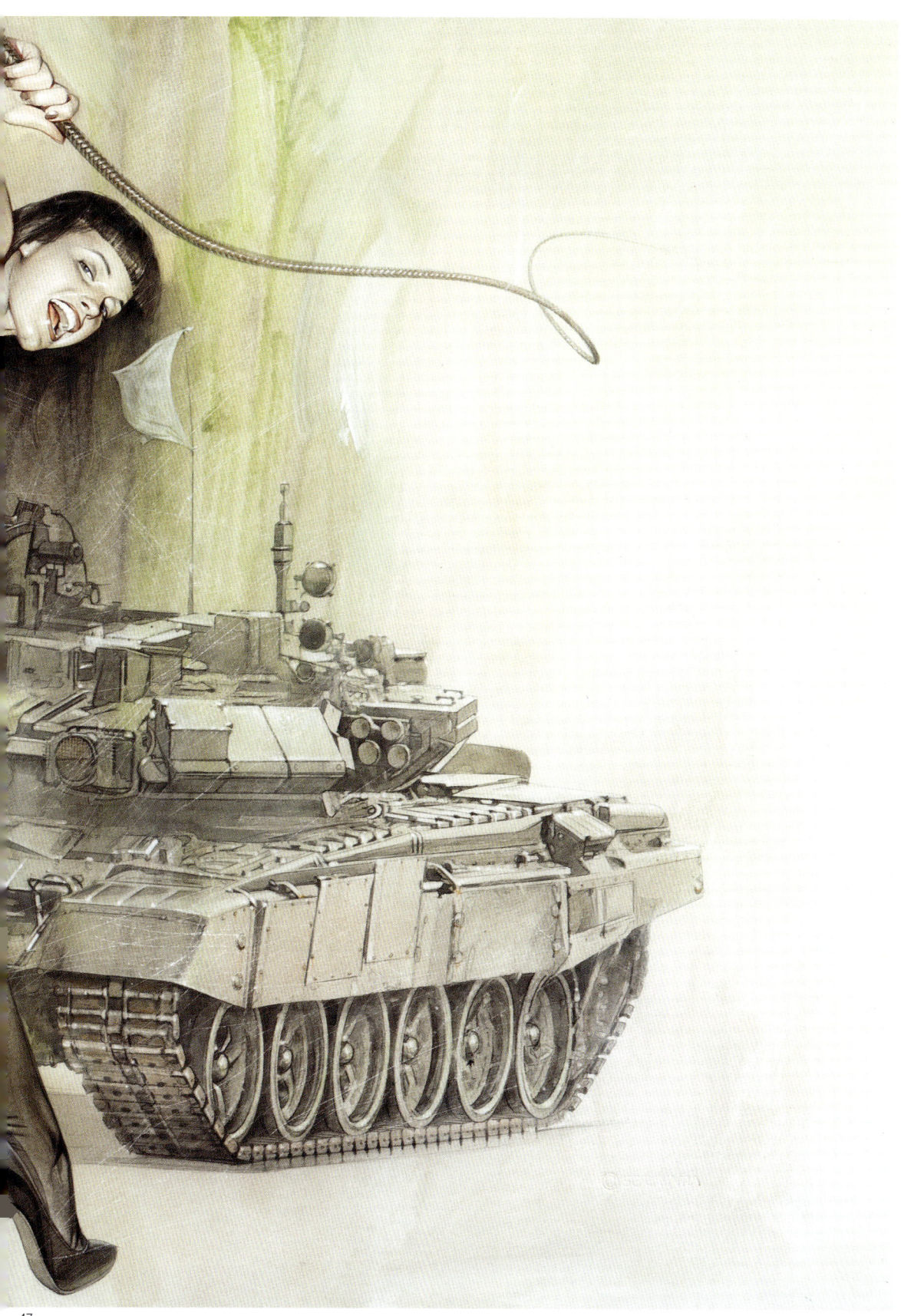

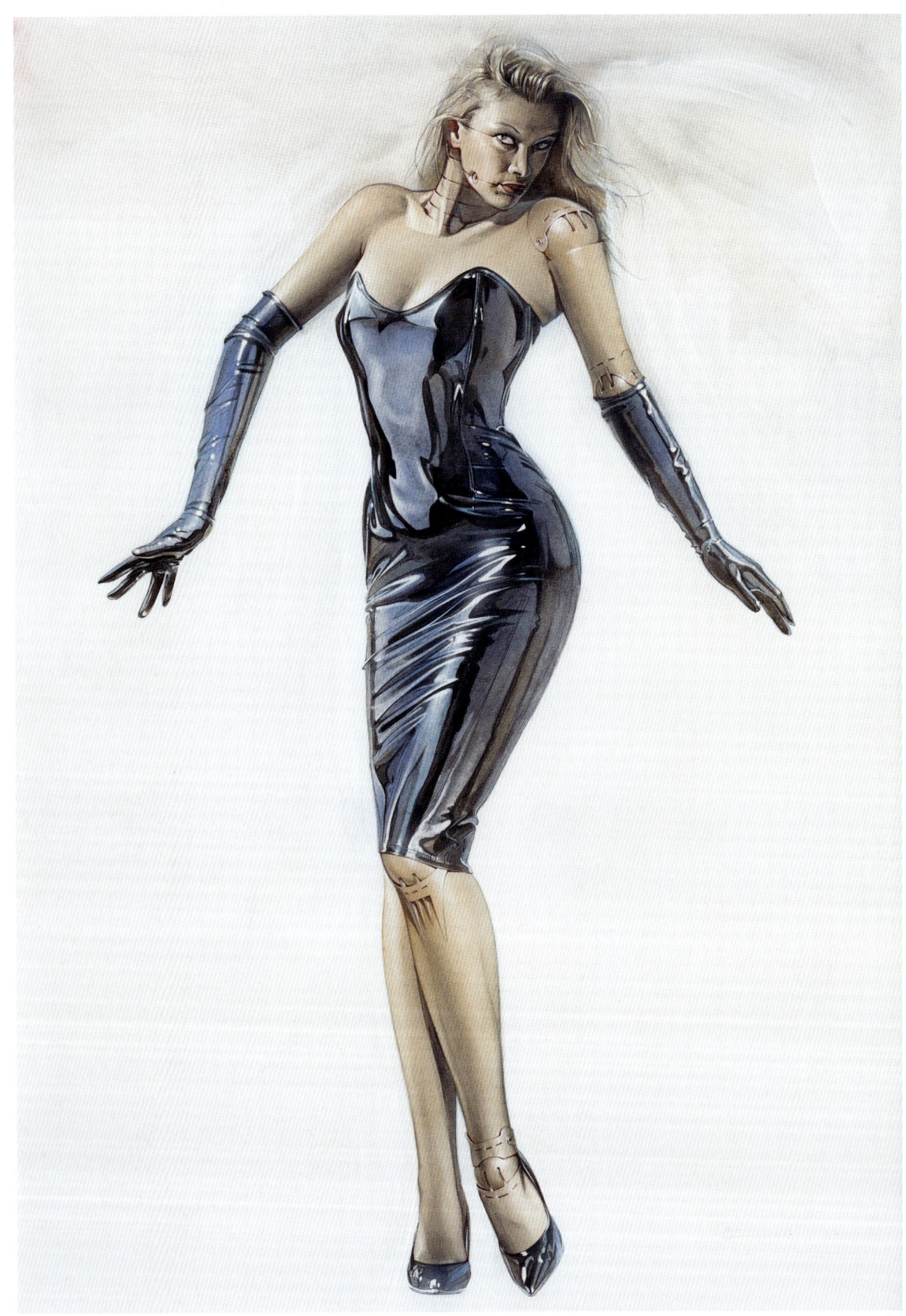

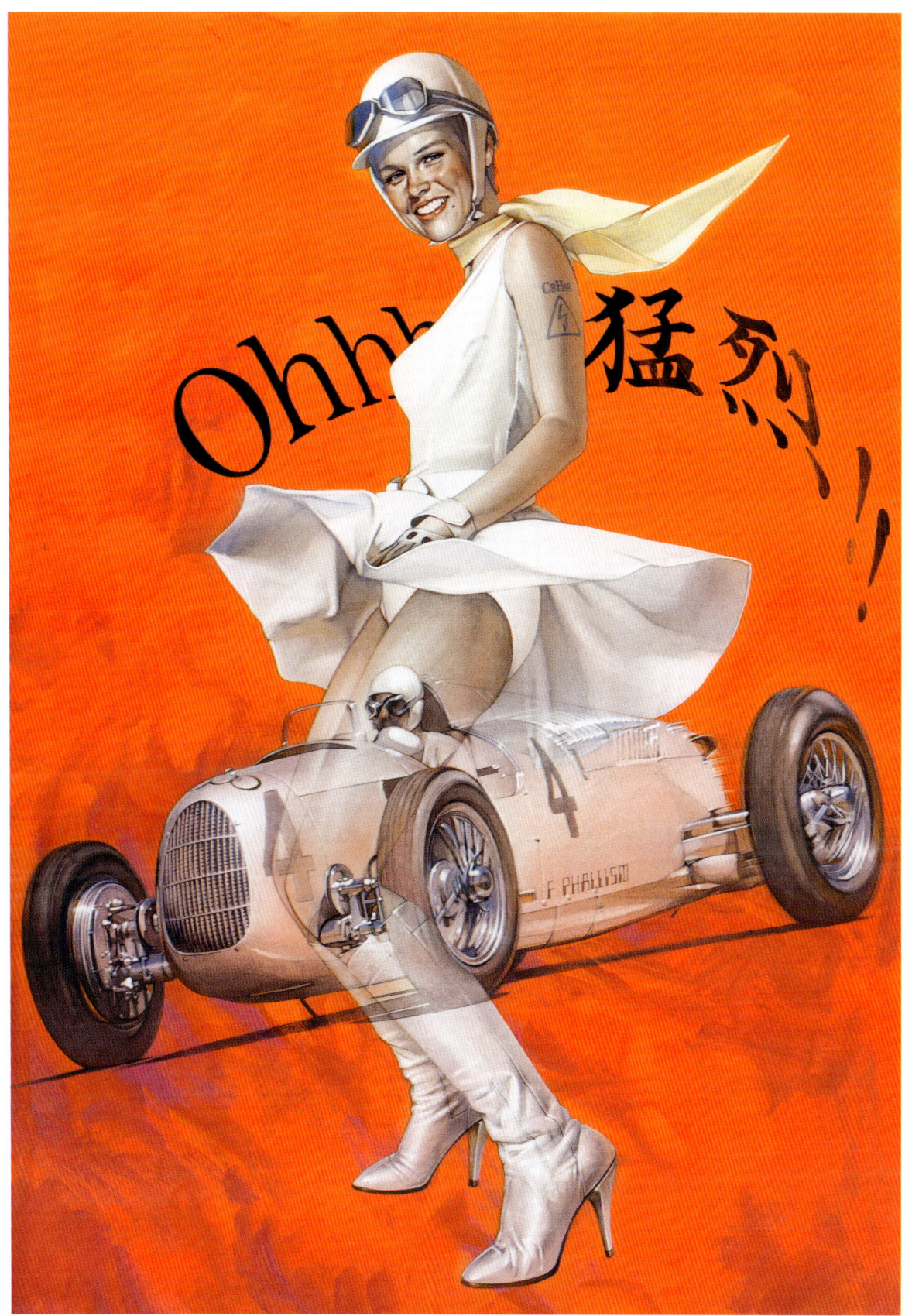

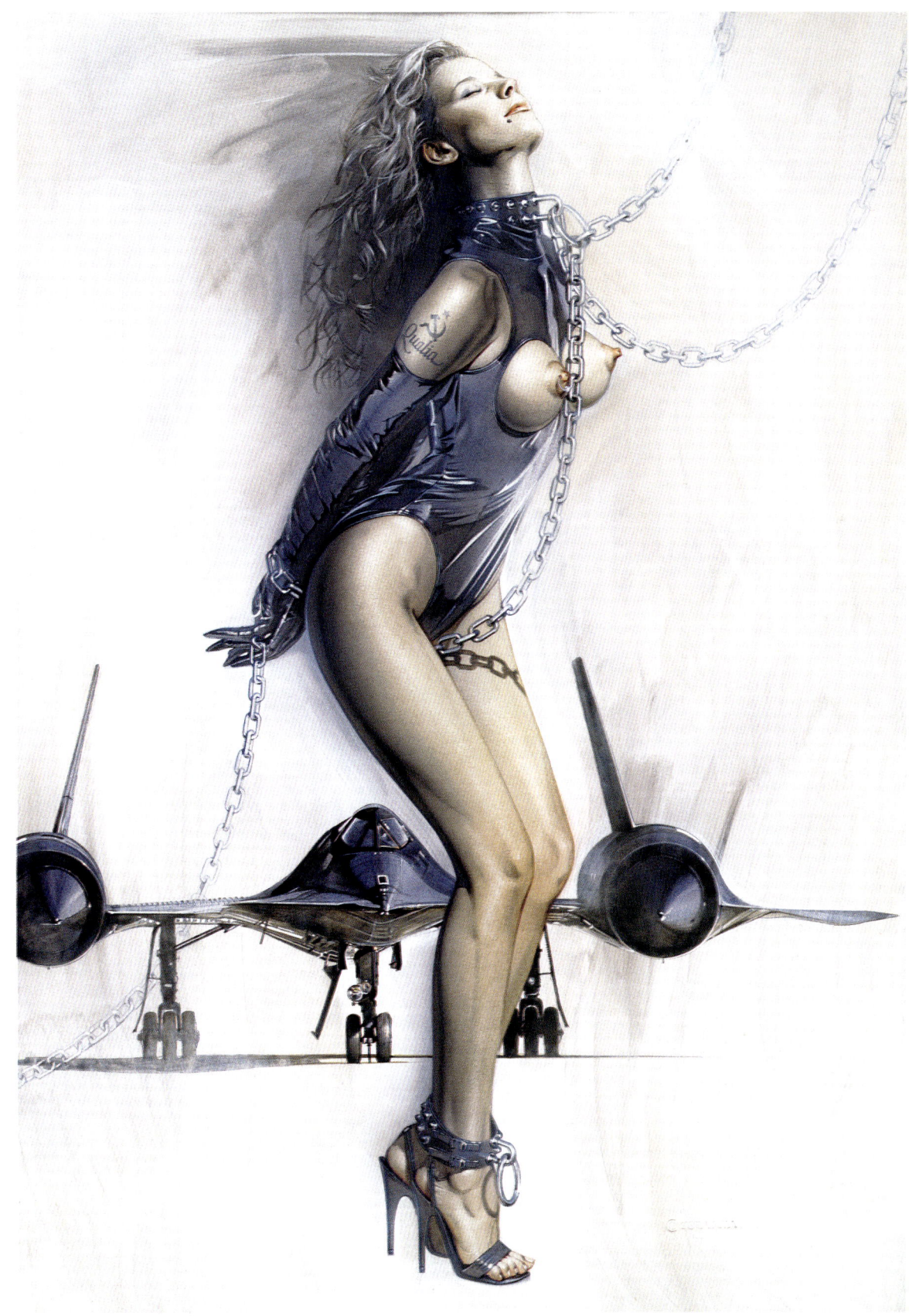

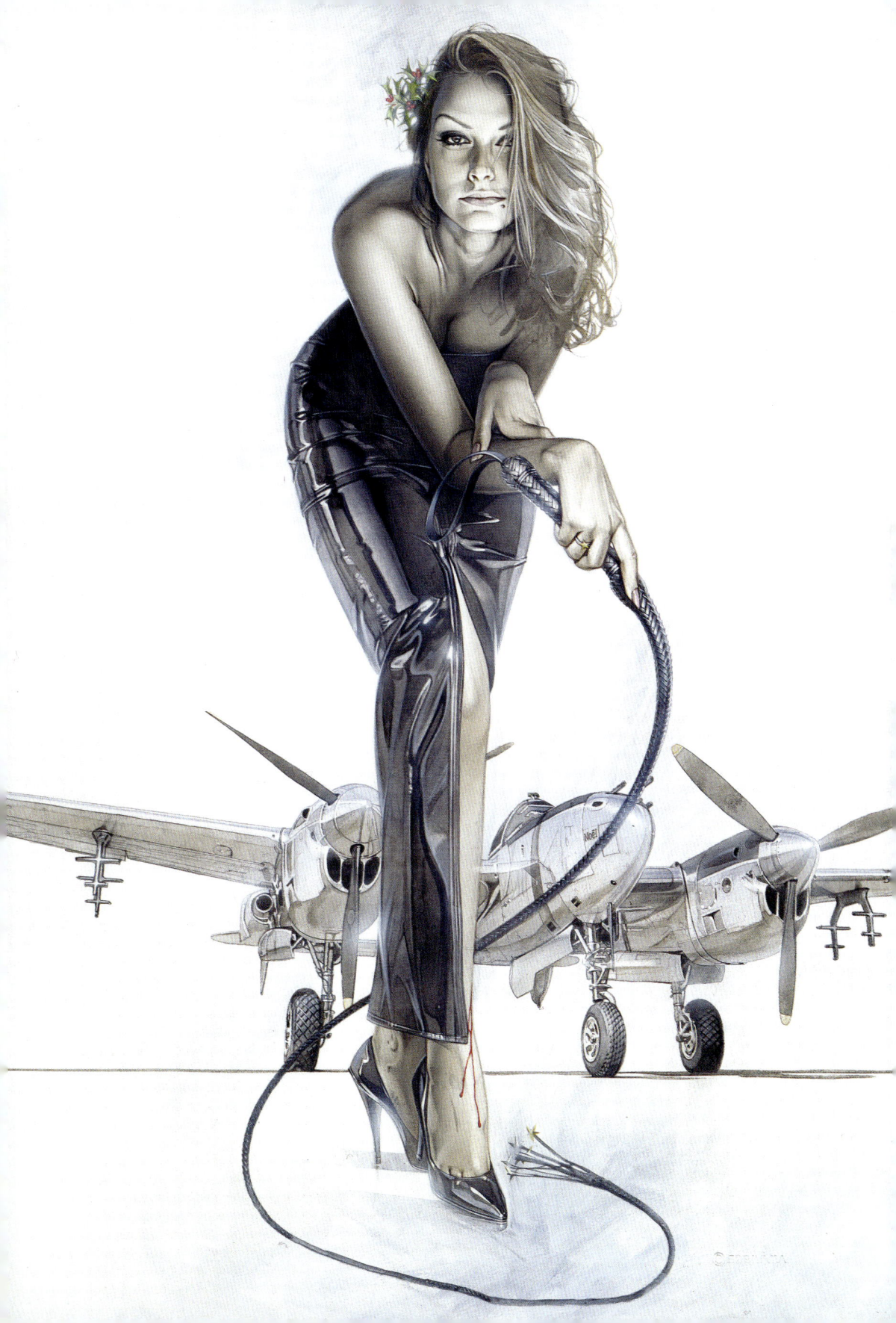

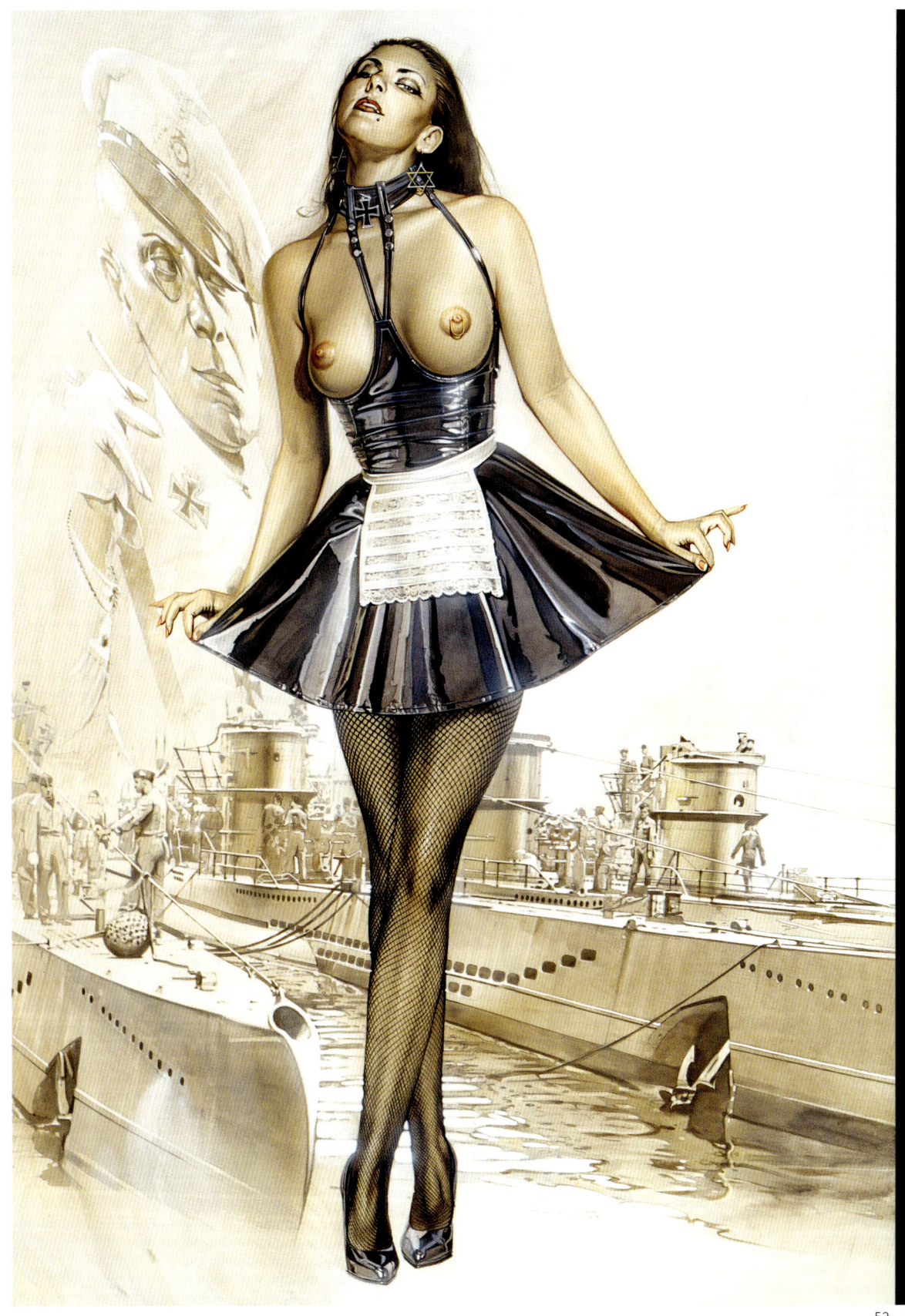

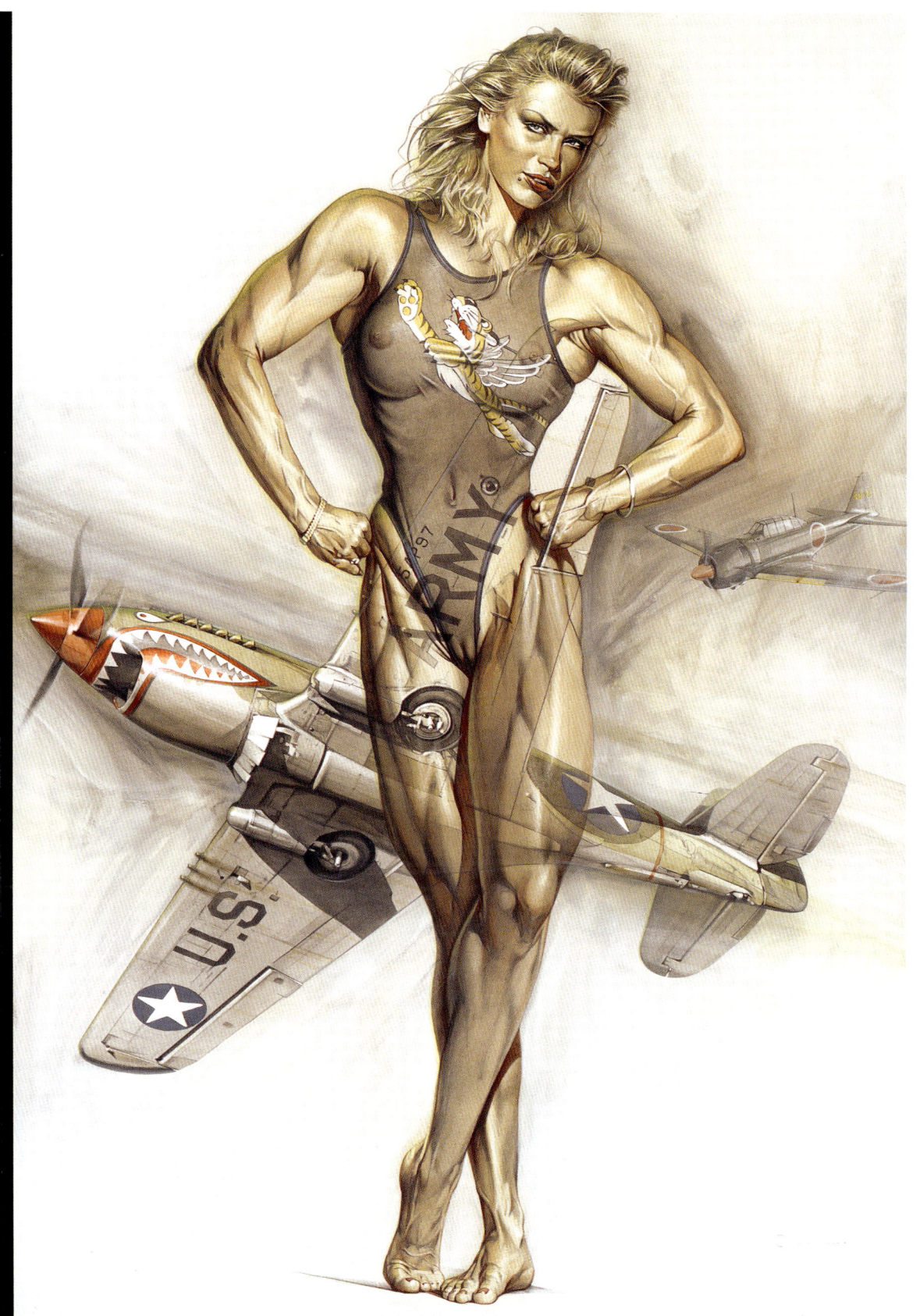

岡田親（変態おじさんお目付役／京ずし主人）

あらッ、あんなところにピアスを付けちゃった。ムッ、そんなところに虫ピン刺しちゃって。……（神様お許し下さい。）2ヶ月もアトリエを尋ねないと、とんでもない事になっている。メガネをかけ、ヒゲを生やかした変態おじさんの描いた絵である。実にとんでもない発想と表現だ。が、不思議とさわやかで明るく、スマートだ。何故か？人柄？とんでもない。30数年前、我々高校生時代、洋書店を夢中で探し、スクラップし、興奮を覚えた、当時の強くかっこいいアメリカが生んだ美しい"PIN UP"。粋でおしゃれなその魅力、さわやかさを、ずっ〜〜と忘れずに今日まで自分の基本に持ち続けているからだ。だから変態おじさんの描いた絵はスマートでさわやかなのだ。私はその絵が大好きだ。
今や世界中の変態アーティストに与えている影響は大変なもの。スマート変態万才‼

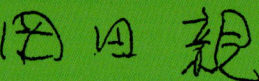

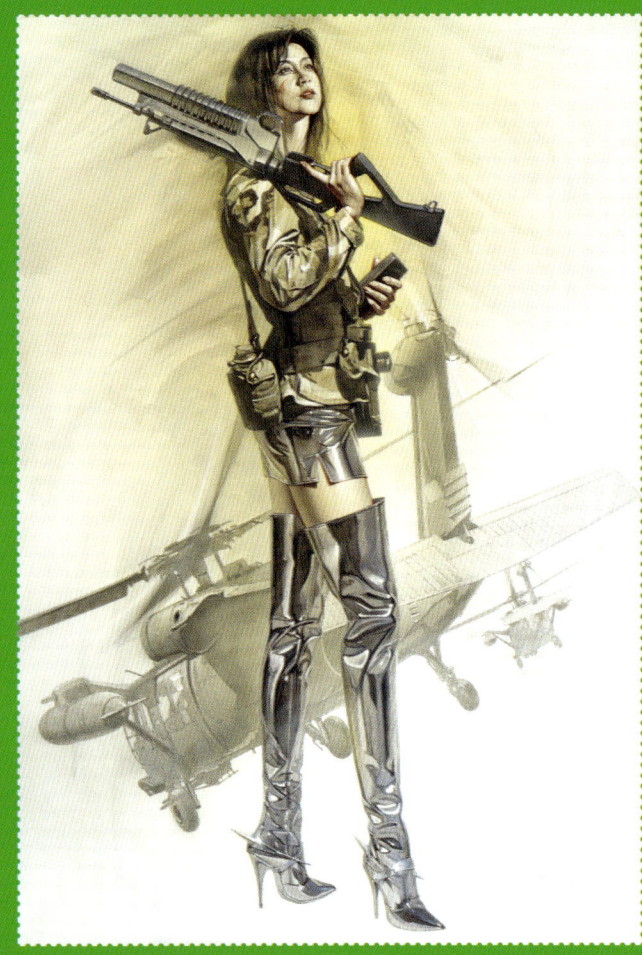

作品集に寄せて

飛行機は誕生以来ずっと、スタイルの良さが性能の証明でした。
カッコいい飛行機はどれもが、高い性能を誇っていたのです。
飛行機の設計や操縦にコンピューターが介在するようになり、
"不細工な高性能機"が多くなったことは嘆かわしいことですが、
空山さんの作品には、いつもカッコいい飛行機が美女と描かれています。
お陰で僕は、今も心穏やかでいられるのです。

『航空ファン』編集長　三井一郎

三井一郎

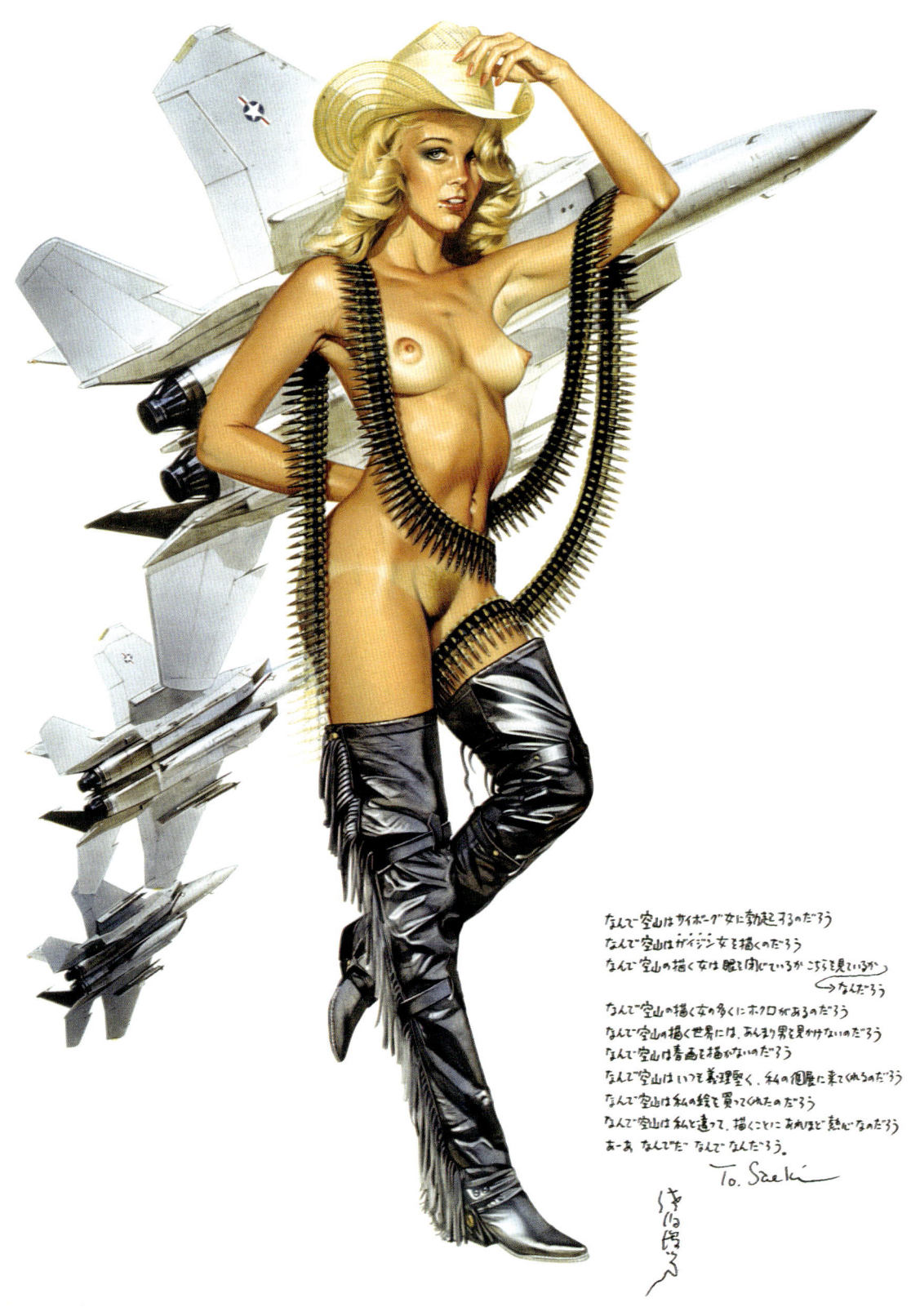

なんで空山はサイボーグ女に勃起するのだろう
なんで空山はガイジン女を描くのだろう
なんで空山の描く女は瞳を閉じているがこちらを見ているか
　　　　　　　　　　　　　　　　　　→なんだろう

なんで空山の描く女の多くにホクロがあるのだろう
なんで空山の描く世界には、あんまり男を見かけないのだろう
なんで空山は春画を描かないのだろう
なんで空山はいつも義理堅く、私の個展に来てくれるのだろう
なんで空山は私の絵を買ってくれたのだろう
なんで空山は私と違って、描くことにあれほど熱心になるのだろう
あーあ　なんでだ　なんでで　なんだろう。

　　　　　　　　　　　To. Saeki

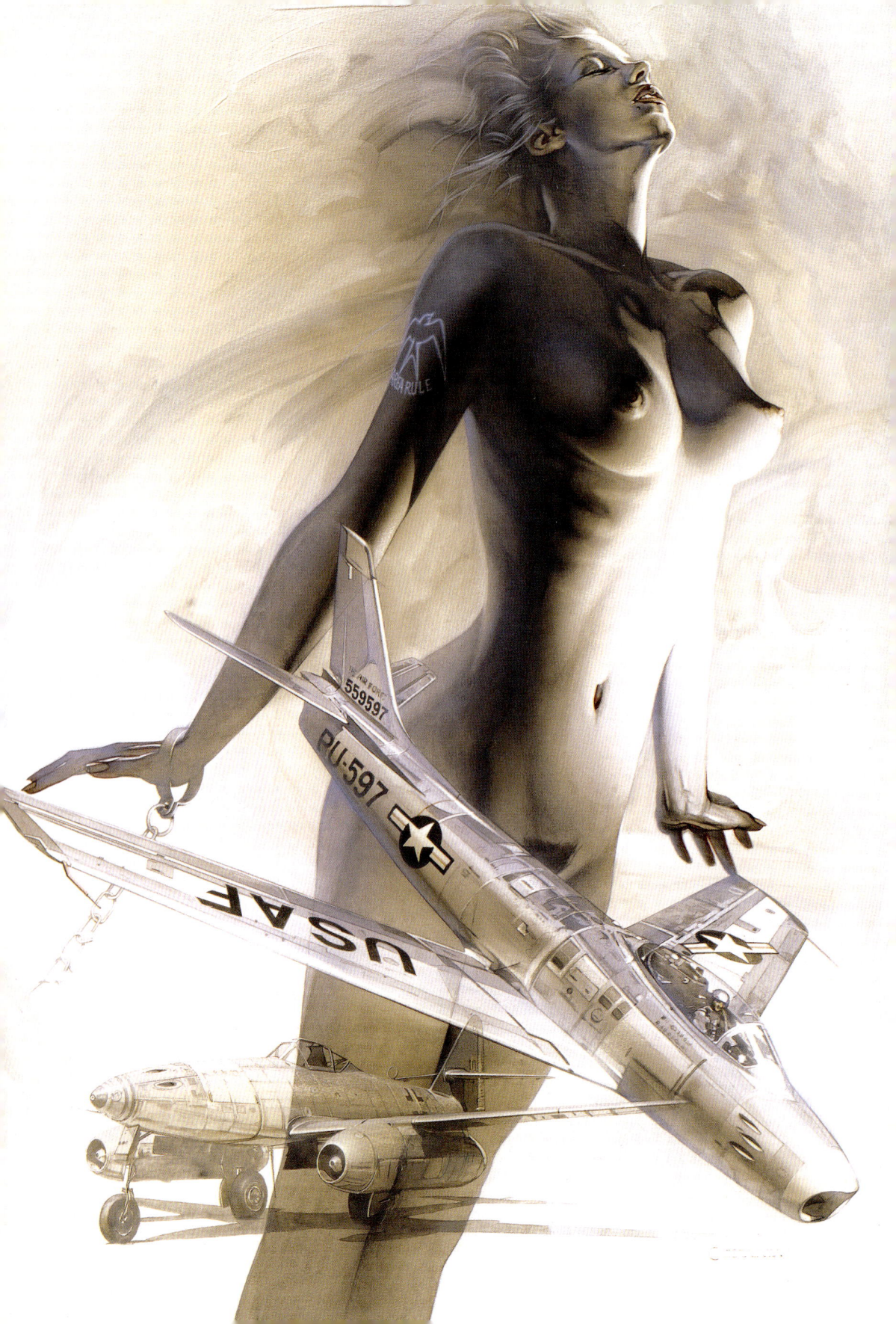

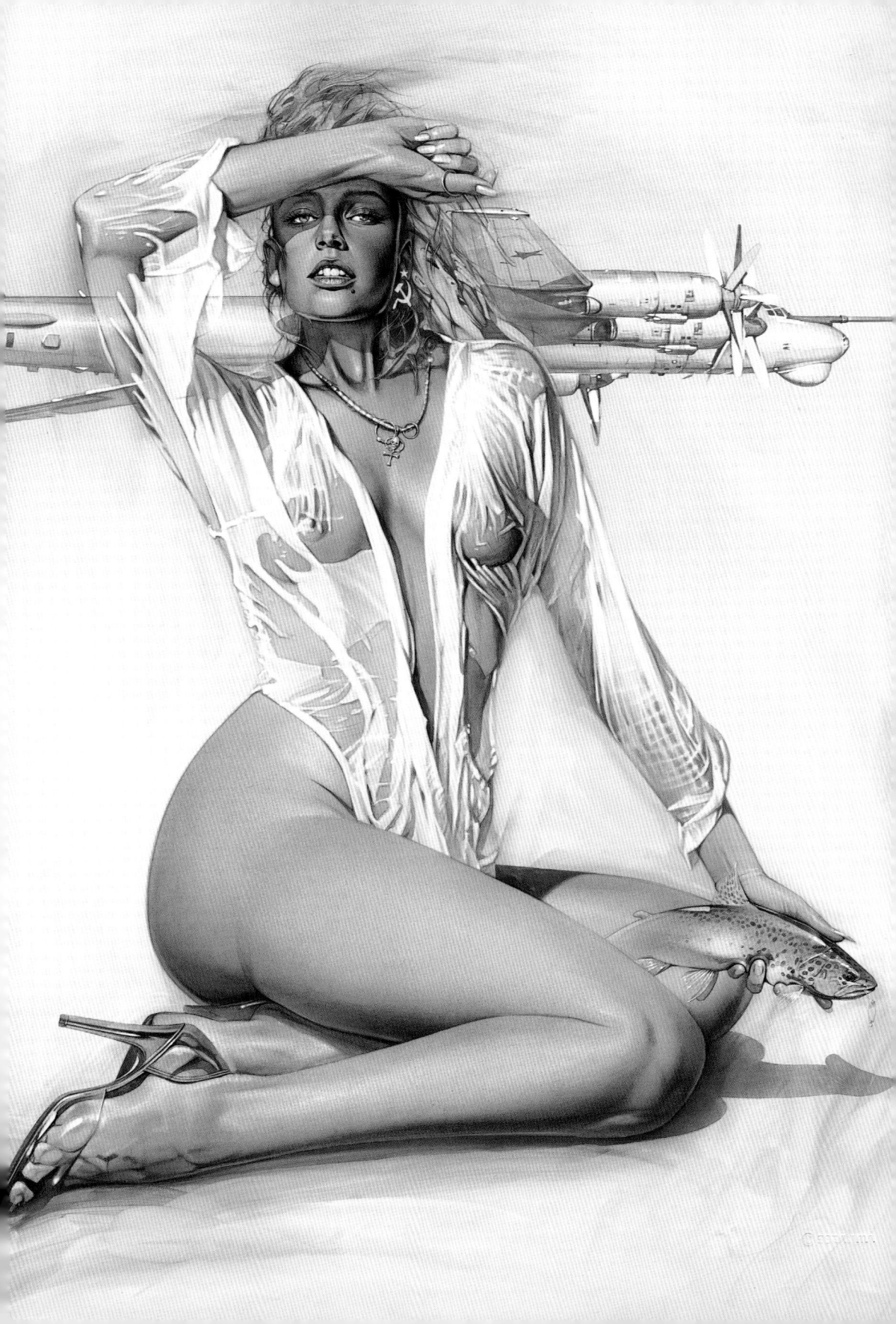

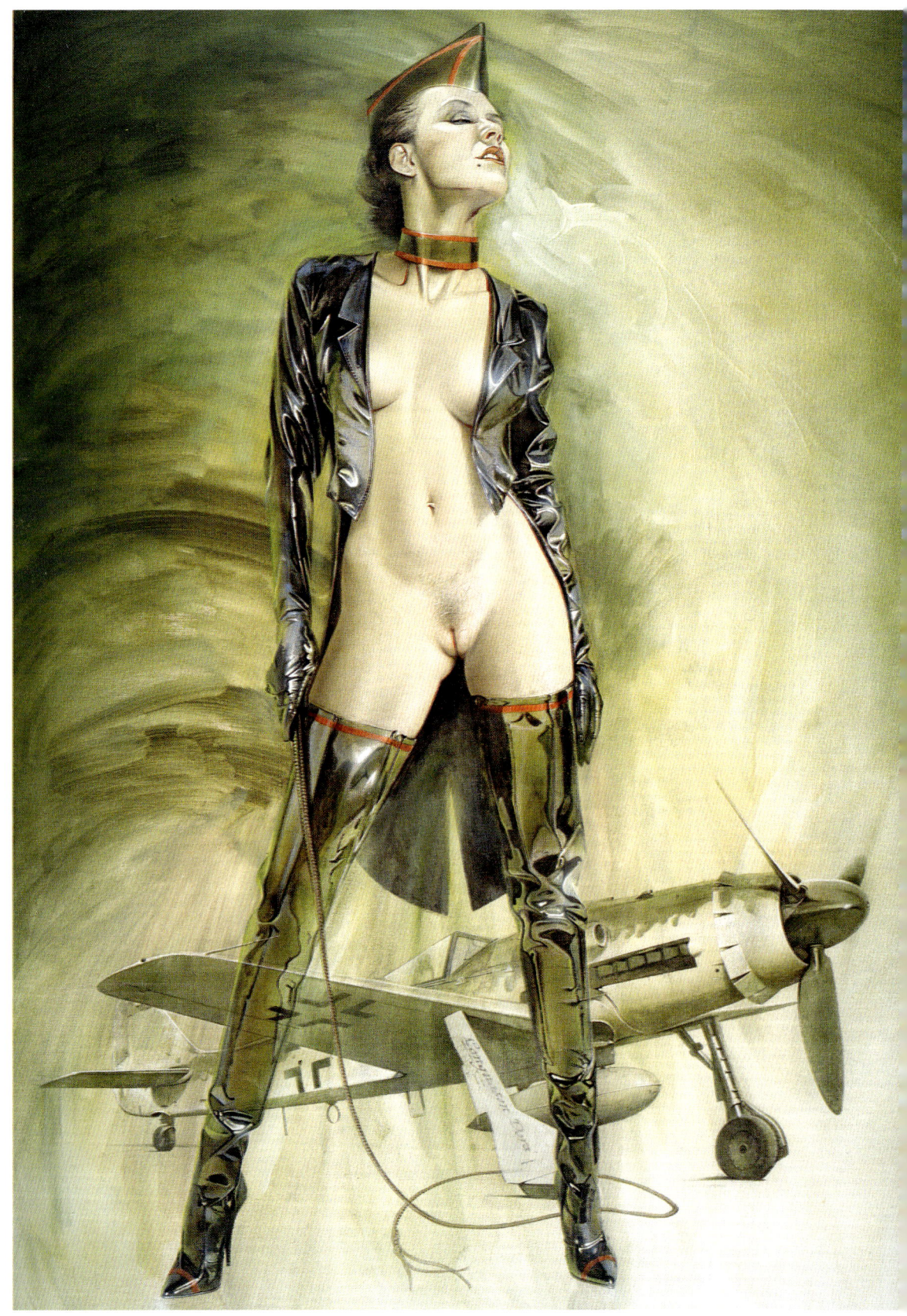

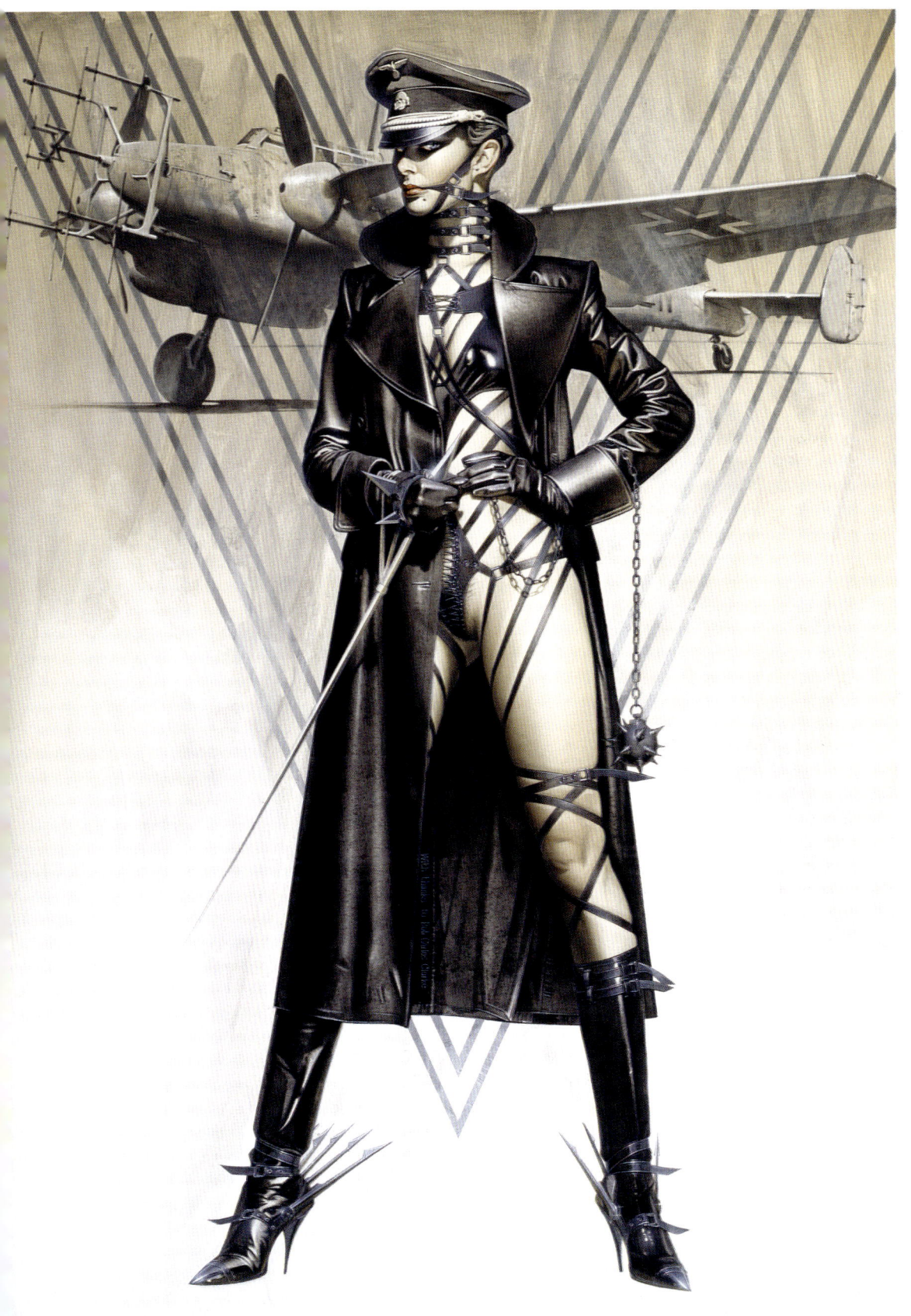

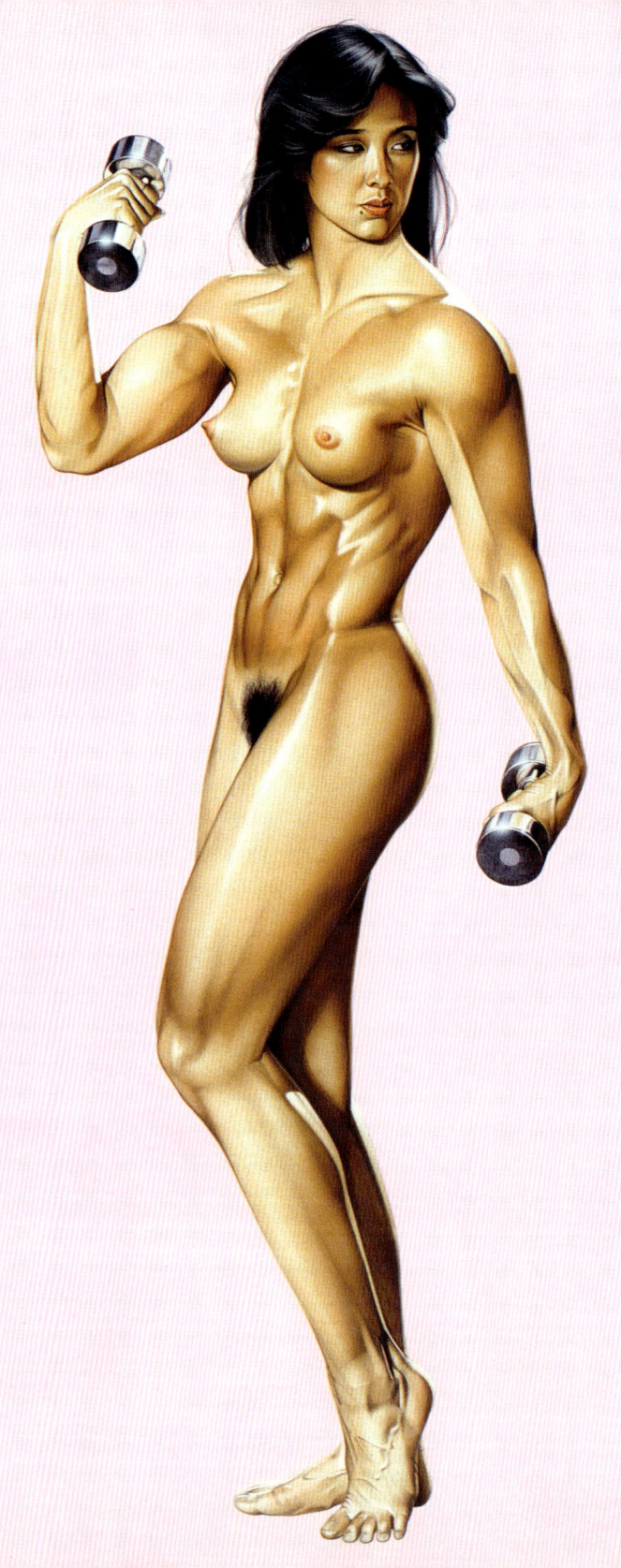

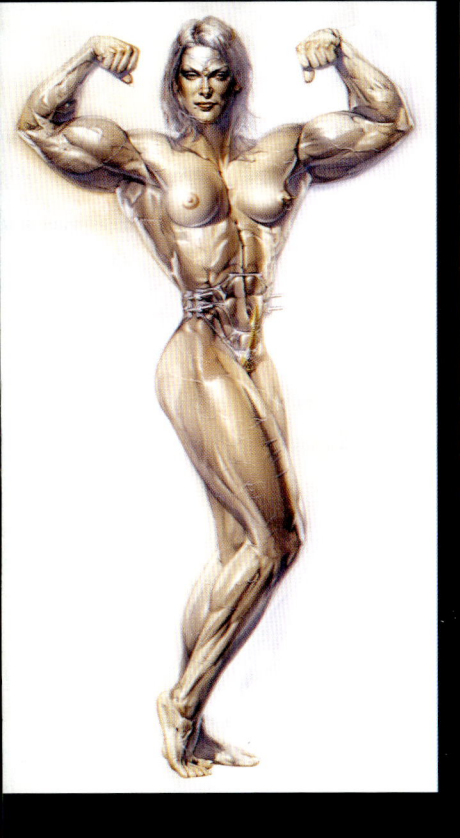
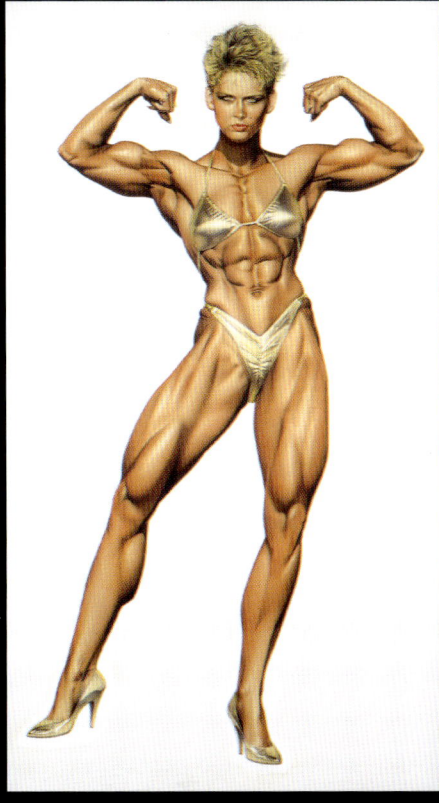
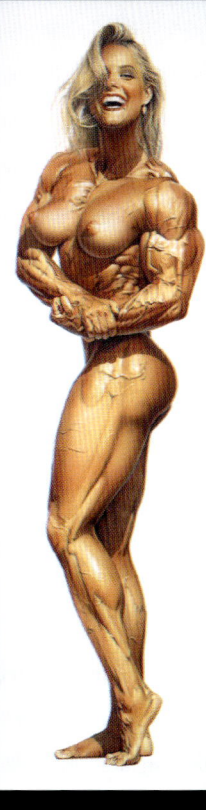

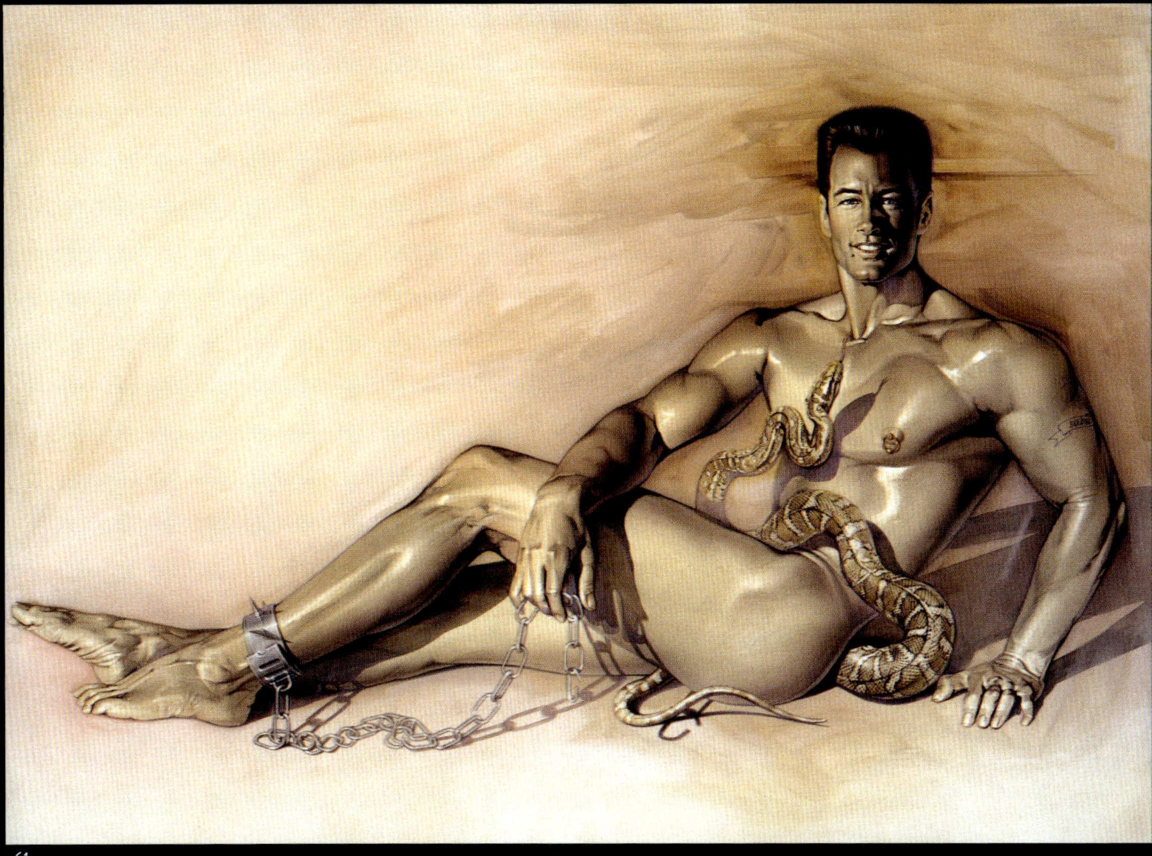

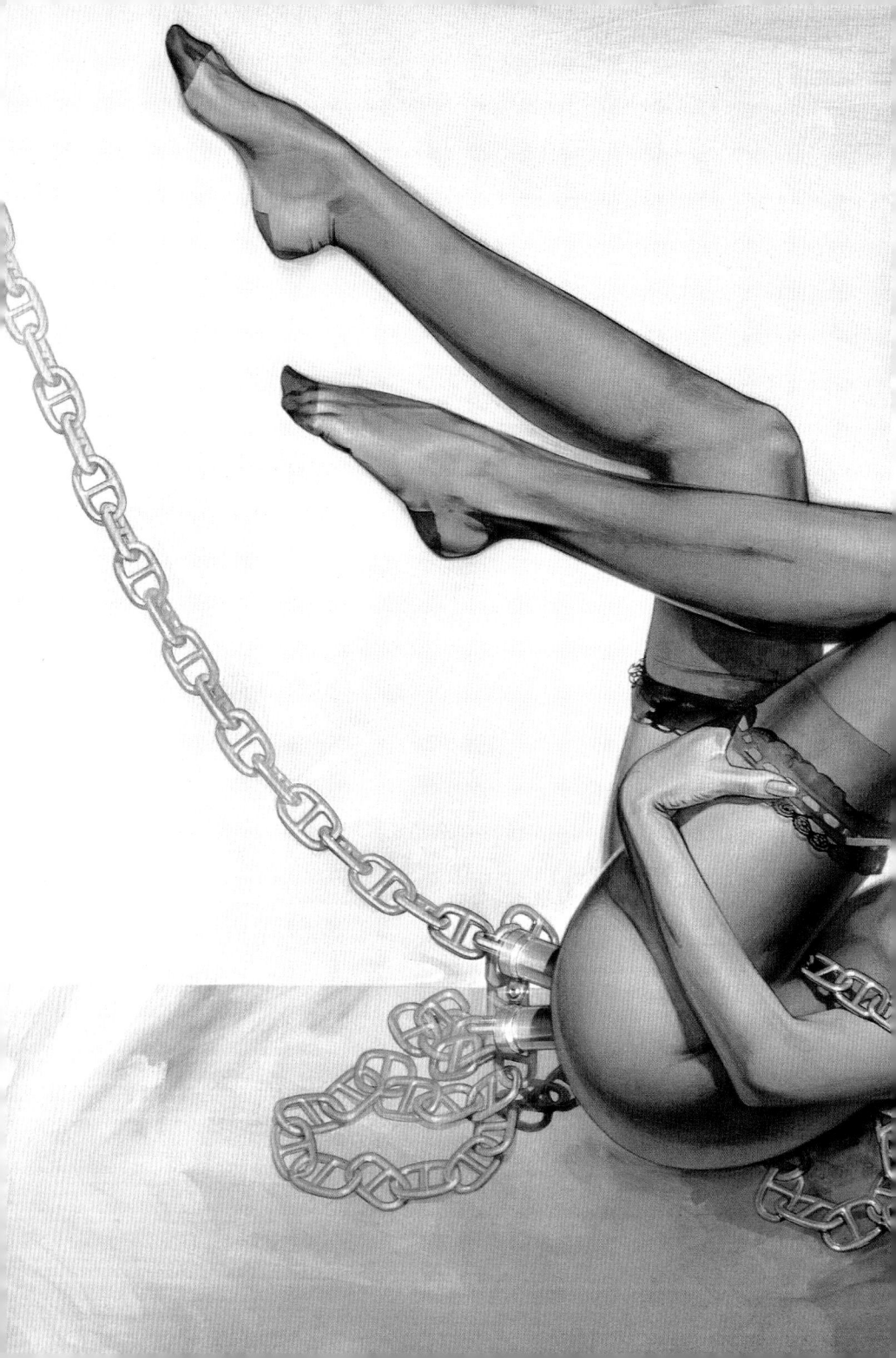

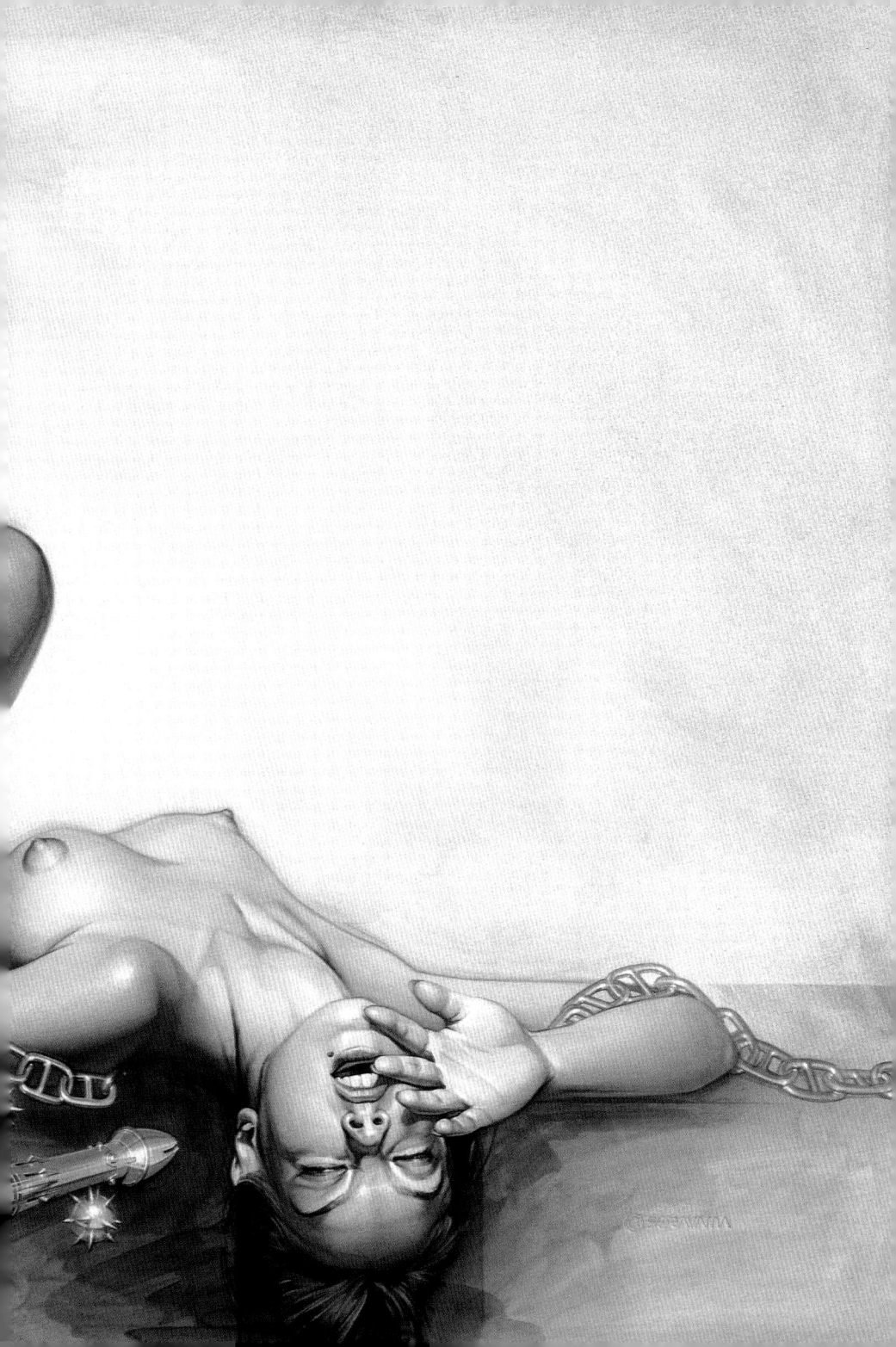

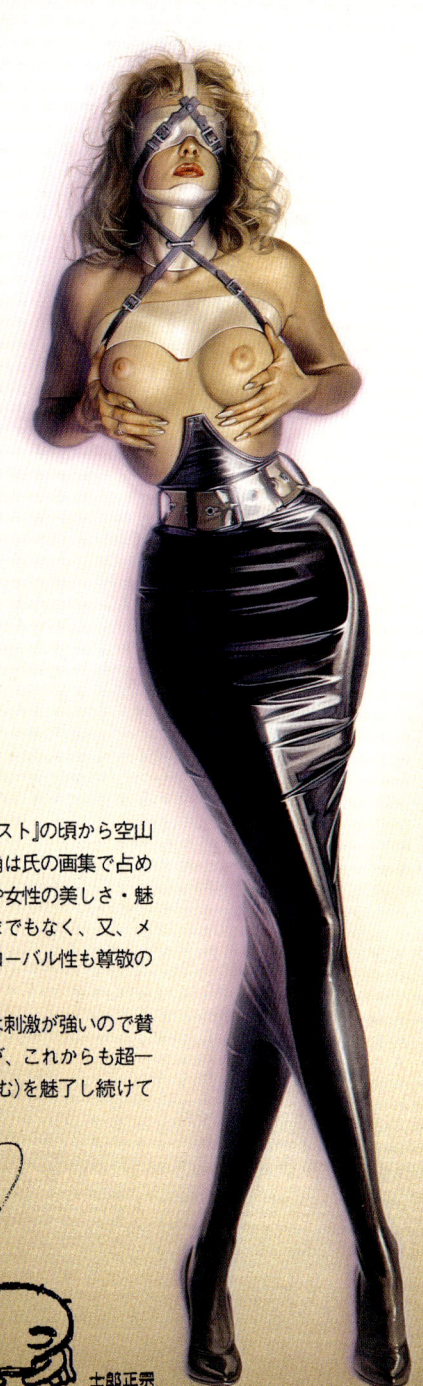

士郎正宗（漫画家）

僕は『サントリー社のイラスト』の頃から空山
氏のファンで、本棚の一角は氏の画集で占め
られている。グロスメカや女性の美しさ・魅
力は僕などが改めて言うまでもなく、又、メ
ディアや国境を越えたグローバル性も尊敬の
一因である。

空山先生、最近の御仕事は刺激が強いので賛
否もあろうかと思いますが、これからも超一
流の品質でファン（僕も含む）を魅了し続けて
下さい。

士郎正宗

大橋歩（イラストレーター）

ずいぶん前に、「コムにちわ、イラストレーターの空山基ですが」って、電話をもらったので、印象をもった。やさしそうですが、ひもさしそうって、同業者とつき合いがまくなった。何故か昔普通の人だった。ひも空山さんに会ったくない、あの私……

れび、イラストレーターもオ……れたのだった。クシーで、緻密な絵を描く人とは思えない。だったり、昔通恐い男、電話の声のよう唯一オトも多チになり、同業者っオト、モ多くは空山……

やさしい発言もあったりしゃべり方もやわらかると、男？といますお声が・え？とでもせっこうな……かっ風しい必得しいと話しようがらしゃわると……男？のように……学のように……わなを思って何はませんはいいかない新はま山さんしありしない。

大橋歩

宇野亜喜良（イラストレーター）

数年前のある夜、ファクシミリがカタカタと鳴った。送られてくる画像は、女性の乳房につけたピアスから、ヴァギナの回りの無数のリングや貴金属類、クリトリスにつけたアクセサリーというようなしろもの。密度のある写真類だからファックスも時間がかかる。50枚くらいを受信し終るのに30分もかかったような気がした。

送り主は空山基で、東欧のこういう趣味の人たちの大会にゲストとして出席したときの資料だそうで、当然それは、ぼくにとっても貴重な資料で紙袋に入れて大事にしているのだけれど、それにしても、空山基に好色な仲間の一種にされたことは嬉しい。好色も好きだが、空山基も好きだからだ。

Aquirax

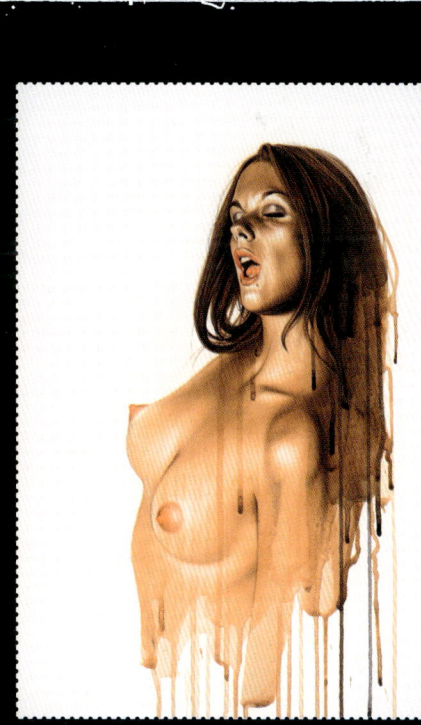

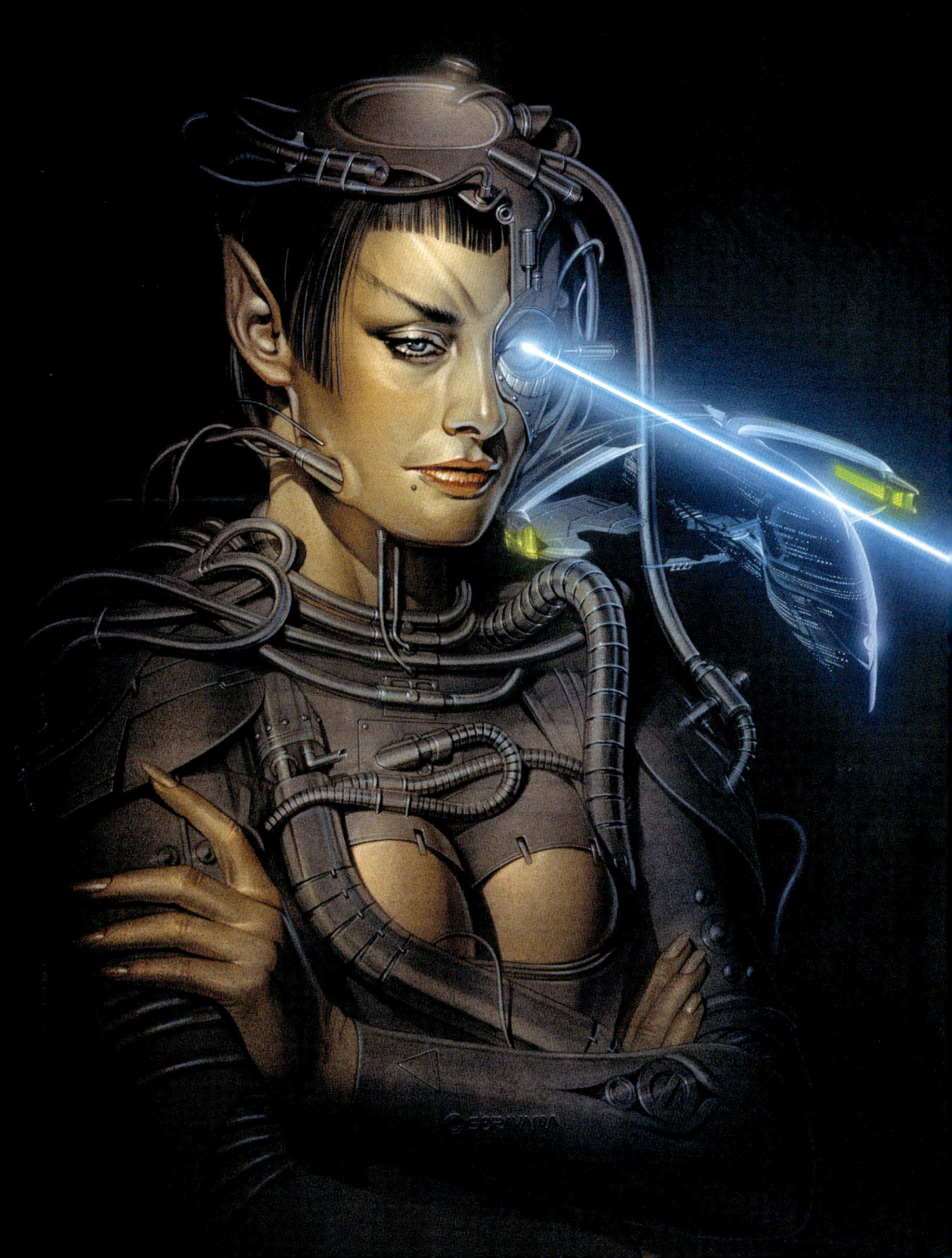

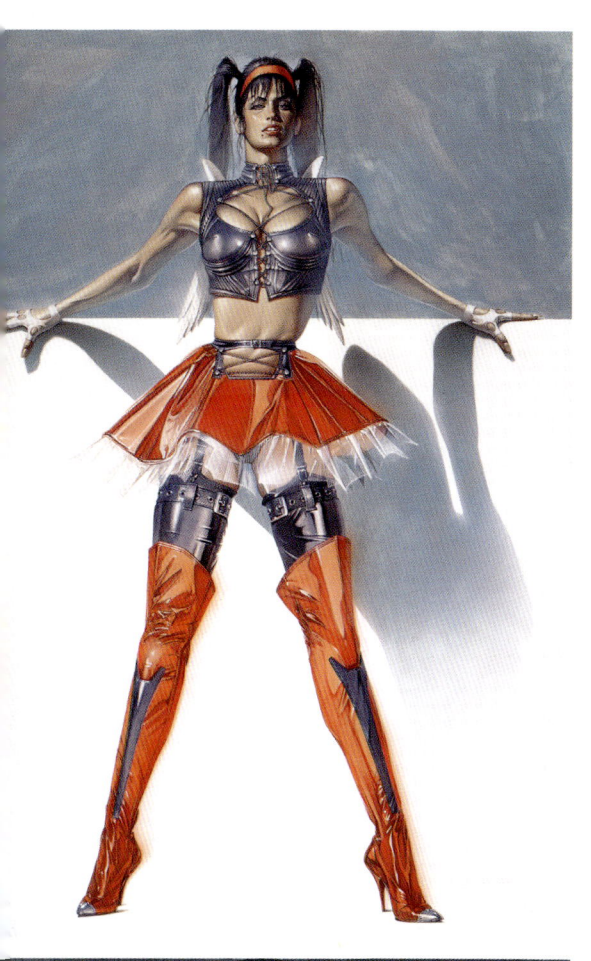
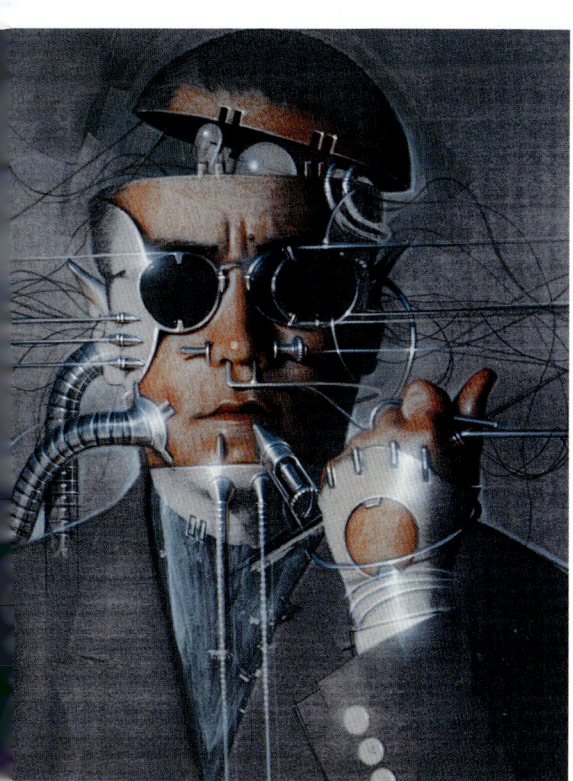

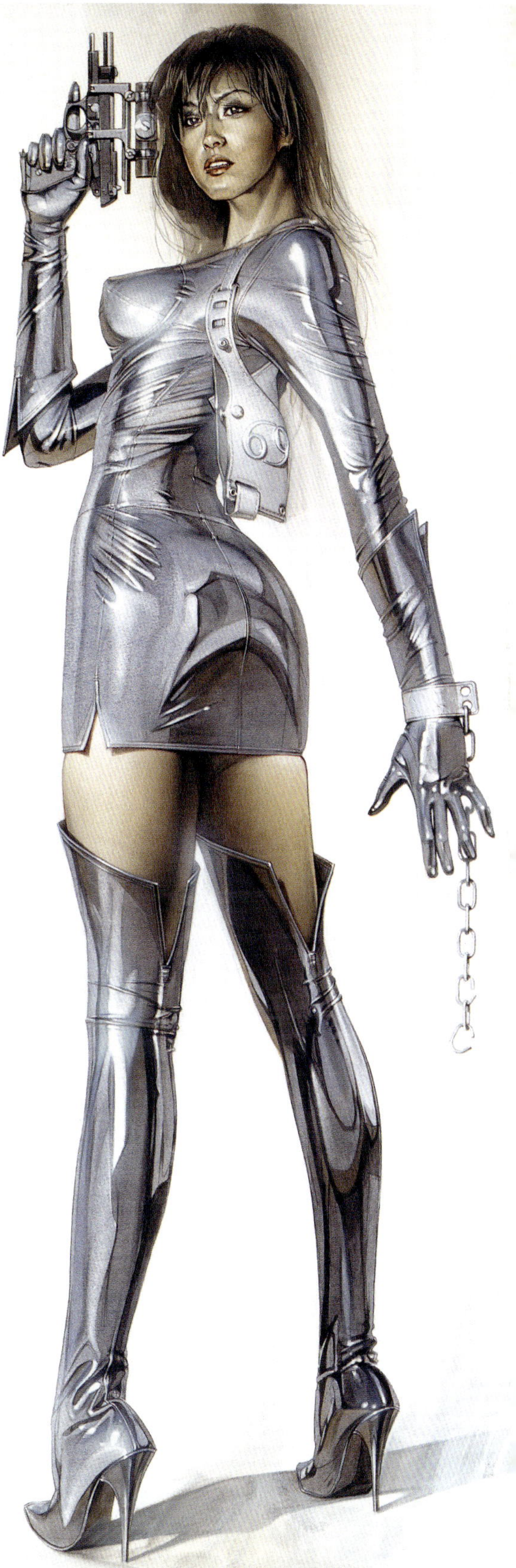

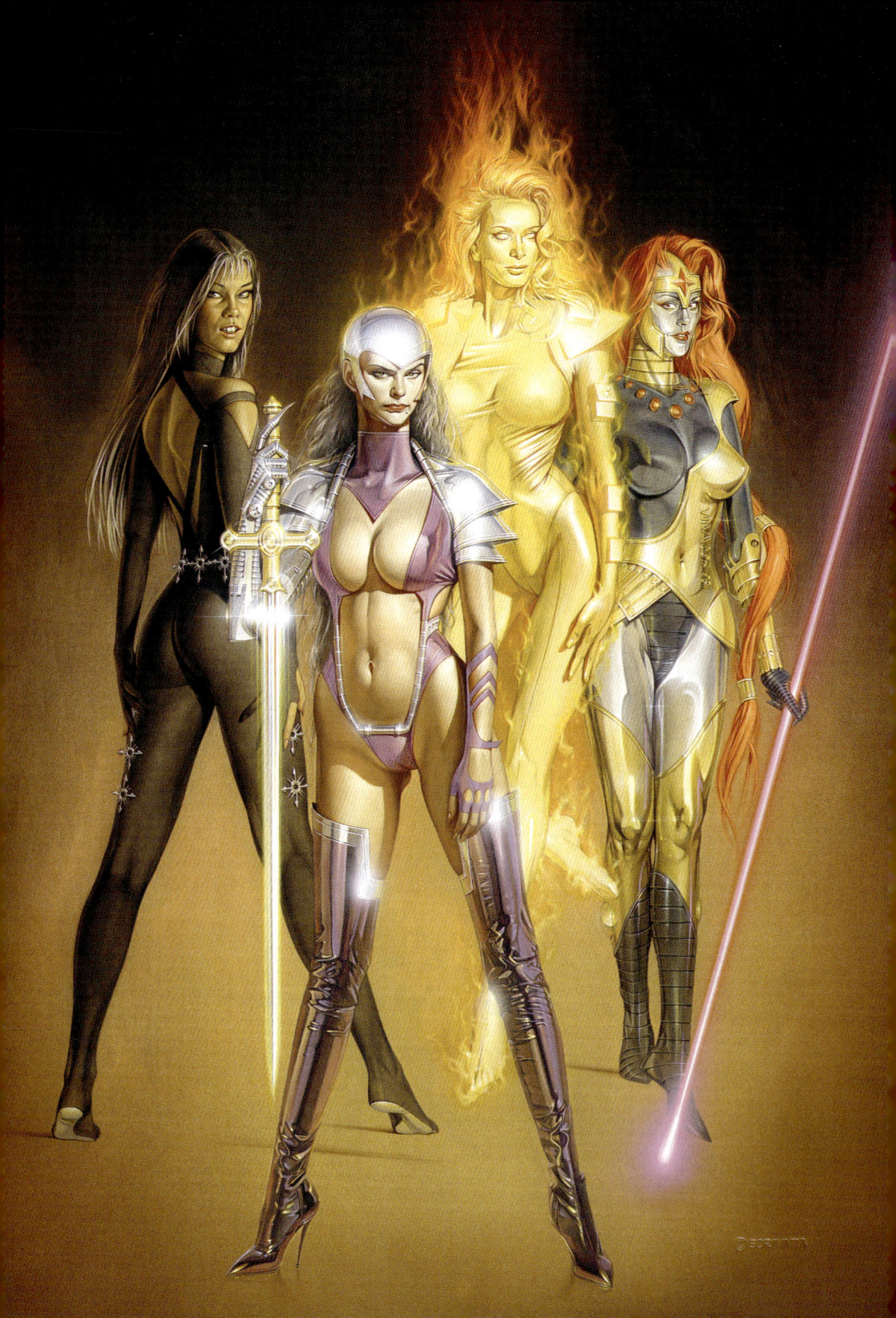

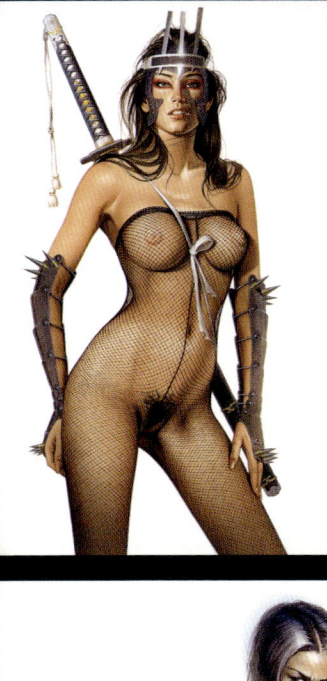
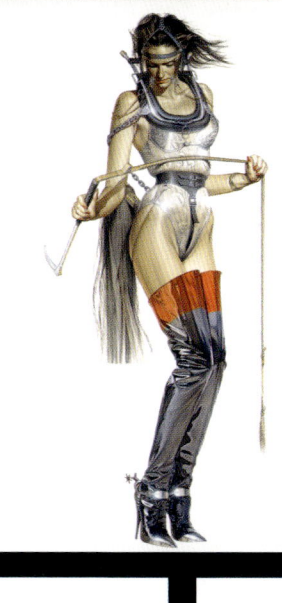
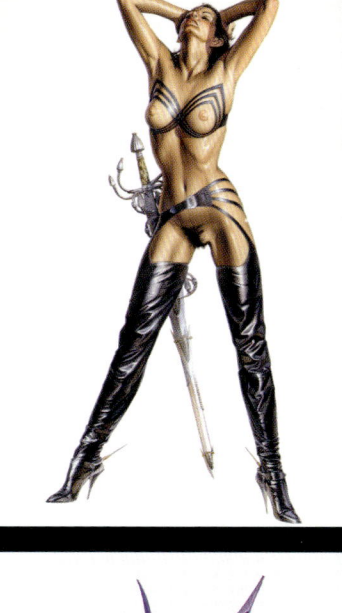
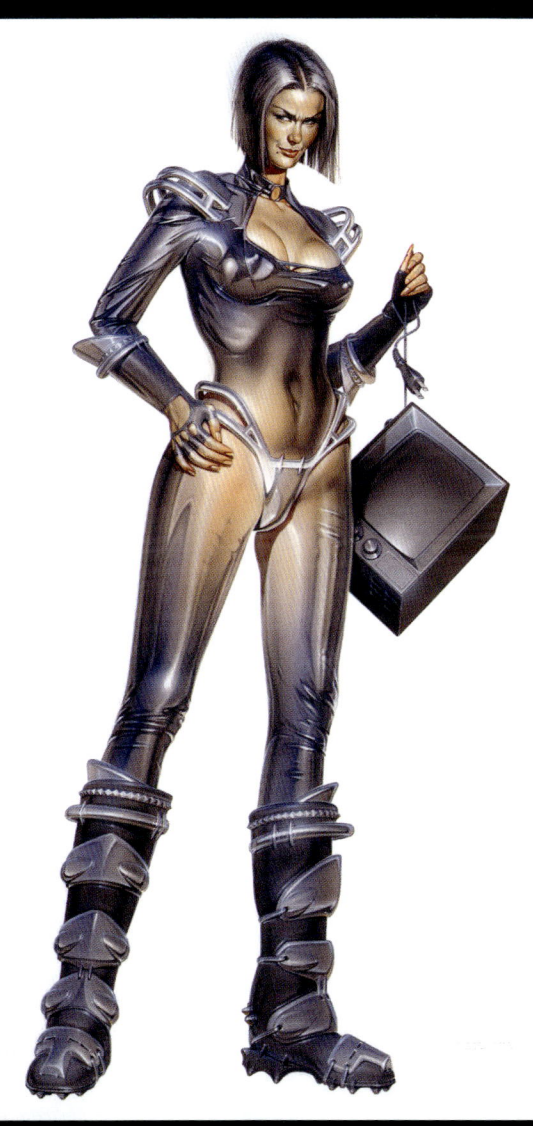
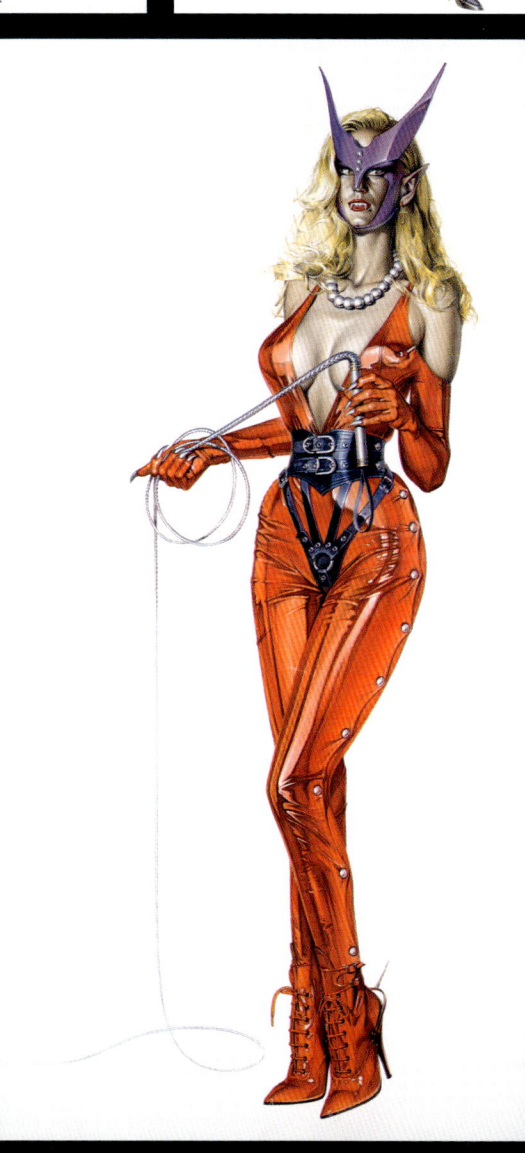

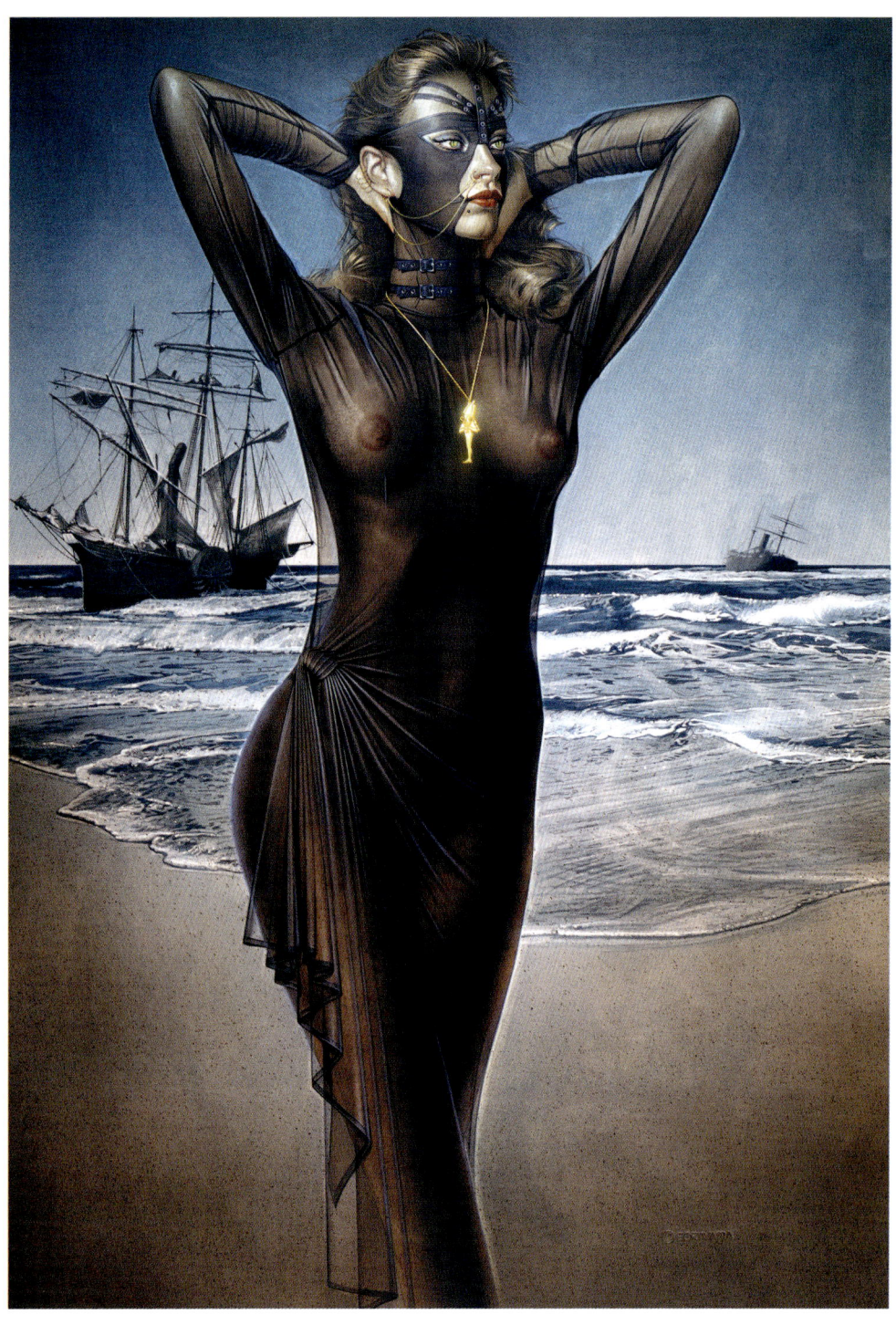

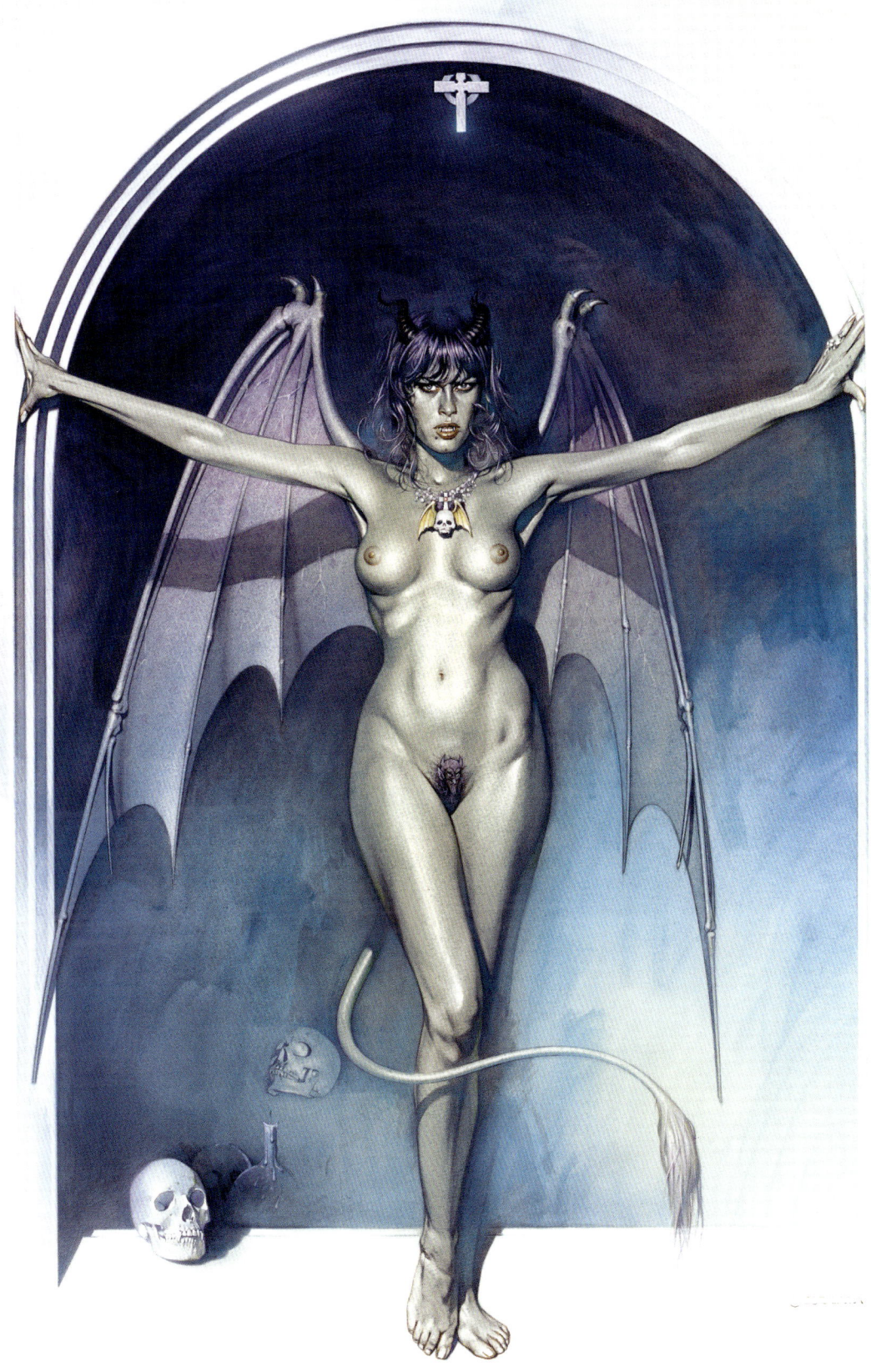

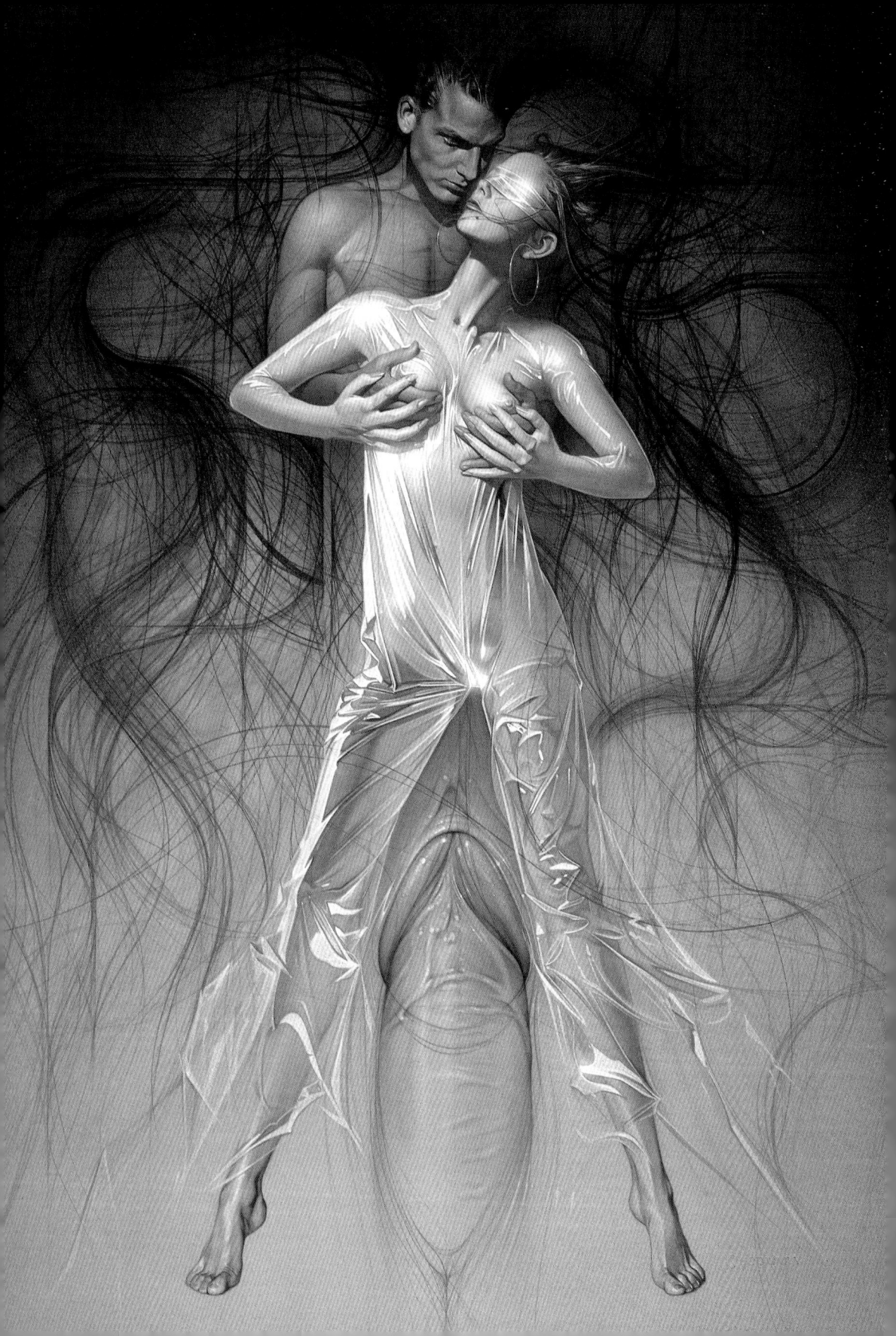

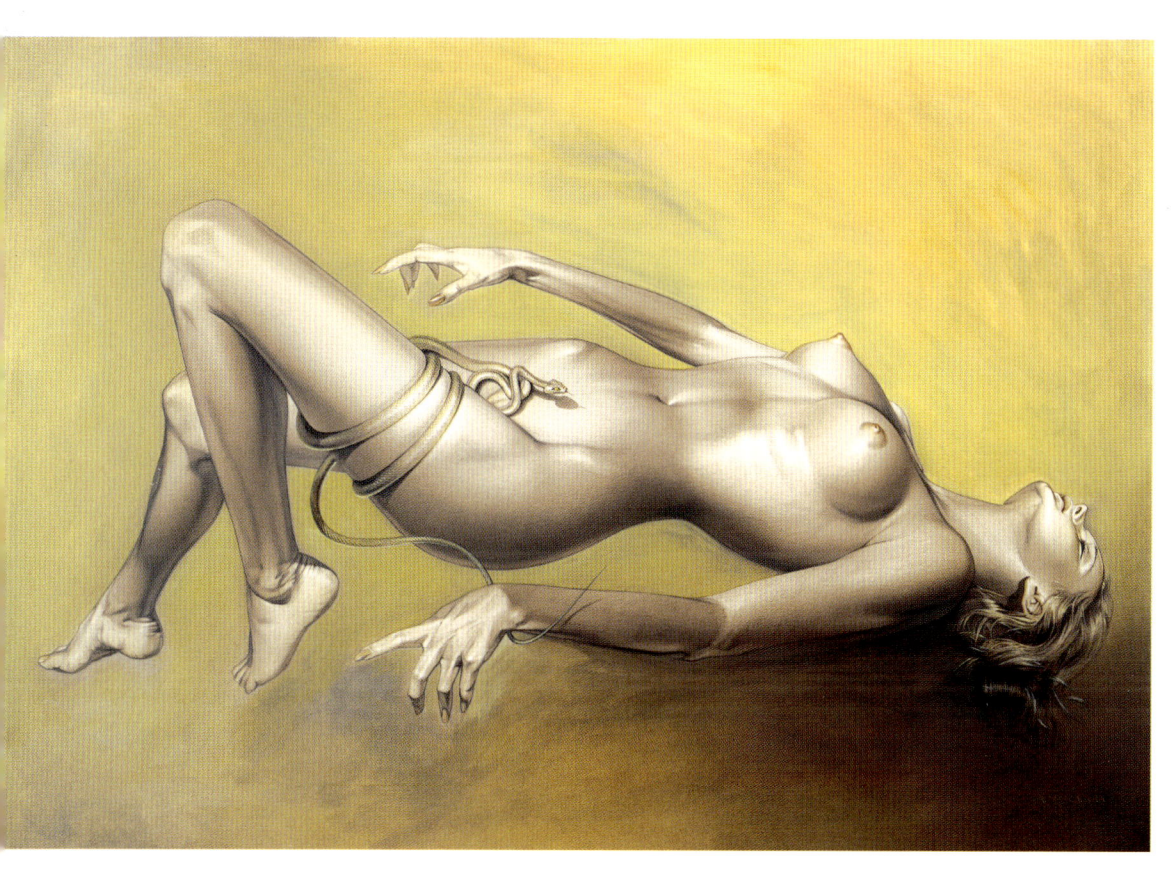

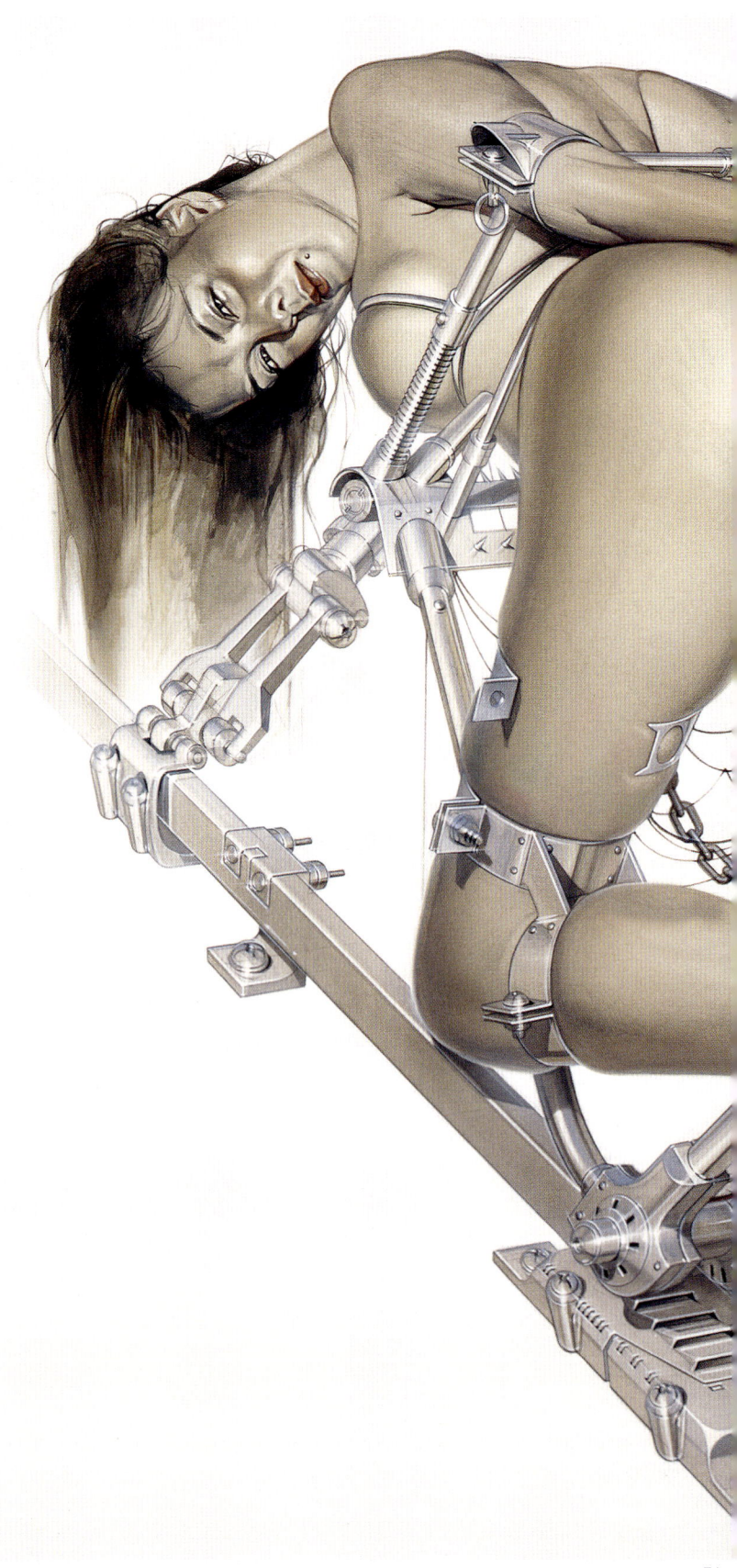

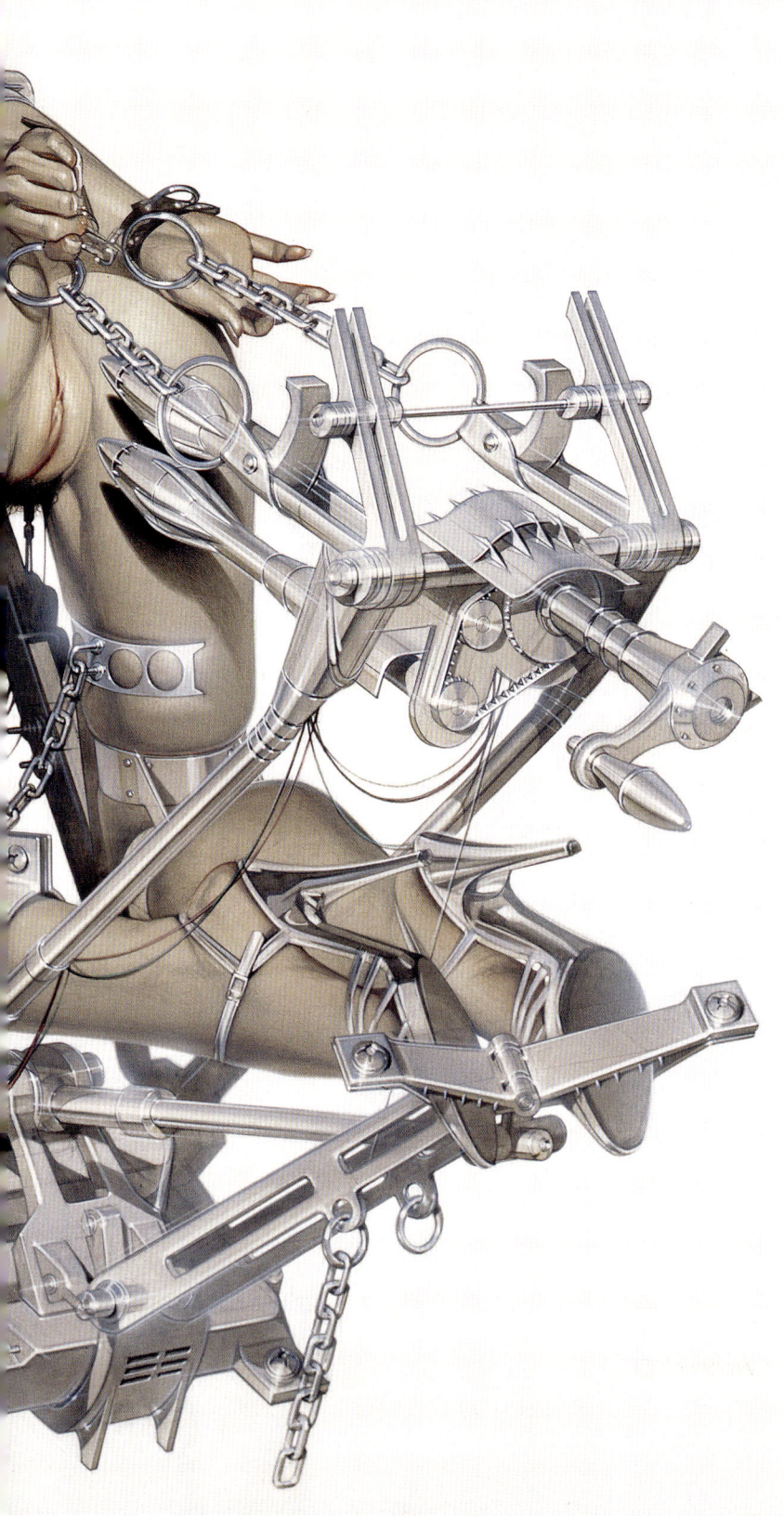

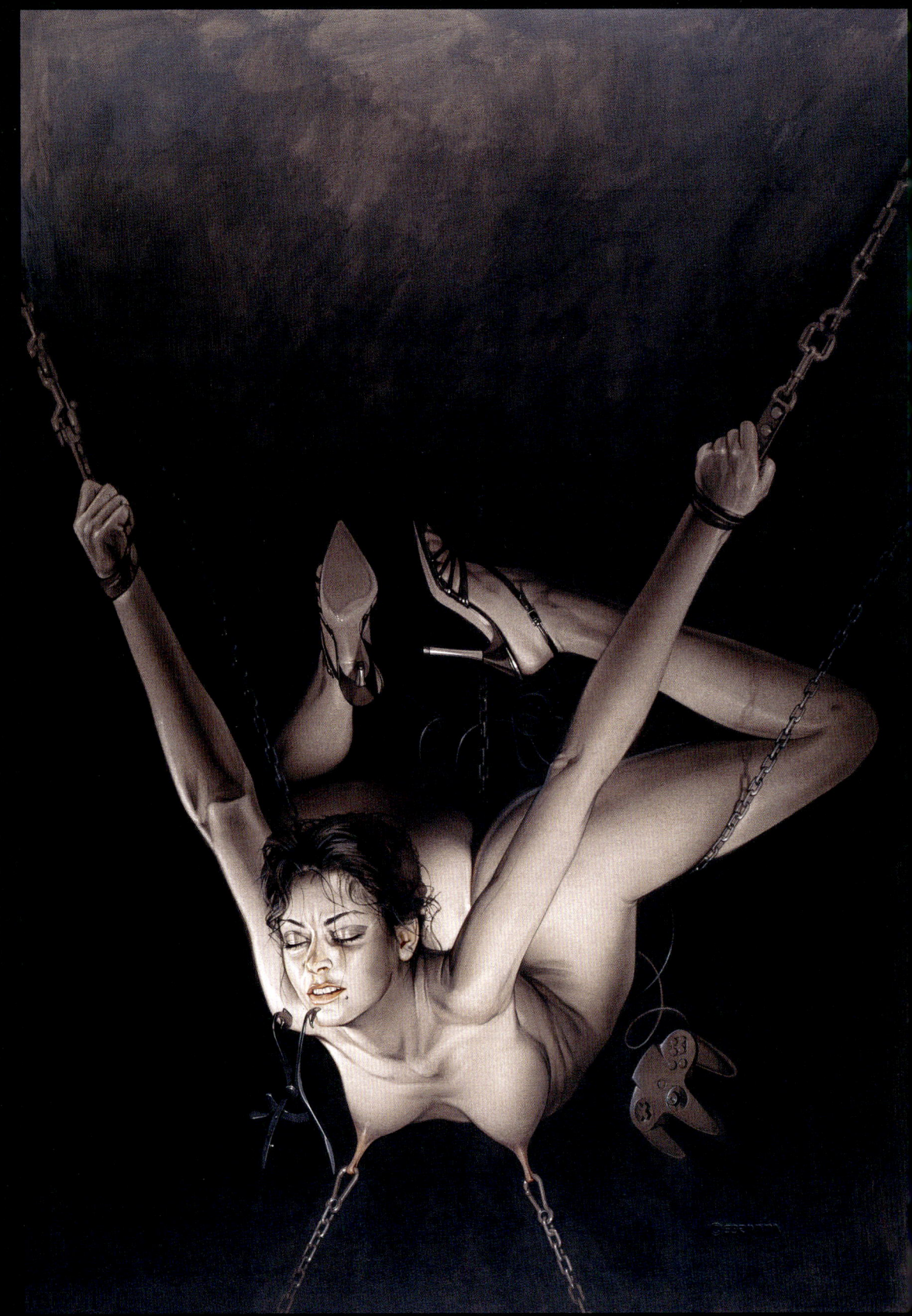

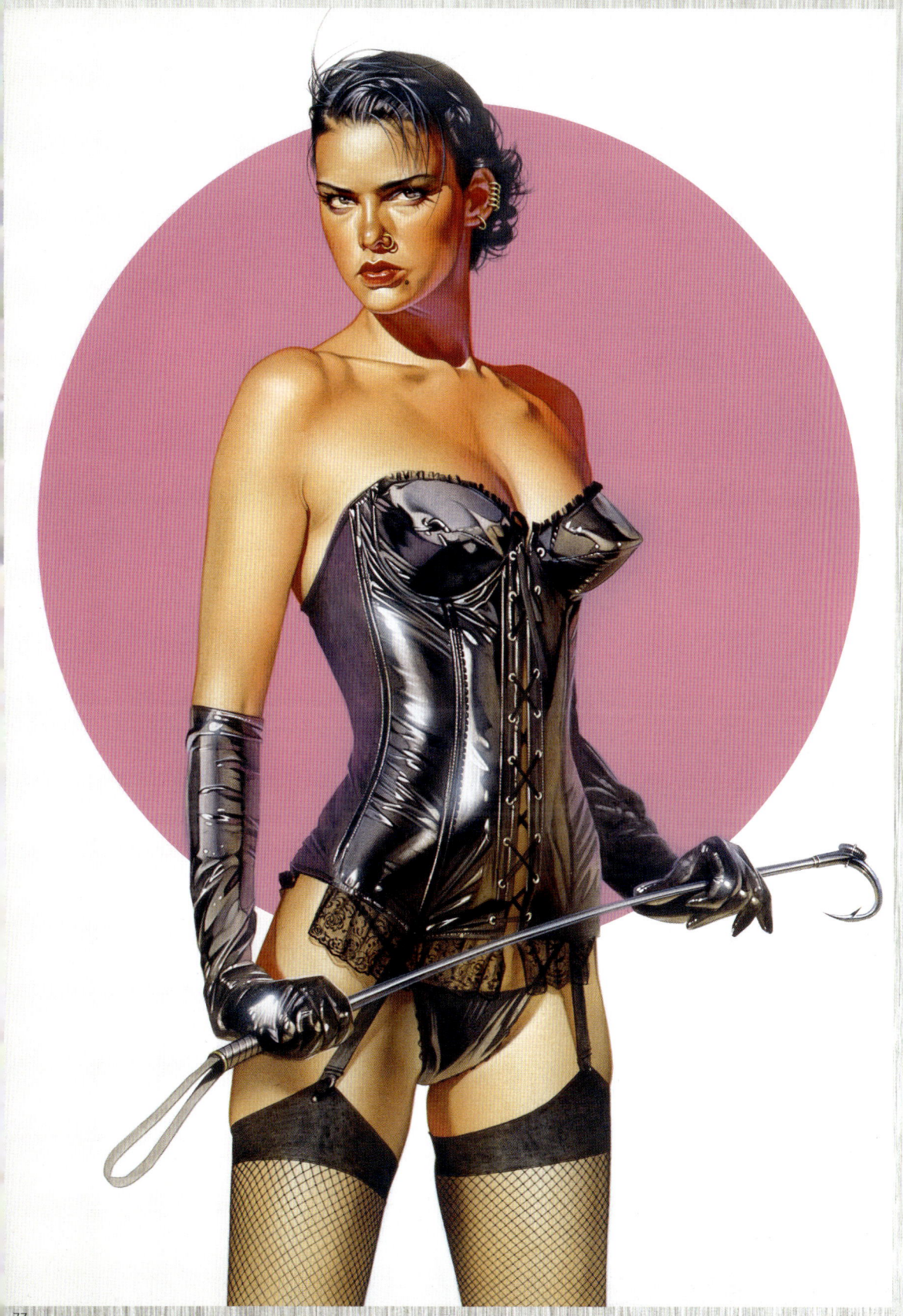

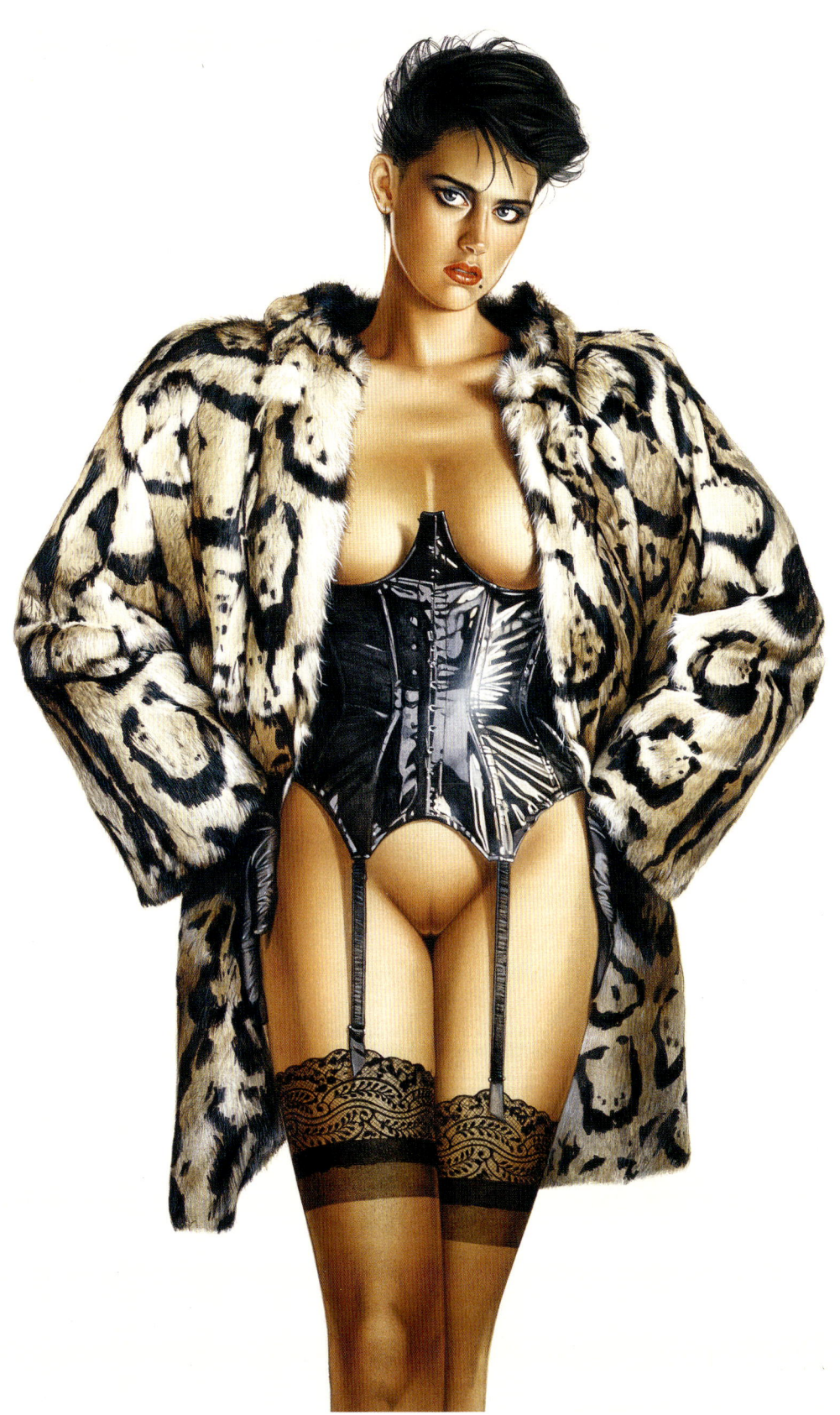

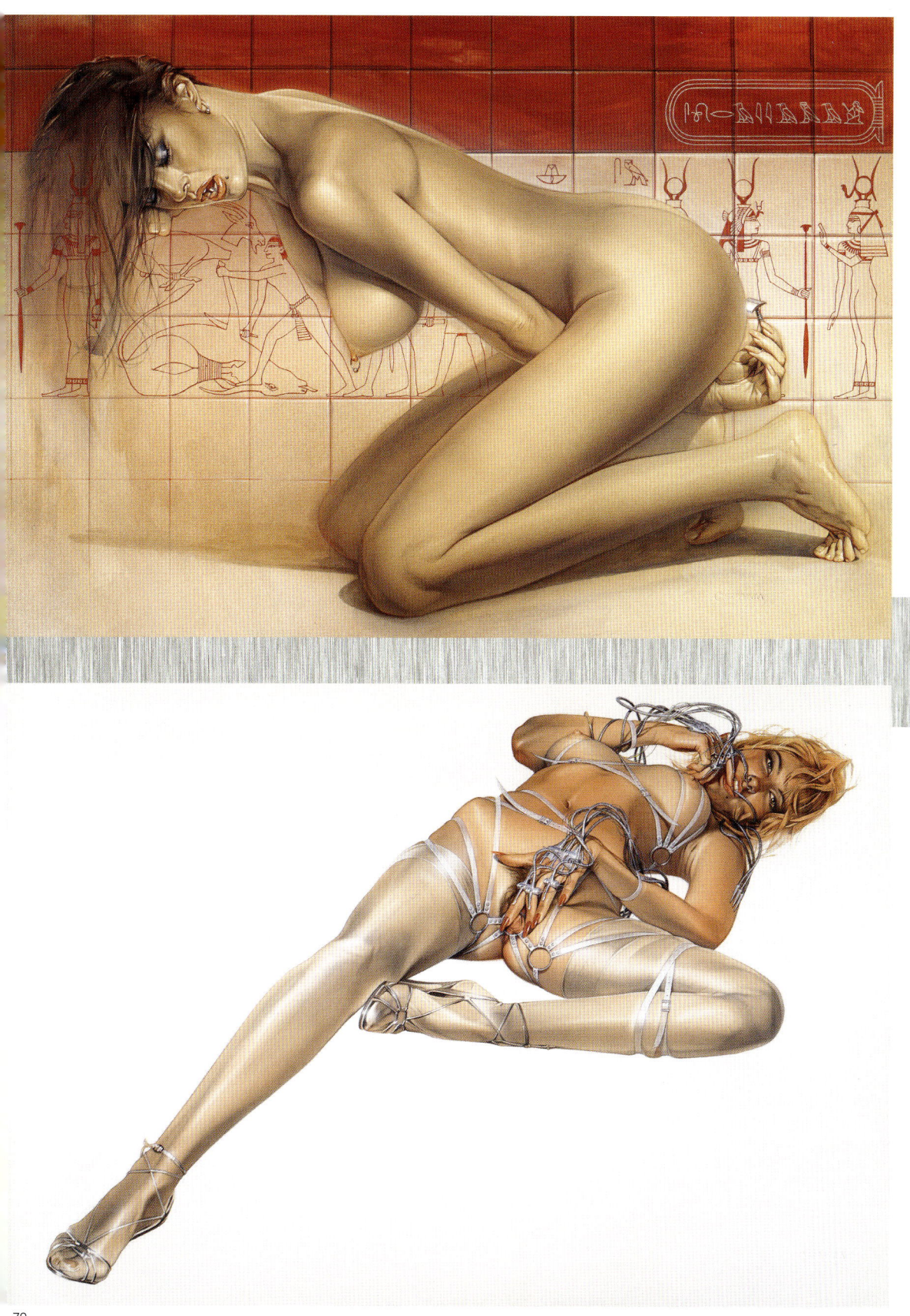

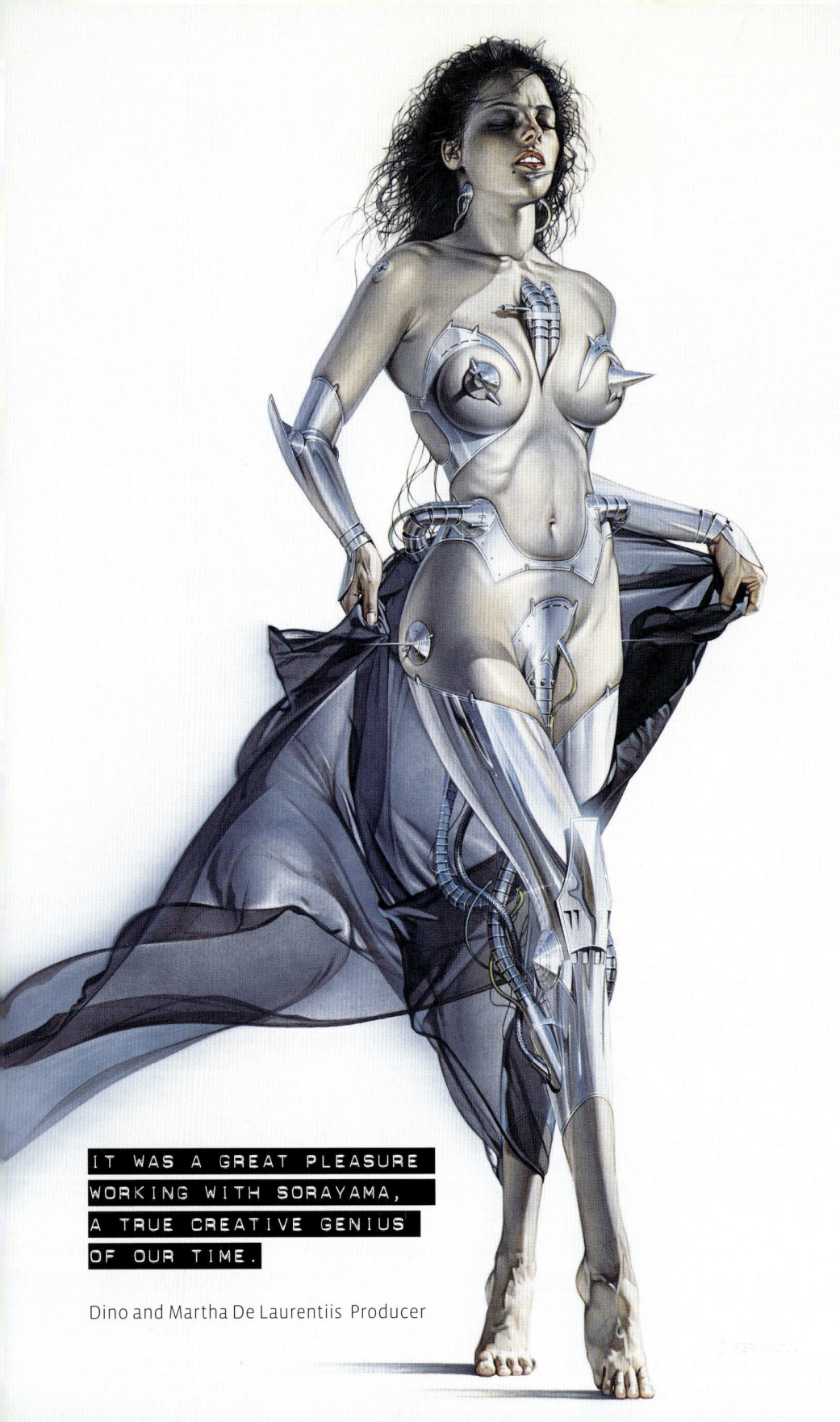

IT WAS A GREAT PLEASURE
WORKING WITH SORAYAMA,
A TRUE CREATIVE GENIUS
OF OUR TIME.

Dino and Martha De Laurentiis Producer

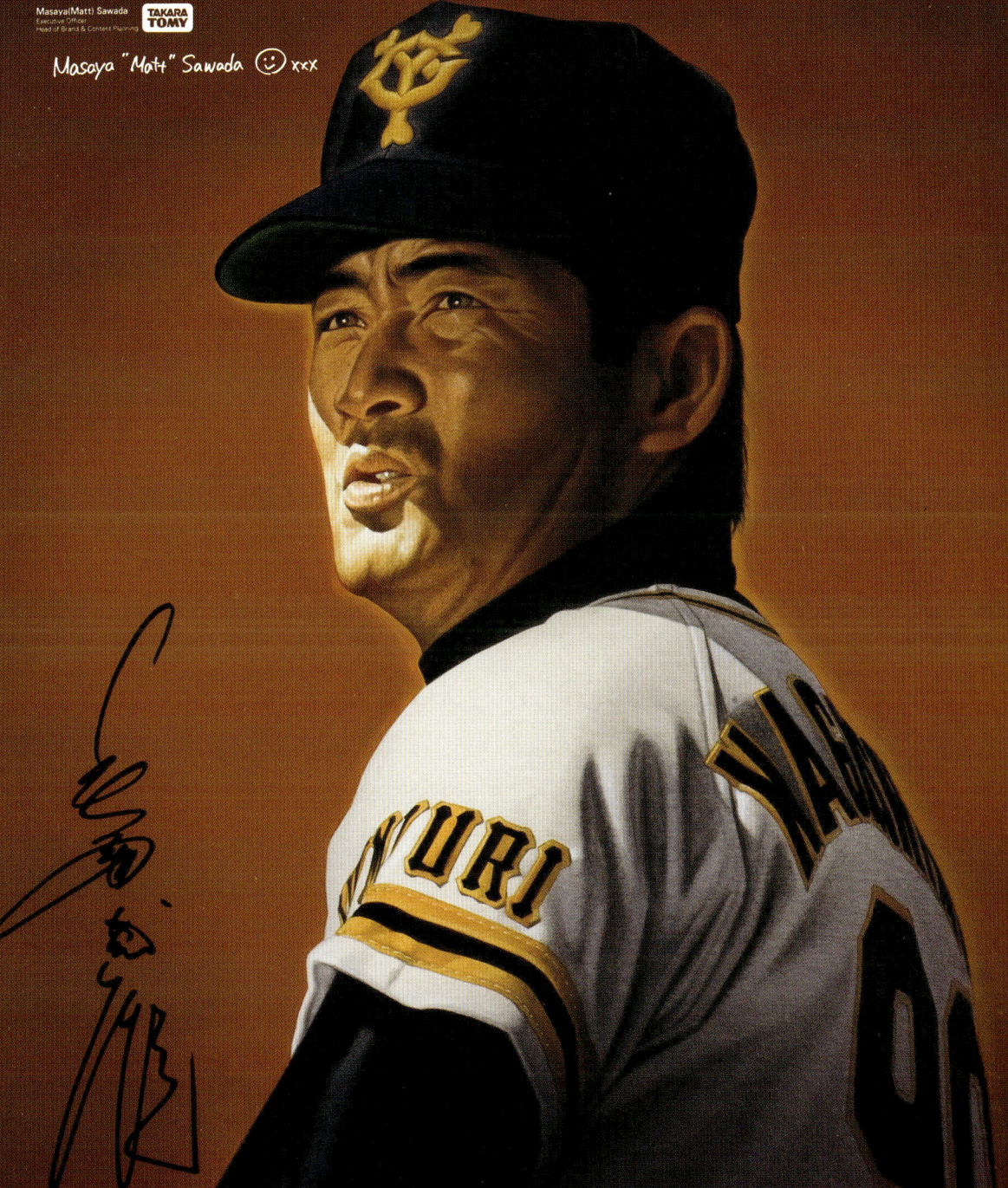

Sorayama-San is a
  remarkable artist, who has
  every feature of successful people
  namely selfishness, stinginess and
  impatience.
May the force be with him!

Masaya(Matt) Sawada
Executive Officer
Head of Brand & Content Planning

Masaya "Matt" Sawada ☺ xxx

すばらしい作品の創作、
その一方で、
ヨットの上での凍りつくような「オヤジギャグ」の連発、
その理解を超えたギャップが魅力…

ヨット戦旅のクルー（奴隷部員）より
㈱ファイ・マイクロテック
取締役
山川兄 裕之

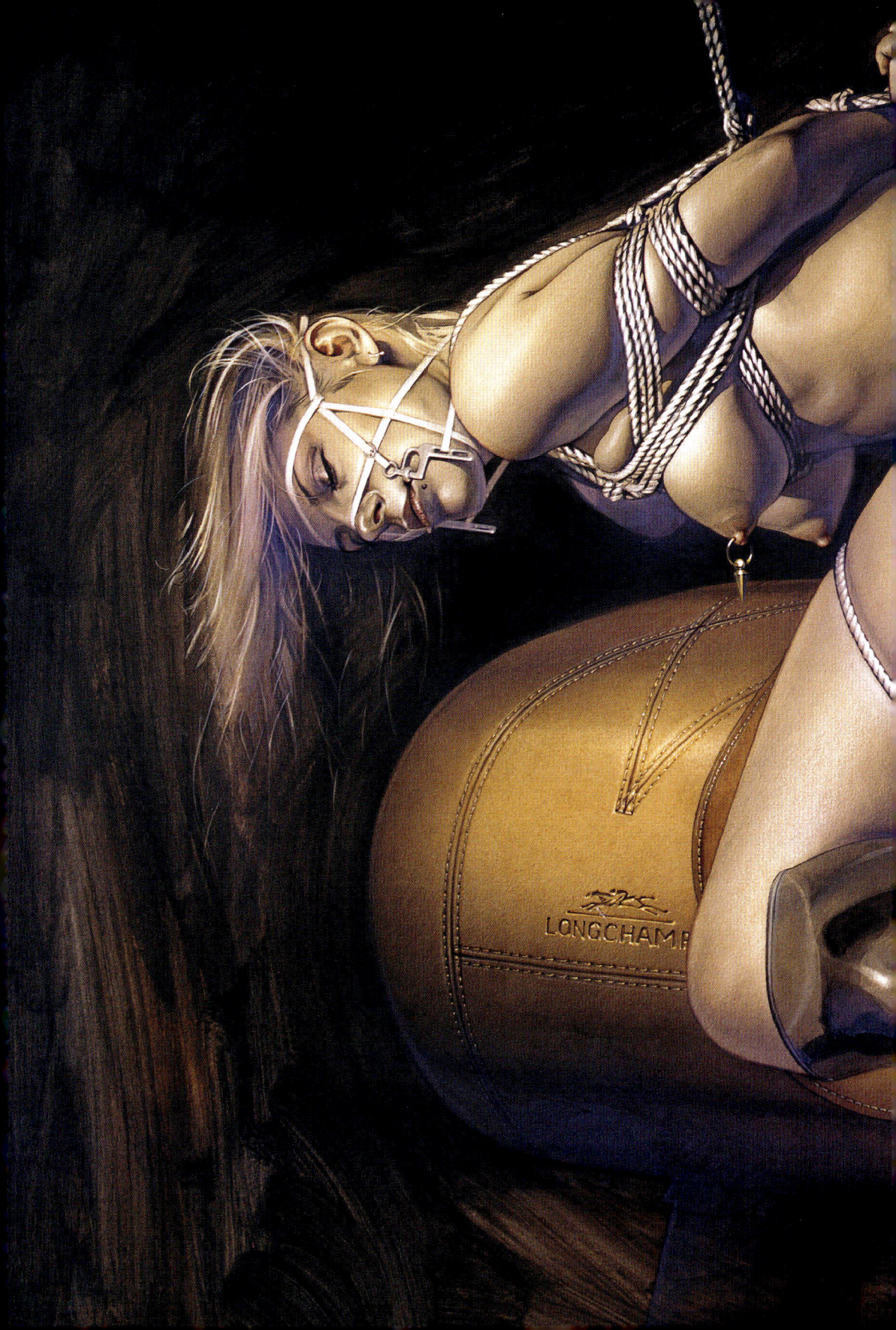

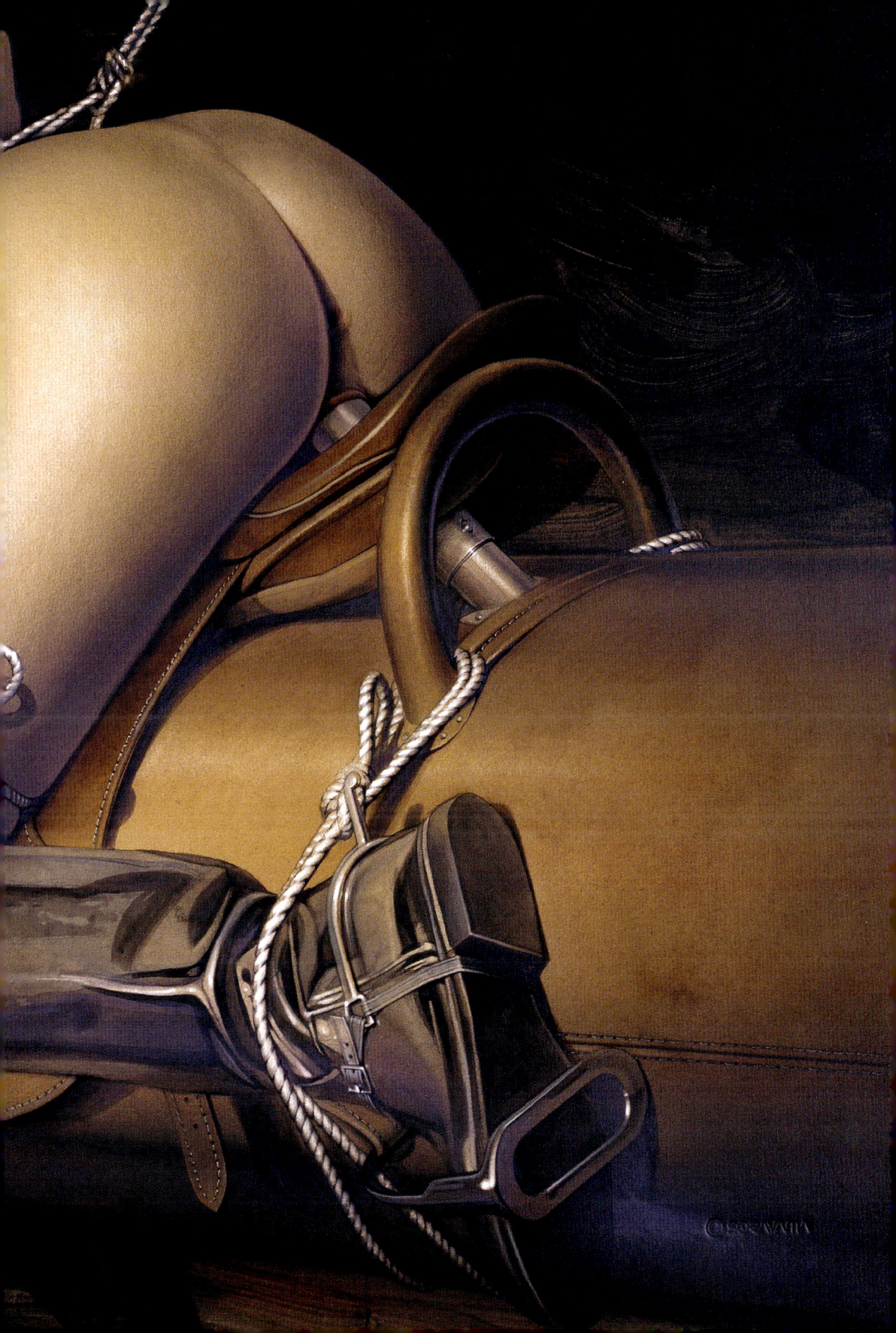

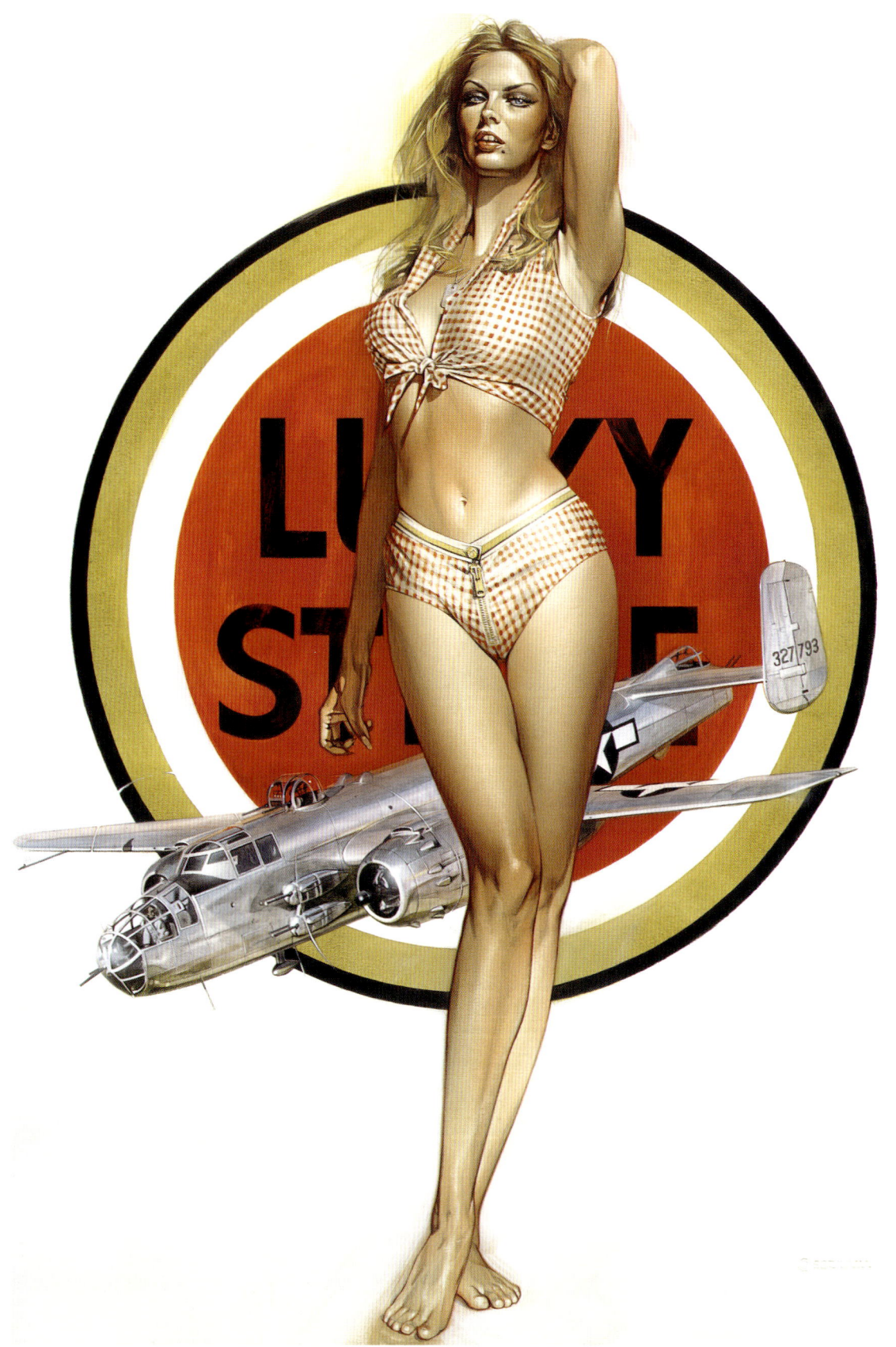

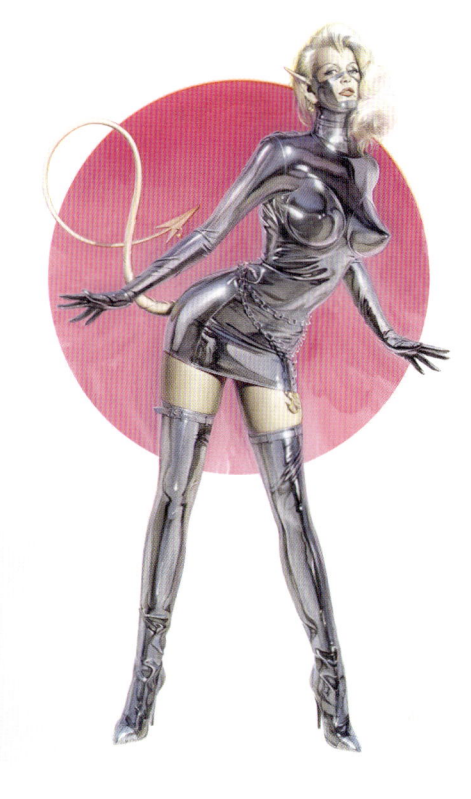

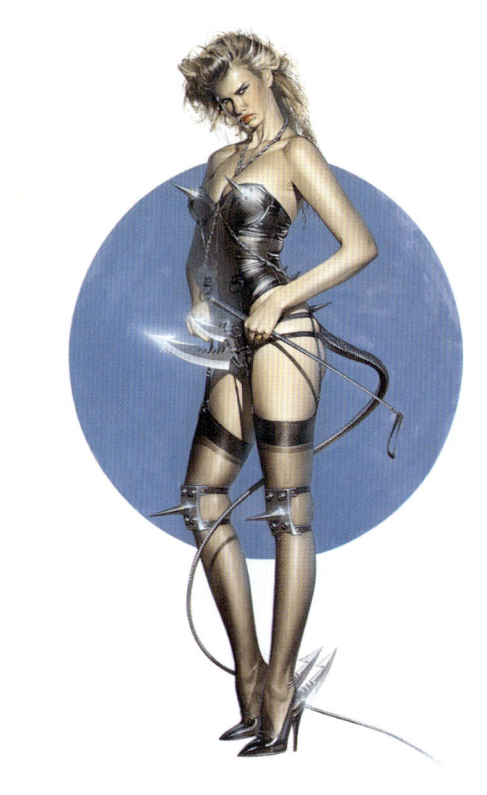

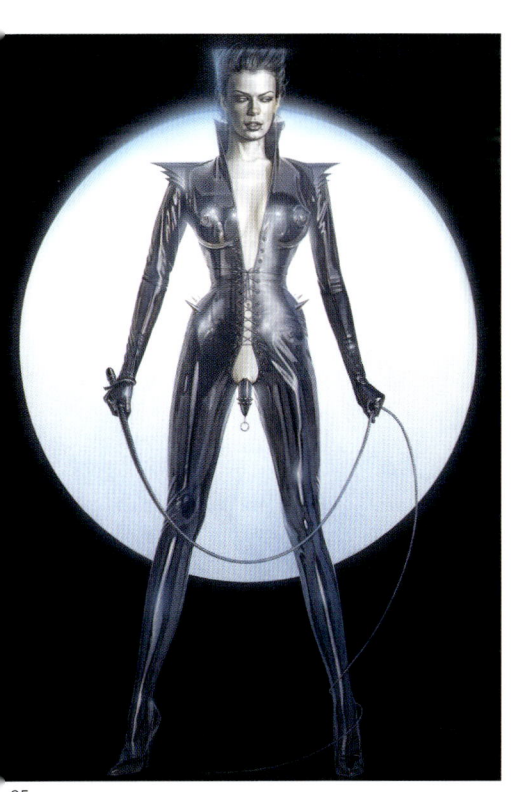

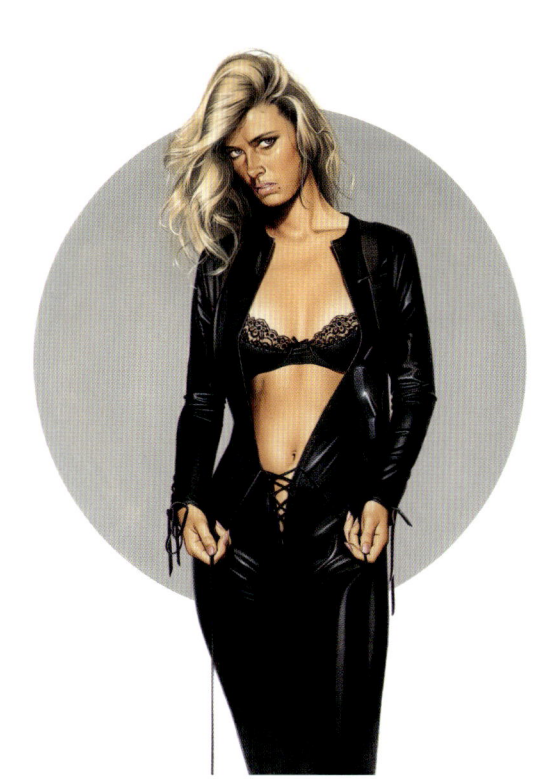

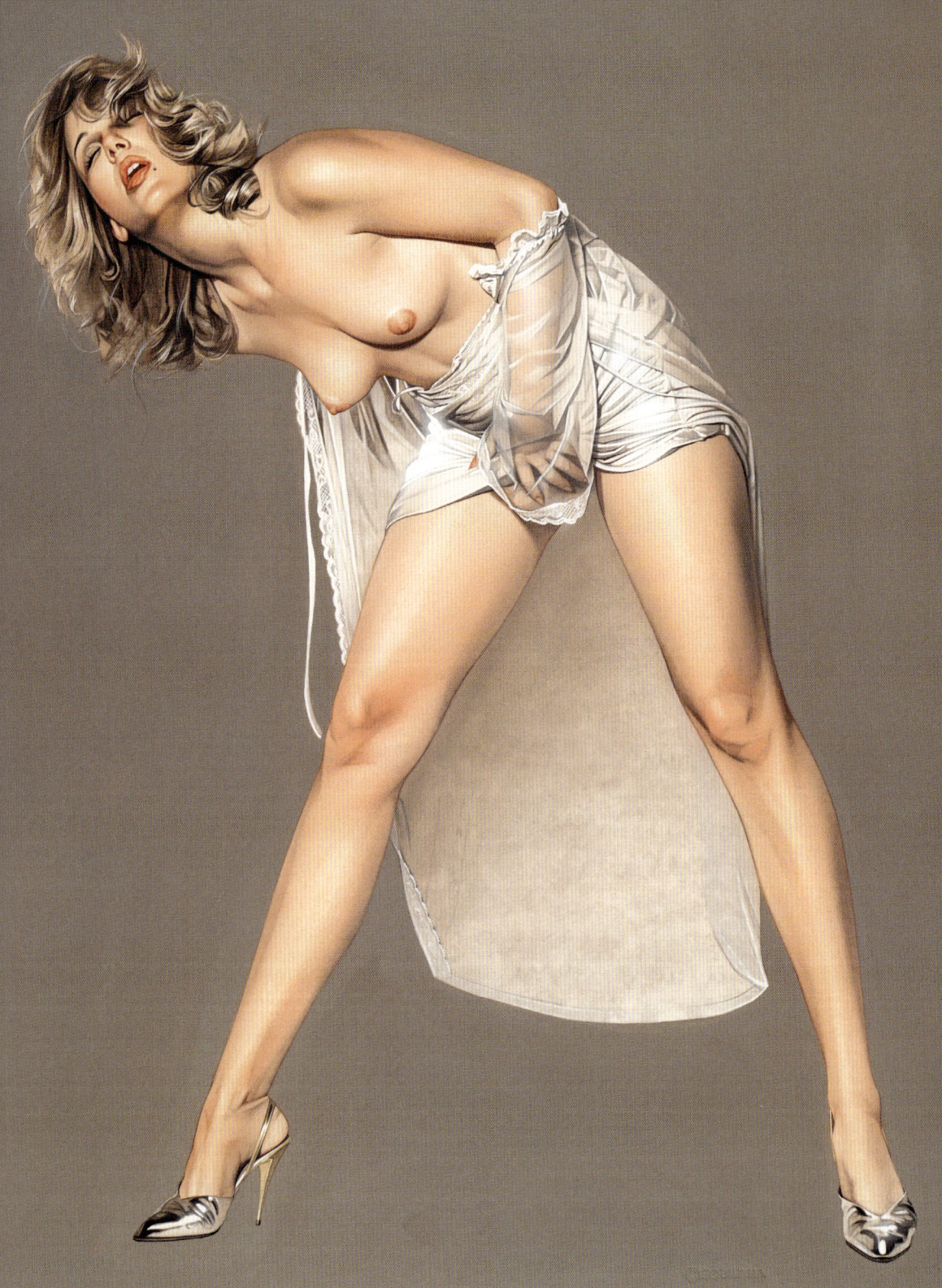

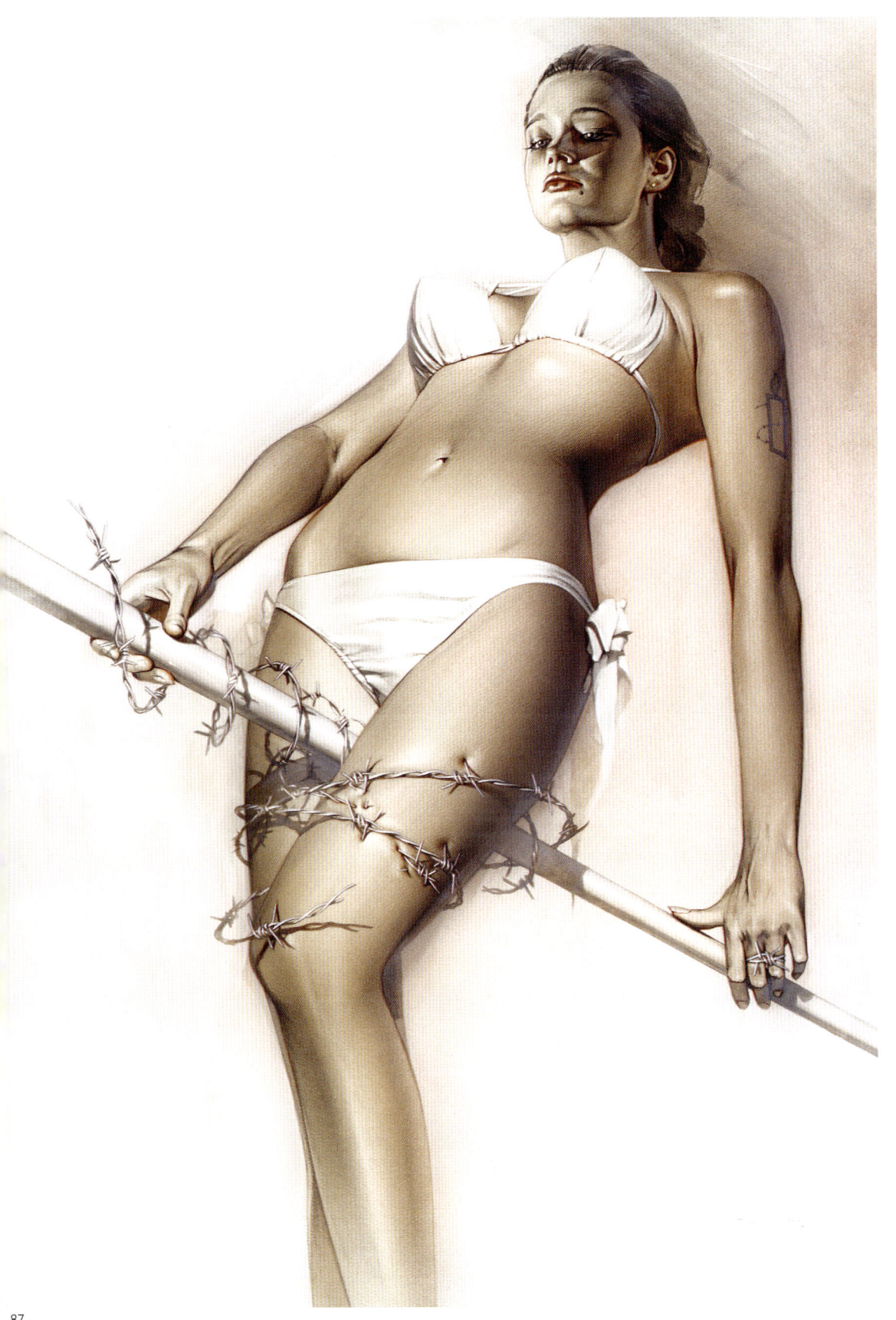

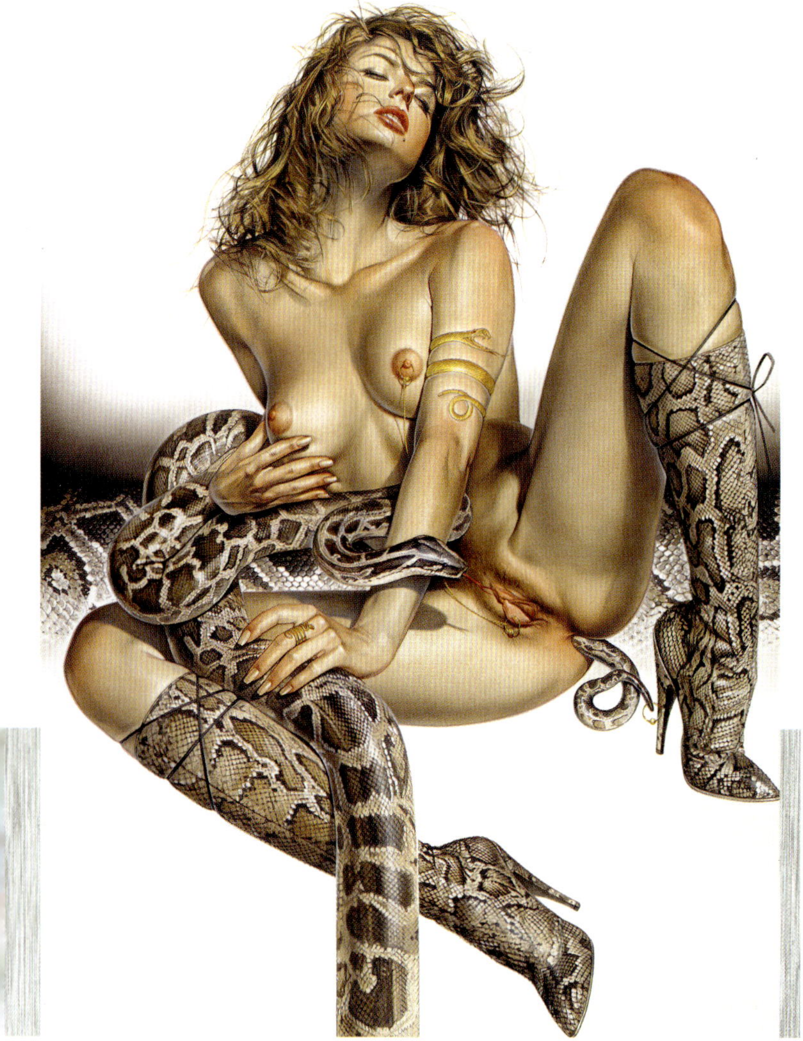

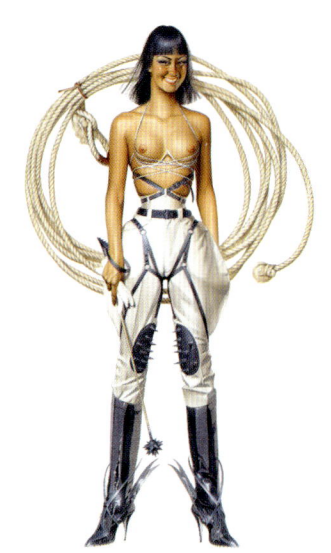

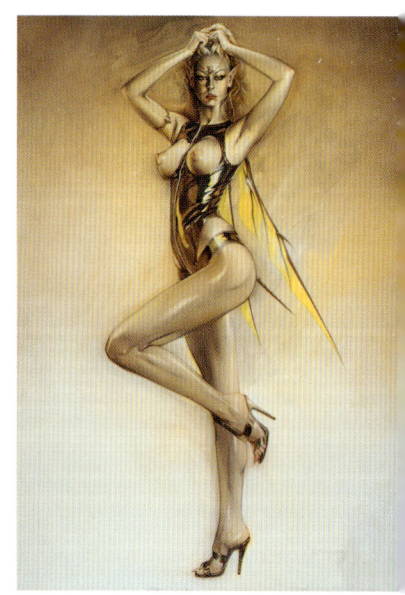

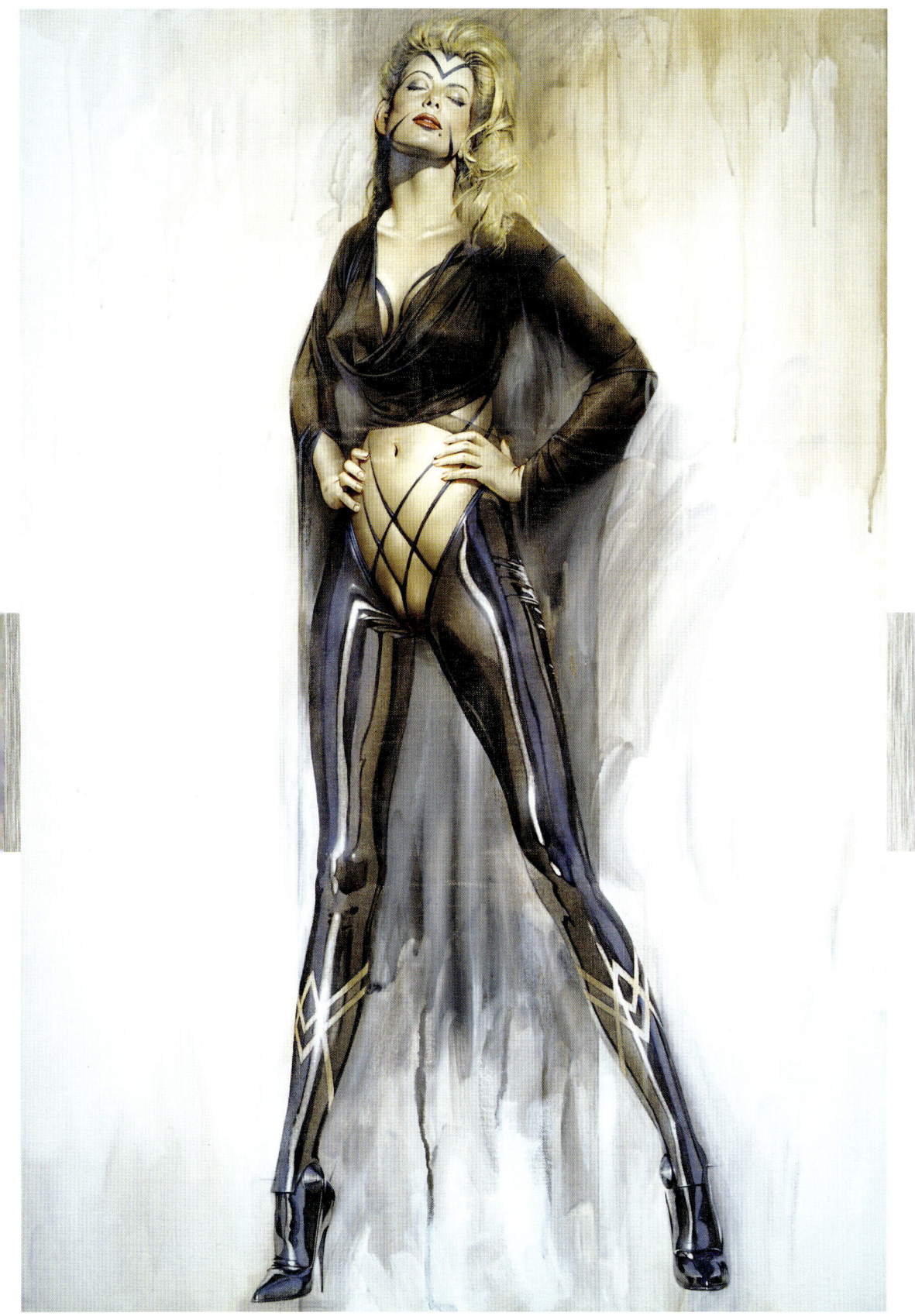

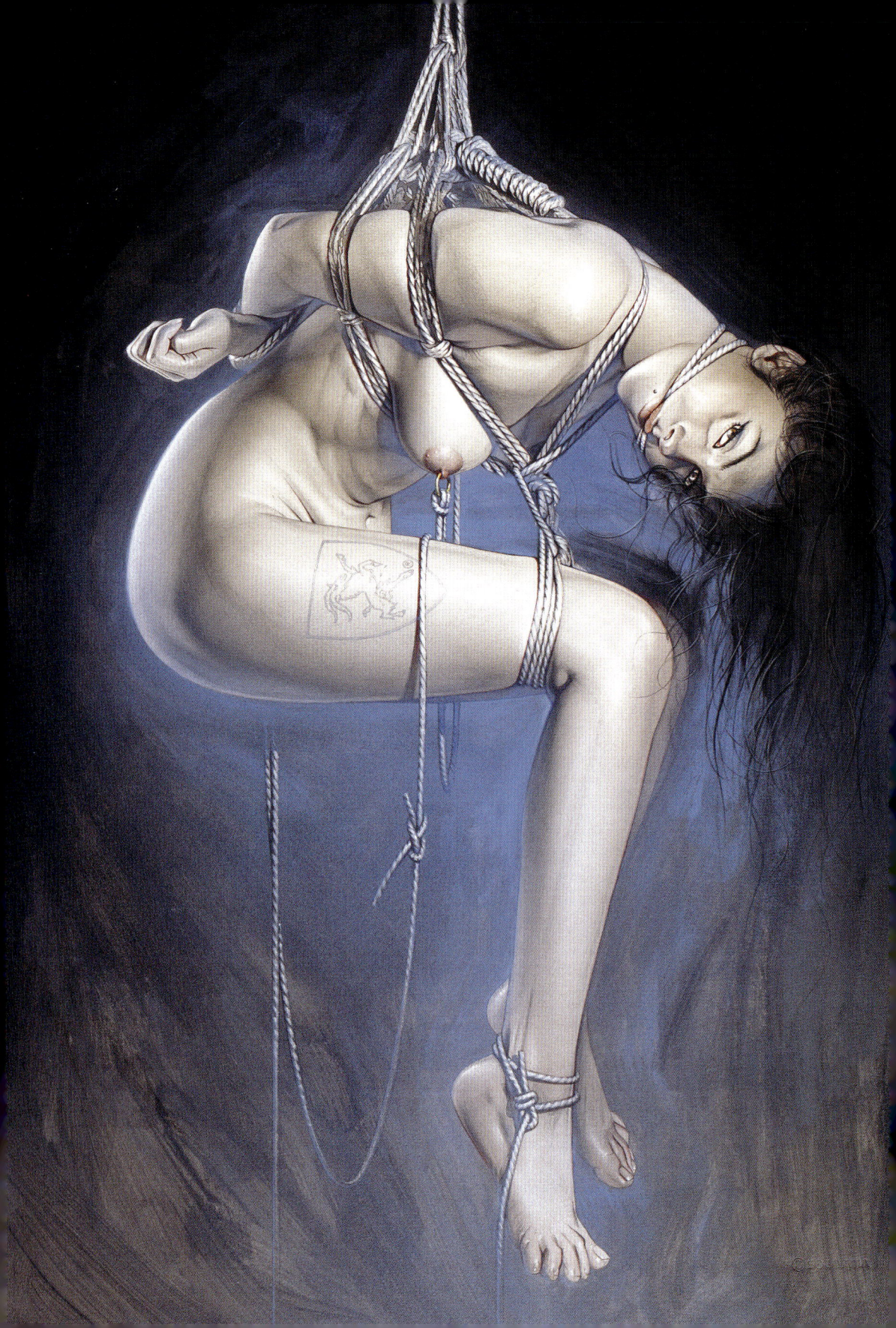

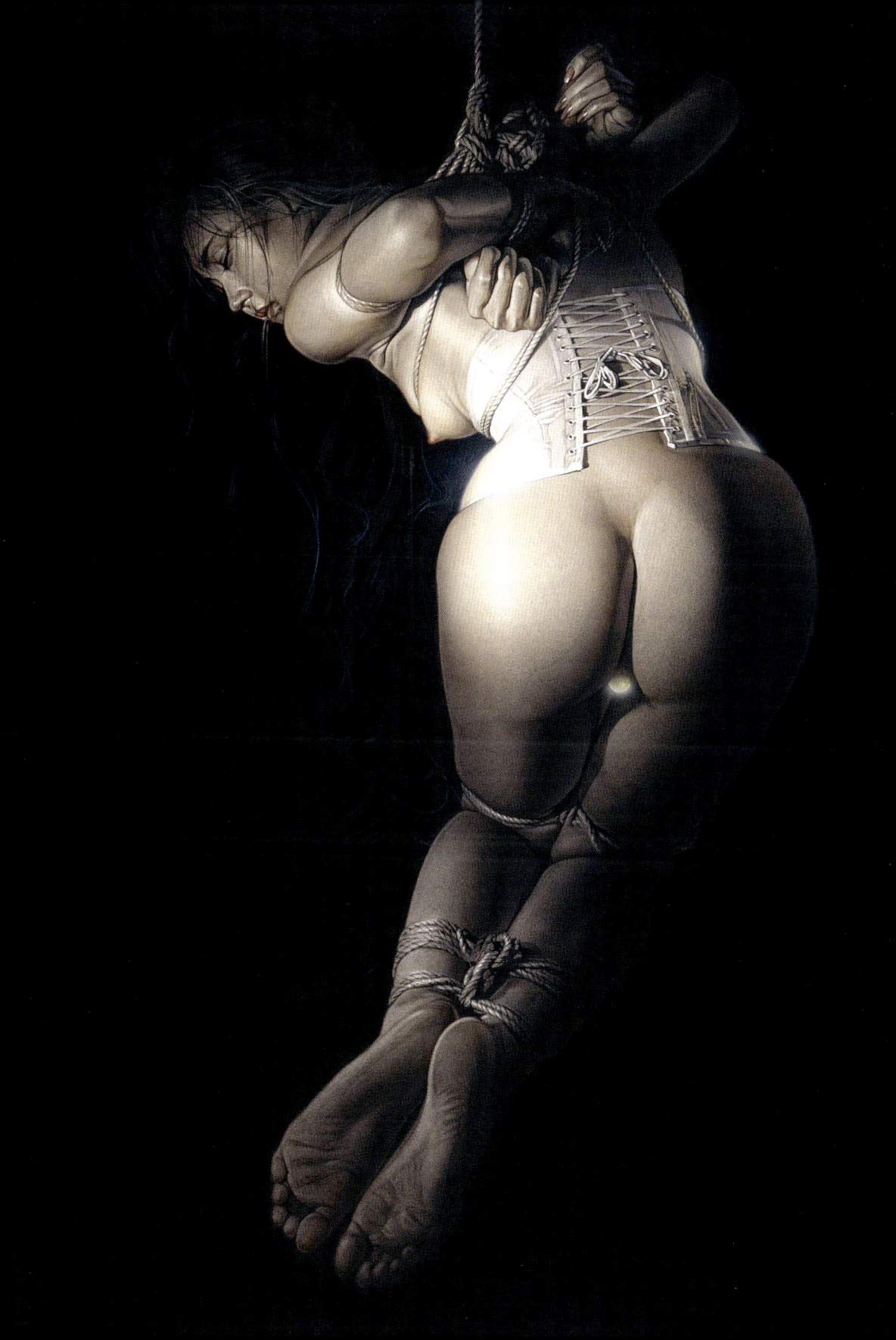

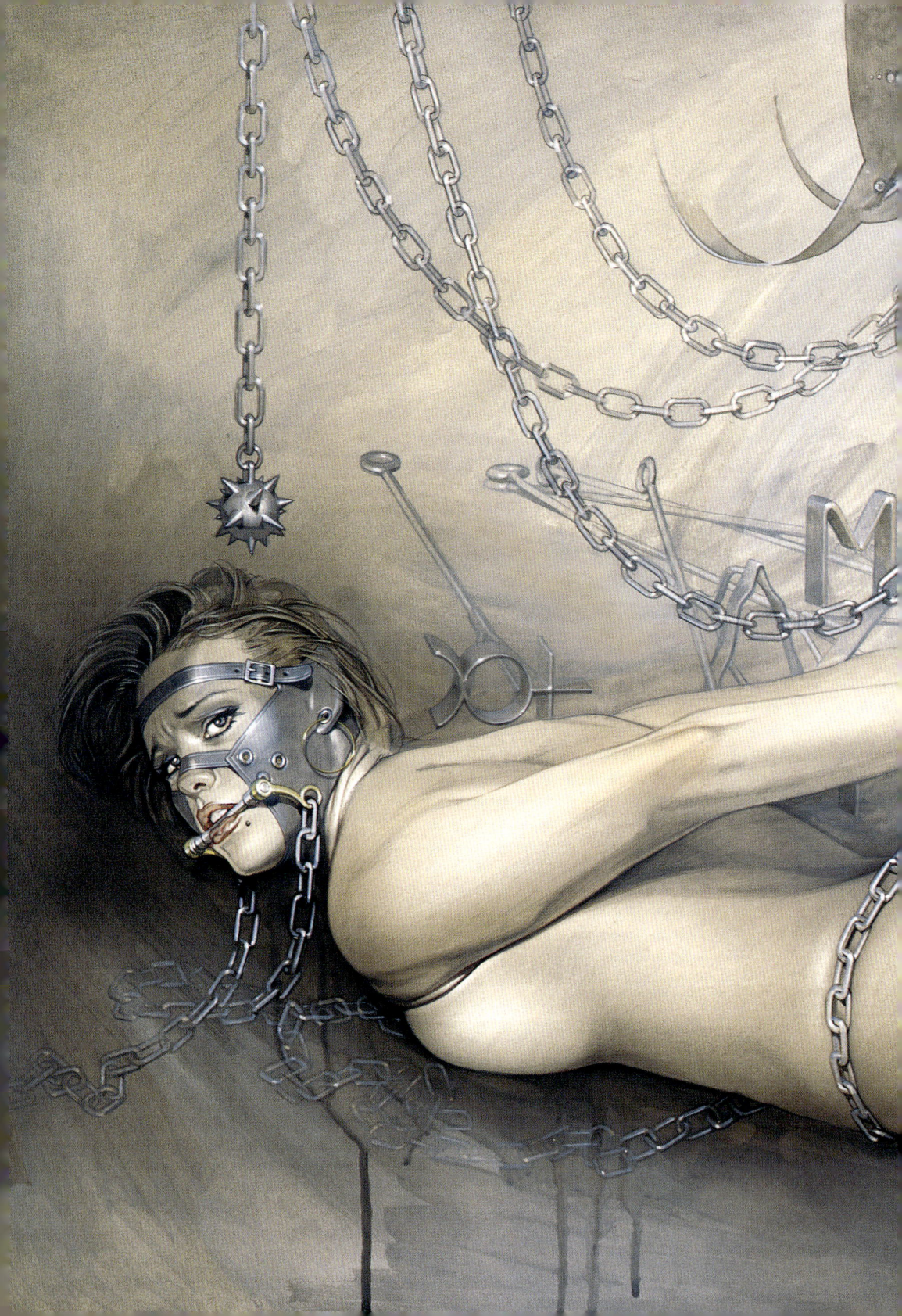

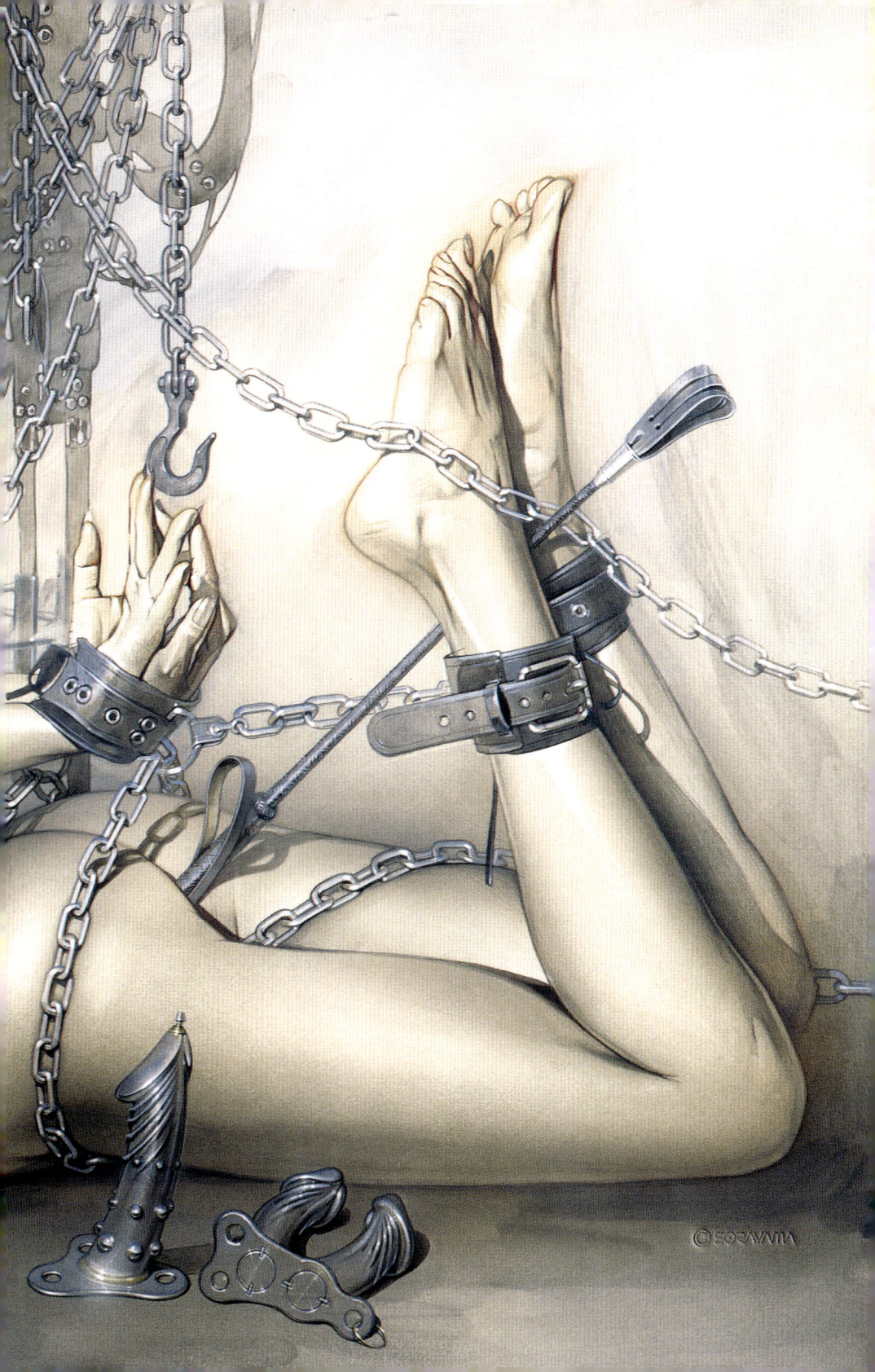

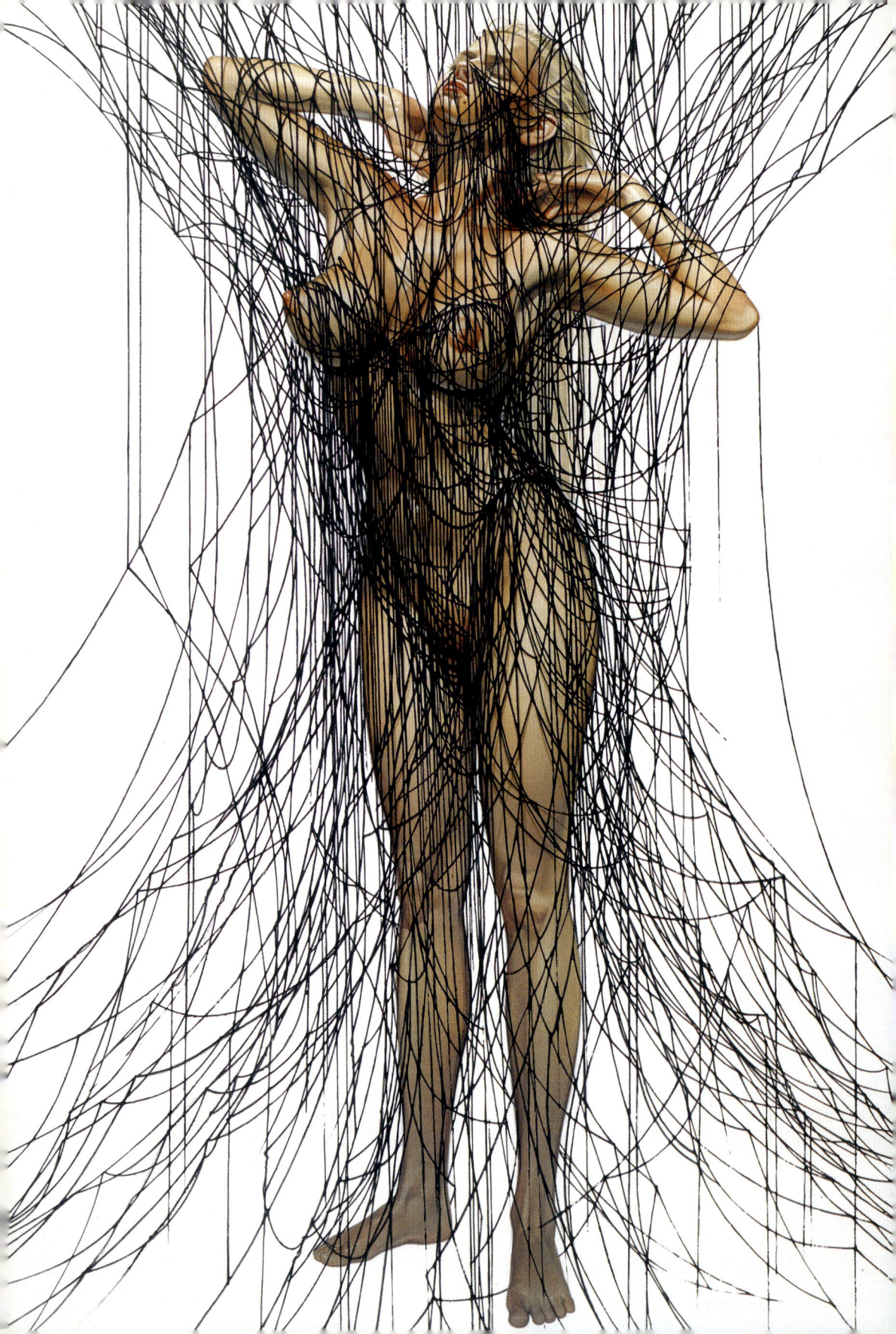

Craig Fraser（クレイグ・フレイザー：オートモーティヴ・エアーブラッシャー）

Hajime Sorayama is one of those artists that comes around once in a lifetime, and inspires us for the rest of our lifetimes. His study of the living form, as well as technical rendering of metallic surfaces is duplicated by many, but rivaled by none. With his deep use of imagery as an equally important tool along with his mixed media, Hajime has created an enviable style that bridges the gaps that often isolate art forms to specific venues. From ad illustration, to fine art, to comic books, Hajime has successfully made the transition to any industry he's attempted. While sometimes shocking in it's portrayal, Hajime's work never ceases to amaze me with it's current grasp of what the artist can handle, and how far to push the envelope. As a fellow artist, I am proud to say he has a distinct influence in my work, but more so, I am proud to call him a friend.

"Onegaishimasu"

吉村則人（カメラマン）

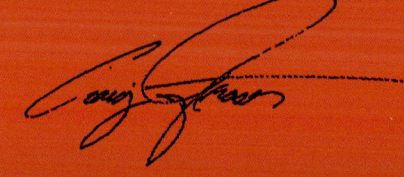

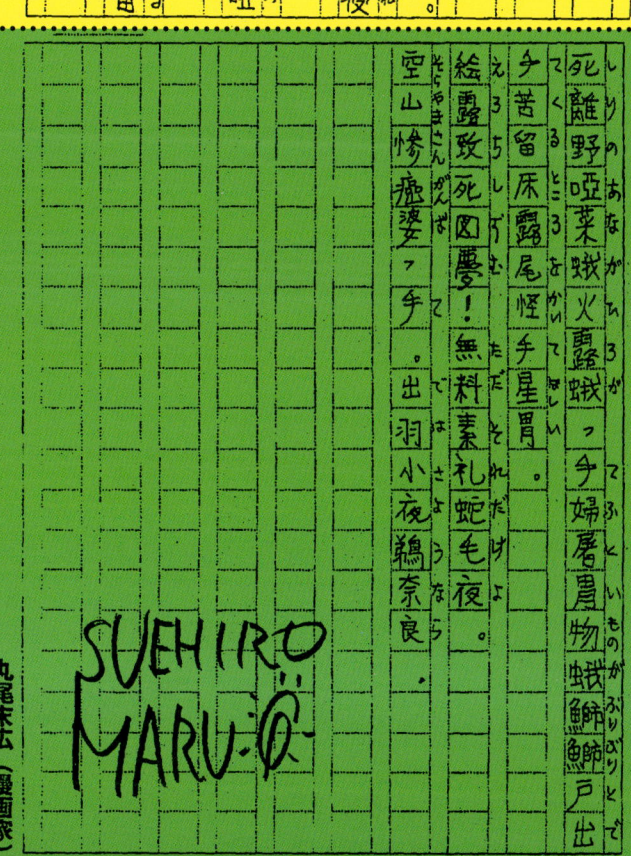

95

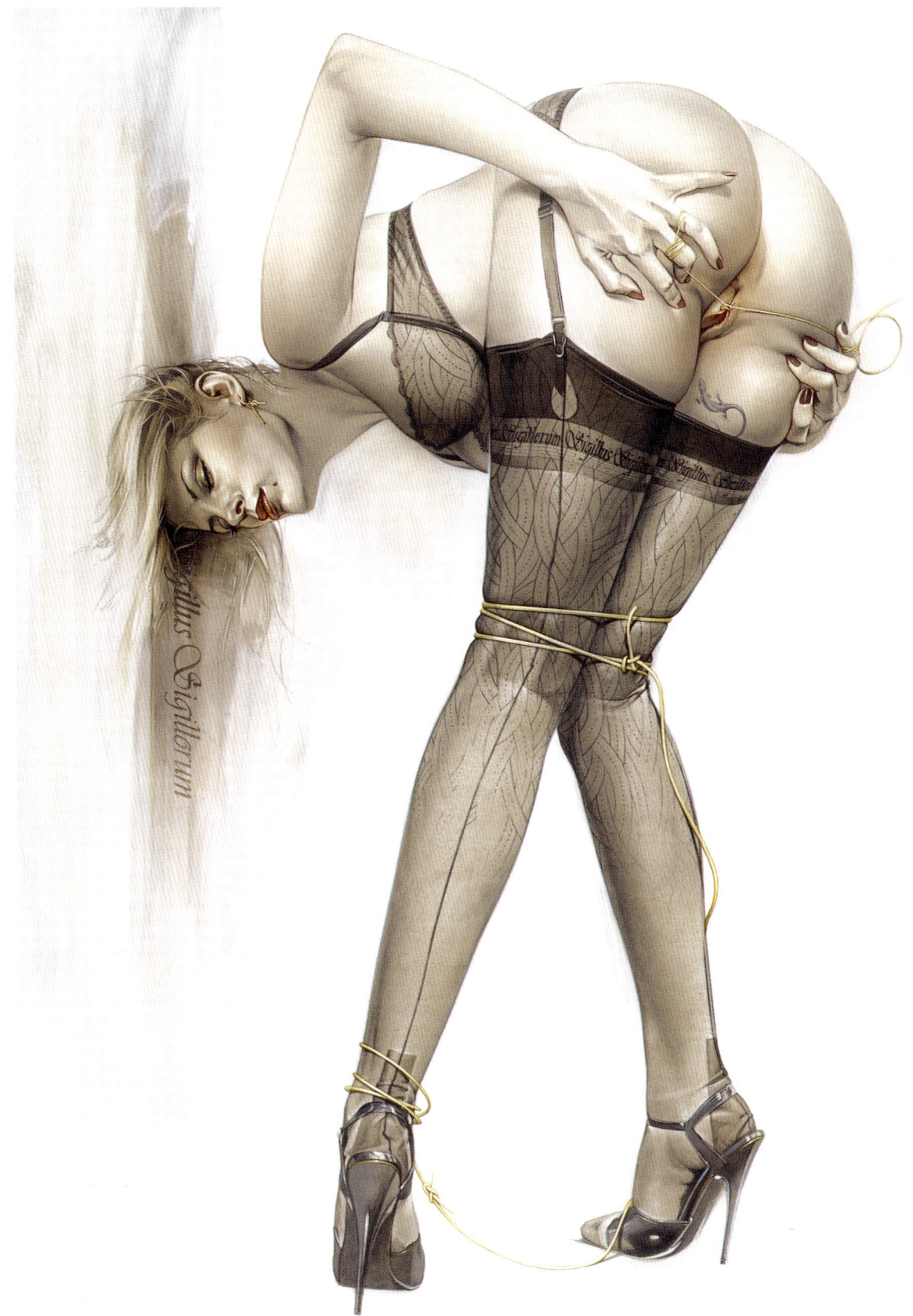

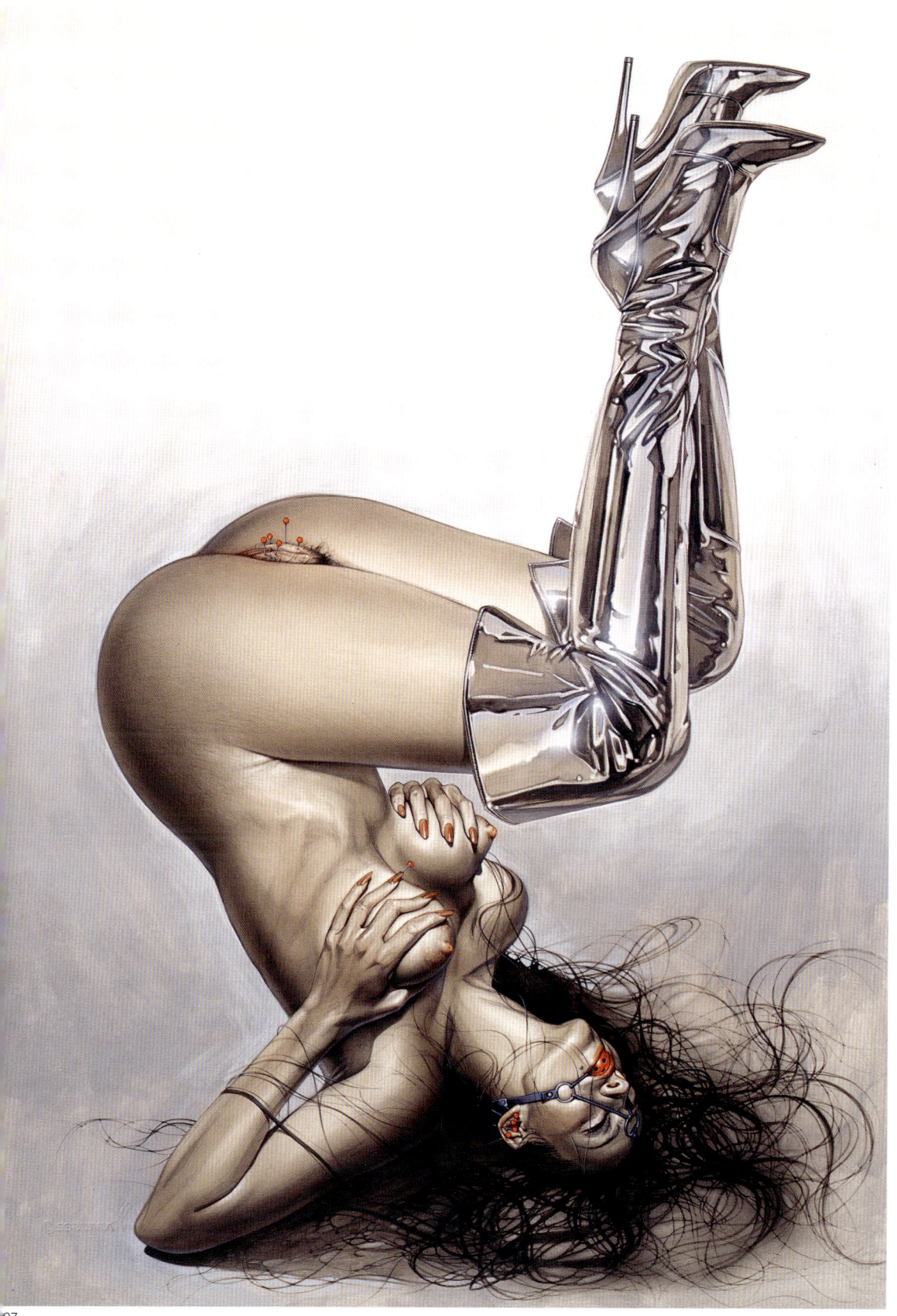

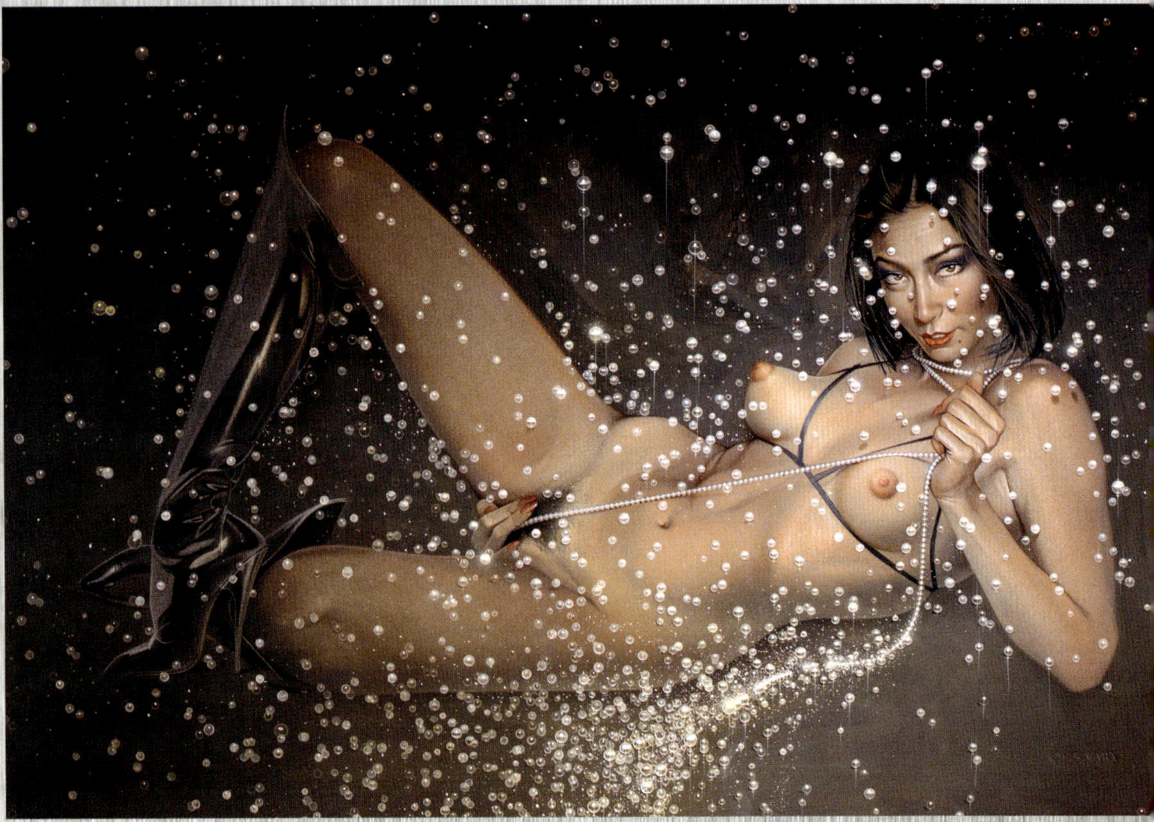

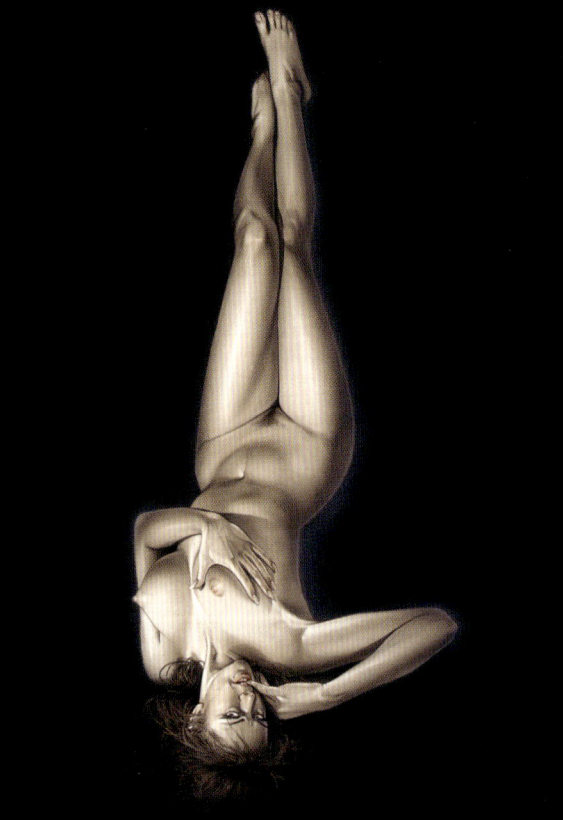

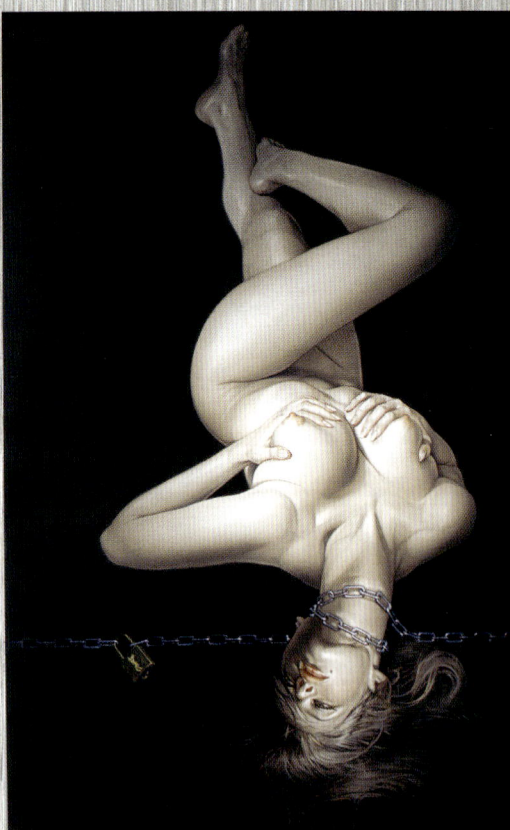

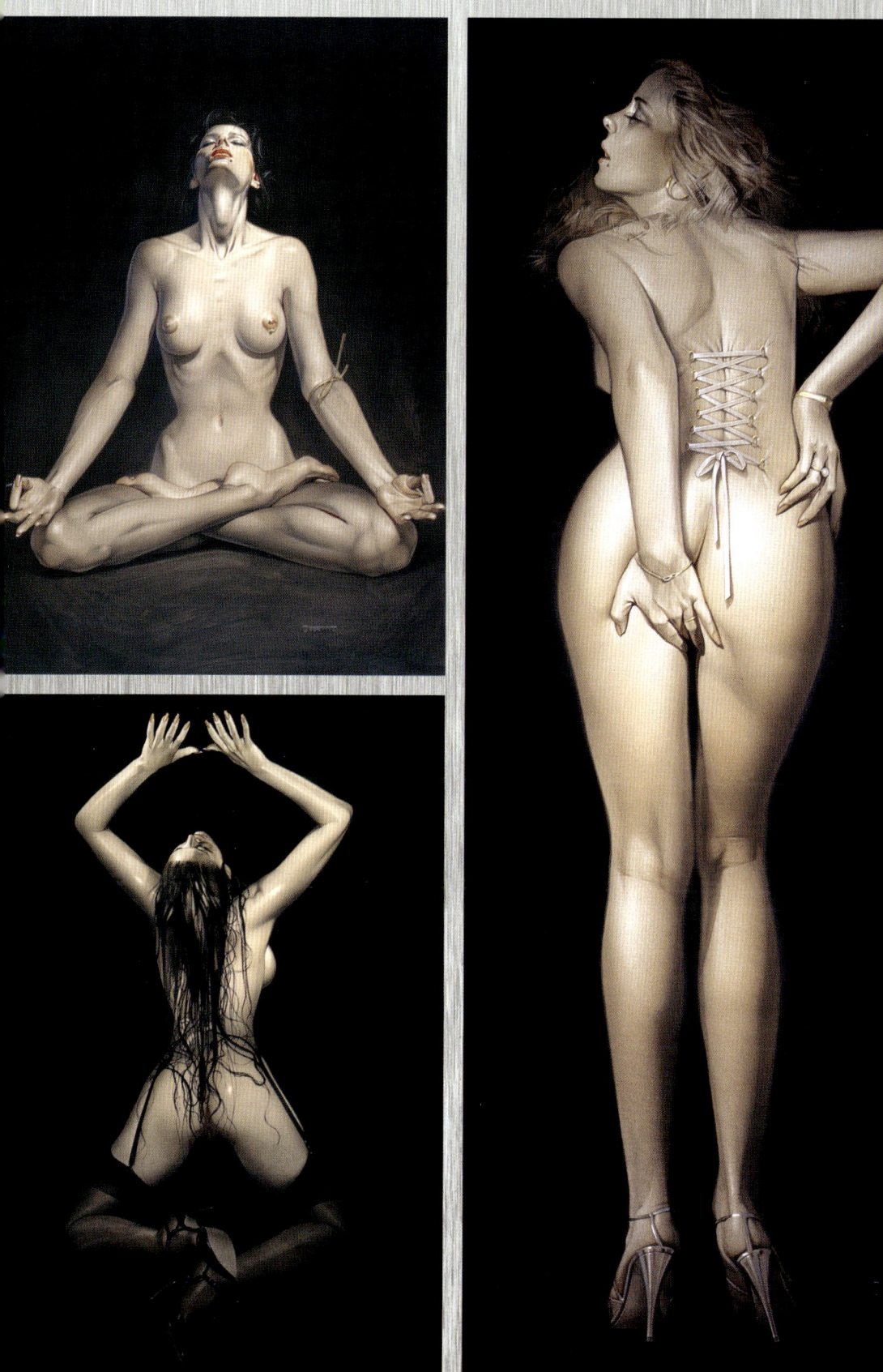

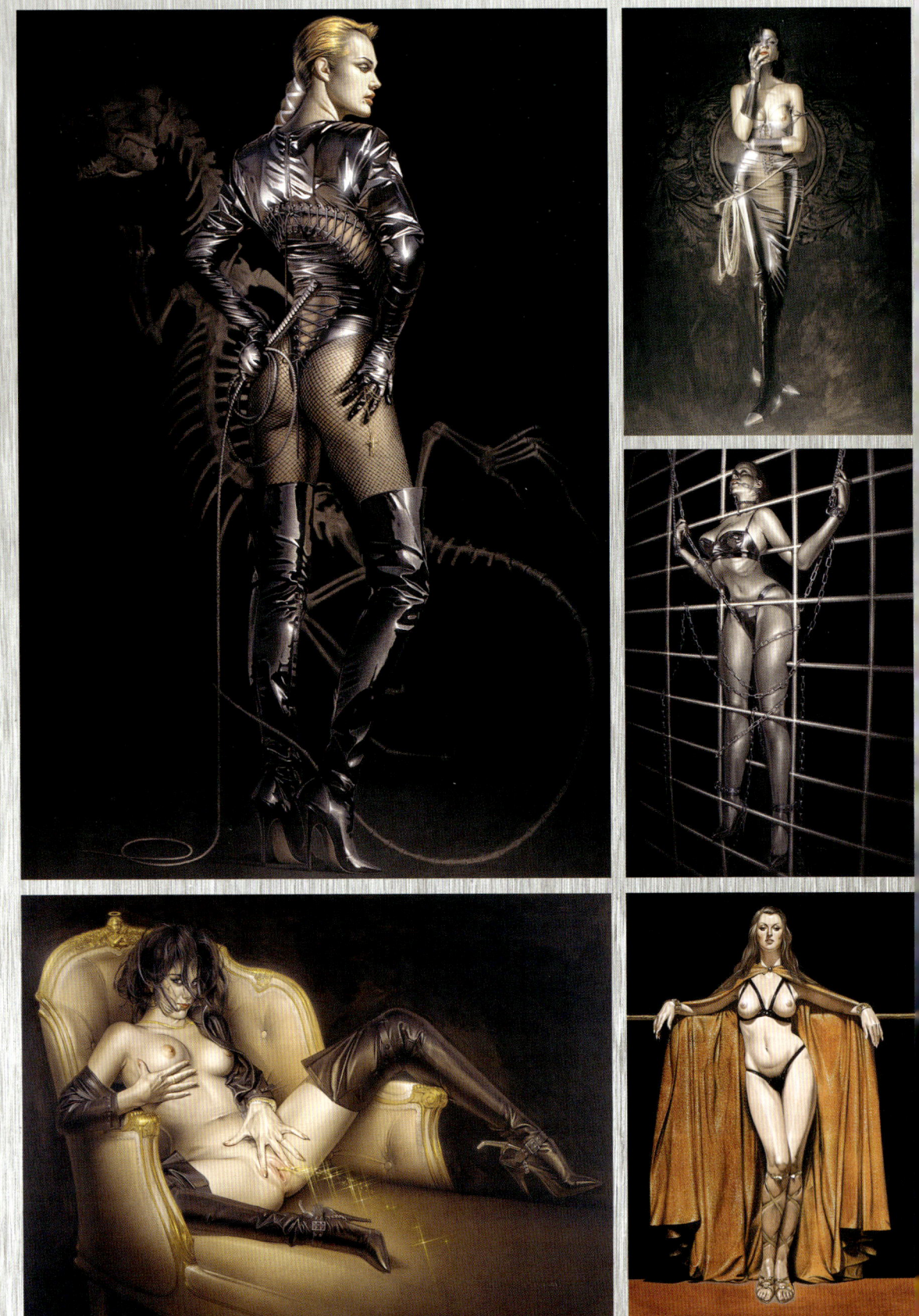

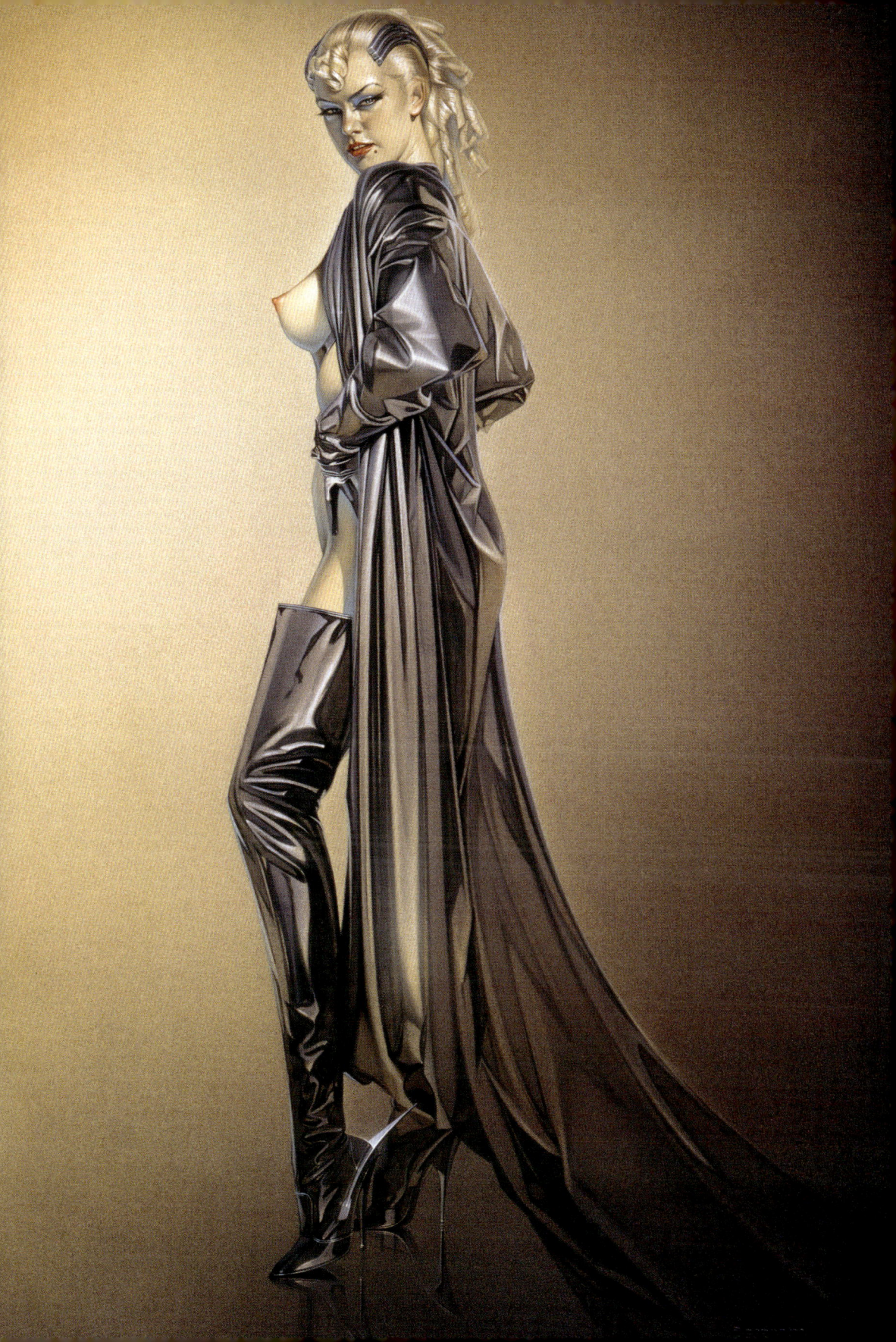

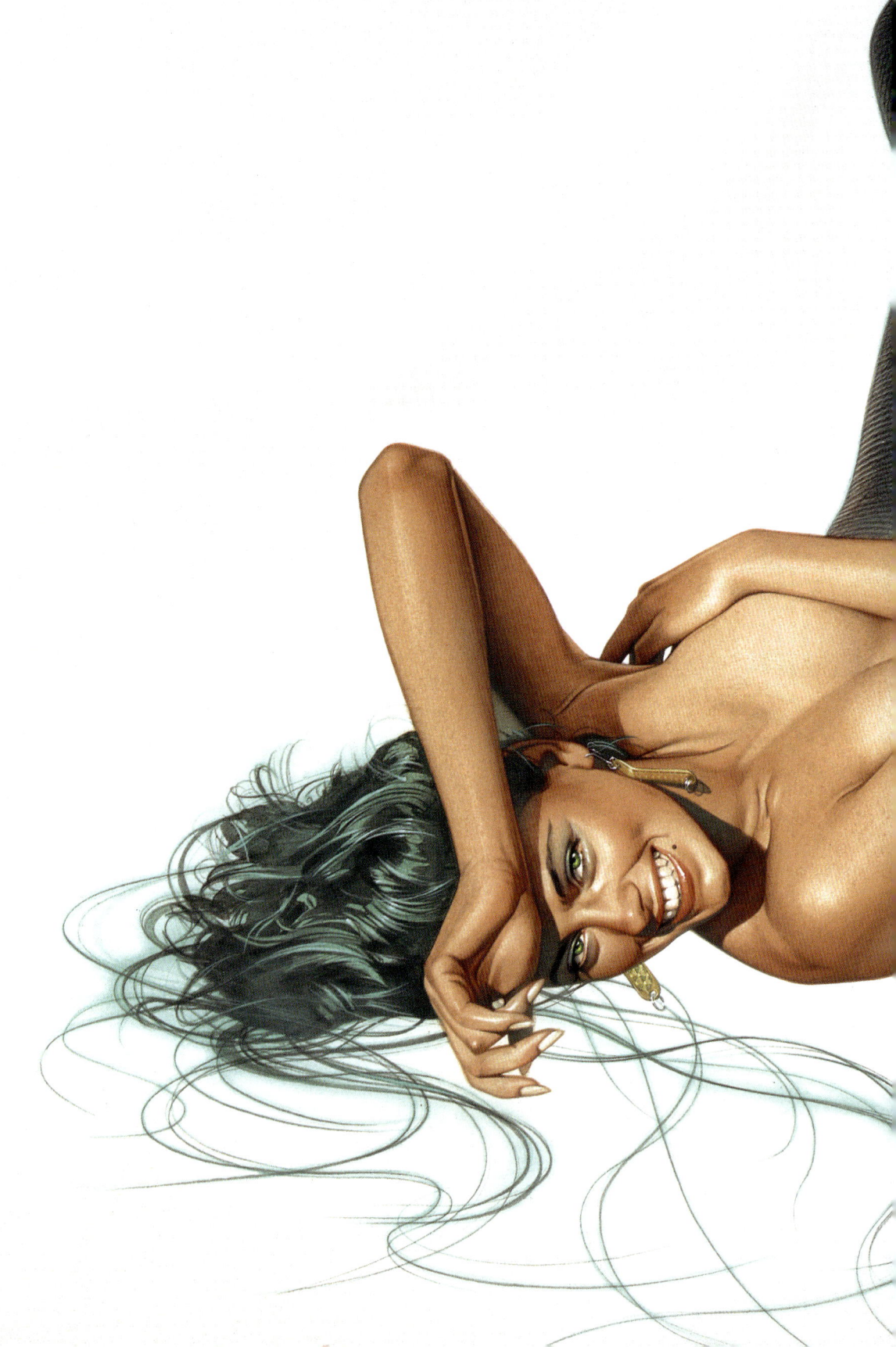

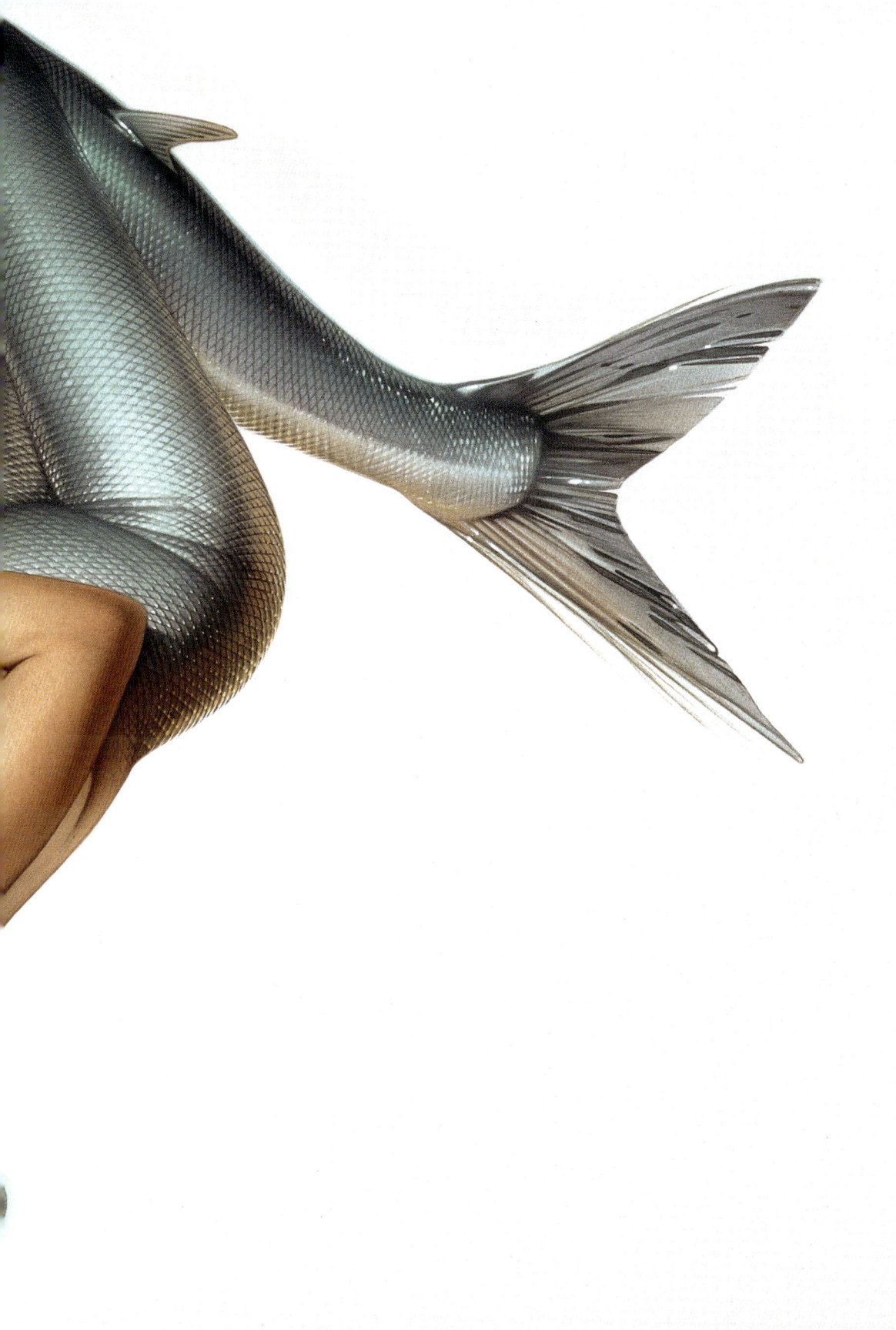

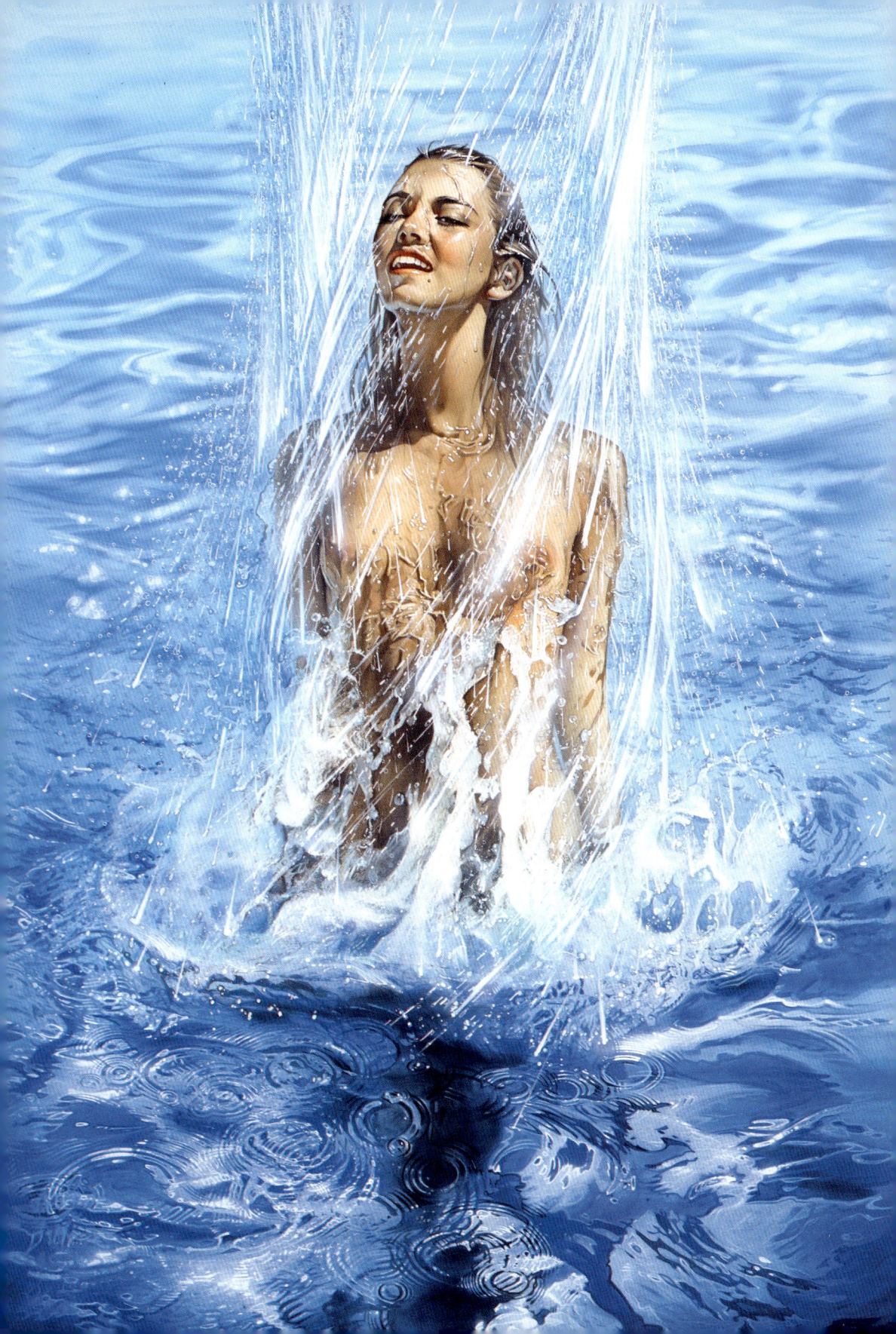

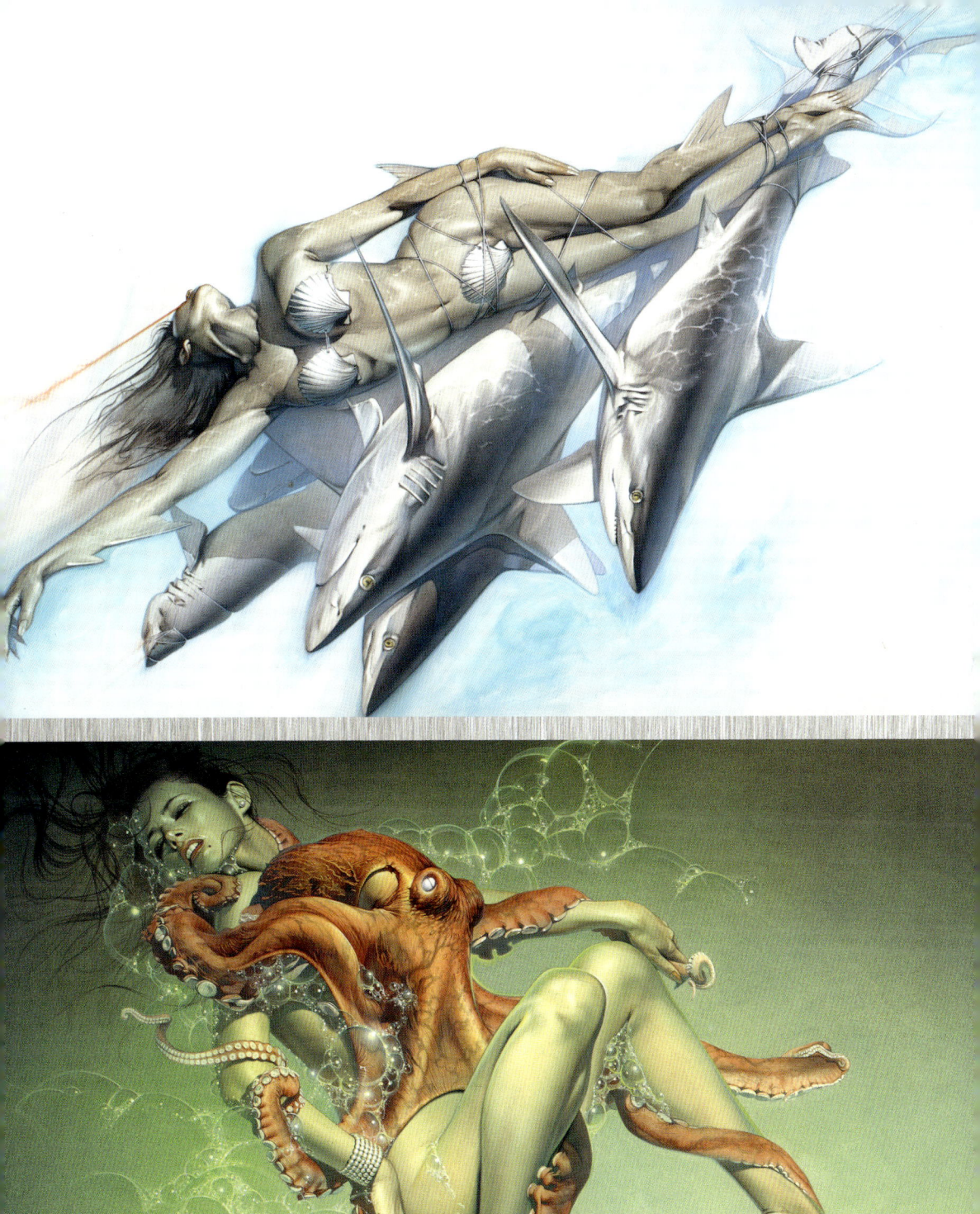

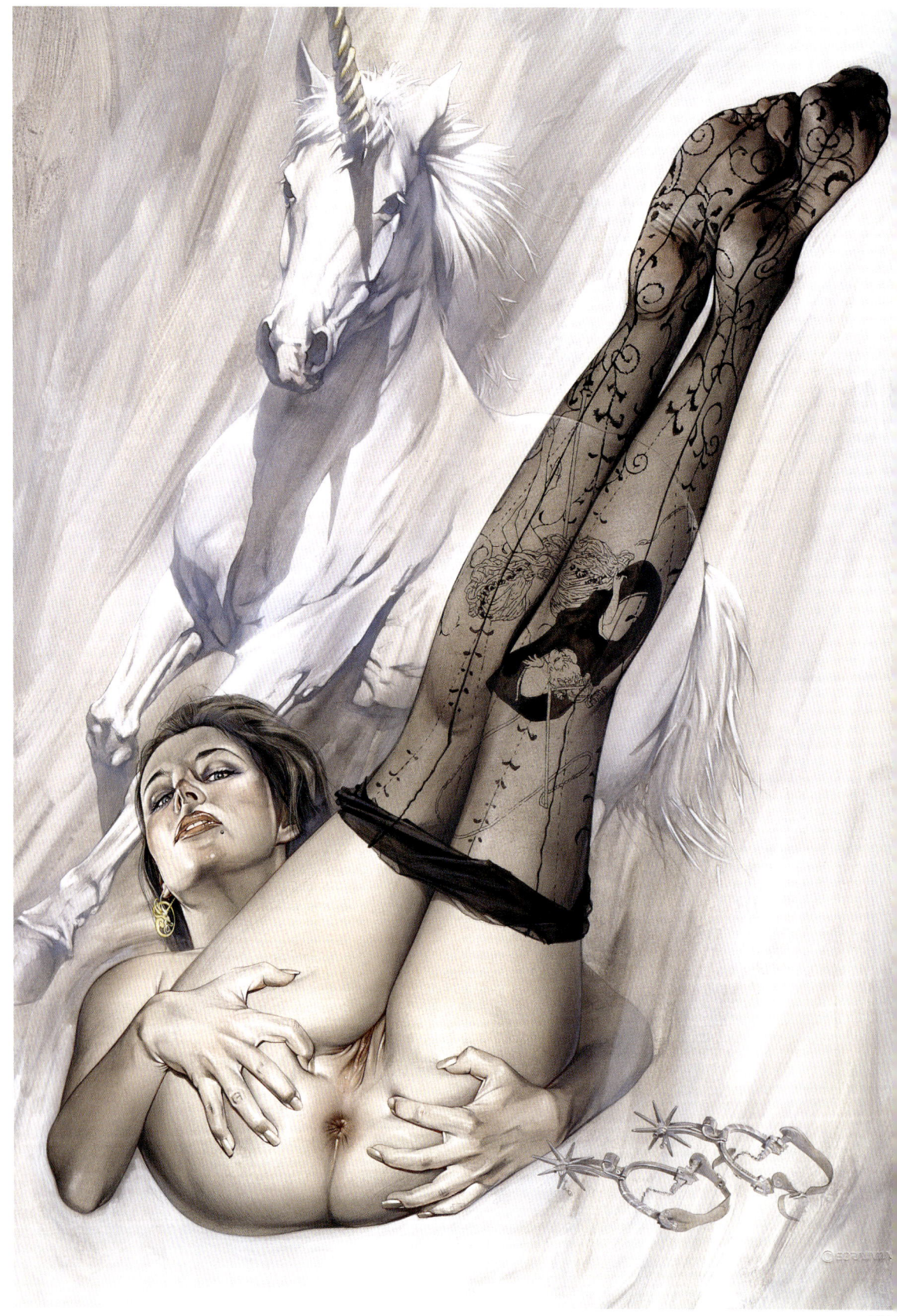

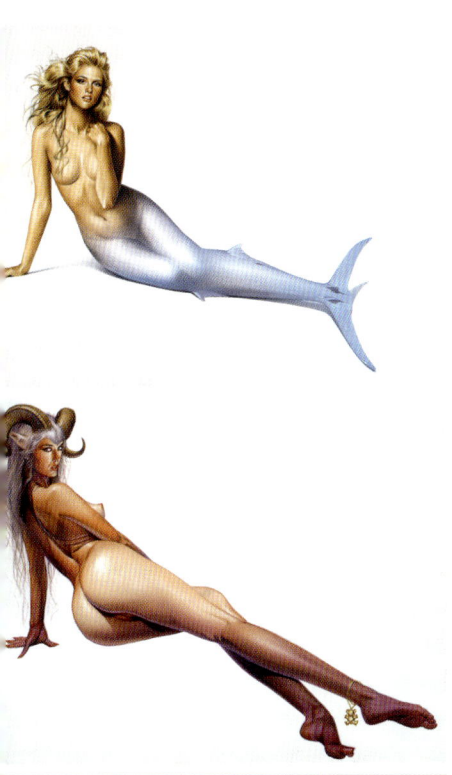

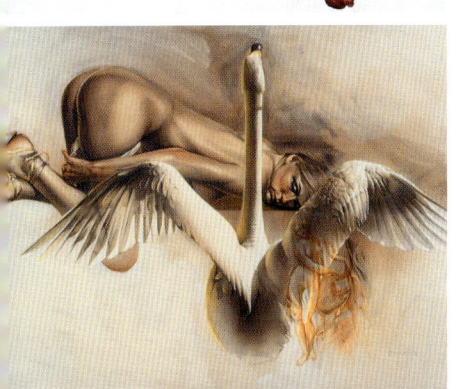

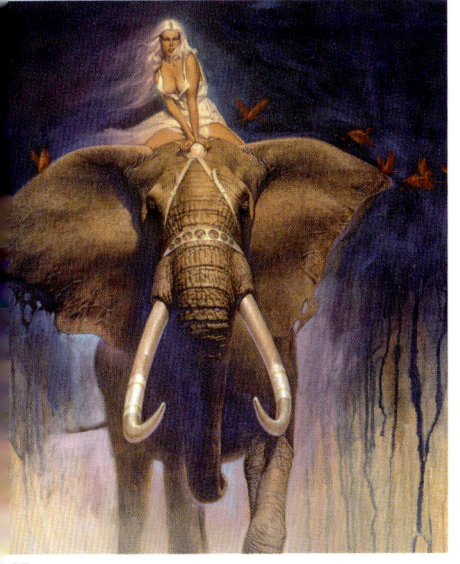

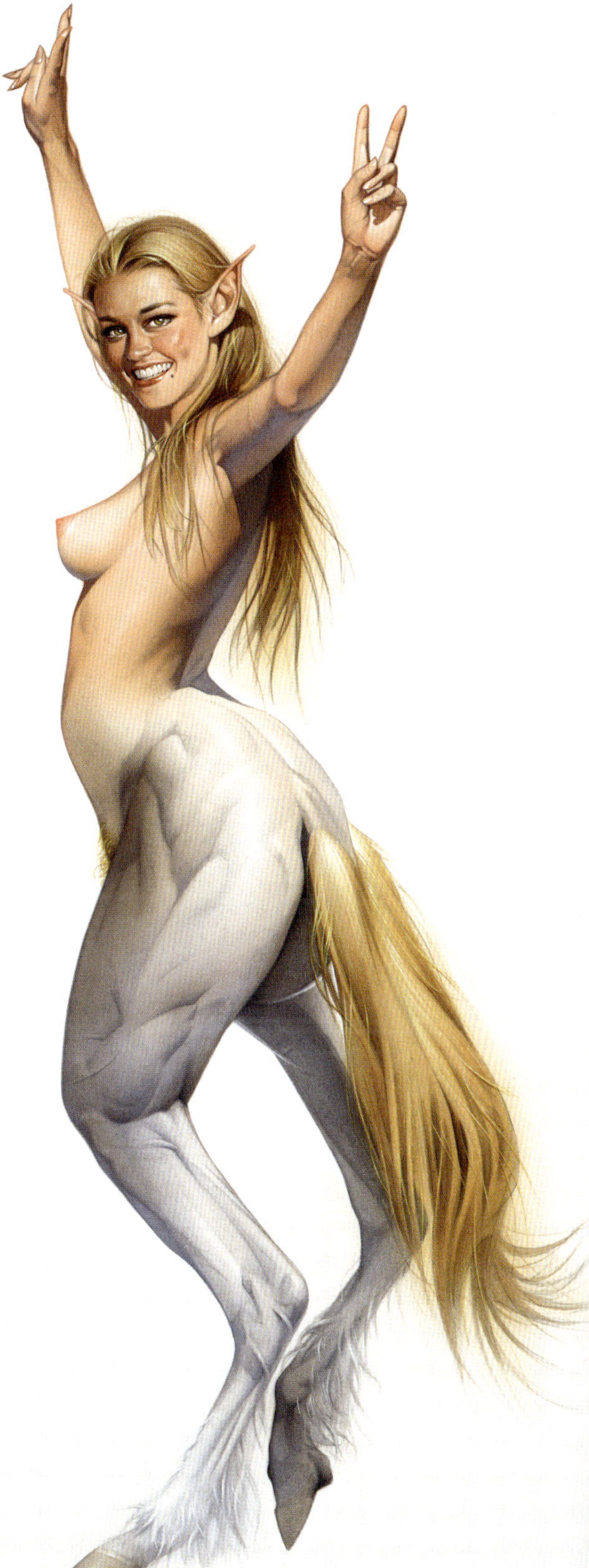

苦痛は陶酔への入口である。

肉体のねじれや変形や歪みによって、苦痛と快楽という境界が失効してゆく。

人間が物や光と化し、感覚のフレームが変調するさまを精緻に、大胆に写しとる空山 基のヴィジョンは、そうした境界を超え、冒険する肉体の王国なのである。

Ito Toshiharu

伊藤俊治

（いとうとしはる、美術史家・多摩美術大学教授）

SORAYAMAのはじまり。

SORAYAMA仕事は原画のサイズの10倍くらいの大きさで見たいと思わせる乾いた熱がある。

お台場にカジノが出来たらぜひ空山の作品を10m×5mくらいの壁画にしてほしい。壁画を見た石原知事も乾いた熱のあるSORAYAMAは気に入ると思う。

渡辺和博 イラストレーター

Dru Blair
（デュルー・ブレアー：イラストレーター）

Erotic, provocative, and often controversial, Sorayama's paintings are a testament to the passion the artist has for his subject. Looking beyond the intricate and subtle brushstrokes, one discovers thoughtful and often humorous details, and realizes that the intent of the artist is not a portrayal of a woman's torture, but of her ecstasy. Naive observers will not realize this, and will continue to register the shock of their erroneous conclusion with a dogmatic contempt for Sorayama's celebration of female erotica. For better or worse, with approval or contempt, few can observe the paintings without reaction, and that's what great art is all about.

Dru Blair

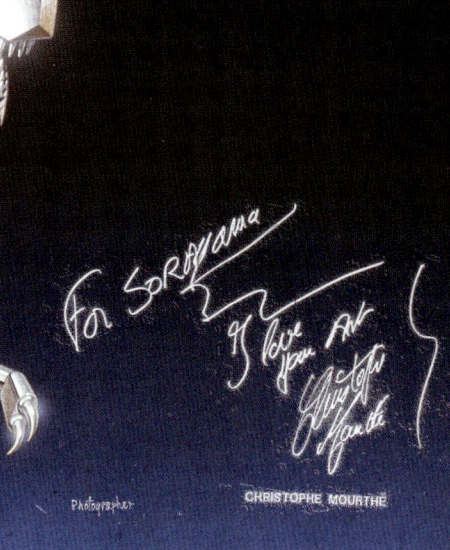

For Sorayama

Photographer

CHRISTOPHE MOURTHÉ

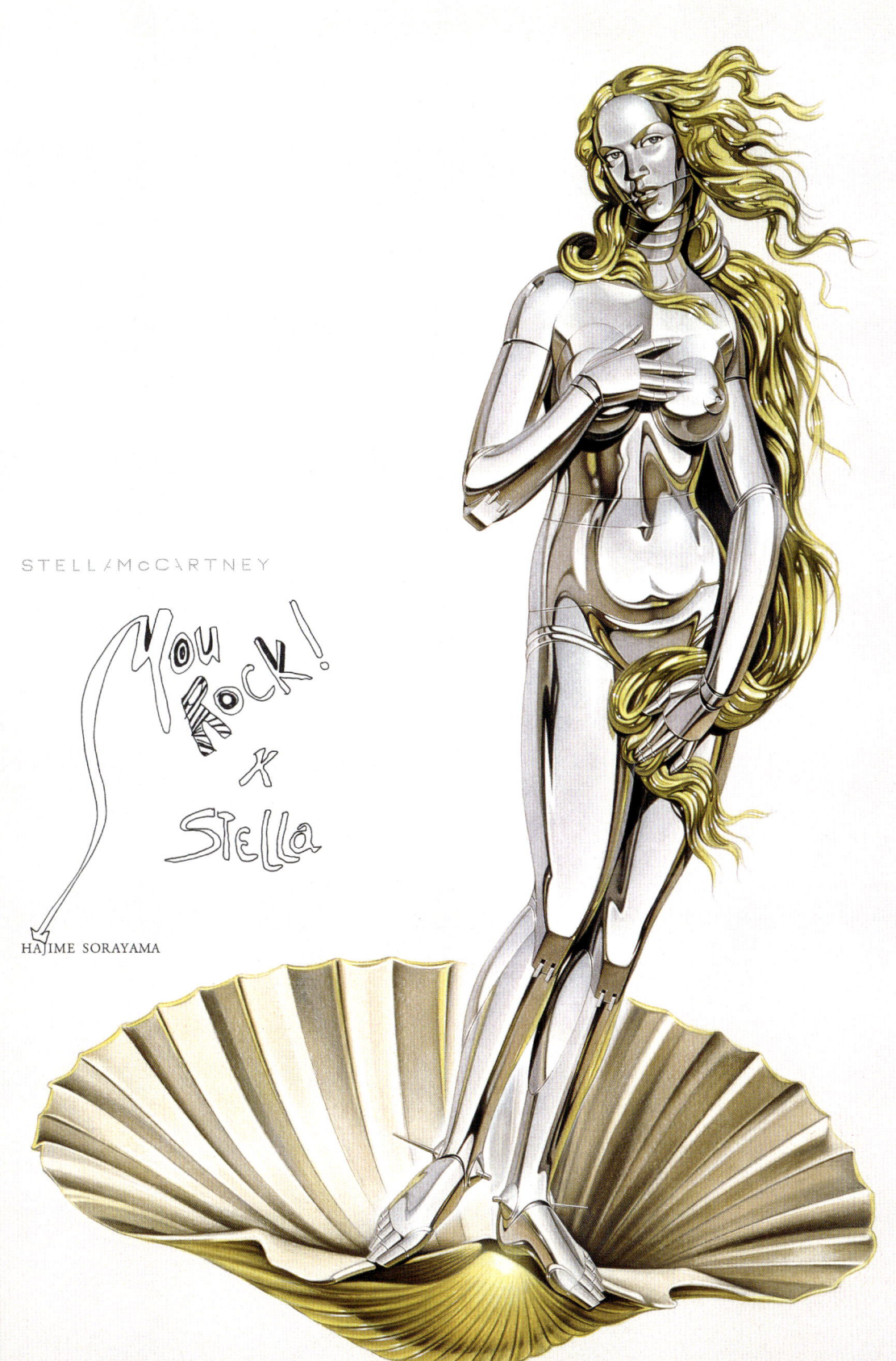

STELLAMcCARTNEY

YOU ROCK!
X
STELLA

HAJIME SORAYAMA

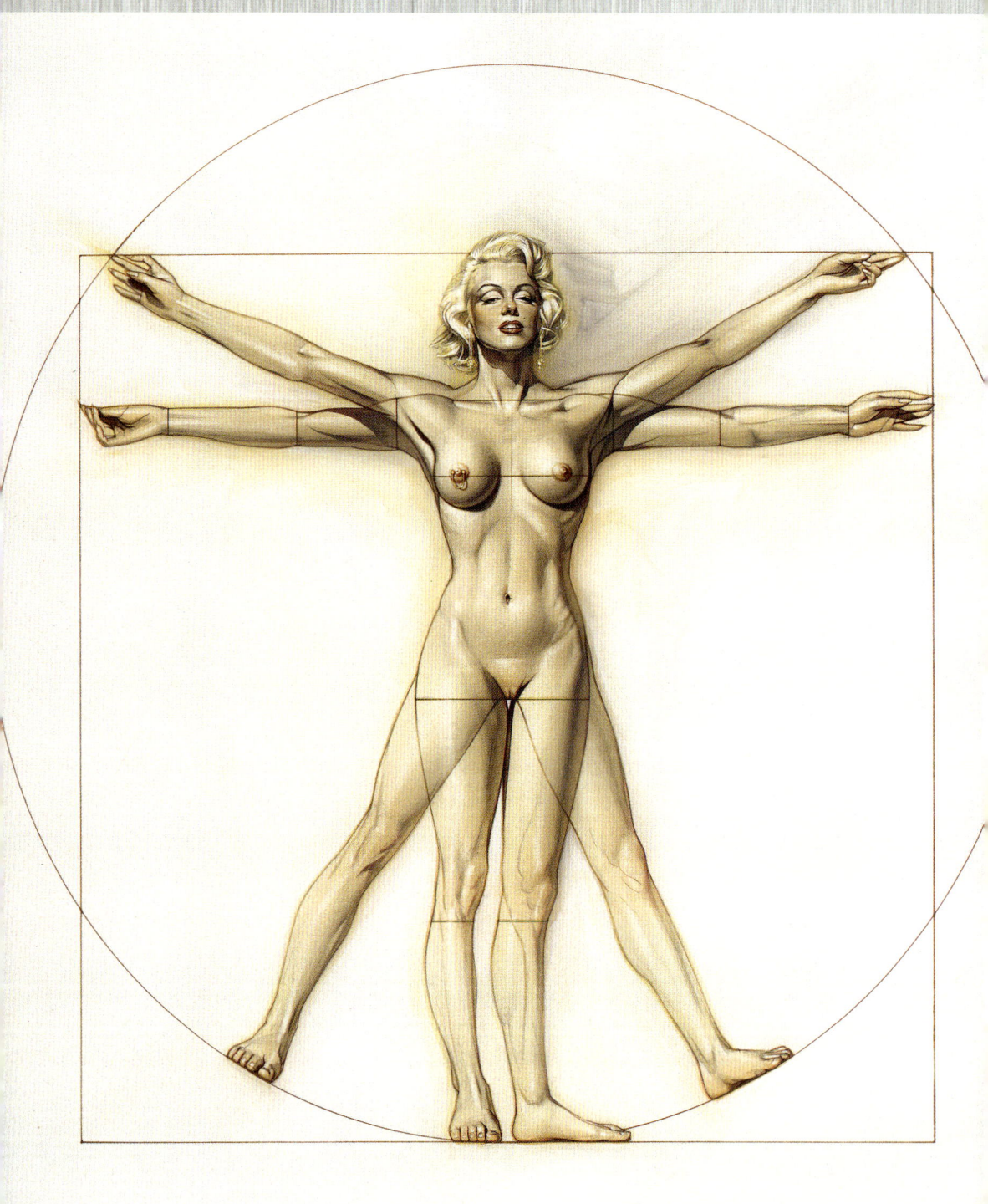

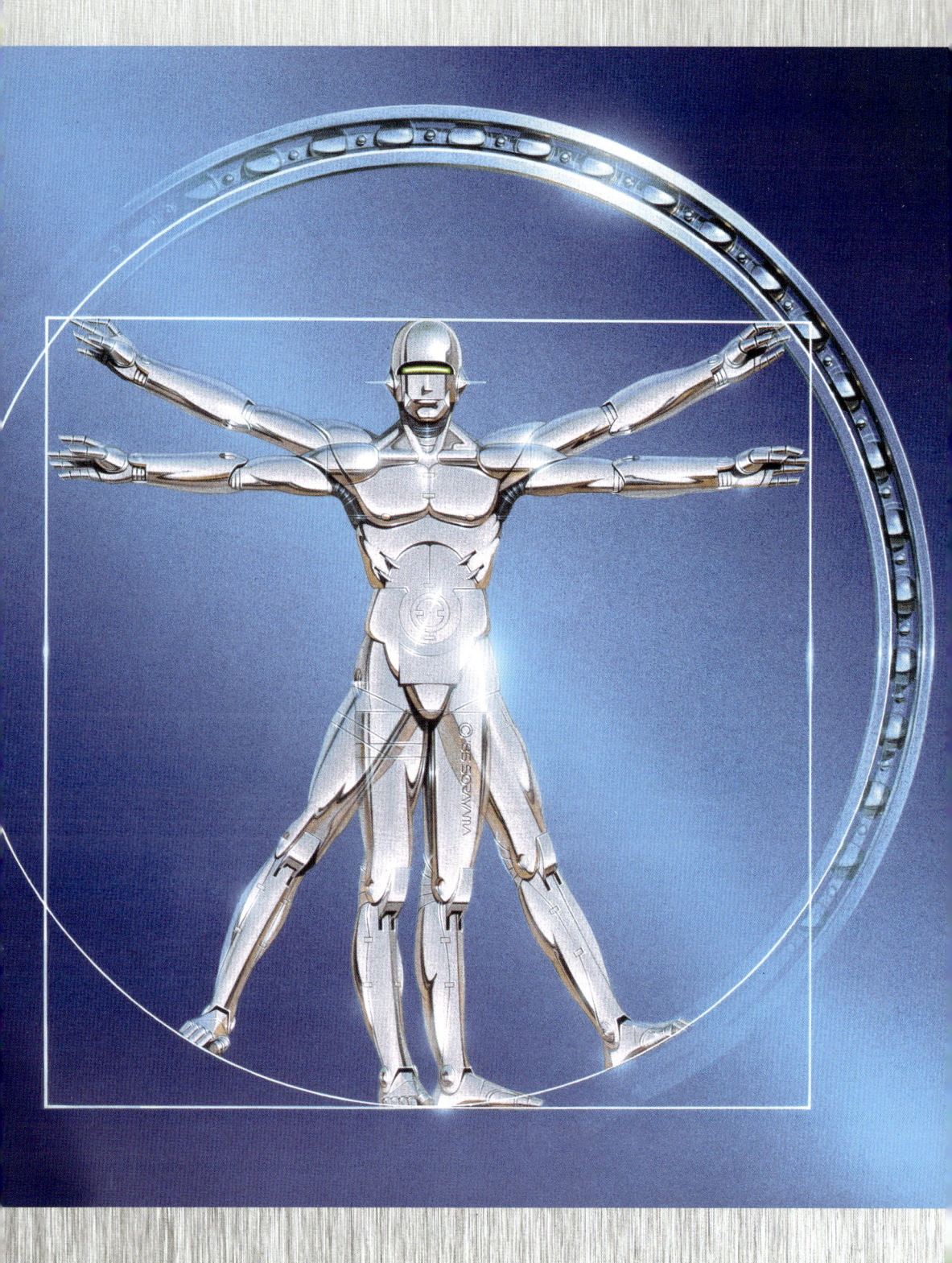

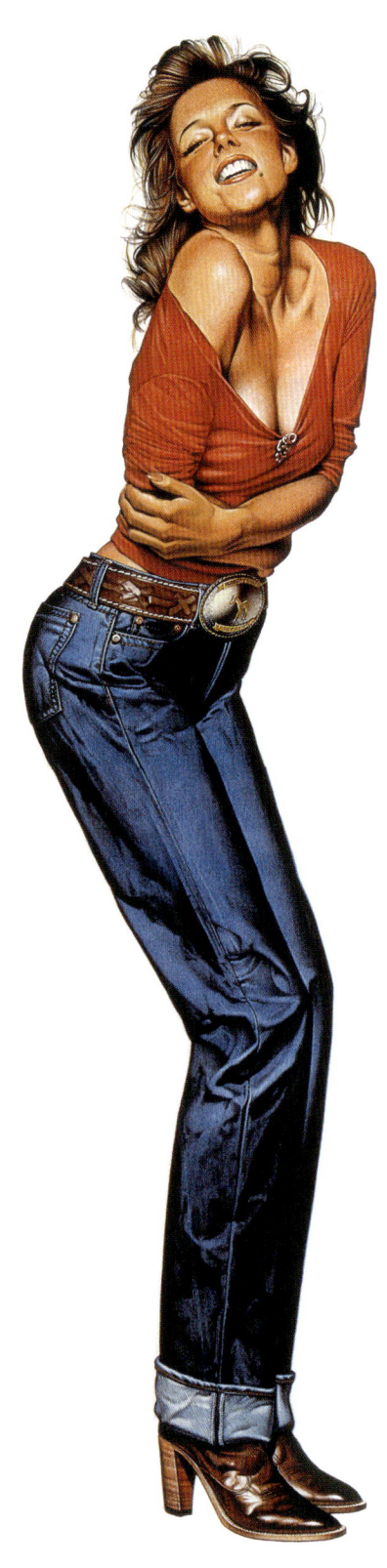

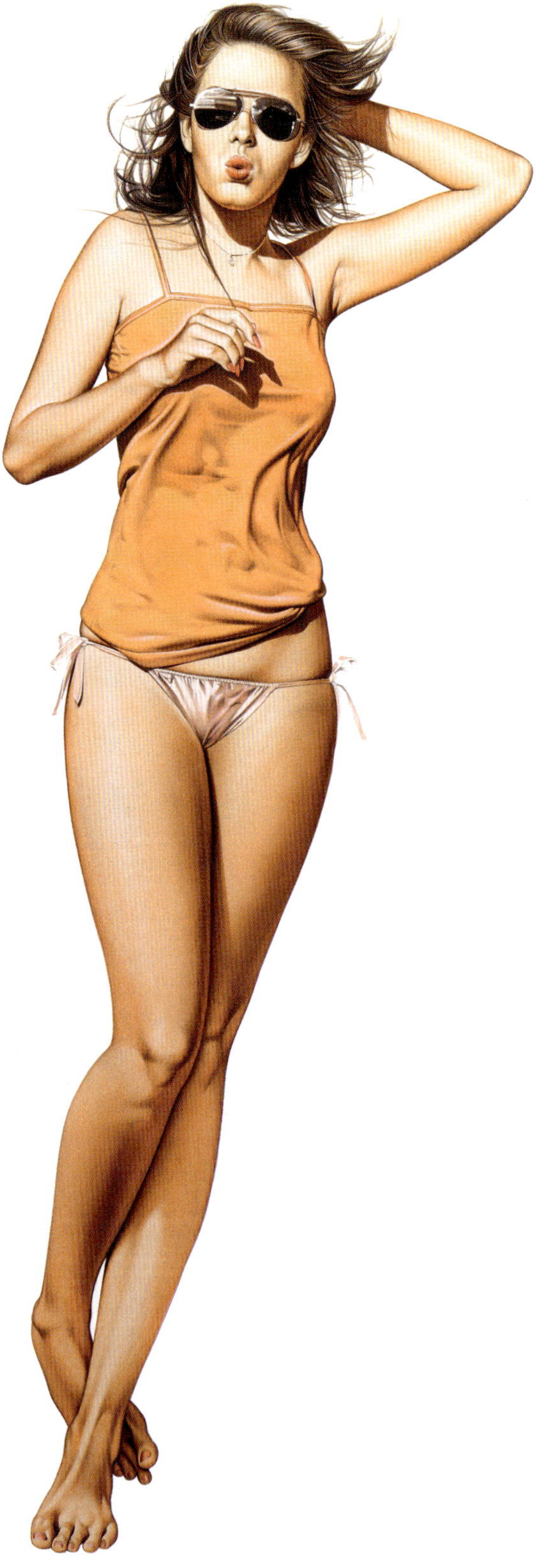

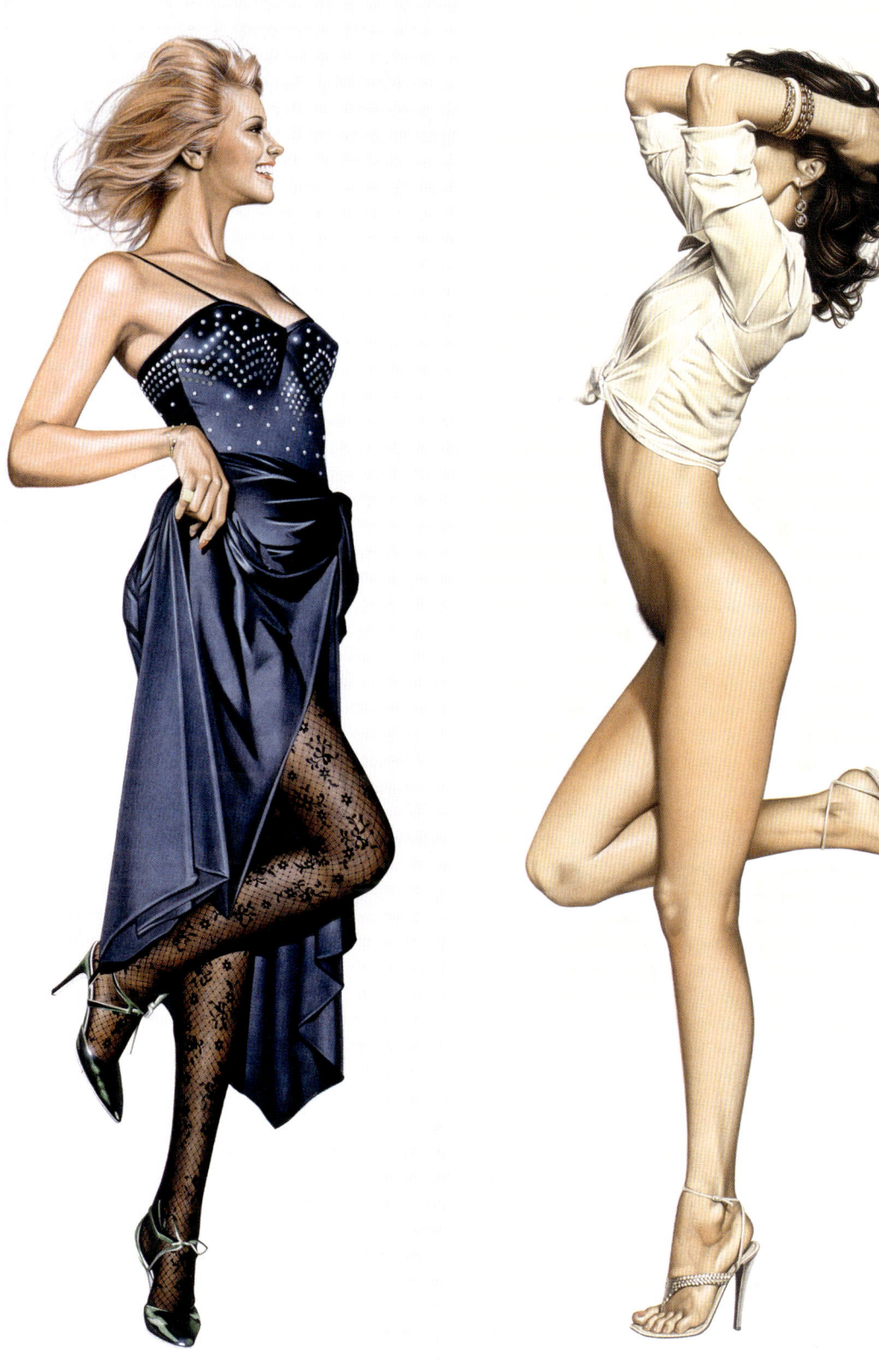

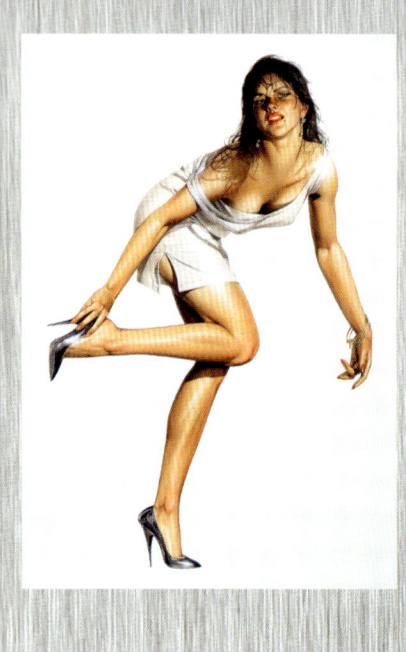
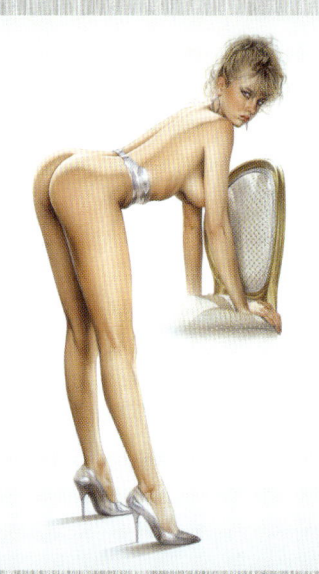
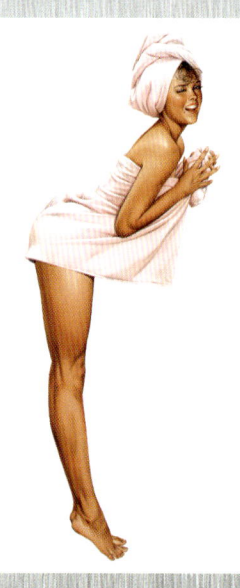

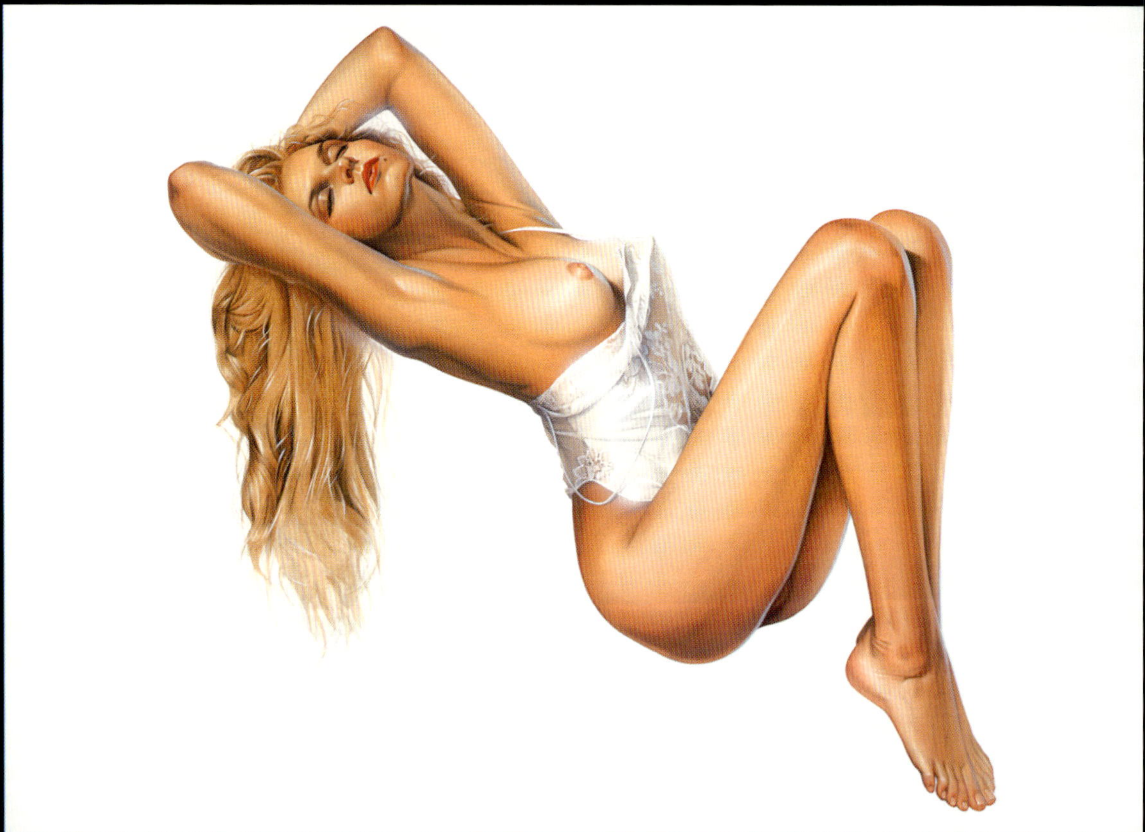

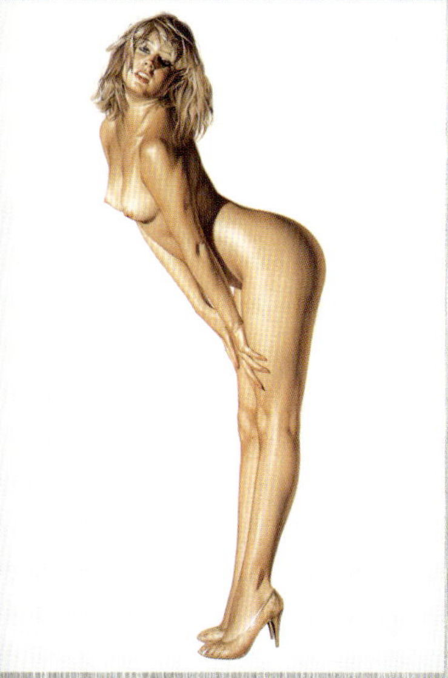

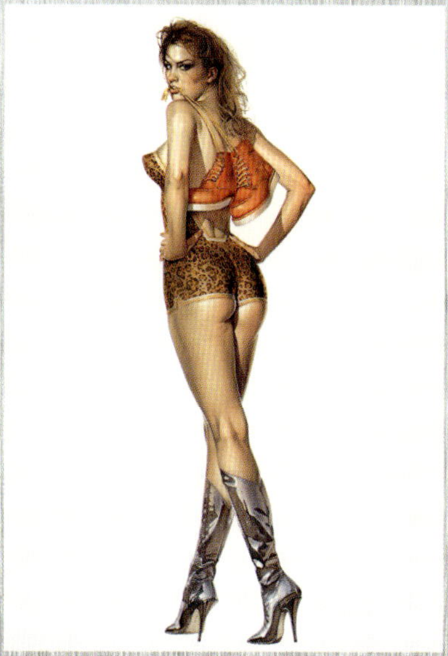

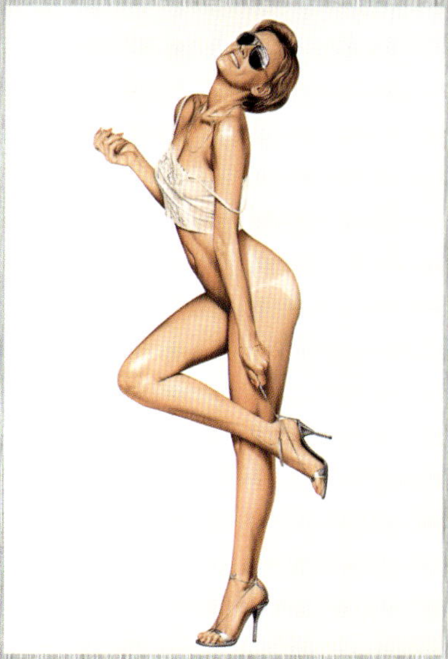

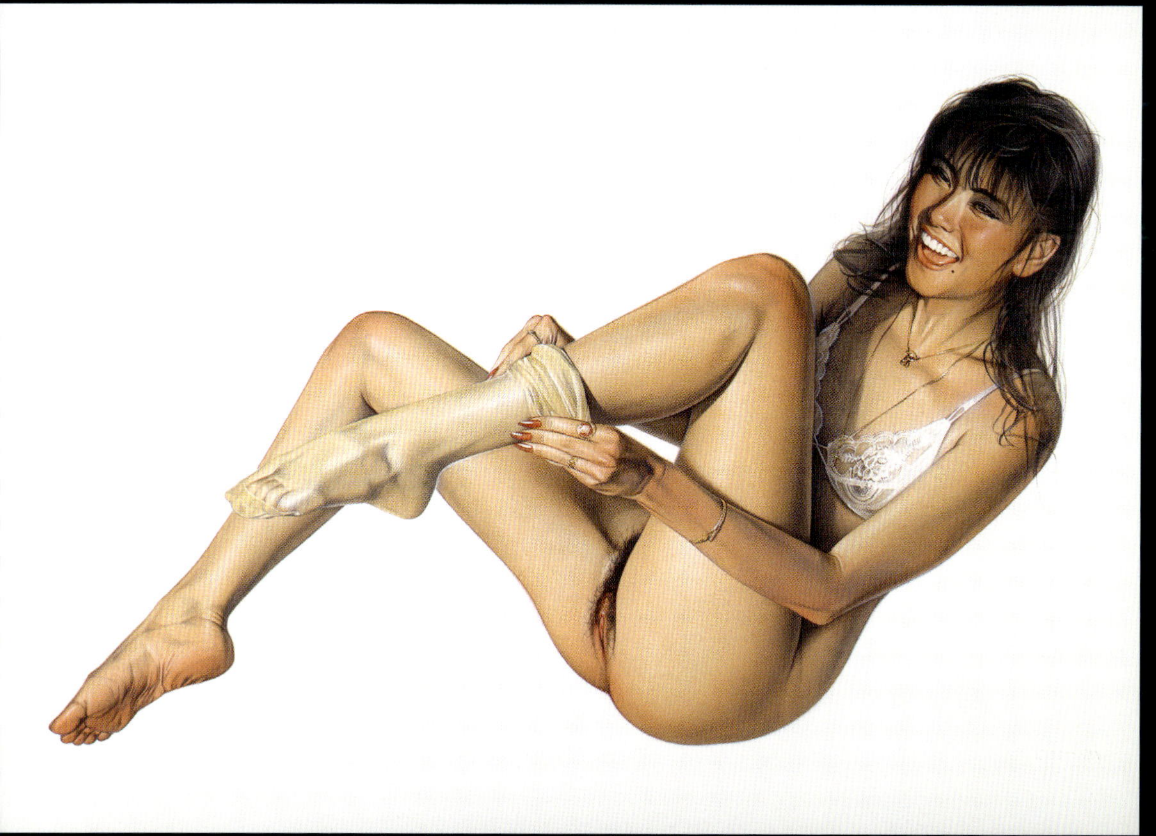

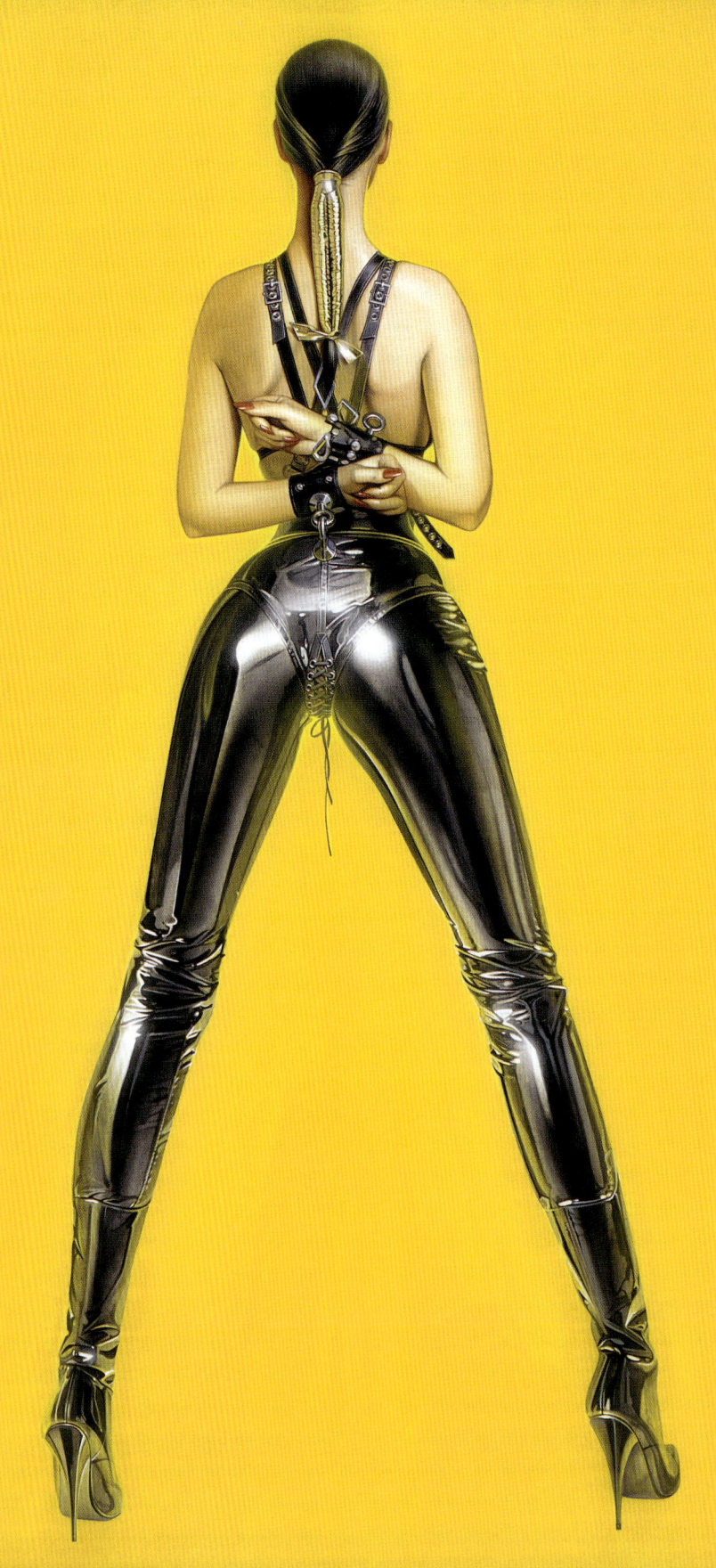

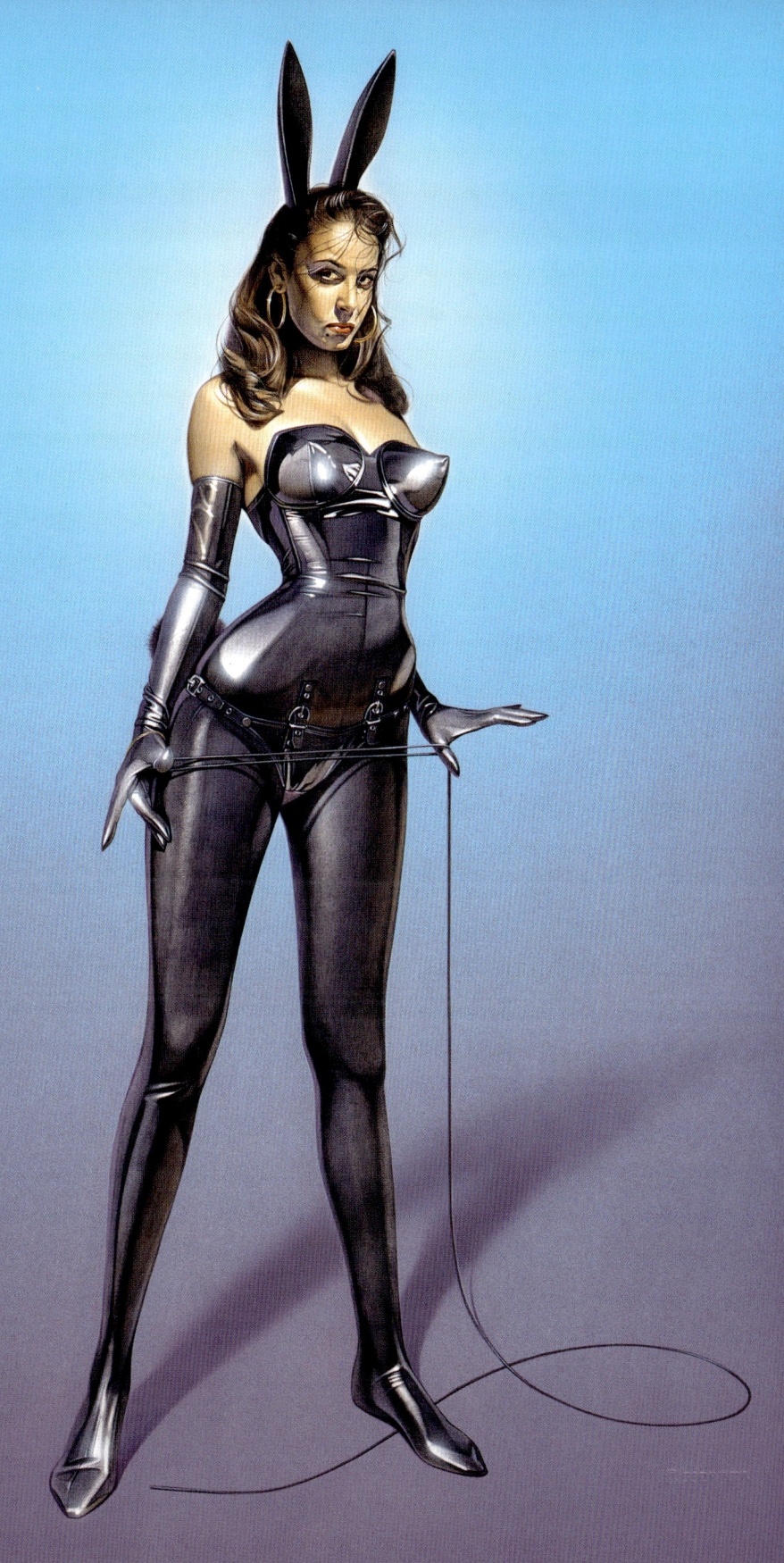

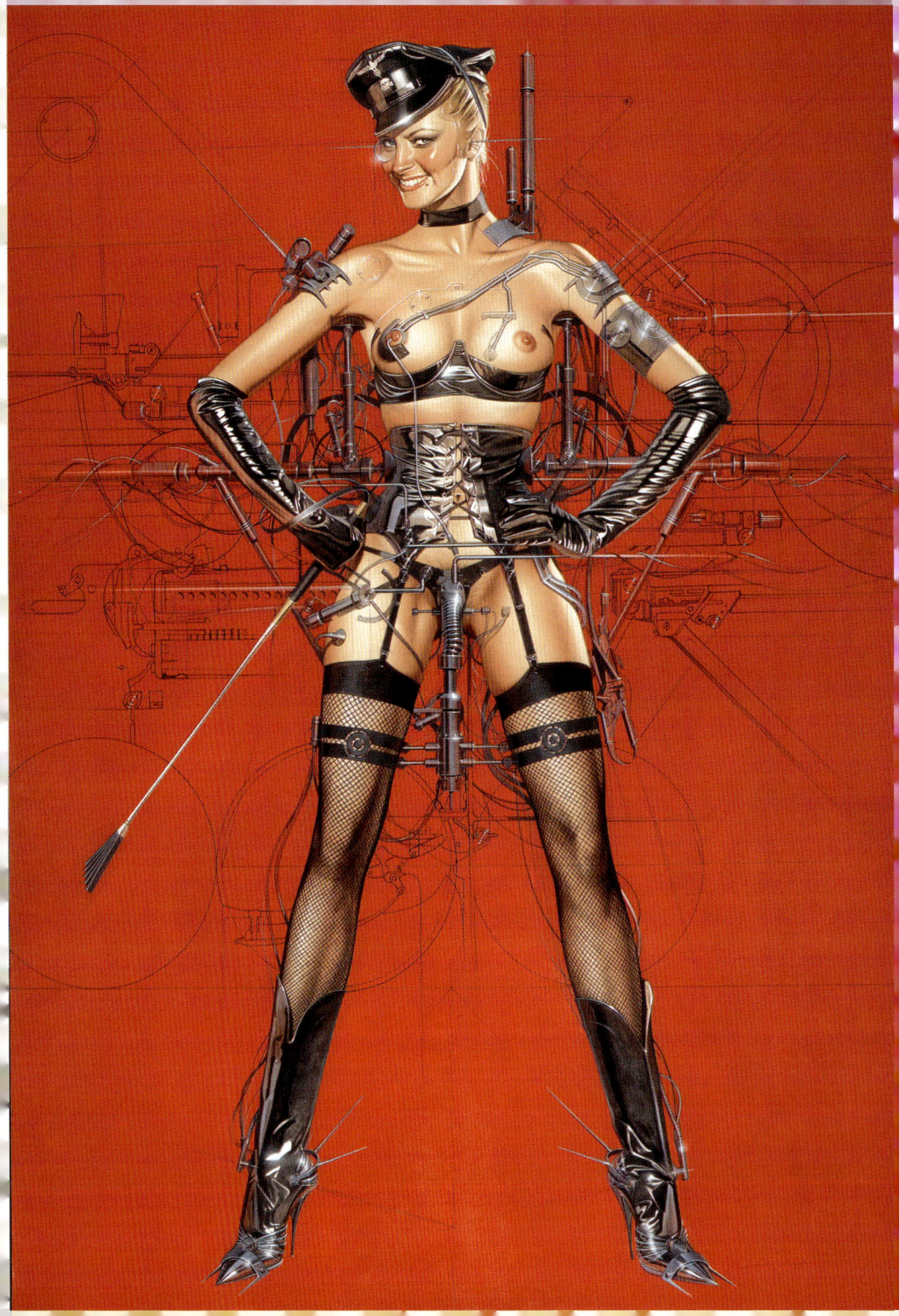

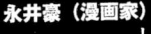

永井豪（漫画家）

空山さんのアダルト好みの女性像に圧倒されっぱなしです。あの、あくなき女性美への追求エネルギーは、いったい空山さんのどこから出てくるのだろうか……？

森豪　Go Nagai '97.12.10

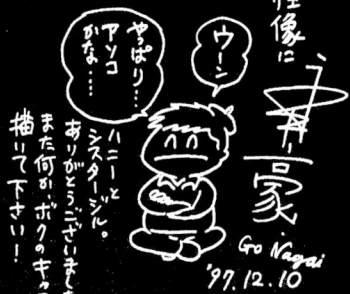

ウーン
やっぱりアソコかな…
ハニーとシスタージル・ありがとうございましたまた何か、ボクのキャラ描いて下さい！

No.1

ミヤ・アーデン・ソラヤマ　福田和彦（美術家）

No.2

福田和彦（美術家）

原耕一（グラフィックデザイナー）

空山さんのかく絵は解りやすい。
とても解りやすい。
これはボクの最高のほめ言葉です。
PARISやNEW YORKのどんなところにあっても、すごく良く見える。そこにいる色々な肌の人にほほえみかけてくる、もちろんボクにも。
なんでこんなにも説得力の有る絵なんだろう、なんでこんなに色々な人が良いとか好きだとかいうんだろう。いろんな事を考えると、空山さんは日本人じゃないんじゃないかな、と思う、思うようにしている。

原 耕一

山口はるみ（イラストレーター）

やさしい空山さんは、今年〈1997〉も私家版CARD.20枚セットを送ってくださいました。うまい。すごい。きつい。えぐい。いたい。きれい。こわい。さむい。かわいい。ずぶとい。おかしい。はずかしい。やばい。んもうまったく空恐ろしいイラストレーターだ!!
空恐ろしい時代の気分が浮立って、MAXに描かれている。それにしても、〈あの事件〉があったこの年に、脳や内臓関係のところまで、良く描けるものだなあ、と、つくづく思いました。基チャンって　ス・ゴ・イ。

HARUMI

飯田コメント

あらゆる画材と資料に溢れた作業机、増殖する観葉植物と古今東西のフェチな珍品の数々・・・・いつもと変わらない風景なのに、行くたびに作業机の上にはドギマギさせられるぶっ飛んだ新作が描きかけで、周りには見たこともないプロジェクトの片鱗が見え隠れする・・・・進化し続ける空山さんに会うことほど、エキサイティングなことはない。師匠、どこまでもついて行きます。
（飯田昭雄／WIEDEN+KENNEDY TOKYO）

Akio E-da

ジェリービーンコメント

情熱的でいてハイ・クオリティー。現代の大美人画師、SORAYAMA 氏の画く摩訶不思議な世界、香り立つ艶気（いろけ）が世界に紹介されることは、我々日本人として最も誇らしいことです。
私も感性の扉を開けられた者の一人です
（覆面画家　Rockin'Jelly Bean）

Bob Guccione（ボブ・グッチョーネ：ベントハウス発行人兼編集長）

SORAYAMA IS AN ARTIST OF
EXTRAORDINARY TALENT, WONDROUS
IMAGINATION AND IMPECCABLE
SKILL. THE FACT THAT HE TILTS
TOWARD THE EROTIC REDOUBLES
MY BELIEF IN SEX AS A SERIOUS
COMMUNICATIONS MEDIUM ~...

BOB GUCCIONE

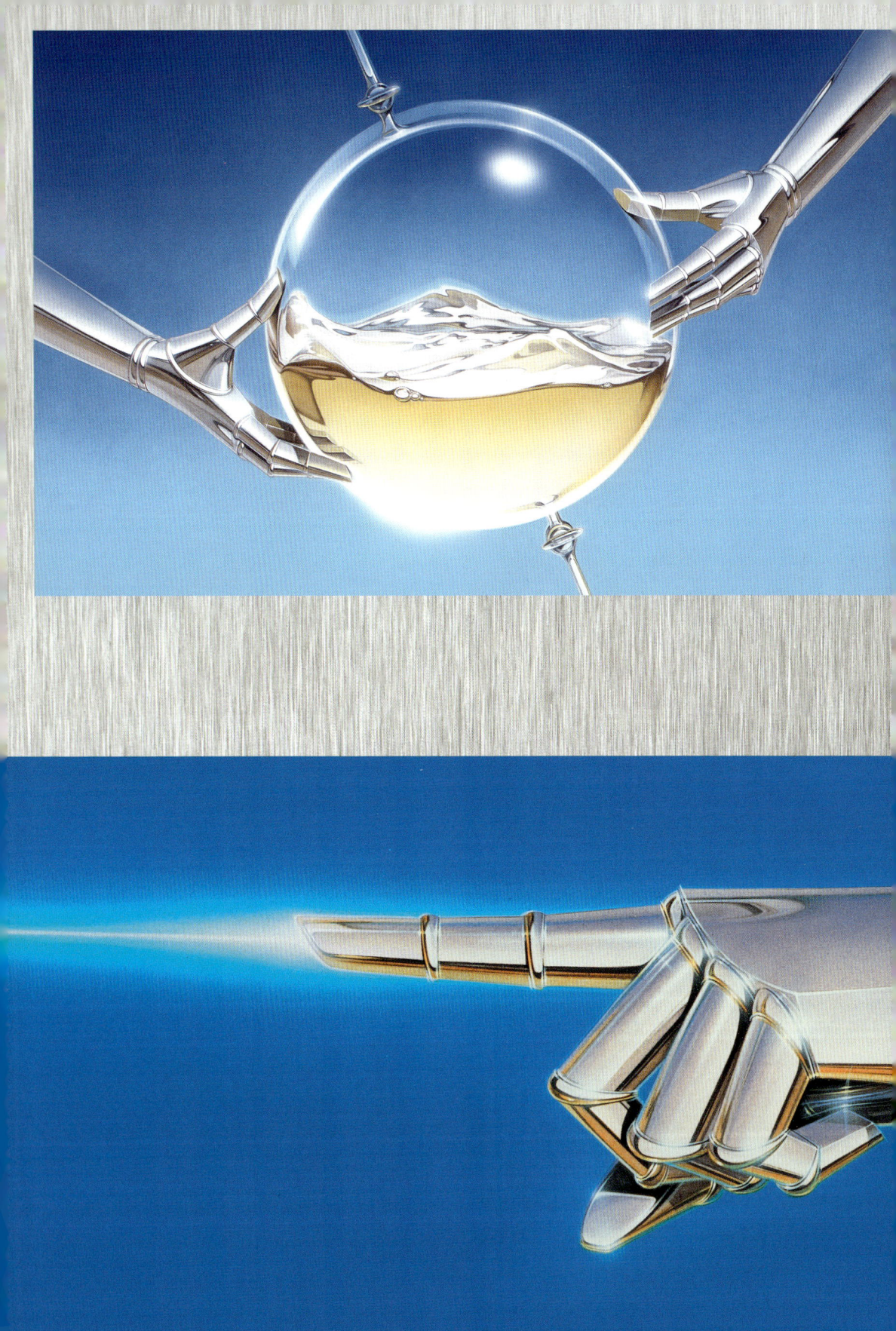

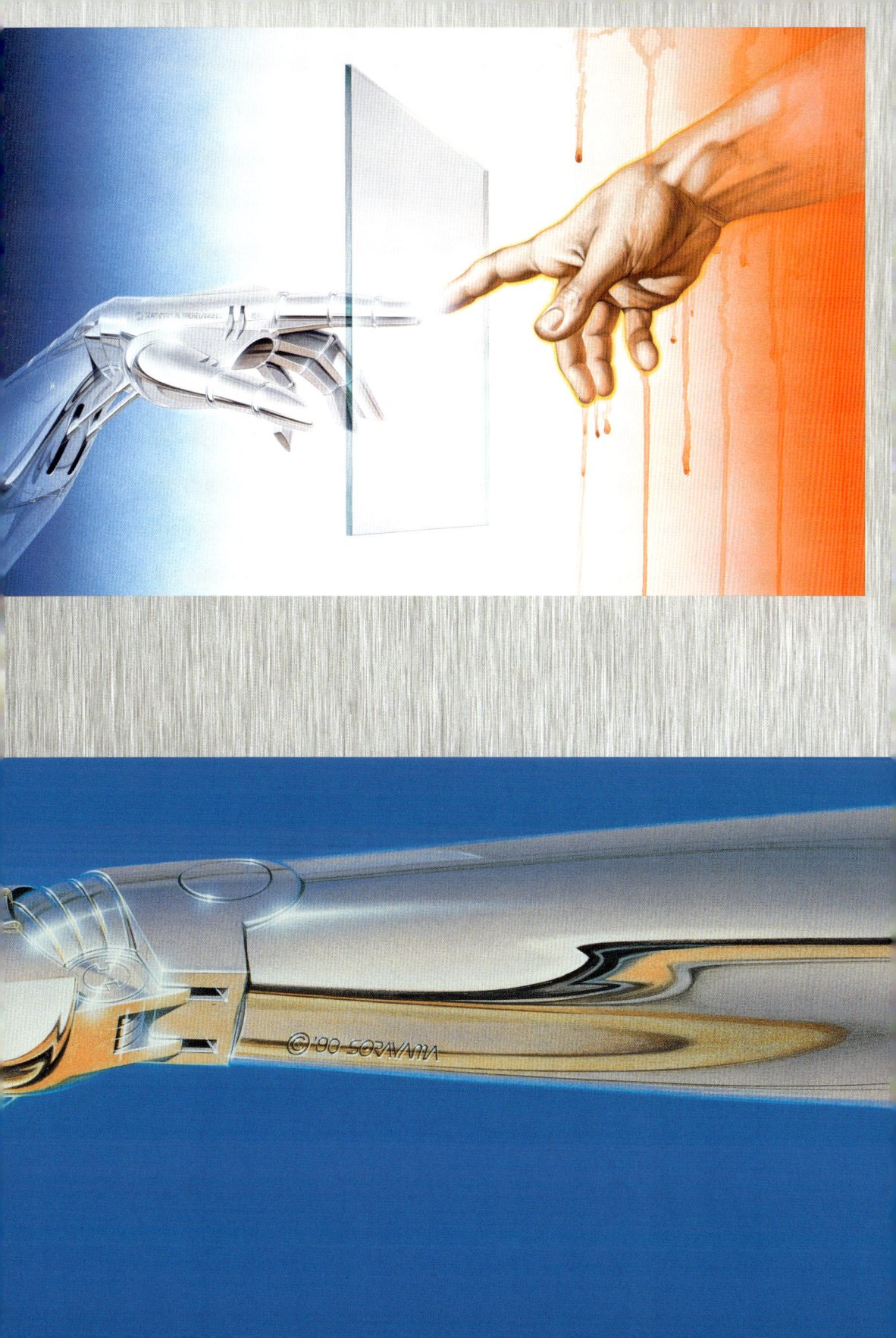

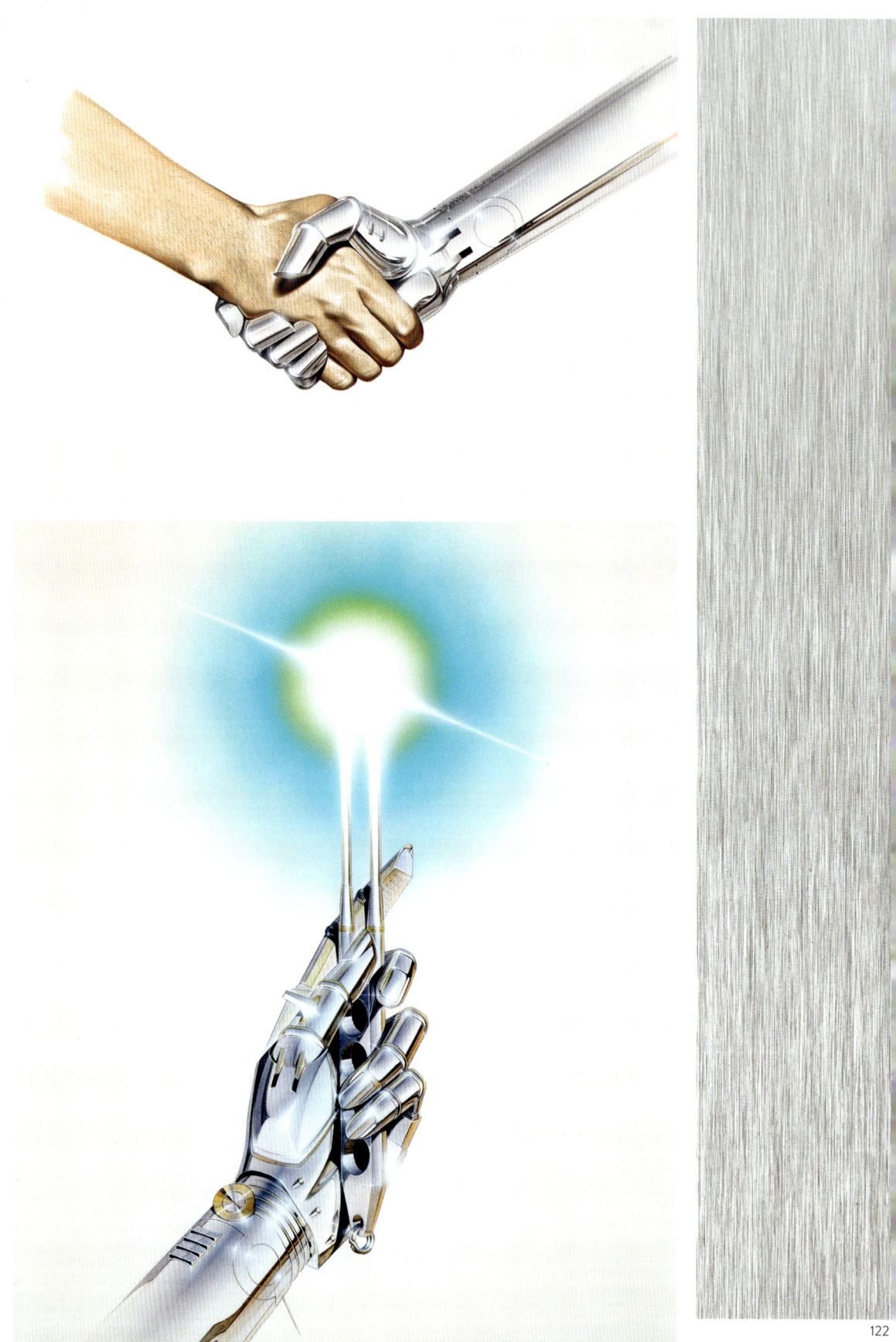

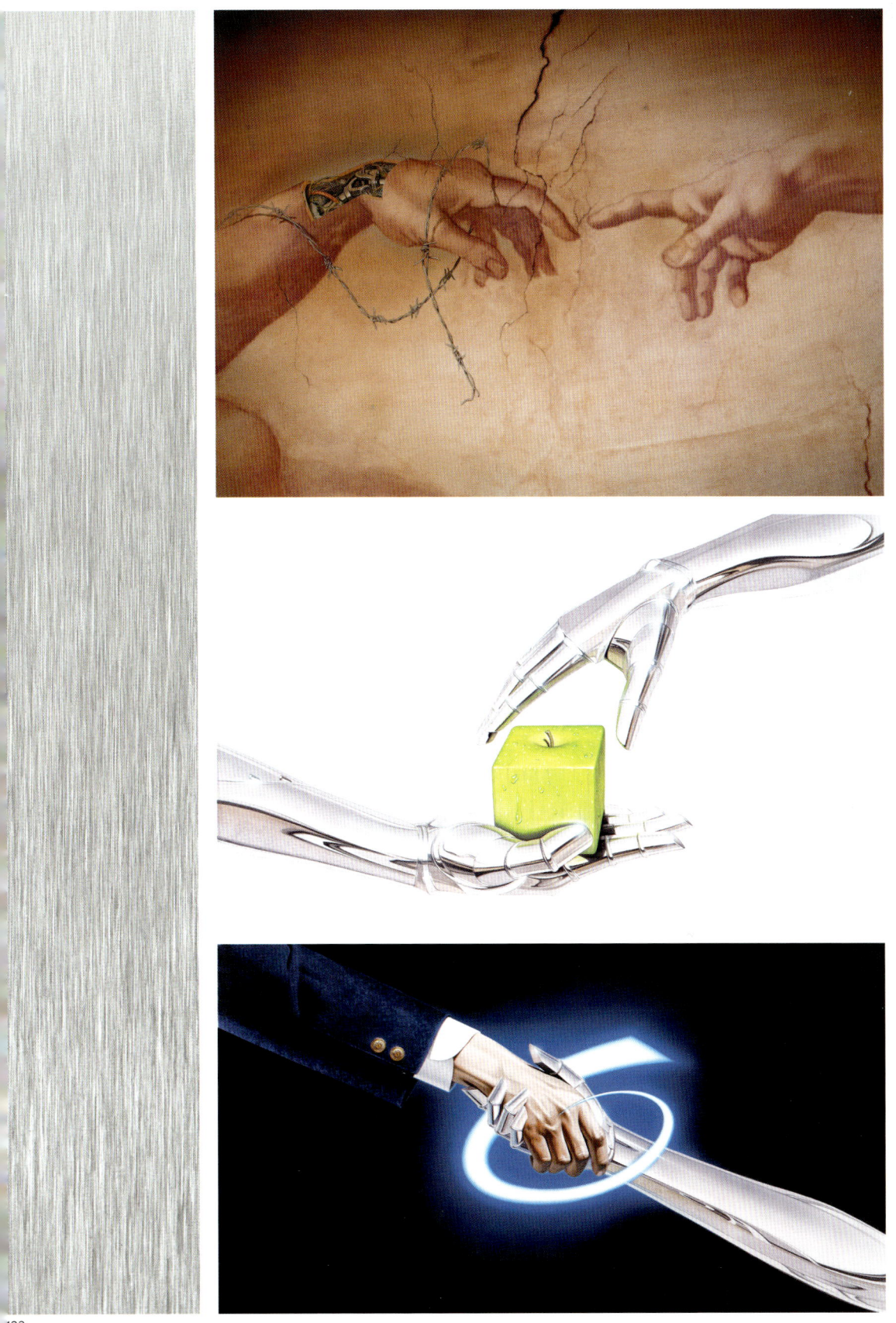

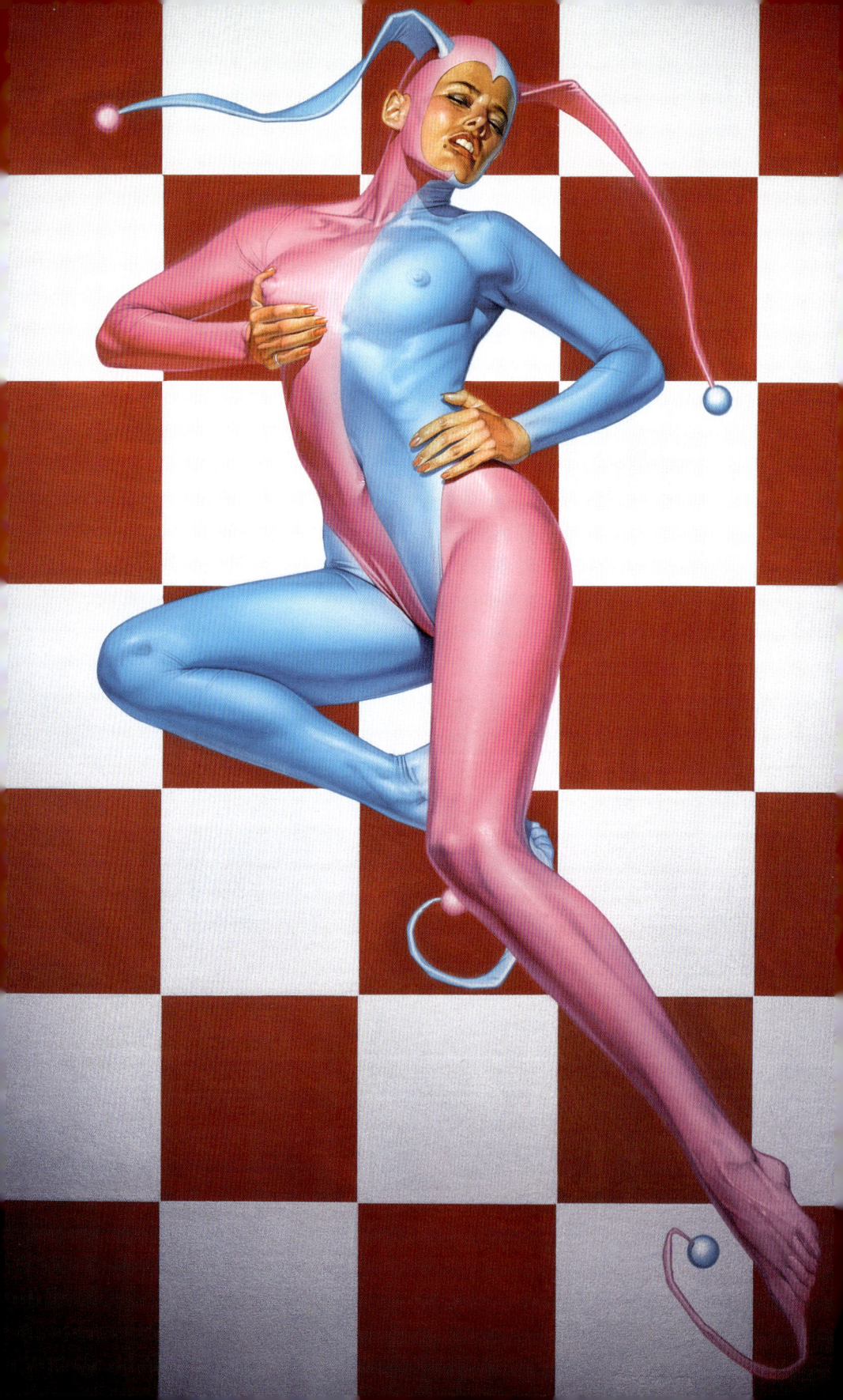

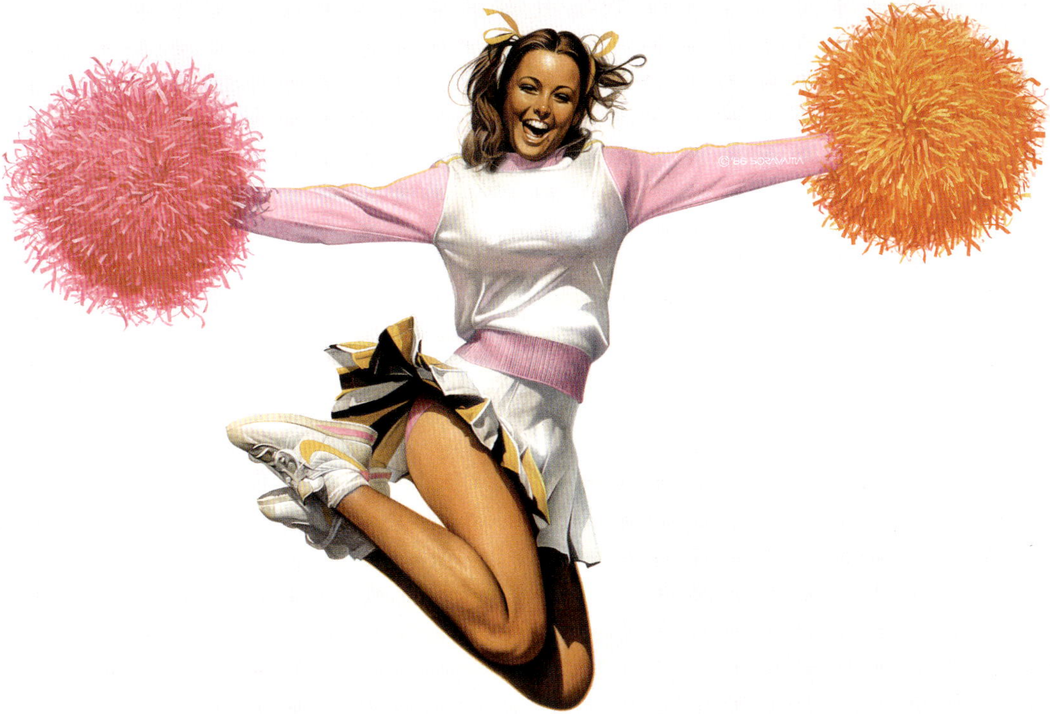

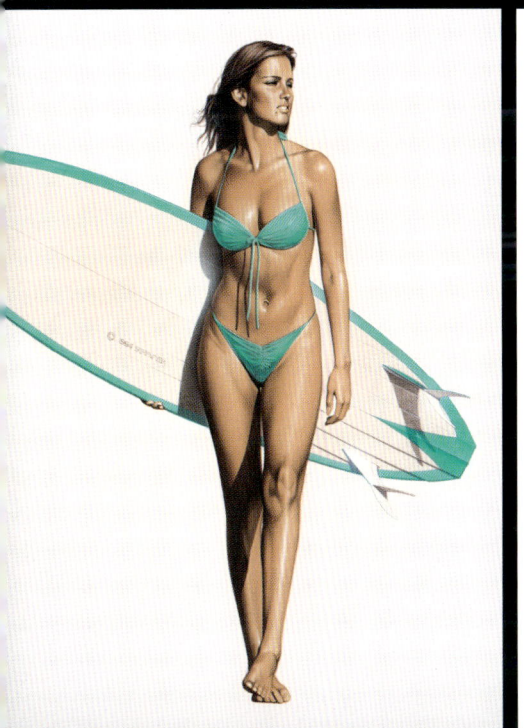
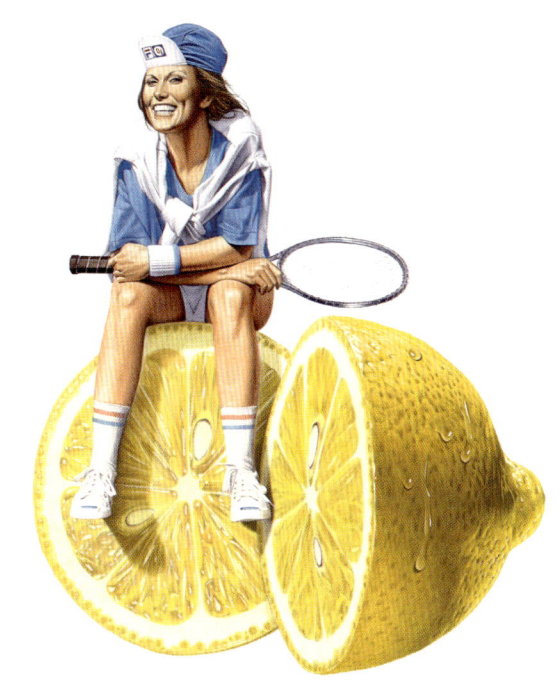

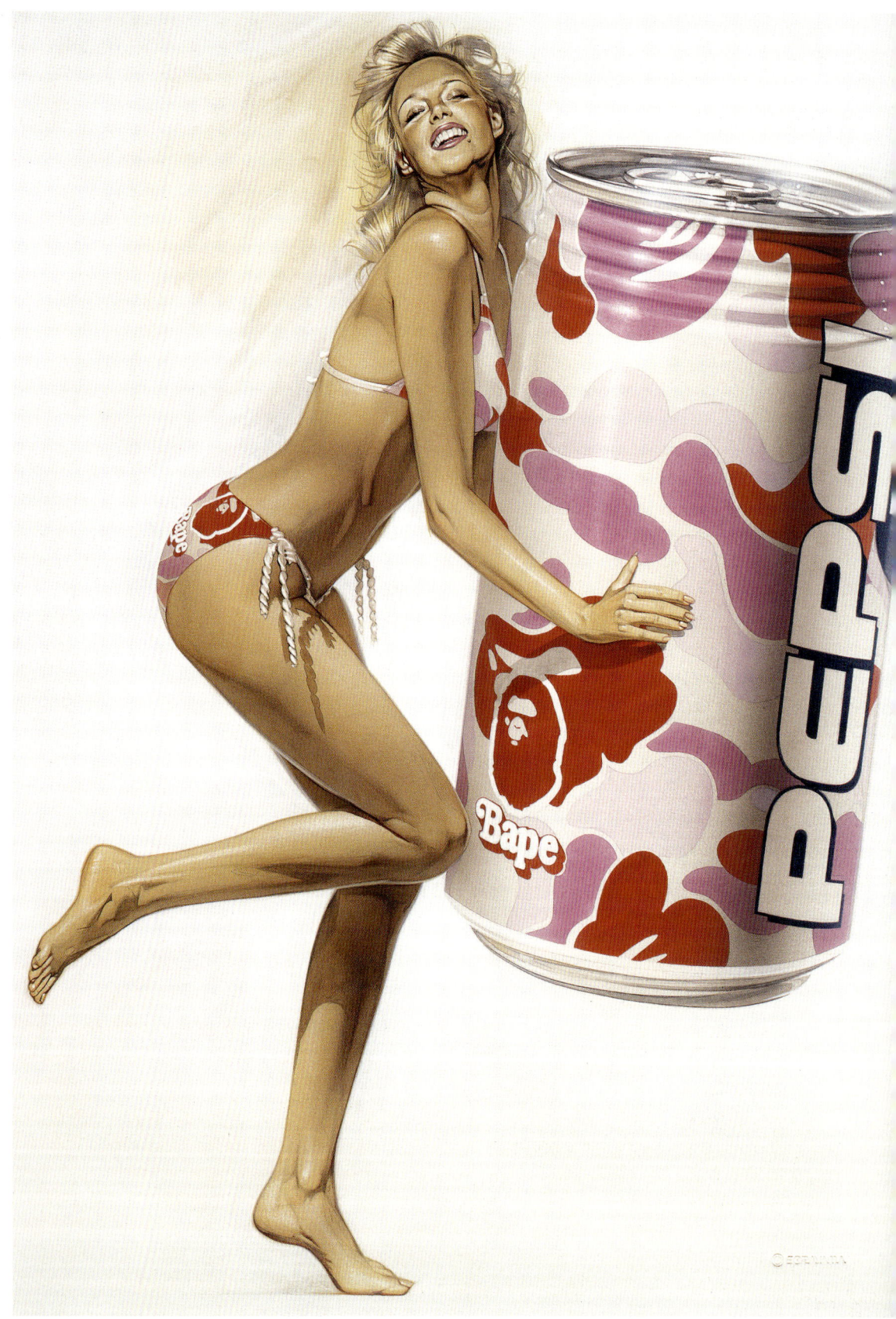

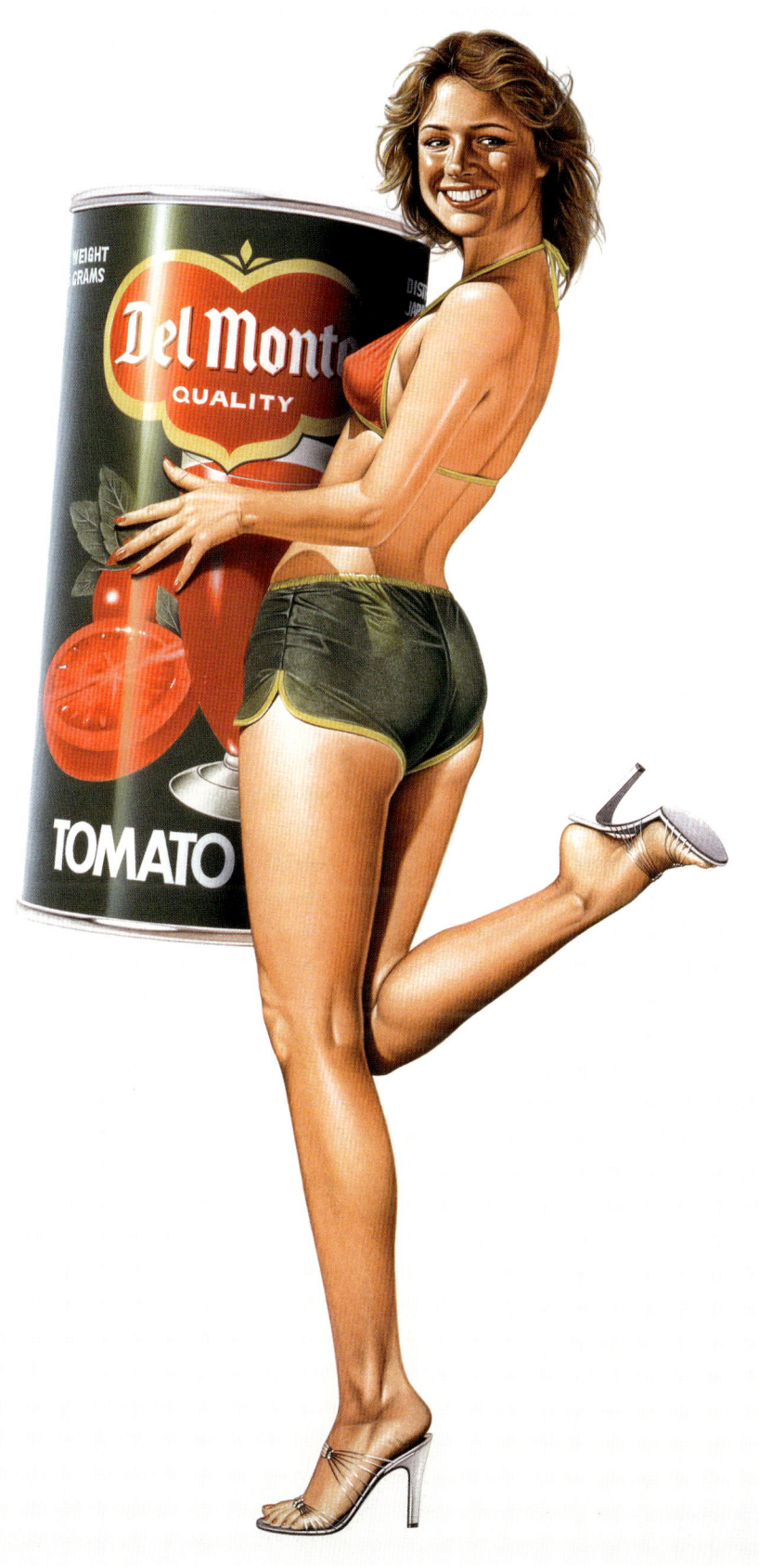

土井利忠（ソニー常務）

空山基さんは、1986年に私がユニックス・ワークステーションのビジネスを始めるときに、シンボル・マークの「ウサギ」のイラストを描いてもらったのが、最初の出会いだった。

その後、「賊族丸」という名の外洋ヨットの共同オーナーにひっぱりこんだので、親しく付き合うようになった。

ごく最近、私は四つ足の犬の格好をしたペットロボットの開発をはじめ、そのキャラクター・デザインをまた彼にお願いすることにした。したがって、彼との付き合いは、海の上や酒の席を中心とした遊びの世界から、キャラクター・デザインをめぐる真剣なやりとりにいたるまで幅が広い。

一般に彼のイラストは、あふれるエロティシズムでよく知られている。あのイラストを見た人のほとんどは、空山基というのは、よほどのスケベ・オヤジではないかと想像すると思う。しかしながら、いや、実は、まったくその通りなのだ。

私は人間には二種類しかいないと思っている。第一の種類は「すけべ人間」だ。もうひとつの種類は「むっつりすけべ人間」と呼ぶ。彼は典型的な前者に分類される。

今後とも、大いに「すけべ人間」の本領を発揮して、お色気あふれる作品を発表して暮れることを期待している。

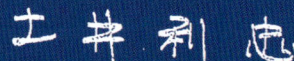

鈴木英人（アーティスト）

ながい間のごぶさたです。
すっかり暗い世の中になりましたね。
できるだけ、この悪くて暗い日本を離れていたいと、アメリカに取材に行くことが多くなっています。日本（アンフェア）よりうんとフェアなアメリカで空さんのイラストカード集をボストンの本屋で見つけました。日本人ではあなたとアラーキーでした。2人ともおんなをモチーフにしているのでおもしろいと思いました。（スバラシイ‼）
いつもぼくの家に送ってくる×××こがちゃんときれいに描いてある空さんのピンナップはもう送ってもらえないのでしょうか。いつも楽しみにしています。
アメリカのほうが空さんのイラストを多くのメディアに生かせる市場があると思います。
いつかアメリカでいっしょに×××の旅行をしたいですね。

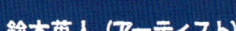

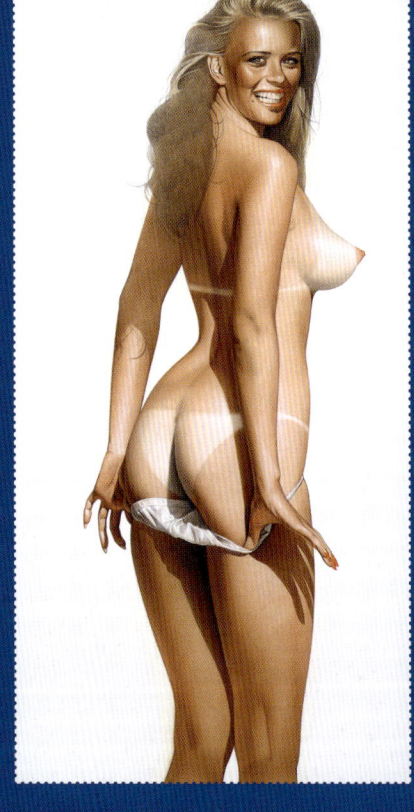

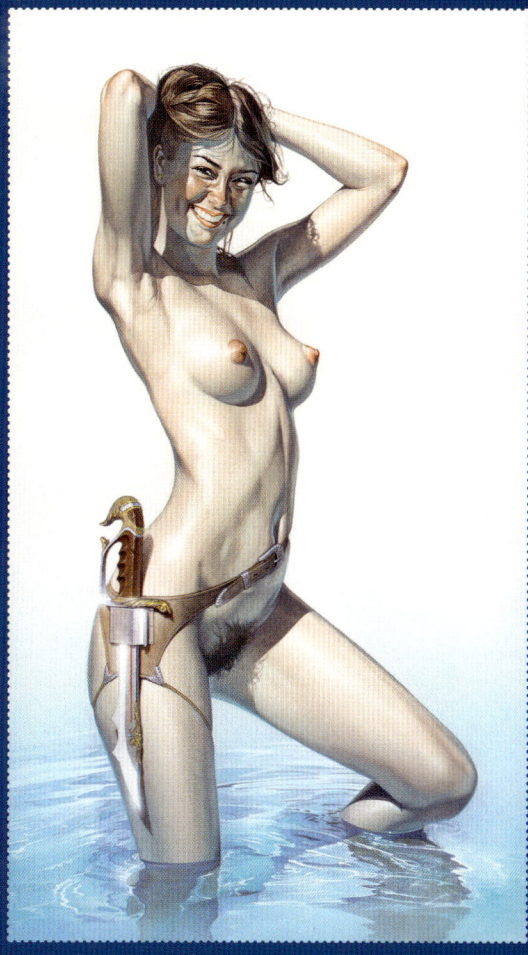

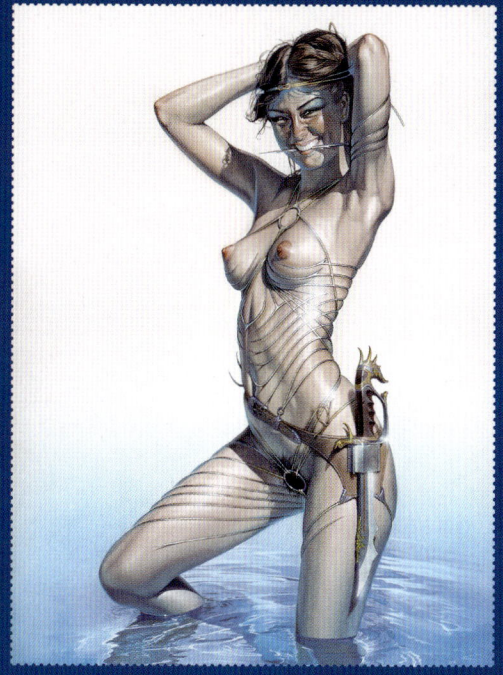

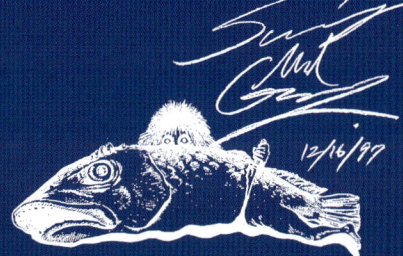

こ、これだっ！と１０代なかばのオレはよろめいたのでした。
輝くクロームの肌に！
唇だけで表情をもつ顔に！
金属なのに柔らかいボディラインに！
女性形ロボットとしてはメトロポリスのマリアもいたがそれは所詮はレト
ロ。
今みたかったんだよ！このカタチで！この質感で！
セクシーロボット万歳！
空山サイコー！！！、と当時
描きたいココロは売るほどあれど、かなしいかな技術ゼロのオレは
指をくわえてセクシーロボットをぼう然とみつめて過ごす日々でありまし
た。
それから月日は２０年あまりも流れたのに、
スクリーンに映るのはクロームの輝きを身にまとった女性形ターミネー
ター。
セクシーロボットのイメージはきらめき、乱反射し、ひろがり、ひろが
り、
そして世界はまだその腕の中にあるのです。

寺田　克也　　漫画家／イラストレーター

空山氏がいったい　どういう人かは、
彼の絵の美しさから想像しくては いけない！！

空山氏がいったい どういう冗談を
いうのかは、
彼の絵からは とうてい 想像できない！！

ただ １つ スケベさに関してだけは
彼の最近の絵から想像される
そのまま ズバリ である！！

12/16/'97

Multi-Media Surreal Productions

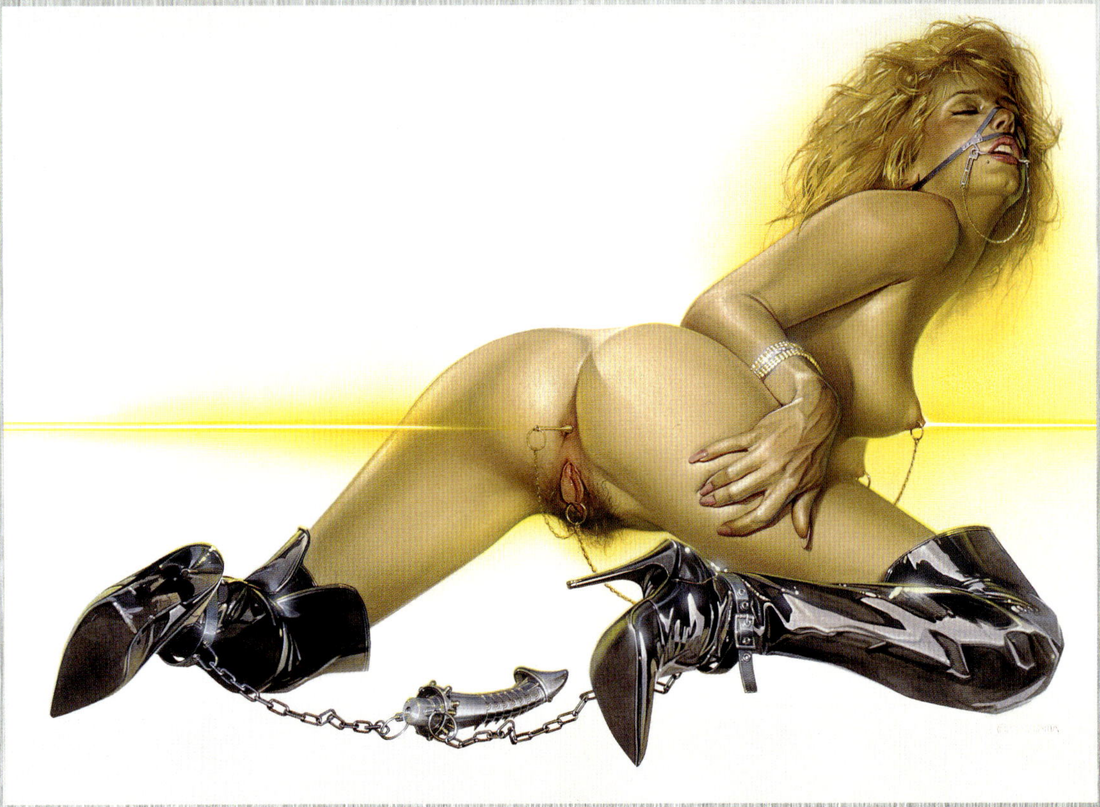

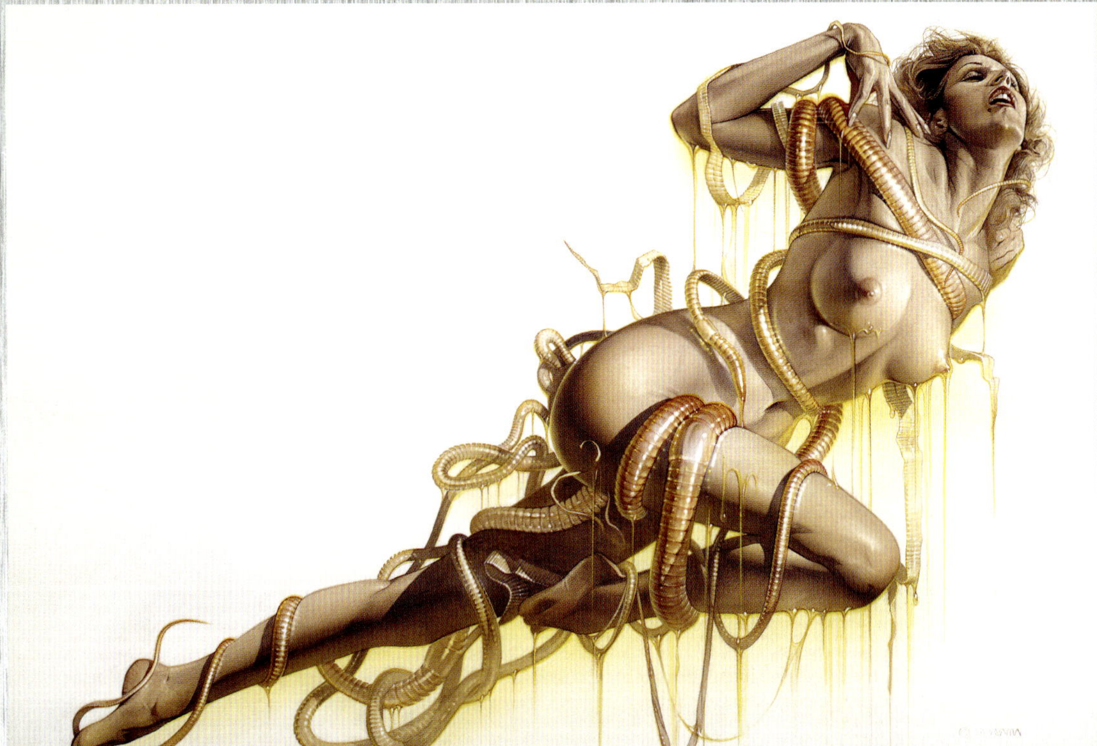

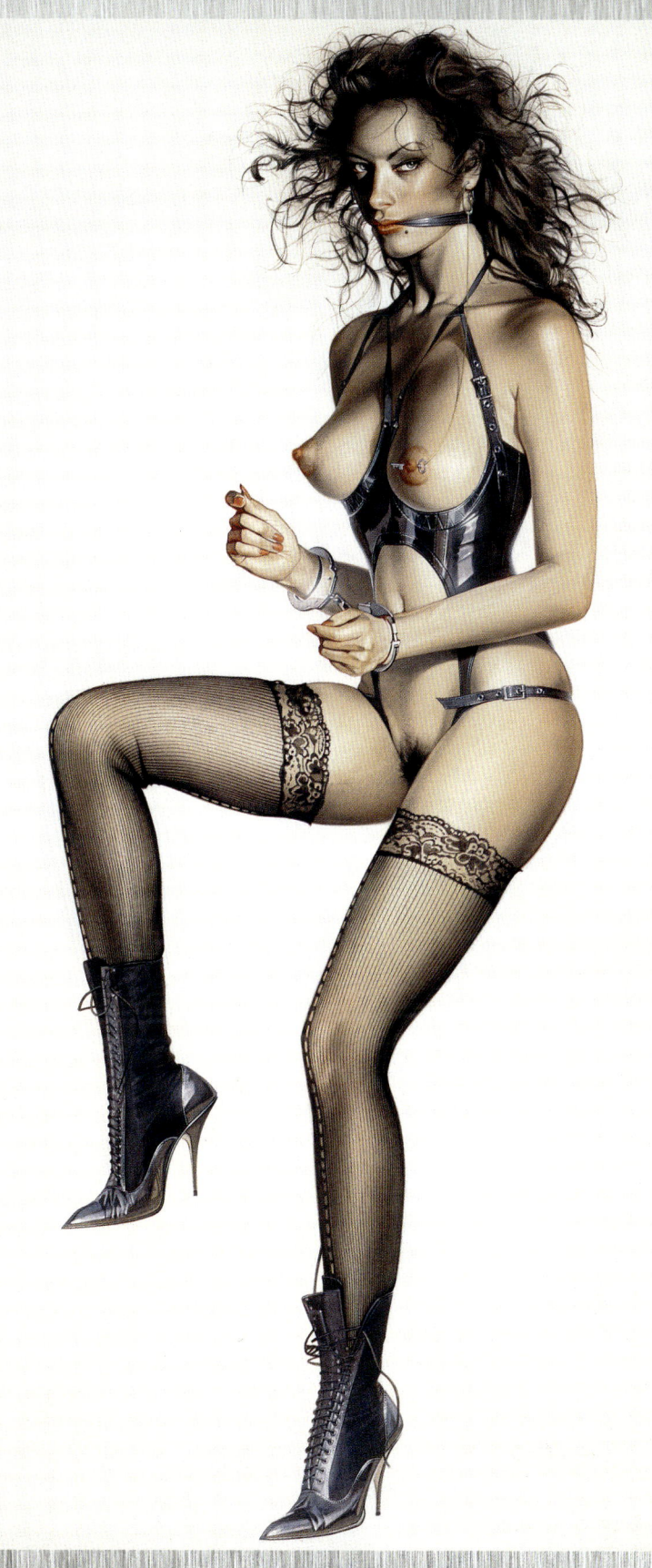

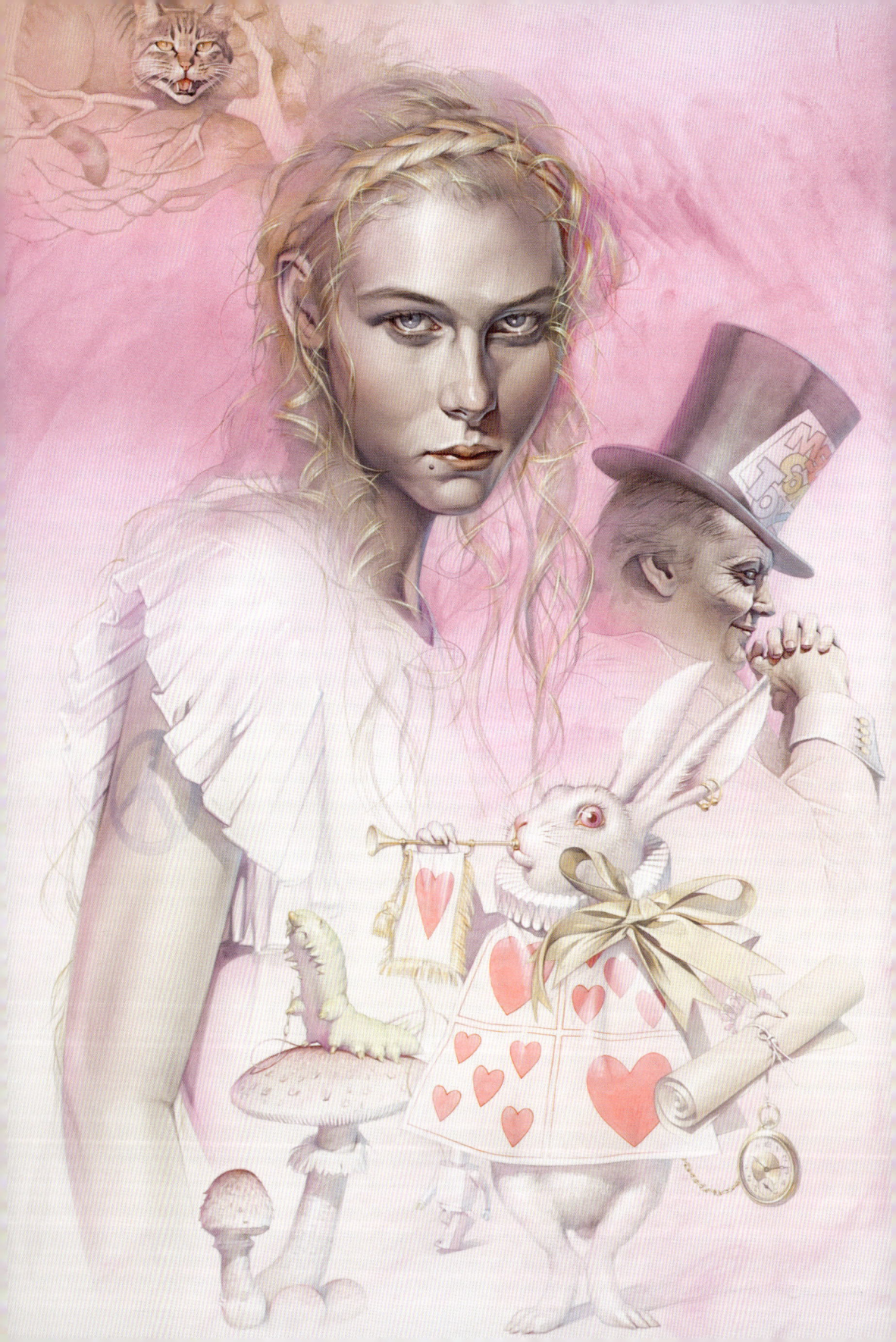

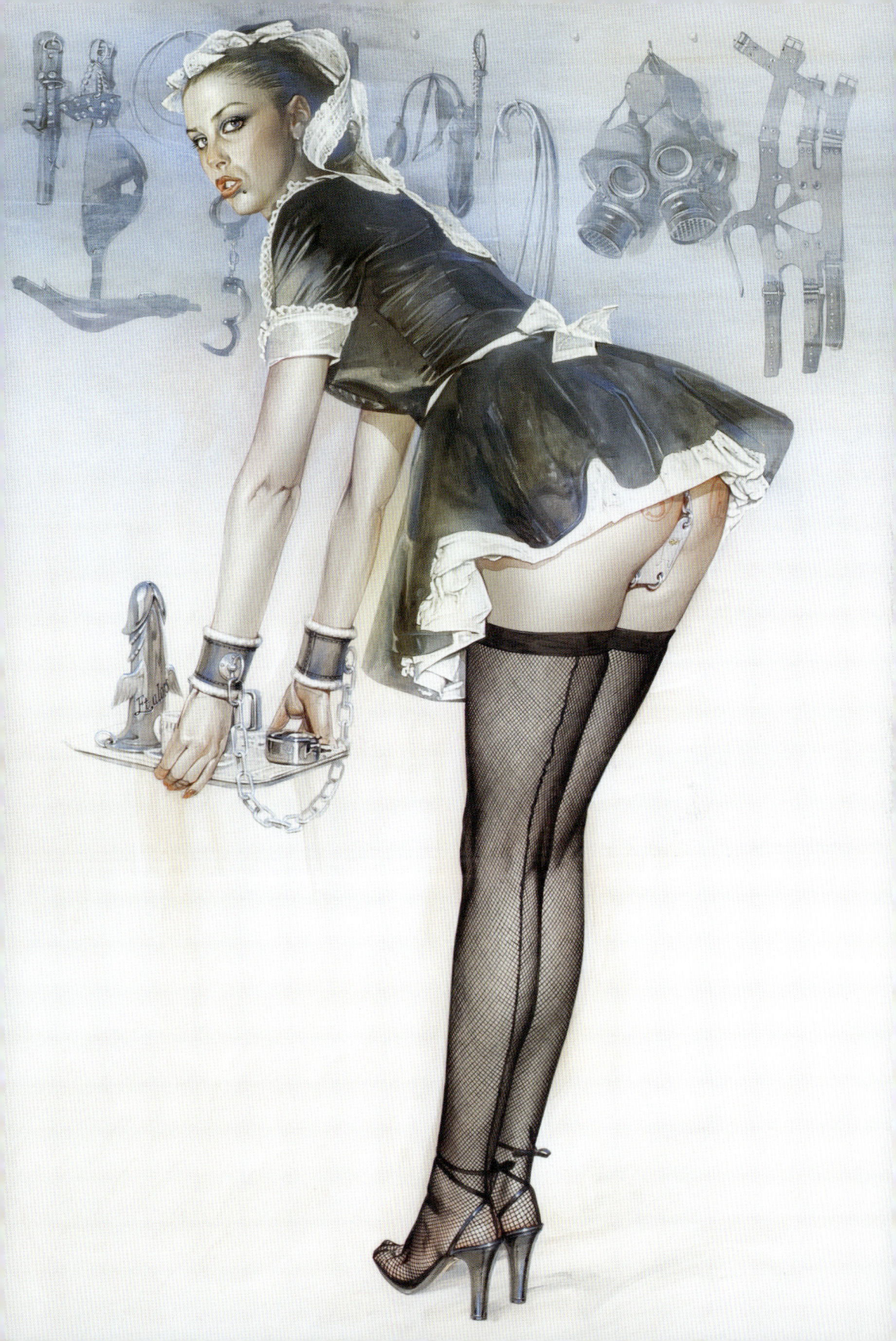

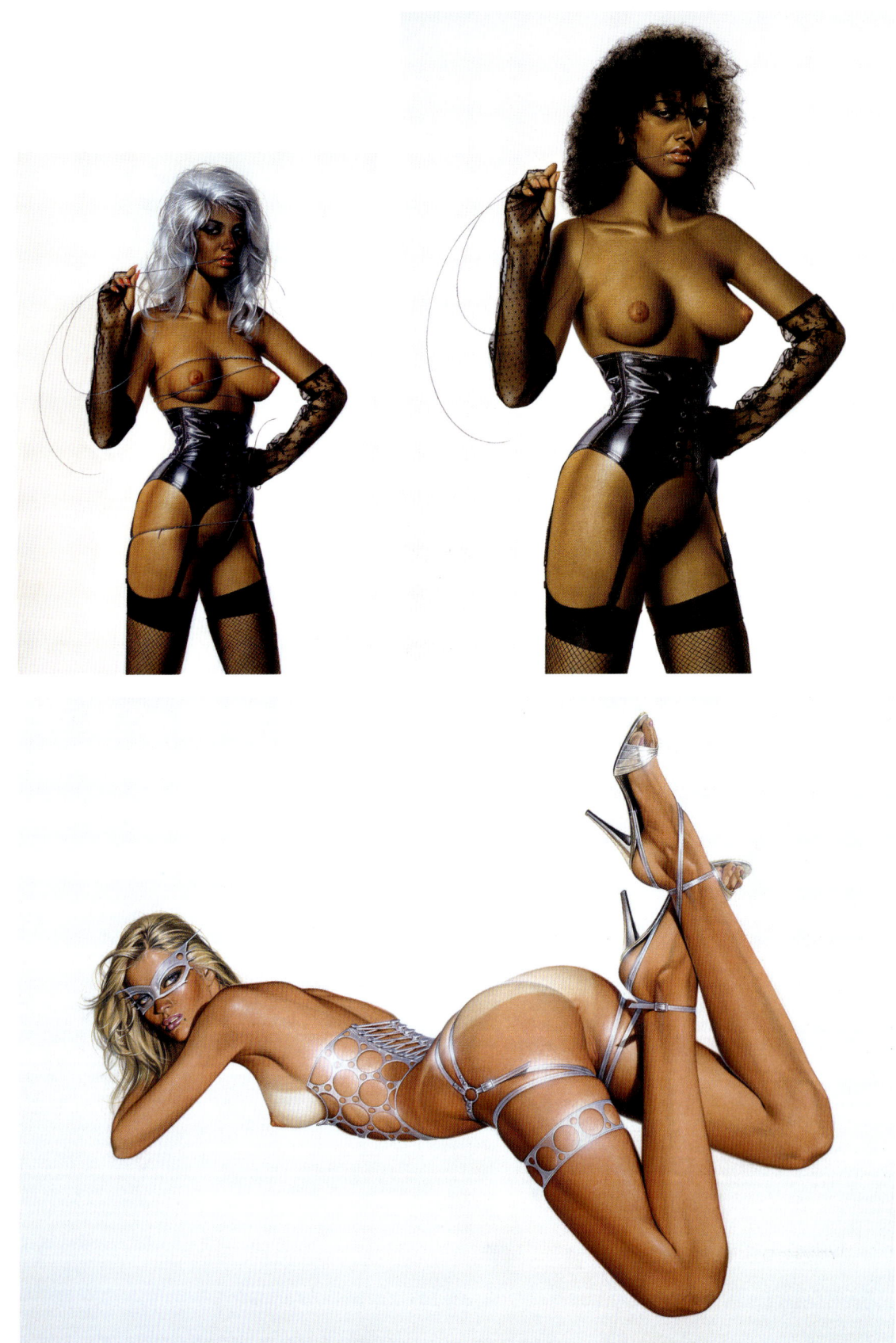

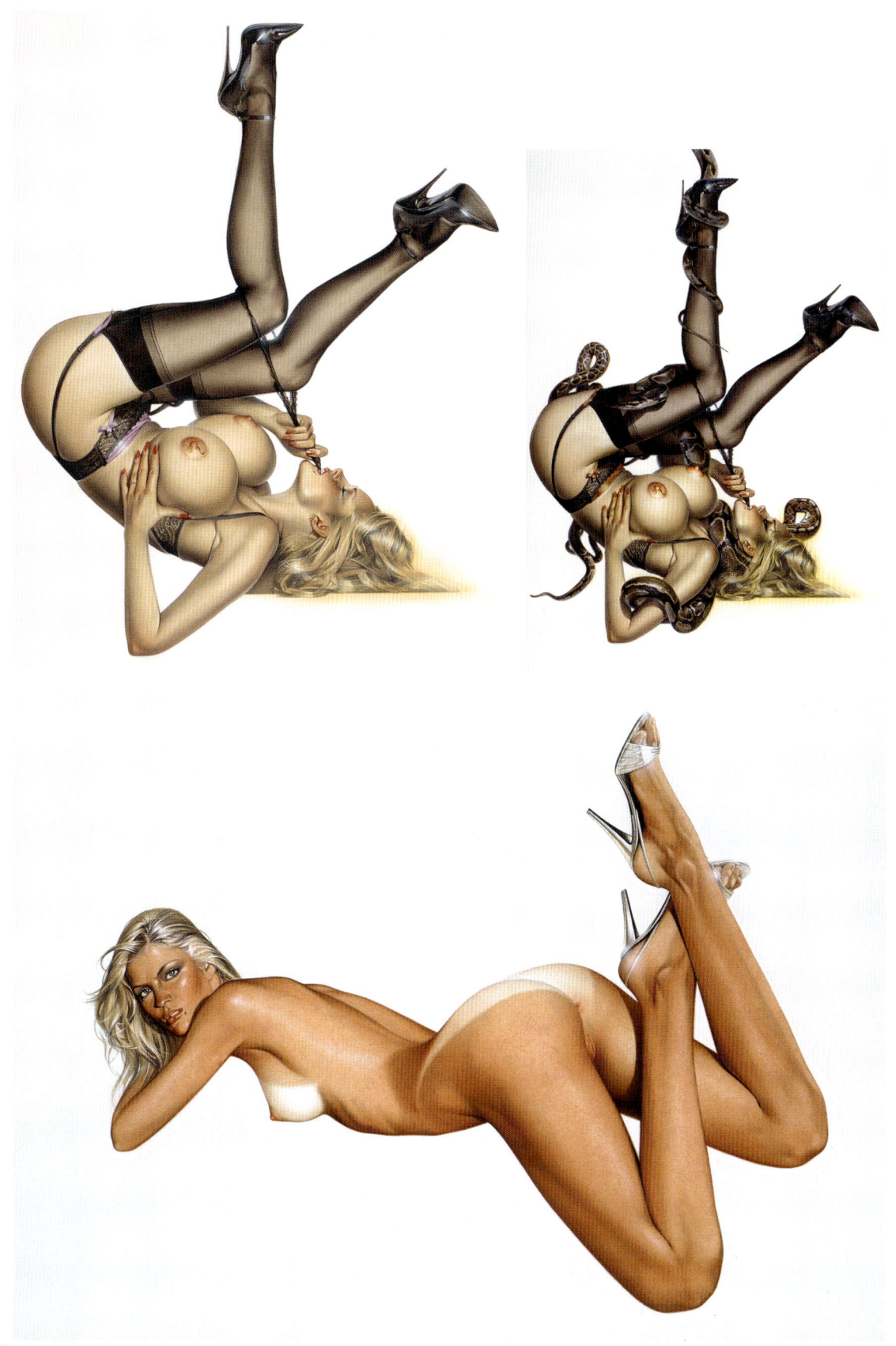

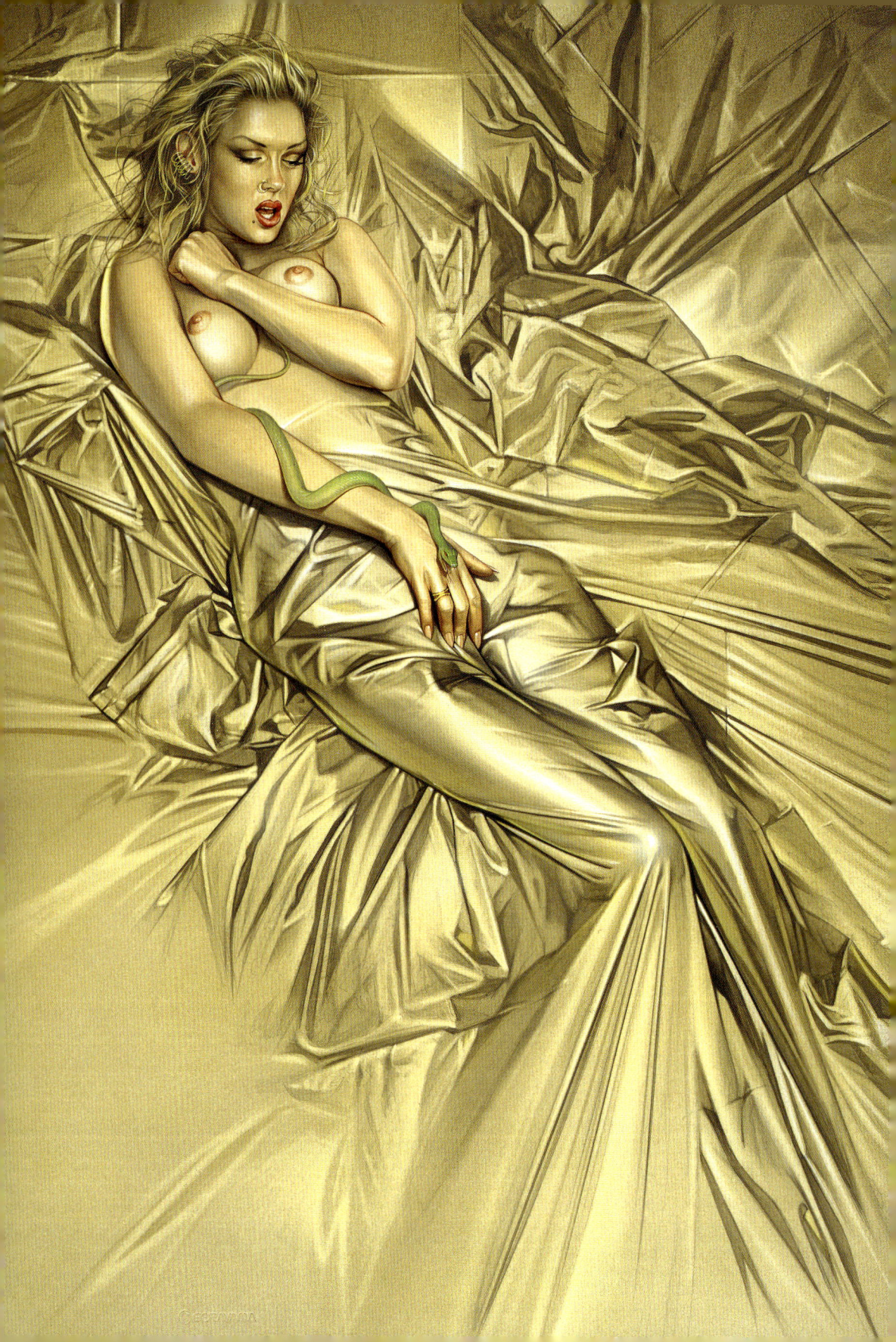

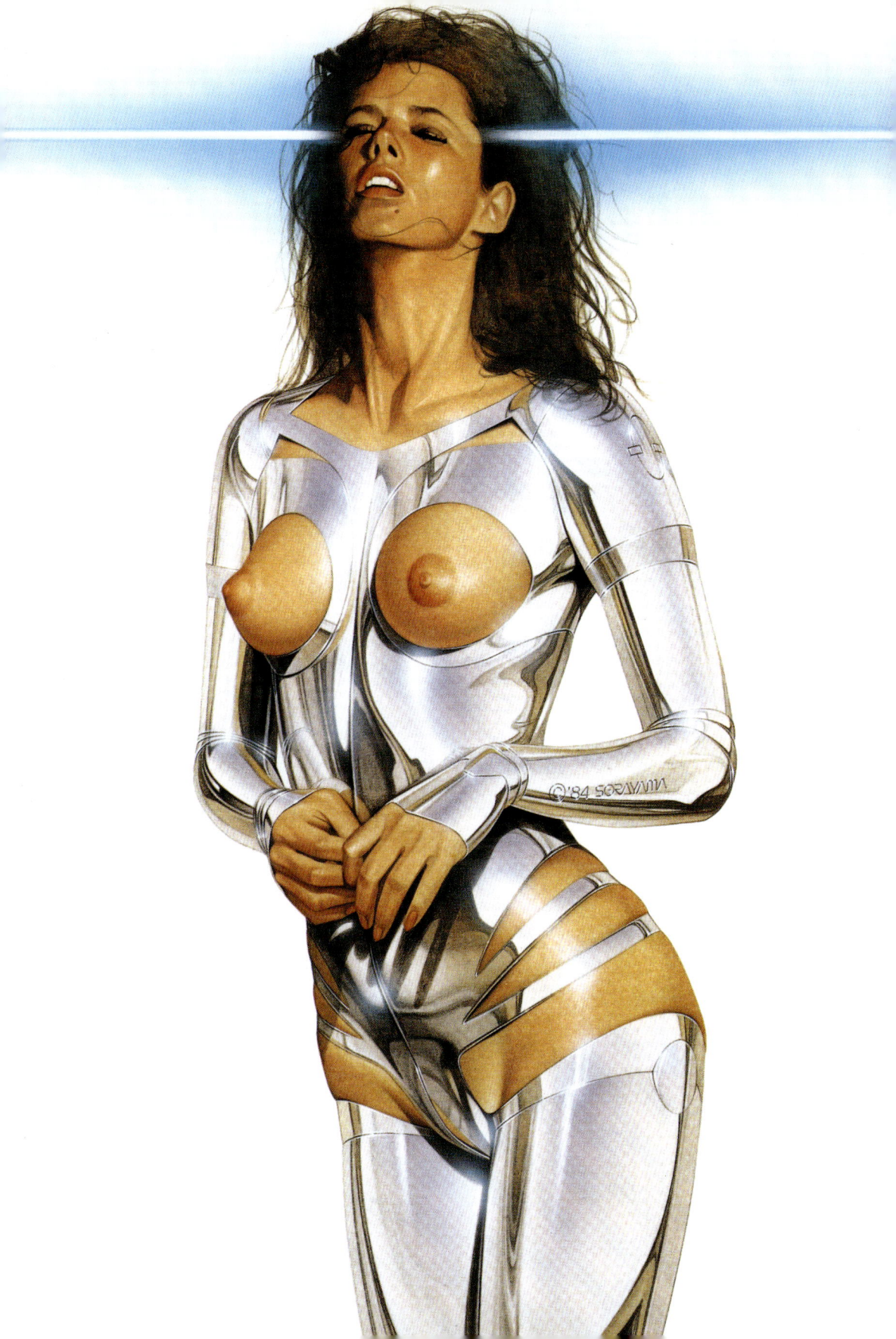

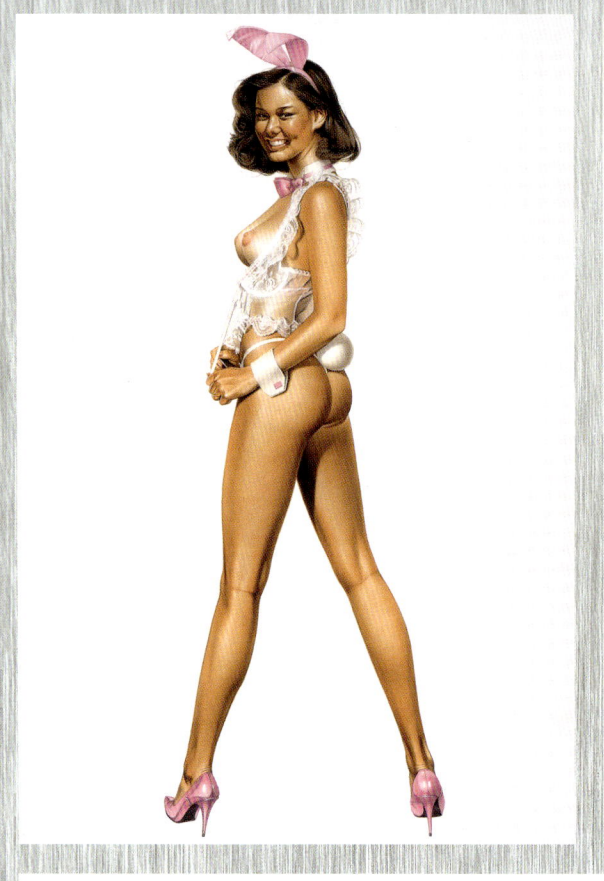

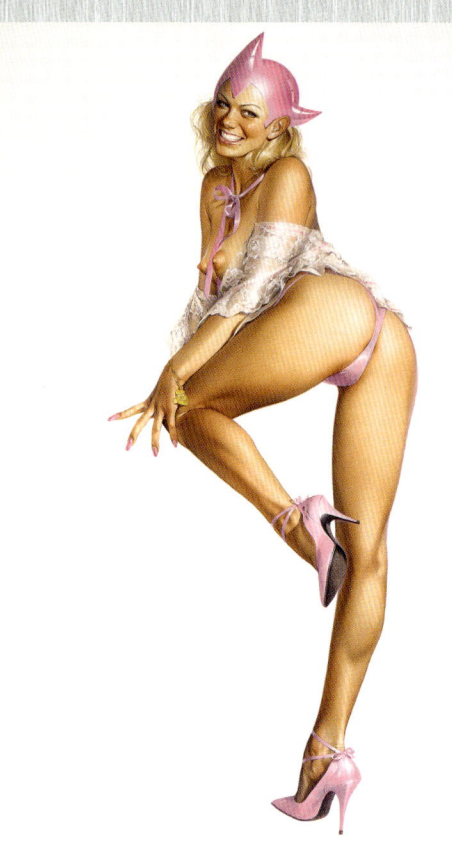

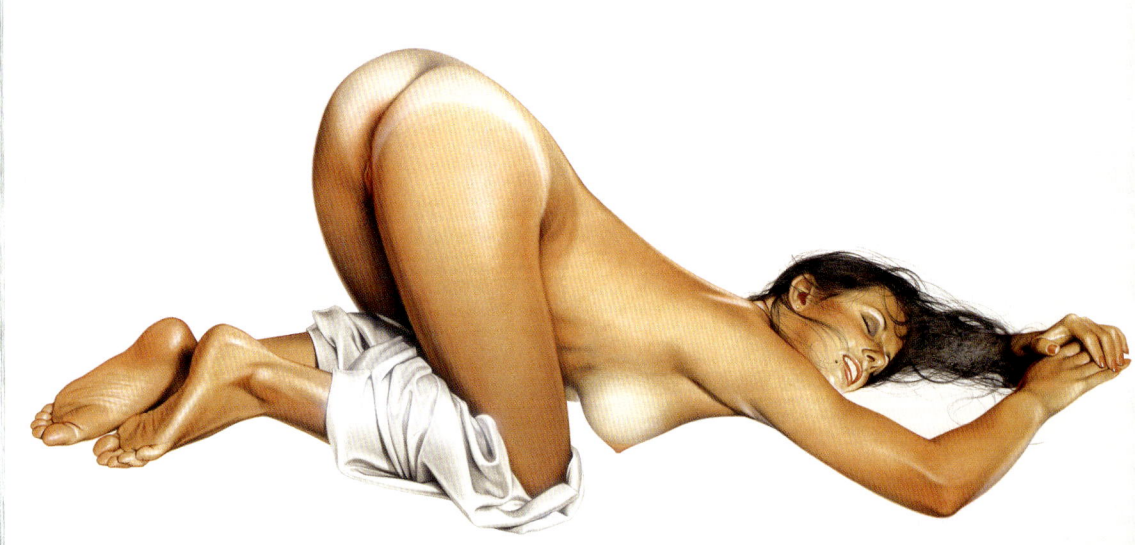

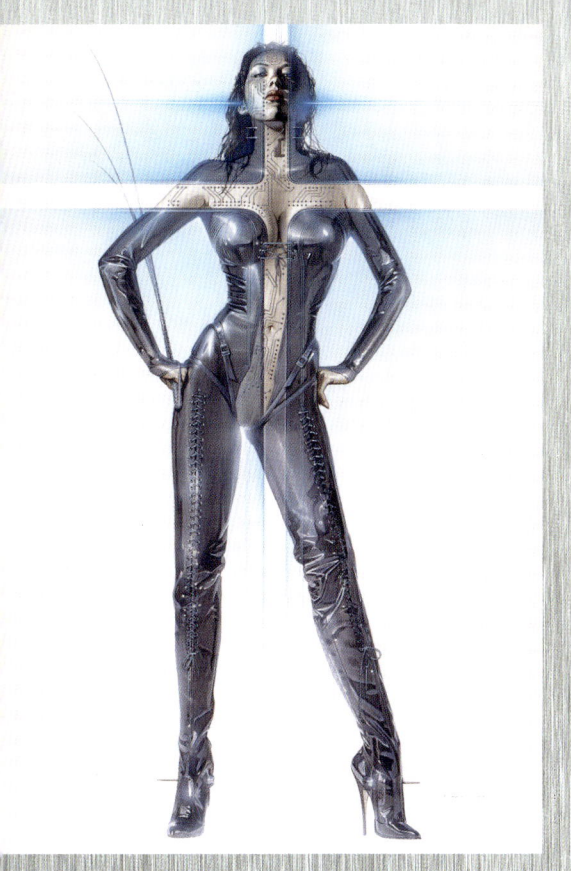

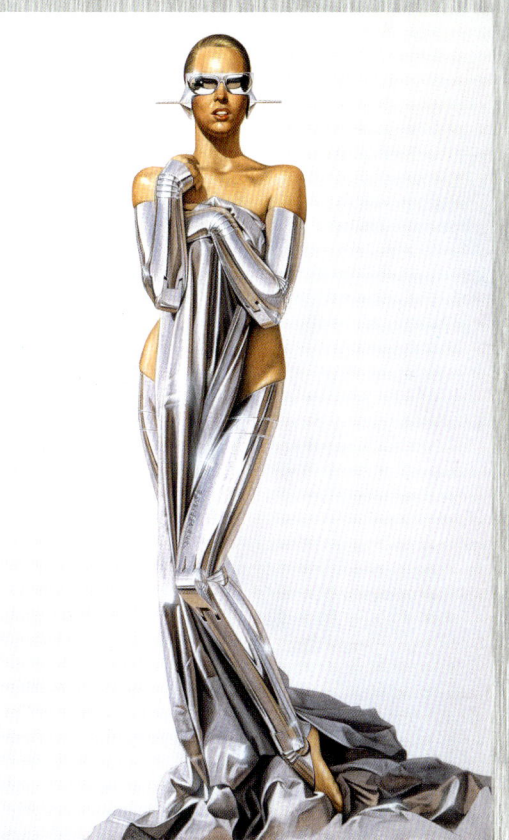

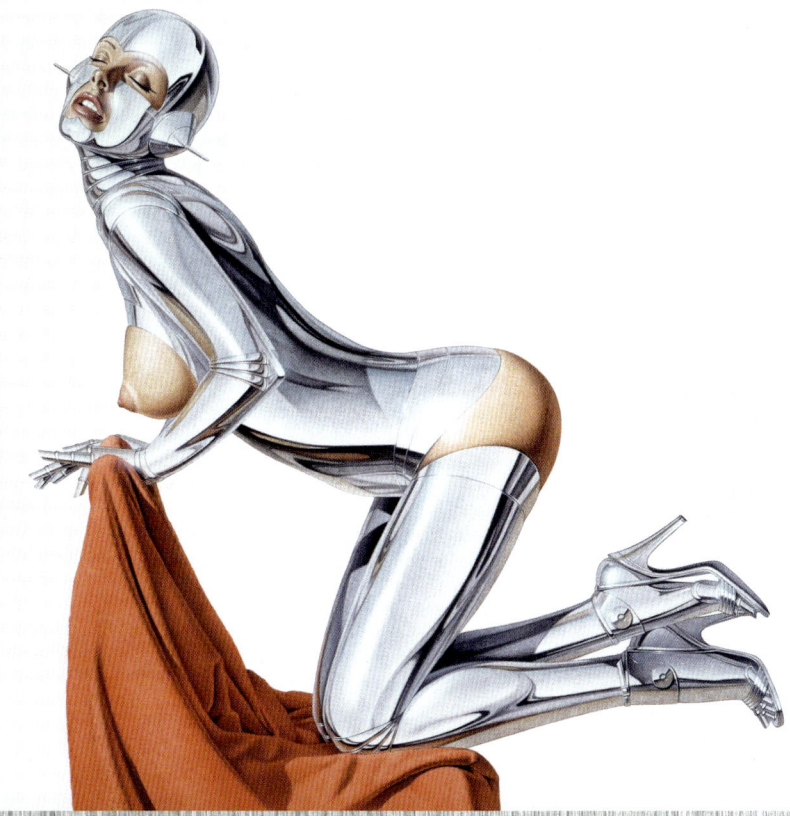

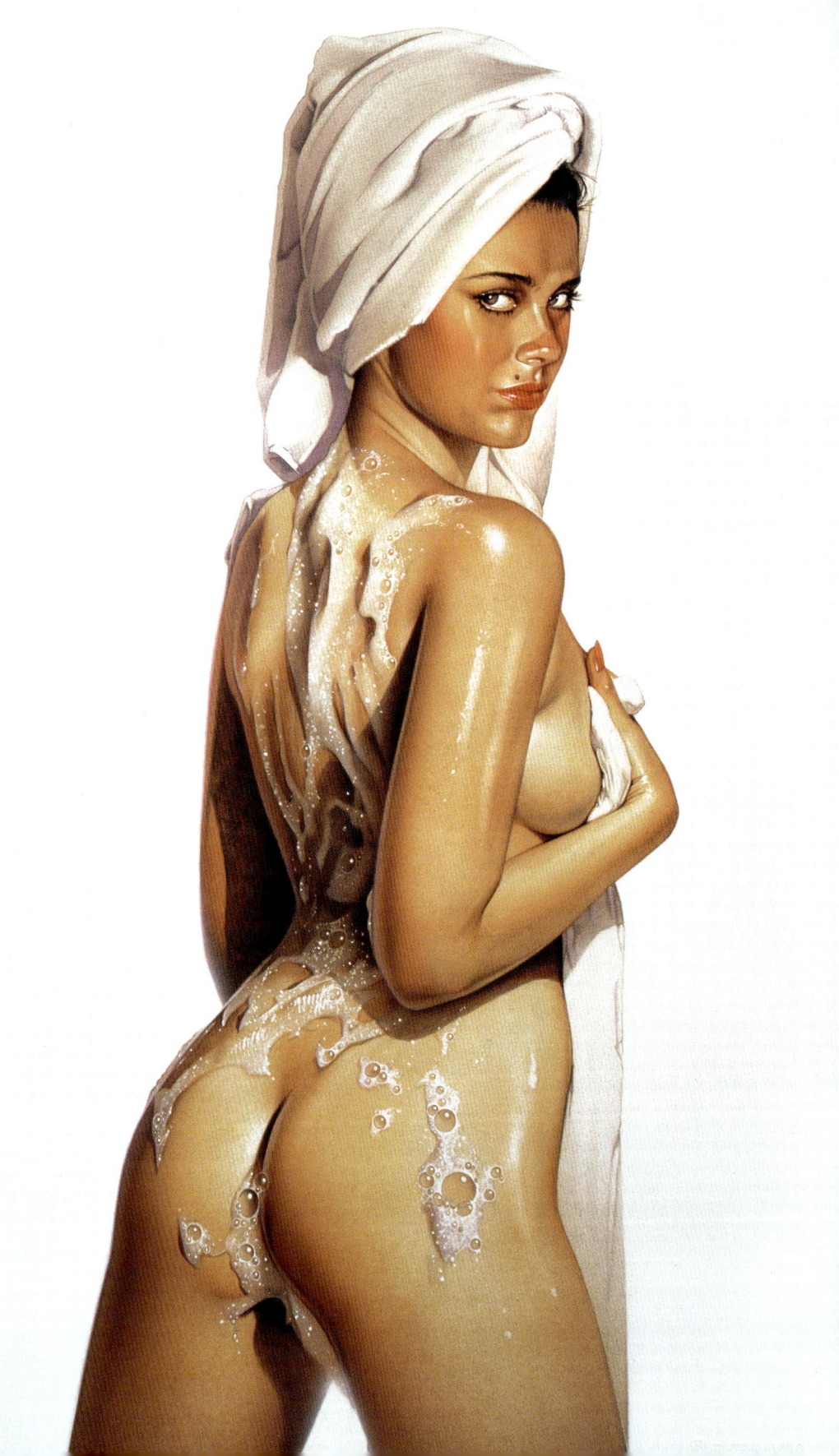

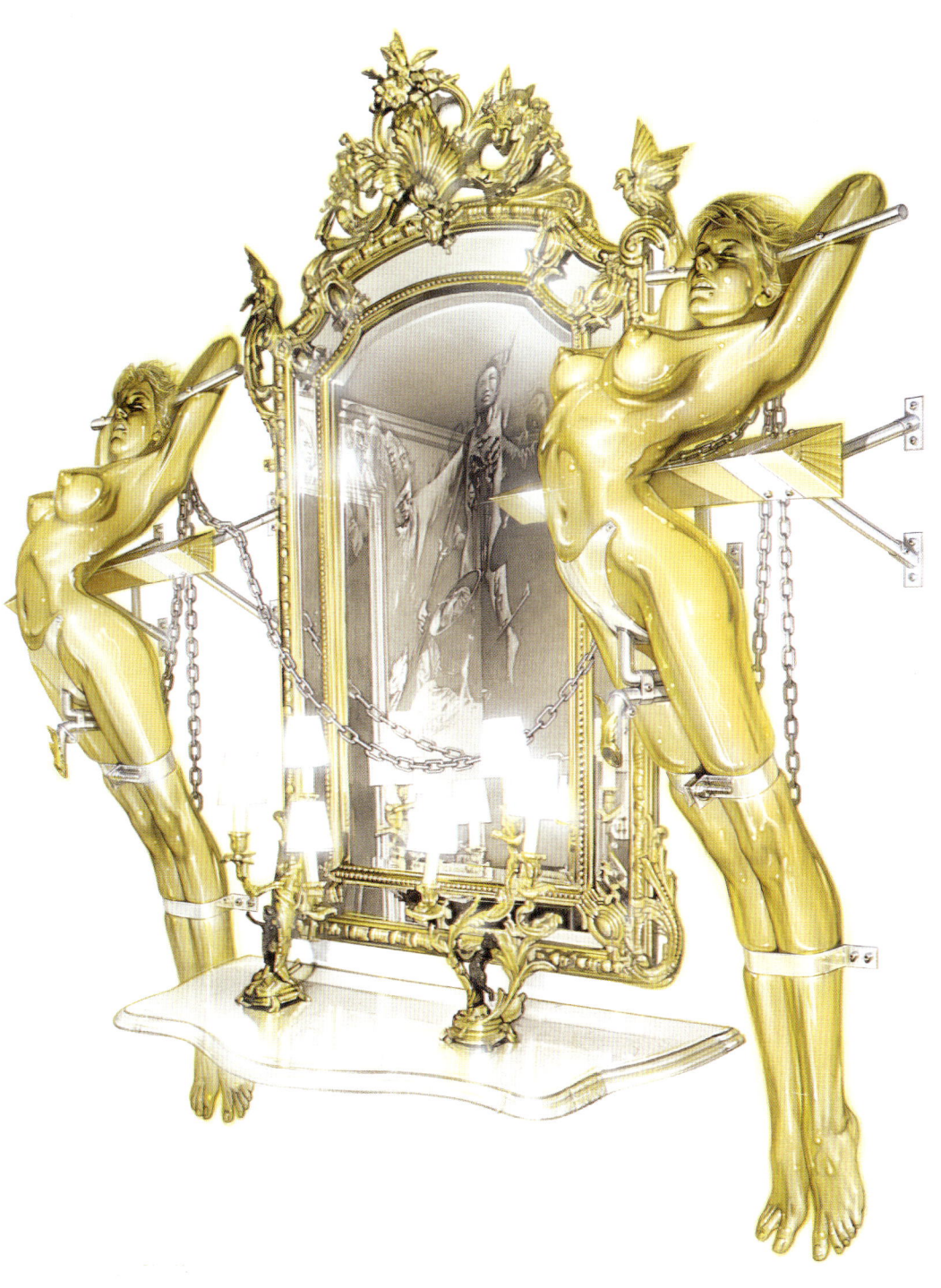

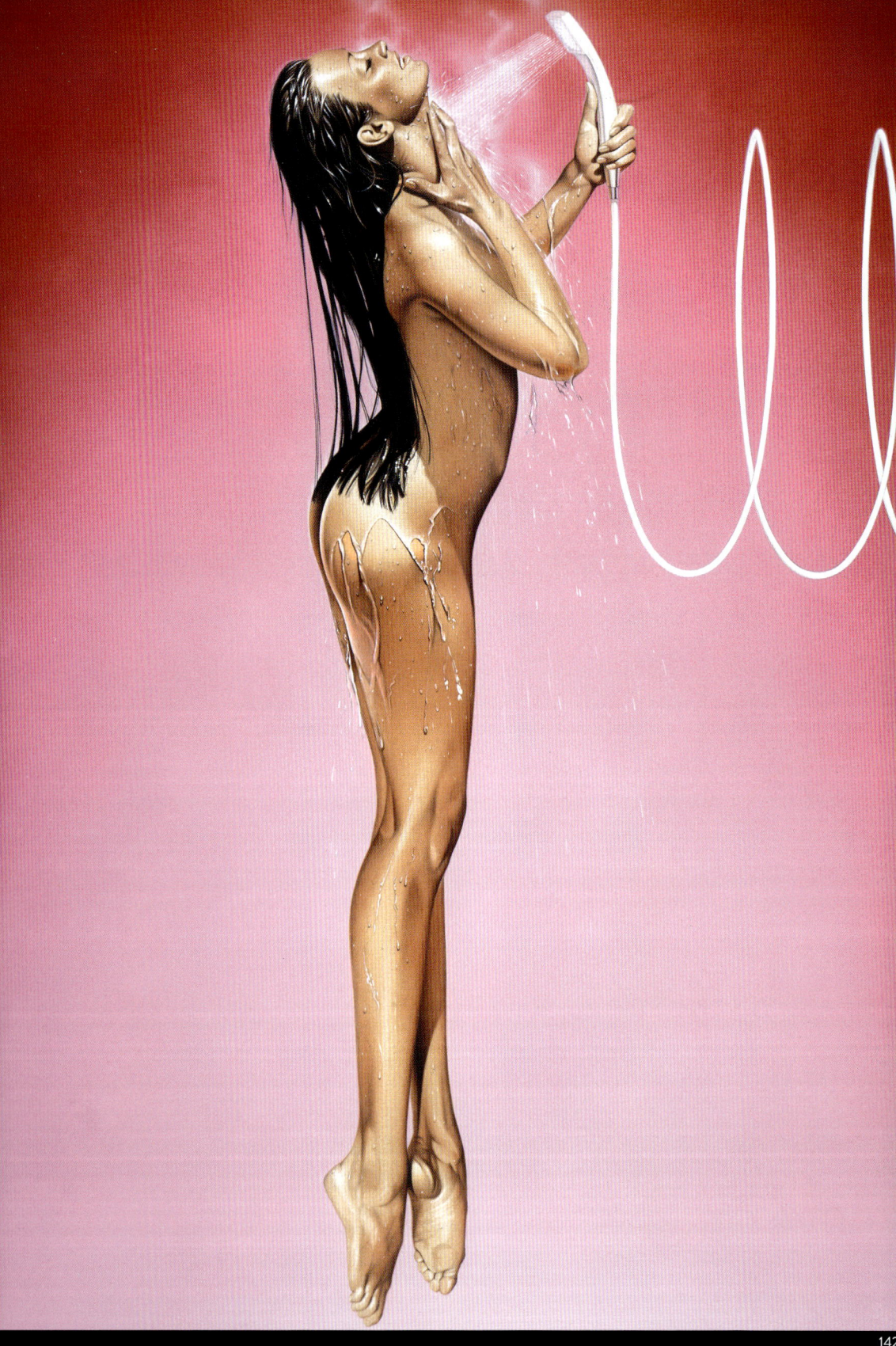

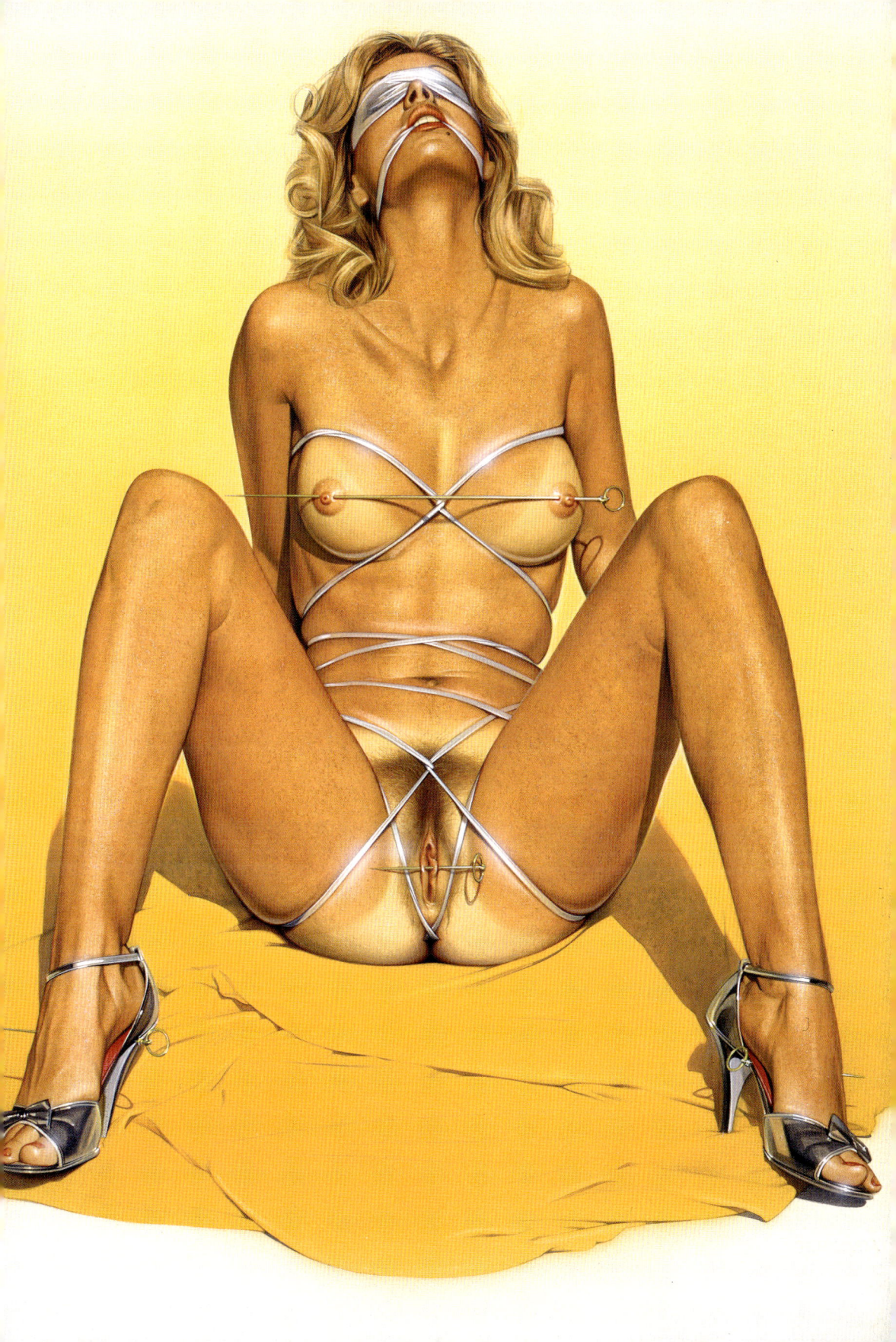

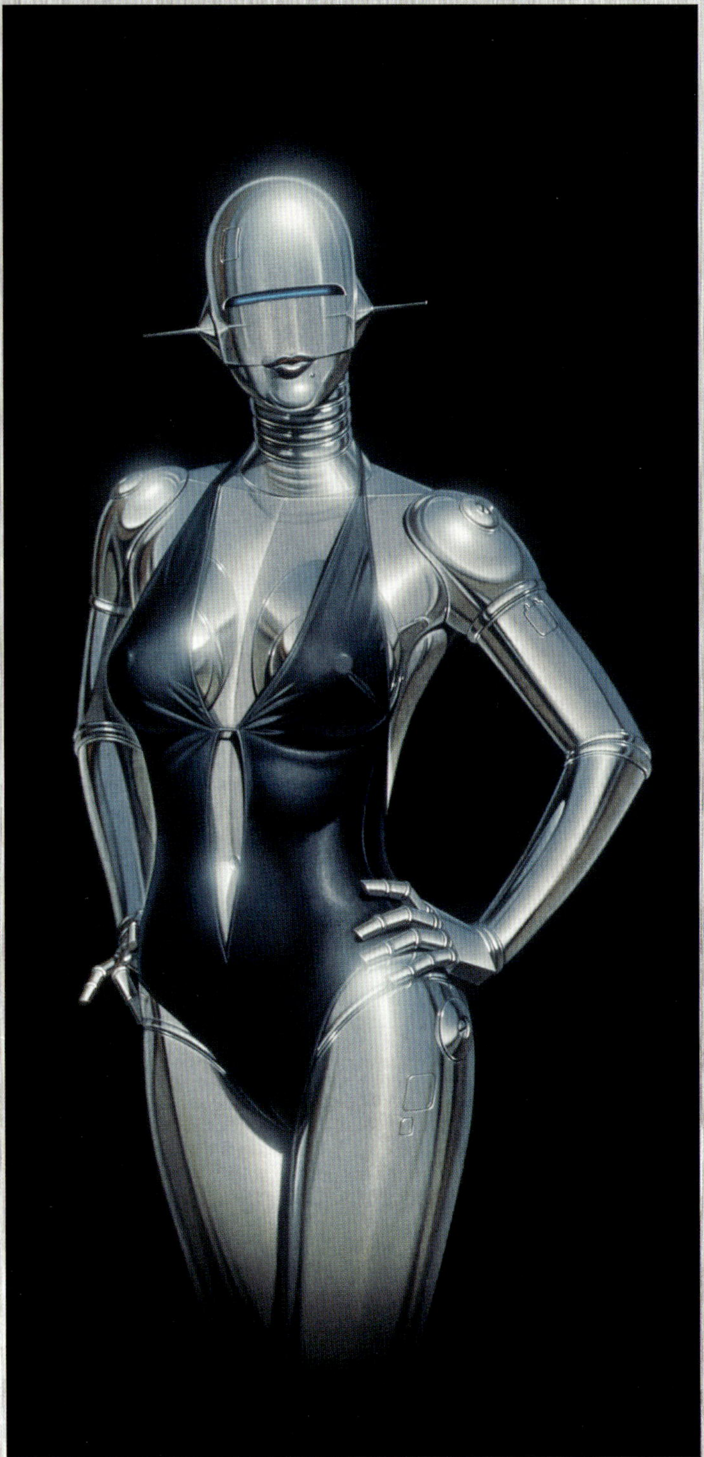

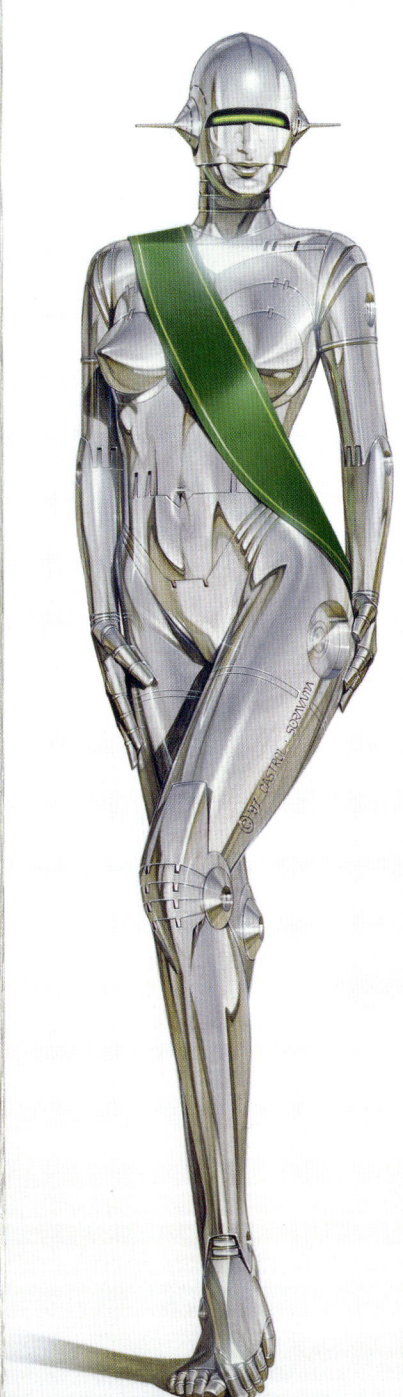

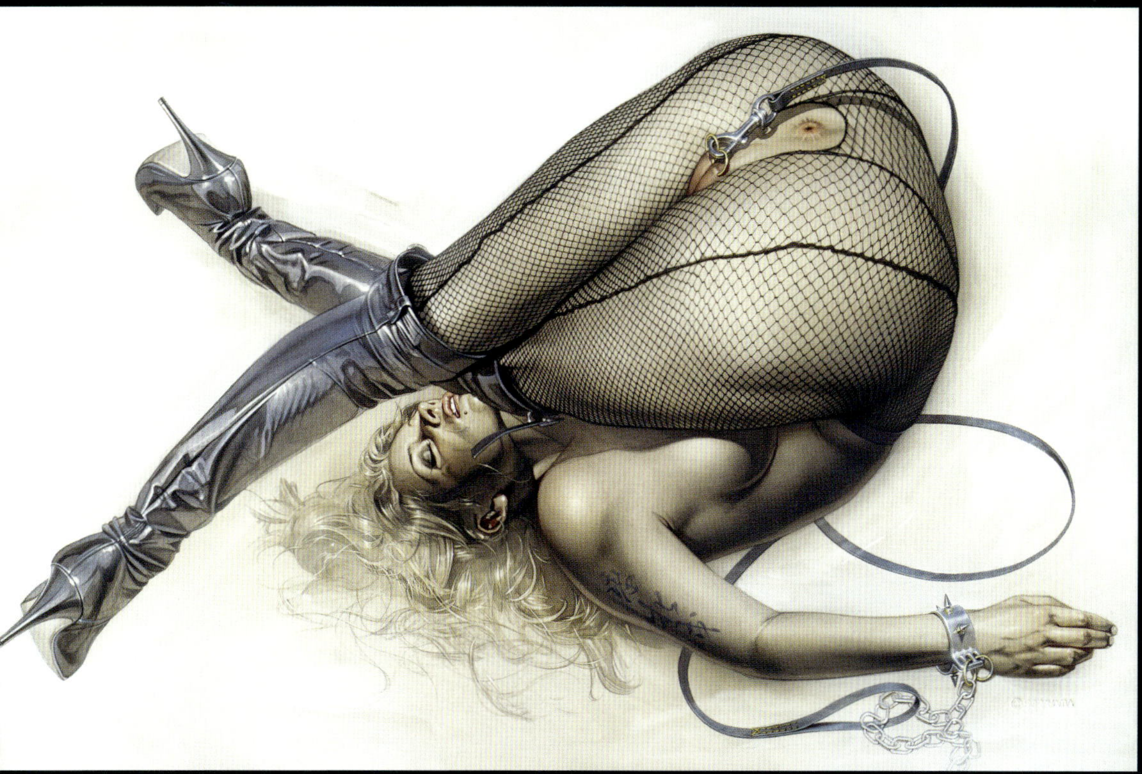

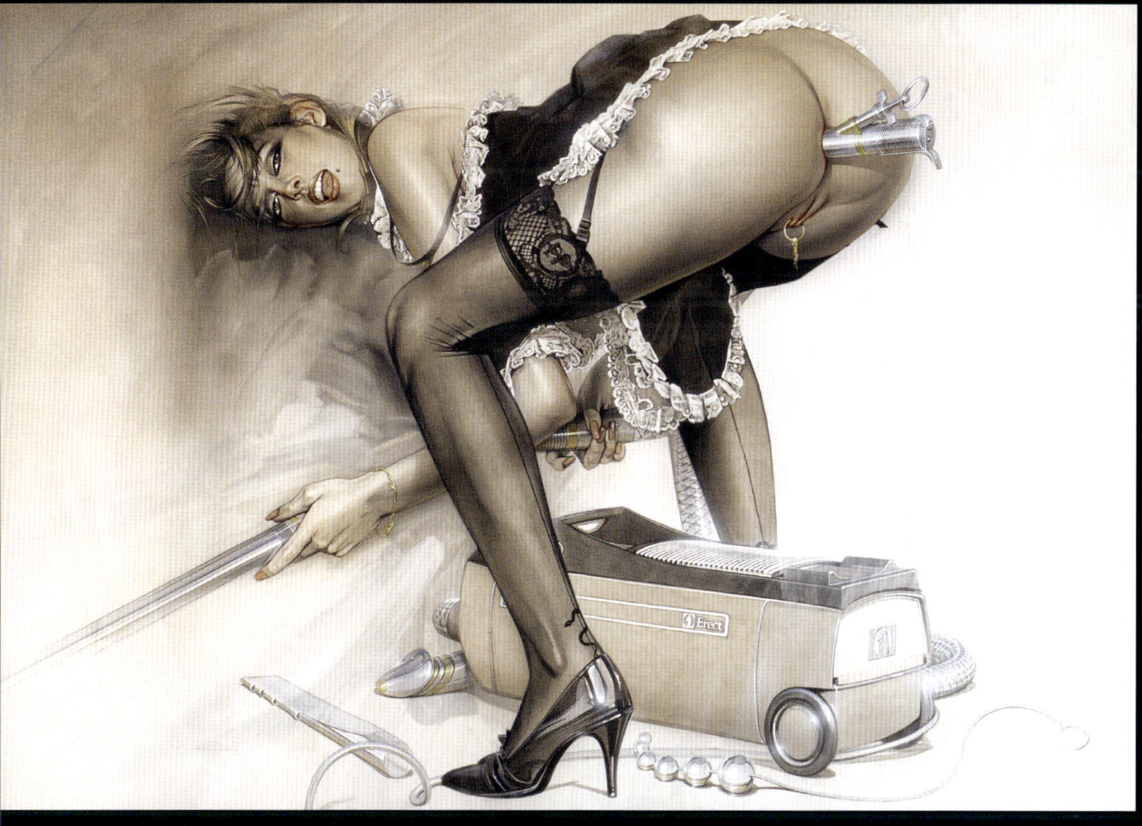
Erect

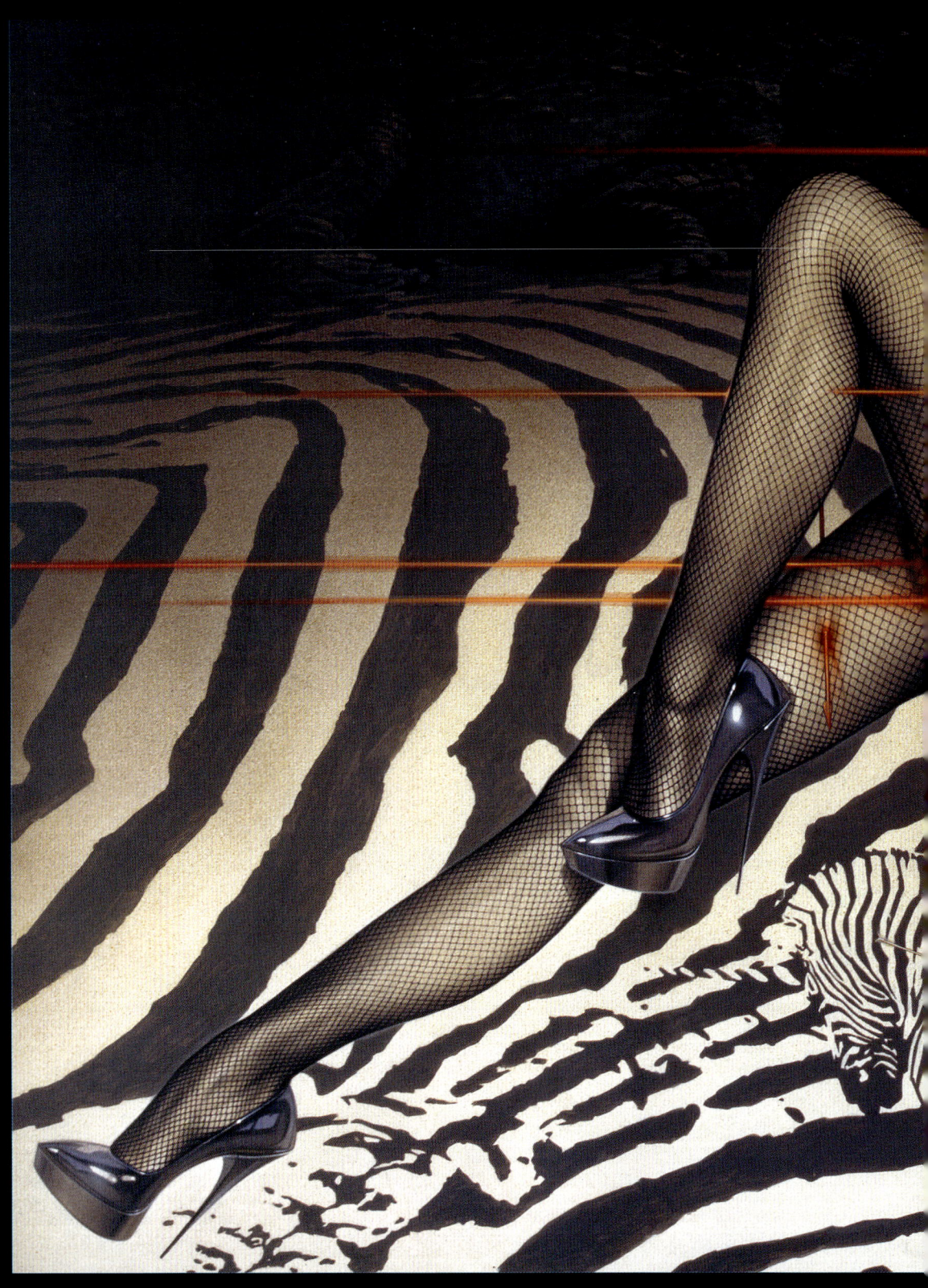

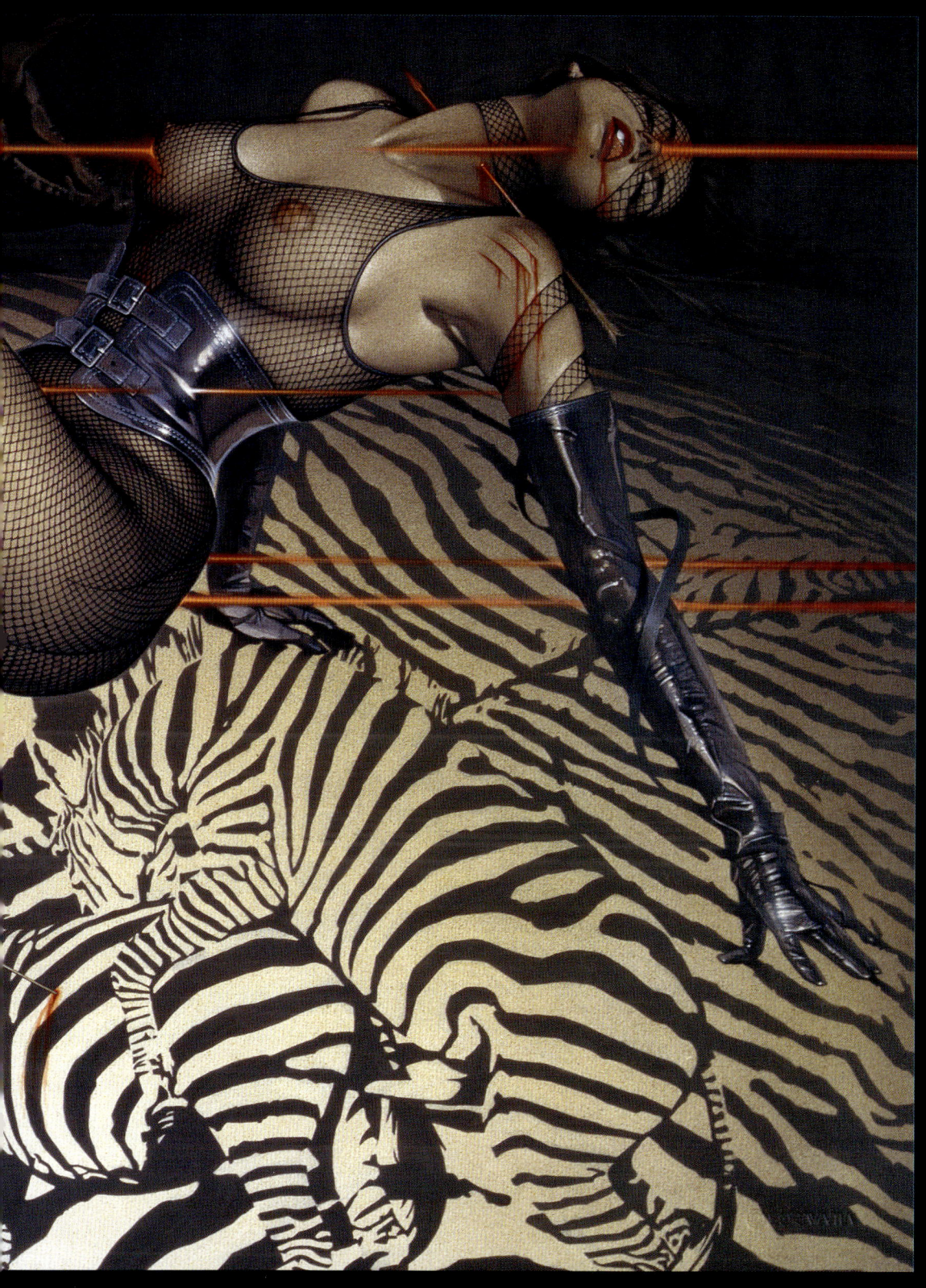

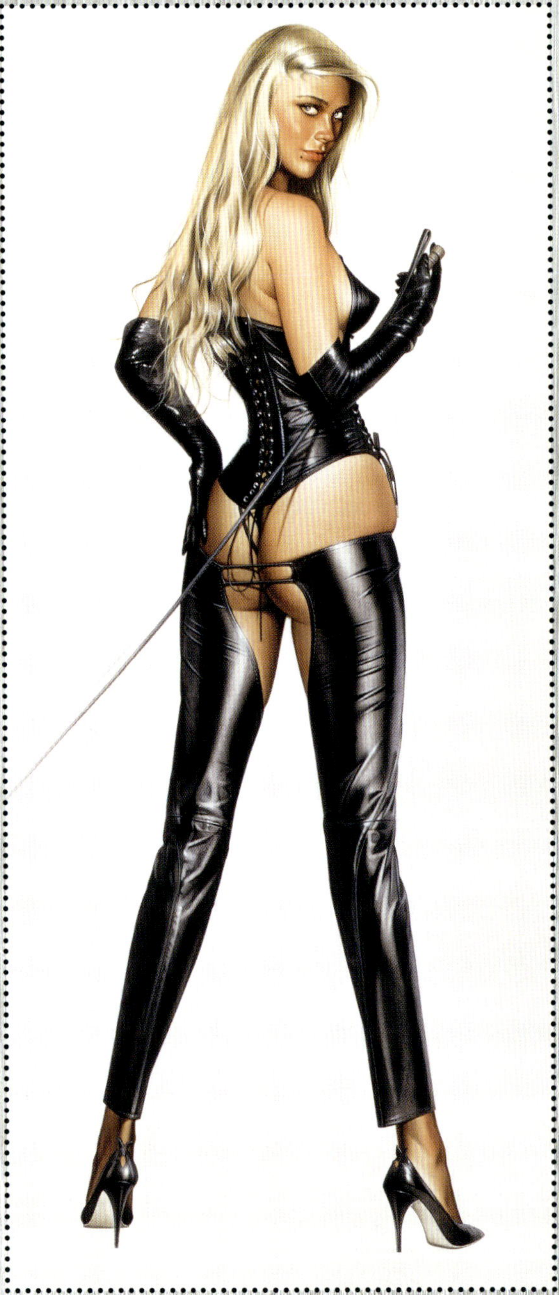

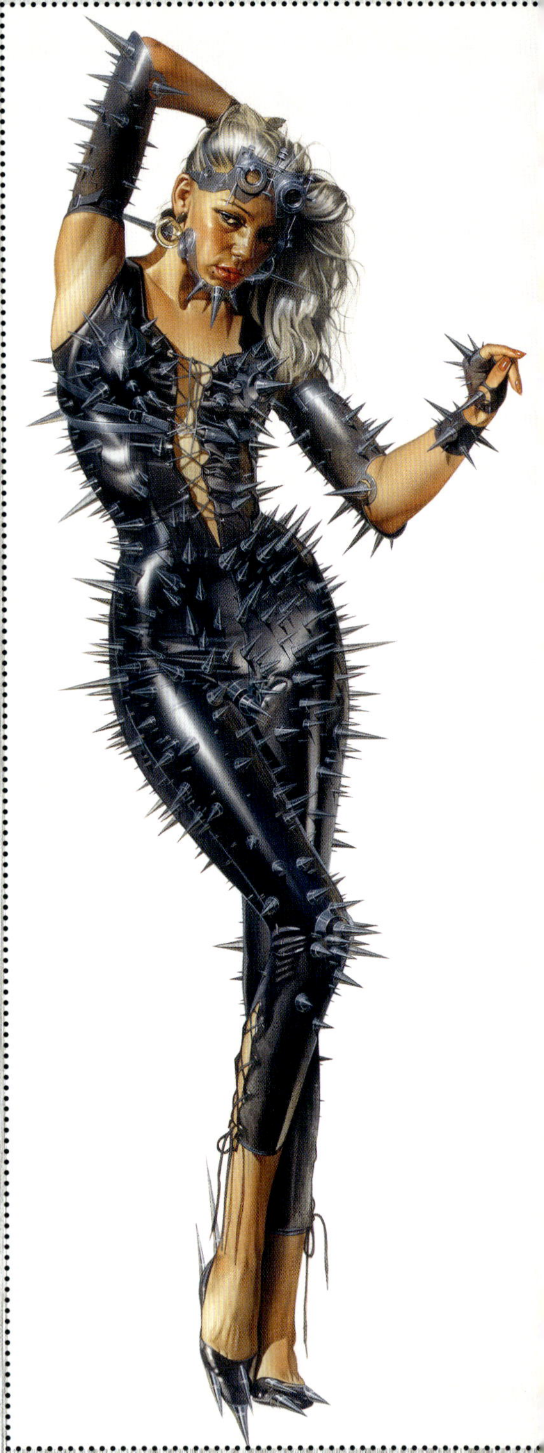

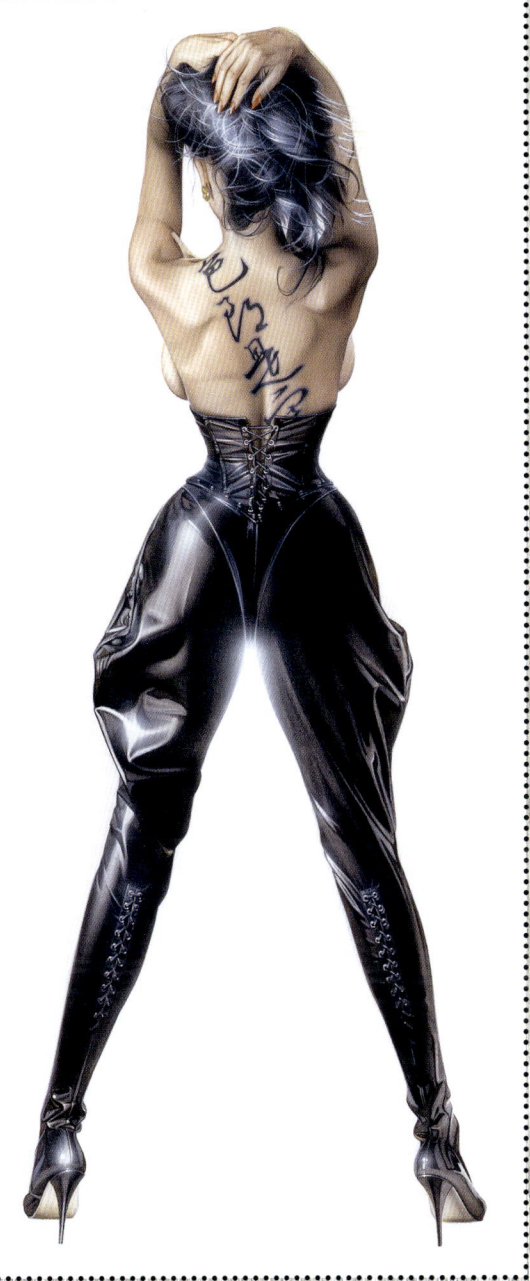

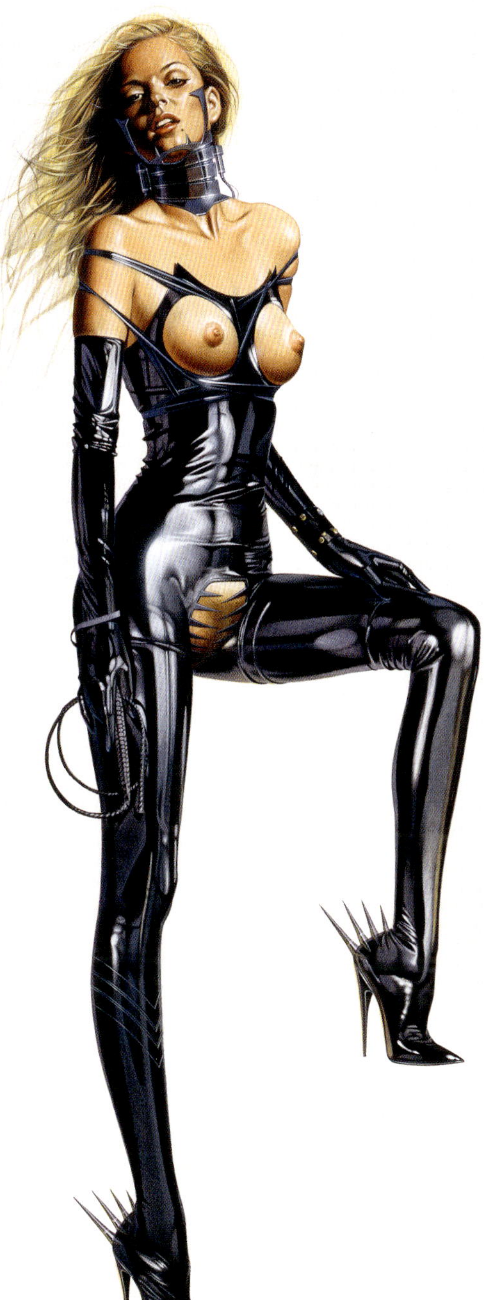

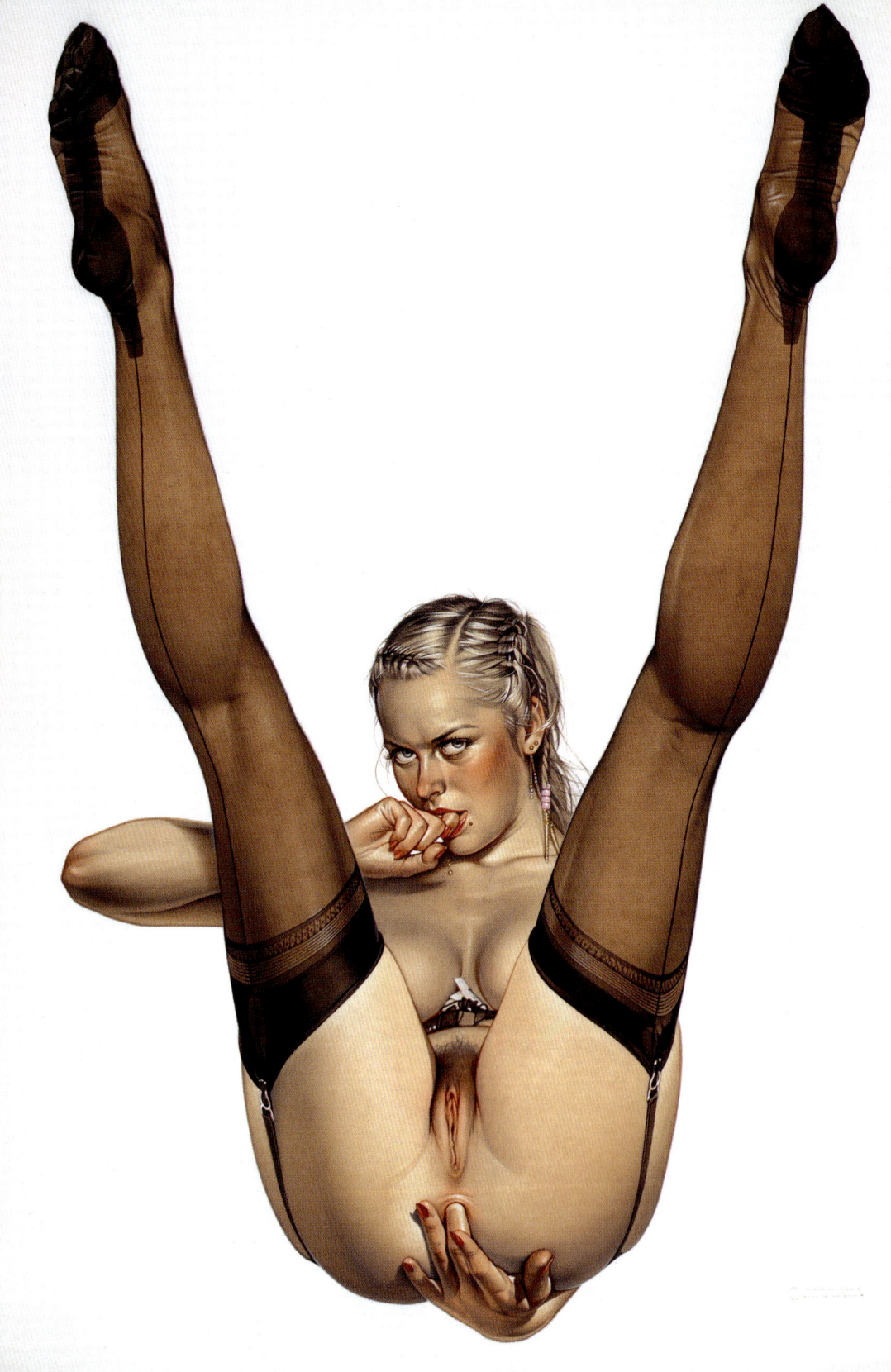

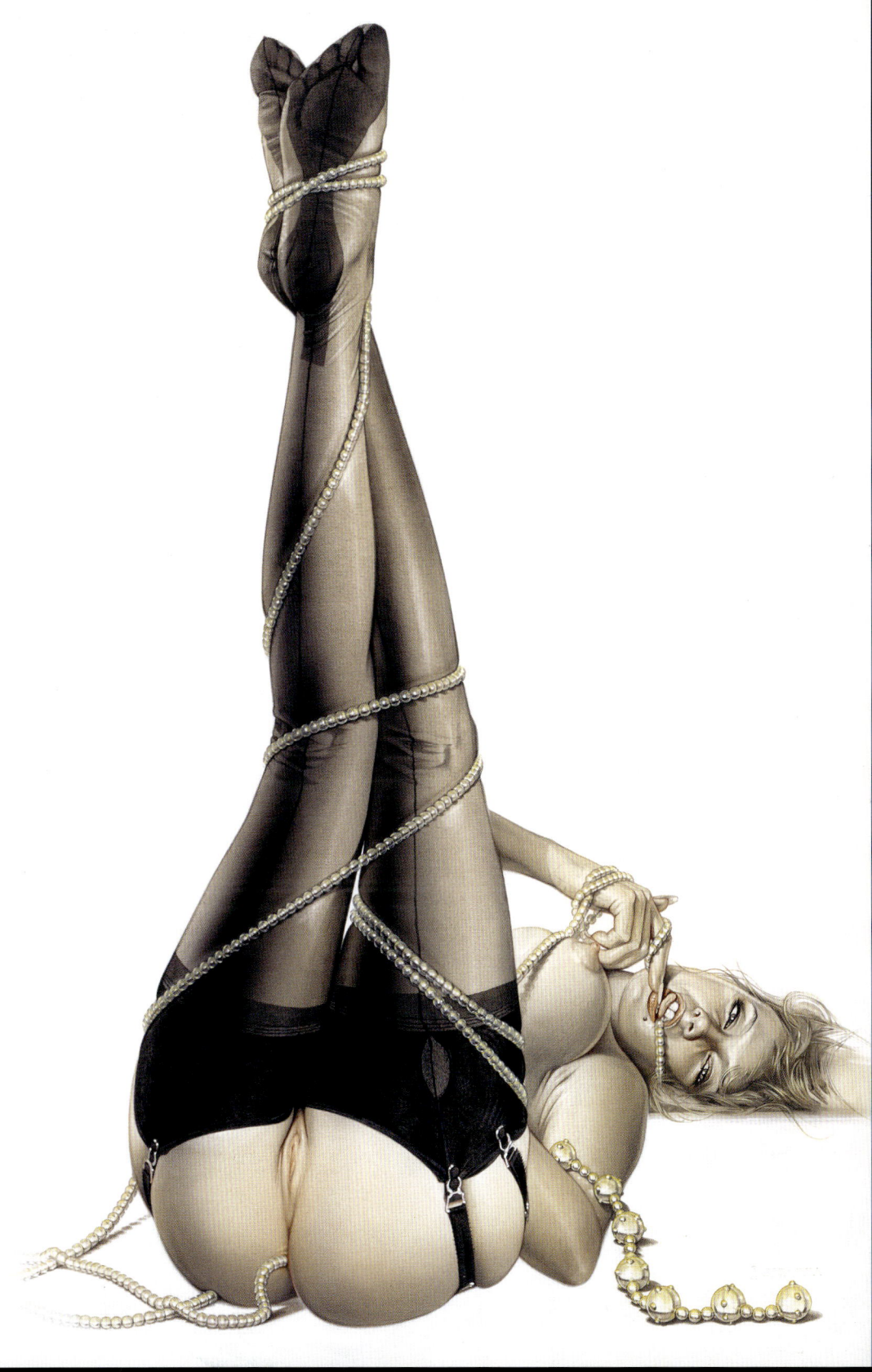

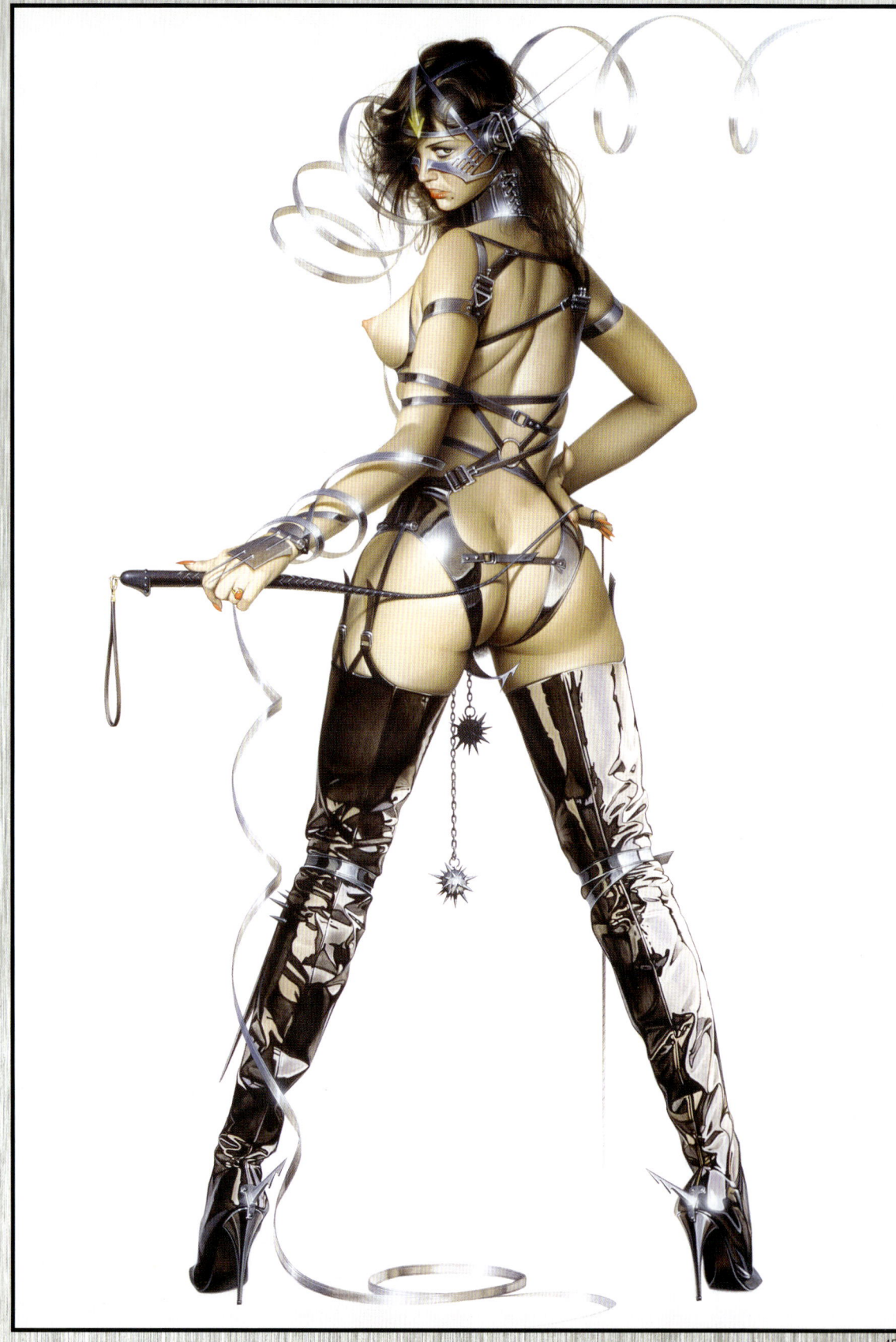

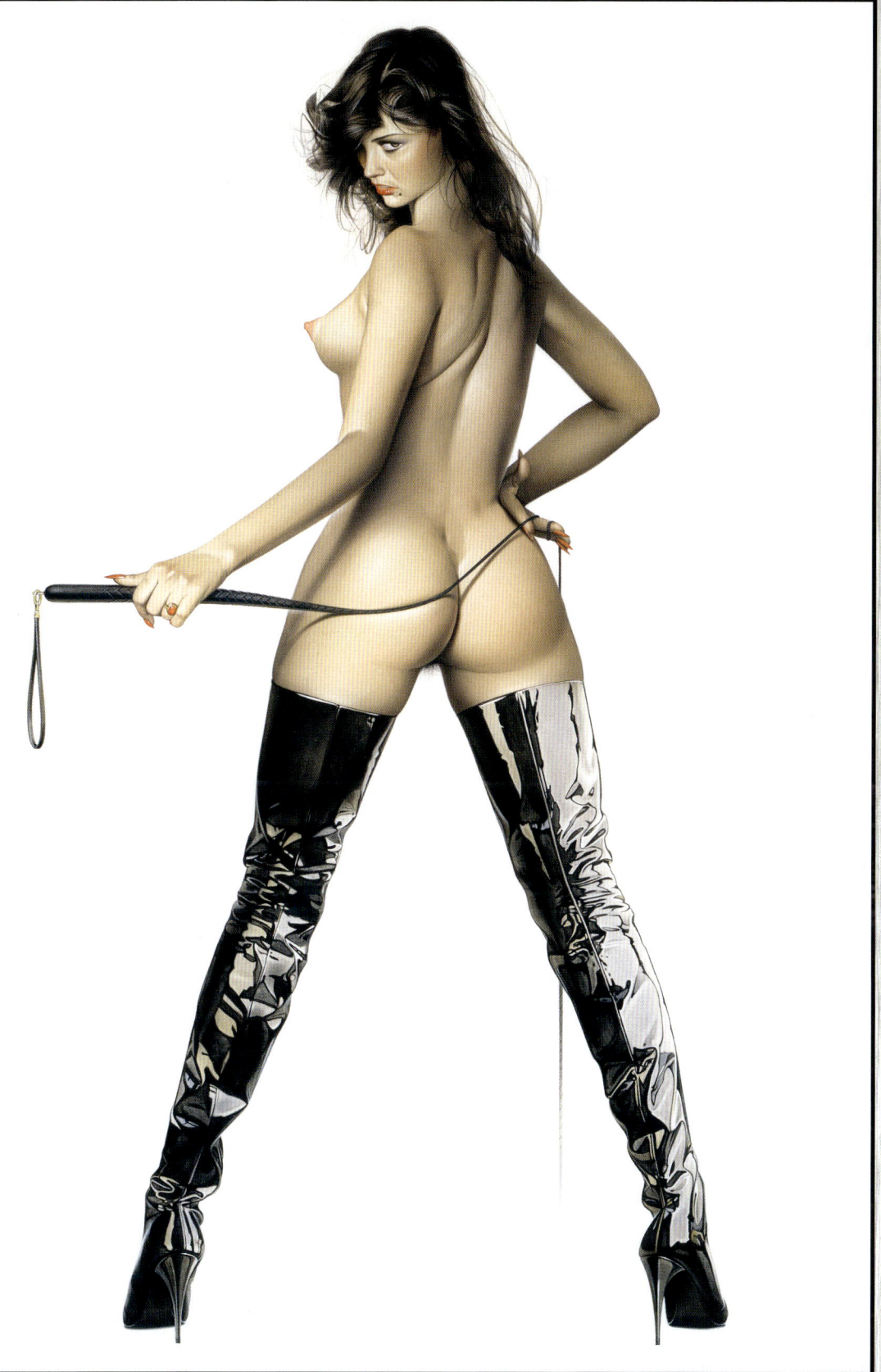

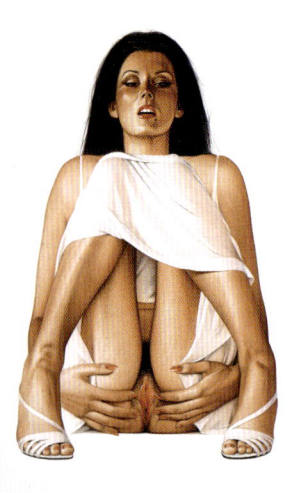
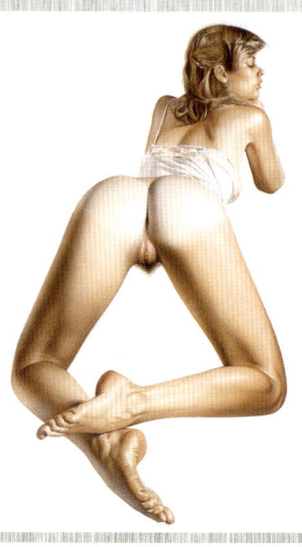
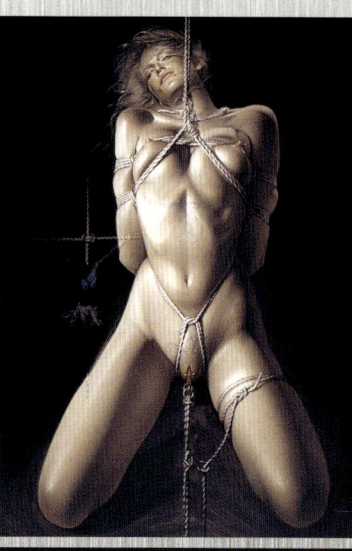
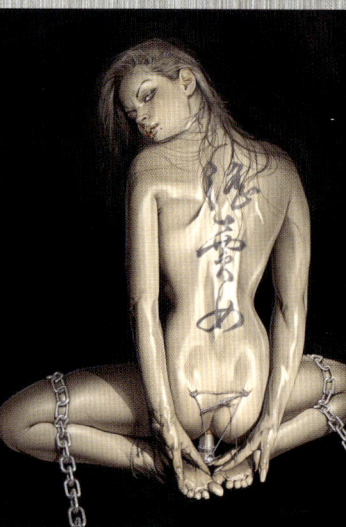
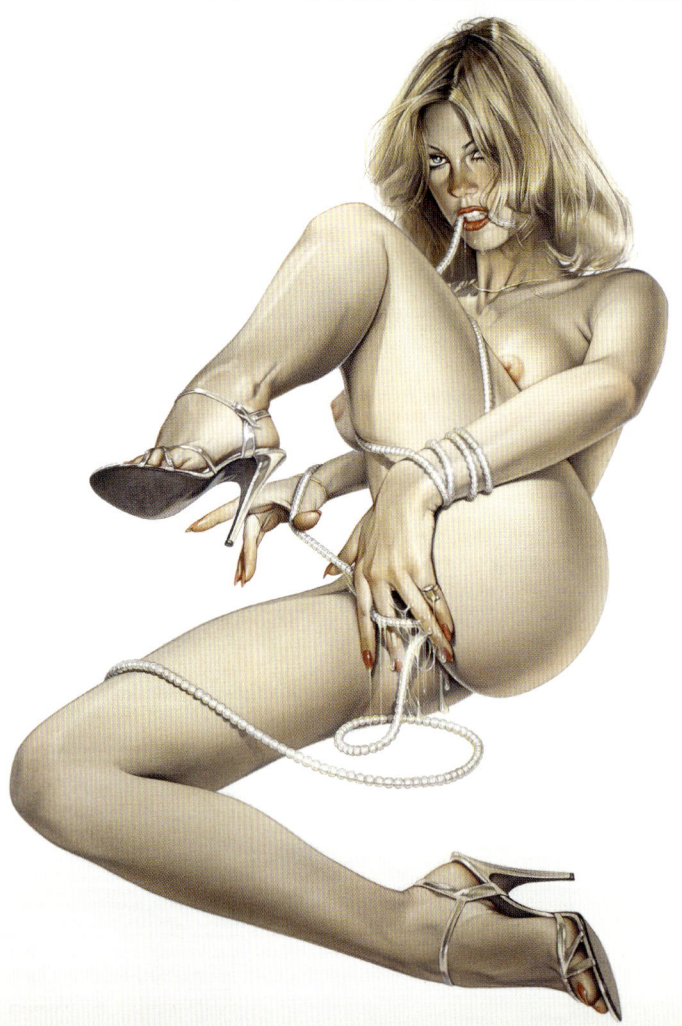
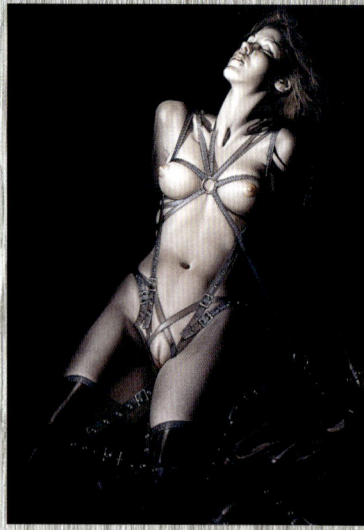

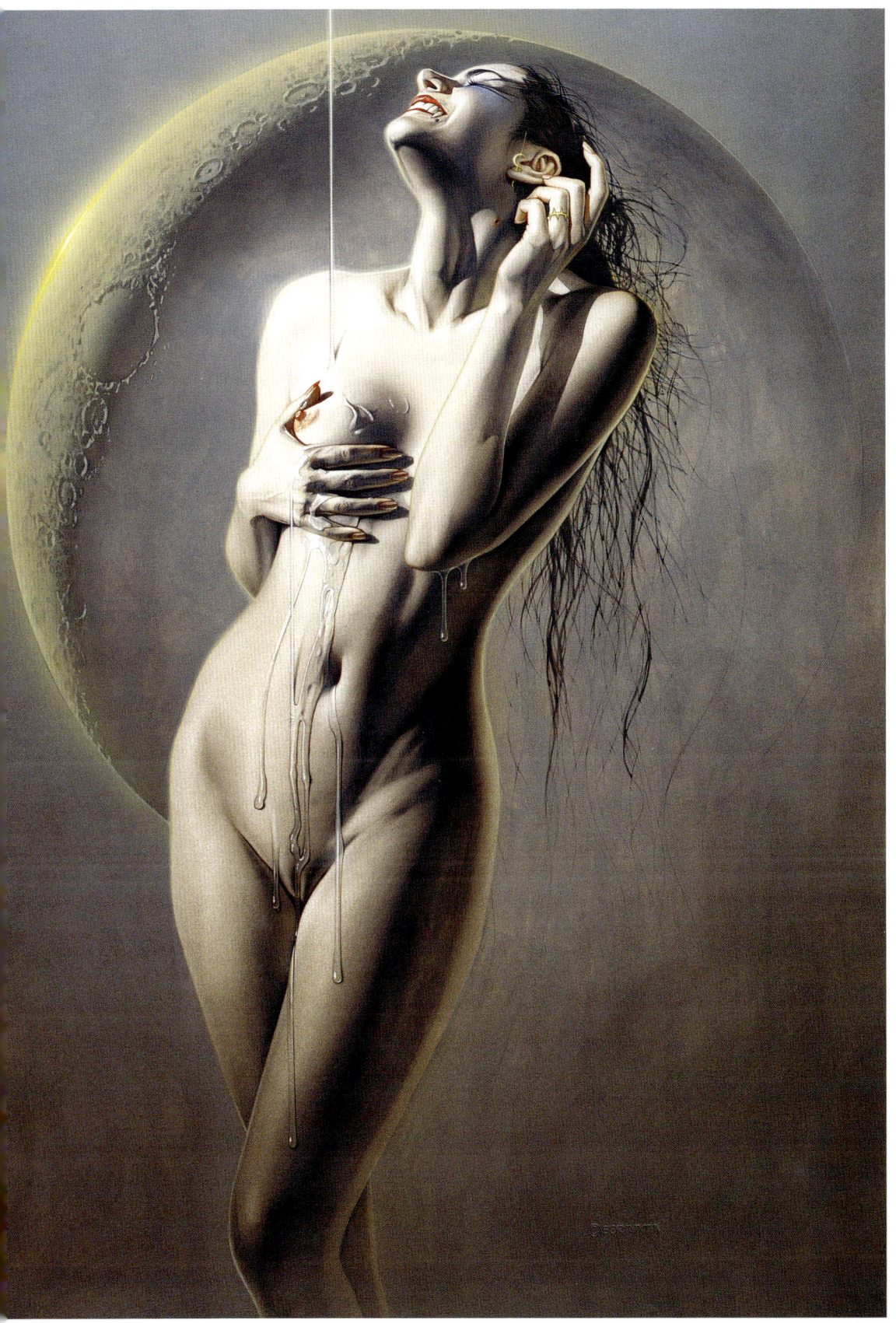

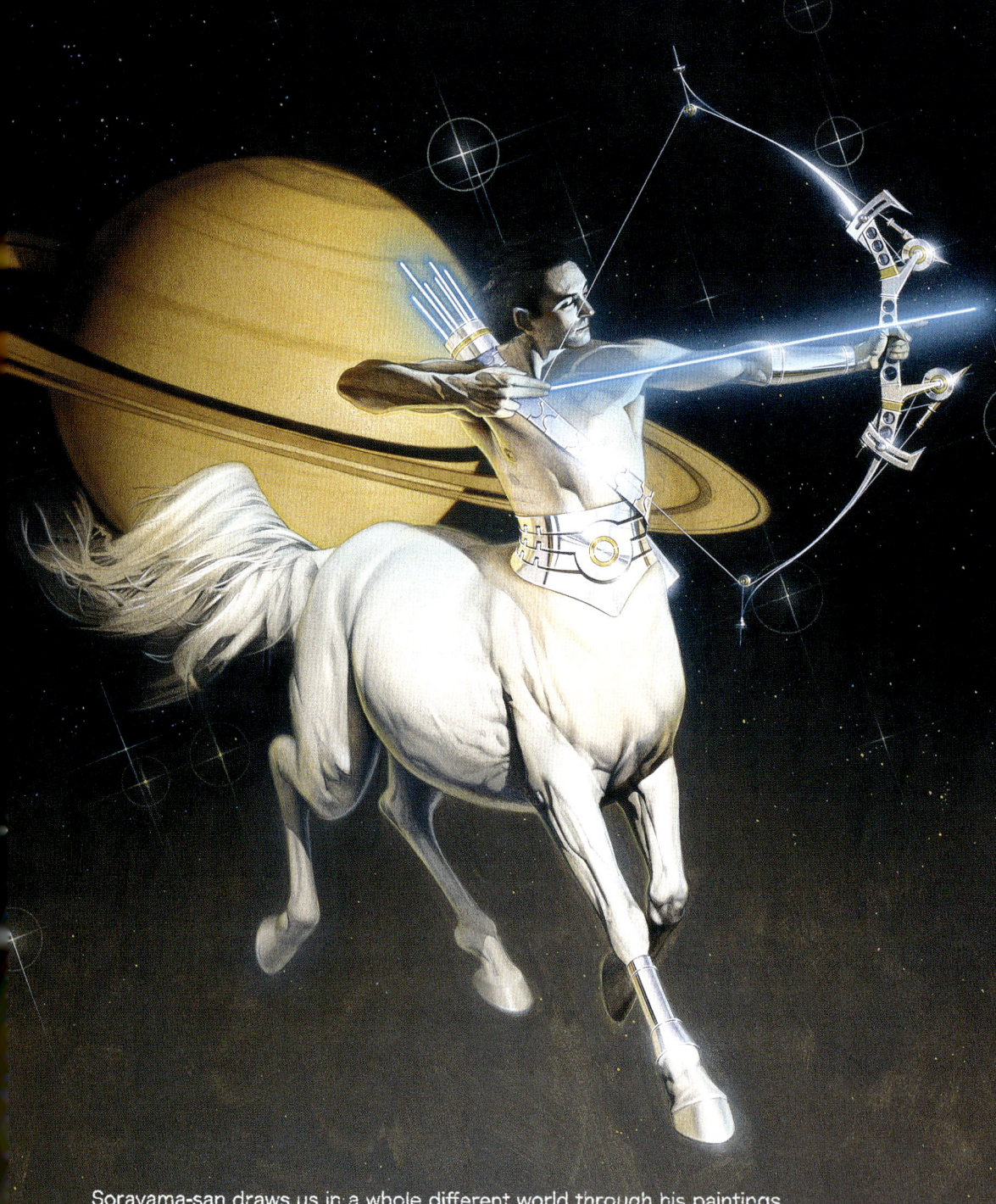

Sorayama-san draws us in a whole different world through his paintings, allowing us to experience the unexpected, which represent that fusion of reality and fantasy that is beyond 'super realism'.

Wonderwall

Masamichi Katayama

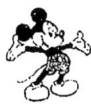

The (Walt Disney) Company (Japan) Ltd.

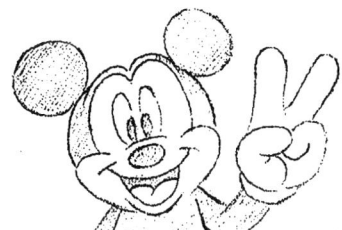

Disney Consumer Products
Walt Disney Japan

Stephen Chianese

Soriyama-san has been a great partner & inspiration of mine since we first met in 2003. My interaction with him while @ Disney consisted of trouble free requests, with 'Art' the priority. That always made my job easy... Well.. Maybe NOT! It often seemed that although Soriyama-san's unique love & passion for Disney, his sole mission in life was to be as difficult as possible, making the creative process a headache — But in the end - we saw to it that his vision was achieved —

Best —

S. Chianese

ARCO TOWER, 1-8-1 Shimomeguro, Meguro-ku, Tokyo 153-8922 Japan

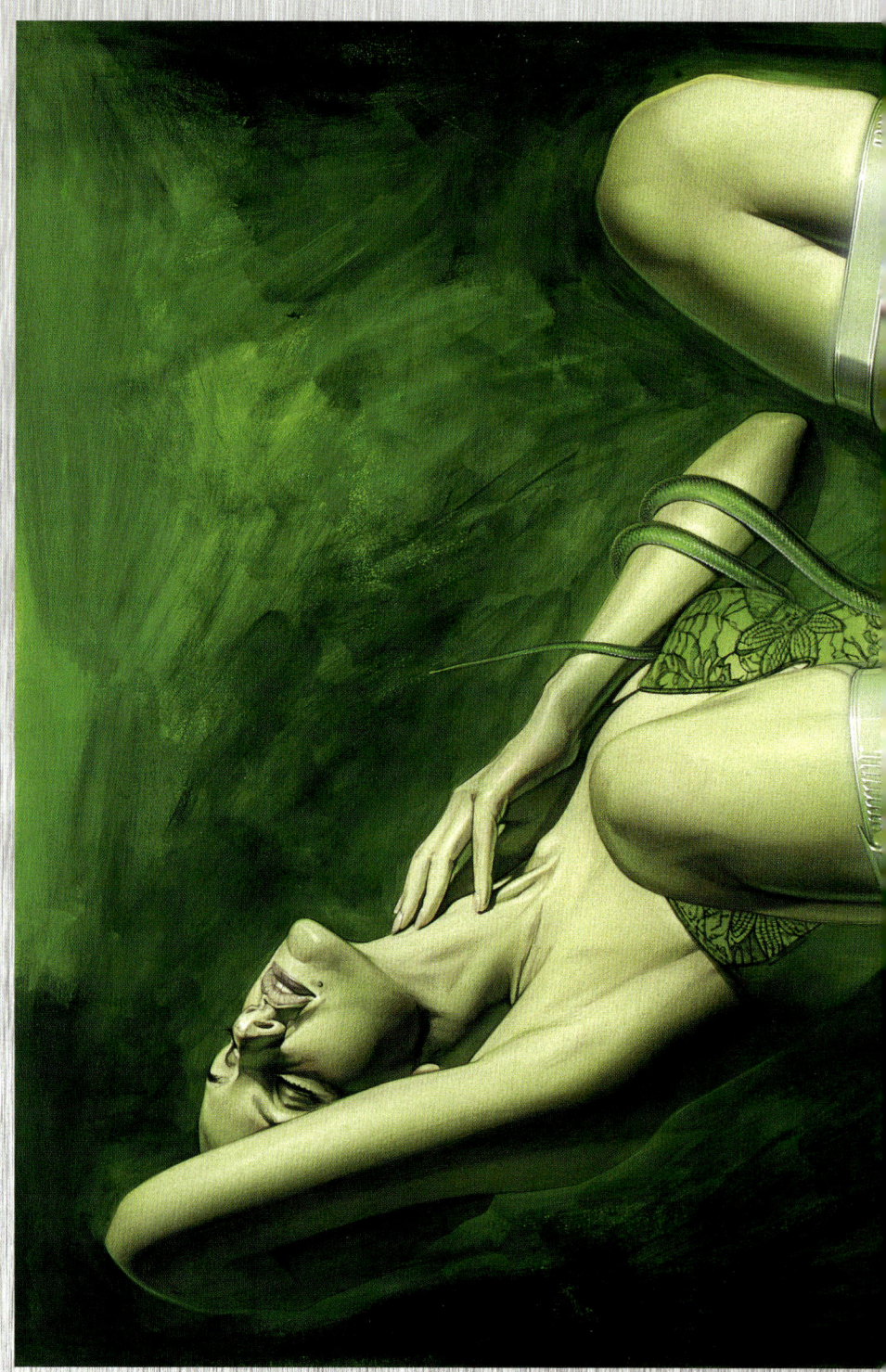

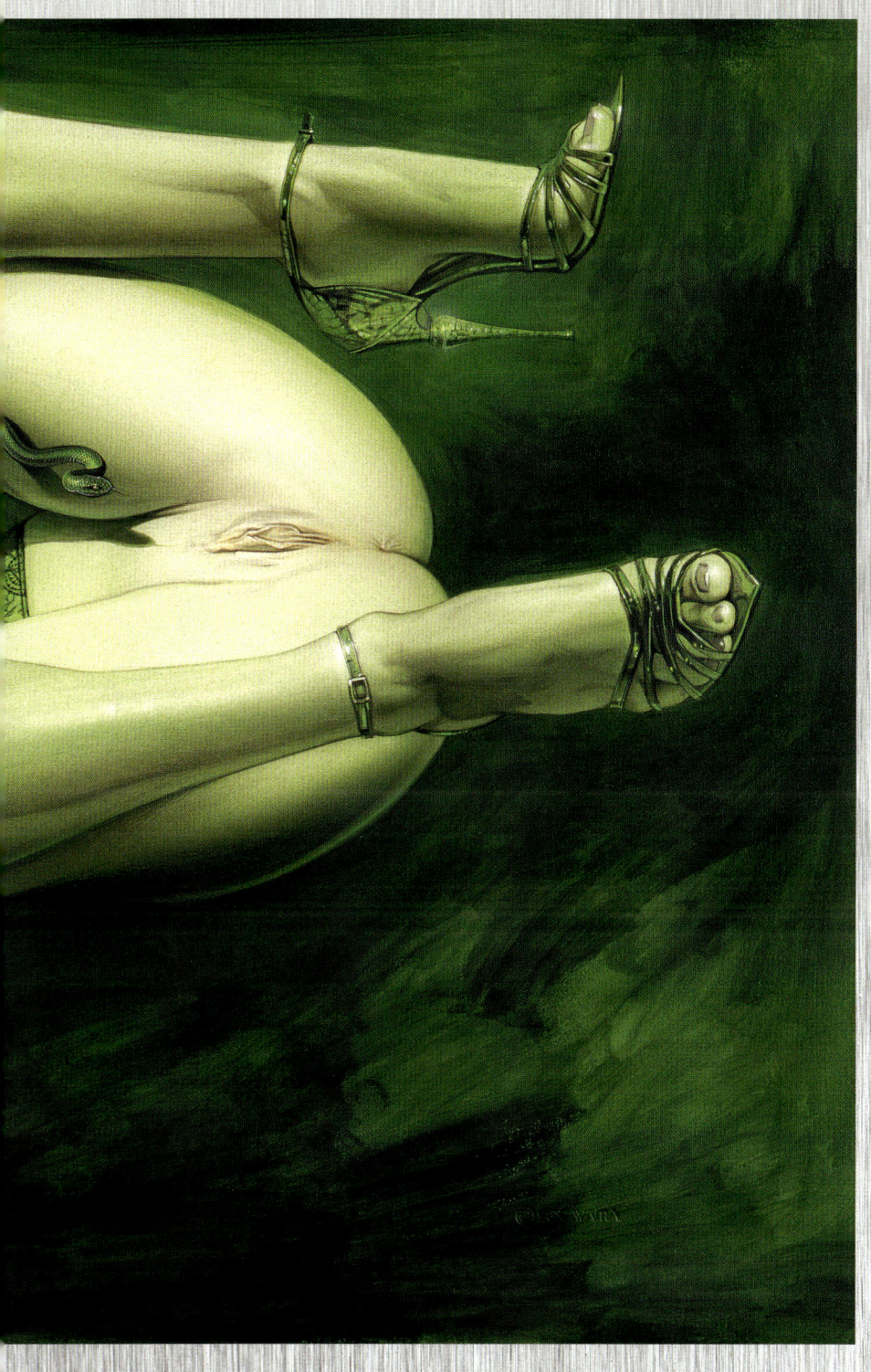

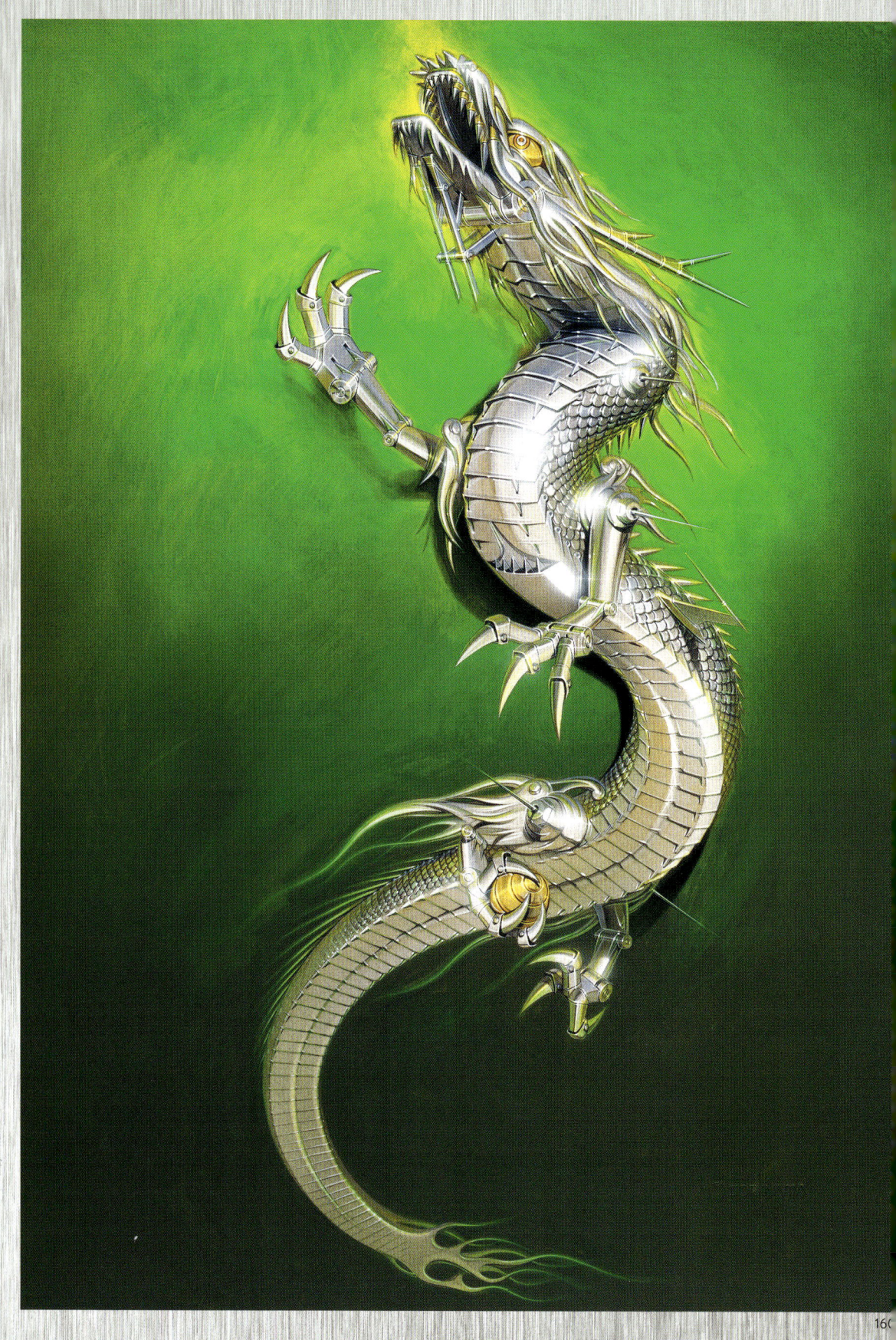

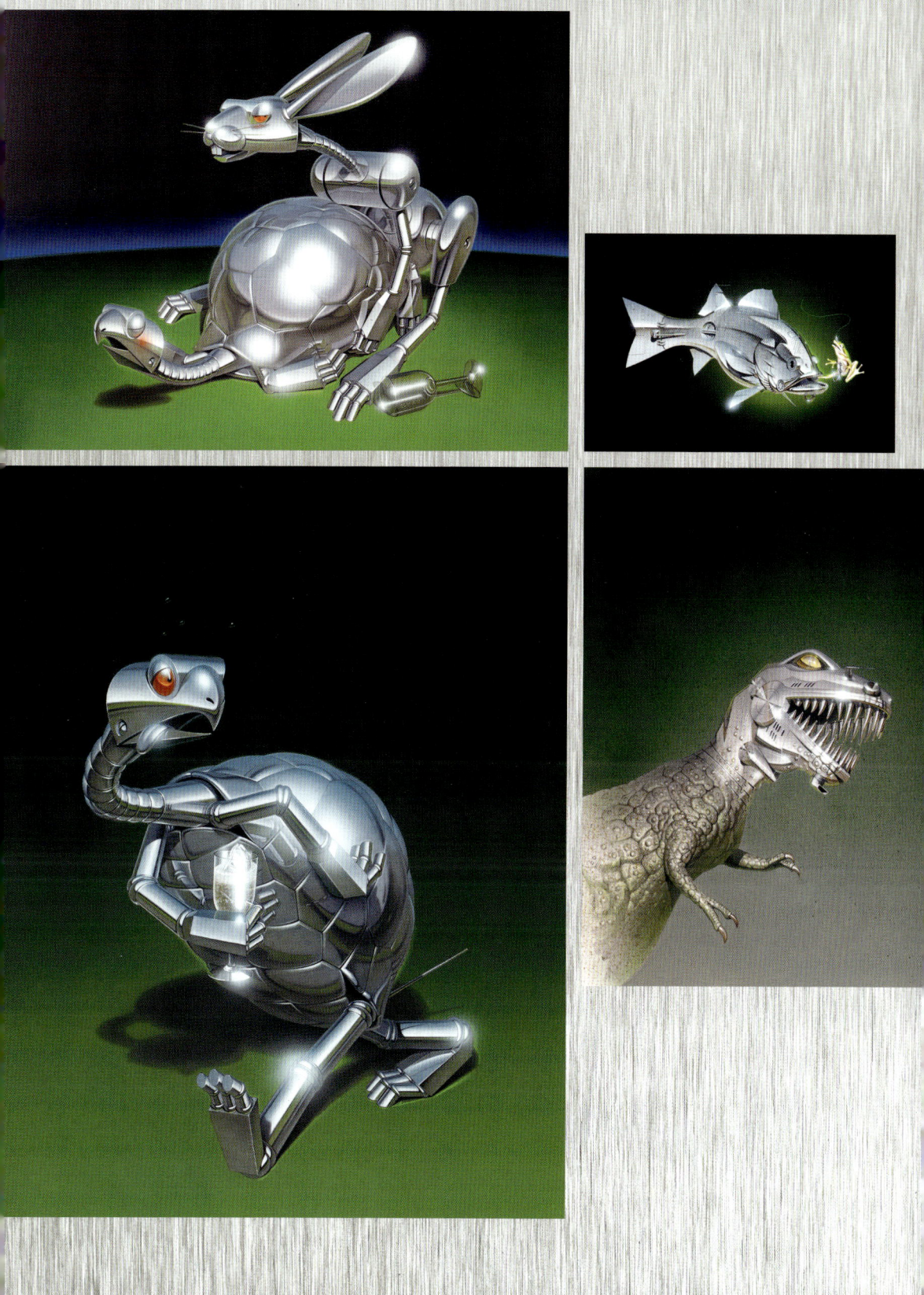

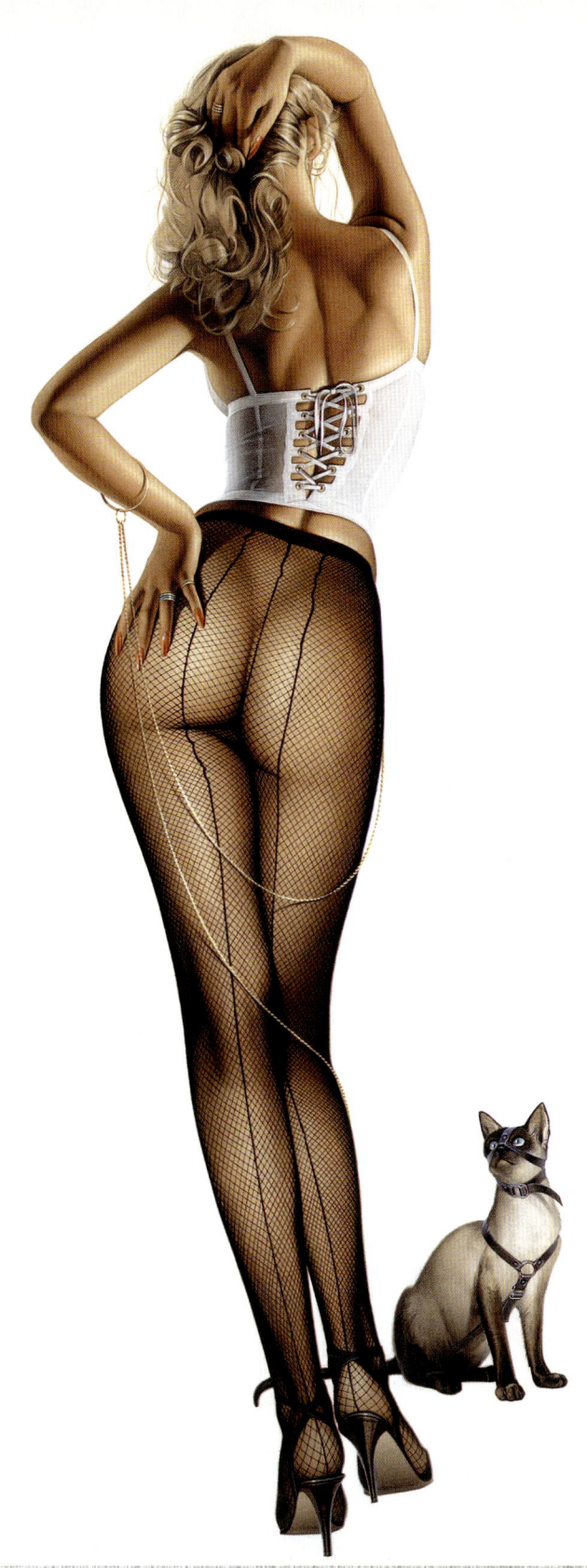

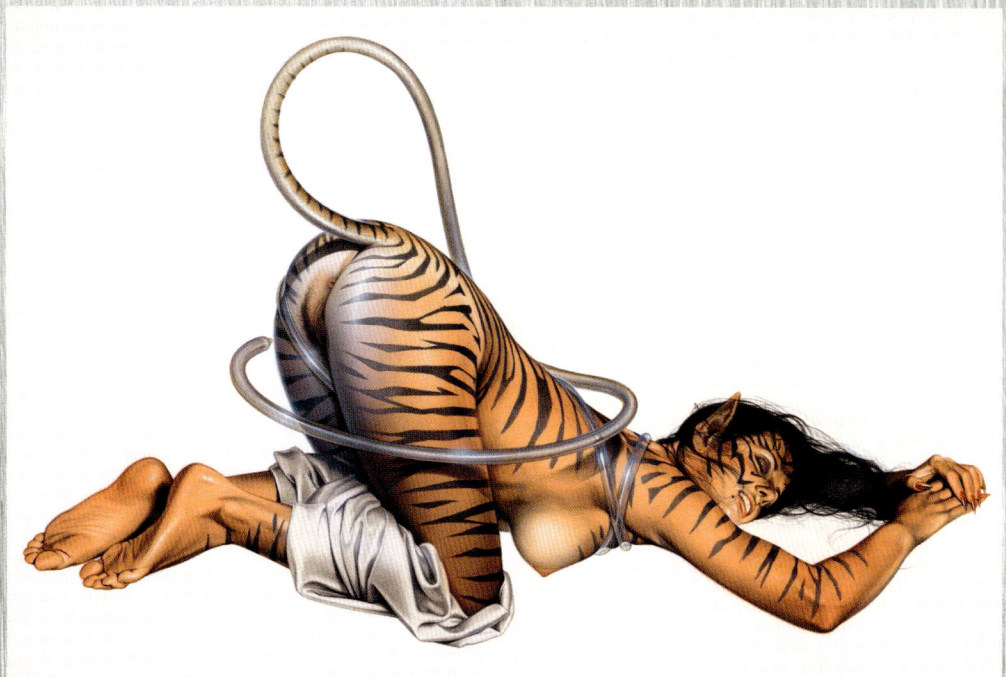

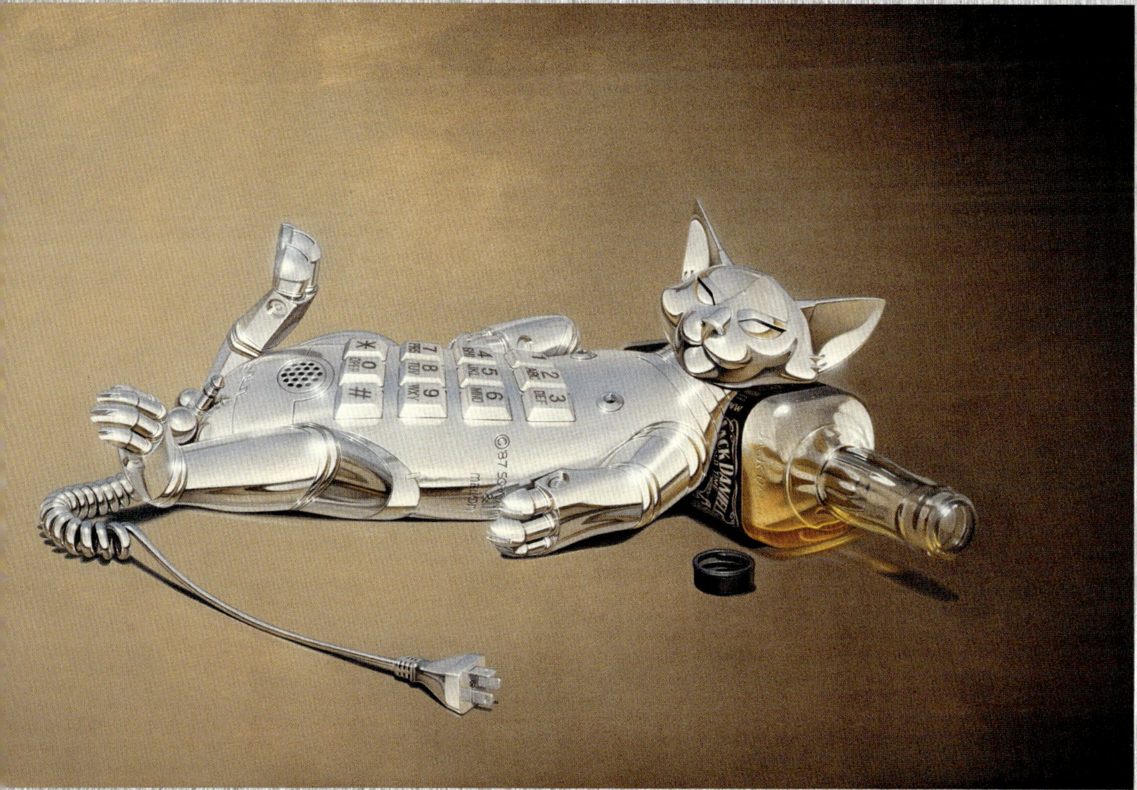

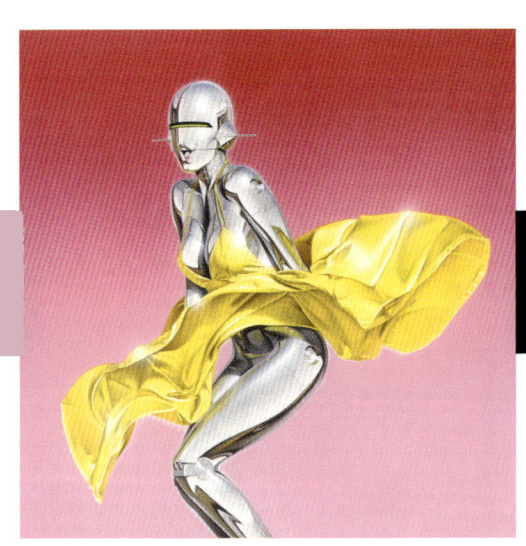

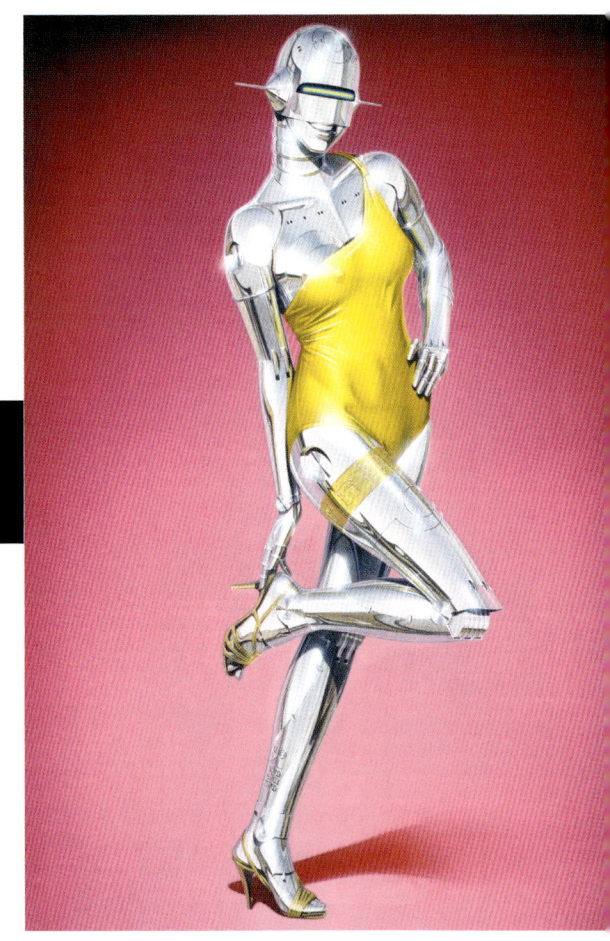

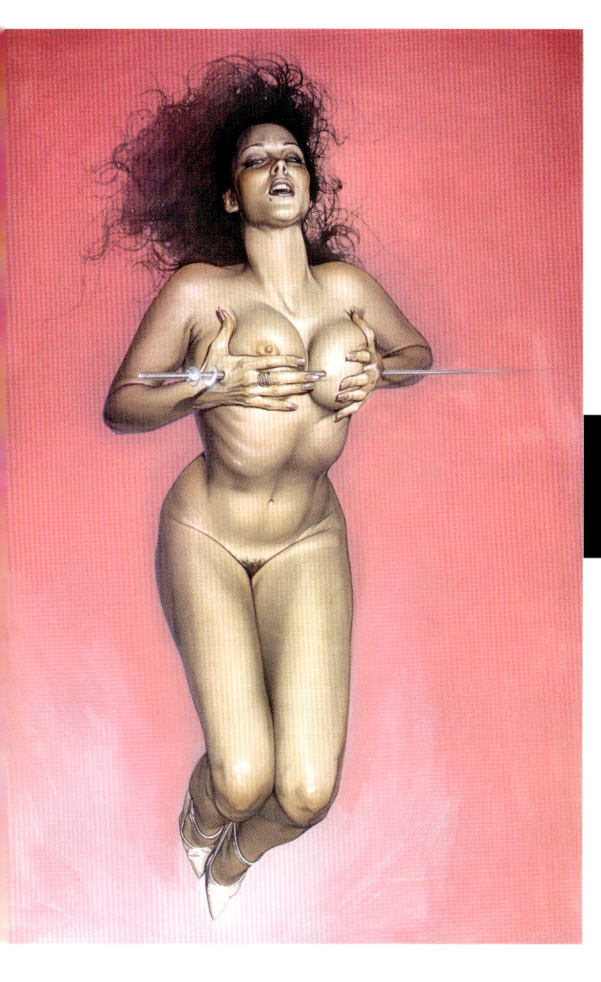

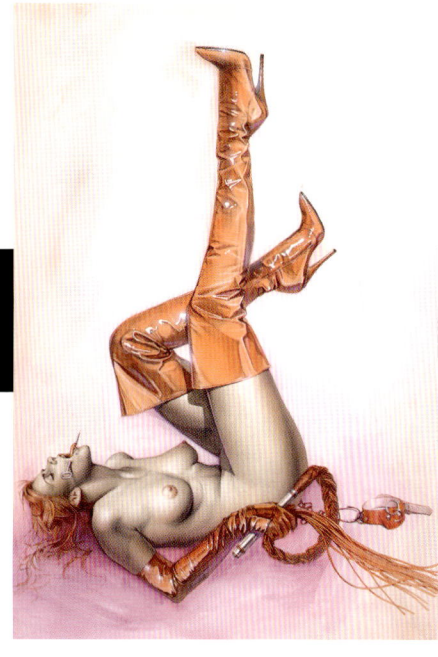

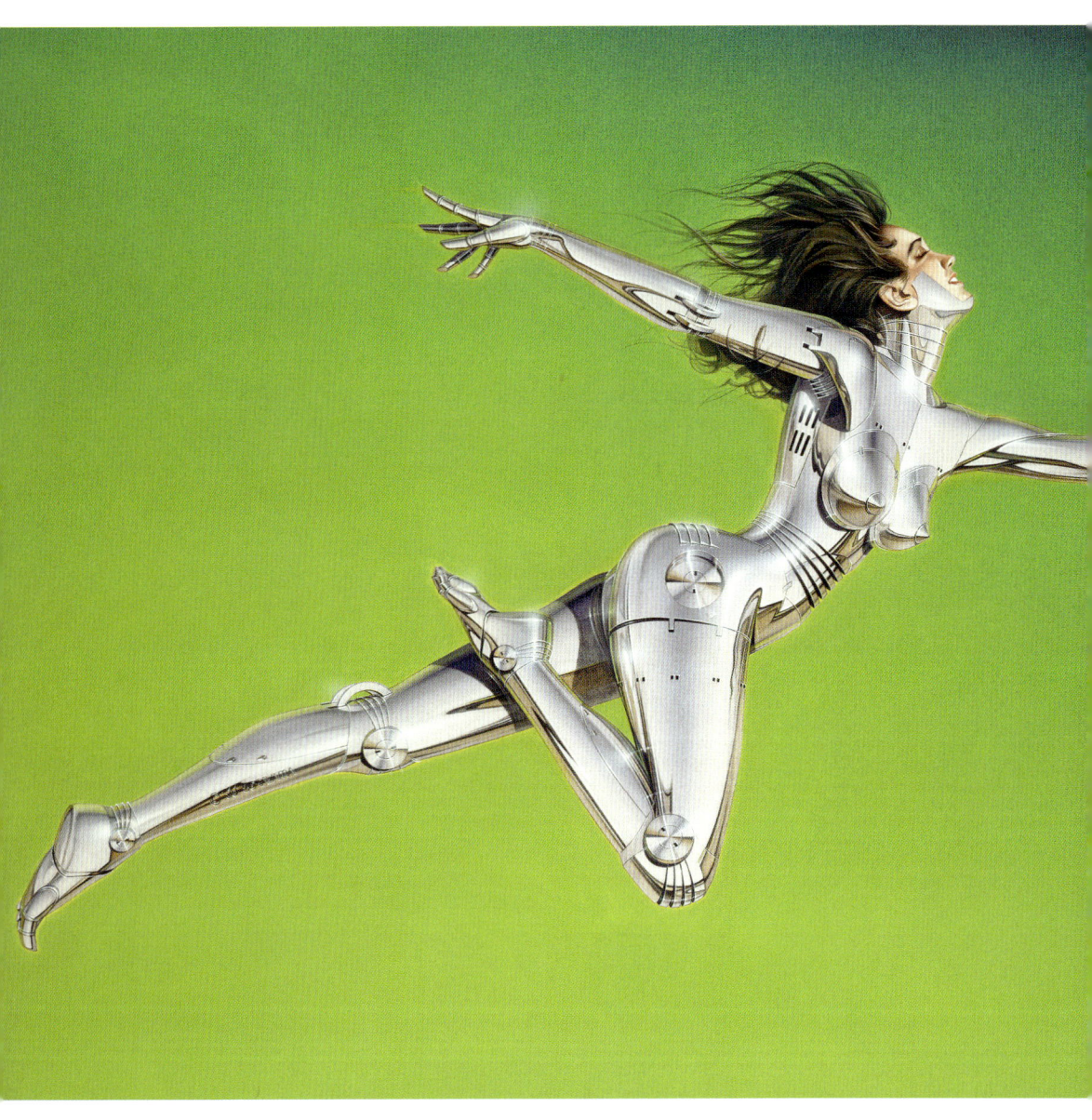

16

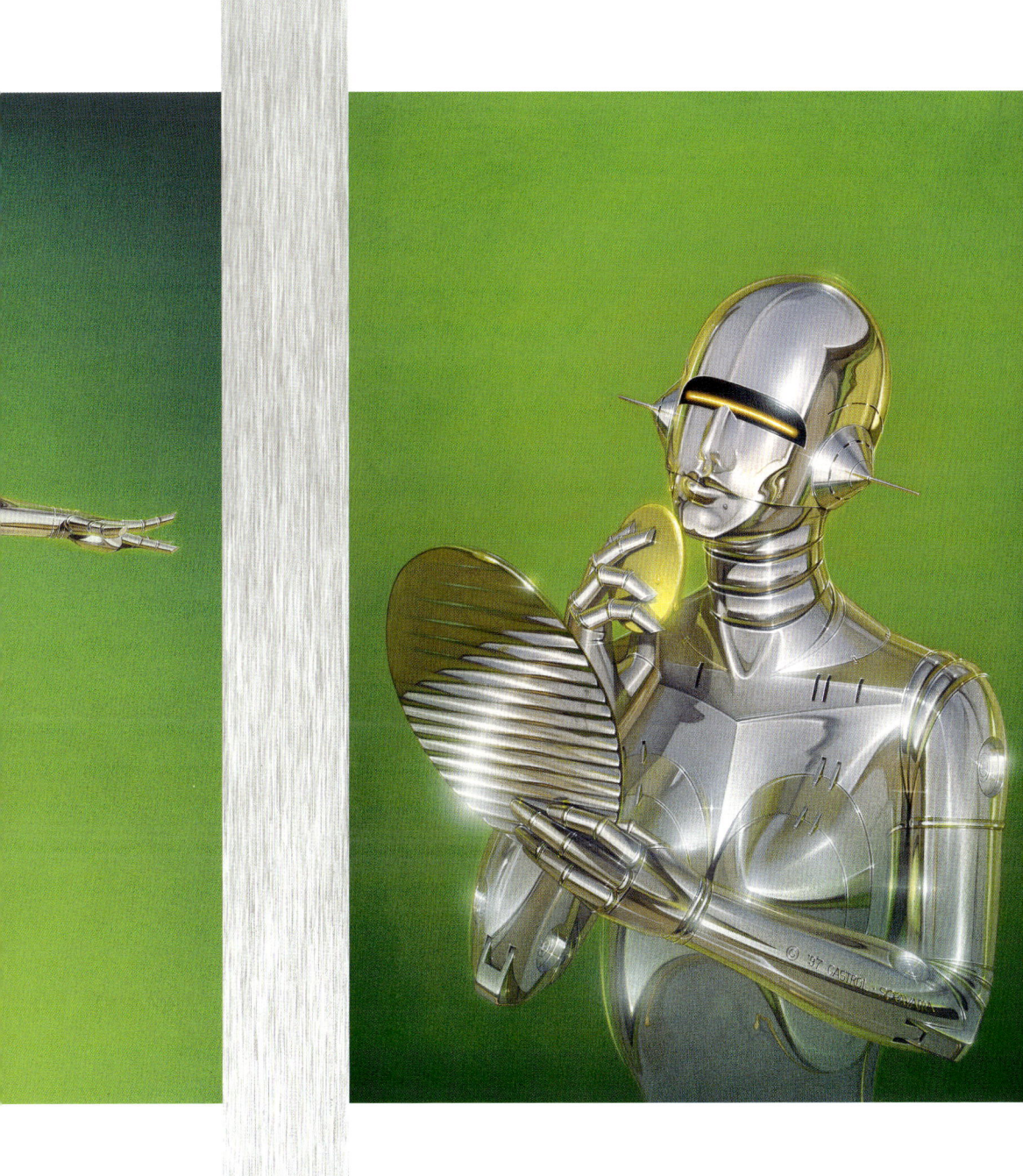

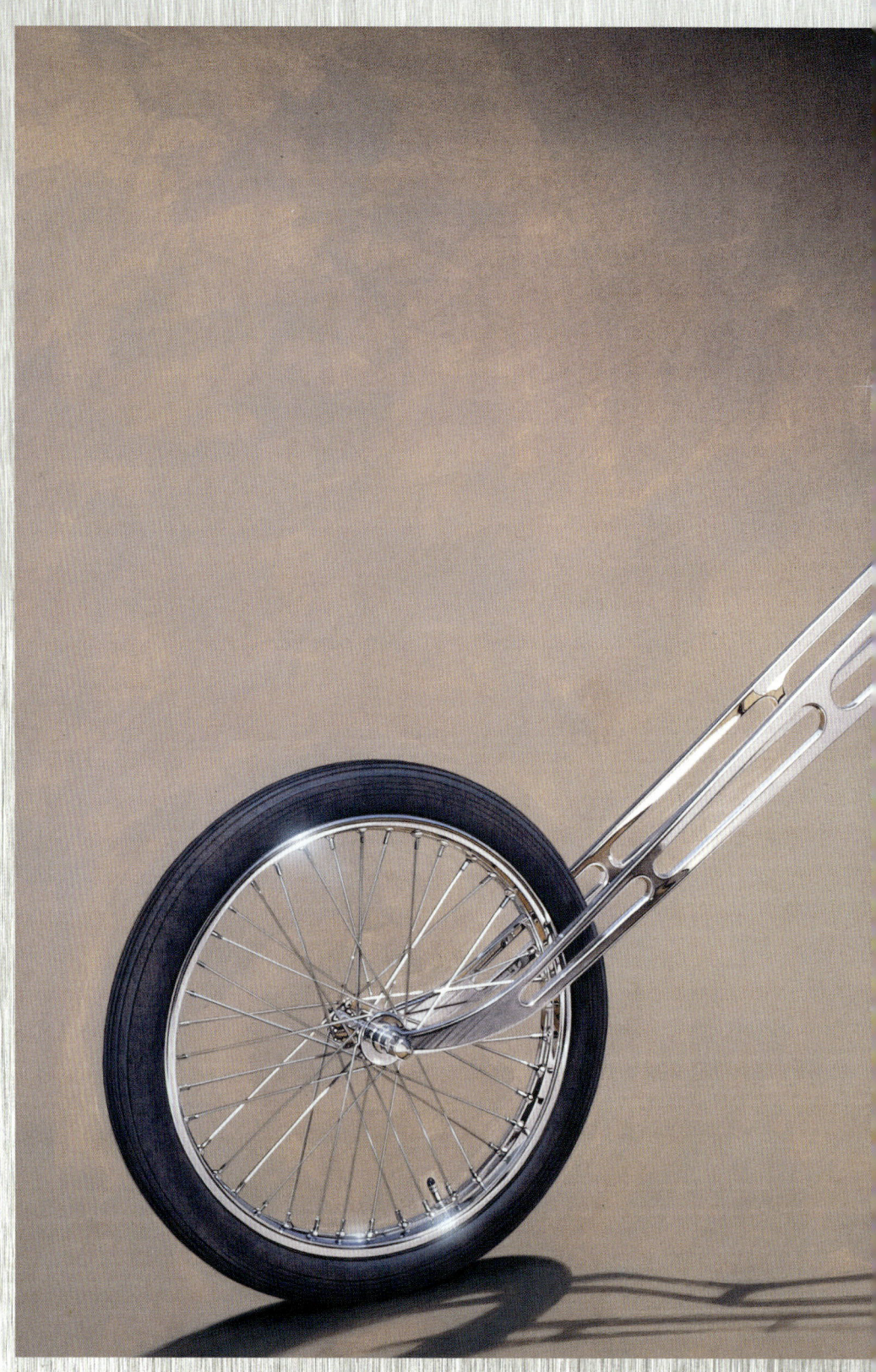

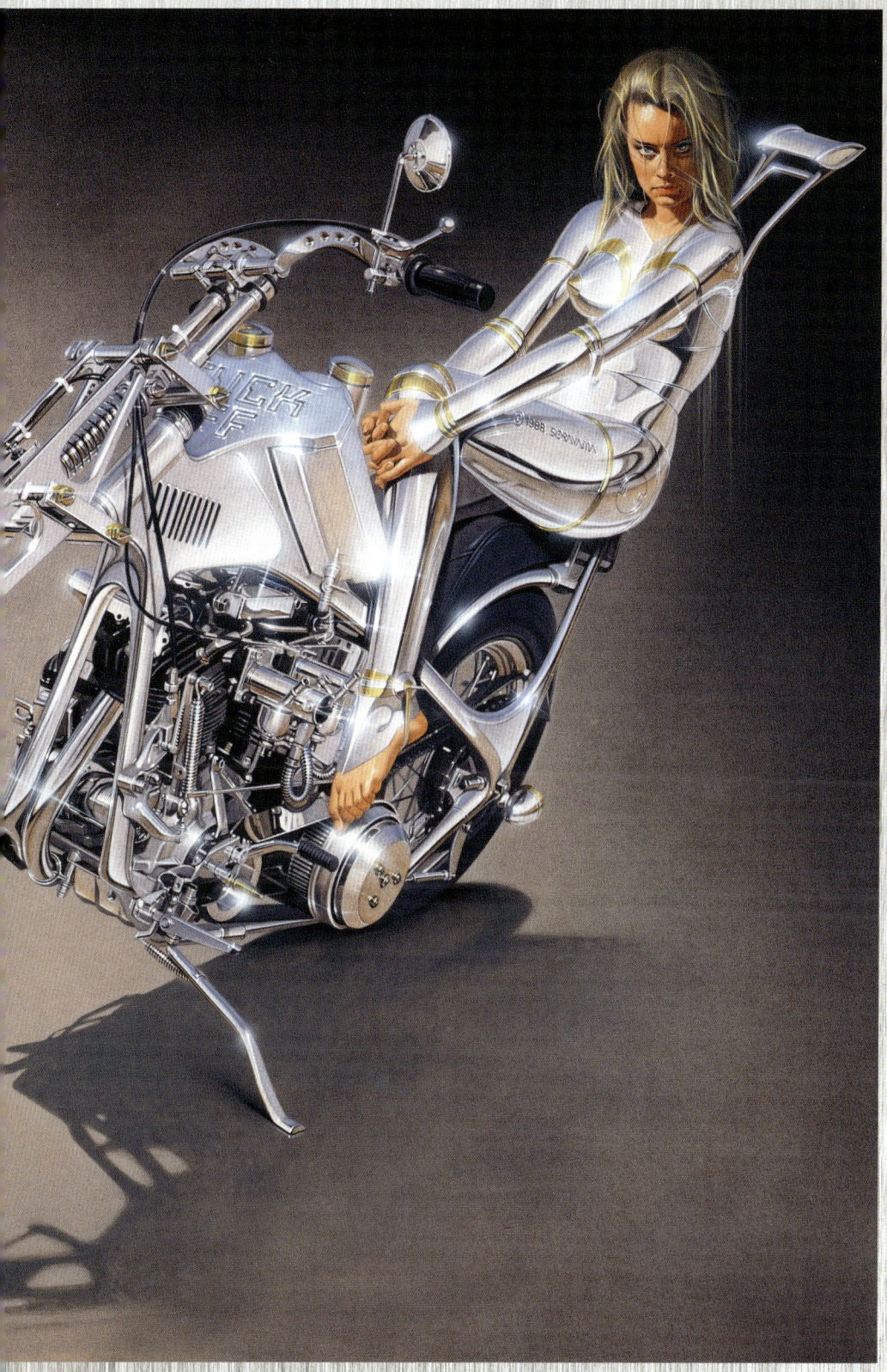

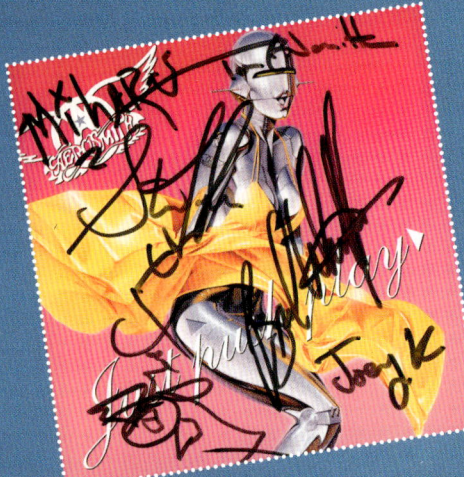

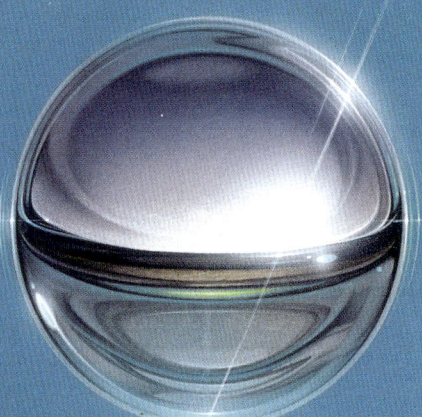

圓句昭浩（造形師）

　空山作品を知った10代の頃、形のない夢ばかりを見ていたようなきがします。造形を職にするようになった20代、空山作品を立体化してみたいと思うようになりました。
　多少腕も上がったかな？　という30代になって、ようやく空山さんにチャレンジ出来るように・・・・・？
　「だって眼に見えていることだけをたよりに造ってても、それはアンコのないモナカの様なモノ・・・・・」
　だから空山さんの描こうとする夢の眼に見えない部分を立体化する作業を心がけています。何がエッチで、何がキッツーイのか？まだまだ奥の奥まで突っ込んでみないことには・・。だって私の目標は、絶え間なく上昇し続けているのですもの。

岡本 博嗣（ザ・トイズ・マッコイズ社長／ザ・リアル・マッコイズ会長）

　この文章をたのまれた時珍人奇人の代表者として私にと言う事らしいけど そのまま そっくり空山のおじさんに返しておいて、空山のおじさんの奇人的変態度を説明しましょう。ひとこと。
　とにかく おじさんからお墨きをなくしたら。タケダテツヤに中野コウイチの顔を付けた奇人の変態おやじでしかないわけど、幸か不幸か、天然のお絵描き病が彼の場合コンプレックスと努力により、変態のふた文字が天才と変わるへだ。でも奇人は、変らないまま奇人の天才となるわけだ。
　変態界をうまく使いようで、真剣に変態を自分の問題として作品に表現しているおじさんは、世知辛い夜の中に関係なく、クソまじめなんだろうと考える。
　この業界でおじさんの絵は、人間が描く事が出来ないテクニックの持ちあわせだ、しかも絵を描くペース女人間進とは思えぬほど早い、やはり奇人の天才（変態）なのだ。
　業種の肩書次第で人間国宝もらえる!! と自分を見る事はダメだが人を見る目は、とってもきびしい私が言うのだからまちがいない。

GENUINE TOYS McCOY QUALITY
売れないおもちゃ屋　社長
おじさんへ♡
おきゃもと じゃが

Stuart Gordon
(スチュアート・ゴードン：映画監督）

It all started when I fell in love with a robot. This was the first time I viewed one of Sorayama's *Sexy Robot* paintings, and her sleek lines and shiny chrome skin made me feel things I'd never felt for a machine before or since. I instantly became a fan and eagerly followed the development of his work which became increasingly more beautiful and outrageous.

When I began work on the science fiction film *Space Truckers* my production designer, Simon Murton, decided to take a Sorayama-like approach on his design of our bio-mechanical warriors (or B.M.W.'s as called them). That very day there was an announcement in the L.A Times that Sorayama himself was in town for an exhibit of his work at a local gallery. I called the gallery and invited the artist to our production office. That afternoon he arrived and was immediately drawn to Simon's sketch. "I would like to redesign this", he told us through an interpreter. Simon and I were both delighted. "But Mr.Sorayama has one question", his interpreter informed us.

"Can it have a penis?"

This took me aback. I hemmed and hawed about this being a family film when Miharu, his agent gave me a polite but firm nudge in the ribs. "Don't forget who you're dealing with", she whispered. "This is Mr.Sorayama."

Simon and I looked at each other for moment and then we both exclaimed, "Of course it can have one." Sorayama smiled and a deal was quickly made.

Sorayama's work on the movie was brilliant. We ended up building the costumes on striking six-foot tall women dancers who could give the creatures the graceful movement that Sorayama's elegant drawings suggested. And yes, they did have penises. Three-foot long affairs that coiled around their left legs. Sorayama suggested that these could be sensory appendages that could peek around corners as the B.M.W.'s advanced.

Working with him is a delight experience. The man combines child-like enthusiasm and limitless imagination with precise craftsmanship and amazing technique unparalleled by any artist working today. And I discovered that his English is excellent, especially after a glass or two of wine.

When as a parting gift he gave me a set of signed *Gynoid* prints I was overcome with emotion, but also a bit nervous (a typical reaction to his work). Where could I hang such astonishing and explicit images? He immediately understood my dilemma.

"When my daughter's friends come over, she makes me take them down and hide them in a closet", he confided with a smile.

So for the time being I will have to be content with viewing his incredible work in books like this after the children are safely in bed, enjoying his fabulous images as they run rampant through my mind.
Anyone for *Gynoids-the Movie?*

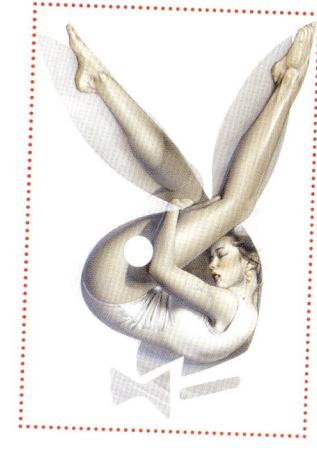

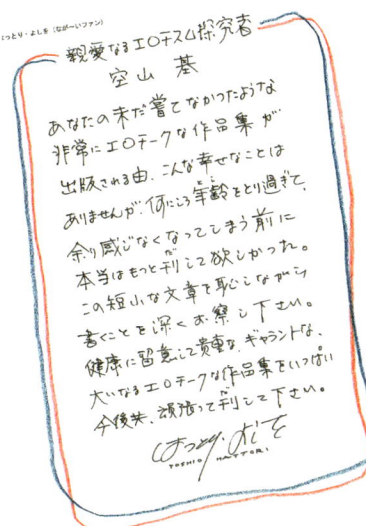

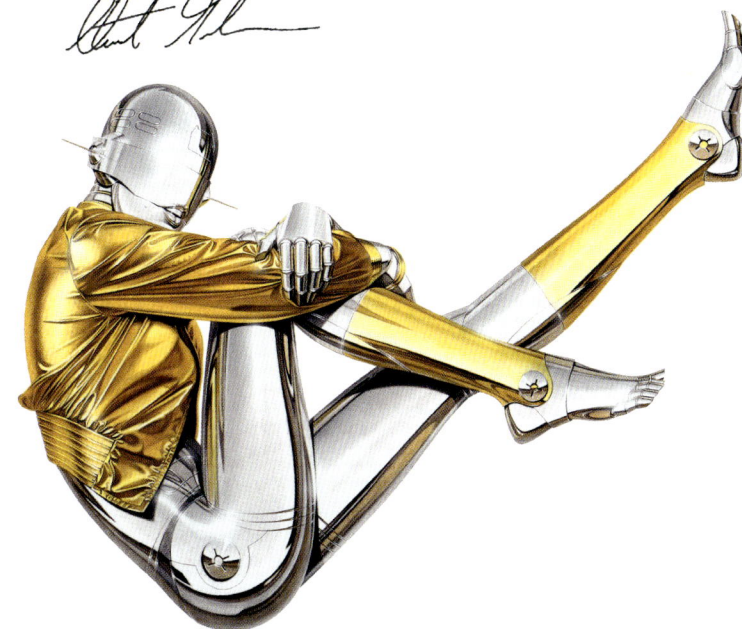

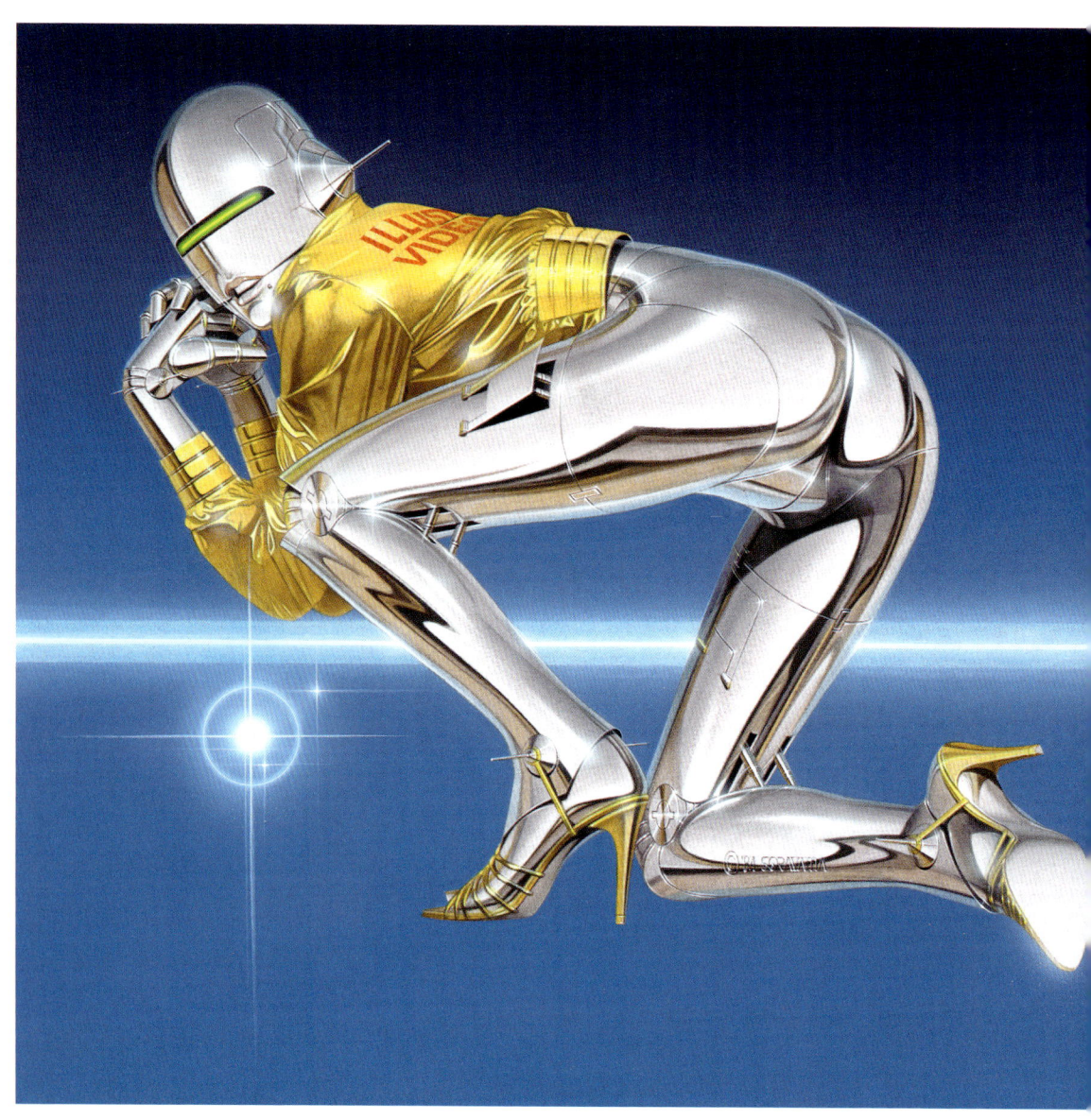

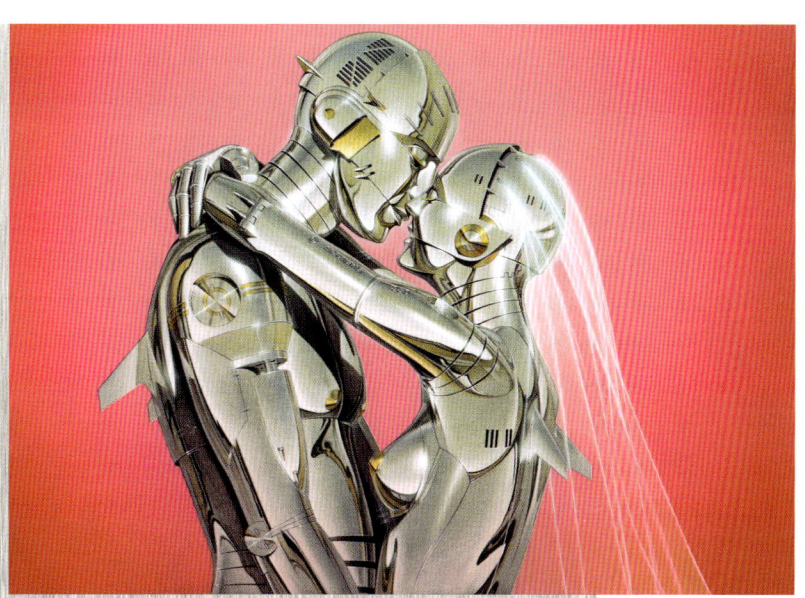
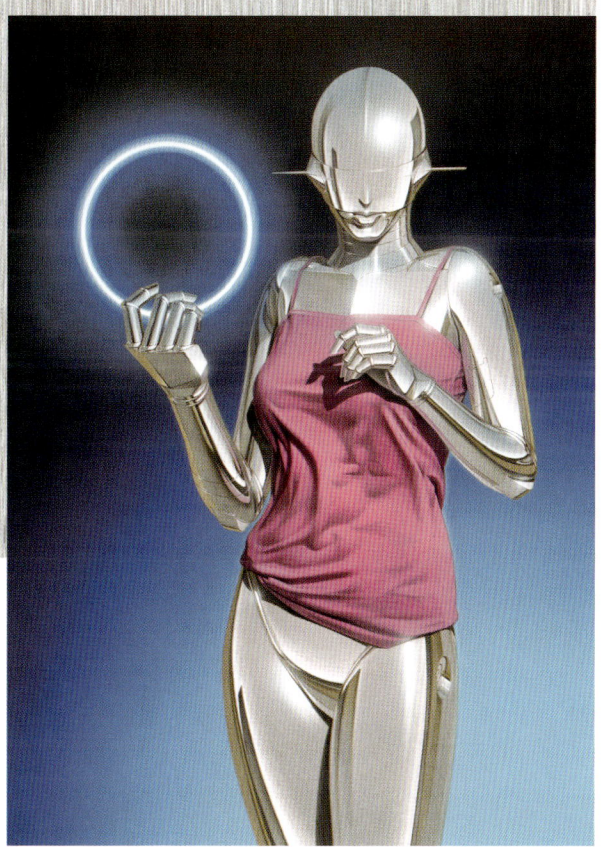

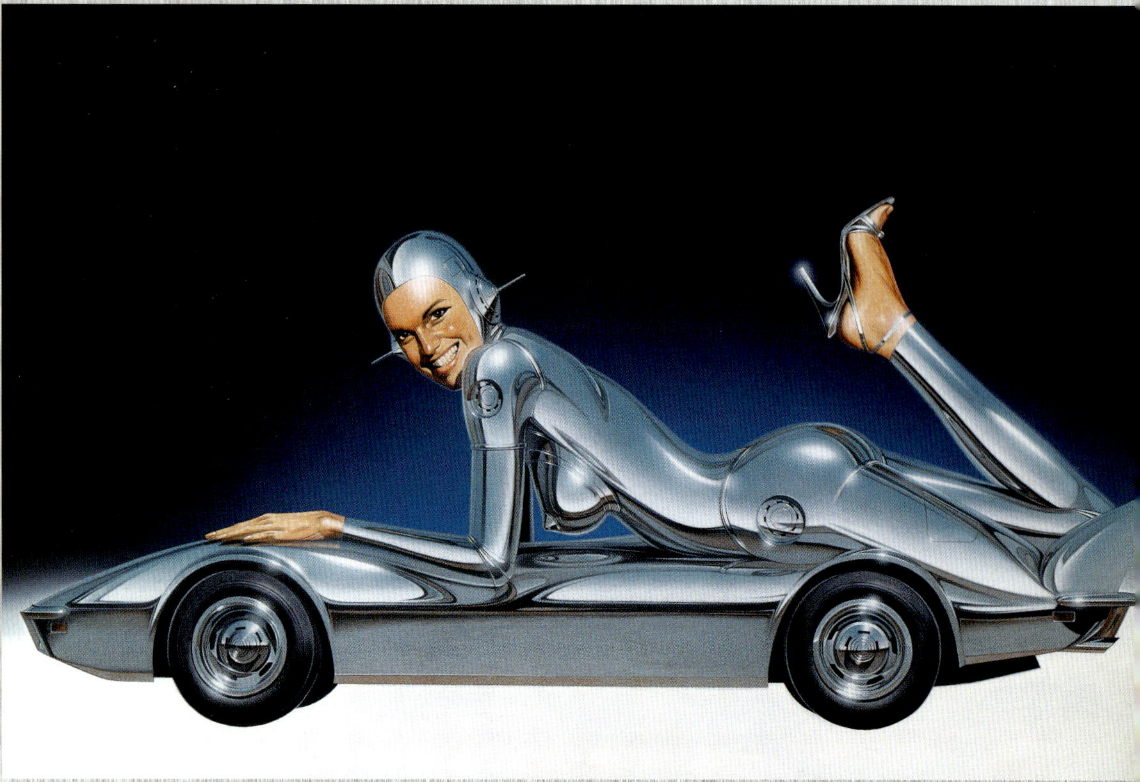

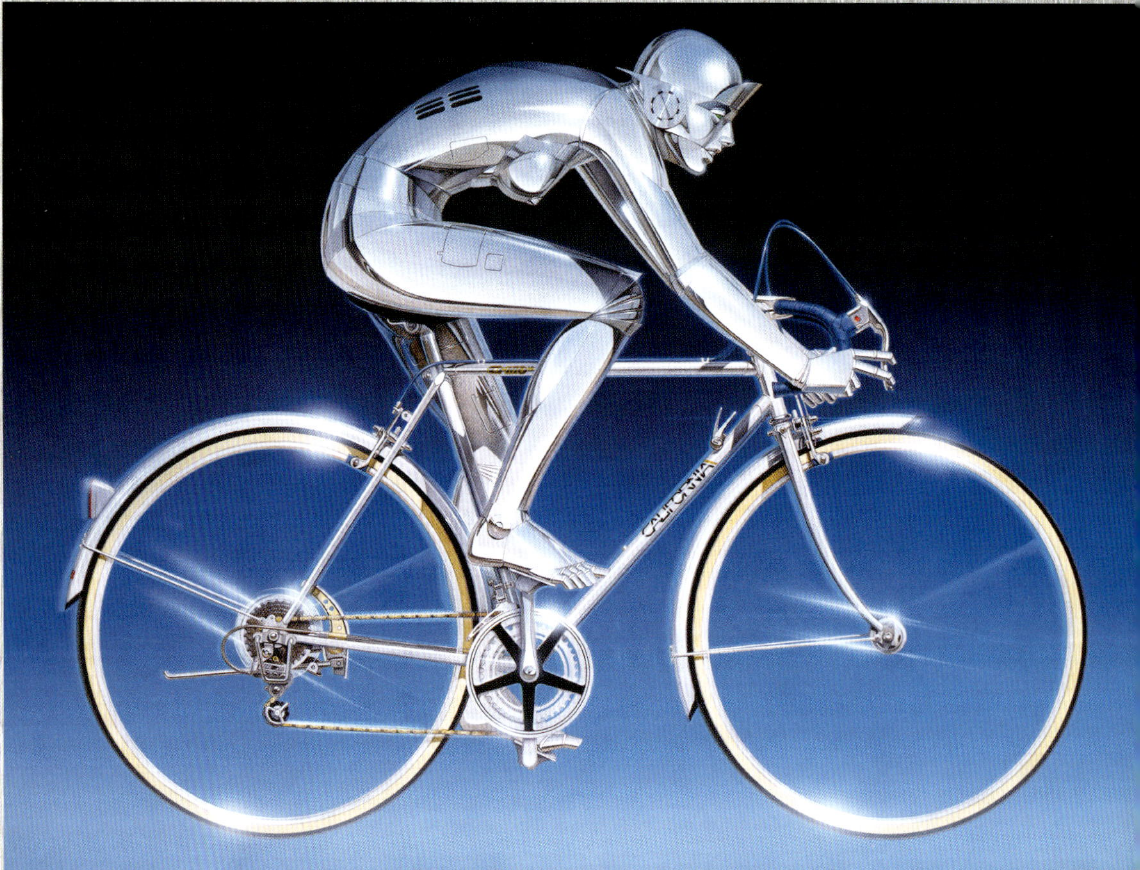
CALIFORNIA

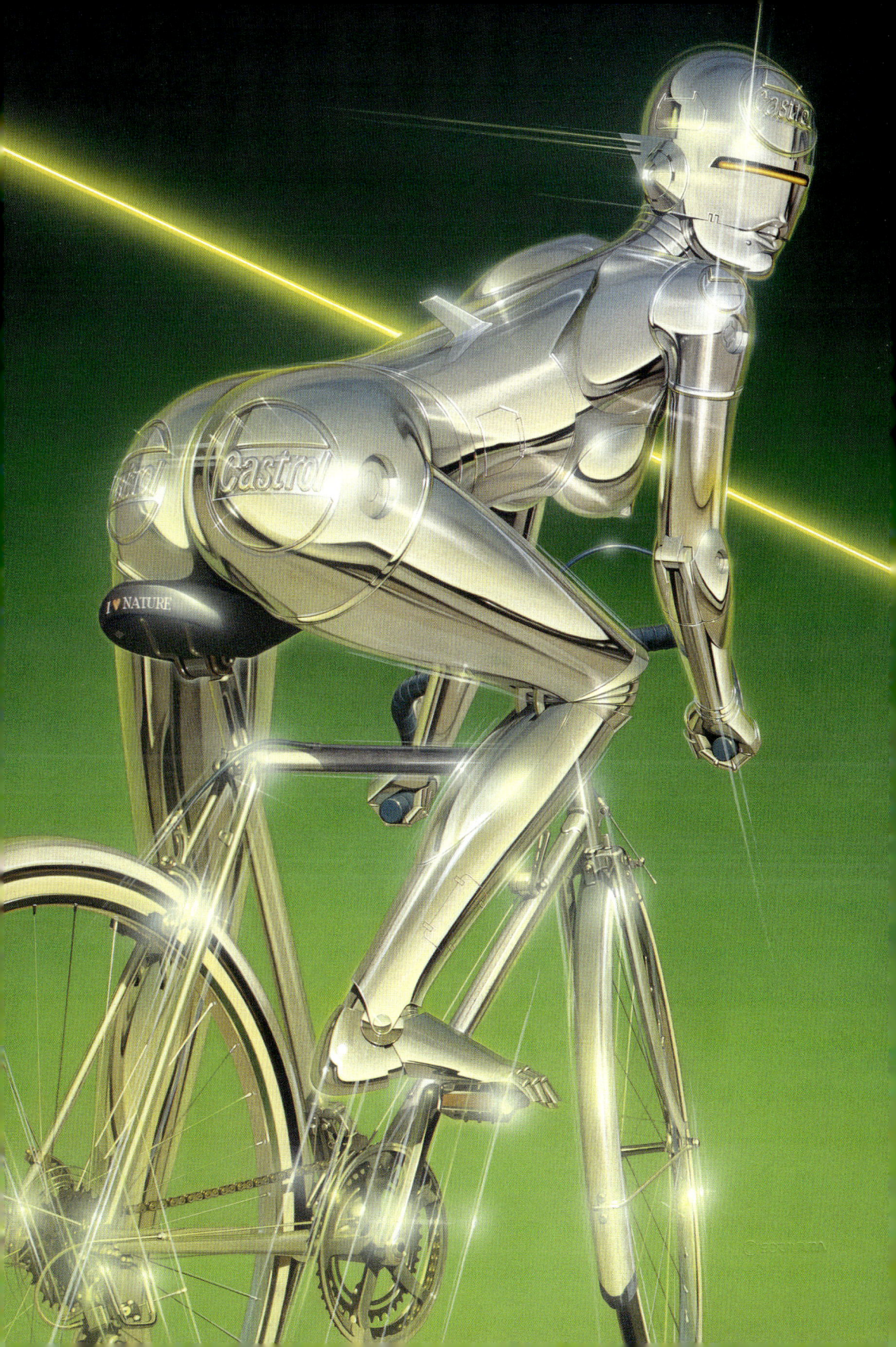

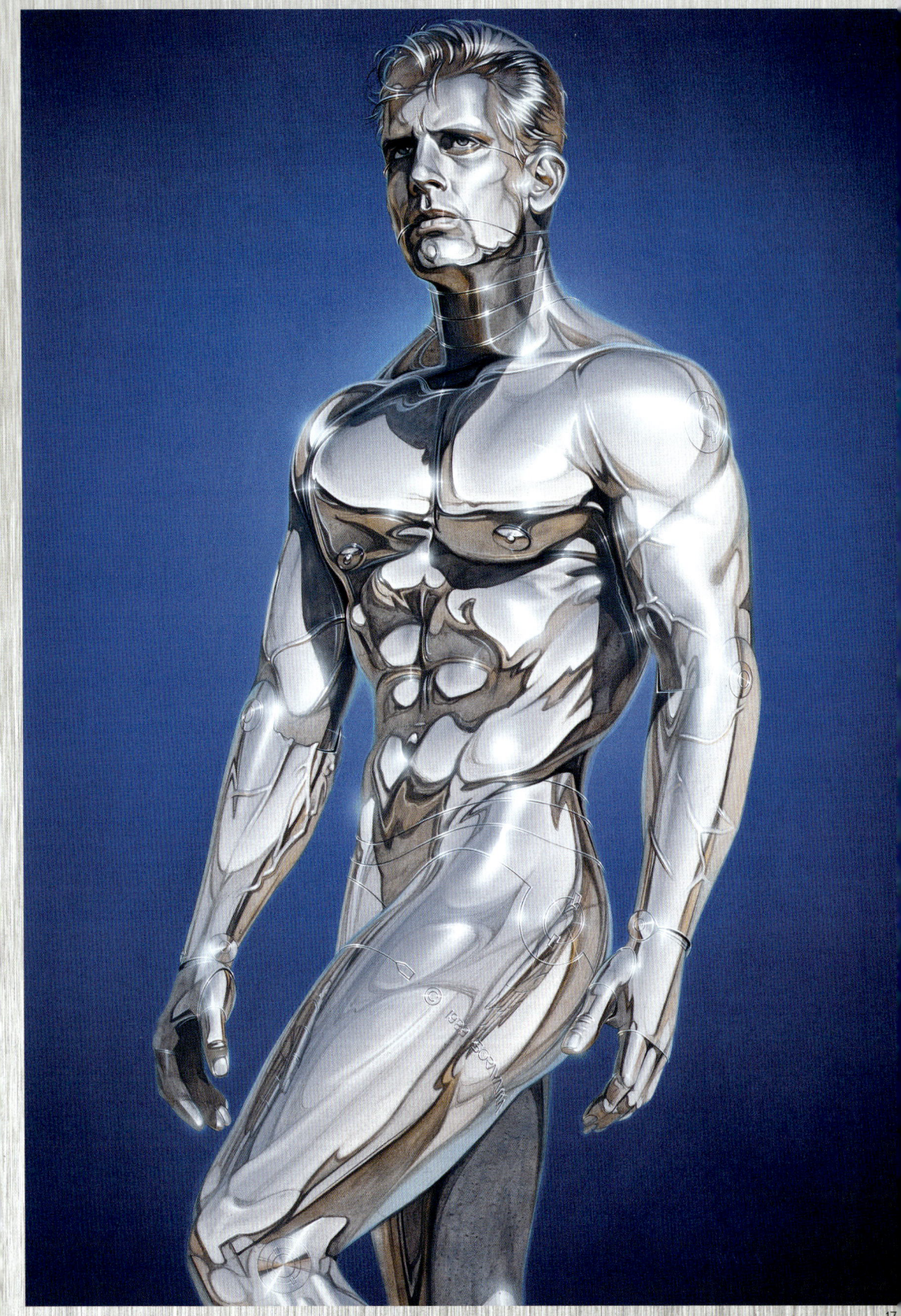

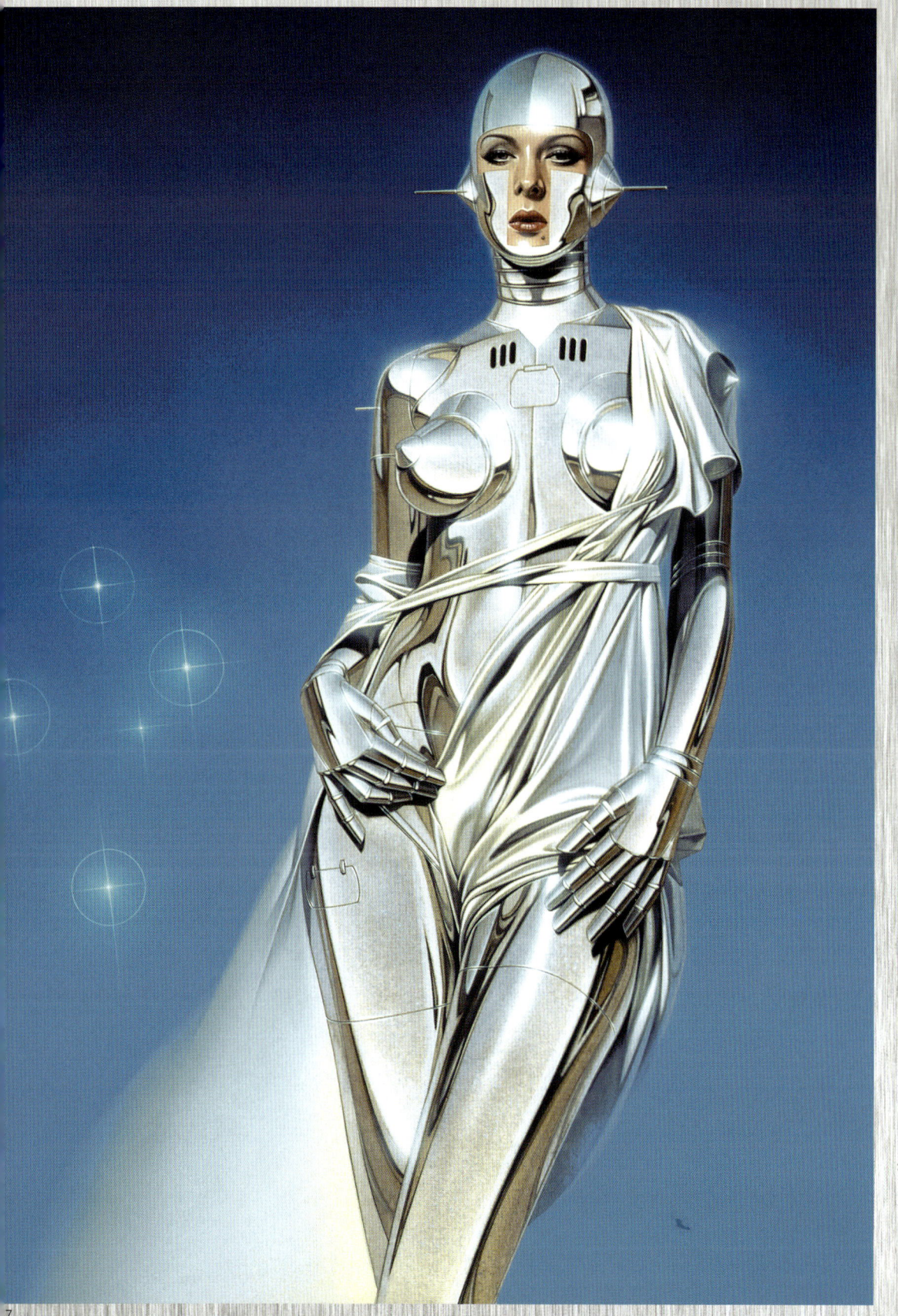

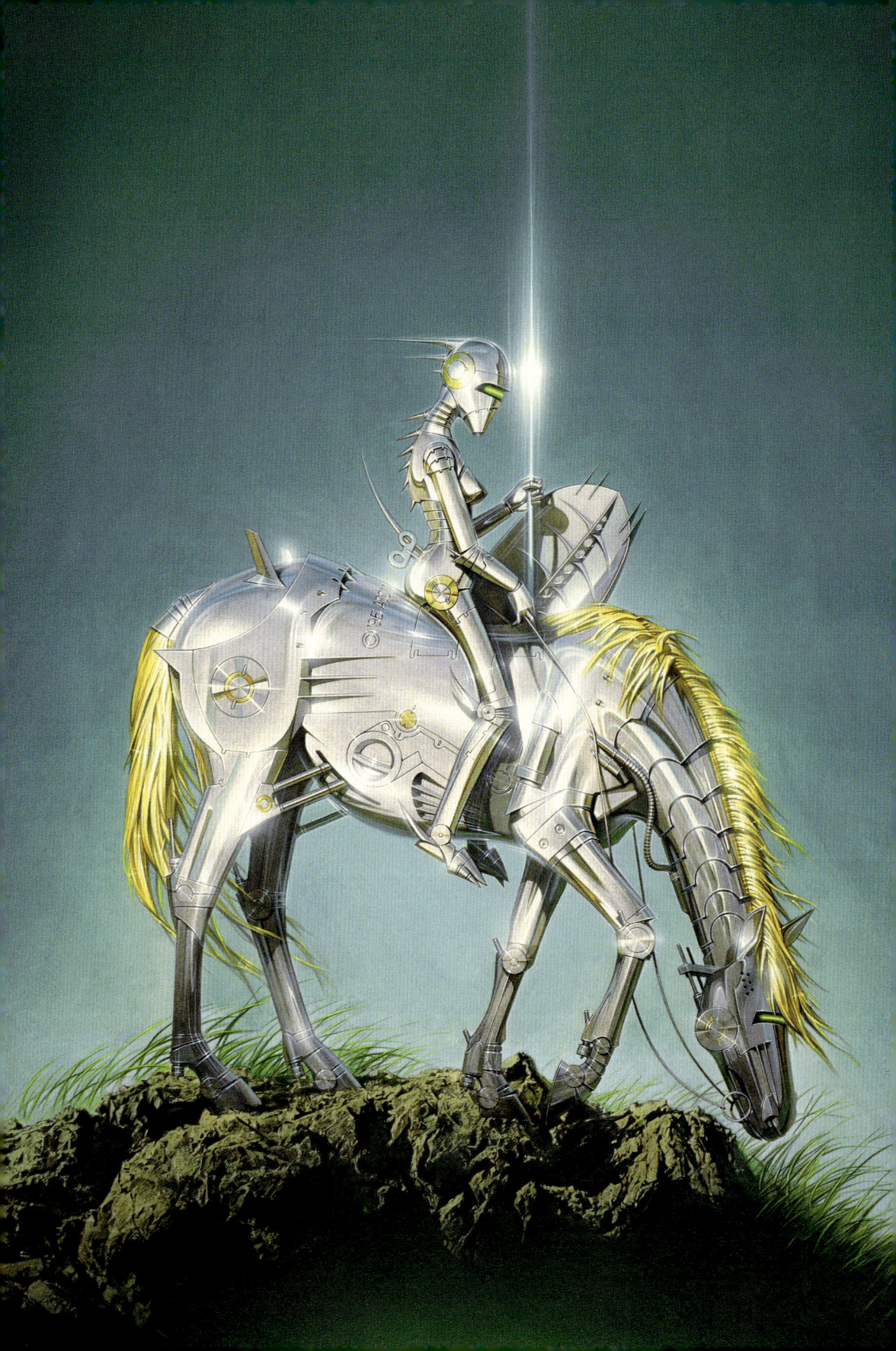

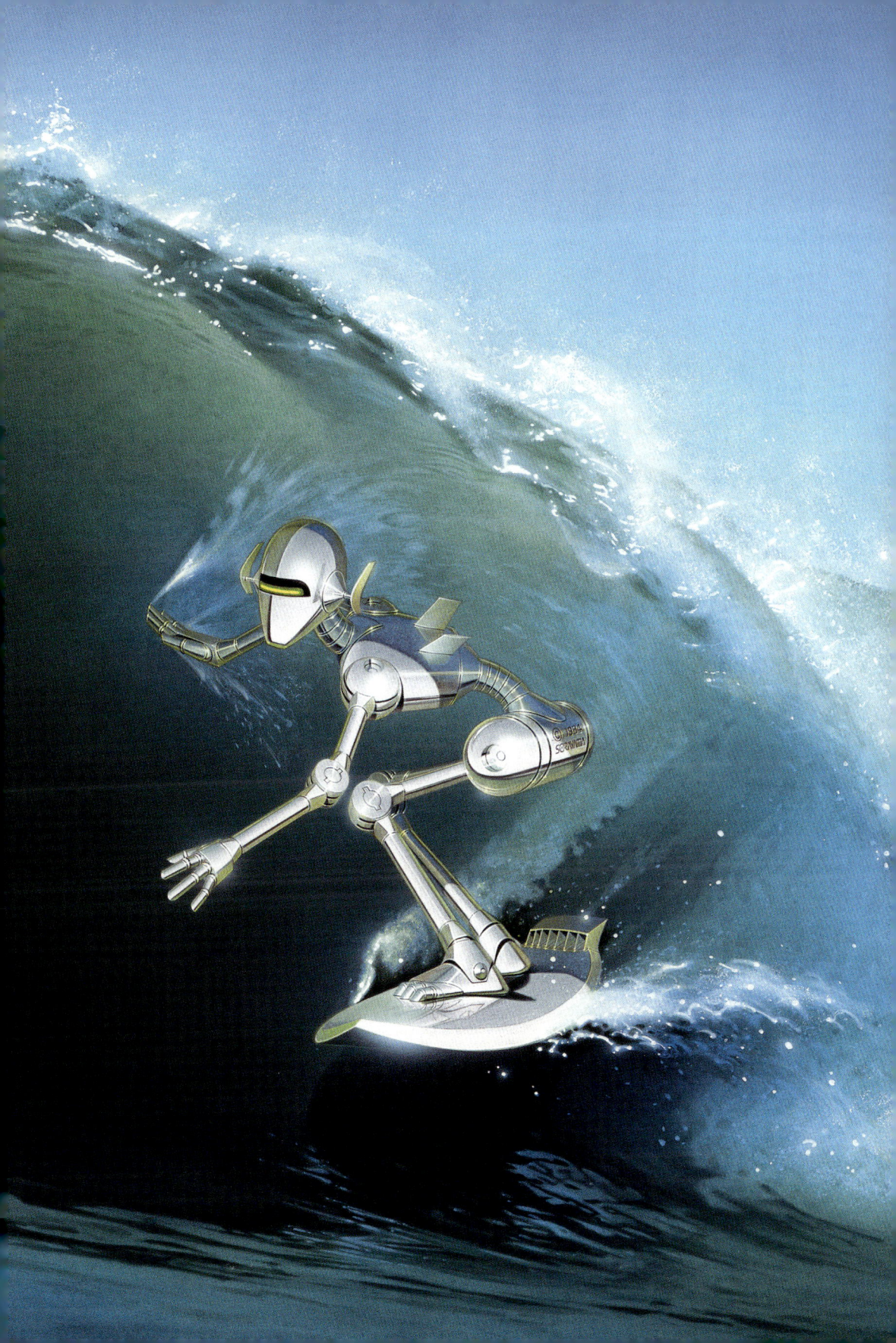

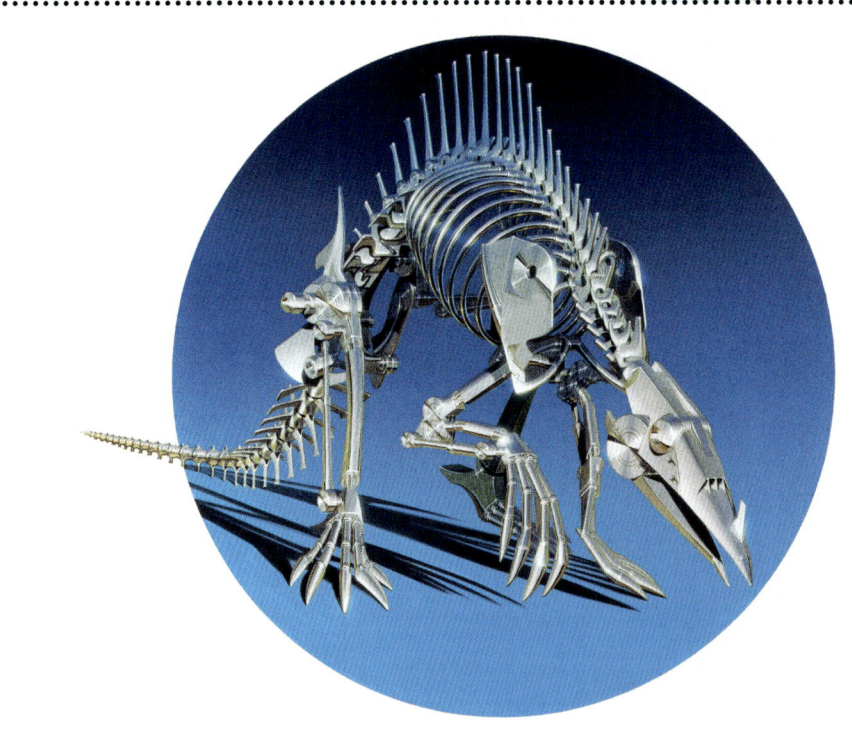

韮沢靖 （フィギュア造形家）

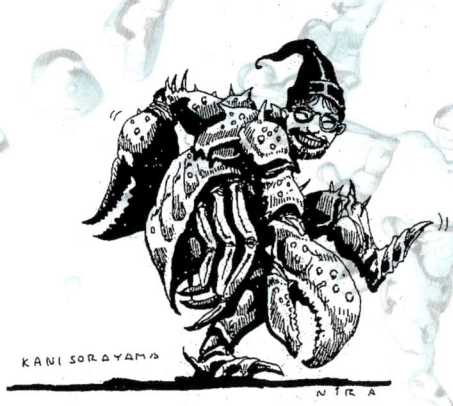

KANI SORAYAMA
NIRA

〝カニ様〟 韮沢 靖

空山氏は、私達デザイン学院生にとって、アイドル…いやいや、神様の様な存在であったのです。イラストボードの中の素材を紙から金属、しかもクロームメッキ仕上げに変えてしまうのですから。そんな氏が5・14年の時を越えて、「会いたい！」との呼び出しがかかったのです。…神様から校庭のウラに呼び出された気分で高円寺に行くと、神様は何とカニ歩きで登場をとったのです。カニ歩きですよ！。そして「いたぁ、いたぁ！」こぉこぉかぁ〜!!」って、まるで小学…いやいや神童の様なピュアな声での登場。私の想像していた神経質で超内向な神様では無く、やんちゃ悪な子鳴をジジイの様なその御姿は、私の中の空山像をさらに不可思議な存在へと登りつめさせました。その後も幾度かお付き合いをさせていただいてますが、氏のピュアな探究心とバイタリティーには尊敬せざるをえません。そのまま走り続けて還暦を手に入れて下さい。私のエロ子鳴きジジイ、韮沢靖〜／NIRA

（カニ）

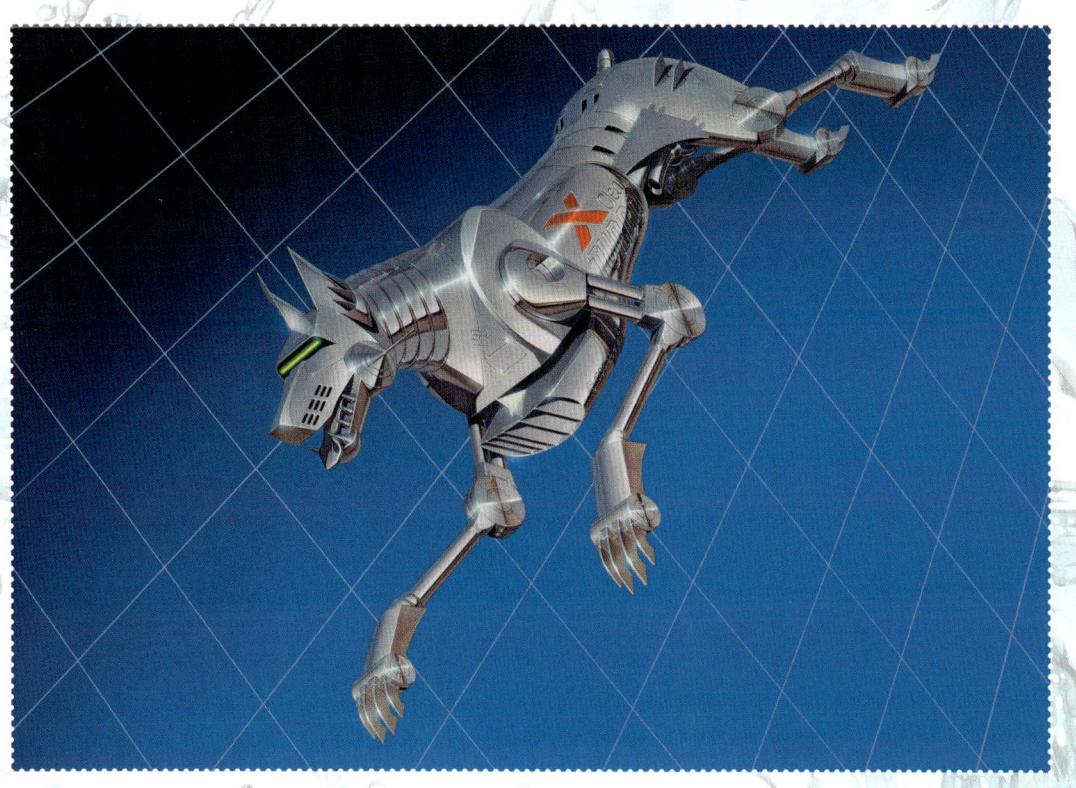

横山明（イラストレーター）

　このところたて続けに出版された空山基さんの画集をみていると、彼のように、ひとつのテーマに向って急傾斜してゆくイラストレーターも珍しいことに気付いた。普通、イラストレーターの扱うモチーフは雑多で、急速に変化する時代色に添寝する「簡便な絵」といった趣がある今日、その点で彼の絵は特異である。かつて、「責め絵」の絵師で伊藤晴雨がいた。

　明治、大正、昭和を生きたこの人の作品集は古書店でも入手困難で、私共の眼に触れる機会が少ないけれど、その特異さはひときわ他を抜いている。SMというテーマが社会的に固く禁忌された時代にありながらも「責め絵」を描き続けた画家に、私は空山さんを重ねてみる。出版規制スレスレ、或はその境を越えたところにスタンスを置いている点ではこの二人は似ているけれど、晴雨のウェットに対して空山さんの絵はドライな感じがする。対象は似ていてもテーマが違う印象がある。ウェットに対してドライという、人間観に於ての対極を感じる。空山さんの描く女性達は、性器に金属を埋められてウットリとしている。刃物で傷つけられて婉然としている。或は性器を露にし乍らも相手を睨みつけている。彼女達は、もはや人間でなく、サイボーグであり、ロボットであり、妖怪であって、晴雨がテーマにした羞恥、苦痛、恐怖というような、自我から発する諸感情が存在していない。「機械化された情緒」とでもいったらよいのであろうか。このようなことを考えていると、空山さんの絵に私は「現代」を痛烈に感じとることができる。ソラヤマサン、アナタハ、コレカラドコヘ、ムカウノデスカ？

横山　明

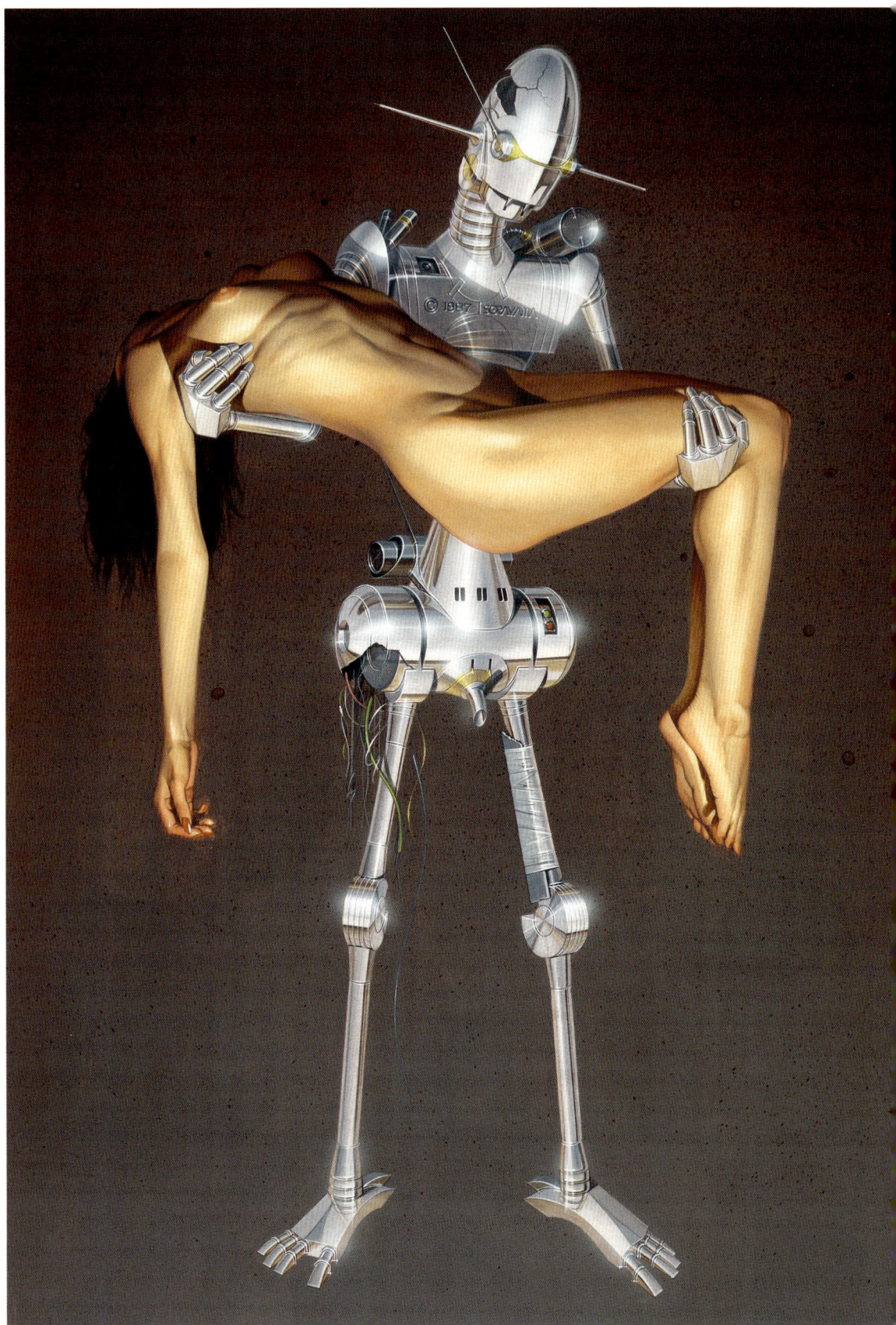

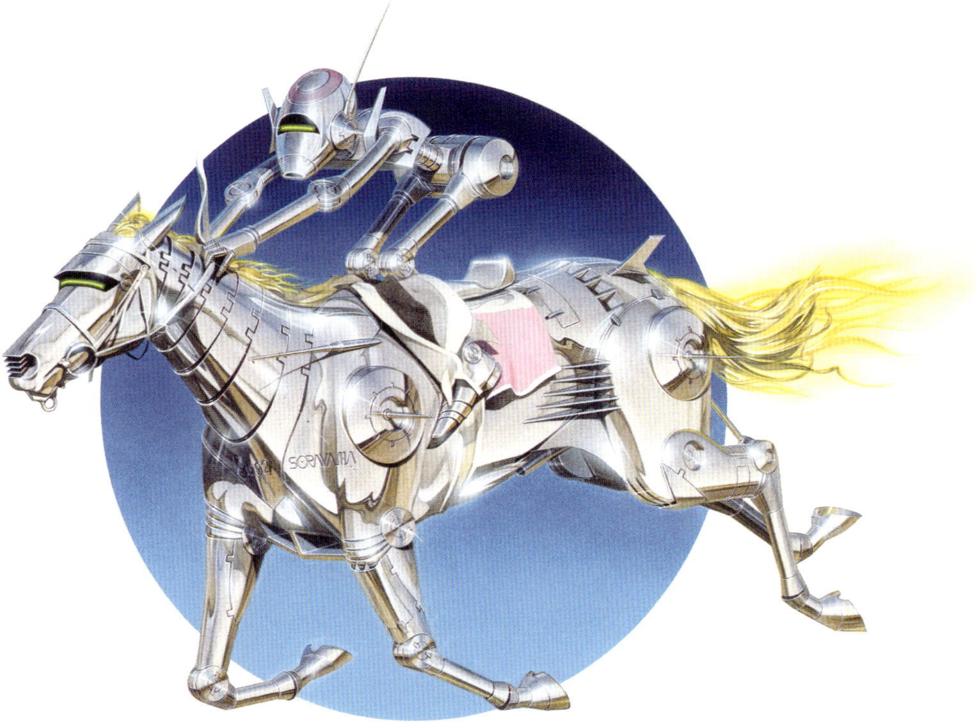

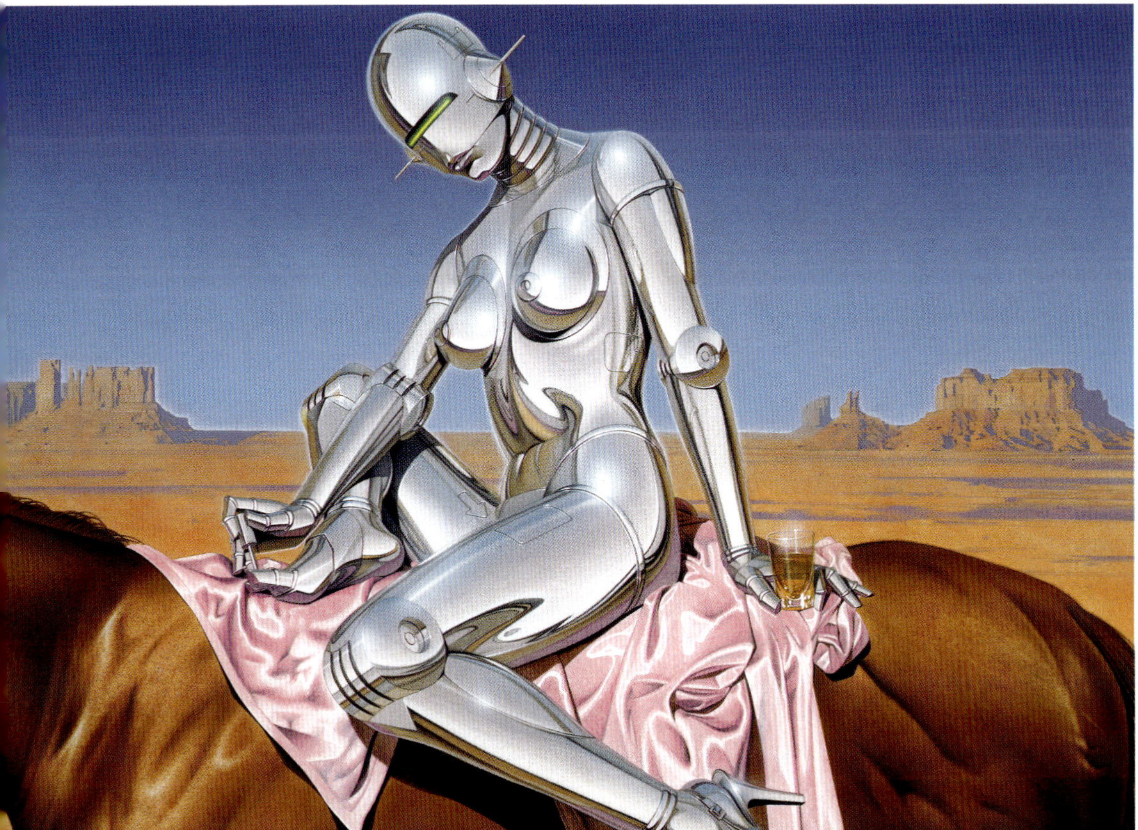

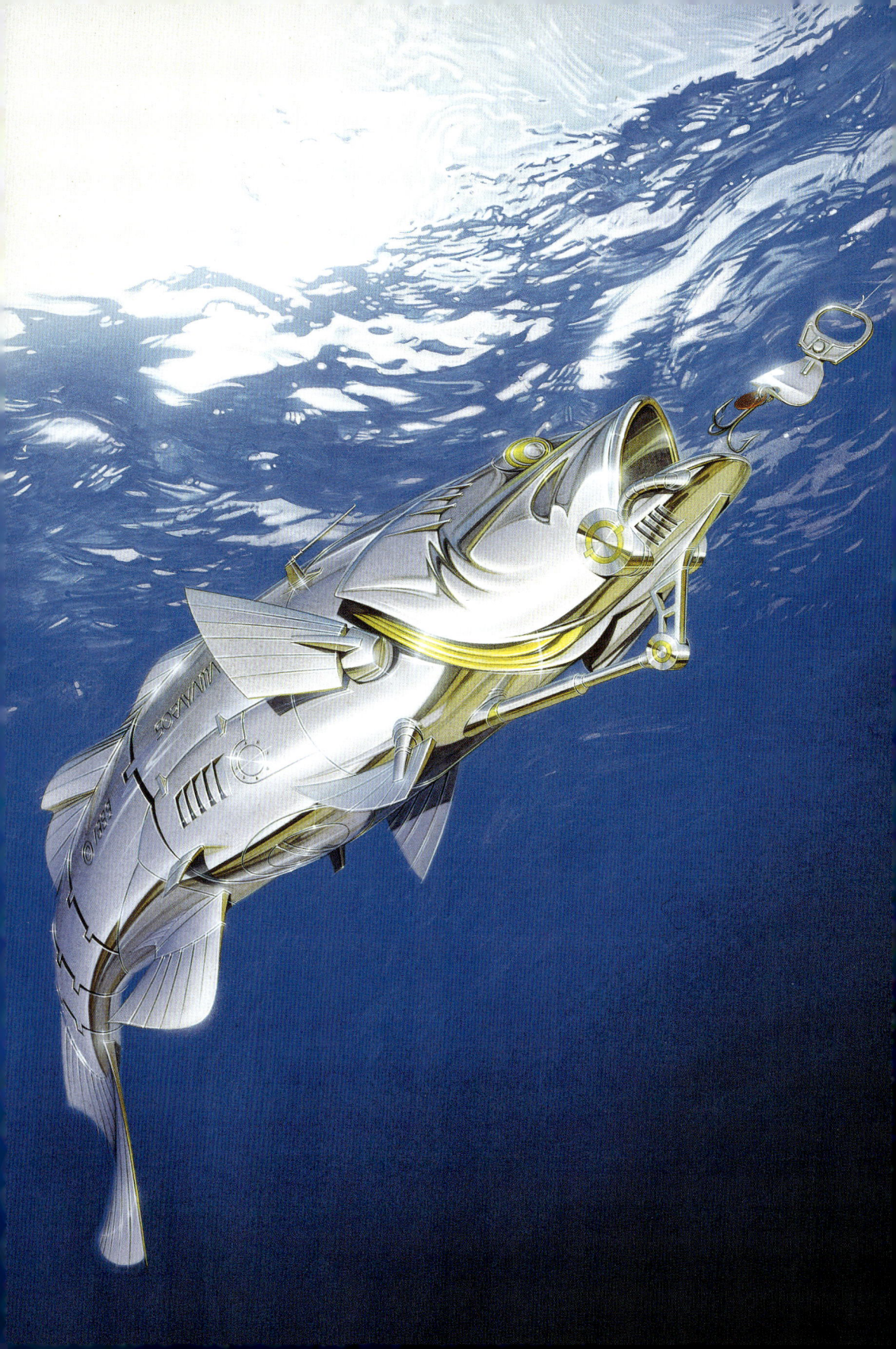

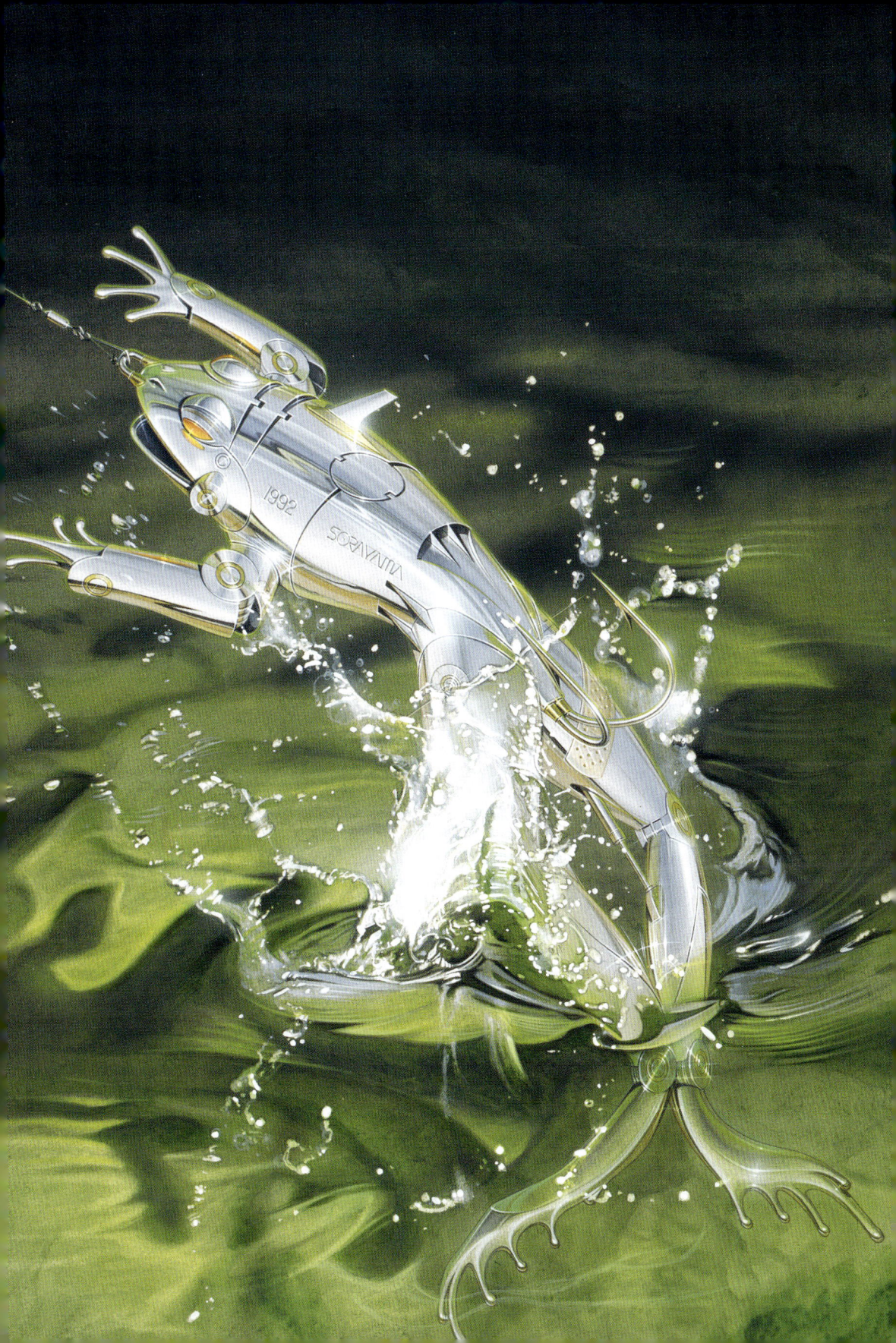

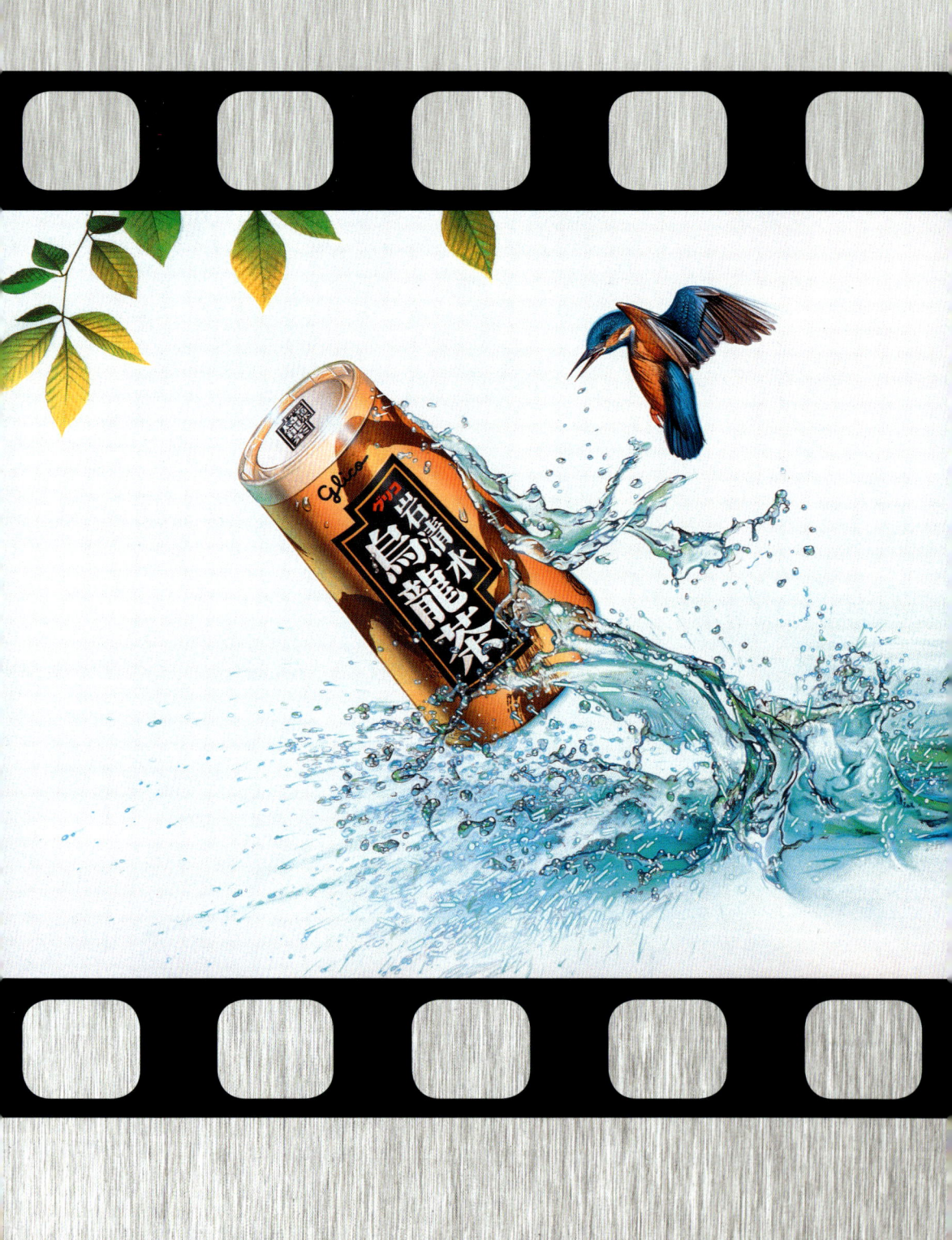

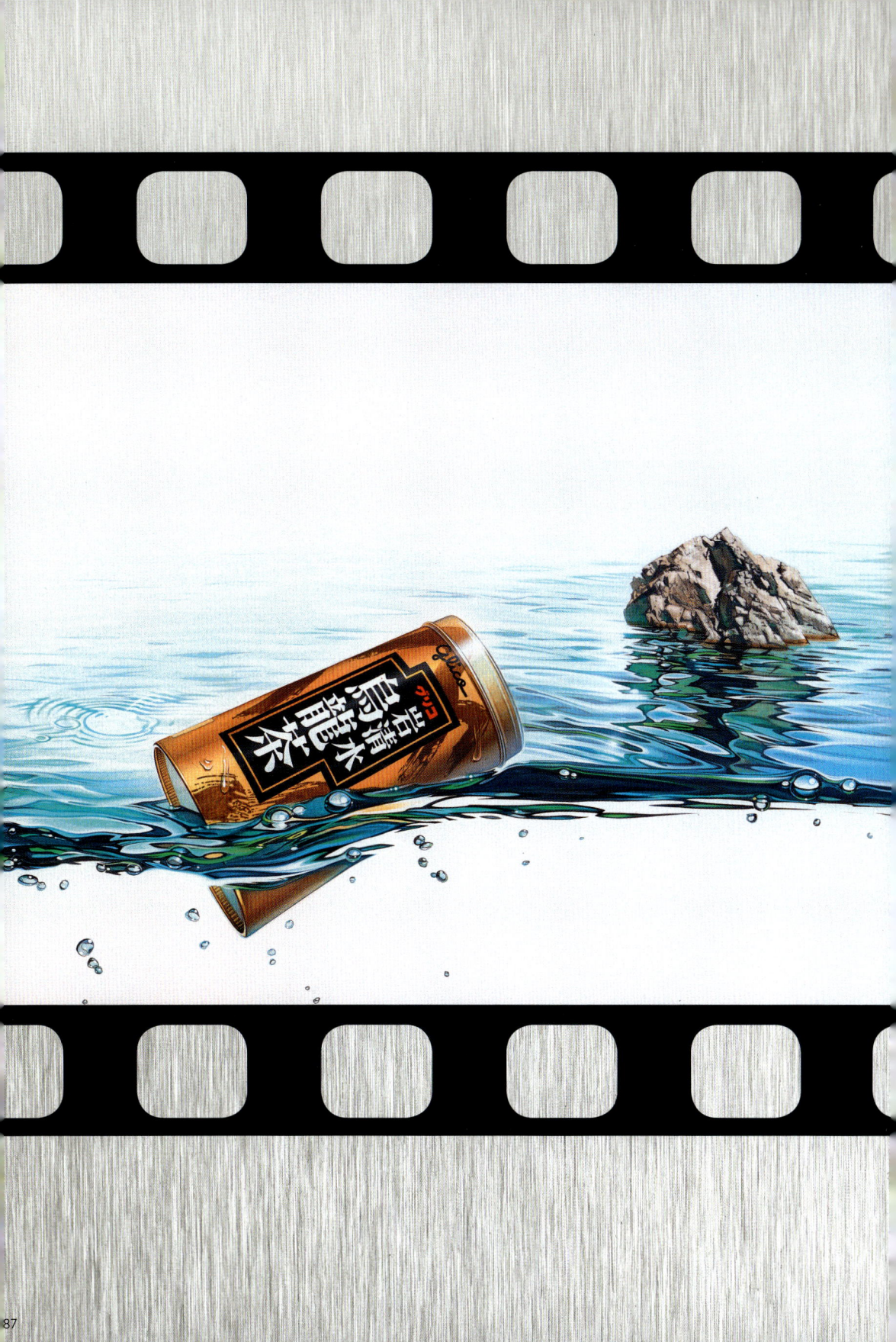

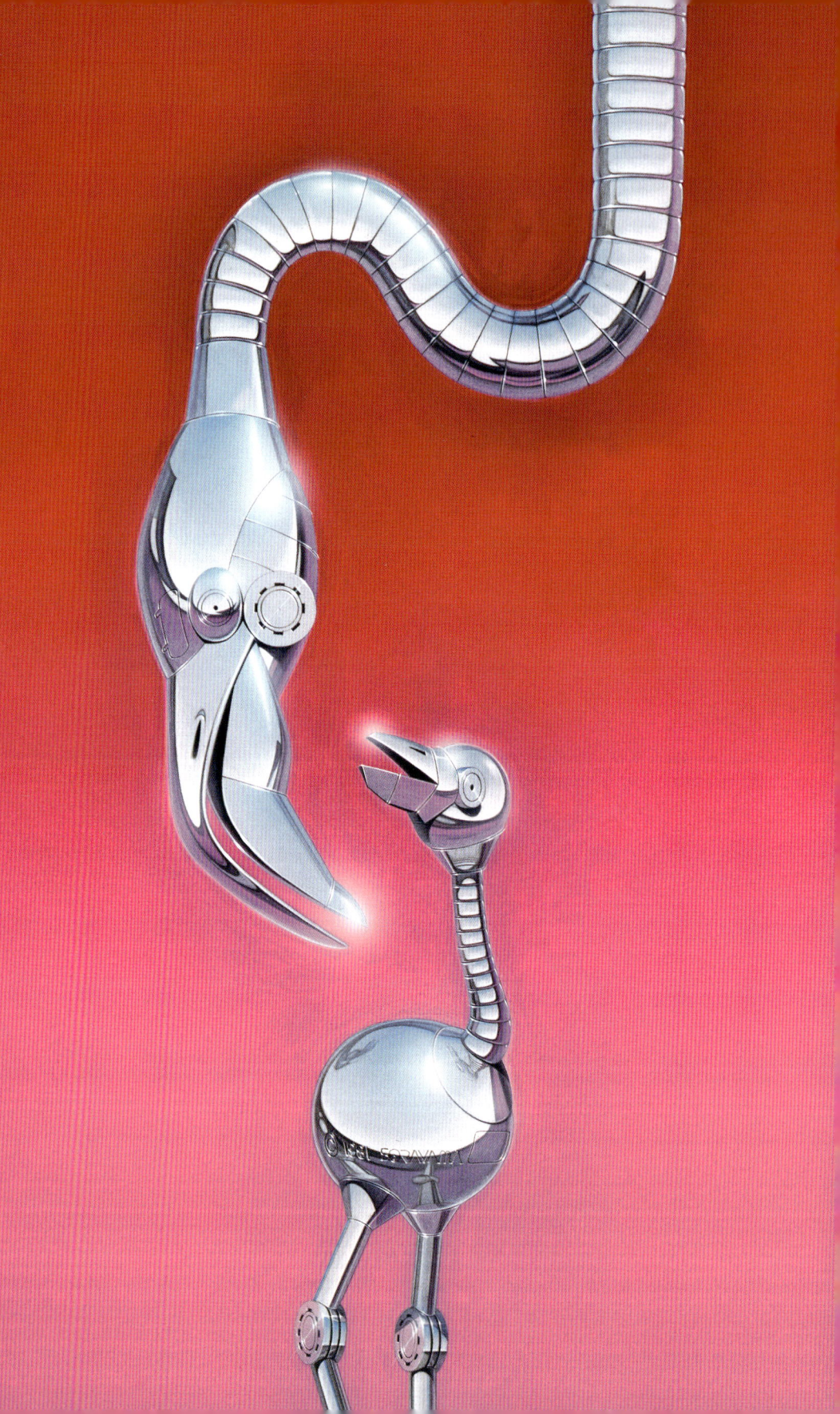

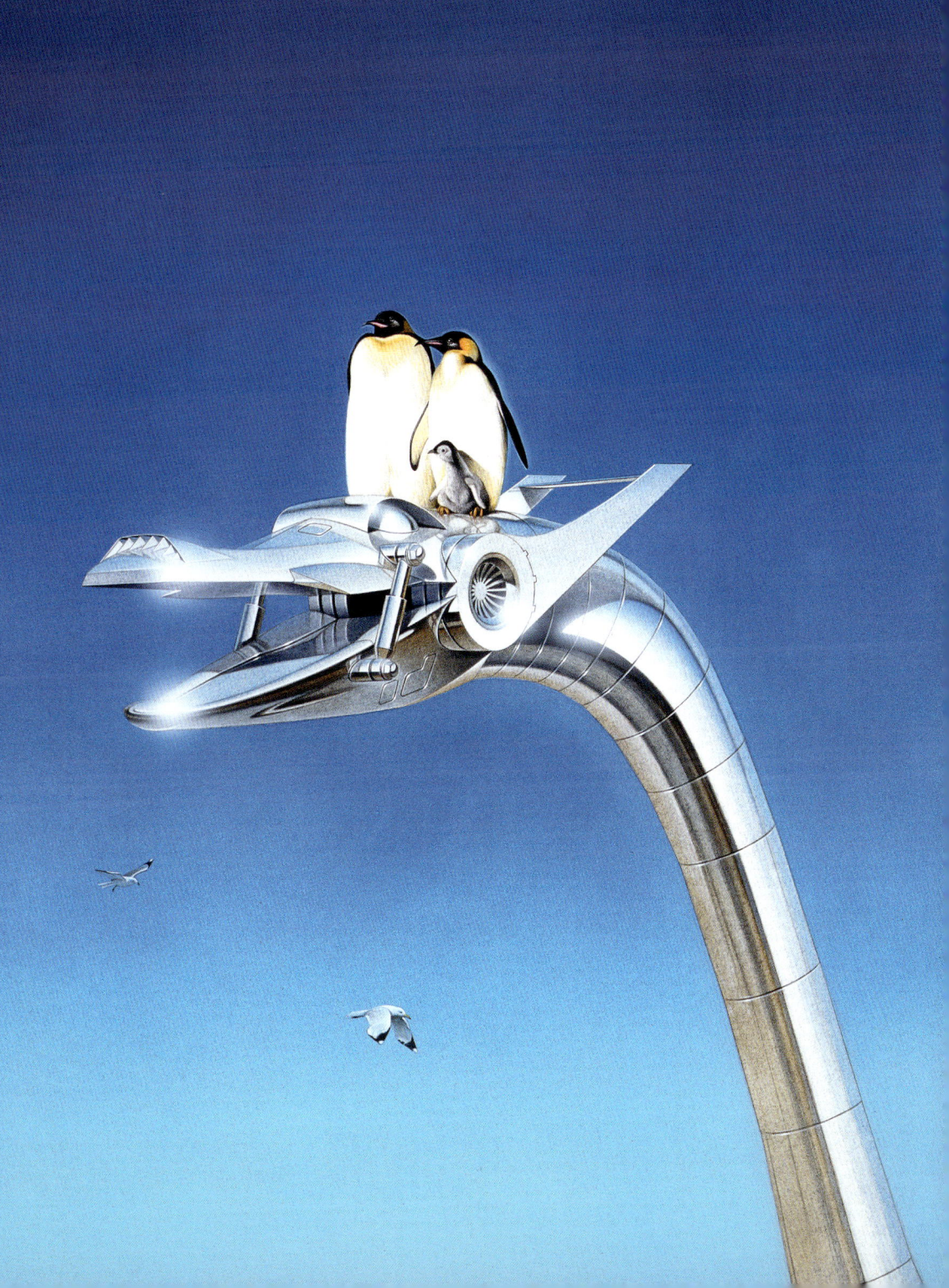

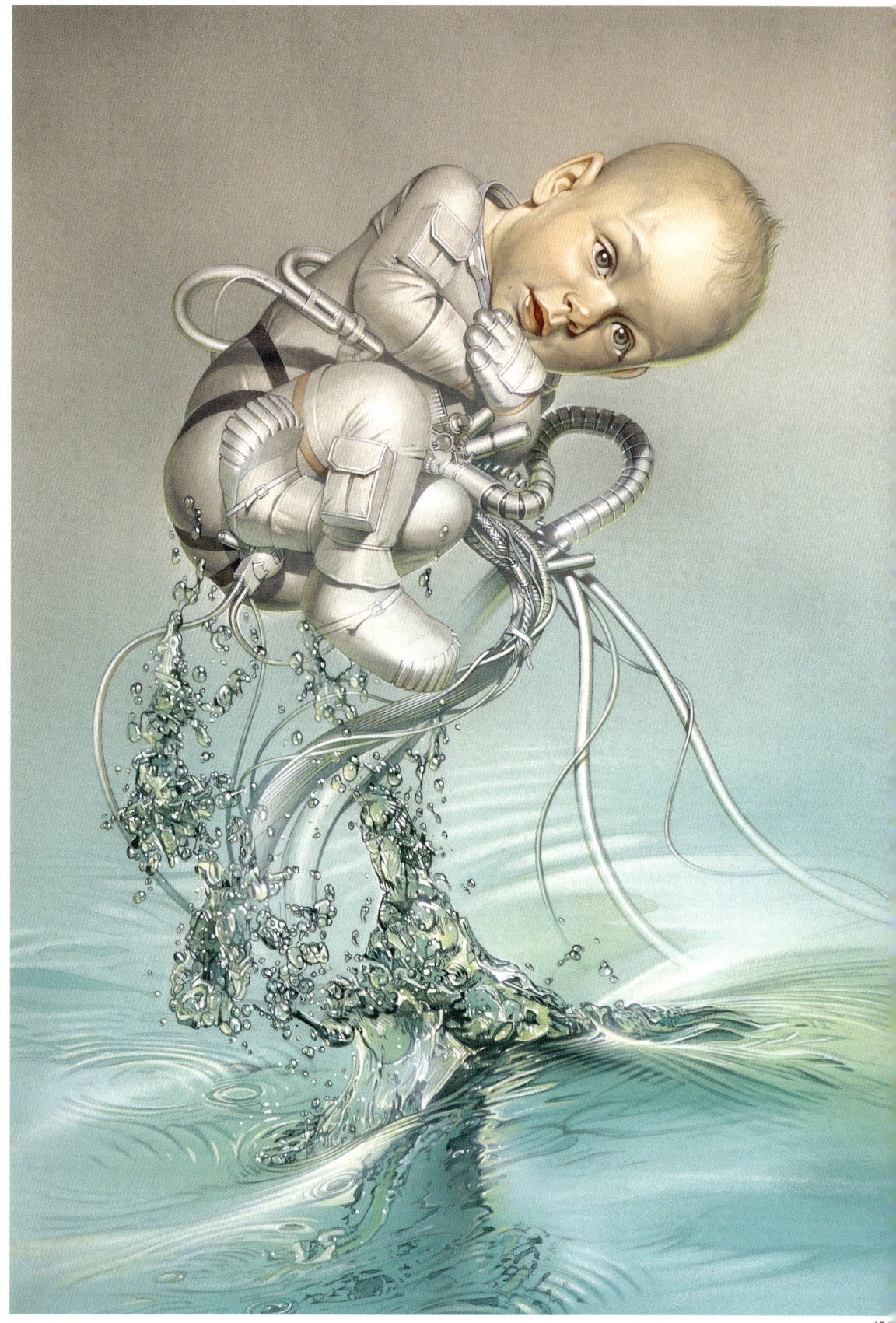

鹿島　茂（フランス文学者・明治大学教授）

サルトル曰く、あまりに美しい女の裸体は猥褻でないがゆえに、
男に欲望を生じさせない、と。
私は、こと、空山基の作品にかぎり、このサルトルのテーゼは
あやまりであると断定する。
空山作品の女たちは、あまりに美しいにもかかわらず、
十分に猥褻であり、欲望をかきたてるからである。
空山ワールドこそは、
美と猥褻さを両立させた奇跡の産物なのである。

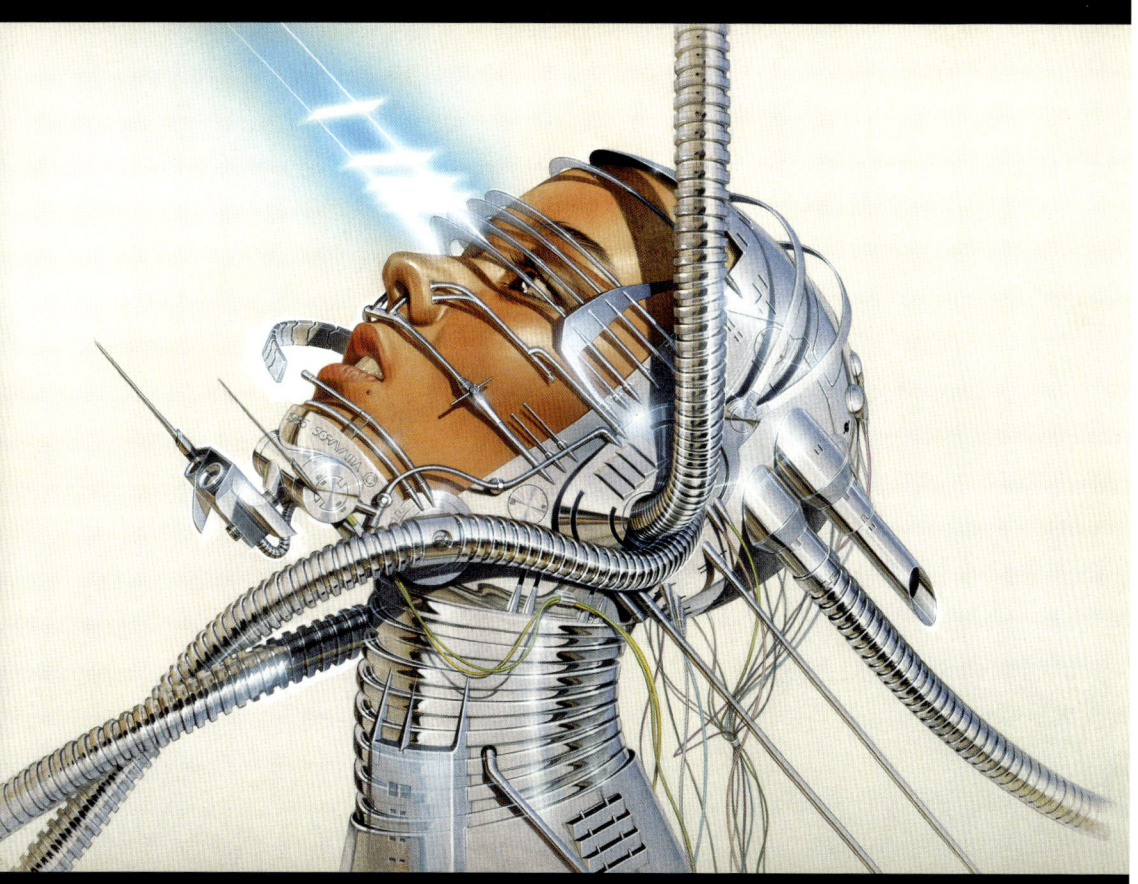

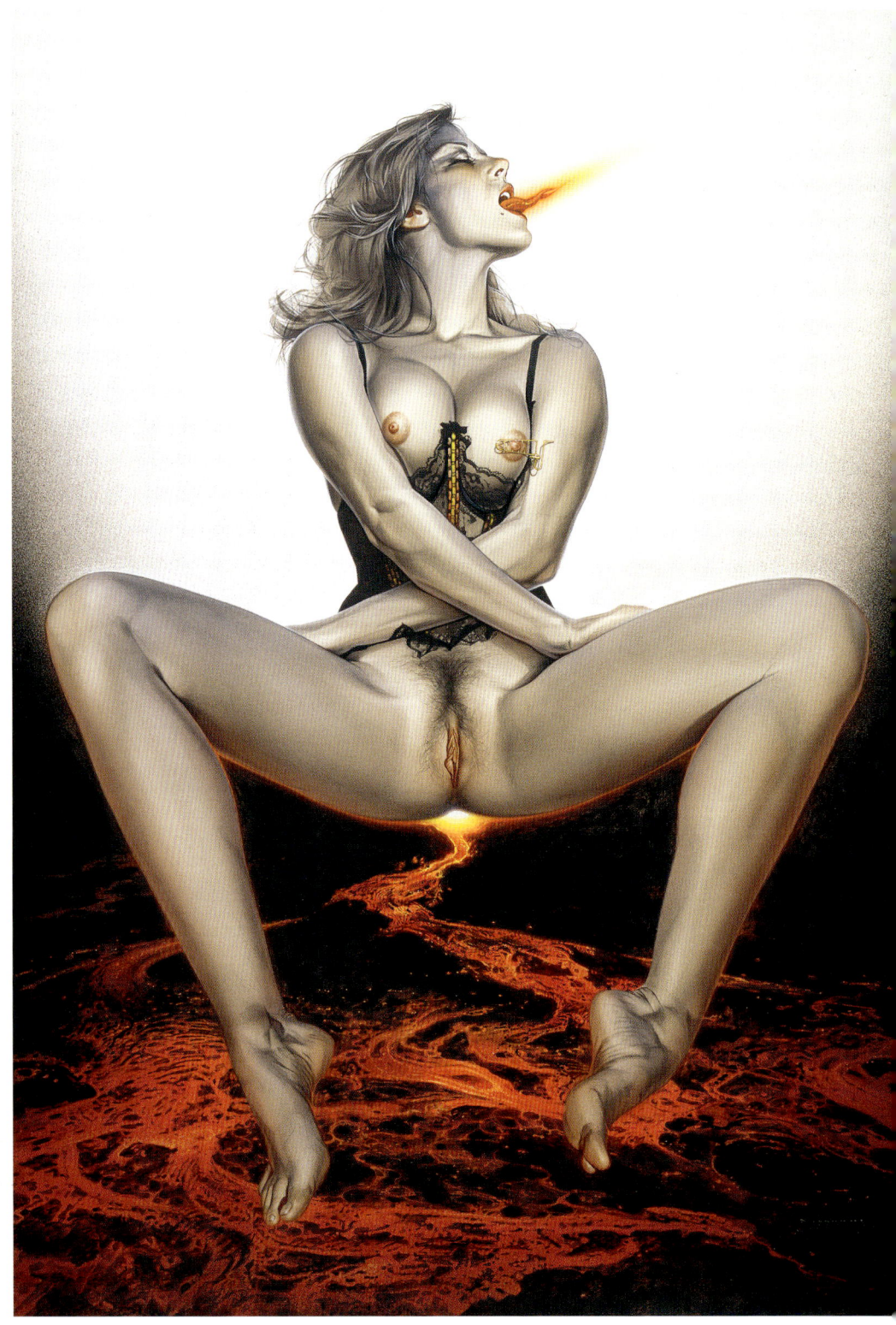

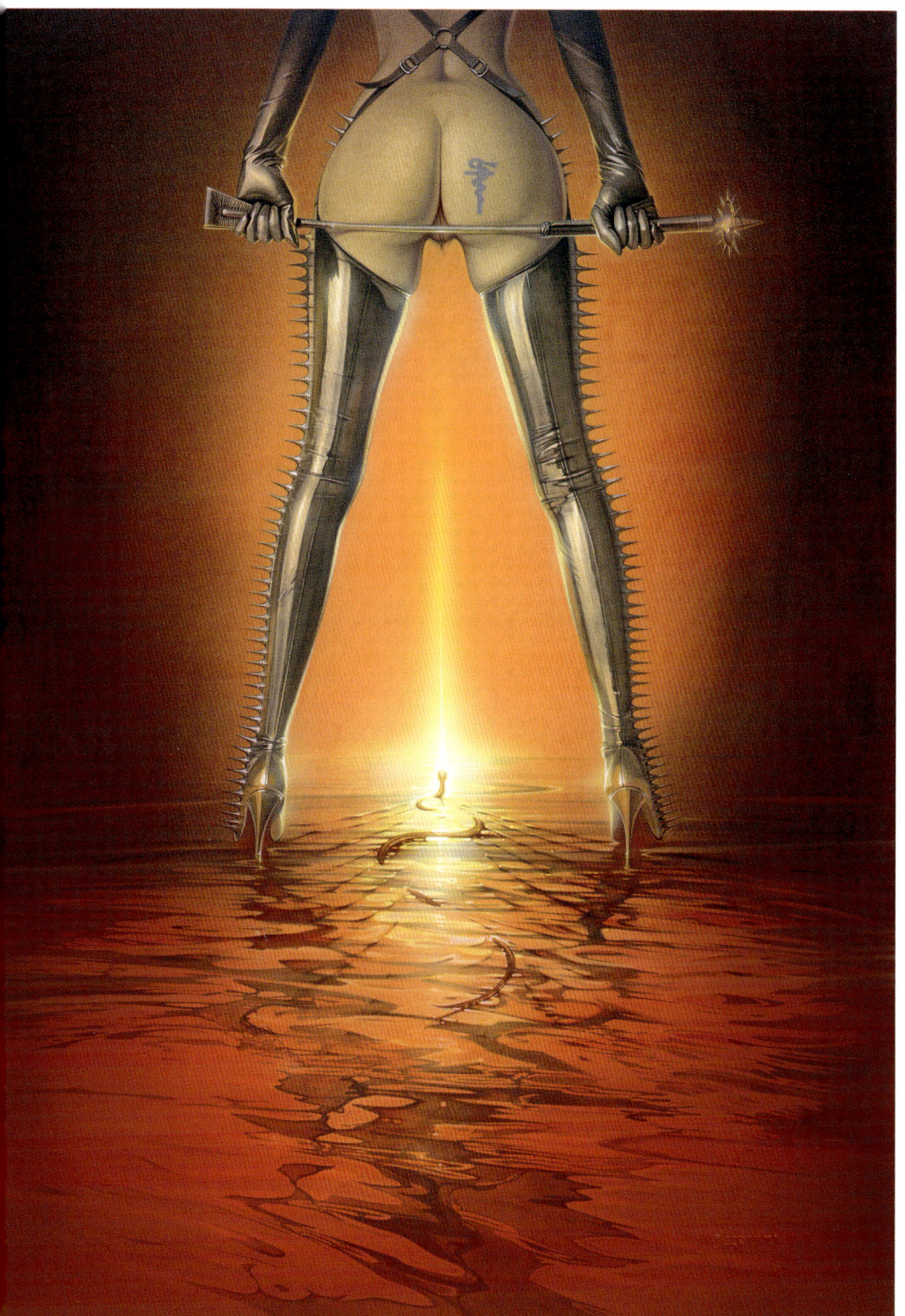

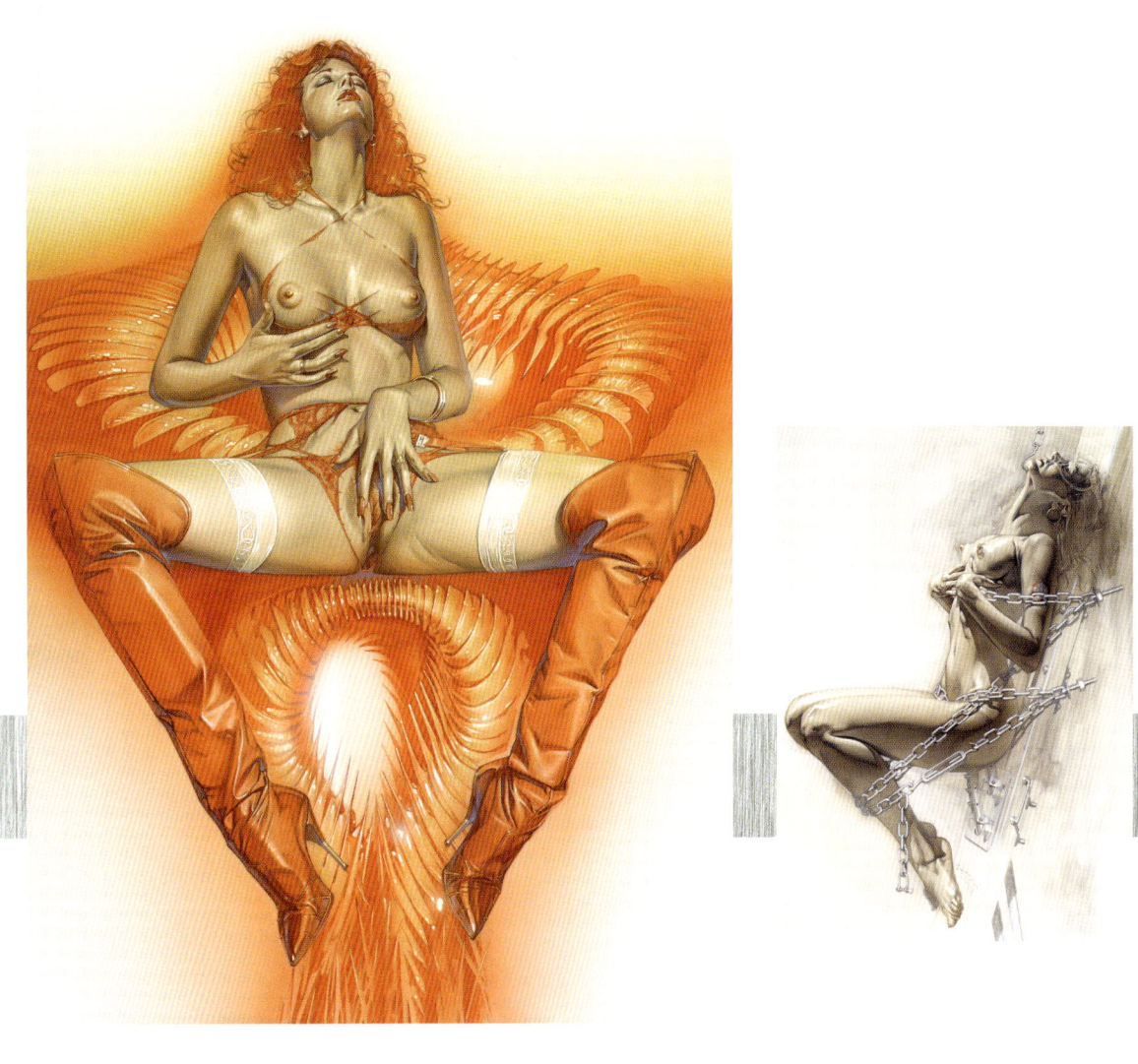

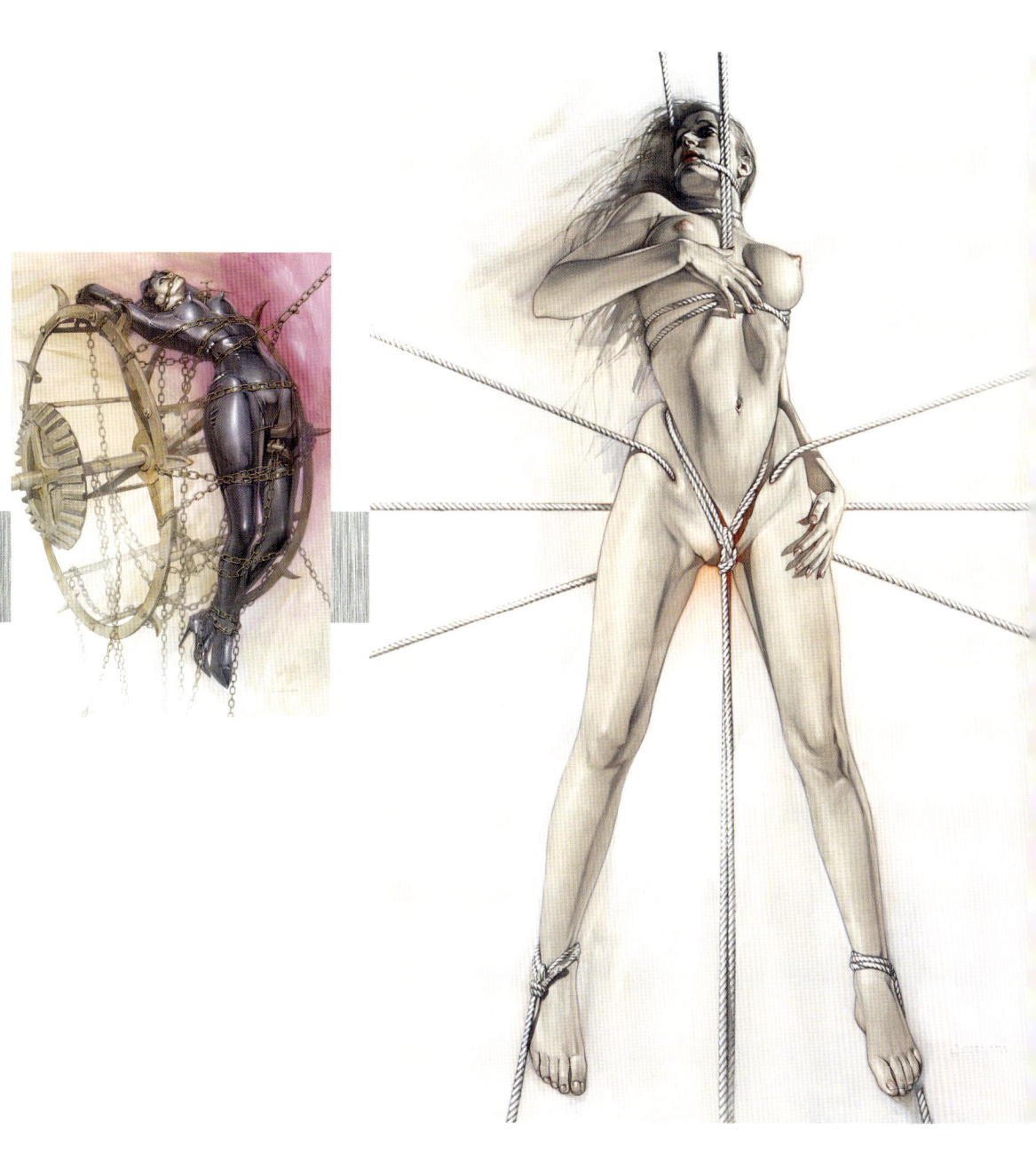

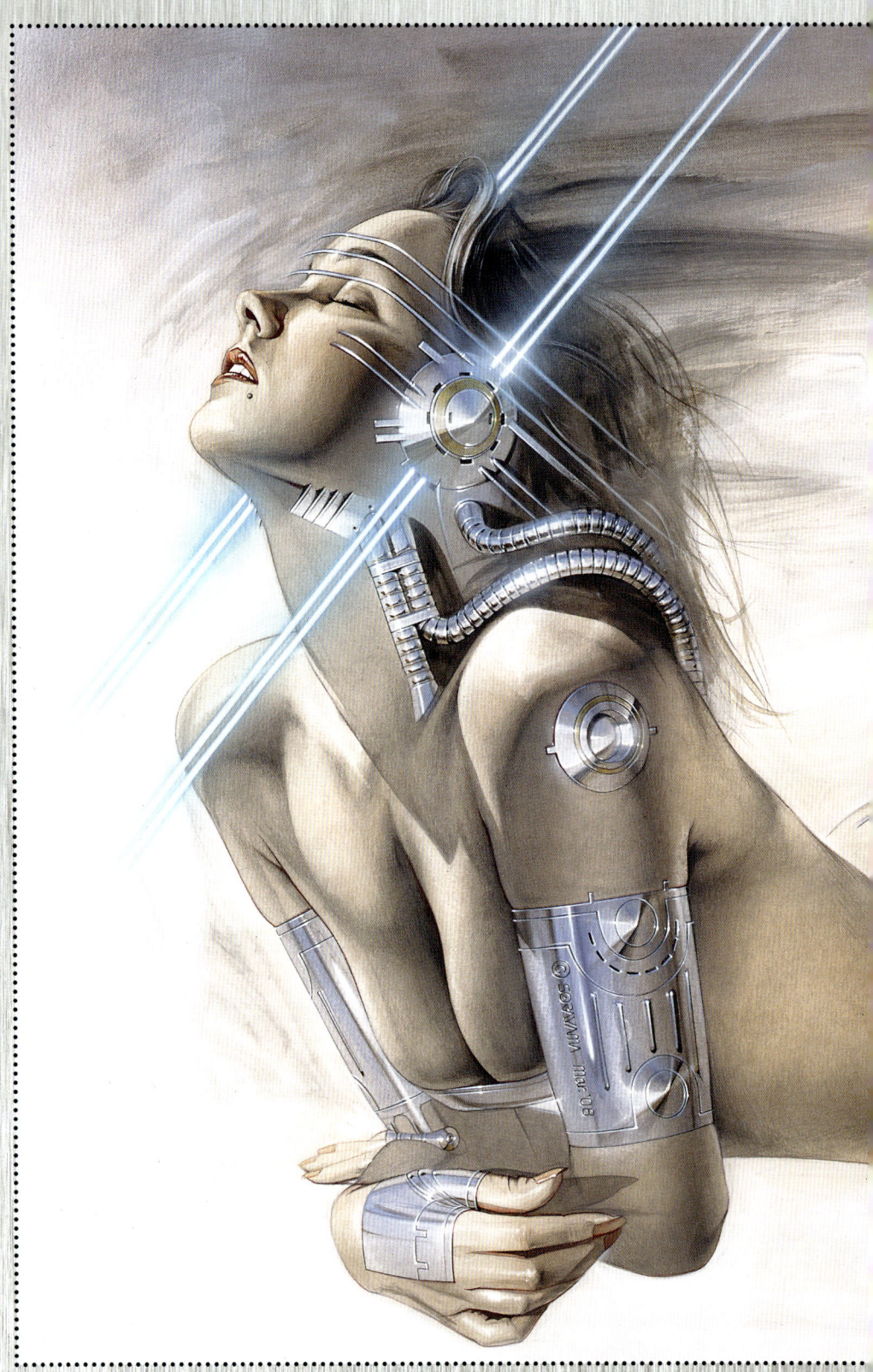

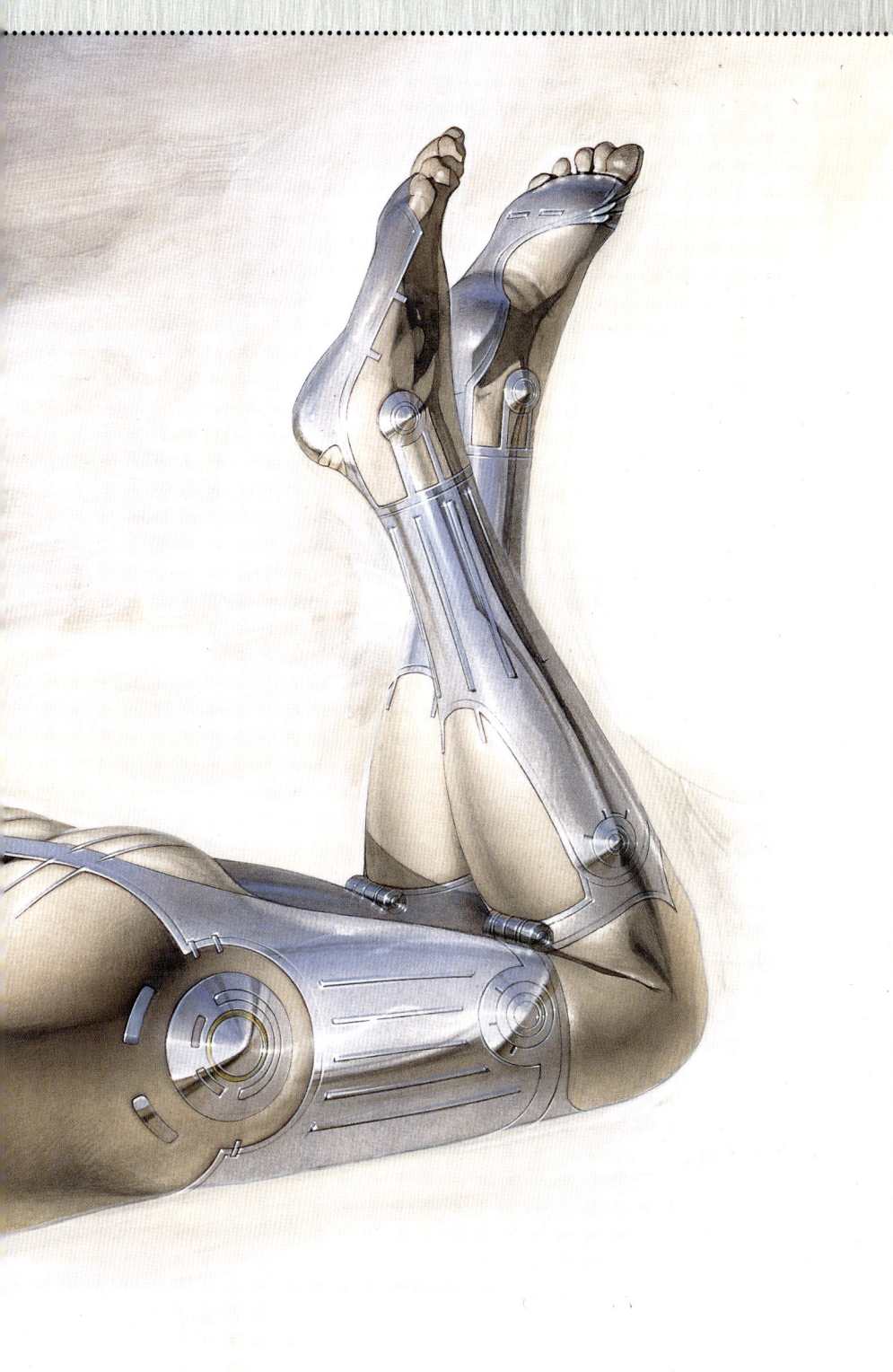

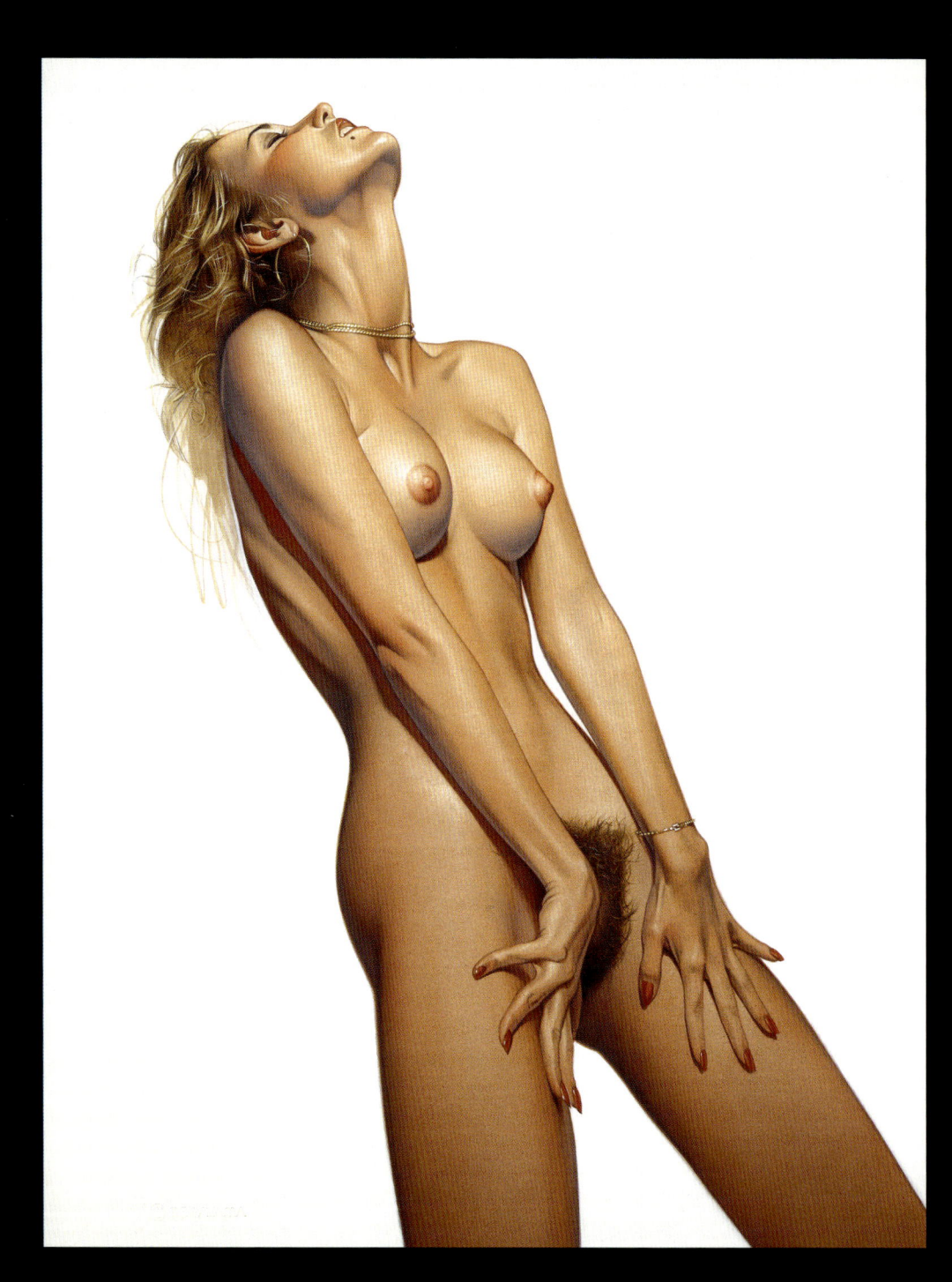

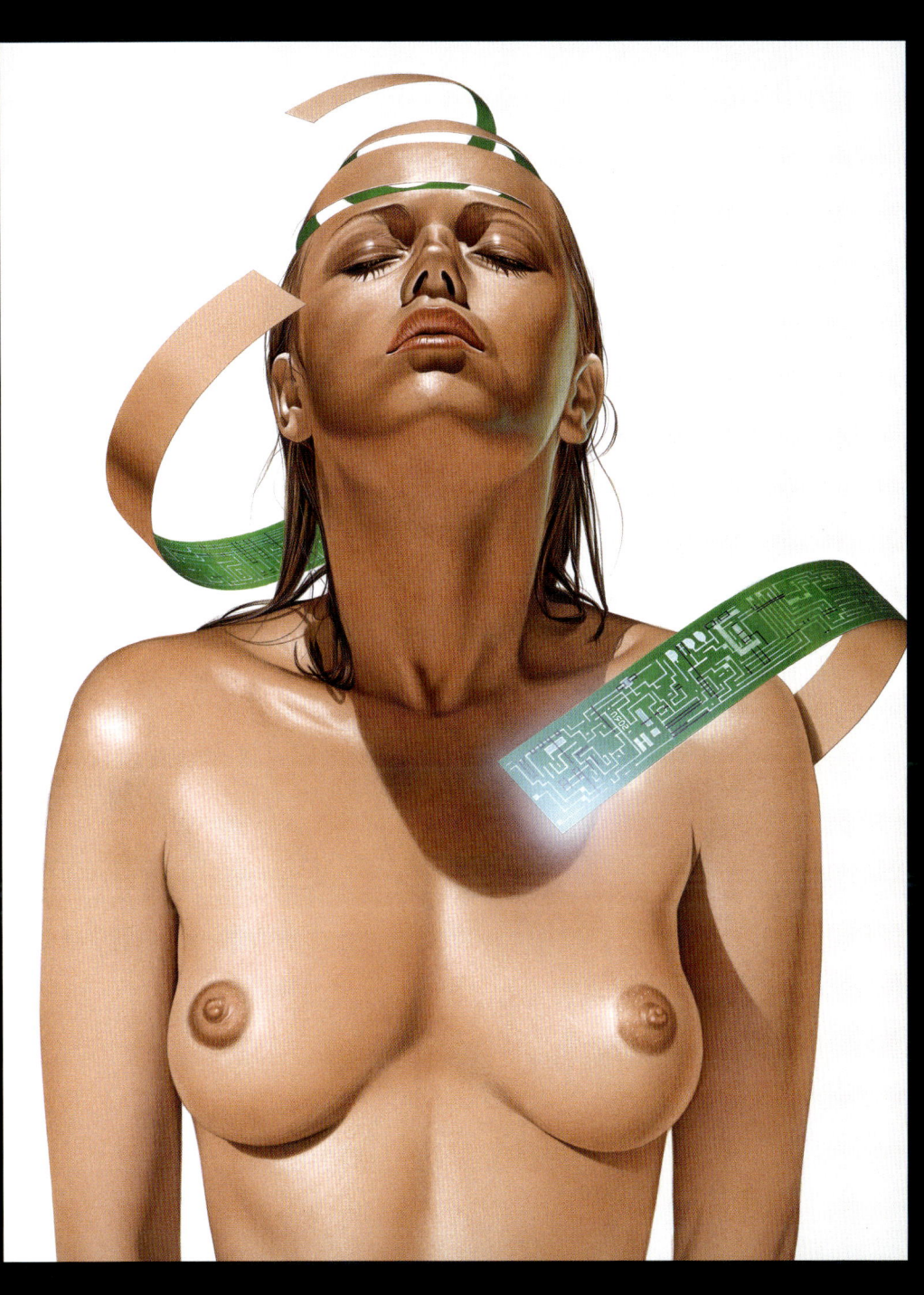

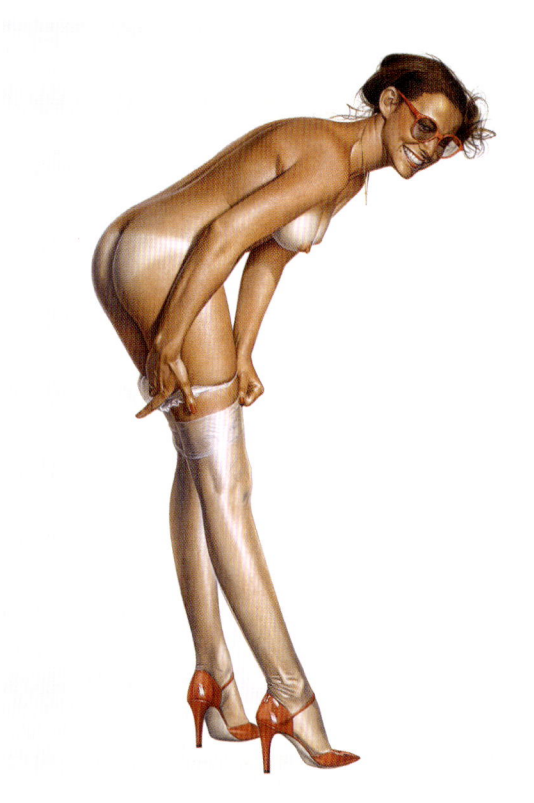
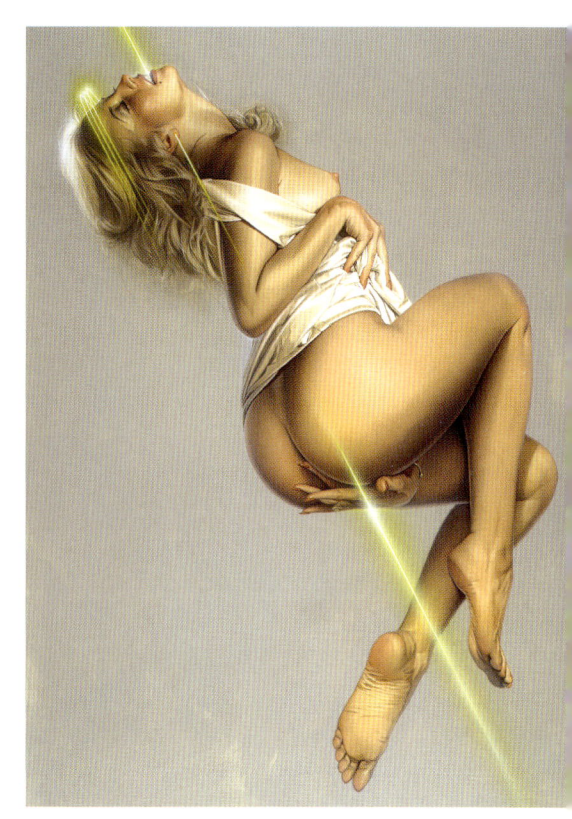
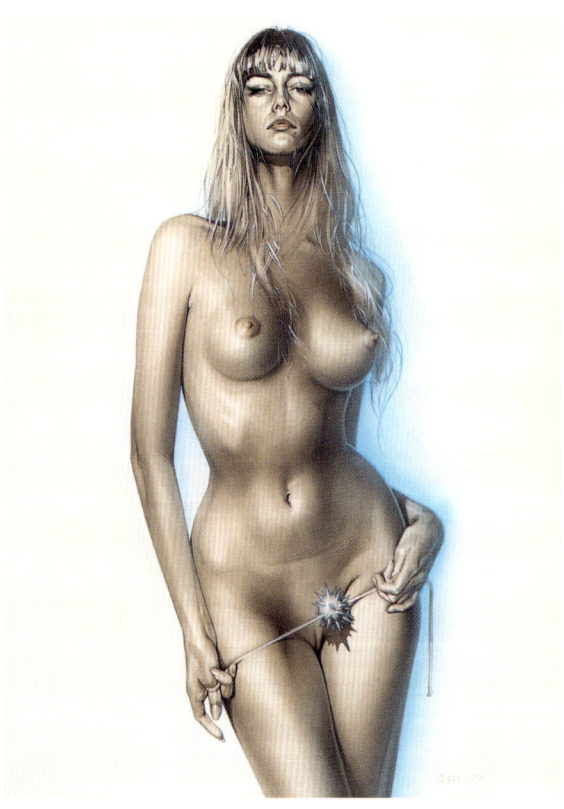
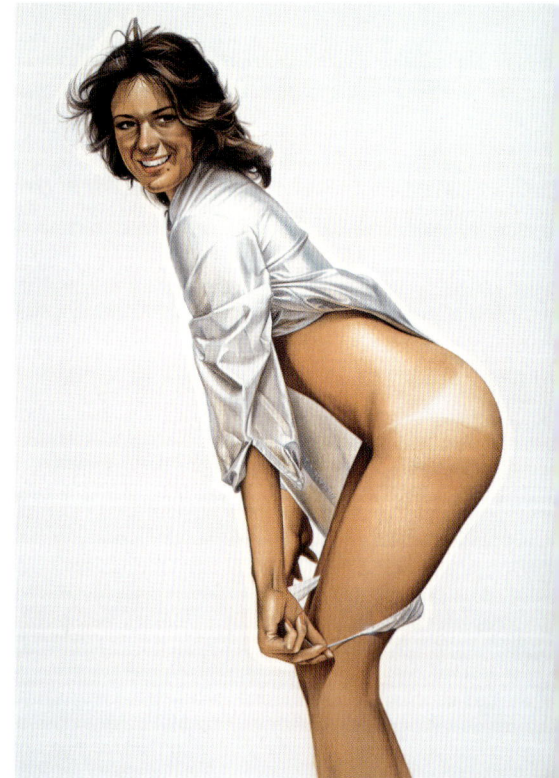

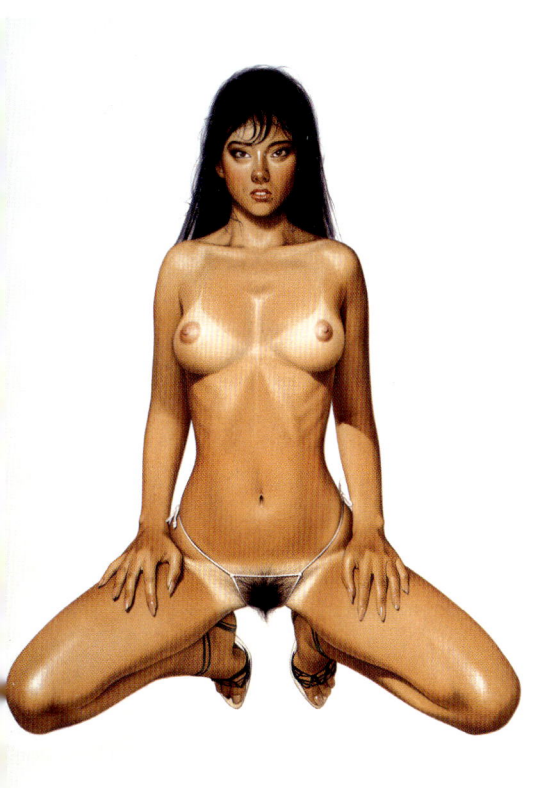
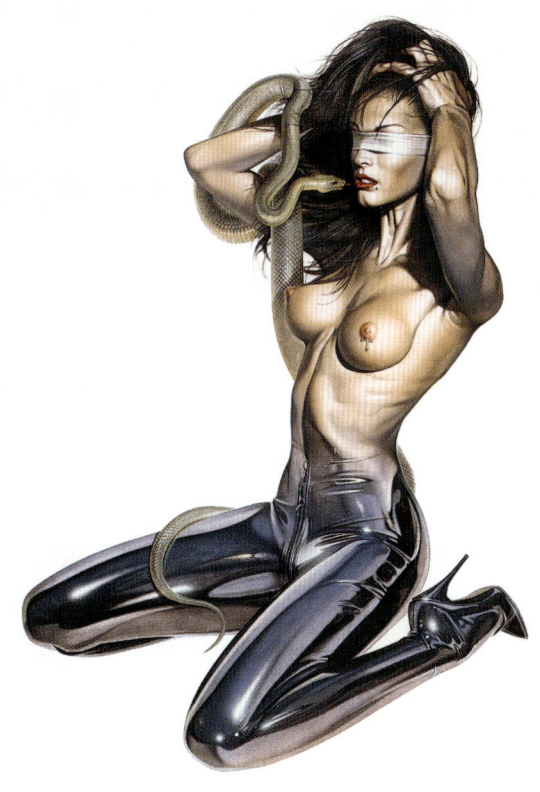
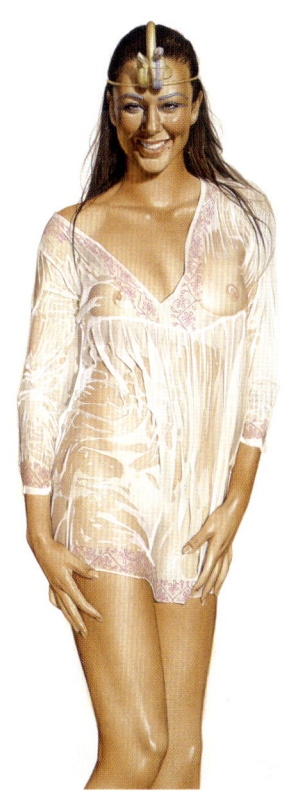
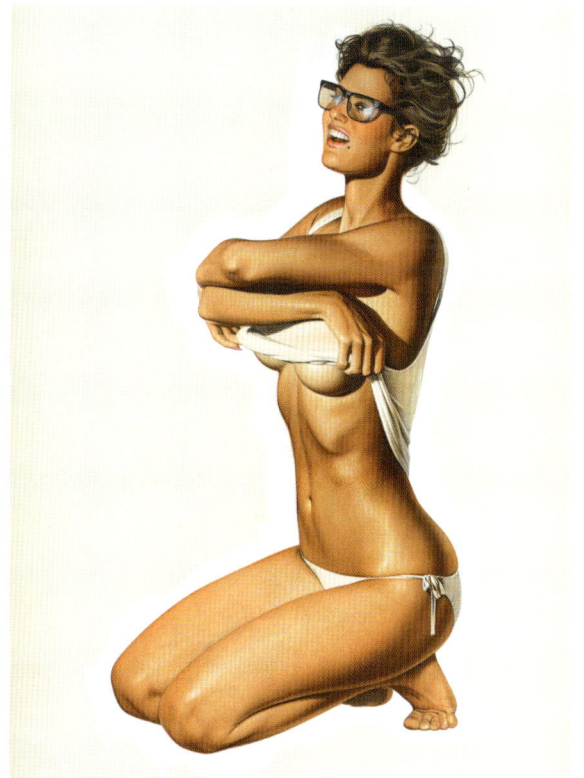

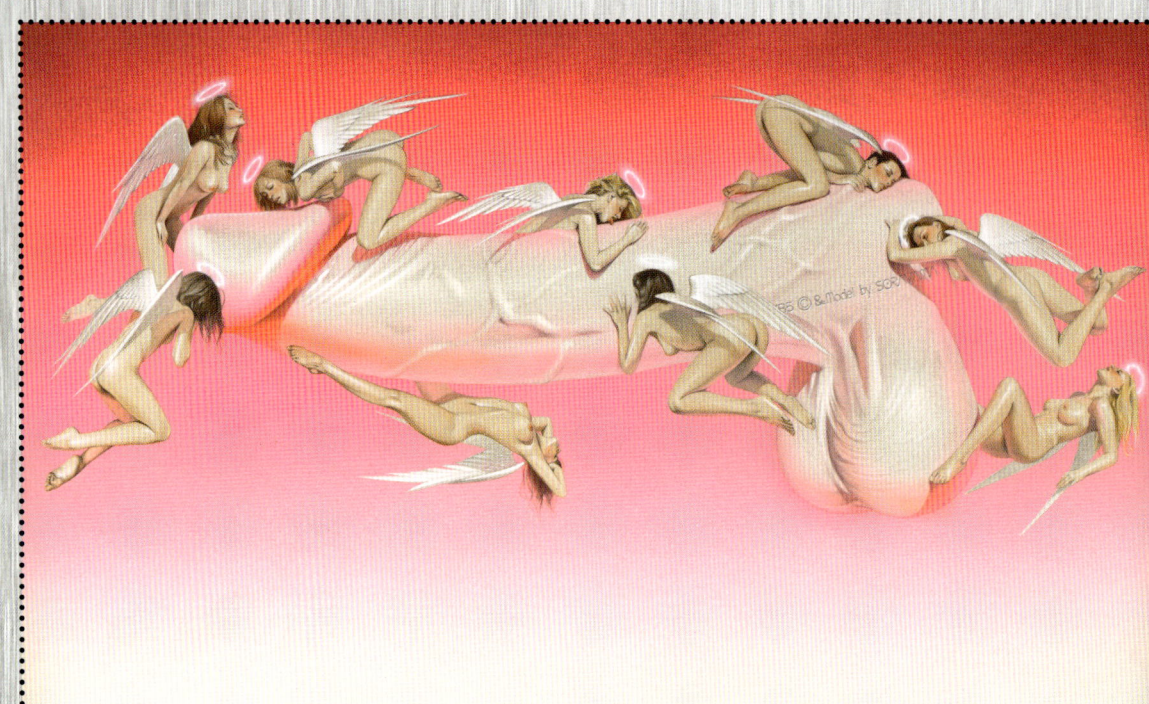

佐々木悟郎（イラストレーター）

空山さんの笑った顔が好きだ。いや、むしろ笑い方が好きだ、と言った方がいいかも知れない。

十年ほど前の事だけど、新年会で初めて御一緒させていただいて、直接お話するまでは少し恐い人なんじゃないかという印象があった。つまんない事言うと叱られそうな…。

確かには、きりした方で、好きなものは好き、嫌いなものは嫌い、とちゃんと言える人なのだ。でもさらっと言うから後をひかない。だ。

今ろ僕も空山さんと話をする時、ちゃんと自分の意見を持っていなくちゃな、と気がつくと背すじをのばしている。

最初は空山さんの方から気さくに声をかけてくれた。少し照れくさそうな感じで話をしていたと思ったら、何か軽いジョークを言って思い、切り声をたてて「ハハハ」等ときたのだ。その時の空山さんの顔がちょっと助平ぽくって、いいなあなんて思った。それでぐっと身近に感じるようになった。

絵は、とても上品だと思います。

佐々木悟郎

以上
12/28/97

Arno Welke （アルノ・ヴェルク：
マーケティング・ディレクター）

Für mich zählt der japanische illustrator und Maler Hajime Sorayama mit seinen hyperrealistischen Werken zu den bedeutendsten Künstlern der Gegenwart. Das unterstreichen nicht zuletzt die Beobachtungen, wie häufig seine Motive entweder unverändert kopiert oder aber leicht modifiziert nachempfunden werden. Ganz zu schweigen von den großen Verkaufserfolgen, die sich mit den zahlreichen Büchern über sein Schaffen eingestellt haben.

Dabei hat mich in den letzten fünfzehn Jahren ganz besonders die Tatsache fasziniert, daß u.a. auch sehr viele Nachwuchskreative aus dem Bereich der Airbrushmalerei in Hajime Sorayama ihr großes Vorbild gesehen haben und sehen. Eine der Ursachen ist zweifellos der Umstand, daß Sorayama seine

Vorliebe für alles Leuchtende und Glänzende sowohl bei den Sexy Robots als auch bei den vielen Pin-Up-Variationen so perfekt mit dem Pinsel umgesetzt hat, daß ihm falschlicher-weise die Spritzpistole als wesentliches Arbeitsmittel zugeschrieben worden ist. Sicher ein Mißverständnis mit dem es sich gut leben läßt.

Ehre wem Ehre gebührt und so kann ich nur hoffen und wünschen, daß Hajime Sorayama seinen unzähligen Vere-hrerinnen und Verehrern in aller Welt auch zükunftig viel Freude mit seinem kreativen Schaffen bereiten wird.

『世界の空山基。そしてコレは世界中が振り向くバイブルです。』

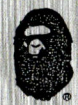

*A BATHING APE   NIGO

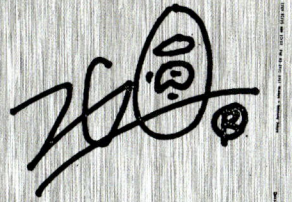

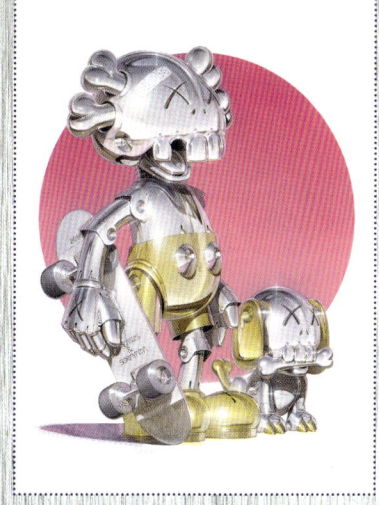

"It has been an honor to be able to work on a project with Hajime Sorayama, I never get tired of looking at his paintings"

artist KAWS

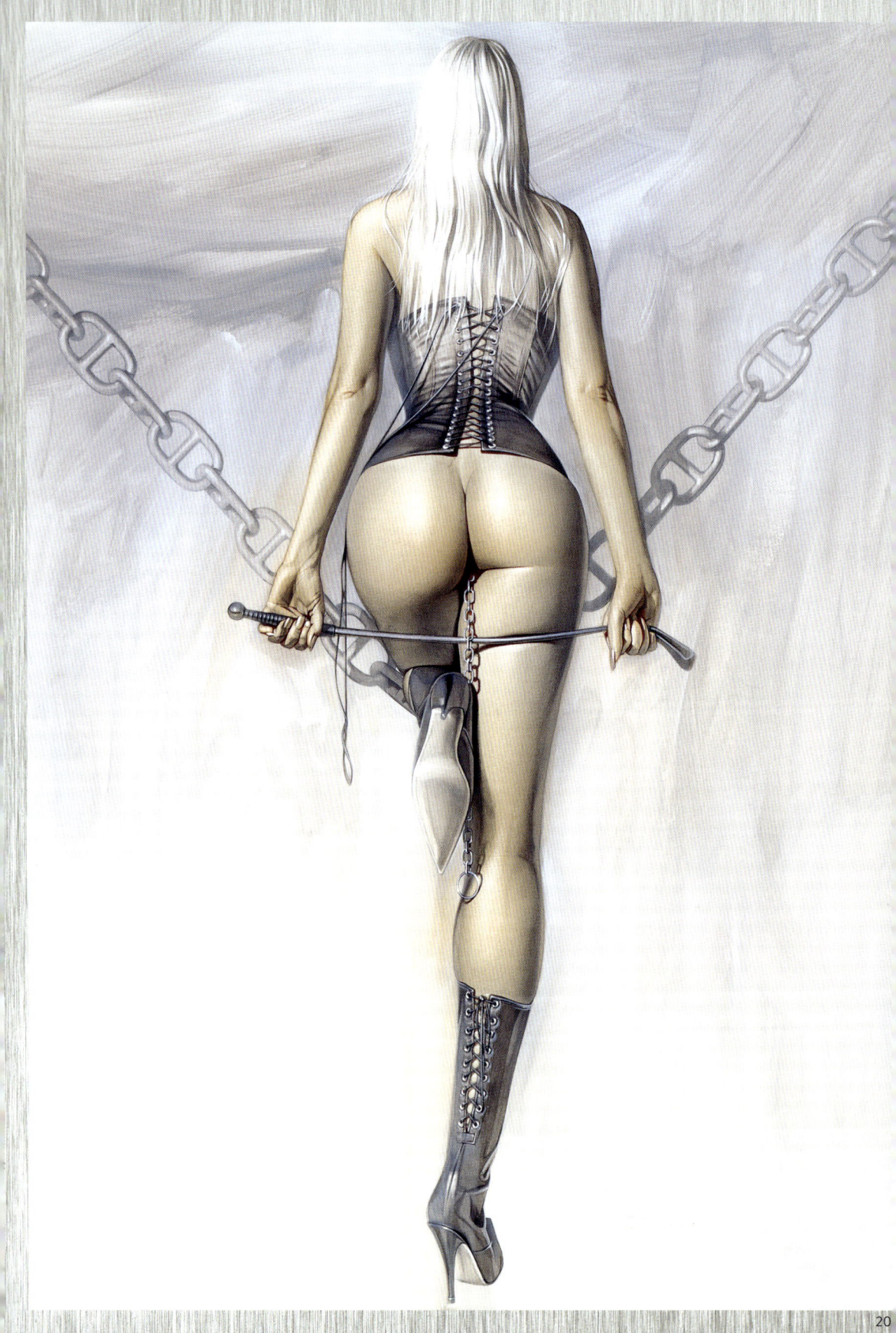

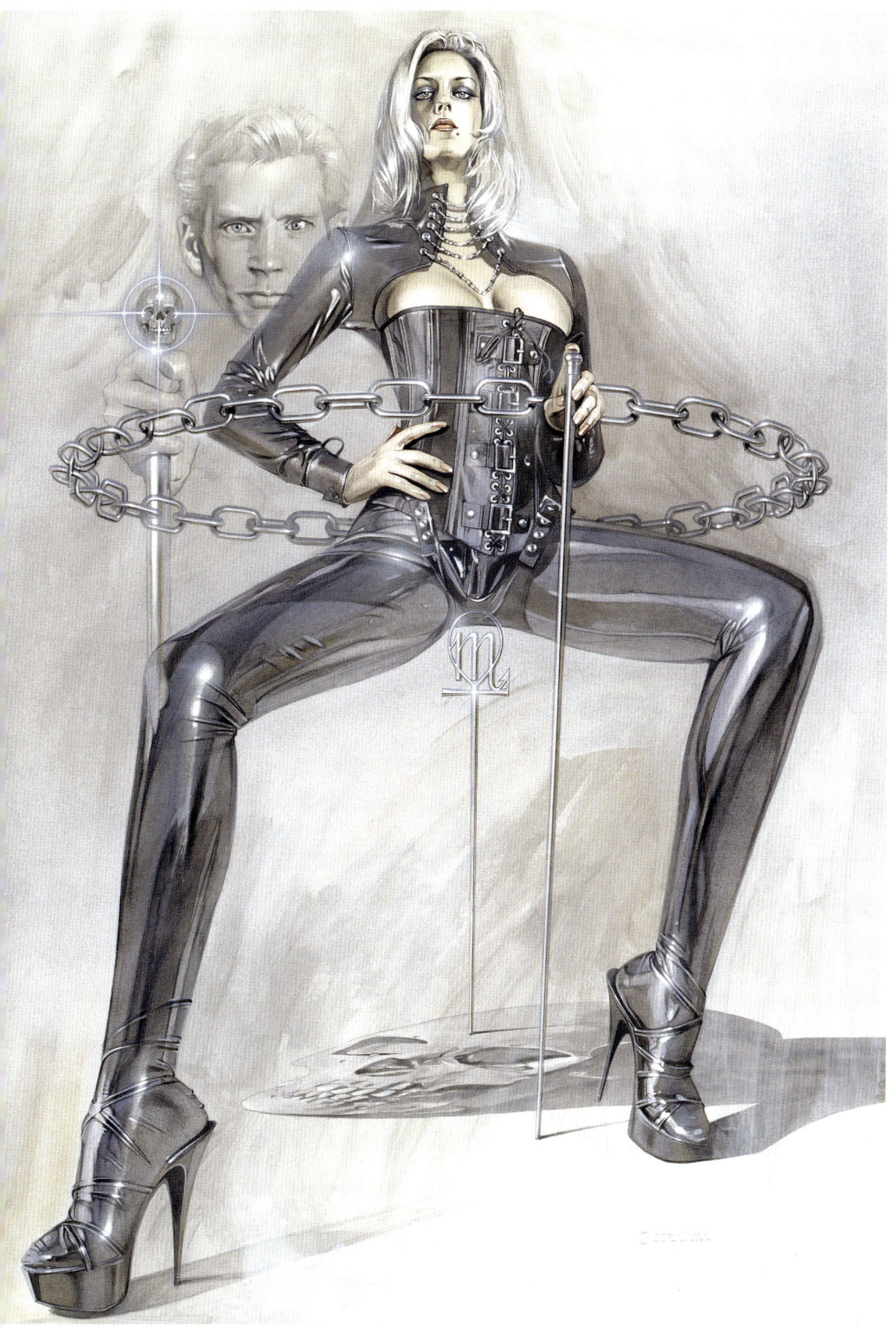

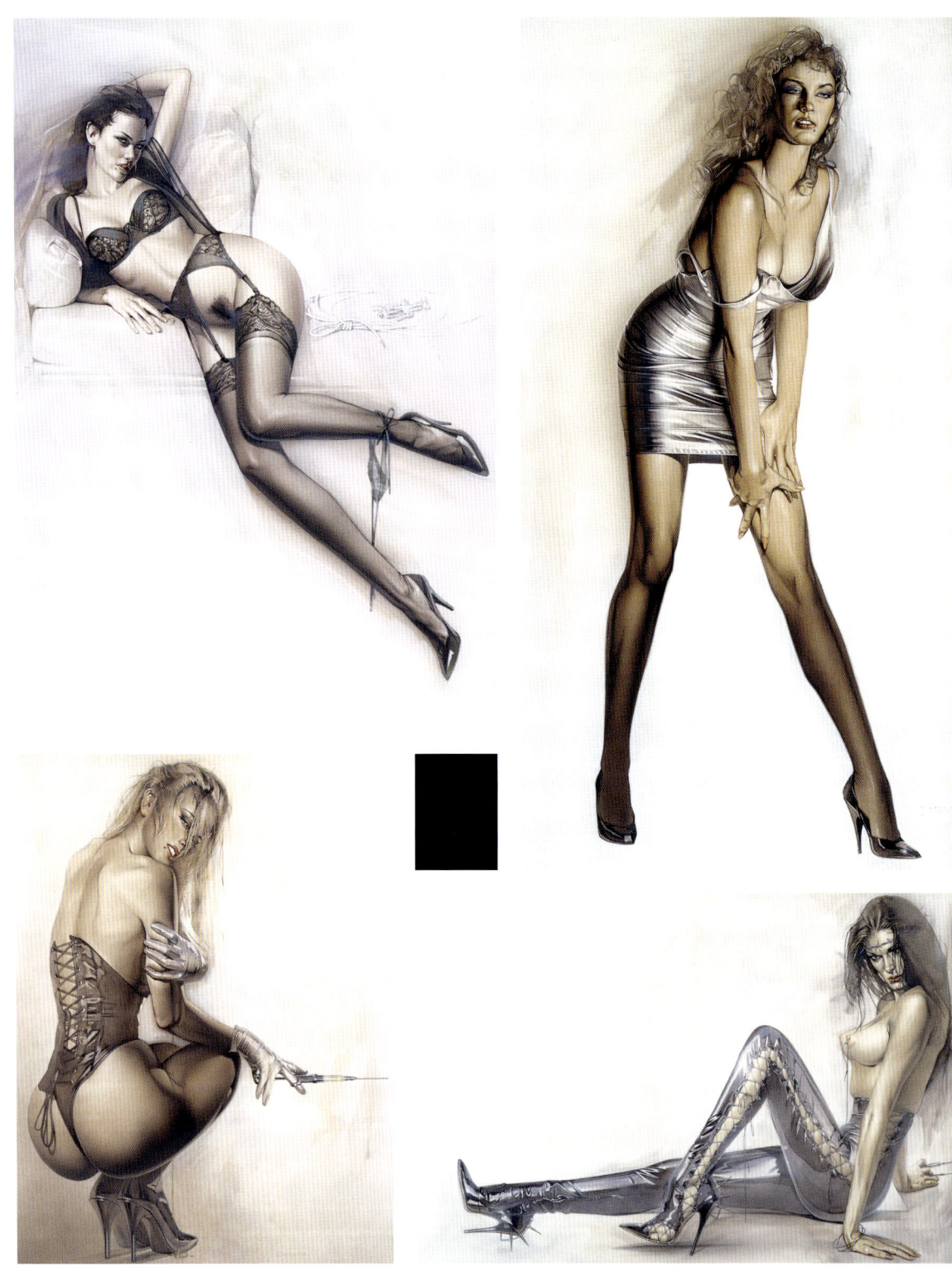

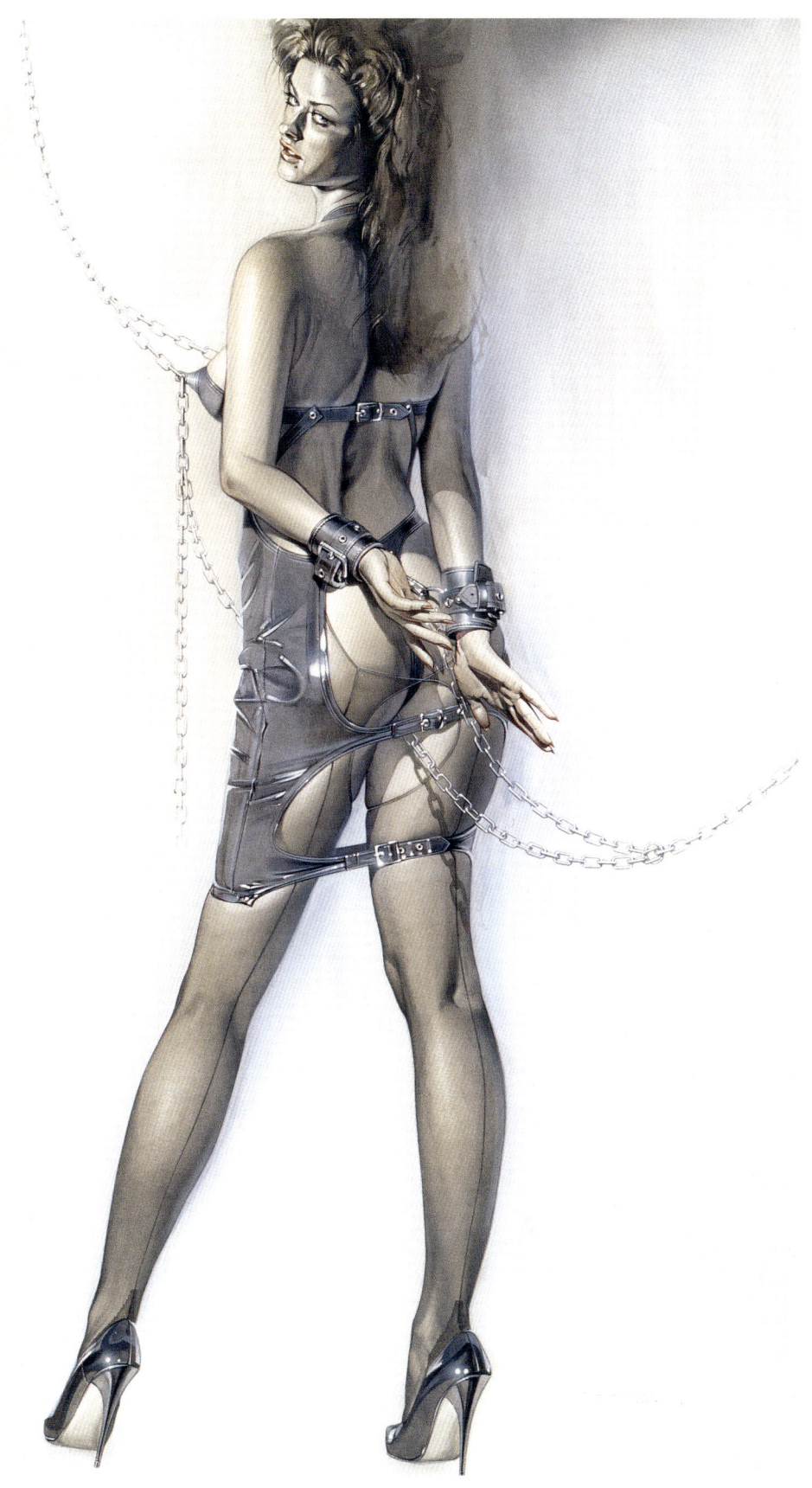

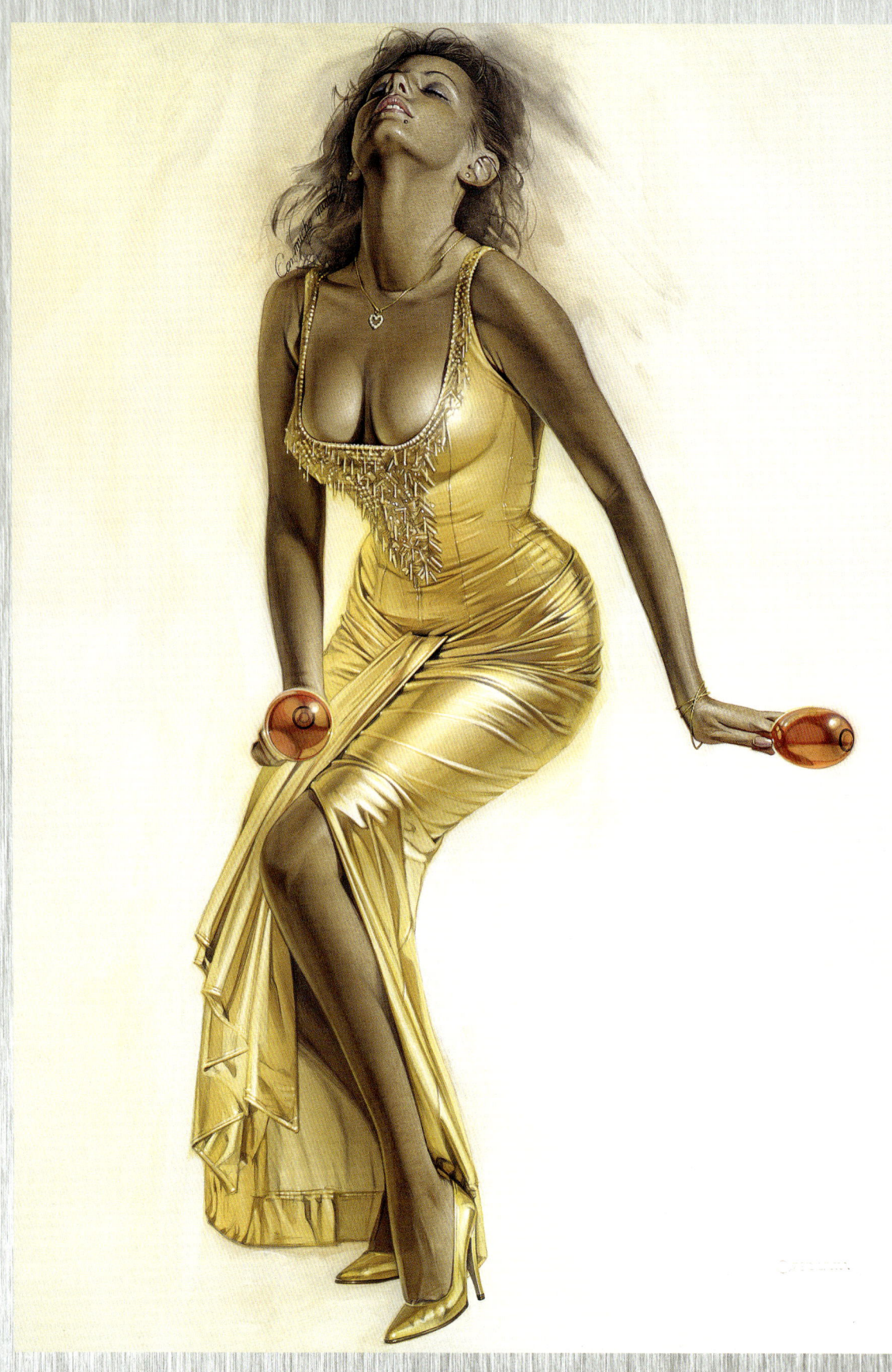

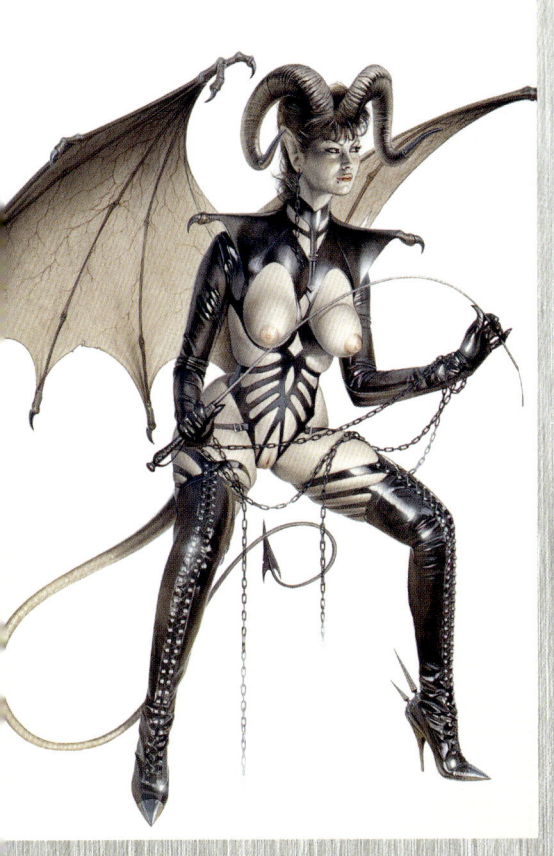
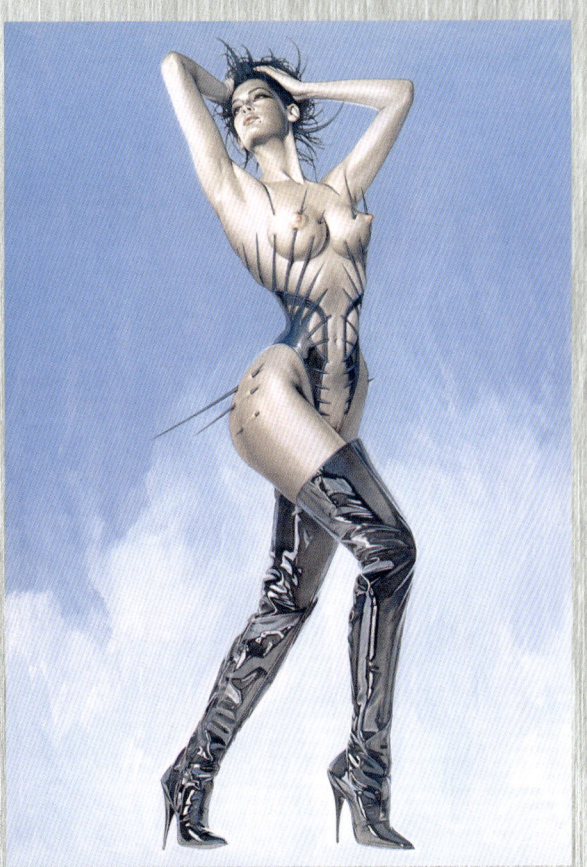

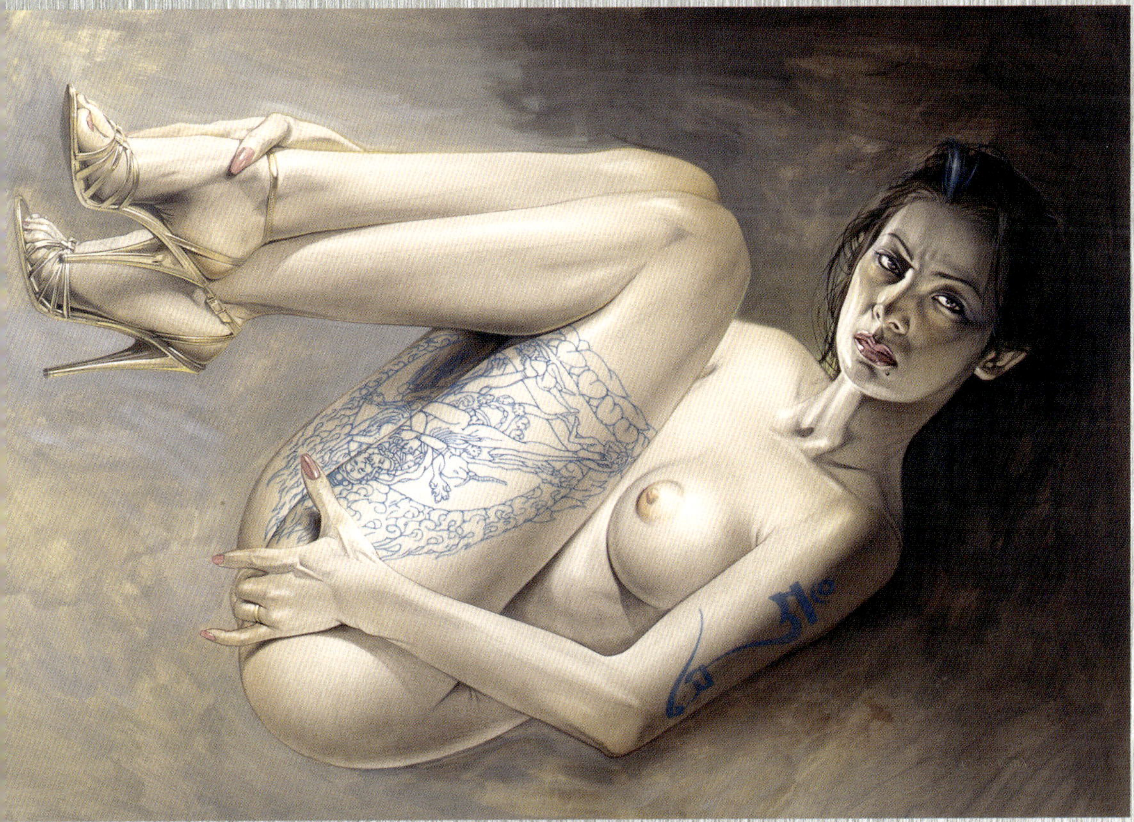

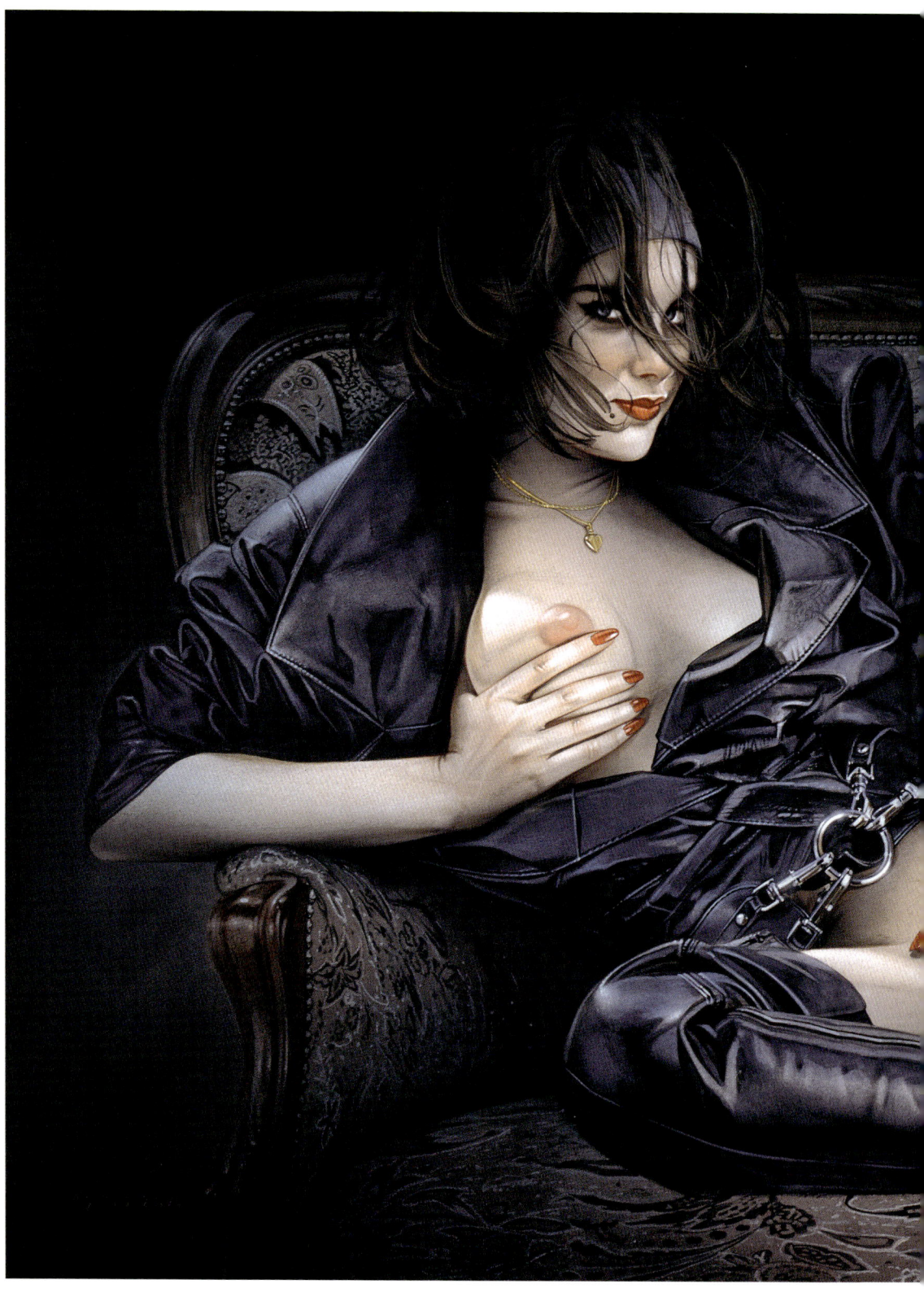

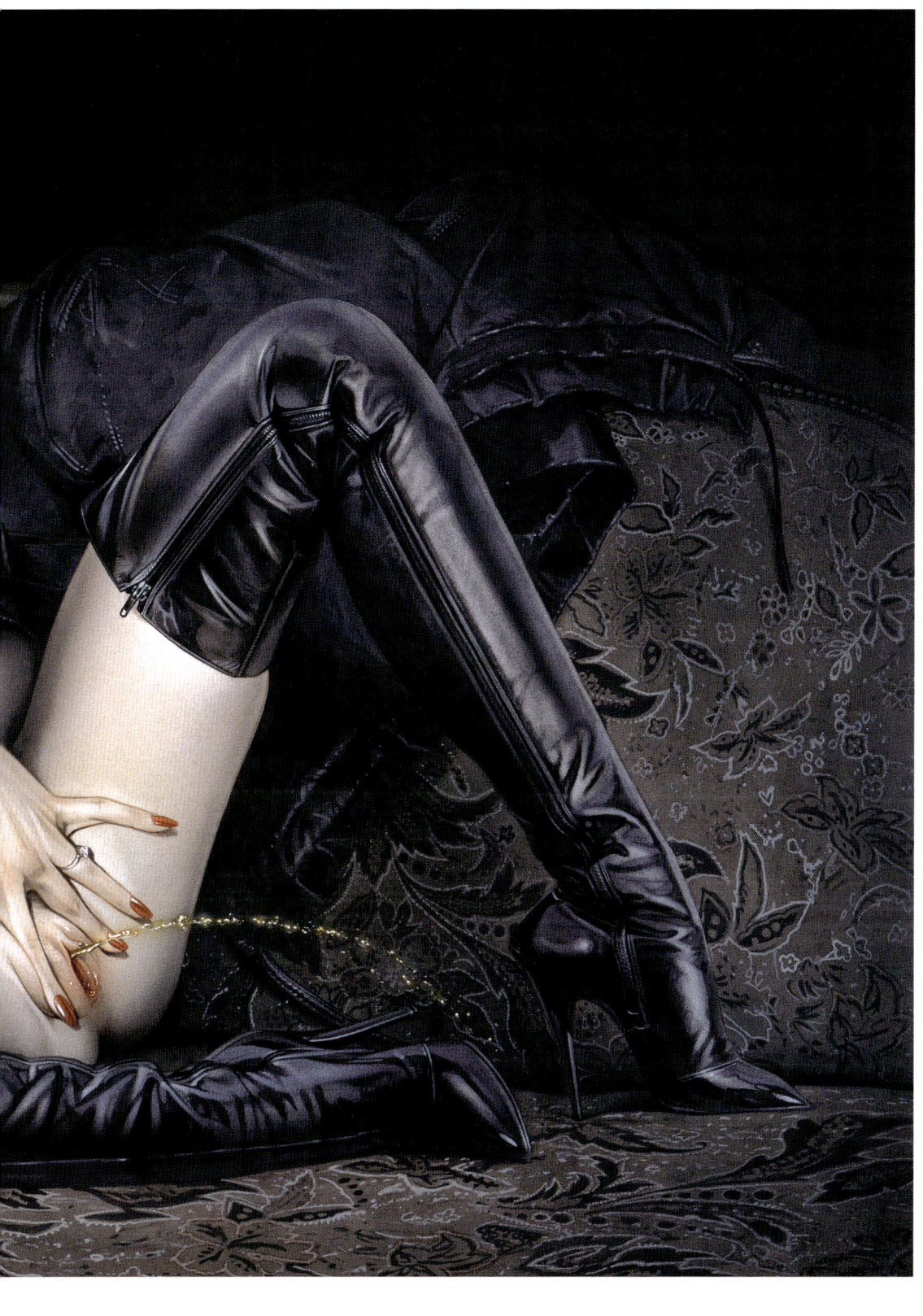

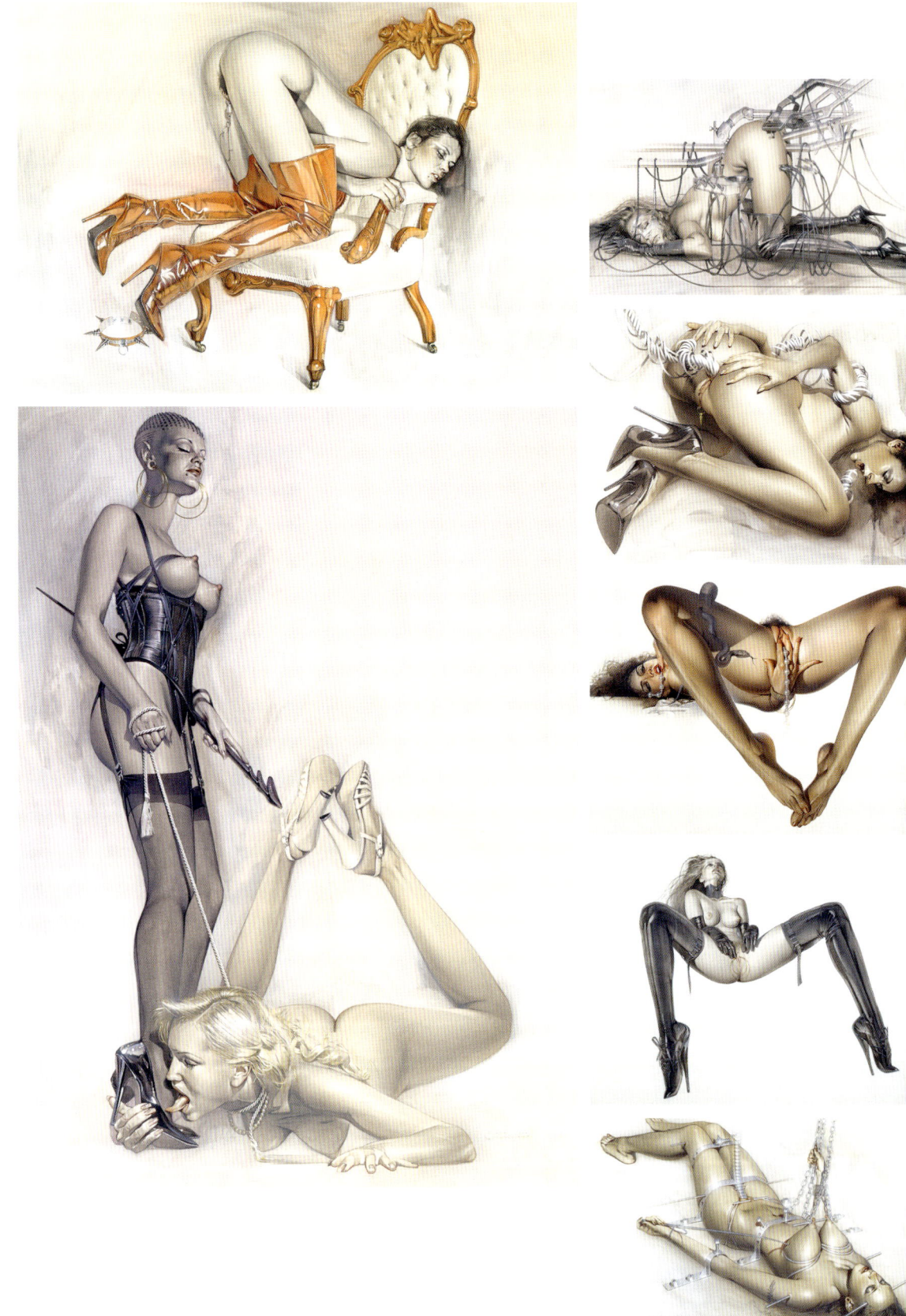

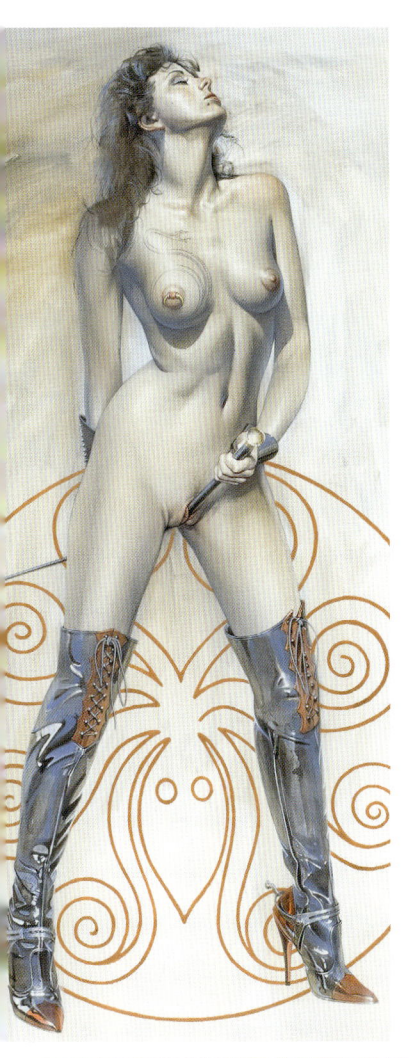
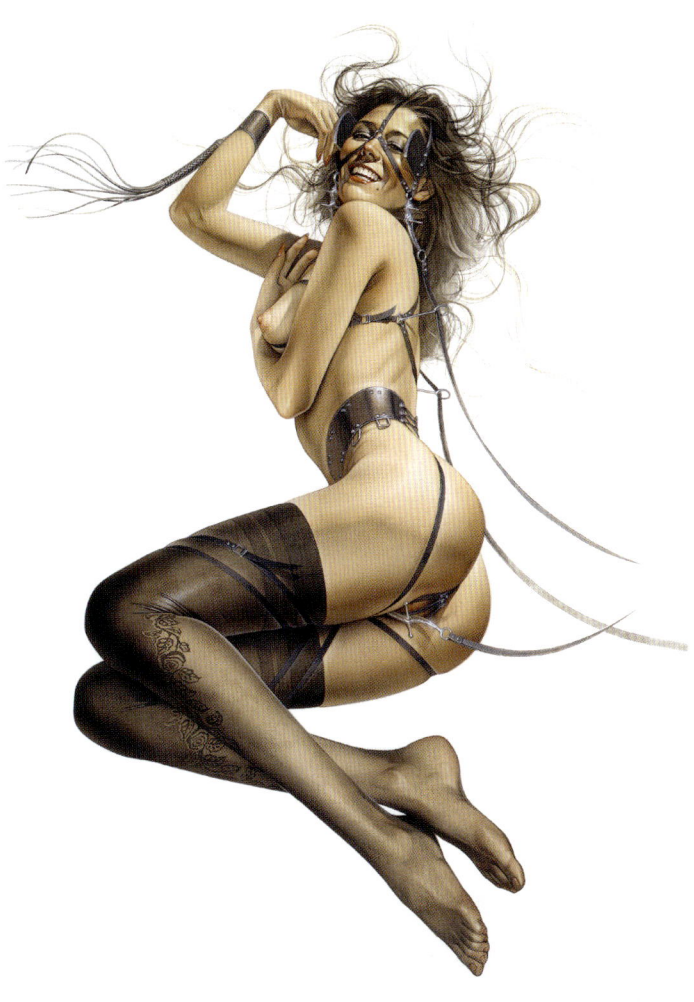
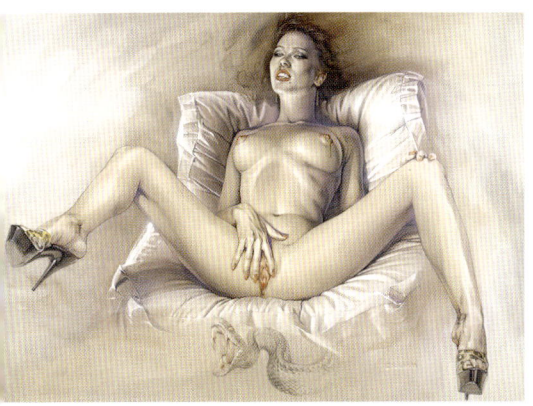
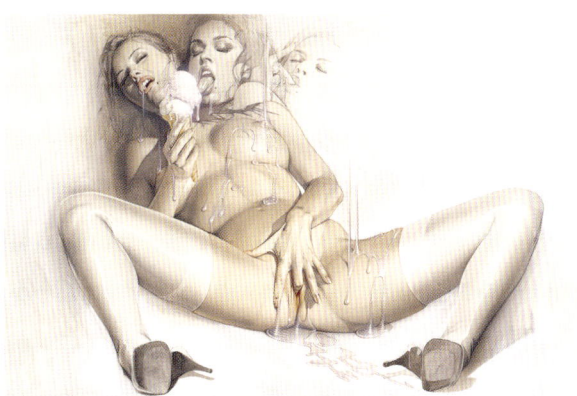

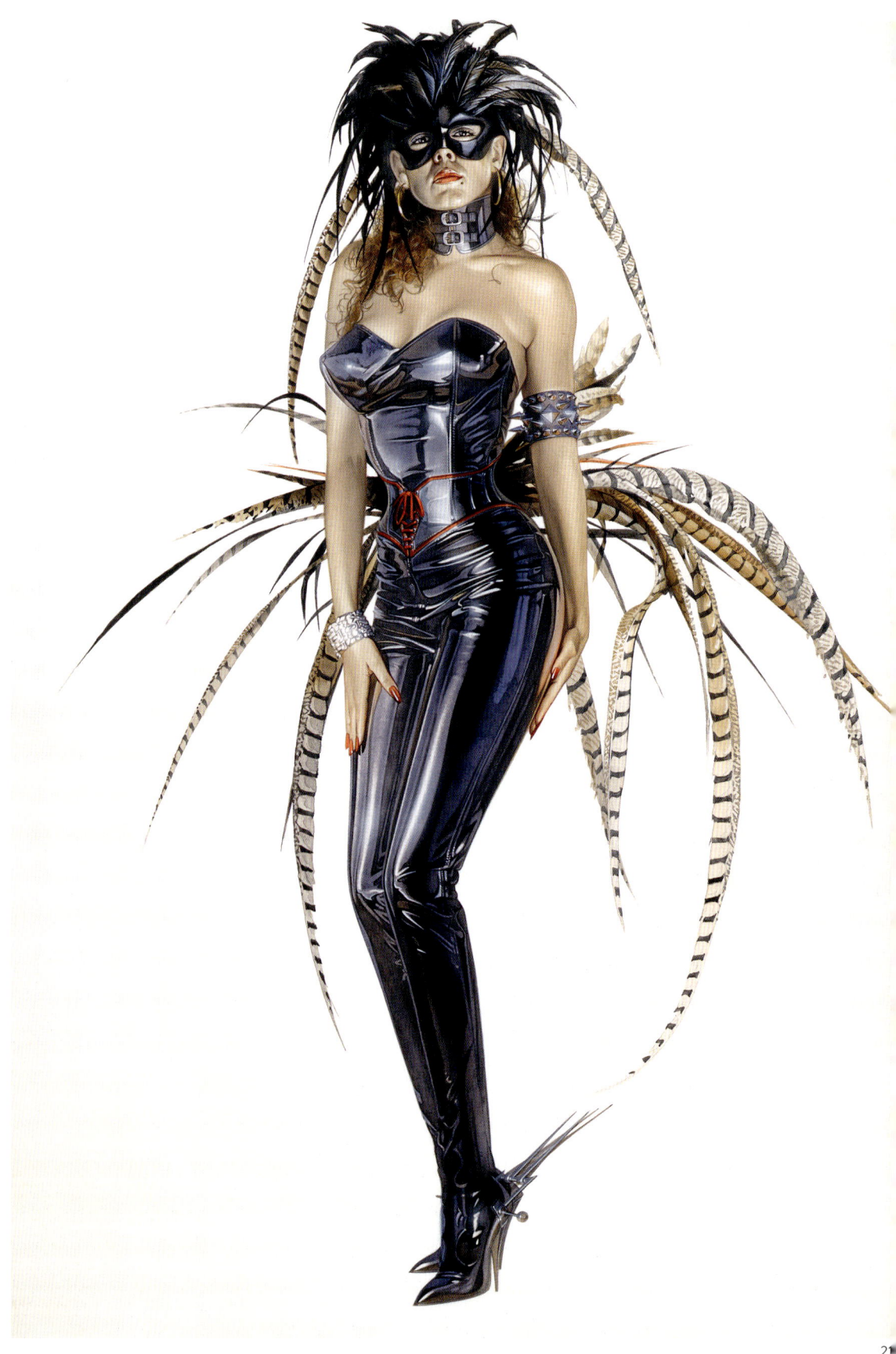

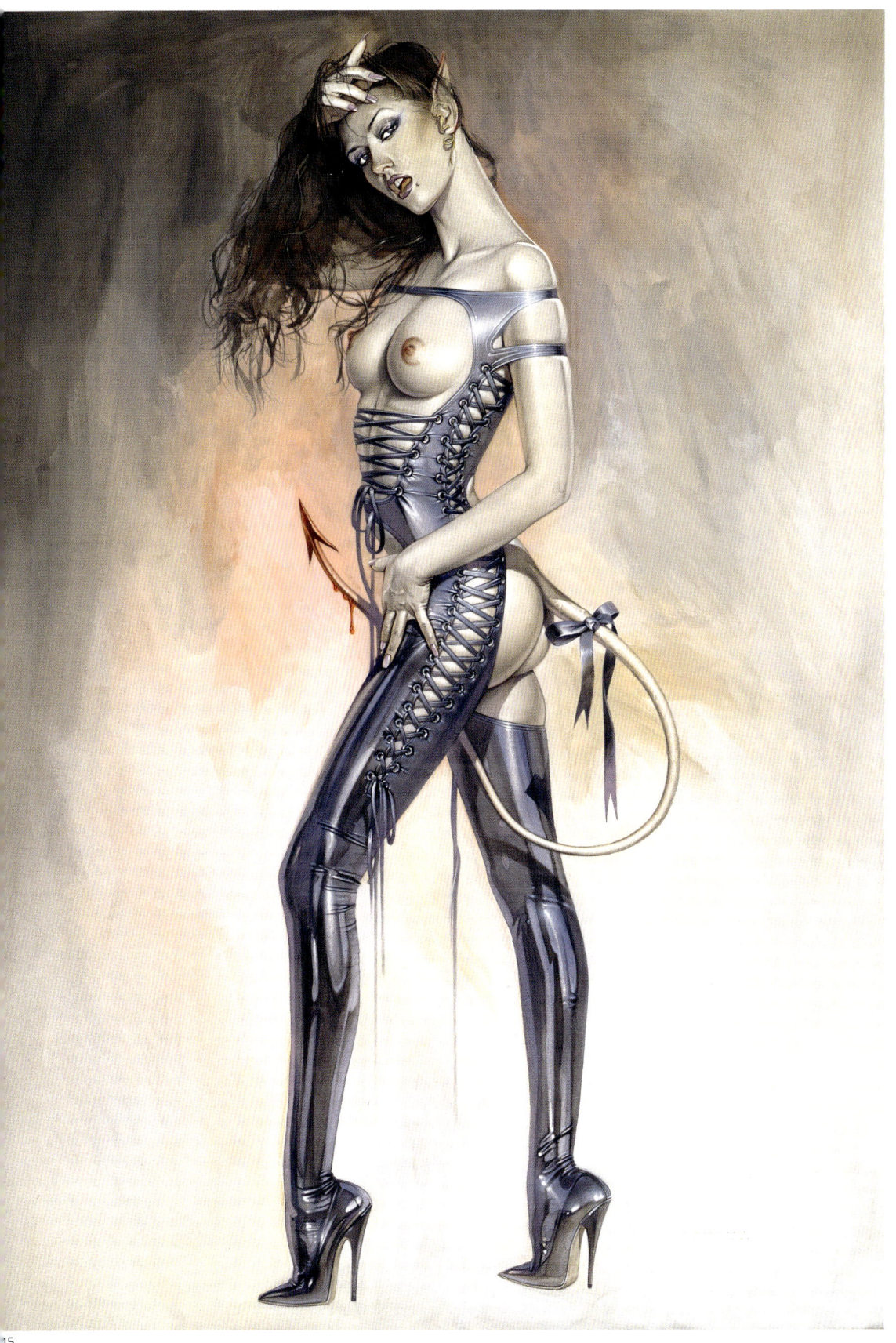

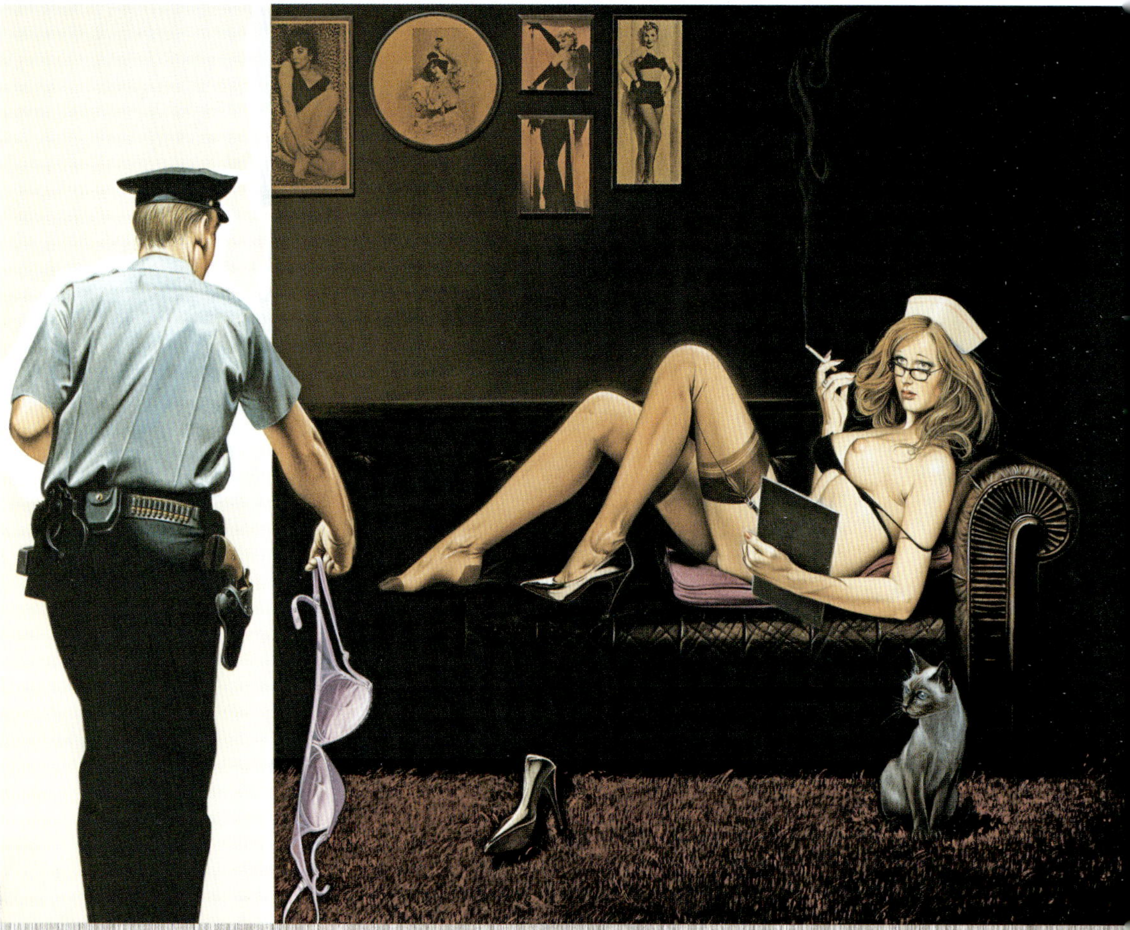

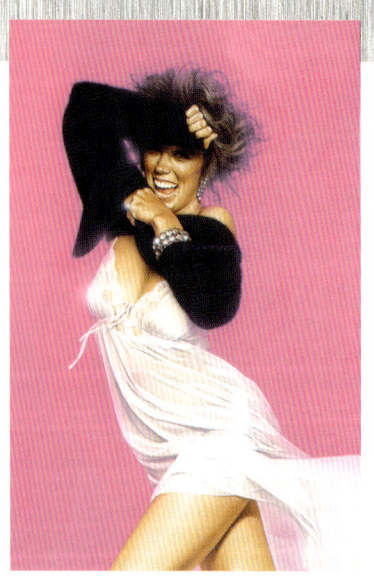

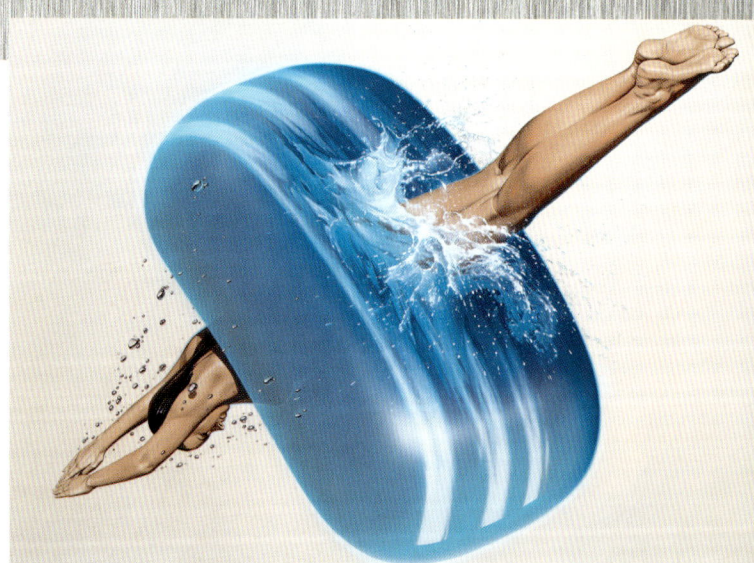

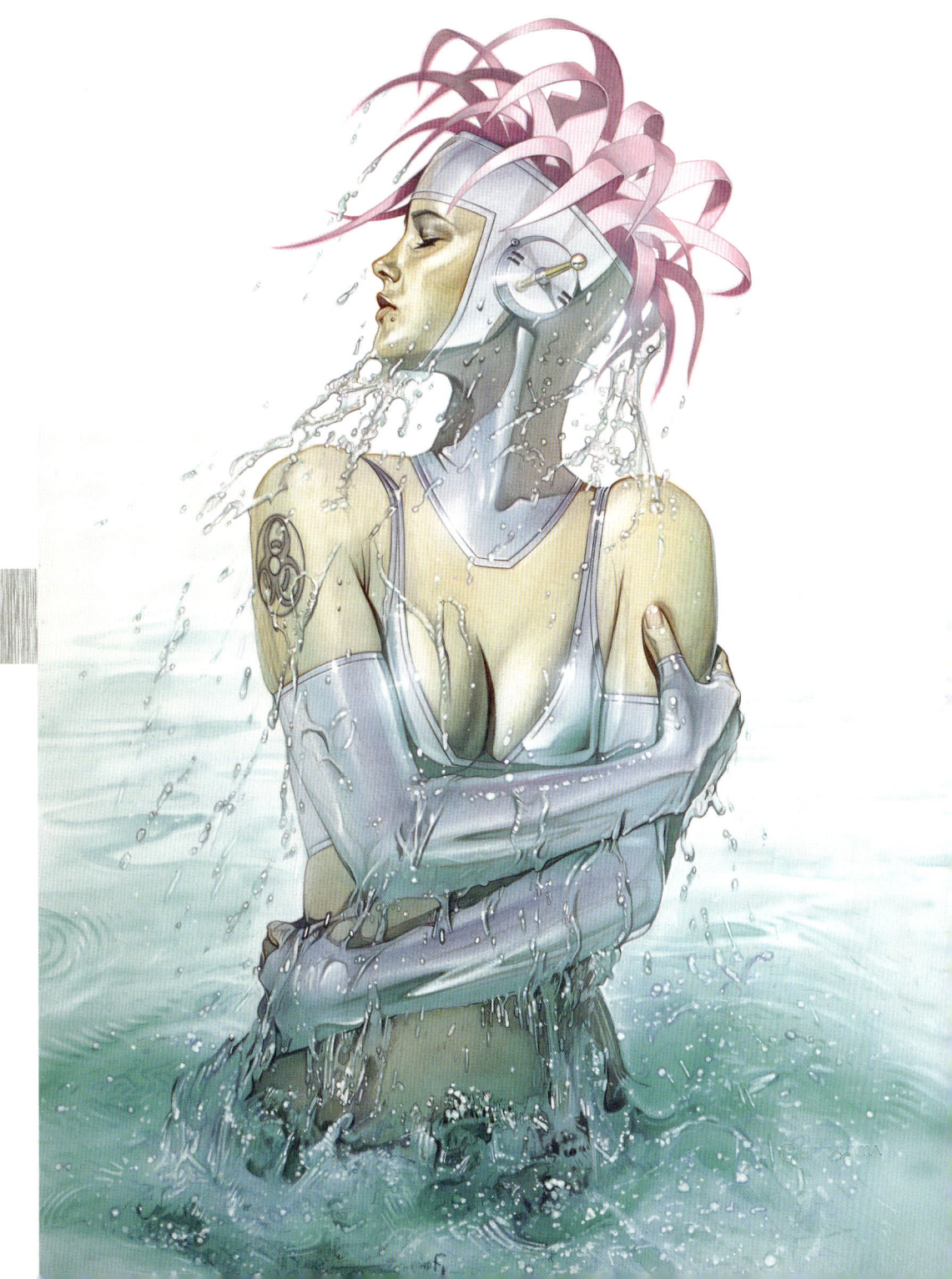

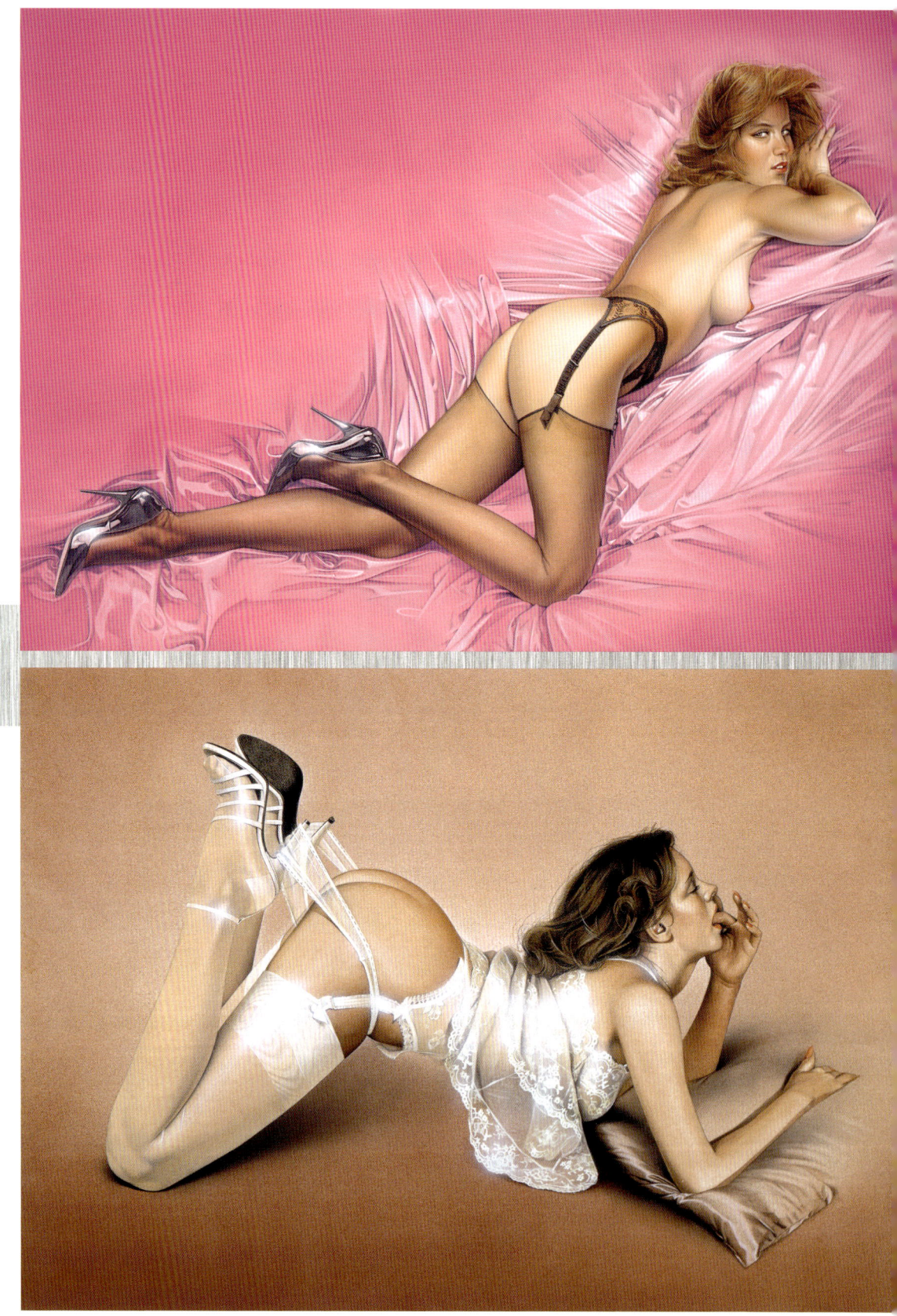

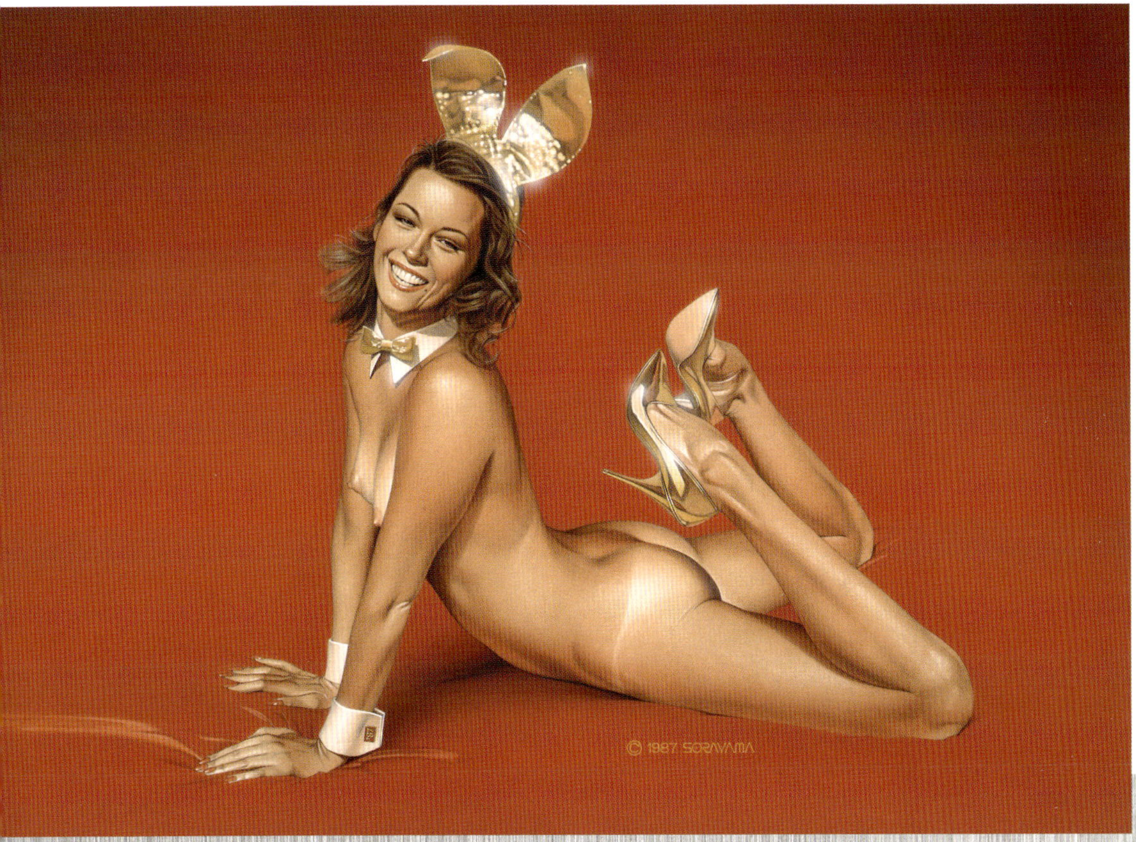

© 1987 SORAYAMA

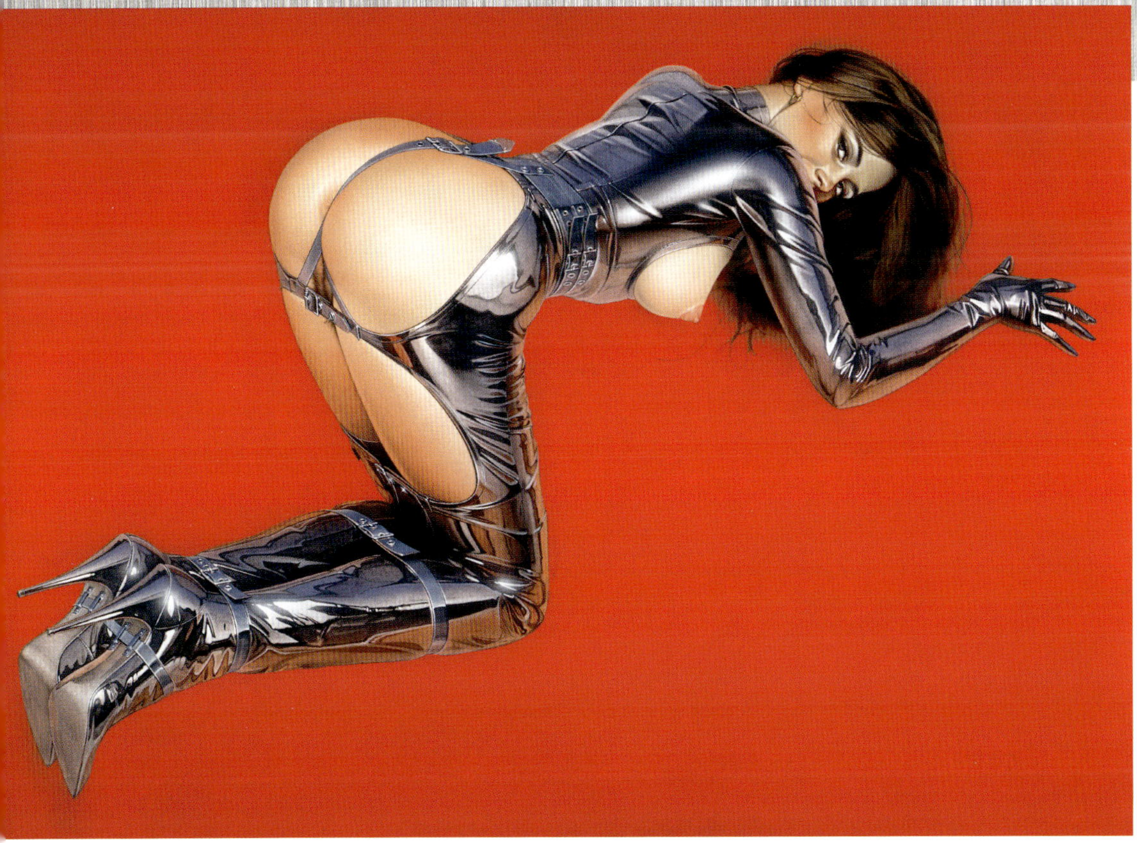

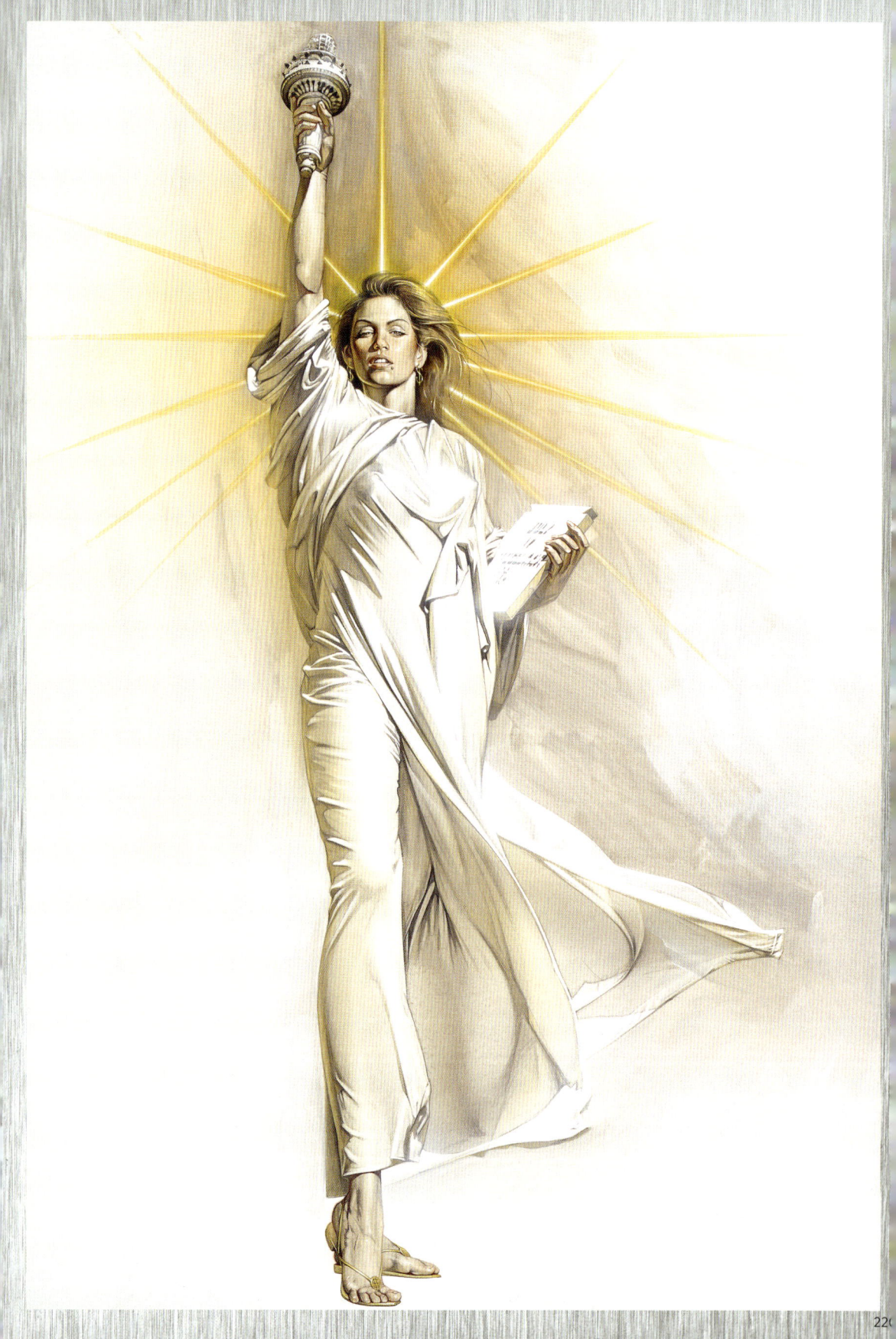

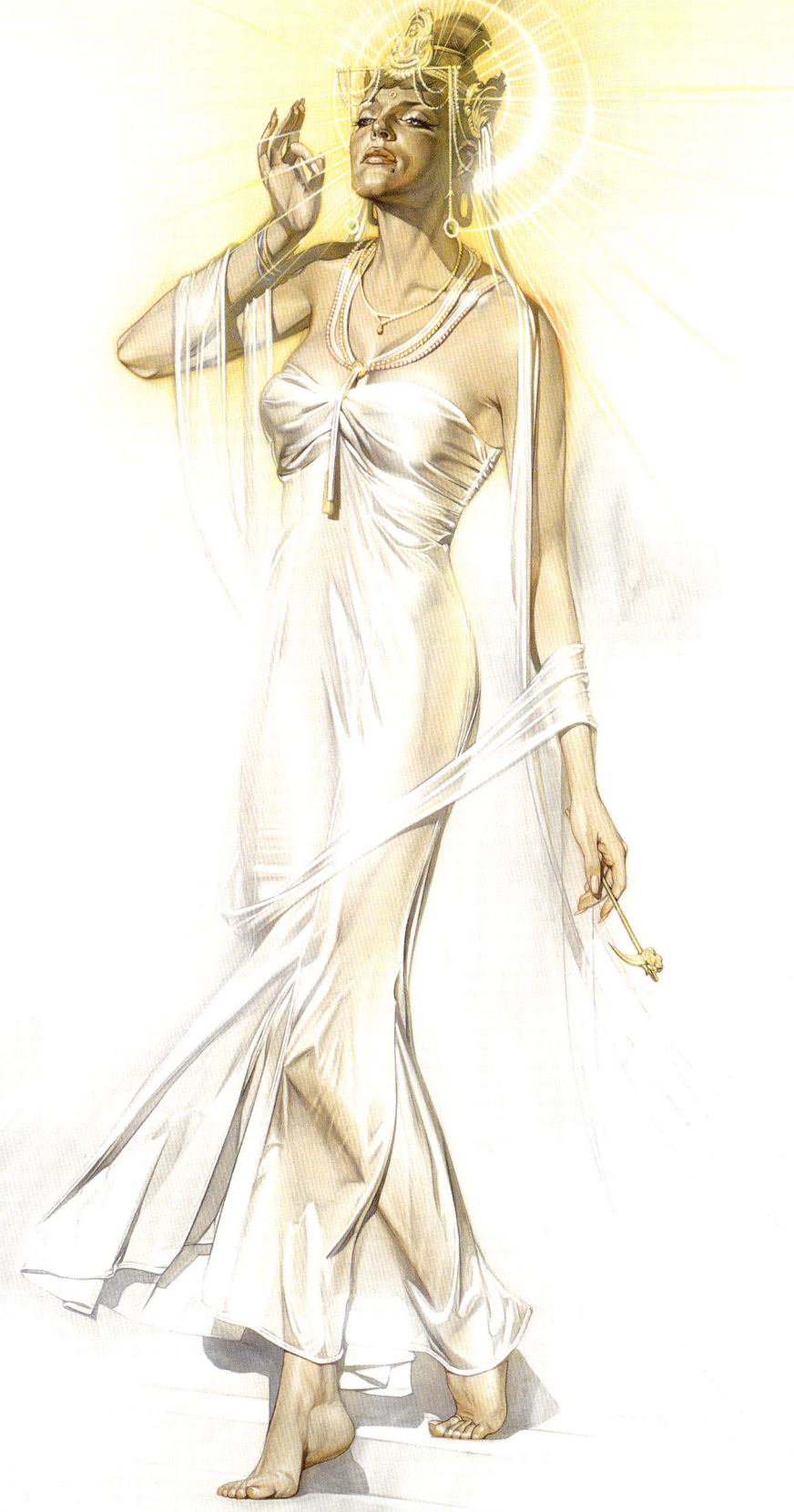

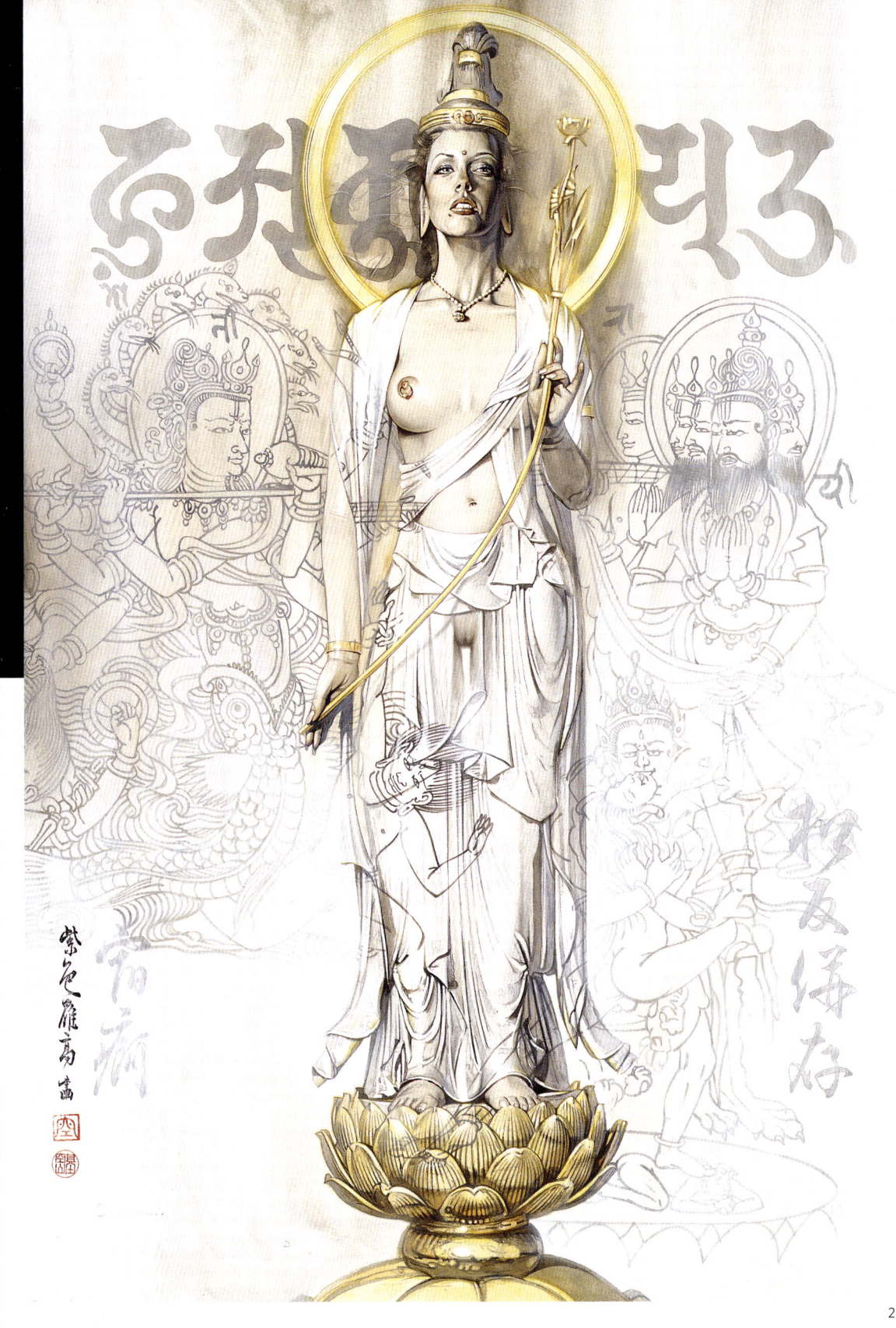

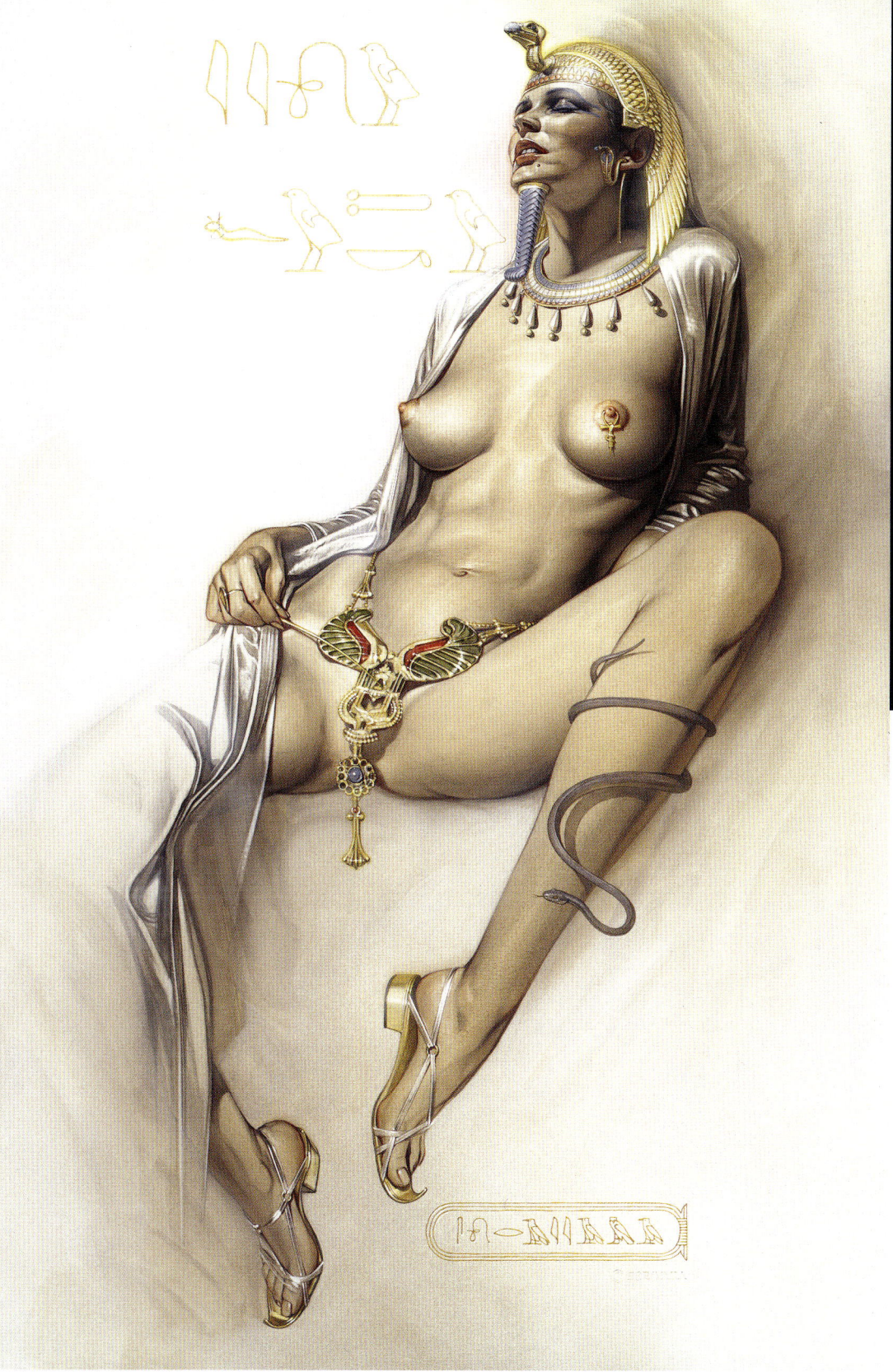

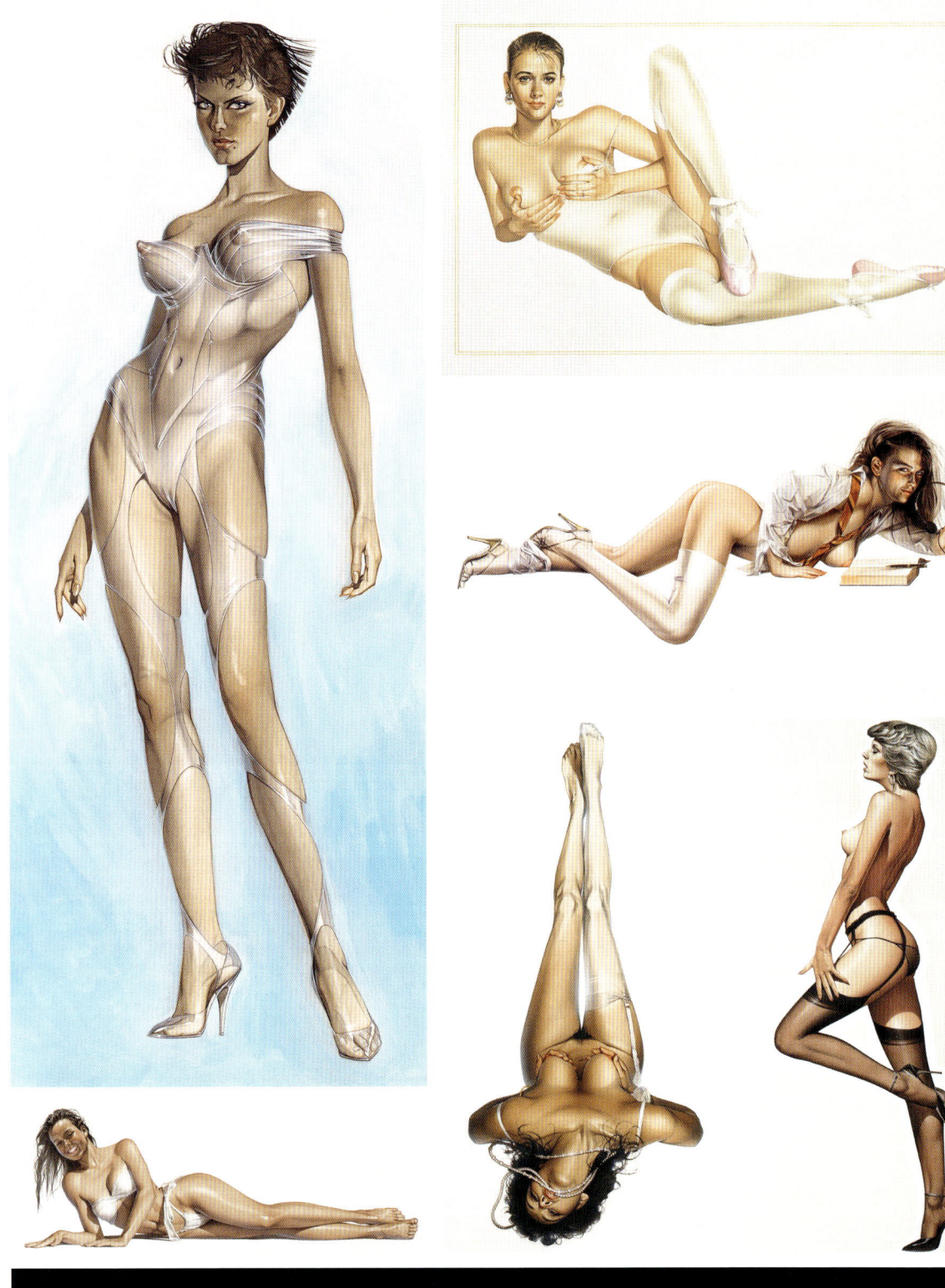

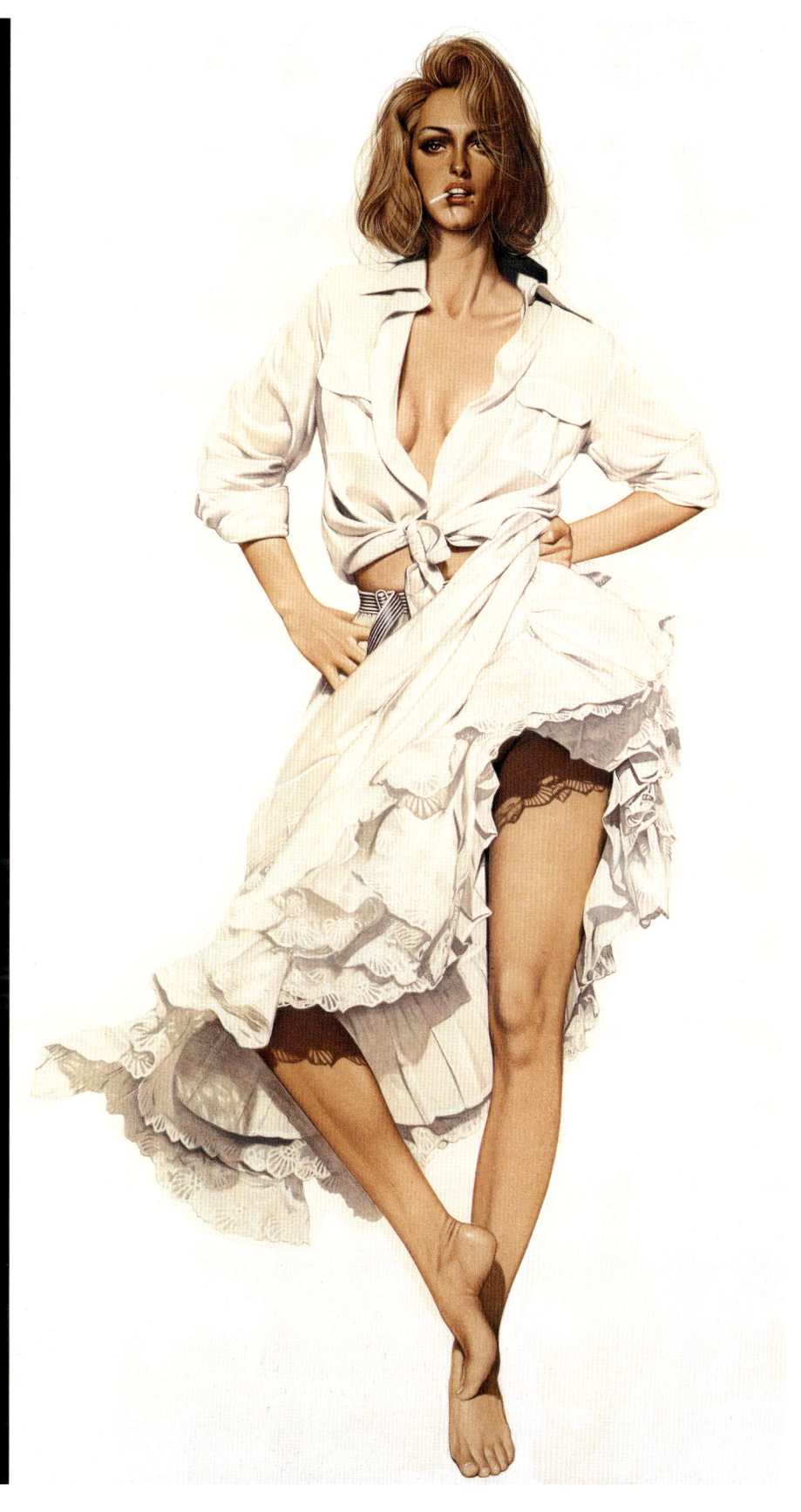

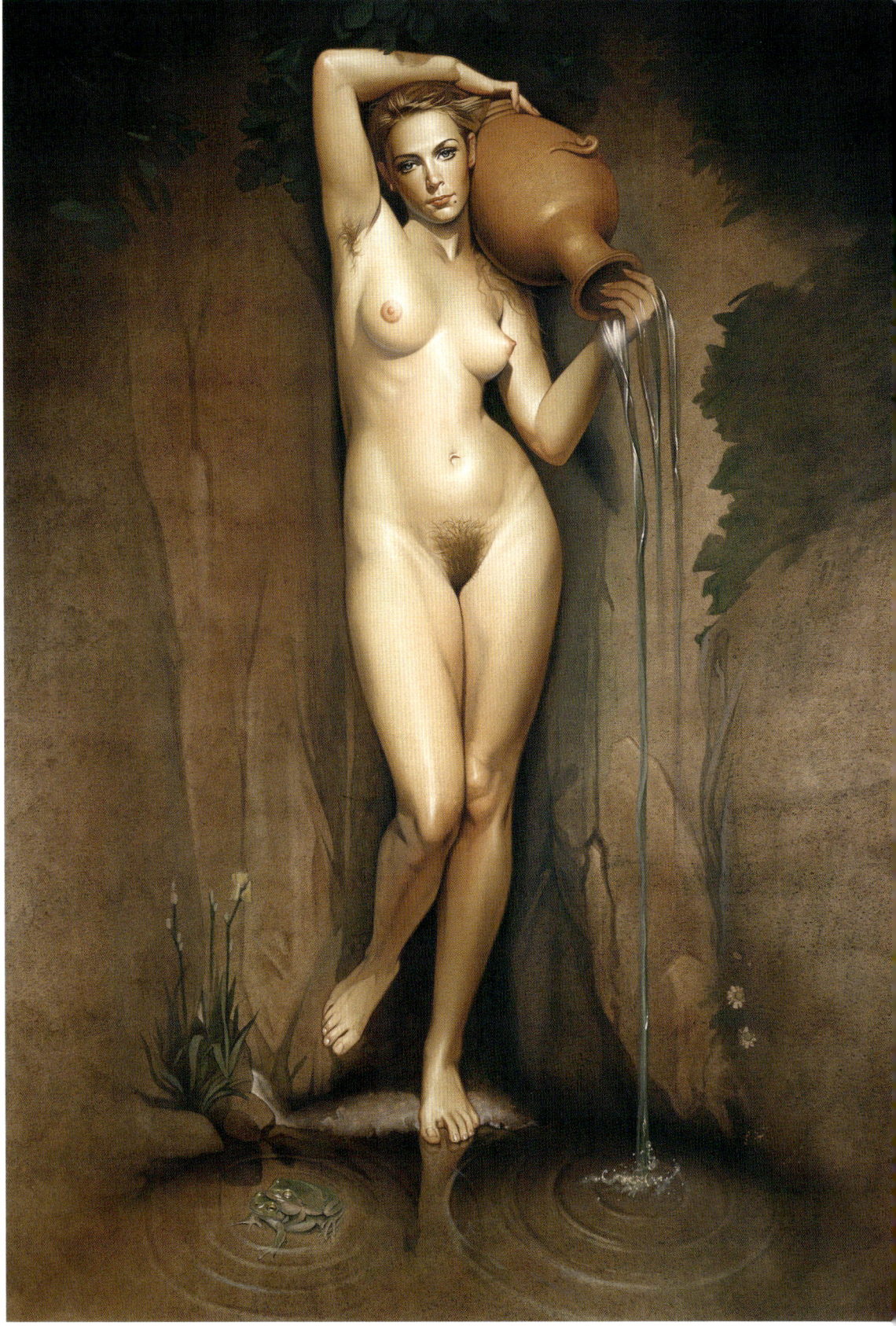

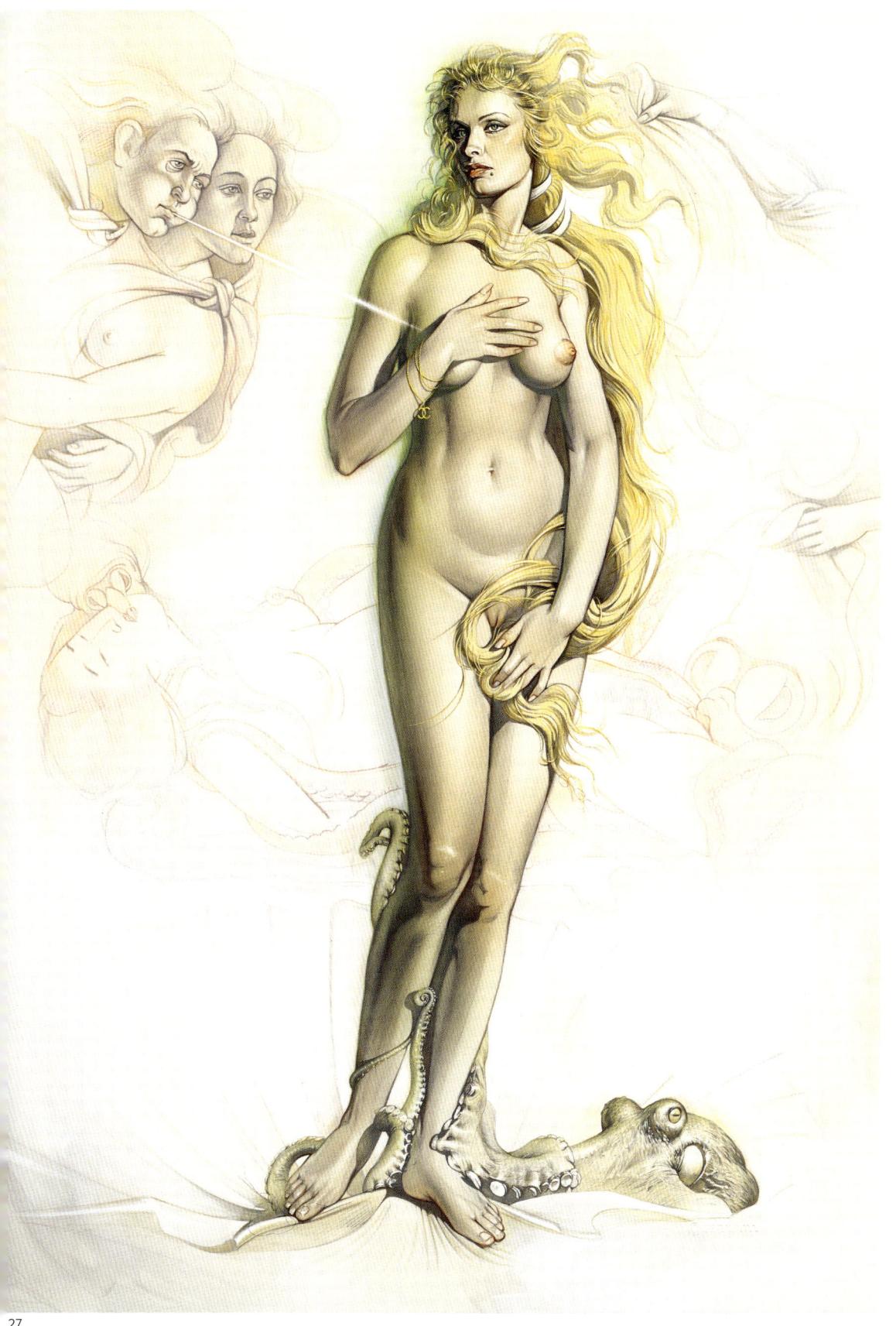

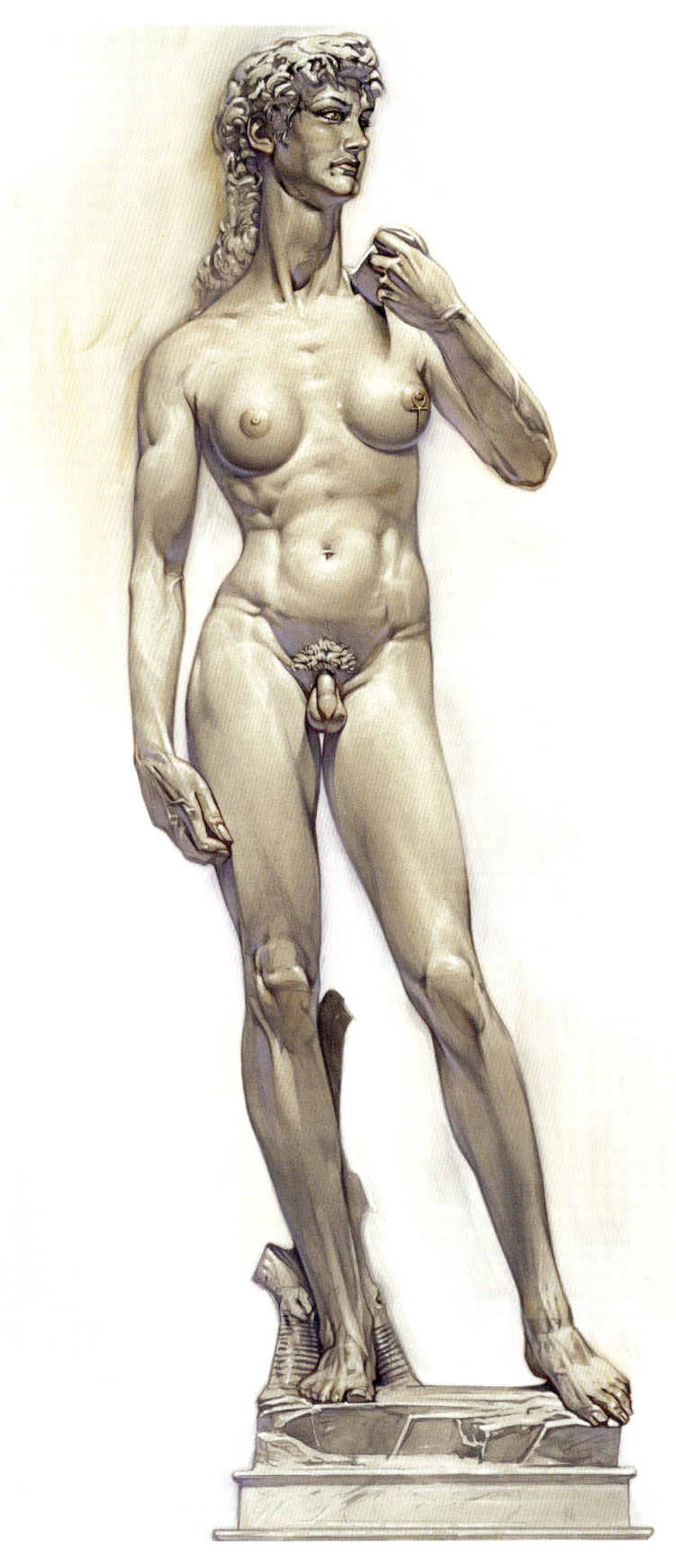

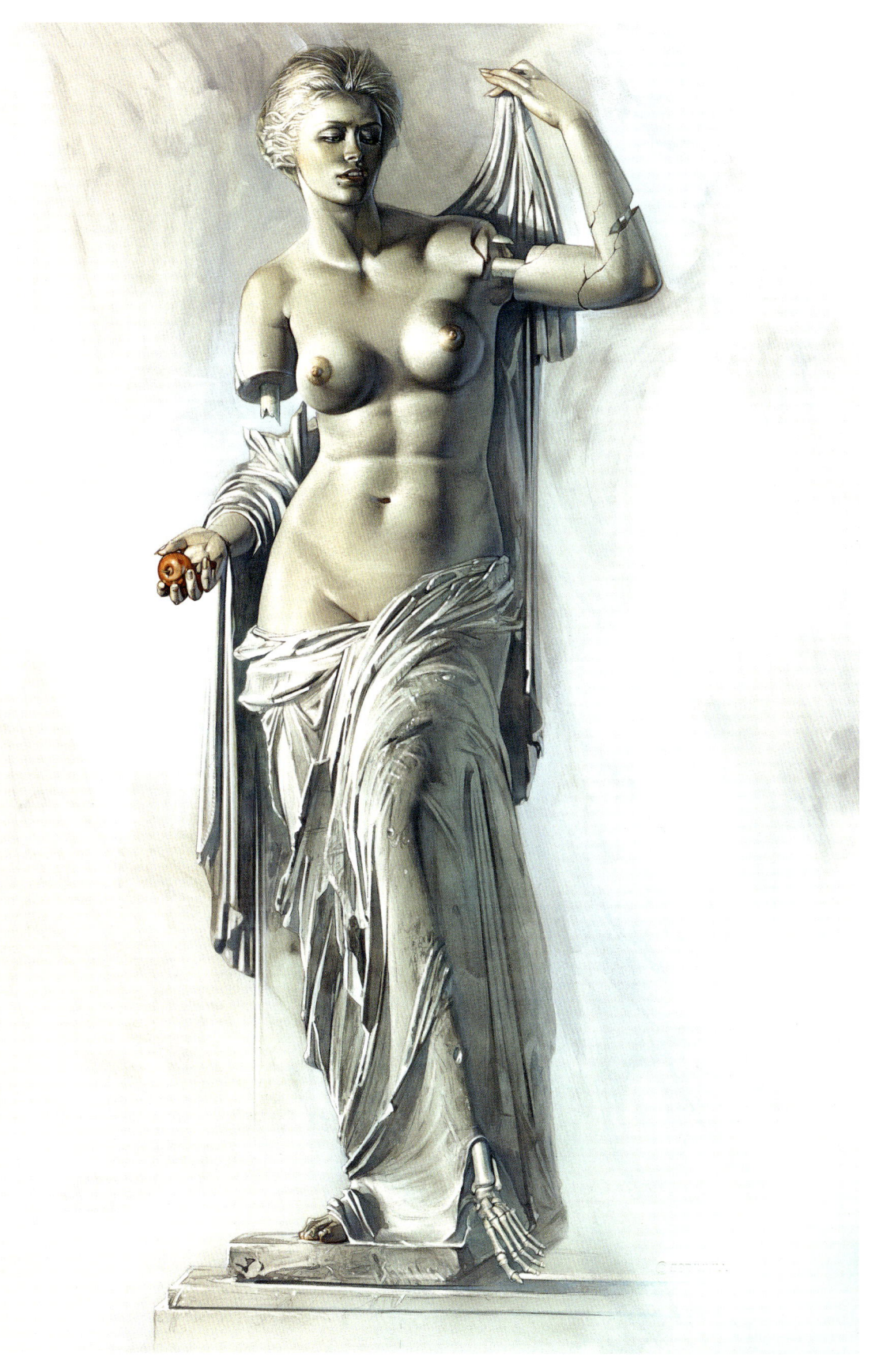

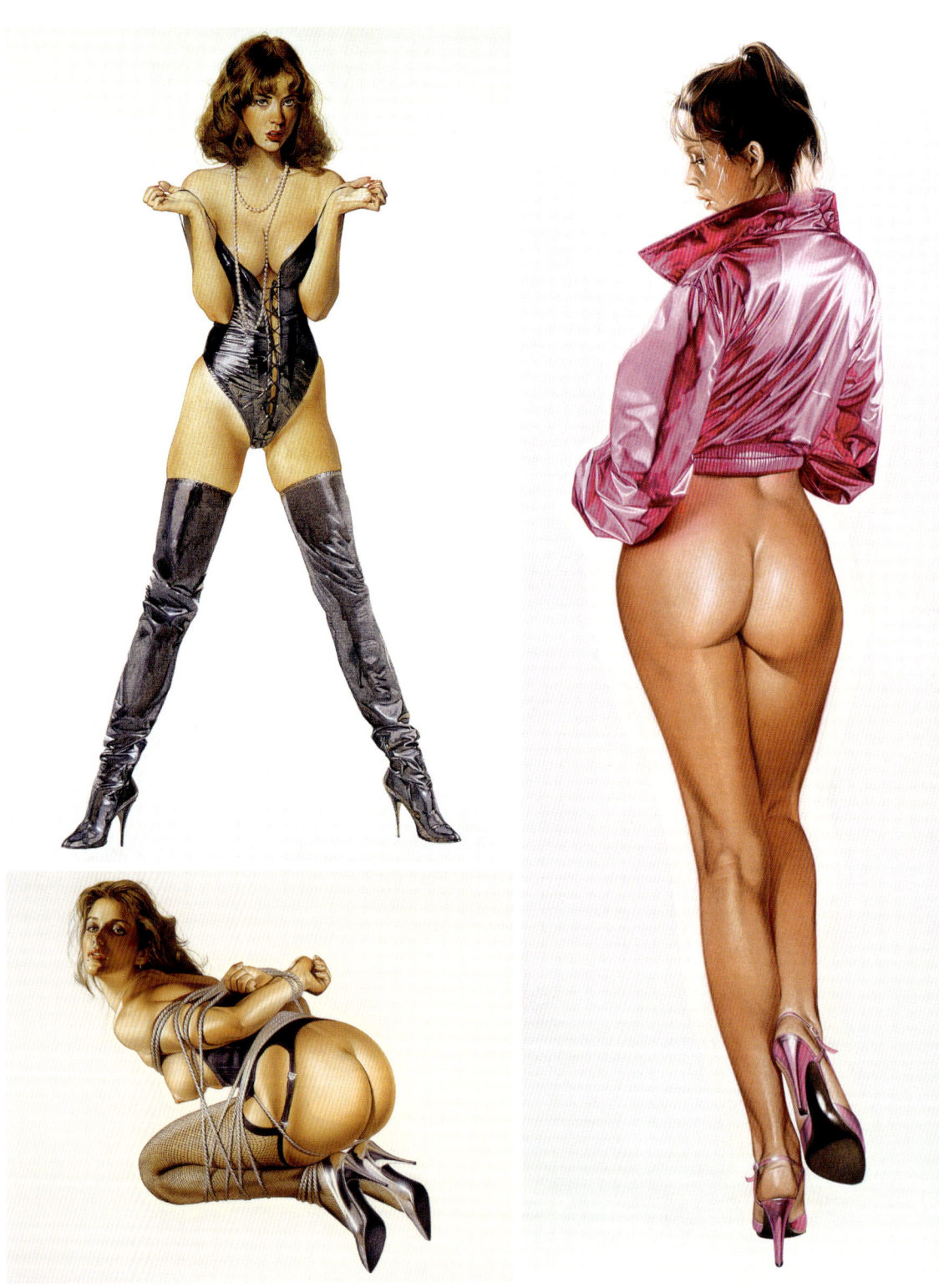

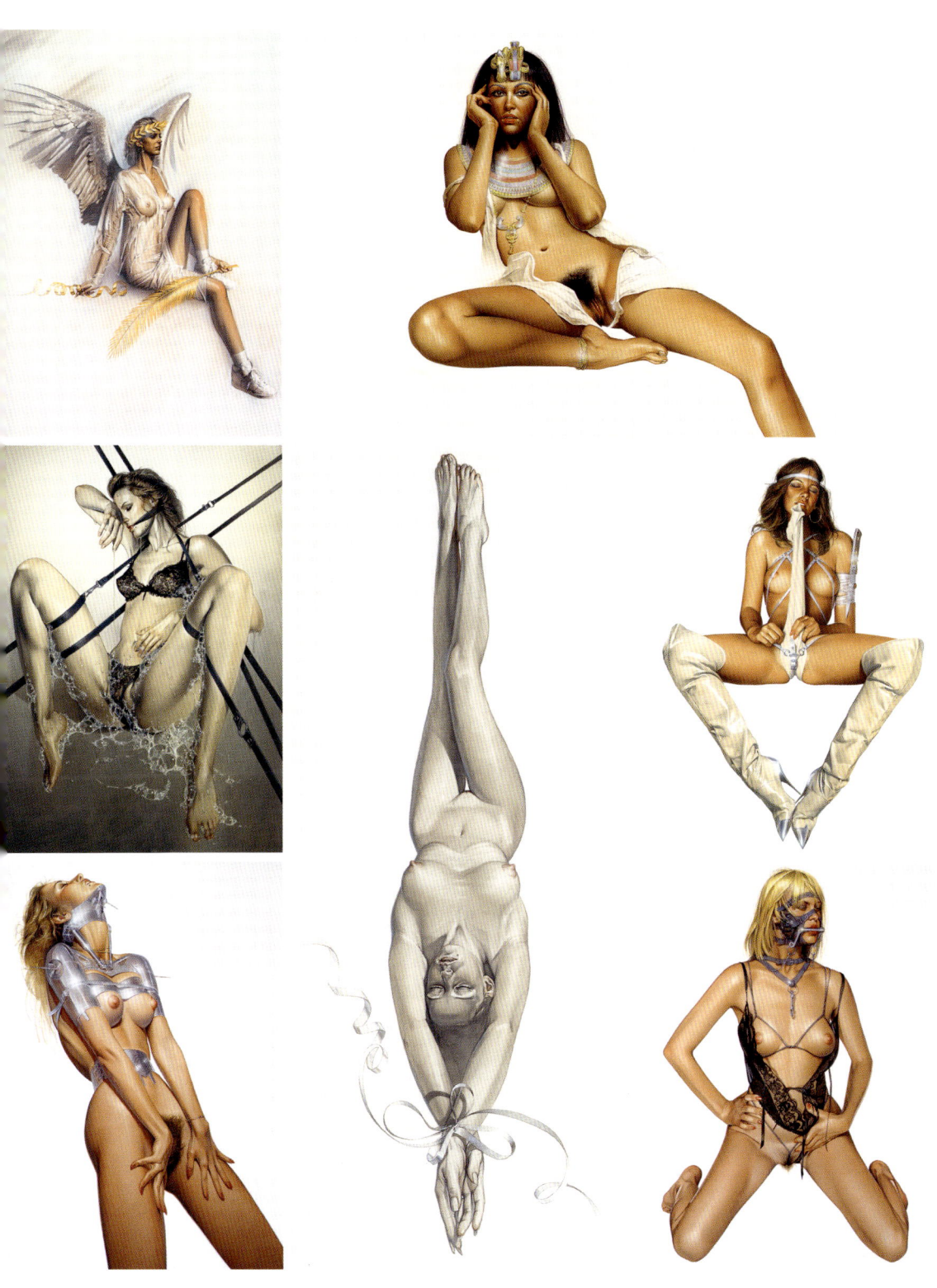

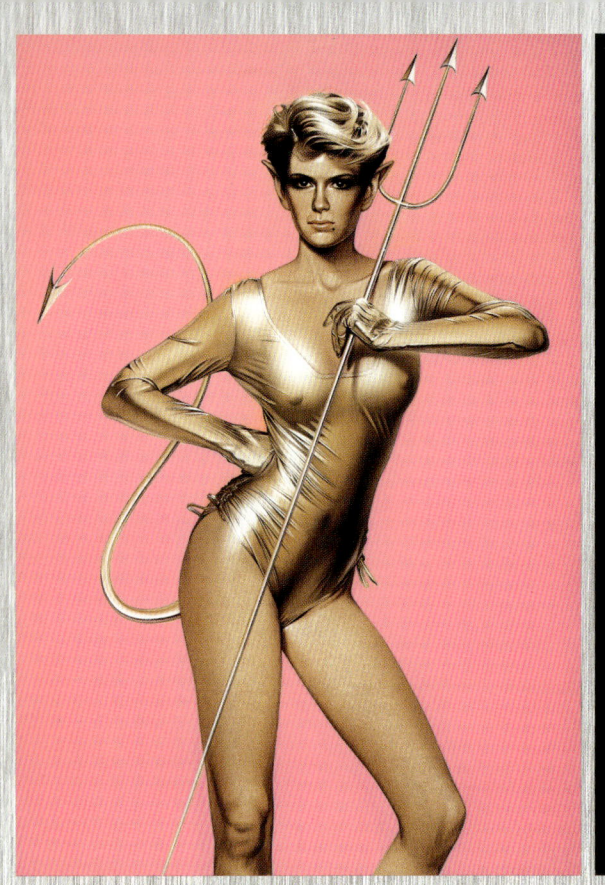

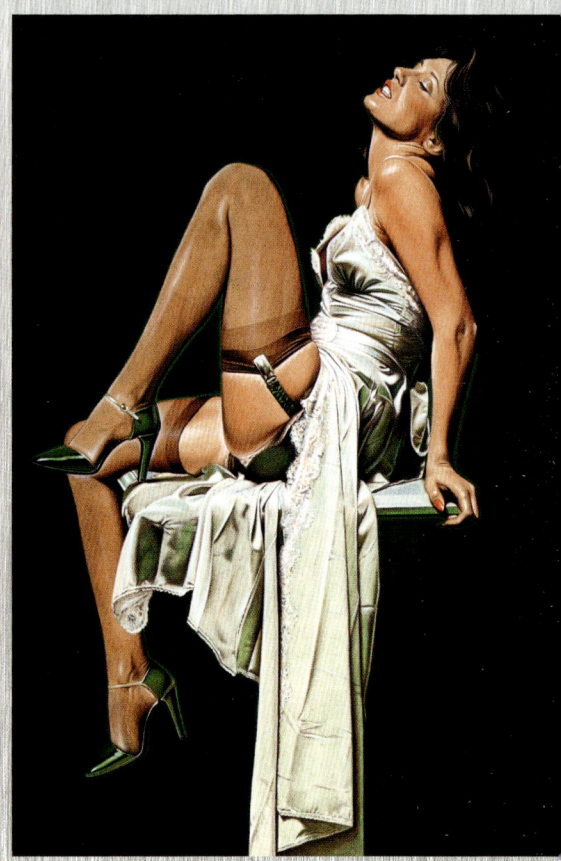

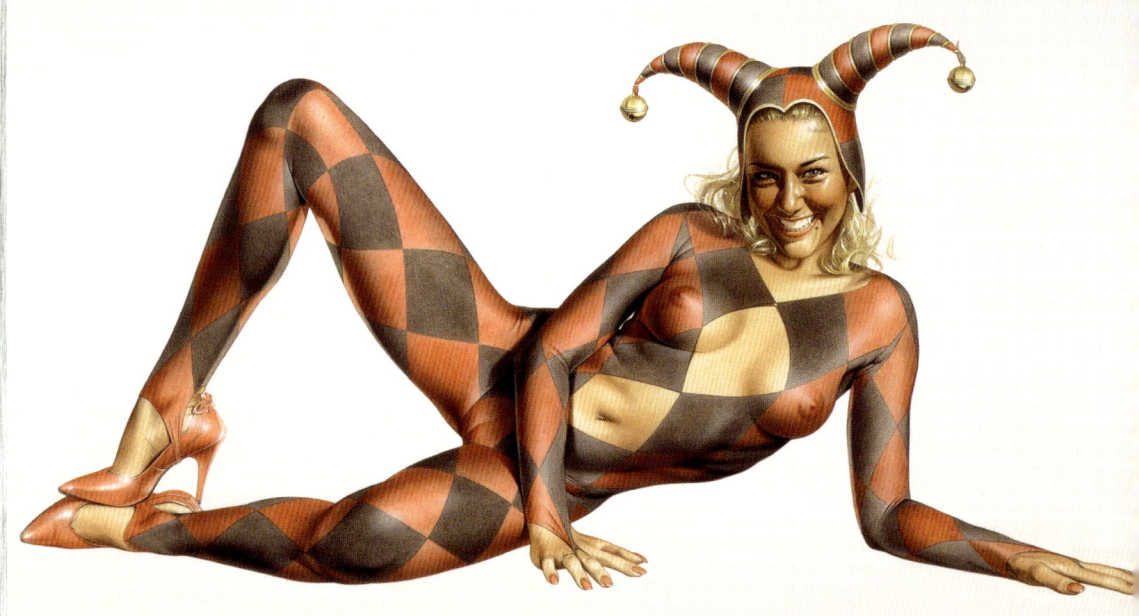

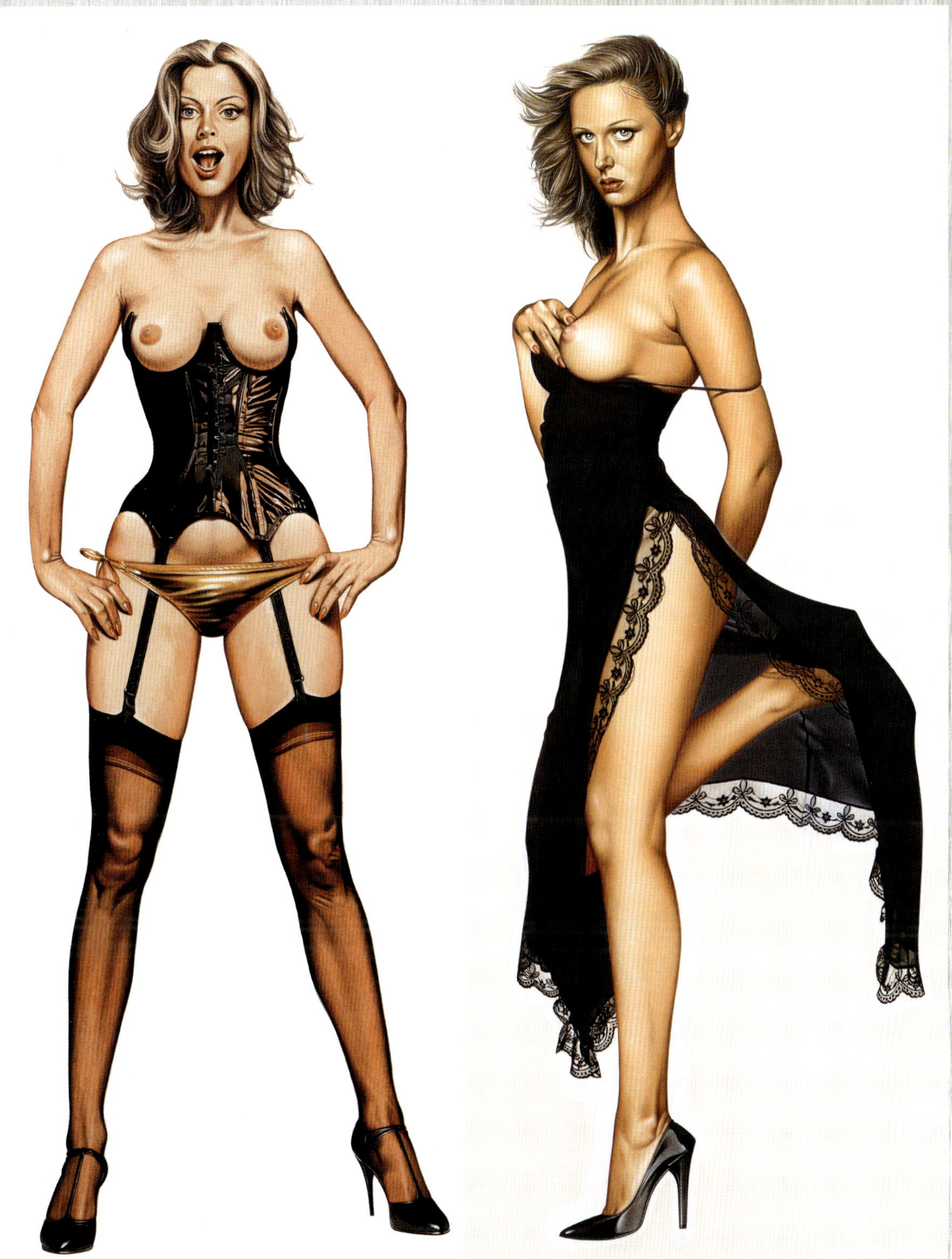

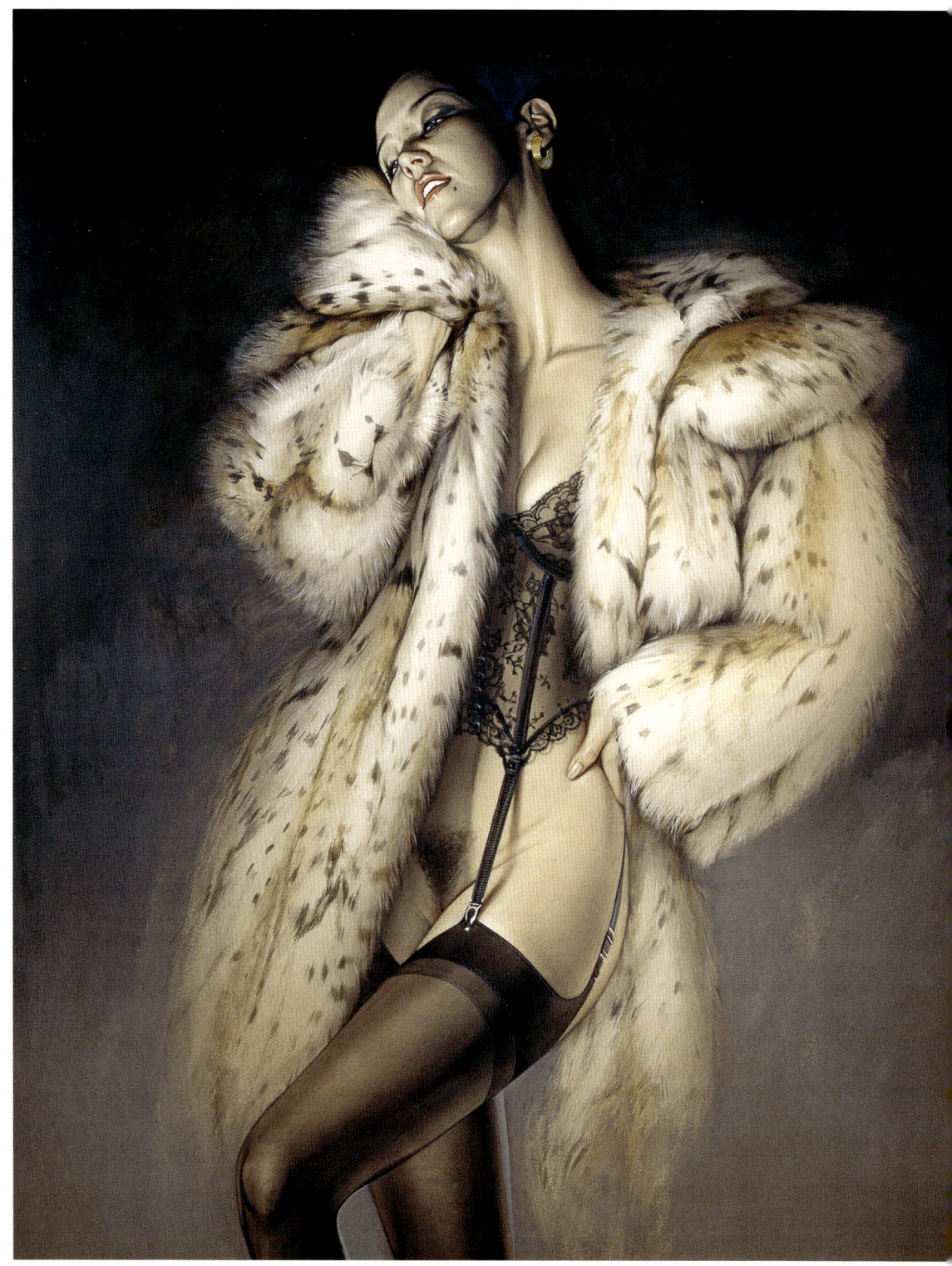

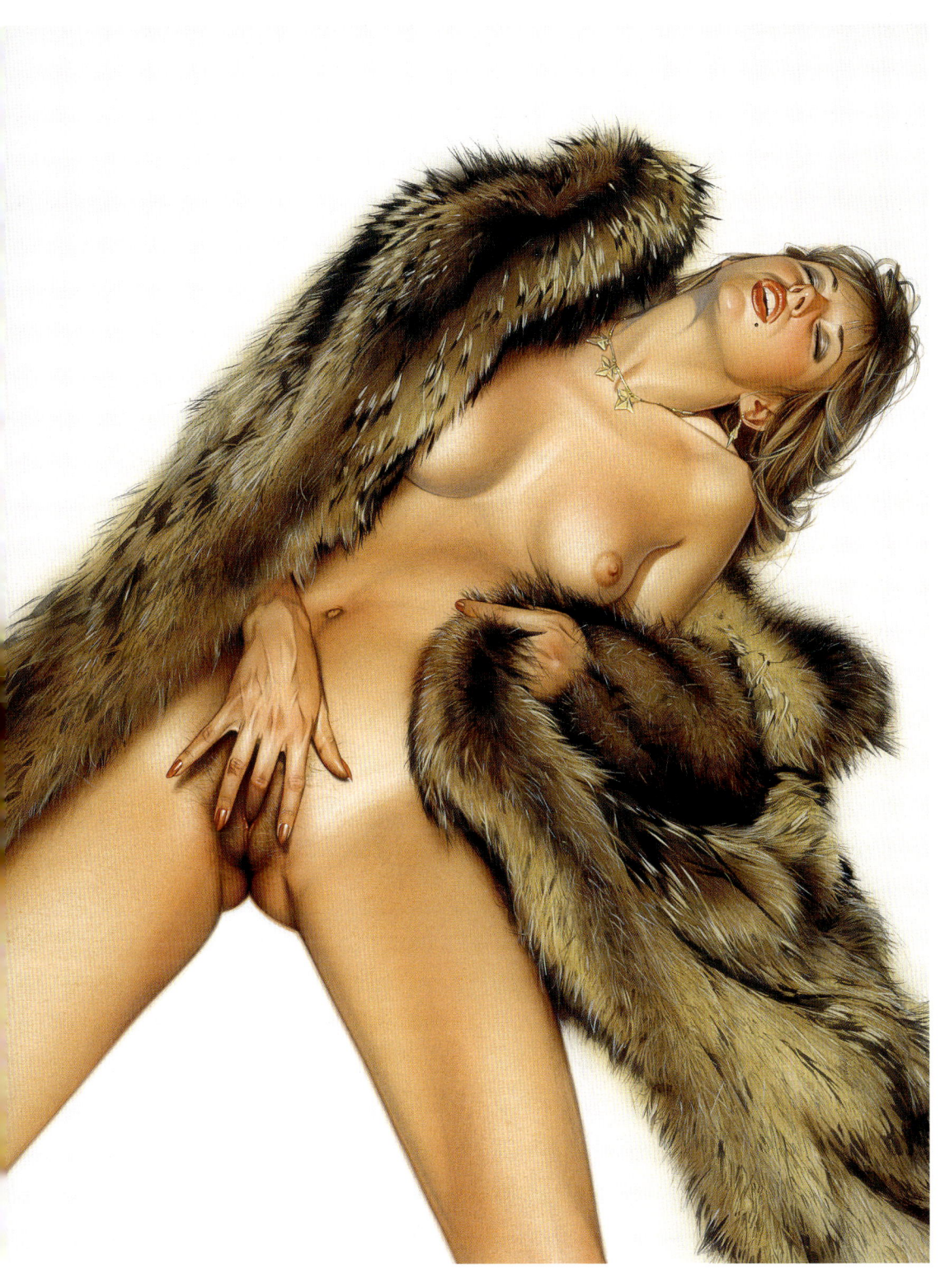

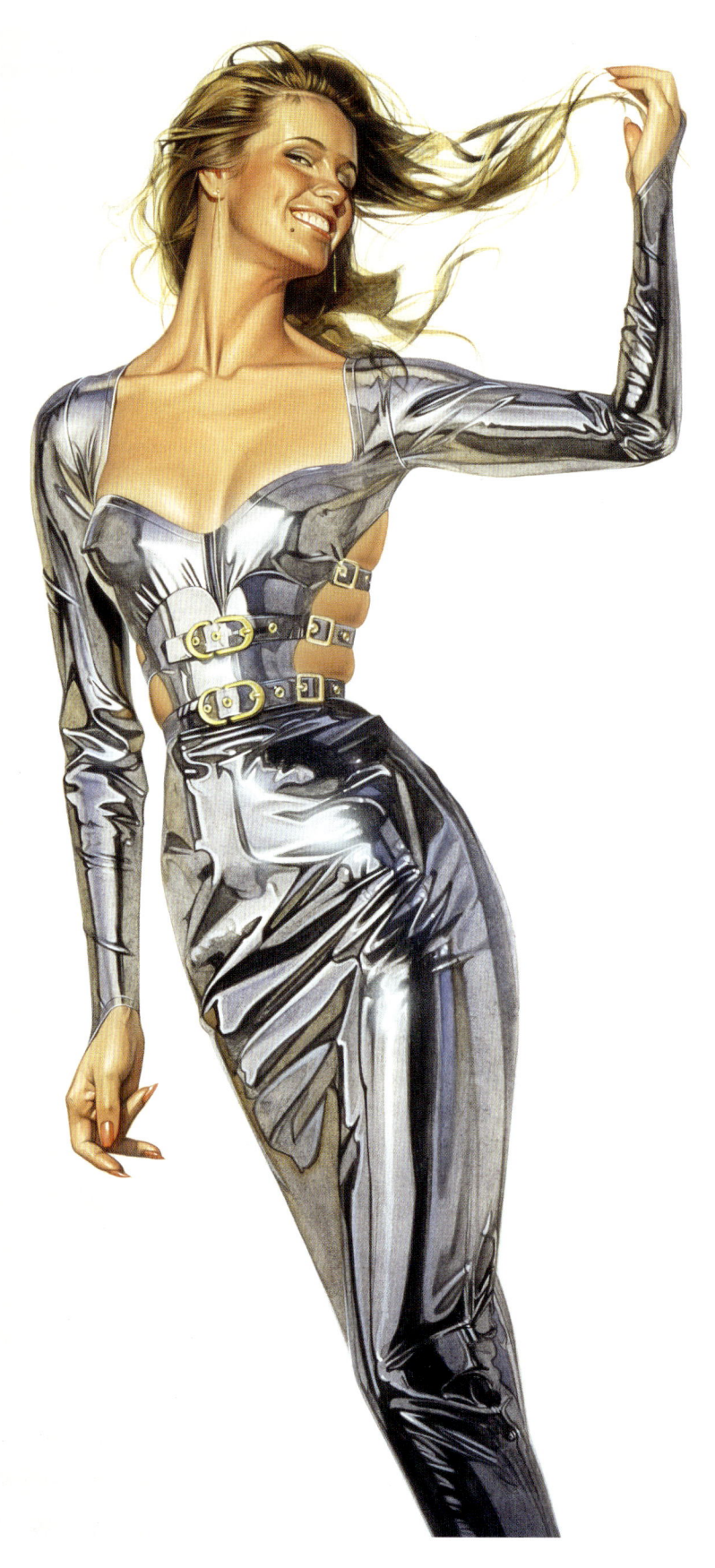

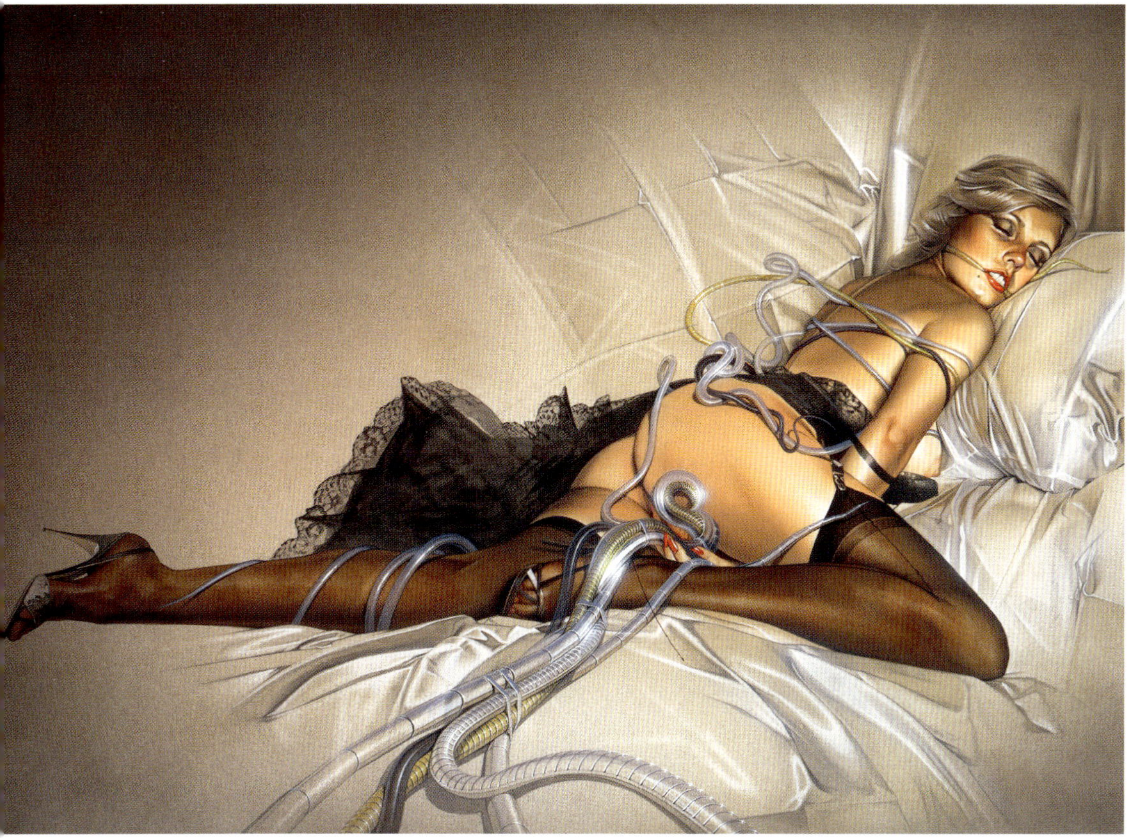

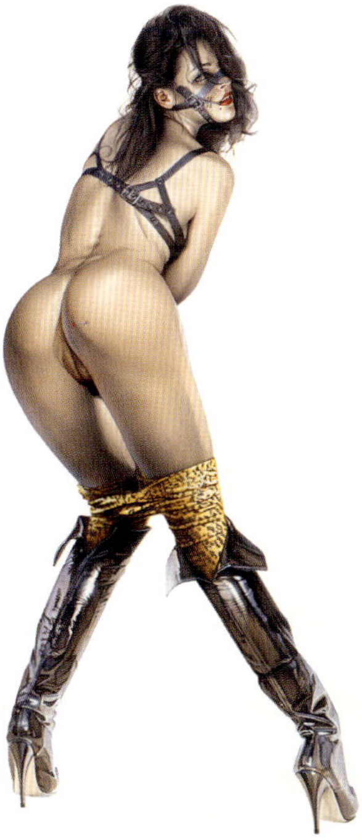

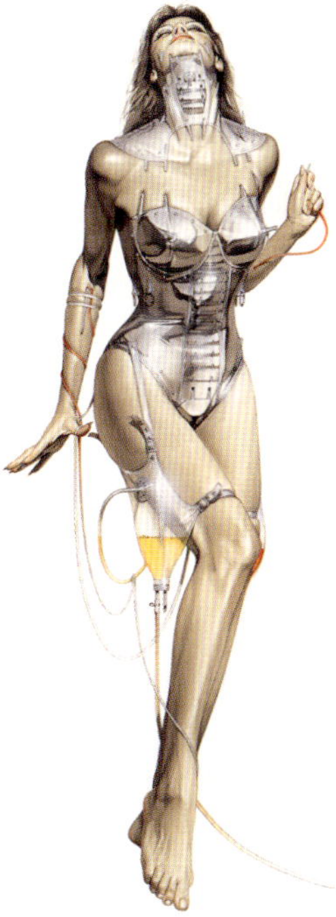

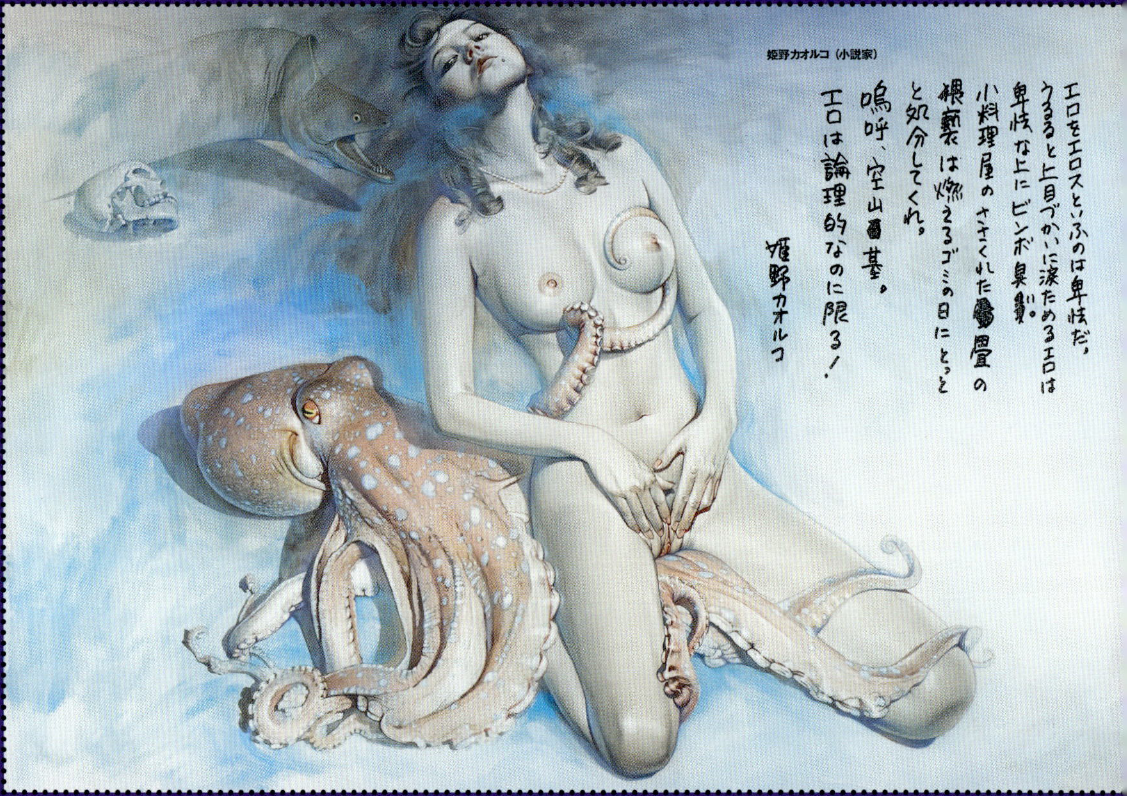

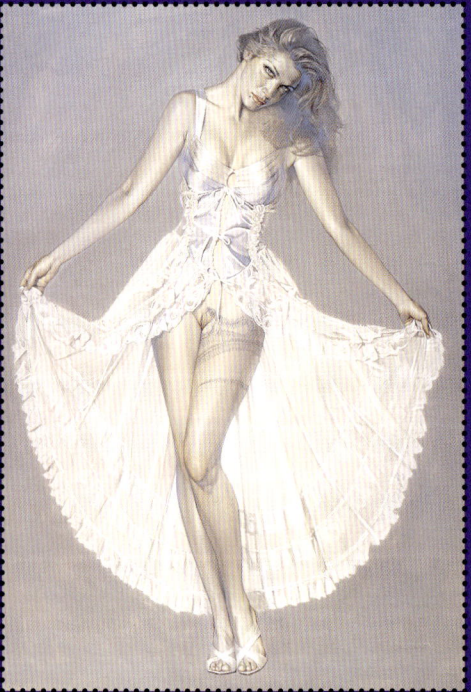

姫野カオルコ（小説家）

エロをエロスといふのは卑怯だ、
うるると上目づかいに流ためるエロは
卑性な上にビンボ臭顔。
小料理屋のささくれた畳の
根薬は燃えるゴミの日にとっと
と処分してくれ。
嗚呼、空山画基。
エロは論理的なのに限る！

姫野カオルコ

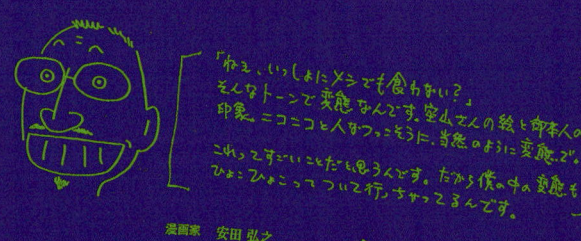

漫画家　安田 弘之

彼の作品を見たとき、どきっとします。
天才は人をどきっとさせます。
空山基は天才です。

BENIHANA ／ ハーバード・ビジネススクール ／ アルテッセ株式会社 オーナー

青木恵子

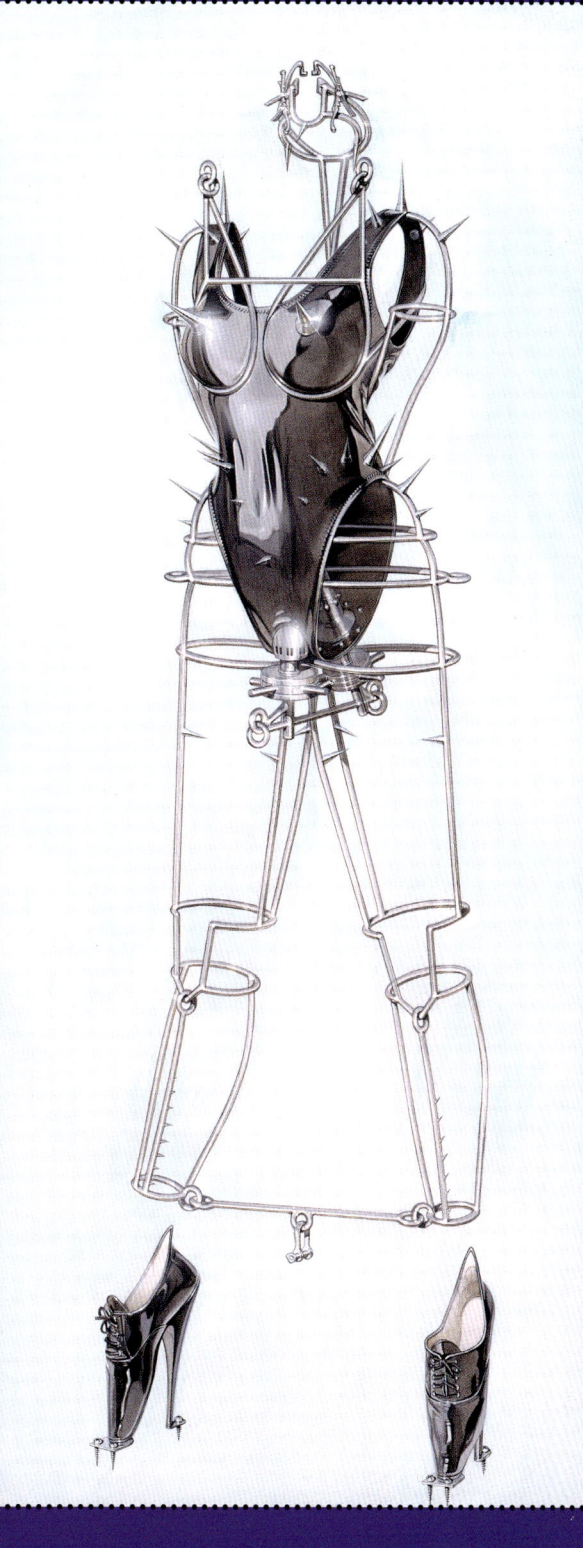

1930年代にアメリカの雑誌のカバーアート「STOLEN SWEET」「Titter」「Spicy」「FILMFUN」を飾ったEnoch Bollesは、若い頃ぼくをともとも魅了したピンナップ・アーティストです。古本屋の店先に置かれていたエロティックなカバーとの出会いは、今でも忘れられないほどの衝撃でした。肉付き豊かで官能的ふくよと弾力のある絵肌は油彩画独特の光彩を放っていて、いつまでみていても飽きることがありません。Bollesアートの最大の見せ場は、脚の大胆な組み方です。逆立ちをしたような不自然で異常ポーズの美女の不思議なエロティシズムは彼の評価を決定的にしたのです。そして古き良き時代を象徴しているともいえるBollesアートの対極にあるのが空山基の描くサディスティックともいえる究極のアート表現です。特に脚の艶やか清豊かな仕草は、金髪紅毛碧眼の欧米人女性エイジャンの官能美をも際立

たせているのです。その迫った足の指先の描写などに、どんなセックスシーンよりも生の快感を描ききる空山の超絶技法には舌を巻くばかりです。リアル過ぎるほどの性器と陰毛のゆらめき、金色の柔らかな産毛がおおう脚、精液を暗示させる水滴が垂れてゆく肉感的な脚、それらひとつが空山アートの視覚めるエクスタシーの源泉なのかもしれません。ほとんどの場合、人間の生きる欲望は、自身が考えるほどにノーマルで平凡なものではなく、常に変質的になろうとする衝動があり、異常ともいえる妄想や性欲に蝕まれることがあります。性器だけでなく、脚や背中や首筋、毛髪に、ふとした興奮を感じてしまっても異常とはみもこないのです。空山アートの見どころは、常に変質的になろうとする人間の、はしたない欲望をみごとに図像化したものであり、これを超えるほどの性美術のアートは他にありません。空山基は、ぼくが認める天才の一人です。

田名網敬一

Keiichi Tanaami

9

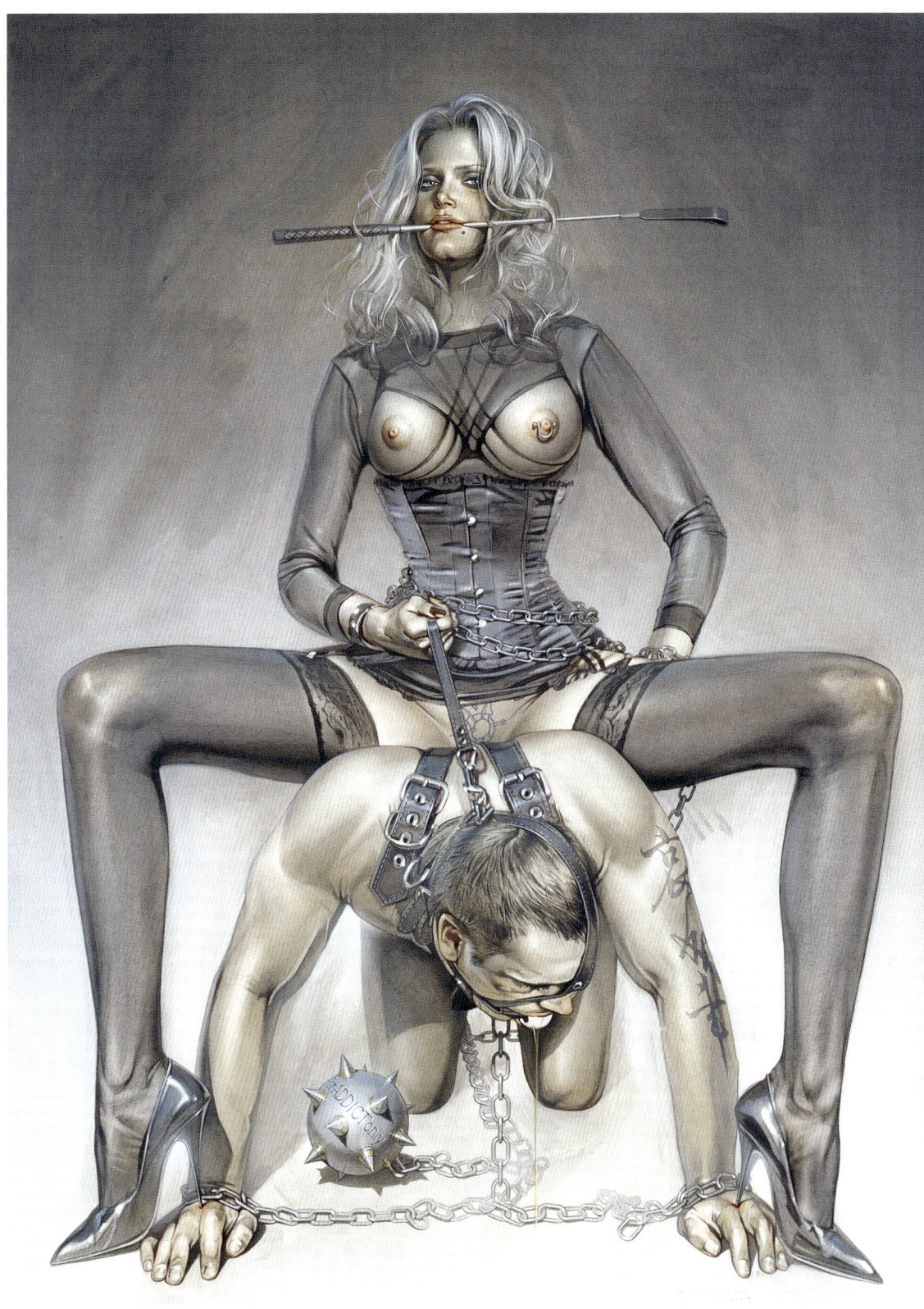

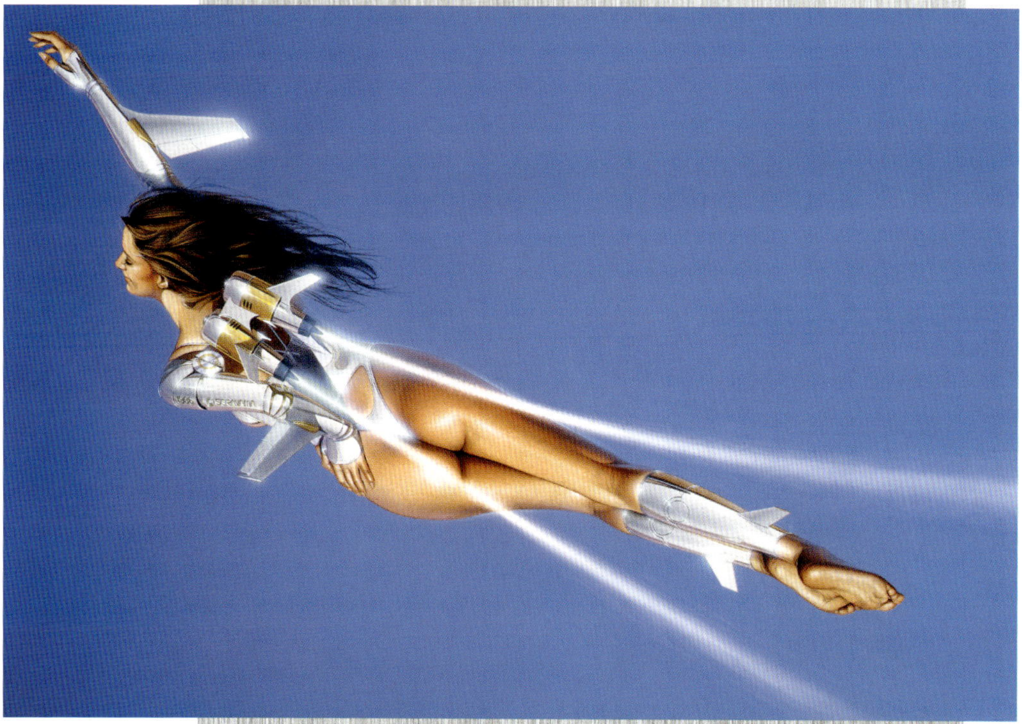

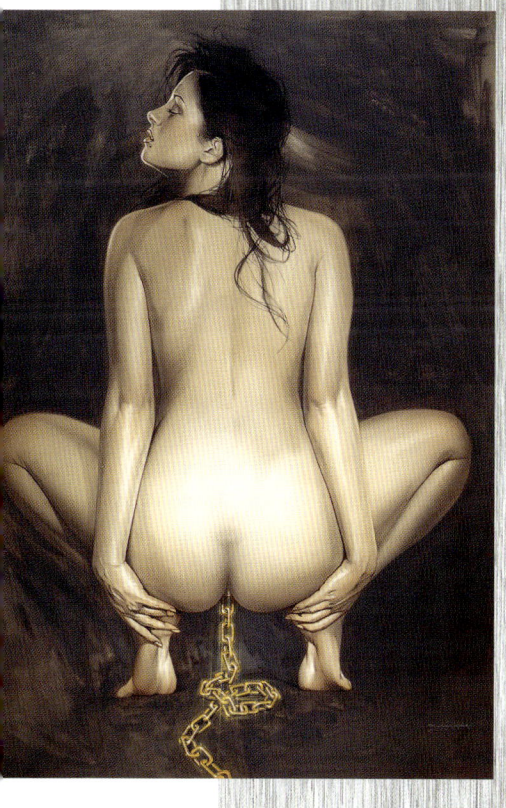
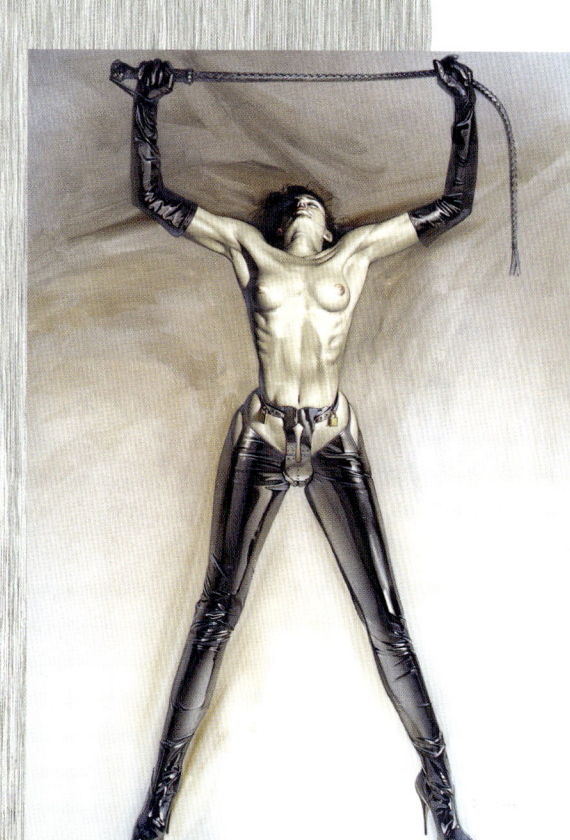

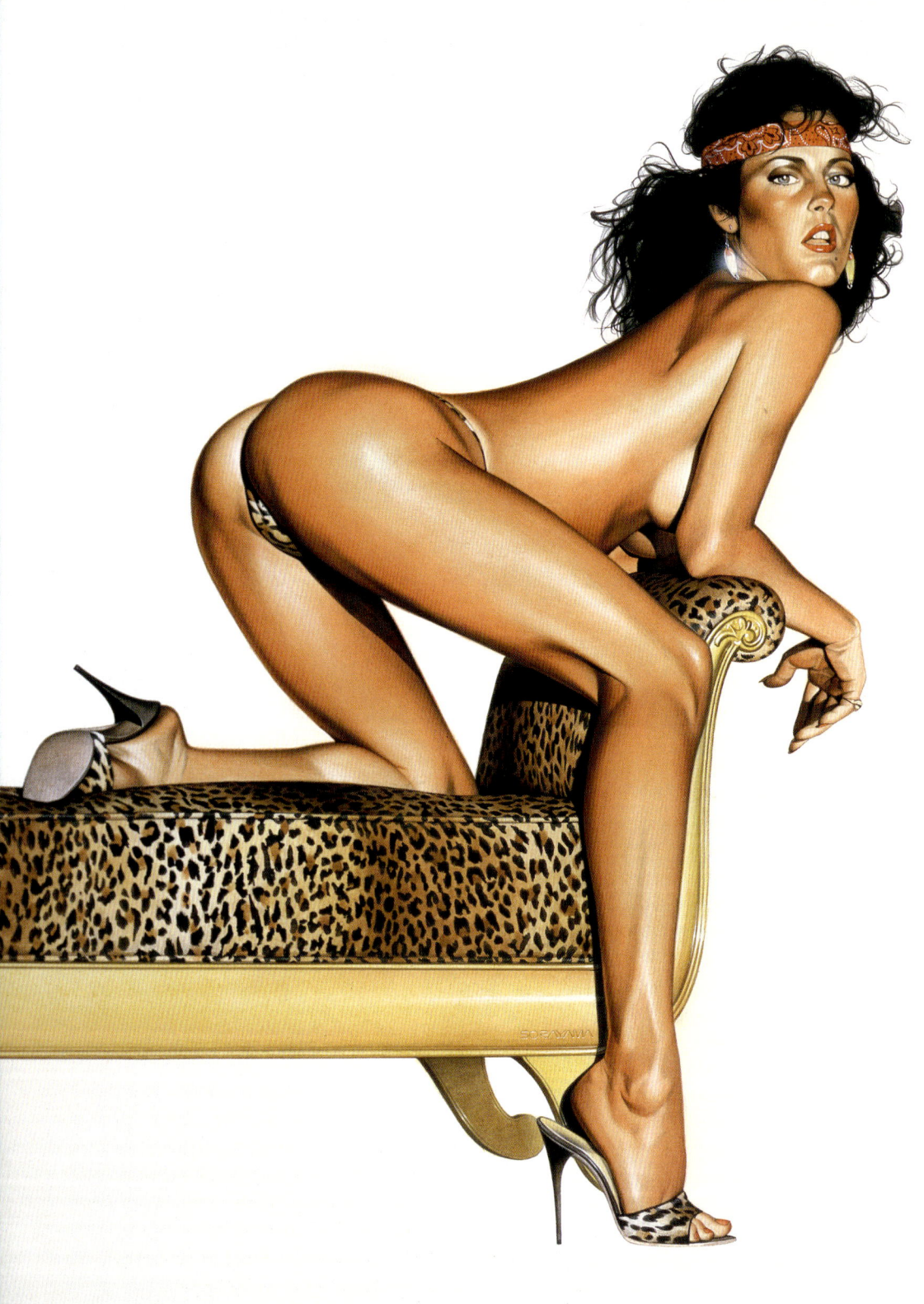

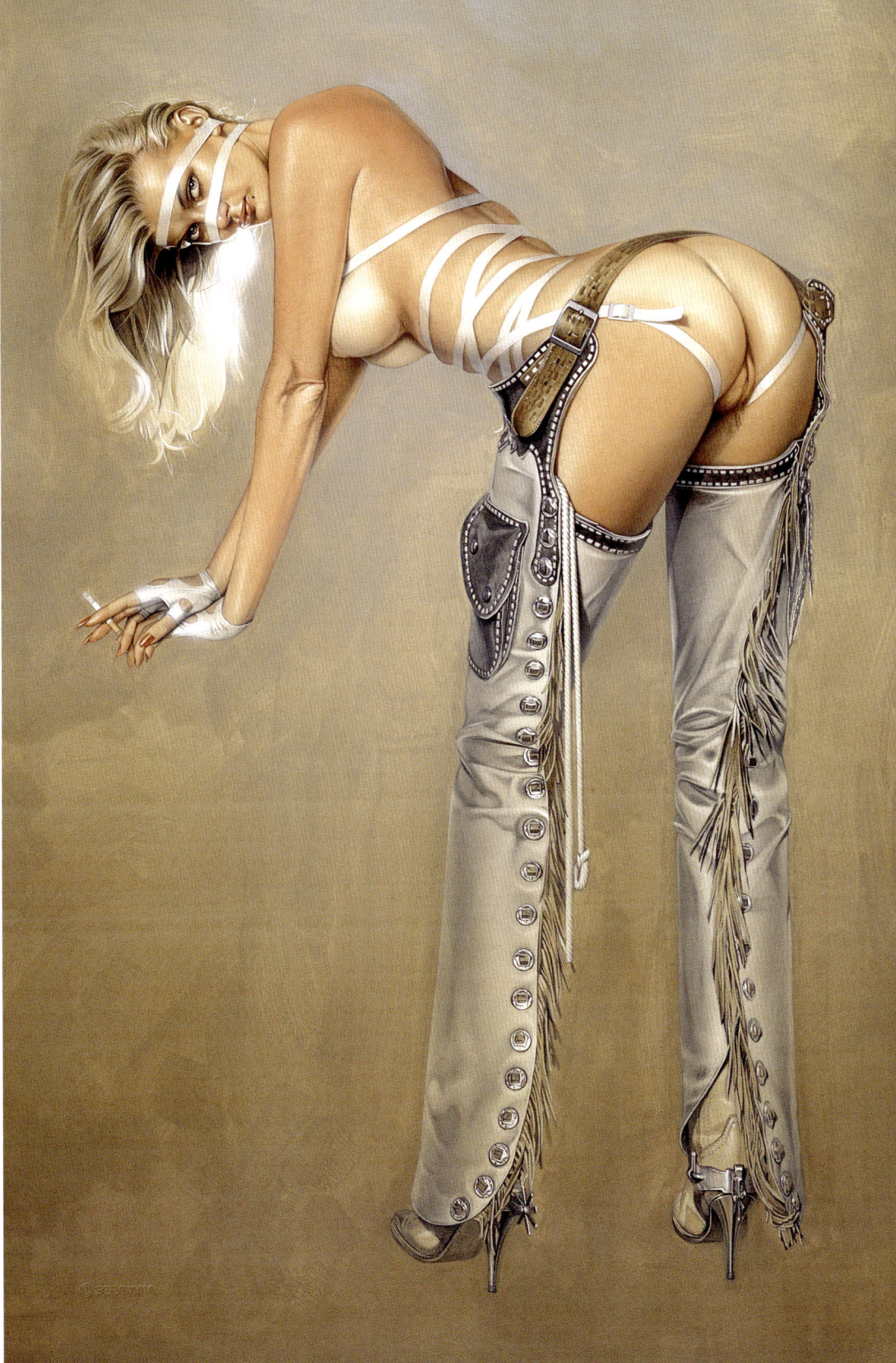

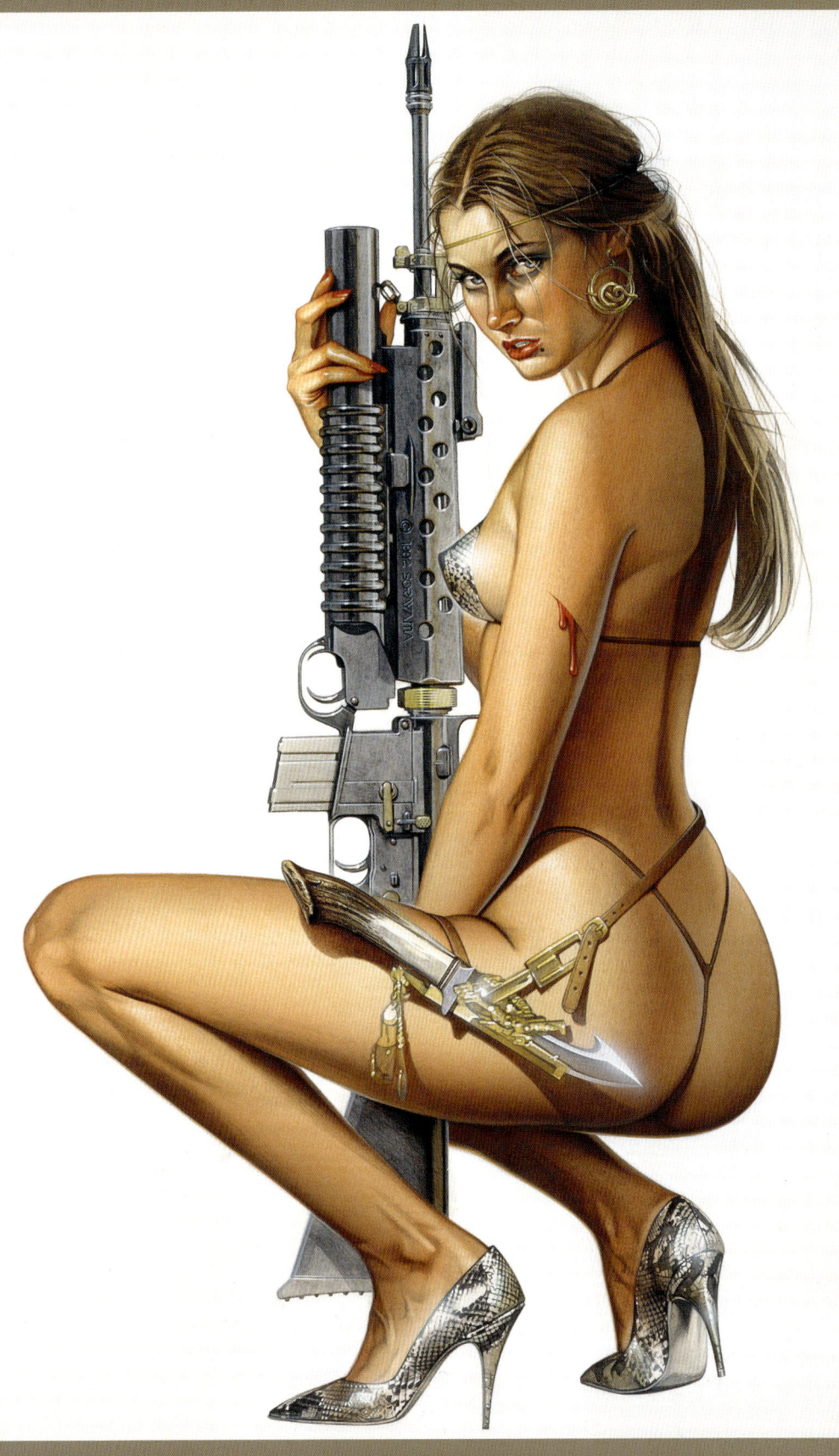

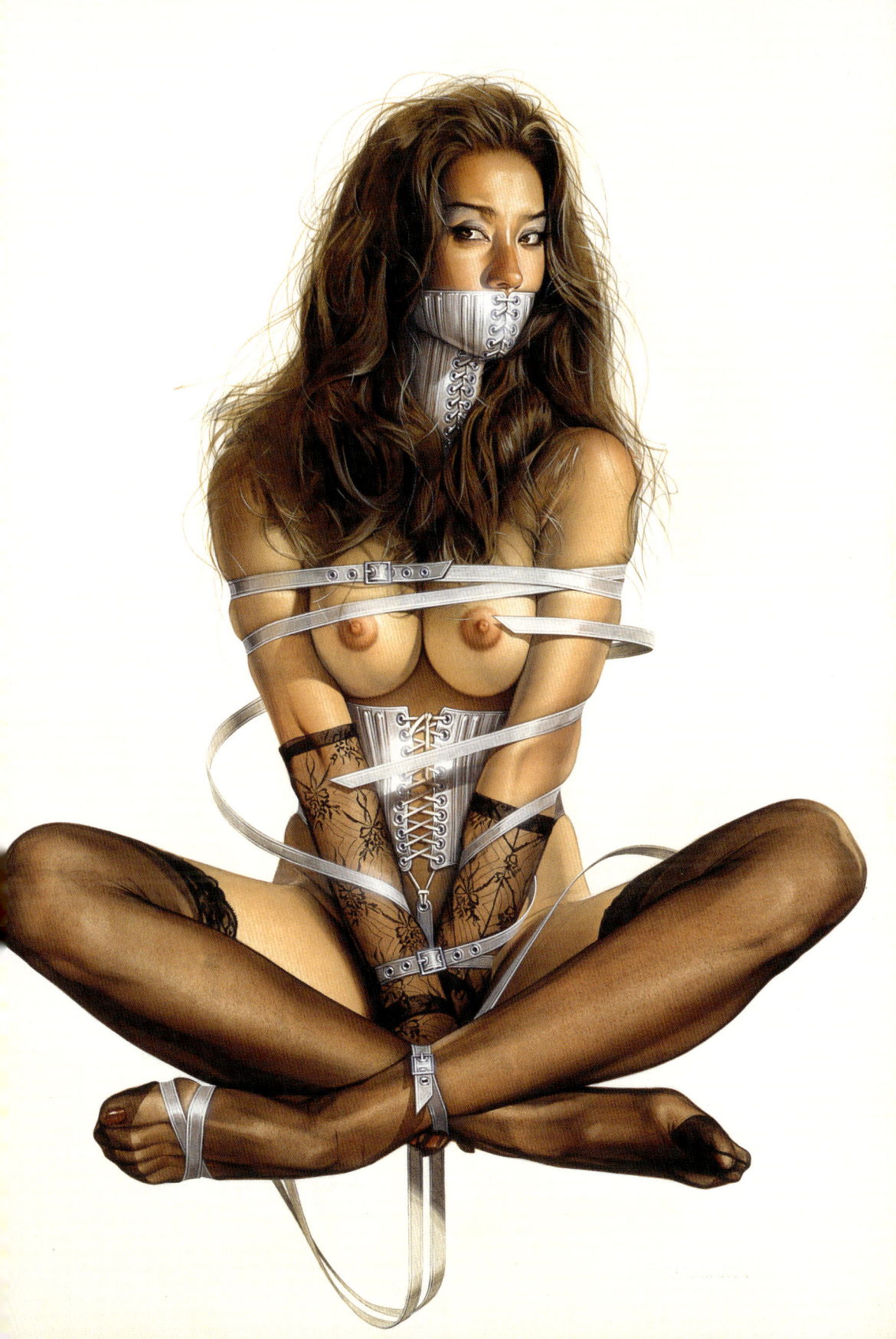

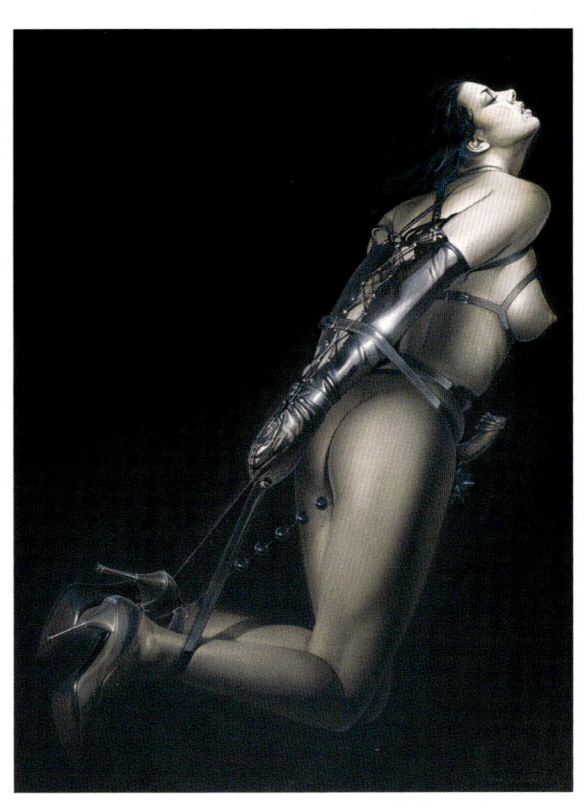
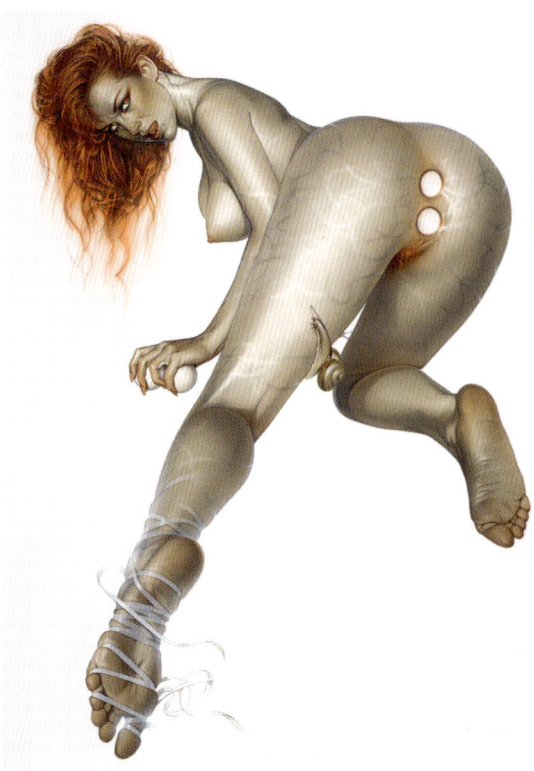

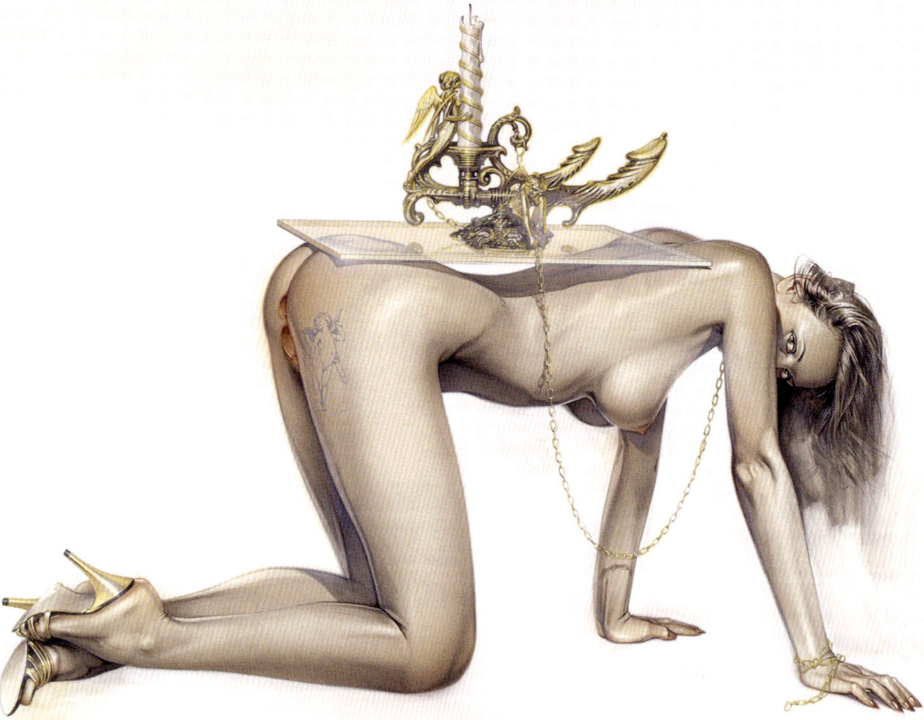

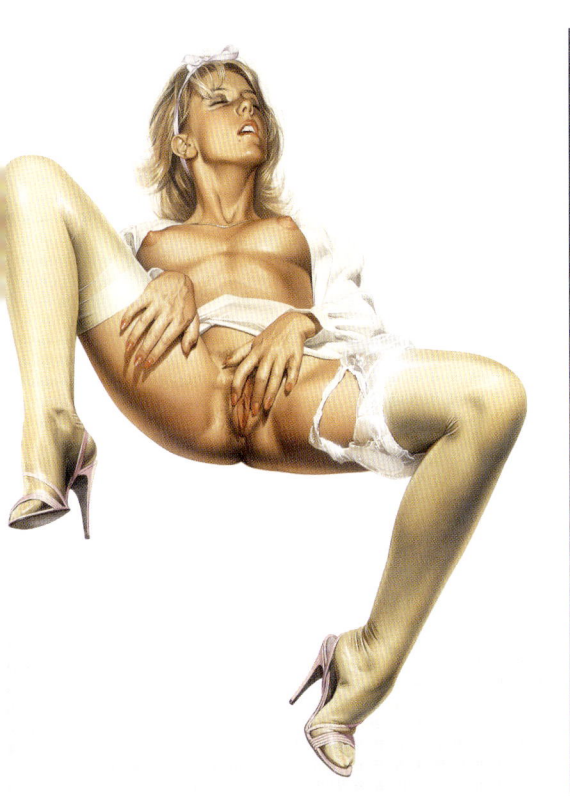
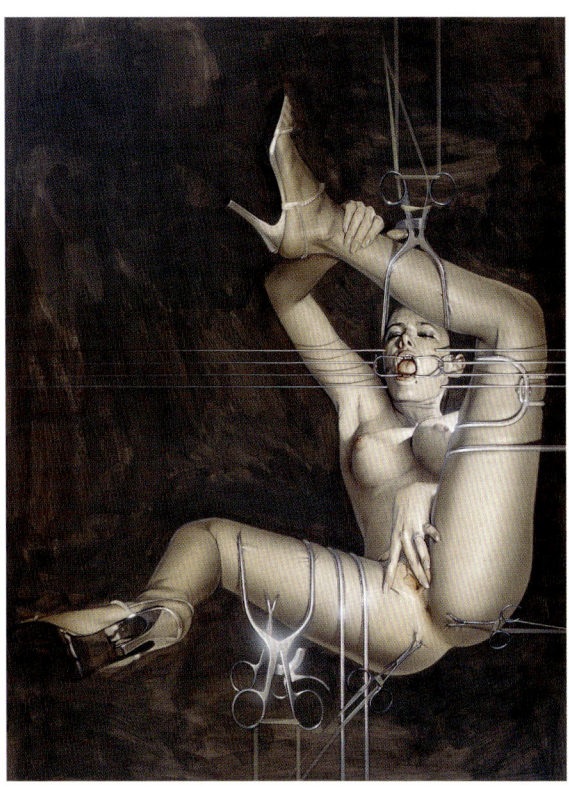

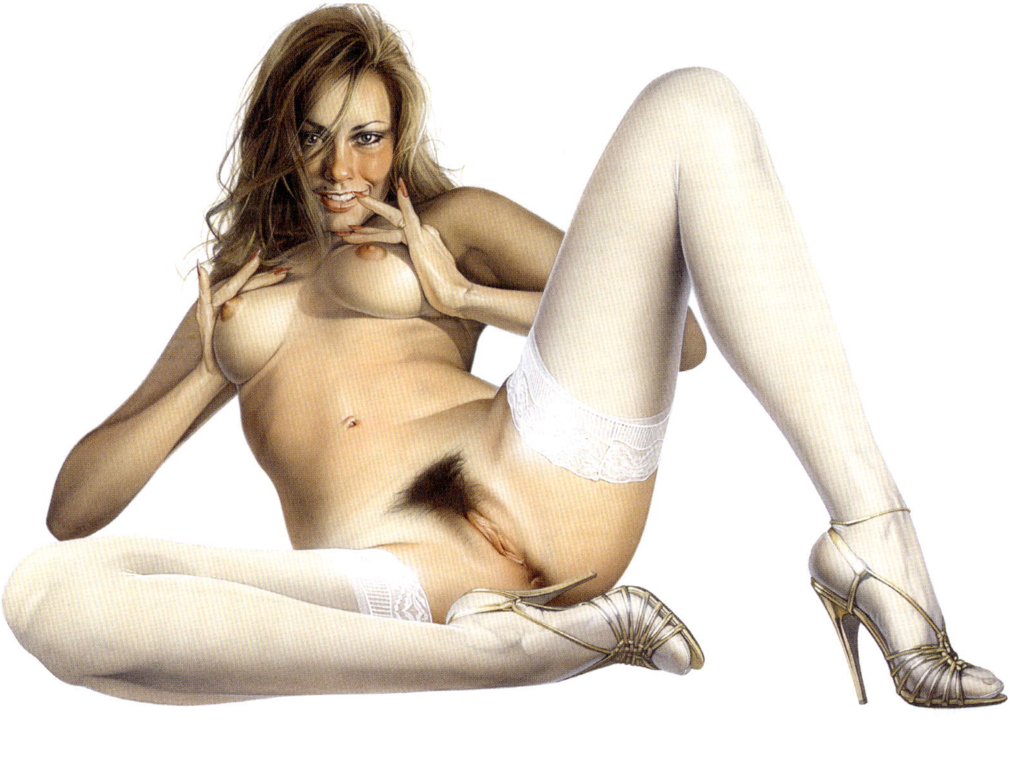

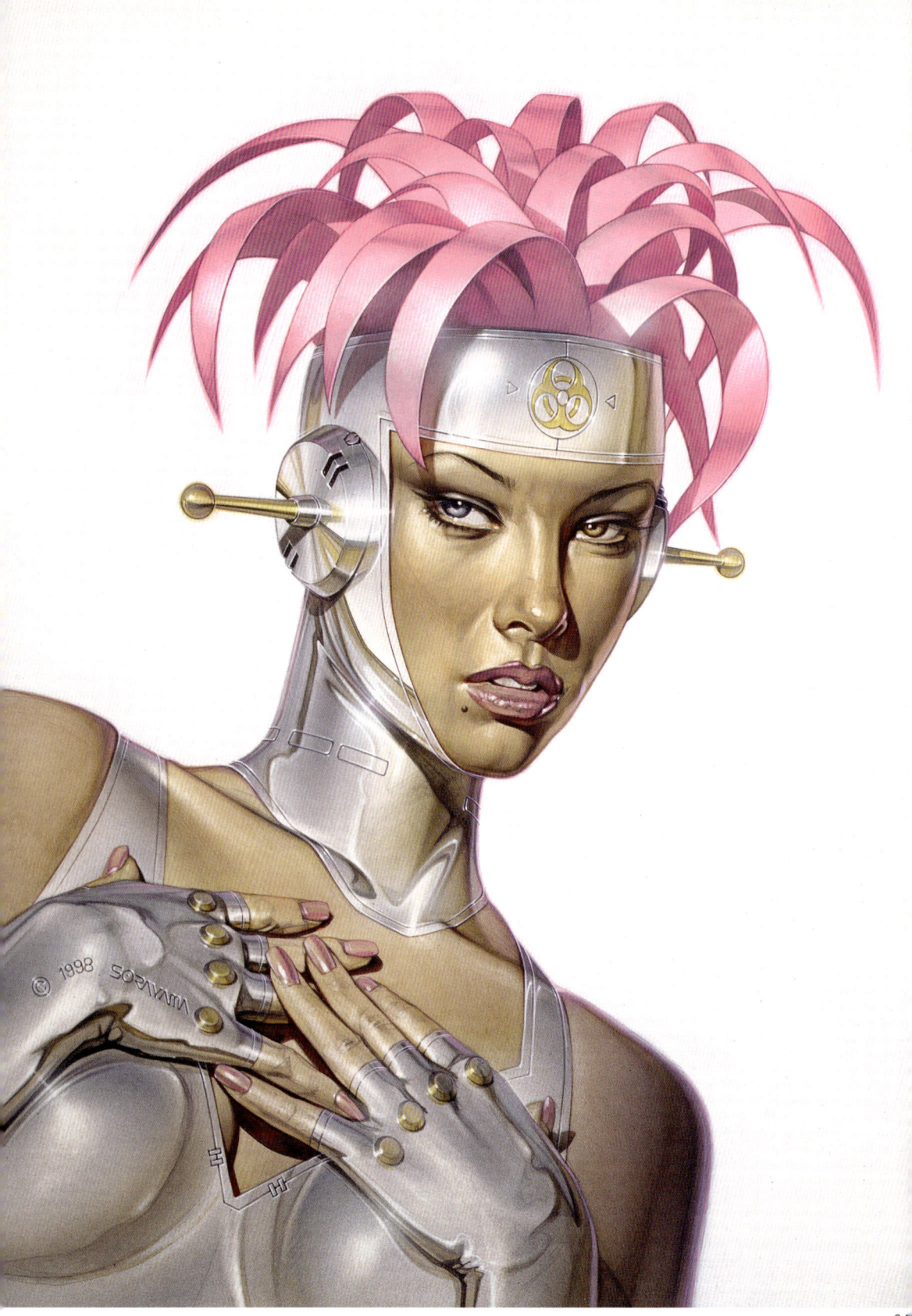

24

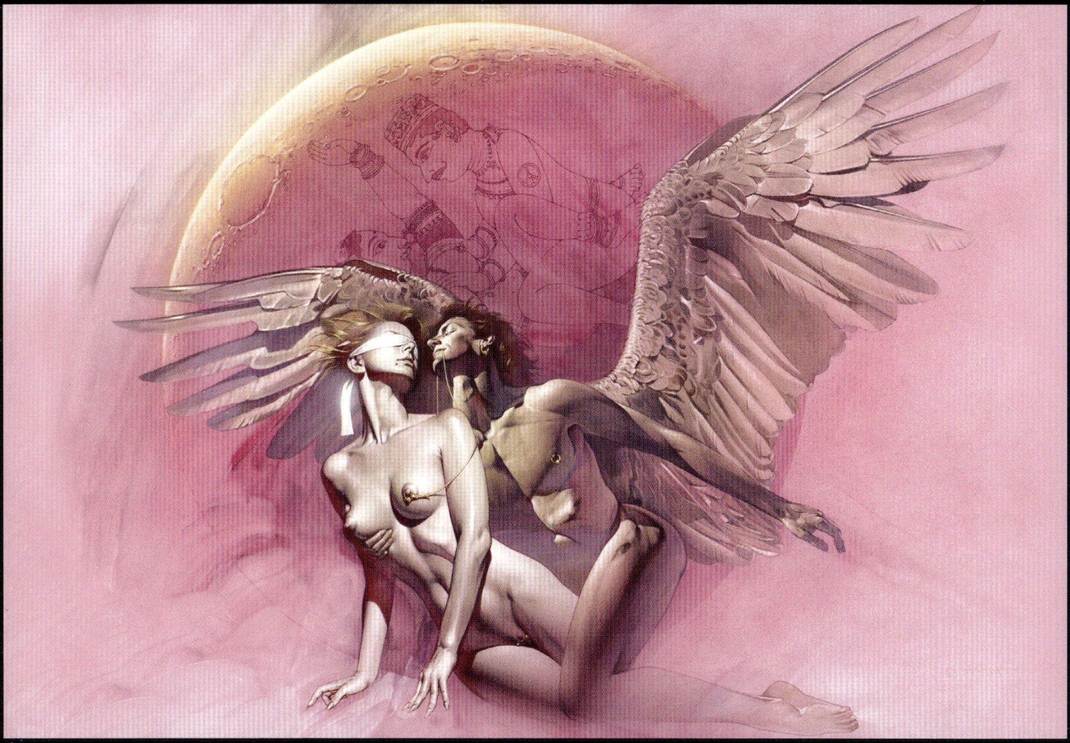

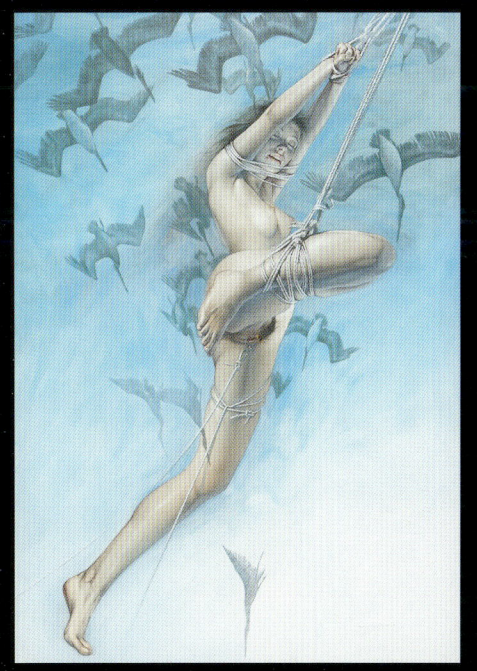
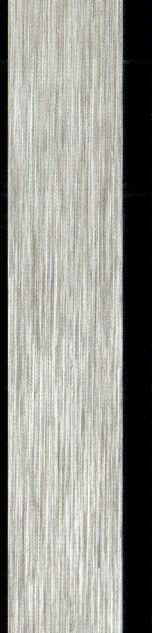
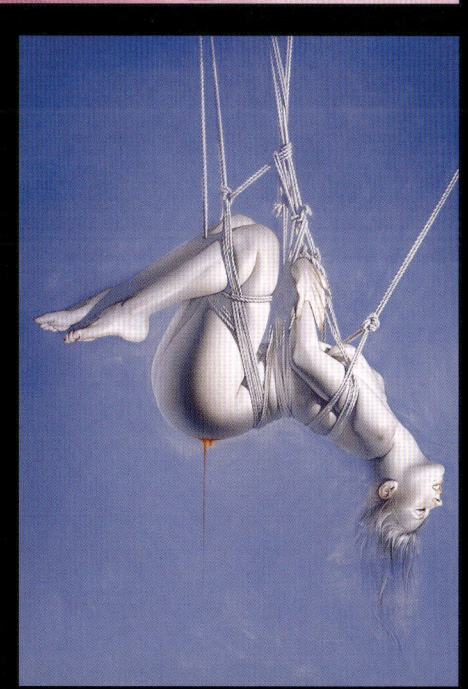

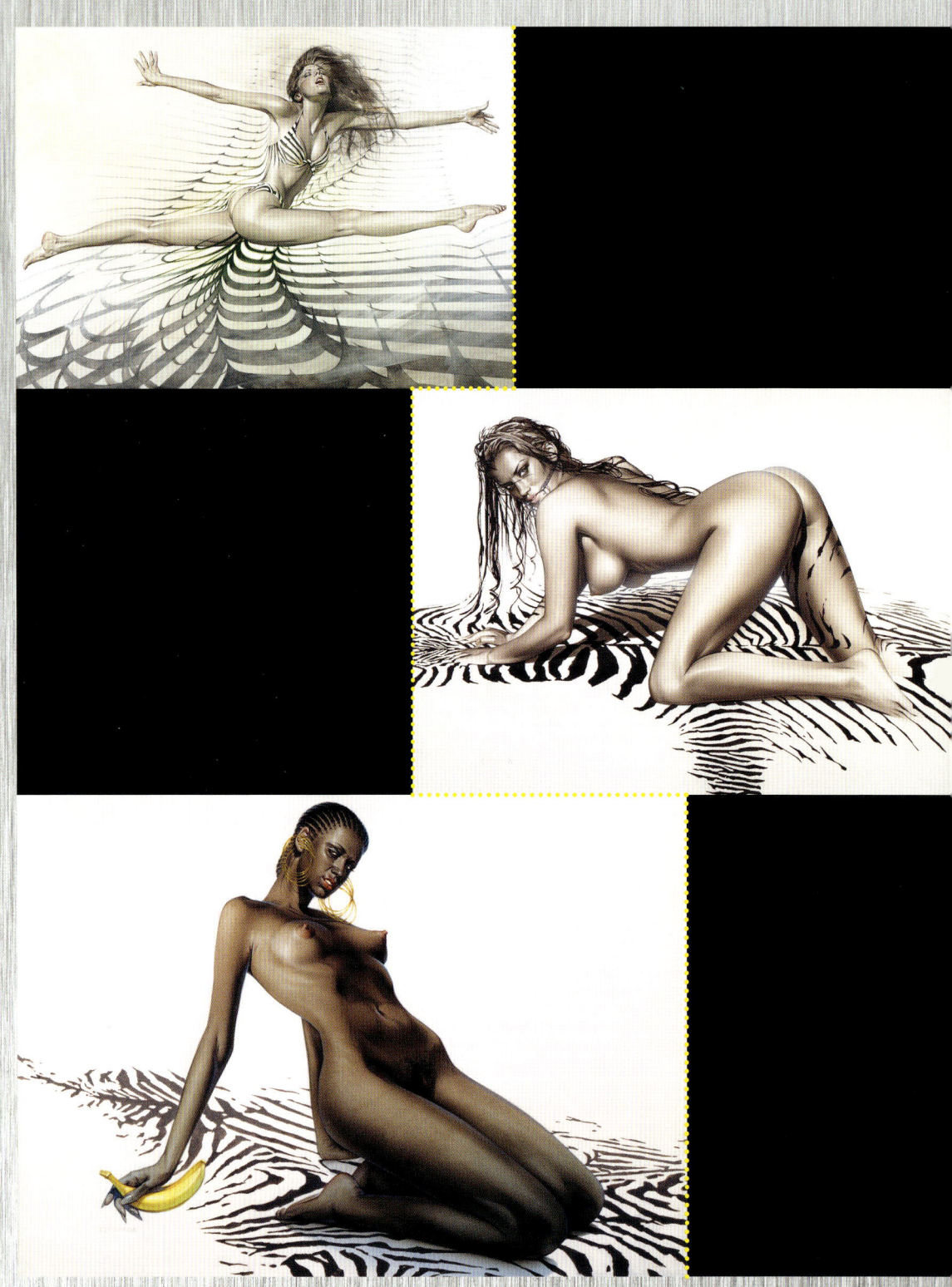

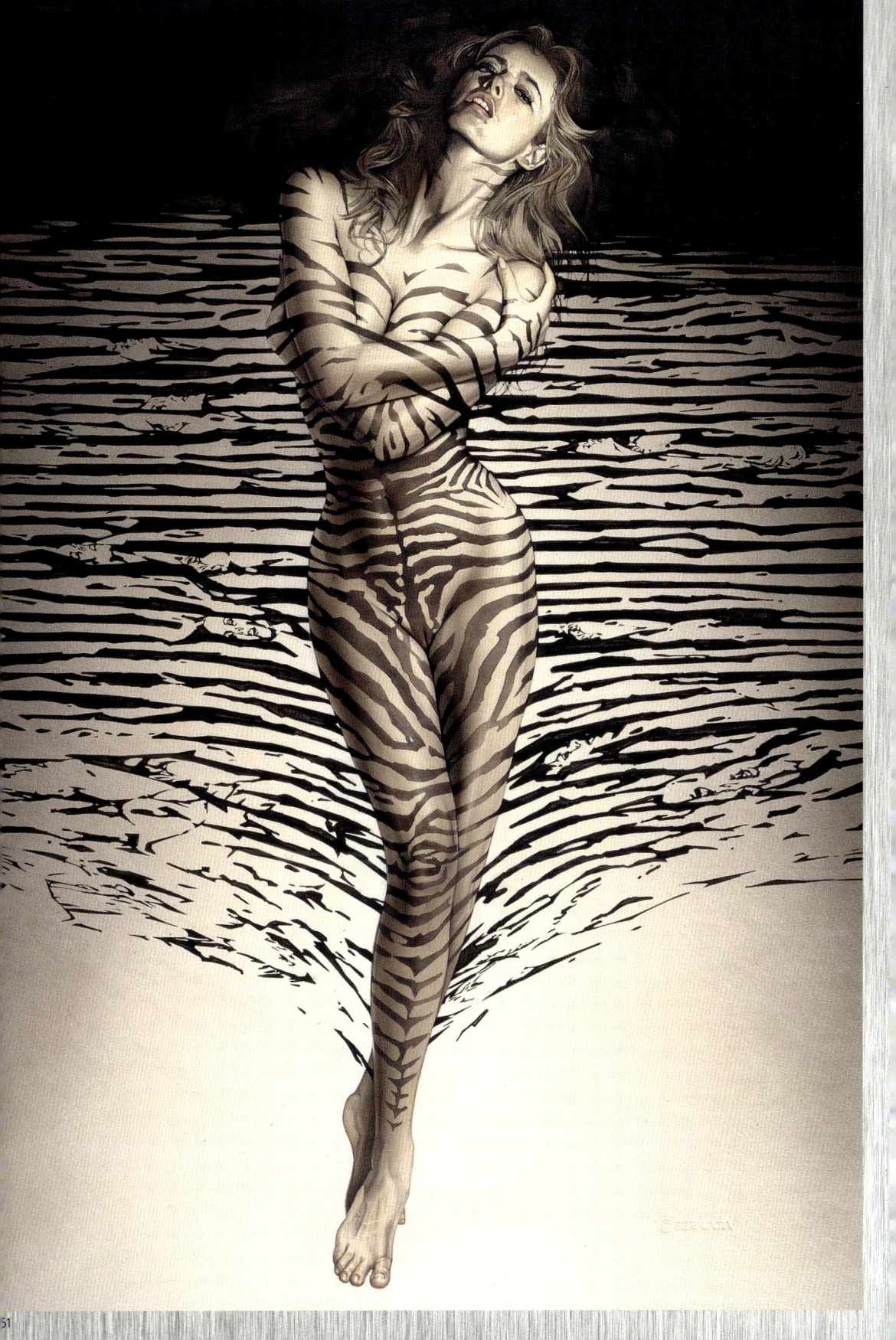

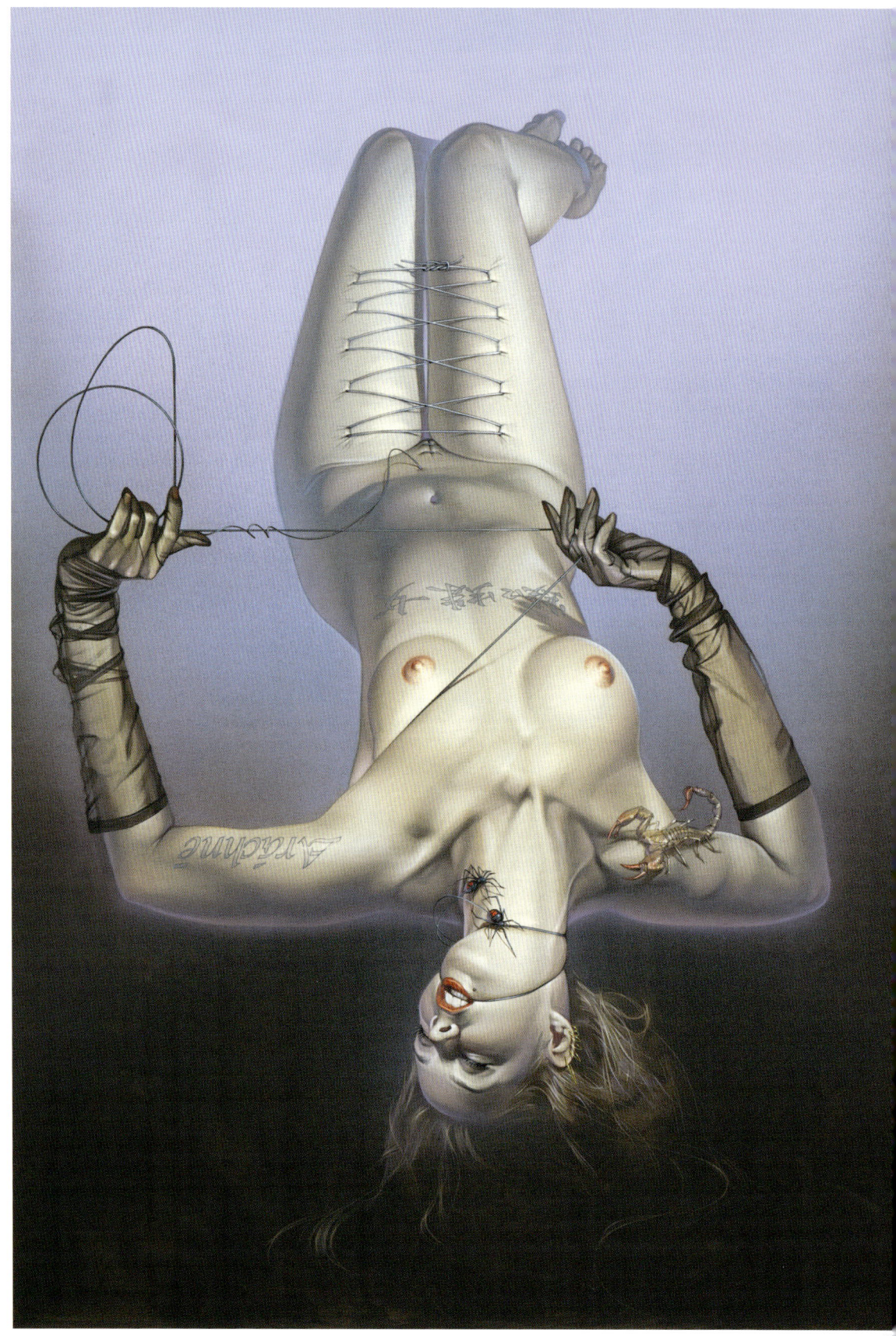

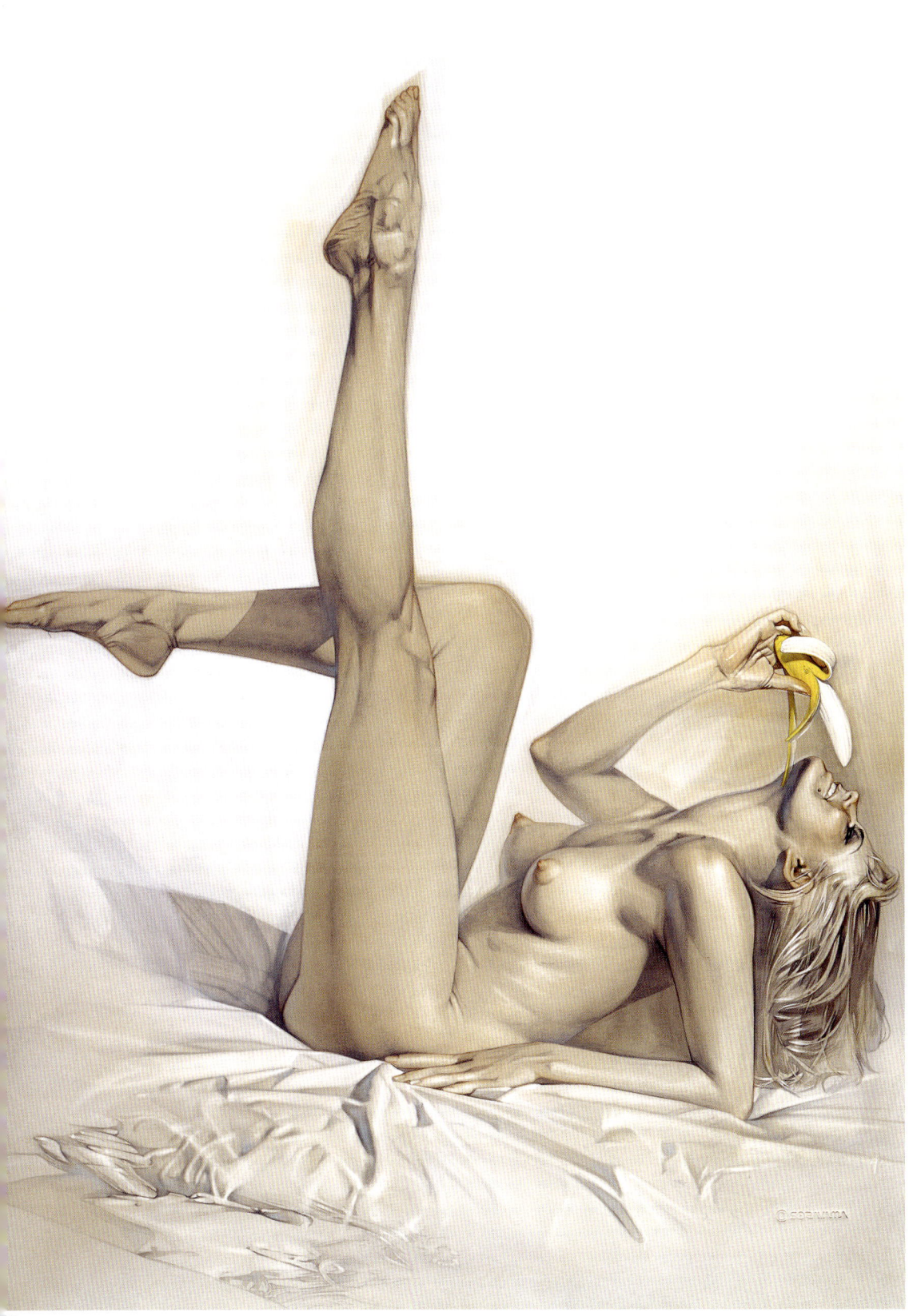

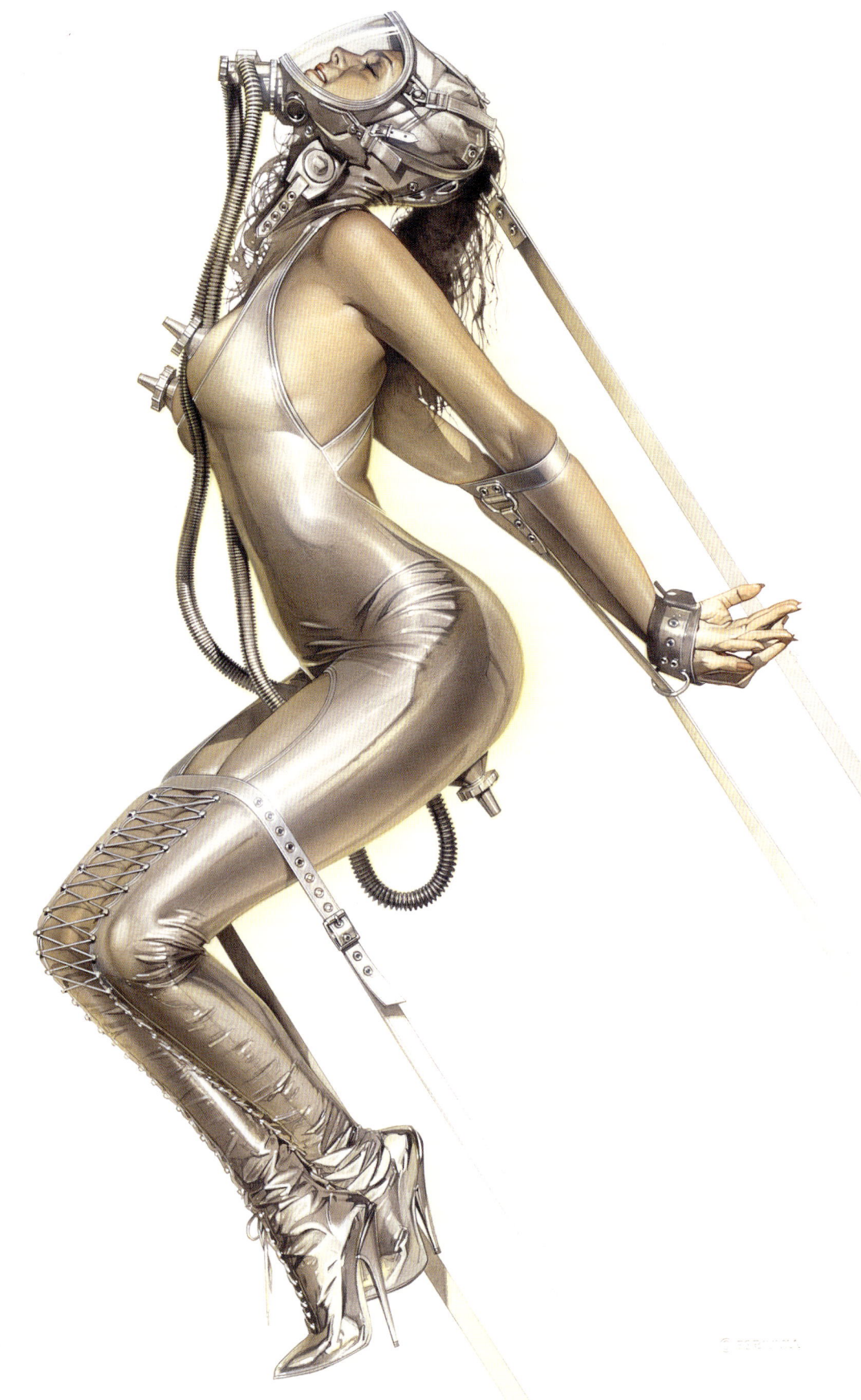

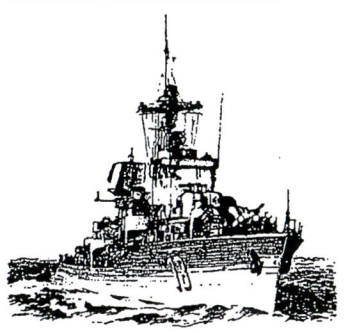

スエーデン駆逐艦ハルランド Halland

……空山 基……

投書規定

● 「読者交歓室」への投稿には必ず原稿用
紙を使用し、これに横書きすること。こ
の規定に満たない投稿は内容の如何にか
かわらず不採用とする。

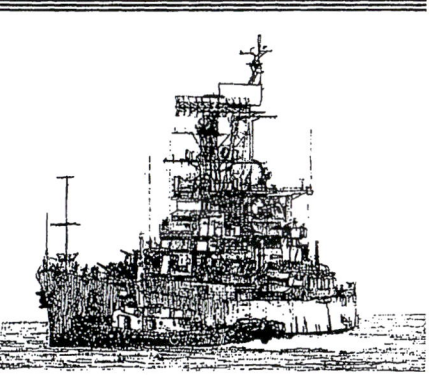

米ミサイル巡洋艦ガルヴェストン Galveston CLG-3 ……空山 基……

す。地味ではあっても正に昼夜を分
かたず活躍する海上保安庁船艇の記
事を、軍艦のそれに決して押される
ことなく取り上げてほしいと思うの
は、私だけではないと考えます。そ
れから読者諸兄のなかで海上保安庁
船艇(巡視船艇はもちろん水路、灯
台関係のものでも)のネガか写真を
お贈り下さる方がおられましたら、
御一報下さい。
(神戸市灘区森昭木町3丁目39
河崎昭男)

◆ "世界の艦船"をここ2年ほど毎

ています。

内容もますます充実しつつあ
特に5月号は、自衛艦の訓練シ
や洋上補給の場面など、実にす
しいものでした。

私は現在自衛艦 "わかば" に
んでいますが、どうもなかなか
の写真を写せません。

学生時代から写真には興味を
ていましたので、出勤時は常に
ラを身近かに置いておくのです
変った船影を発見して、用意し
るうちに、シャッターチャンス

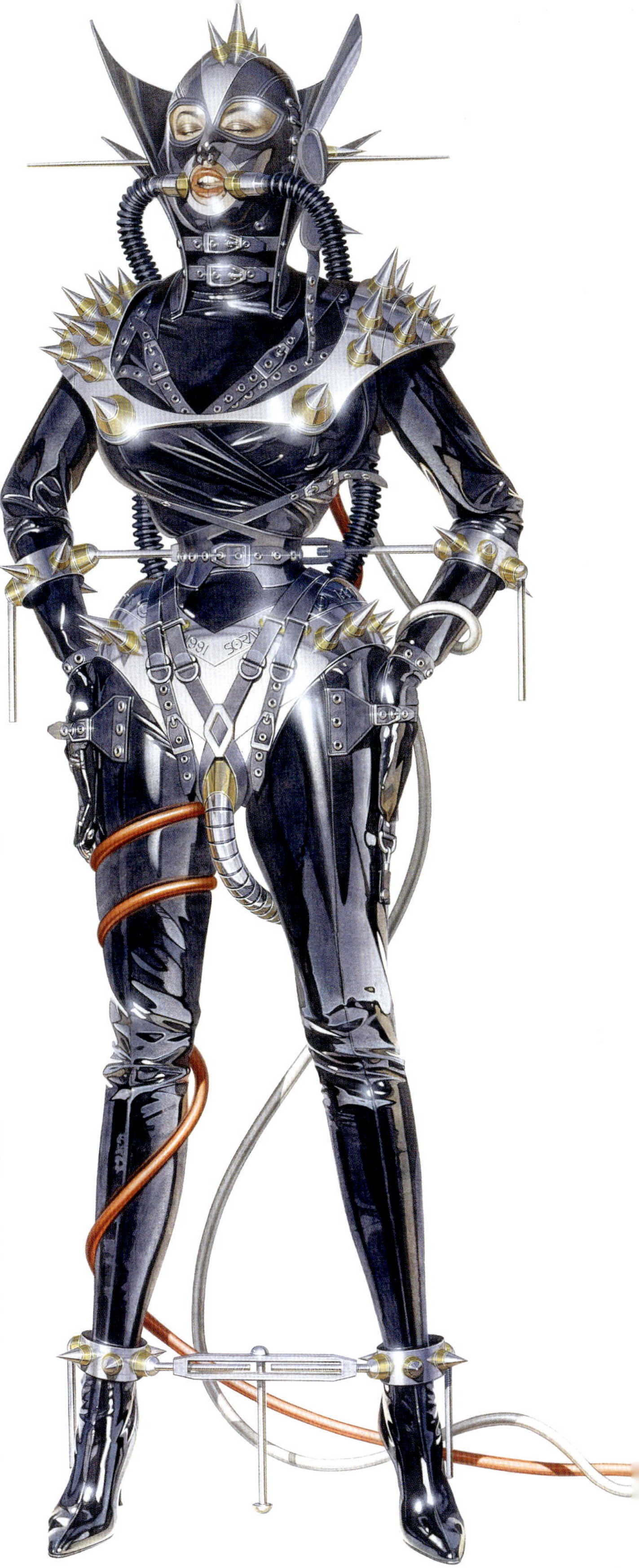

1964

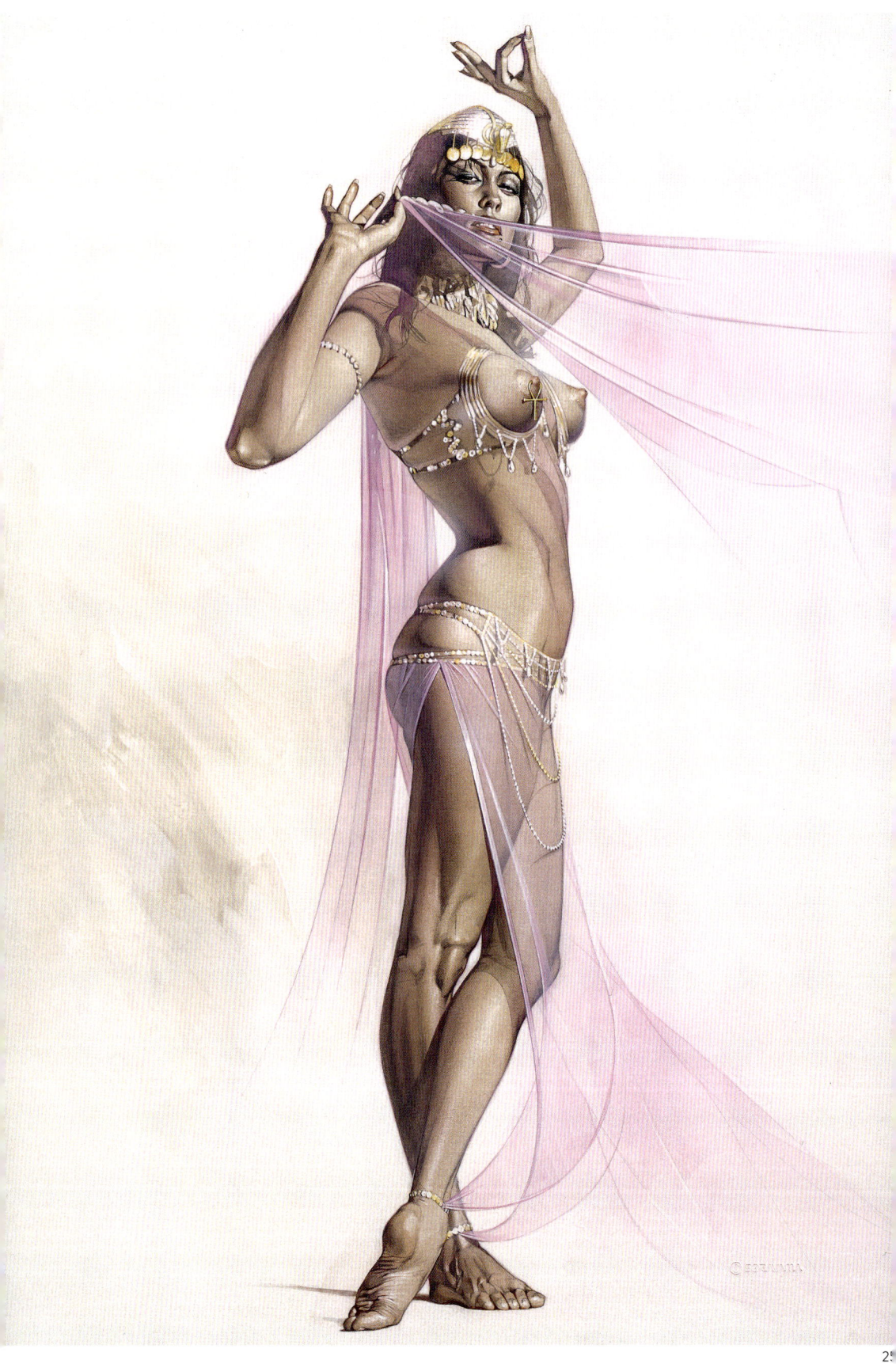

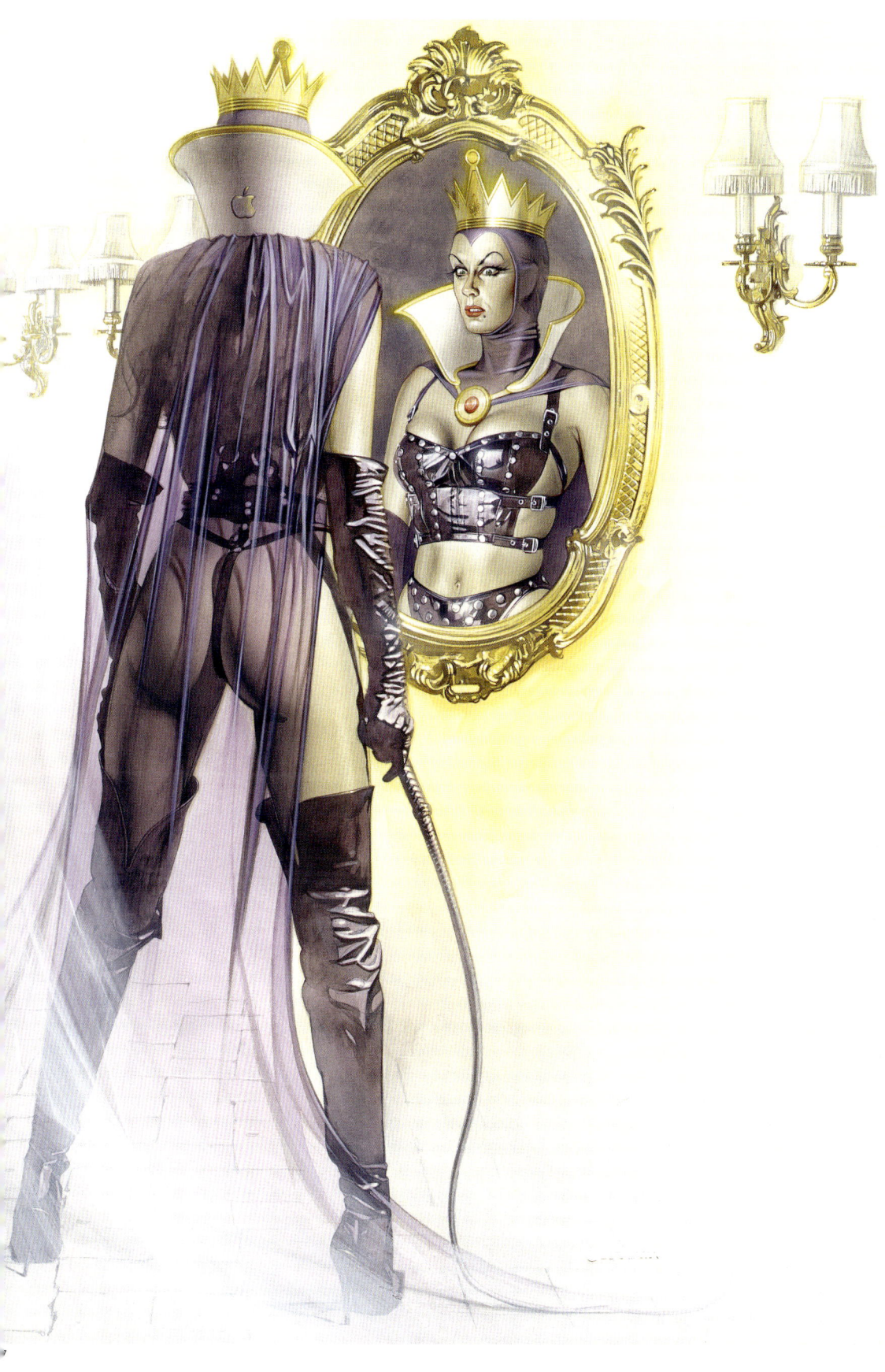

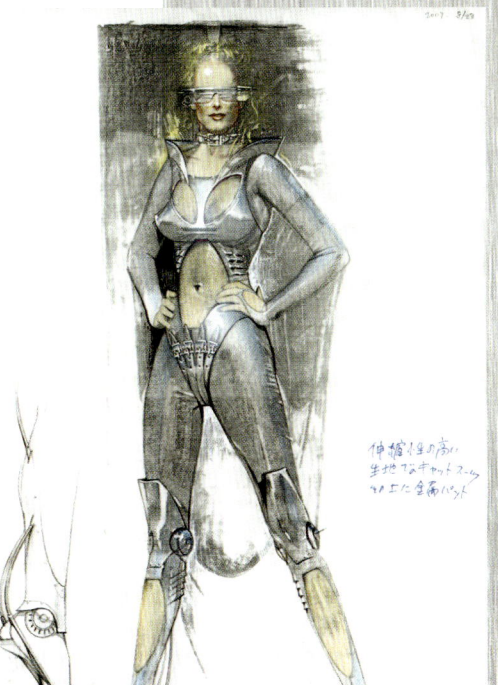

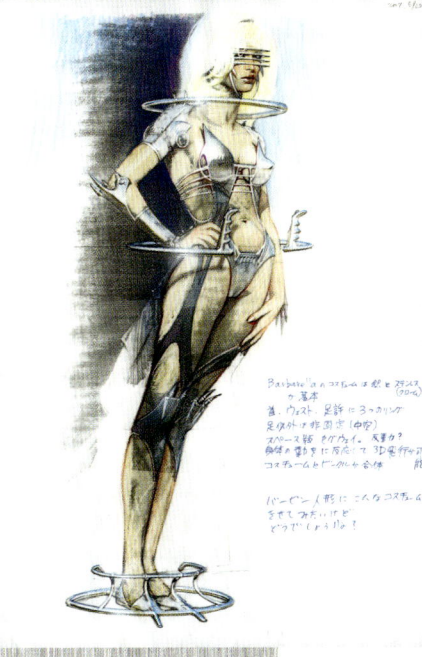

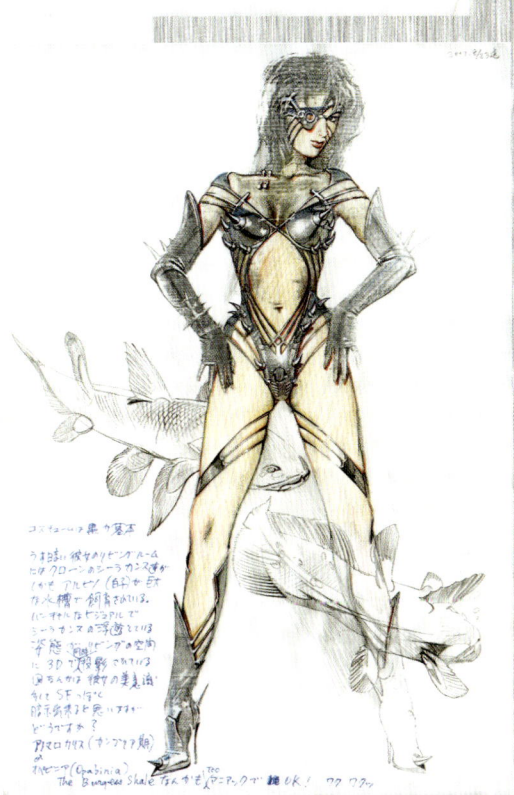

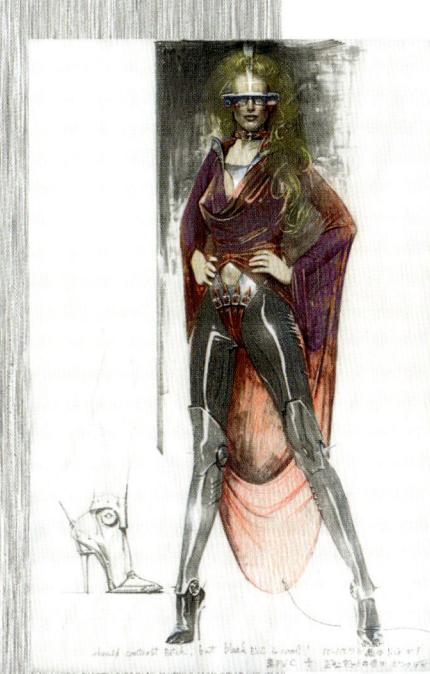

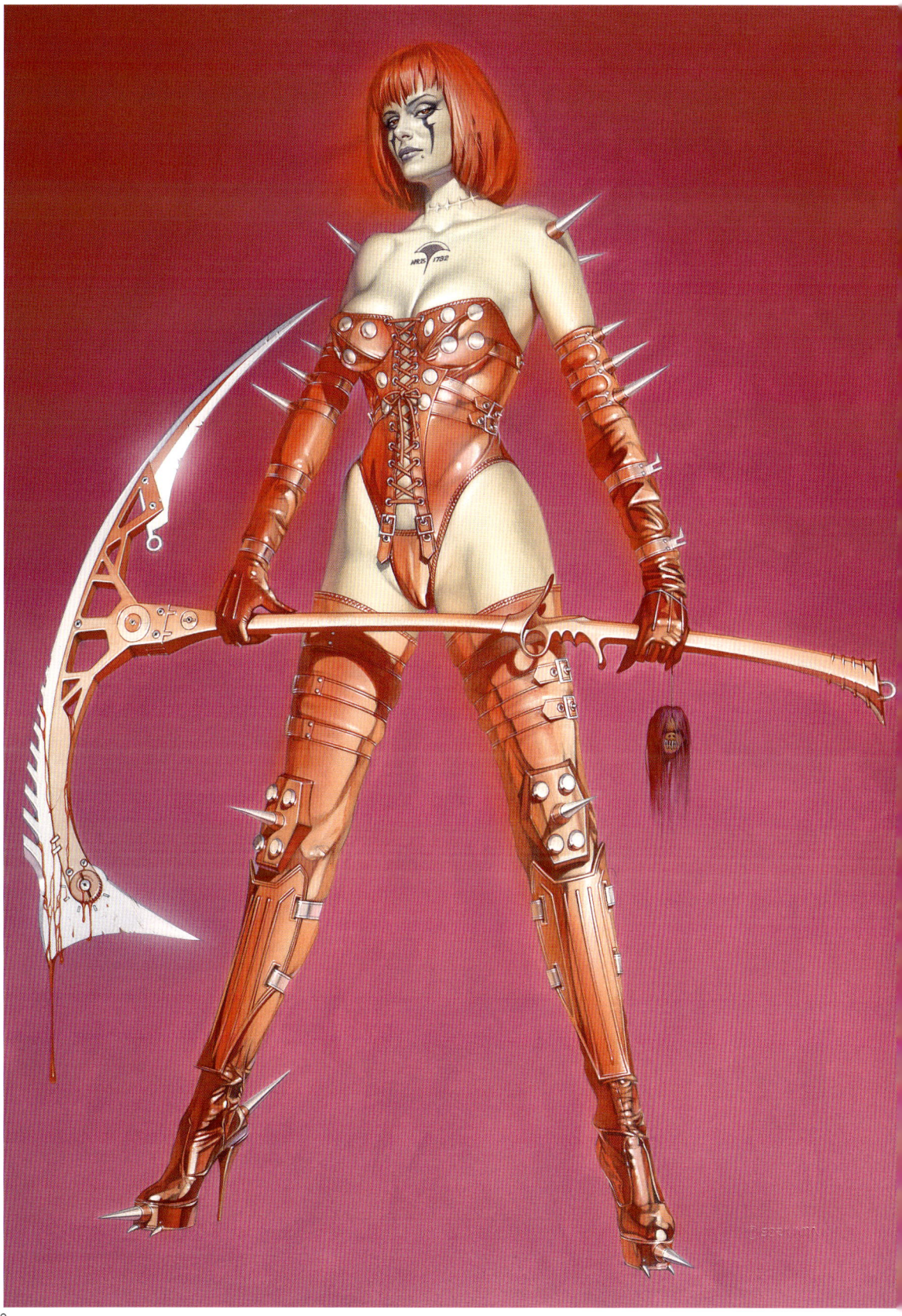

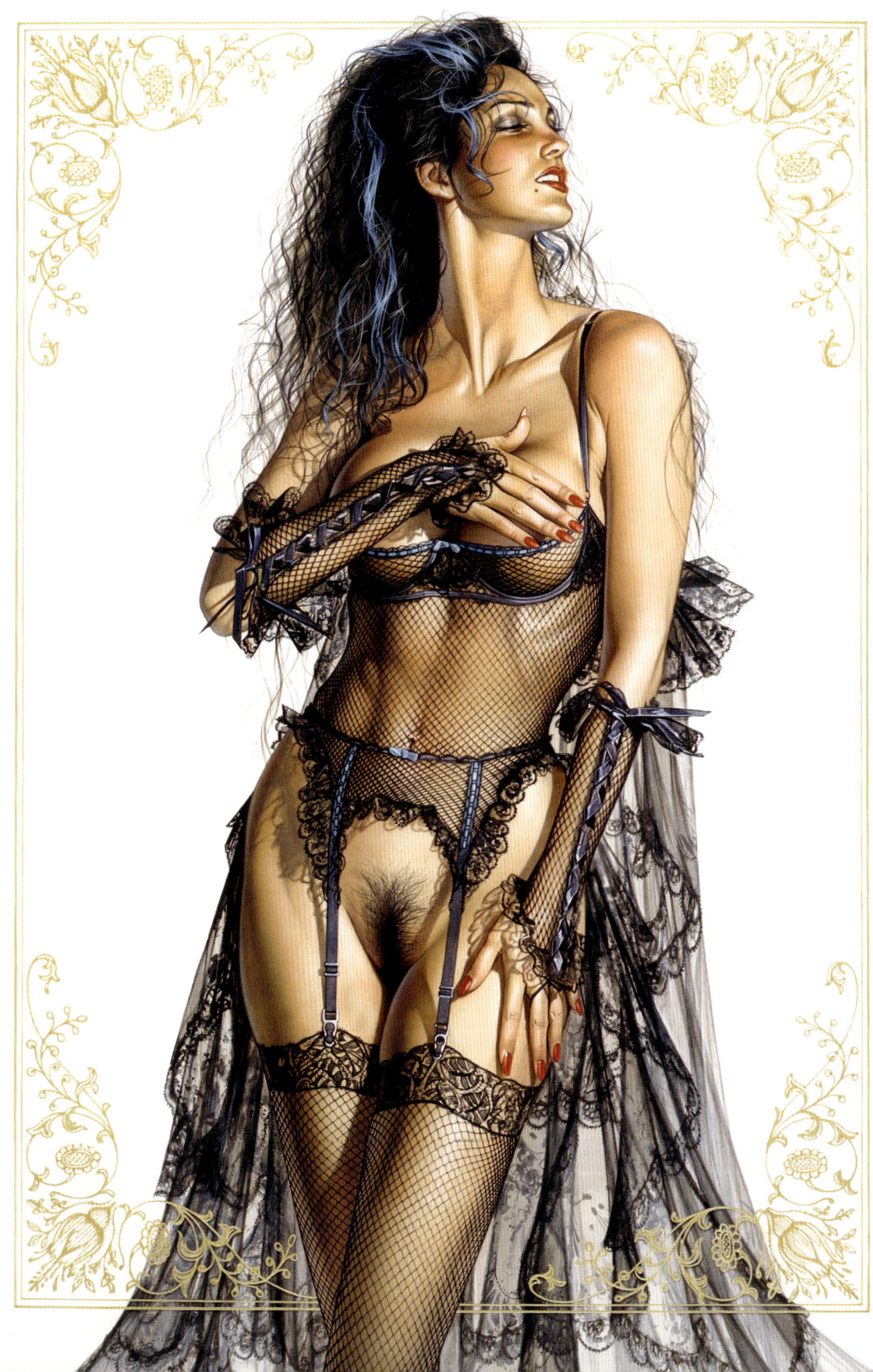

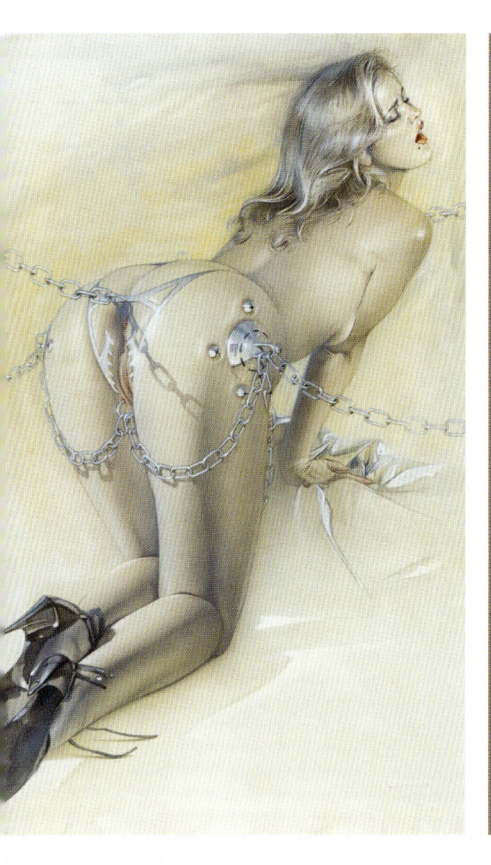
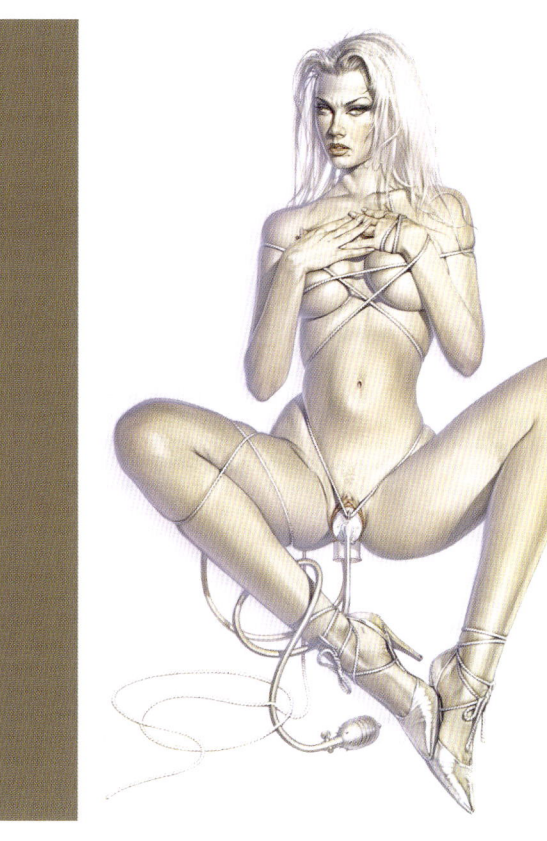

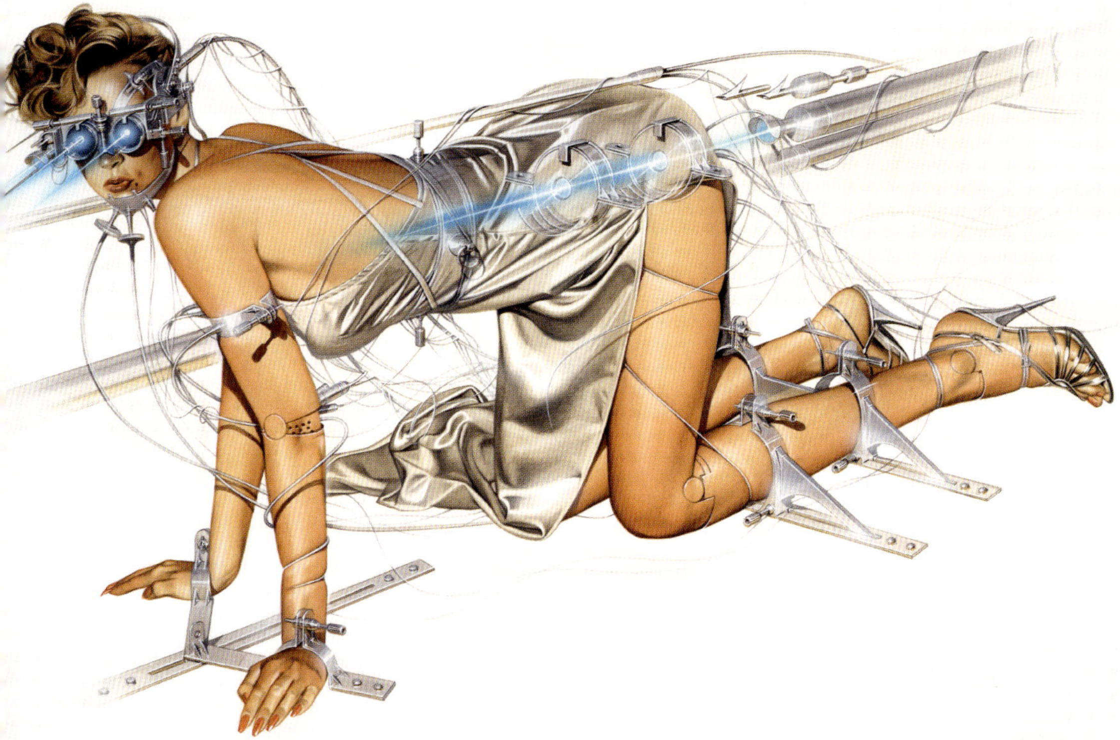

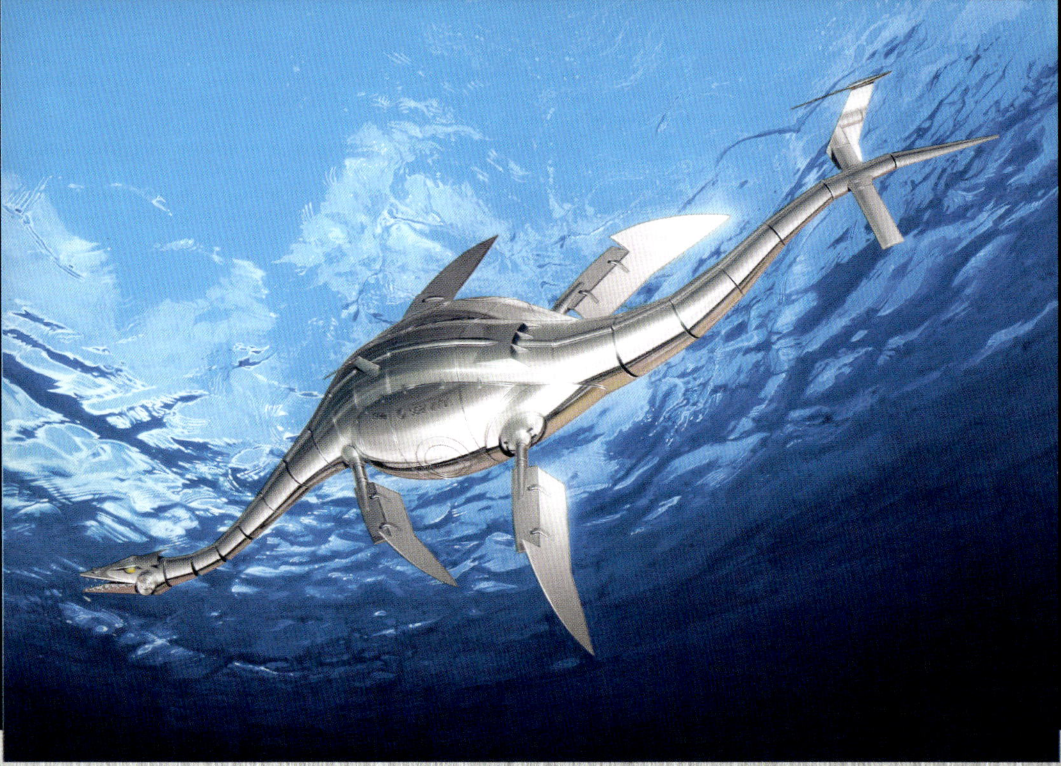

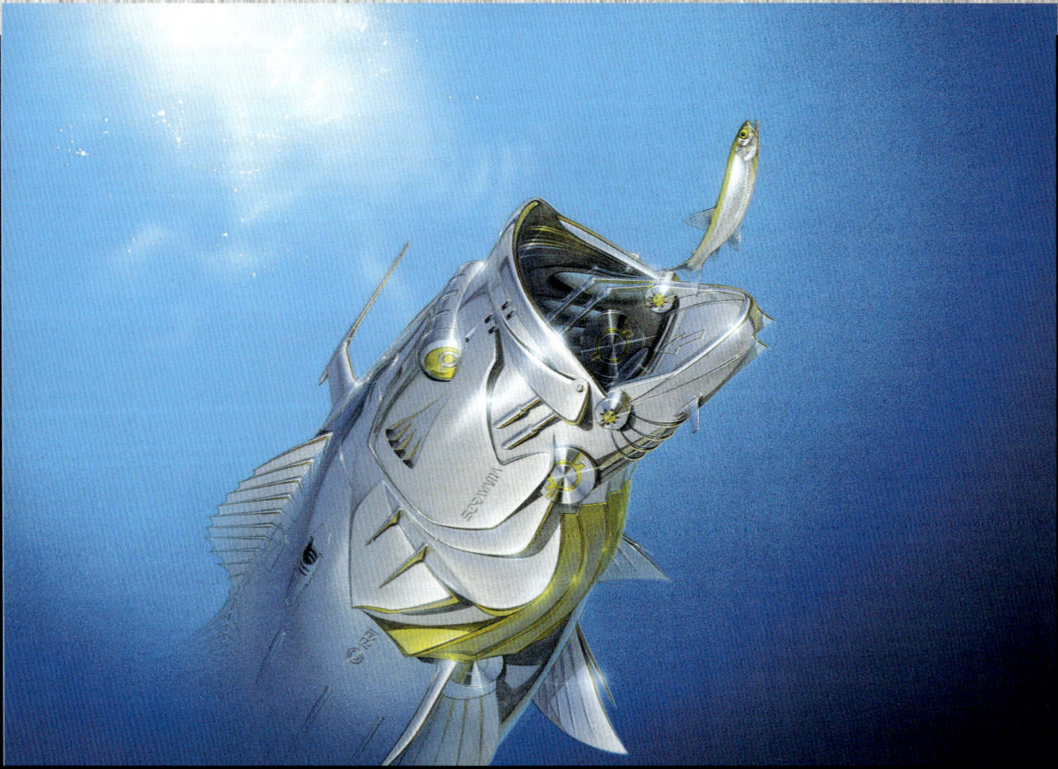

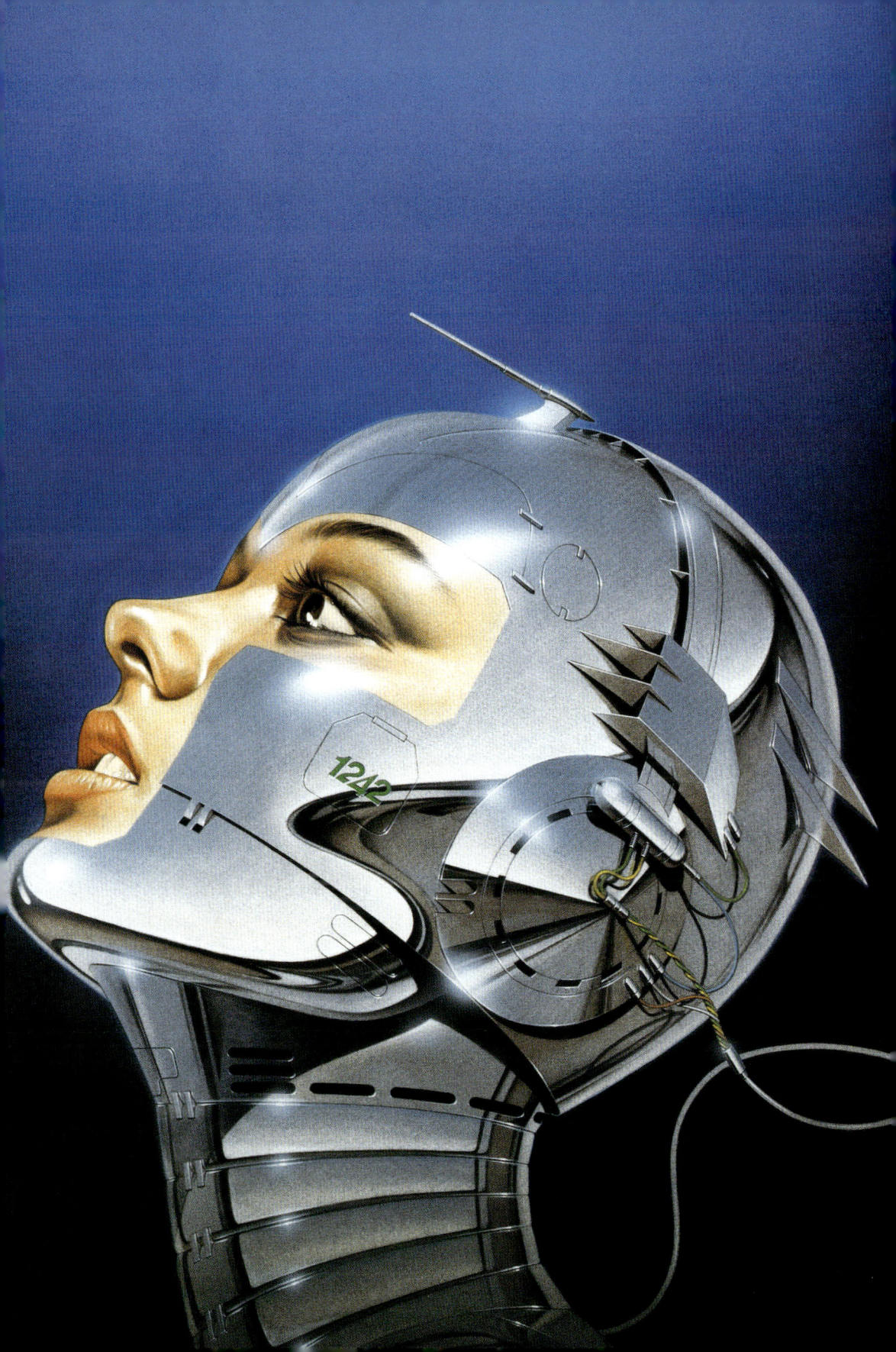

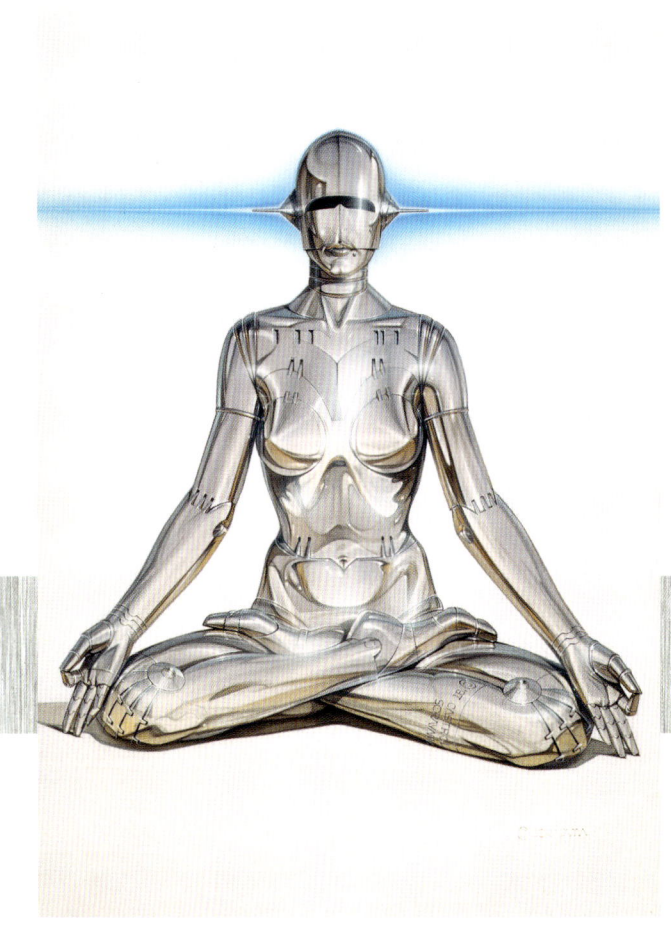

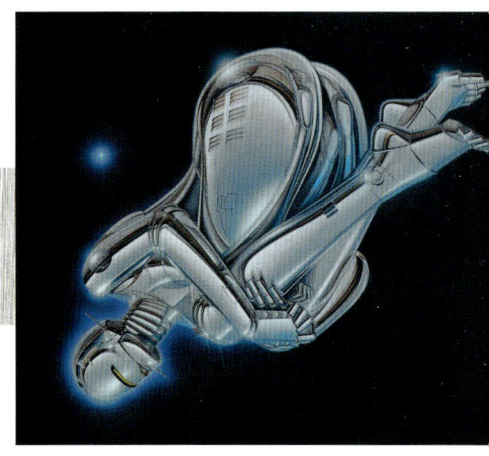

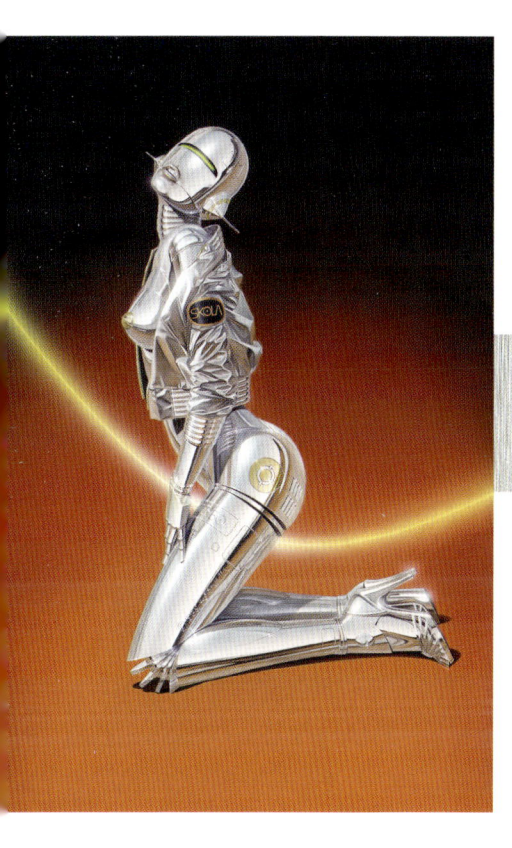
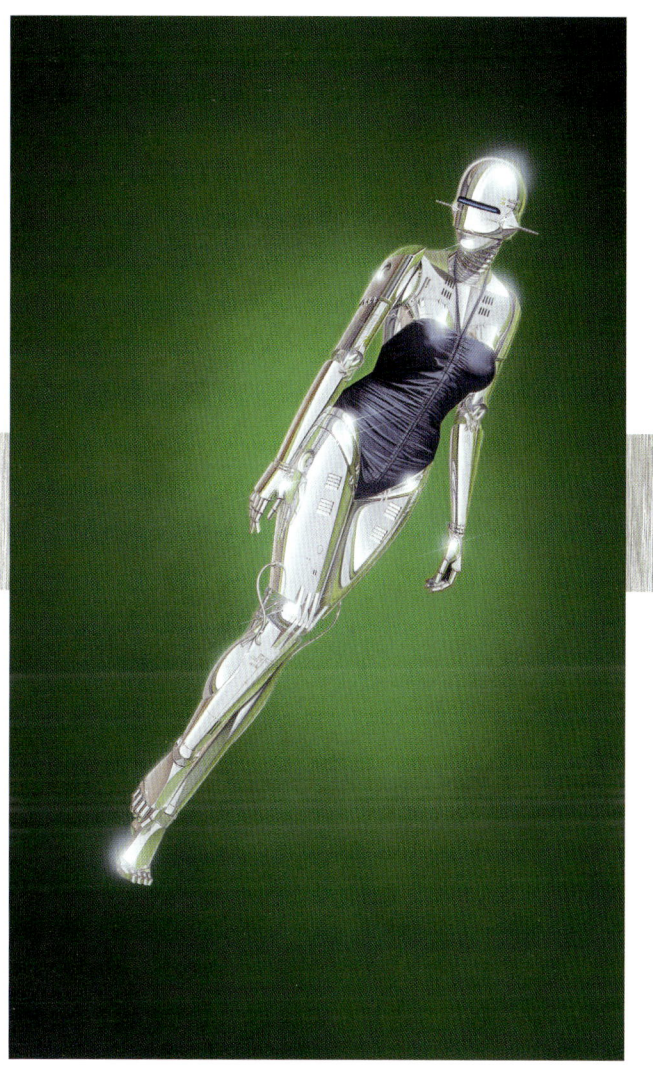

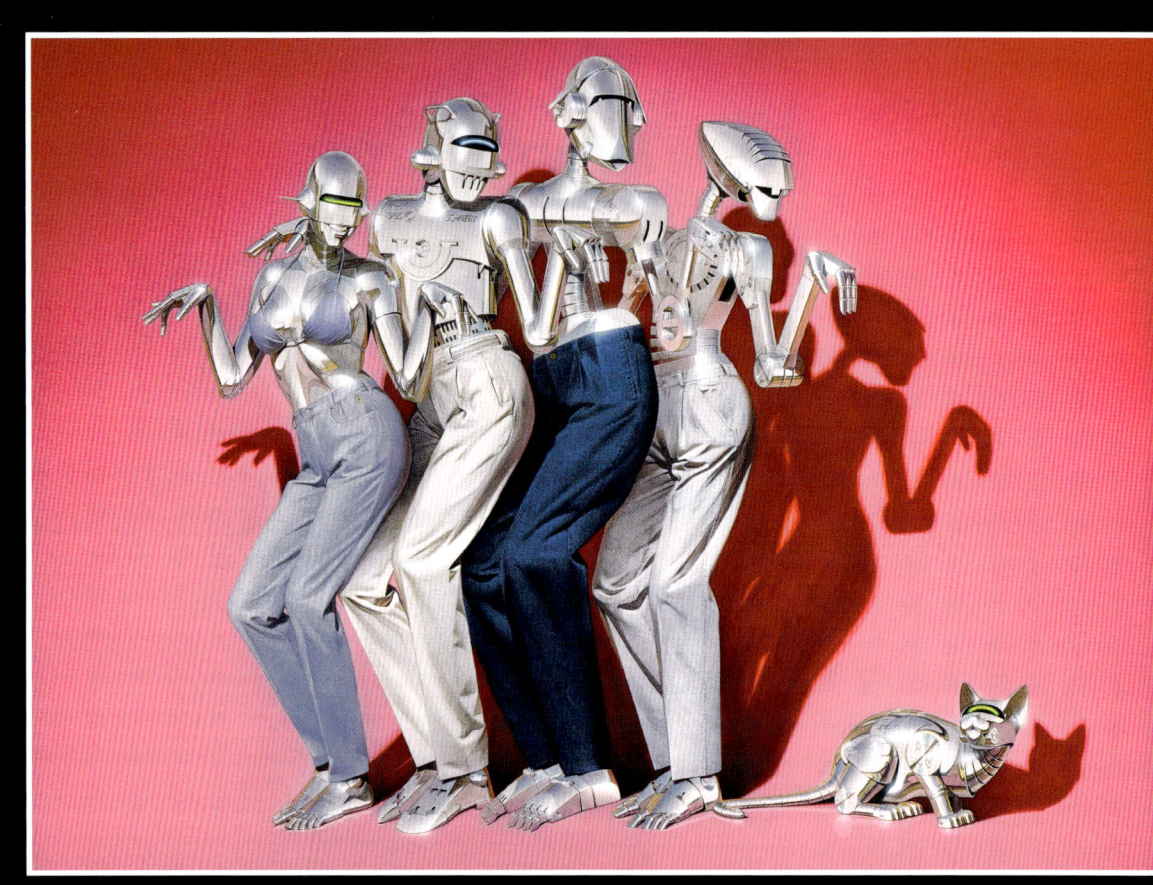

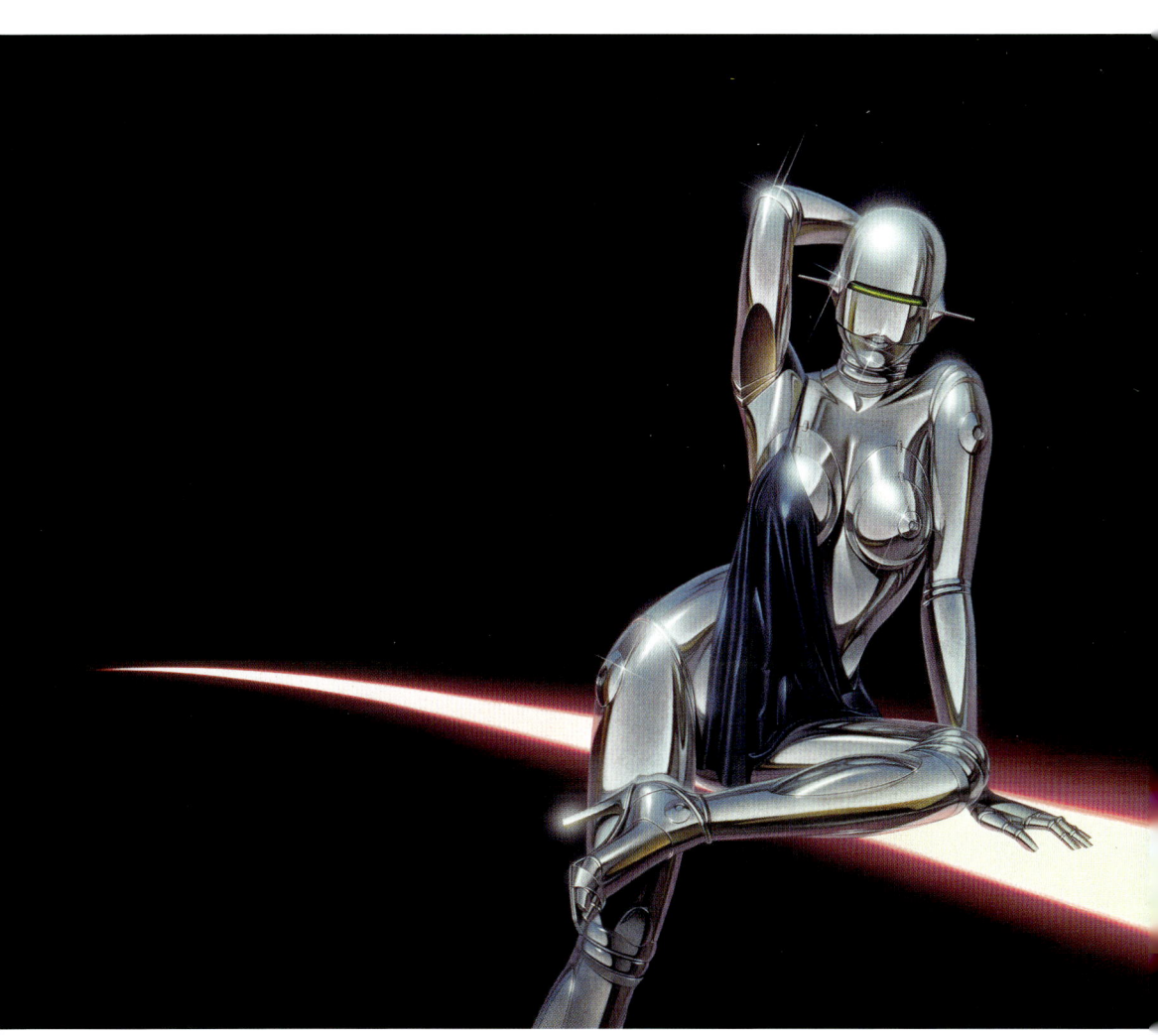

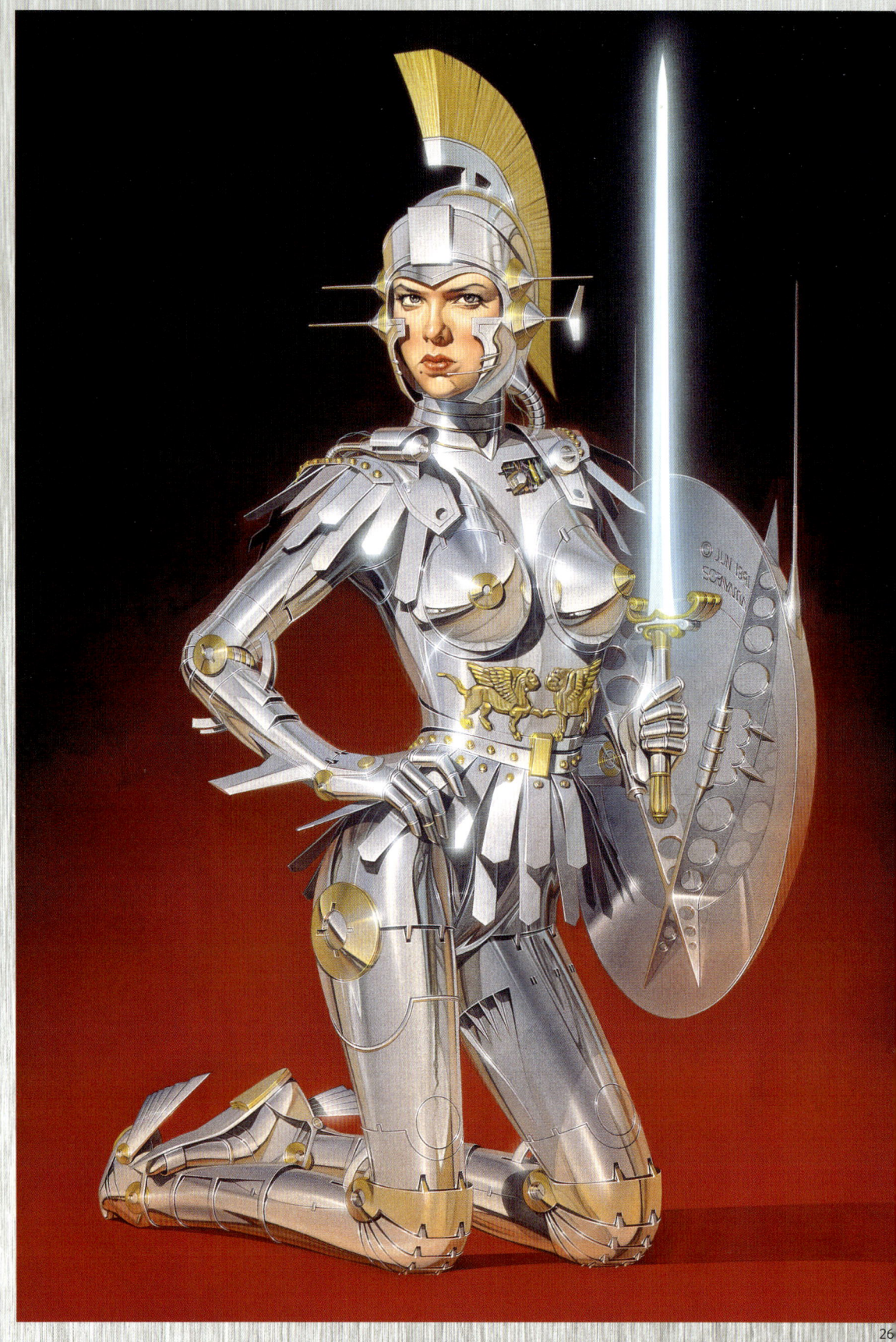

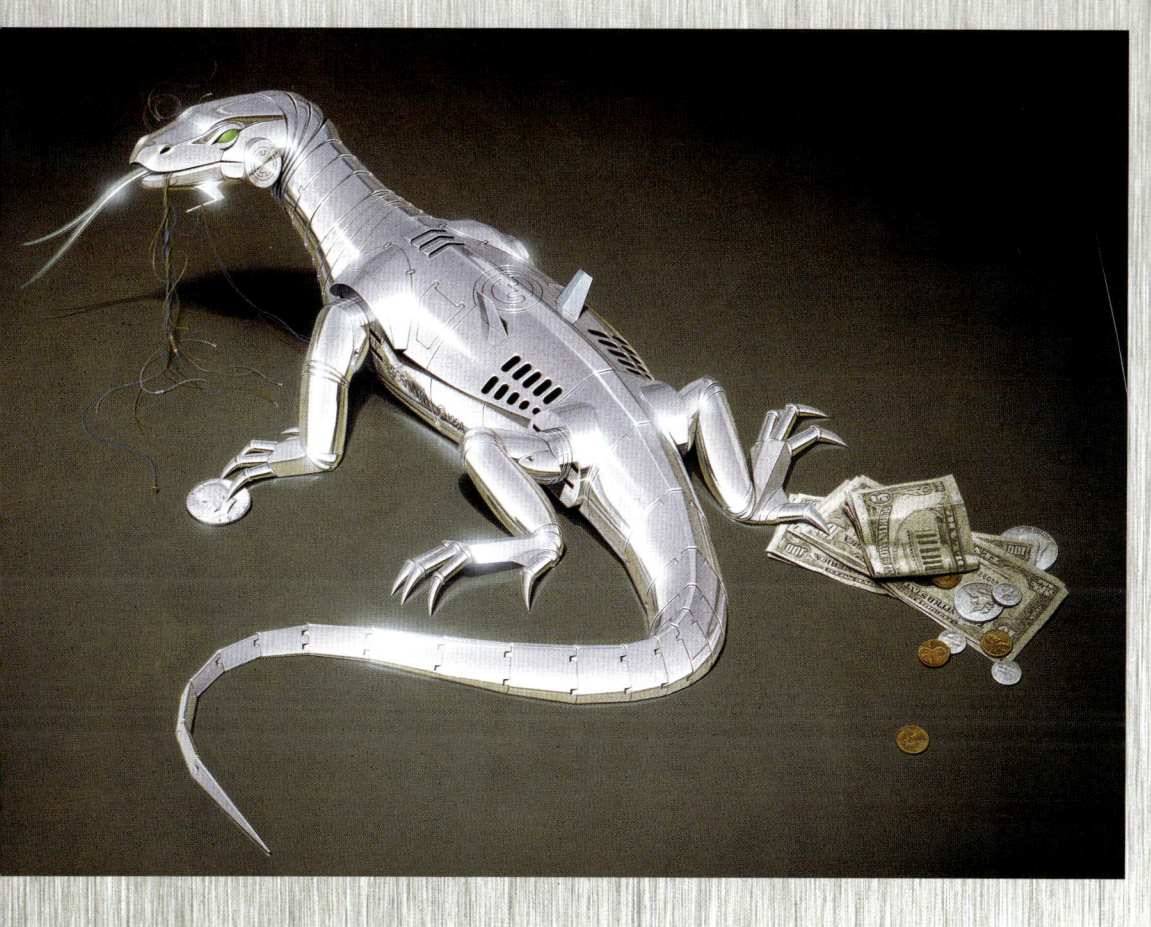

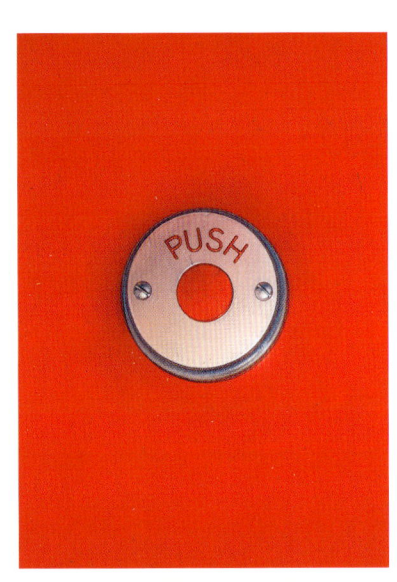
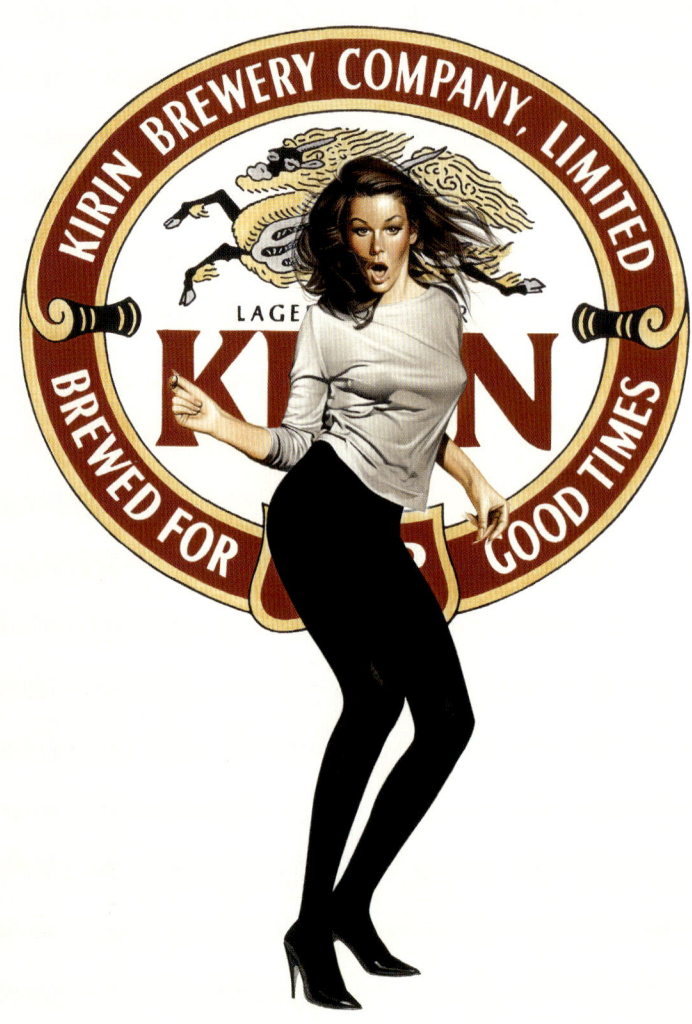
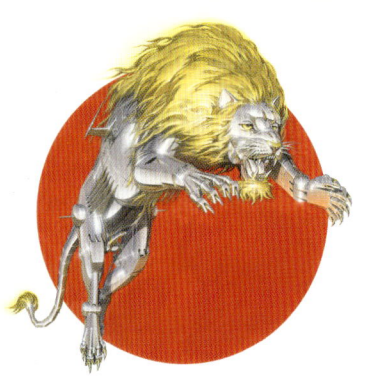
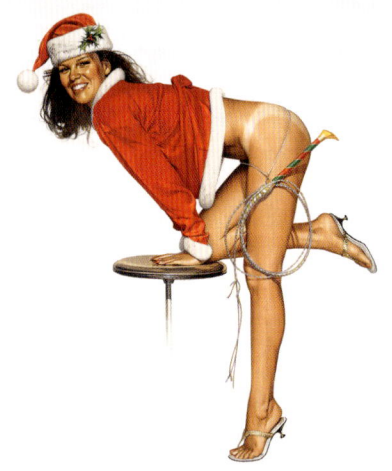
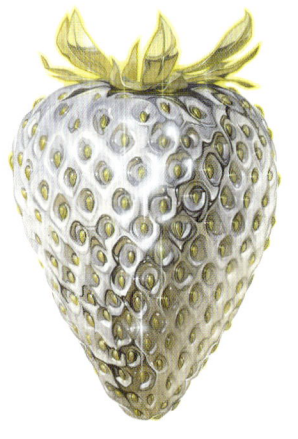
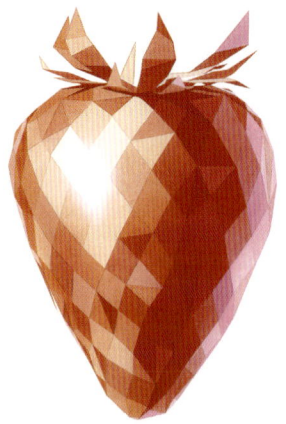

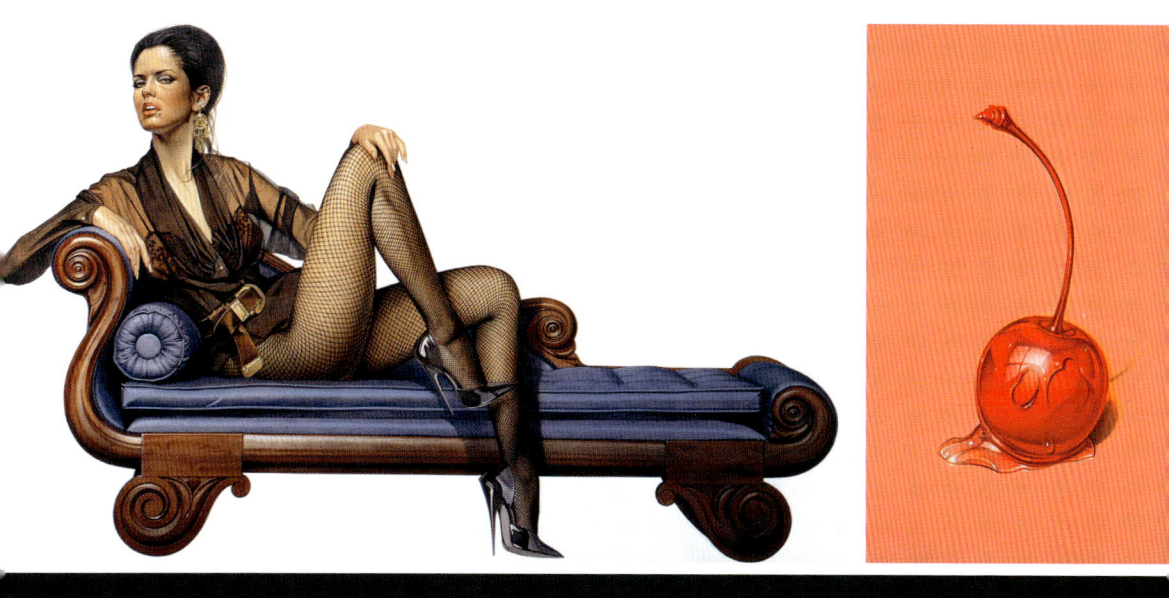

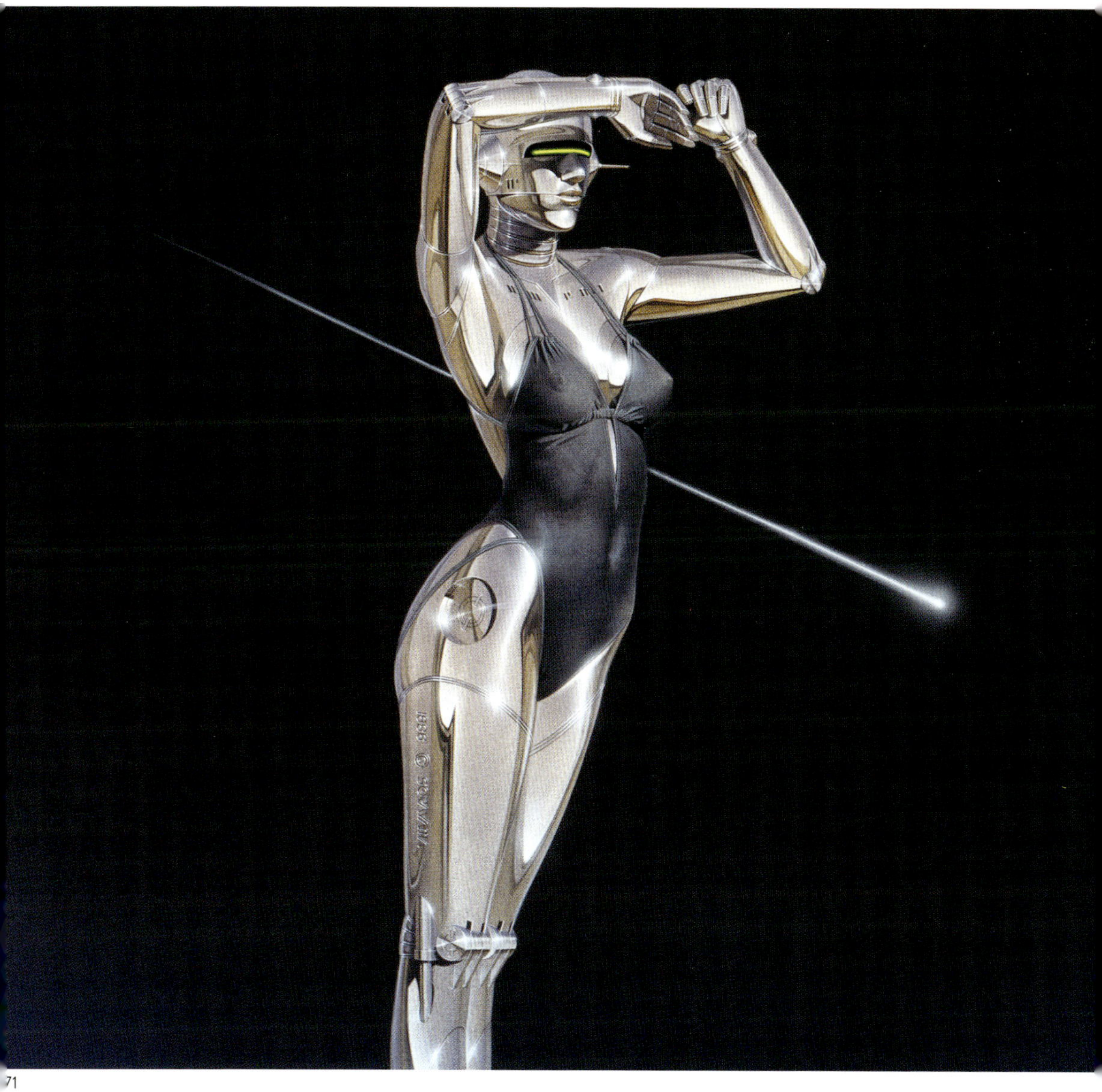

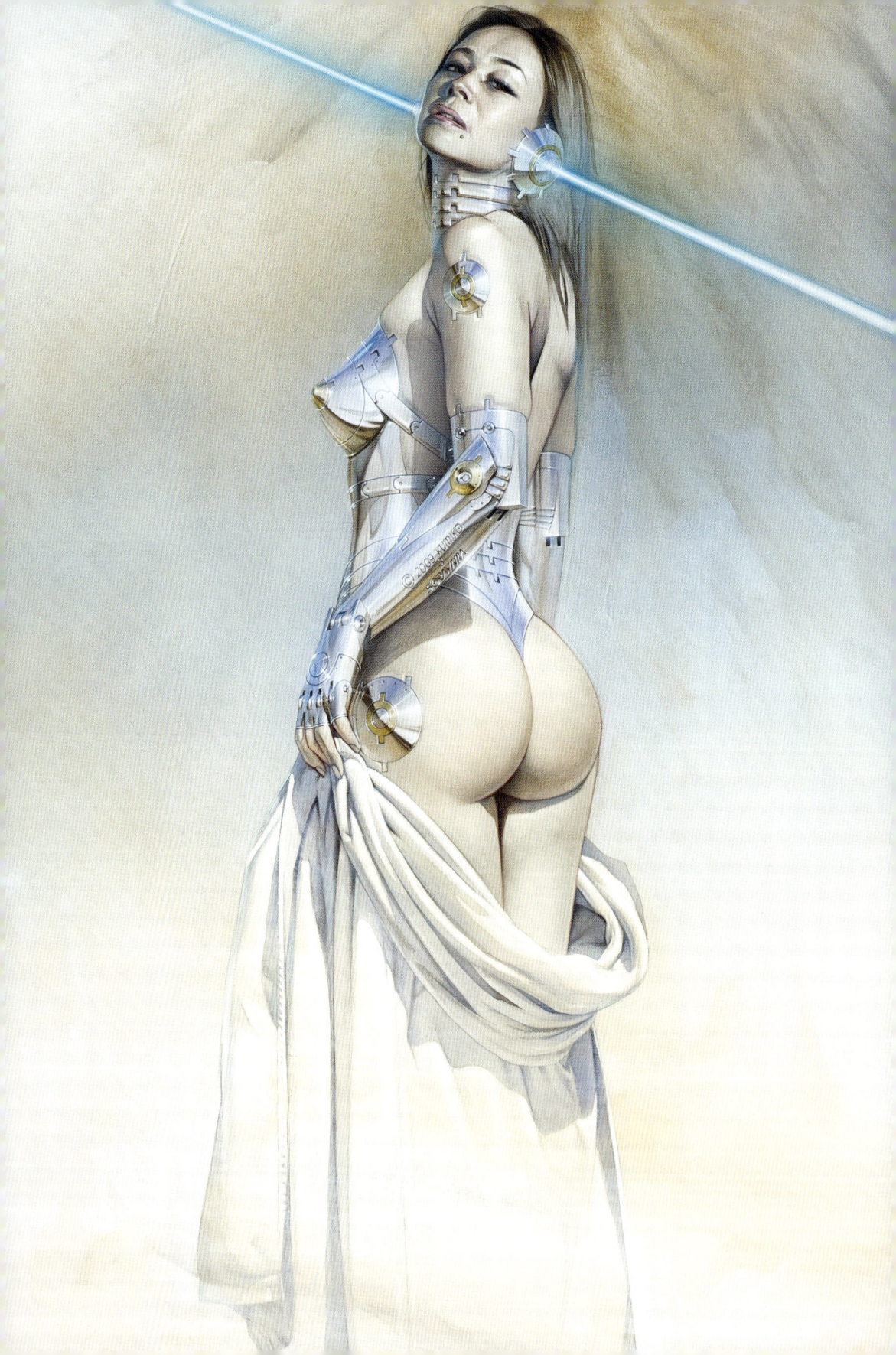

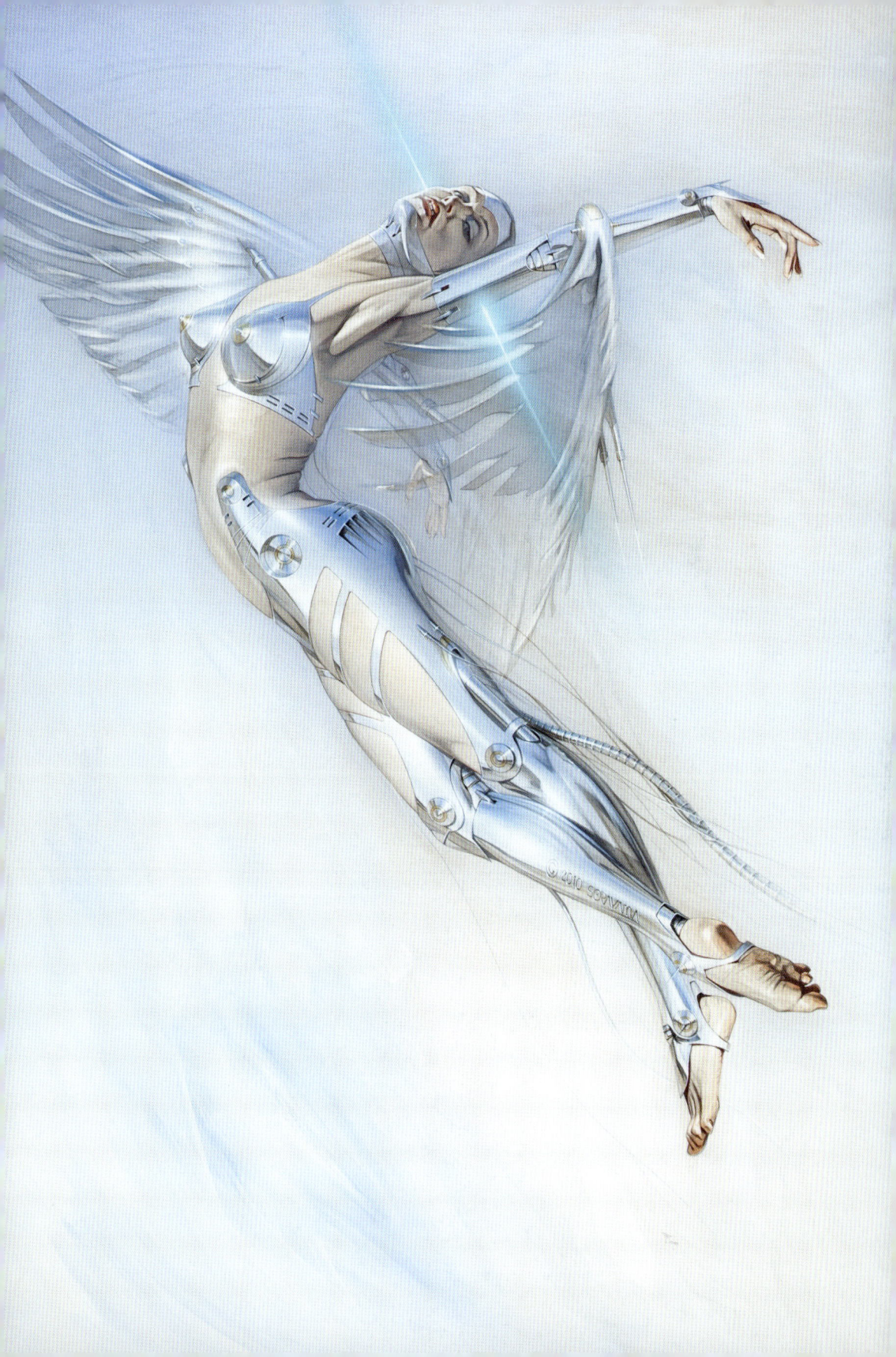

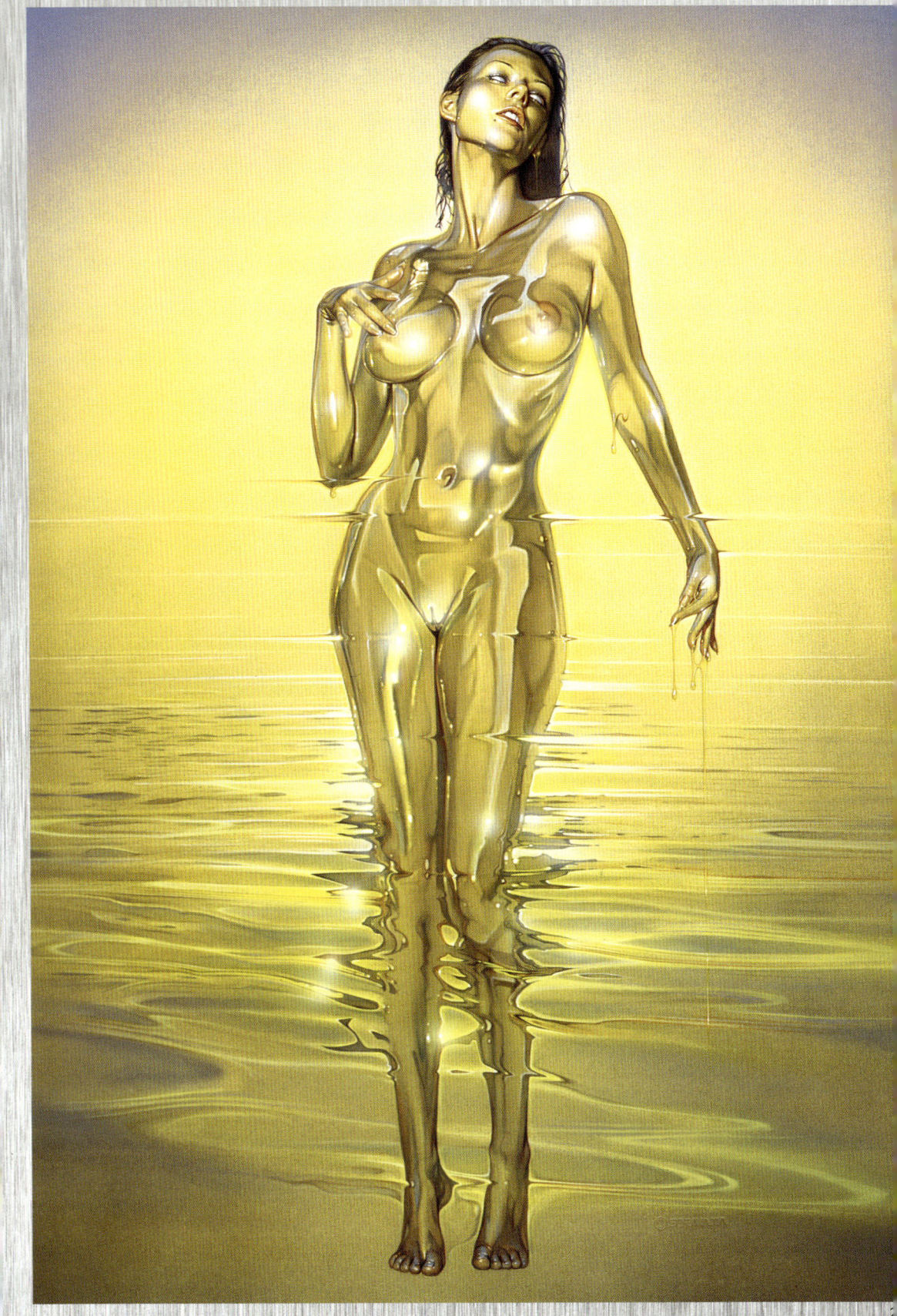

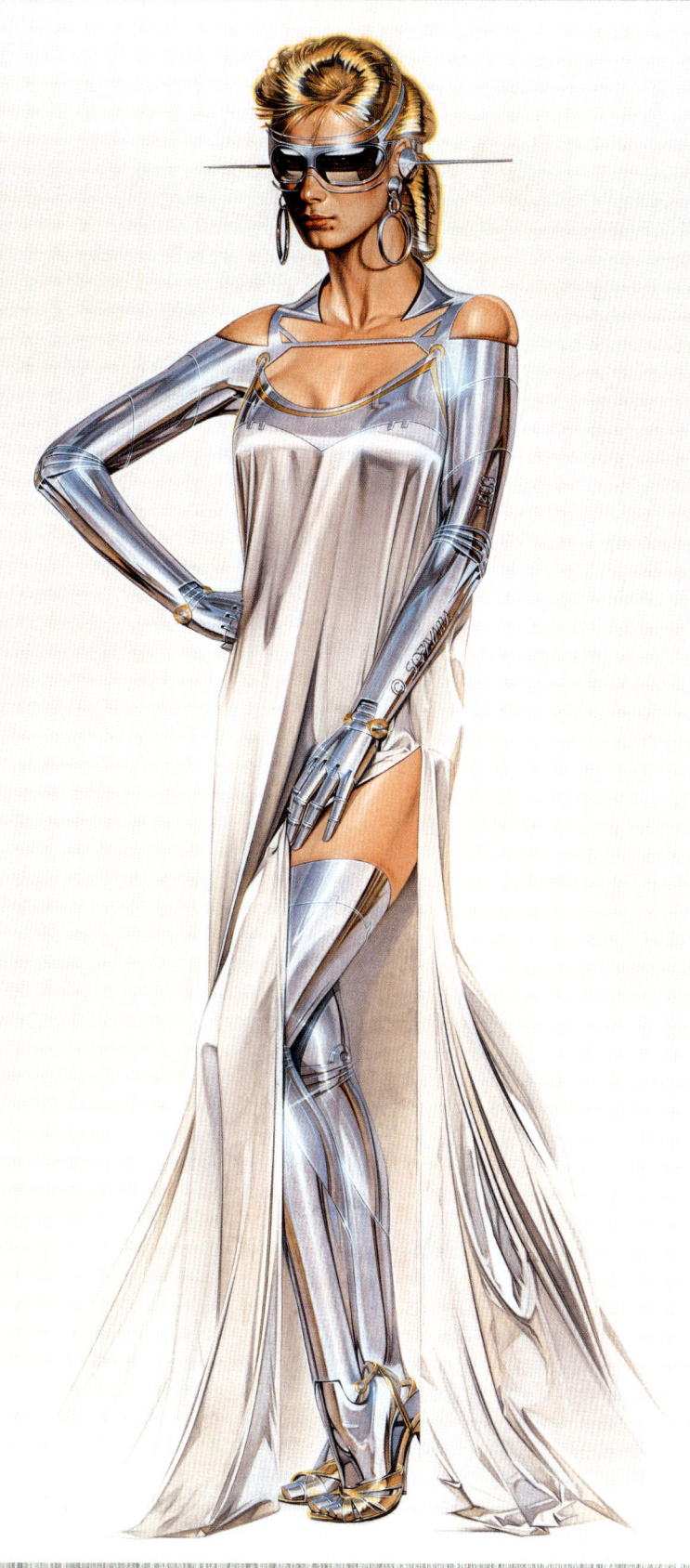

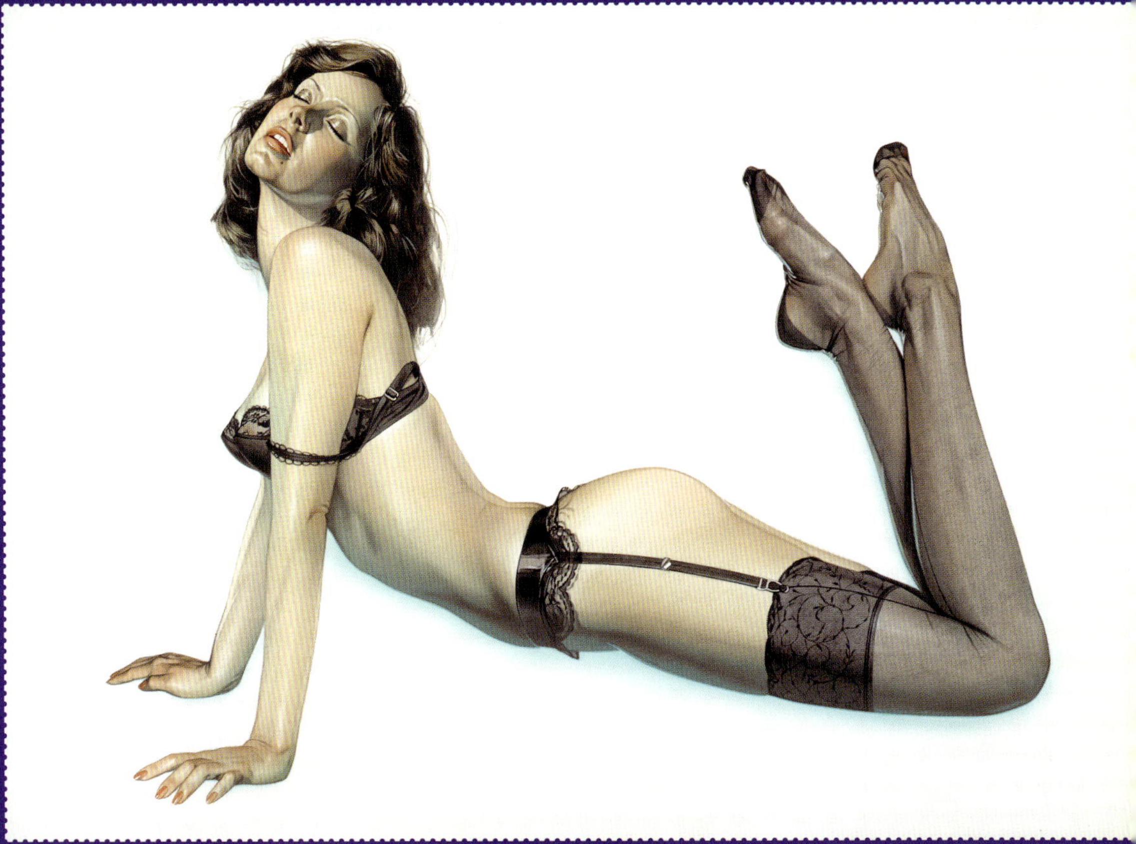

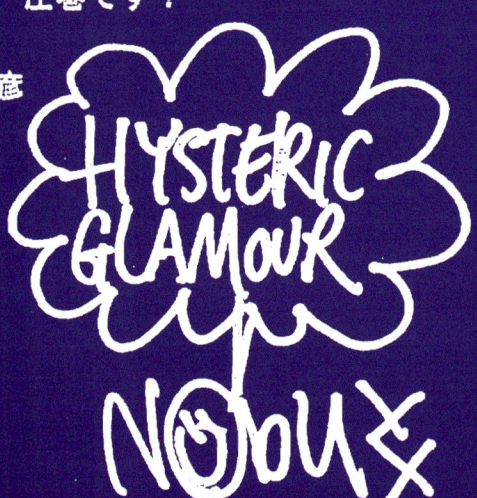

"THE CRIMINAL ART" 。スーパーリアルを超越した空想の世界。恐るべし探究力。
最も繊細で、WIT の効いた、スーパーエロティズムの巨匠。ミスタースケアリーモンスター。 圧巻です！

HYSTERIC GLAMOUR　北村　信彦

HYSTERIC GLAMOUR NOJOUX

YO SHITARA

PRESIDENT
BEAMS CO., LTD.

自宅の地下室に 女を一人飼っている。
全裸に コルセットだけの 金髪の女だ。
空山さんの 部屋から 連れてきた。
今は 私が 主だ。
天窓の下の 煉瓦の壁に いつも繋いでいる
こいつもそうだが…
空山さんの 女達は どれも 私好みだ。
大人の女の フェロモンが 溢れている。
また あの部屋に 選びに 行きたい。
今は 一頭飼いだが…
いずれは 多頭飼いになる気がする。

設楽洋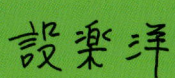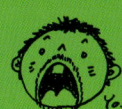

松下進（イラストレーター）

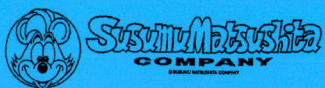

拝啓、空山 基 様

恐らく、空山さんに手紙など書くというのは、初めての事だと想います。
最初に断わっておきますが、僕は空山さんの大ファンなのです。
絵はもちろんの事、御本人のキャラクターも含めてです。
キッチリと自分の行くべき道が見えていると云う事が作品を通して
ストレートに伝わってくるんです。とても明快です。
どう云う事かと云うと、自分が楽しんで描いている事が見事に作品の
見栄えになってしまっているんです。これは、他人から見ると、
とてもうらやましく、そして単純そうに写るかもしれませんが、
なかなか実際にそうやって、仕事として成立出来る事じゃありません。
好きな事を表現するための努力と云うのは、本人にとって意識すること
なく、続けられている事だと想うのですが、他人から見たら、それは
途方もないパワーが必要な事であり、驚異的な事に思えるハズです。
空山アートは完全無欠なエンターテインメントです。空山さんの描く
女性は○○○○などと、もう今さら当り前の事を云うつもりもありません。
とにかく、これほどカッコ良く描けるエンターテインメント・クラフツマン
（オールドマン?!）は日本の、いや、世界の宝です。
ひとつお願いがあるんですけど…
空山さん、今度こっそり、絵の描き方教えて！

12月26日　1997年

イラストレーター
松下　進

窪田真弓

　空山氏のエージェントという仕事をさせて
戴くという事。その苦労。それはもう皆様お
察しの通りでございますから…。何ぜあのような方
でございますから…
　しかし一方、彼の仕事はおもしろい。メジ
ャーでインターナショナル。スケールがデカ
いのであります。
　イラストレーションという枠を易々と越
え、他の誰にも取り替えのきかない作品を、
次々と生み出して来る空山の仕事を通じ
て、人生勉強をさせていただいている私であ
ります。そして個人に立ち返れば、氏の作品
の熱烈な崇拝者であることは言うまでもご
ざいません。

**Hank Rose（ハンク・ローズ：
Comic Imagesディレクター）**

One need only glance at a Sorayama figure to know who created the image.
Sorayama pulls no punches. There are
no secrets in his characters. Bizarre.
Bold. Erotic. Beautiful. However, even
his images with the hardest edge - tubes,
metal and leather - have a mysterious
delicacy about them. Though we are
shocked by these images, we are drawn
in to study them. Sorayama, therefore,
shows us the Yin the yang of erotic
art. The three trading card sets we published of his art have been well received
and highly successful.

Hank Rose

たむらしげる（イラストレーター）

　空山基とぼくはお互いにファンタジーを描く
イラストレーターだ。
　彼は架空の国のハーレムの王を夢想し、ぼく
は架空の惑星の神を夢見る。共に実現不能な
ファンタジー。
　ぼくは子供たちの夢を描いて家族の尊敬を得
ているが、空山基は男たちの夢を描いて家族
のひんしゅくを買っているようだ。
　「ちぇっ、同じようにファンタジーを描いて、
この違いはなんだよ？　たむらはうまいこと、女、子供はだまくらかしてるな…」
　空山基はちょっと不満。
　空山基はまぎれもない変態だ。たいていの変
態はそれを隠そうとするが、彼は隠そうとし
ない。彼は嘘をつきながら生活するのが嫌い
なのだ。空山基は自分の好きな女を、高度な
プロのテクニックを駆使して、愛情を持って
描く。それは異常すぎる情熱。変態でなけれ
ば描けない絵だ。
　「どうだい、いい女だろ？」
　空山基は気に入った絵ができると人に見せた
がる。それが時として社会的に問題になるこ
ともある。
　「はは…！　空山基がまたやっちゃった」
　世の中、いろんな人間がいるから楽しい。み
んな暖く眼で彼を見てやって欲しい。仲
間じゃないよ。ぼくもあなたも変態なのだ。
　空山基は純粋だ。純粋な変態！
　そんな彼の生き方をぼくは好きだ。

河原敏文（CGアーティスト）

　空山さんは数少ない日本が誇れる国際的スー
パースターなのである。

　日本においてもたいへん有名なアーティスト
ではあるが、ヨーロッパやアメリカにおける
空山さんの作品に対する評価とは比べ物にな
らない。特にプロのアーティストやクリエイ
ター、すなわち目利きの連中に圧倒的なファン
が多い。
　1980年代中頃、私は当時ハリウッドで最も
有名なコンピュータ・グラフィックス・プロ
ダクションであったロバート・エイブル・ア
ンド・アソシエイツの日本代表をしていた。
世界中のCGアーティストがその
出来栄えにど肝を抜かれた。
　その"SEXY ROBOT"に登場するロボットの
原型（というかそのもの）が、空山さんの描
いた「セクシーロボット」だったのである。
当時からハリウッドではSORAYAMAは超
有名だったのである。西洋のアーティストの
マネをする日本人はたくさんいるが、西洋の
アーティスト達にマネされる日本人はなかな
かいない。多くのアーティストやデザイナー
は常に空山さんの次の作品や著書を心待ちに
していた。

　その後、ドイツの○誌やアメリカのペントハ
ウス誌でレギュラーの頁を持つだけでなく、
何度かSORAYAMA特集が組まれた。

　今、ボクは空山さんから送られてきた最新作
品集NAGAを何度も繰り返し見ている。ヒン
ドゥー教・ジャイナ教に出てくる蛇の姿を
した女神がテーマになった作品集である。
　ハイパーリアルな絵を描くアーティストの多
くは、ハイパーリアルに描く事が目的化して
いる為、表現内容におけるイマジネーション
に欠ける。
　いったい空山さんのこのイマジネーションは
どこから出てくるのだろうか？
　空山さんの描く女性はエロティック、セクシ
ー、官能的、妖艶、等々どんな言葉を使って
もその何万分の一も説明できない。又、その
女性達の繰り広げる行為のとんでもない危な
さをどうしてこれほどまでに美しく、エレガ
ントに描けるのだろうか？
　天才、鬼才、どんな言葉を持っても空山さん
のイマジネーションとテクニックの絶妙な組
み合わせを説明することはできない。

　悪魔のイマジネーションを天使が描いている
のかもしれない。

河原　敏文

Kevin Eastman（ケヴィン・イーストマン："Heavy Metal Magazine"）

"I HAVE BEEN A FAN OF FANTASY ART
AND ARTISTS FOR 25 OF MY 35 YEARS.
OF THE THOUSANDS I RESPECT, NINE HUNDRED:
I COLLECT, AND THE MANY I'VE SEEN CHANGE
IT'S FACE FOREVER, THERE ARE FEW WHOM
I THINK ARE TRUE GENIUS'... SORAYAMA
IS ONE OF THEM."
SIGNED,
Kevin EASTM
- HEAVY METAL MAGAZINE -

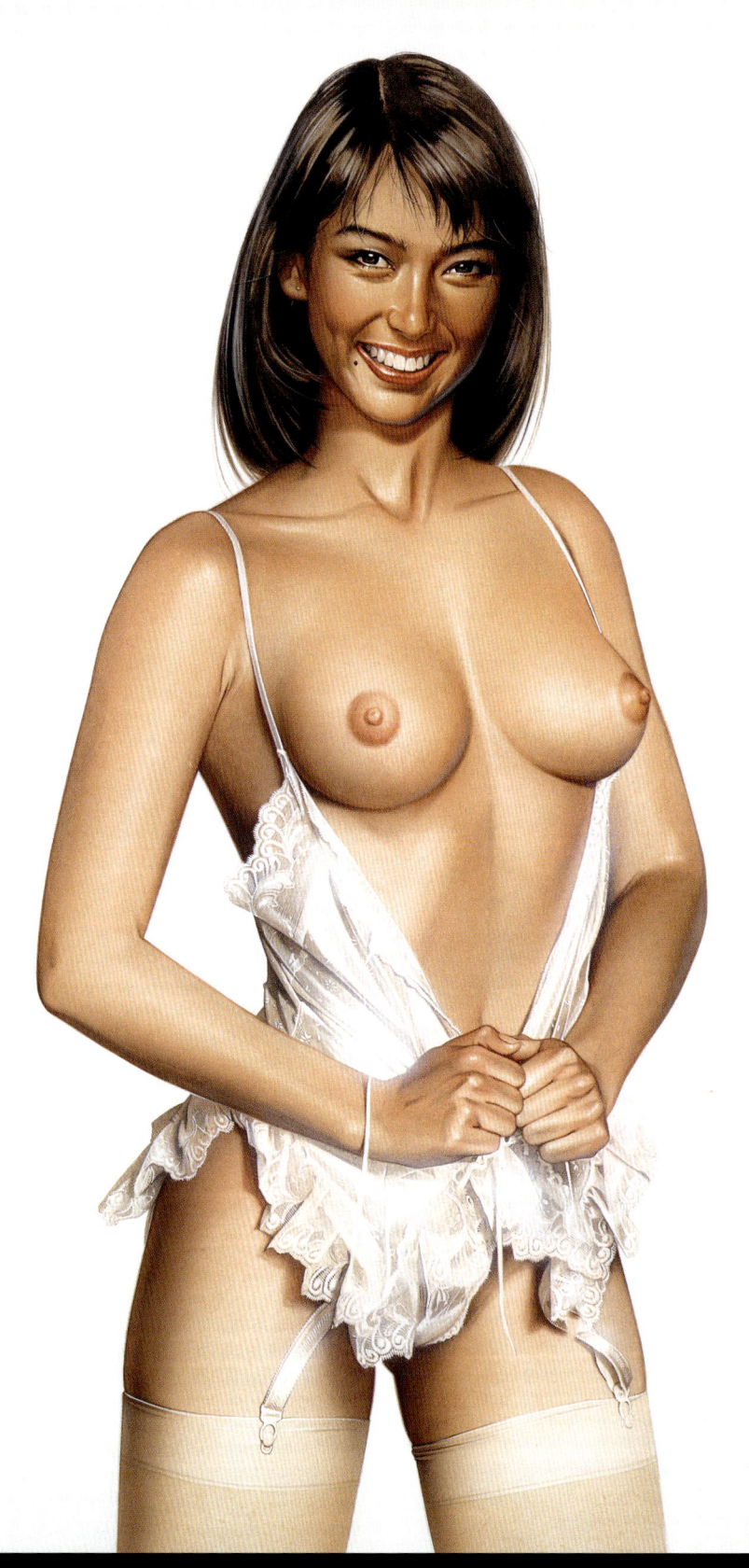

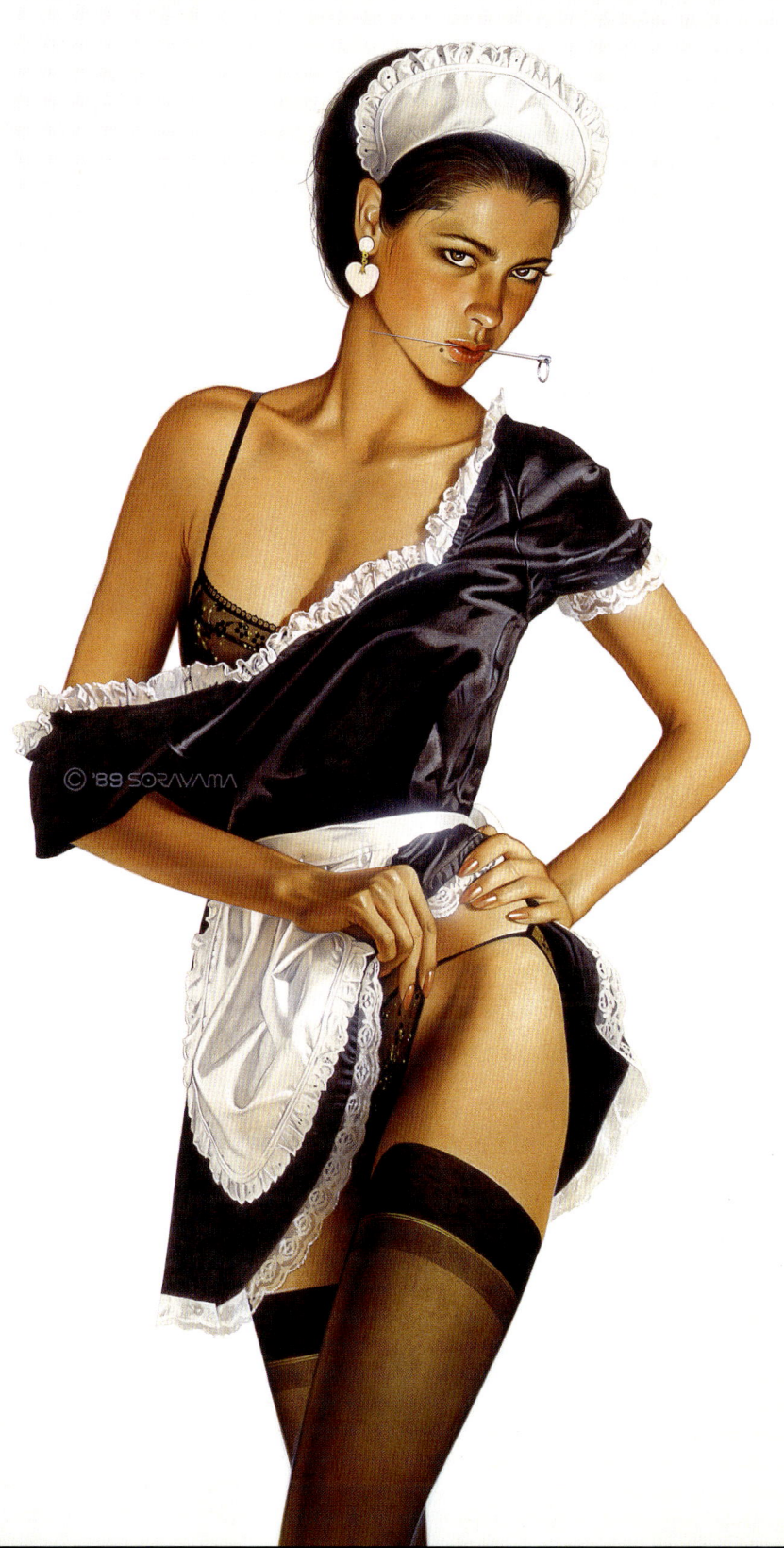

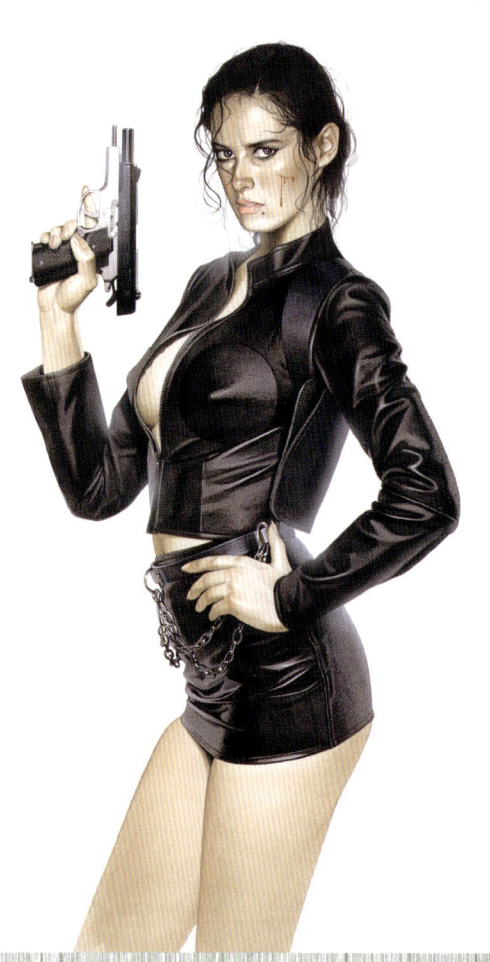
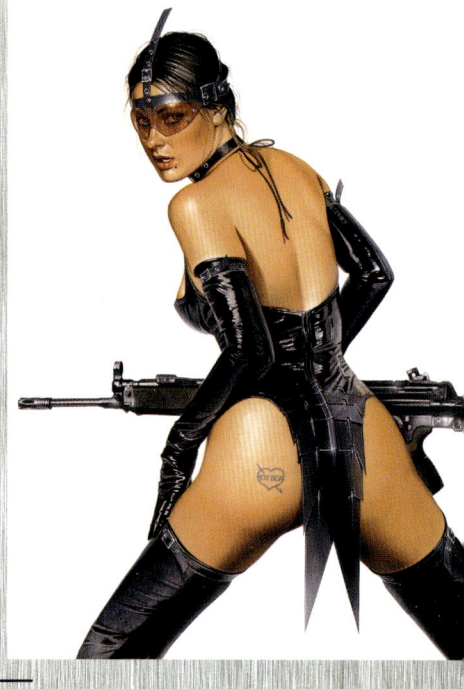
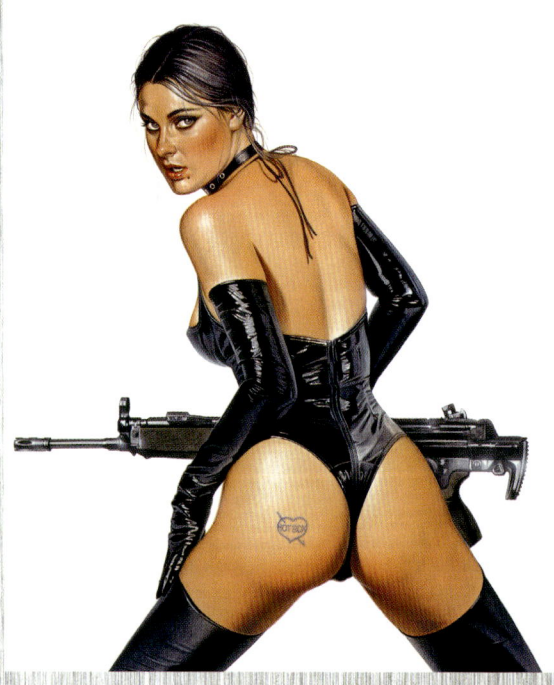
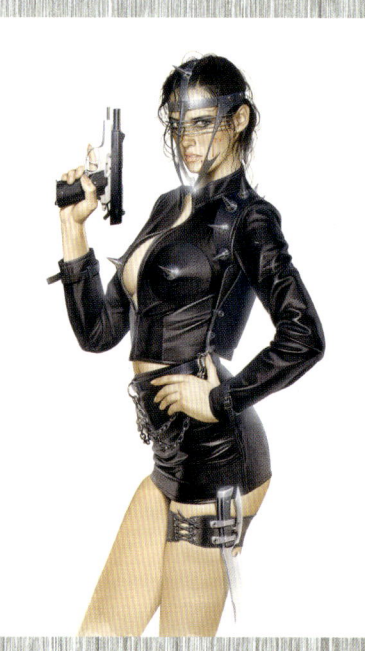

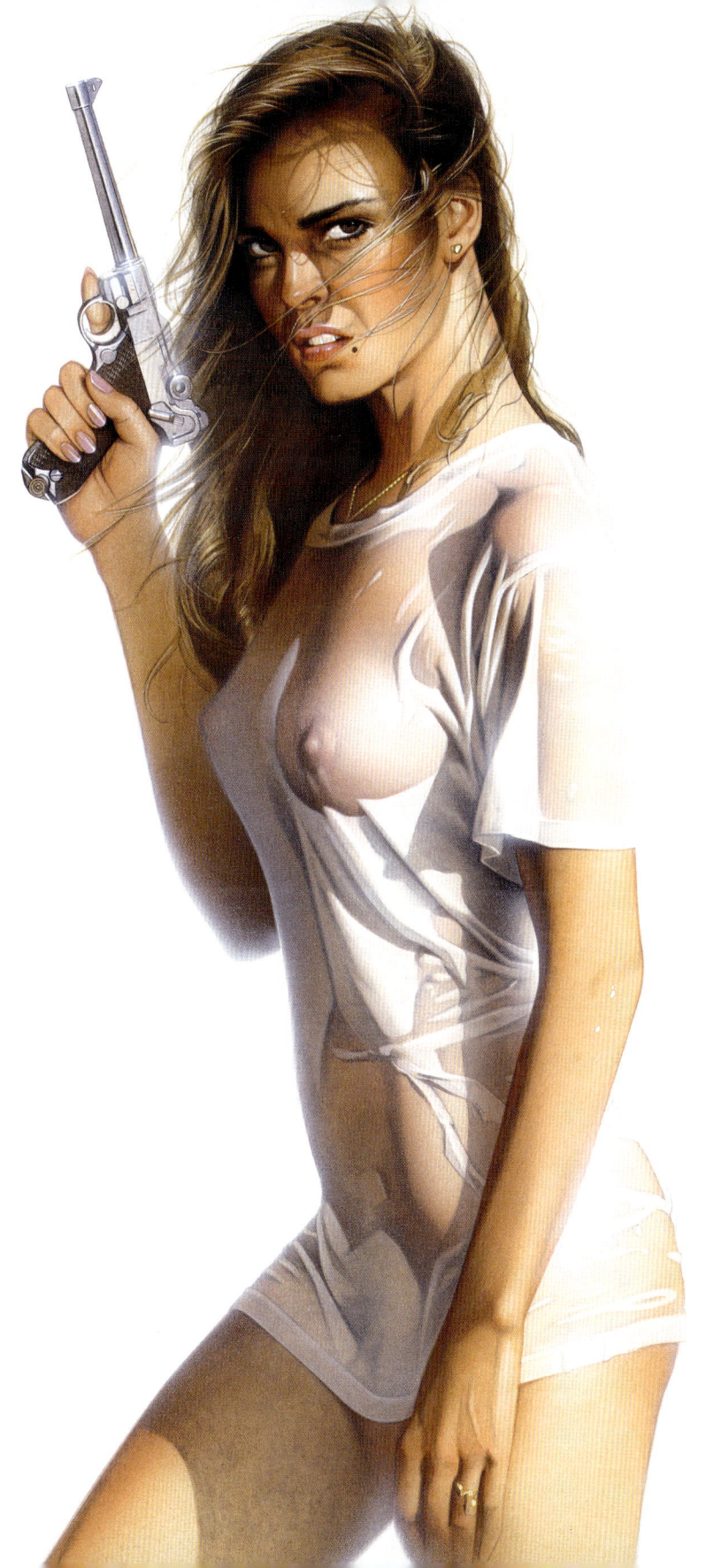

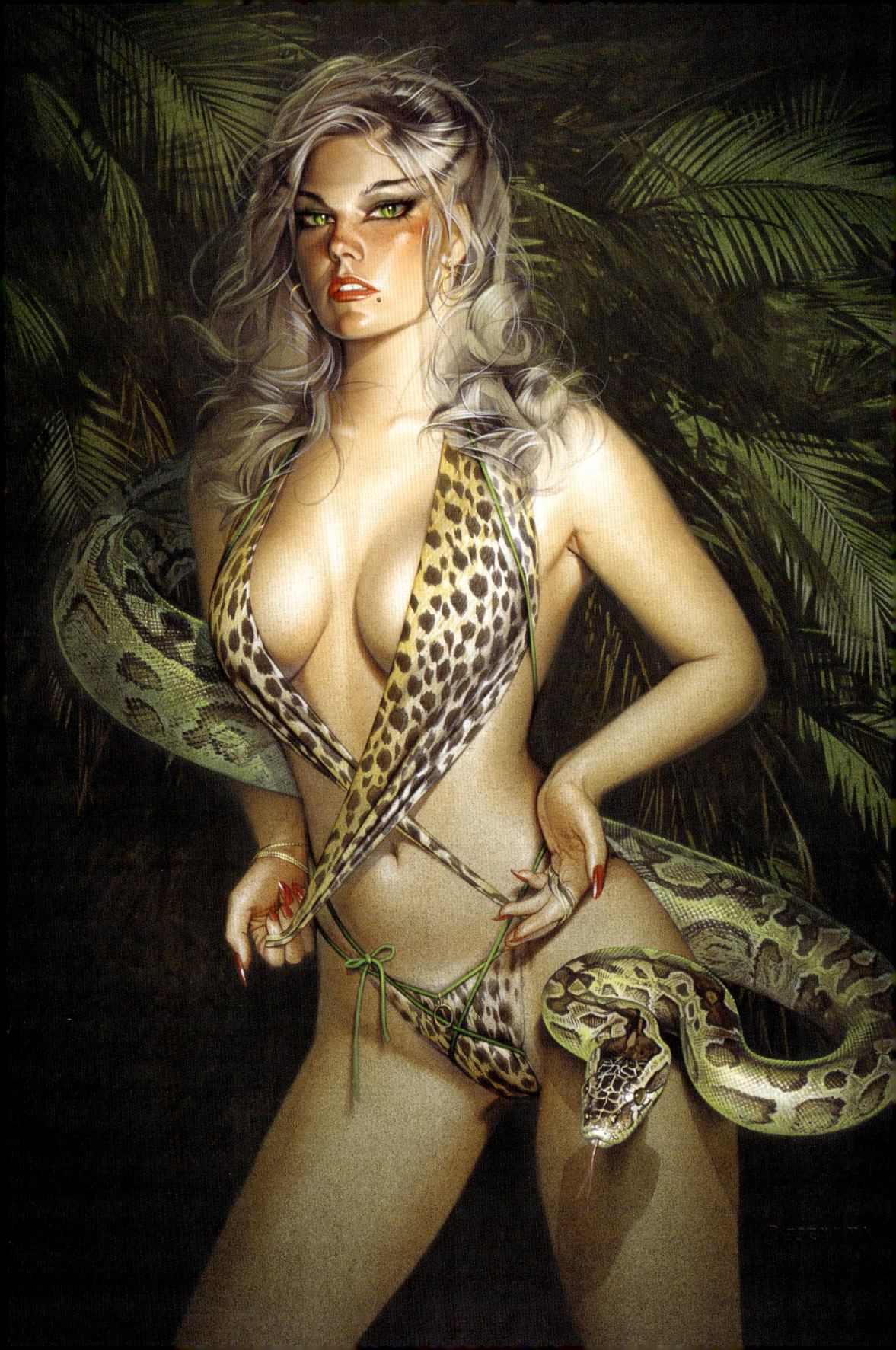

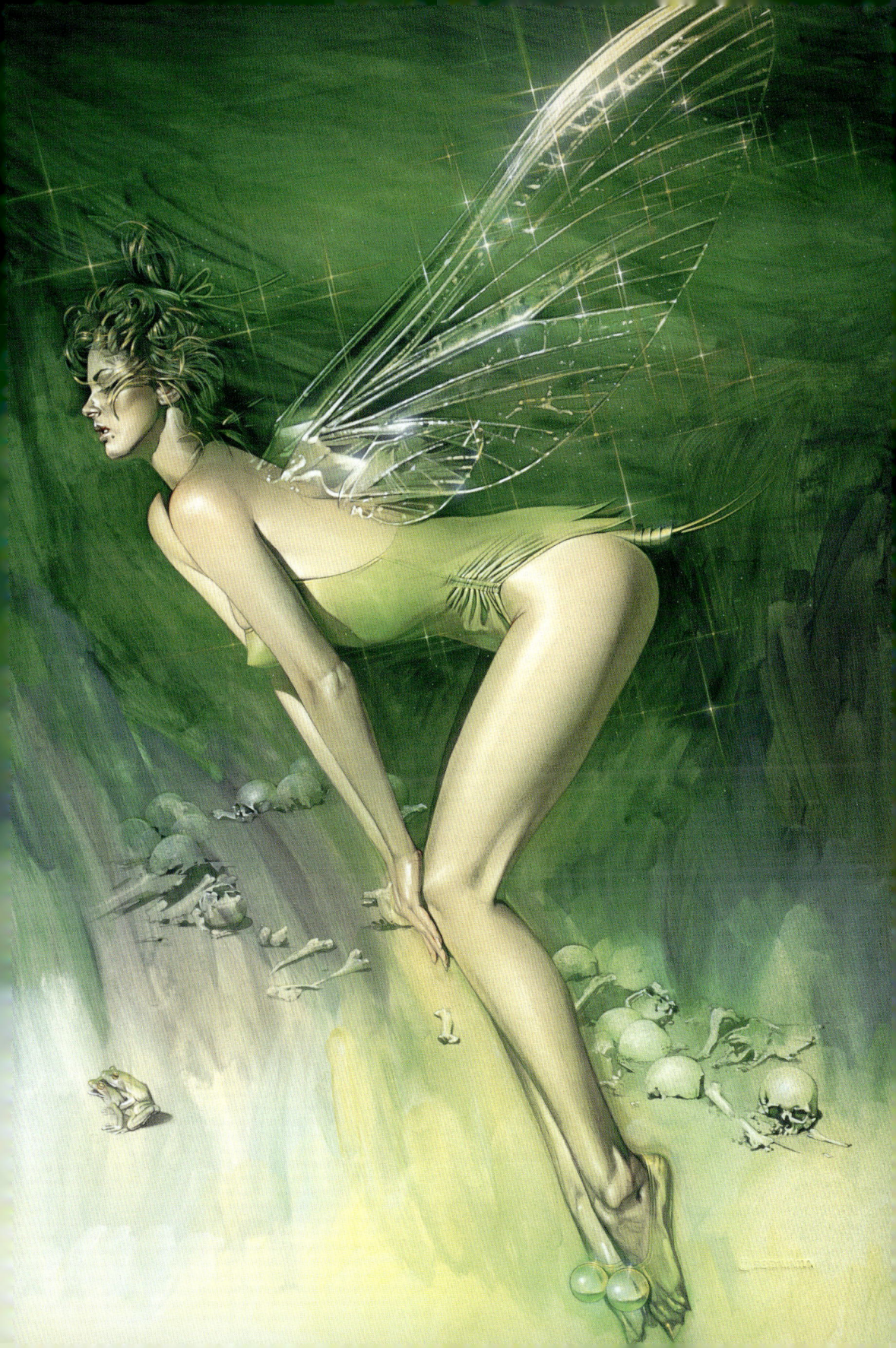

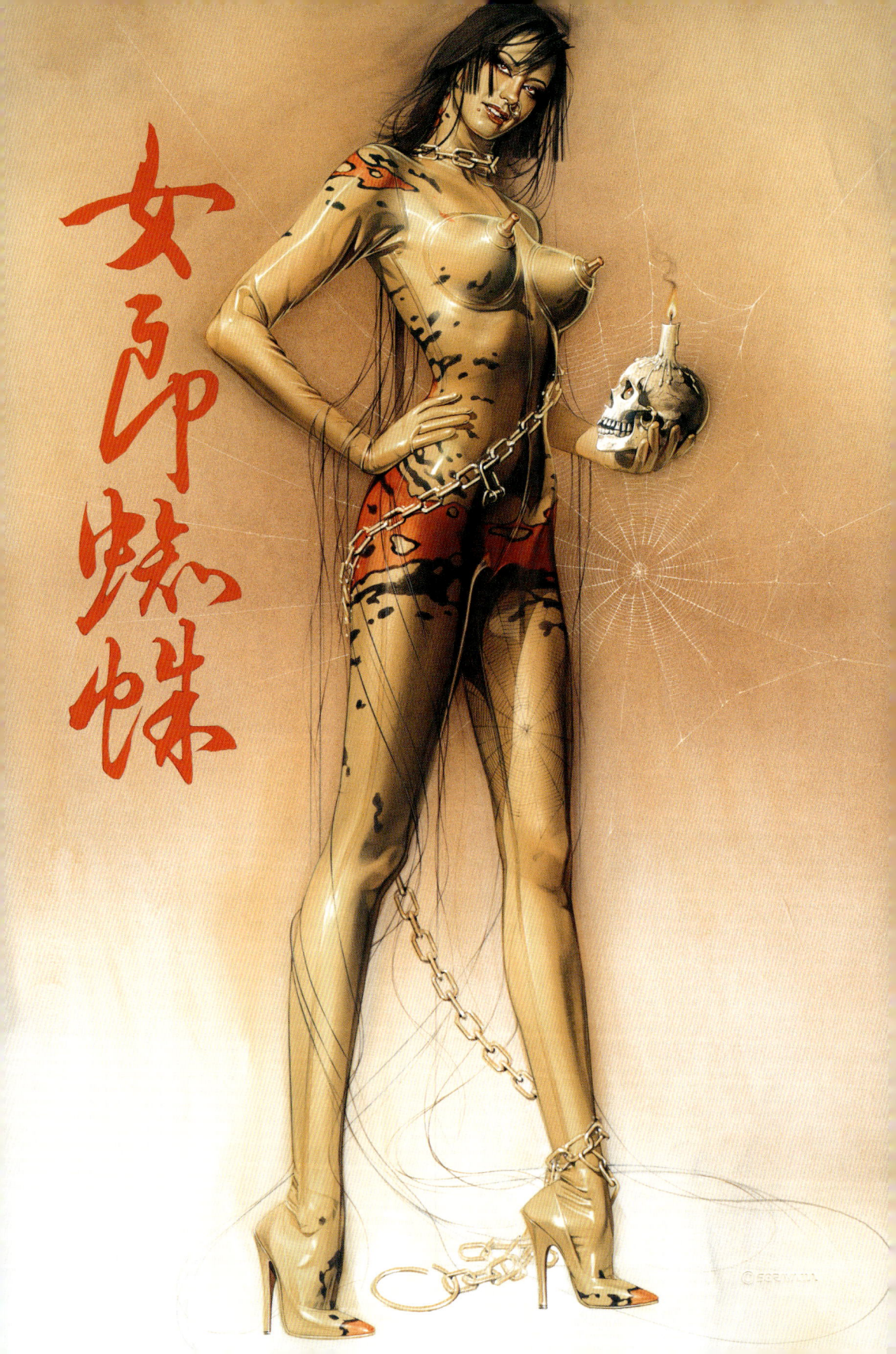
女印蜘蛛

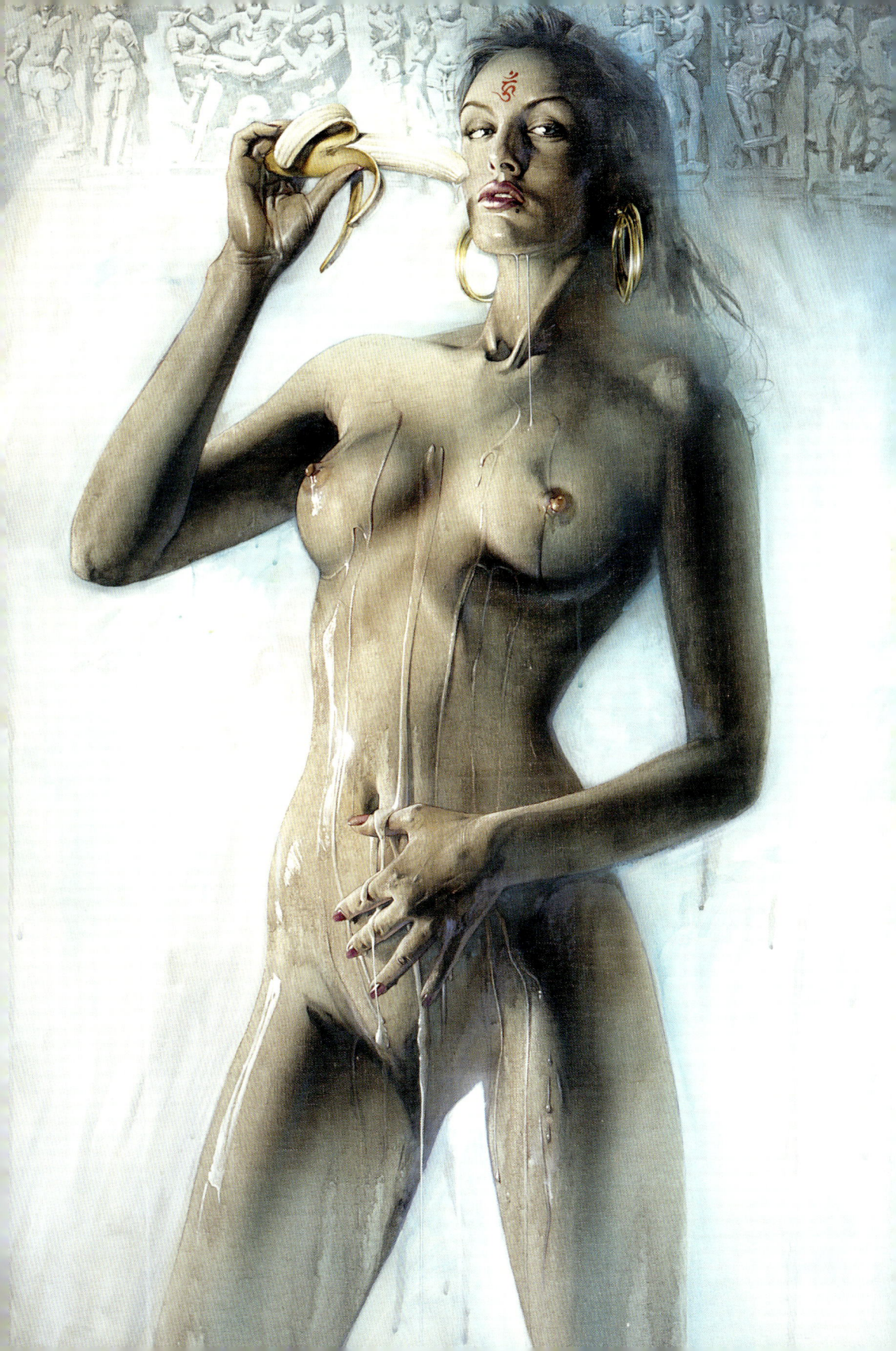

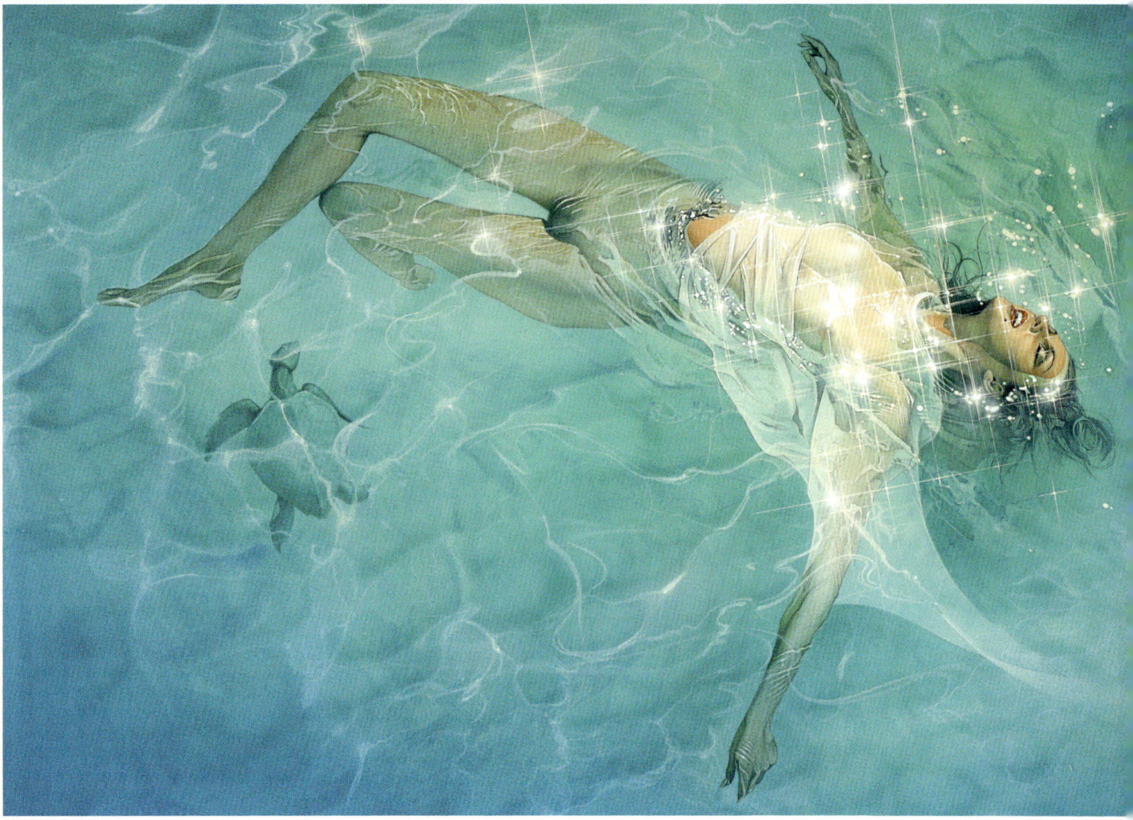

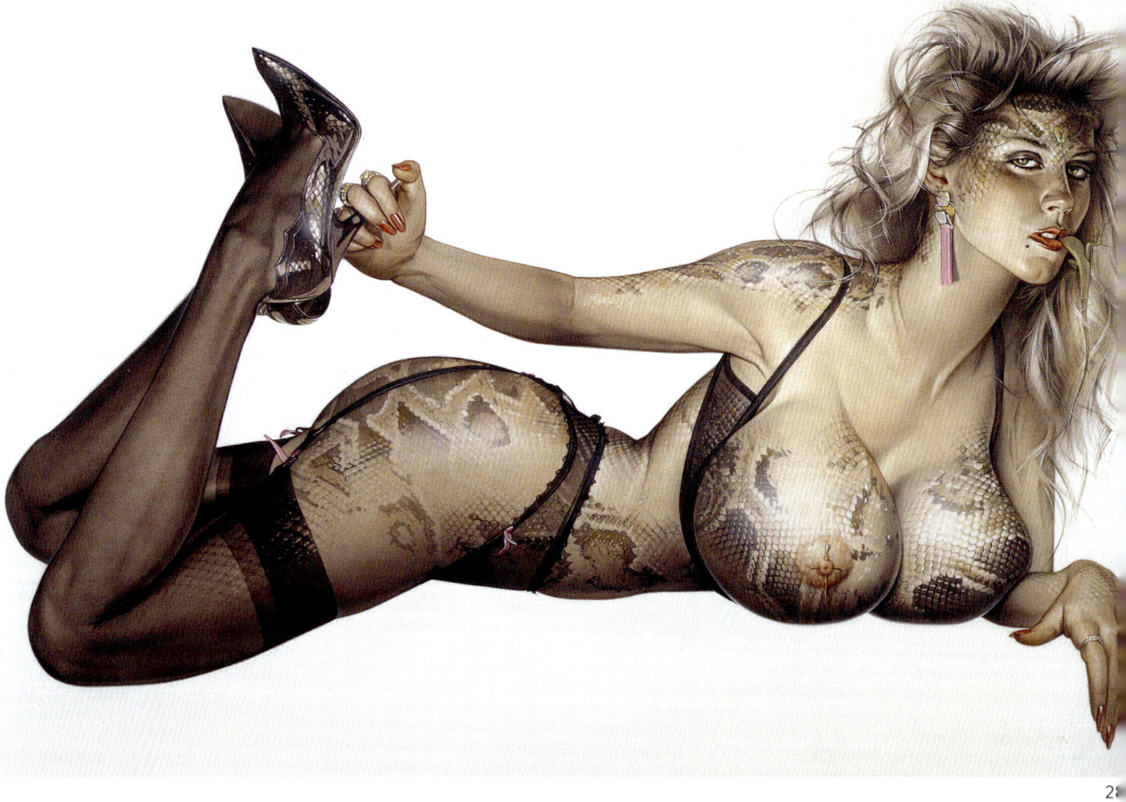

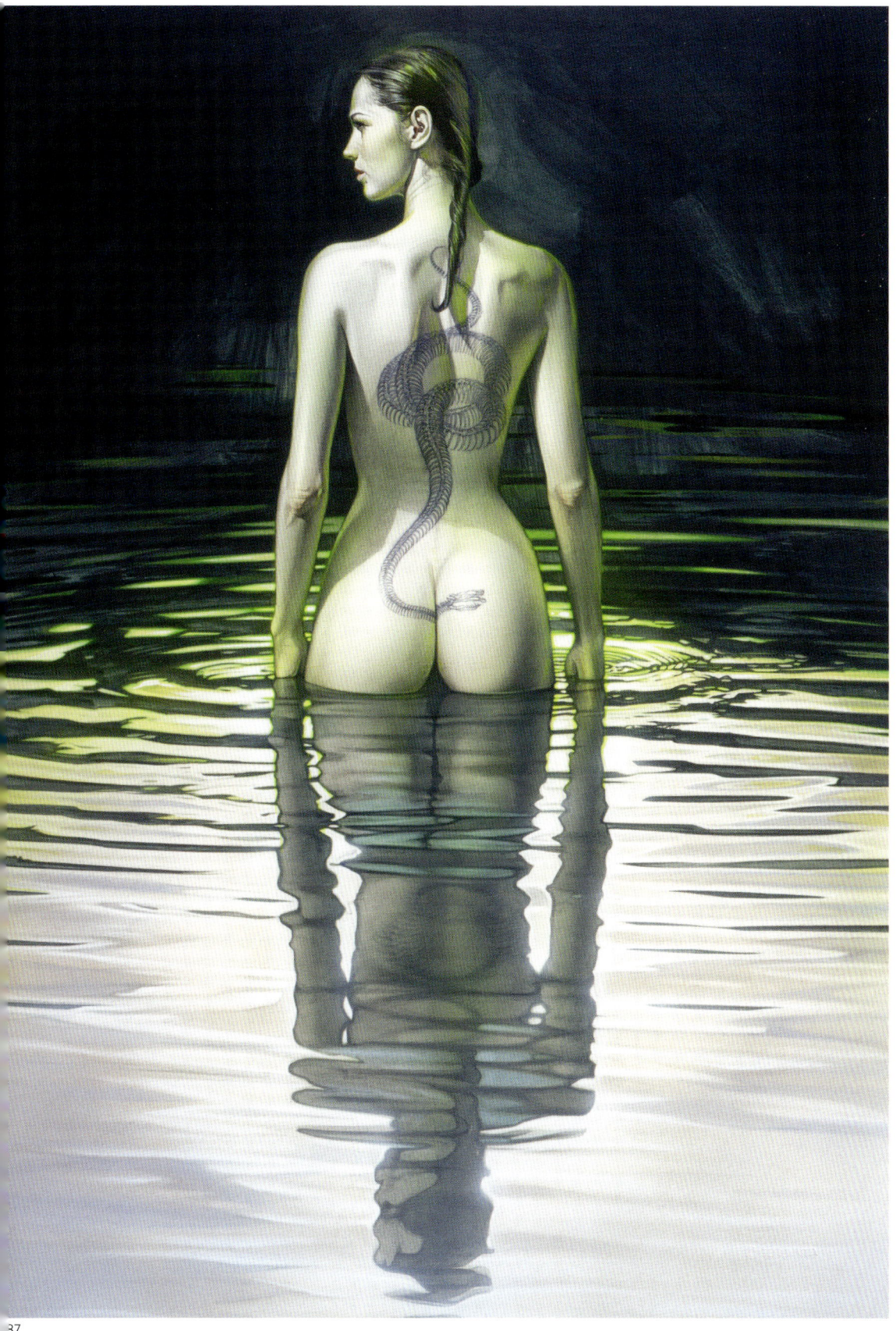

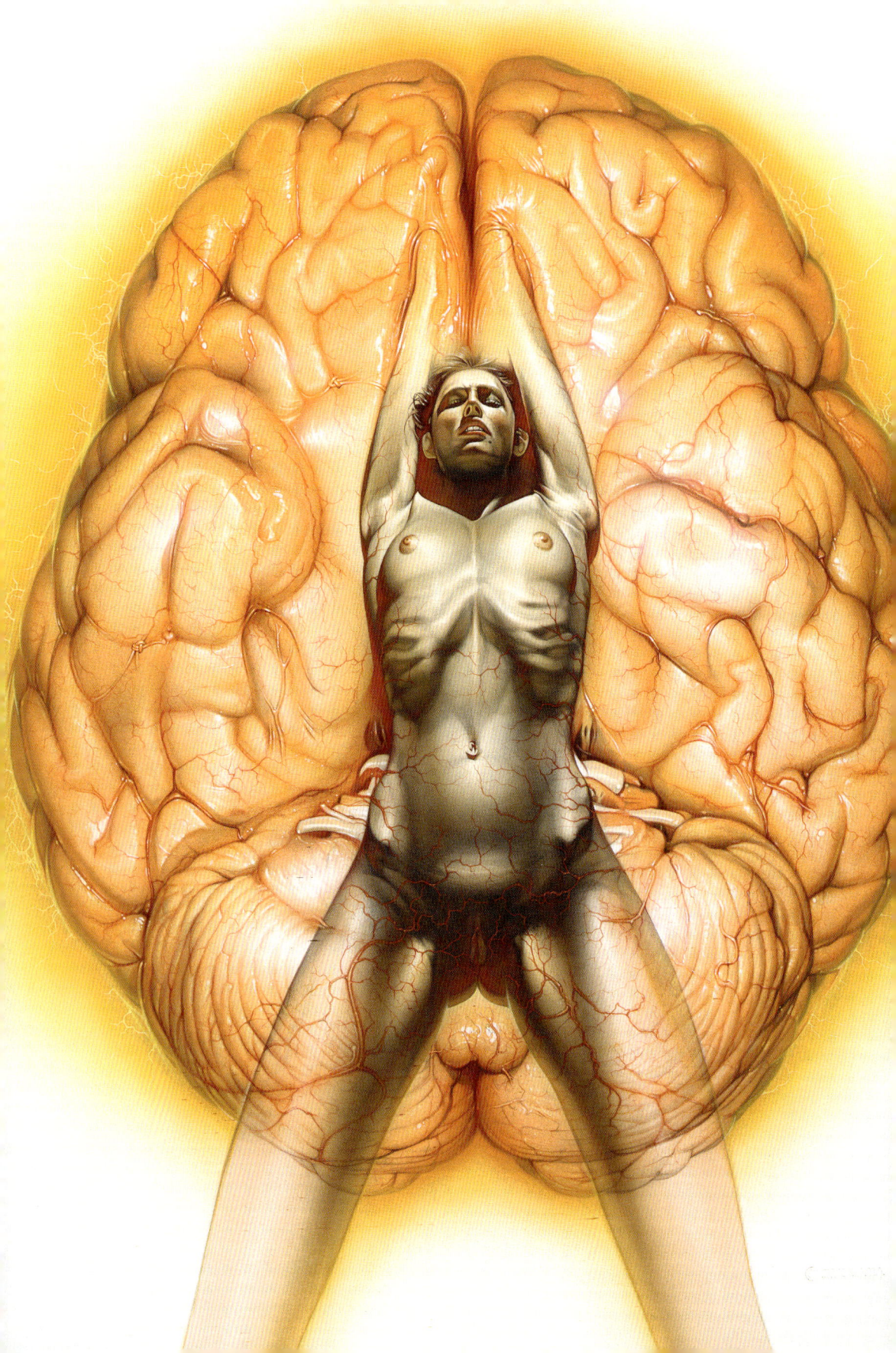

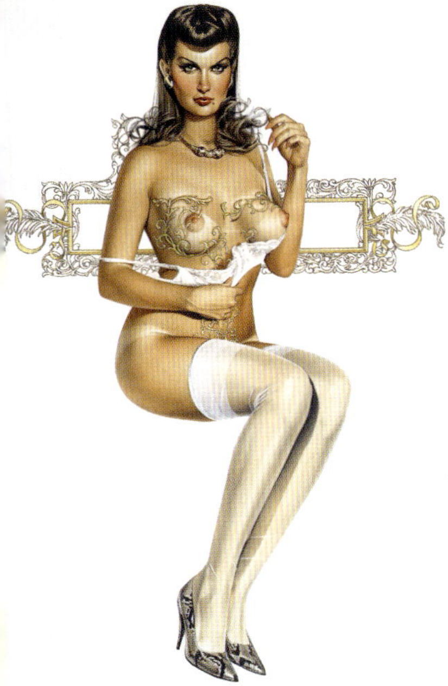

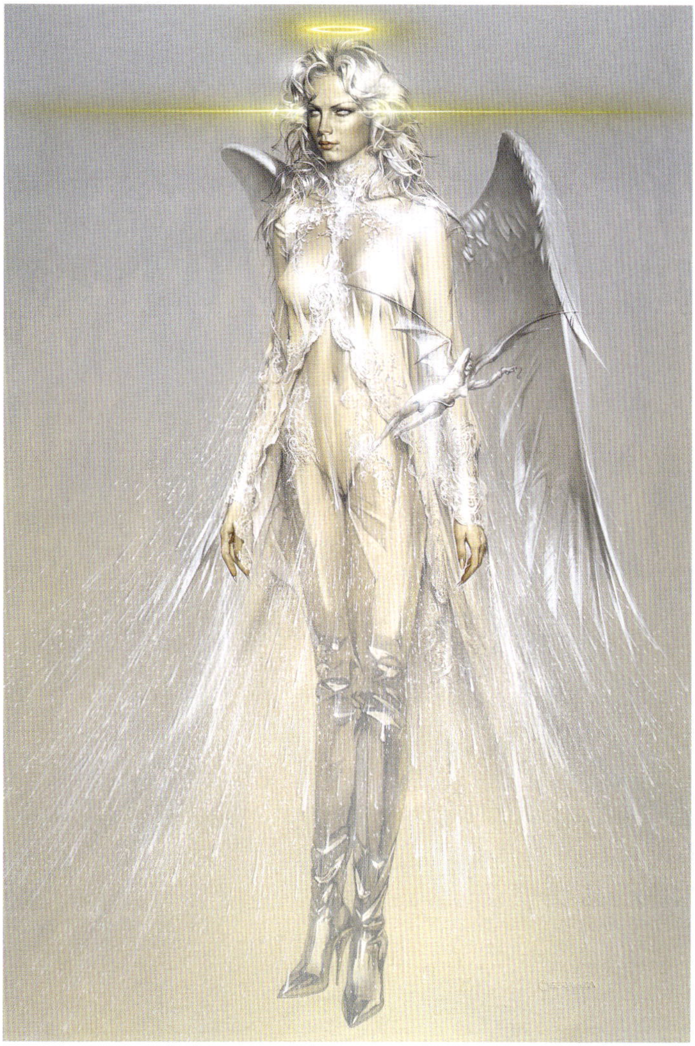

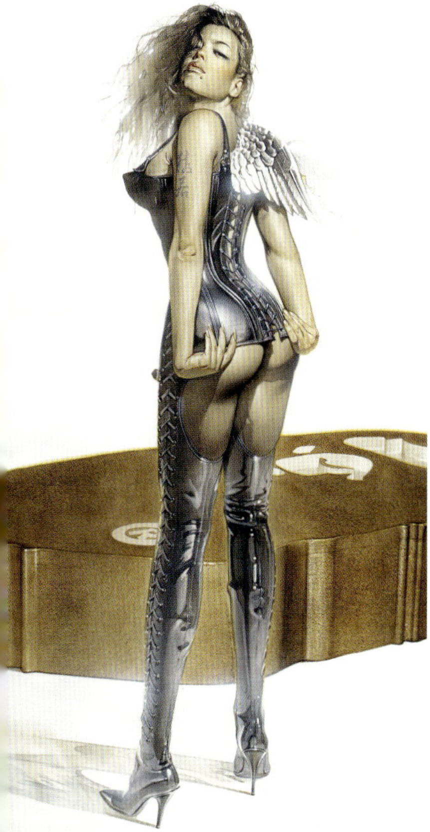

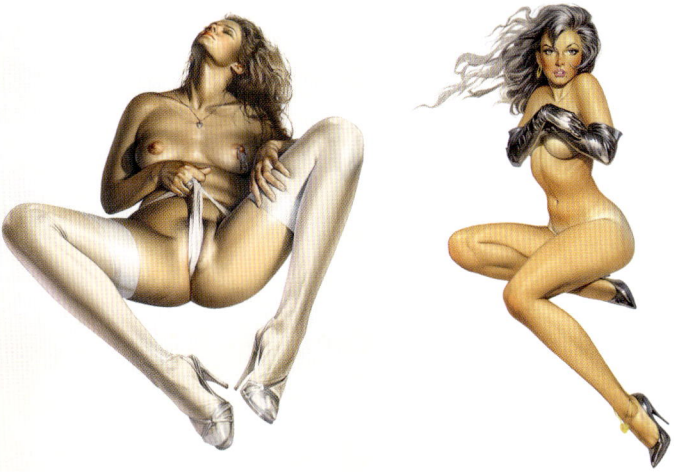

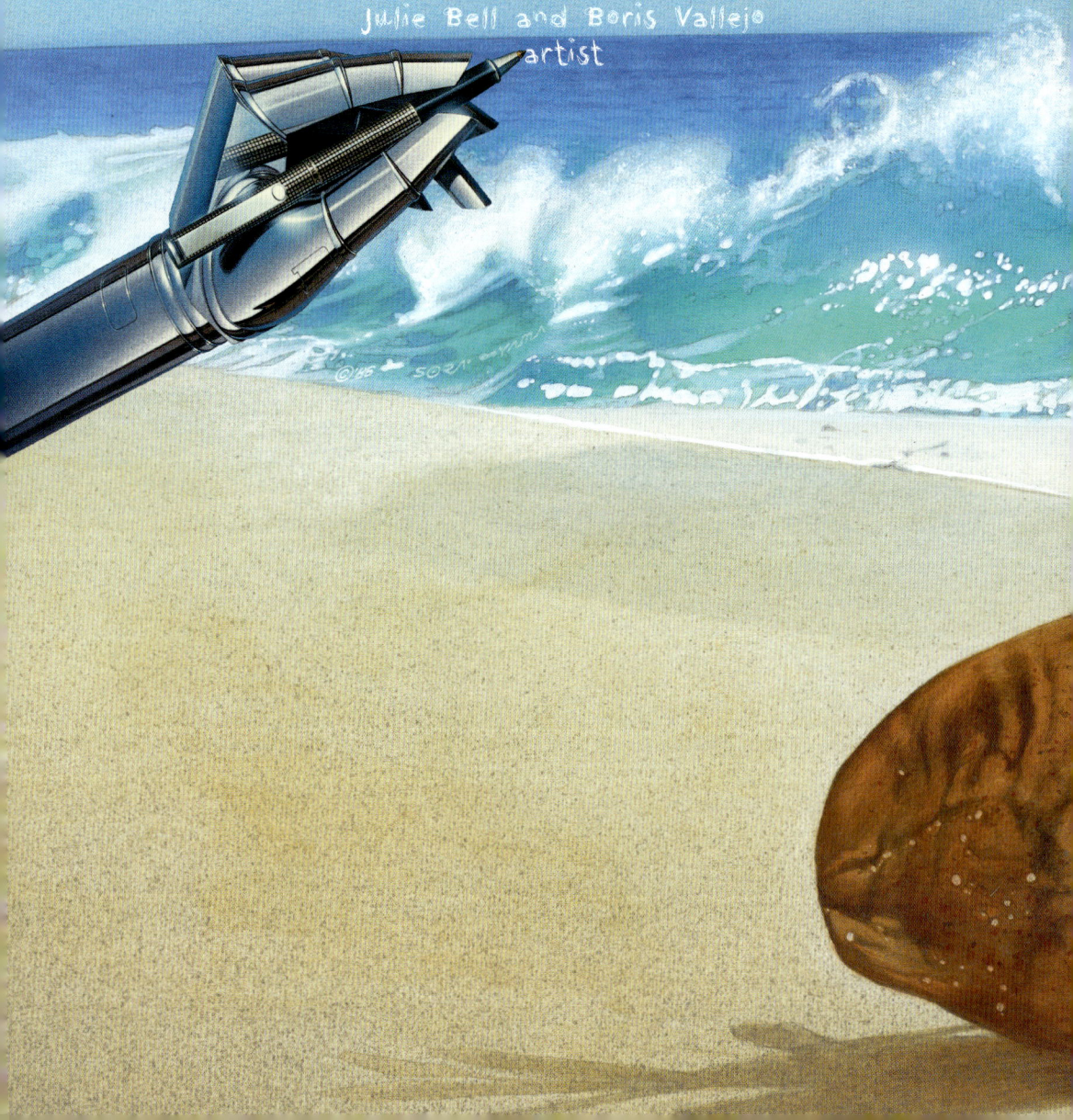

Hajime Sorayama is among a select group of professionals that have been influential in shaping the face of contemporary illustration. Hajime's imagination, skill and style are truly amazing. His innovative approach to stylizing and painting the female figure has been of inspiration to scores of other artists. His understanding of the rendering of various textures in his mind-blowing way, particularly, of course, his famous stainless steel has pushed all of us to work towards new heights in our own work. It's just so fun to look at a painting that combines so many different types of surface - soft skin and hair, shiny vinyl, hard metal - all painted in such a convincing way! The work takes the viewer into an unexpected tactile experience.

Each new book of his collected works is eagerly received by his legions of fans. We are among them!

Julie Bell and Boris Vallejo
artist

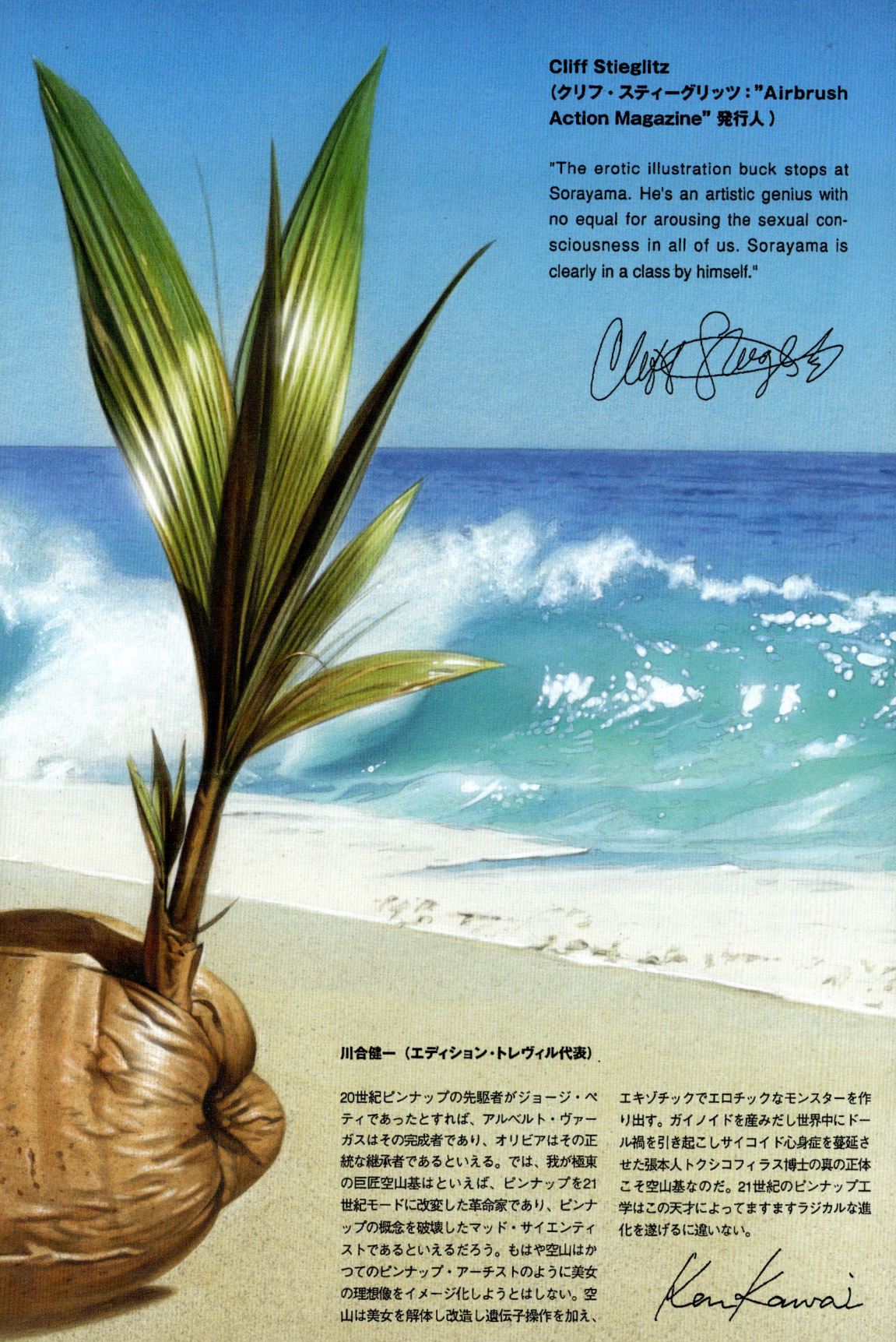

Cliff Stieglitz
（クリフ・スティーグリッツ："Airbrush Action Magazine" 発行人 ）

"The erotic illustration buck stops at Sorayama. He's an artistic genius with no equal for arousing the sexual consciousness in all of us. Sorayama is clearly in a class by himself."

川合健一（エディション・トレヴィル代表）

20世紀ピンナップの先駆者がジョージ・ペティであったとすれば、アルベルト・ヴァーガスはその完成者であり、オリビアはその正統な継承者であるといえる。では、我が極東の巨匠空山基はといえば、ピンナップを21世紀モードに改変した革命家であり、ピンナップの概念を破壊したマッド・サイエンティストであるといえるだろう。もはや空山はかつてのピンナップ・アーチストのように美女の理想像をイメージ化しようとはしない。空山は美女を解体し改造し遺伝子操作を加え、エキゾチックでエロチックなモンスターを作り出す。ガイノイドを産みだし世界中にドール禍を引き起こしサイコイド心身症を蔓延させた張本人トクシコフィラス博士の真の正体こそ空山基なのだ。21世紀のピンナップ工学はこの天才によってますますラジカルな進化を遂げるに違いない。

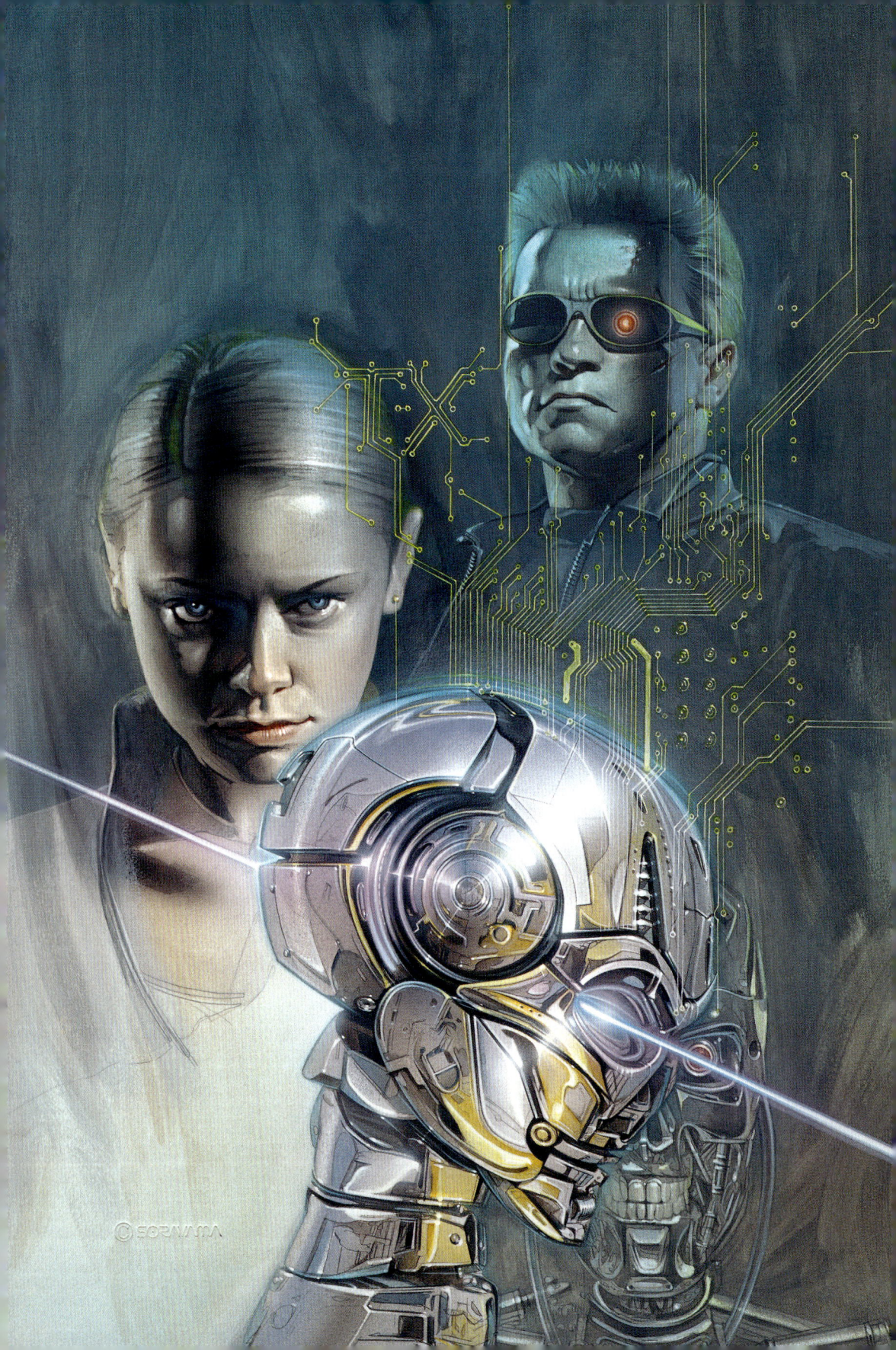

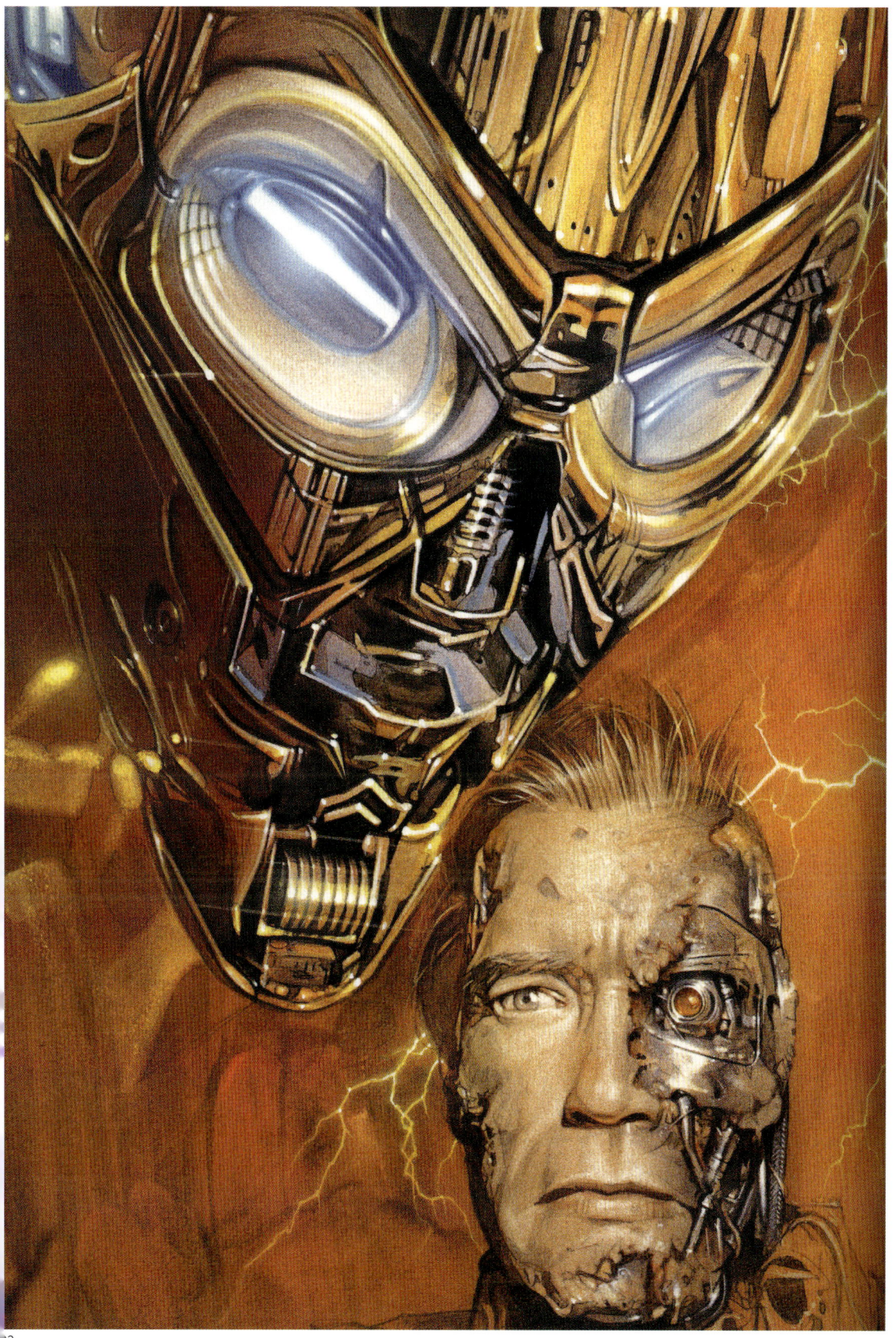

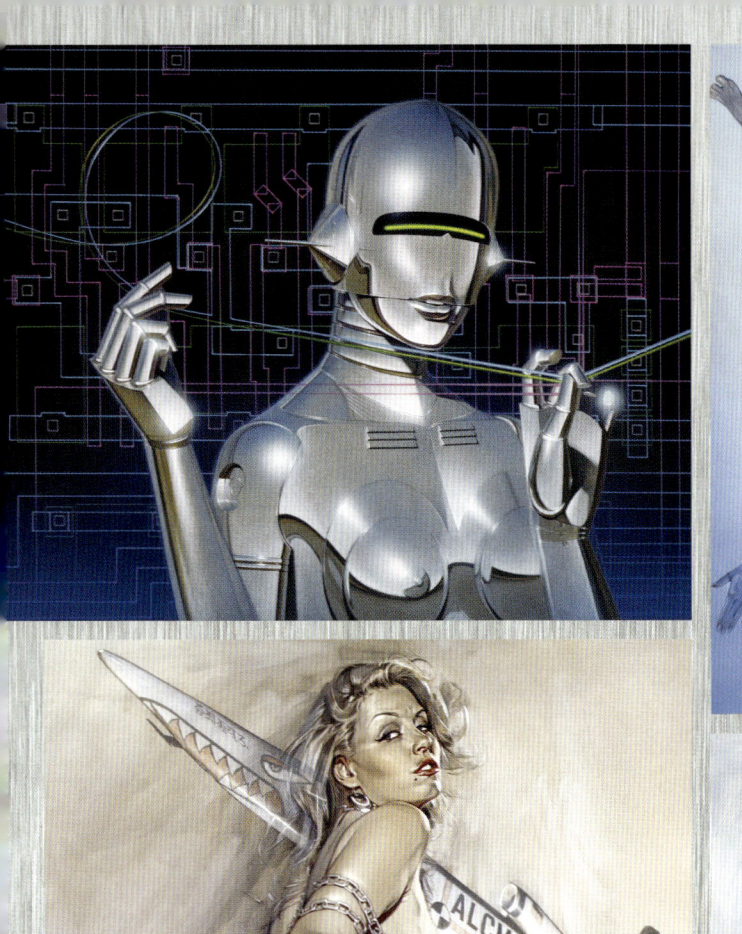
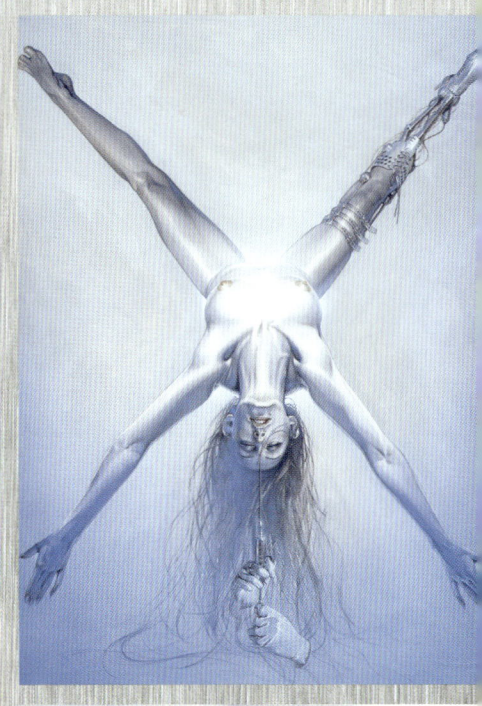
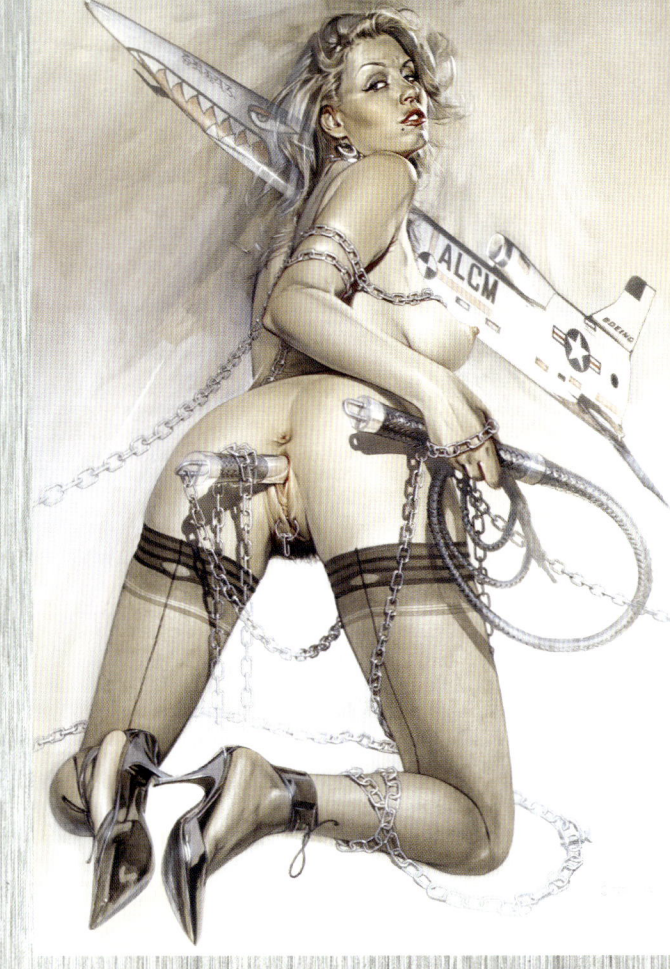
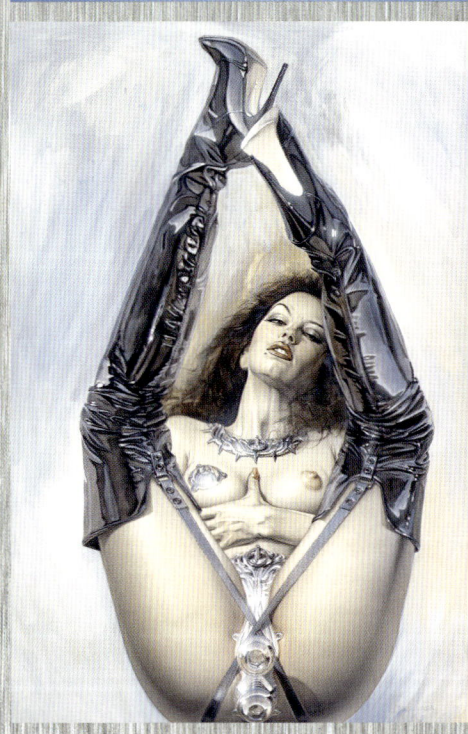
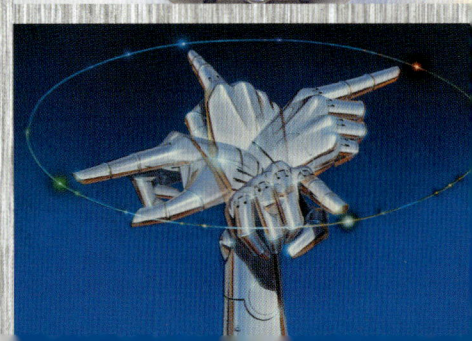

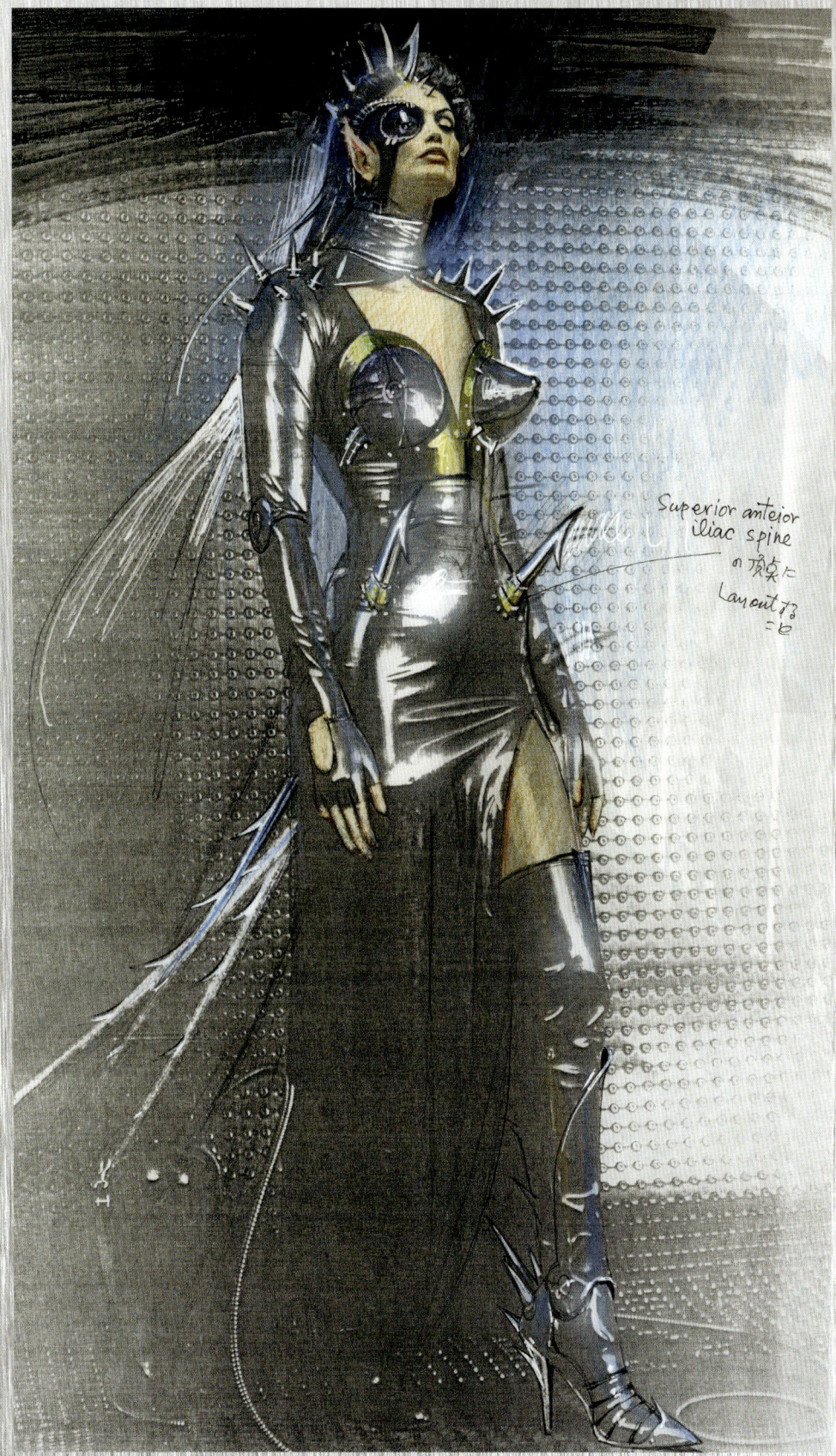

Superior anterior
iliac spine
の下あたに
Layout する
二d

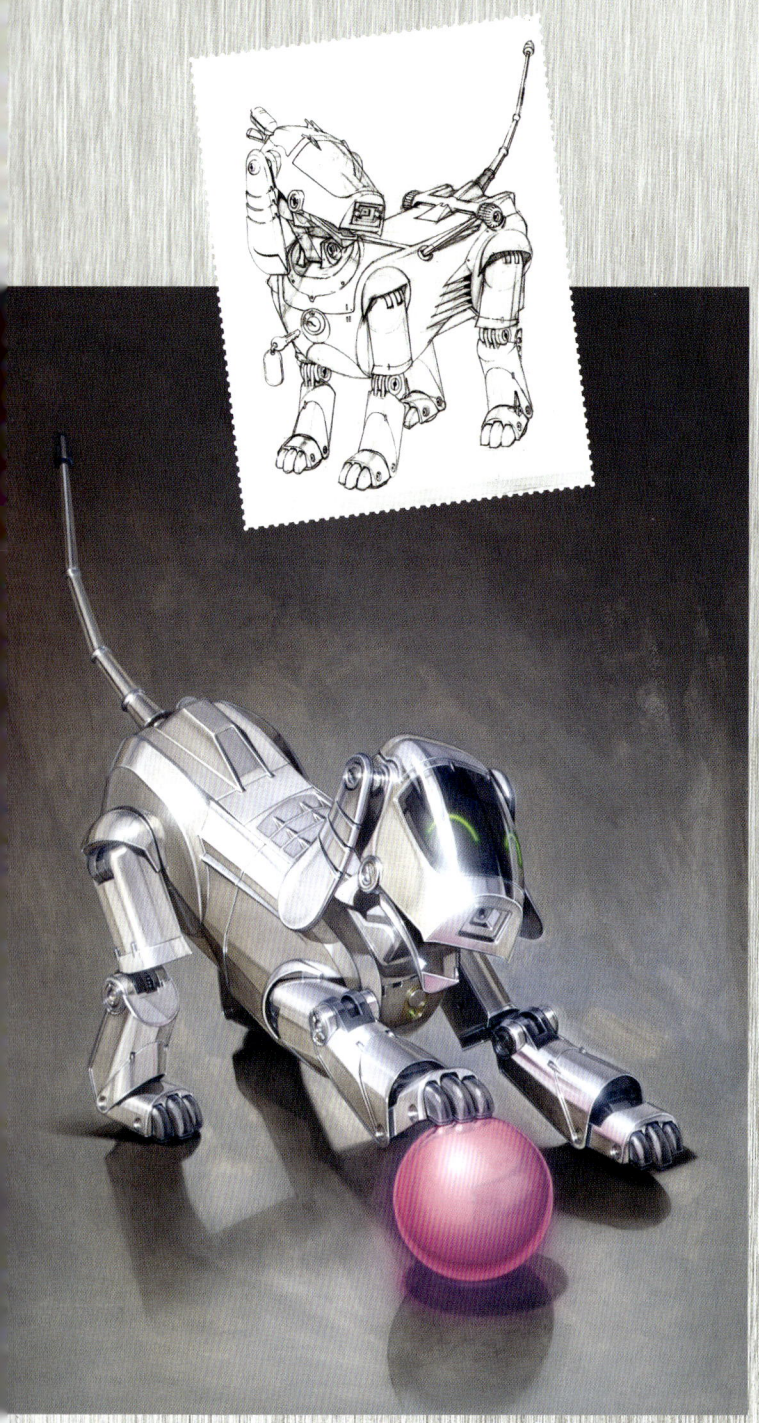

鵜野義嗣（データハウス代表）

ボクは空山さんの絵は何枚か持っています
グロっぽいものばかりで、ボクの宝物です。
でも、空山さんはいやがっています。
伊集院健くんやセシールの下着をつけてい
麗華ちゃんといっしょにかざってあるのか
すごくいやなようです。
ぼくはどっちも好きなのに……。
空山さんは今、観葉植物にこっています。
先日、電話で「目黒の花屋さんにソテツの
なザミアがあるが、枯れさせてしまうと嫌
ので、どうしようかと迷っている。」等と
っていました。
ボクはすぐにそのザミアを先廻りして買っ
来て空山さんに
「ザミアみろ、私が買ってしまったからも
迷わなくっていいよ！」と電話しました。
空山さんは怒っていました。
残念ながらそのザミアが今彼の心配どおり
れかけています。
そんな空山さんが大好きです。

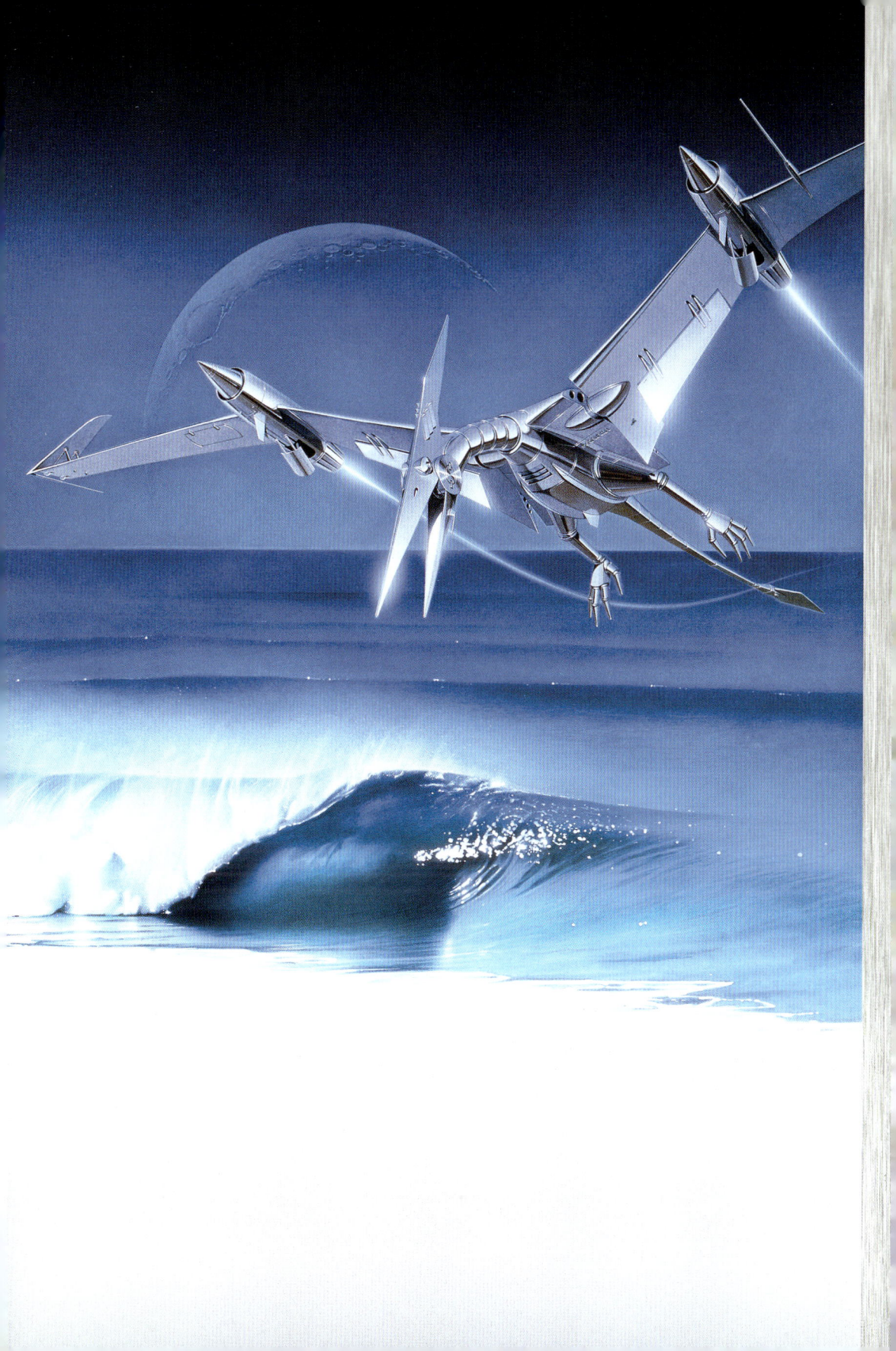

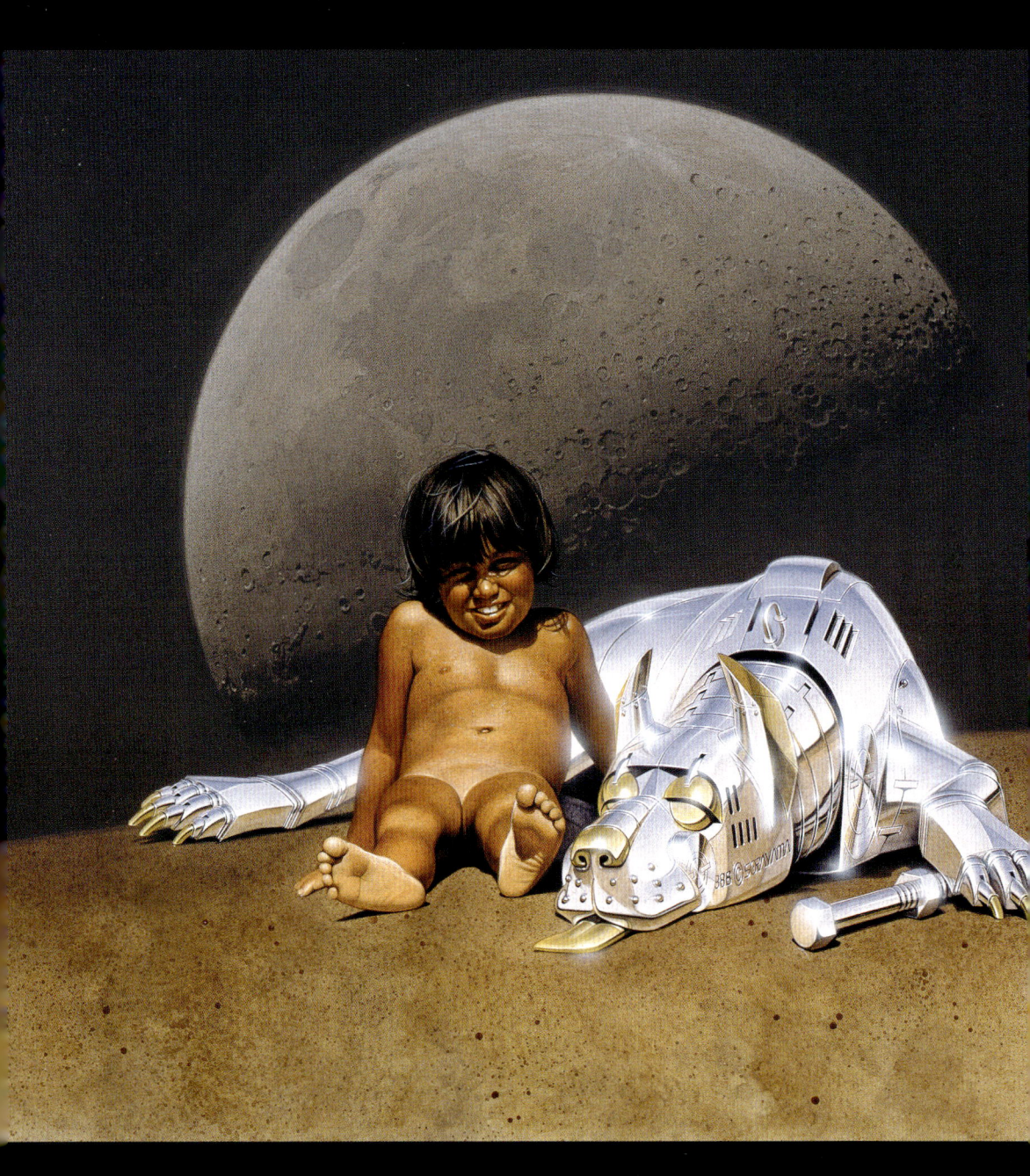

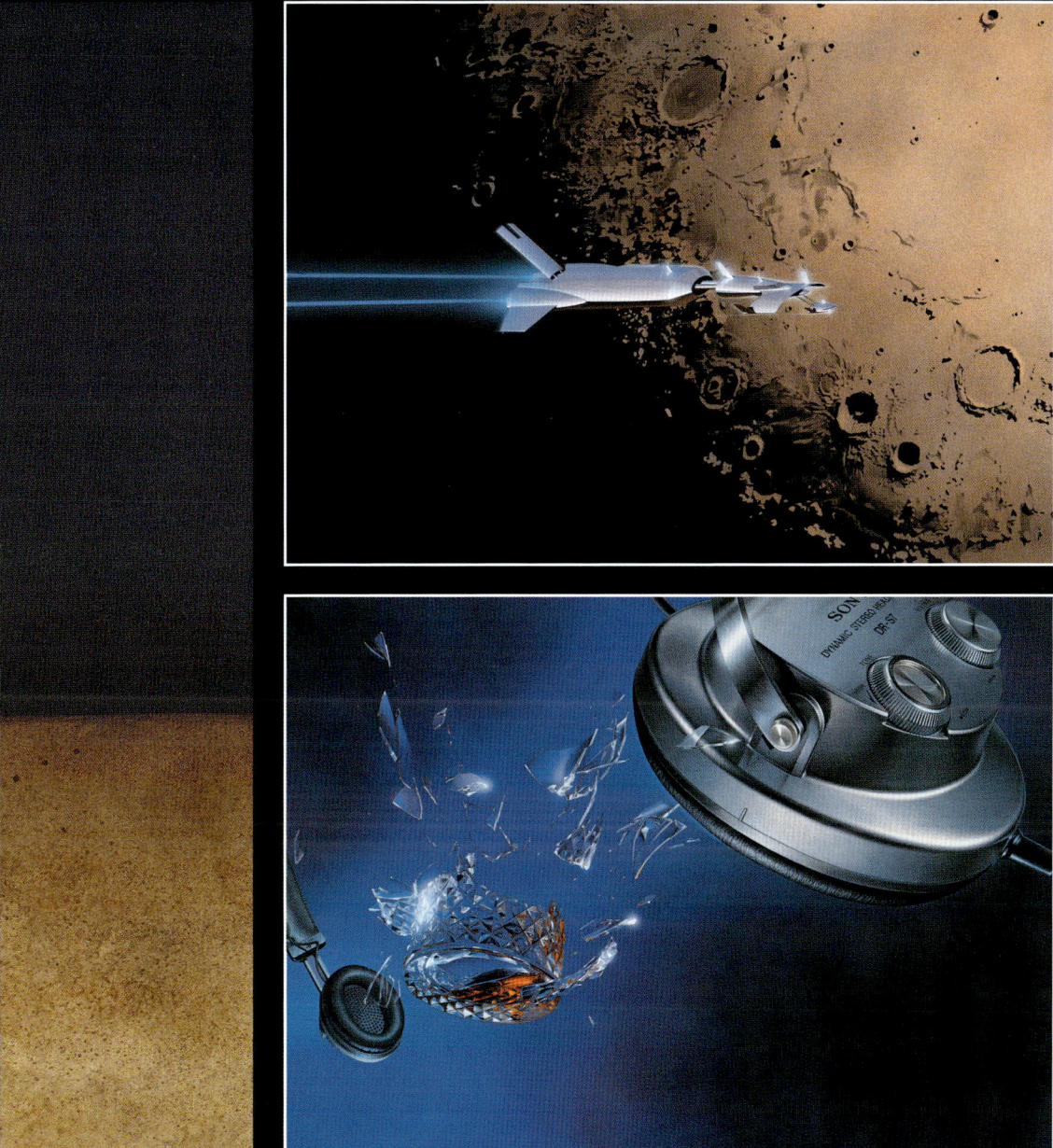

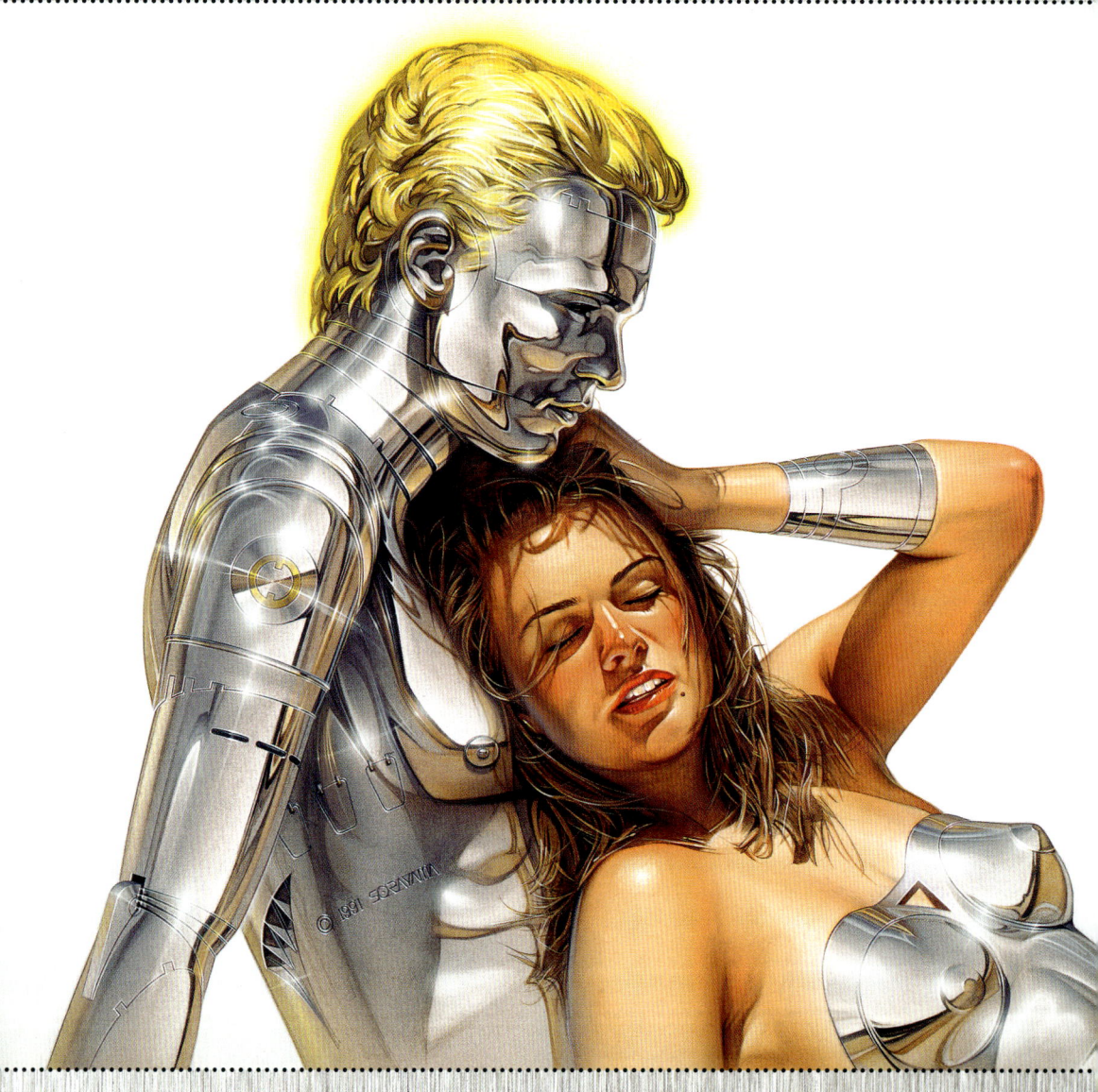

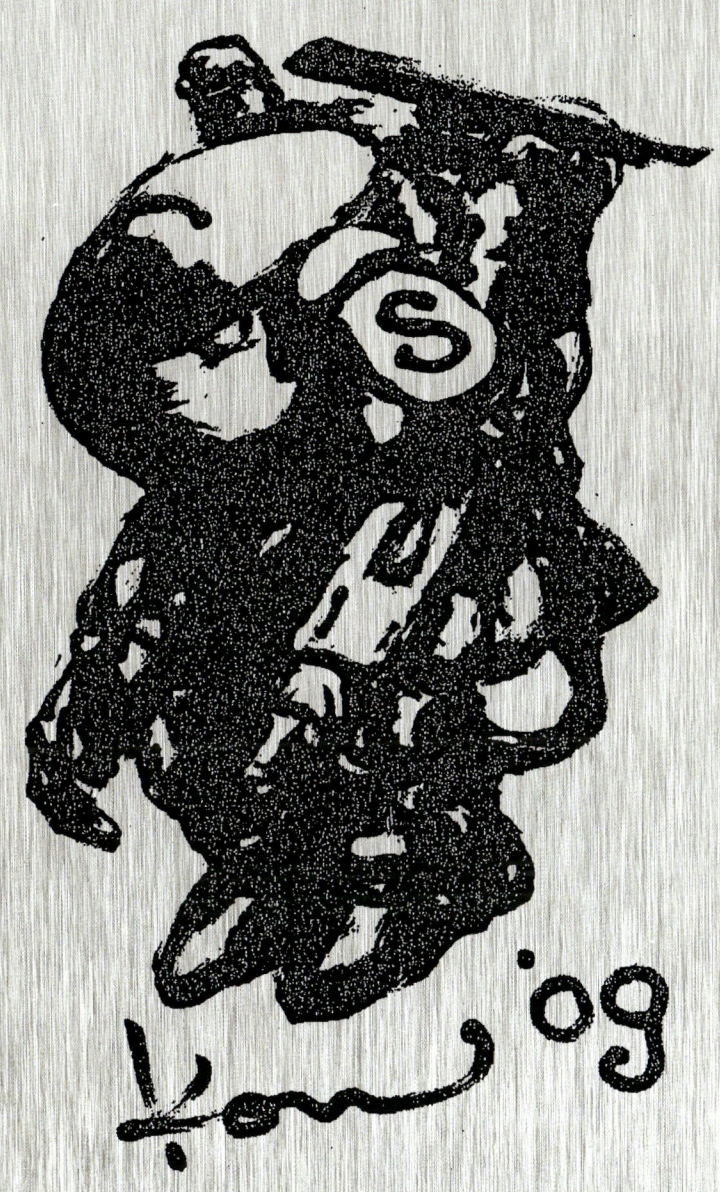

'09
Kom

Maschinen Krieger   Kow YOKOYAMA

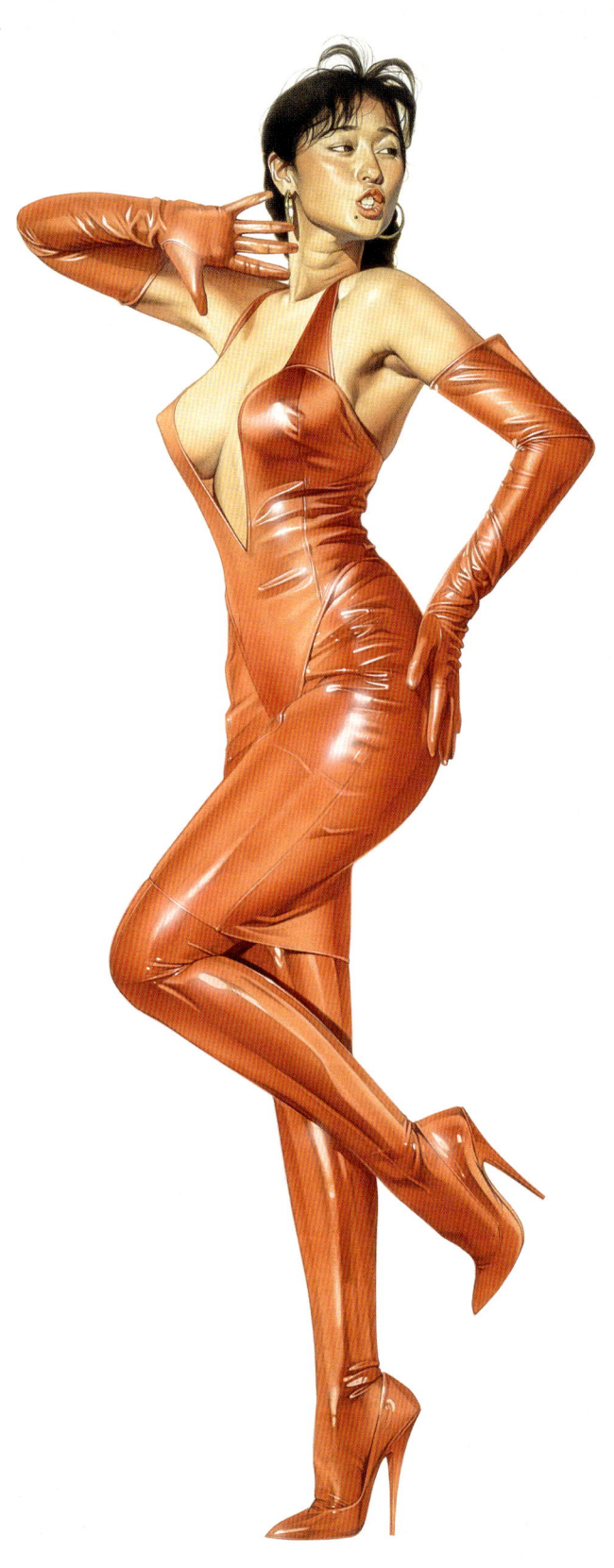

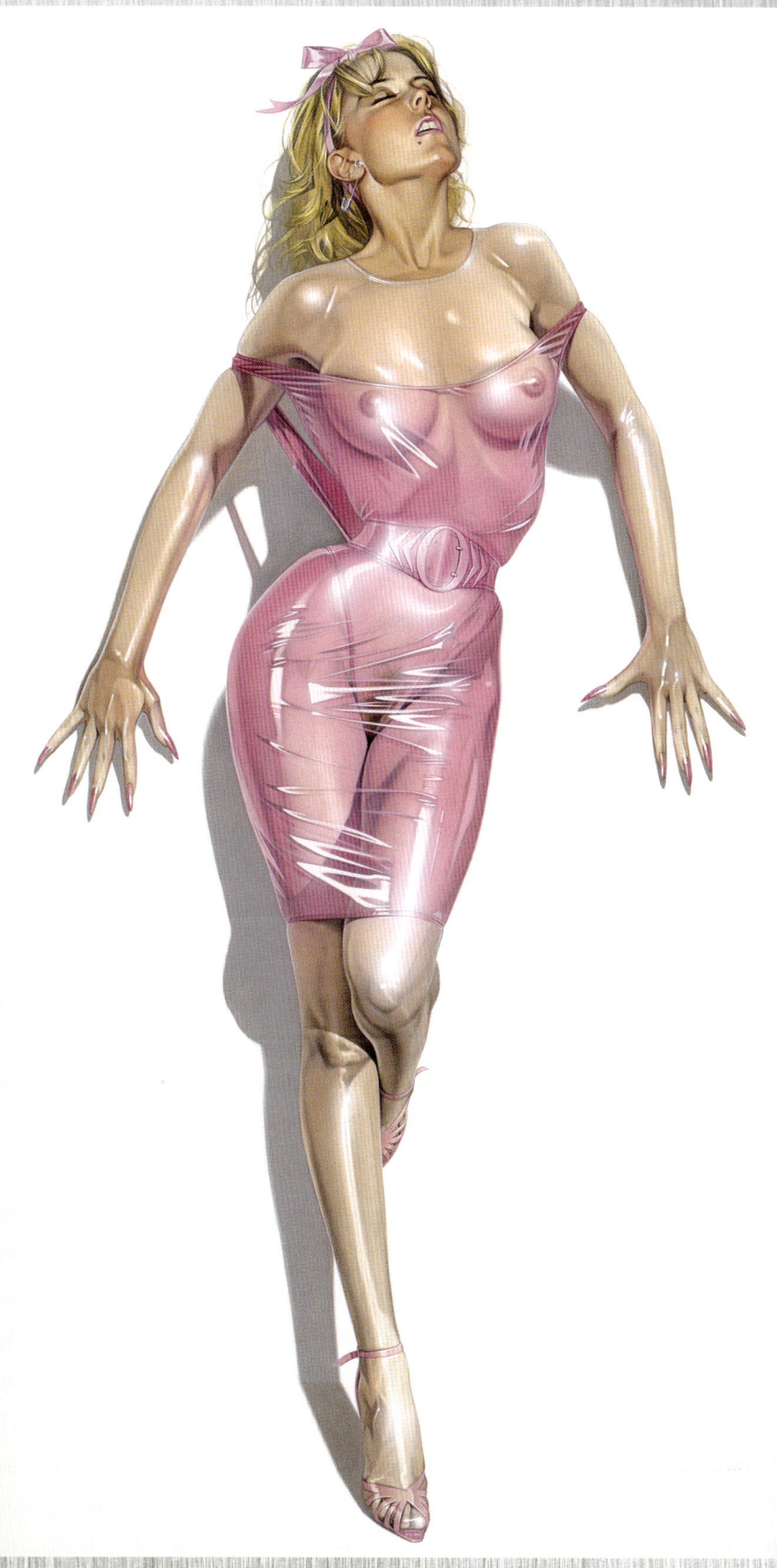

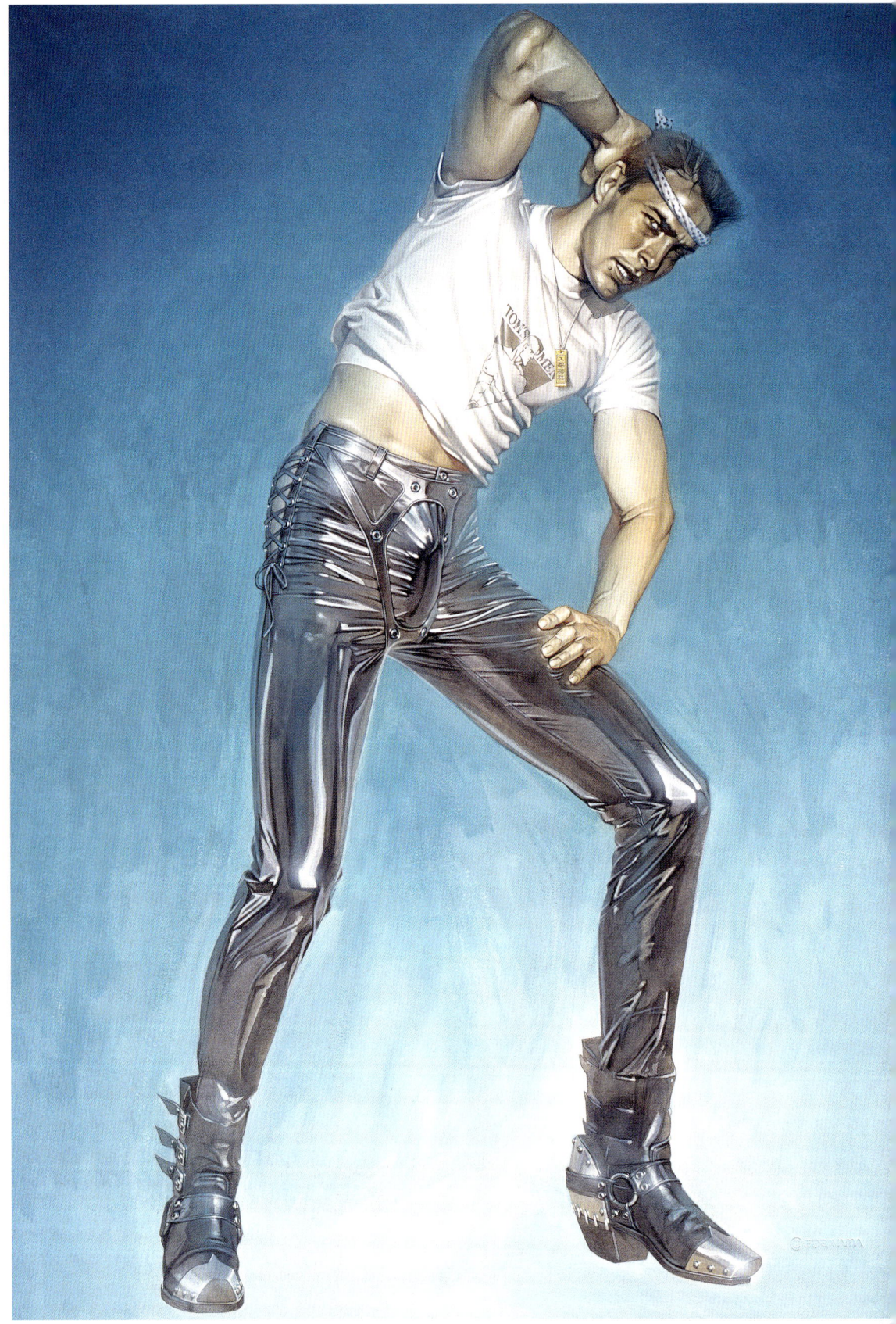

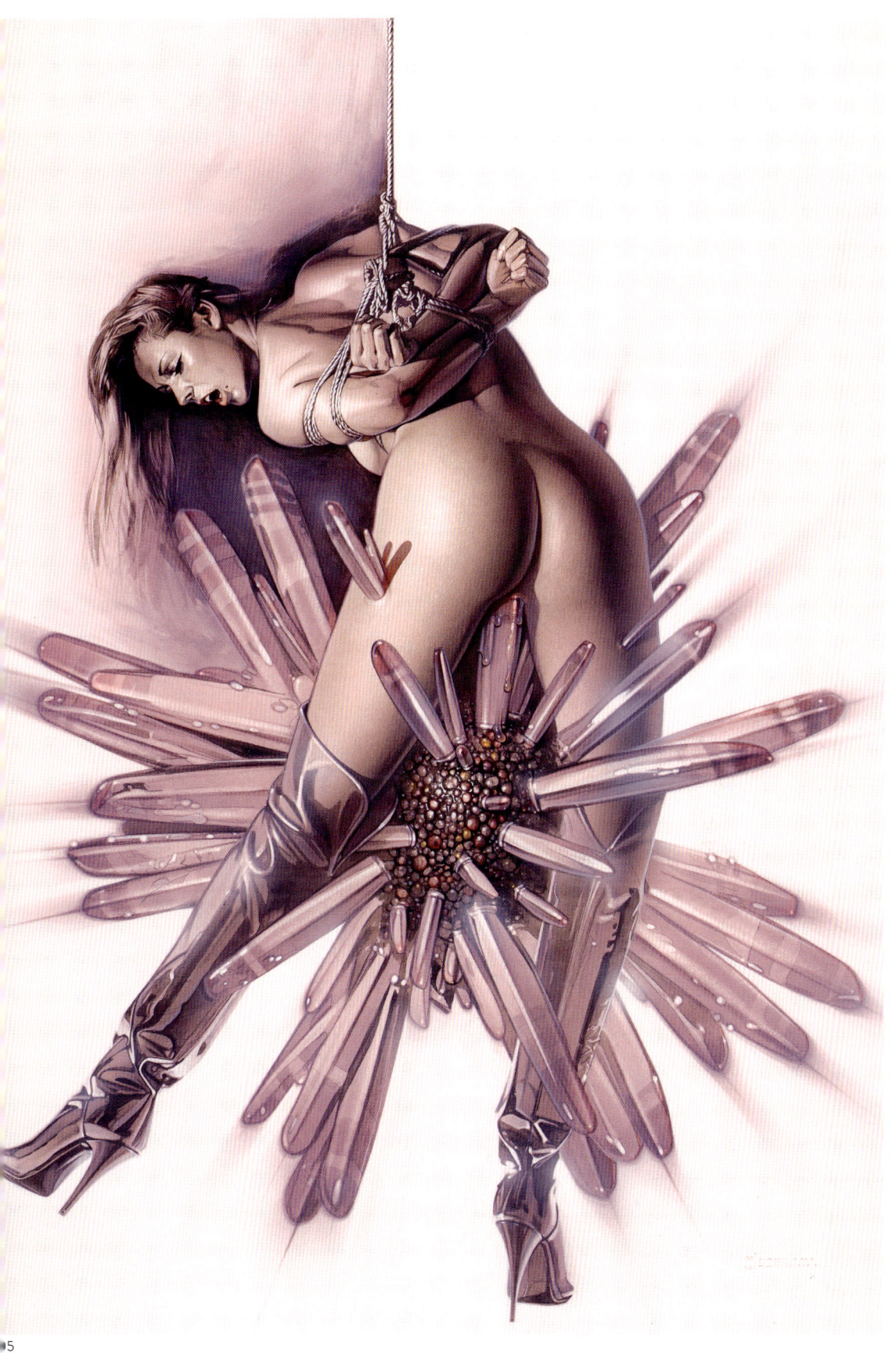

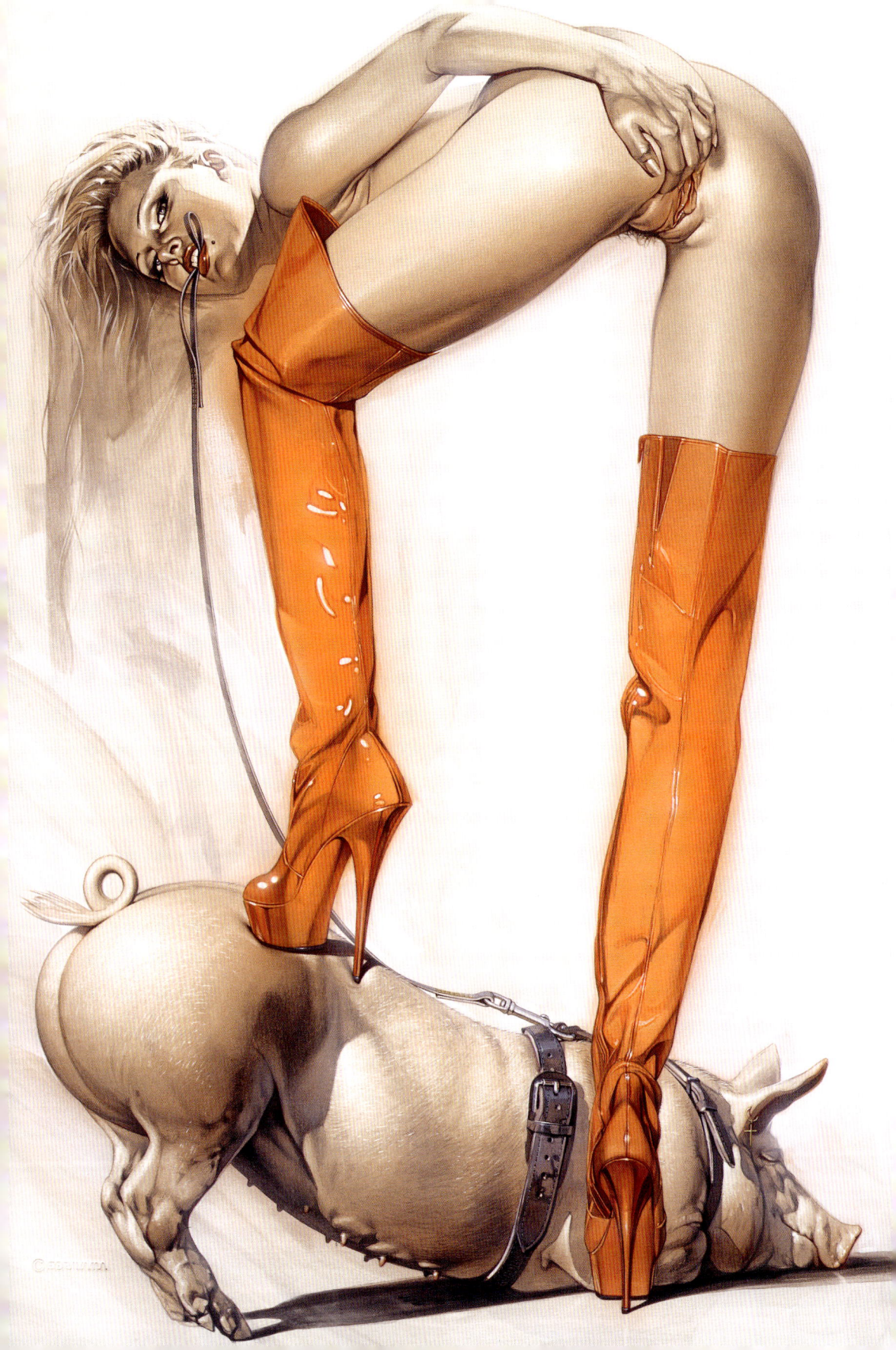

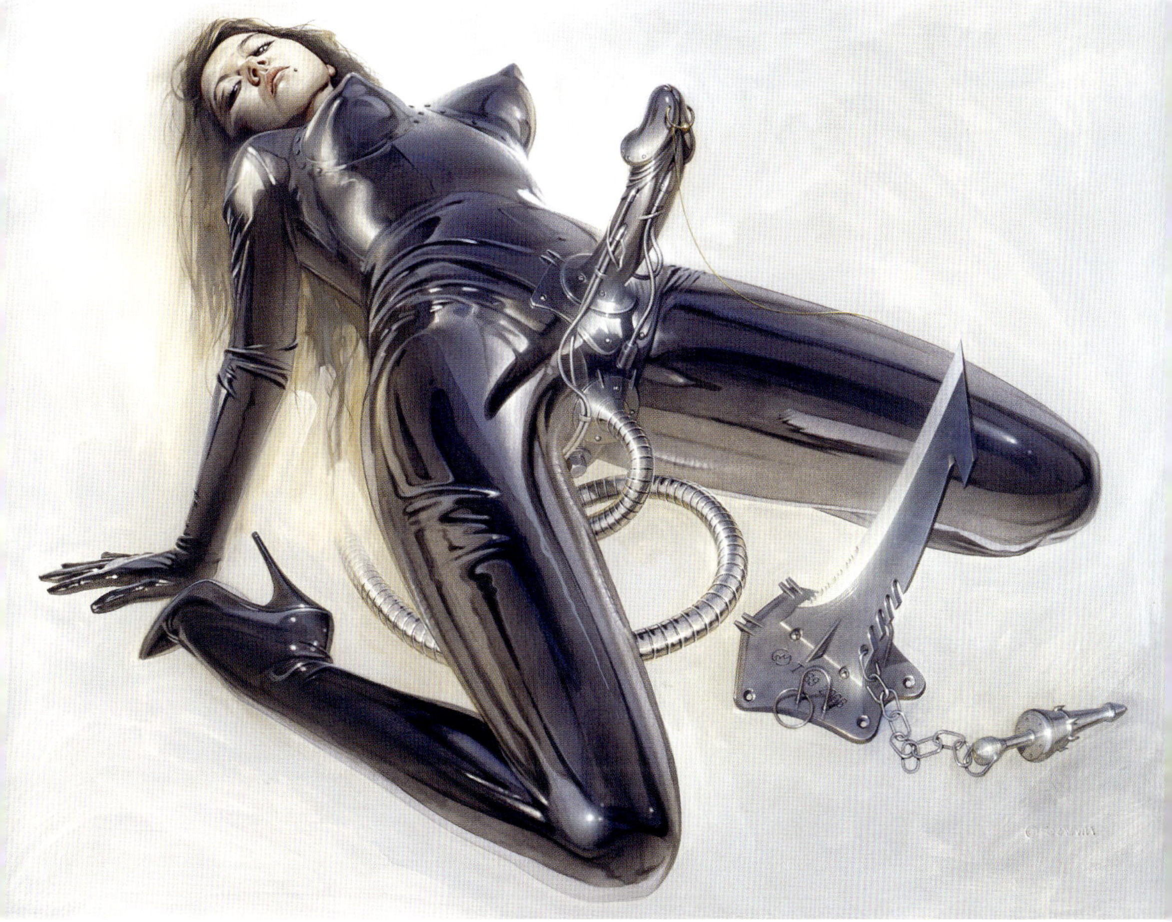

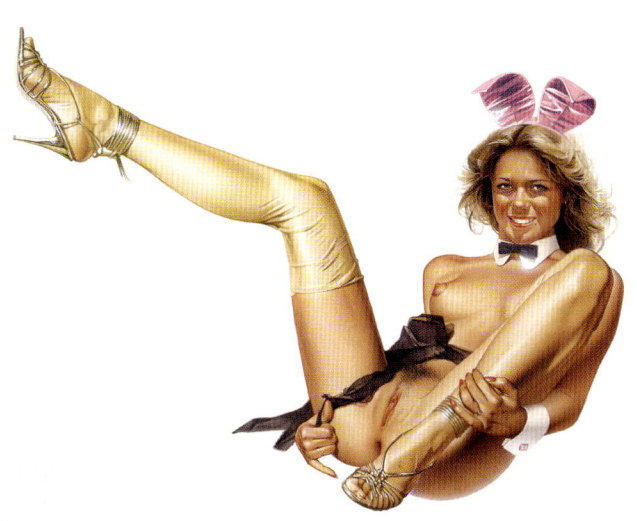
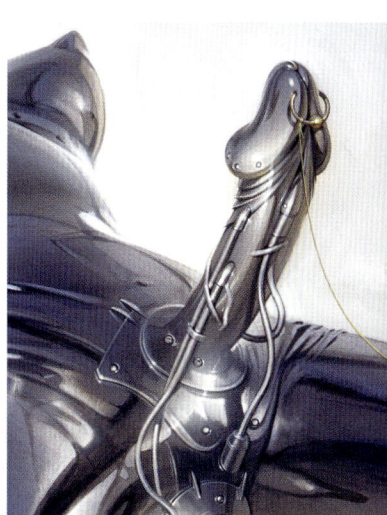

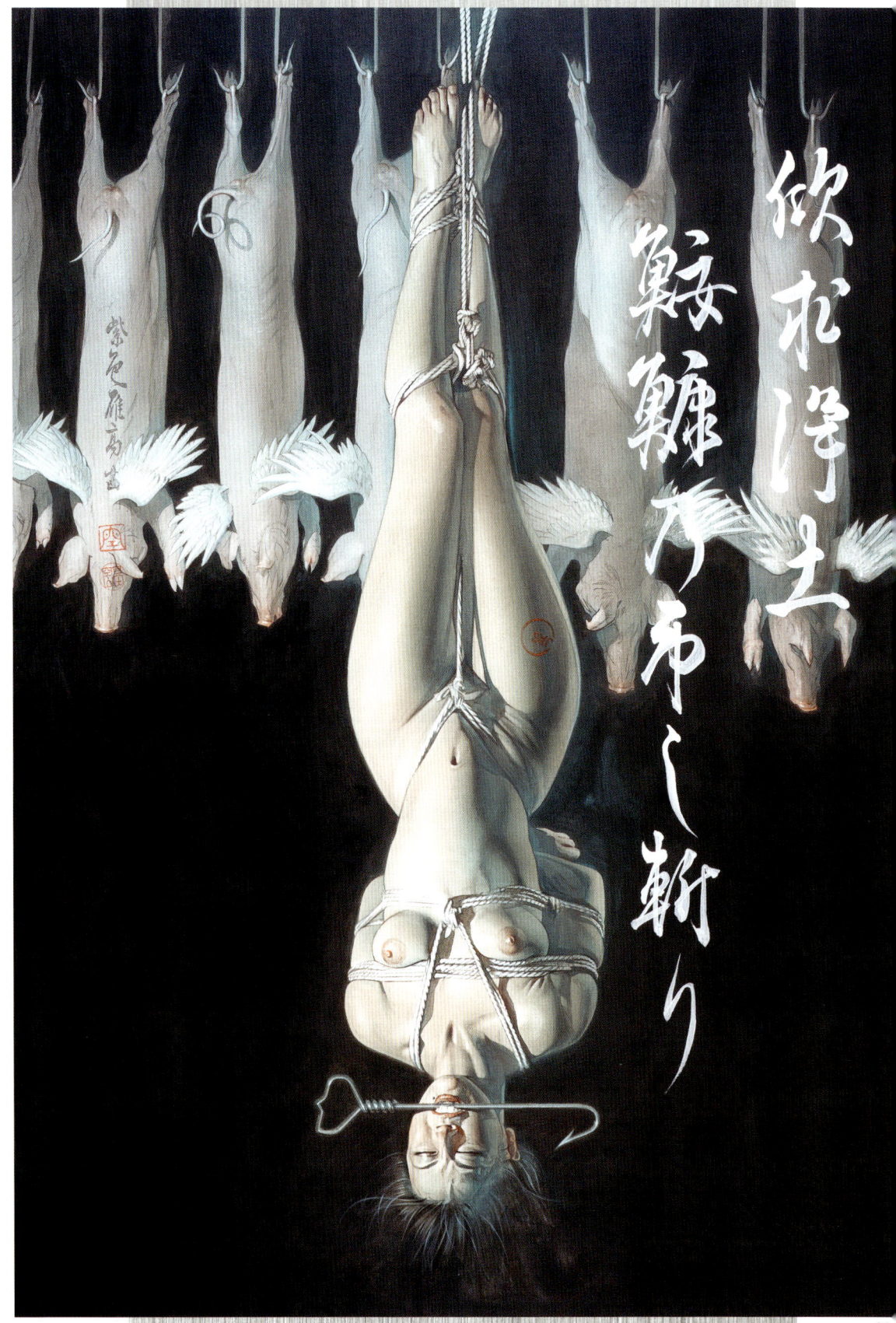

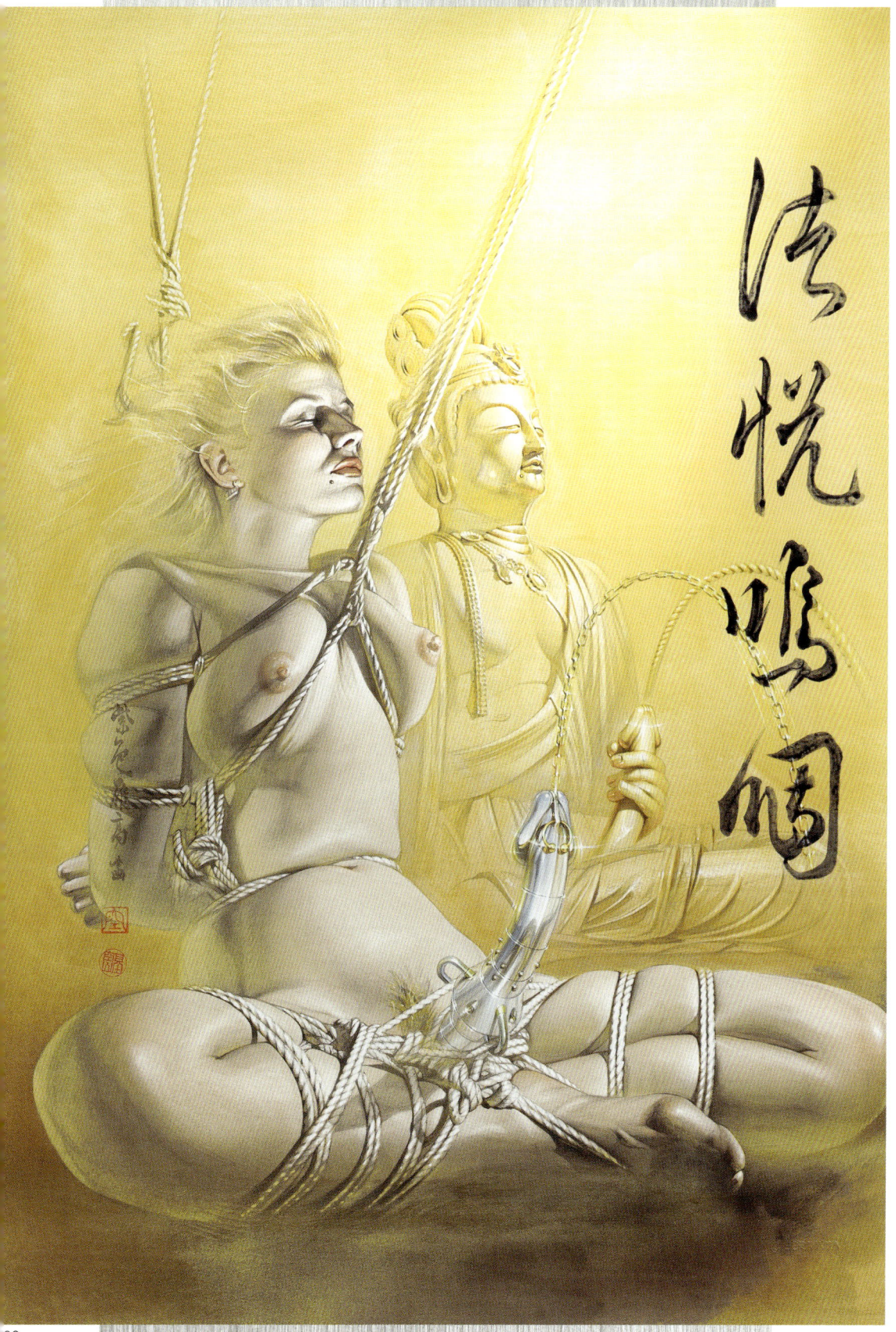

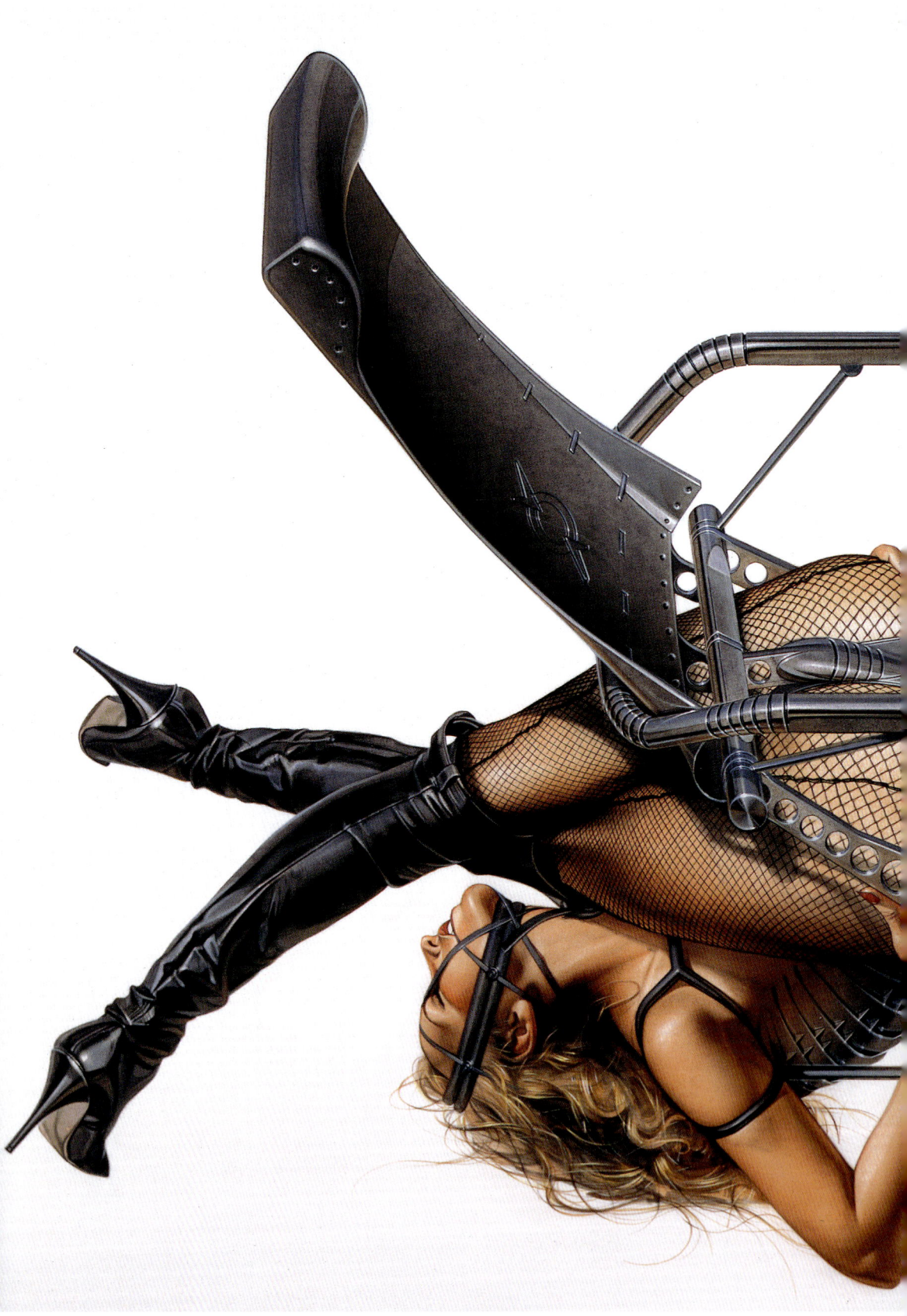

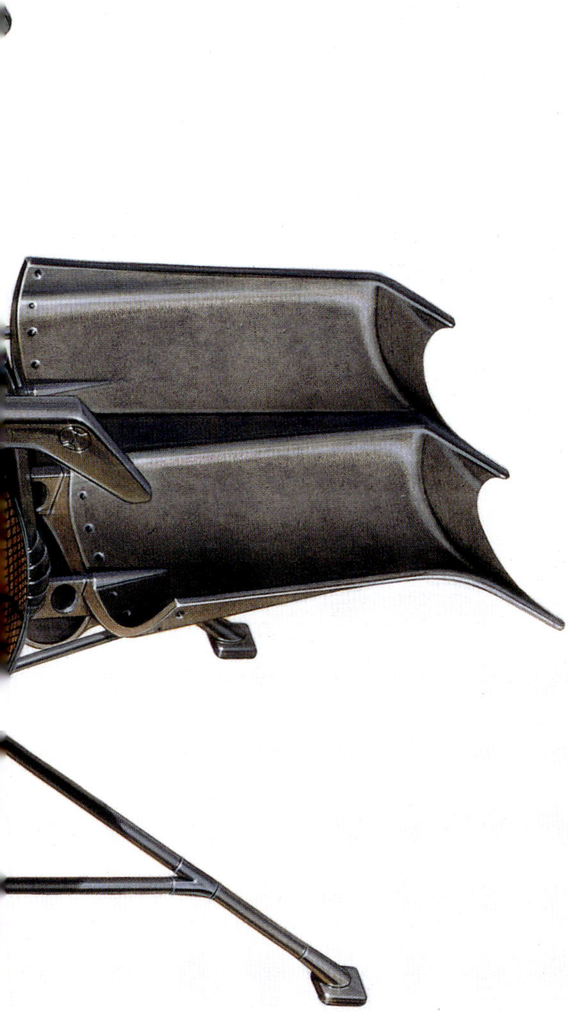

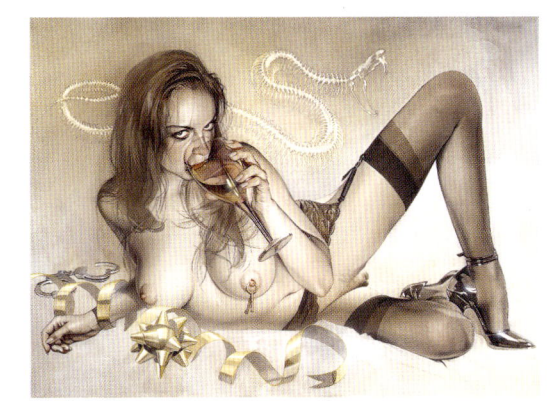

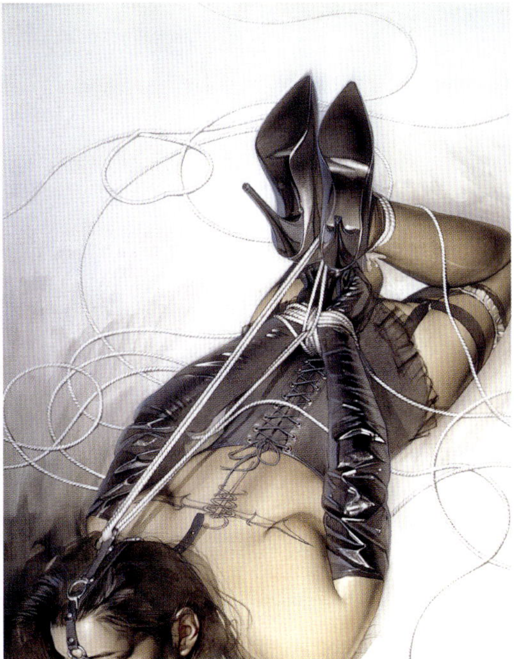

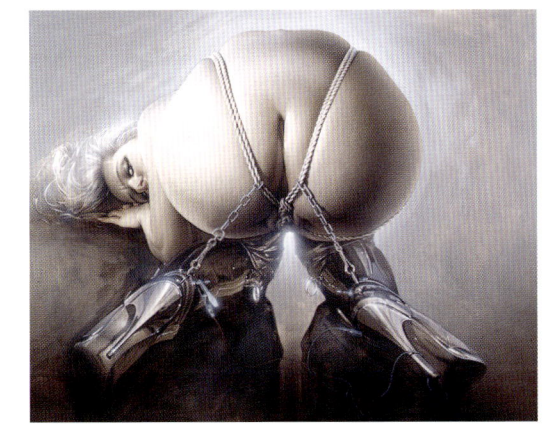

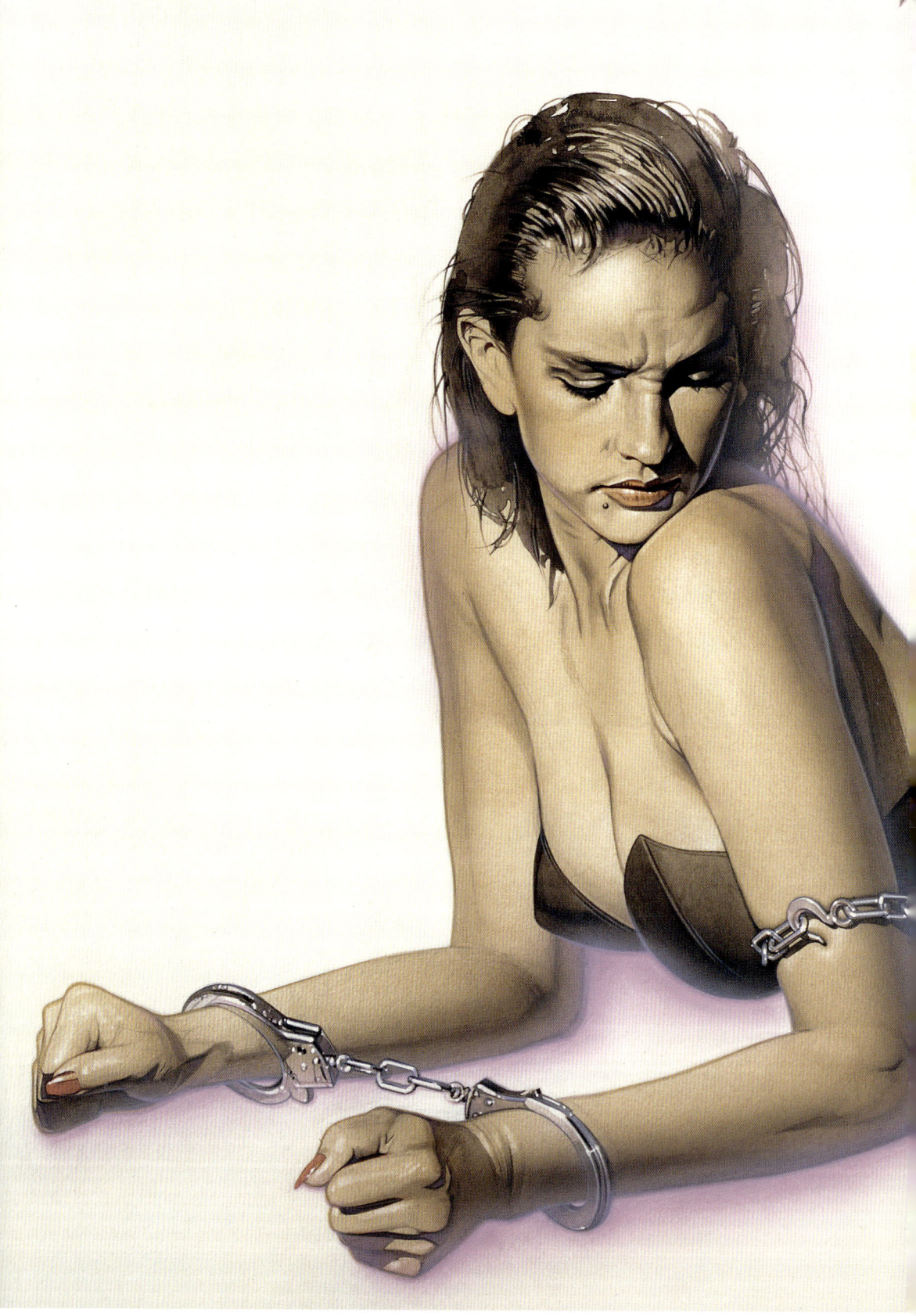

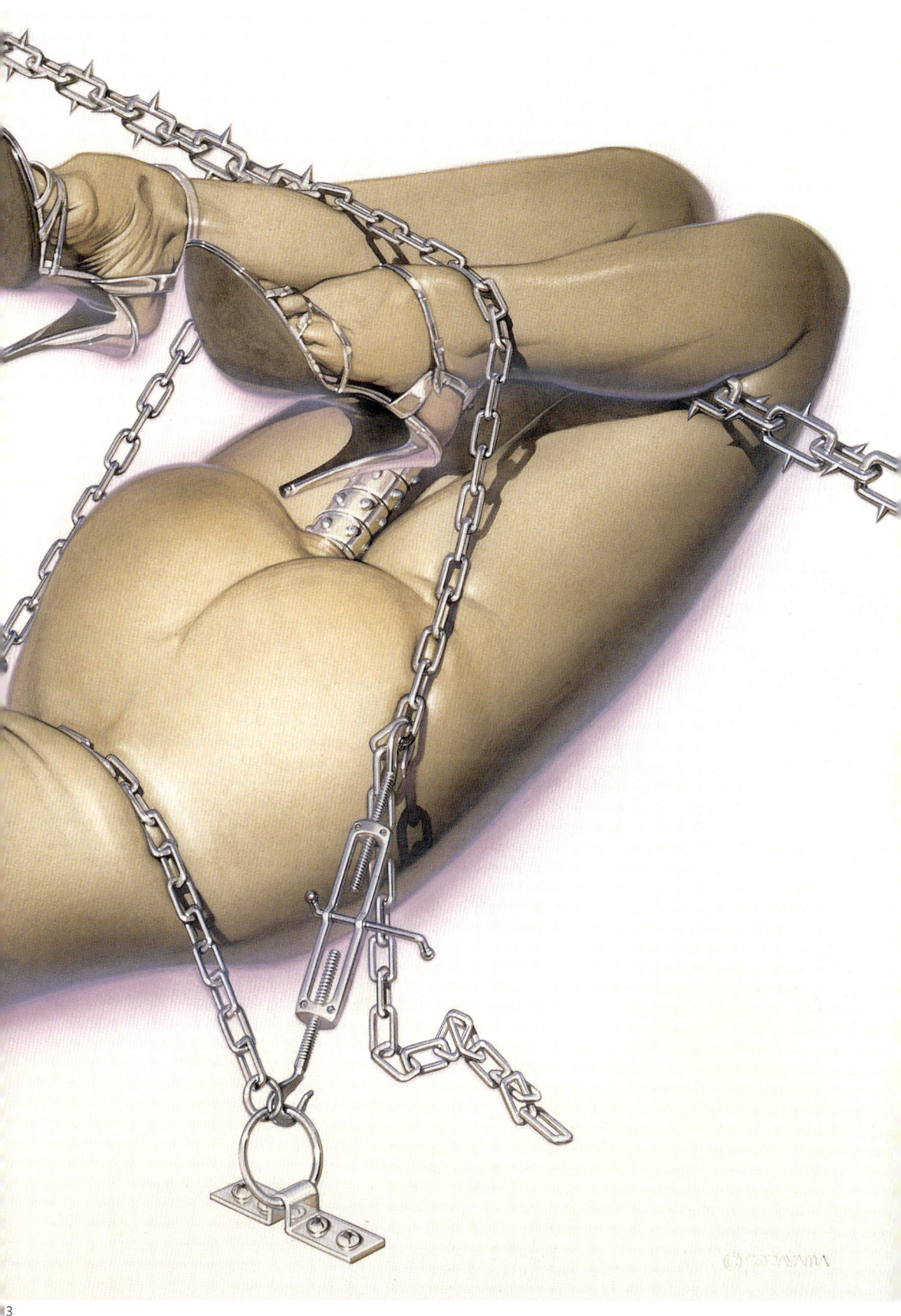

The works of Sorayama were well received by the South Beach, Miami, art community. In addition to the month long exhibition which brought in record crowds, we have purchased three unique Sorayama works which are prominently displayed in our permanent museum collection. We have also included four of his books in our erotic art research library.

Naomi Wilzig
Curator/owner
World Erotic Art Museum
South Beach, Florida

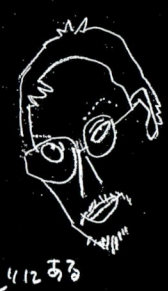

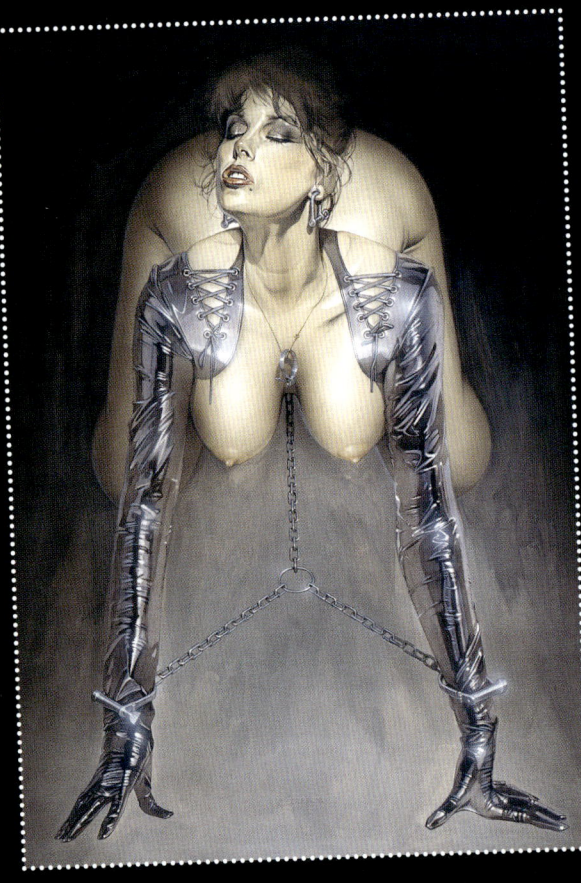

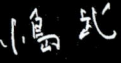

小島武 (イラストレーター)

たとえば
ロサンゼルスのメルローズ通りにある
書店などで、空山の作品集が
目立つ棚に置いてあるのに出会ったりすると
やはり胸のなかで 日の丸の旗が
のぼってくる。
いやらしく、みだらで、いかがわしいと
言われがちな主題のキワドさ、ケバさを
空山はみごとに聖化してきた。
主題のいかがわしさとはまったく逆の
描法の気品ーすずしさ、りりしさ、に
よってである。

小島 武

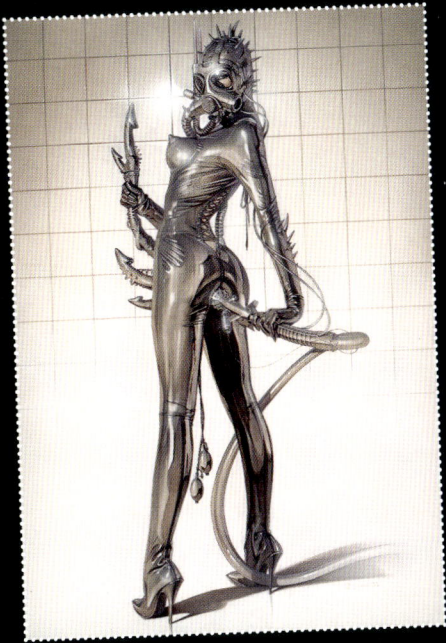

Peter Leth
(ピーター・レス：アーティスト)

I immediately recognised a fantastic talent when I for the first time saw a Sorayama illustration on the cover of the magazine OMNI about 1980.

A photographic painting of a chrome steel girl - a fantasy image, Amazing. The steelfigure caught in a moment of beauty and cast into eternity.
A very realistic style for a very unrealistic image. The very essence of erotic fantasy. That's when Hajime is at his best I think.

Later I got the book Sexy Robot Girls which I think is a milestone in erotic imagery. Noone - and I mean noone has his perfection in technique. Many walk in his footsteps - but they never get ahead.
But technique doesn't do it alone. The sense of style, beauty and humor is the spice in his work. He has broken taboos very elegantly, so that we hardly feel there was one. He gets away with it with unique style.

I known Sorayama will continue to explore the borders of sexual behaviour. And he shows us what we cannot imagine or dare to imagine, so clearly as a photo form the subconsious mind.
I have met Hajime at two occations in Germany, and I felt at once a mutual sympathy. We have faxed, written and exchanged ideas regularly over the years and he have been so kind to say that I have given him a little inspiration, and I can say for my part that his work has ment A LOT to me.
The way he can make a figure shine in rubber, vinyl and steel, and the fetishistic approch to the clothing and ridgidness shows a deep understanding of the feeling for this side of erotisism. He makes everything so aesthetically beautiful - innocent in away - even the strongest image, so that one doesn't feel embarrassed over ones fantasy. I think that shows he is a warm and gentle and humorous man at heart - that is the way I known him.

Peter

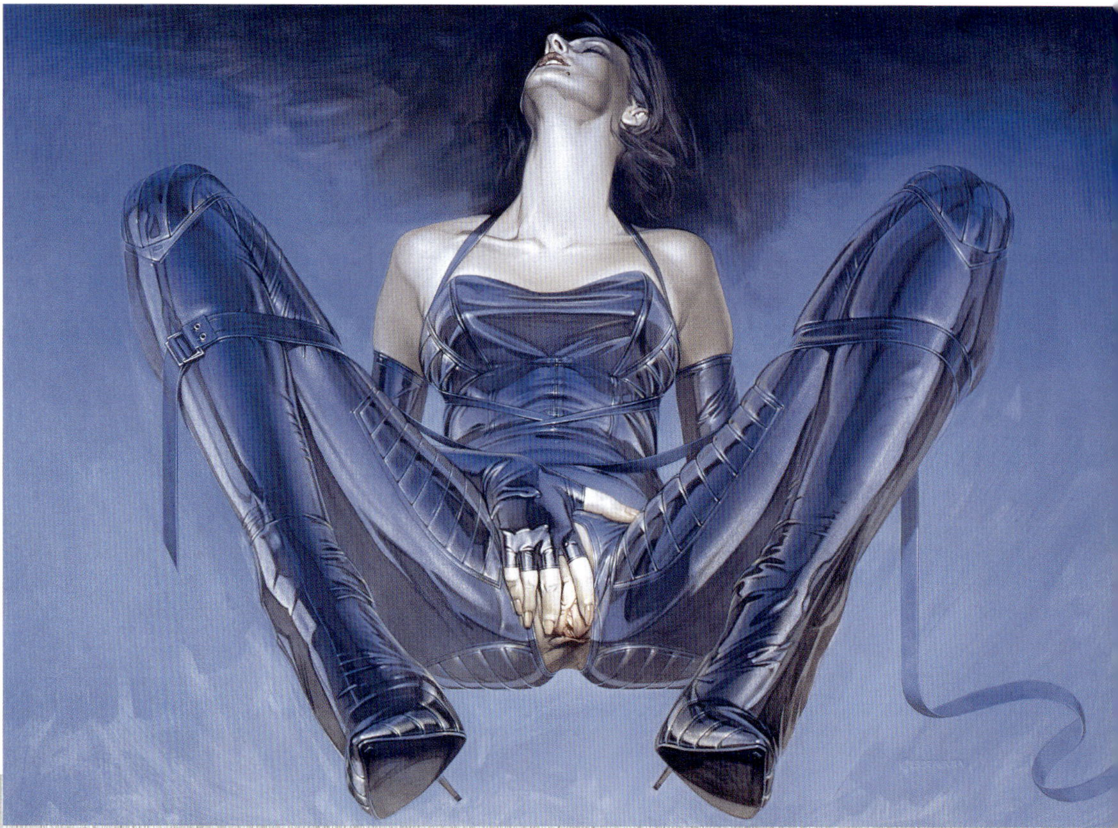

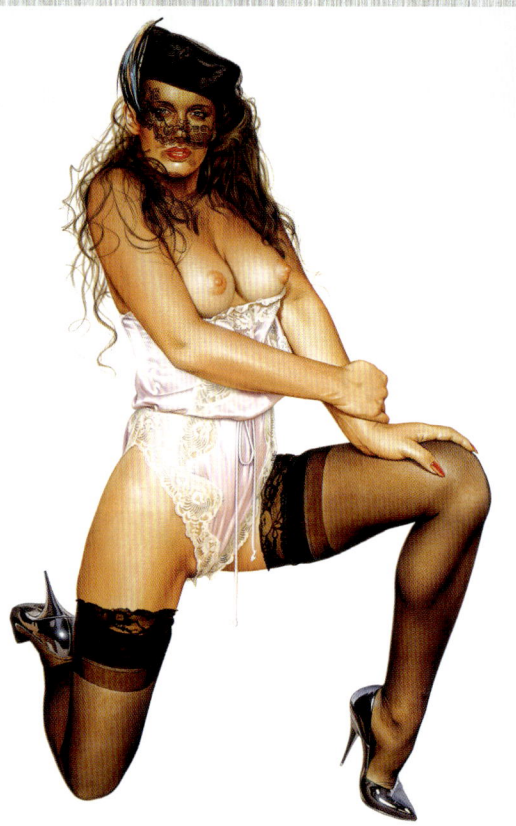
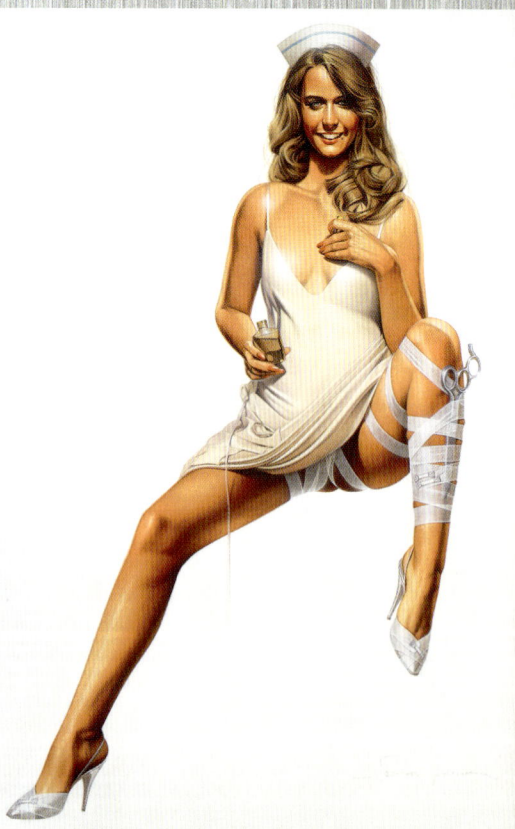

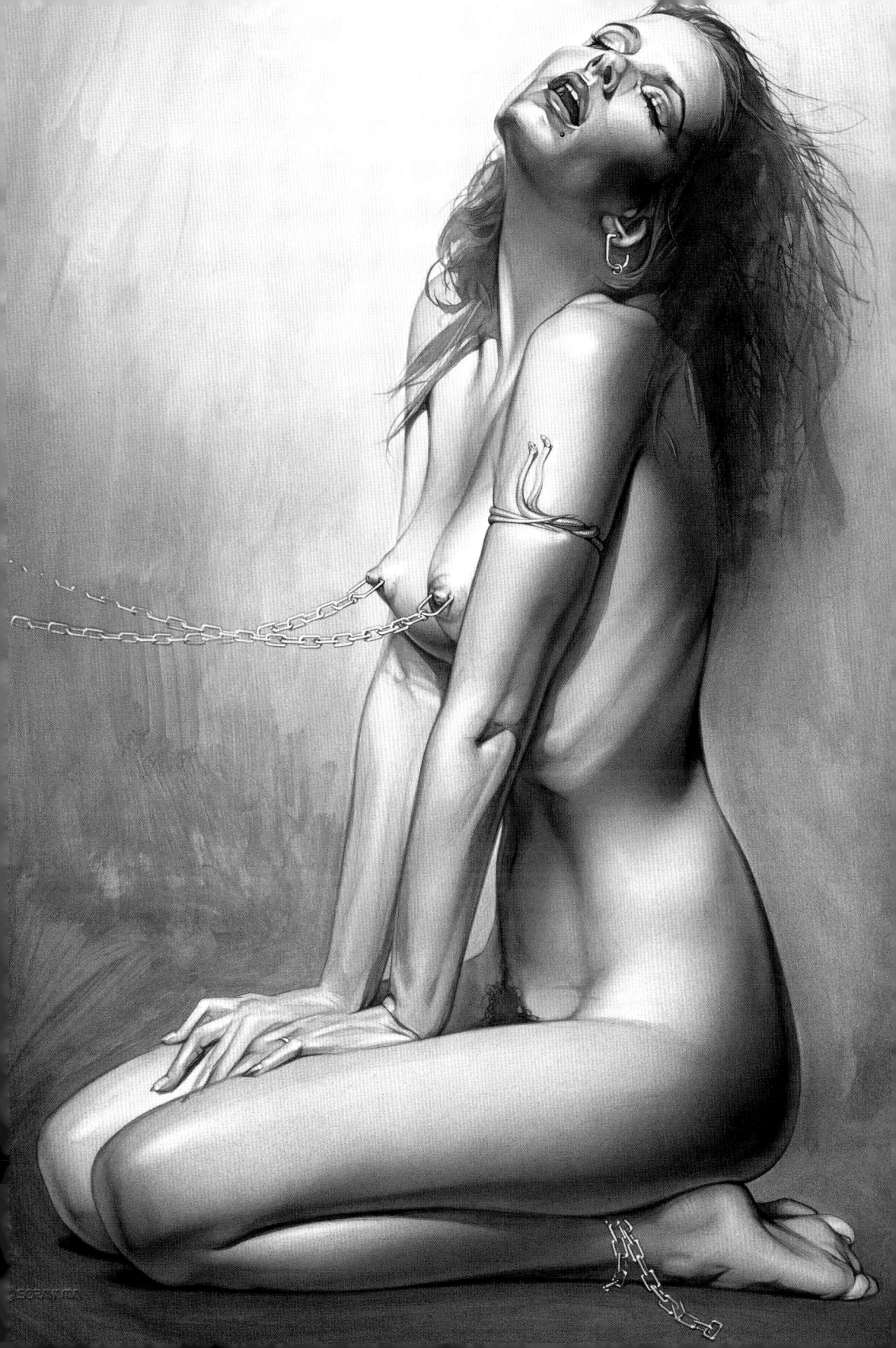

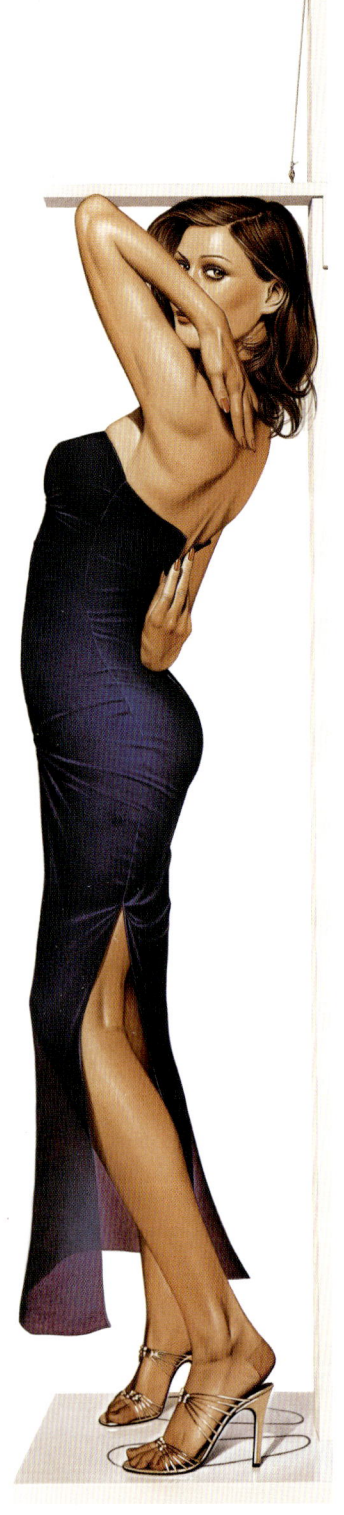

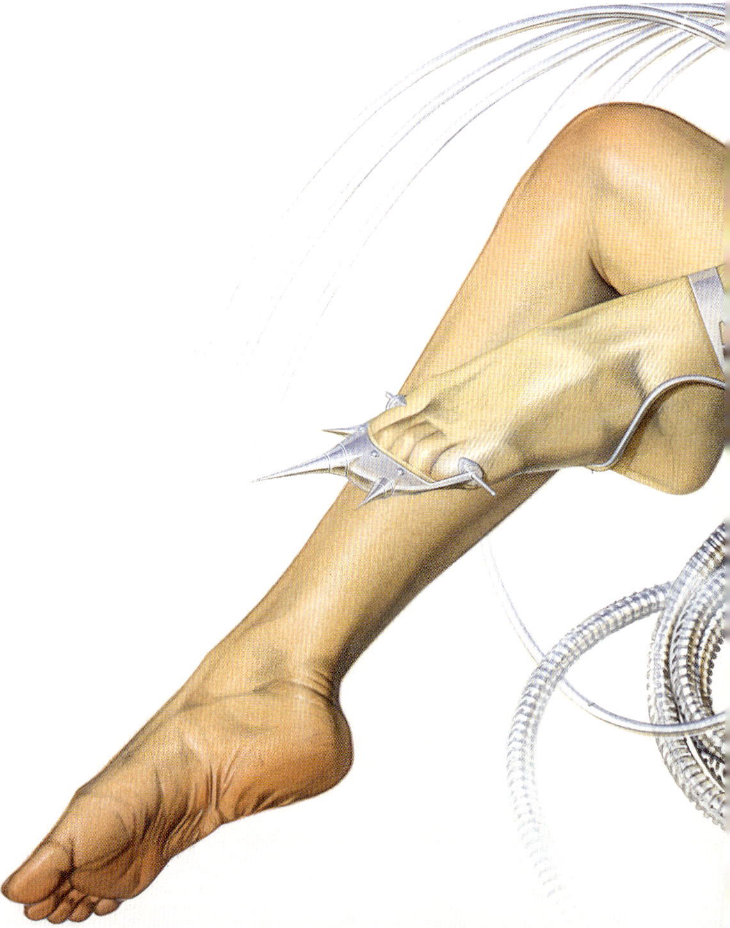

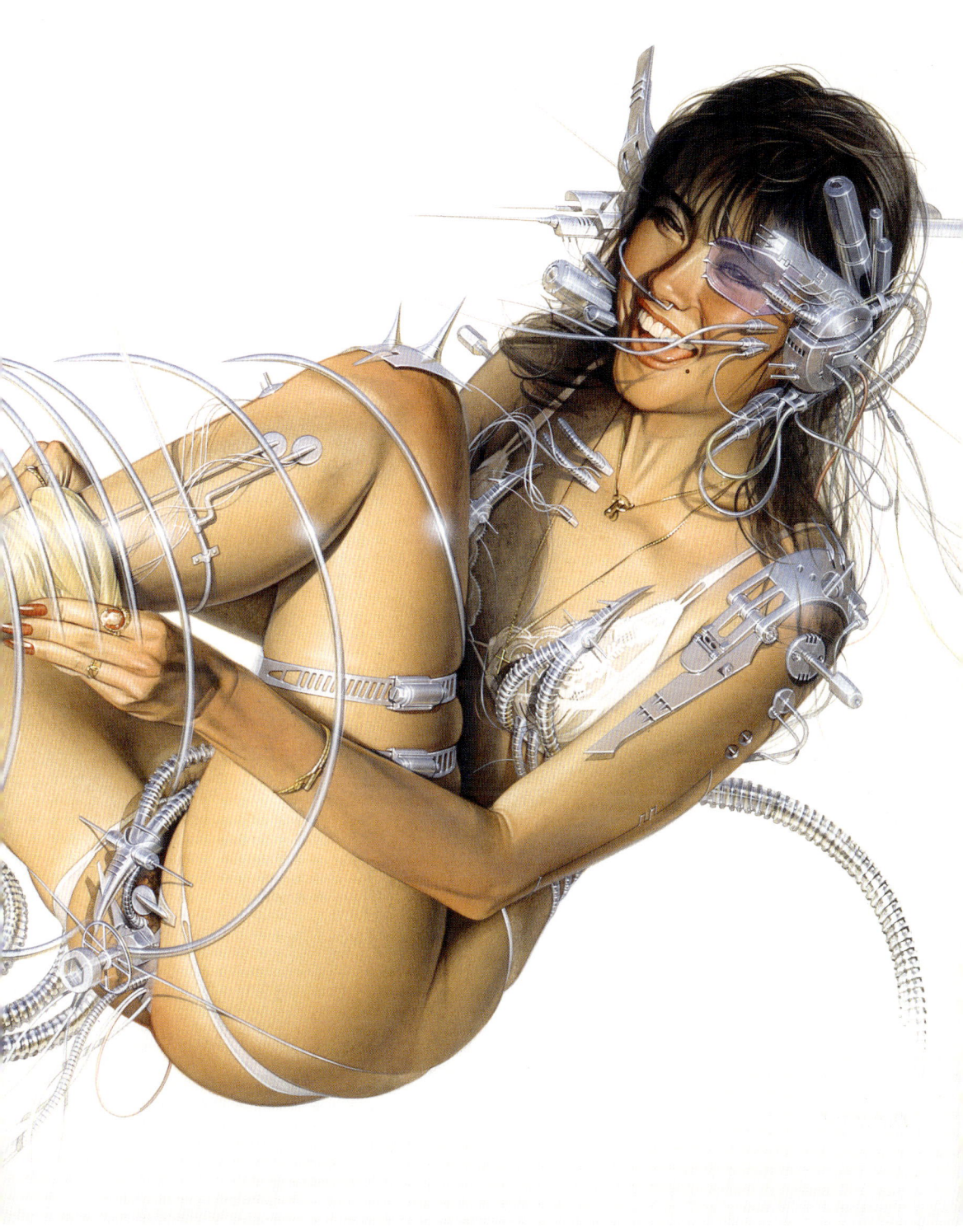

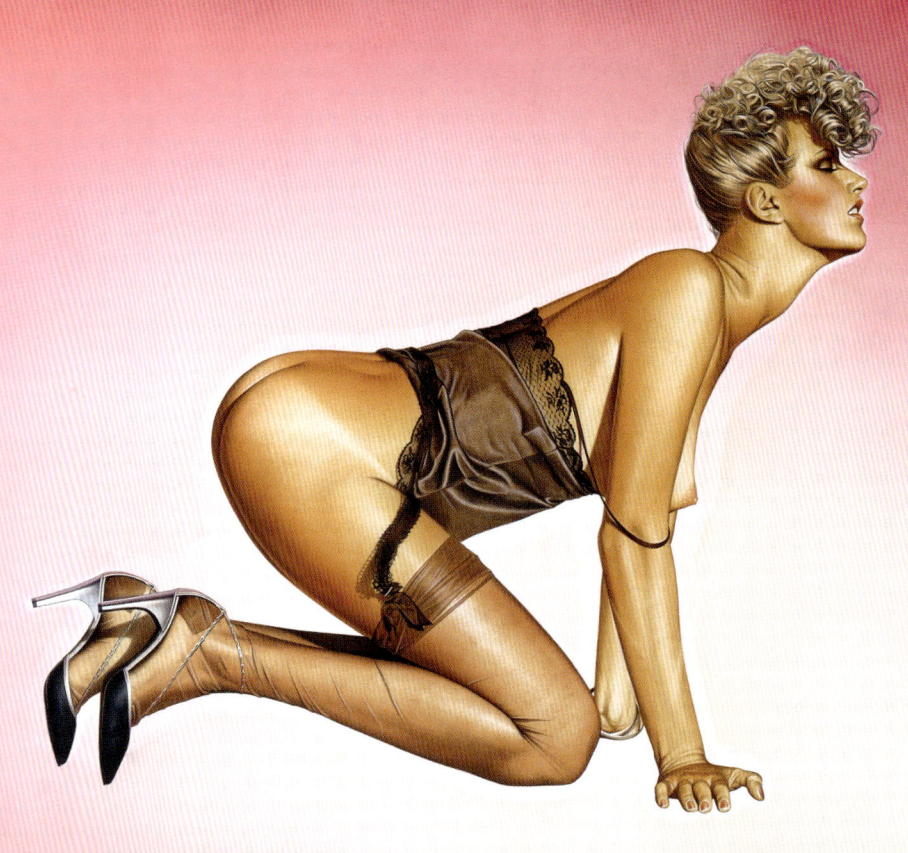

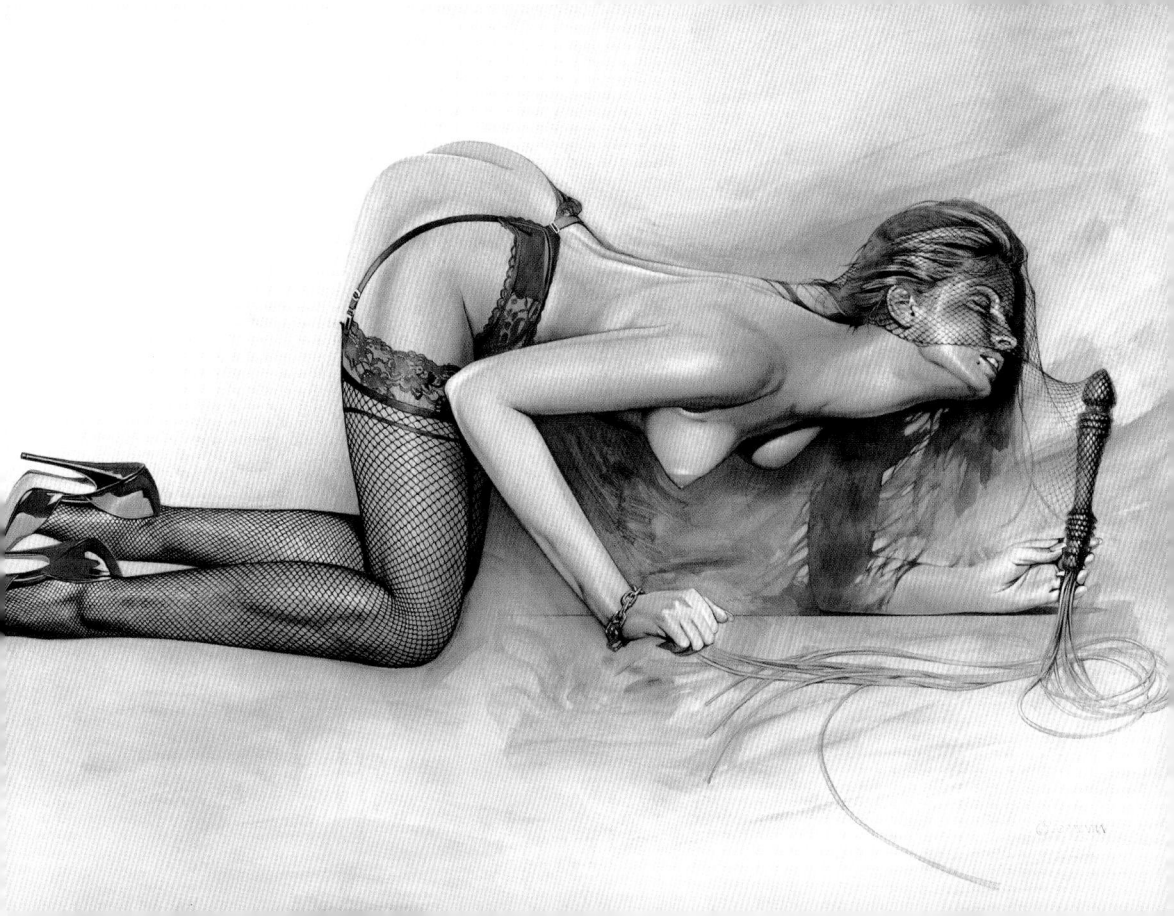

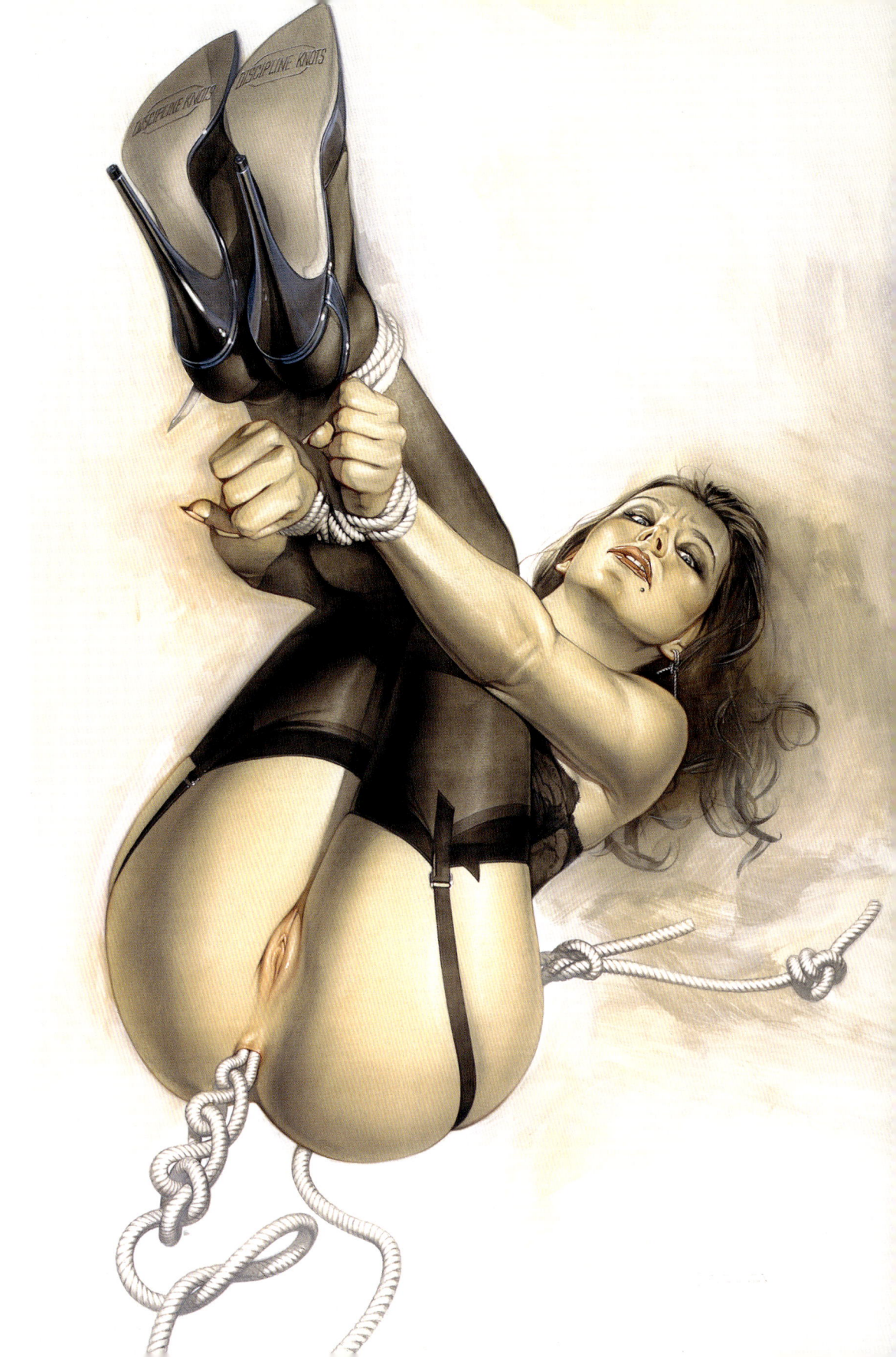

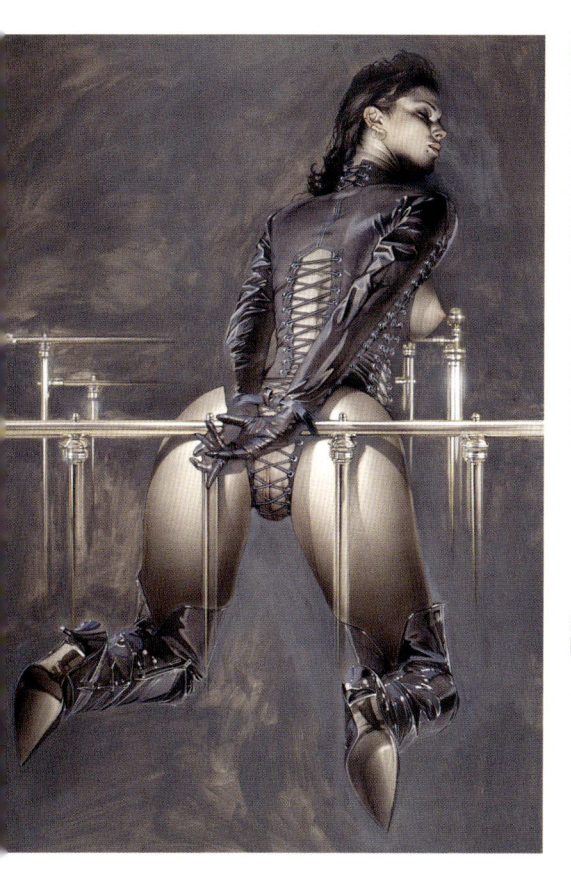
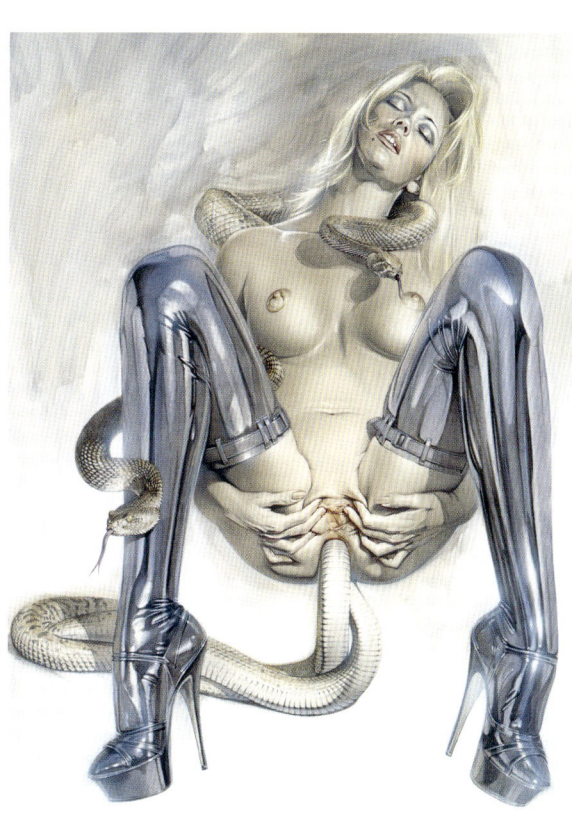
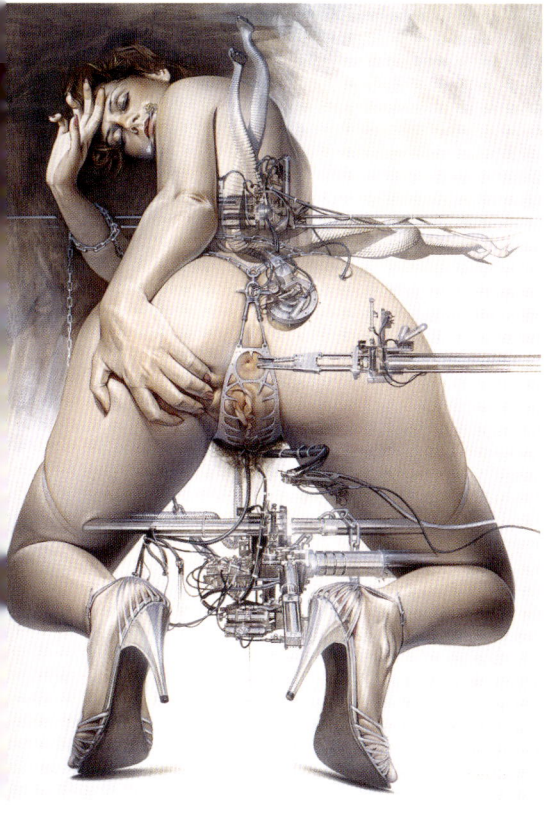
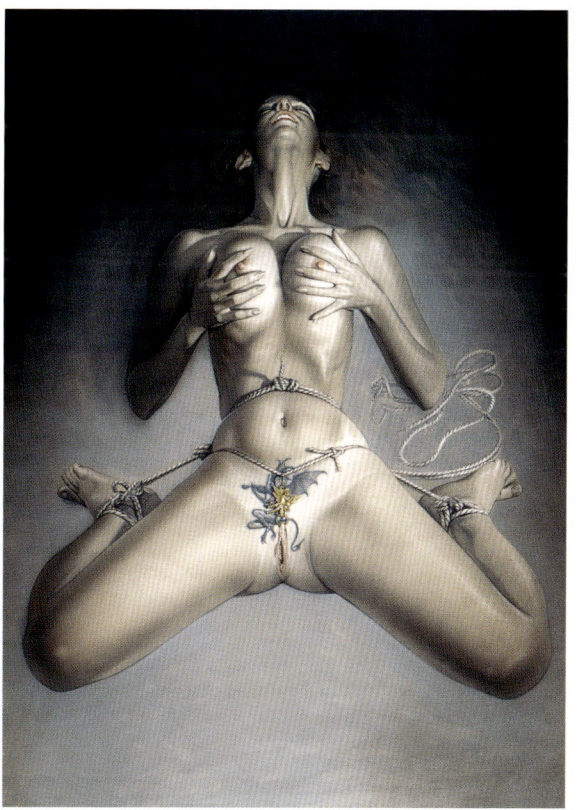

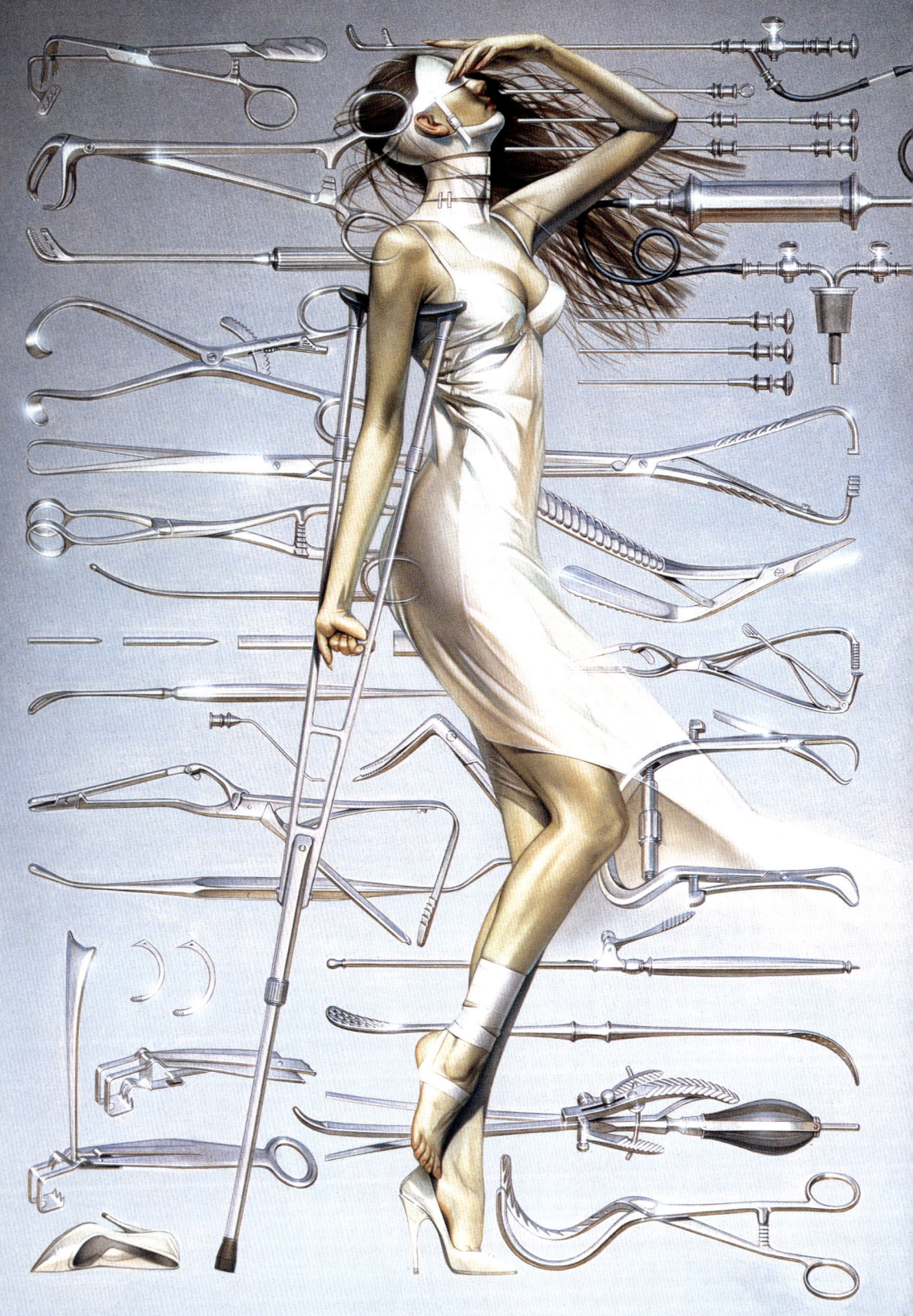

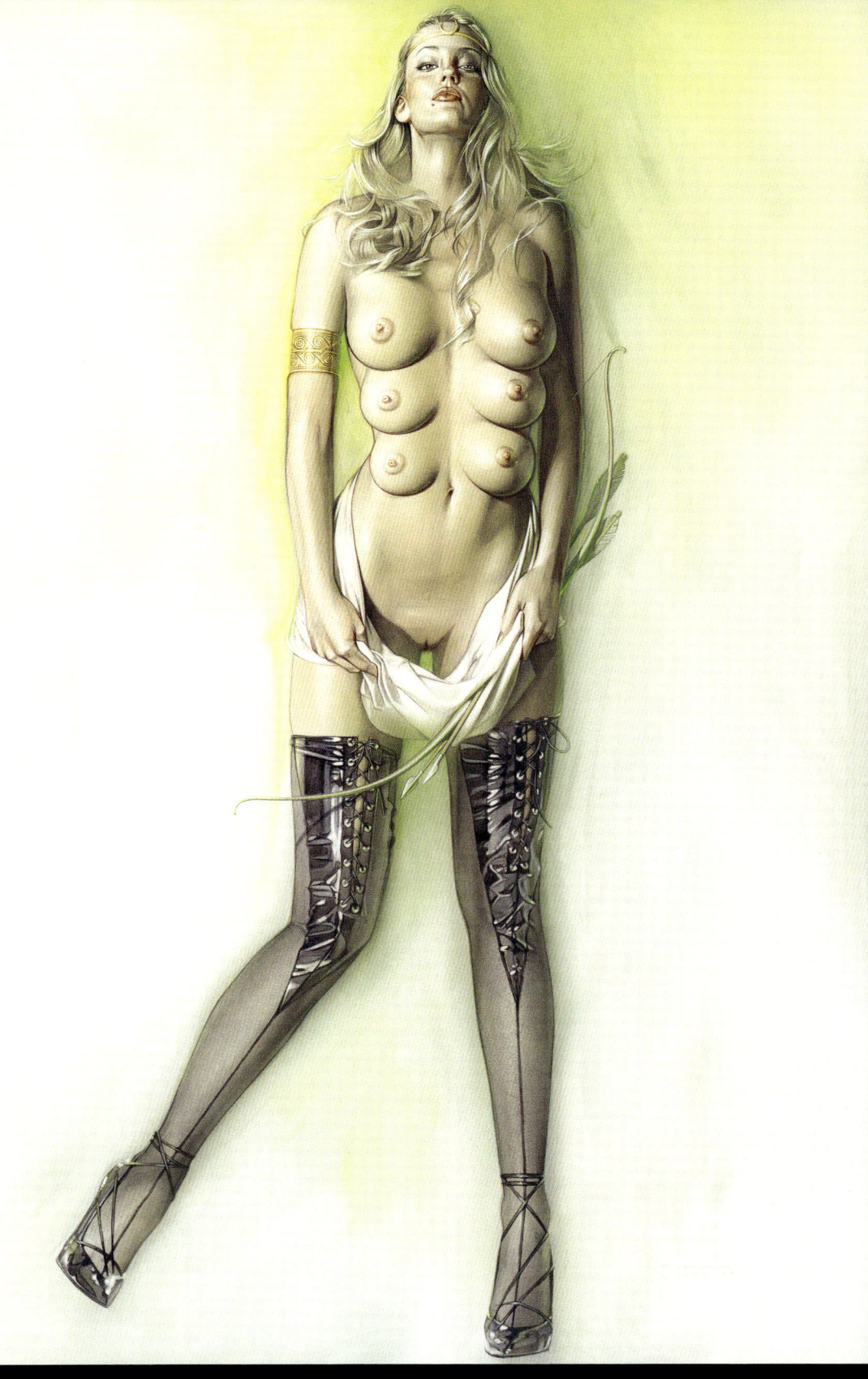

Hajime Sorayama: artist who depicts
powerful women's beauty by using
astonishing tecnics.

Minko Tanaka

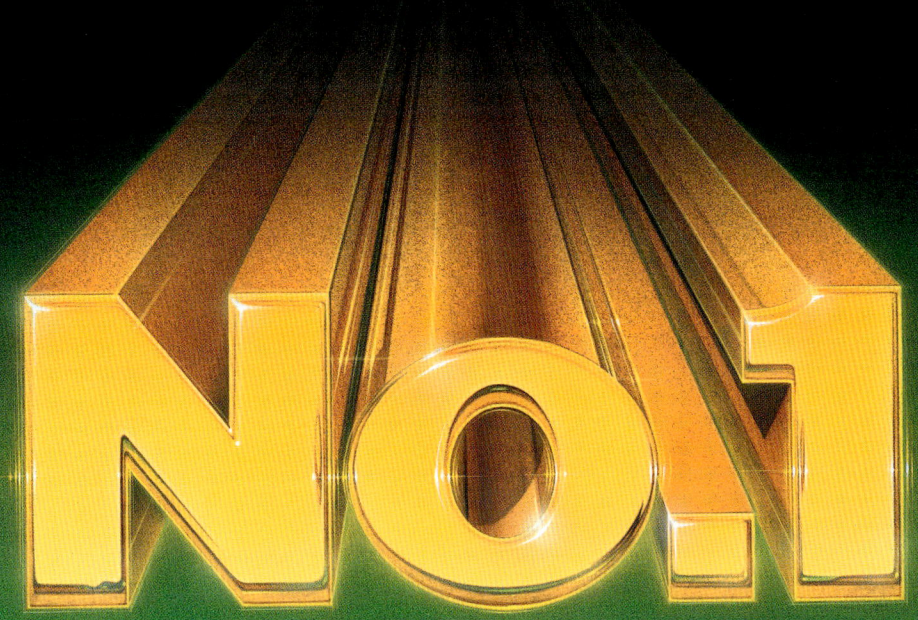

No.1

Olivia De Berardinis (オリビア・デ・ベラルディニス：アーティスト)

I feel a unique kinsip with Hajime. Over the last 25 years we have been working in parallel worlds, crisscrossing between fantasy, pin-up, and erotica. In '94 I finally had the pleasure to meet Hajime in Tokyo. I was having my first shows in Japan and, ironically, he was having his first U.S.show, the very next week, at the *Tamara Bane Gallery*, my US art dealer/publisher/gallery. I have gone from explicit illustration for the sex magazines to pin-up. Hajime had a family and held off his erotic work till his children were adults. We are two ships passing in the night. My husband, Joel, and I have been collecting his books since we found *Sexy Robots* in the early 80's. This book has some of my favorite Sorayama pin-ups. His molding of cold, reflective metal and forging it into warm, flirtatious images, combined with flesh, this was sheer brilliance to me. I also love the sense of humor which permeates his work. And I get great joy from his animals, the attention to detail, particularly the ones with chrome genitalia.

I was amused recently when I was looking at his book, *NAGA*, among a group of people. The work was so beautiful, some concepts pushed the audience over the edge. I was amused. I somehow enjoy this, in my own perverse way. I think art should push the boundaries, push buttons. This is ultimately what makes it interesting. It forces a reaction, good or bad.

Once I get past the initial "wow" of the painting, the concept, the execution, and the success of it, I get into the inner workings, the details, which I identify with in my own work. There is this Zen-like place where rendering and painting is done in a trance state where time ceases to exist. I enjoy imagining his pencil, stroking incessantly, maddeningly, delicately on the paper, a form of insanity, the fight for total control of all the elements it takes to make a successful work of art. This struggle is what I find most erotic in his paintings; his delicate touch and how he obsesses everything into perfection, a form of masturbation, something all artists could be accused of. Sorayama has already gotten us to stare at the sensuous shine of his metal, the maddening reflections in the boot. Now, he is almost violently pushing us into sensing what the flesh does when it is impaled with heavy pneumatic plumbing, gadgets, jewelry, penises, horns, stitching, all done hyper realistically. It twists my brain. Pushing taboos, painting them so beautifully, the subversive, the perverse, nearly escape my attention, but only for a moment.

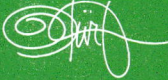

松本秀実 (アーティスト)

驚異的勃起持続力に脱帽！
— 惚けた —
松本秀実

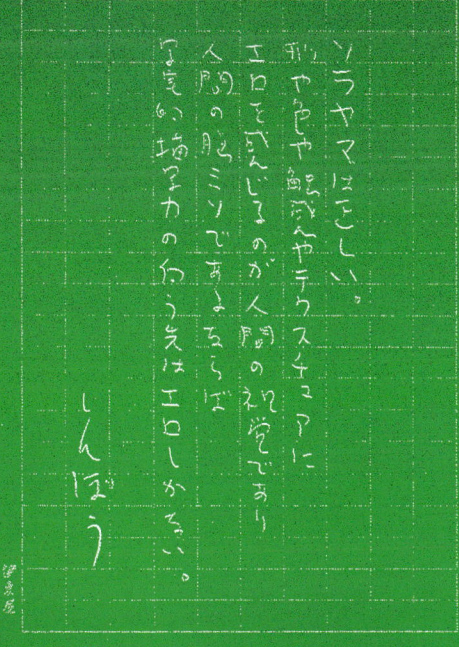

ソラヤマはこい、
私や色や触感やテクスチュアに
エロを感じるのが人間の初覚であり
人間の脳ミソであるならば
宮山の塗力の向うえはエロしかない。

しんぼう

空山脩

ILLUSTRATOR 南 伸坊

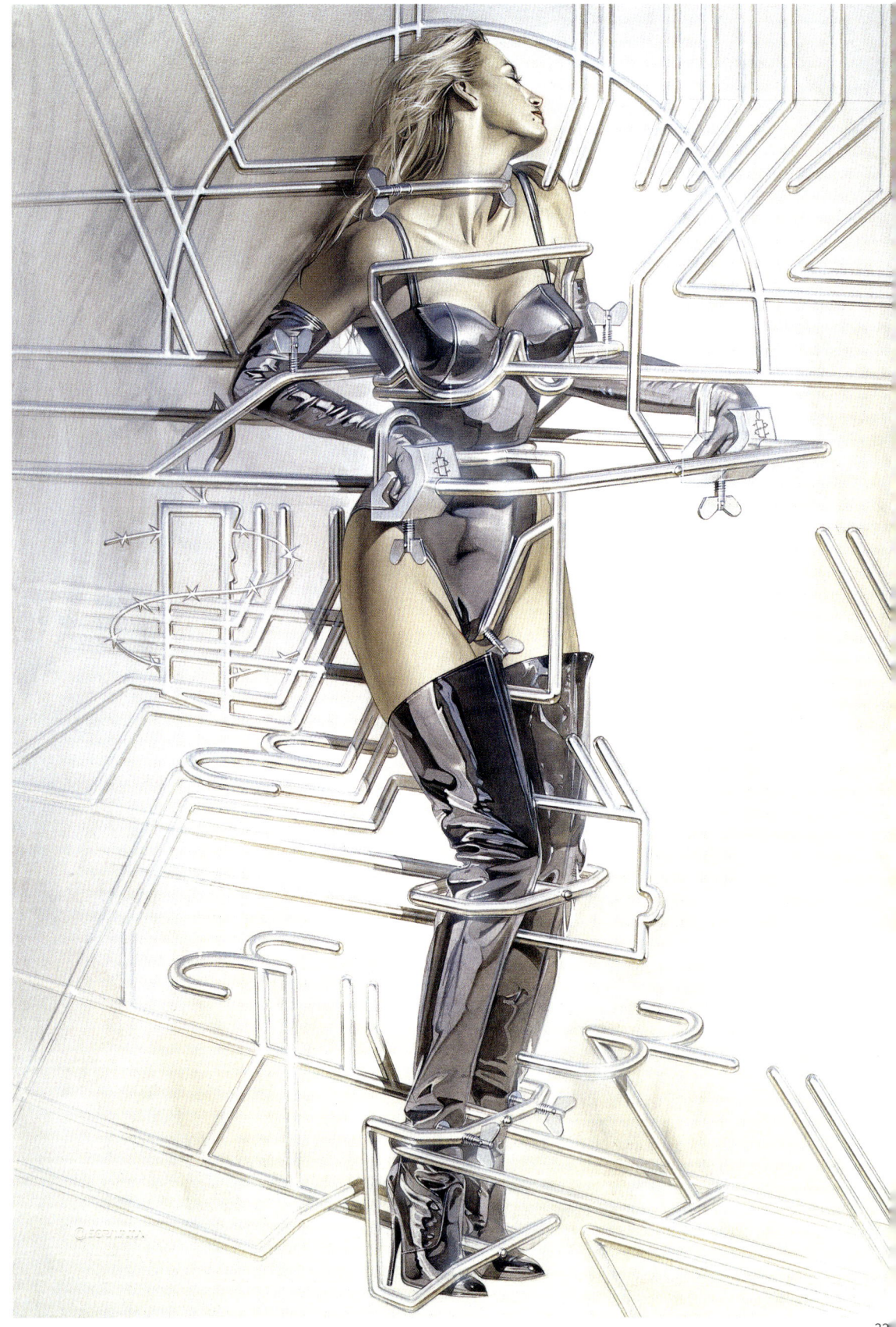

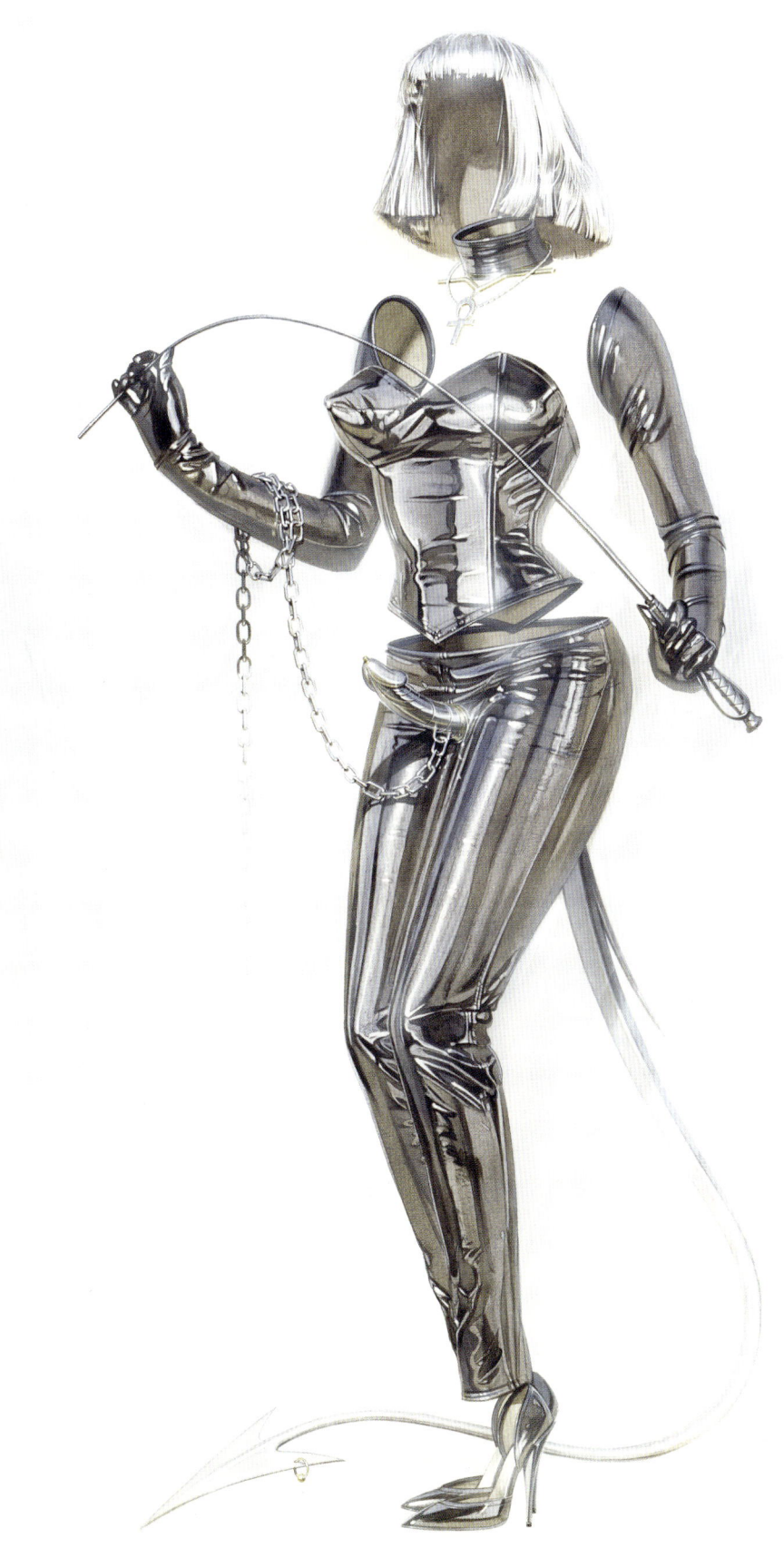

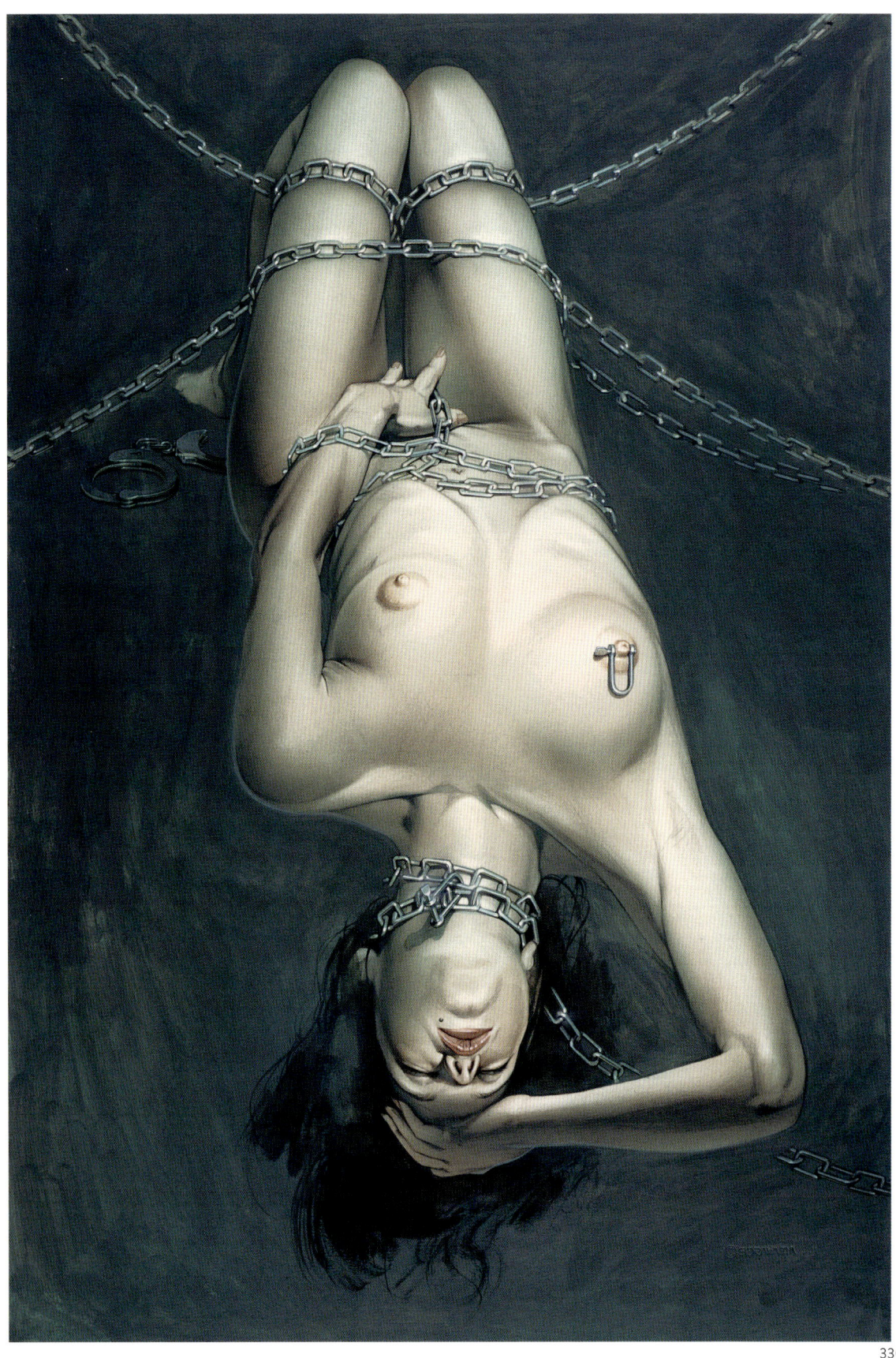

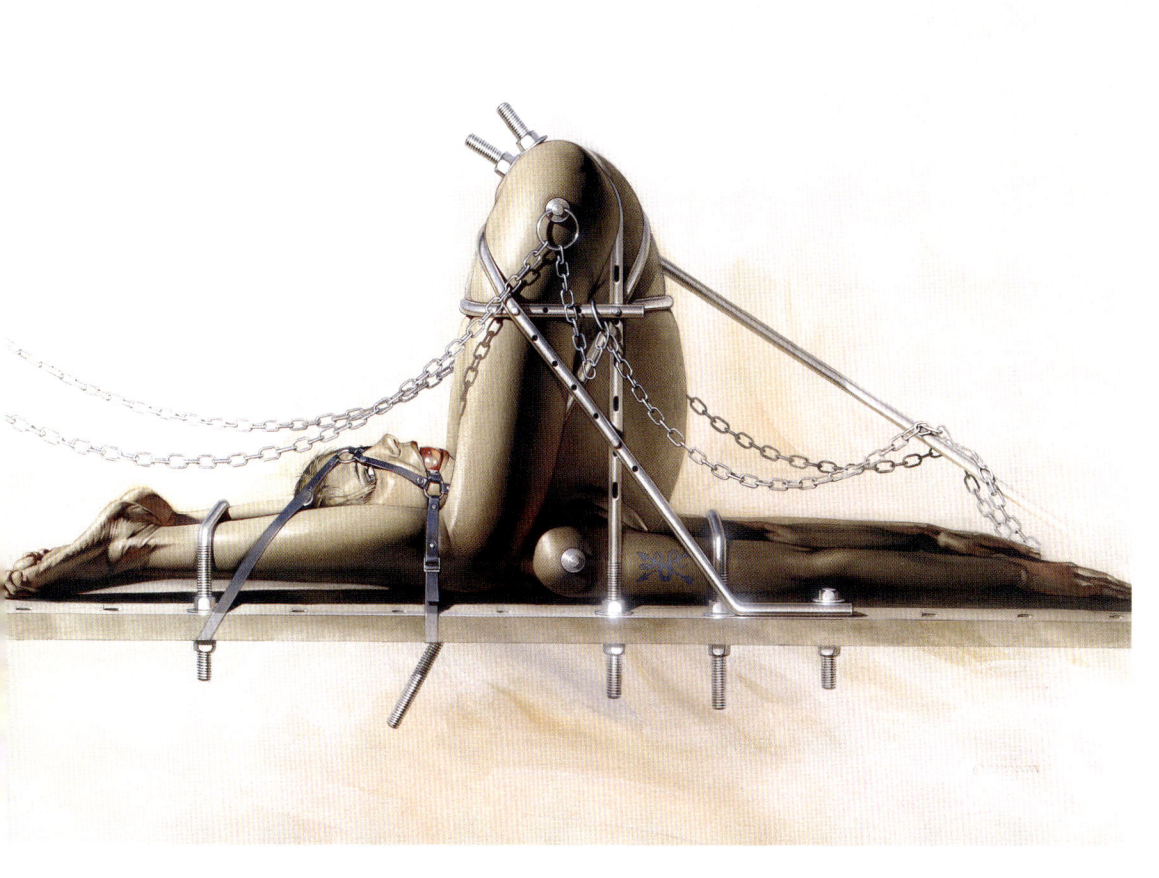

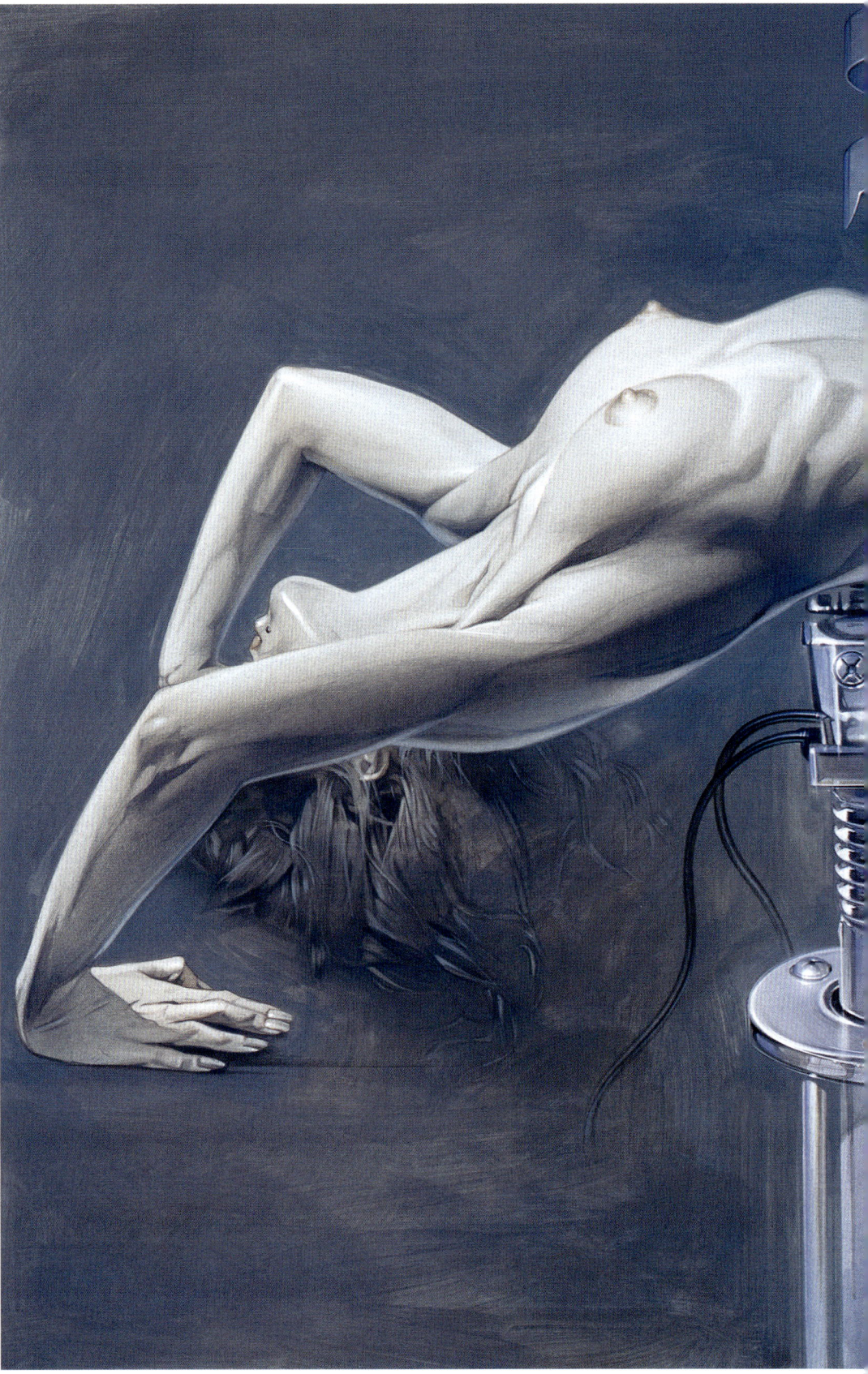

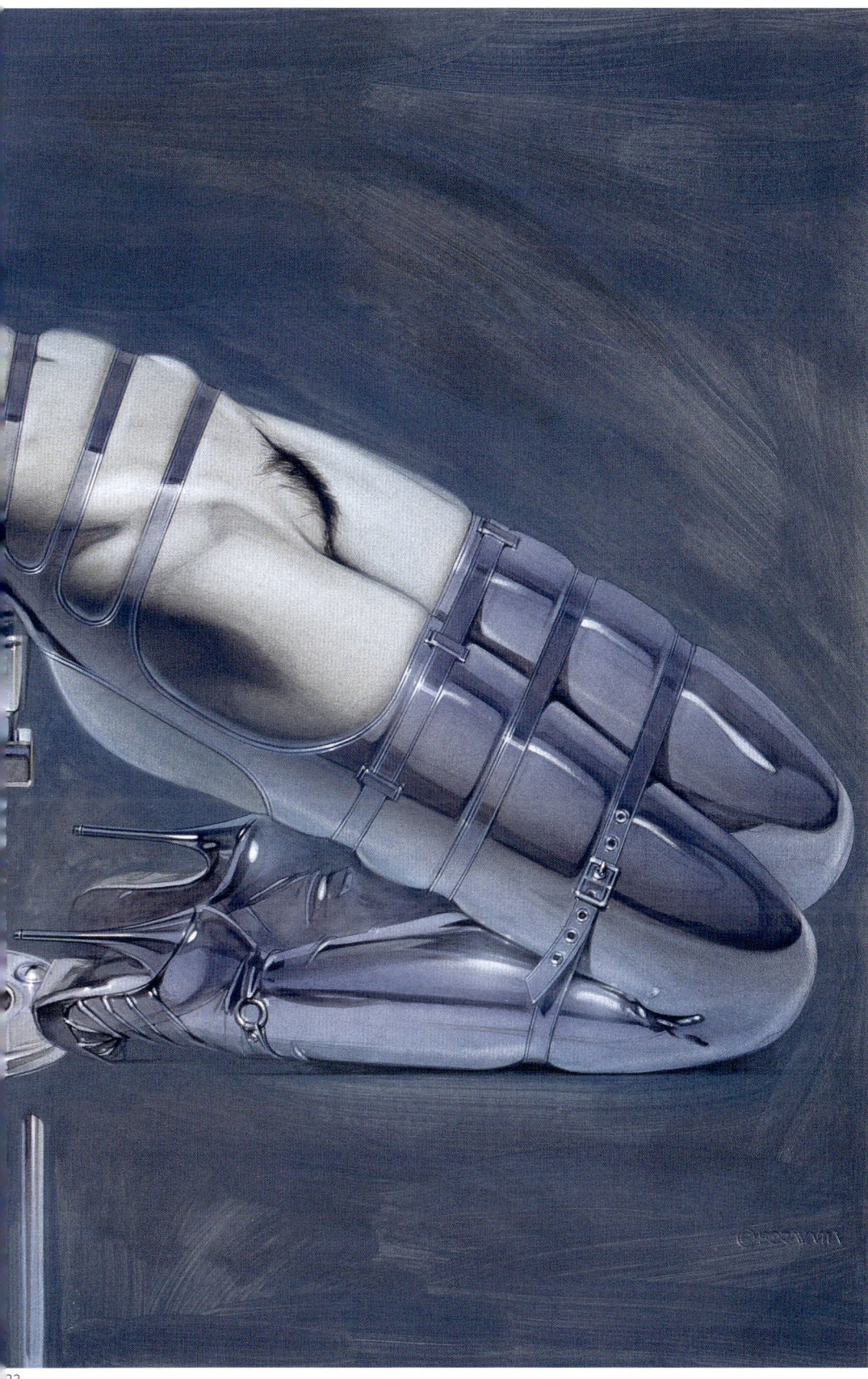

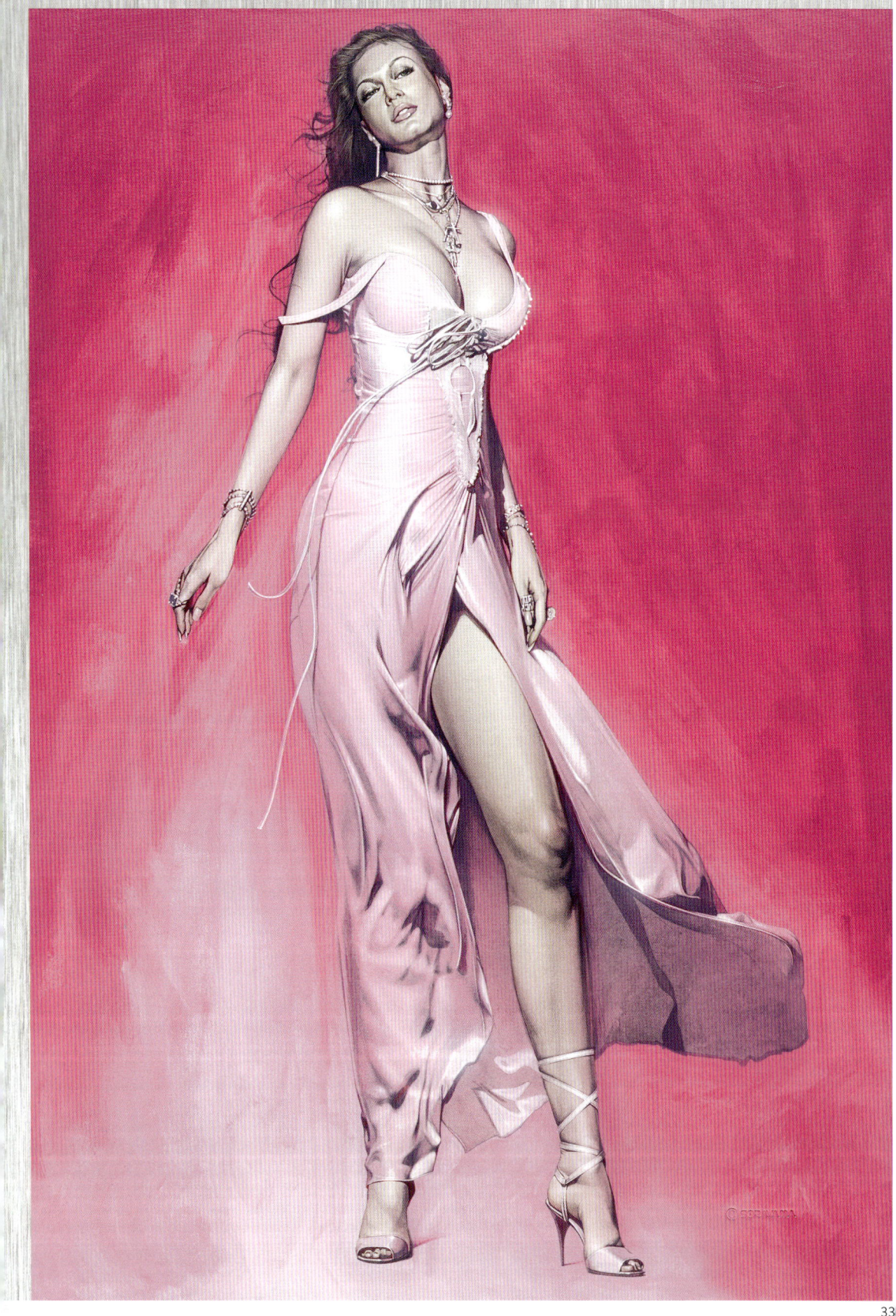

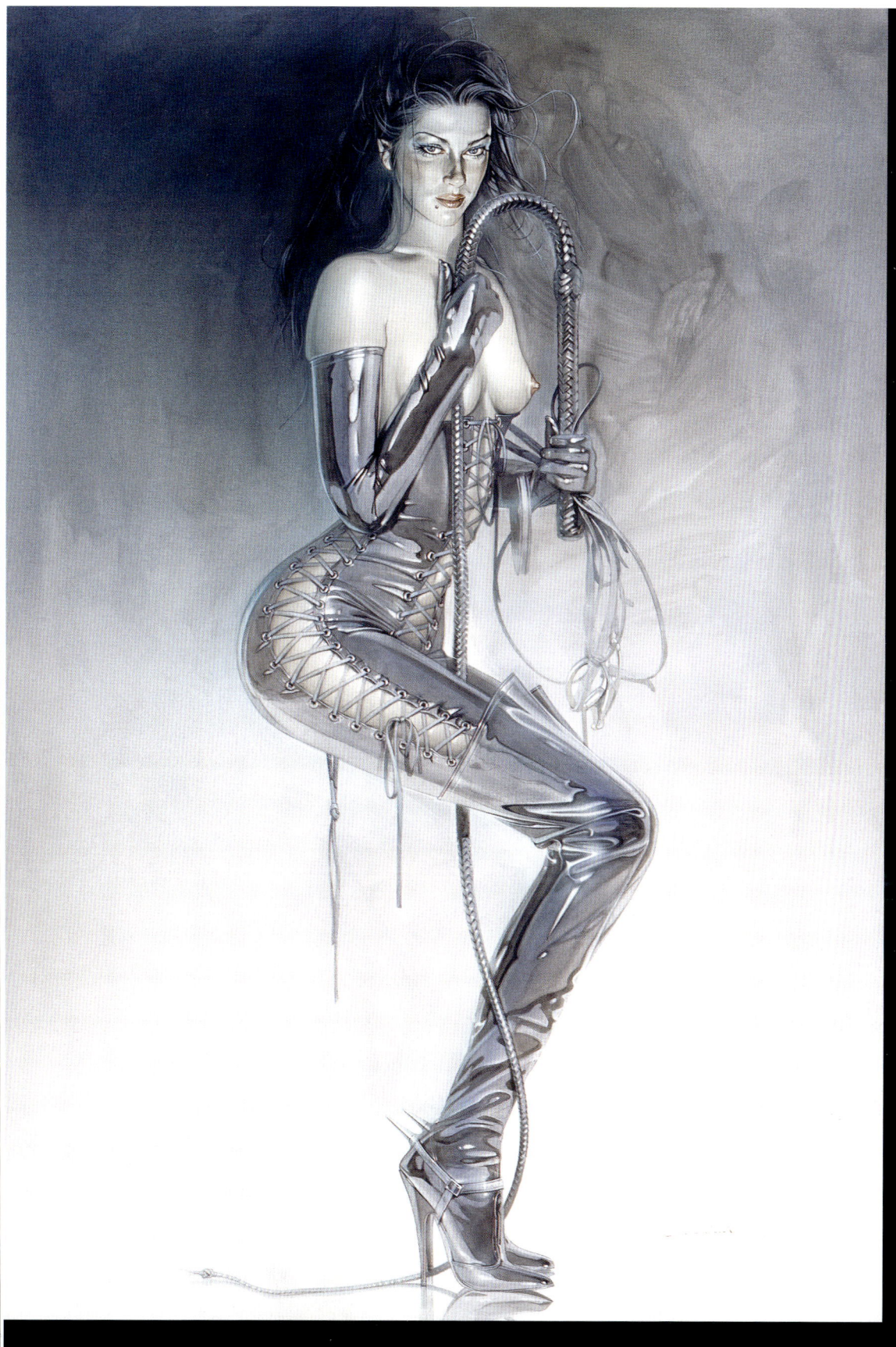

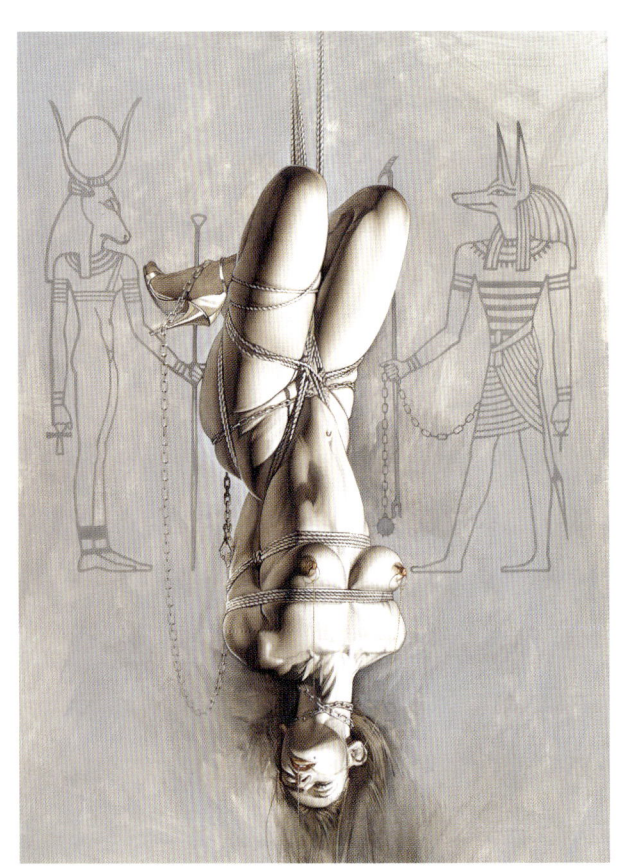
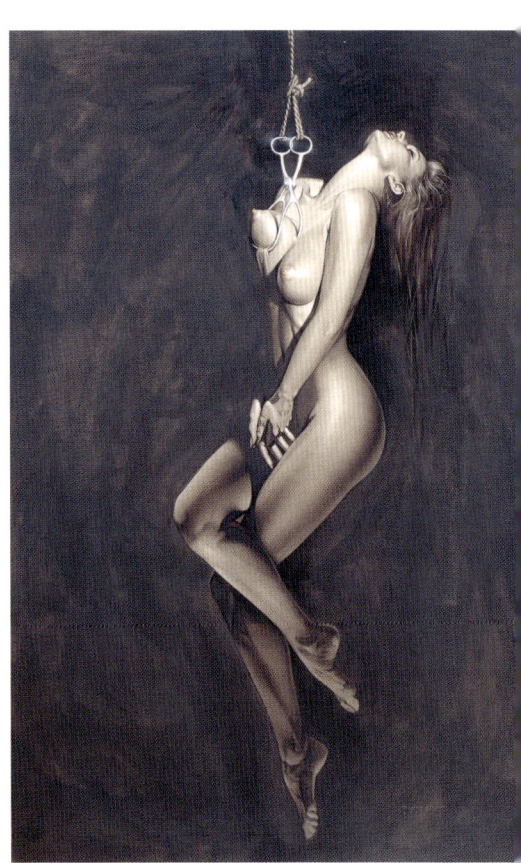

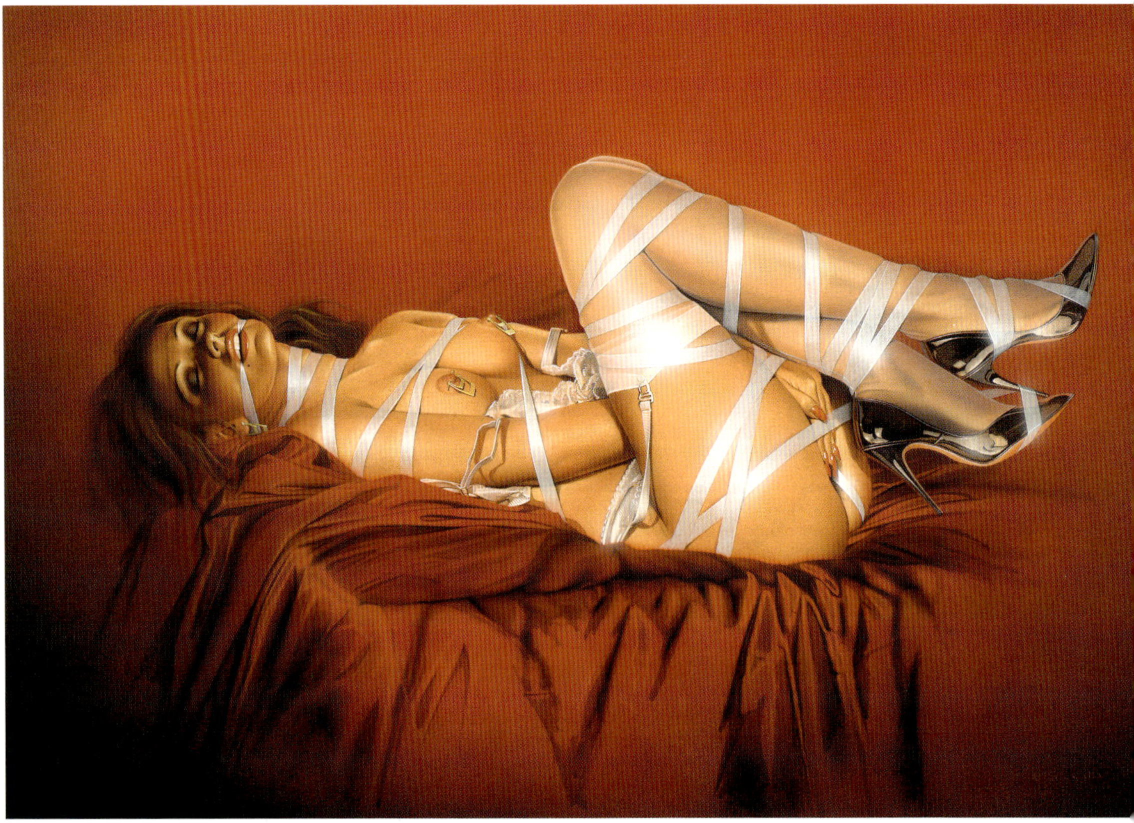

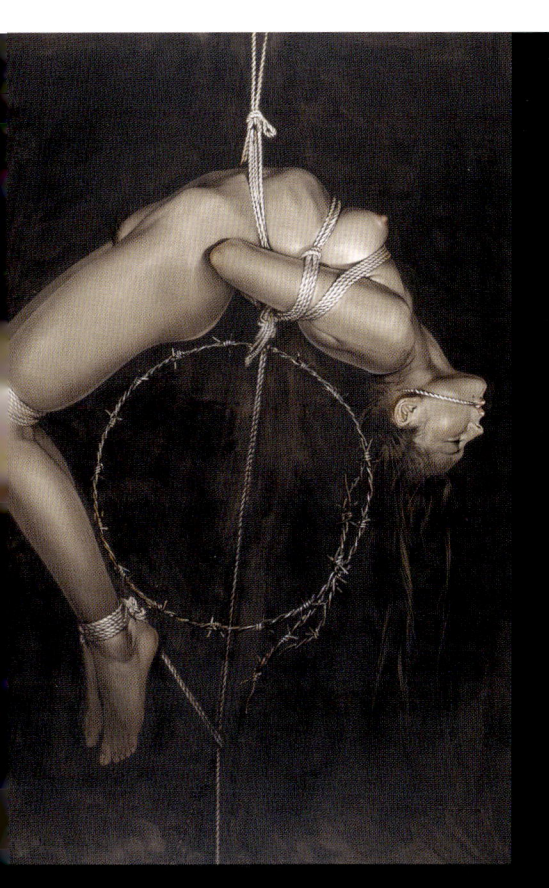
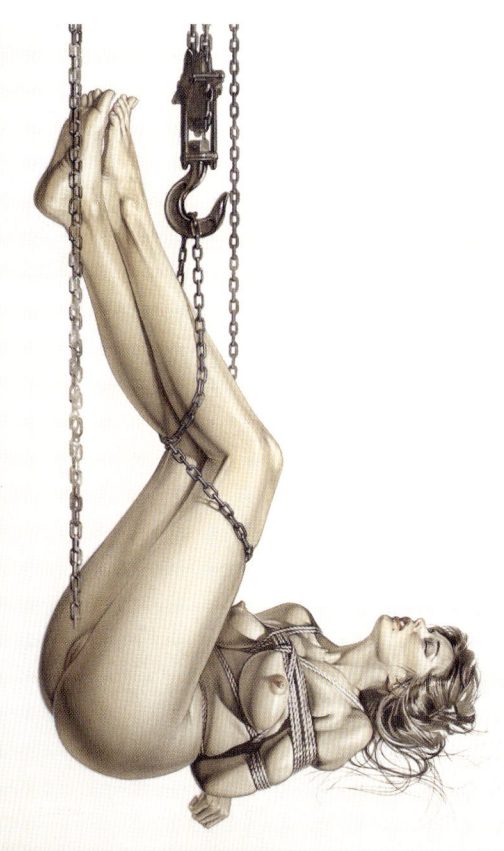

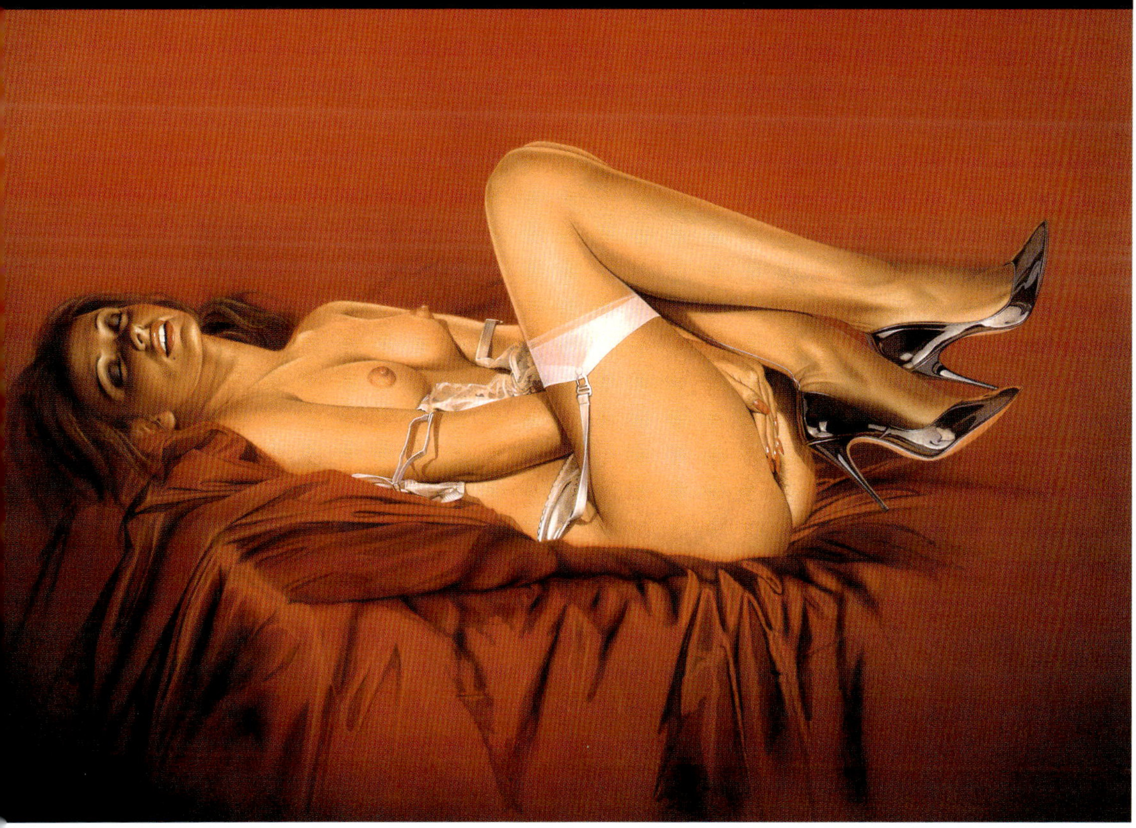

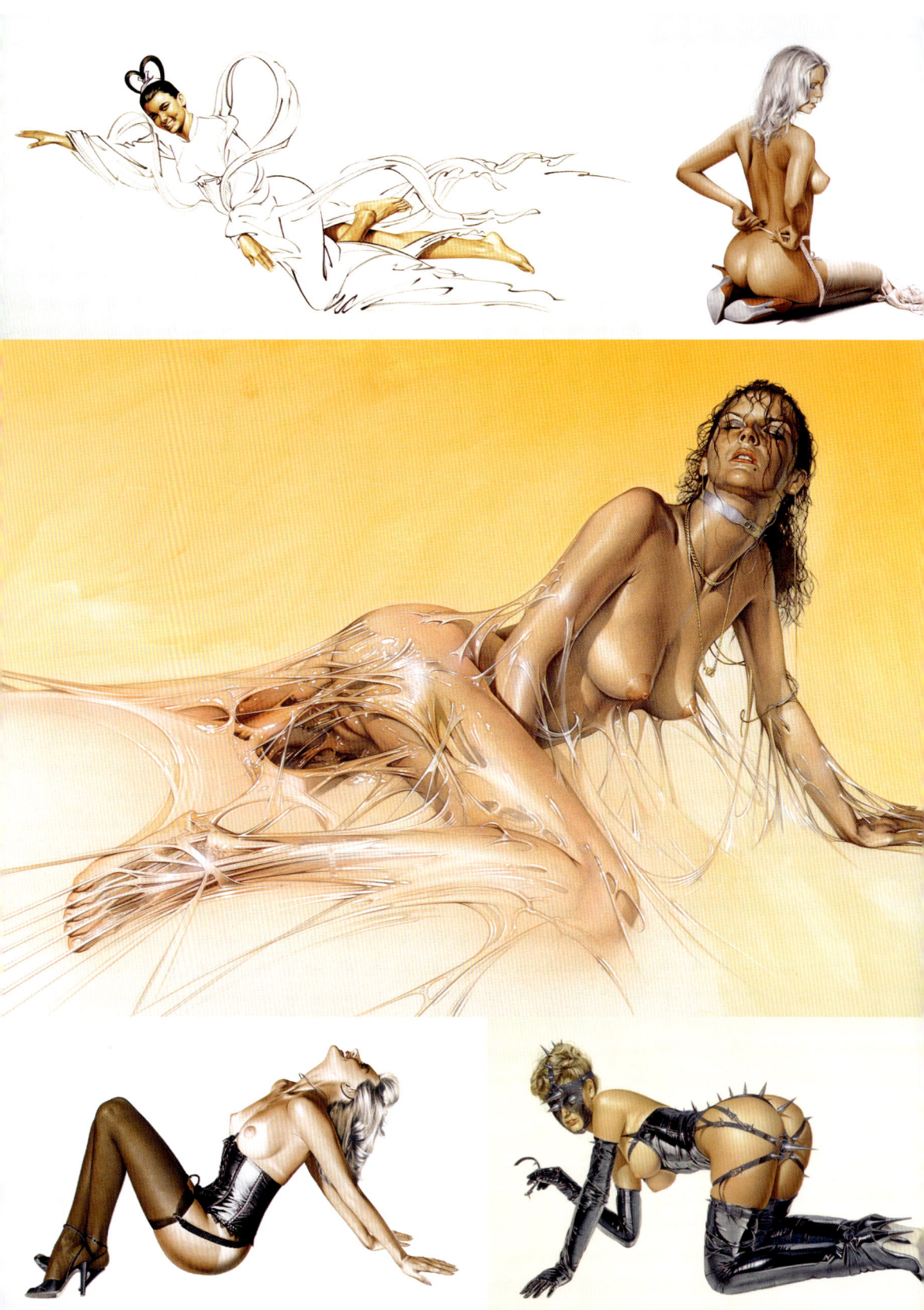

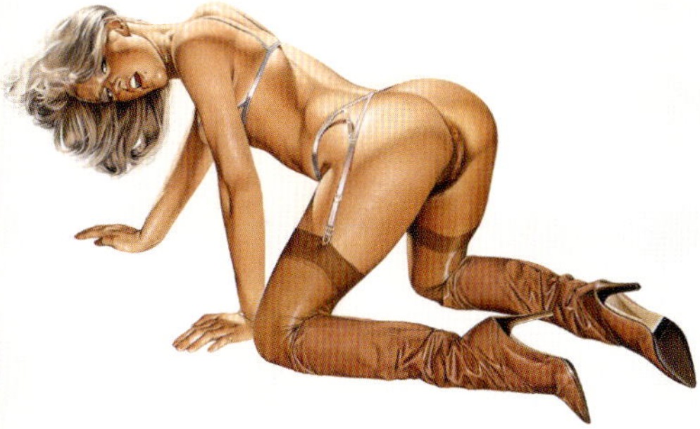

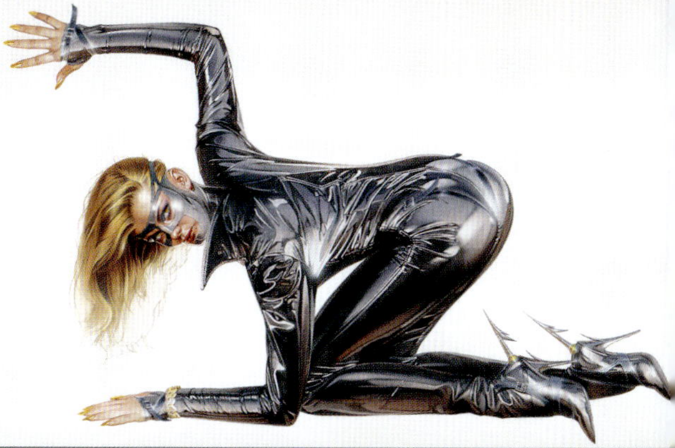

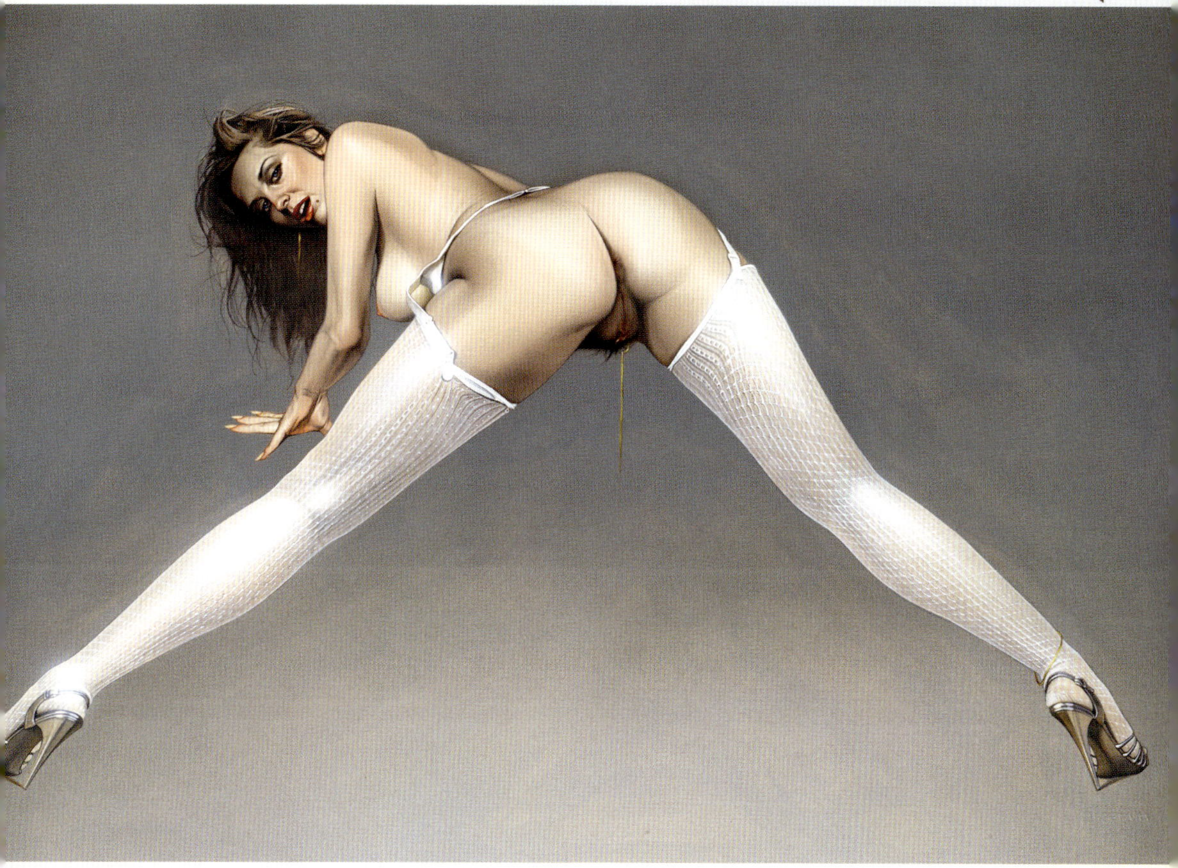

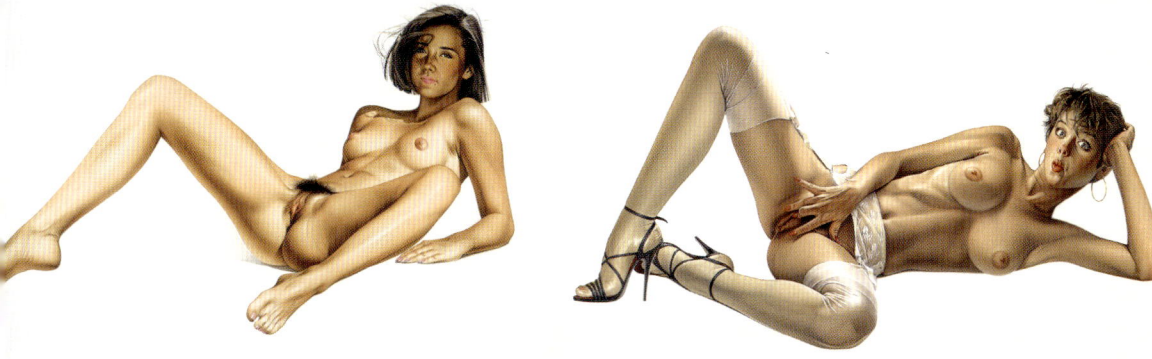

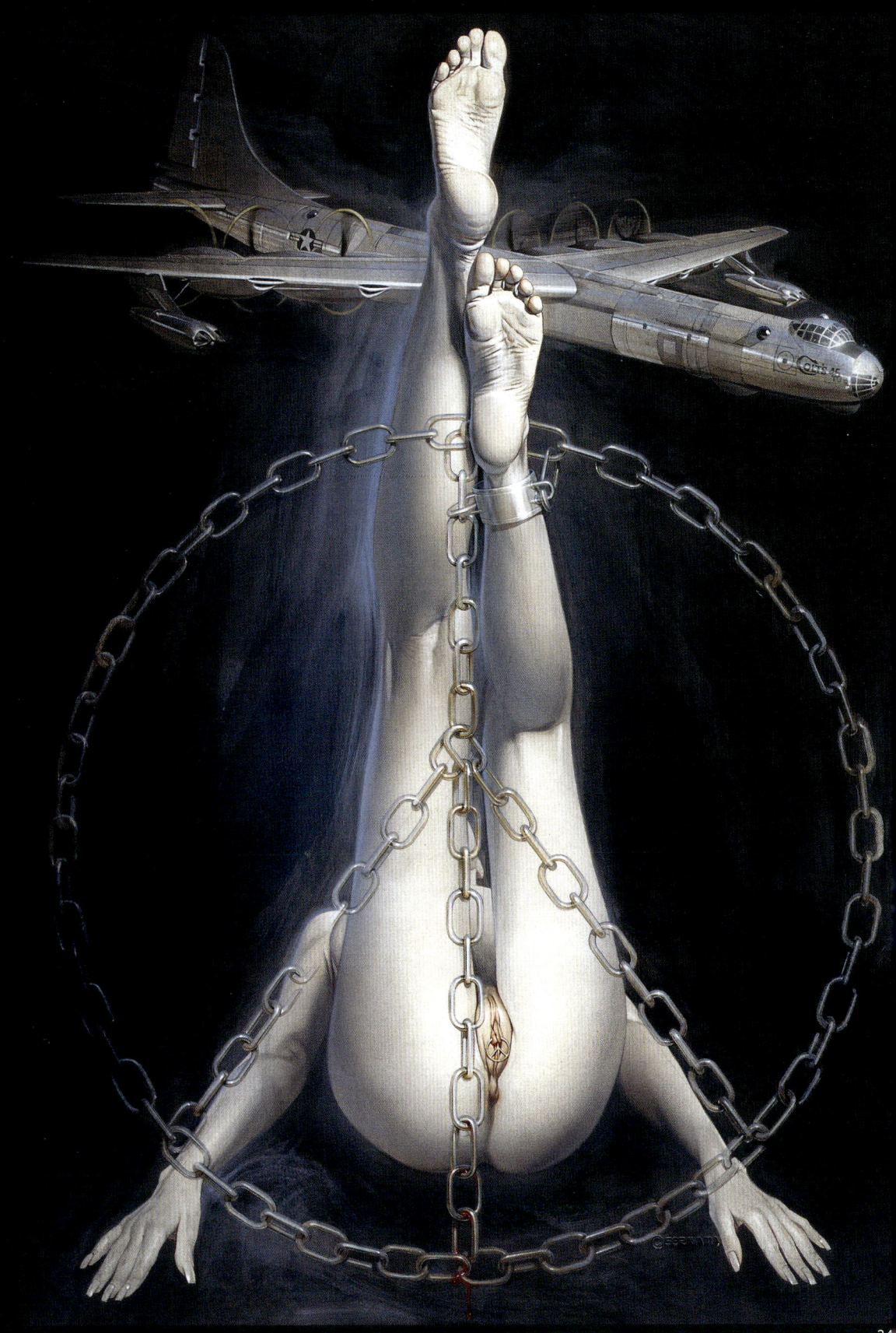

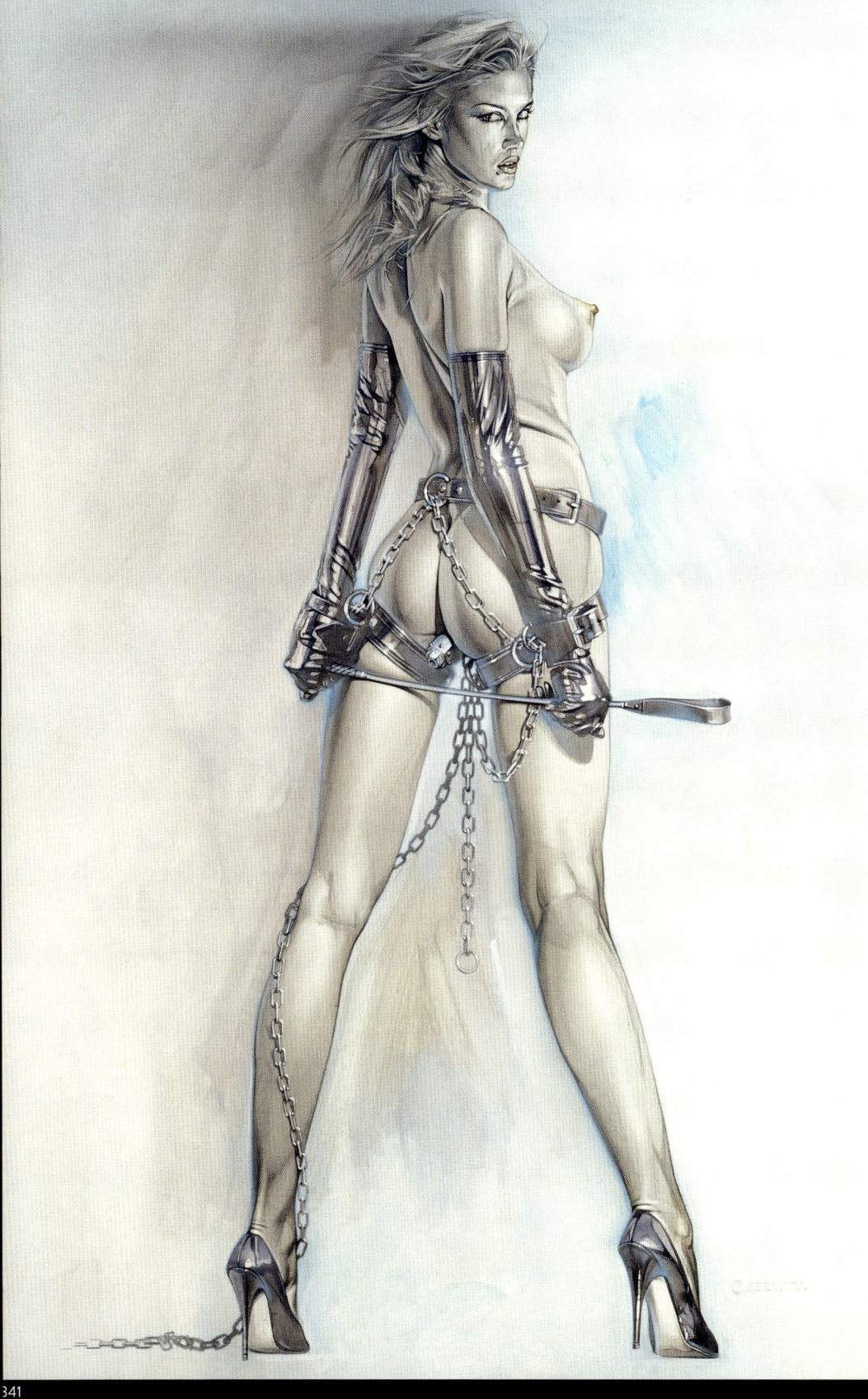

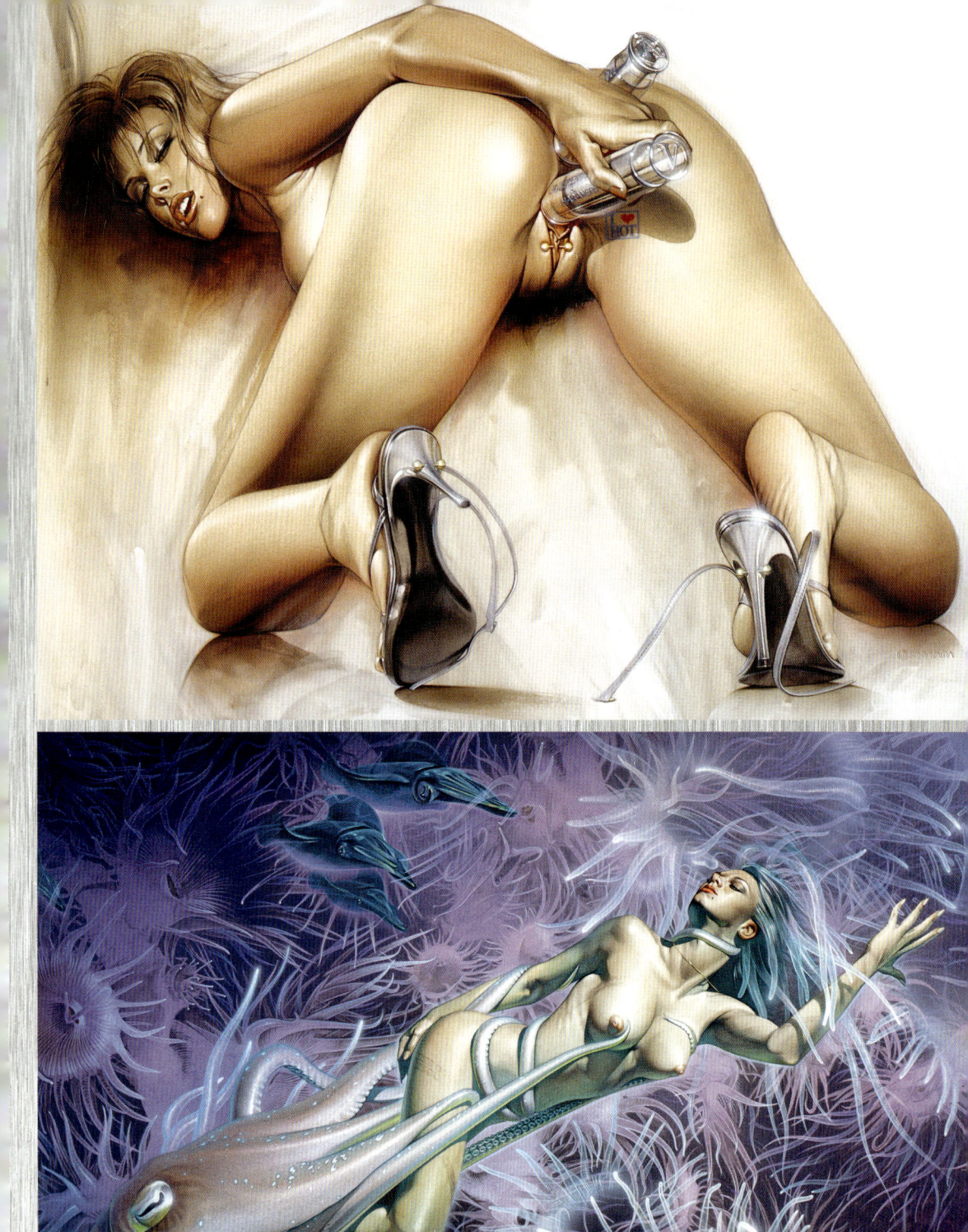

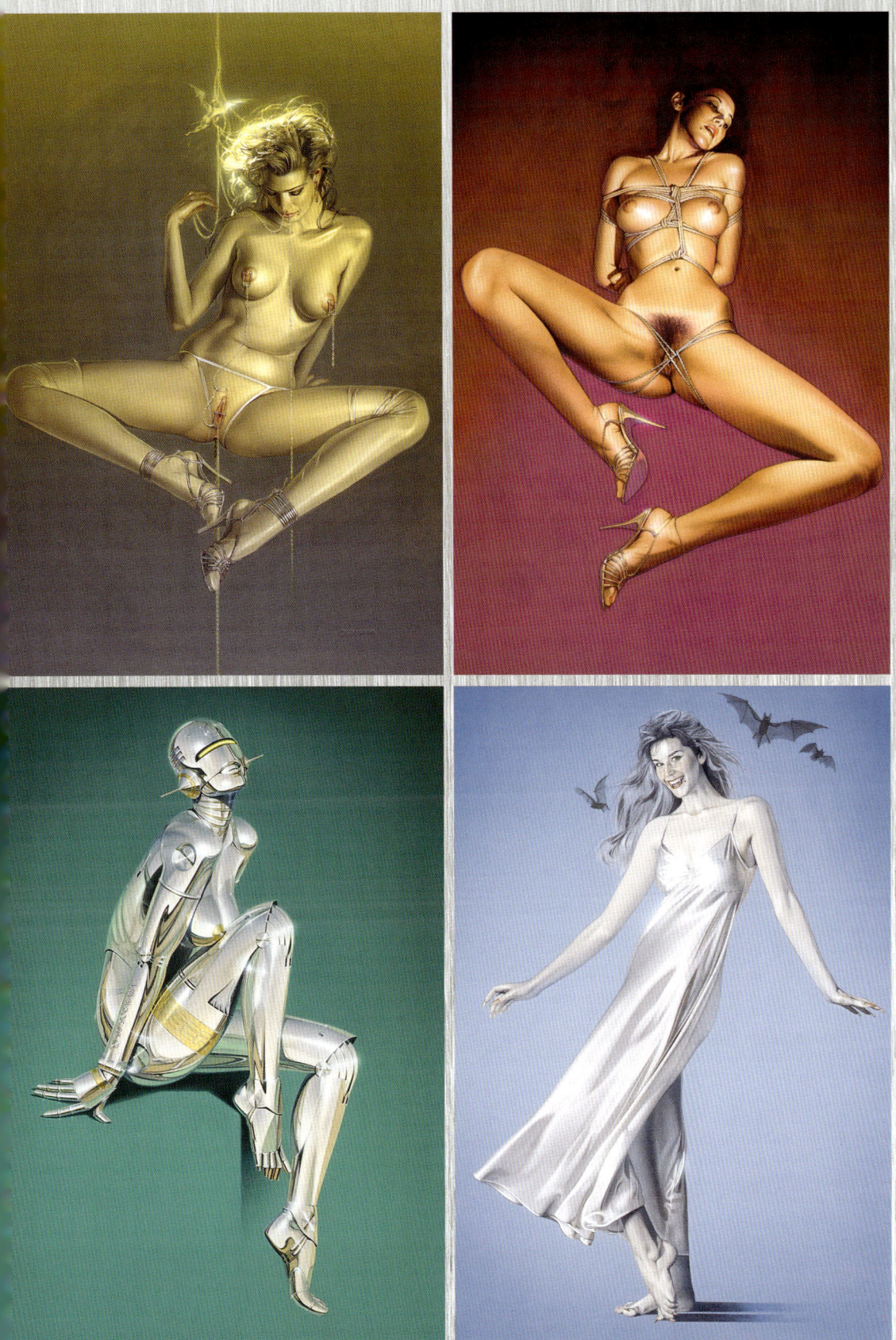

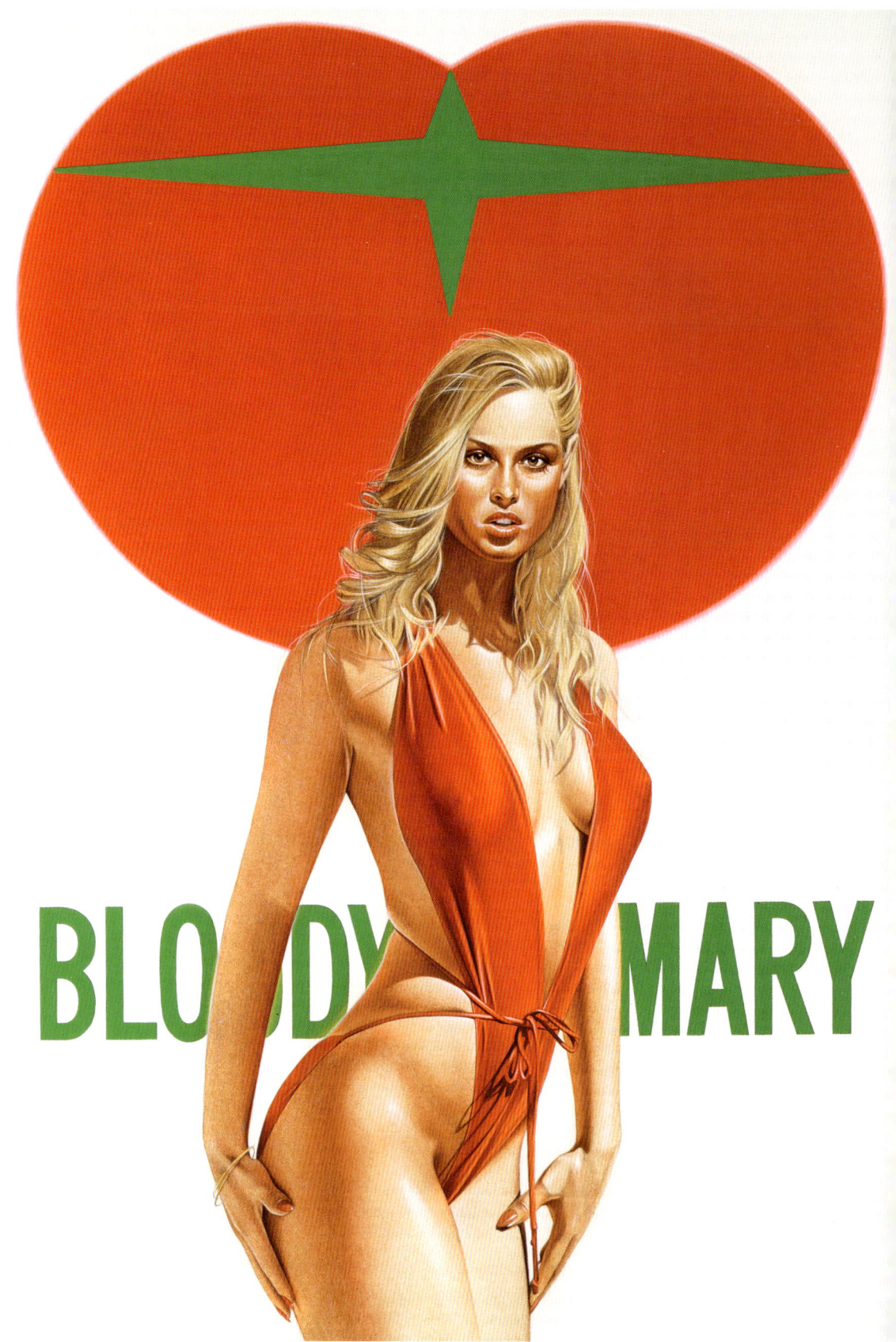

BLOODY MARY

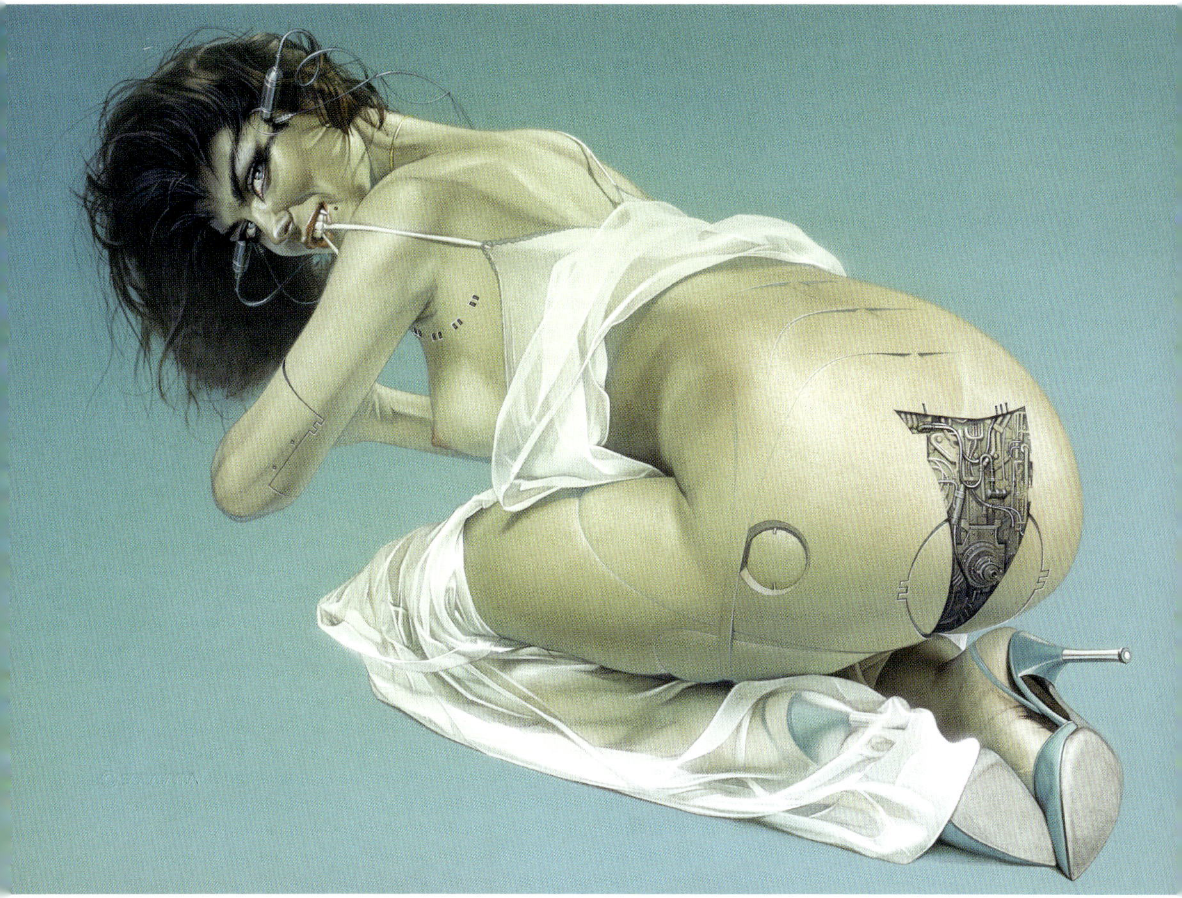

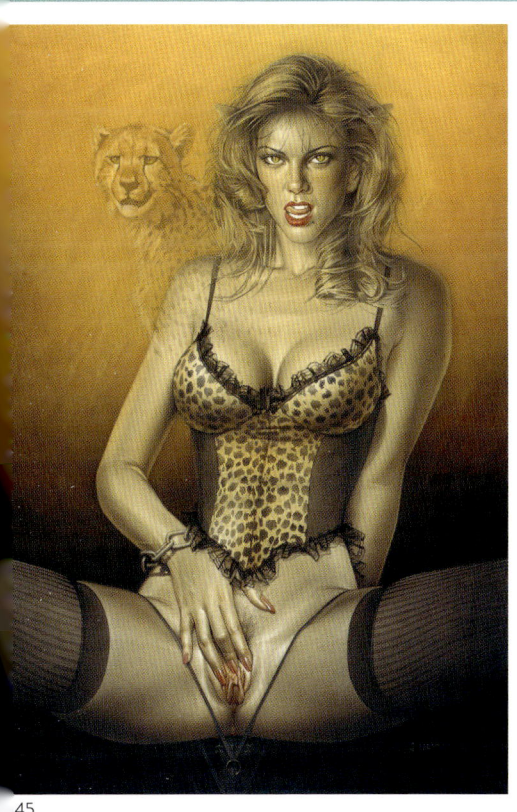

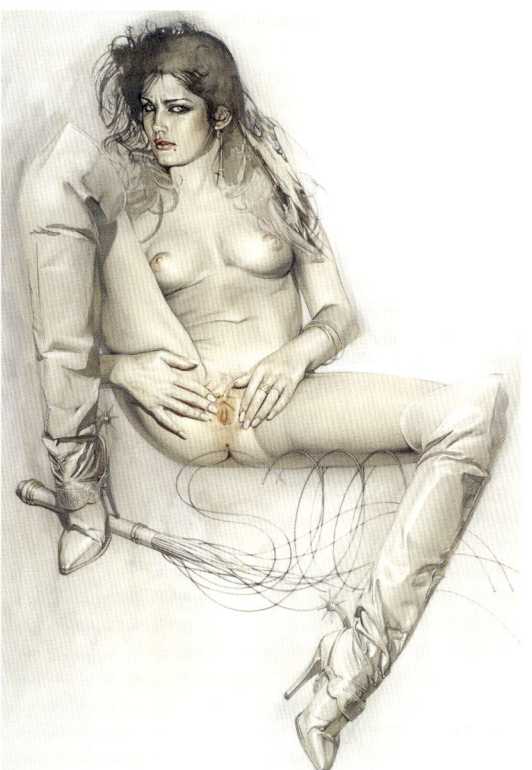

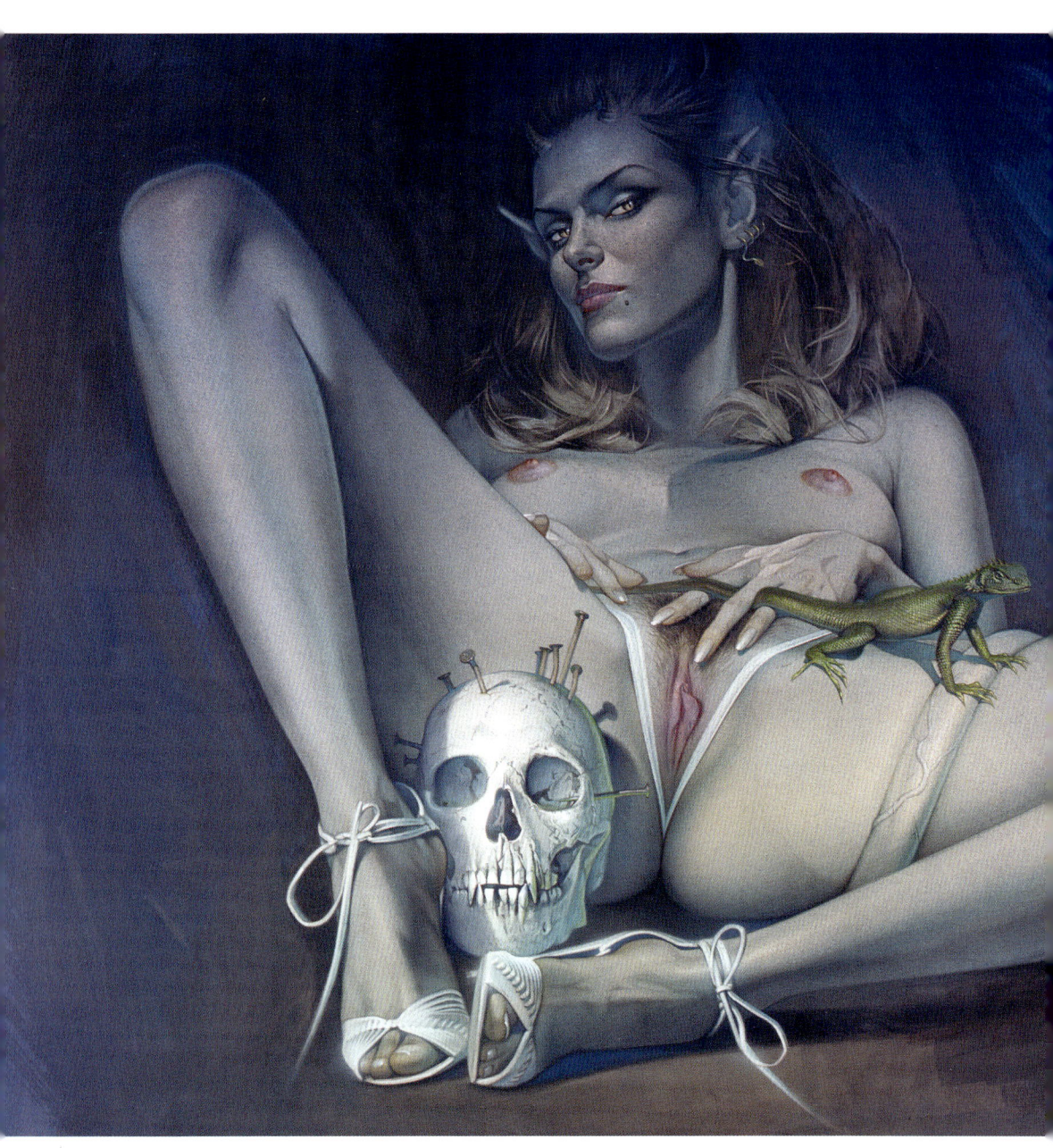

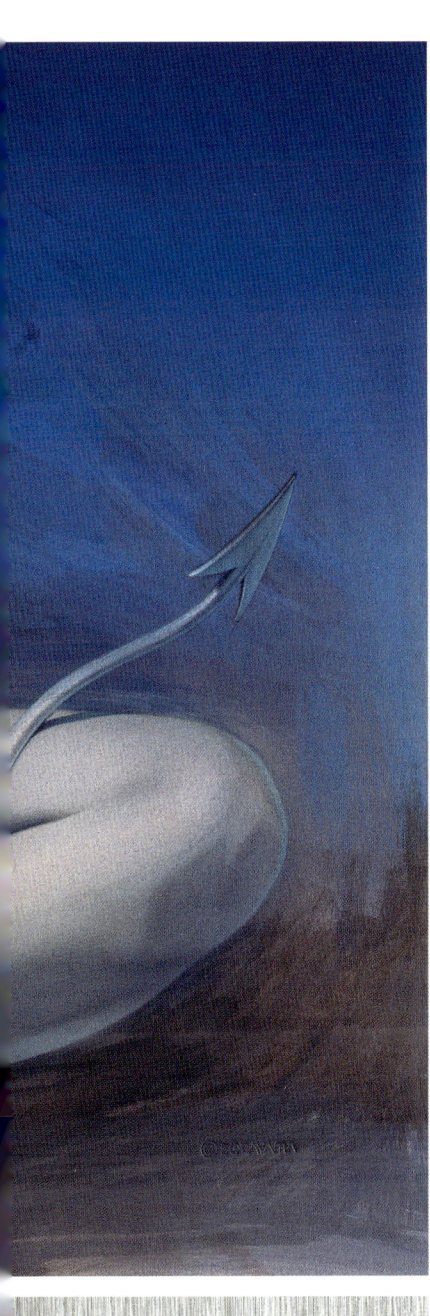

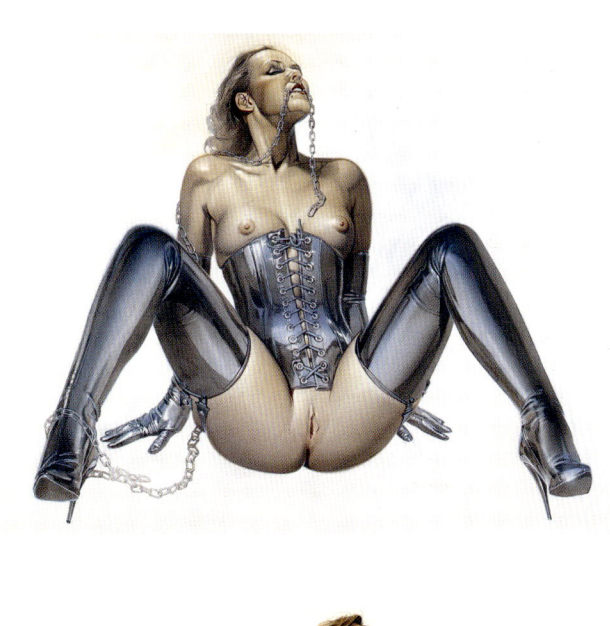

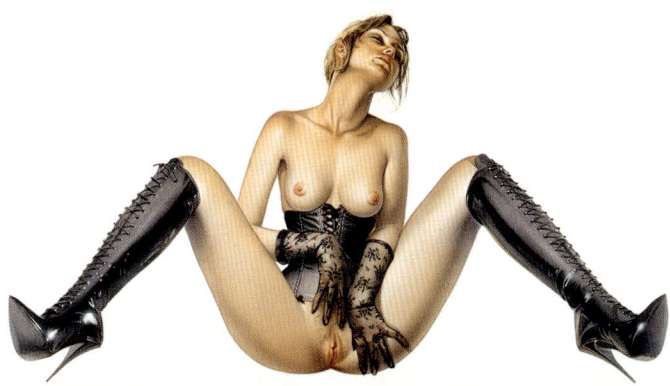

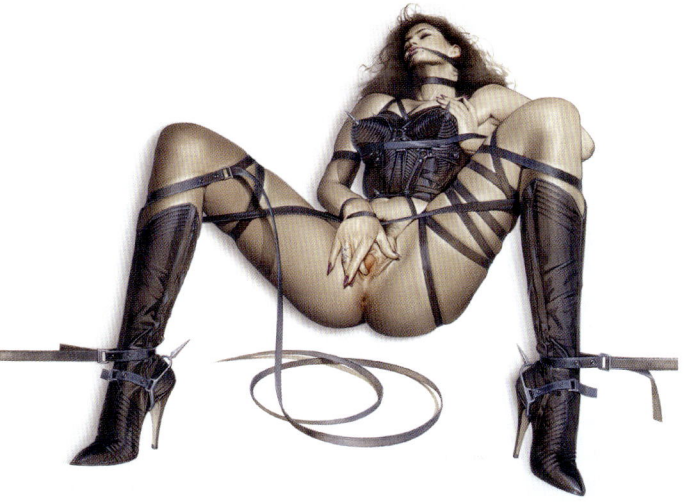

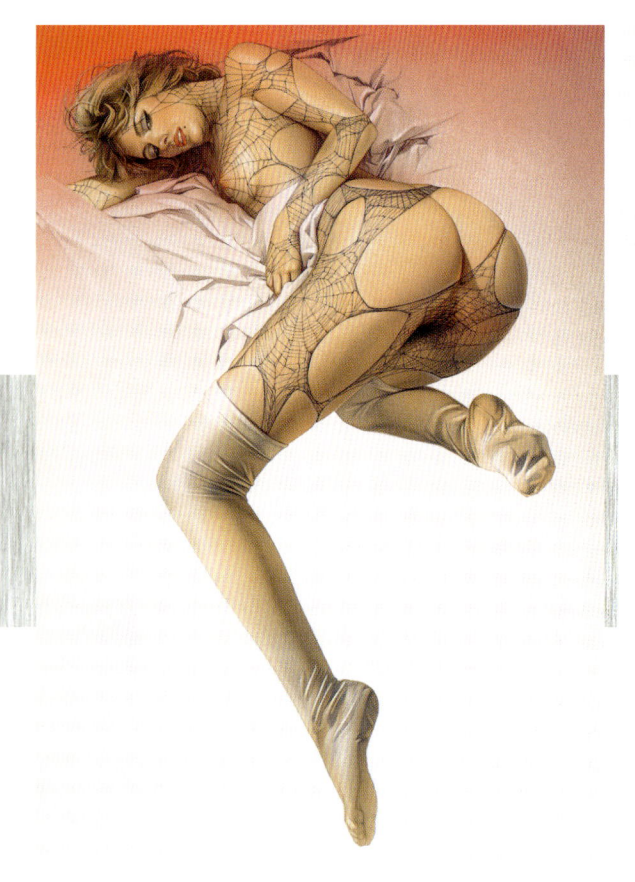
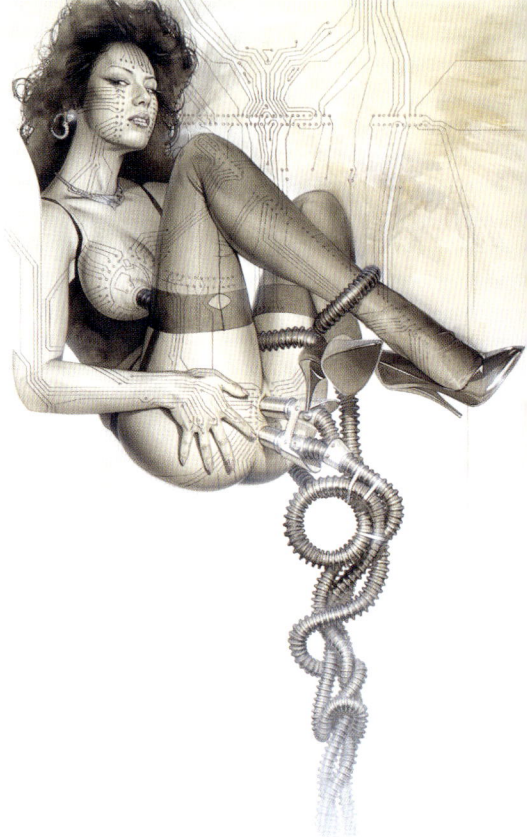

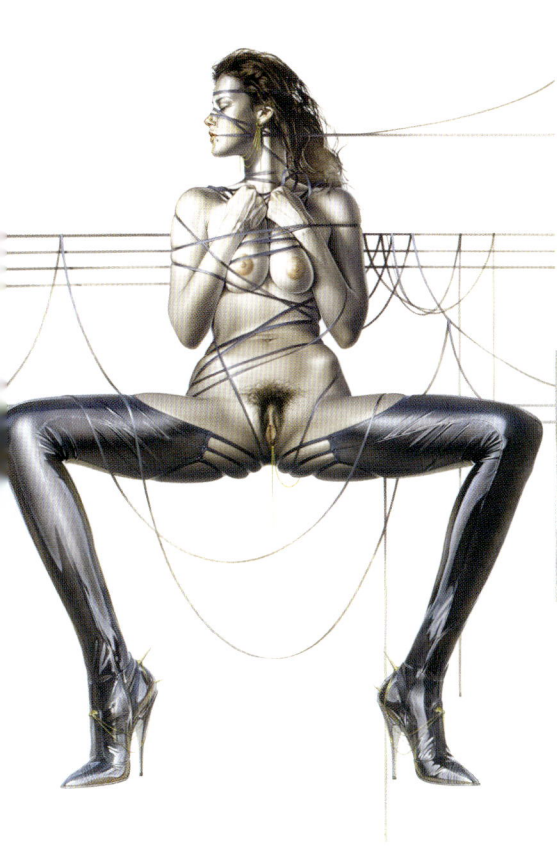

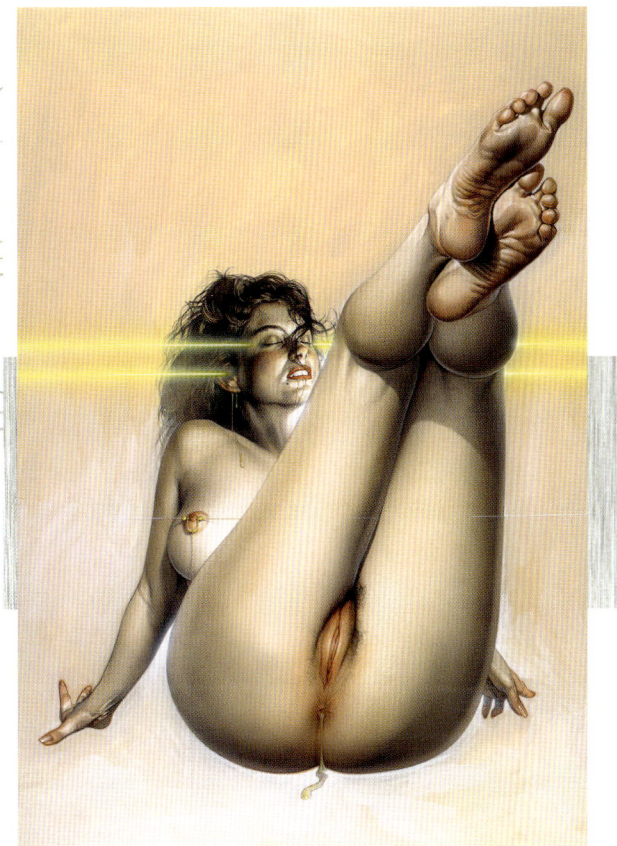

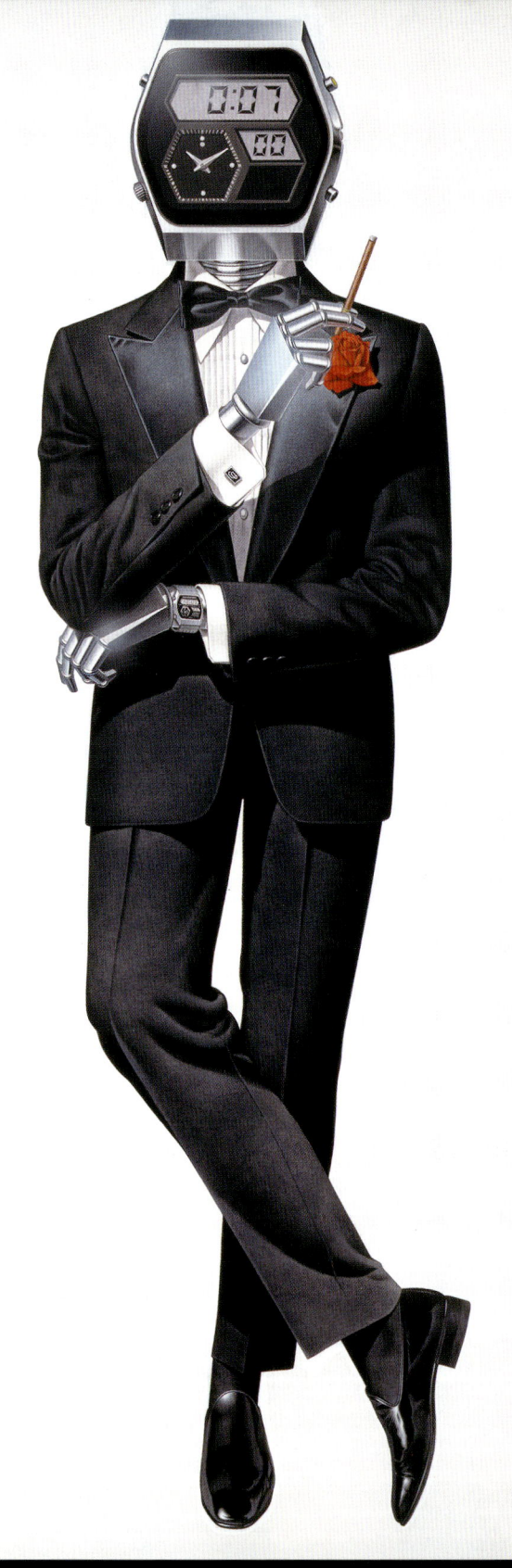

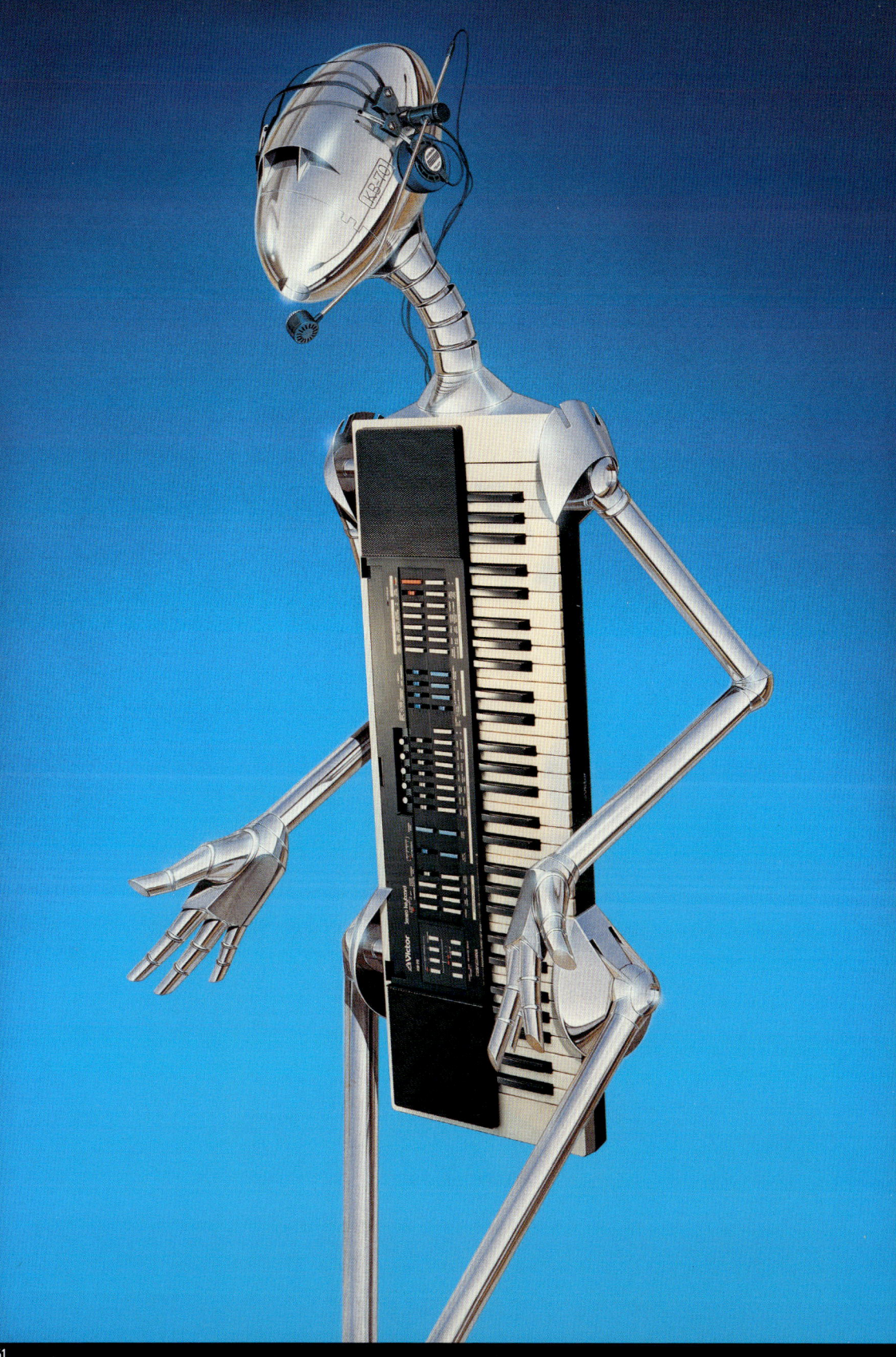

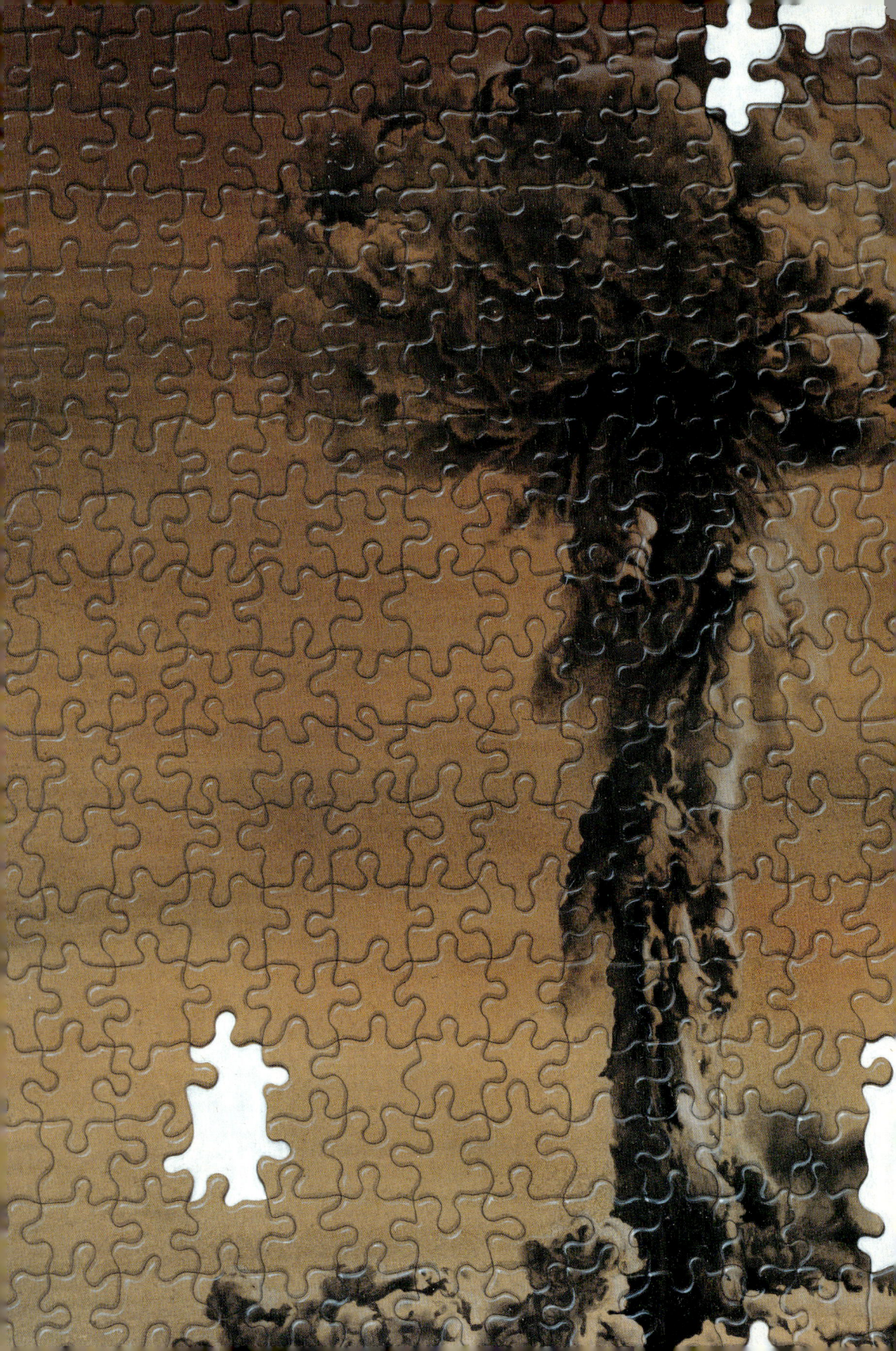

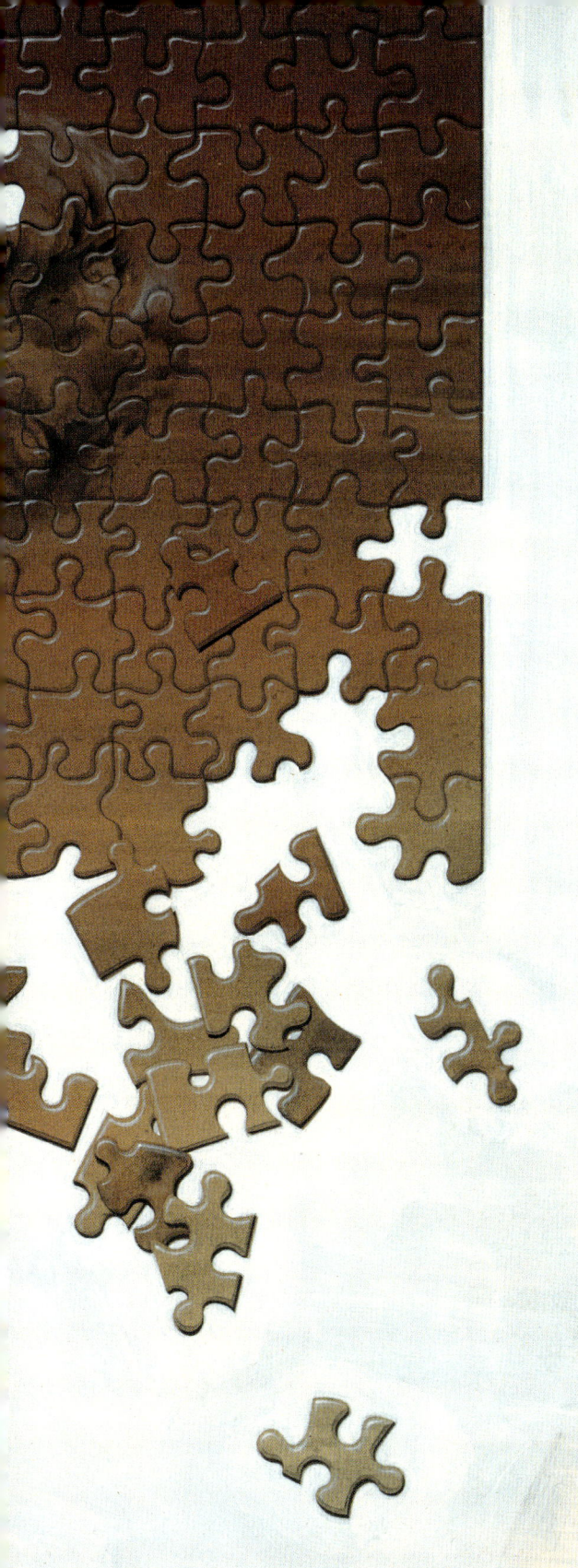

上田三根子（イラストレーター）

　同じ女を描いているのに、何で表現の仕方一つで、こんなにも違っちゃうんだろうって、空山さんのイラストレーションを見るたびに私は思う。

　エロチックで、変態ぽくて、官能的、男が100人いたとしたら、そこにいるすべての男の眼を釘付け状態にしてしまうであろう、空山さんの描く女性と違って、私の描く女のコは180度違う世界に住んでいるみたいだ。「エッチなことなんてなーんにも知らないの。世の中に闇の部分なんてあるの？　私の眼に映るのは明るくて、オシャレなことだけだもん」っていうような女のコばかりだもんなあ。

　官能性なんてものは、限りなくゼロに近い。

　たまには、裸を描くこともあるけれど、あくまでもサッパリ、スッキリって感じだし。

　もしもだけれど、私の描く女のコに官能を感じる男がいたとしたら、空山さんの描く女性になにも反応を示さない男がいたとしたら、そっちの方が、よっぽど重症な変態だ。

　エッチな下着から透けて見える豊かな乳房や性器（ときどきは、丸見えだったりする）に、ちゃんと反応してこそやっぱり正しい男だと思うし、それがいくら、変態っぽいセックスを描いていたとしても正しい反応なのだ。

　みんな（男女関係なく）が心の奥底で、見てみたいやってみたいと密かに思っているような世界を白い紙の上に造り上げていく空山さんは、世紀末の正しい「愛の伝道師」なのだ。

　これからも、いっぱいエッチなのを描いて、楽しませて欲しいなって思ってる。

上田三根子

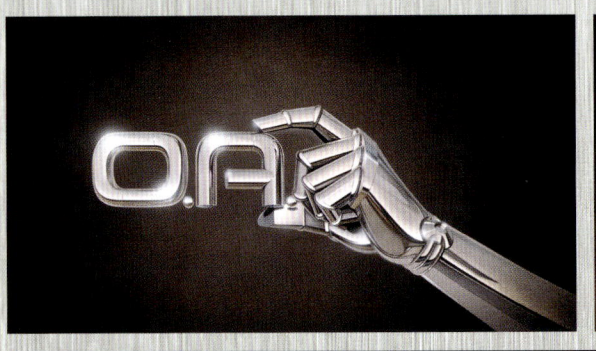

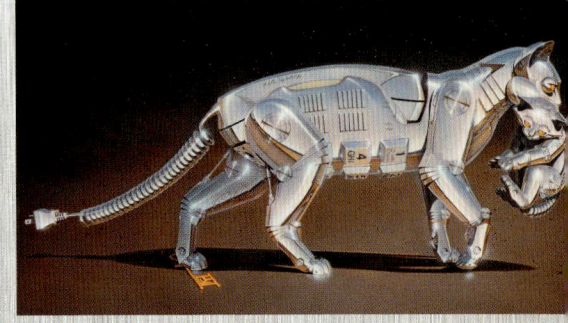

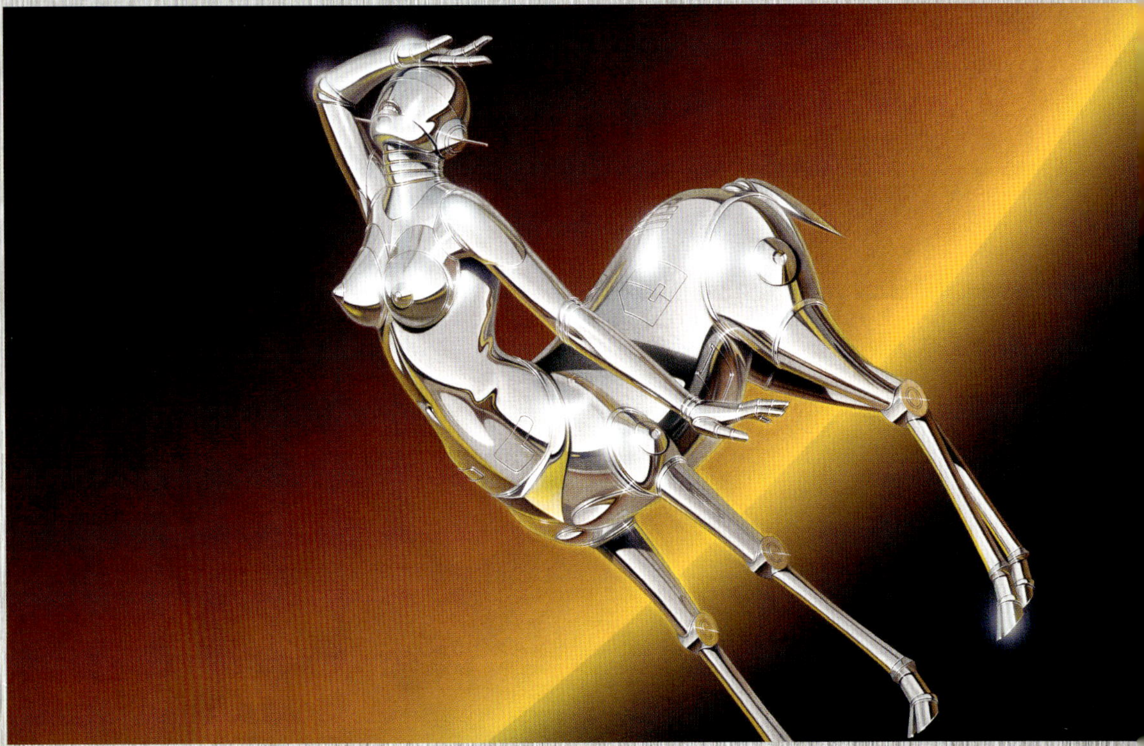

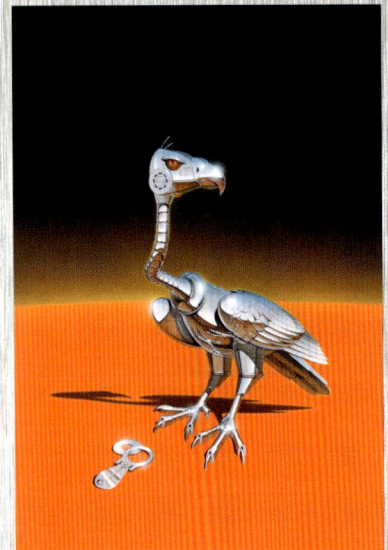

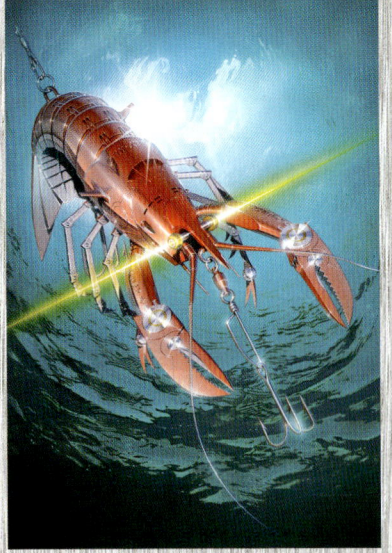

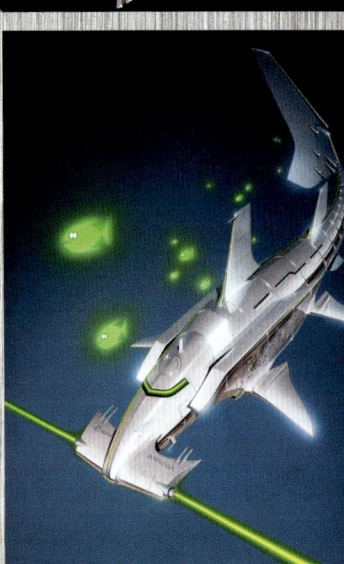

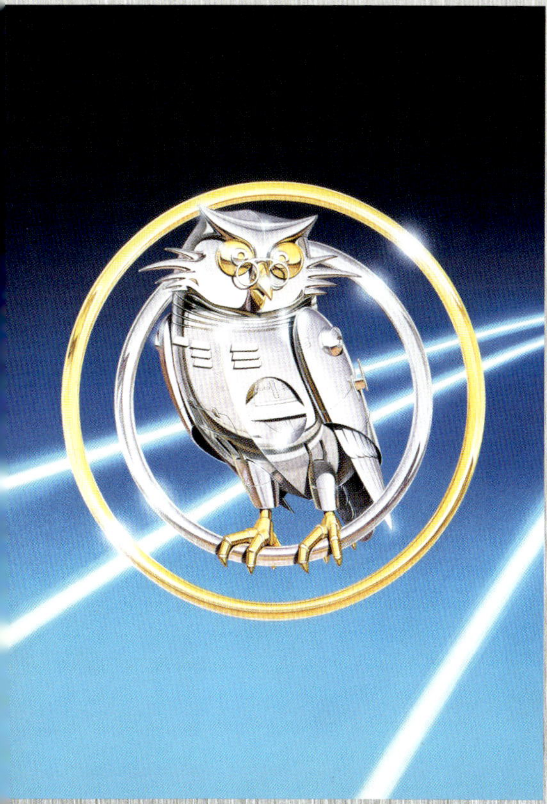

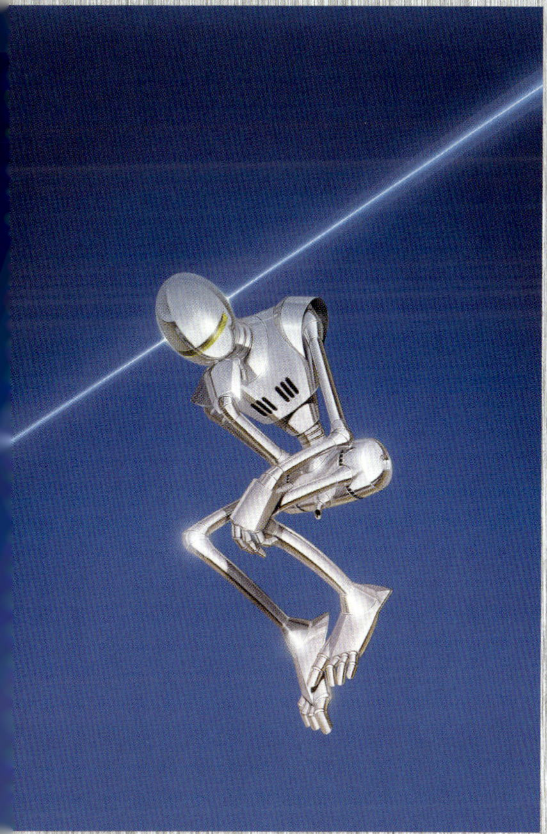

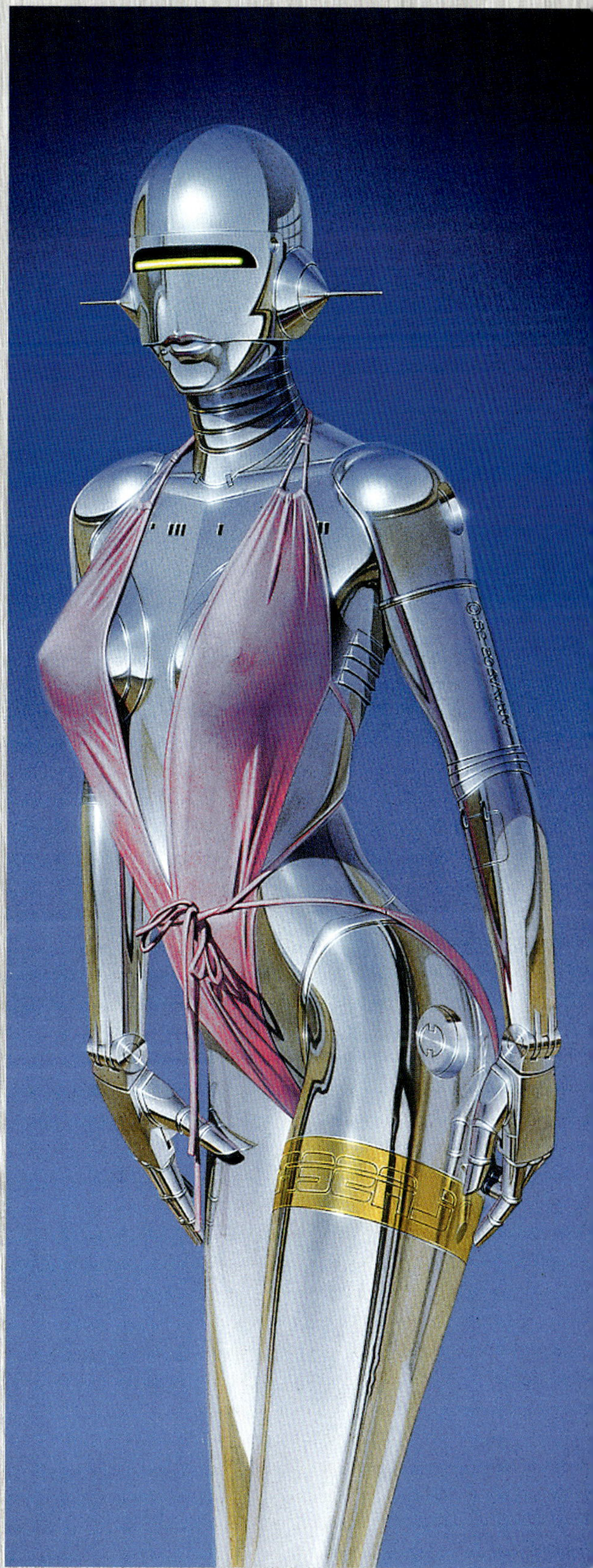

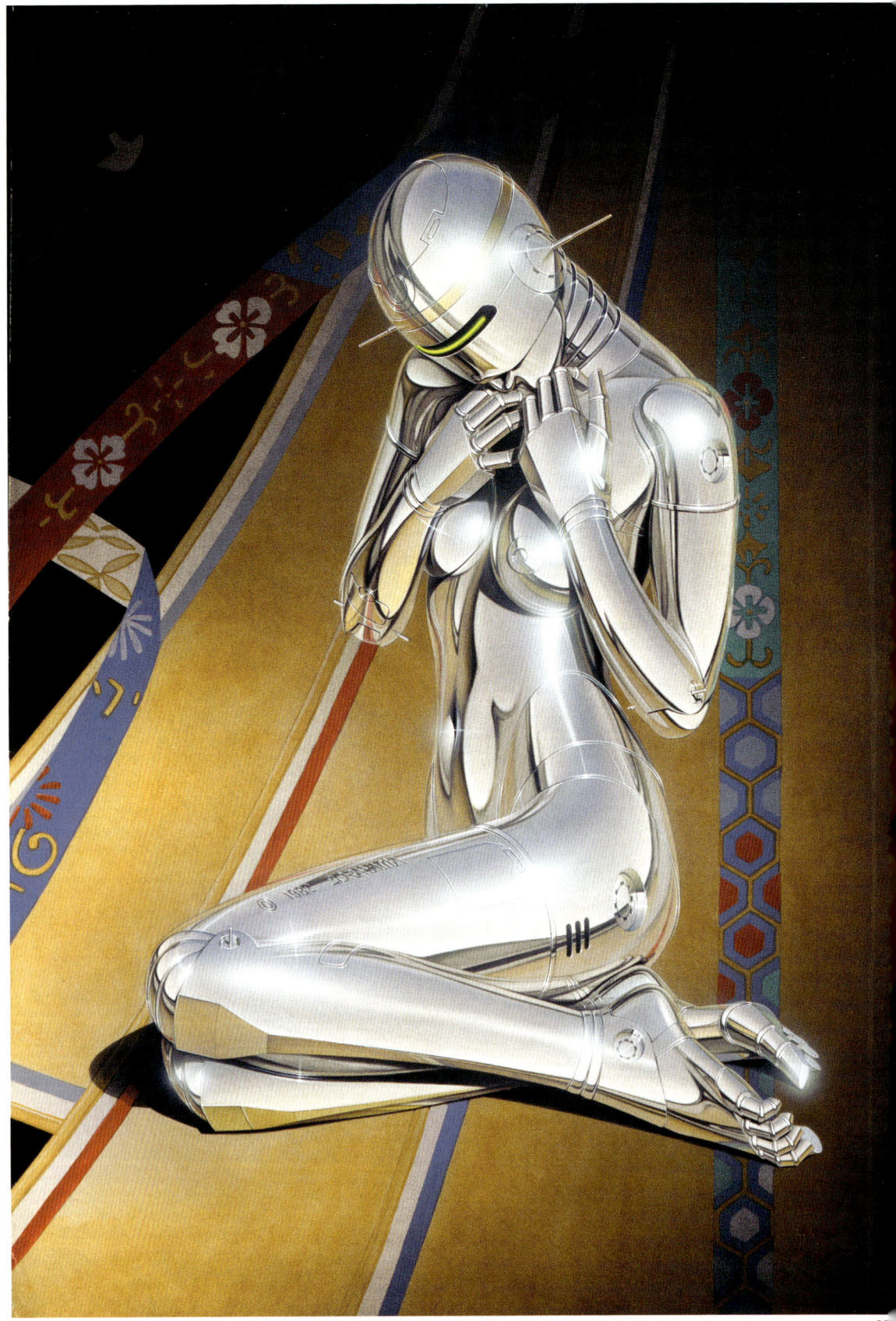

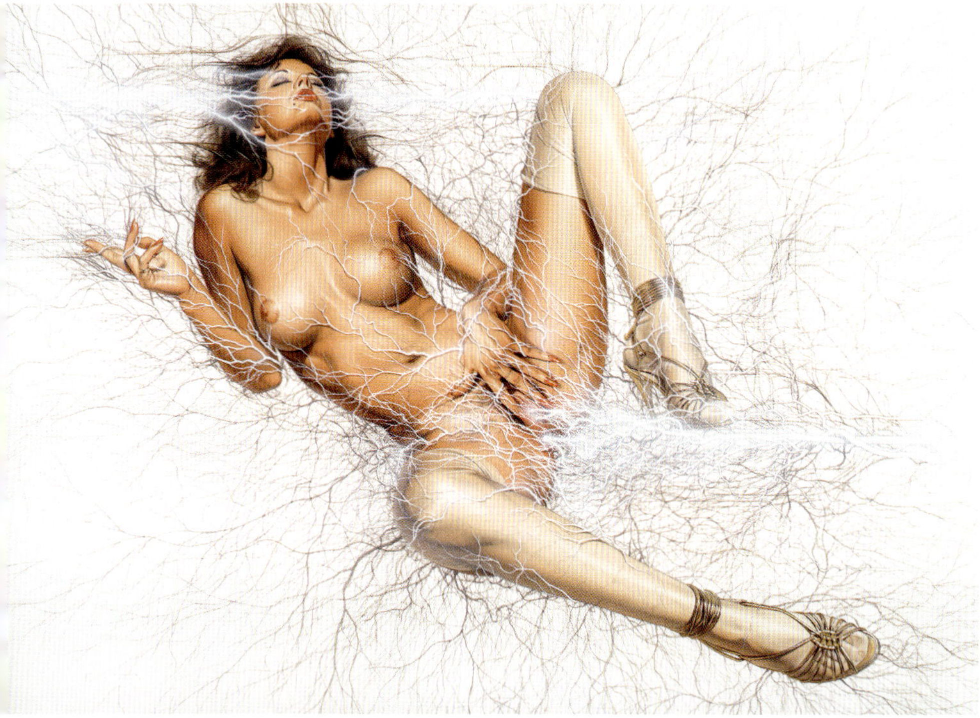

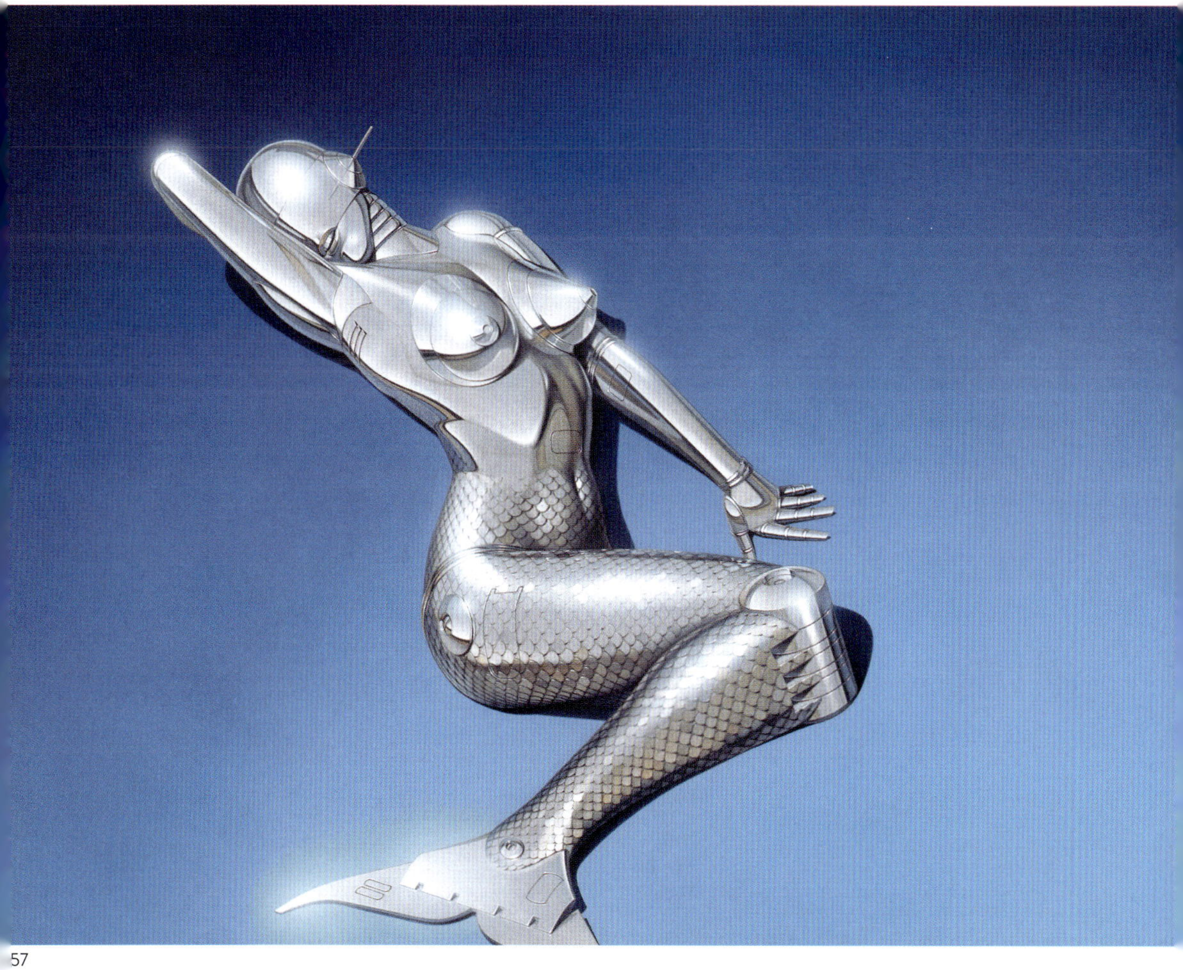

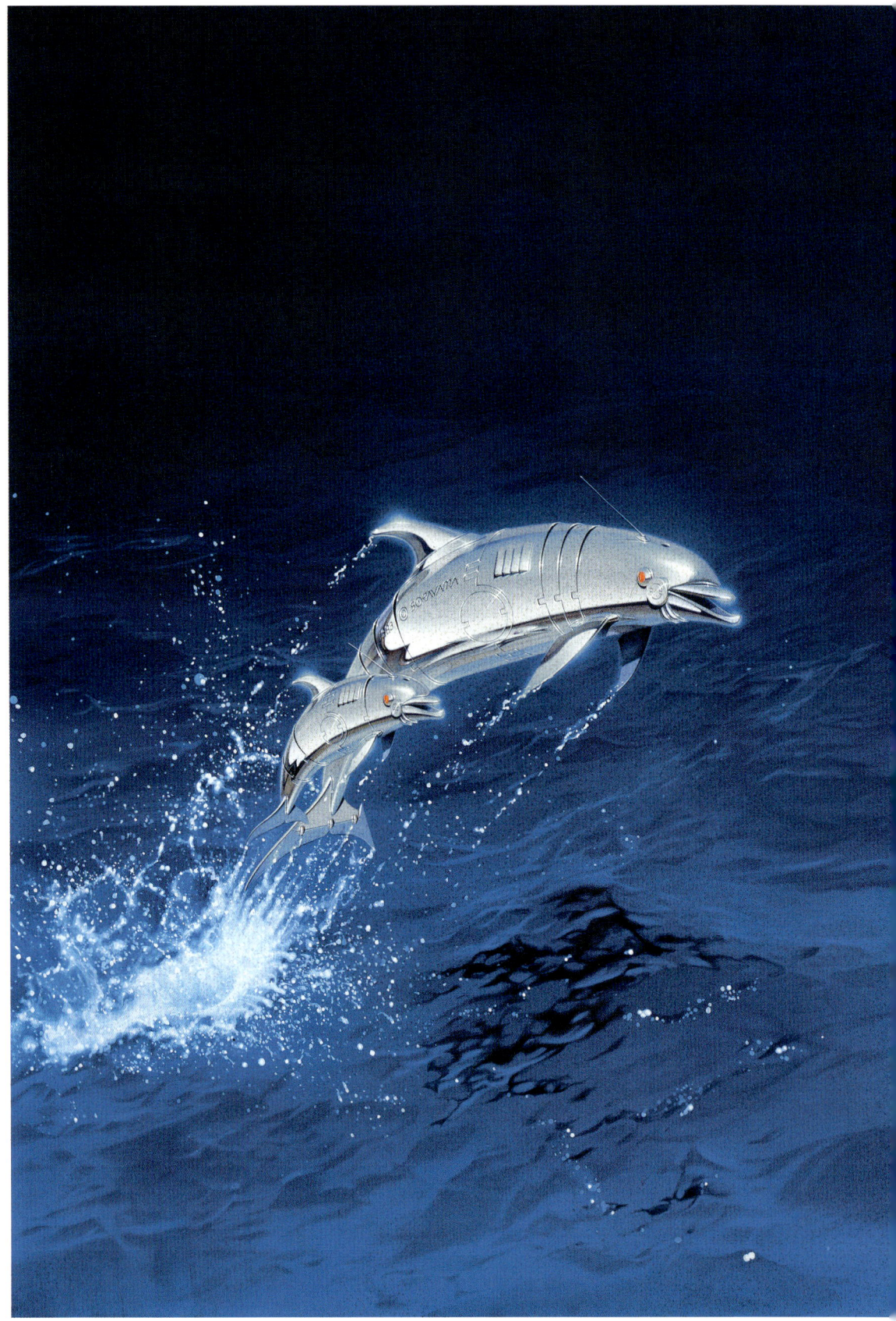

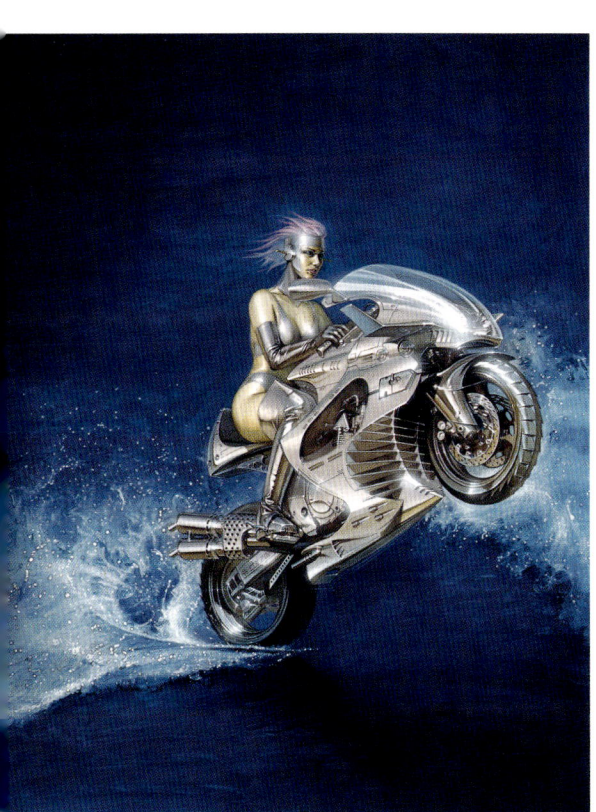
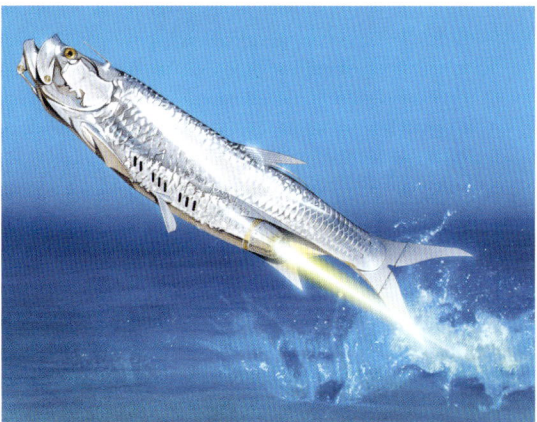
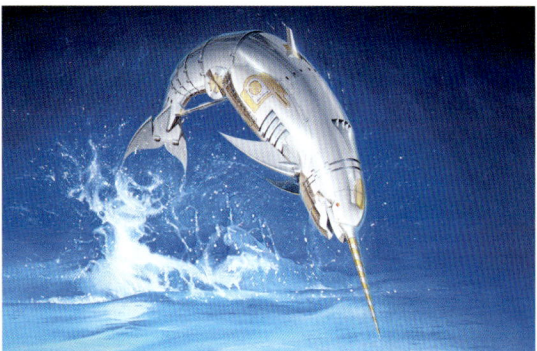

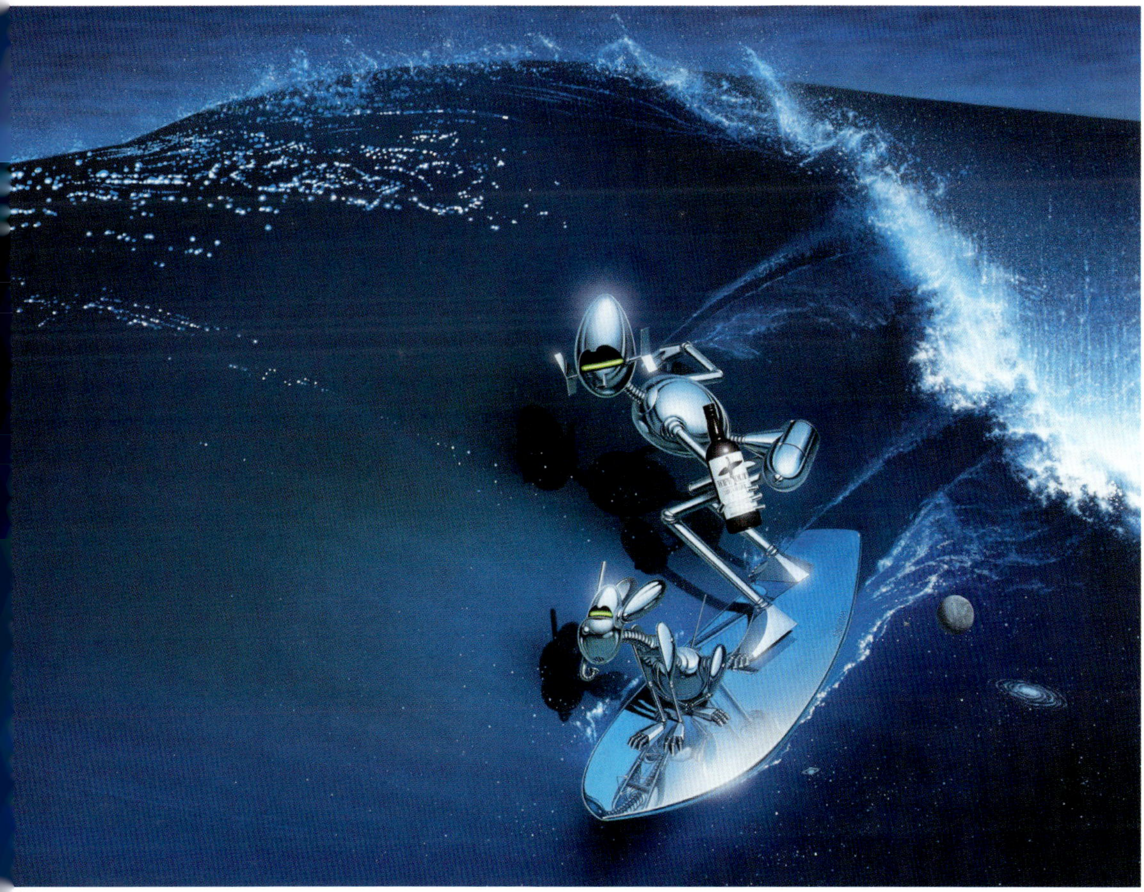

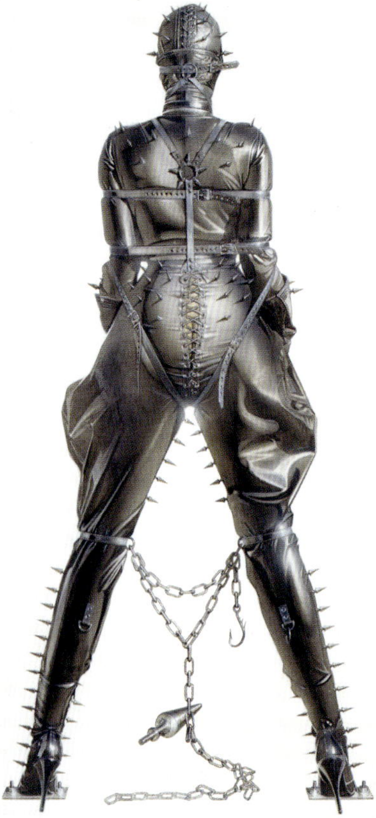

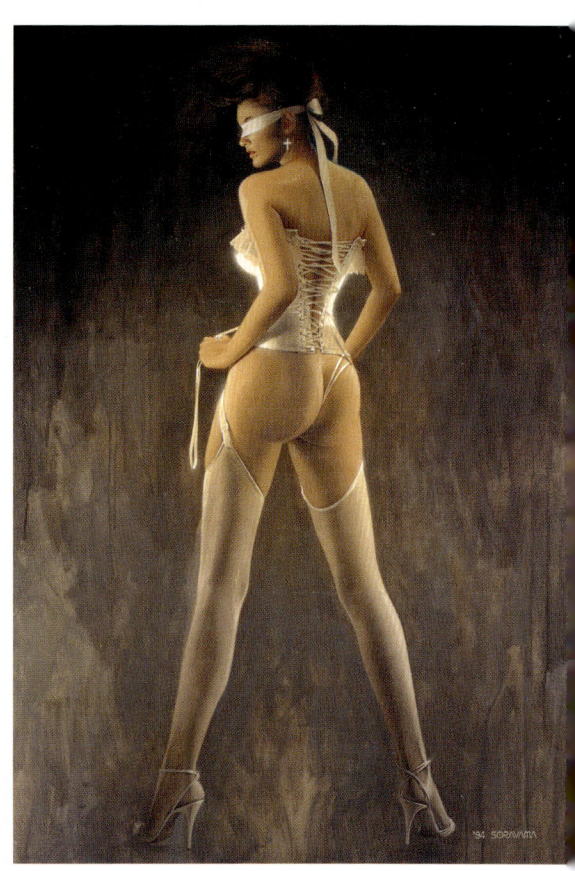

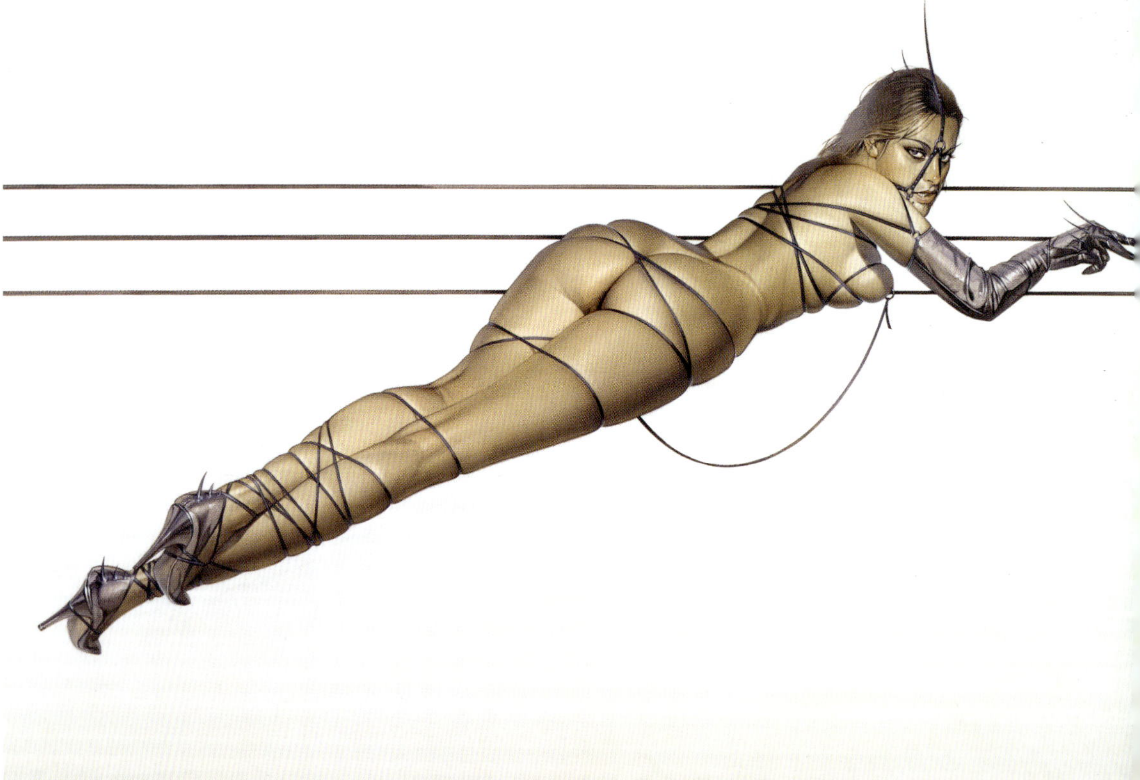

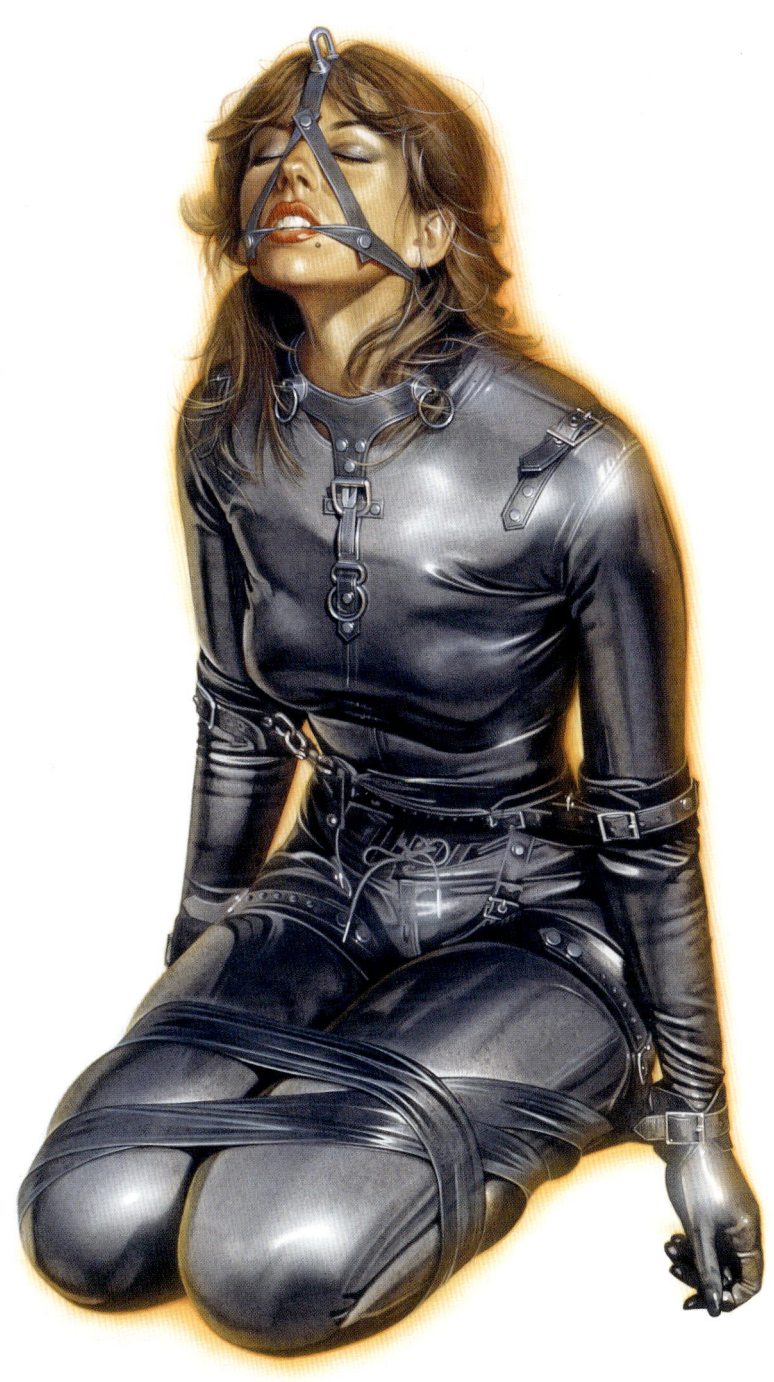

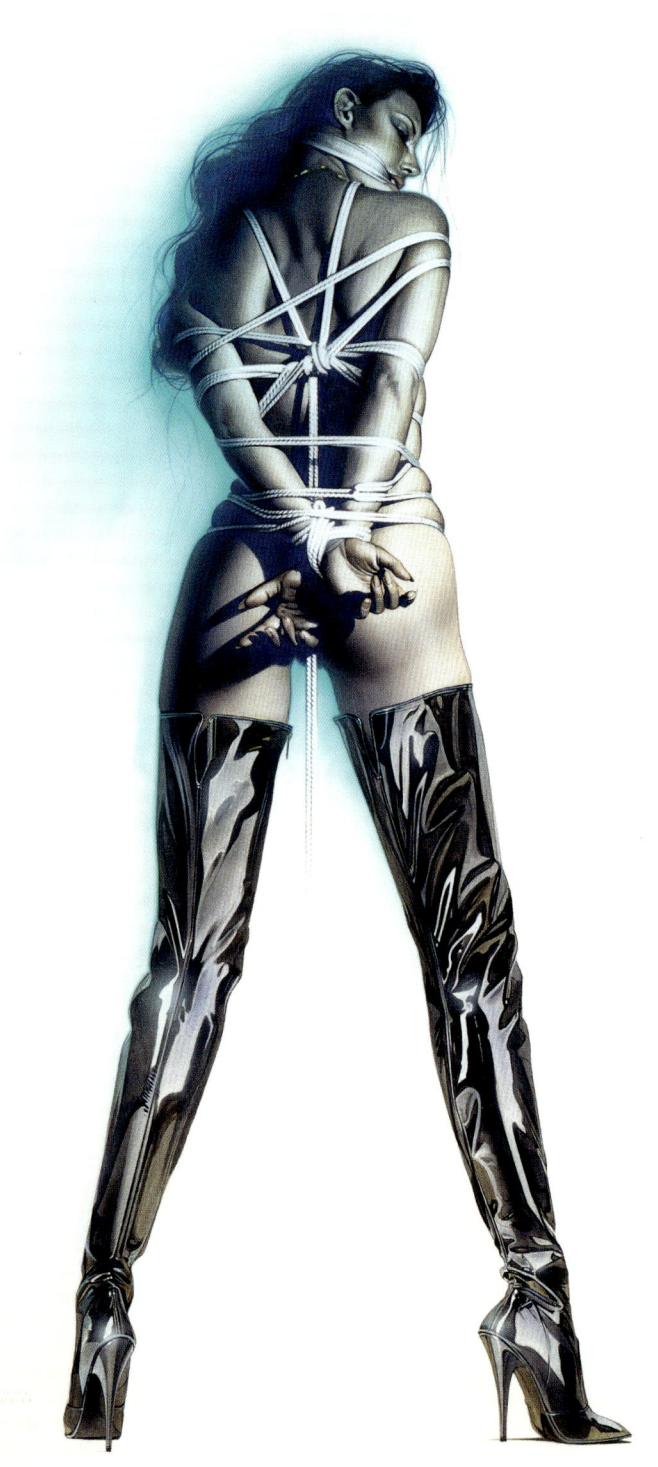

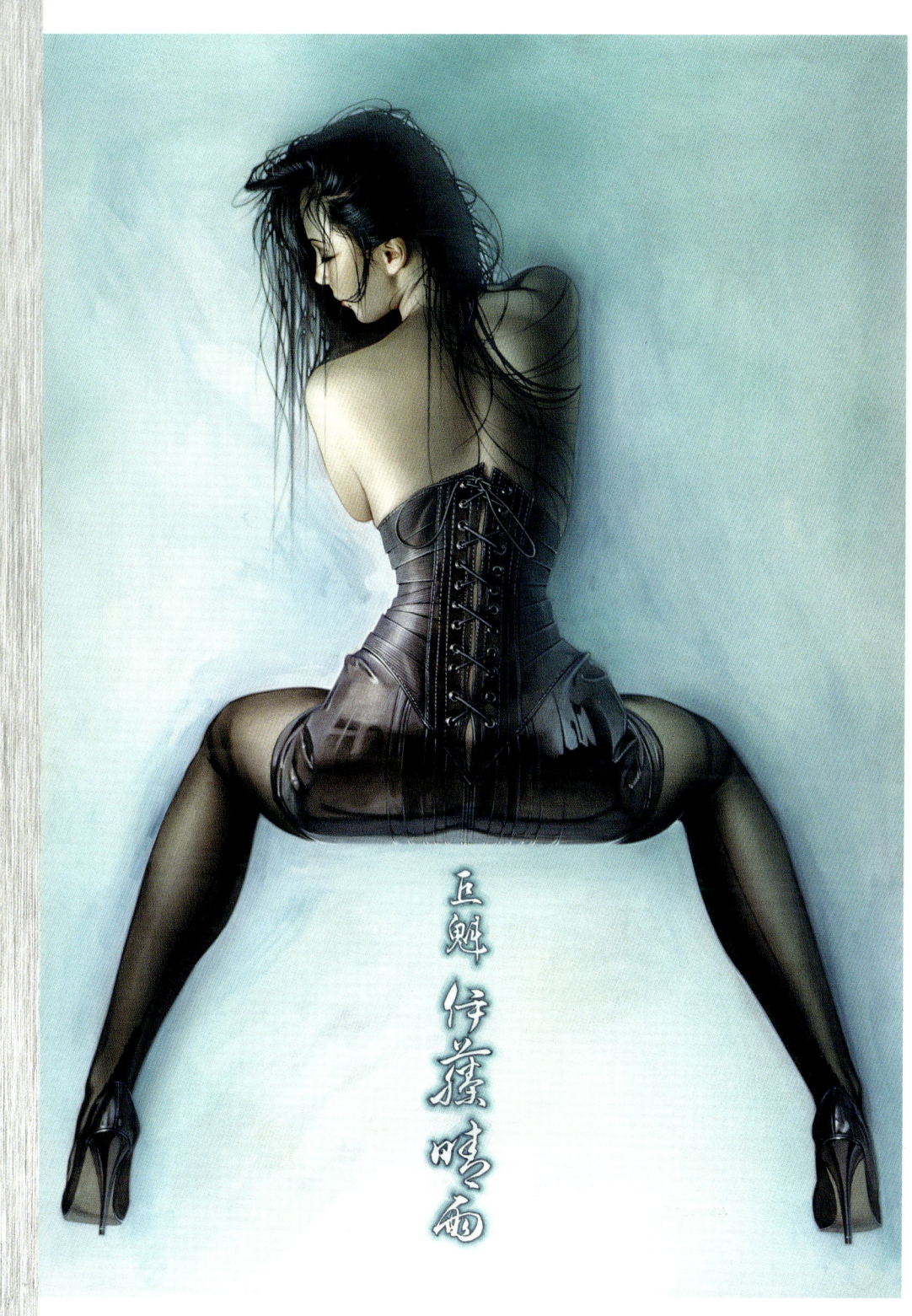

魁

伊藤晴雨

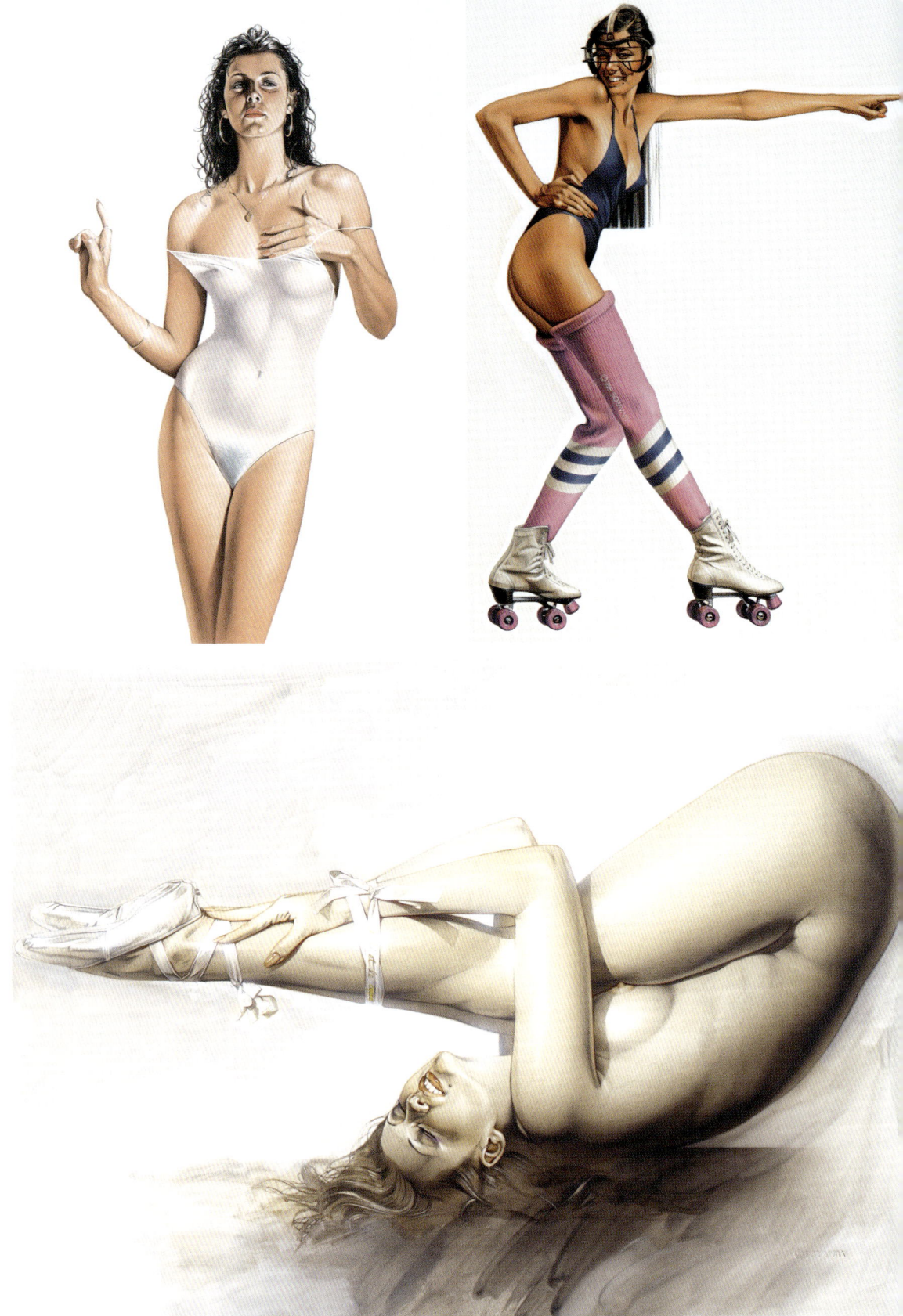

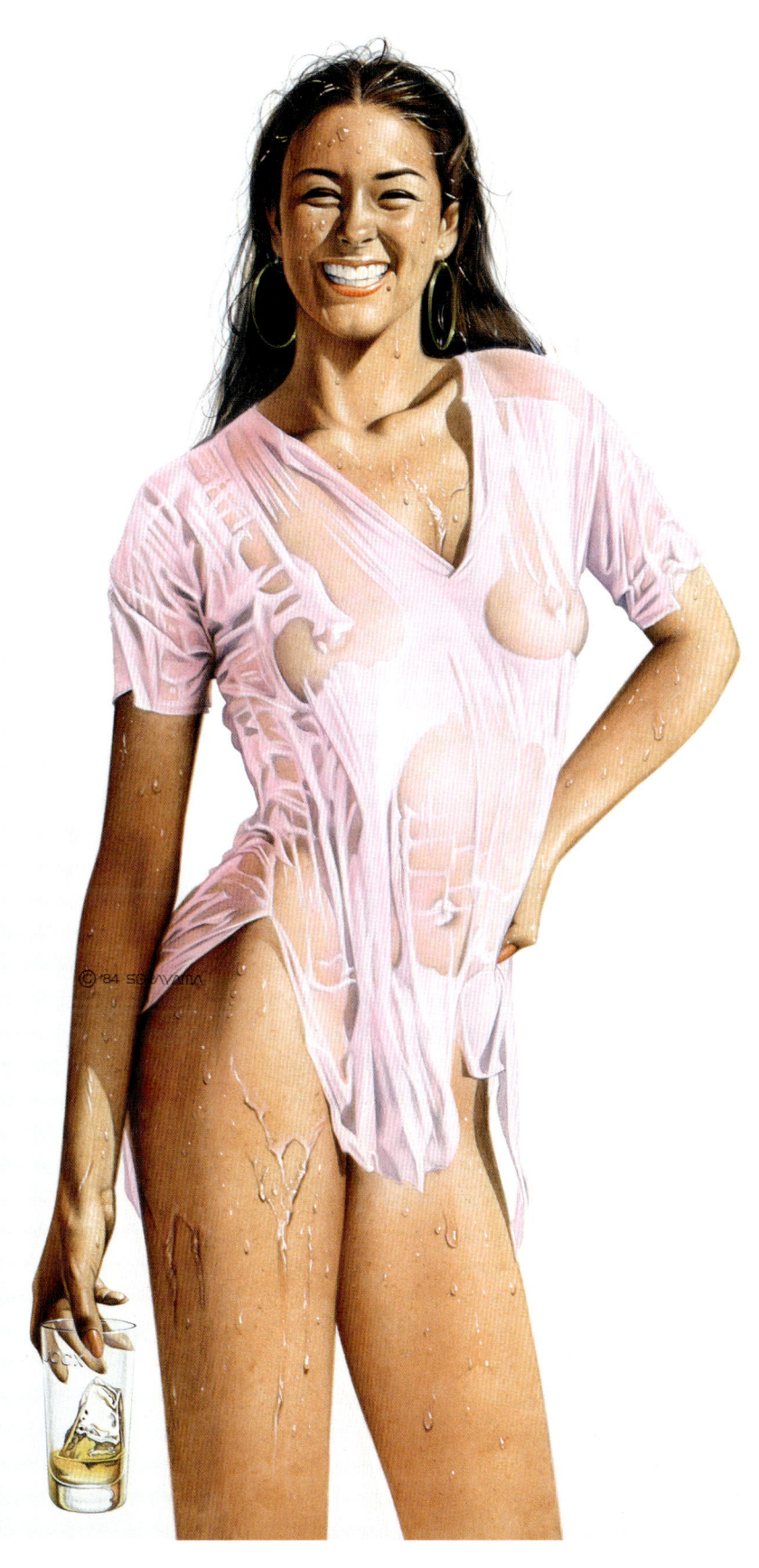

65

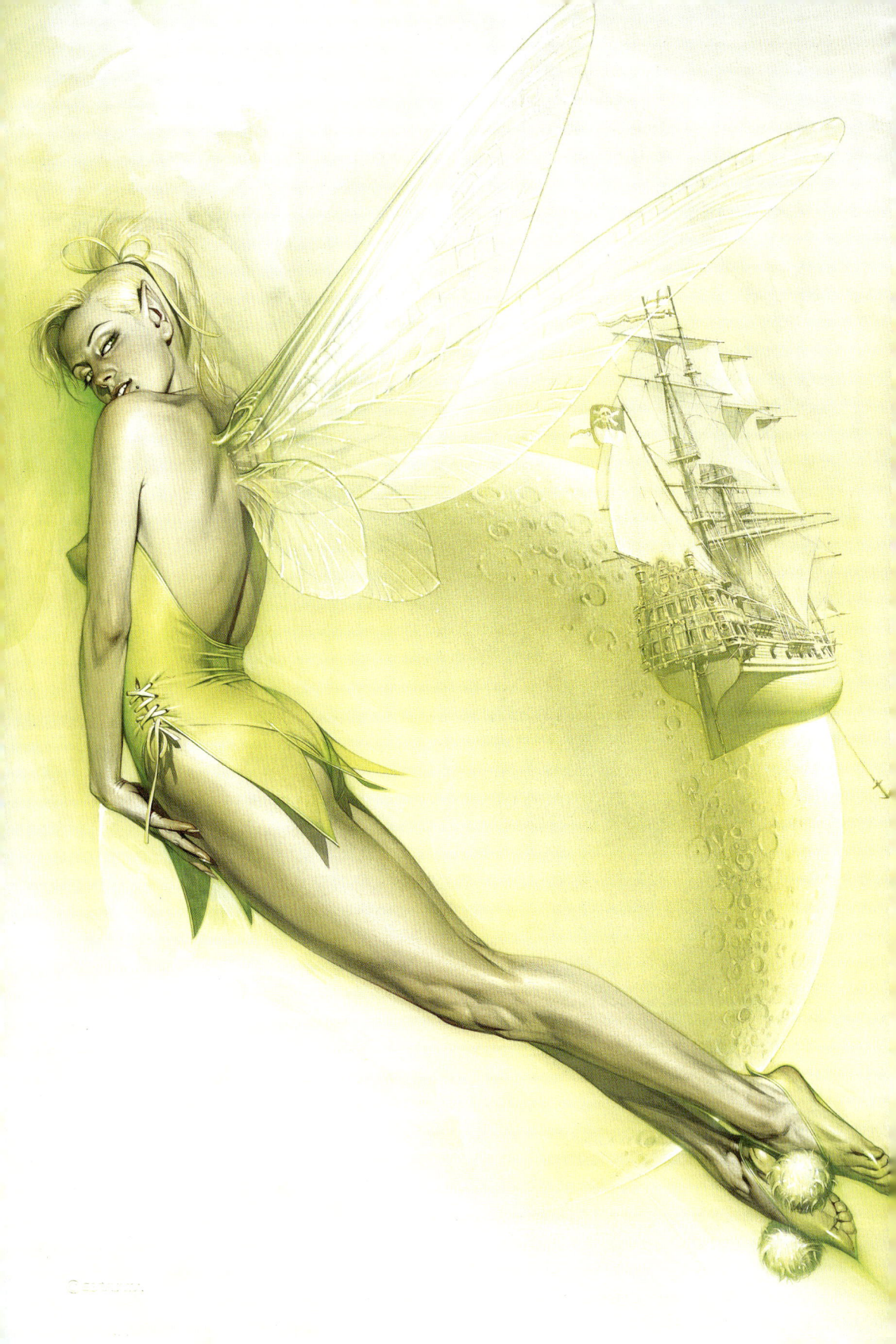

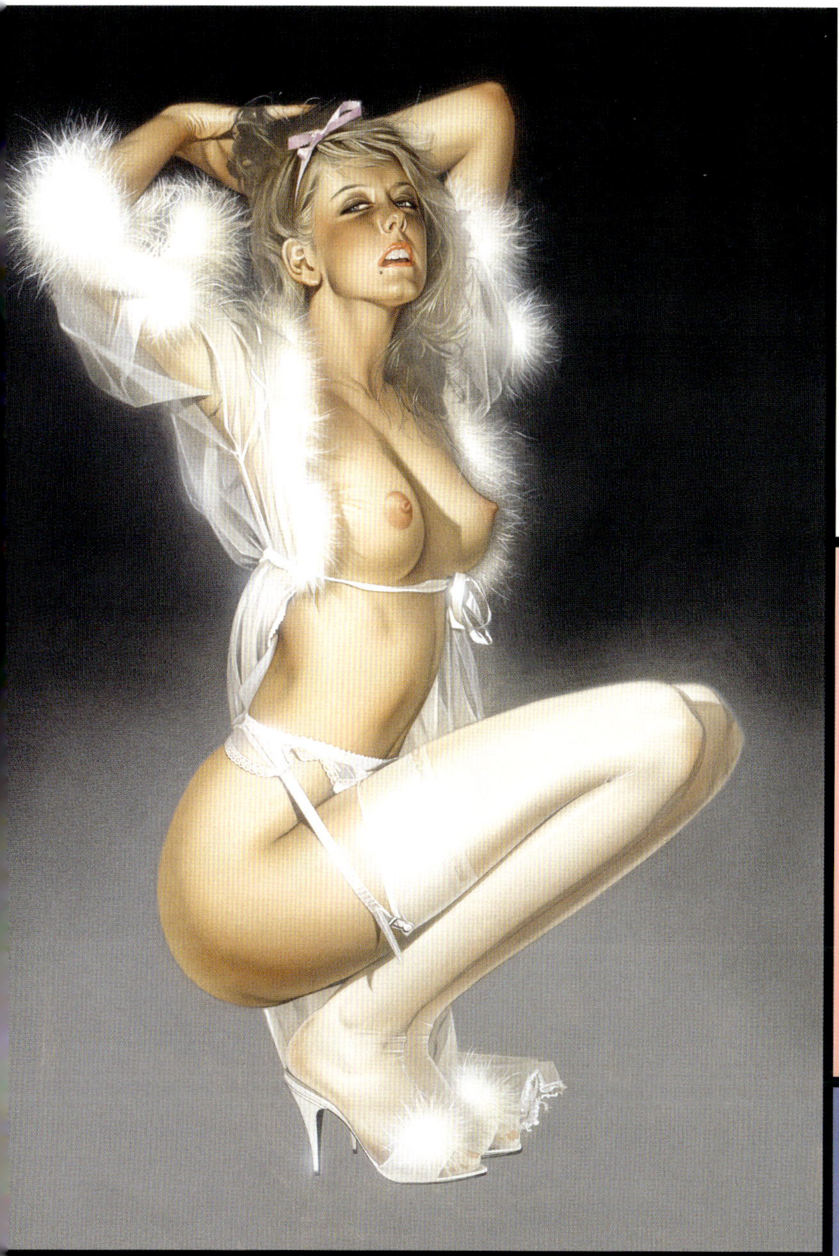

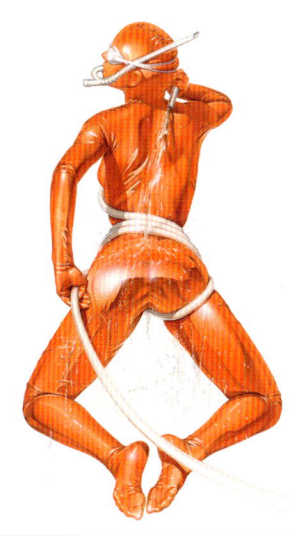

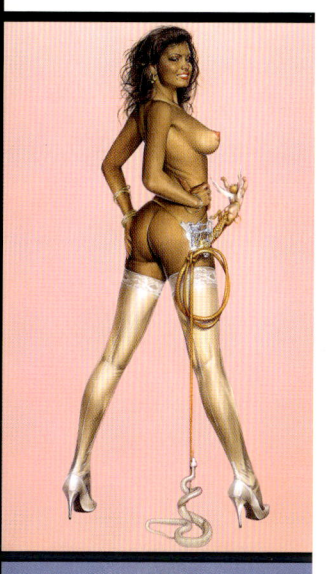

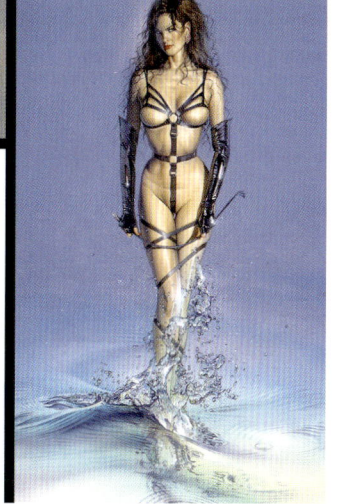

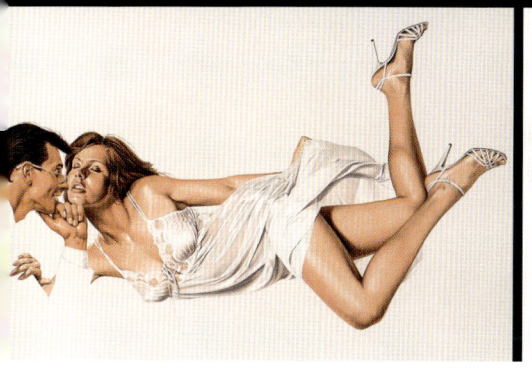

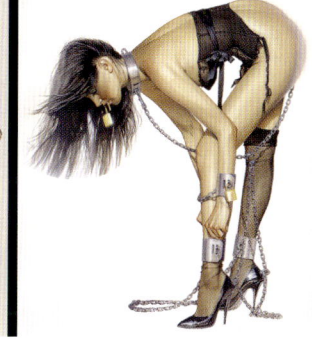

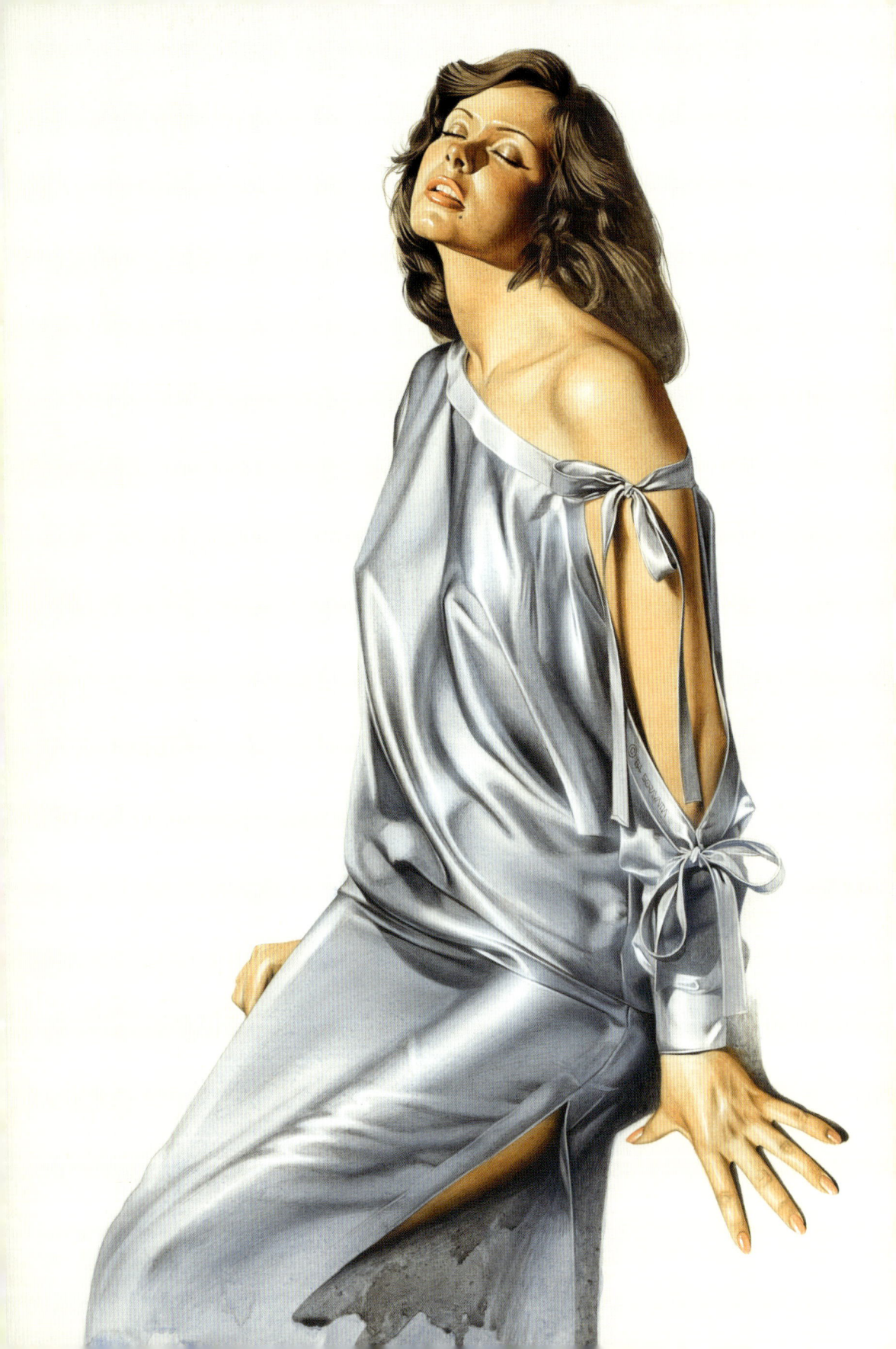

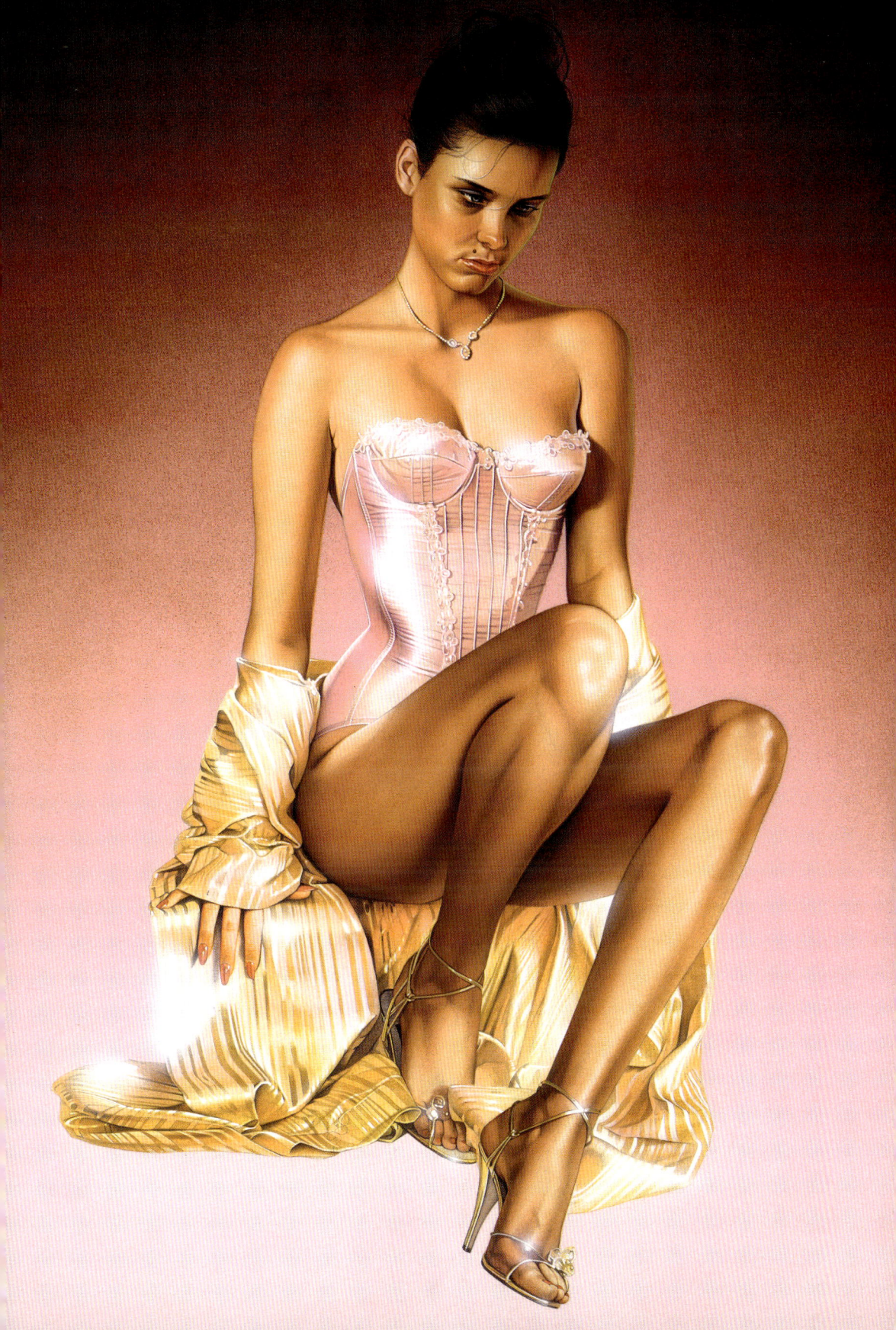

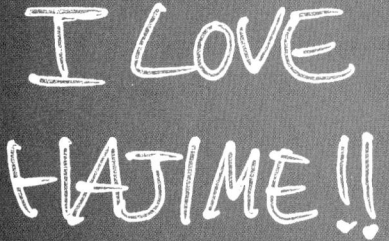

I LOVE HAJIME !!

MEDICOM TOY CORPORATION
President & CEO
Tatsuhiko"Ryu"Akashi

Of course I am a great admirer of Hajime Sorayama. He creates the ultimate, unattainable fantasy female-the one that exists only in our dreams. Hajime Sorayama captures it on paper, for our pleasure.

Bob Carlos Clarke (Photographer,

Tom Porta （トム・ポルタ：カメラマン／アーティスト）

Milano, February 1998

At the end of the images century, the computers can make us live in virtual realities, we can modify average pictures into rasor sharp perfect beauty and probably soon we will have Digital toothbrushes—

There he is—

As a pencils and brushes Samurai, Hajime Sorayama represents a higher point in today's art world. He's the King—

Before startin' my career as illustrator, I was amazed by his technique—

As any other student of Art Institutes I could'nt ignore the way Sorayama was able to create materials, from flesh to metal—

Growing up I discovered his best kept secret—

Hajime Sorayama is pure soul—Period—

His body construction, expressions, renderings are all about inspiration and beauty—

Just lookin' and wondering only about his amazing technique is offensive—

I feel deeply honoured to be asked to write few lines about a guy I consider among the best artists of this century—Long live the King—

Tom Porta

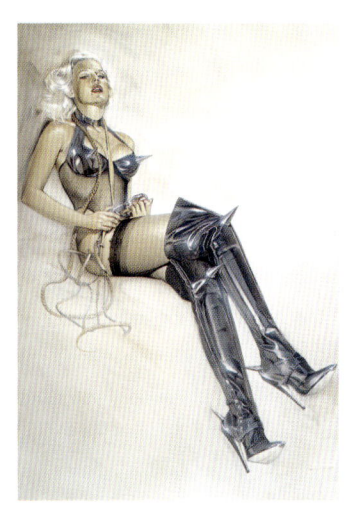
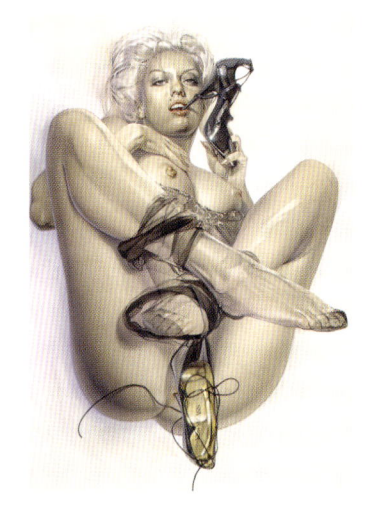
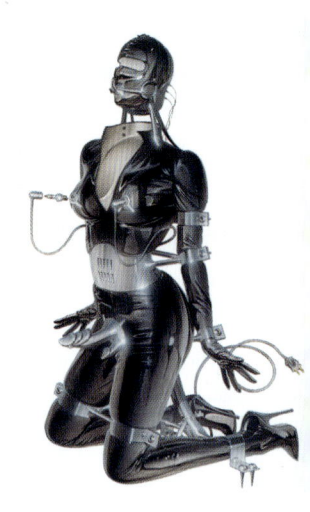

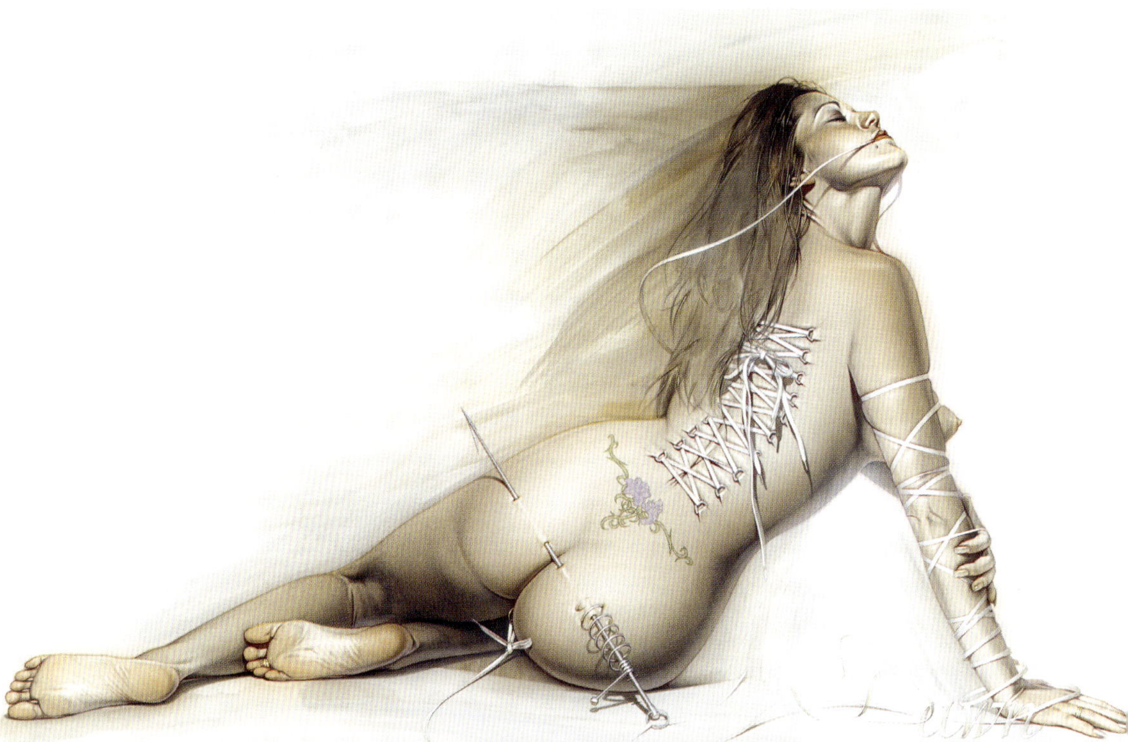

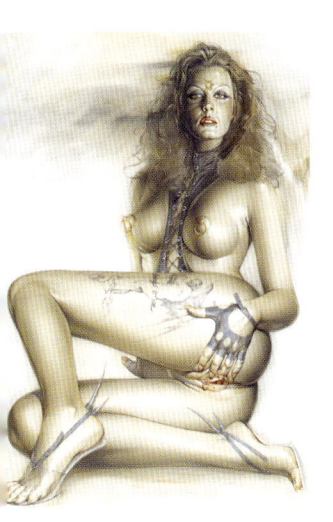
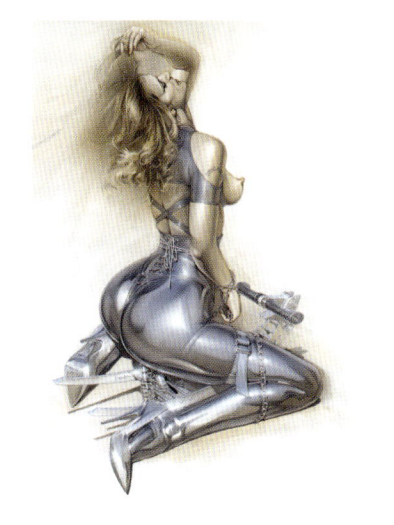
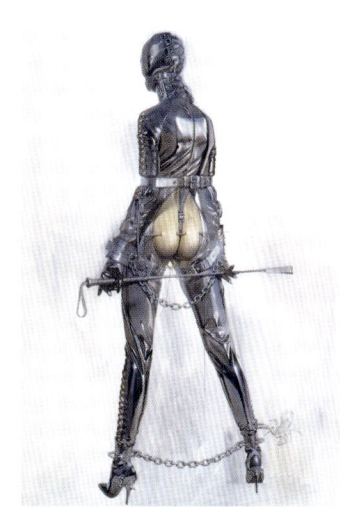

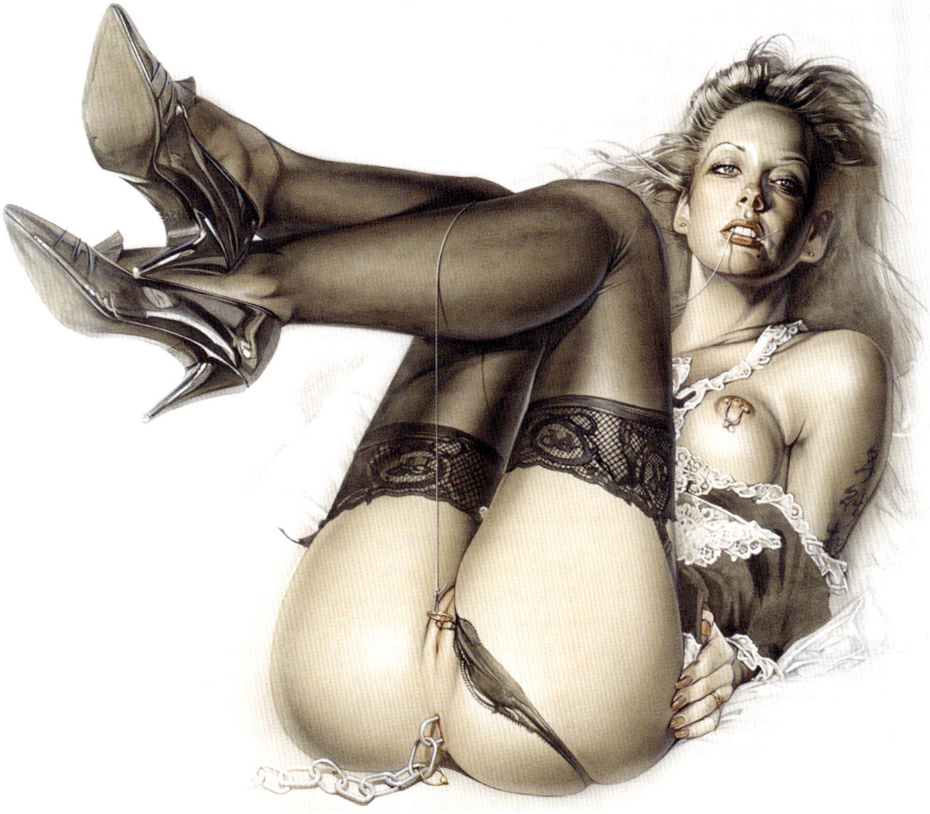

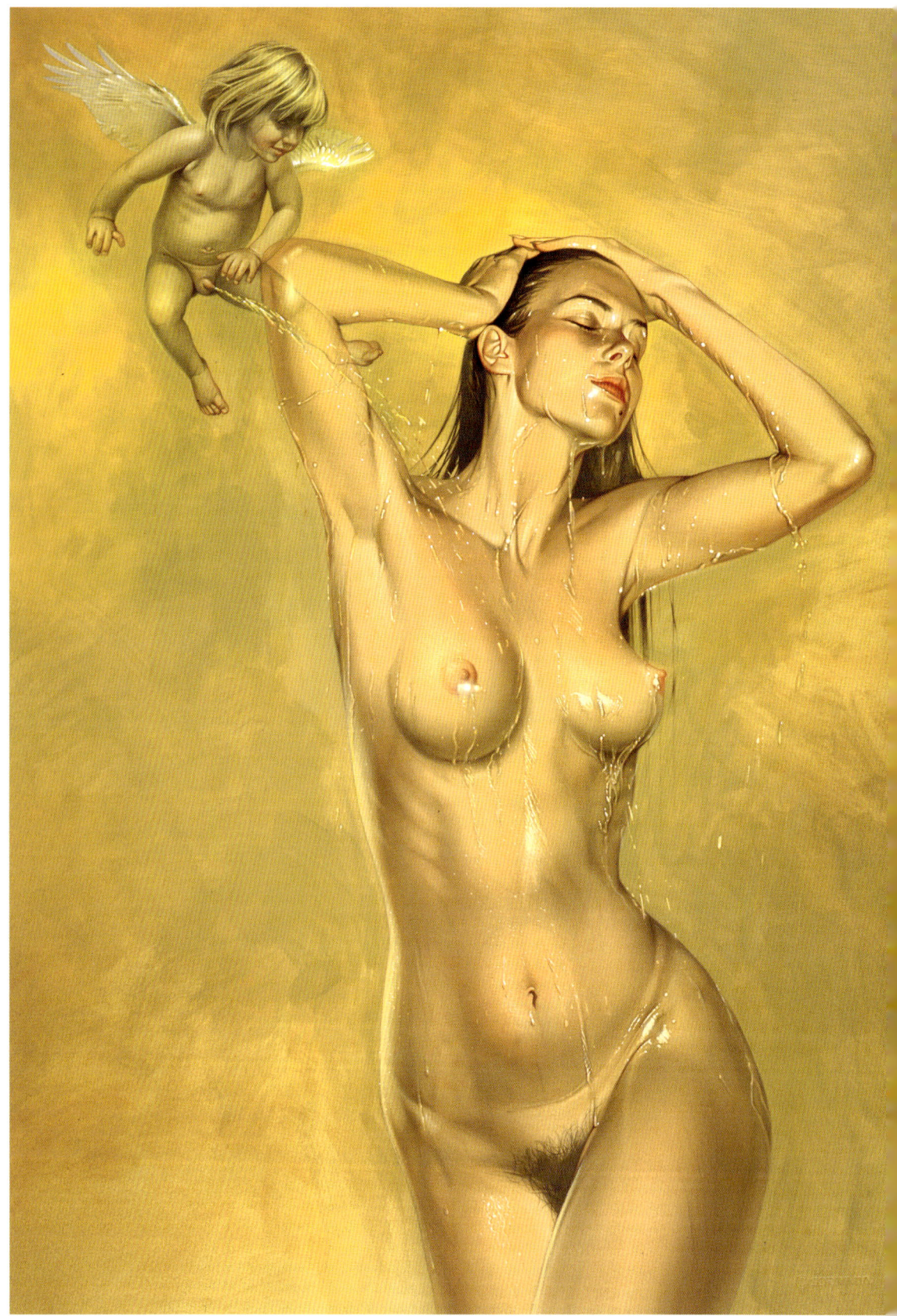

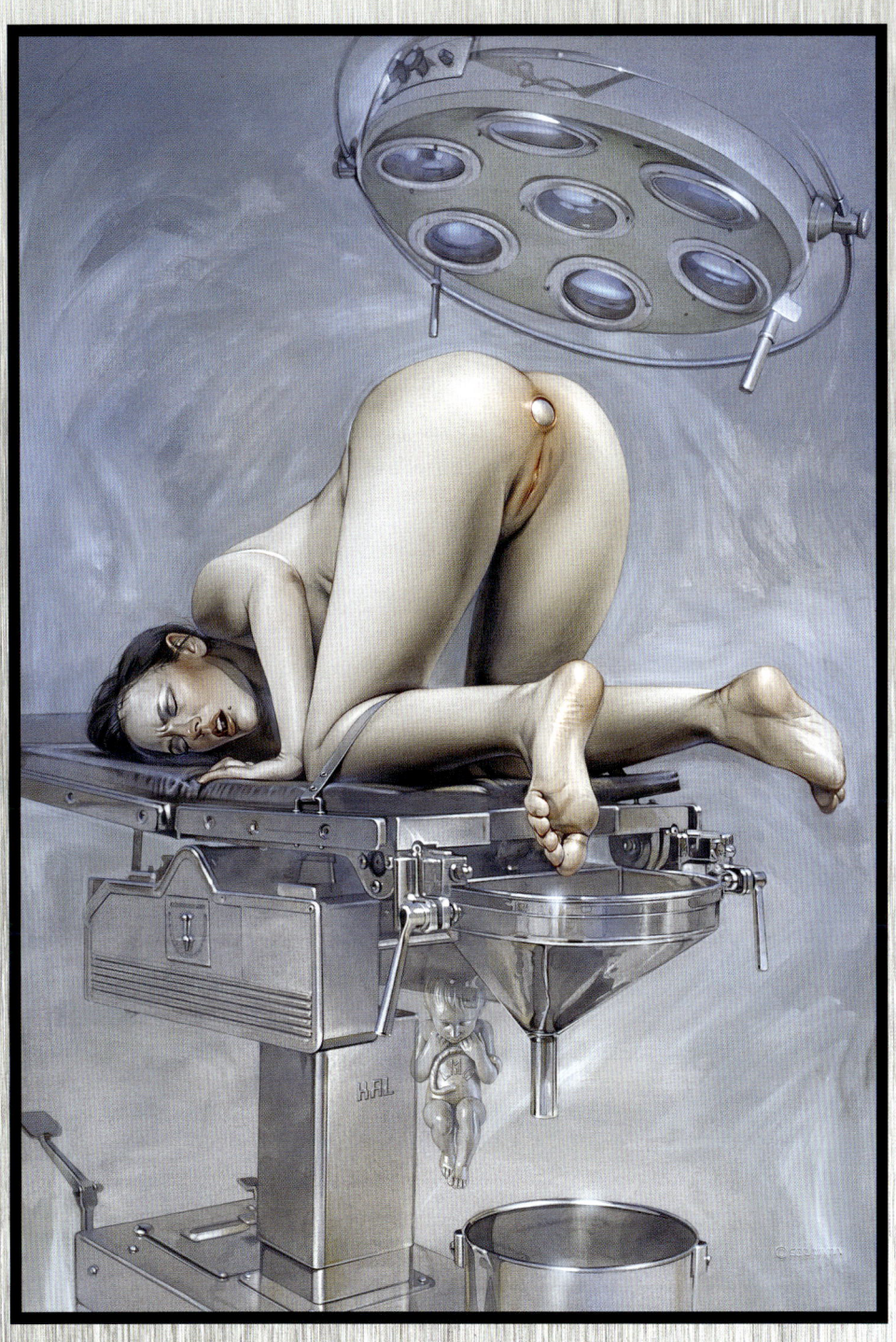

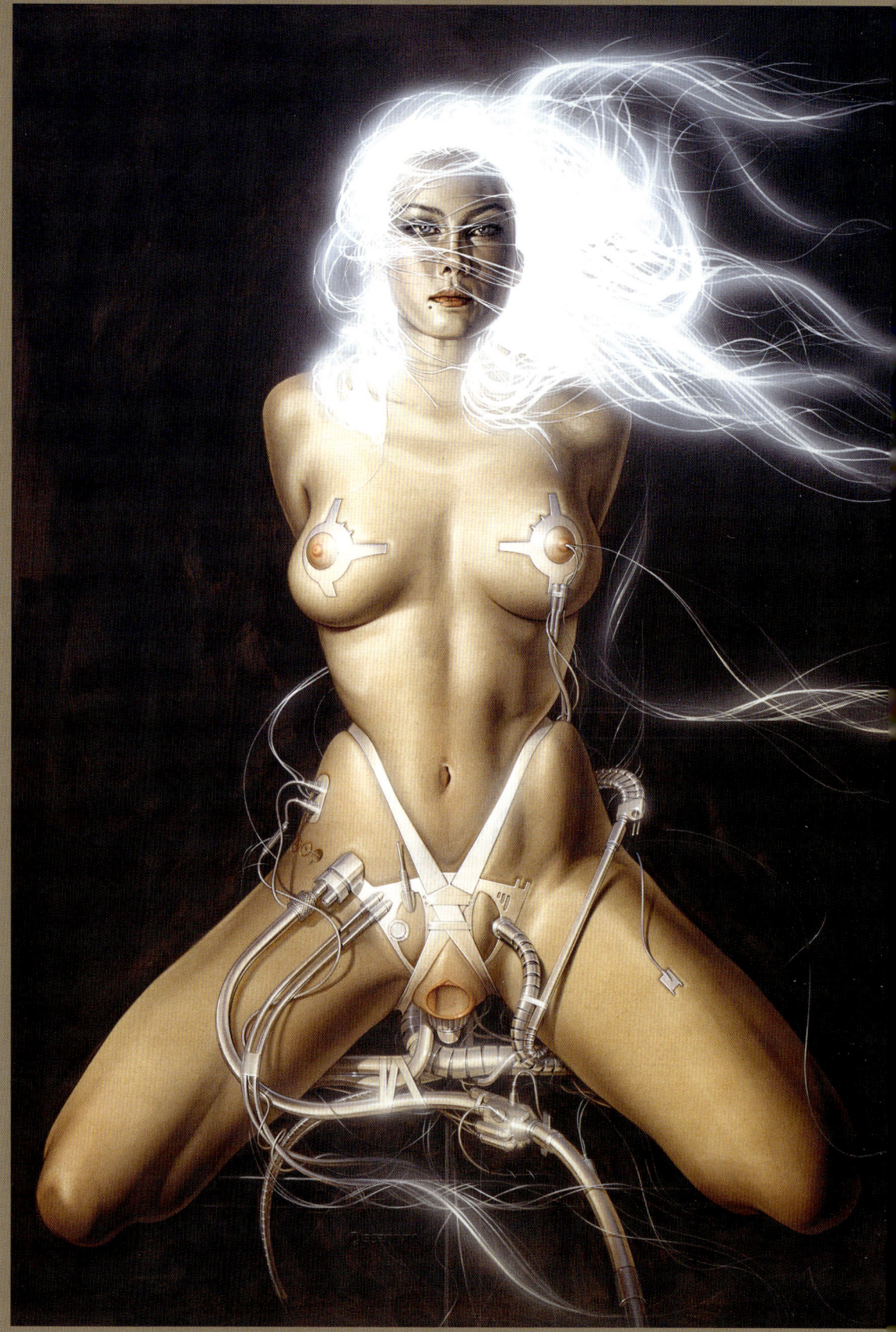

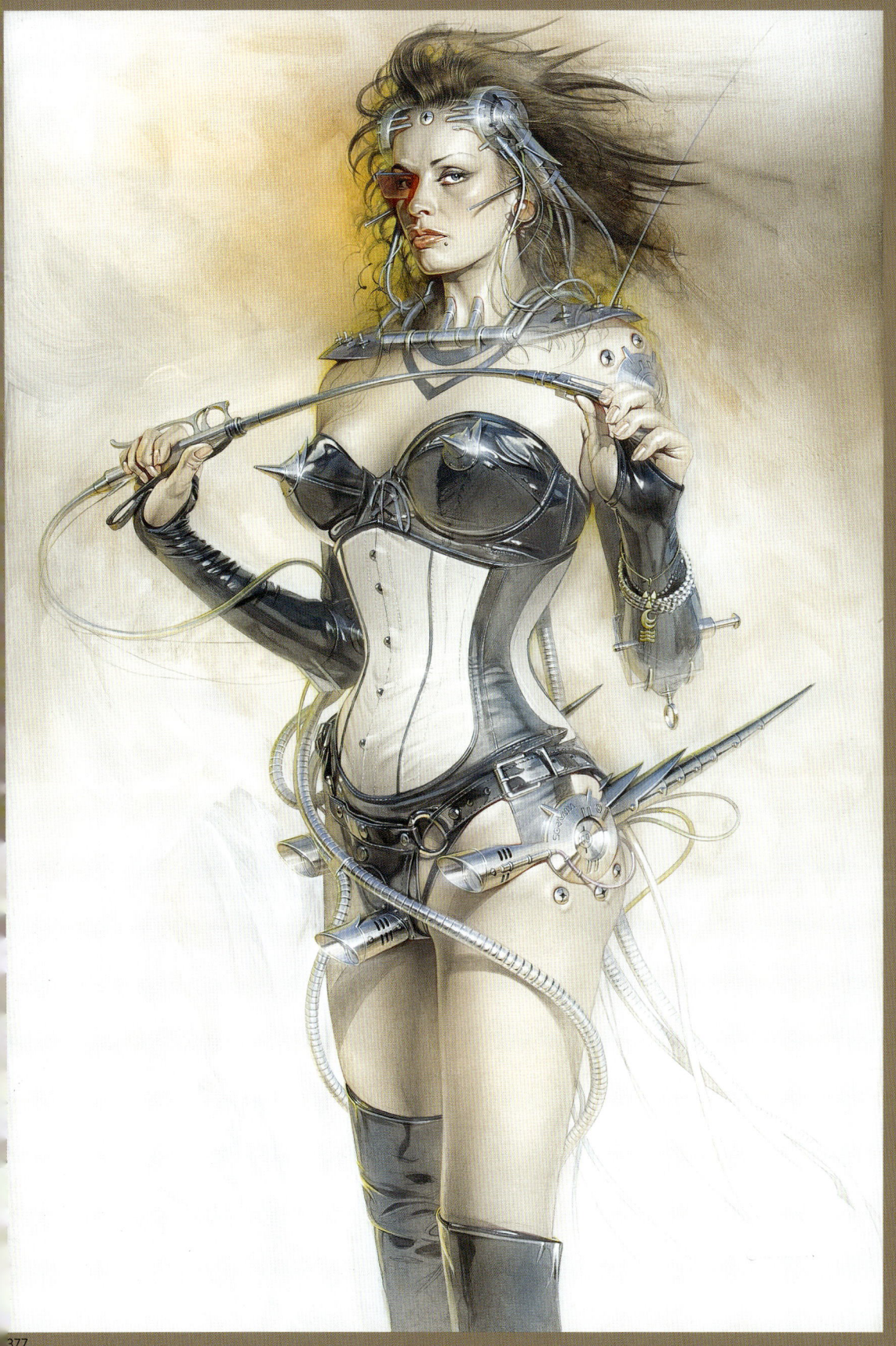

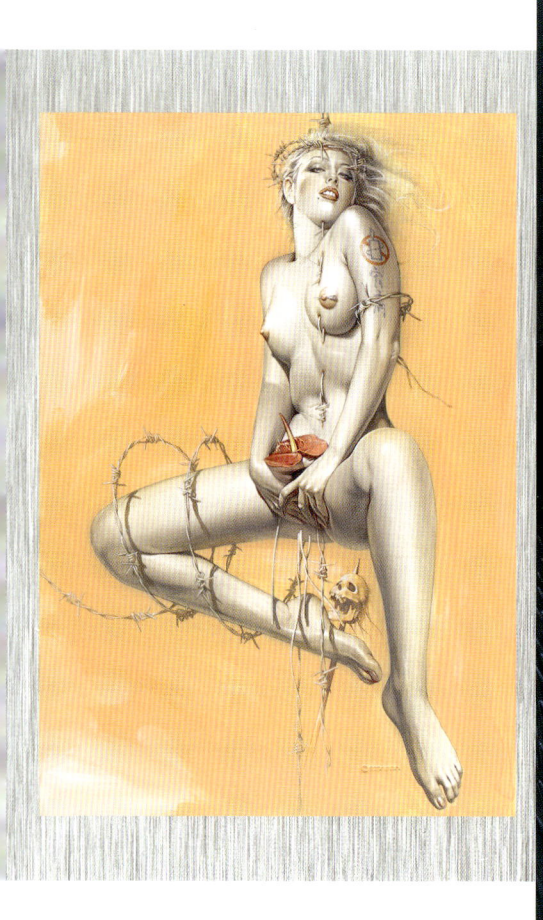

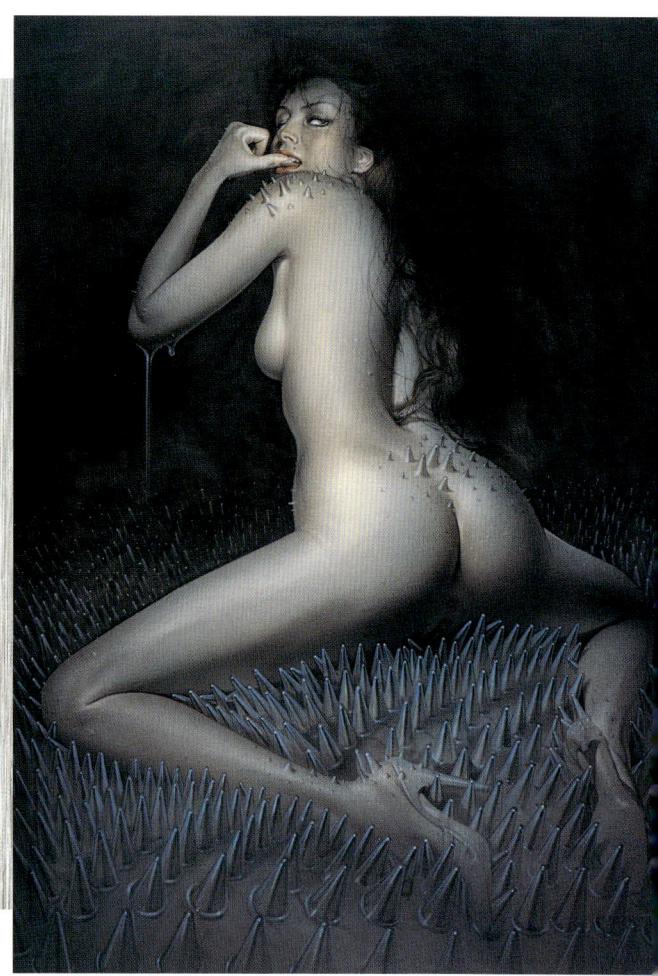

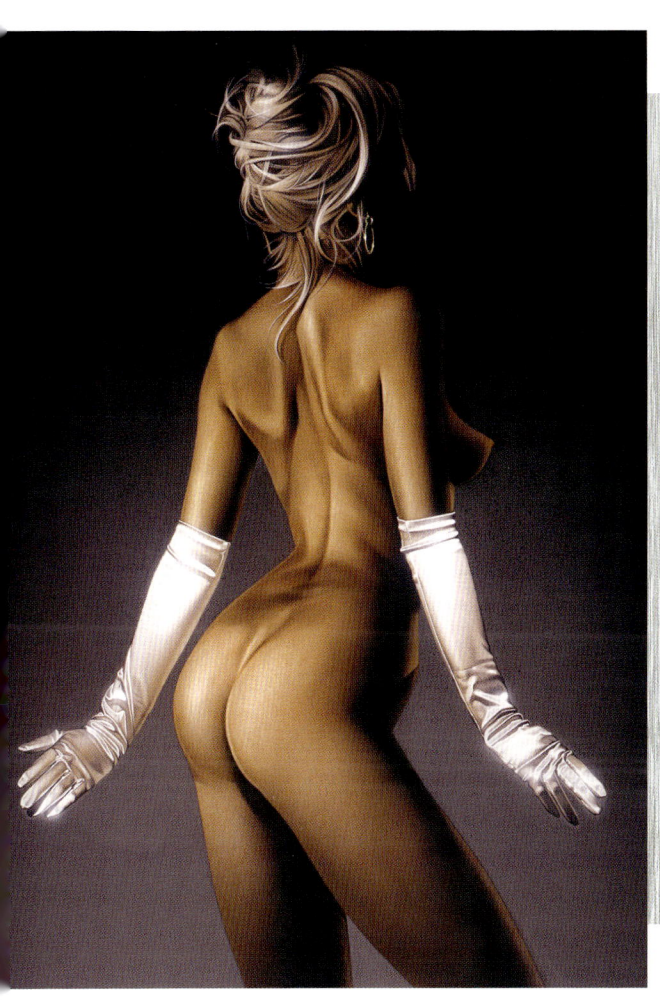

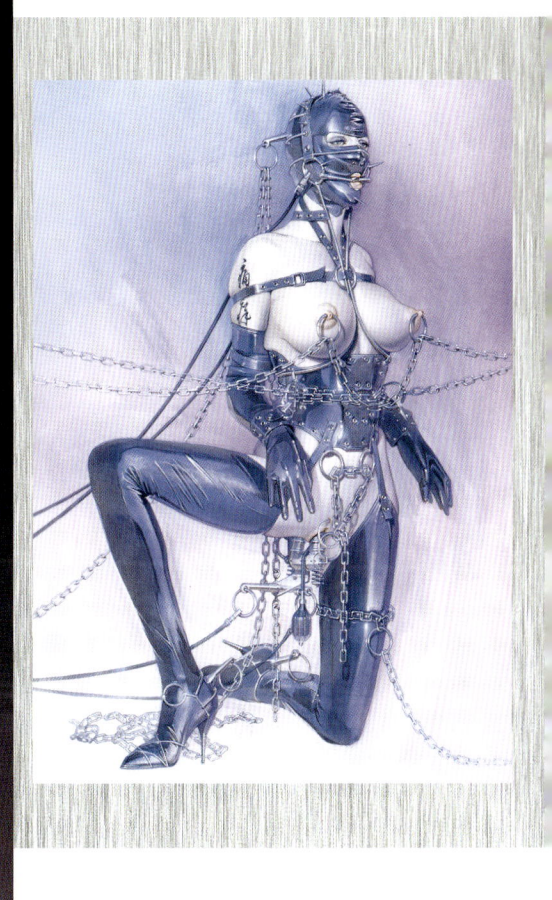

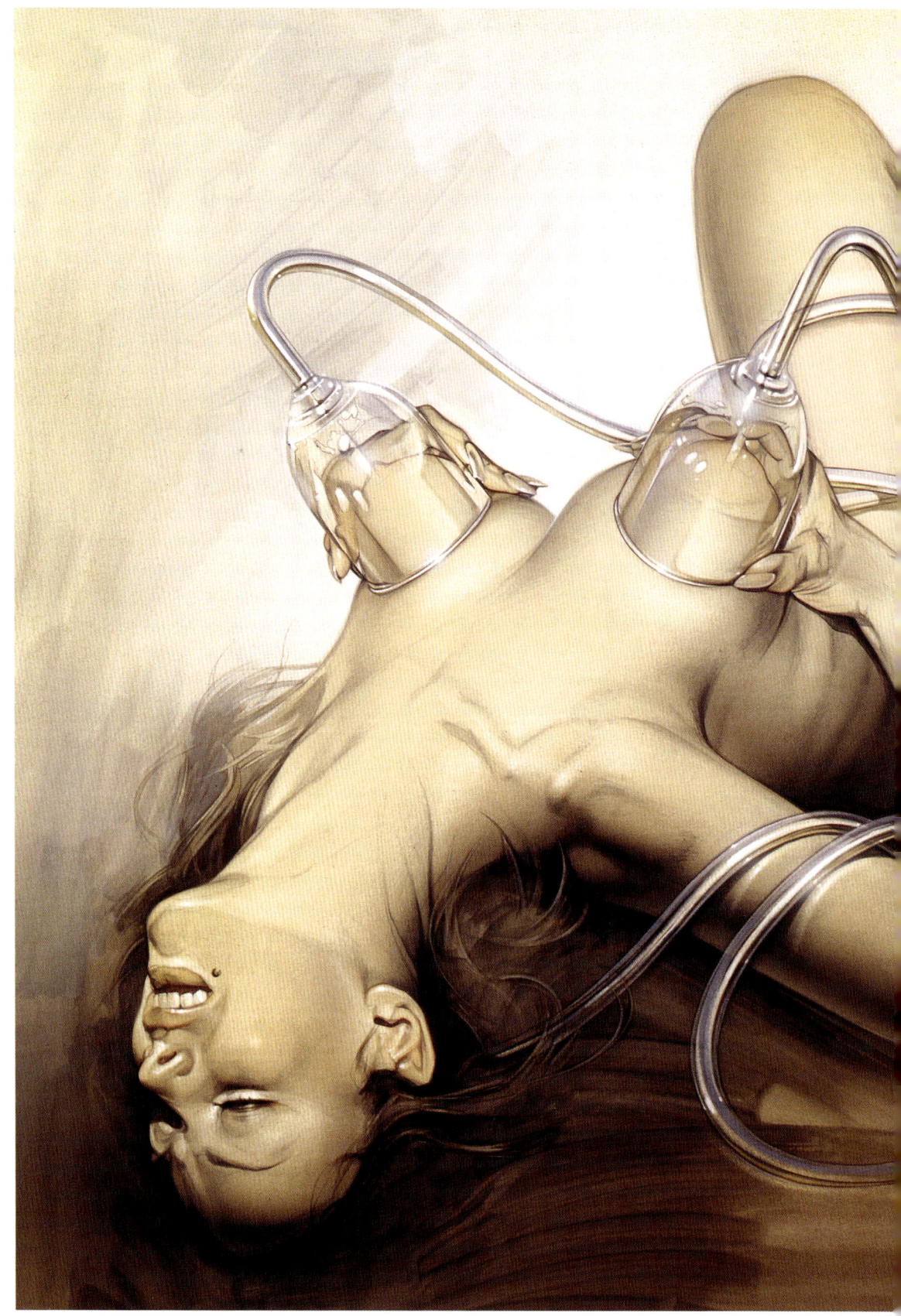

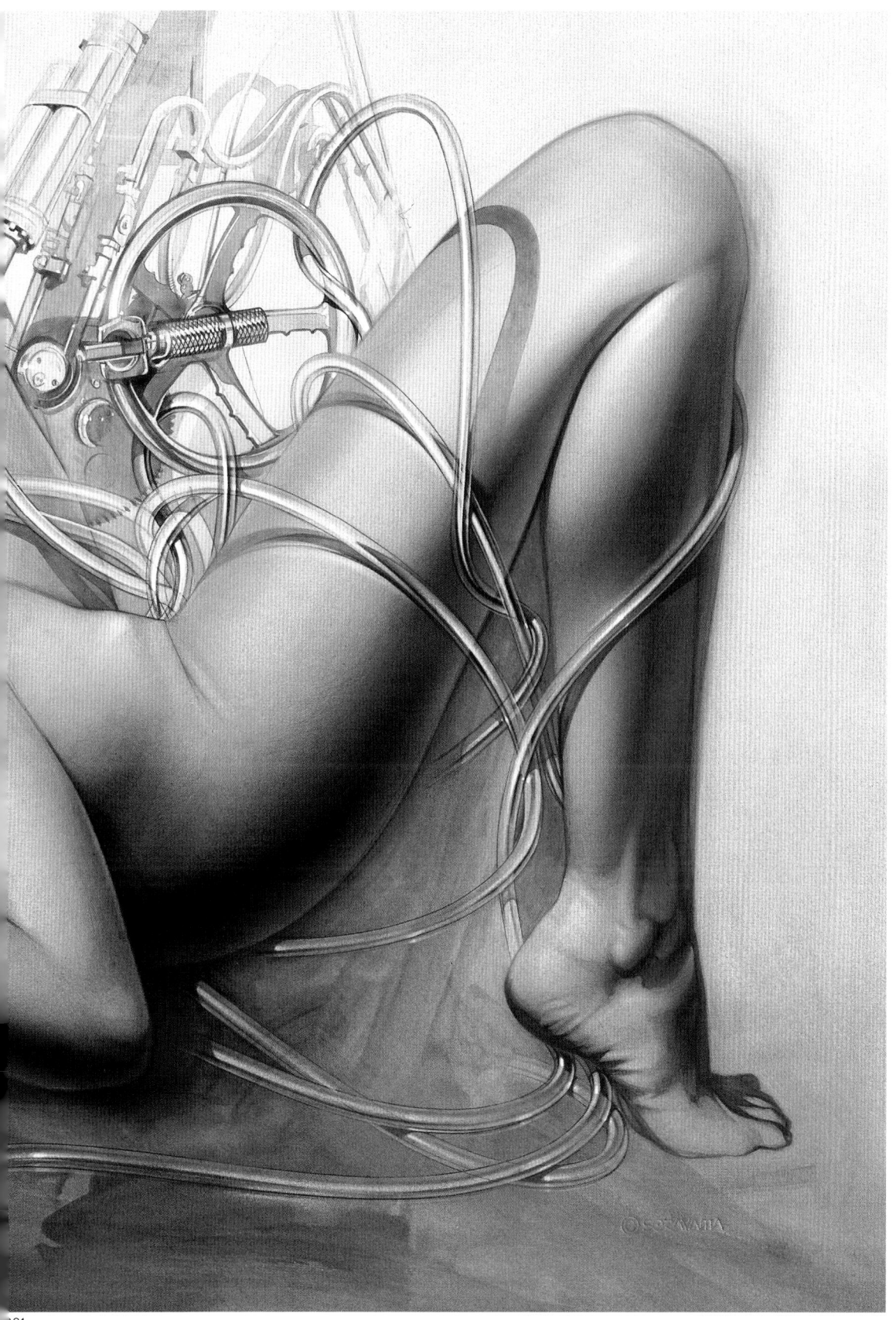

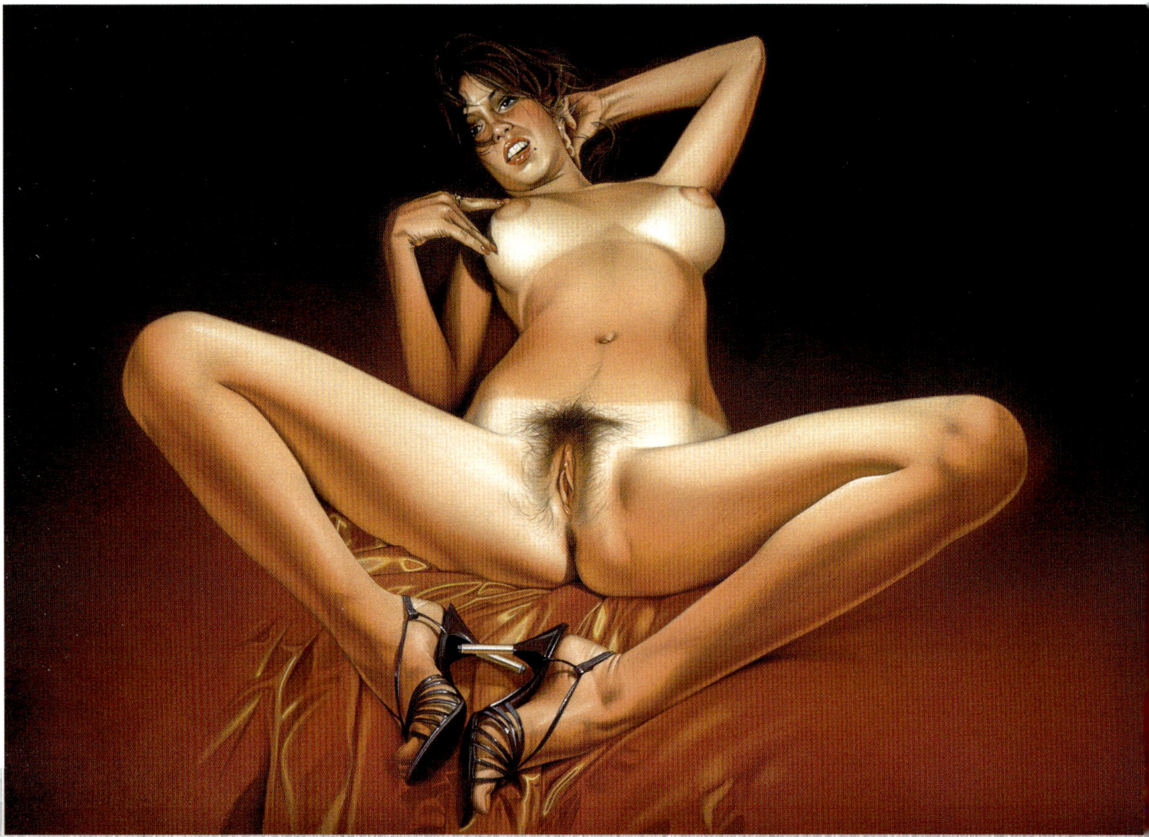

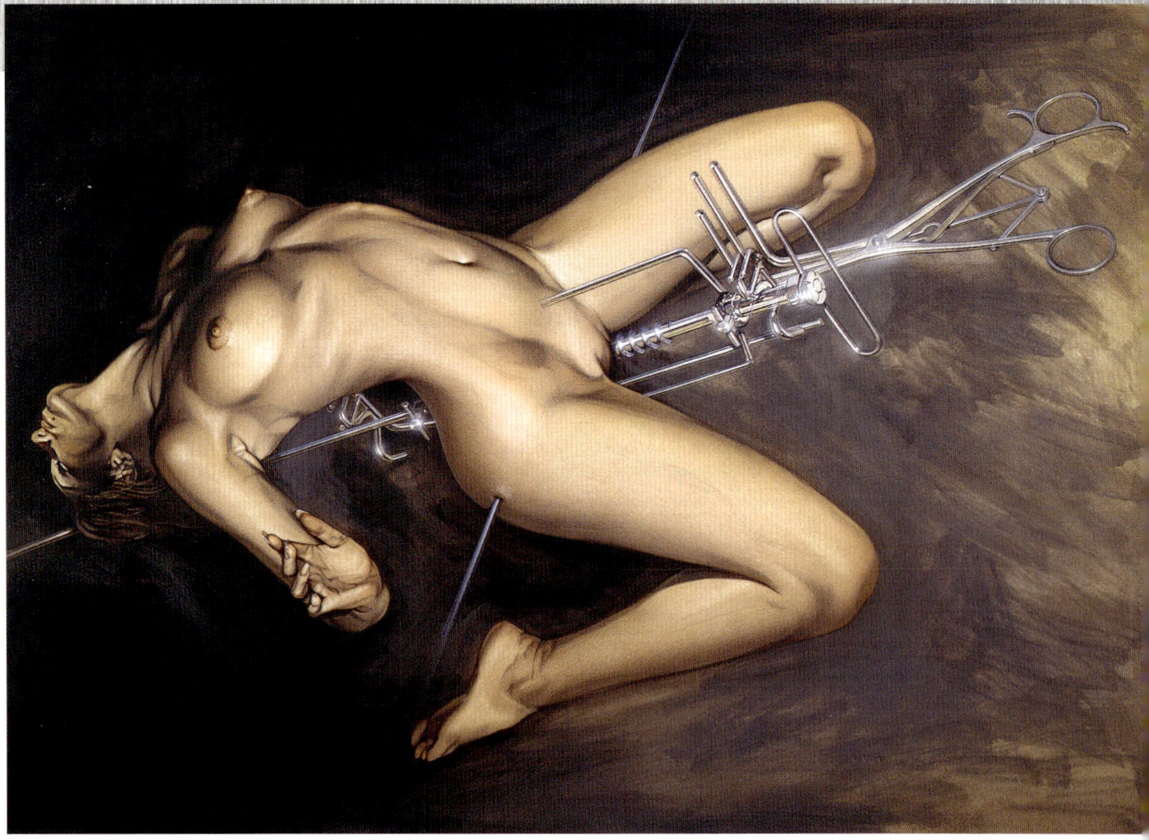

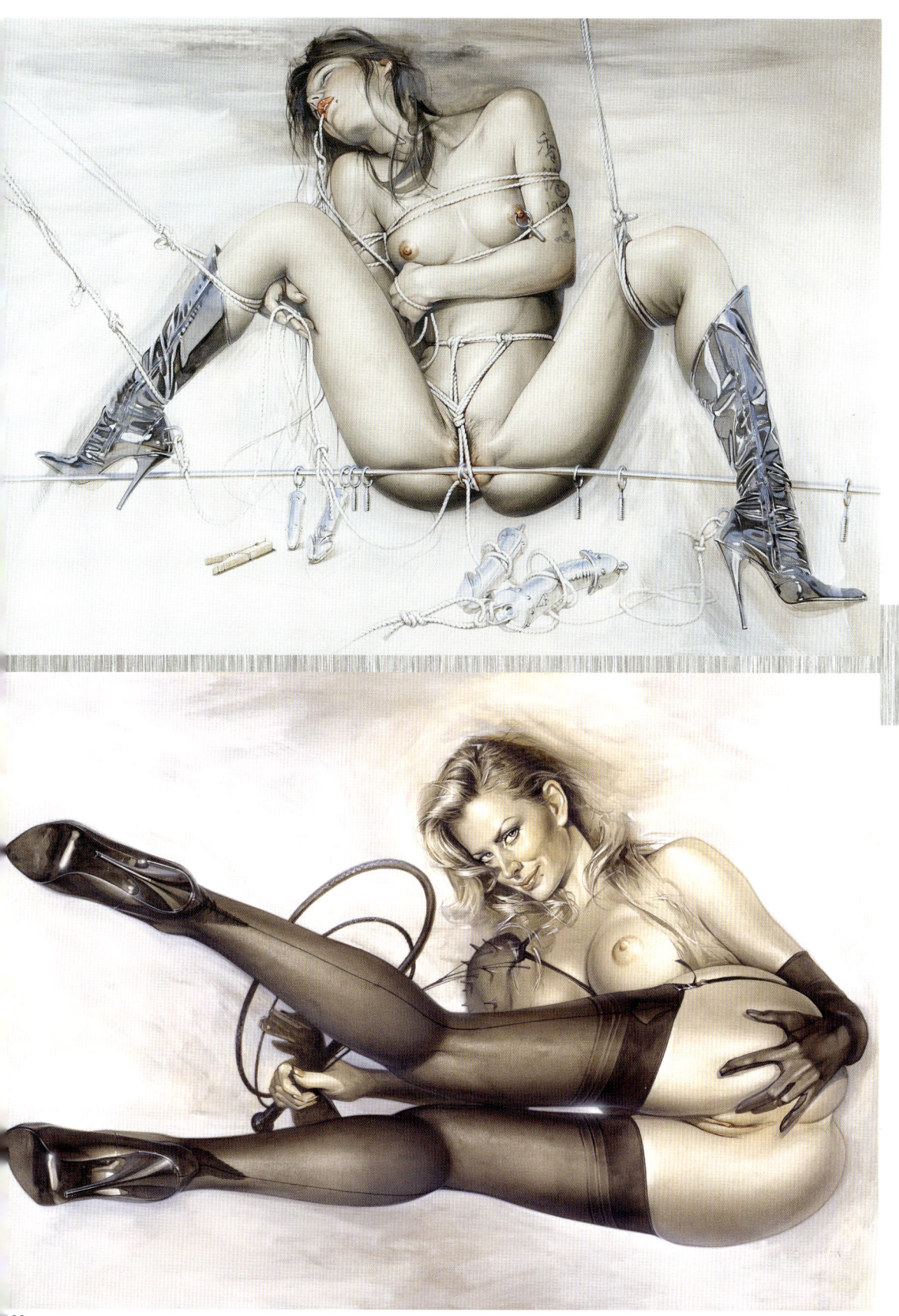

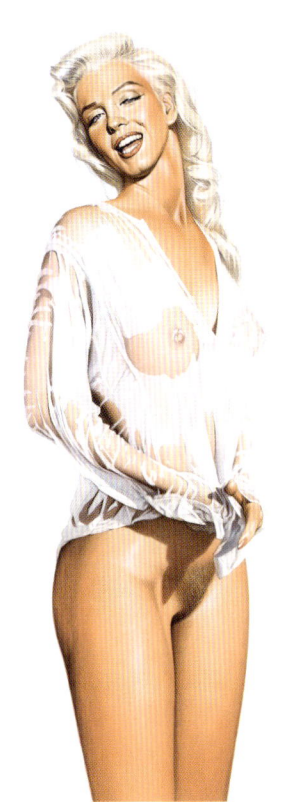
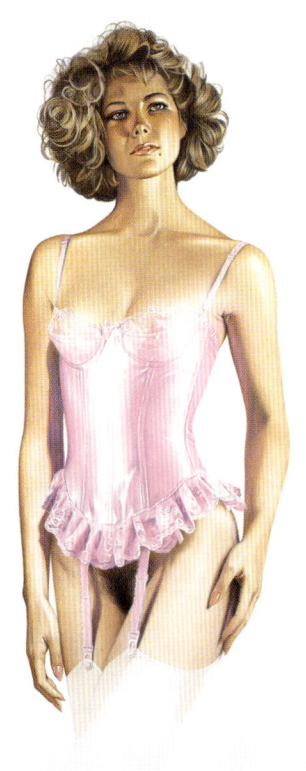
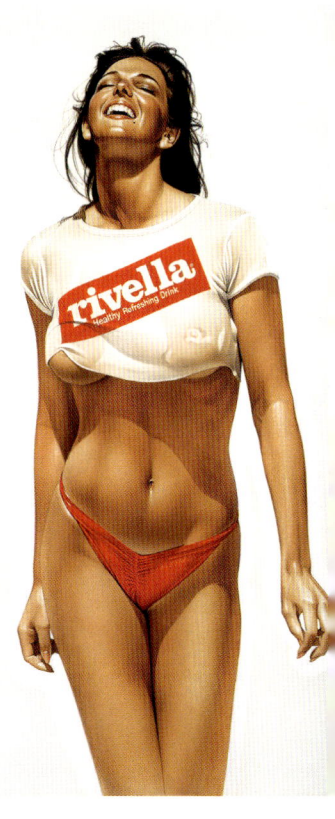

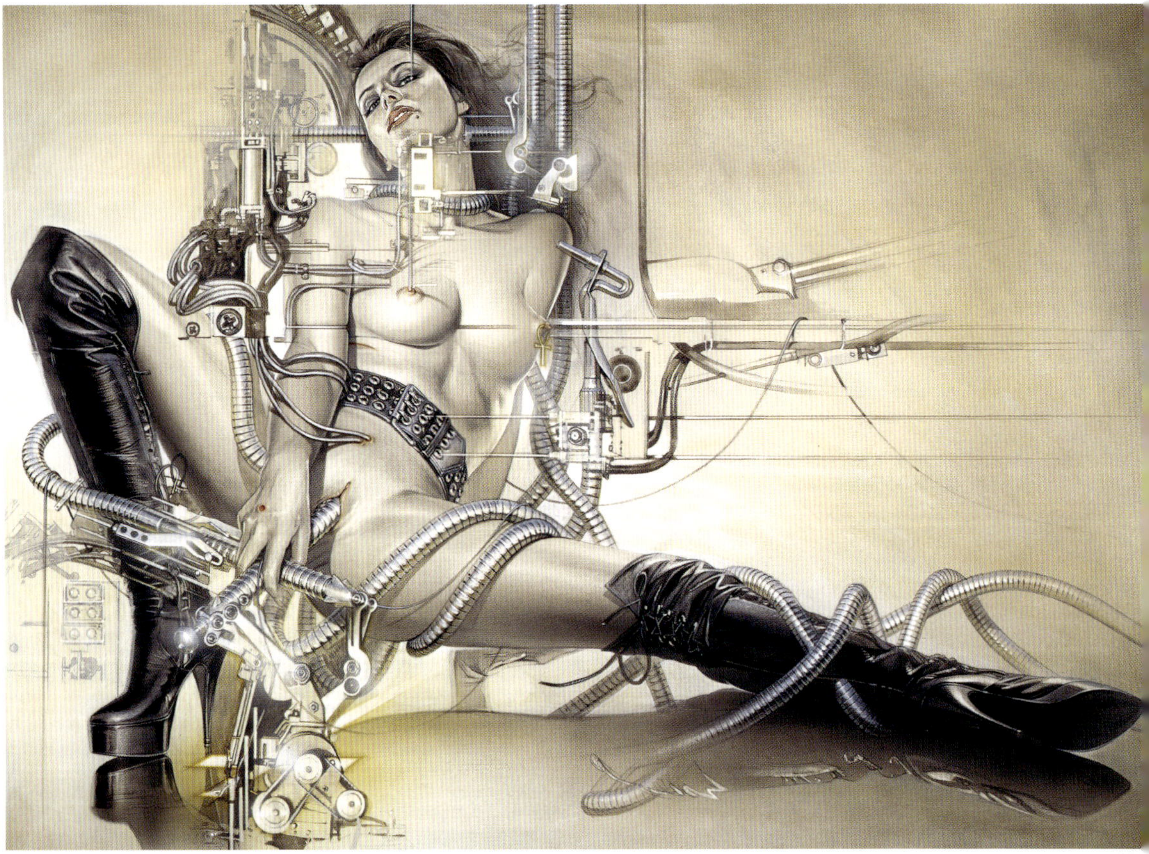

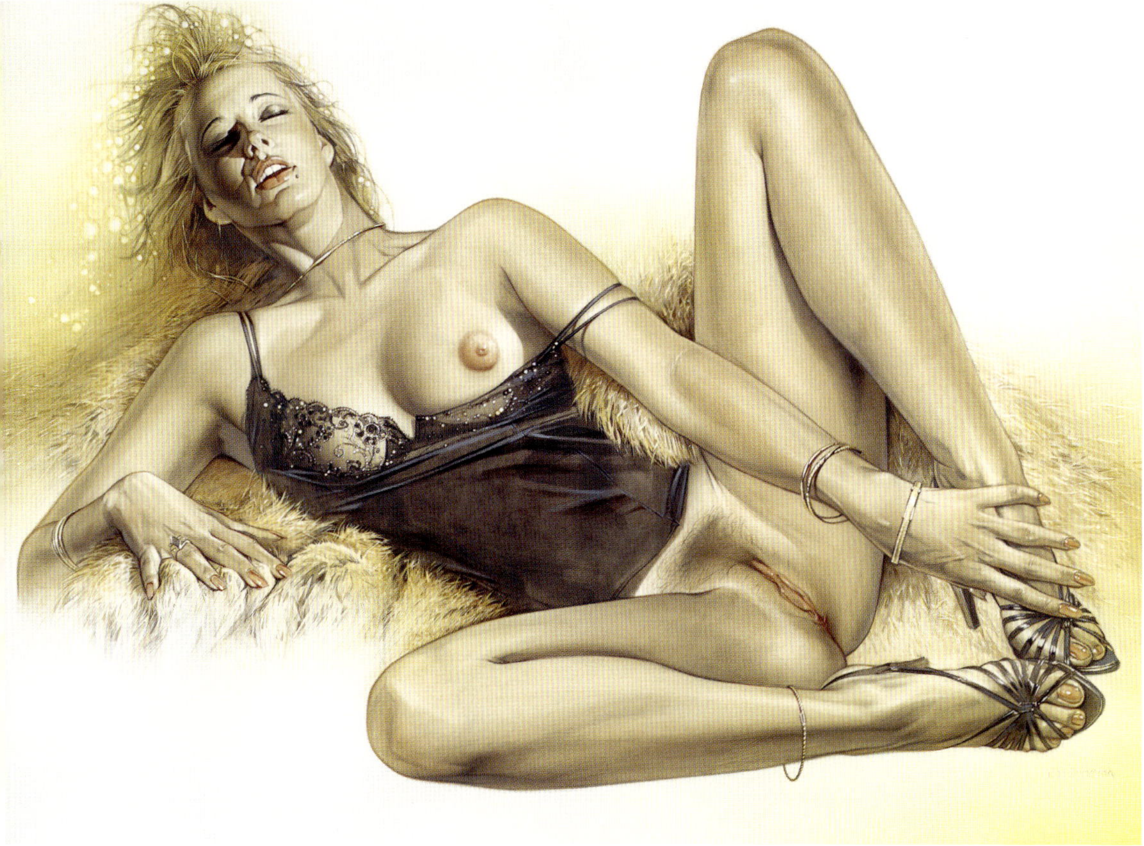

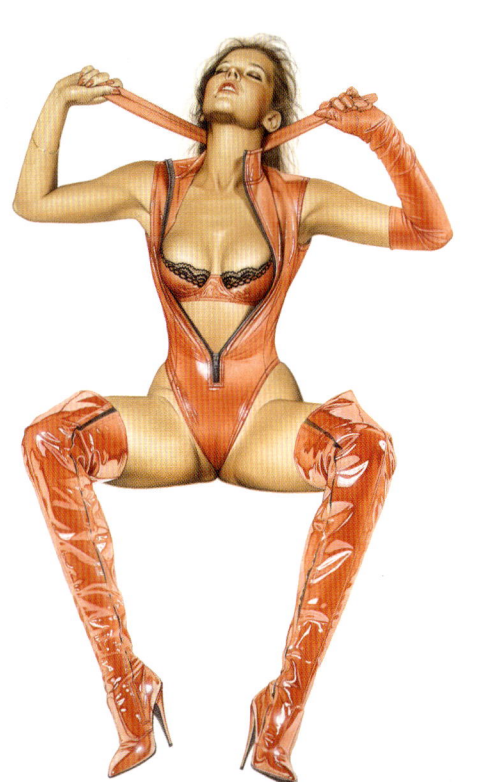

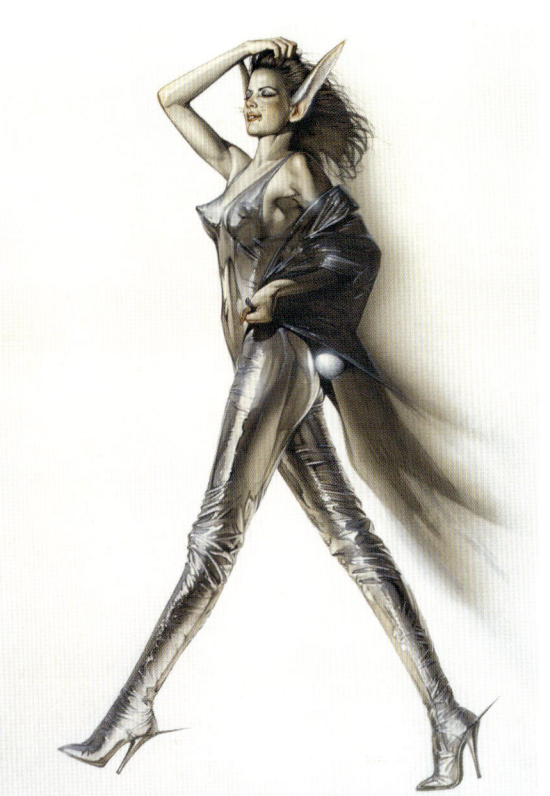

Sorayama is a male artist.

While female nudes have served as the subject for many of his works, he is also renowned for depicting all kinds of robotic forms from human beings (male and female) to animals, dinosaurs, and machinery.

It is not out of the ordinary for a male artist to depict female nudes. Rather, when reflecting upon the history of art spanning from ancient Greece to the Renaissance and to the present, it could be considered as the mainstream. There are indeed tens of thousands of artists who are insistent on pursuing the beauty, complexity, and sheer profundity of the human body.

One actively refutes the argument that Sorayama's works are misogynistic and illustrate disrespect for women, as it is by no means the case. In truth, Sorayama continues to be a good father to his two daughters, and currently lives an "ordinary and happy" life in the company of his wife and his three grandchildren. Although his paintings consist of fetishistic motifs, he himself does not express sexual preference for this realm. His work is based on an extremely intensified curiosity and a sense of universal worship.

Sorayama's works are a testament to the fact that life is conceived through the presence of men and women in this world. Furthermore, he recognizes that human dignity and evolution are at times brought about by mortal desires and curiosity. It is no exaggeration to say that his entire oeuvre is a reflection of intellectual curiosity and eternal life. In fact, Sorayama's depictions have gained significant support from people of all ages, regions, and genders in their treatment of themes such as body modification, the post-human body, and AI.

Sorayama is in denial of things that are deemed taboo. For instance, he is unable to understand at all the reasons why human nudity is socially oppressed. In the same way, he also boldly challenges political and religious taboos.

This is not about being 'punk', but is an act of honesty. Sorayama is convinced that issues must be resolved through voicing one's thoughts and opinions rather than remaining silent, and for that reason he at times strives to maintain a sense of child-like innocence. As a result, he tries to be more radical. Sorayama deliberately attempts to engage in modes of expression that people tend to avoid or distance themselves from.

Having said that, at the same time his works are highly personal. Sorayama never intends for his work to be appreciated as "high art." Quite the contrary, he regards the framework of art to be nothing but a constraint.

Text: Shinji Nanzuka (NANZUKA)

古川タク（イラストレーター）

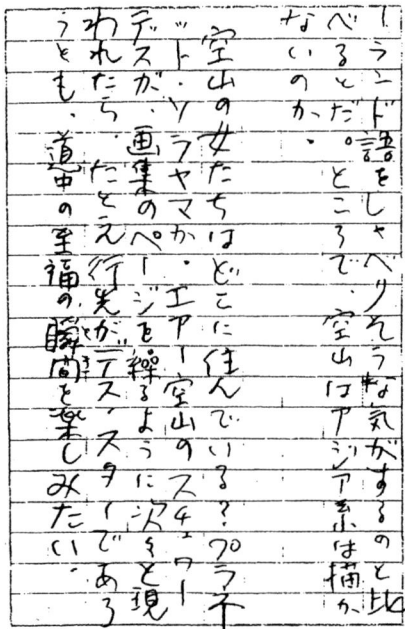
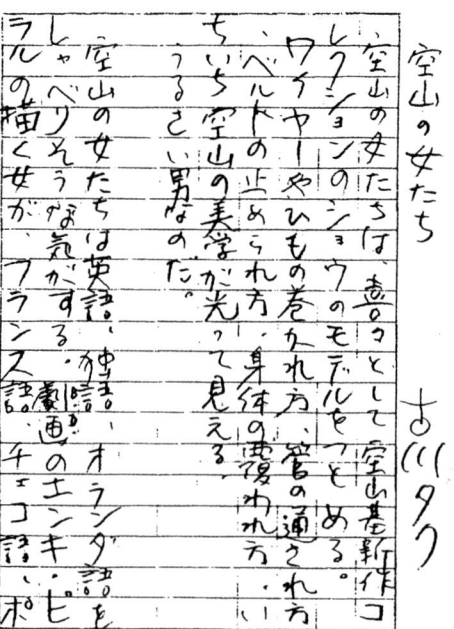

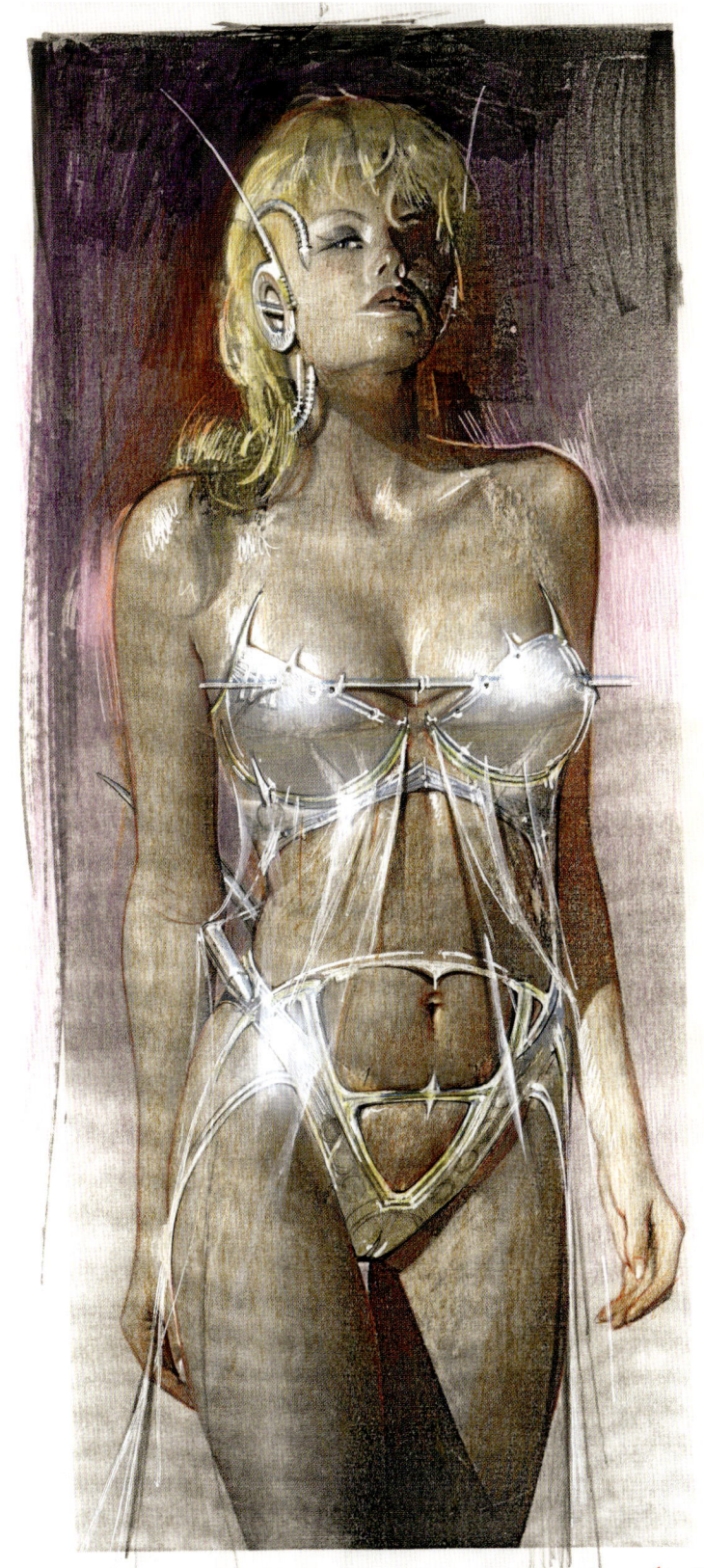

花のドレープ・花のドレス on cyber elements, where the metal cling right to her skin.

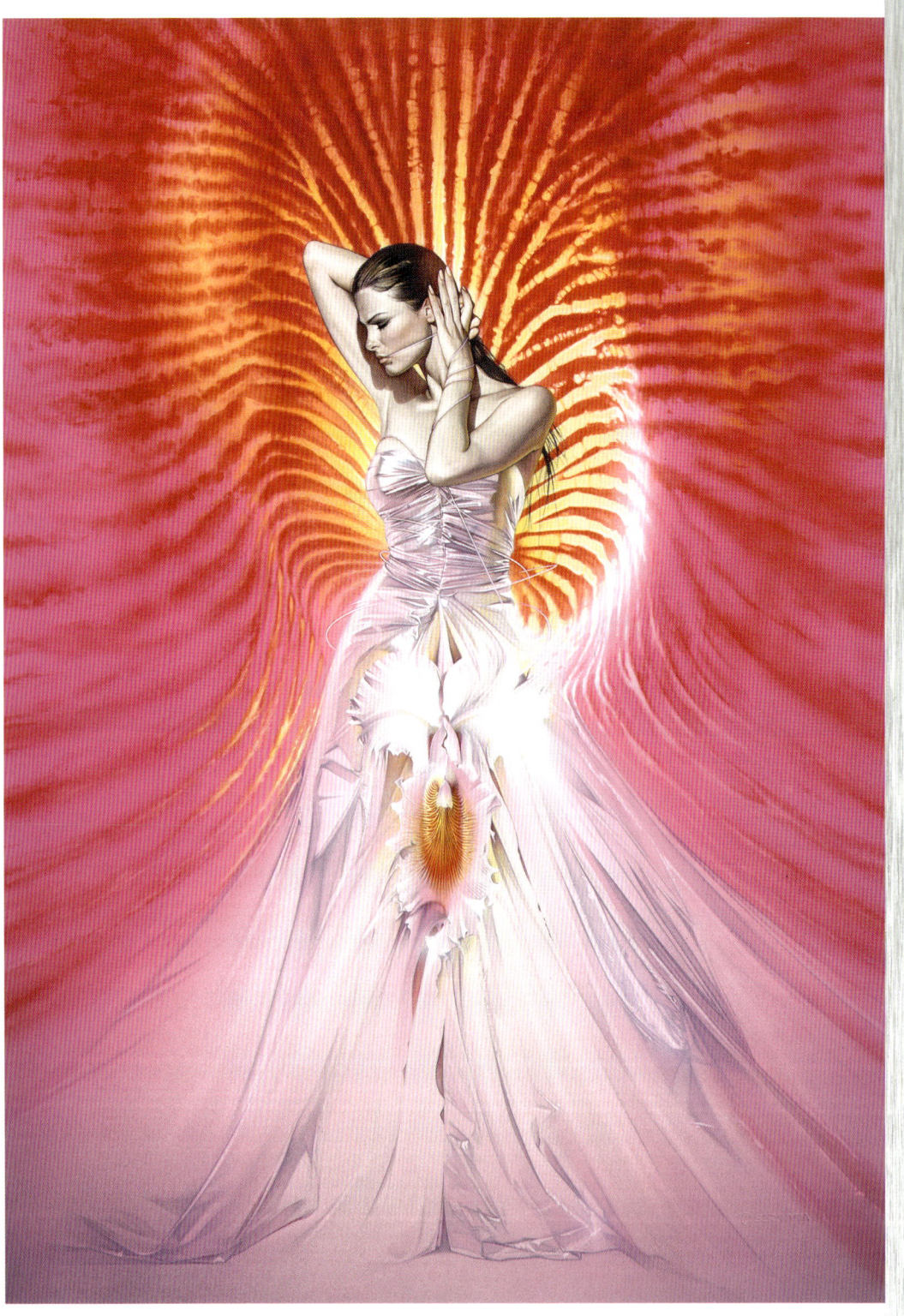

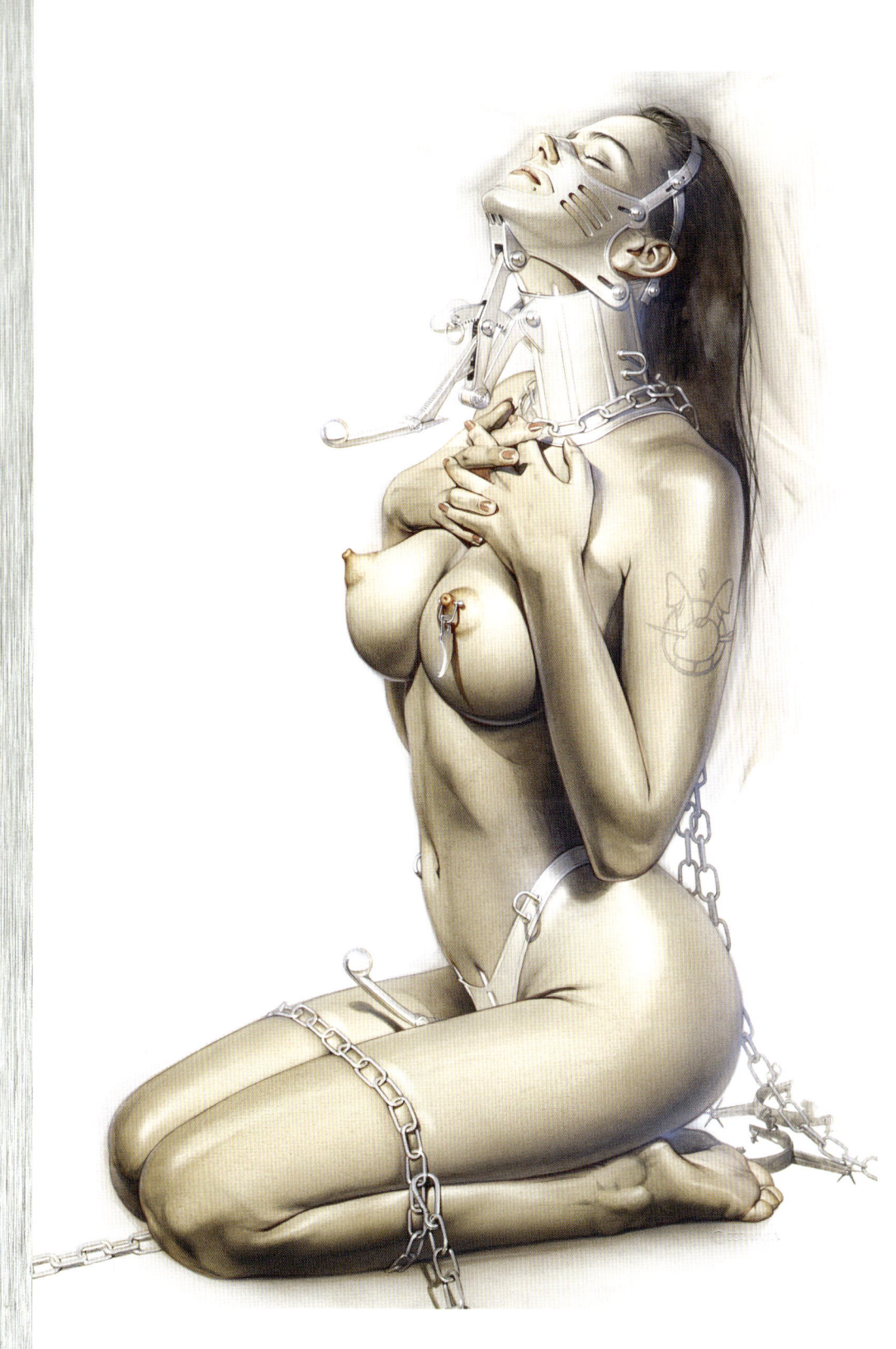

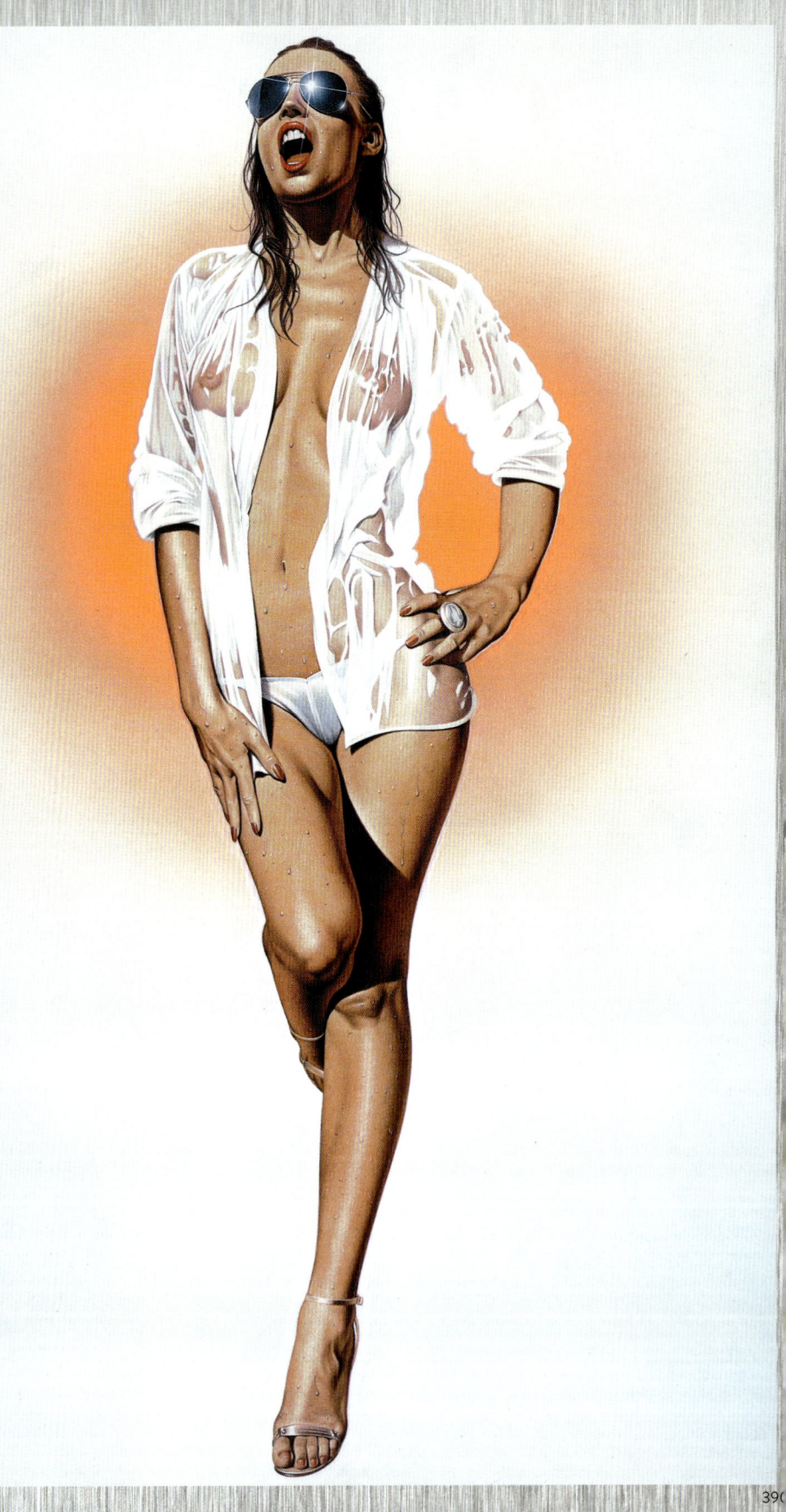

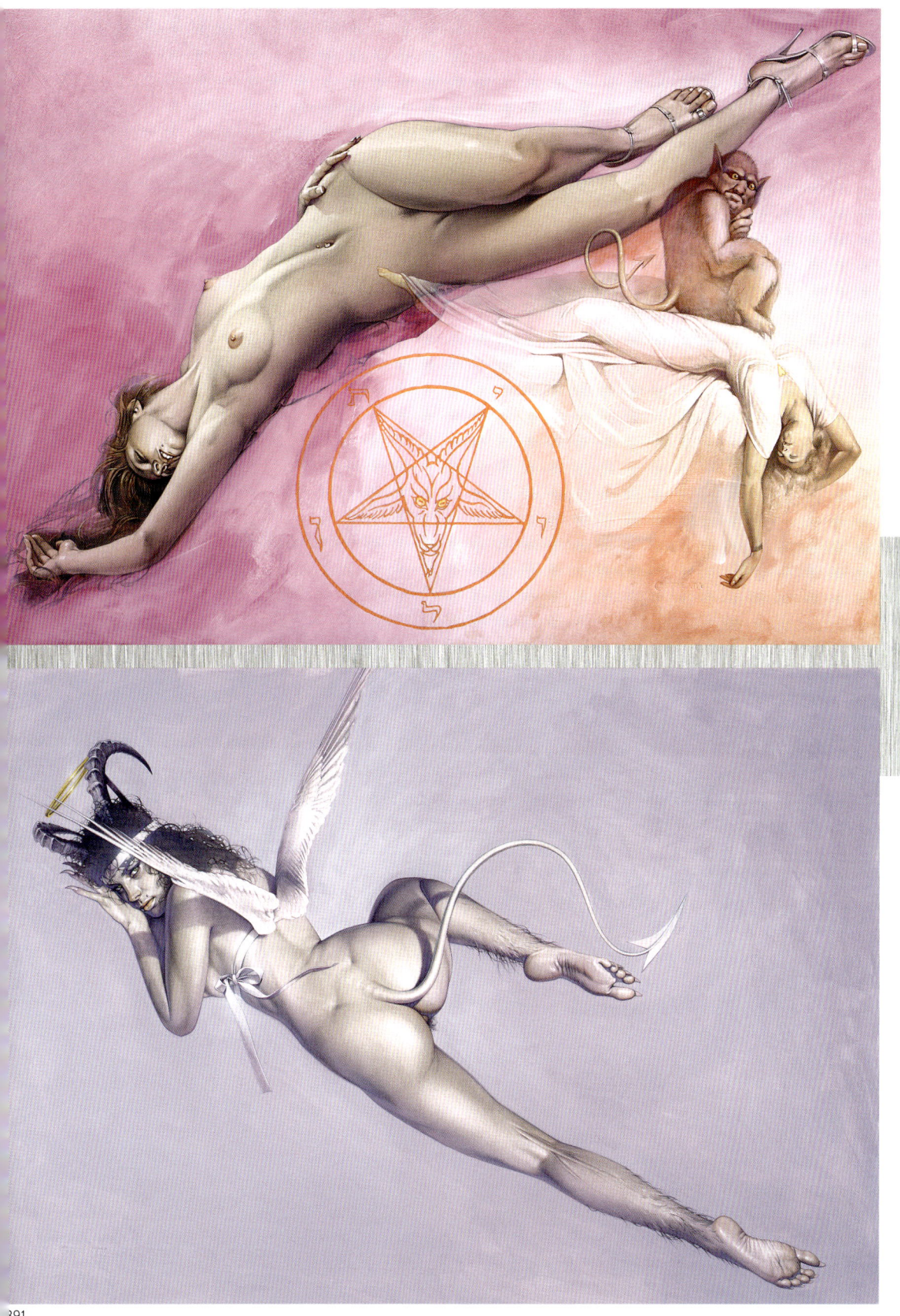

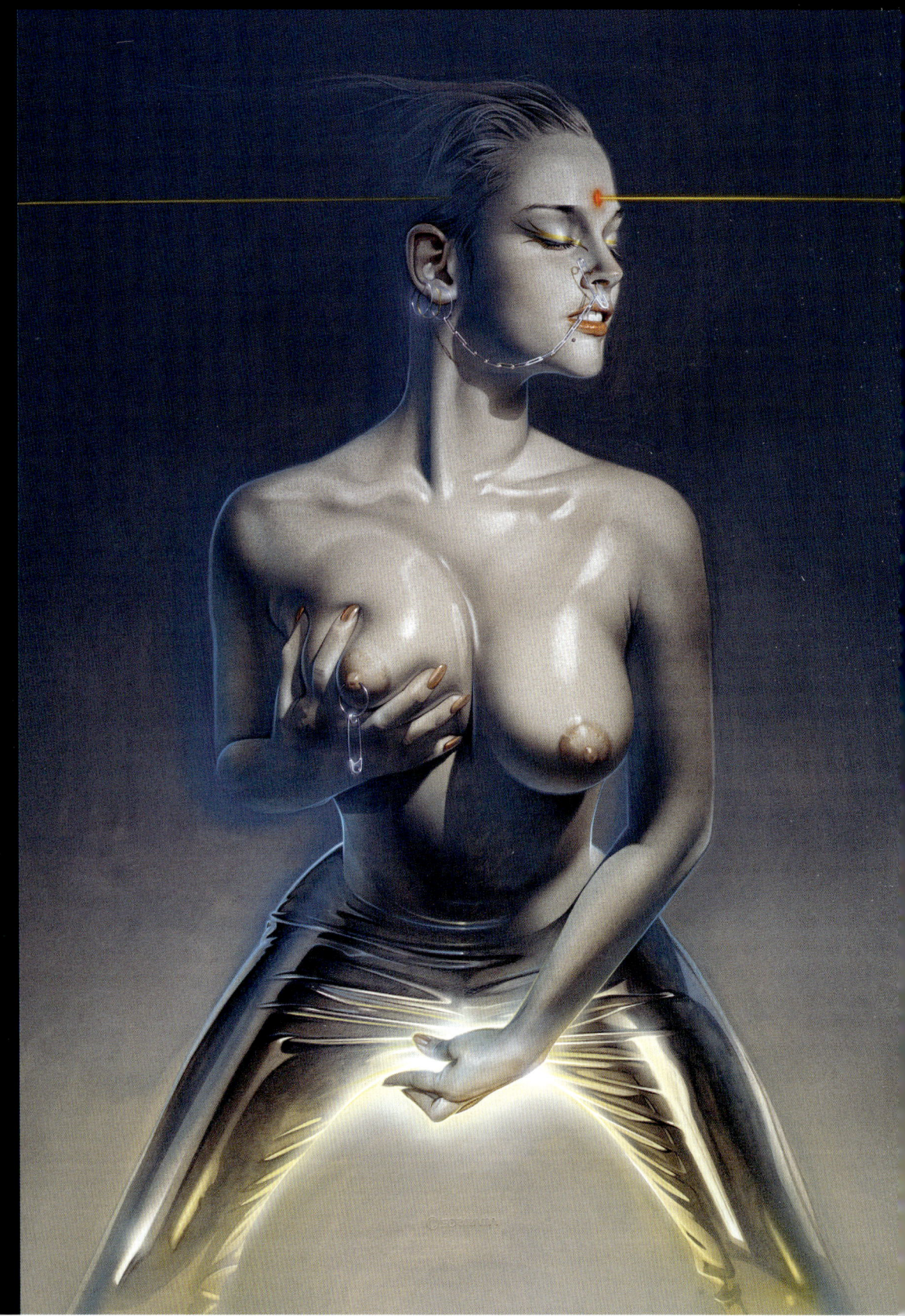

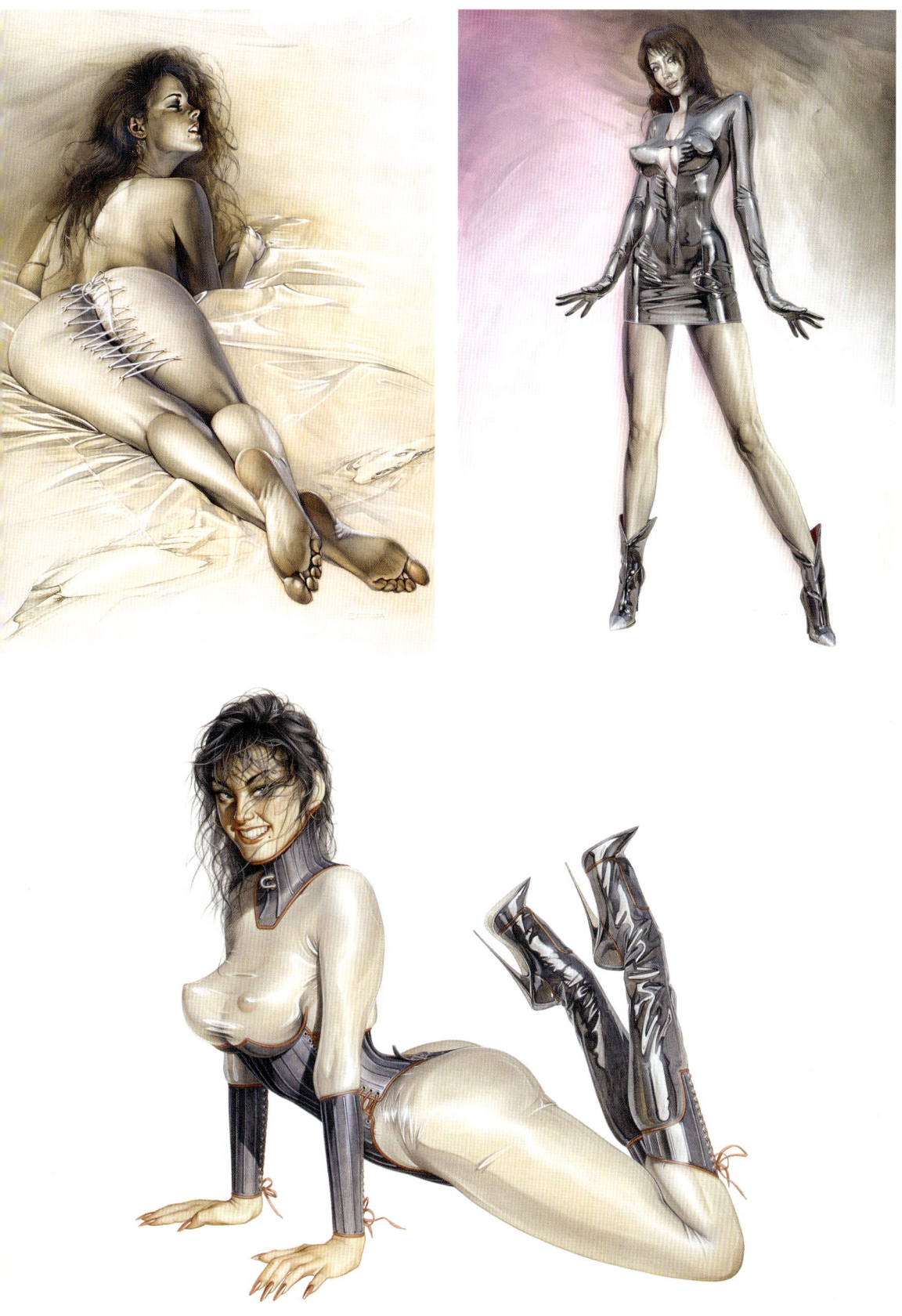

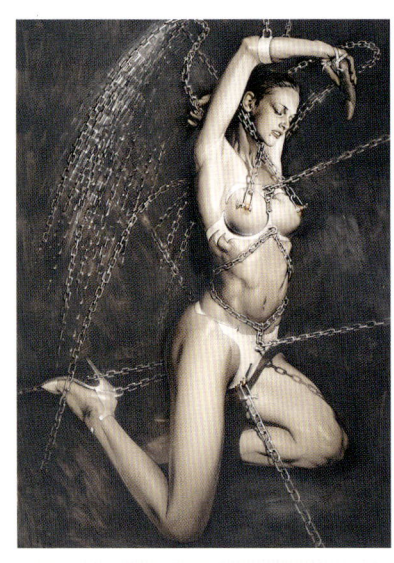
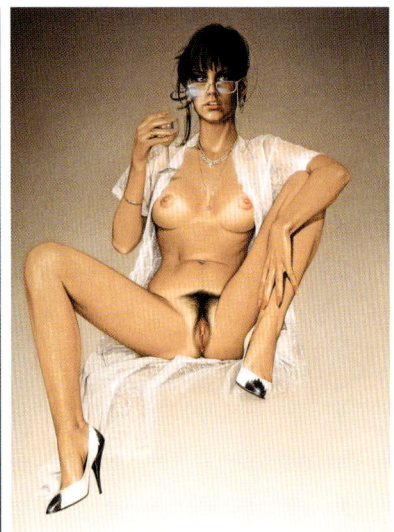
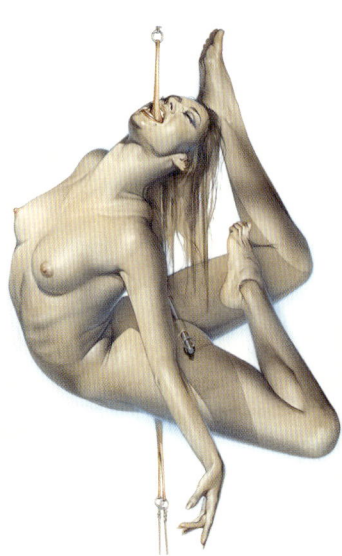
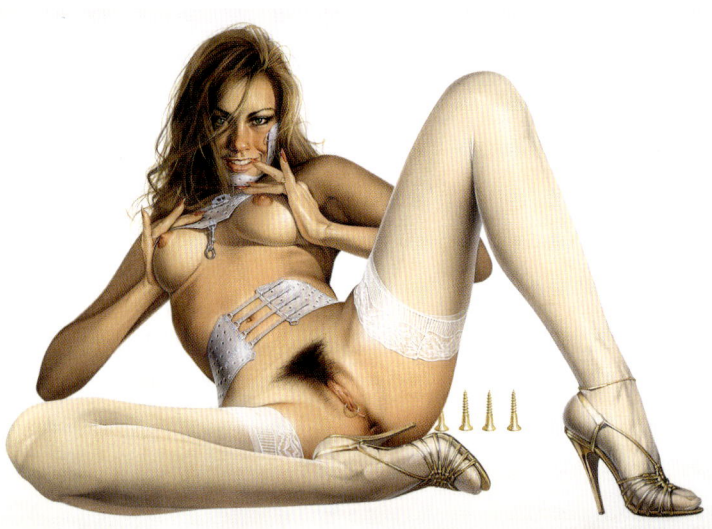
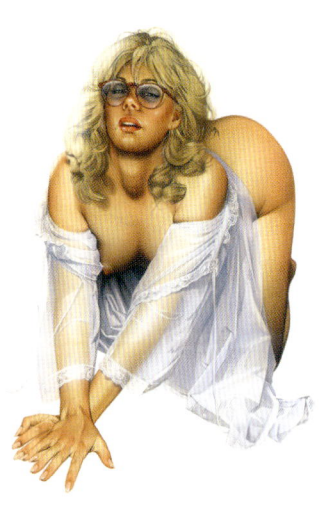
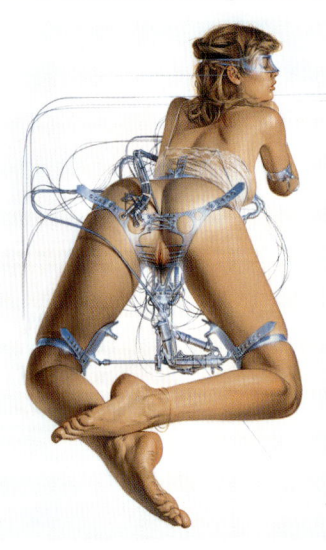
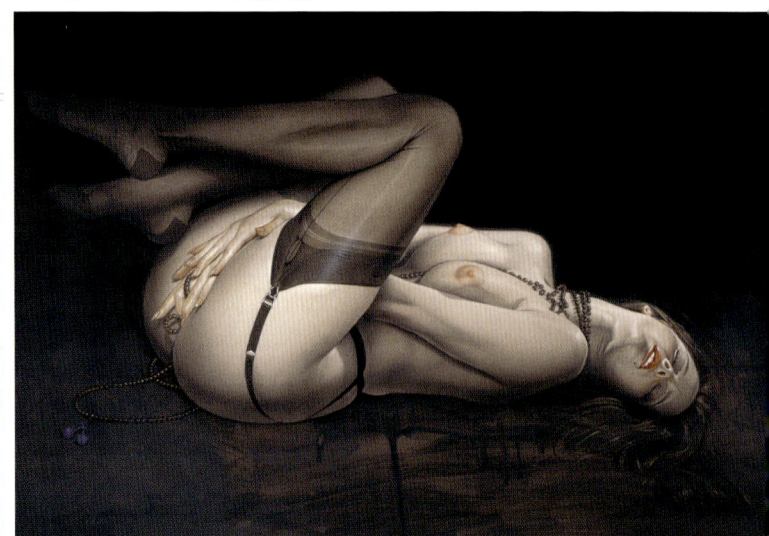

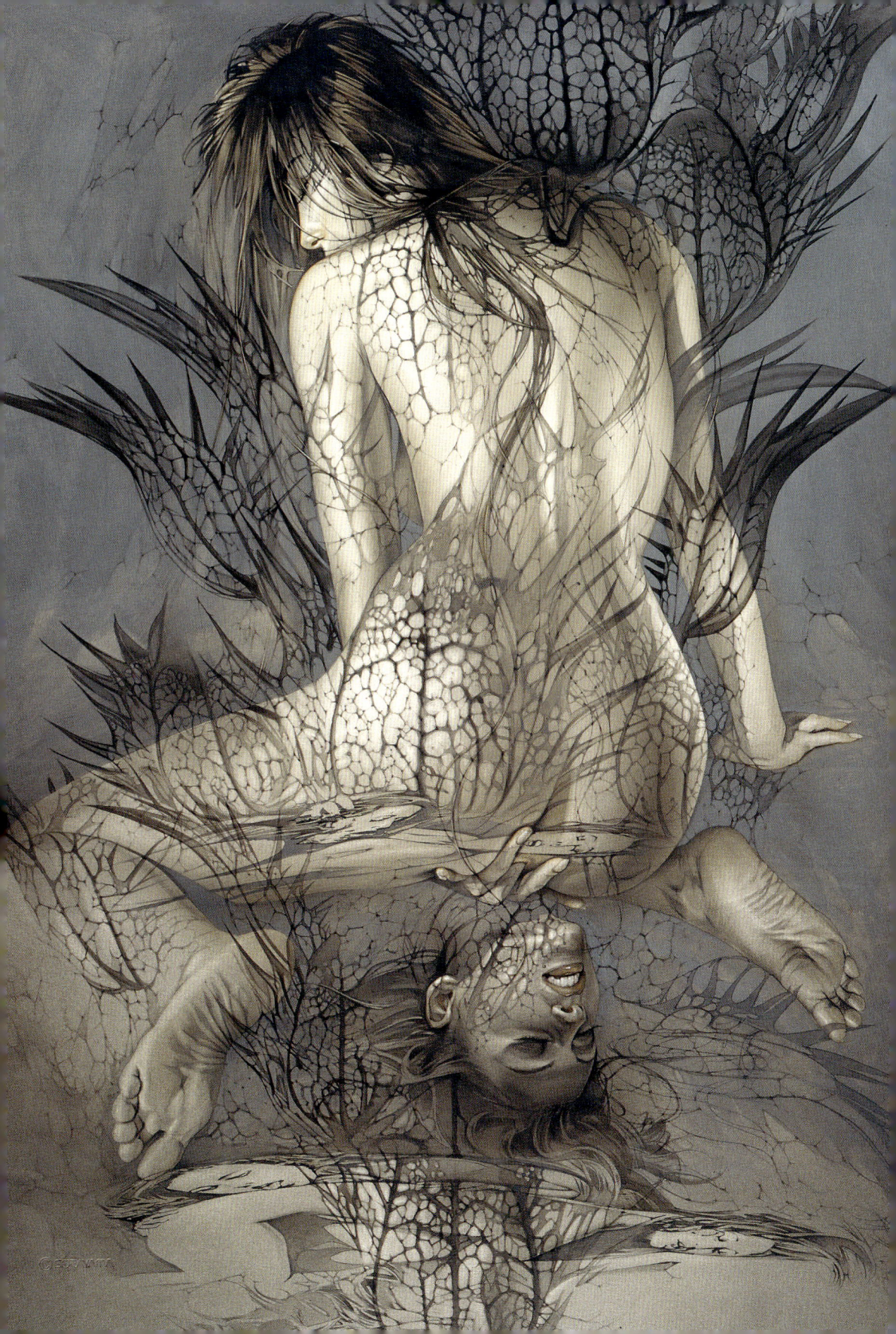

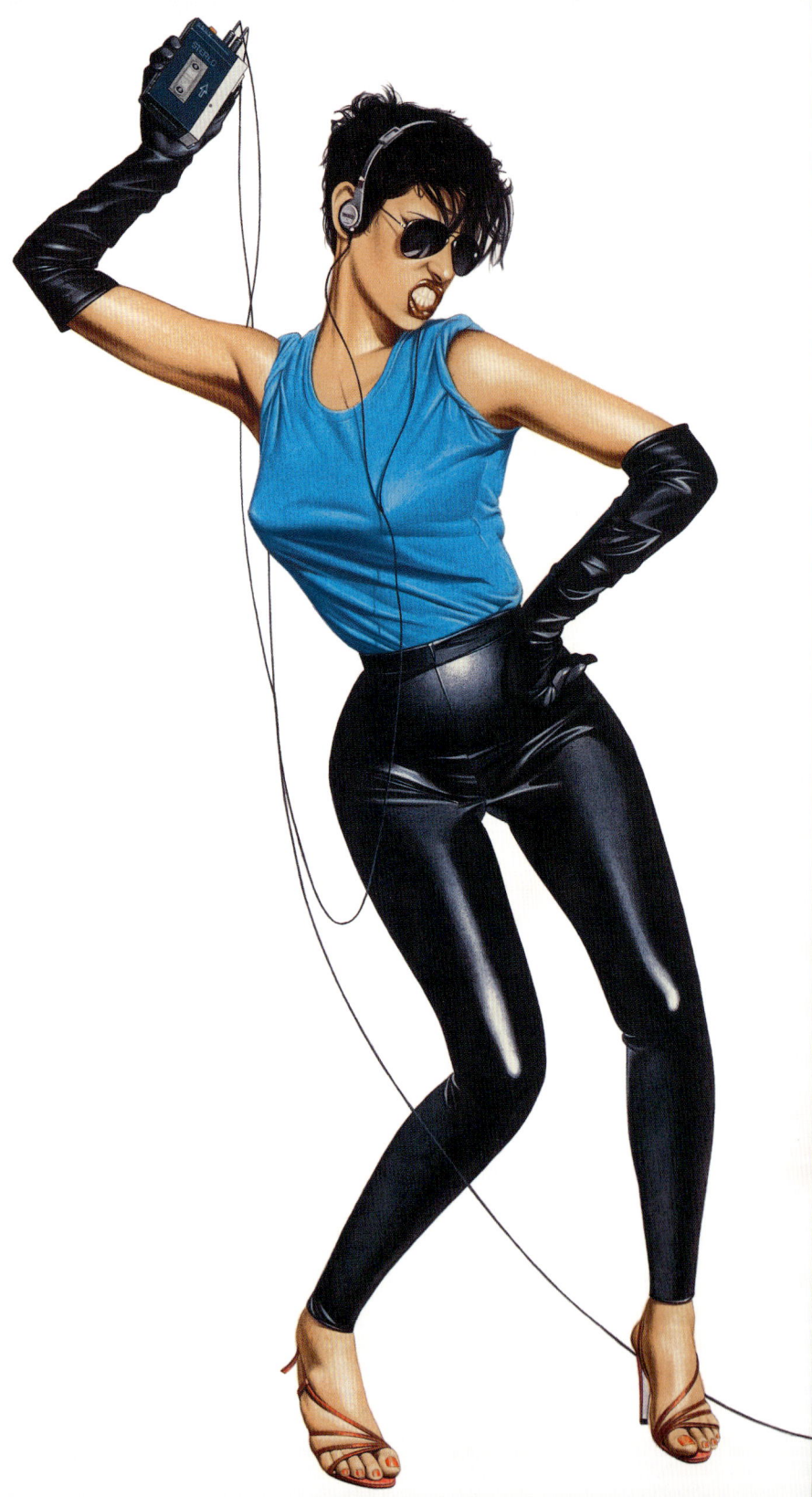

湯村輝彦（イラストレーター）

エロ・スーパー・リアリズム絵画の王様、空山基氏
と、エロ・ヘタうま絵画の王様、テリー・ジョンスン（私）
とは手法こそいちぢるしく違うものの、そこはどっこい、エロを追
究する者同志どこか心が通じ合うから、道ですれ違えば、お互い熱
い視線を投げかけ合う関係なのである。いずれ機会があれば、鬼エ
ロいコラボレーションなんかをズボズボやってみたいものだ。
その節はヨロシク‼
P.S. 股、エロVIDEO送ってネ♡

T-Back Agency.
a Division of Ryashiga Studio Inc.

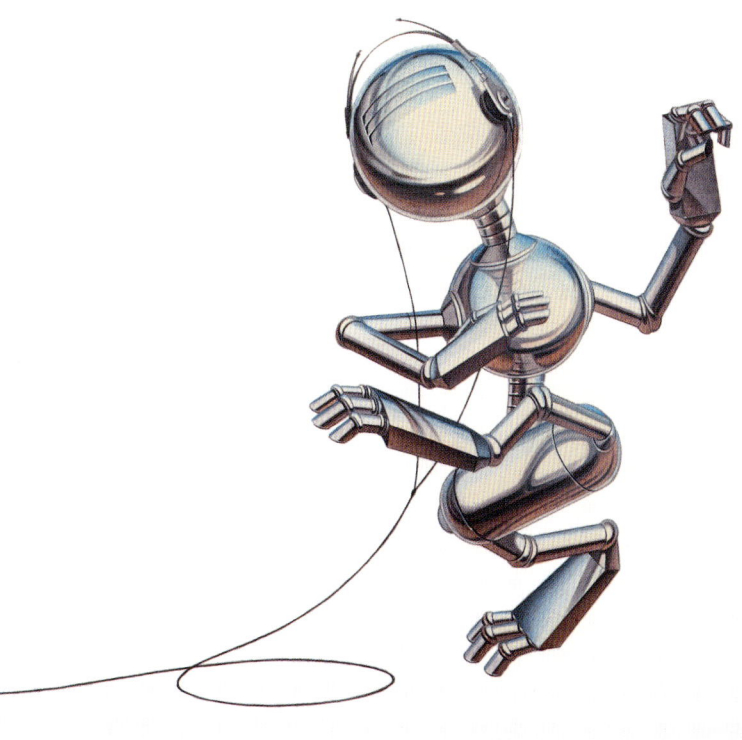

397

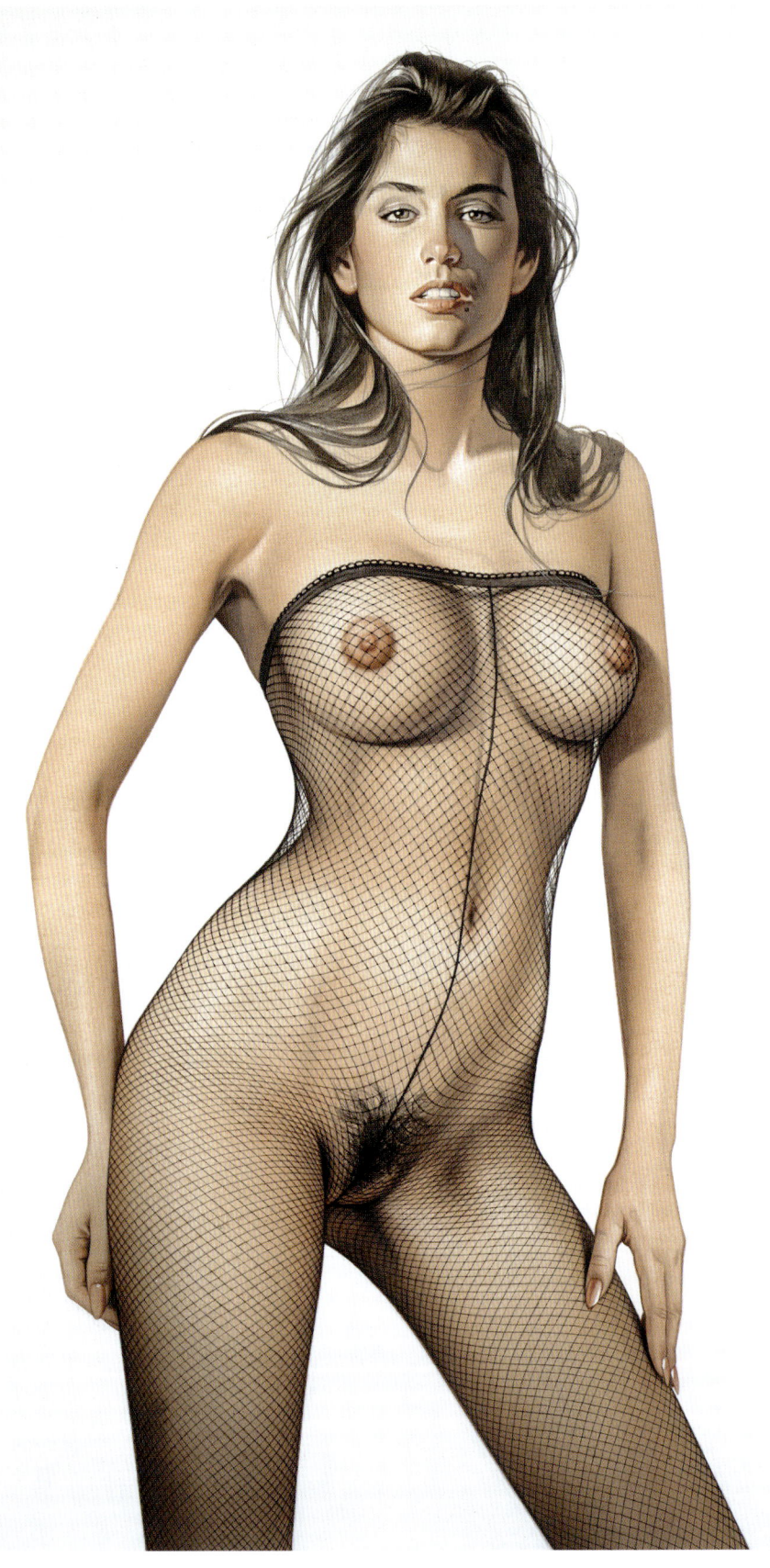

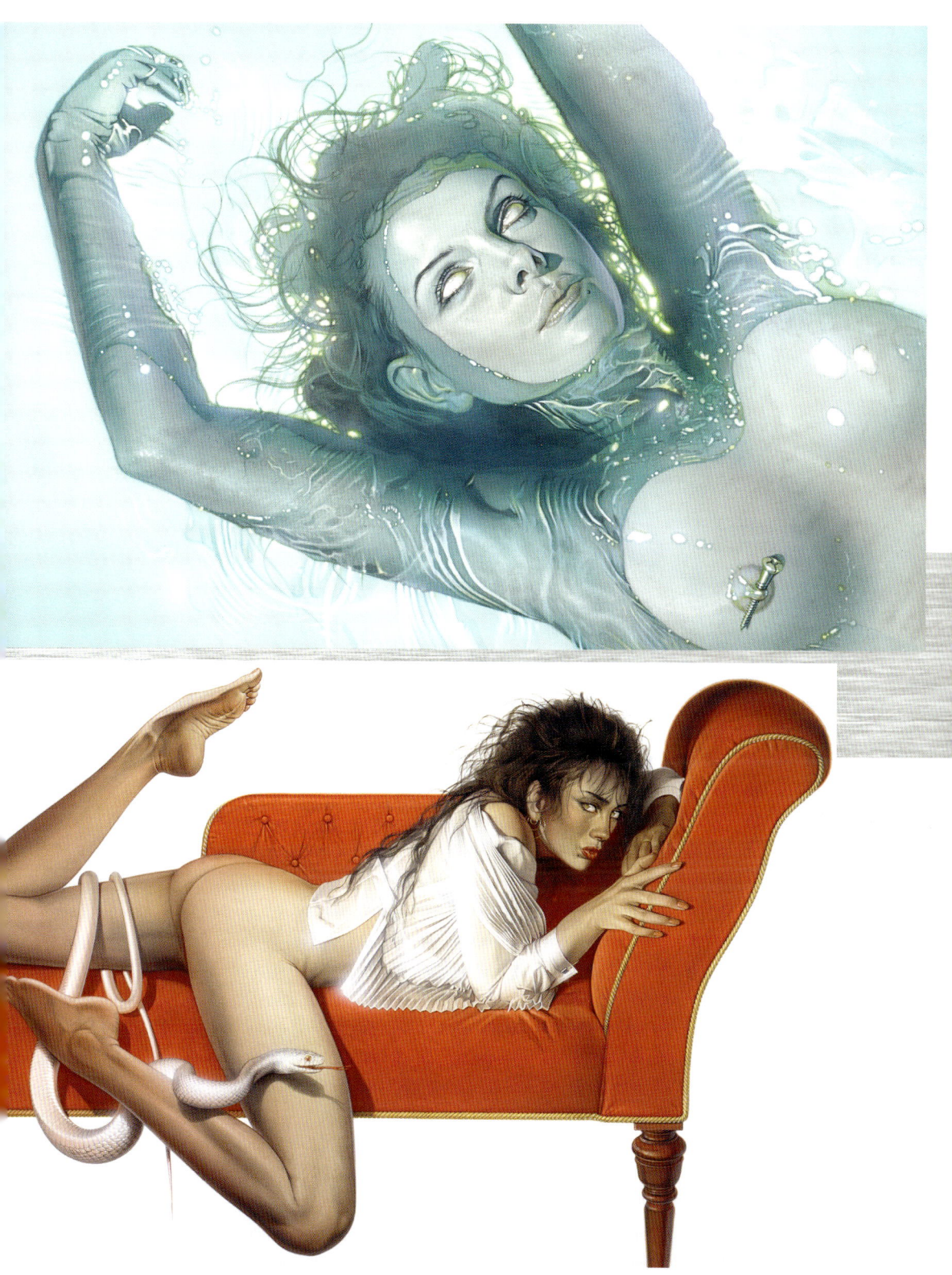

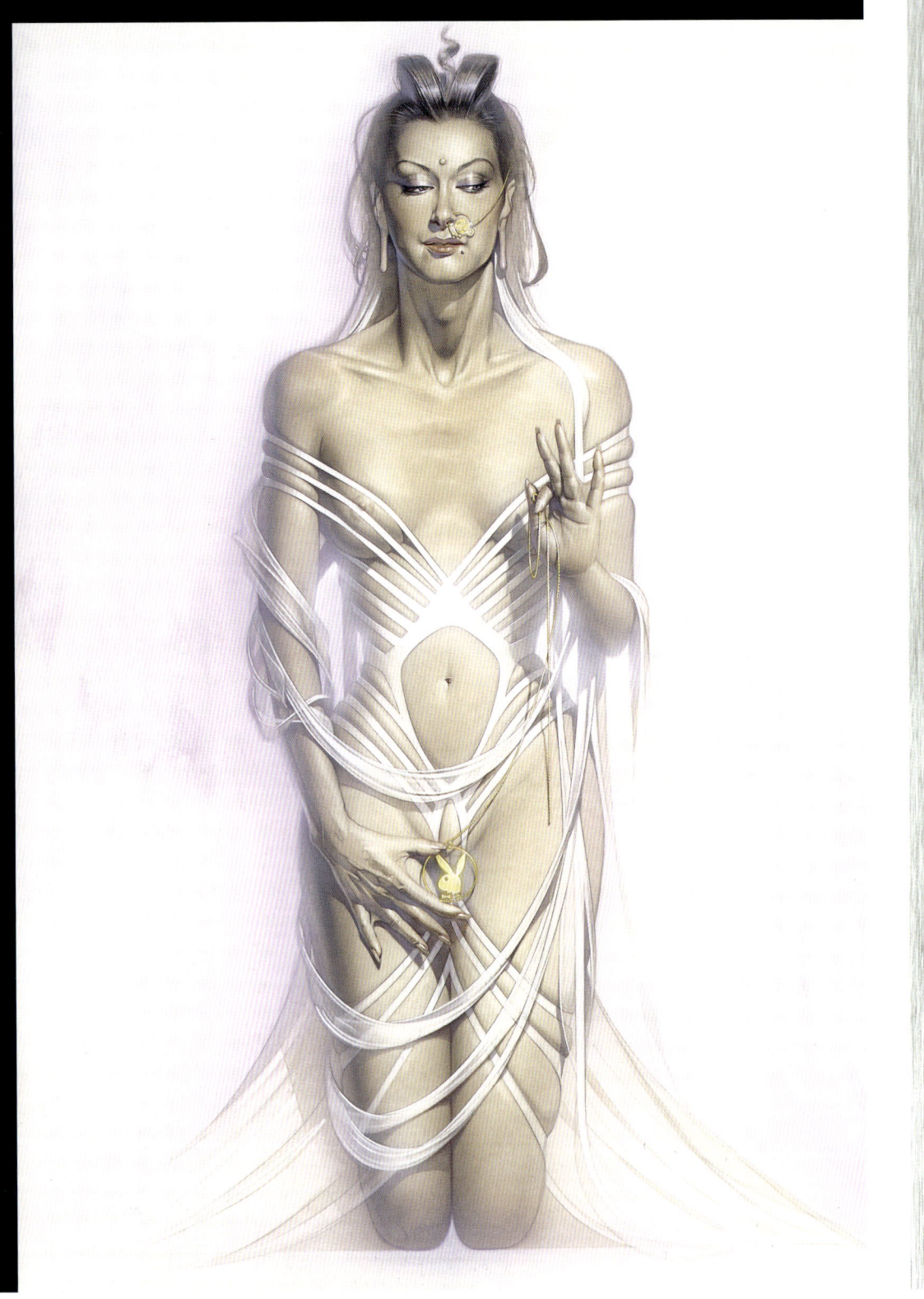

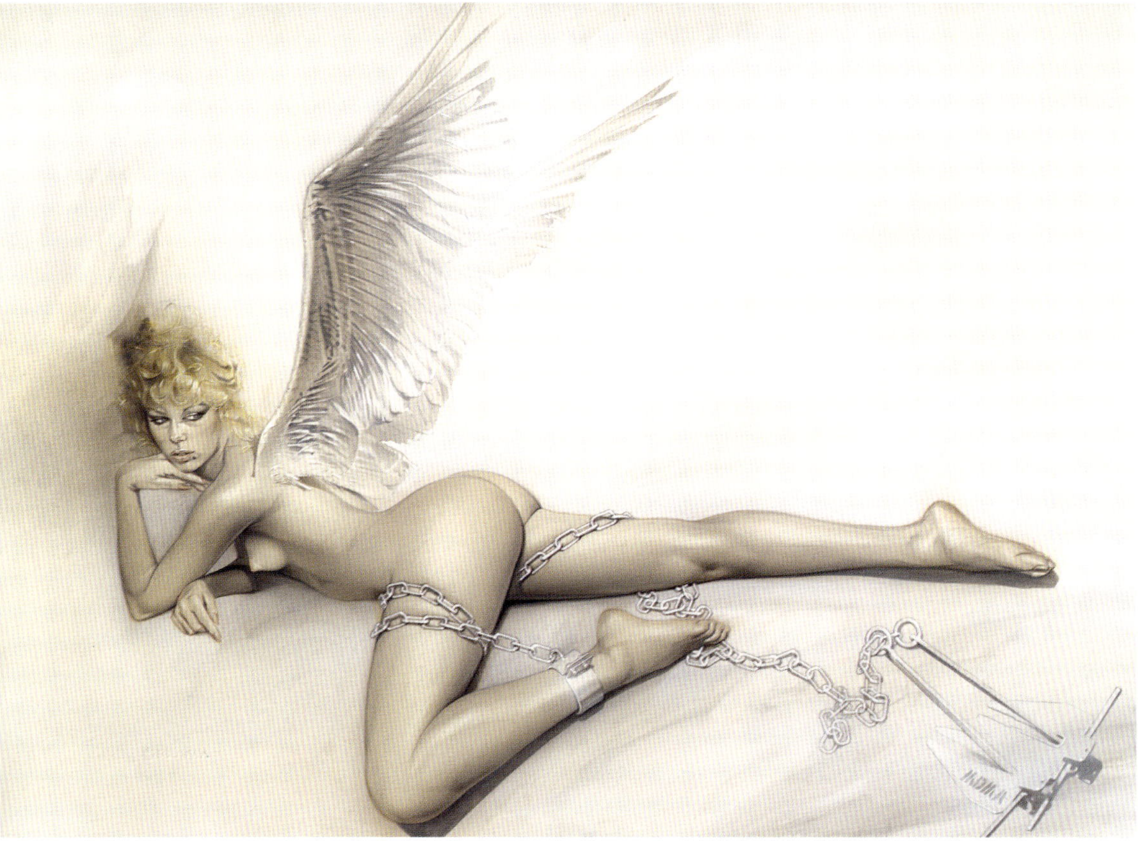

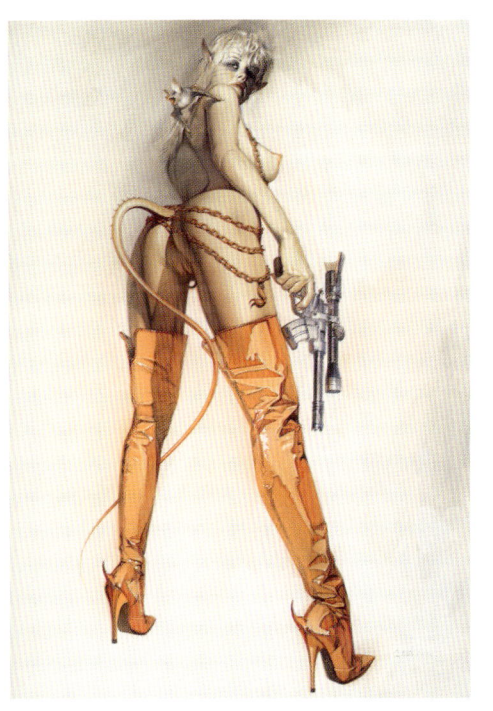

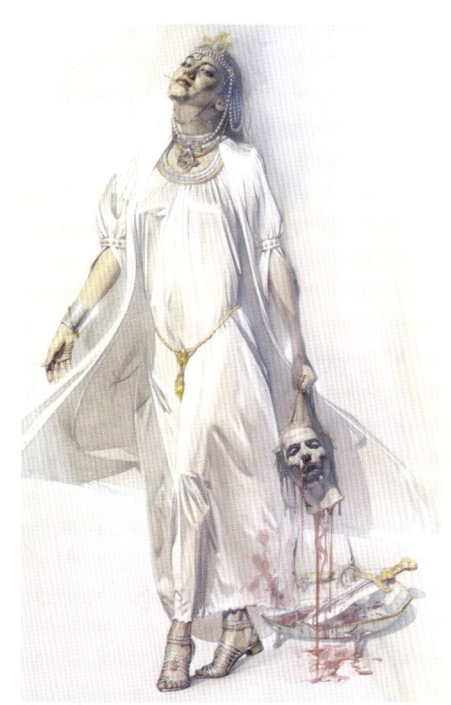

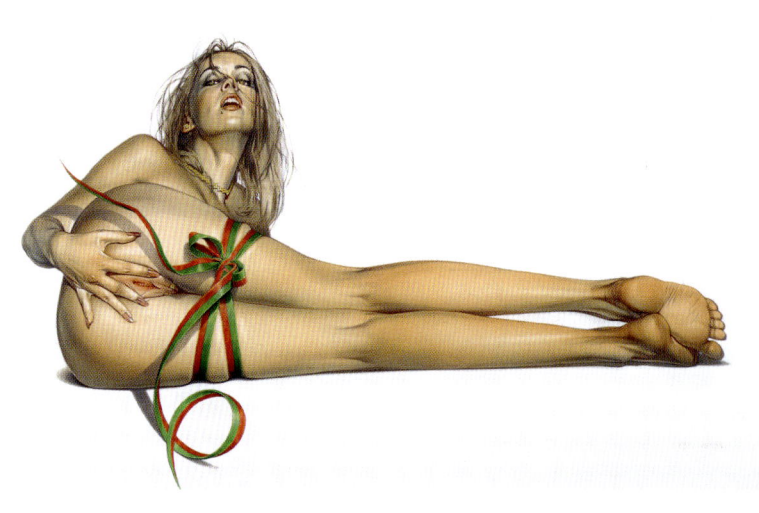
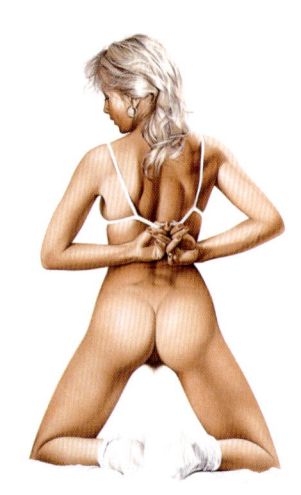
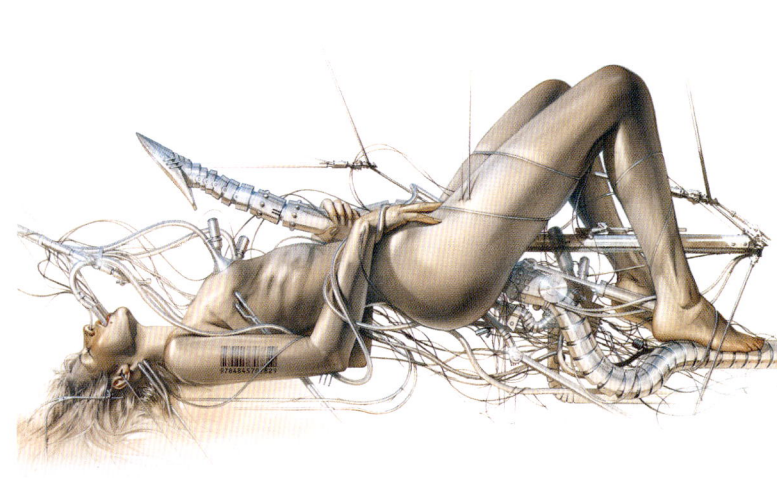
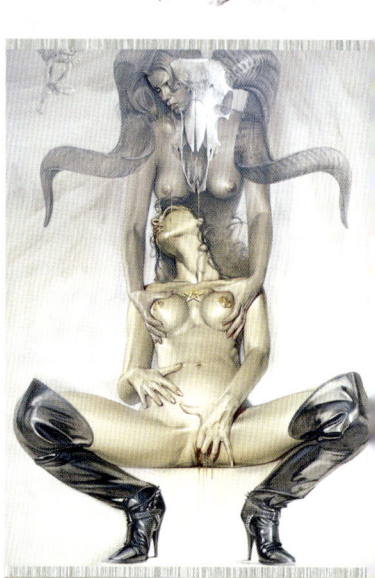
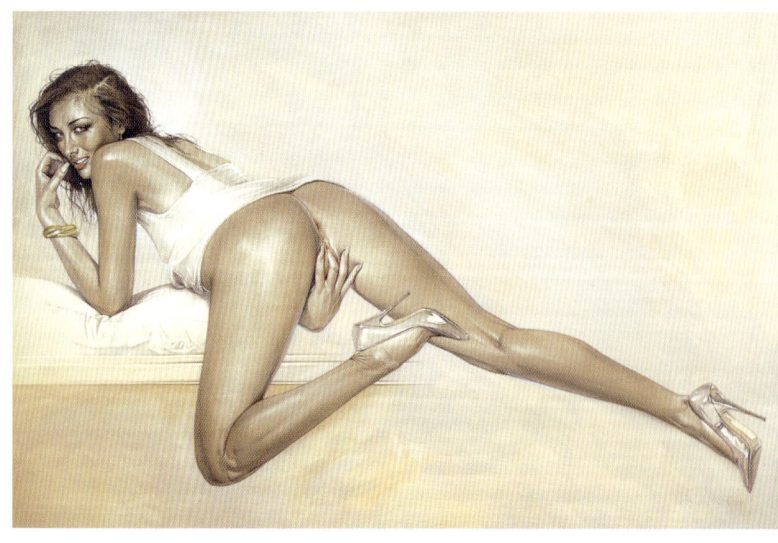
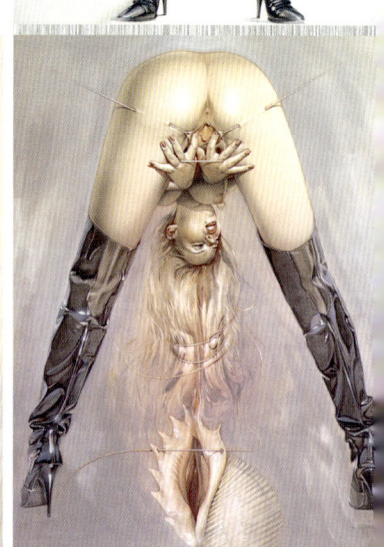

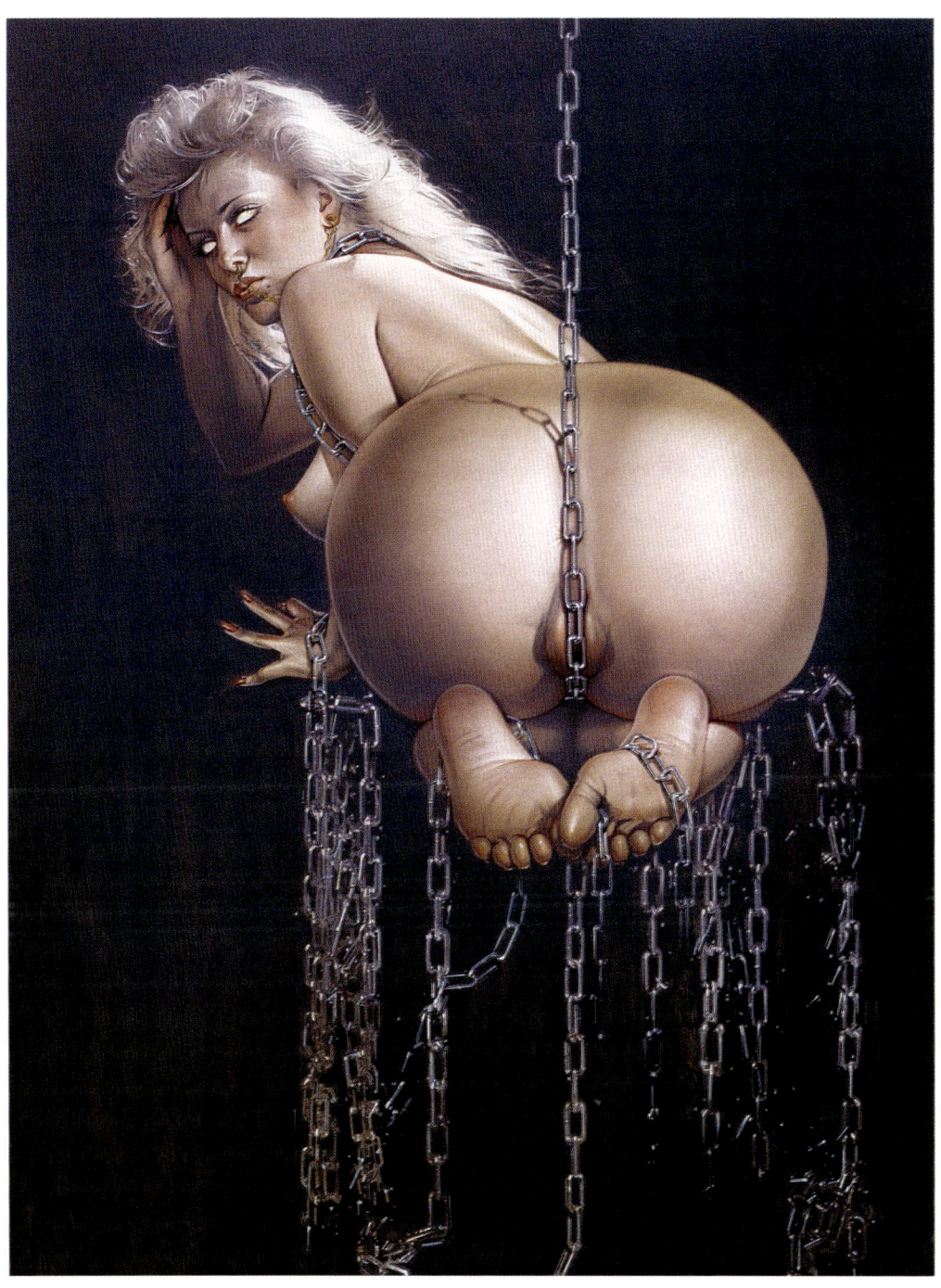

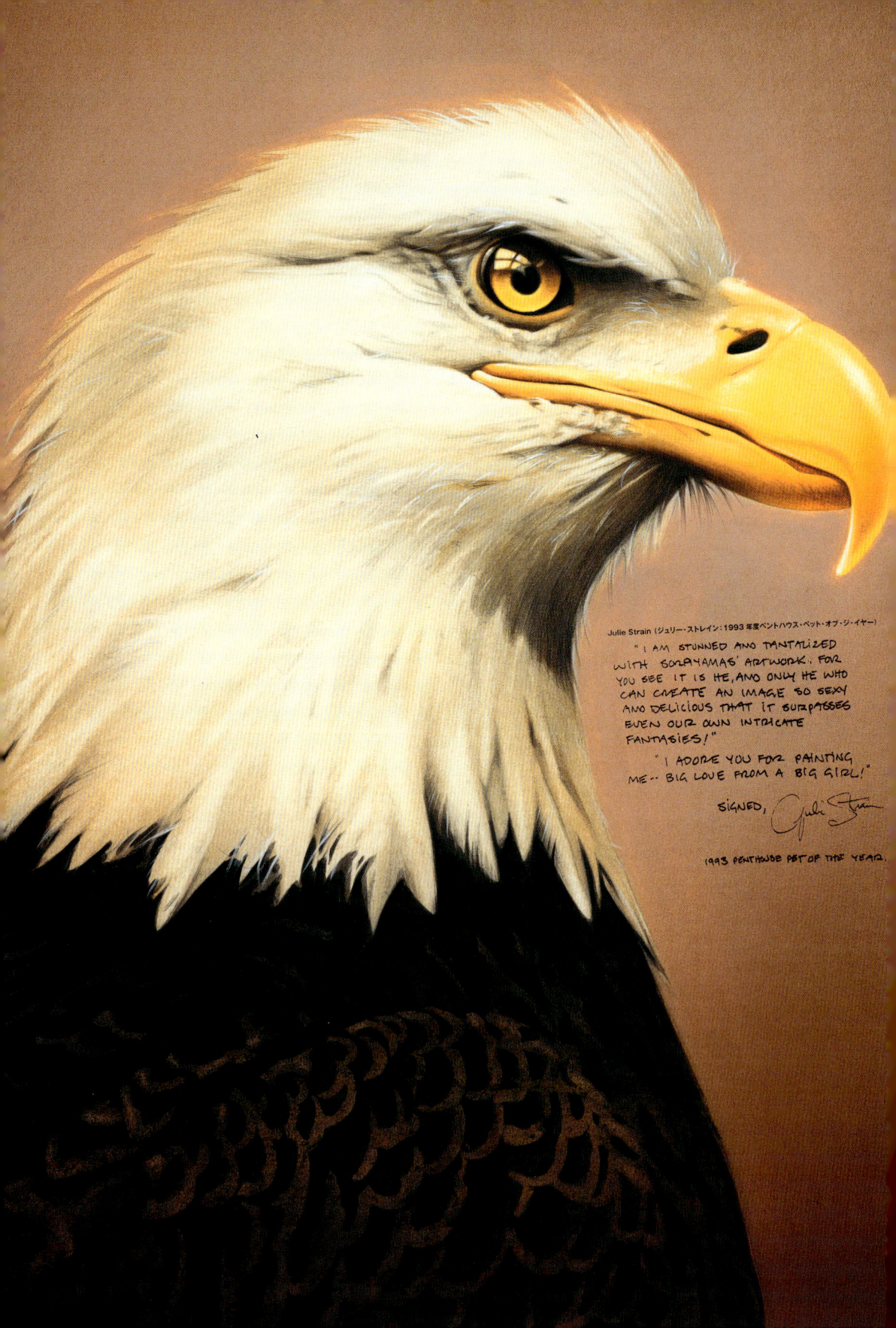

Julie Strain (ジュリー・ストレイン：1993 年度ベントハウス・ペット・オブ・ジ・イヤー)

"I AM STUNNED AND TANTALIZED
WITH SORAYAMAS' ARTWORK, FOR
YOU SEE IT IS HE, AND ONLY HE WHO
CAN CREATE AN IMAGE SO SEXY
AND DELICIOUS THAT IT SURPASSES
EVEN OUR OWN INTRICATE
FANTASIES!"

"I ADORE YOU FOR PAINTING
ME -- BIG LOVE FROM A BIG GIRL!"

SIGNED, Julie Strain

1993 PENTHOUSE PET OF THE YEAR.

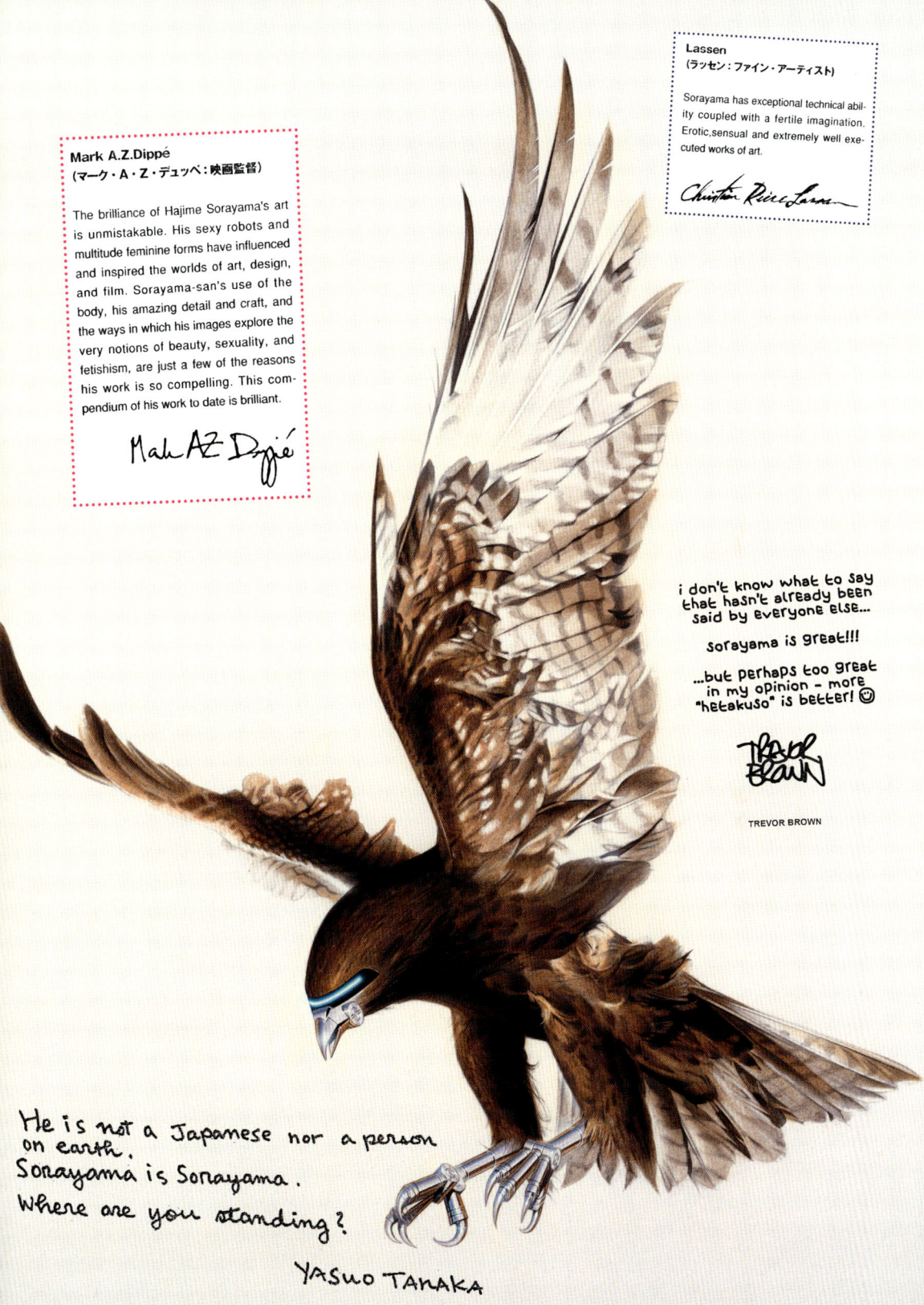

Mark A.Z.Dippé
（マーク・A・Z・デュッペ：映画監督）

The brilliance of Hajime Sorayama's art
is unmistakable. His sexy robots and
multitude feminine forms have influenced
and inspired the worlds of art, design,
and film. Sorayama-san's use of the
body, his amazing detail and craft, and
the ways in which his images explore the
very notions of beauty, sexuality, and
fetishism, are just a few of the reasons
his work is so compelling. This com-
pendium of his work to date is brilliant.

Lassen
（ラッセン：ファイン・アーティスト）

Sorayama has exceptional technical abil-
ity coupled with a fertile imagination.
Erotic,sensual and extremely well exe-
cuted works of art.

i don't know what to say
that hasn't already been
said by everyone else...

sorayama is great!!!

...but perhaps too great
in my opinion - more
"hetakuso" is better! 🙂

TREVOR BROWN

He is not a Japanese nor a person
on earth.
Sorayama is Sorayama.
Where are you standing?

YASUO TANAKA

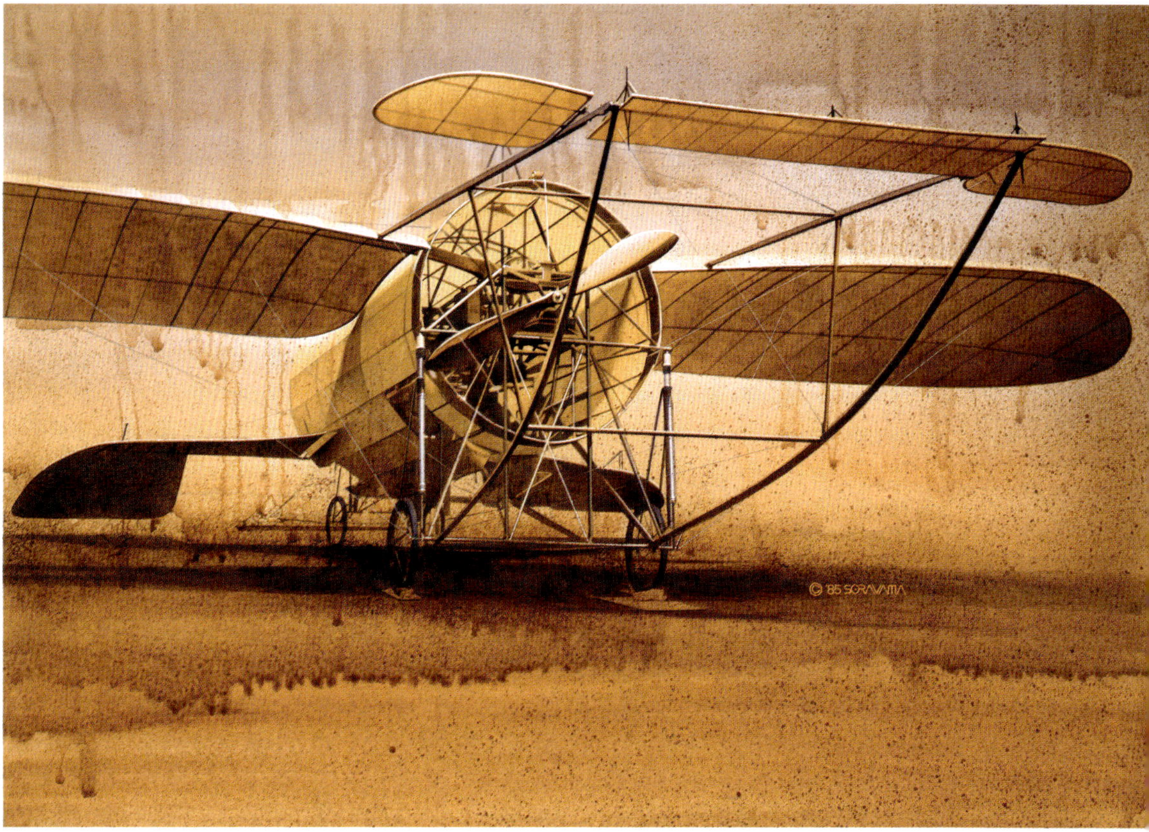

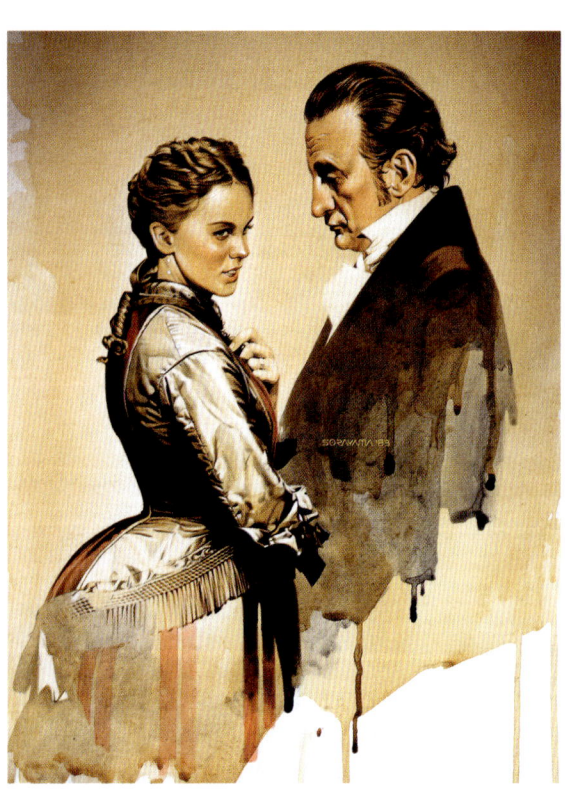

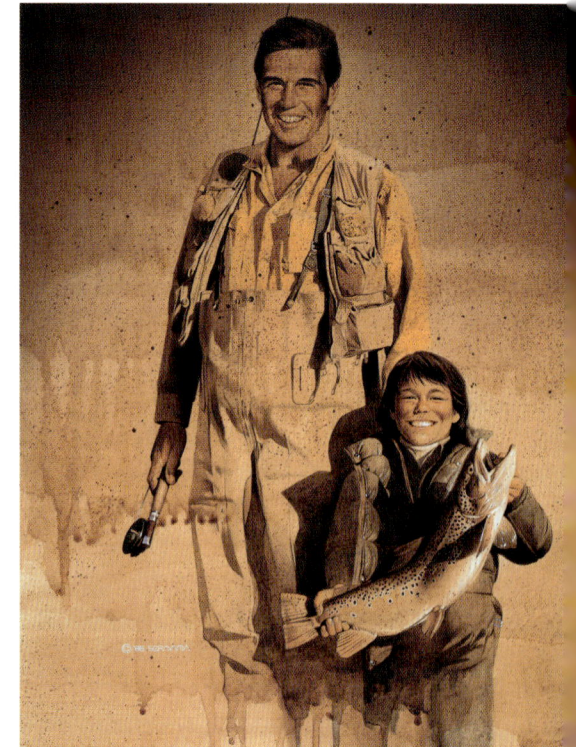

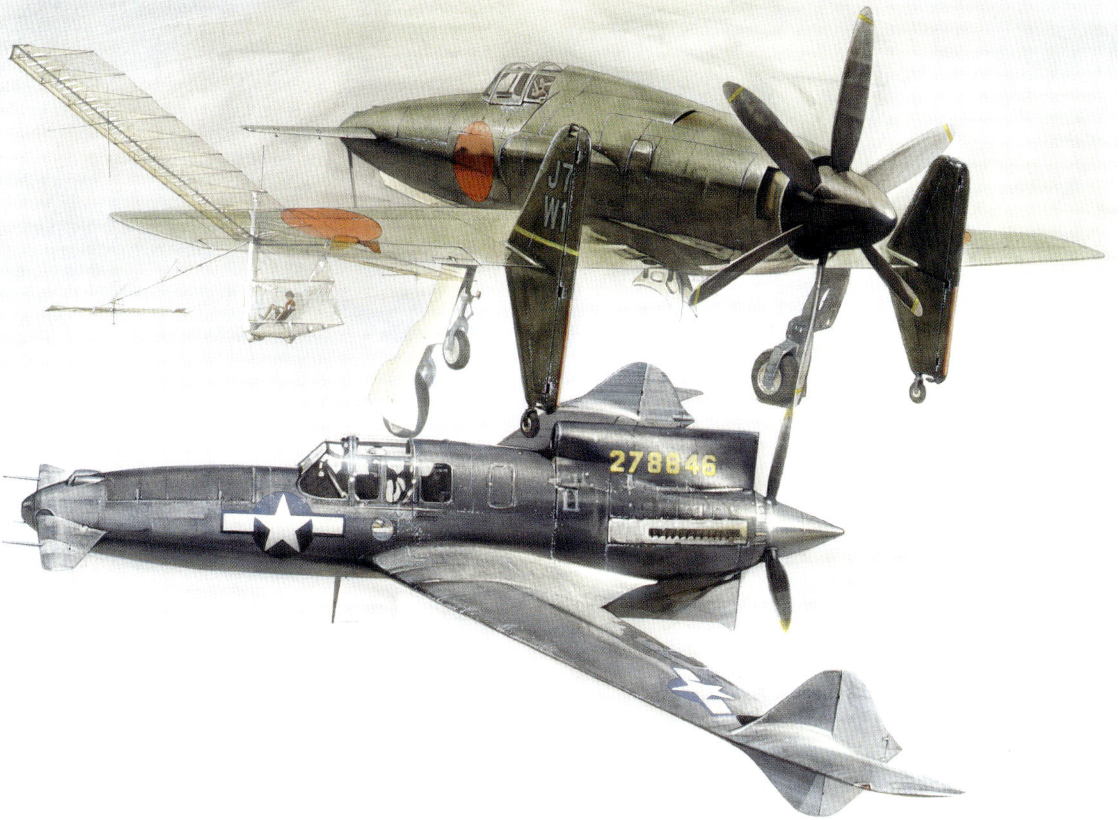

MIKE & RAIN   Fan-site Webmaster

空山基教信徒の待望なる新画集の発行を
極東より御祝い申し上げます。
珠玉の最新作に加えて幻の未発表作から
秘蔵の逸品までも収録された有難い新経典。
貧しく迷える子羊を導き給え。

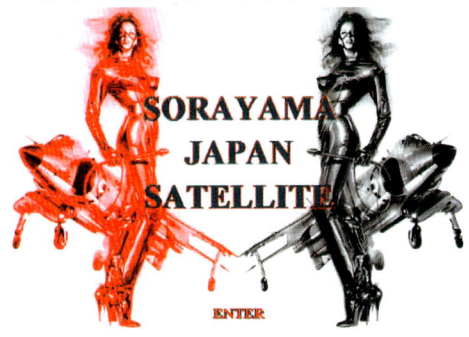

Fan-site
空山・ジャパン・サテライト
SORAYAMA JAPAN SATELLITE
http://sorayama-japan.net

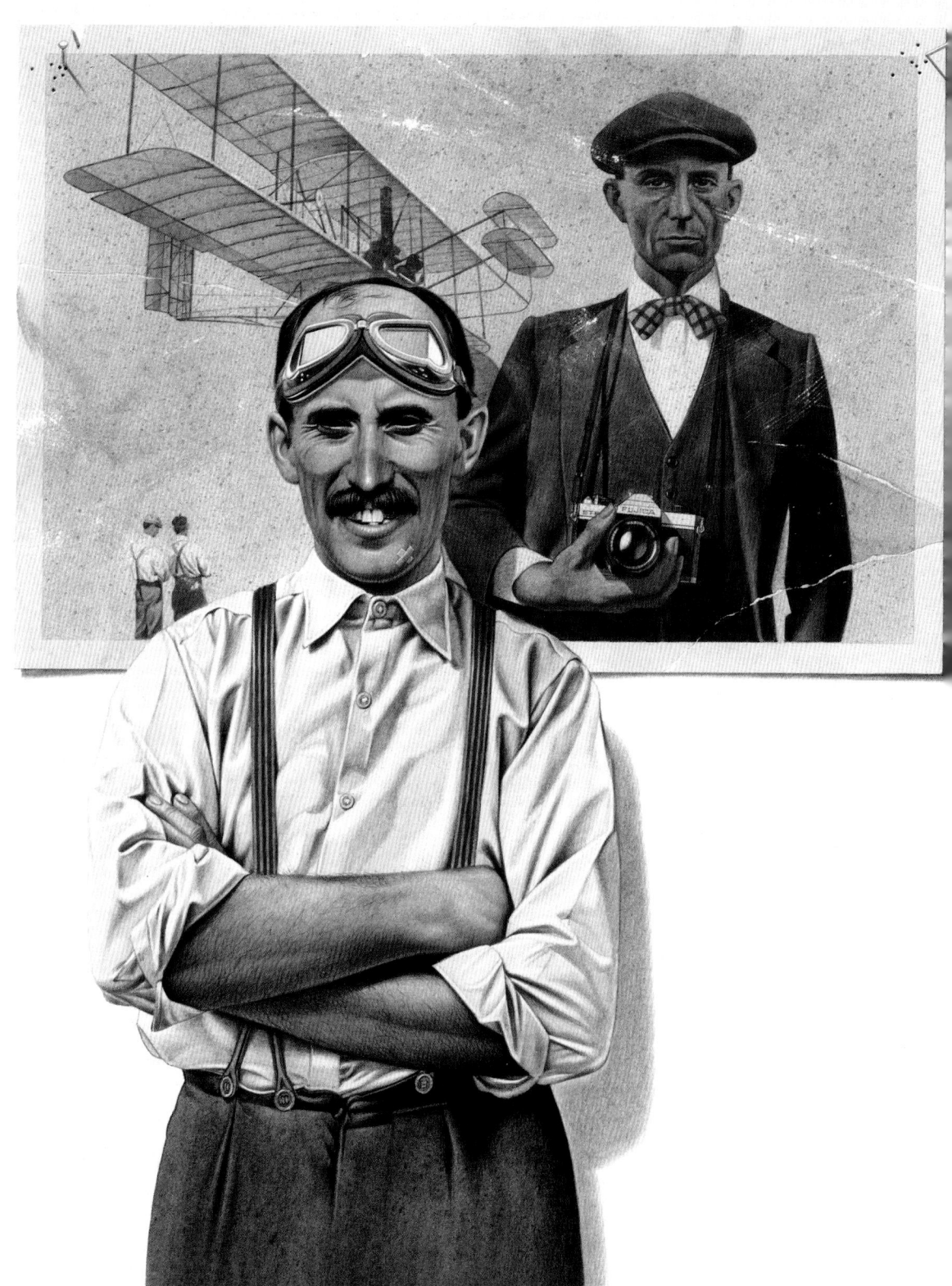

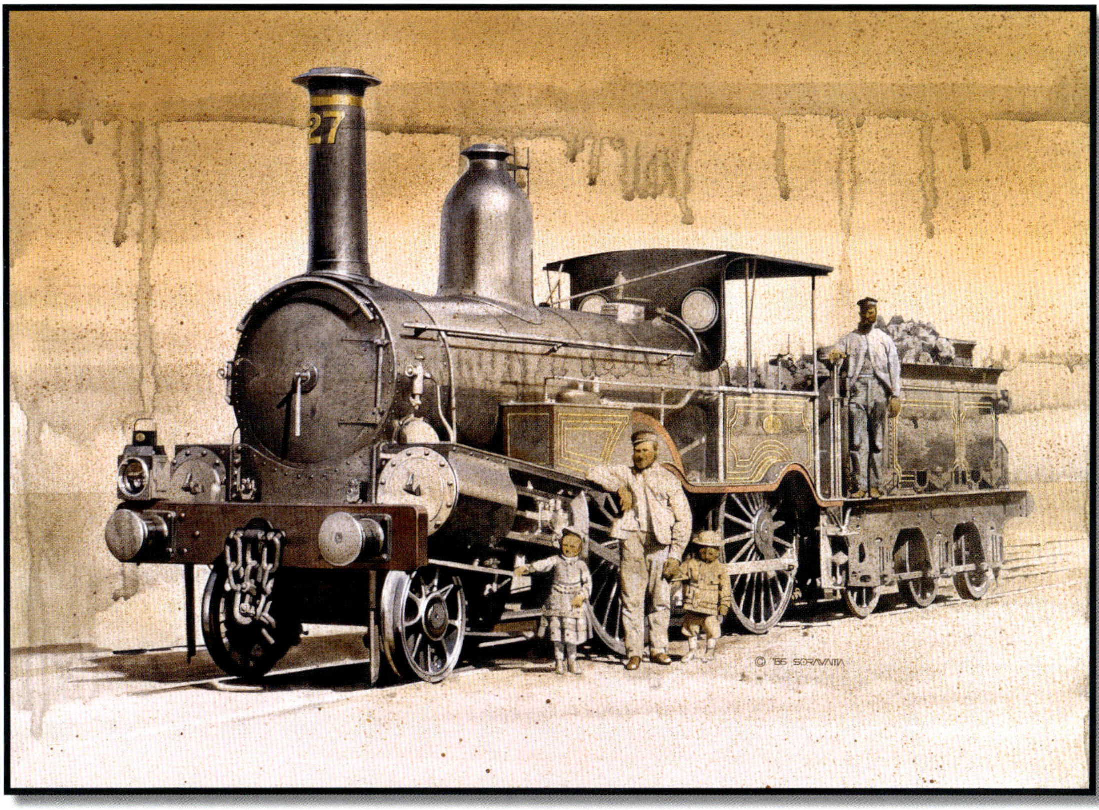

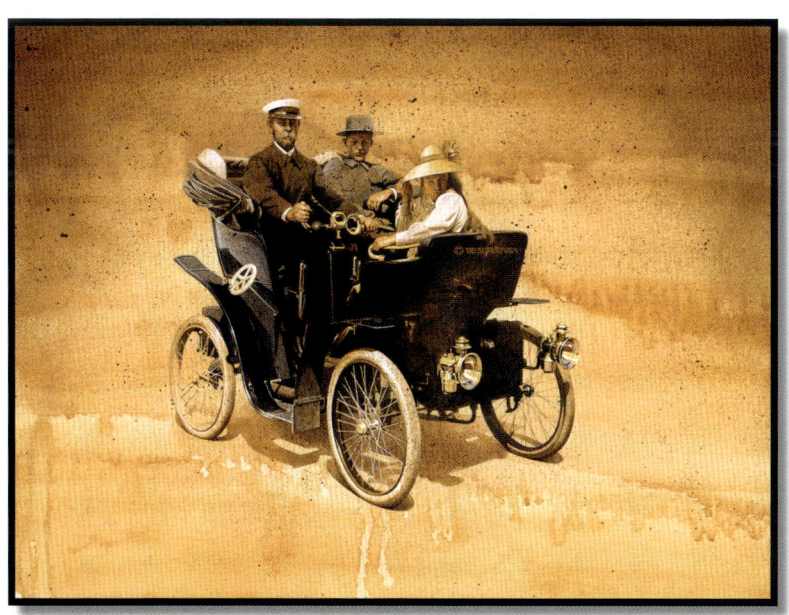

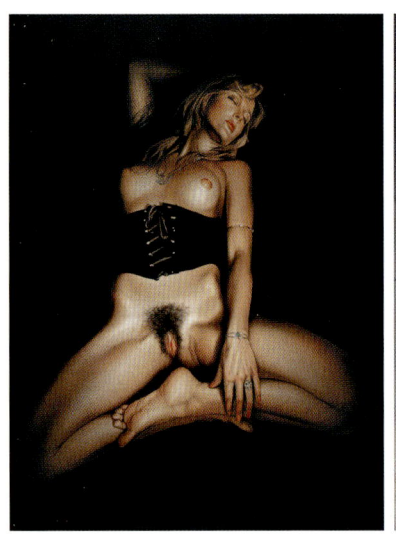
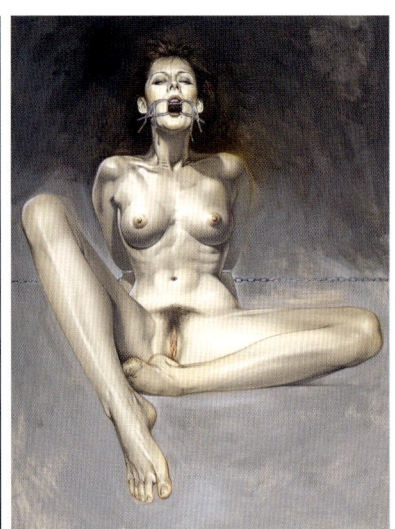
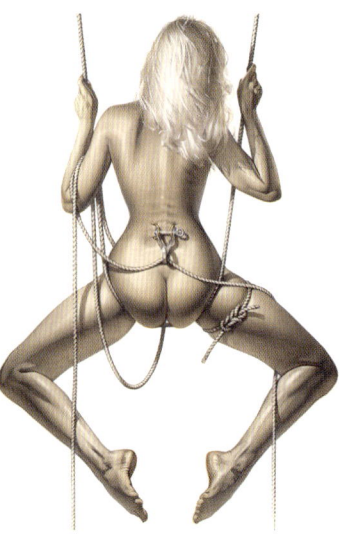

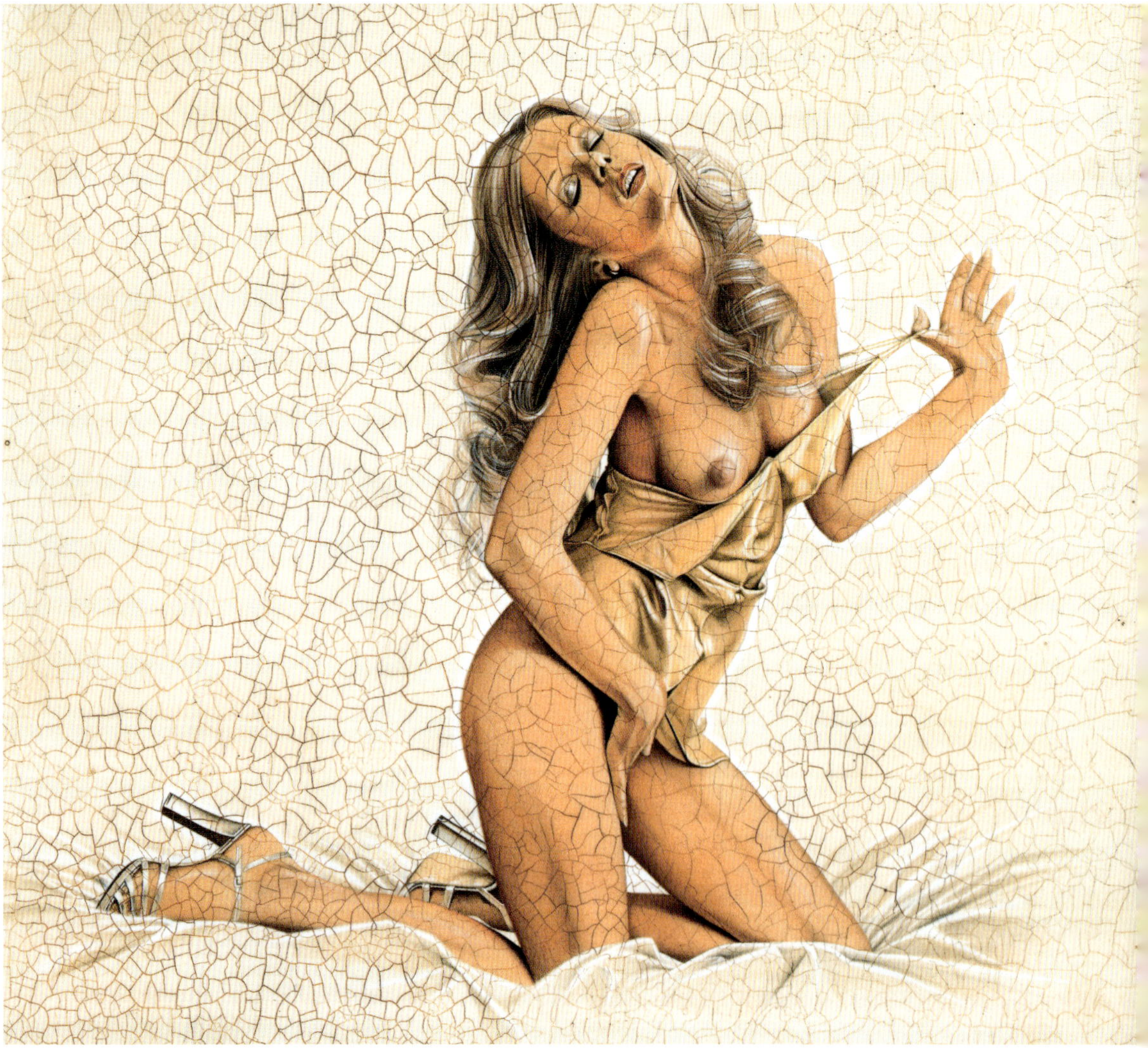

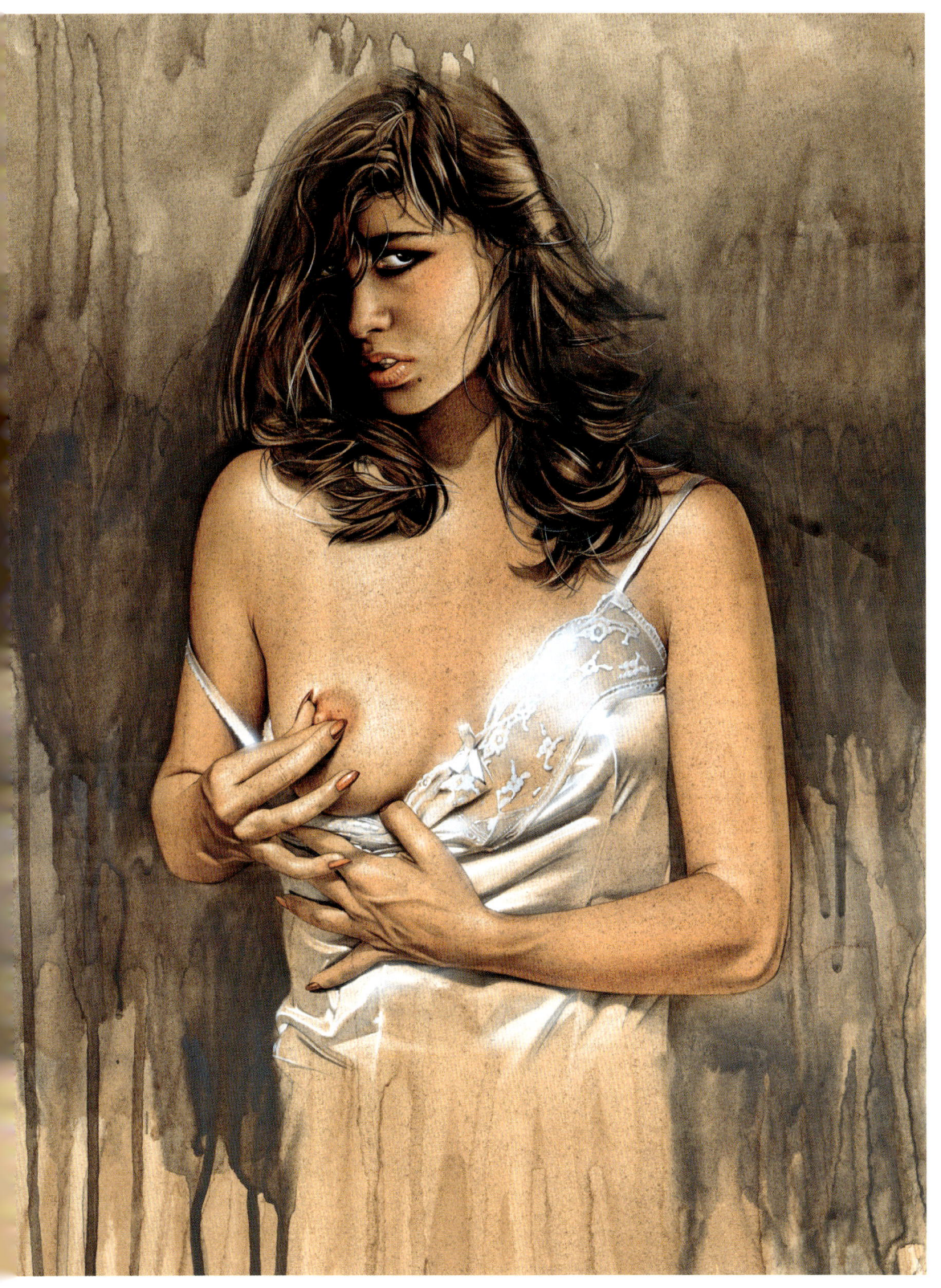

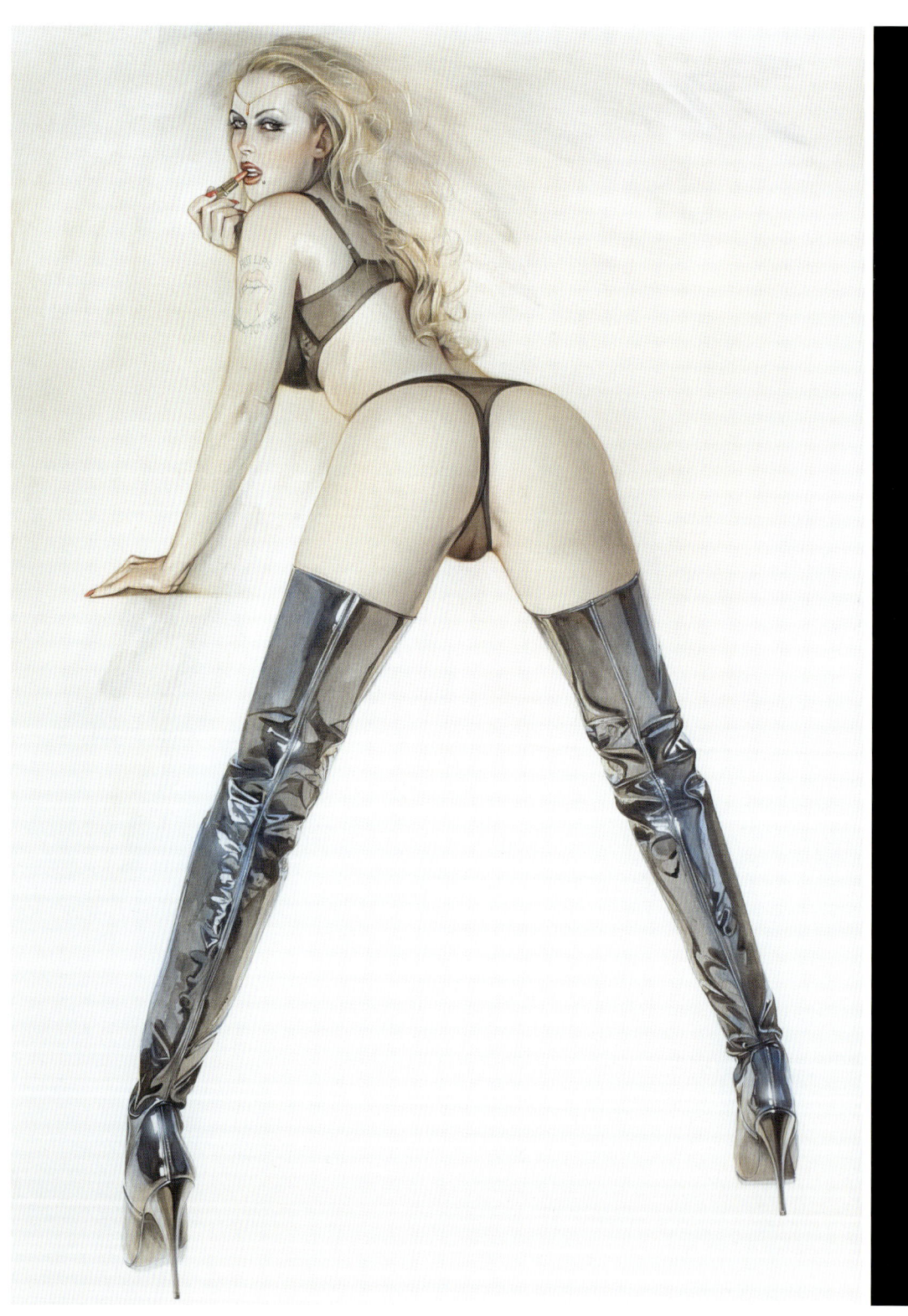

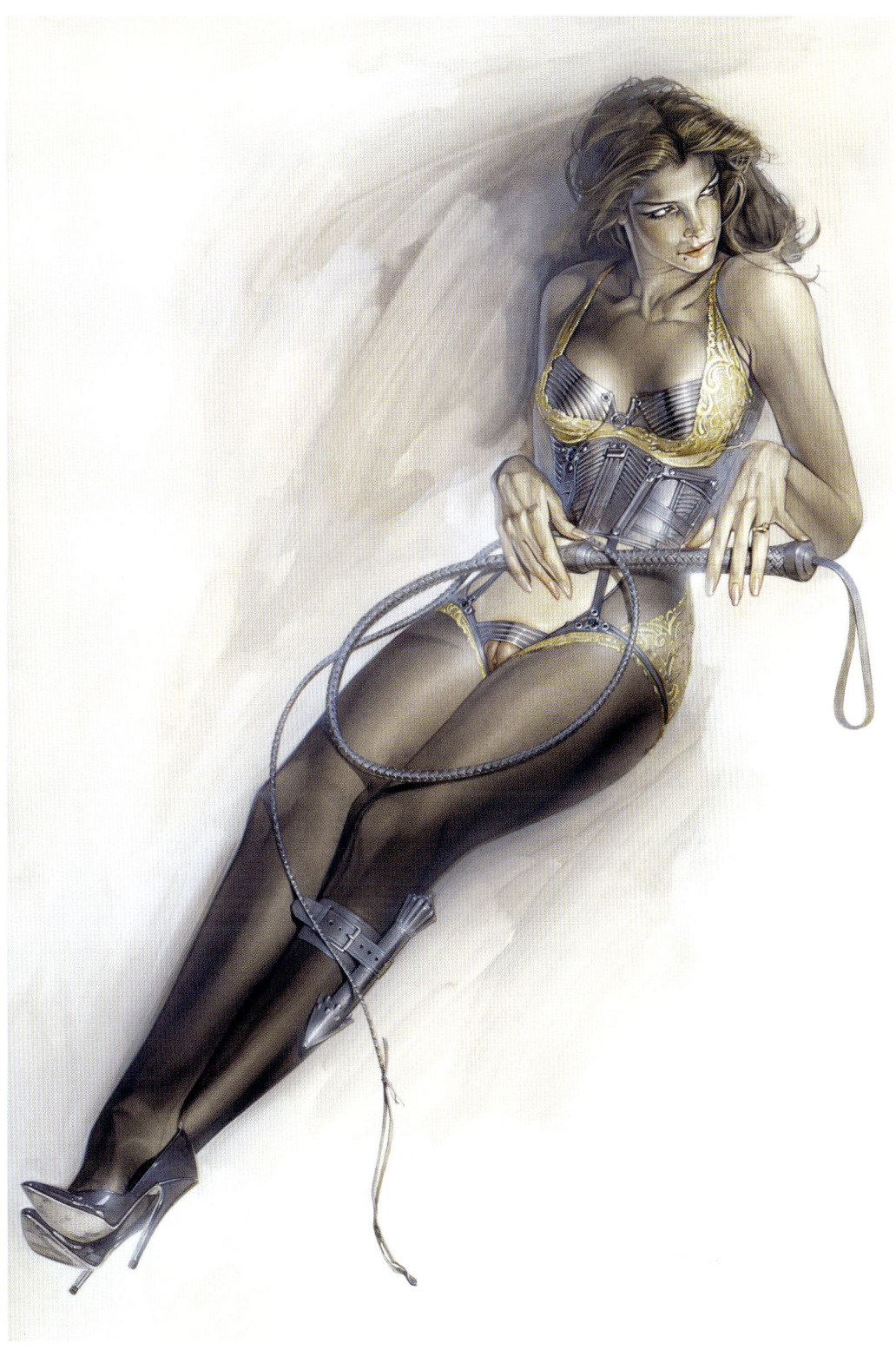

ニューヨークの「SORAYAMA」ショーのあと、ミッドナイトが近いソーホーのレストランで、空山さんやみんなとワインを飲んでたら、ぼくの記憶の中のニューヨークが1984年の夏にタイムスリップしていた。

その夏、ぼくは、絵を描いて生きていくのなら、ここで仕事をしたいと思っていて、レップを本気で探していた。そこで肌で感じたのは、あまりにもニューヨークのアーティストの層が厚いことだったのは、想像するのは容易いと思うが、結局、日本での仕事が忙しくなったことを理由に実現することはなかったが、ぼくの中には、いつまでもその願望が残り続けていた。

そんなぼくのような、ここに居ることのできなかった無数のアーティストたちを横目に、ソーホーのギャラリーのウインドウに掛けられた「SORAYAMA」の作品は、いまここで生きている希有なアーティストのひとりであることを物語っていた。

HOSAKA

保坂英孝
株式会社 枻（えい）出版社　取締役
ピークス株式会社　代表取締役

Robt. Williams （ロバート・ウィリアムズ：アーティスト）

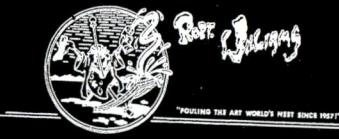

"FOULING THE ART WORLD'S NEST SINCE 1937!"

EMINENCE AND ELOQUENCE,
THAT DEFINES THE STYLE OF HAJIME
SORAYAMA, ONE OF THE FINEST, IF NOT
THE PREEMINENT FETISH CHEESE CAKE
MASTER PAINTER OF OUR TIME.
    HE IS TECHNICALLY AND GRAPHICALLY
SUPERIOR TO THE FOREFATHERS, VARGAS,
PETTY & ETC. OF THE PAINTED PIN-UP
GIRL TRADITION.

3·25·98

R. Williams

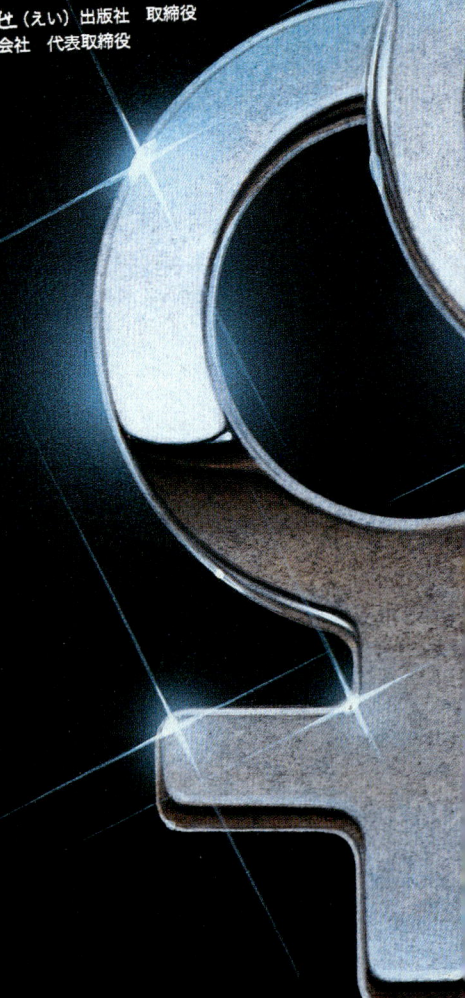

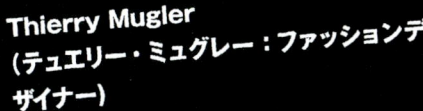

Thierry Mugler
（テュエリー・ミュグレー：ファッションデ
ザイナー）

Sorayama's surreal and futuristic DADA
images not only provoke incredible sen-
sations, but also melt into a unique
homage to life. With joyful freedom he
amalgamates and morphs fear with happiness, pain with pleasure, repulsion with
attraction, past with future, flesh with
metal, the organic with the ethereal.
Stronger than any constraint, the energy
of life and love that goes through his
work is what I admire most in his amaz-
ingly perfect technique.

Thierry Mugler

My idea of success and happiness has nothing to do with money.
It has to do with surrounding myself with things I love that stir unique emotions in
me. I have over 40 original Sorayama paintings hanging in my house.
He is the only artist that touches my inner feelings in such a unique way. I
consider myself a very lucky person.

AA / collector

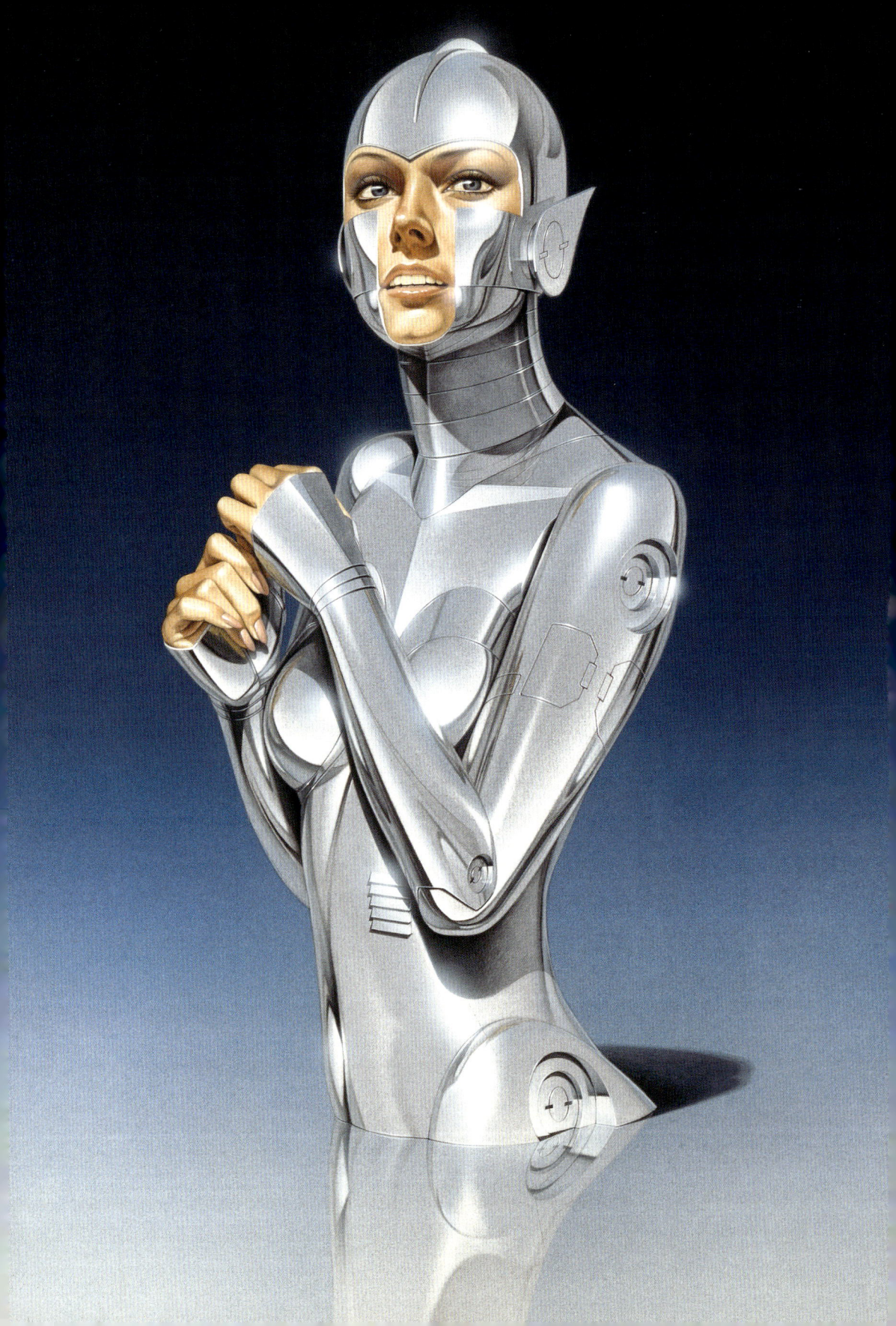

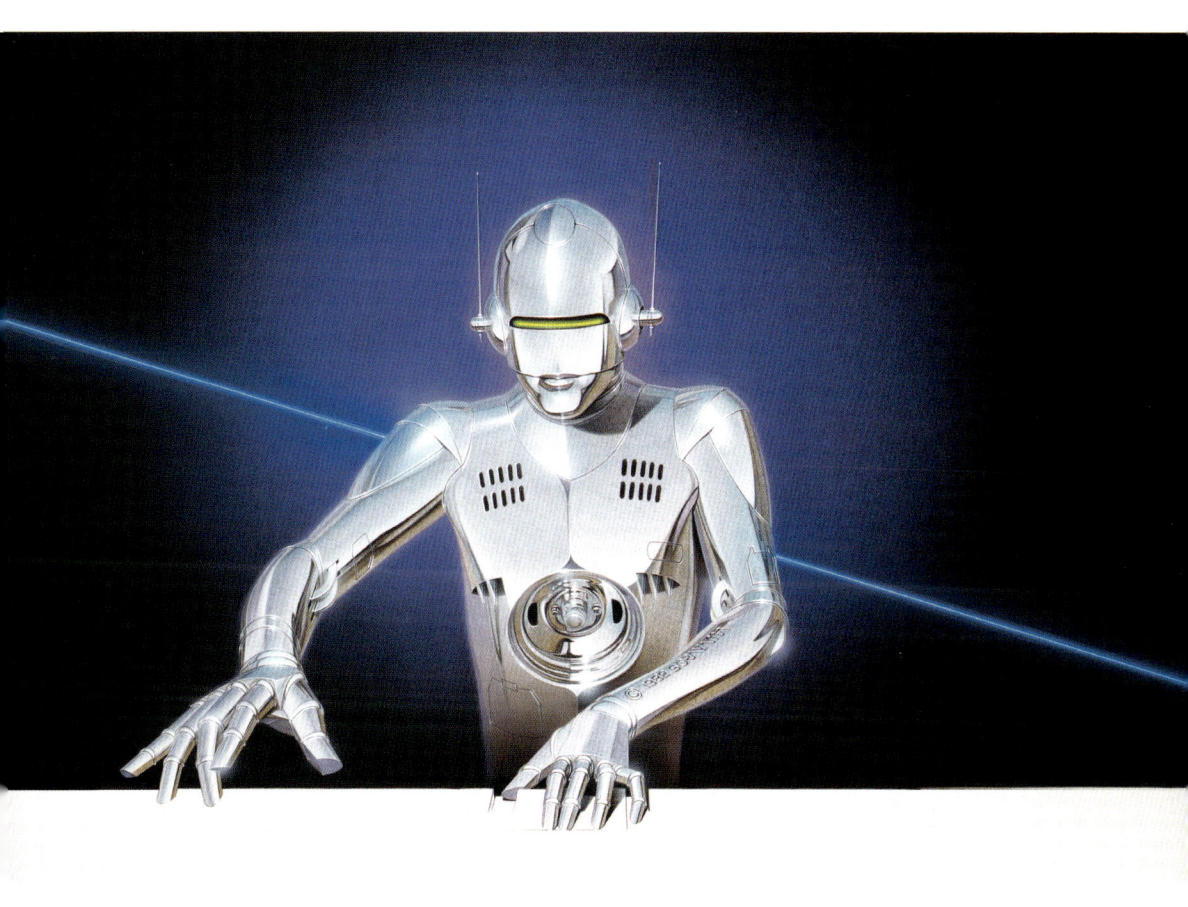

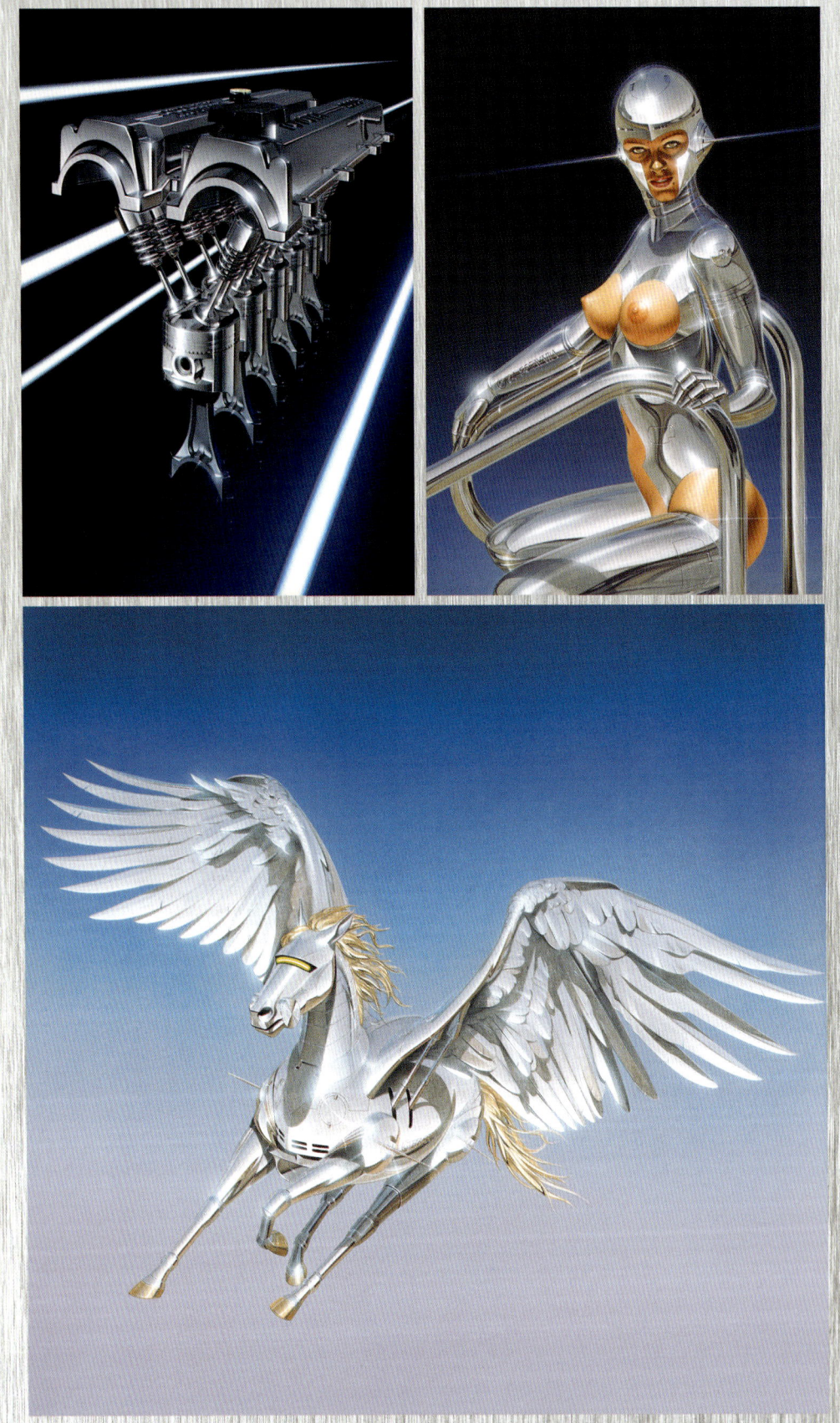

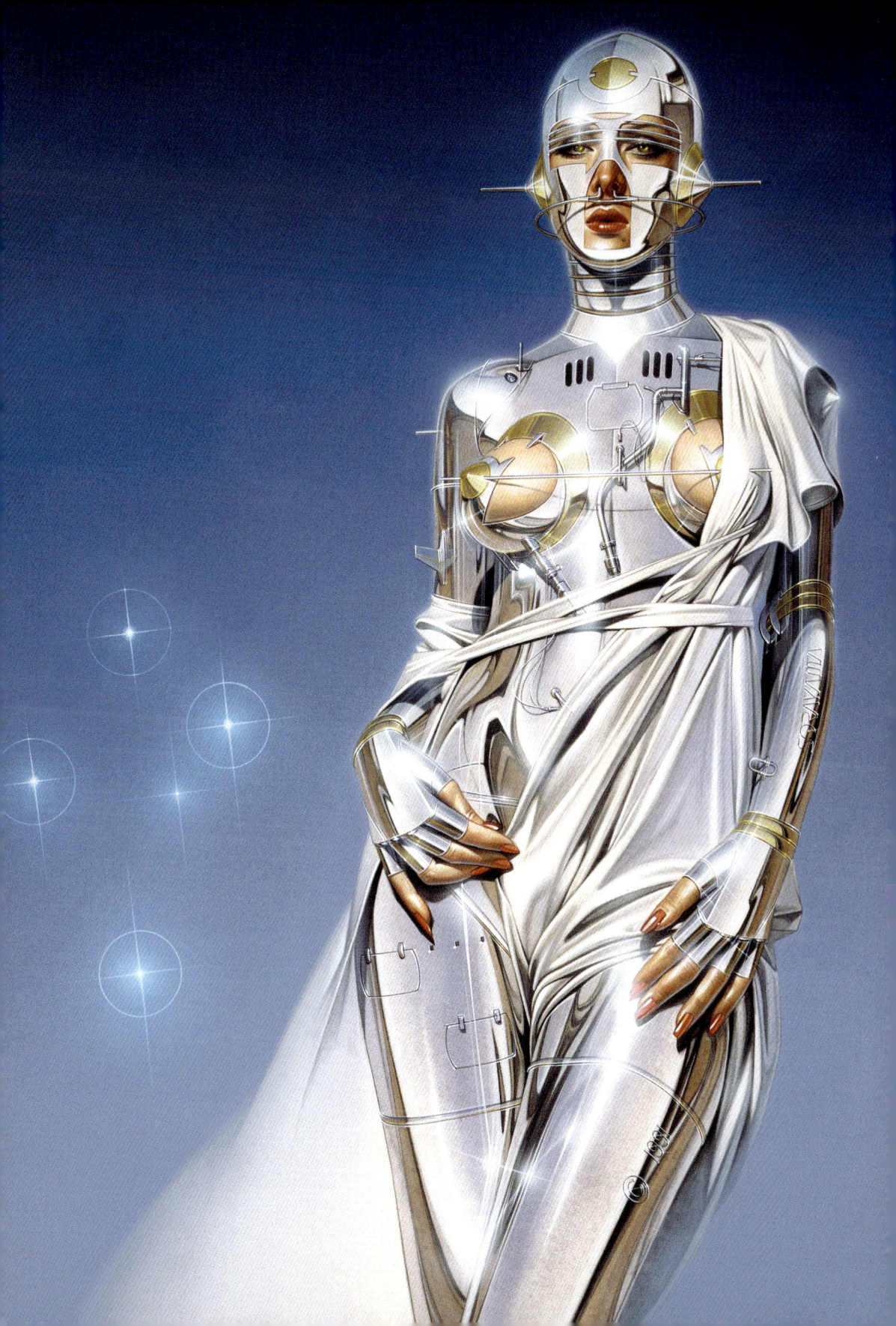

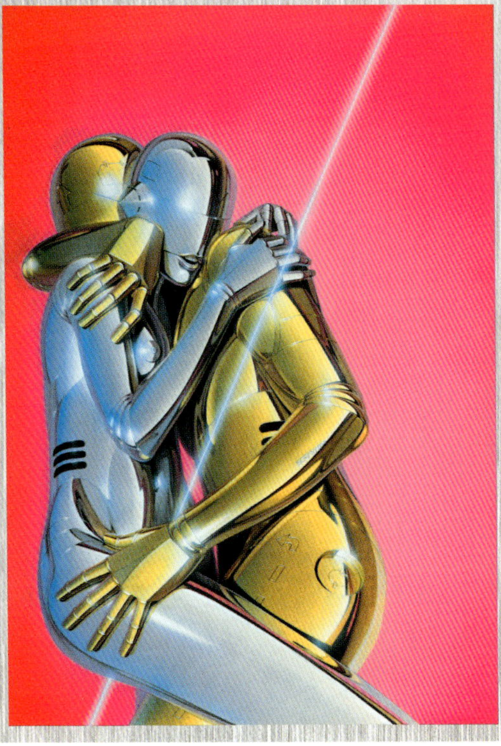

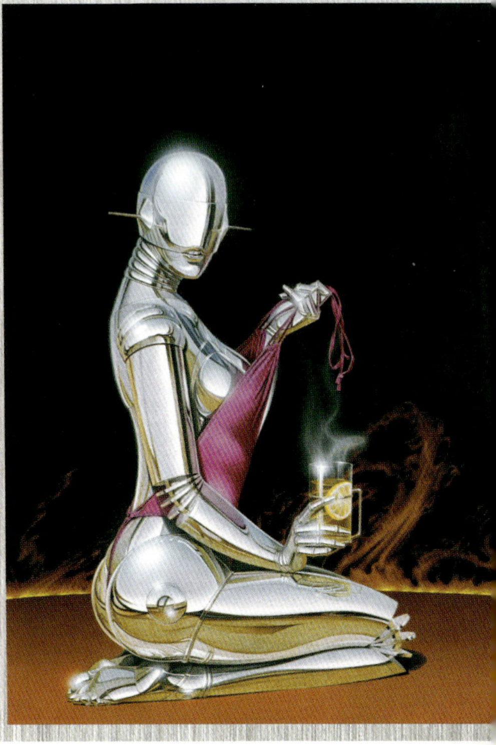

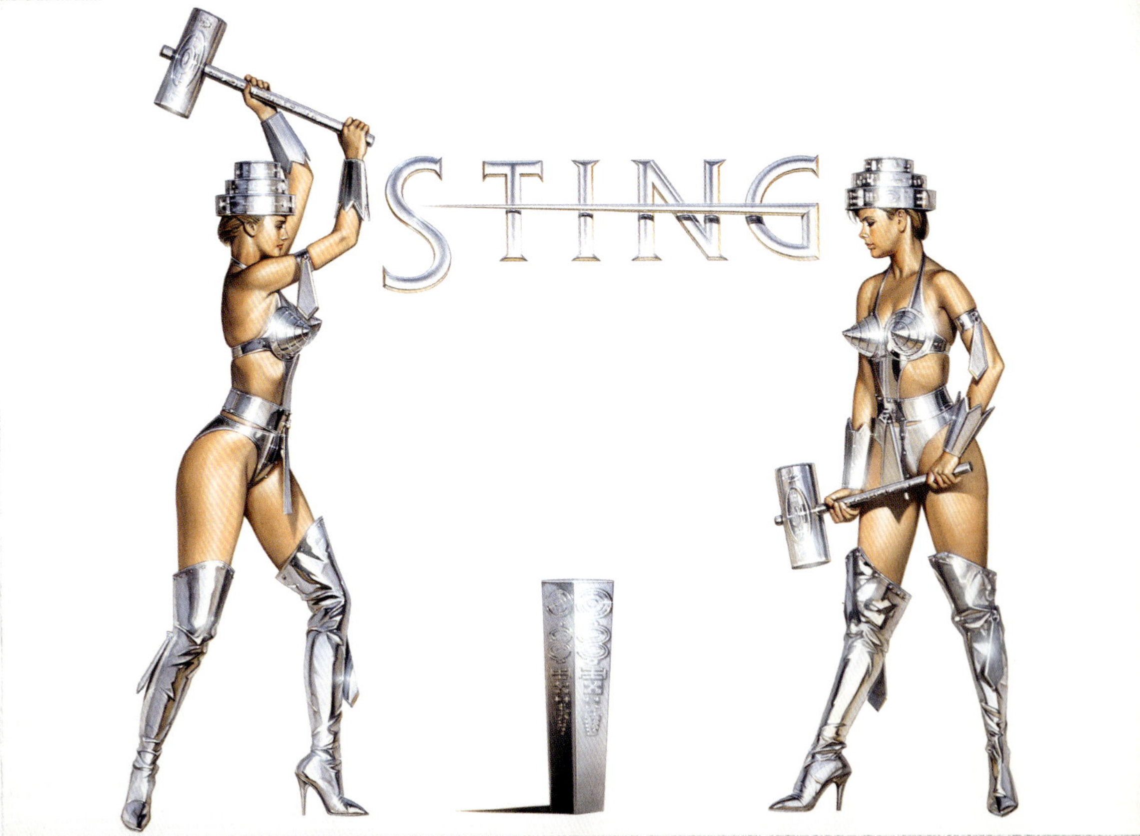

STING

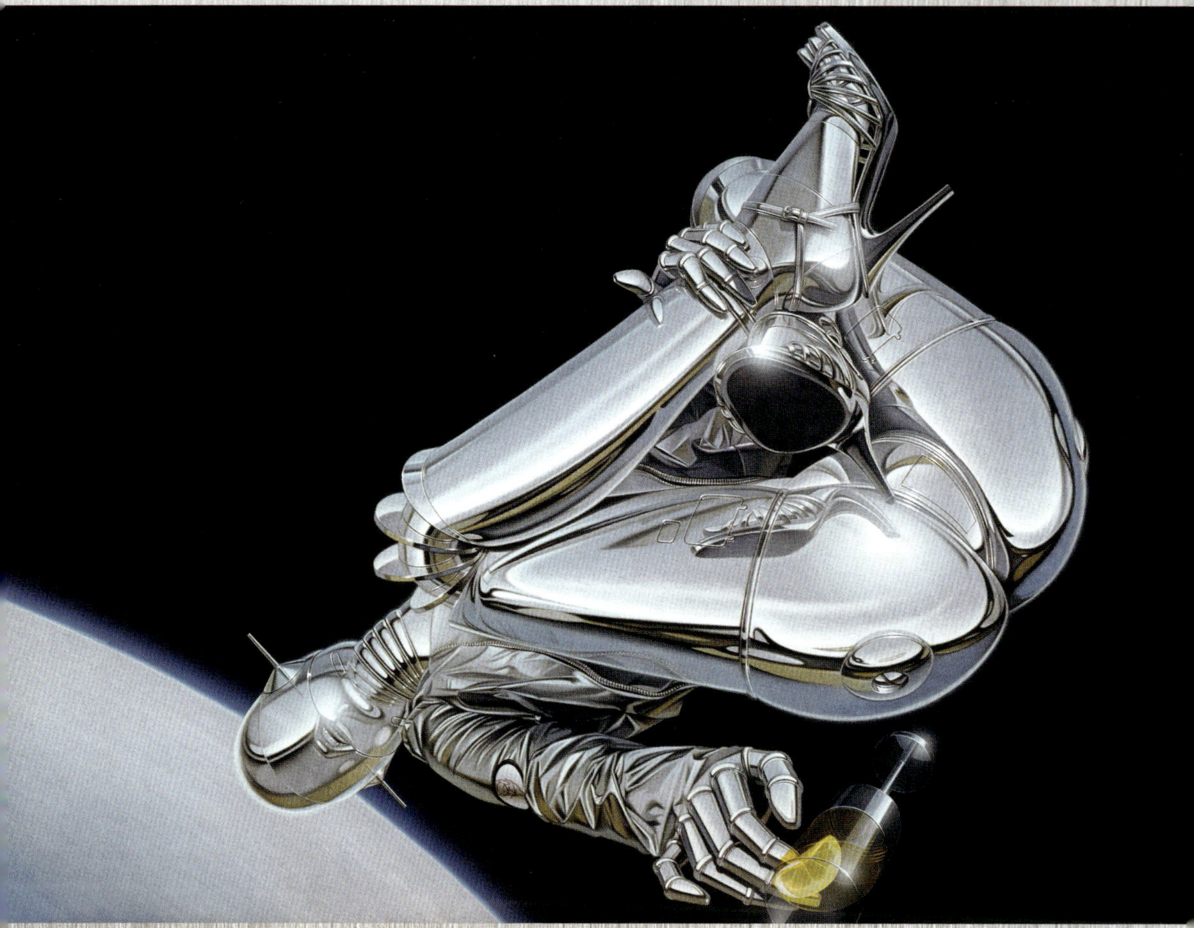

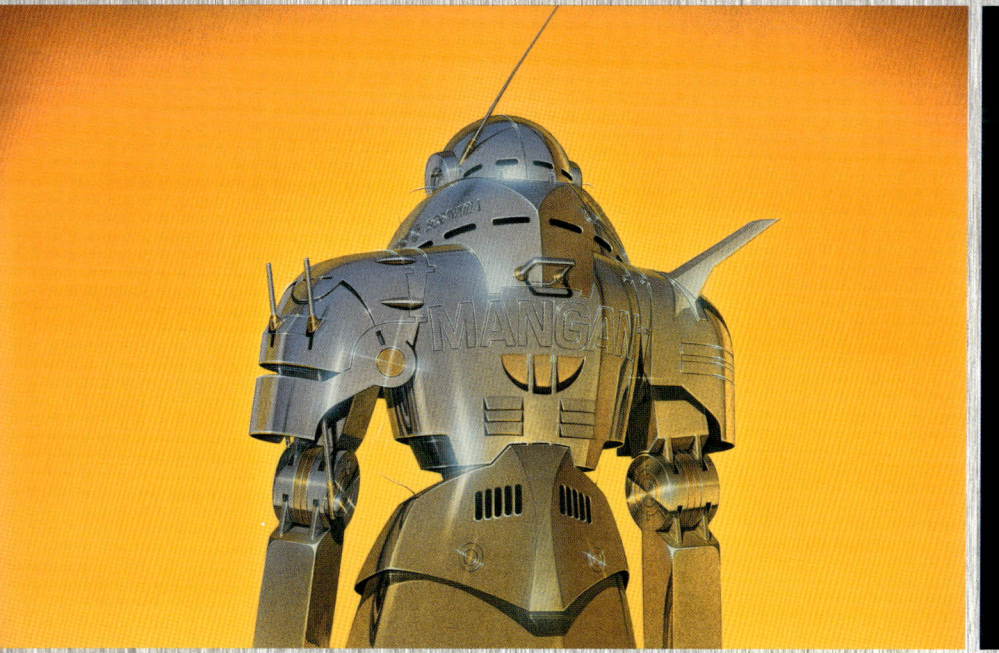

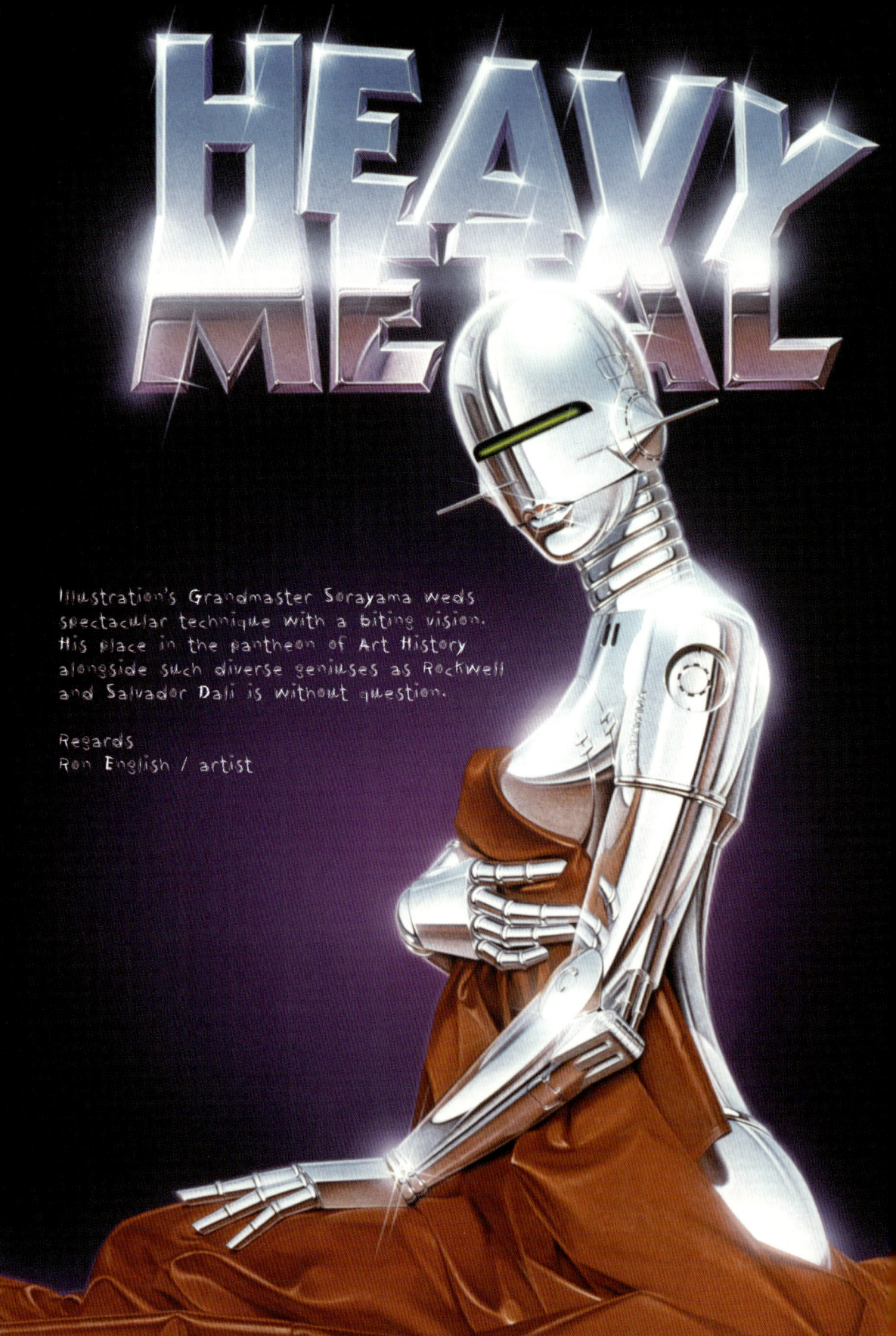

Illustration's Grandmaster Sorayama weds
spectacular technique with a biting vision.
His place in the pantheon of Art History
alongside such diverse geniuses as Rockwell
and Salvador Dali is without question.

Regards
Ron English / artist

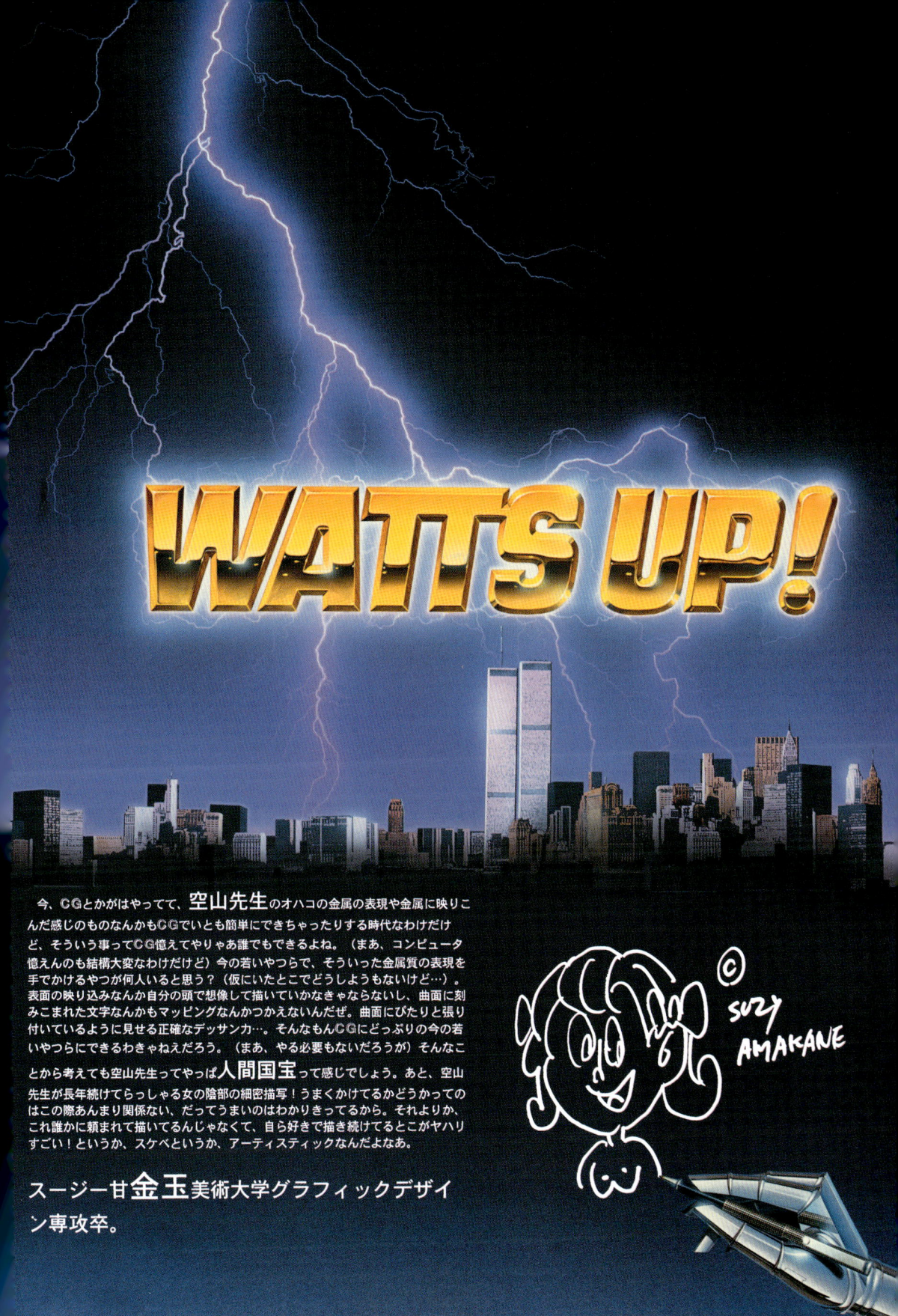

WATTS UP!

今、CGとかがはやってて、空山先生のオハコの金属の表現や金属に映りこんだ感じのものなんかもCGでいとも簡単にできちゃったりする時代なわけだけど、そういう事ってCG憶えてやりゃあ誰でもできるよね。（まあ、コンピュータ憶えんのも結構大変なわけだけど）今の若いやつらで、そういった金属質の表現を手でかけるやつが何人いると思う？（仮にいたとこでどうしようもないけど…）。表面の映り込みなんか自分の頭で想像して描いていかなきゃならないし、曲面に刻みこまれた文字なんかもマッピングなんかつかえないんだぜ。曲面にぴたりと張り付いているように見せる正確なデッサン力…。そんなもんCGにどっぷりの今の若いやつらにできるわきゃねえだろう。（まあ、やる必要もないだろうが）そんなことから考えても空山先生ってやっぱ人間国宝って感じでしょう。あと、空山先生が長年続けてらっしゃる女の陰部の細密描写！うまくかけてるかどうかってのはこの際あんまり関係ない、だってうまいのはわかりきってるから。それよりか、これ誰かに頼まれて描いてるんじゃなくて、自ら好きで描き続けてるとこがヤハリすごい！というか、スケベというか、アーティスティックなんだよなあ。

© SUZY AMAKANE

スージー甘金玉美術大学グラフィックデザイン専攻卒。

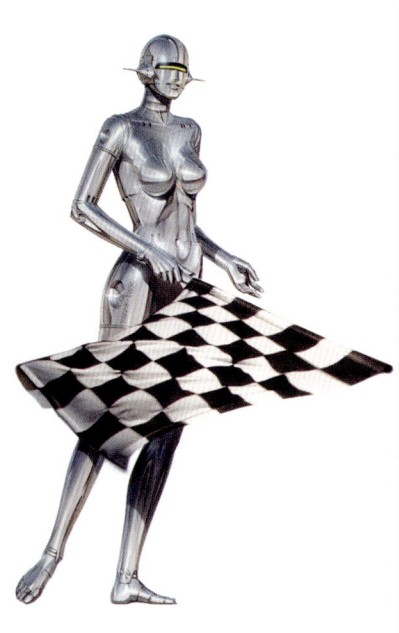

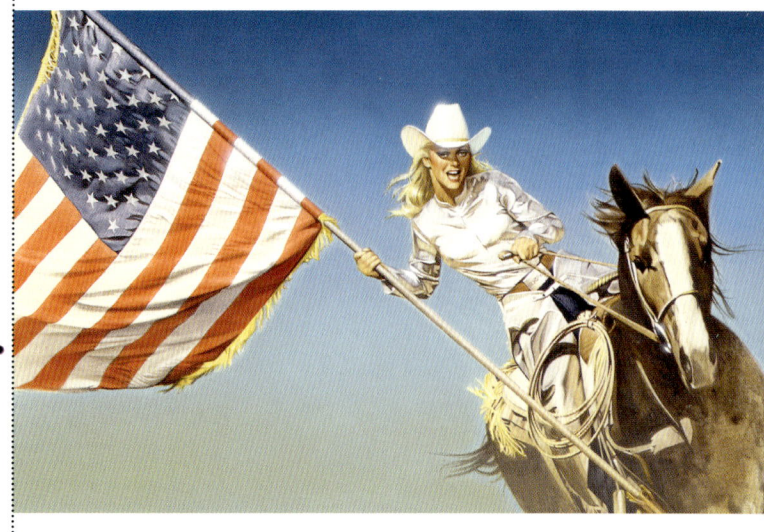

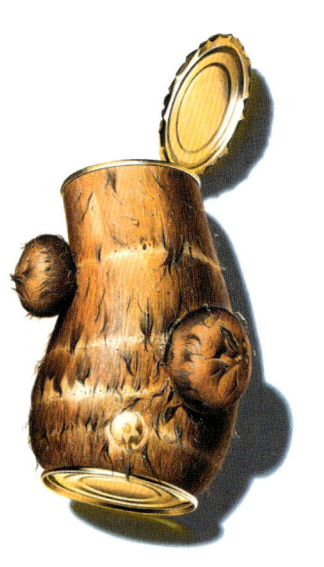

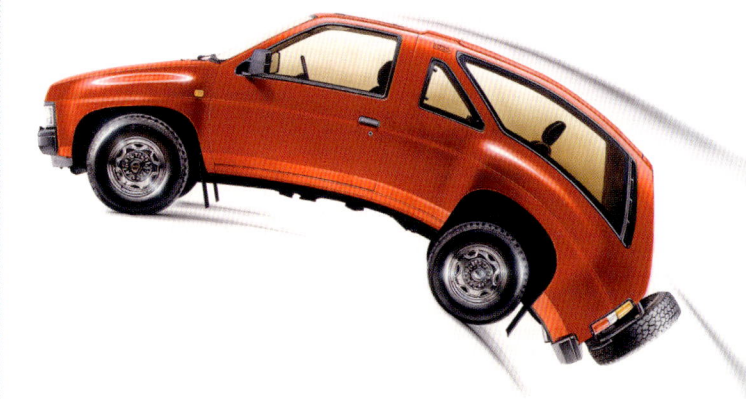

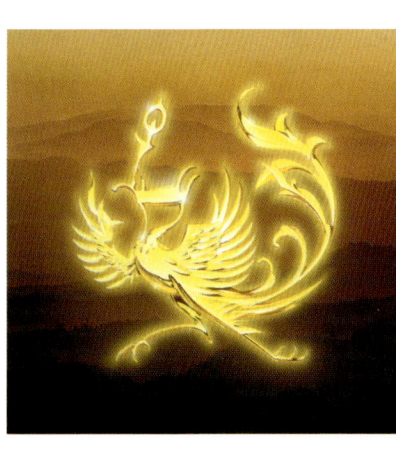

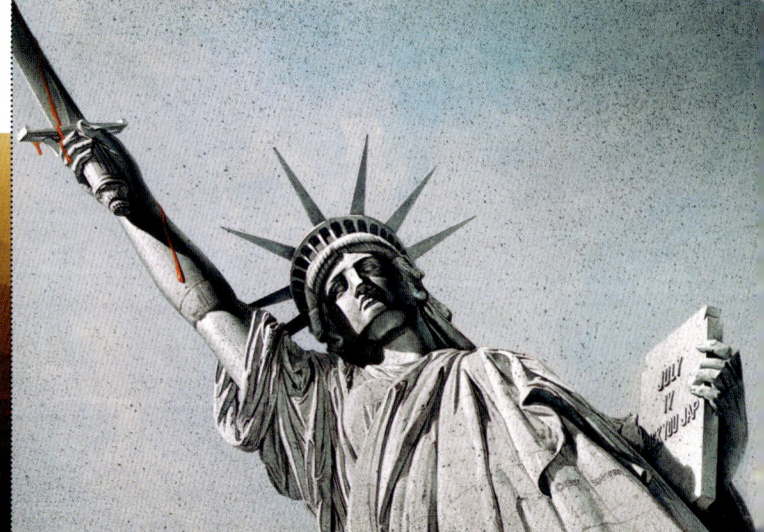

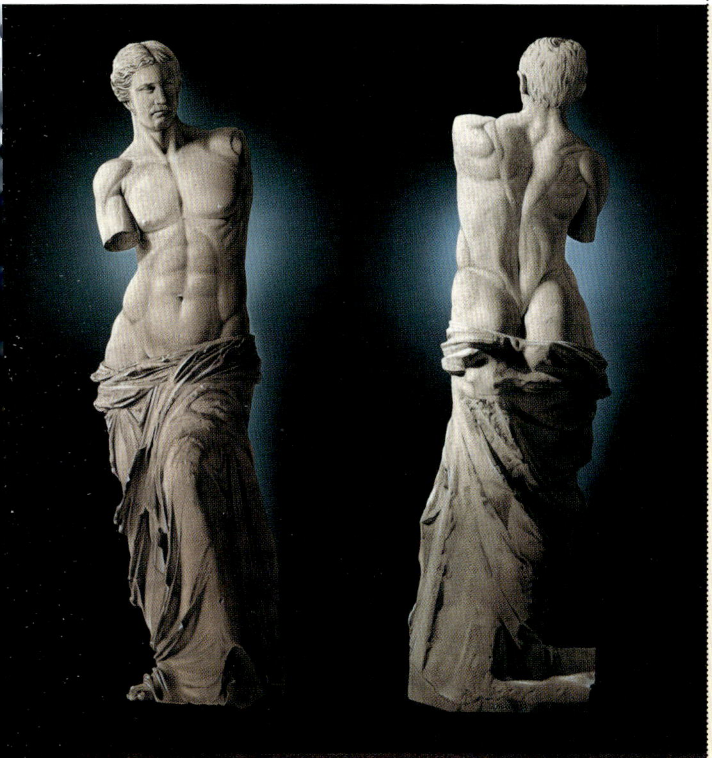

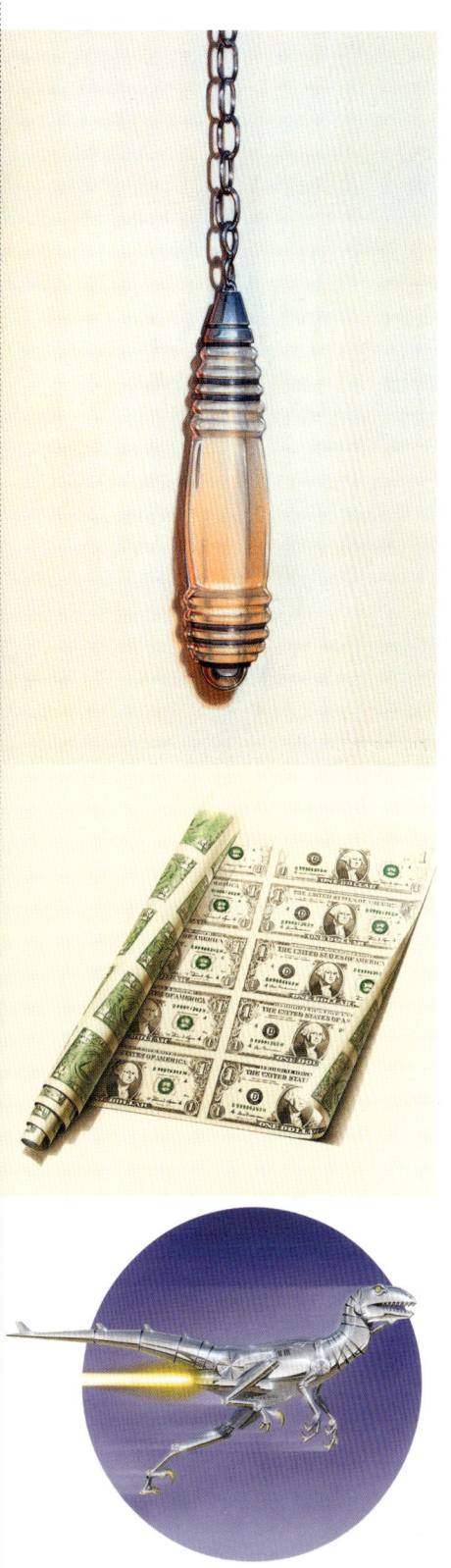

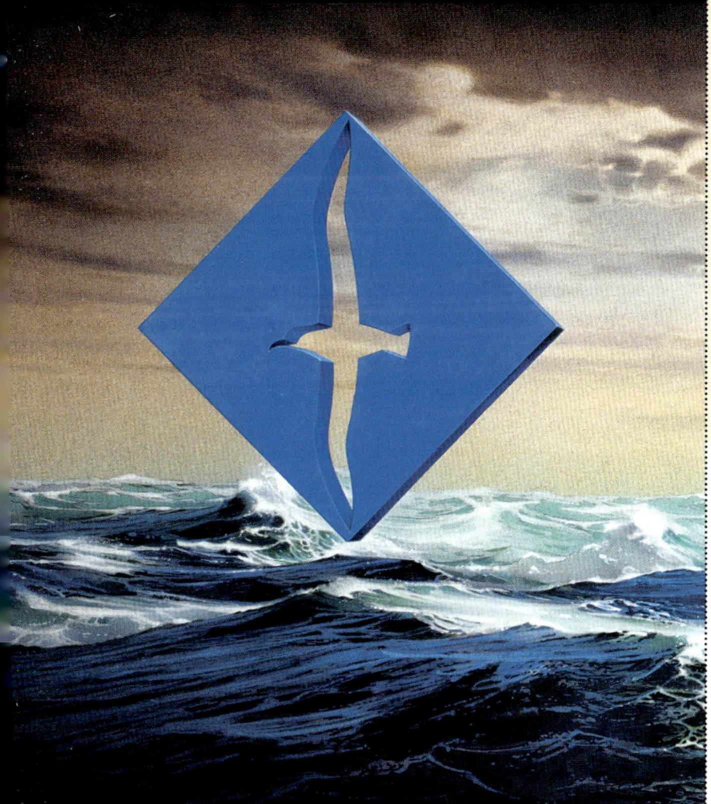

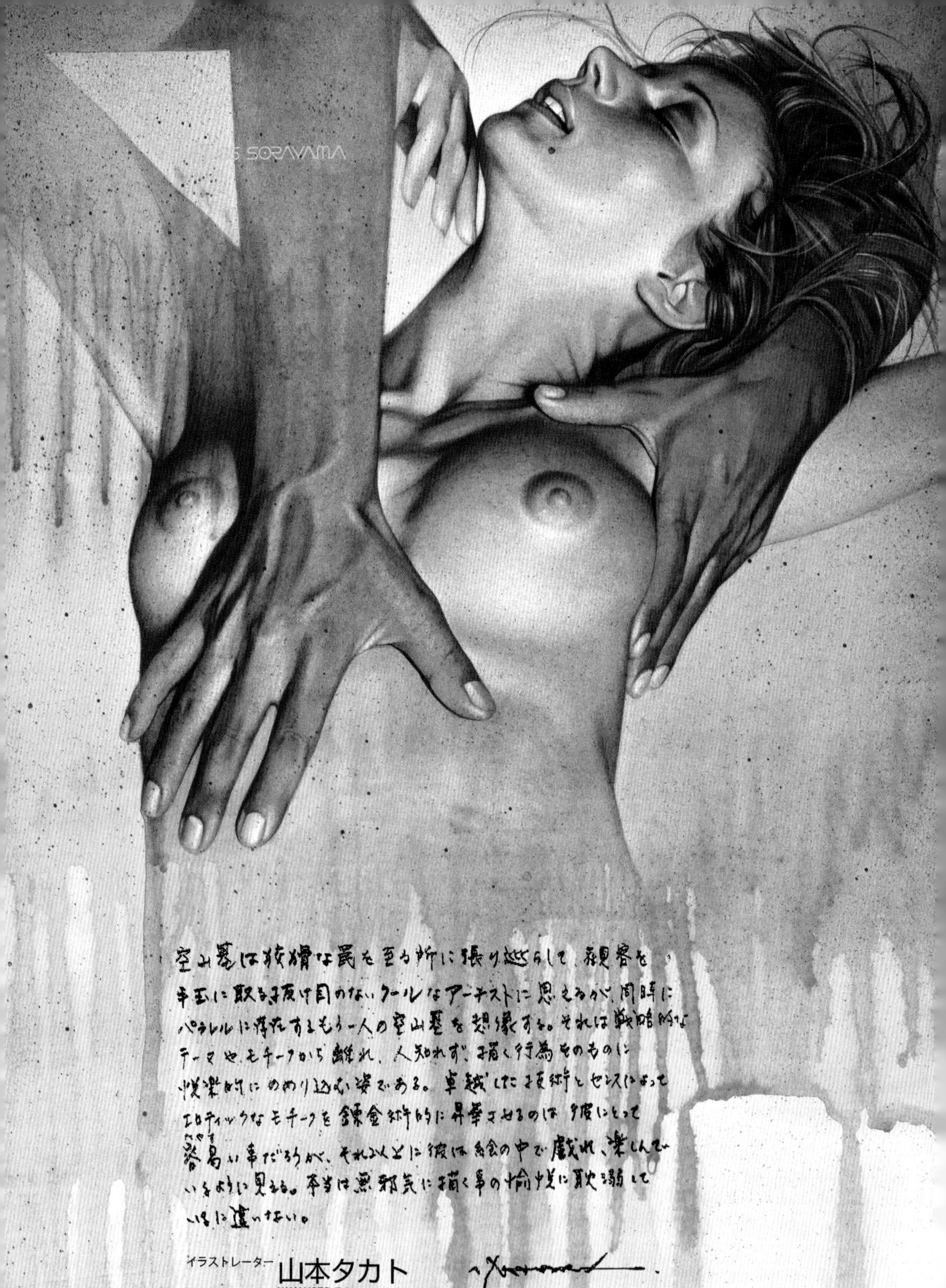

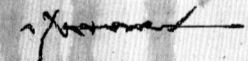

イラストレーター 山本タカト
YAMAMOTO, Takato

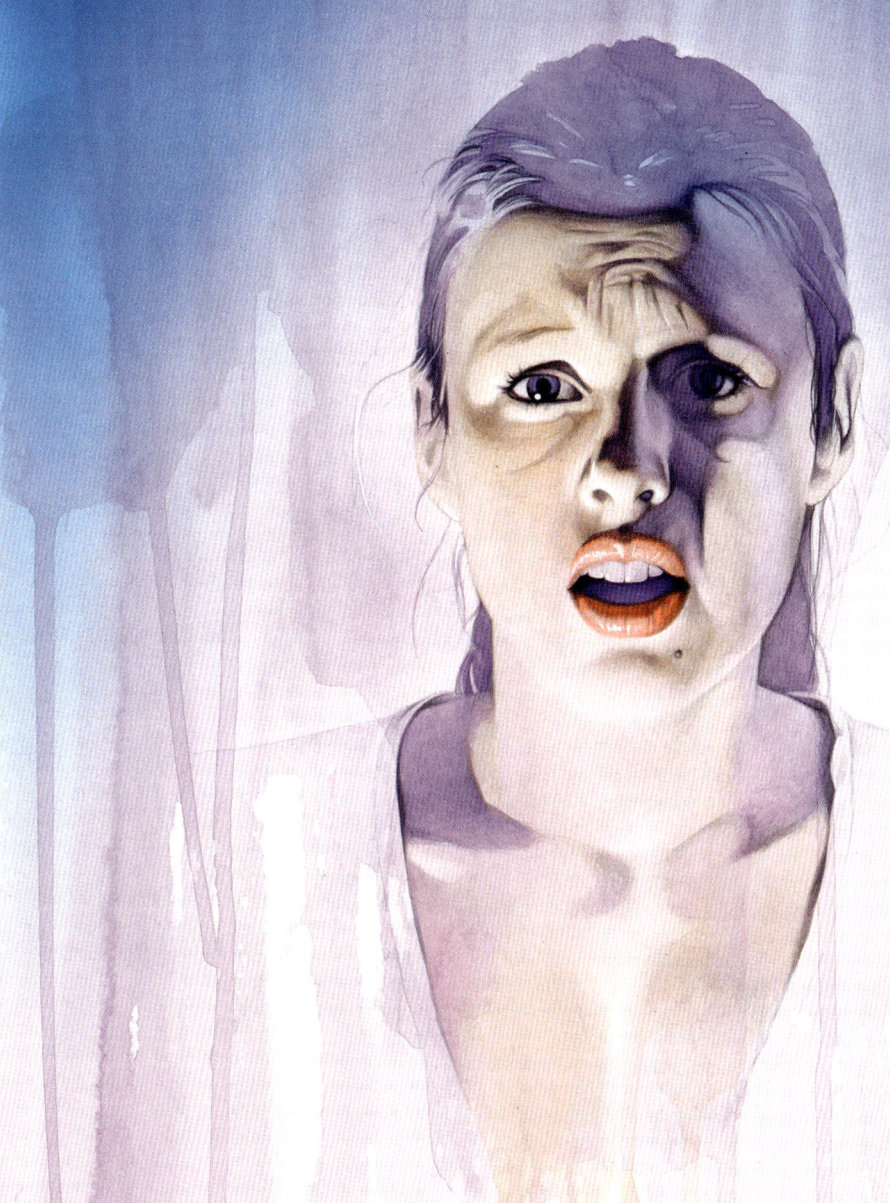

Paul Virilio has made a claim that a physical body cannot be separated from the unique world of its own. He has further stated that one particular body can be positioned in relation to its individual world.

The world that actually existed as 'right here, right now' has transformed itself to a mere information behind the small screen of CRT. Artificial human organs and microchips have begun to colonize a human body if such horrifying nihilistic scene is indeed our future and the loss of physical body is inevitable, it may also be necessary to dream the self-contained female beauty fused with machine in the world of sexual fantasy.

Virilio has also made the following statements: There is no existence beyond men. Men are the end of the line and the ultimate goal of the world. I simply wonder what those cables attached to the Sorayama's Gynoids are connected to, beyond the frame.

Mamoru Oshii (Movie Director)

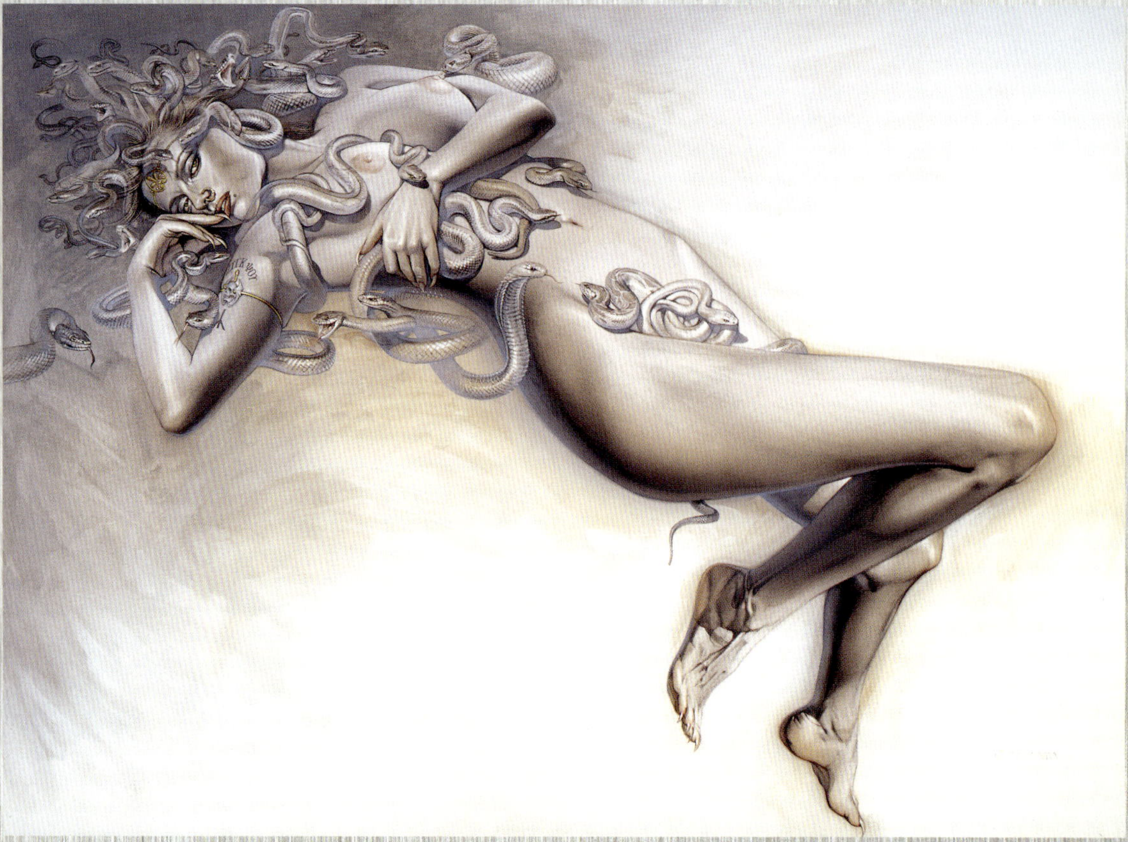

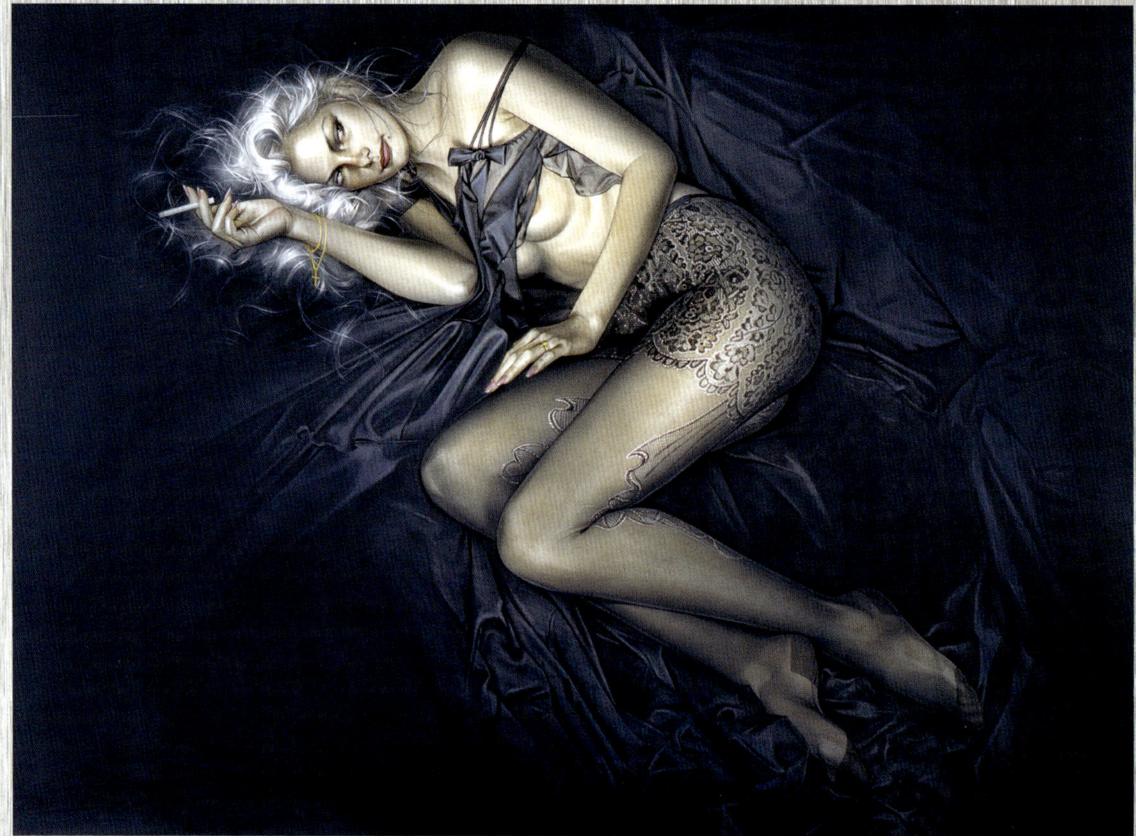

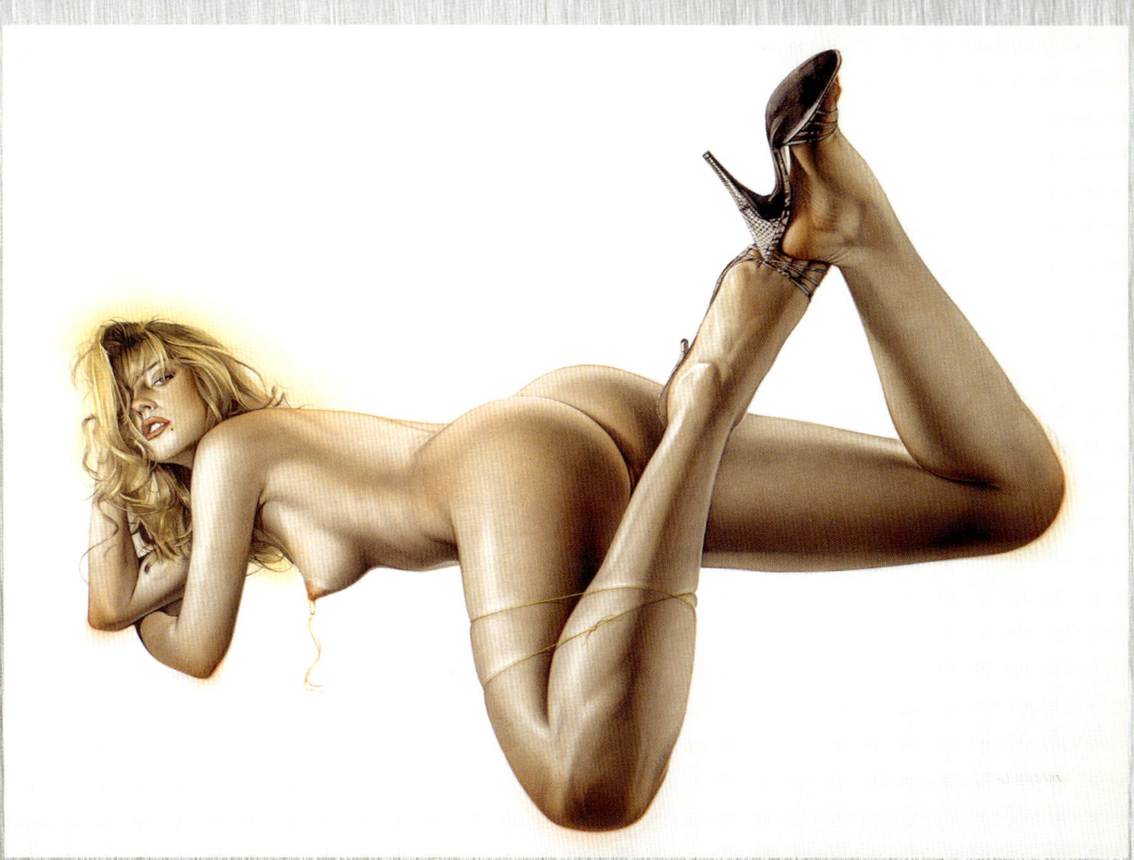

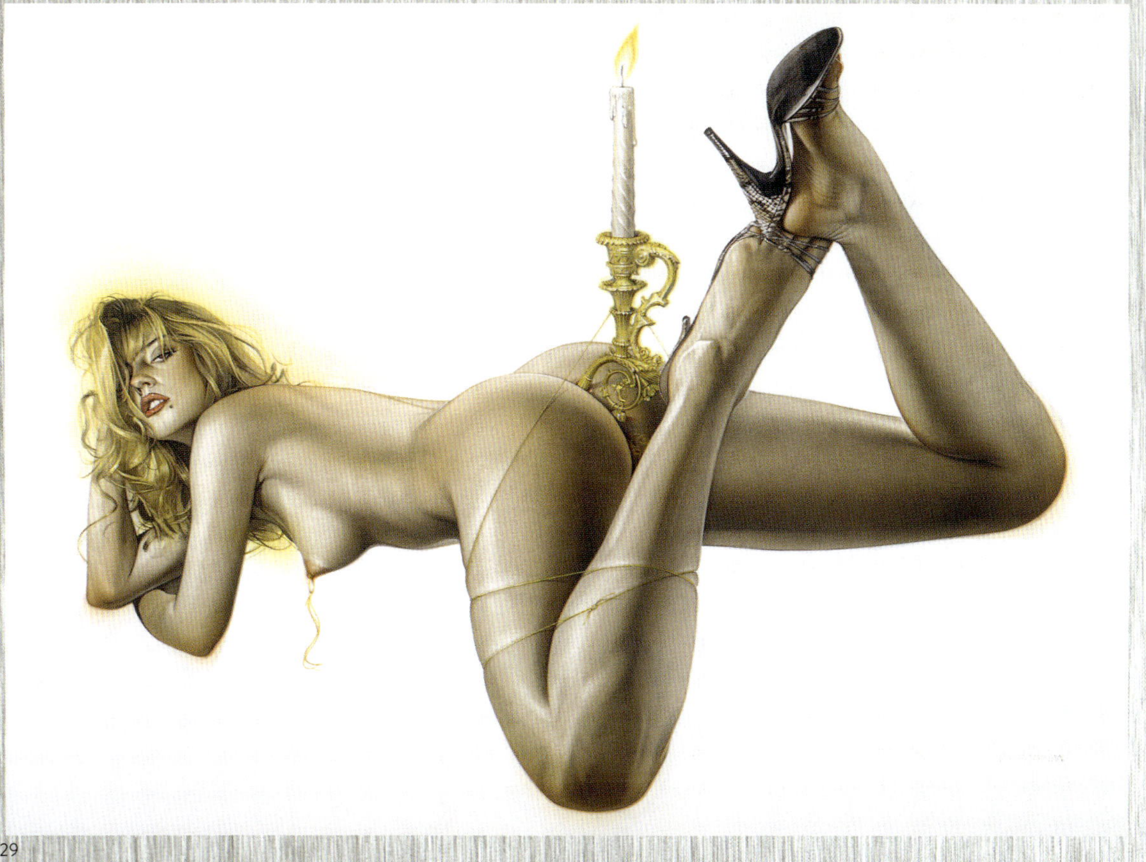

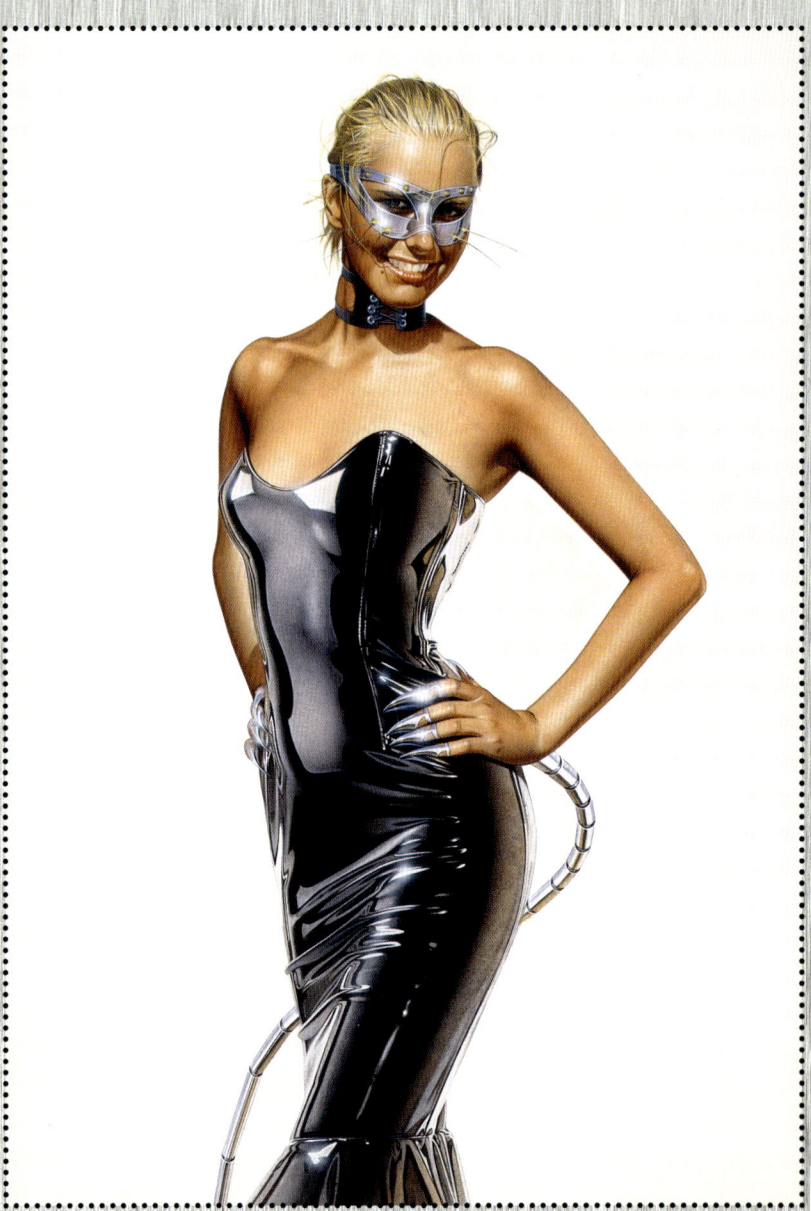

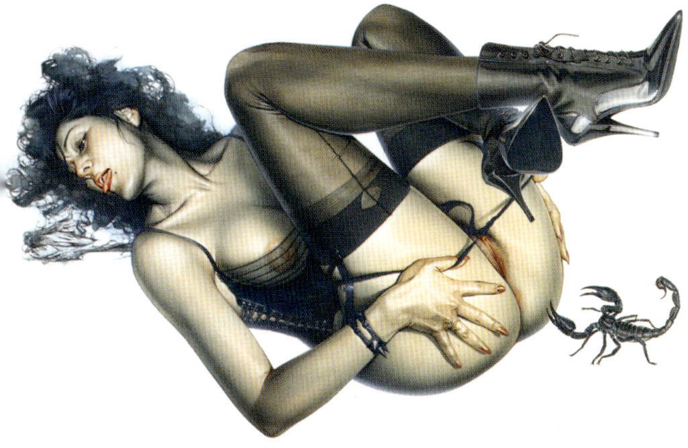

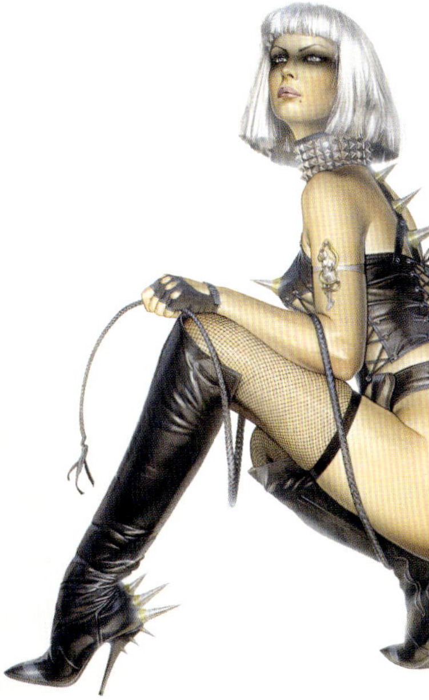

[redacted]

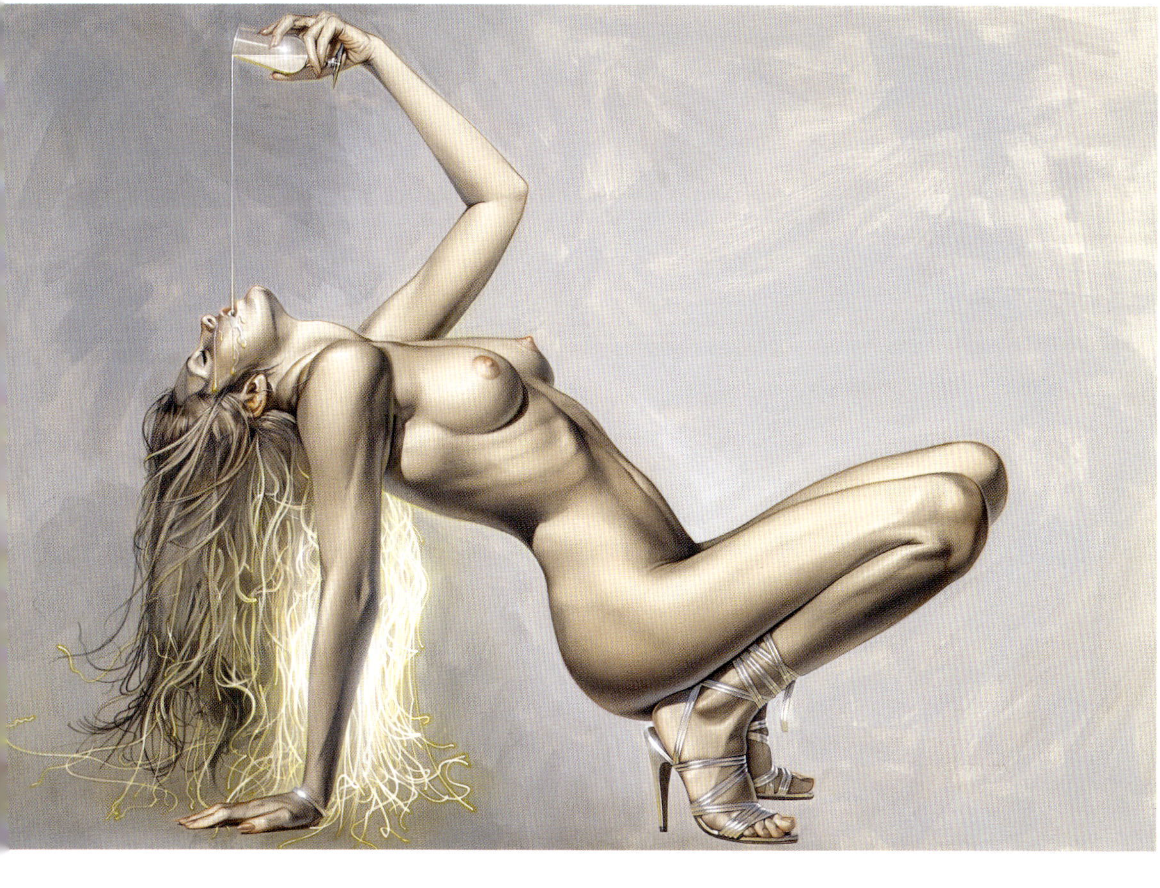

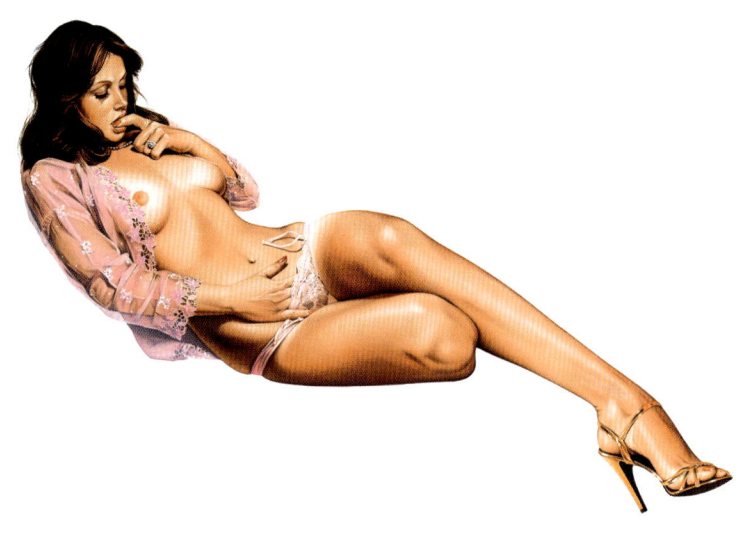

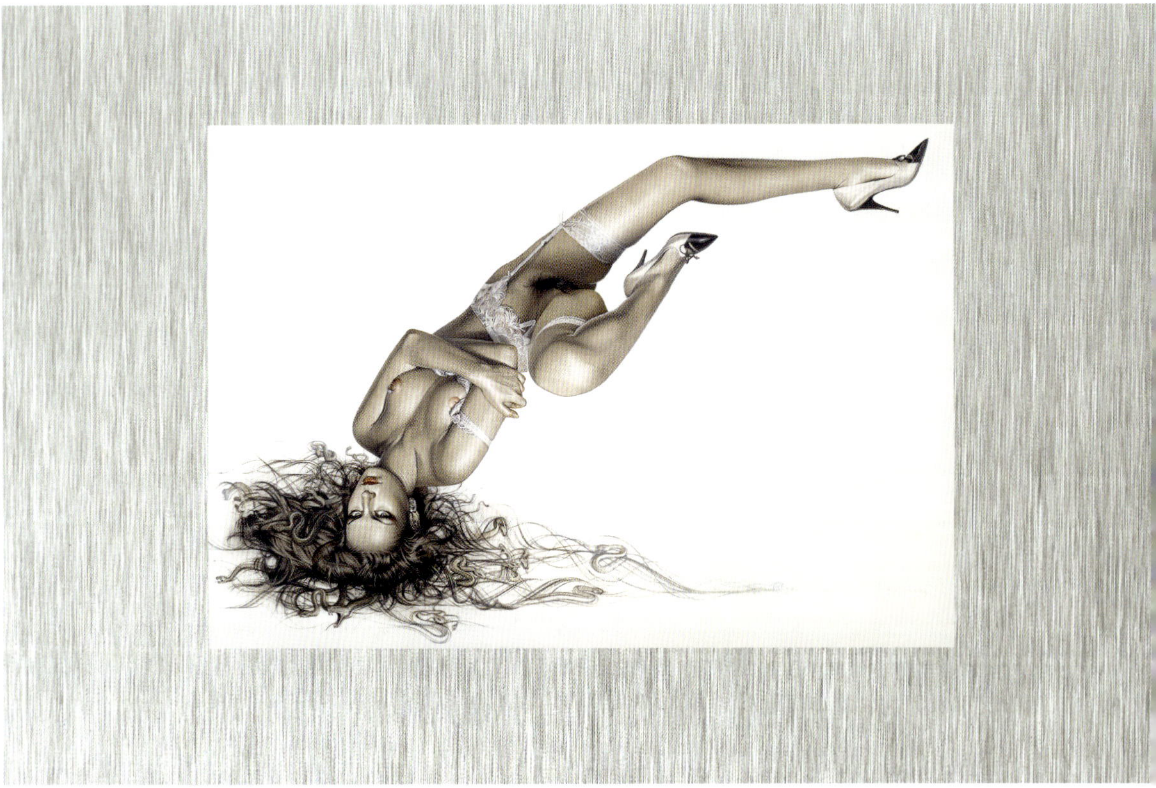

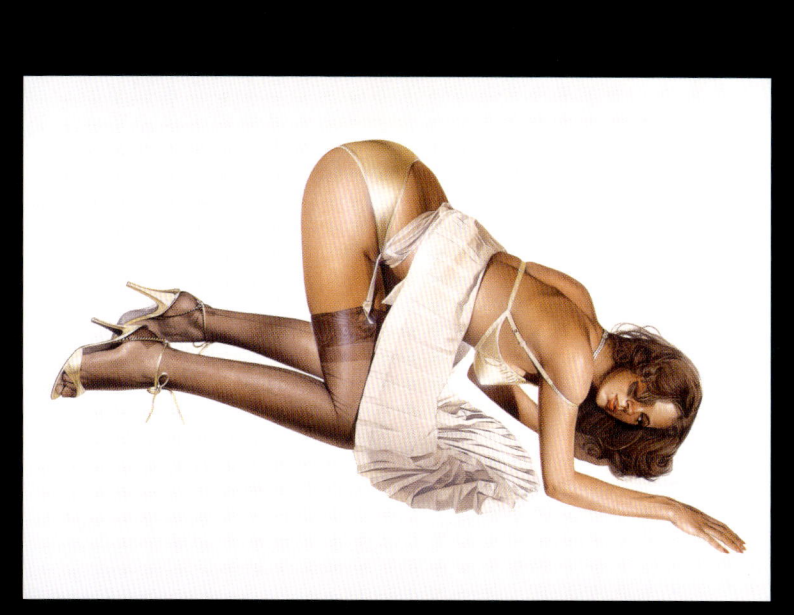

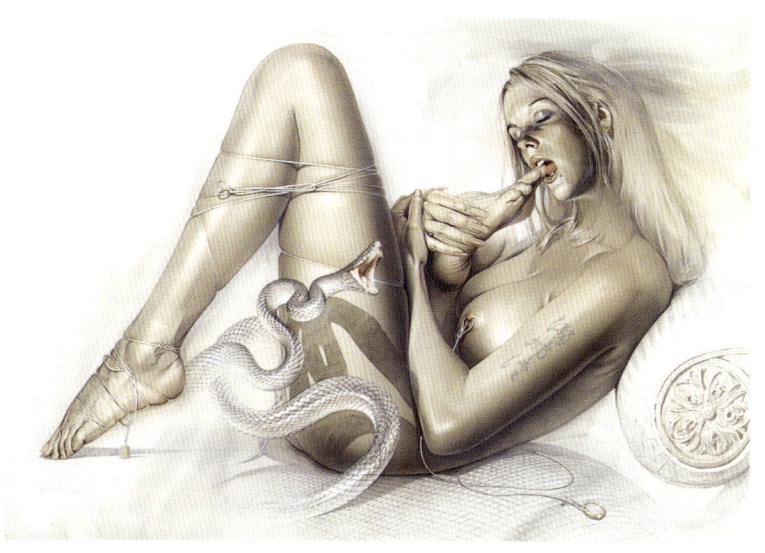

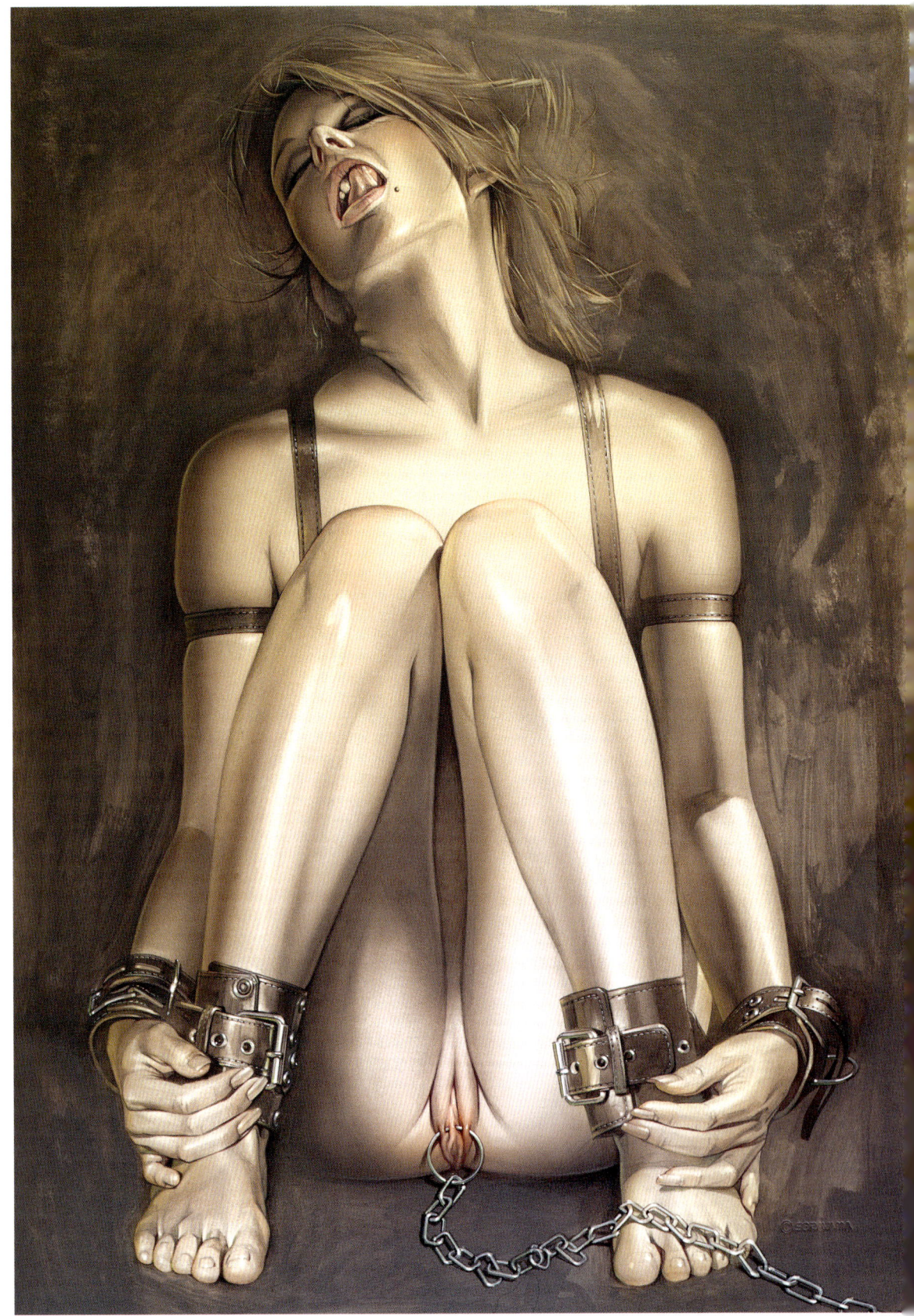

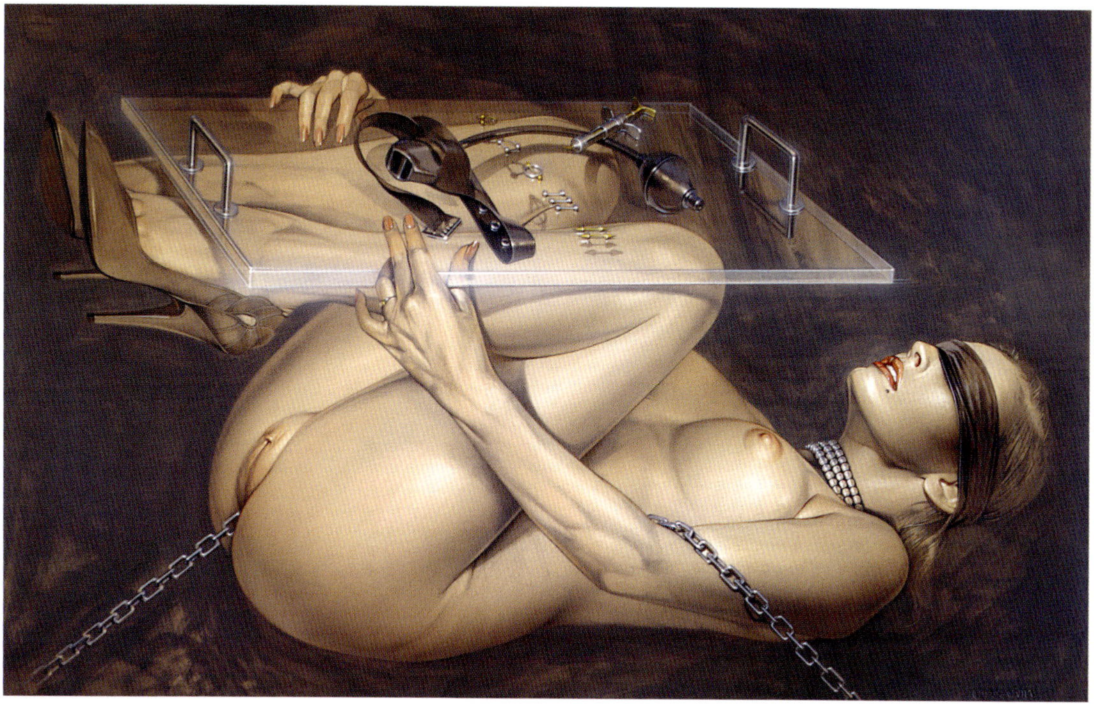

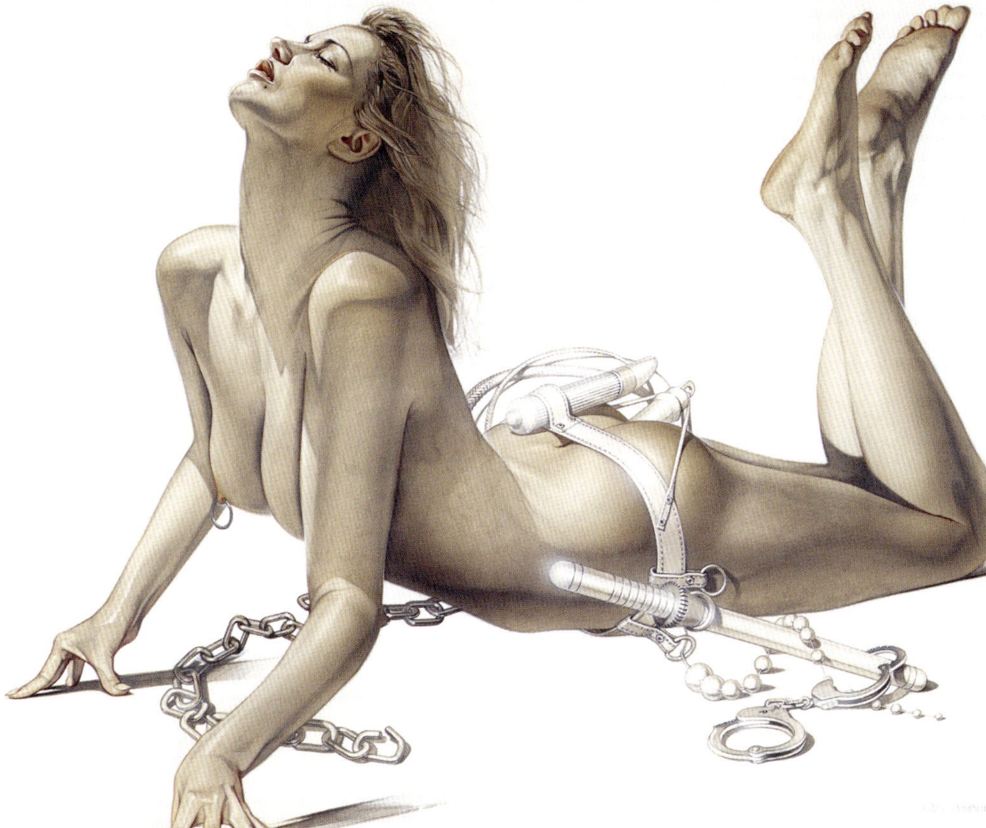

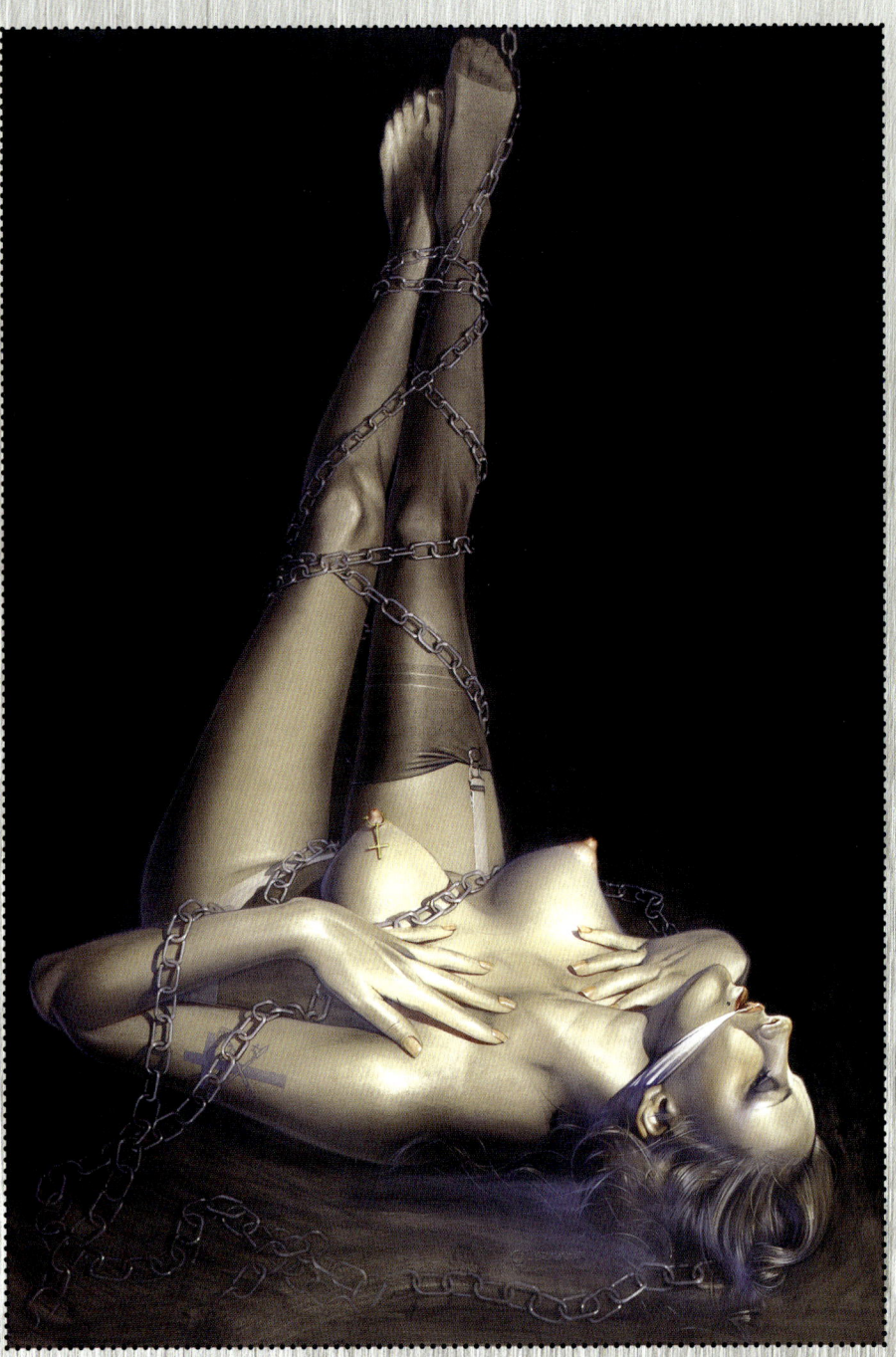

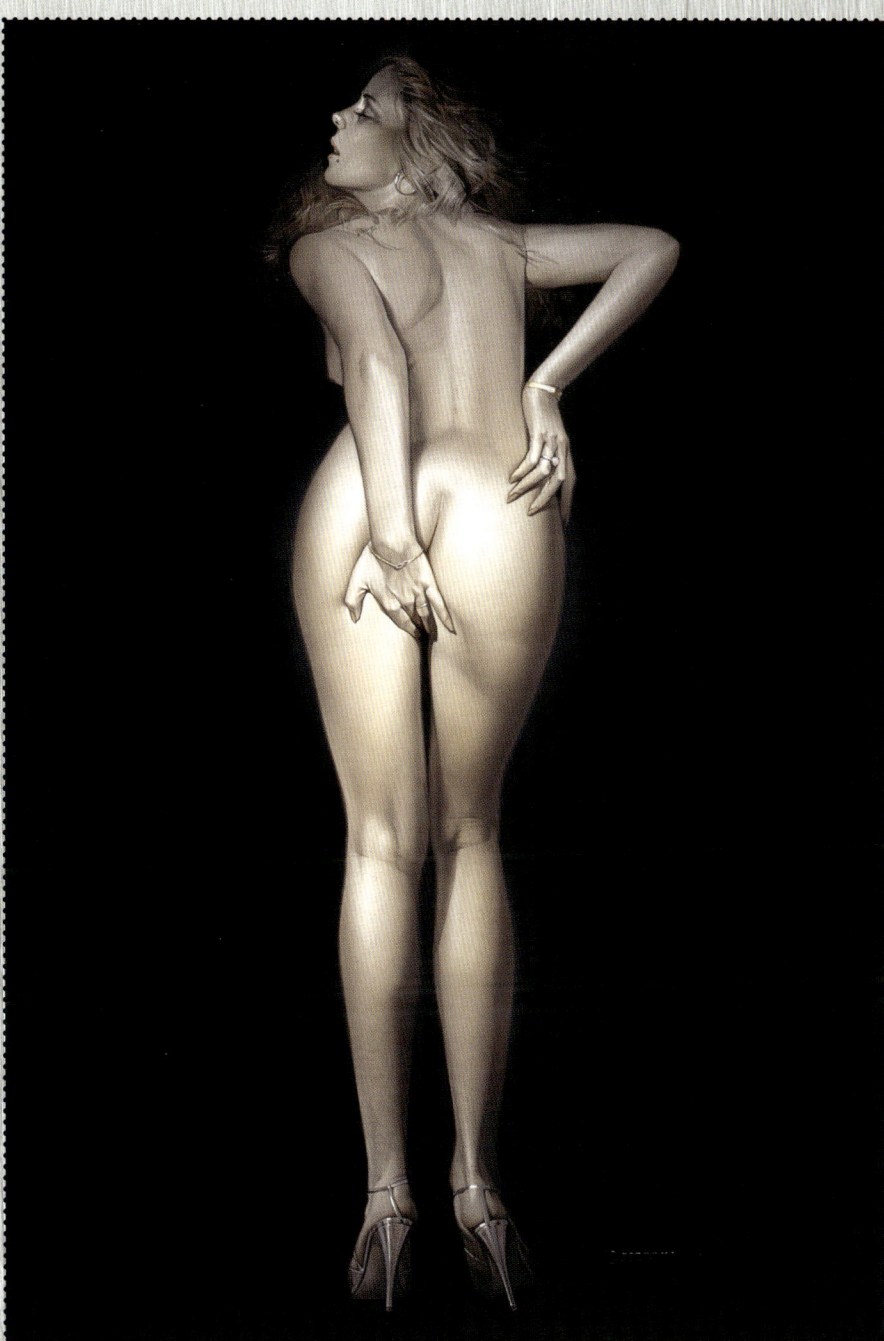

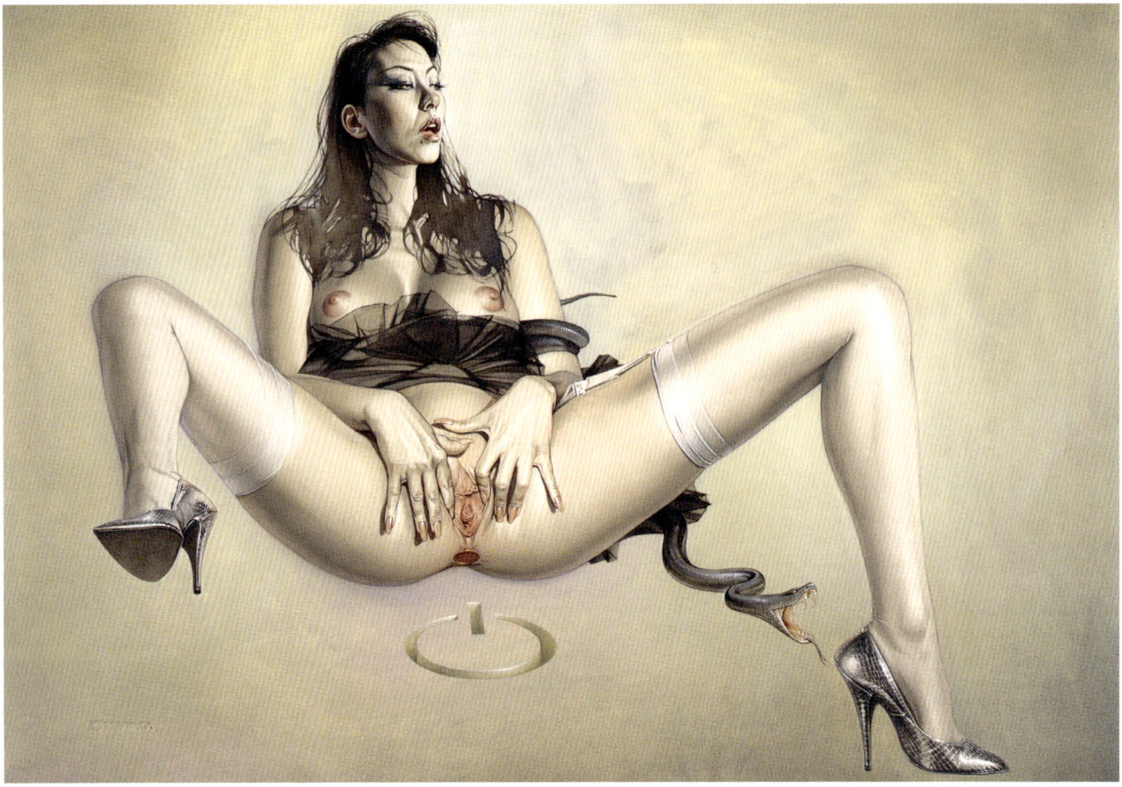

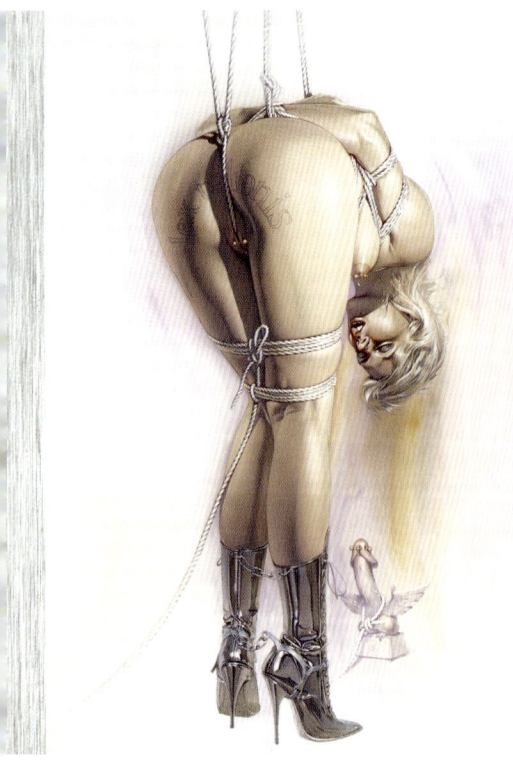
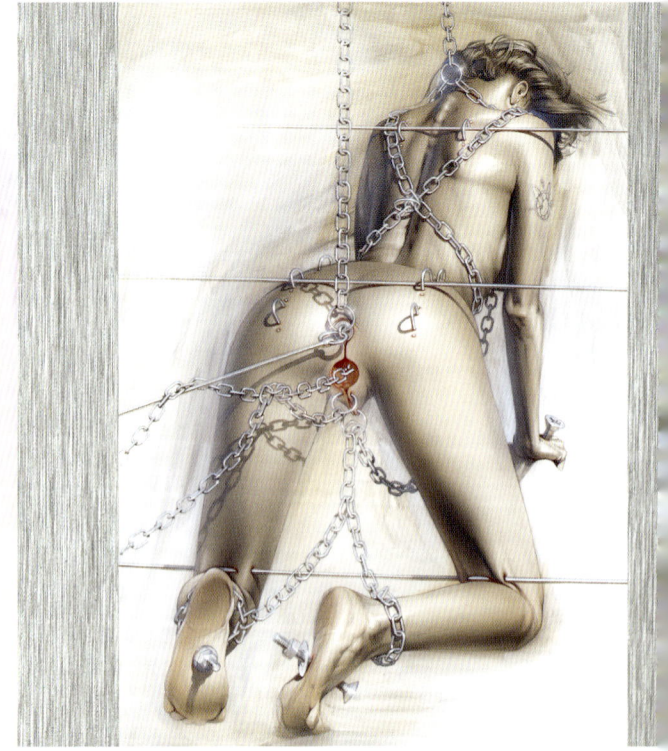

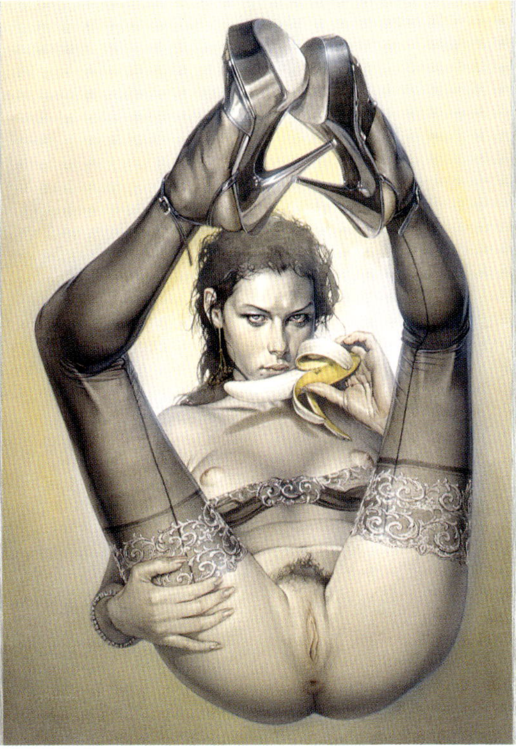

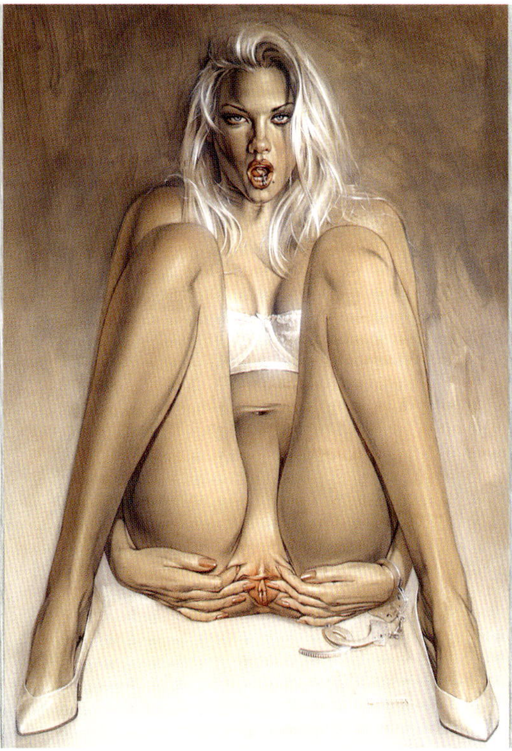

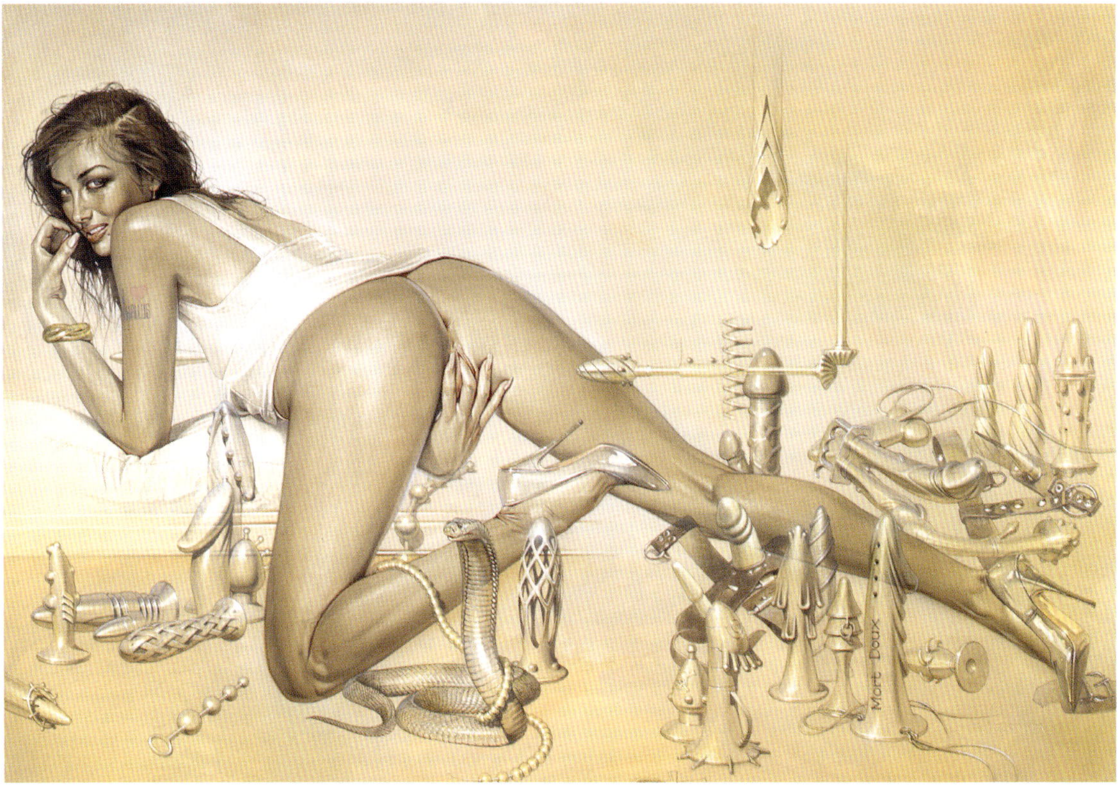

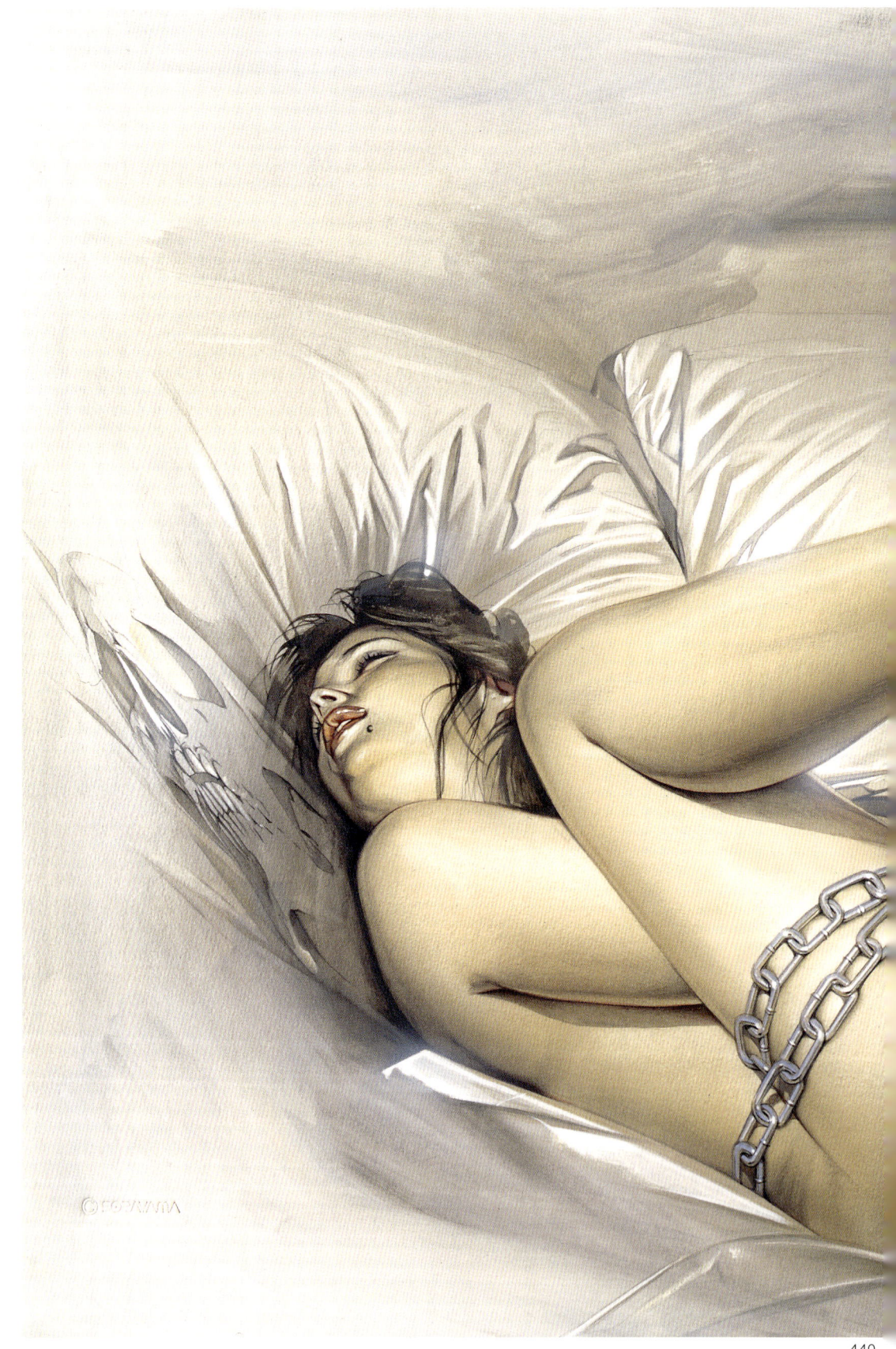

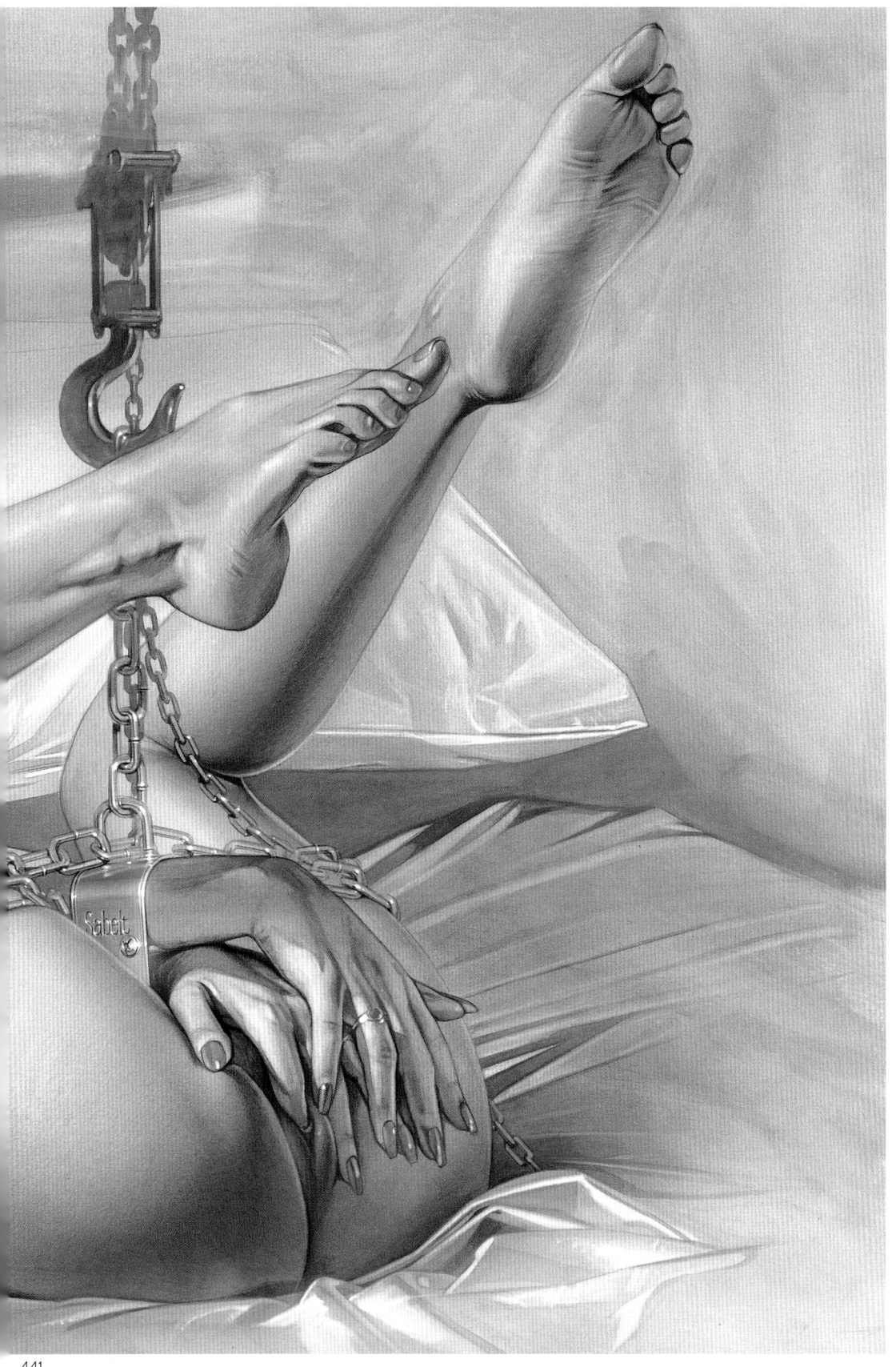

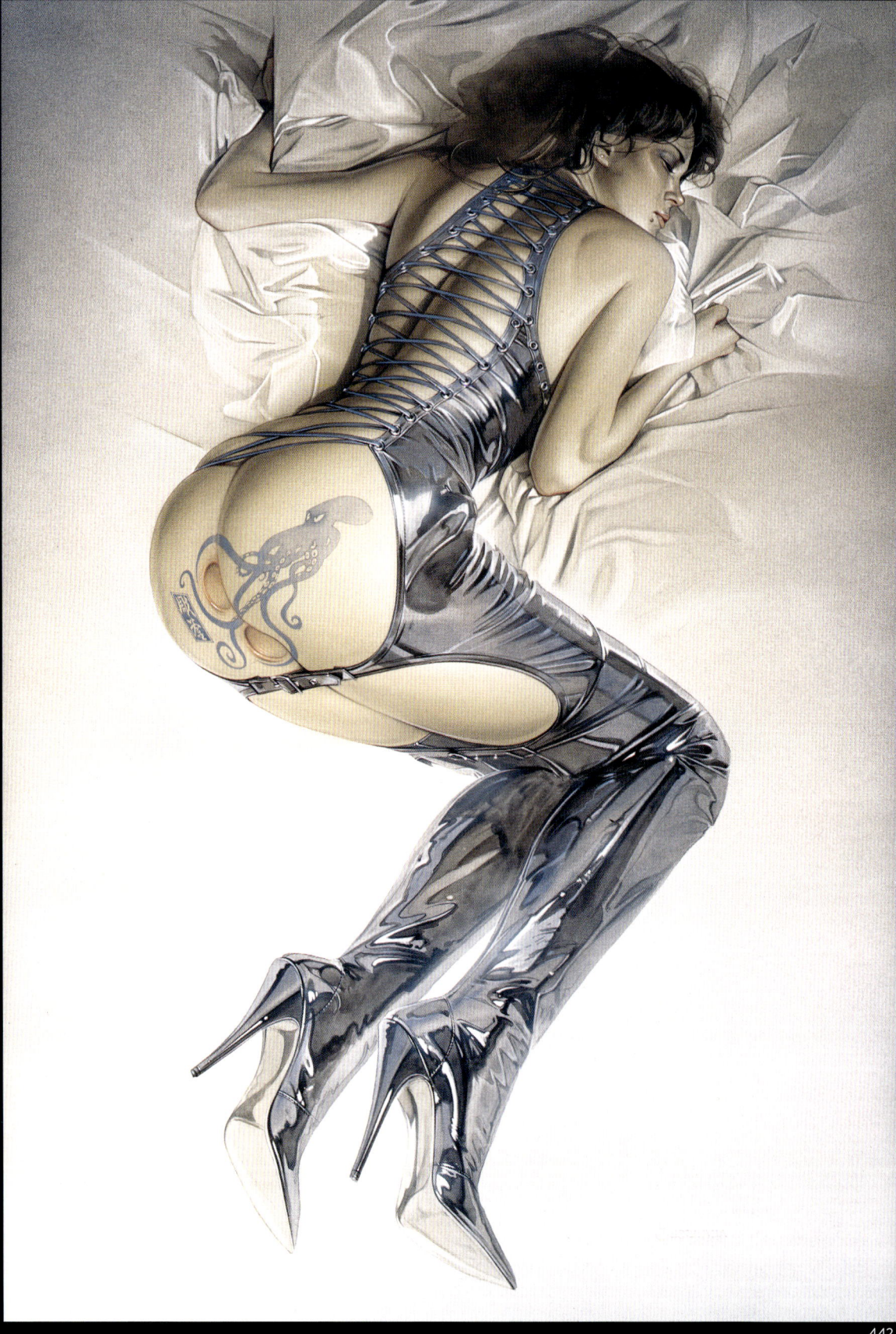

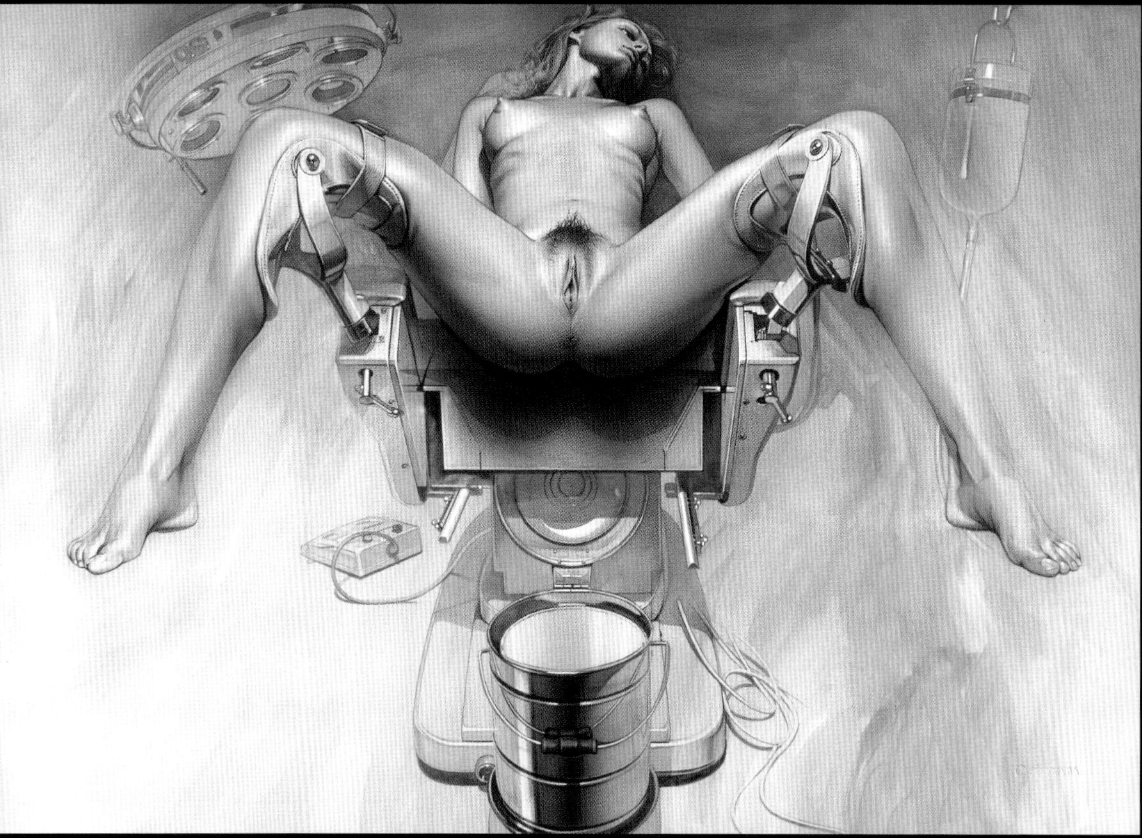

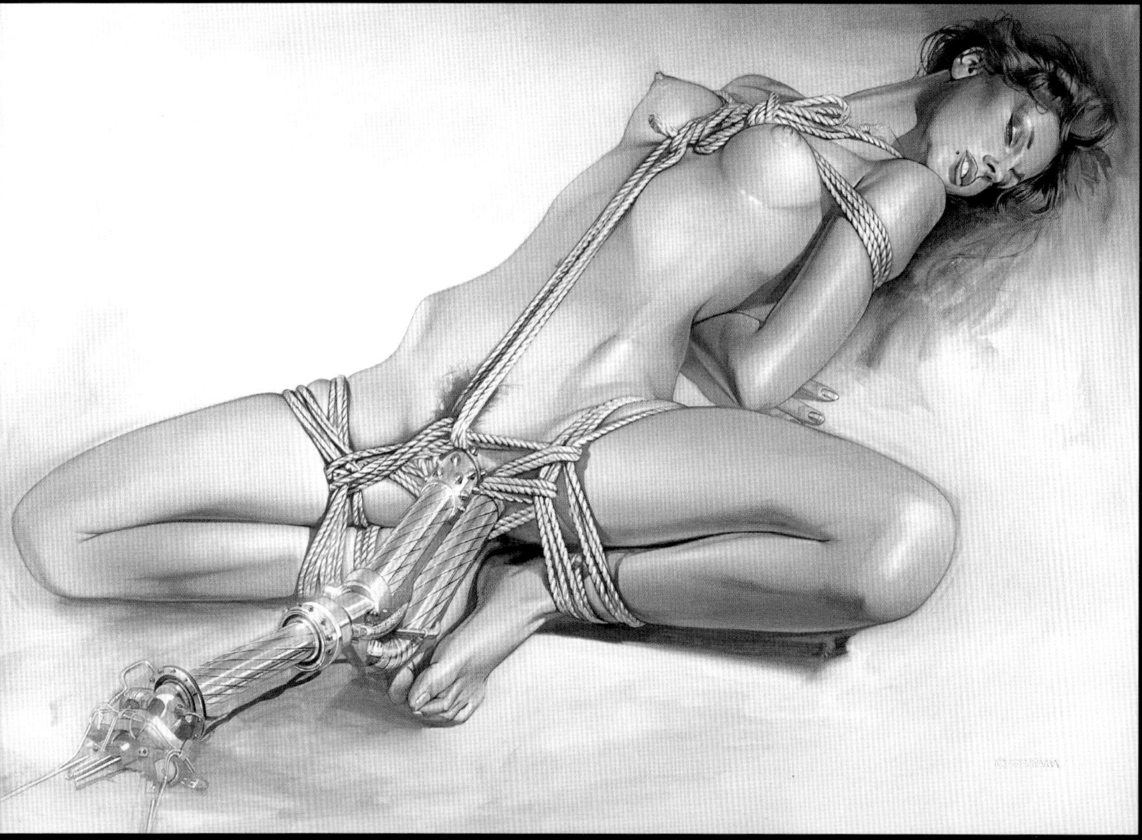

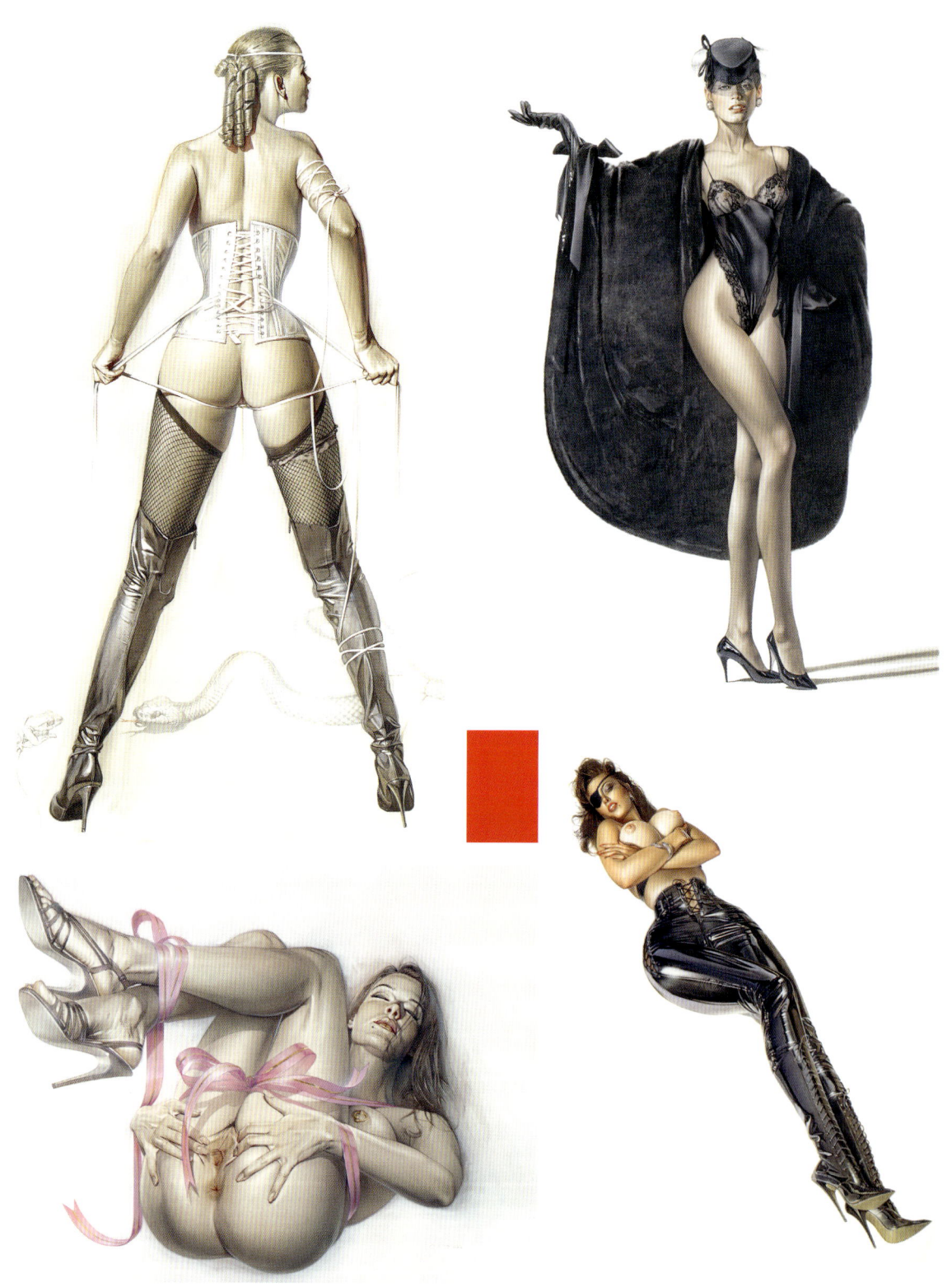

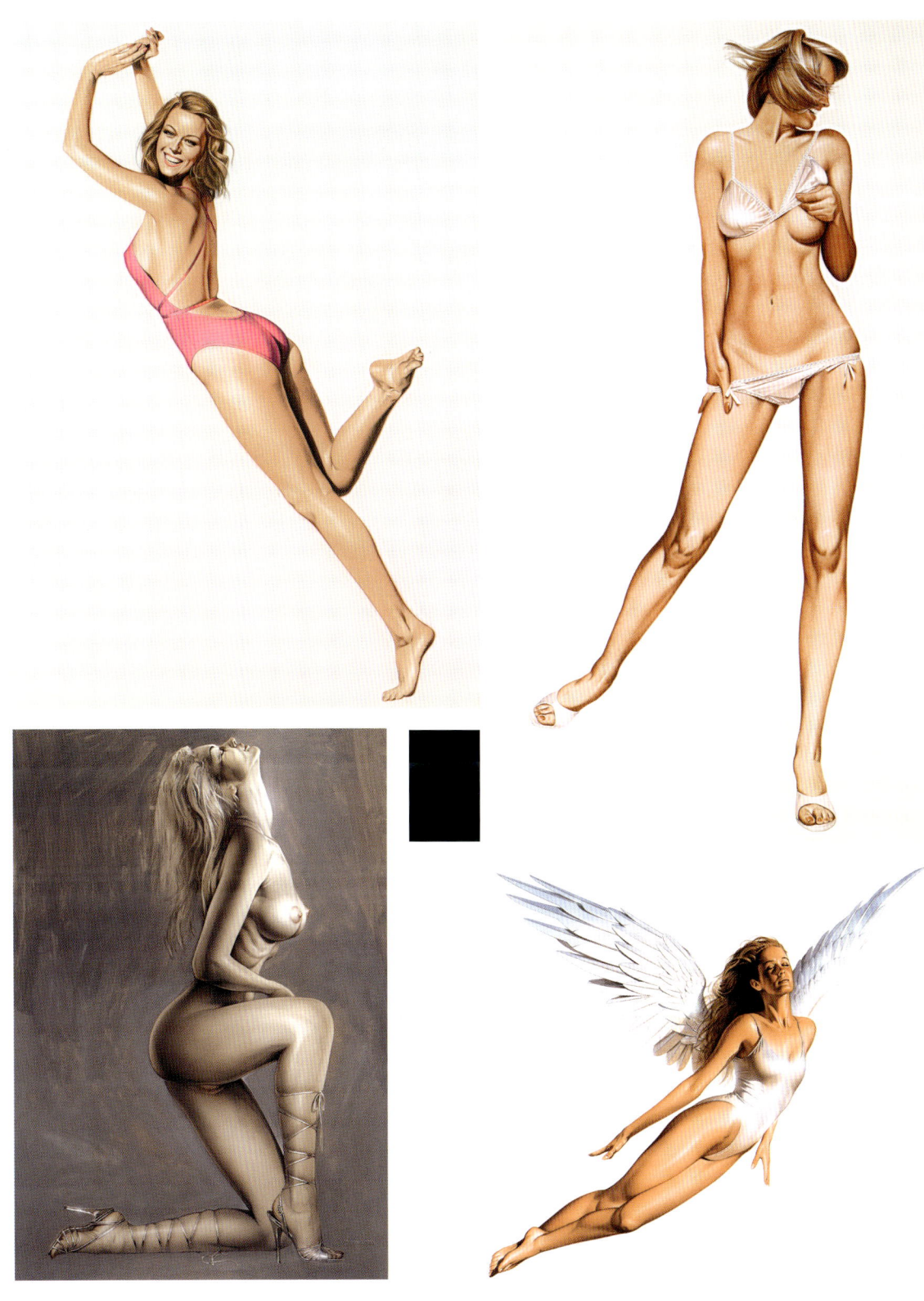

445

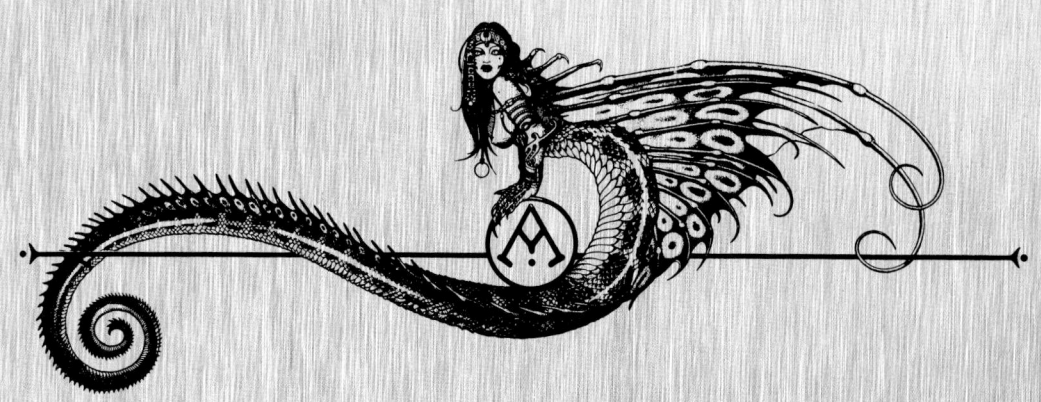

A few words by: Chris Achilleos

I have known Haijime Sorayama, or Hi-Jime, as I call him, for some
years now and we have become good friends, but I have been aware
of his work for a much longer time, before the publication of
"SEXY ROBOTS" which launched him to the world.

Like so many other people, I became an instant fan, inspite my
annoyance that he has made one of my ideas, a robot girl, rather
redundant and not worth finishing off. What can I do now? How can
I possibly follow that? and what will people say? "He,s just copying
Sorayama" Oh to hell with it!!
It was some years later that I eventualy got round to painting it,
and just to make it clear to everyone that this is intended as a
tribute to the "crome master", I included Hi-Jimes trade mark of the
time, the golden garters on the robot girls thighs. For those anoraks
of you out there, you can see this picture in my "SIRENS" book,page
46, "model 2000"

Because we live so far away from each other, Japan and England, we
tend to meet up only at conventions and art shows anywhere in the
world and have a great time together. At one of these shows where
we both exhibited work, Hi-Jime surprised me by suggesting that
we should swap pictures. I am now the proud owner of one of his
wonderfull originals, and oh yes, he has one of my old sketches!

I will say this about Hi-Jime, as a man he,s charming and friendly
with a wicked sense of humour, always ready to share a joke, even if
it is at his own cost sometimes. As an illustrator/Artist, he is a
spur that makes me, and i,m sure many other illustrators to try
harder and harder. Simply, Hi-Jime is the measuring stick of technical excellence that we all try and measure up to.

Chris Achilleos
December 1997

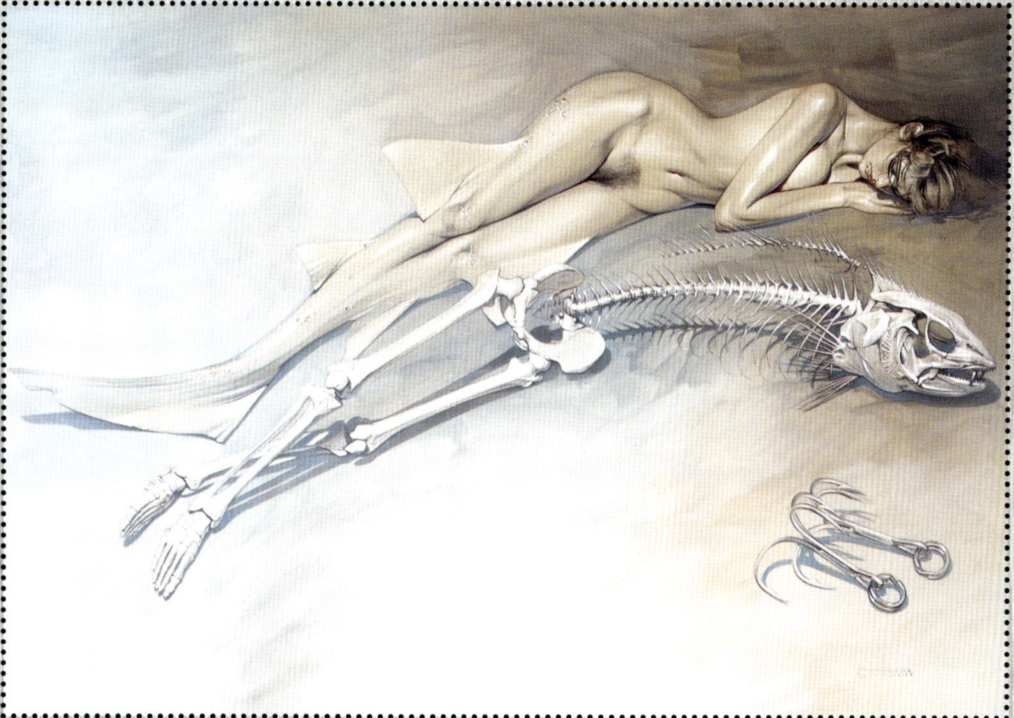

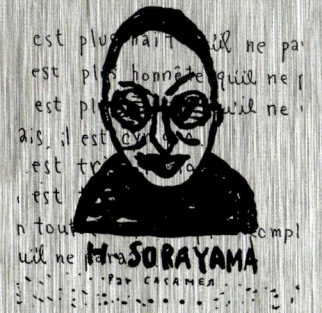

積算

Il est plus naïf qu'il ne paraît
Il est plus honnête qu'il ne paraît
Il est plus gentil qu'il ne paraît
Mais, il est cynique
Il est très ironique
Il est trop passionné
En tout cas il est plus compliqué
qu'il ne paraît

par cacamea

painter   SASAMEYA, Yuki

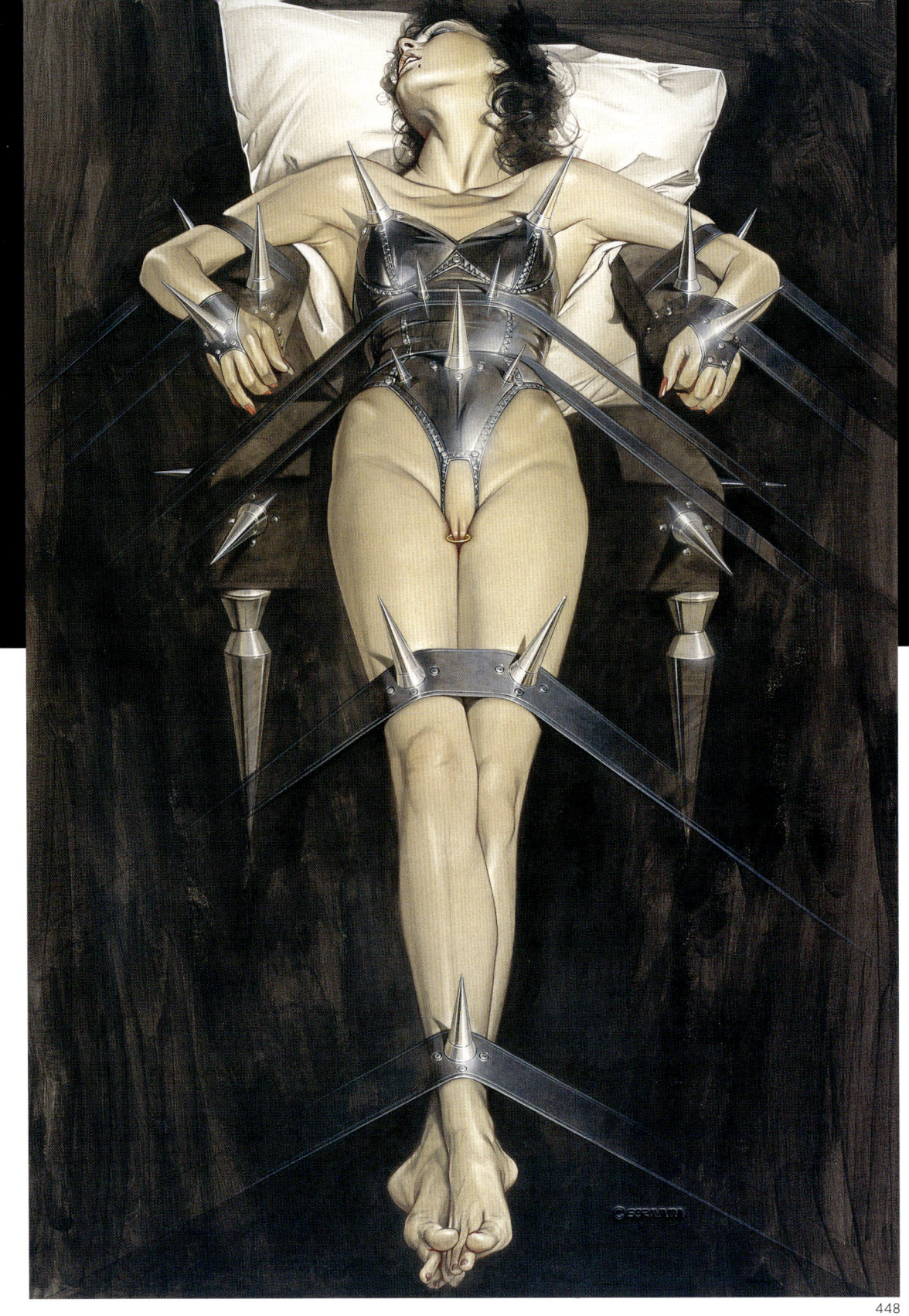

448

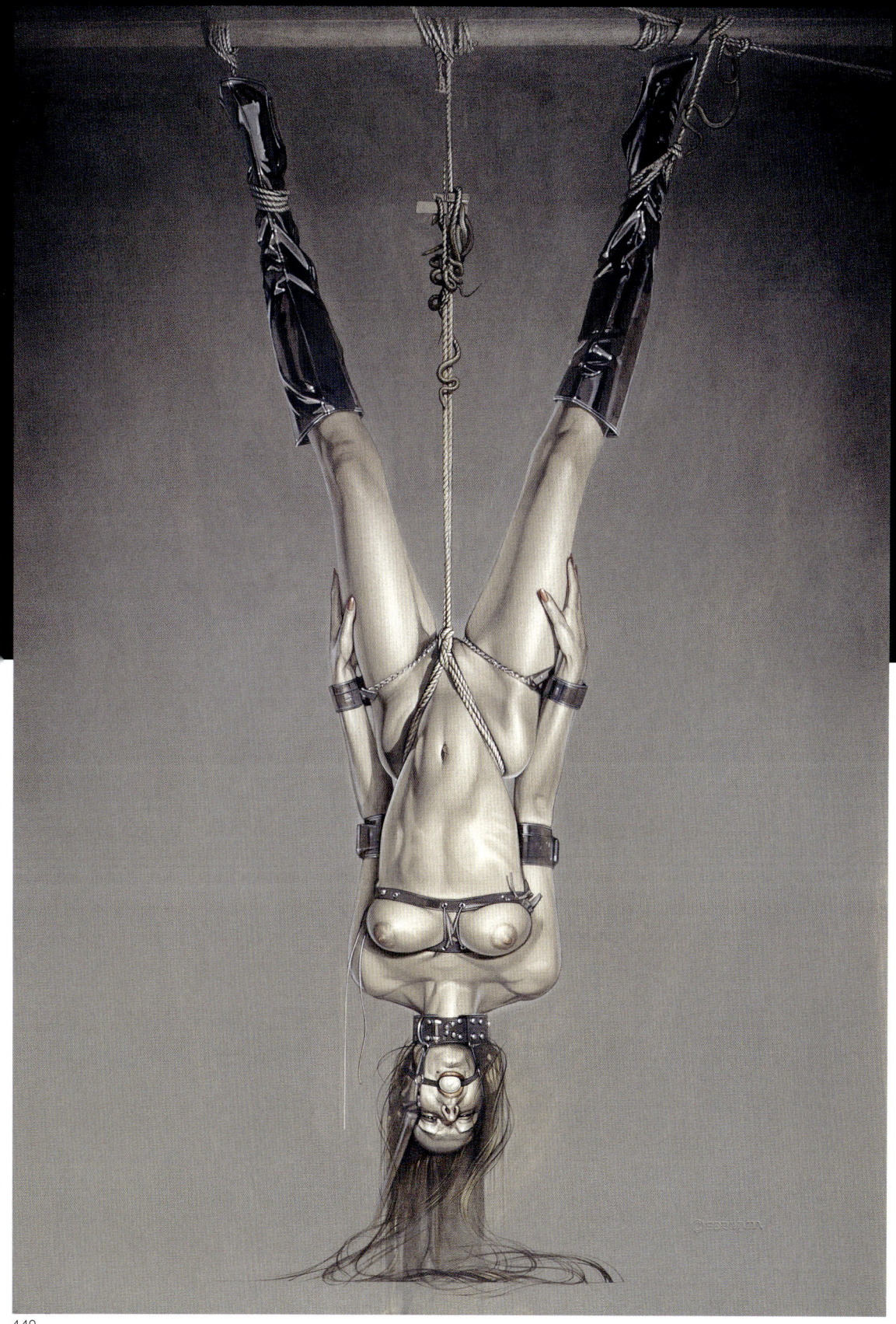

449

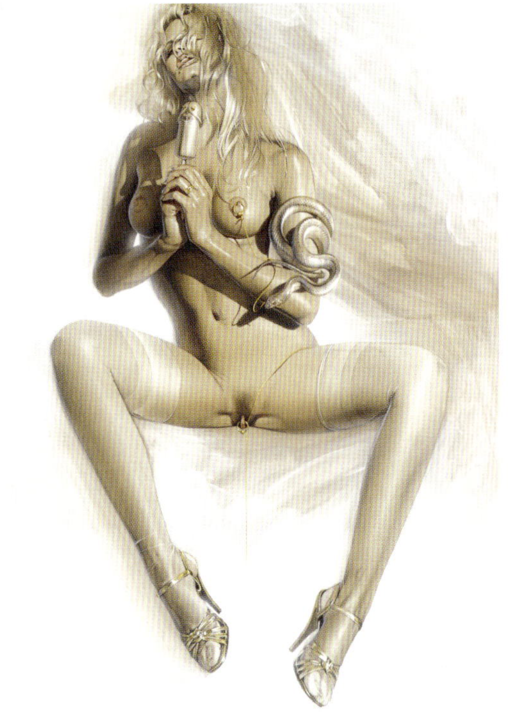

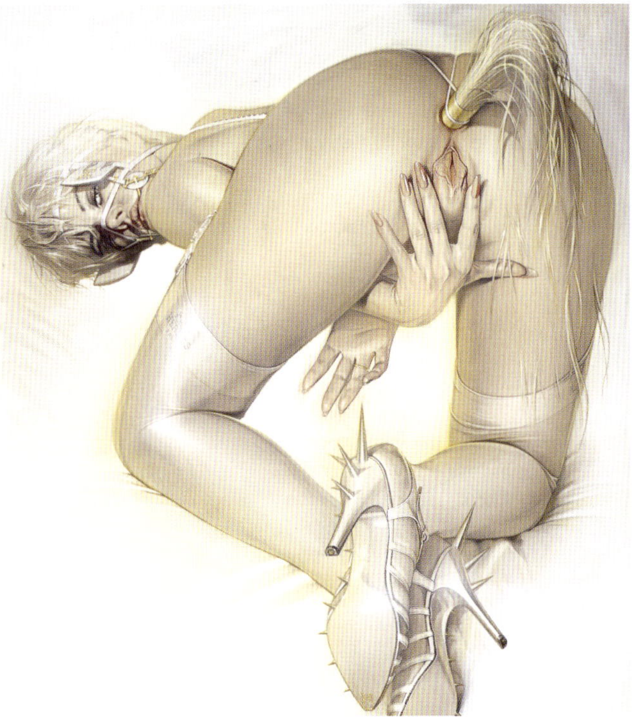

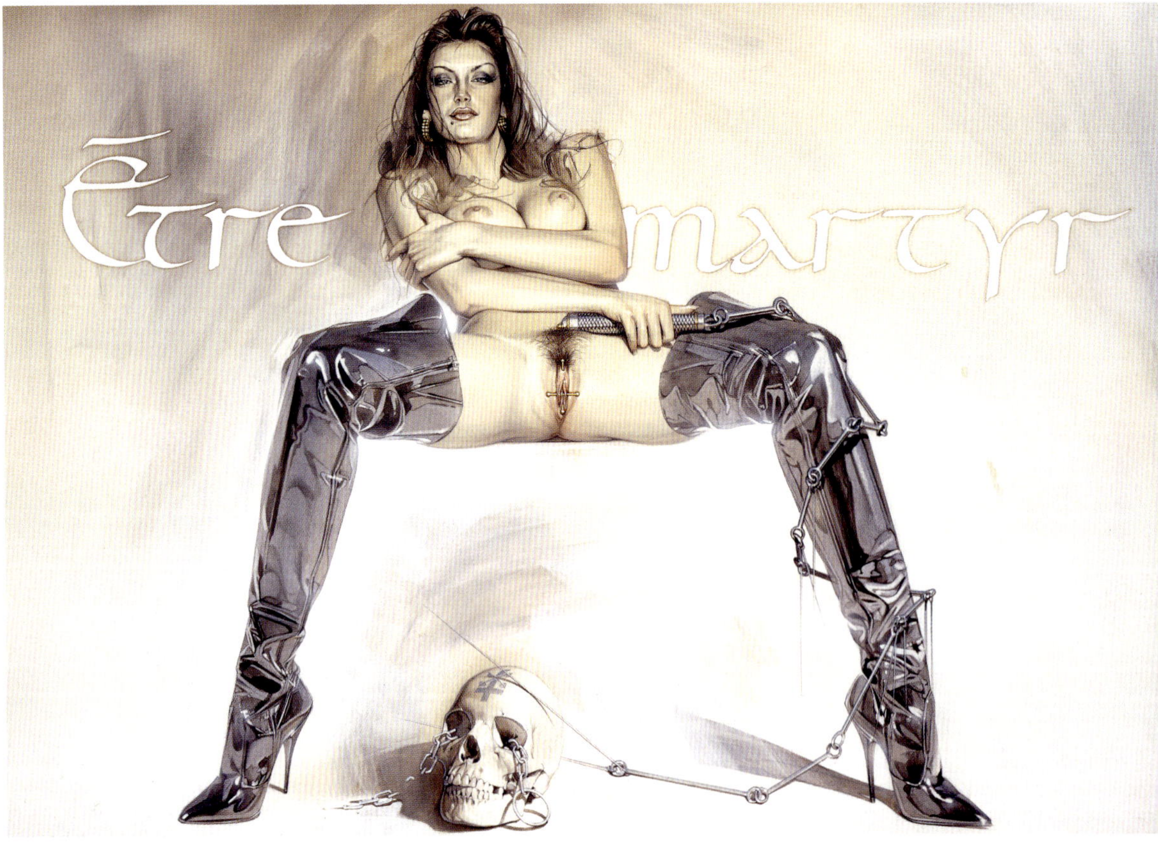

ÊTRE martyr

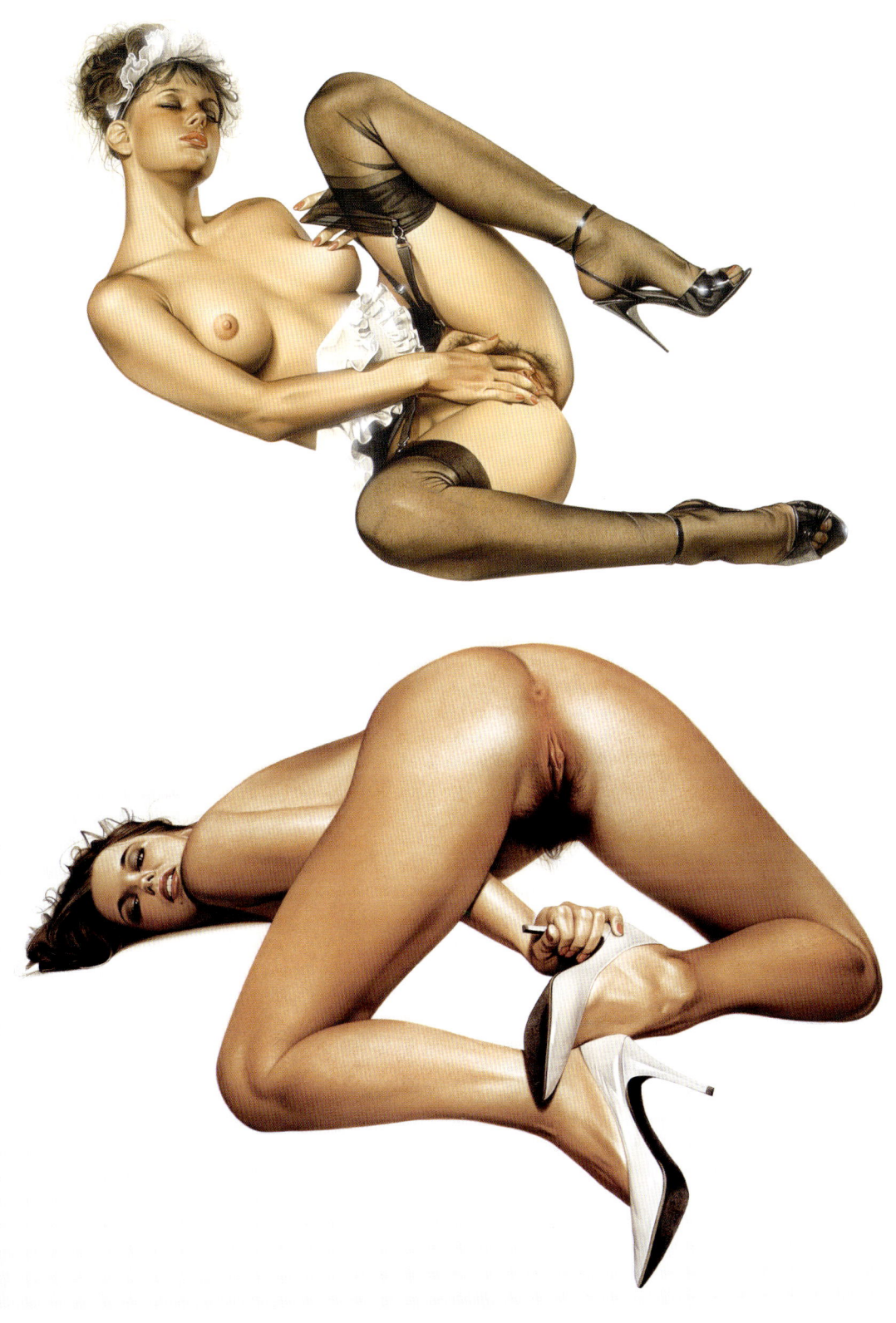

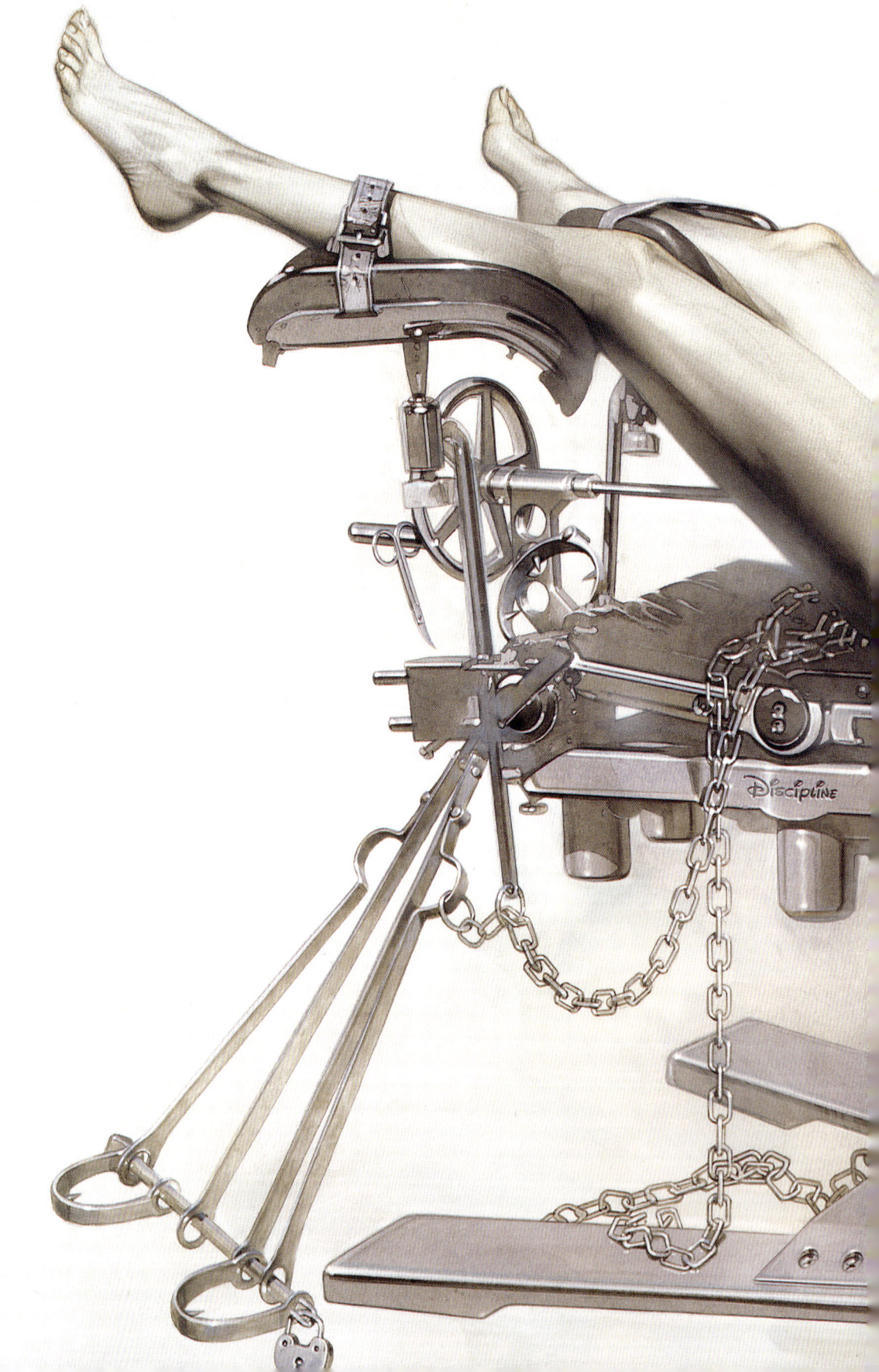

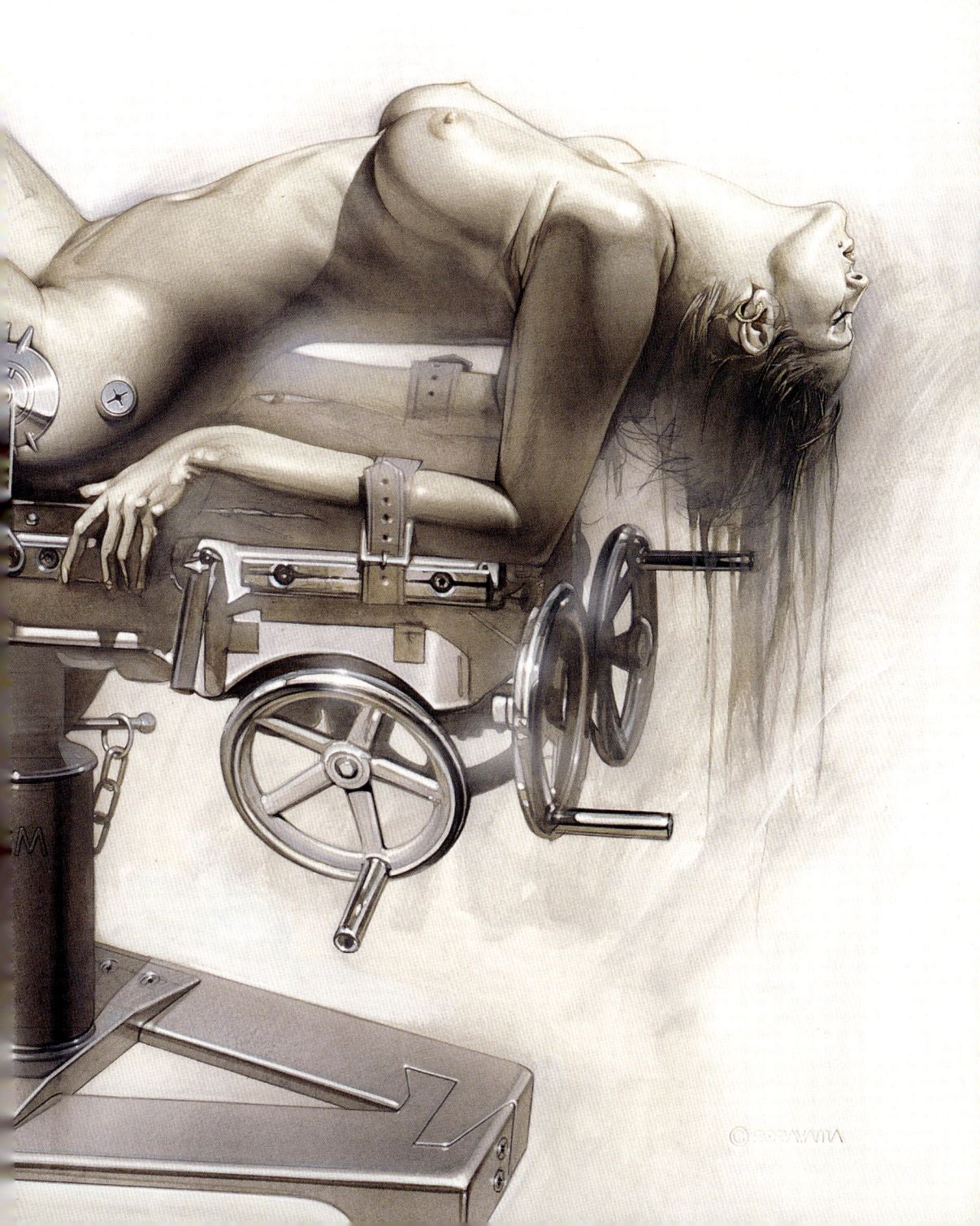

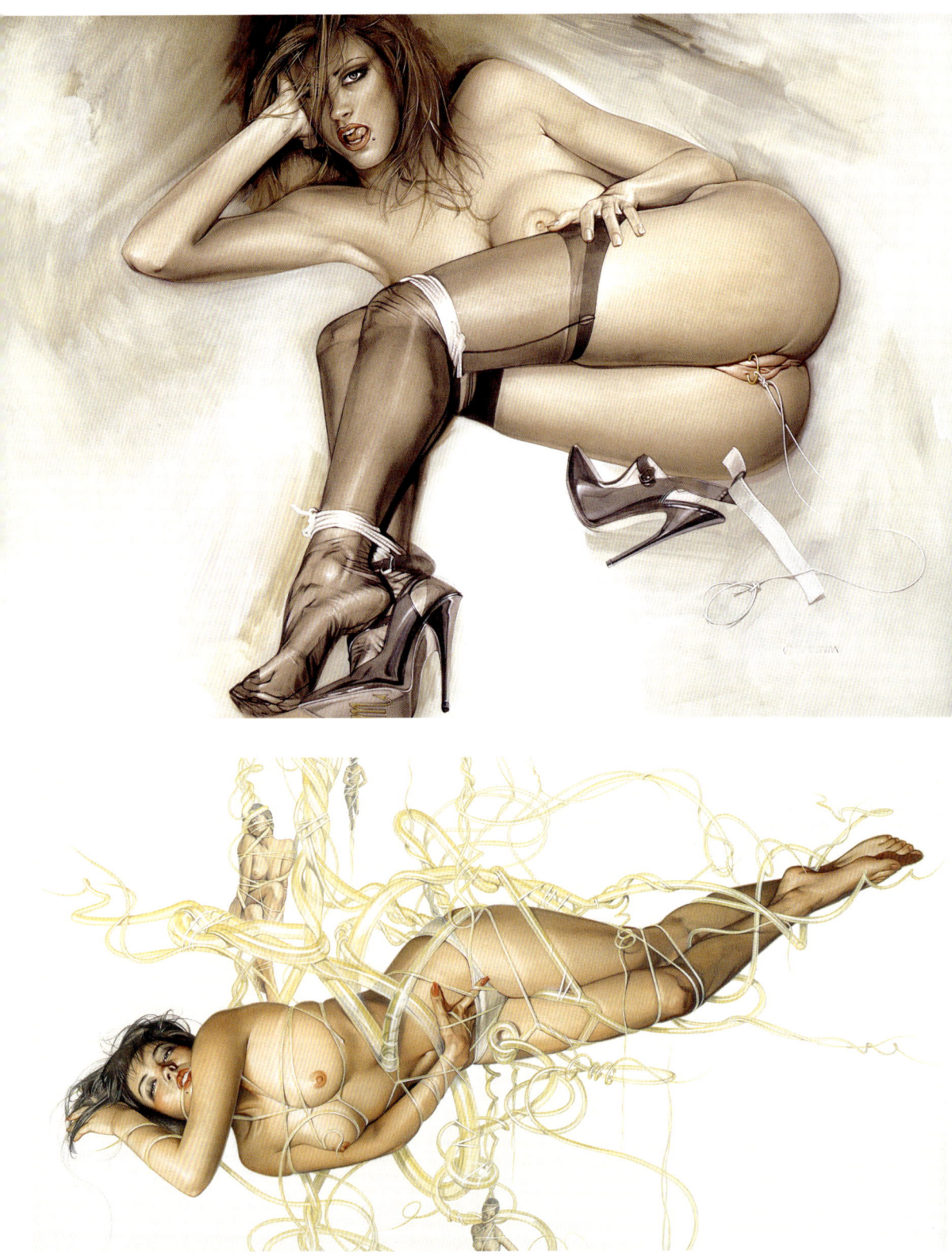

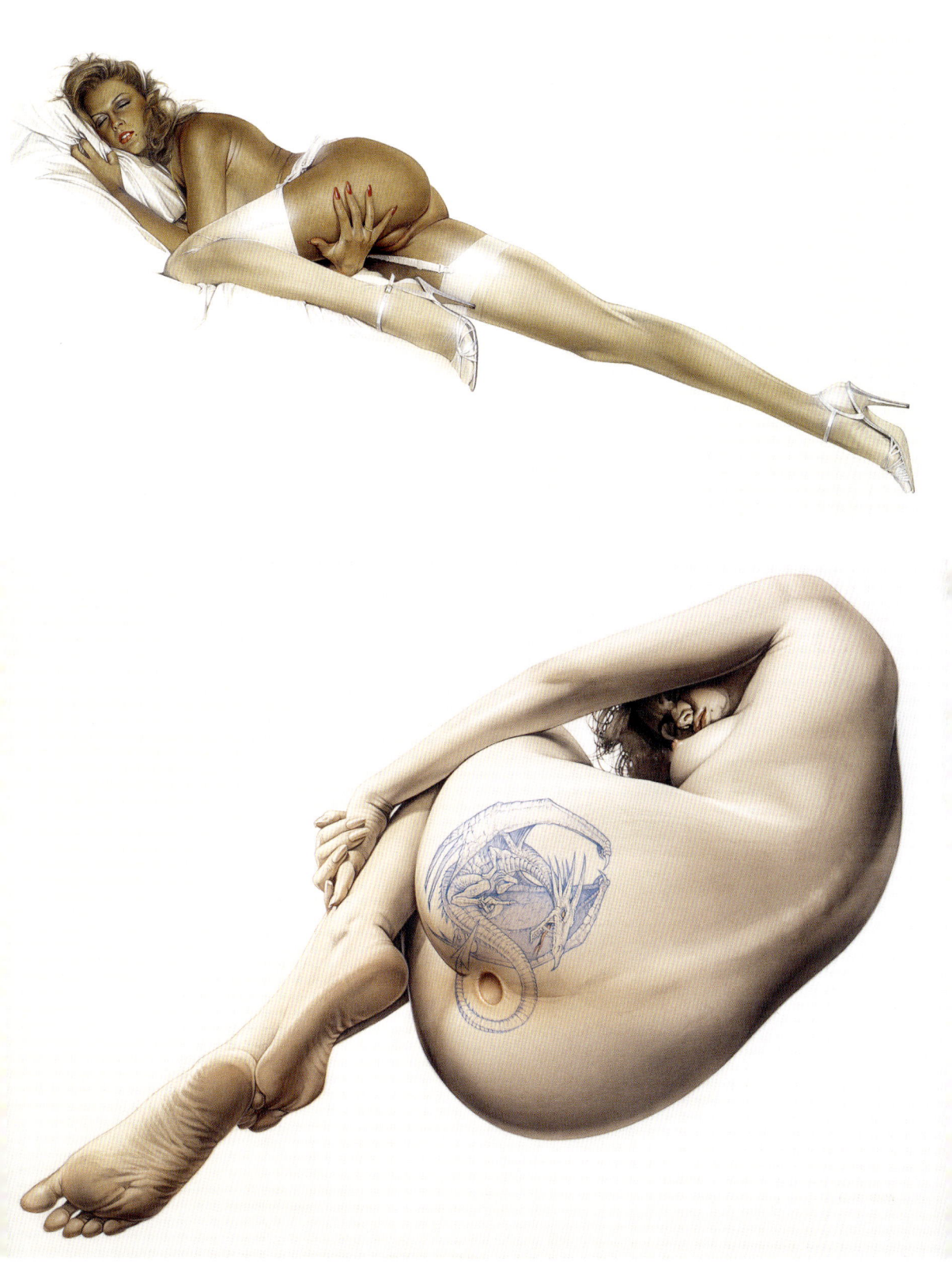

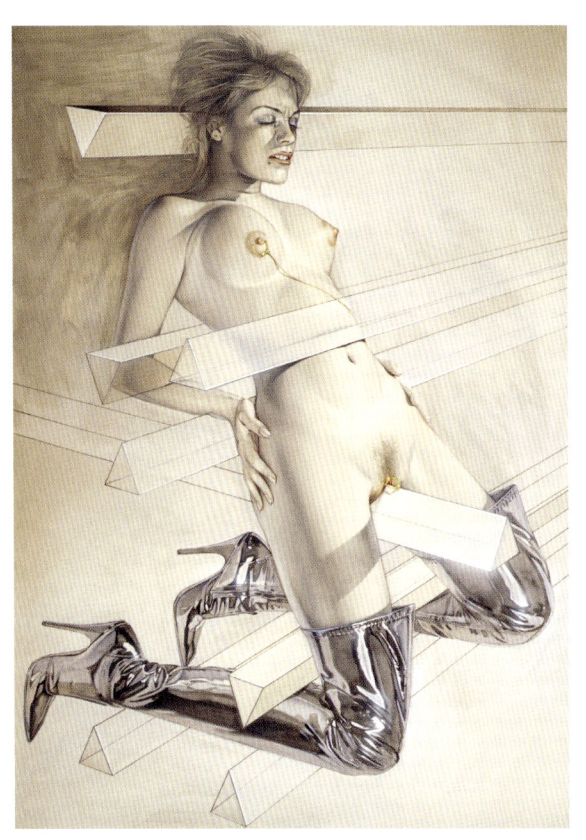
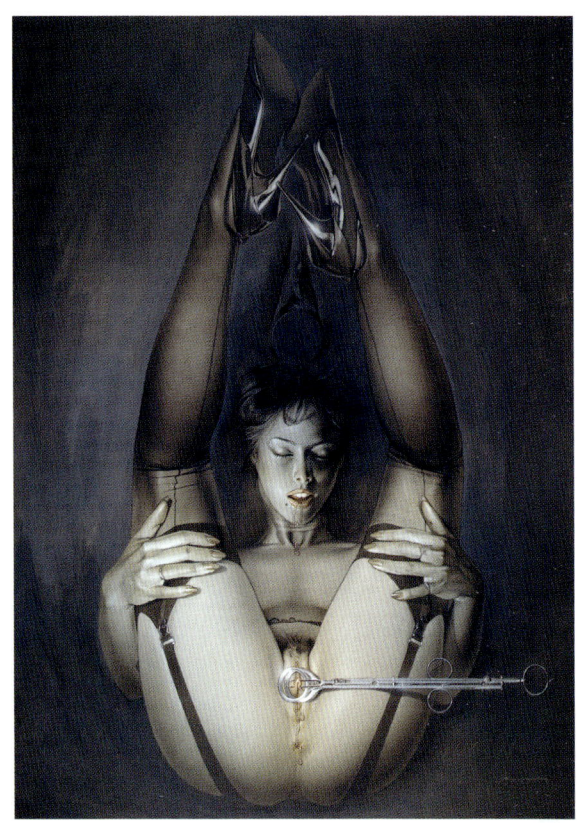

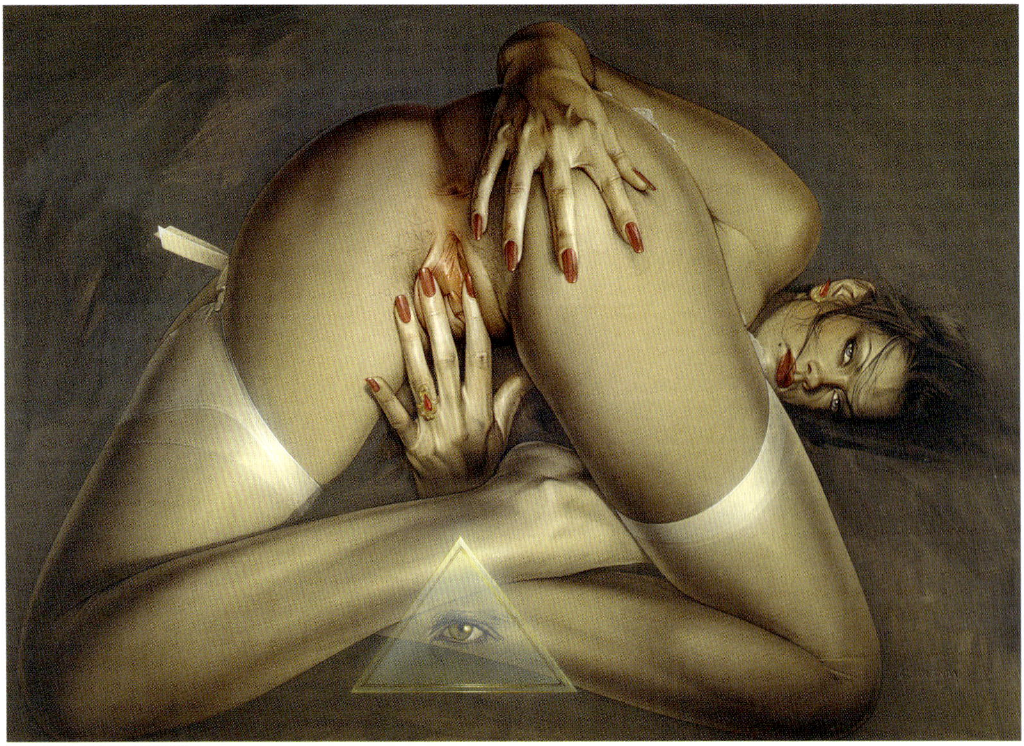

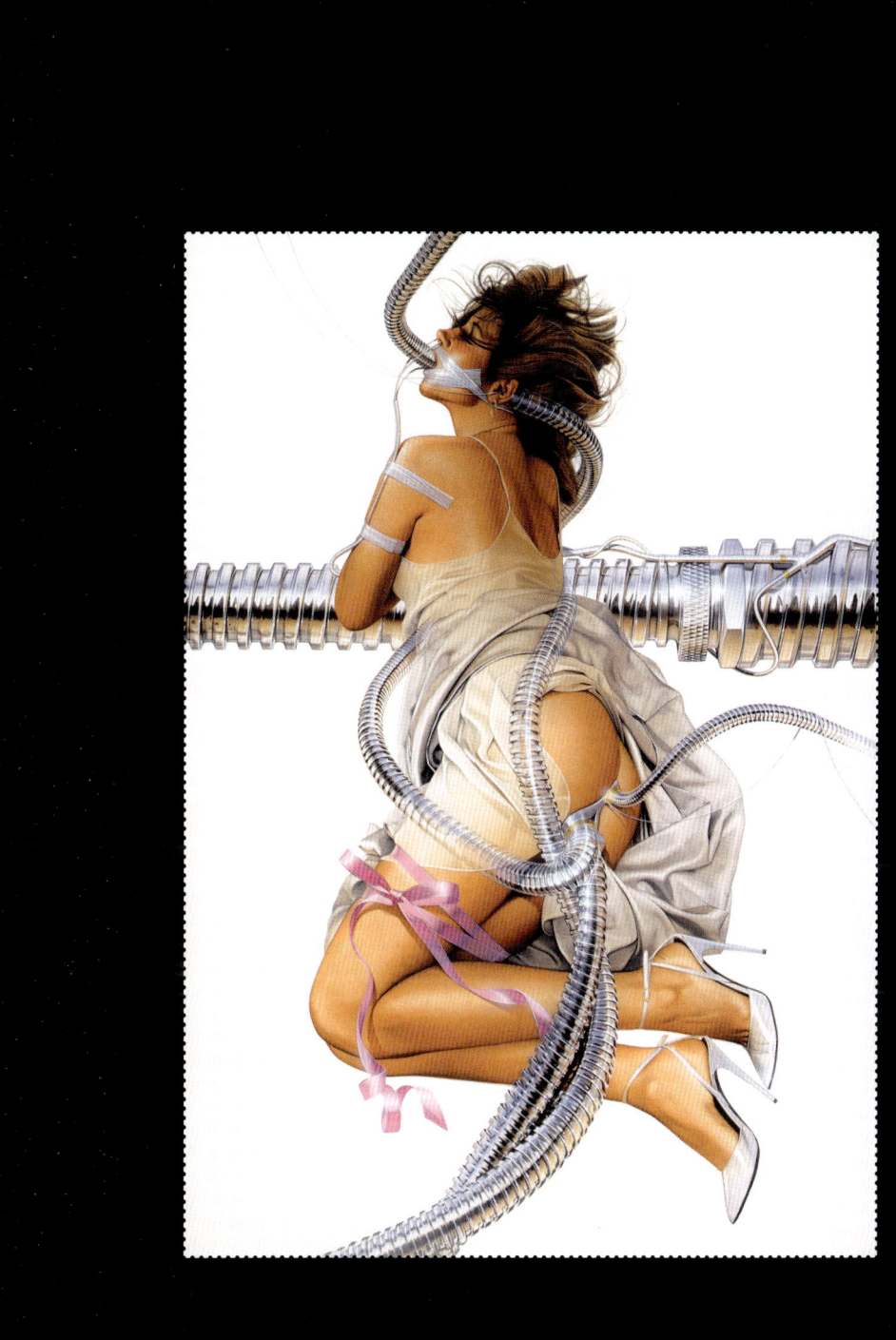

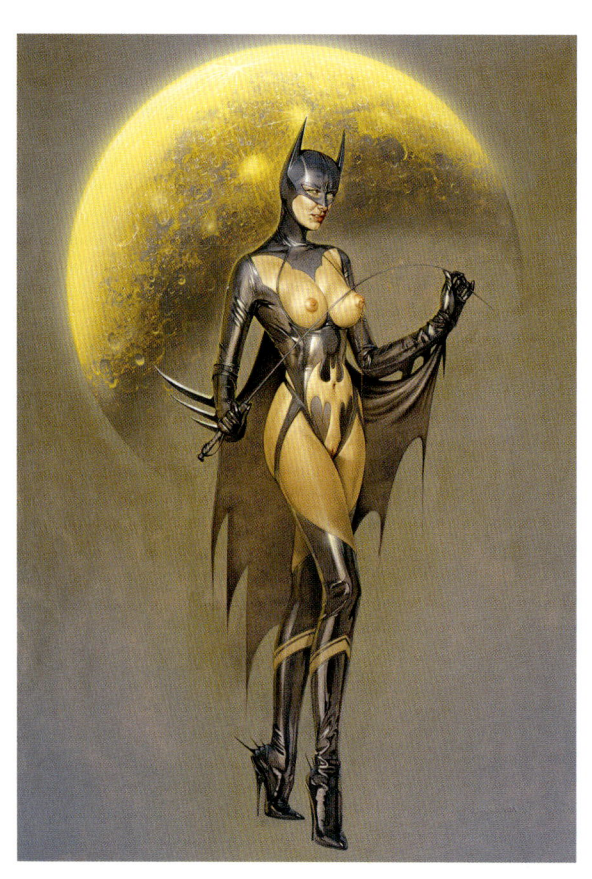

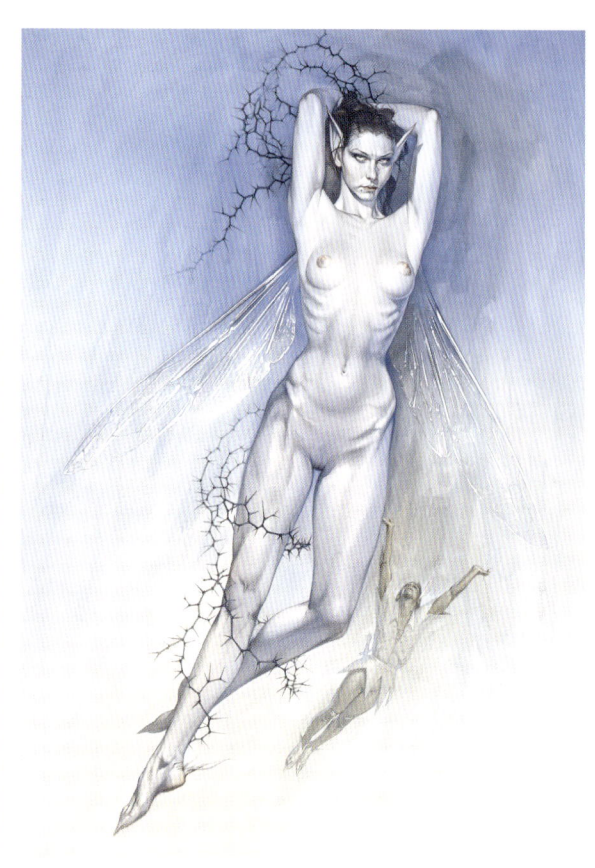

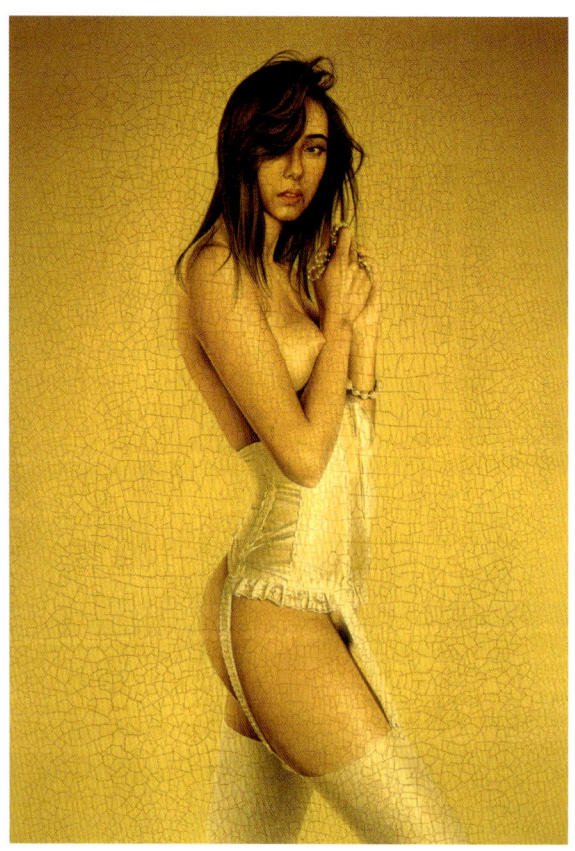

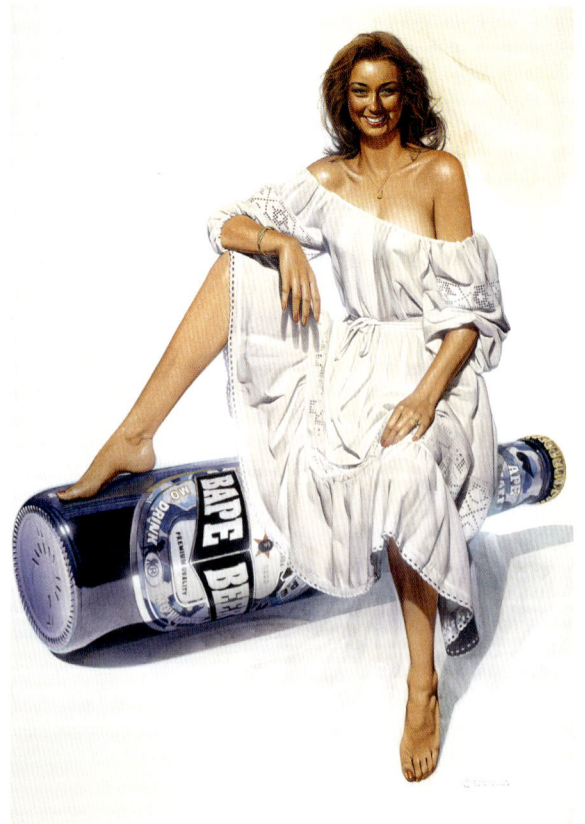

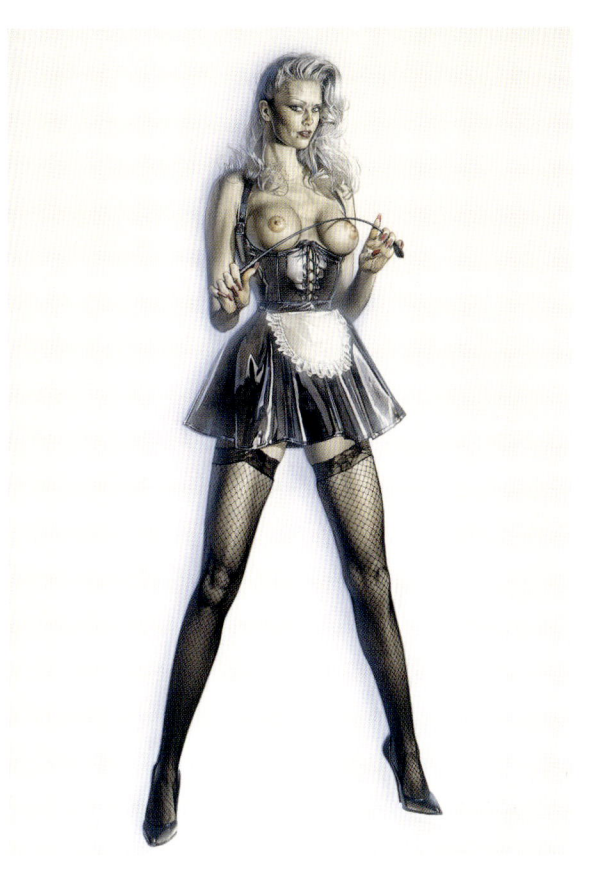
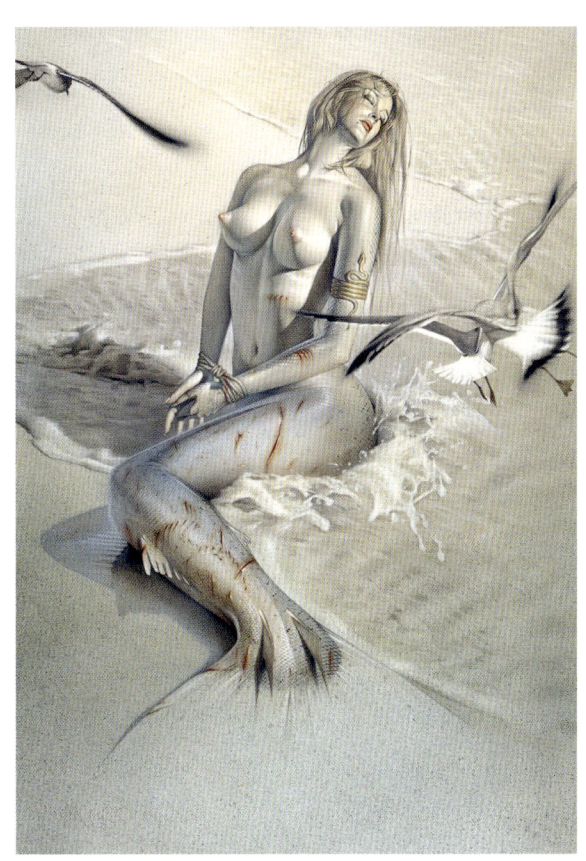
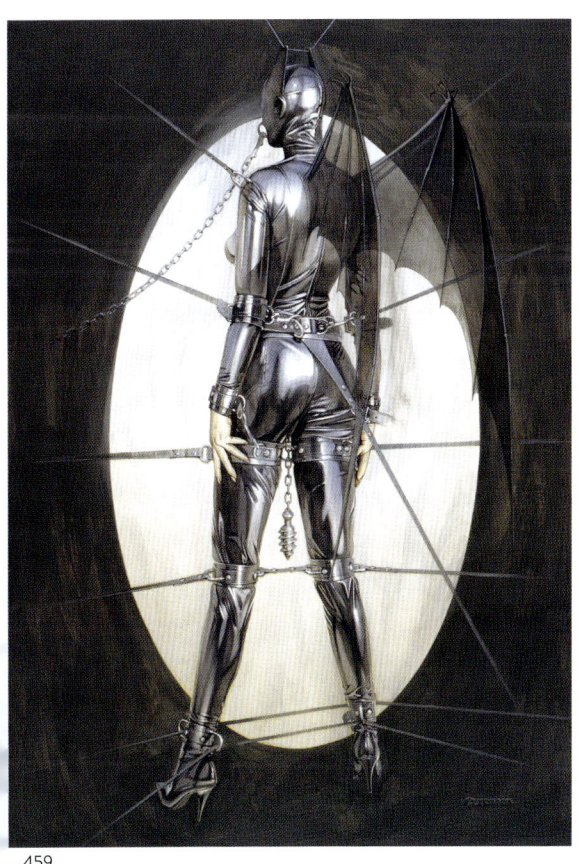
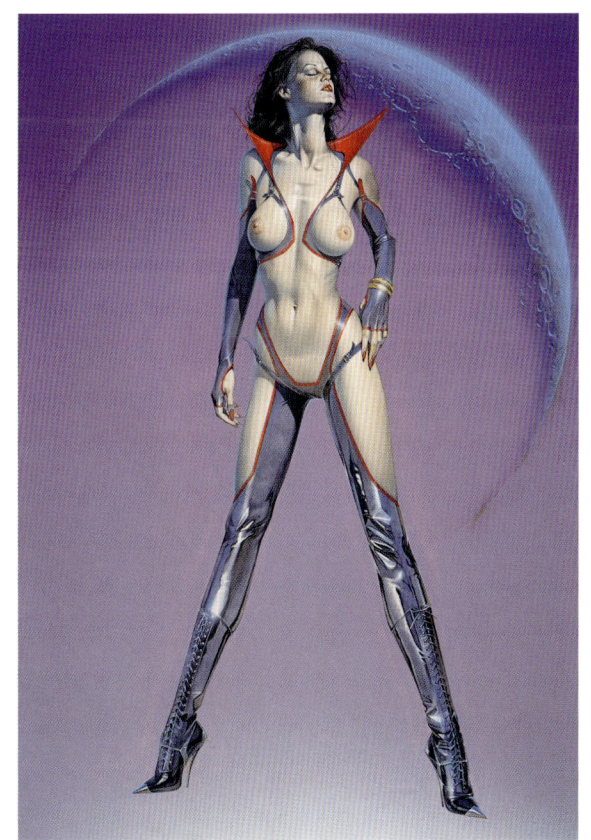

459

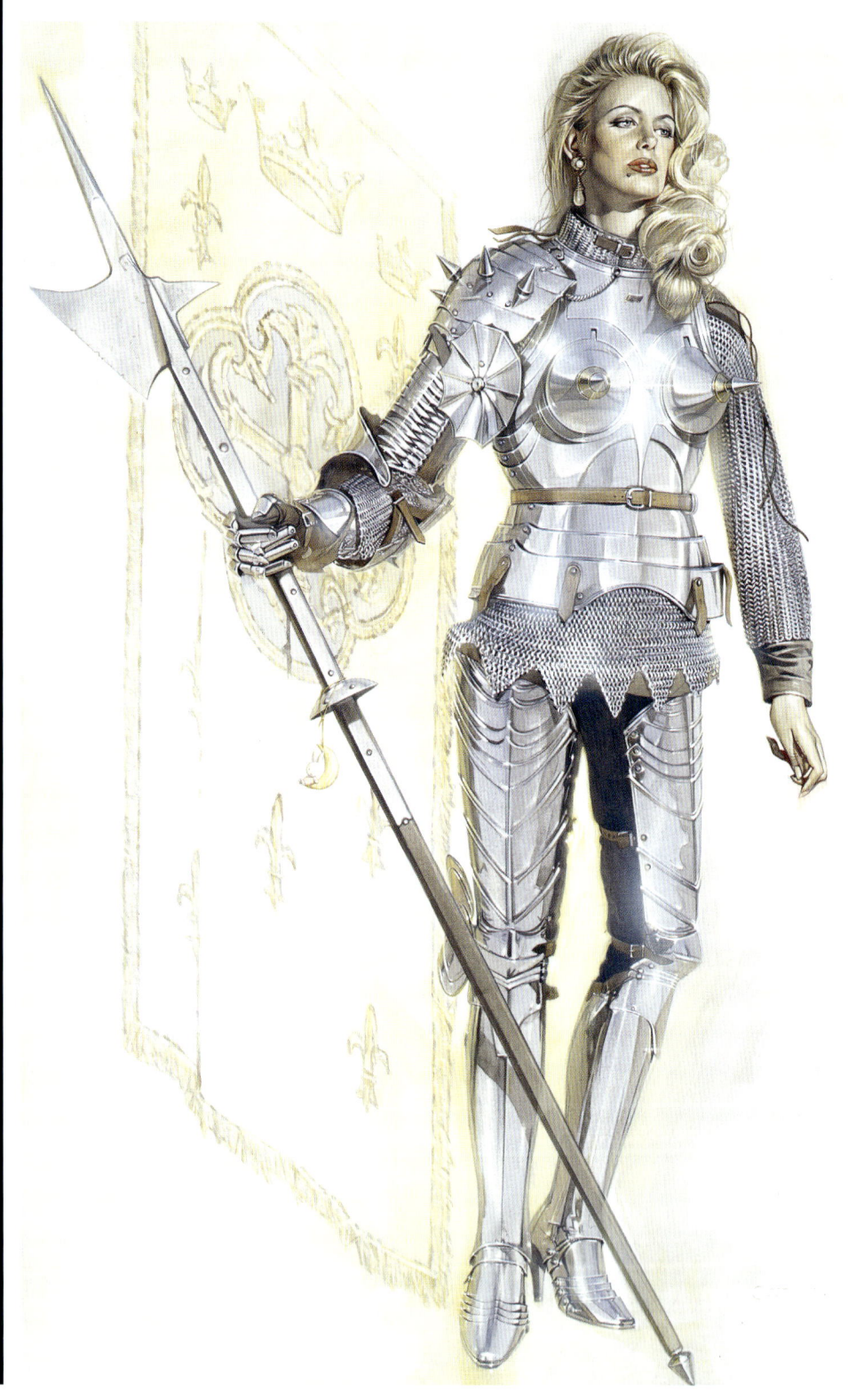

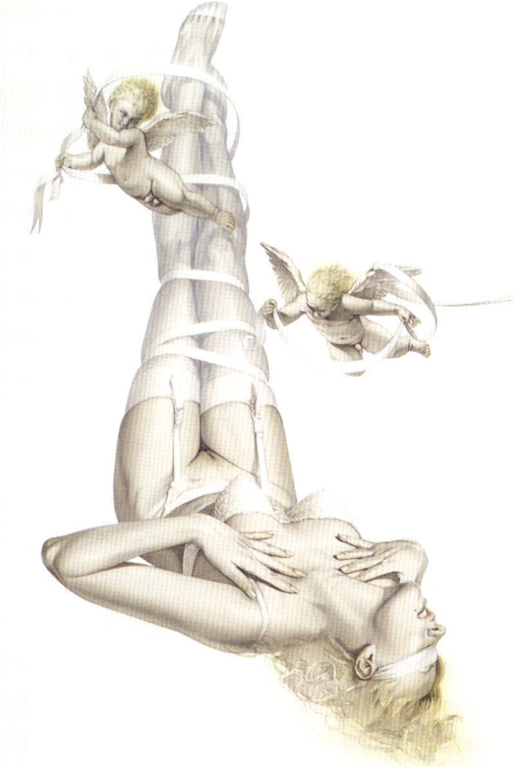

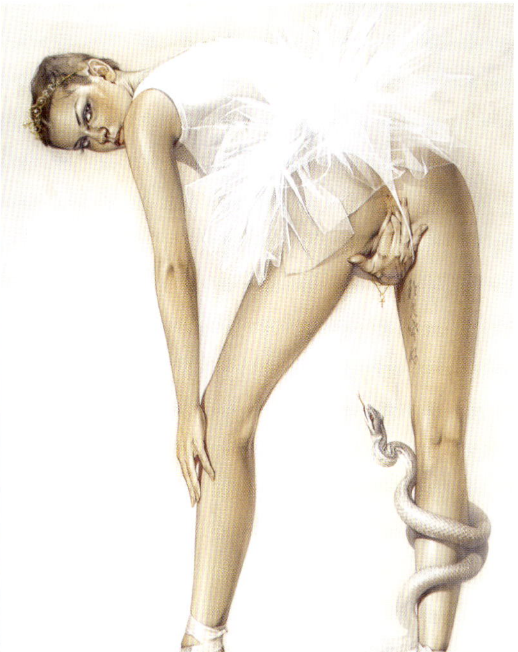

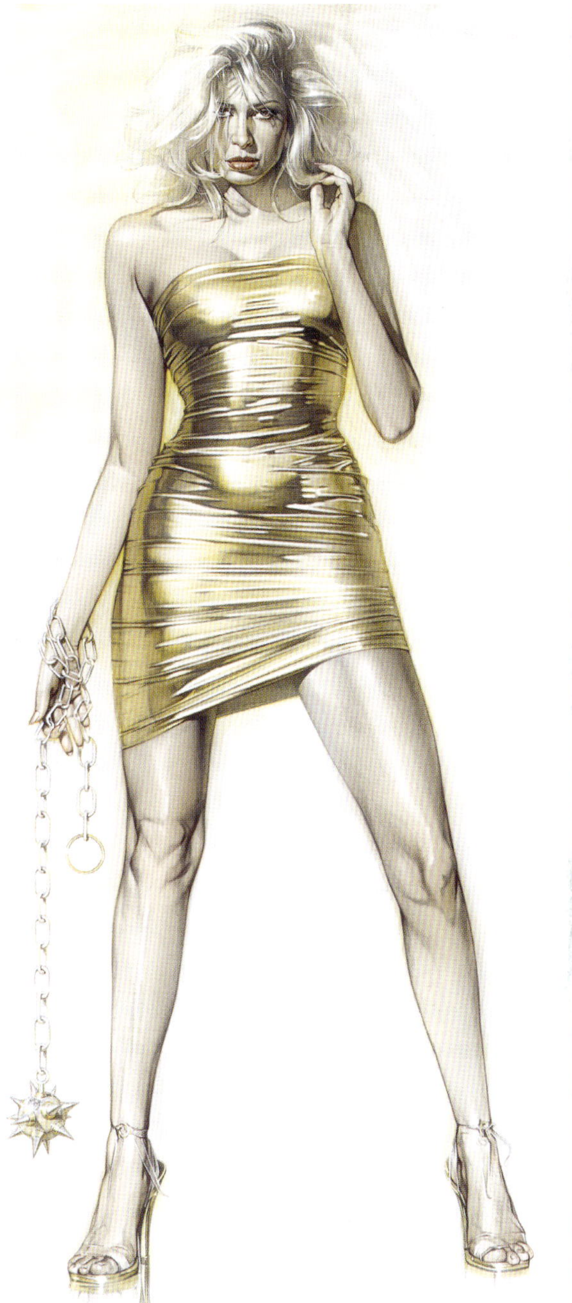

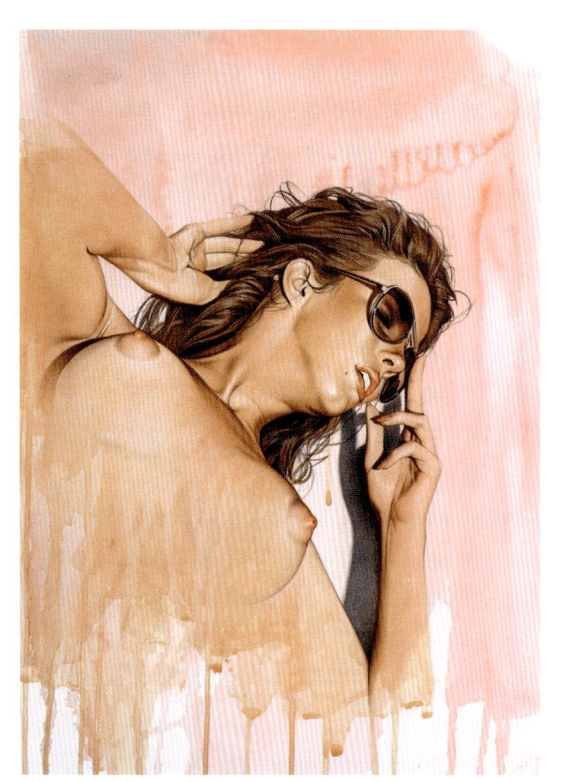
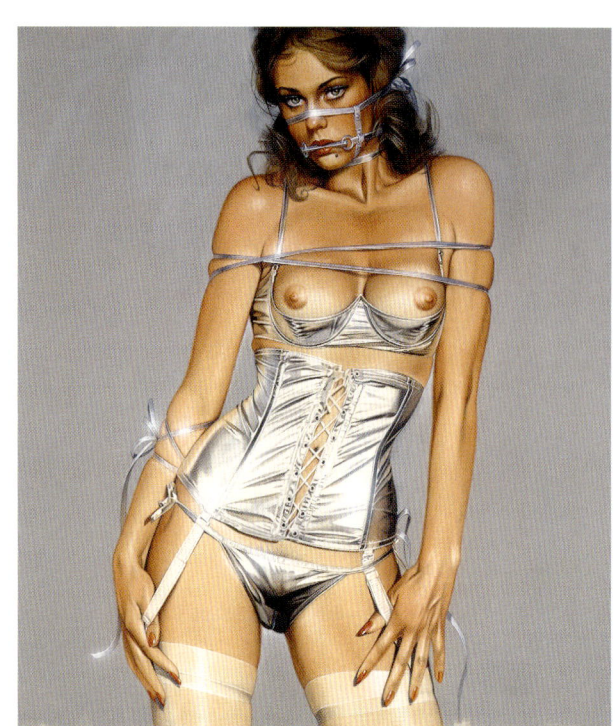

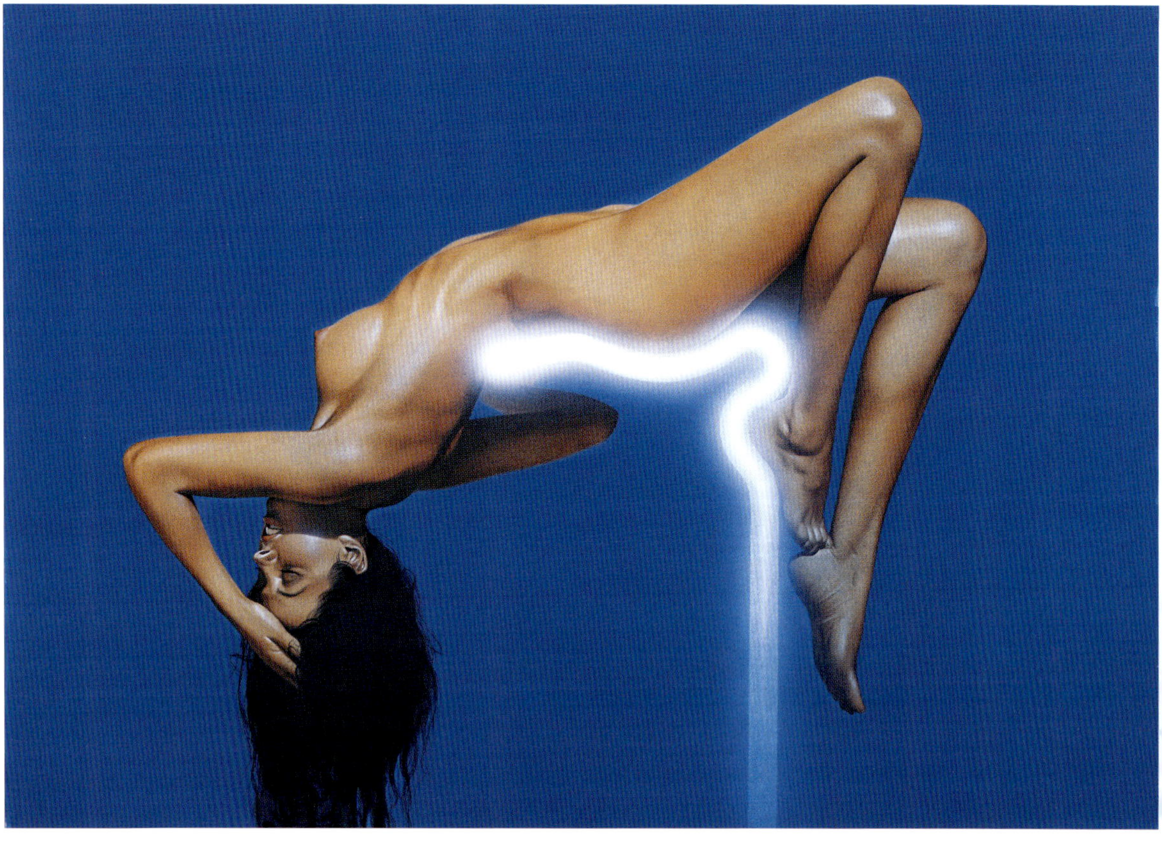

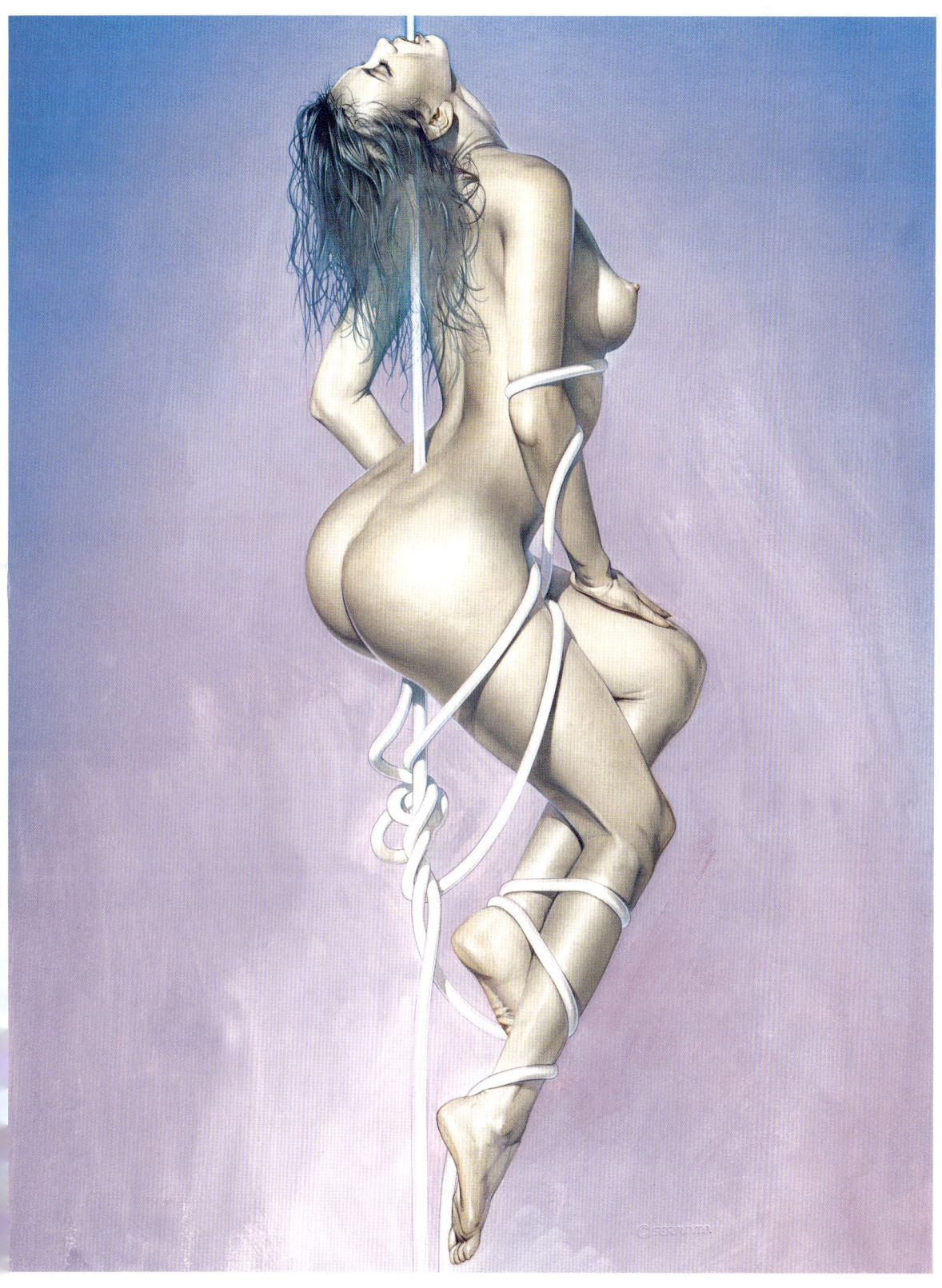

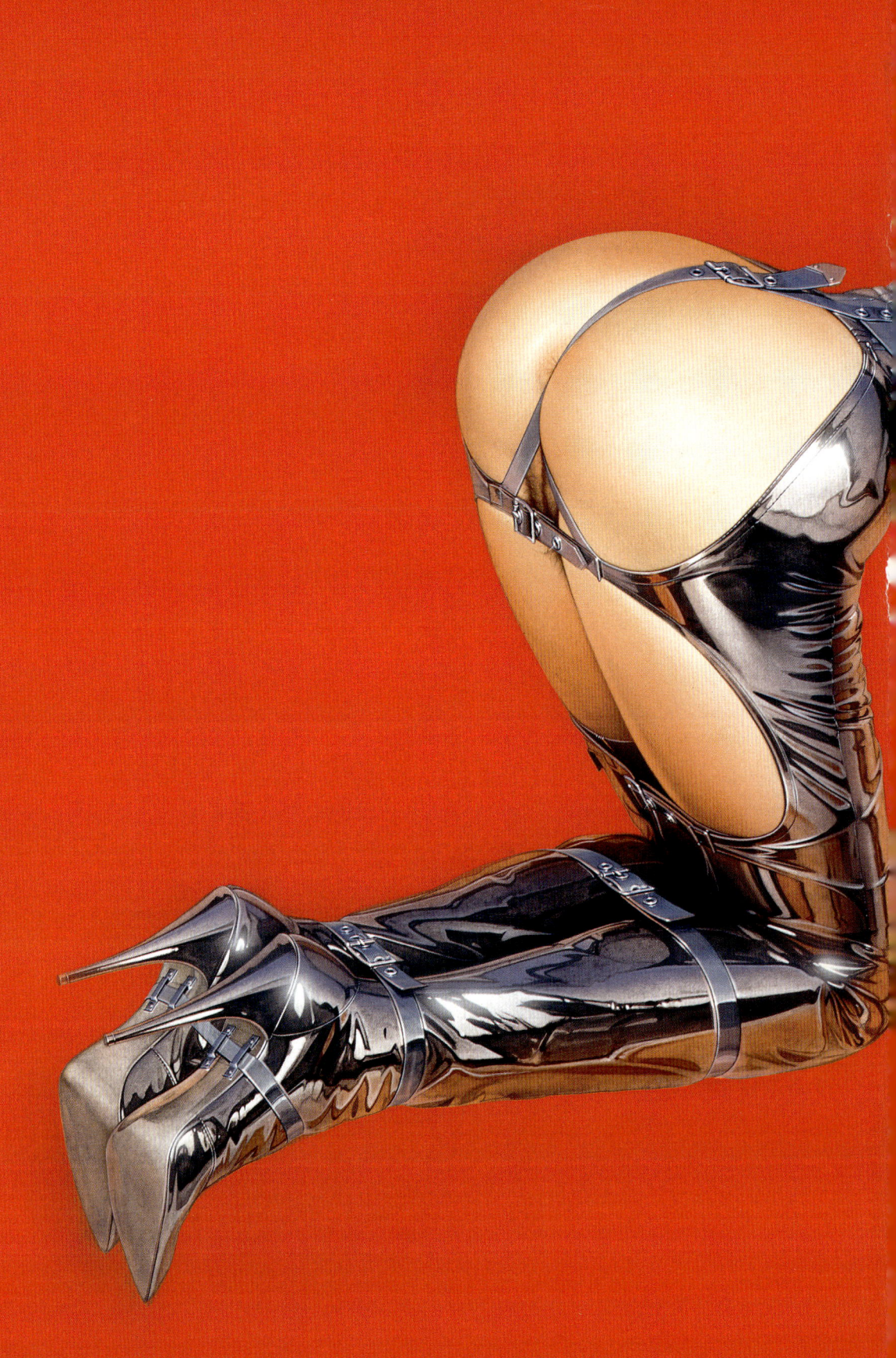

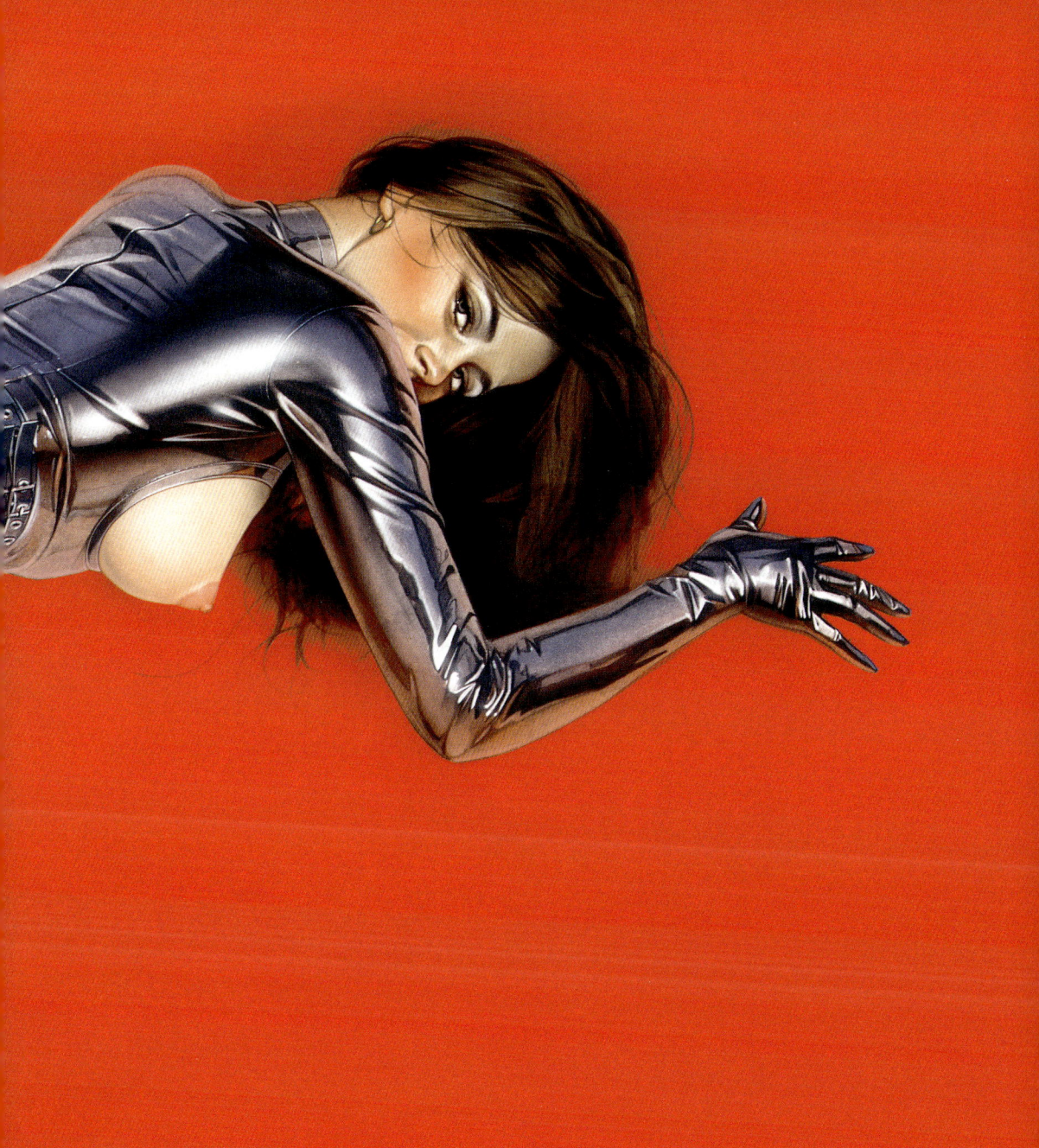

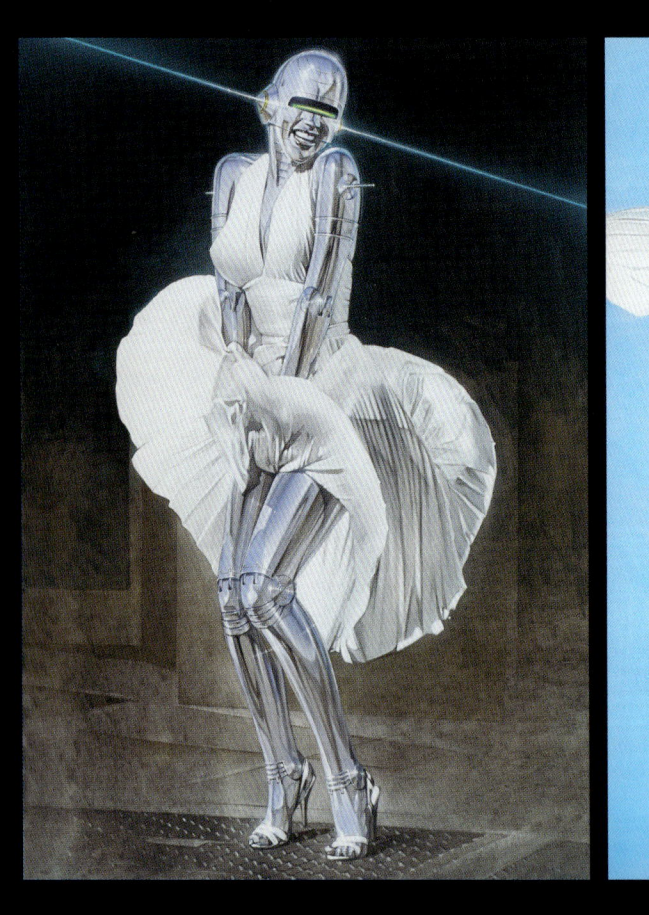
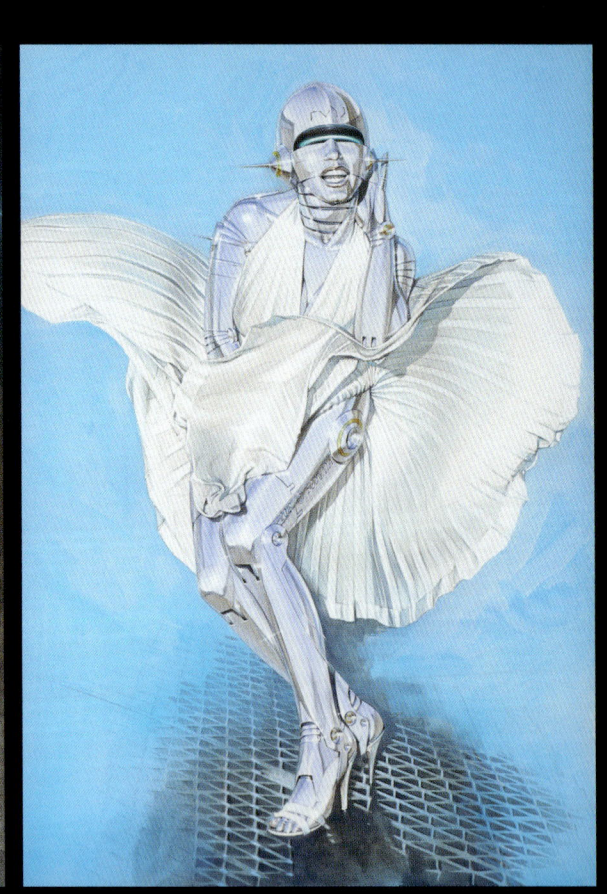

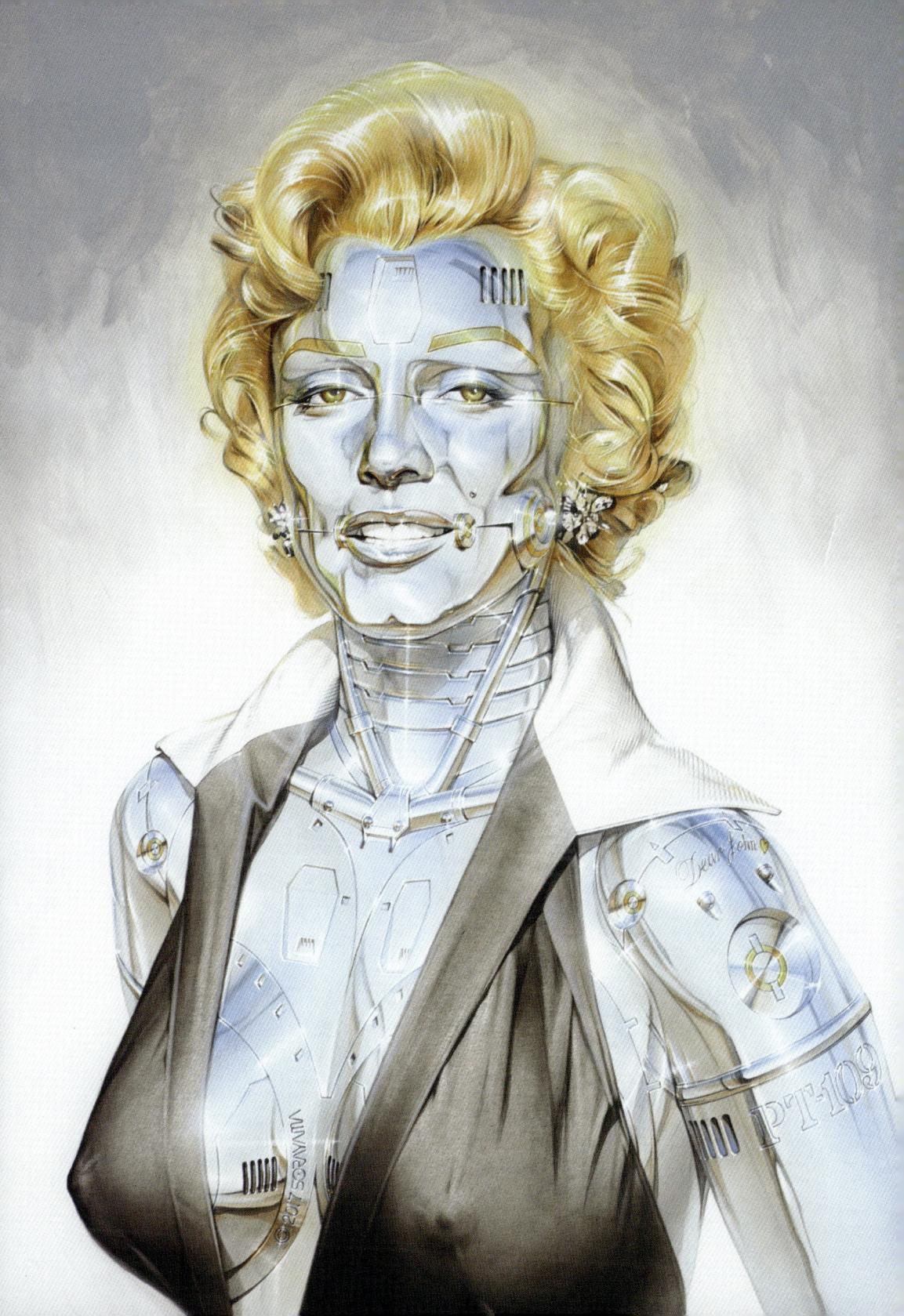

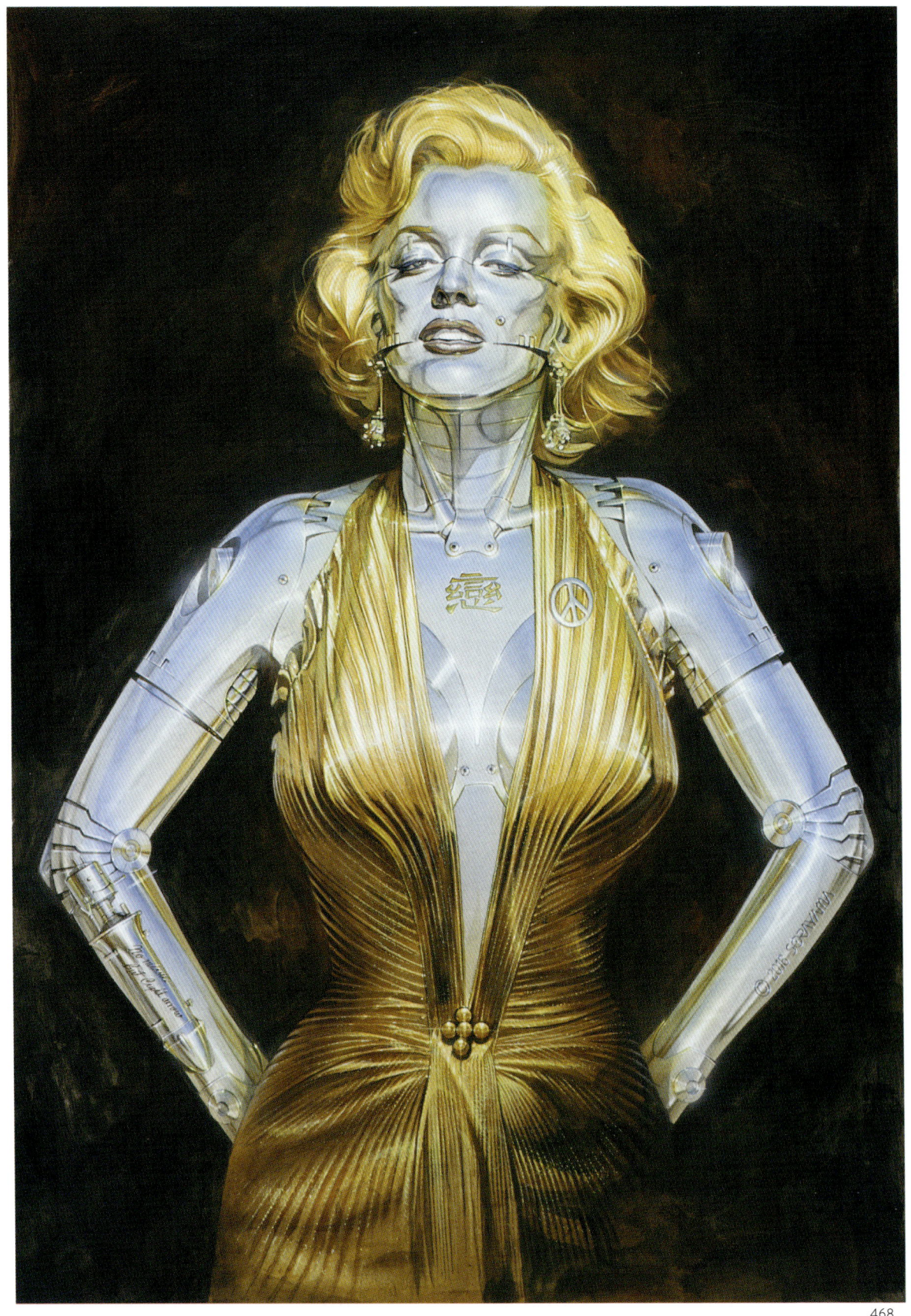

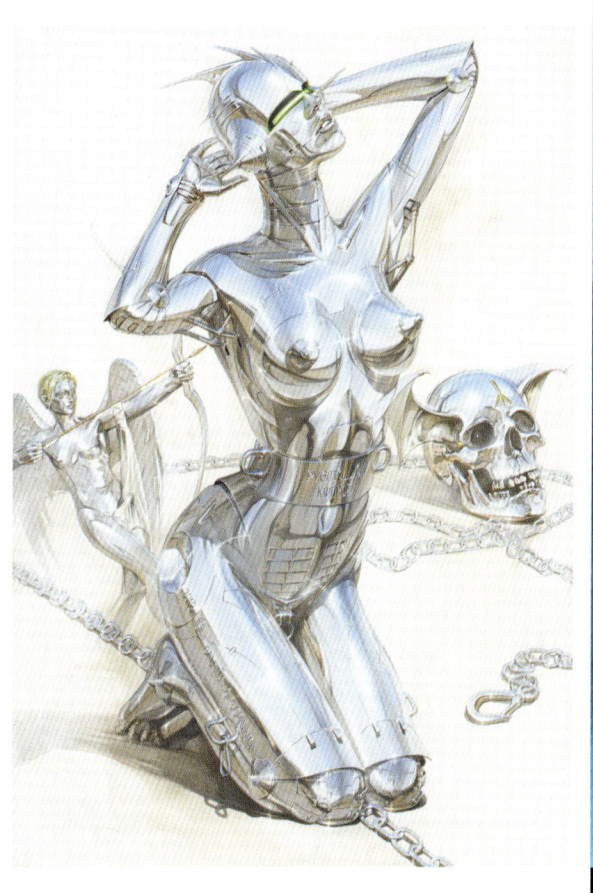
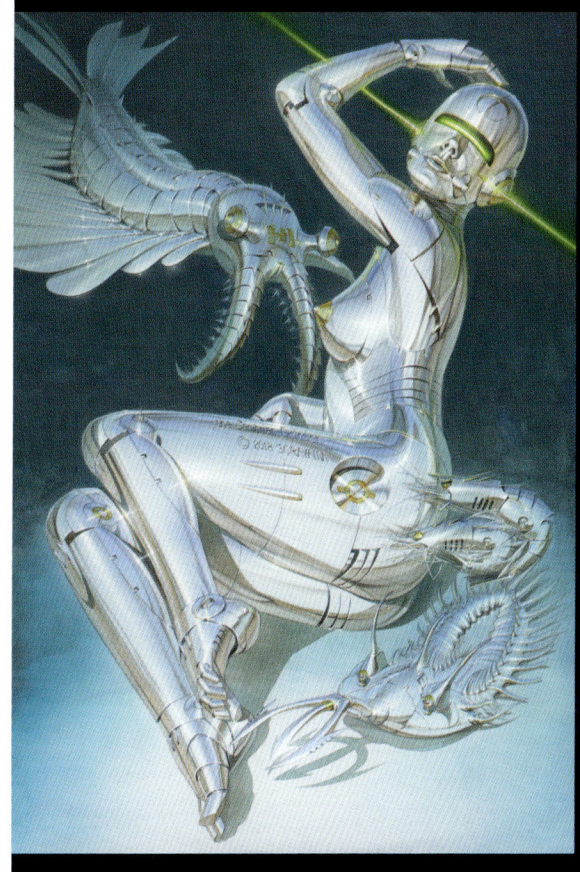

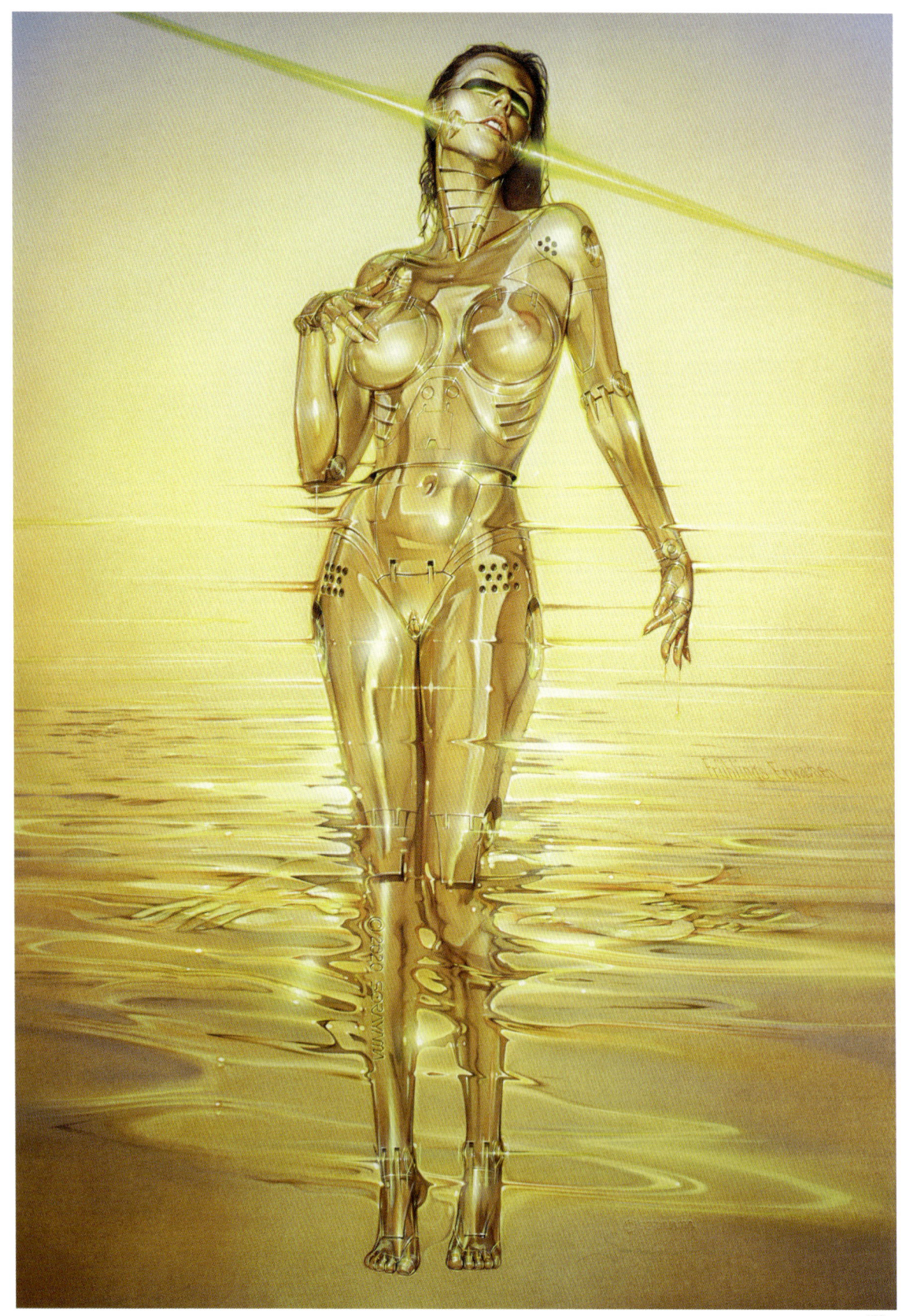

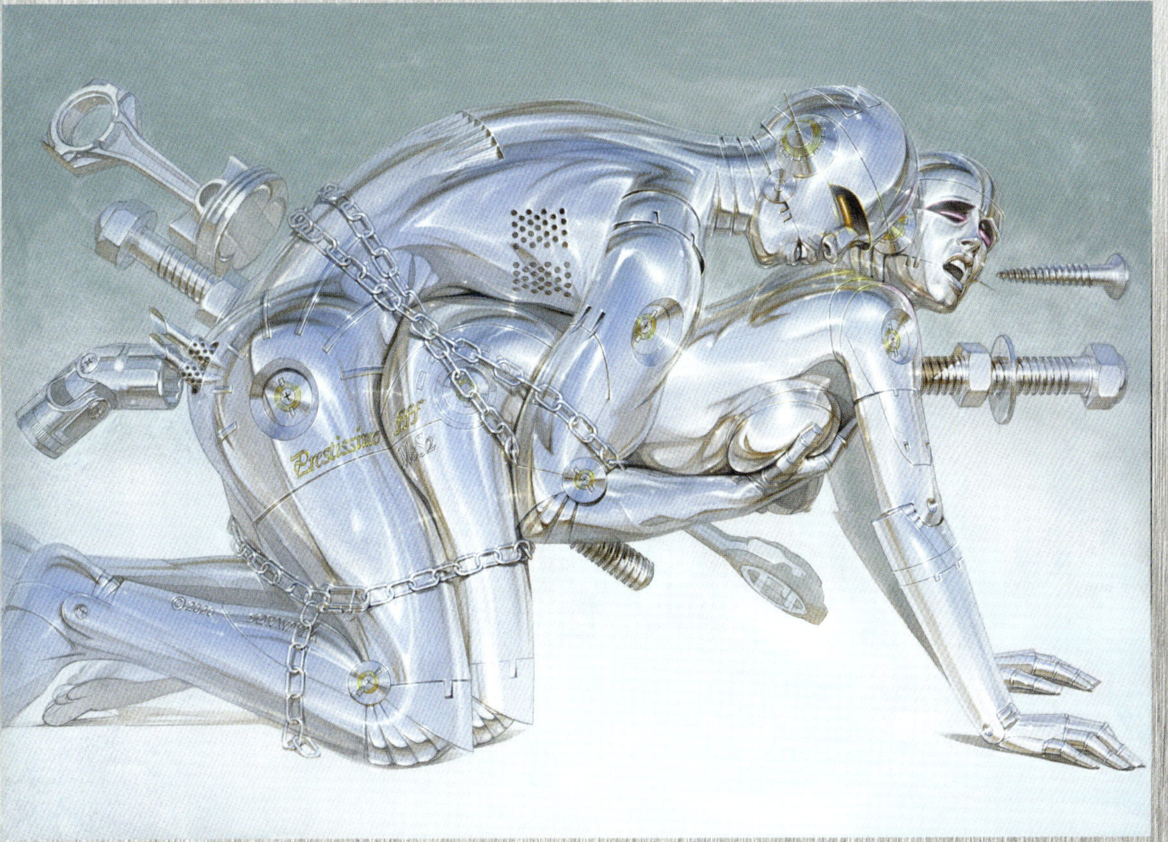

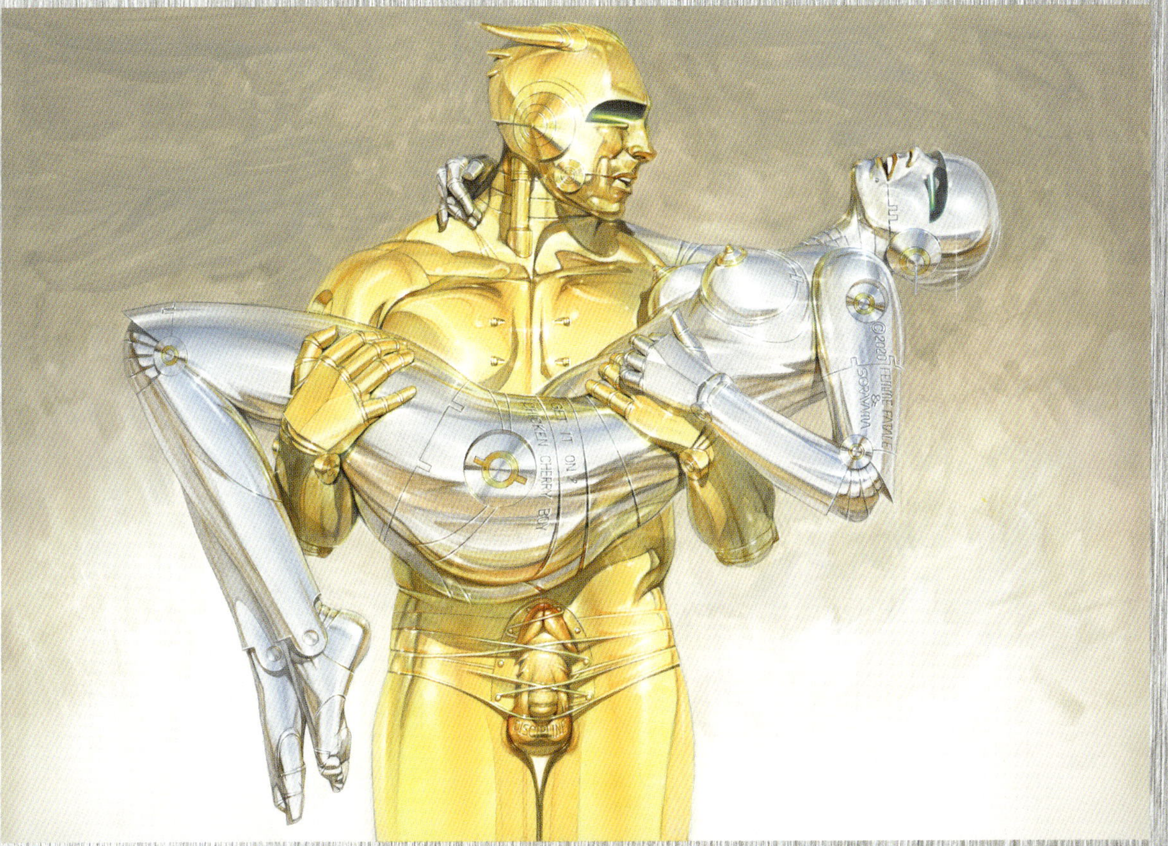

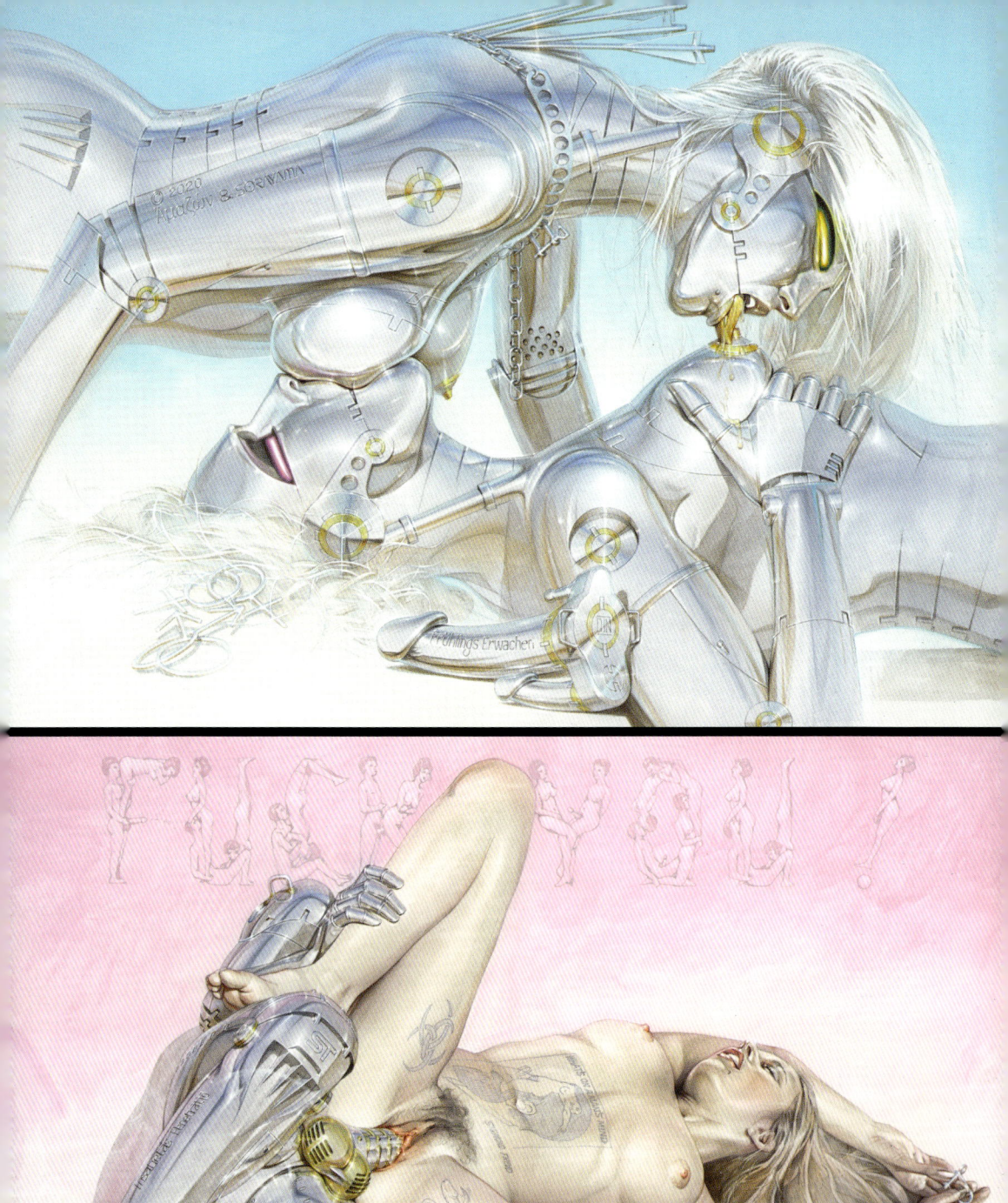

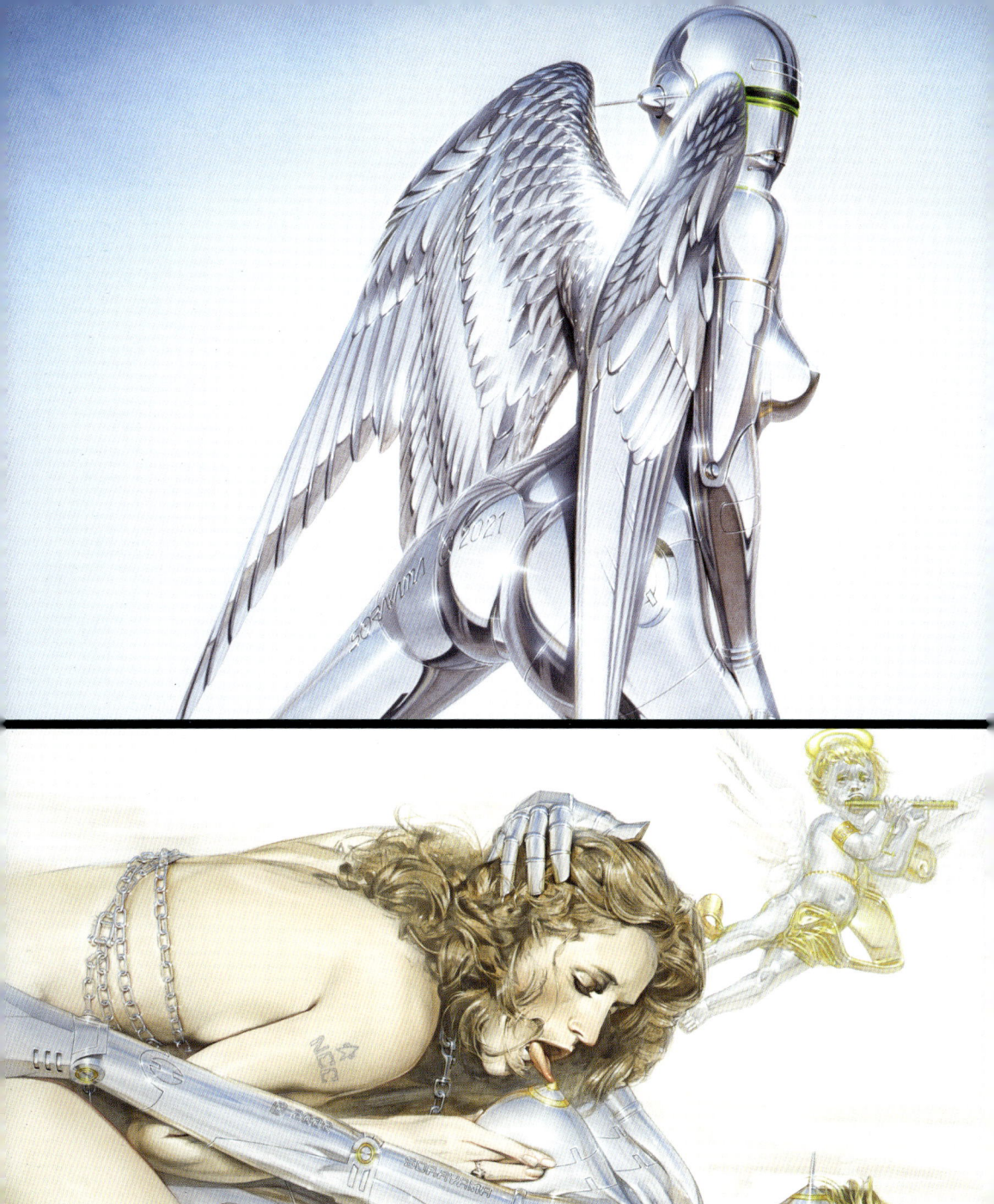

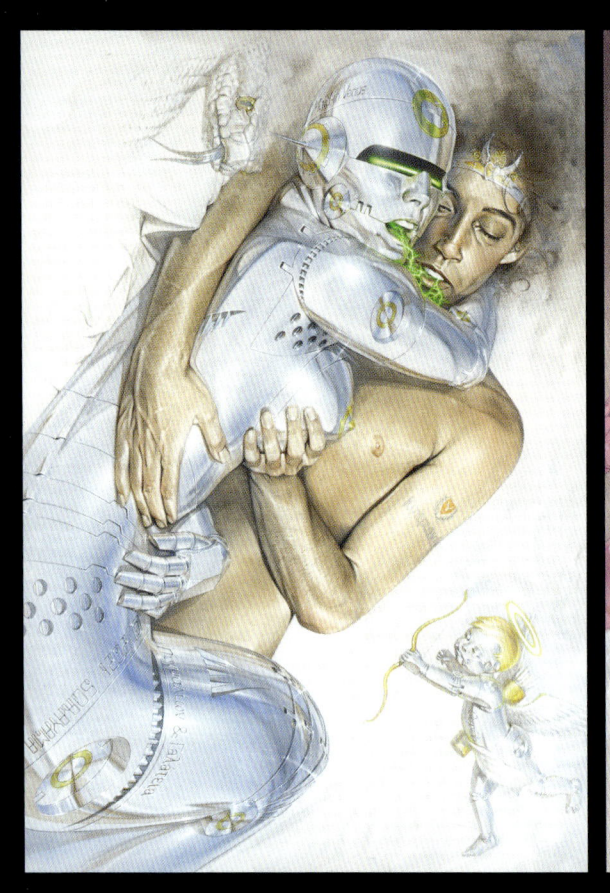
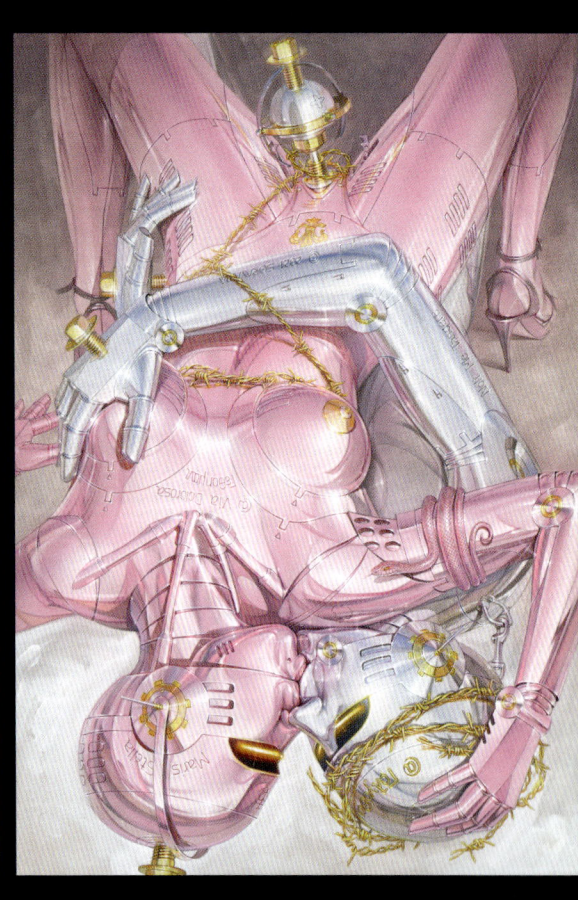

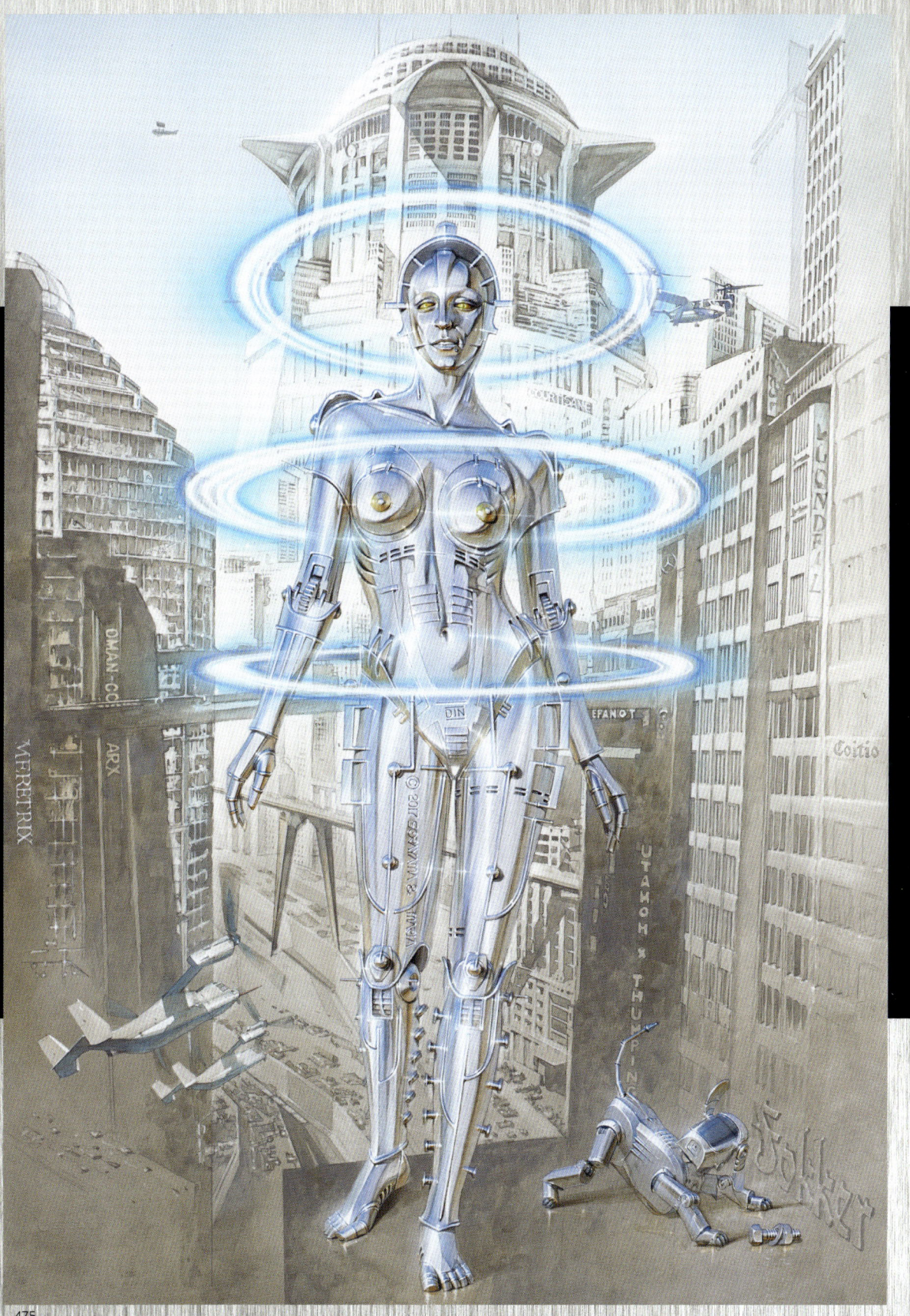

475

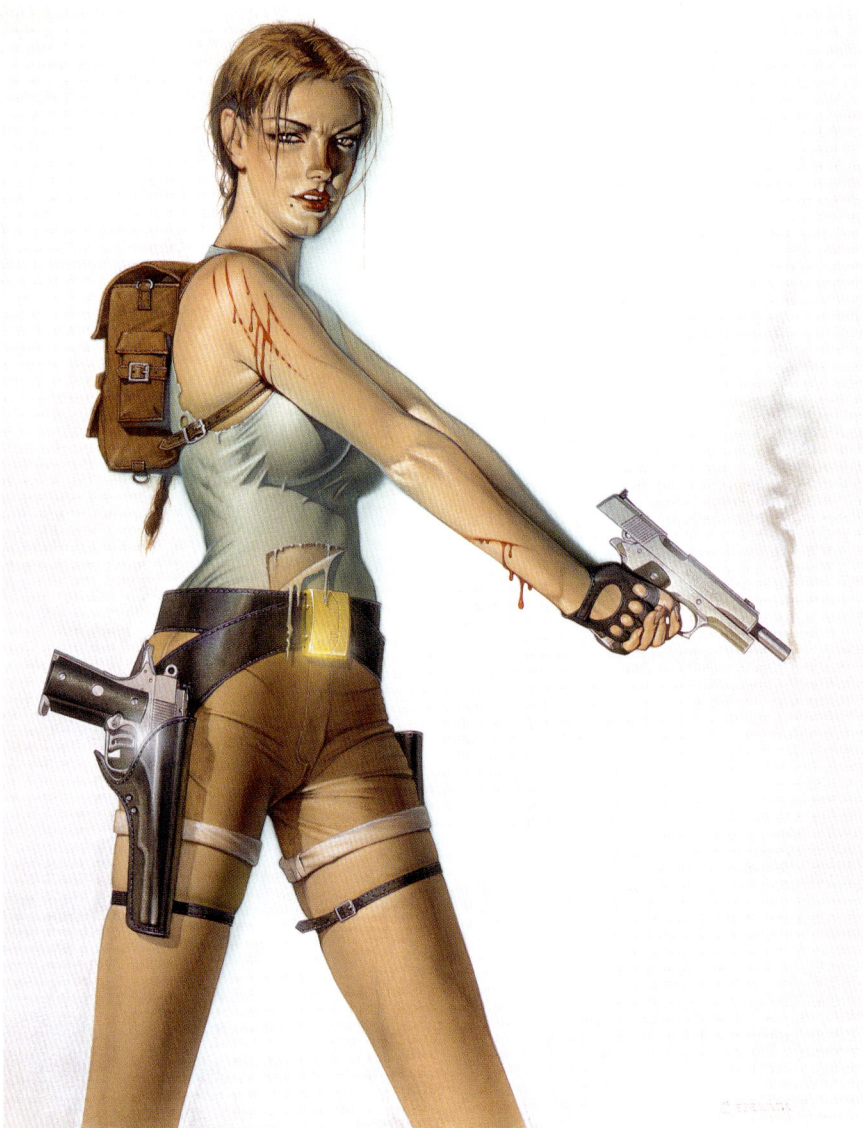

CREDITS

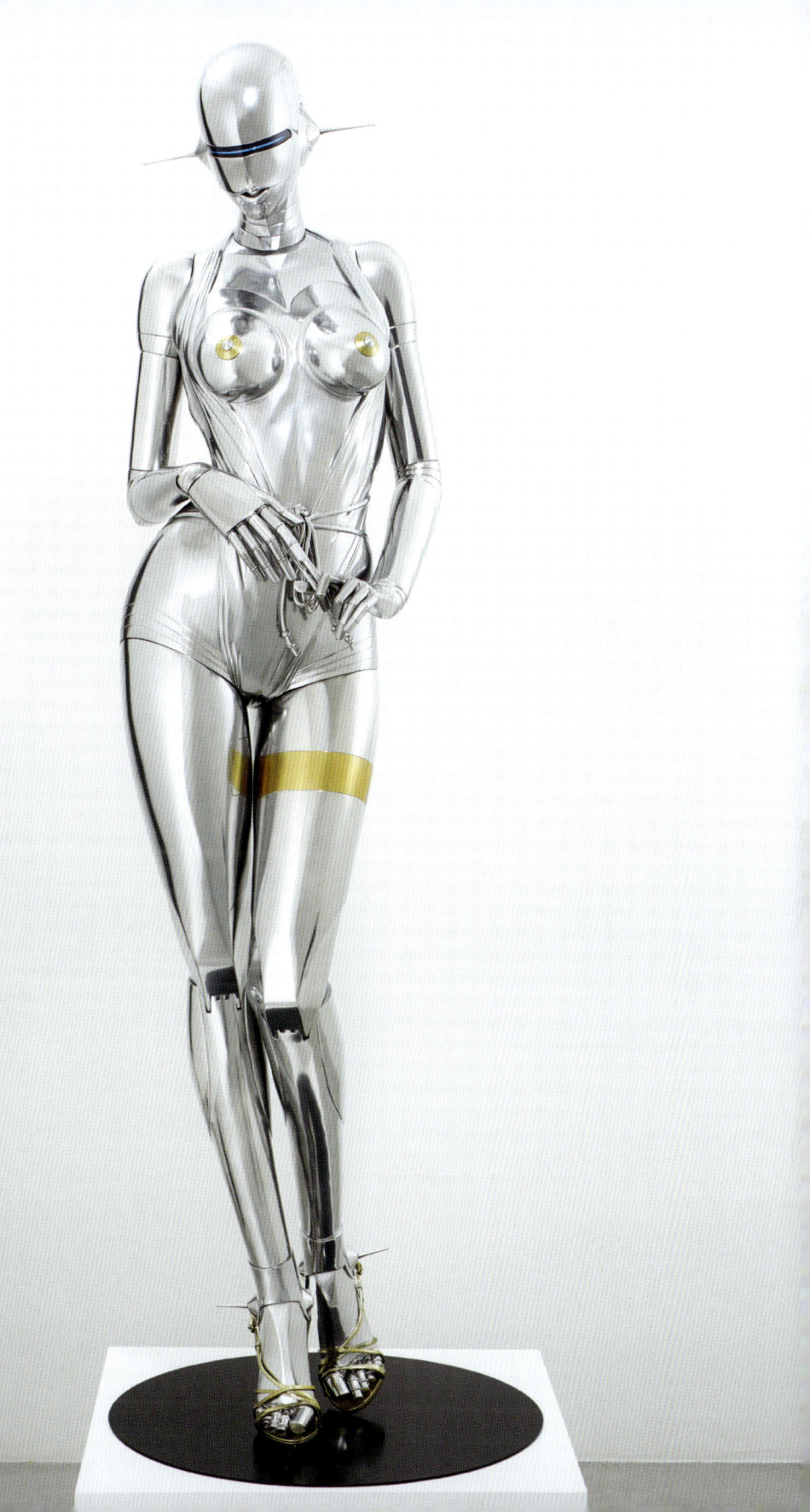

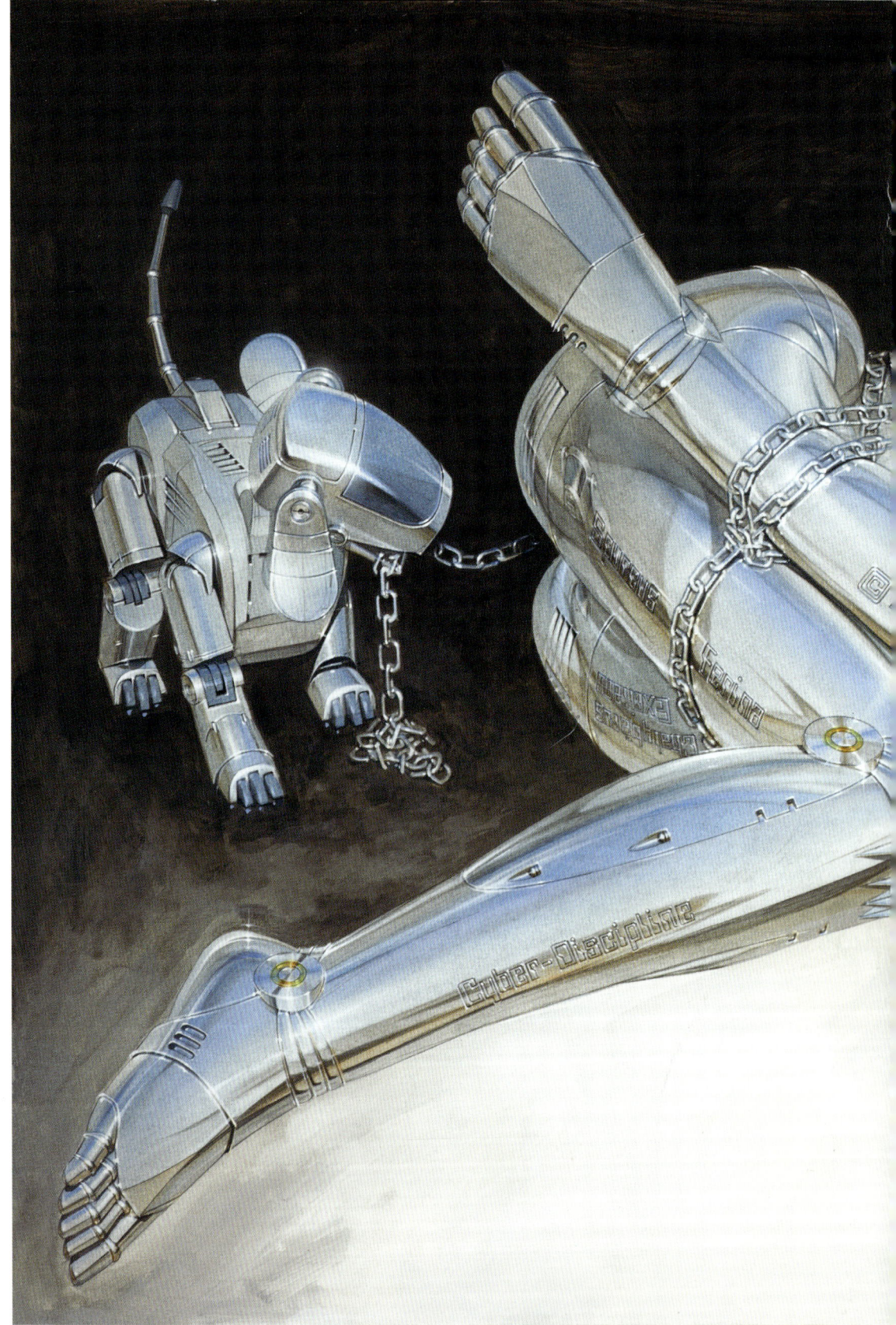